Essentials of Understanding Psychology

THIRTEENTH EDITION

Robert S. Feldman

University of Massachusetts Amherst

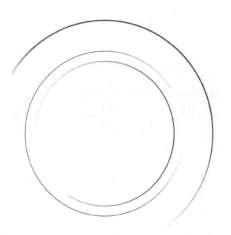

Mc
Graw
Hill
Education

ESSENTIALS OF UNDERSTANDING PSYCHOLOGY, THIRTEENTH EDITION

Published by McGraw-Hill Education, 2 Penn Plaza, New York, NY 10121. Copyright © 2019 by McGraw-Hill Education. All rights reserved. Printed in the United States of America. Previous editions © 2017, 2015, and 2013. No part of this publication may be reproduced or distributed in any form or by any means, or stored in a database or retrieval system, without the prior written consent of McGraw-Hill Education, including, but not limited to, in any network or other electronic storage or transmission, or broadcast for distance learning.

Some ancillaries, including electronic and print components, may not be available to customers outside the United States.

This book is printed on acid-free paper.

4 5 6 7 8 9 LWI 21 20

Bound:
ISBN 978-1-259-92272-5
MHID 1-259-92272-3

Loose Leaf:
ISBN 978-1-260-19461-6
MHID 1-260-19461-2

Portfolio Manager: *Nancy Welcher*
Product Development Manager: *Dawn Groundwater*
Product Developer: *Cara Labell*
Marketing Manager: *Augustine Laferrera and Olivia Kaiser*
Content Project Managers: *Mary E. Powers* (Core), *Jodi Banowetz* (Assessment)
Buyer: *Sandy Ludovissy*
Design: *David W. Hash*
Content Licensing *Specialist: Melisa Seegmiller*
Cover Image: *©Chayantorn Tongmorn/Shutterstock, ©Indypendenz/Shutterstock*
Compositor: *Aptara®, Inc.*

All credits appearing on page or at the end of the book are considered to be an extension of the copyright page.

Library of Congress Cataloging-in-Publication Data

Names: Feldman, Robert S. (Robert Stephen), 1947- author.
Title: Essentials of understanding psychology / Robert S. Feldman, University of
   Massachusetts Amherst.
Description: Thirteenth edition. | New York, NY : McGraw-Hill Education, [2019]
Identifiers: LCCN 2018022599 | ISBN 9781259922725 (soft cover : alk. paper) |
   ISBN 1259922723 (soft cover : alk. paper)
Subjects: LCSH: Psychology.
Classification: LCC BF121 .F337 2019 | DDC 150–dc23 LC record available at
https://lccn.loc.gov/2018022599

The Internet addresses listed in the text were accurate at the time of publication. The inclusion of a website does not indicate an endorsement by the authors or McGraw-Hill Education, and McGraw-Hill Education does not guarantee the accuracy of the information presented at these sites.

mheducation.com/highered

Dedication
To
Jon, Leigh, Alex, Miles, Josh, Julie, Naomi,
Sarah, Jeff, Lilia, and Kathy

About the Author

ROBERT S. FELDMAN is Professor of Psychological and Brain Sciences and Senior Advisor to the Chancellor of the University of Massachusetts Amherst. A recipient of the College Distinguished Teacher Award, he teaches psychology classes ranging in size from 15 to nearly 500 students. During the course of more than three decades as a college instructor, he has taught undergraduate and graduate courses at Mount Holyoke College, Wesleyan University, and Virginia Commonwealth University in addition to the University of Massachusetts.

©Robert S. Feldman

Professor Feldman, who initiated the Minority Mentoring Program at the University of Massachusetts, also has served as a Hewlett Teaching Fellow and Senior Online Teaching Fellow. He initiated distance-learning courses in psychology at the University of Massachusetts.

A Fellow of the American Psychological Association, the Association for Psychological Science, and the American Association for the Advancement of Science, Professor Feldman received a BA with High Honors from Wesleyan University and an MS and PhD from the University of Wisconsin-Madison. He is a winner of a Fulbright Senior Research Scholar and Lecturer Award and the Distinguished Alumnus Award from Wesleyan. He is past President of the Federation of Associations in Behavioral and Brain Sciences (FABBS) Foundation, which advocates for the field of psychology, and is on the board of the Social Psychology Network (SPN).

He has written and edited more than 250 books, book chapters, and scientific articles. He has edited *Development of Nonverbal Behavior in Children, Applications of Nonverbal Behavioral Theory and Research*, and *Improving the First Year of College: Research and Practice*, and co-edited *Fundamentals of Nonverbal Behavior*. He is also author of *P.O.W.E.R. Learning: Strategies for Success in College and Life*. His textbooks, which have been used by more than 2 million students around the world, have been translated into Spanish, French, Portuguese, Dutch, German, Italian, Chinese, Korean, and Japanese. His research interests include deception and honesty in everyday life, work that he described in *The Liar in Your Life*, a trade book published in 2009. His research has been supported by grants from the National Institute of Mental Health and the National Institute on Disabilities and Rehabilitation Research.

Professor Feldman loves music, is an enthusiastic pianist, and enjoys cooking and traveling. He serves on the Executive Committee and Board of New England Public Radio. He and his wife, also a psychologist, live in western Massachusetts in a home overlooking the Holyoke mountain range.

Brief Contents

connect   McGraw-Hill Education Psychology APA Documentation Style Guide

Contents

CHAPTER 4

States of Consciousness 122

©Eugenio Marongiu/Shutterstock

©MJTH/Shutterstock

CHAPTER 5

Learning 160

©Eugenio Marongiu/Shutterstock

©Chris Robbins/Moodboard/Glow Images

CHAPTER 8

Motivation and Emotion 271

©Yasuyoshi Chiba/AFP/Getty Images

©Nancy Mao Smith/Shutterstock

CHAPTER 9

Development 309

©santypan/Shutterstock

©Fancy Collection/SuperStock

©Andrey_Popov/Shutterstock

CHAPTER 12

Psychological Disorders 426

©urbancow/Getty Images

©Ingram Publishing/SuperStock

©Shutterstock/Rawpixel.com

connect   McGraw-Hill Education Psychology APA Documentation Style Guide

Students—study more efficiently, retain more and achieve better outcomes. **Instructors**—focus on what you love—teaching.

SUCCESSFUL SEMESTERS INCLUDE CONNECT

FOR INSTRUCTORS

You're in the driver's seat.

Want to build your own course? No problem. Prefer to use our turnkey, prebuilt course? Easy. Want to make changes throughout the semester? Sure. And you'll save time with Connect's auto-grading too.

65%
Less Time Grading

They'll thank you for it.

Adaptive study resources like SmartBook® help your students be better prepared in less time. You can transform your class time from dull definitions to dynamic debates. Hear from your peers about the benefits of Connect at **www.mheducation.com/highered/connect**

Make it simple, make it affordable.

Connect makes it easy with seamless integration using any of the major Learning Management Systems—Blackboard®, Canvas, and D2L, among others—to let you organize your course in one convenient location. Give your students access to digital materials at a discount with our inclusive access program. Ask your McGraw-Hill representative for more information.

©Hill Street Studios/Tobin Rogers/Blend Images LLC

Solutions for your challenges.

A product isn't a solution. Real solutions are affordable, reliable, and come with training and ongoing support when you need it and how you want it. Our Customer Experience Group can also help you troubleshoot tech problems—although Connect's 99% uptime means you might not need to call them. See for yourself at **status.mheducation.com**

Effective, efficient studying.

Connect helps you be more productive with your study time and get better grades using tools like SmartBook, which highlights key concepts and creates a personalized study plan. Connect sets you up for success, so you walk into class with confidence and walk out with better grades.

©Shutterstock/wavebreakmedia

"I really liked this app—it made it easy to study when you don't have your text-book in front of you."

- Jordan Cunningham,
Eastern Washington University

Study anytime, anywhere.

Download the free ReadAnywhere app and access your online eBook when it's convenient, even if you're offline. And since the app automatically syncs with your eBook in Connect, all of your notes are available every time you open it. Find out more at **www.mheducation.com/readanywhere**

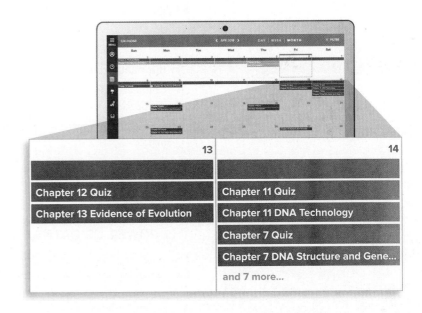

No surprises.

The Connect Calendar and Reports tools keep you on track with the work you need to get done and your assignment scores. Life gets busy; Connect tools help you keep learning through it all.

13	14
Chapter 12 Quiz	Chapter 11 Quiz
Chapter 13 Evidence of Evolution	Chapter 11 DNA Technology
	Chapter 7 Quiz
	Chapter 7 DNA Structure and Gene...
	and 7 more...

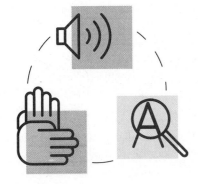

Learning for everyone.

McGraw-Hill works directly with Accessibility Services Departments and faculty to meet the learning needs of all students. Please contact your Accessibility Services office and ask them to email accessibility@mheducation.com, or visit **www.mheducation.com/accessibility** for more information.

Preface

Students First

If I were to use only two words to summarize my goal across the 13 editions of this introduction to psychology, as well as my teaching philosophy, that's what I would say: Students first.

I believe that an effective introduction to a discipline must be oriented to students–informing them, engaging them, and exciting them about the field and helping them connect it to their worlds. To achieve these goals, *Essentials of Understanding Psychology*, 13/e, includes these features:

A PERSONALIZED EXPERIENCE THAT LEADS TO IMPROVED LEARNING AND RESULTS

How many students *think* they know everything about introductory psychology, but struggle on the first exam?

Students study more effectively with Connect and SmartBook.

- SmartBook helps students study more efficiently by highlighting where in the chapter to focus, asking review questions and pointing them to resources until they understand.

- Connect's assignments help students contextualize what they've learned through application, so they can better understand the material and think critically.

- Connect will create a personalized study path customized to individual student needs.

- Connect reports deliver information regarding performance, study behavior, and effort. So instructors can quickly identify students who are having issues, or focus on material that the class hasn't mastered.

THE POWER OF DATA

Essentials of Understanding Psychology harnesses the power of data to improve the instructor and student experiences.

Better Data, Smarter Revision, Improved Results For this new edition, data were analyzed to identify the concepts students found to be the most difficult, allowing for expansion upon the discussion, practice, and assessment of challenging topics. The revision process for a new edition used to begin with gathering information from instructors about what they would change and what they would keep. Experts in the field were asked to provide comments that pointed out new material to add and dated material to review. Using all these reviews, authors would revise the material. But now, a new tool has revolutionized that model.

McGraw-Hill Education authors now have access to student performance data to analyze and to inform their revisions. This data is anonymously collected from the many students who use SmartBook, the adaptive learning system that provides students with individualized assessment of their own progress. Because virtually every text

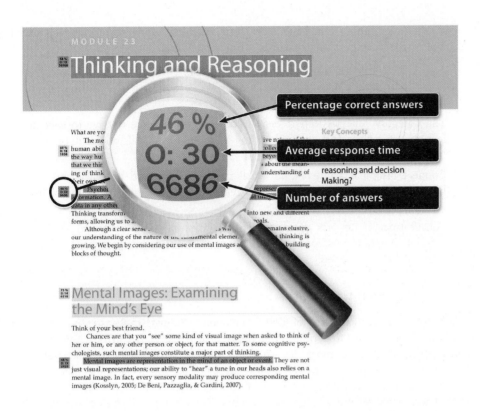

paragraph is tied to several questions that students answer while using the SmartBook, the specific concepts with which students are having the most difficulty are easily pinpointed through empirical data in the form of a "Heat Map" report.

The Power of Student Data

Step 1.

Over the course of 2 years, data points showing concepts that caused students the most difficulty were anonymously collected from SmartBook for *Essentials of Understanding Psychology, 12e.*

Step 2.

The data was provided to the author in the form of a *Heat Map,* which graphically illustrated "hot spots" in the text that impacted student learning.

Step 3.

The author used the *Heat Map* data to refine the content and reinforce student comprehension in the new edition. Additional quiz questions and assignable activities were created for use in Connect Psychology to further support student success.

4. RESULT:

Because the *Heat Map* provided empirically based feedback at the paragraph and even sentence level, the author was able to develop the new edition using precise student data that pinpointed concepts that caused students the most difficulty.

POWERFUL REPORTING

Whether a class is face-to-face, hybrid, or entirely online, Connect provides the tools needed to reduce the amount of time and energy that instructors must spend to administer their courses. Easy-to-use course management tools allow instructors to spend less time administering and more time teaching, while reports allow students to monitor their progress and optimize study time.

- The At-Risk Student Report provides instructors with one-click access to a dashboard that identifies students who are at risk of dropping out of the course due to low engagement levels.
- The Category Analysis Report details student performance relative to specific learning objectives and goals, including APA Learning Goals and Outcomes and levels of Bloom's taxonomy.
- Connect Insight is a one-of-kind visual analytics dashboard–now available for both instructors and students–that provides at-a-glance information regarding student performance.
- The LearnSmart Reports allow instructors and students to easily monitor progress and pinpoint areas of weakness, giving each student a personalized study plan to achieve success.

STUDENT CRITICAL THINKING SKILLS

At the apply and analyze levels of Bloom's taxonomy, **Scientific Reasoning Activities** found in Connect offer in-depth arguments to sharpen students' critical thinking skills and prepare them to be more discerning consumers of psychology in their everyday lives. For each chapter, there are multiple sets of arguments accompanied by auto-graded assessments requiring students to think critically about claims presented as facts. These exercises can also be used in Connect as group activities or for discussion.

New to the 13th edition, **Power of Process,** now available in McGraw-Hill Connect™, guides students through the process of critical reading, analysis, and writing. Faculty can select or upload their own content, such as journal articles, and assign analysis strategies to gain insight into students' application of the scientific method. For students, Power of Process offers a guided visual approach to exercising critical thinking strategies to apply before, during, and after reading published research. Additionally, utilizing the relevant and engaging research articles built into Power of Process, students are supported in becoming critical consumers of research.

STUDENT ACTIVE ENGAGEMENT

Concept Clips help students comprehend some of the most difficult ideas in introductory psychology. Colorful graphics and stimulating animations describe core concepts in a step-by-step manner, engaging students and aiding in retention. Concept Clips can be used as a presentation tool in the classroom or for student assessment. New in the 13th edition, Concept Clips are embedded in the ebook to offer an alternative presentation of these challenging topics.

Interactivities, assignable through Connect, engage students with content through experiential activities. New and updated activities include: Perspectives in Psychology; Correlations; Neurons; The Brain and Drugs; The Stages of Sleep; Levels of Processing; Maslow's Hierarchy of Needs; Naturalistic Observation; Observational Learning; Defense Mechanisms; Stereotypes and Prejudice; Heuristics; Personality Assessment; and First Impressions and Attraction.

Through the connection of psychology to students' own lives, concepts become more relevant and understandable. Powered by McGraw-Hill Education's Connect Psychology, **NewsFlash** exercises tie current news stories to key psychological principles and learning objectives. After interacting with a contemporary news story, students are assessed on their ability to make the link between real life and research findings.

Psychology at Work videos, assignable and assessable within McGraw-Hill Connect™, highlight nine careers in which knowledge of psychology is beneficial in the workplace. Each video introduces a person at work, who specifies how knowledge gained from taking introductory psychology in college is applied to the work environment.

Student Tools: Mastering the Material

Student success in psychology means mastering the material at a deep level. These are some of the tools that help students maximize their performance:

STUDY ALERTS

Throughout, marginal notes point out important and difficult concepts and topics. These Study Alerts offer suggestions for learning the material effectively and for studying for tests.

FROM THE PERSPECTIVE OF . . .

Every chapter includes questions to help students connect psychological concepts with career realities. Called "From the Perspective of . . .," this feature helps students understand how psychology relates to various career fields.

Study Alert
Differentiate the stages of sleep (stage 1, stage 2, stage 3, and REM sleep), which produce different brain-wave patterns.

From the perspective of . . .

An Educator How might you use the findings in sleep research to maximize student learning?

©Andersen Ross/Blend Images/Getty Images

NEUROSCIENCE IN YOUR LIFE

This updated feature emphasizes the importance of neuroscientific research within the various subfields of the discipline and in students' lives. Representative brain scans, with both caption and textual explanation, illustrate significant neuroscientific findings that increasingly influence the field of psychology. For example, one *Neuroscience in Your Life* feature explains why people are so emotional when they don't get enough sleep

NEUROSCIENCE IN YOUR LIFE: WHY ARE WE SO EMOTIONAL WHEN WE DON'T GET ENOUGH SLEEP?

After a restless night, many people feel increased stress and overreact to events in their lives the next day. Recent research has now identified the neural basis for these reactions. For example, in one study, participants were kept awake all night and then asked to perform an experiment involving exposure to emotional and neutral images. Participants who were sleep deprived reacted to the neutral images as if they were emotional, and they had less connectivity between the amygdala (a region of the brain that processes emotion) and the anterior cingulate cortex (a region of frontal cortex important for emotional regulation). The green in the scan below shows the area of anterior cingulate that has greater connectivity to the amygdala for sleep-rested than sleep-deprived participants. These findings suggest that sleep loss increases emotional reactivity by interfering with our ability to control our emotions (Simon et al., 2015).

Left

Student Learning: Content and Concepts

A major change in this new edition is an increased commitment to covering diversity. A new concluding module called "Epilogue: Diversity, Culture, Conflict, and Cooperation" addresses questions of how diversity affects individual behavior, how we observe and understand other people, and how our understandings (and misunderstandings) of our differences can lead to cooperation and/or conflict. Beyond the Epilogue, every chapter has a section called "Exploring Diversity," which examines how diversity affects psychology and vice-versa. These sections address ways to incorporate the concepts of diversity and culture across the curriculum as well as ways we can interact more effectively in this country and the world. In addition, the following information about new and revised topics and textual changes, including new definitions based on heat map data, provides a good indication of the content's currency and clarification for students.

Chapter 1-Introduction

- Added new figure on where psychologists work
- Clarified introspection
- Redefined structuralism
- Expanded graphical timeline on developments in psychology
- Discussed discrepancy in salary and prestige between male and female psychologists
- Clarified definition of theory
- Clarified experimental manipulation
- Added new Neuroscience and Your Life feature

Chapter 2-Neuroscience and Behavior

- Explained hydrogel-embedding methods of brain scanning
- Added new information on using computers to assist movement in quadriplegics
- Added research on cortical thickness and student income level differences
- Clarified definition of dendrite
- Redefined terminal button
- Clarified process of neurotransmission
- Redefined neurotransmitter
- Added new definition of reuptake
- Clarified acetylcholine description
- Clarified description of motor neurons
- Clarified transcranial magnetic stimulation
- Clarified reticular formation
- Added new definition of neuroplasticity
- Reorganized description of lateralization of hemispheres of brain
- Added information on brain-computer interface

Chapter 3 Sensation and Perception

- Clarified description of light waves
- Clarified feature detection and specialization of receptors of visual information

- Clarified afterimage implications for trichromatic theory
- Clarified place theory of hearing
- Clarified auditory neurons specialization
- Defined reflex sympathetic dystrophy syndrome
- Clarified gate-control theory
- Clarified biofeedback as a means to control pain
- Clarified synesthesia
- Redefined motion parallax
- Updated information on cognitive factors in pain perception
- Added feature on use of dogs' sensory capabilities for detection
- Enhanced discussion of echolocation
- Updated statistics on chronic pain
- Introduced new synesthesia cases
- Inner speech and daydreaming

Chapter 4-States of Consciousness

- Included information on the opioid epidemic
- Added new figure for sleep needs by age
- Discussed reverse learning and synaptic pruning as function of sleep
- Clarified definition of nightmares
- Added information on frequency of nightmares
- Changed stages of sleep from four to three, reflecting American Academy of Sleep Medicine change
- Clarified experience of waking consciousness while daydreaming
- Clarified changes in electrical activity during hypnosis
- Clarified controversy regarding nature of hypnosis
- Clarified use of hypnosis in pain relief
- Discussed long-term effects of meditation on heart disease
- Clarified psychologists' motivation for studying consciousness

- Added example of opioid addict whose addiction started with Percocet
- Clarified reasons for increase in death due to opioid overdoses
- Clarified difference between opioids and opiates
- Clarified reasons why people seek out drug highs
- Discussed Adderall use by college students
- Added new figure on drug use
- Clarified use of cocaine and crack
- Clarified definition of hallucinogens
- Discussed expanded legalization of marijuana
- Clarified MDMA use

Chapter 5-Learning

- Added feature on use of learning principles by Uber and Lyft
- Added new prologue on training dogs for medical purposes
- Clarified classical conditioning figure
- Clarified neutral stimulus
- Clarified description of classical conditioning
- Clarified stimulus generalization definition
- Redefined operant conditioning
- Redefined schedule of reinforcement
- Clarified continuous and partial reinforcement schedules
- Redefined variable-ratio schedule
- Clarified results of exposure to media aggression
- Noted that behavior modification can help students study more effectively
- Added APA task force findings on violent video game play

Chapter 6-Memory

- Discussed highly superior auto-biographical memory (HSAM)
- Added information on the meaning of memories

- Enhanced discussion of false memories
- Clarified sensory memory explanation
- Redefined chunk
- Clarified explanation of chunk
- Redefined mnemonics
- Clarified description of memory stores in working memory
- Clarified procedural memory
- Added implicit memory term
- Clarified description of engram
- Clarified flashbulb memory description
- Clarified similarities and differences between cultures in memory
- Clarified relearning and importance of practice
- Refined description of keyword technique
- Explained the value of forgetting regarding relearning
- Explained conditions under which eyewitness memories are accurate

Chapter 7–Thinking, Language, and Intelligence

- Added information on the value of video gaming for cognitive skills
- Included new definition of reasoning
- Redefined familiarity heuristic, with new example
- Clarified how we represent problems to ourselves
- New examples of enhancing insight in humans
- Clarified definition of functional fixedness
- Removed term mental set
- Redefined divergent thinking
- Redefined cognitive complexity
- Added new definition of convergent thinking
- Clarified telegraphic speech
- Clarified overgeneralization
- Added new contrary evidence to nativist approach
- Clarified definition of interactionist approaches to language development
- Clarified linguistic-relativity hypothesis
- Added new statistics on multilingual students
- Discussed behavioral economics
- Changes in creativity with aging
- Redefined fluid intelligence
- Redefined crystallized intelligence

- Added new definition of reliability
- Added new definition of validity
- Added new definition of familial intellectual disability
- Redefined intellectual disability

Chapter 8–Motivation and Emotion

- Added feature regarding research on biggest losers' inability to maintain weight loss
- Added new prologue on excessive weight loss and social media
- Clarification of Maslow's view of esteem
- Clarified self-determination theory
- Added new definition of need for achievement
- Clarified James-Lange theory of emotions
- Clarified Schachter-Singer theory of emotions
- Updated description of facial-affect program
- Discussed increase in obesity across the globe
- Clarified use of gay and lesbian labels
- Clarified biological and genetic causes of sexual orientation
- Redefined transgender
- Clarified distinction between transgender and intersex persons

Chapter 9–Development

- Discussed use of mitochondria in IVF
- Clarified vision capabilities of neonates
- Clarified the benefits of play
- Clarified Erikson's trust-versus mistrust stage
- Clarified Erikson's autonomy-versus-shame-and-doubt stage
- Clarified Erikson's industry-versus-inferiority stage
- Clarified information-processing approach
- Clarified Vygotsky's view of cognitive development
- Changed presentation of scaffolding
- Clarified presentation of puberty
- Clarified discussion of spermarche
- Clarified Kohlberg's Level 2 morality
- Clarified Kohlberg's Level 3 morality
- Clarified adolescence as a period of relative tranquility
- Redefined personal fables
- Clarified discussion of culture-specific rites of passage
- Clarified emerging adulthood

- Redefined genetic programming theories of aging
- Added new statistics on Alzheimer's disease
- Added new research on slowing the declines of Alzheimer's disease
- Added new statistics on Facebook use by adolescents
- Discussed cyberbullying as a cause of suicide

Chapter 10–Personality

- Added new prologue on Lance Armstrong case
- Discussed stability of personality across generations
- Redefined ego
- Clarified discussion of ego's mediating role
- Clarified discussion of Freud's Oedipal conflict in boys and girls
- Added specificity to influence of psychoanalytic theory
- Added new definition of inferiority complex
- Redefined Allport cardinal trait
- Redefined Allport central trait
- Refined definition of factor analysis
- Clarified criticisms of trait theory
- Clarified distinction between psychodynamic, trait, and learning theories
- Clarified relationship harmony concept
- Clarified temporary reductions in self esteem
- Clarified research studies on twins separated early in life
- Clarified Rogers' notion of self-concept
- Replaced term norm with test norm
- Added new definition of test norm
- Added new definition of projective test
- Clarified projective test criticisms

Chapter 11–Health Psychology: Stress, Coping, and Well-Being

- Added concept of posttraumatic growth
- Added feature on training physicians to convey bad news effectively
- Added data on Facebook as a source of negative health outcomes
- Updated medical error death statistics
- Discussed nontraditional forms of PTSD for combat veterans

- Discussed eHealth communication
- Added statistics on e-cigarette use statistics
- Added discussion on how e-cigarette use can make it easier to quit traditional cigarette smoking
- Discussed link between social relationships and health
- Clarified biological and psychological consequences of stress
- Clarified critique of general adaption syndrome
- Clarified effects of stress on lymphocytes
- Clarified techniques for coping with stress
- Included data on incidence of smoking and disease, among whites versus African Americans
- Clarified social causes of smoking
- Discussed relationship between poverty and sadness
- Added information on buying time savers leads to greater happiness than buying goods
- Added new figure on smoking incidence

Chapter 12-Psychological Disorders

- Added new case study of woman with anxiety disorder
- Added references to magic, spells as explanations for abnormal behavior
- Added feature on increase in self-reported psychological disorders
- Removed explication of historical change in DSM
- Discussed epigenetic approaches to schizophrenia
- Discussed relationship between homelessness and psychological disorders
- Added new statistics on mentally ill homeless population
- Clarified deviation from typical definition of abnormality
- Clarified deviation from an ideal definition of abnormality
- Clarified discussion of insanity
- Explicitly defined abnormal behavior
- Clarified importance of neurological basis of psychological disorders
- Clarified criticisms of psychoanalytic theory
- Added new example of rationality of negative emotions regarding cognitive perspectives

- Clarified discussion of the humanistic perspective
- Added new definition of sociocultural perspective
- Clarified the atheoretical, descriptive approach of DSM
- Clarified lack of objective danger in phobic stimuli
- Redefined compulsion
- Clarified definition of illness anxiety disorder
- Clarified discussion of dissociative identity disorder
- Redefined mood disorder
- Clarified causes of gender differences in depression in women
- Clarified label and explanation of internal unconscious conflicts as a cause of depression
- Changed "inappropriate emotional displays" to "inappropriate emotions" in discussion of schizophrenia
- Added explanation of action of glutamate in treating schizophrenia
- Added material on genes responsible for schizophrenia
- Discussed gray matter differences in brains of people with schizophrenia
- Clarified and qualified psychoanalytic explanations of schizophrenia
- Clarified the predispositional model schizophrenia
- Clarified lack of distress for those with personality disorders
- Clarified explanation of borderline personality disorder
- Redefined neurocognitive disorders
- Clarified statistics on prevalence of psychological disorders
- Condensed and clarified discussion of cross-cultural influences on definitions of abnormal behavior

Chapter 13-Treatment of Psychological Disorders

- Redefined psychotherapy
- Redefined biomedical therapy
- Reframed discussion of psychodynamic therapies (versus psychoanalysis)
- Redefined psychoanalysis
- Clarified free association
- Redefined behavioral approaches to therapy
- Clarified aversive therapy
- Revised discussion of aversion therapy
- Clarified definition of systematic desensitization

- Revised discussion of contingency contracting
- Added new definition of observational learning
- Reframed discussion of behavioral techniques
- Expanded definition of unconditional positive regard
- Clarified discussion of contemporary versions of client-center therapy
- Revised discussion of interpersonal therapy effectiveness
- Revised discussion of the goals of family therapy
- Clarified definition of self-help therapy
- Clarified discussion of effectiveness of therapy in general versus specific kinds of therapy
- Added new case study on use of DBS
- Discussed use of online therapy
- Reframed distinction between biomedical approaches and other treatments
- Updated definition of drug therapy
- Clarified inhibition of neurotransmitter transmission
- Discussed virtual reality exposure therapy
- Added psychotherapy to biomedical treatments for schizophrenia
- Added discussion of brain scan neurofeedback for treatment
- Clarified prefrontal lobotomy discussion
- Clarified drawbacks to biomedical therapies
- Revised definition of deinstitutionalization
- Added material on drug treatments that is more explicitly linked to neuroscience chapter
- Discussed cognitive appraisal retraining on academic tasks
- Added information on memory deficits as side effect of antidepressant drugs
- Referenced Satir's family therapy work

Chapter 14-Social Psychology

- Added new prologue on Dylann Roof in South Carolina
- Discussed mentoring approaches to reducing self-stereotyping
- Clarified description of warm-cold person perception experiment

- Clarified example of fundamental attribution error
- Redefined norms
- Clarified description of foot-in-the-door technique
- Clarified door-in-the-face technique
- Clarified effect of proximity on liking

- Clarified mere exposure effect
- Clarified effect of similarity on liking
- Clarified relationship between physical attractiveness and ageneral attraction
- Clarified frustration-aggression approaches

- Clarified diffusion of responsibility explanations of helping
- Added information on global warming and aggression
- Added research on microaggression

Supporting Instructors with Technology

With McGraw-Hill Education, you can develop and tailor the course you want to teach.

McGraw-Hill Campus (www.mhcampus.com) provides faculty with true single sign-on access to all of McGraw-Hill's course content, digital tools, and other high-quality learning resources from any learning management system. McGraw-Hill Campus includes access to McGraw-Hill's entire content library, including e-books, assessment tools, presentation slides, and multimedia content, among other resources, providing faculty open, unlimited access to prepare for class, create tests or quizzes, develop lecture material, integrate interactive content, and more.

With **Tegrity,** you can capture lessons and lectures in a searchable format and use them in traditional, hybrid, "flipped classes," and online courses. With Tegrity's personalized learning features, you can make study time efficient. Its ability to affordably scale brings this benefit to every student on campus. Patented search technology and real-time learning management system (LMS) integrations make Tegrity the market-leading solution and service.

Easily rearrange chapters, combine material from other content sources, and quickly upload content you have written, such as your course syllabus or teaching notes, using McGraw-Hill Education's **Create.** Find the content you need by searching through thousands of leading McGraw-Hill Education textbooks. Arrange your book to fit your teaching style. Create even allows you to personalize your book's appearance by selecting the cover and adding your name, school, and course information. Order a Create book, and you will receive a complimentary print review copy in 3 to 5 business days or a complimentary electronic review copy via email in about an hour. Experience how McGraw-Hill Education empowers you to teach *your* students *your* way: http://create.mheducation.com.

TRUSTED SERVICE AND SUPPORT

McGraw-Hill Education's Connect offers comprehensive service, support, and training throughout every phase of your implementation. If you're looking for some guidance on how to use Connect or want to learn tips and tricks from super users, you can find tutorials as you work. Our Digital Faculty Consultants and Student Ambassadors offer insight into how to achieve the results you want with Connect.

INTEGRATION WITH YOUR LEARNING MANAGEMENT SYSTEM

McGraw-Hill integrates your digital products from McGraw-Hill Education with your school learning management system (LMS) for quick and easy access to best-in-class content and learning tools. Build an effective digital course, enroll students with ease, and discover how powerful digital teaching can be.

Available with Connect, integration is a pairing between an institution's LMS and Connect at the assignment level. It shares assignment information, grades and calendar items from Connect into the LMS automatically, creating an easy-to-manage course for instructors and simple navigation for students. Our assignment-level integration is available with **Blackboard Learn**, **Canvas by Instructure,** and **Brightspace by D2L,** giving you access to registration, attendance, assignments, grades, and course resources in real time, in one location.

INSTRUCTOR SUPPLEMENTS

Instructor's Manual The instructor's manual provides a wide variety of tools and resources for presenting the course, including learning objectives and ideas for lectures and discussions.

Test Bank By increasing the rigor of the test bank development process, McGraw-Hill Education has raised the bar for student assessment. A coordinated team of subject-matter experts methodically vetted each question and set of possible answers for accuracy, clarity, effectiveness, and accessibility; each question has been annotated for level of difficulty, Bloom's taxonomy, APA learning outcomes, and corresponding coverage in the text. Organized by chapter, the questions are designed to test factual, conceptual, and applied understanding. All test questions are available within TestGen™ software and as Word documents.

PowerPoint Presentations The PowerPoint presentations, available in both dynamic, lecture-ready and accessible, WCAG-compliant versions, highlight the key points of the chapter and include supporting visuals. All of the slides can be modified to meet individual needs.

Image Gallery The Image Gallery features the complete set of downloadable figures and tables from the text. These can be easily embedded by instructors into their own PowerPoint slides.

Acknowledgments

One of the central features of *Understanding Psychology* is the involvement of professionals as well as students in the review process. The 13th edition of *Essentials of Understanding Psychology* has relied heavily–and benefited substantially–from the advice of instructors and students from a wide range of backgrounds.

Many teachers along my educational path have shaped my thinking. I was introduced to psychology at Wesleyan University, where several committed and inspiring teachers–and in particular, Karl Scheibe–conveyed their sense of excitement about the field and made its relevance clear to me. Karl epitomizes the teacher-scholar combination to which I aspire, and I continue to marvel at my good fortune in having such a role model.

By the time I left Wesleyan, I could envision no other career but that of psychologist. Although the nature of the University of Wisconsin, where I did my graduate work, could not have been more different from the much smaller Wesleyan, the excitement and inspiration were similar. Again, a cadre of excellent teachers–led, especially, by the late Vernon Allen–molded my thinking and taught me to appreciate the beauty and science of the discipline of psychology.

My colleagues and students at the University of Massachusetts Amherst provide ongoing intellectual stimulation, and I thank them for making the university a fine place to work. Several people also provided extraordinary research and editorial help. In particular, I am especially grateful to my superb students, past and present, including Erik Coats, Ben Happ, Sara Levine, Chris Poirier, Jim Tyler, and Matt Zimbler. John Bickford, in particular, provided invaluable editorial input that has enhanced the content considerably. Finally, I am grateful to John Graiff and Michelle Goncalves, whose hard work and dedication helped immeasurably on just about everything involving this material.

I am also grateful to Erika Nyhus of Bowdoin College, who provided exceptional support in helping identify appropriate neuroscientific research to include in the *Neuroscience in Your Life* features. I thank her for her fine work.

I offer great thanks to the McGraw-Hill Education editorial and marketing teams that participated in this new edition. Vice President and General Manager Mike Ryan and Senior Portfolio Manager Nancy Welcher foster a creative, energetic, and environment. I am in awe of their enthusiasm, commitment, and never-ending good ideas. I also thank my award-winning Marketing Managers AJ Laferrera and Ann Helgerson for their enthusiasm and commitment to this project and for being so great to work with. I'm also happy that the indefatigable, inventive Cory Reeves provided input about all sorts of things, and I especially thank him for his mentorship in the realm of all things musical. I thank these folks not only for their superb professionalism, but also for their friendship.

I am very grateful to Susan Messer, product developer on this edition. Susan did a superb job of managing a myriad of details (as well as me), bringing motivation, intelligence, and a fine literary sense to the project. Finally, every reader of this book owes a debt to Rhona Robbin and Judith Kromm, developmental editors on earlier editions of *Understanding Psychology*. Their relentless pursuit of excellence helped form the essence of this book, and they taught me a great deal about the craft and art of writing. Central to the design, production, and marketing process were Program Manager Kelly Heinrichs, Text Content Licensing Specialist Melisa Seegmiller, Image Content Licensing Specialist Shawntel Schmitt, and Designer David Hash, as well as Marilynn Taylor and Mary Powers, key members of the production group. I am proud to be a part of this world-class McGraw-Hill team.

Finally, I remain completely indebted to my family. My parents, Leah Brochstein and Saul Feldman, provided a lifetime foundation of love and support, and I continue to see their influence in every corner of my life. My extended family also plays a central role in my life. They include, more or less in order of age, my nieces and nephews, my terrific brother, my brothers- and sisters-in-law, and the late Ethel Radler. My mother-in-law, the late Mary Evans Vorwerk, had an important influence on this book, and I remain ever grateful to her.

Ultimately, my children, Jonathan, Joshua, and Sarah; my daughters-in-law Leigh and Julie; my son-in-law Jeffrey; my grandsons Alex and Miles; my granddaughters Naomi and Lilia; and my wife, Katherine, remain the focal points of my life. I thank them, with immense love, and thank my lucky stars that they are in my life.

Robert S. Feldman
Amherst, Massachusetts

Making the Grade: A Practical Guide to Smarter Studying

No matter why you are taking introductory psychology, it's a safe bet you're interested in maximizing your understanding of the material and getting a good grade. And you want to accomplish these goals as quickly and efficiently as possible.

Good news: Several subfields of psychology have identified different ways to help you learn and remember material you will study throughout college. Here's my guarantee to you: If you learn and follow the guidelines in each of these areas, you'll become a better student and get better grades. Always remember that *good students are made, not born*.

Adopt a General Study Strategy: Using the Power Framework

Psychologists have devised several excellent techniques to improve study skills. One of the best, based on a substantial body of research, is "P.O.W.E.R." or *P*repare, *O*rganize, *W*ork, *E*valuate, and *R*ethink

P.O.W.E.R. system entails the following steps:

- **Prepare.** In *Essentials of Understanding Psychology*, 13th Edition, read the broad questions called *Learning Outcomes* to *Prepare* yourself for the material that follows. *Learning Outcomes* are at the start of each chapter and each module.

- **Organize.** The *Organize* stage involves developing a mental roadmap of where you are headed. *Essentials of Understanding Psychology* includes an outline at the beginning of each chapter. Read it to get an idea of what topics are covered and how they are organized.

- **Work.** Because of your effort in the *Power* and *Organize* stages, the *Work* stage will be easier. You know what questions the material will answer based on the *Learning Outcomes*, and you know how it is organized based on the outline. Read everything in the content, including the material in boxes and the margins, to fully understand the material.

- **Evaluate.** *Evaluate* provides the opportunity to determine how effectively you have mastered the material. In *Essentials of Understanding Psychology*, questions at the end of each module offer a rapid check of your understanding of the material. *Evaluate* your progress to assess your degree of mastery.

- **Rethink.** This final stage, *Rethink*, entails reanalyzing, reviewing, questioning, and challenging assumptions. Rethinking allows you to consider how the material fits with other information you have already learned. Every major section of *Essentials of Understanding Psychology* ends with a *Rethink* section. Answering its thought-provoking questions will help you think about the material at a deeper level.

©Comstock/PunchStock

Using the P.O.W.E.R. framework will help you maximize the efficiency and effectiveness of your study. In addition, the P.O.W.E.R. framework can be applied beyond the classroom, helping you to achieve success in your career and life.

Manage Your Time

Managing your time as you study is a central aspect of academic success. But remember: The goal of time management is to permit us to make informed choices about how we use our time. Use these time management procedures to harness time for your own advantage.

SET YOUR PRIORITIES. First, determine your priorities. *Priorities* are the tasks and activities you need and want to do, rank-ordered from most important to least important.

The best procedure is to start off by identifying priorities for an entire term. What do you need to accomplish? Rather than making these goals too general, make them specific, such as, "studying 10 hours before each chemistry exam."

IDENTIFY YOUR PRIME TIME. Are you a morning person or do you prefer studying later at night? Being aware of the time or times of day when you can do your best work will help you plan and schedule your time most effectively.

MASTER THE MOMENT. Here's what you'll need to organize your time:

- A *master calendar* that shows all the weeks of the term on one page. It should include every week of the term and seven days per week. On the master calendar, note the due date of every assignment and test you will have. Also include important activities from your personal life, drawn from your list of priorities. Add some free time for yourself.

- A *weekly timetable* that shows the days of the week across the top and the hours, from 6:00 A.M. to midnight, along the side. Fill in the times of all your fixed, prescheduled activities—the times that your classes meet, when you have to be at work, the times you have to pick up your child at day care, and any other recurring appointments. Add assignment due dates, tests, and any other activities on the appropriate days of the week. Then add blocks of time necessary to prepare for those events.

- A *daily to-do list* using a small calendar or your smartphone. List all the things that you intend to do during the day and their priority. Start with the things you *must* do and that have fixed times, such as classes and work schedules. Then add in the other things that you *should* accomplish, such as researching an upcoming paper or finishing a lab report. Finally, list things that are a low priority, such as taking in a new movie.

CONTROL YOUR TIME. If you follow the schedules that you've prepared, you've taken the most important steps in time management. Things, however, always seem to take longer than planned.

When inevitable surprises occur, there are several ways to take control of your days to follow your intended schedule:

- **Say no.** You don't have to agree to every favor that others ask of you.
- **Get away from it all.** Adopt a specific spot to call your own, such as a corner desk in a secluded nook in the library. If you use it enough, your body and mind will automatically get into study mode as soon as you get there.

©Stockbyte/Getty Images

- **Enjoy the sounds of silence.** Studies suggest that we are able to concentrate most when our environment is silent. Experiment and work in silence for a few days. You may find that you get more done in less time than you would in a more distracting environment.
- **Take an e-break.** Take an e-break and shut down your communication sources for some period of time. Phone calls, text messages, IMs, and e-mail can be saved on a phone or computer. They'll wait.
- **Expect the unexpected.** You'll never be able to escape from unexpected interruptions and surprises that require your attention. But by trying to anticipate them and thinking about how you'll react to them, you can position yourself to react effectively when they do occur.

Take Good Notes in Class

Let's consider some of the basic principles of notetaking:

- **Identify the instructor's–and your–goals for the course.** The information you get during the first day of class and through the syllabus is critical. In addition to the instructor's goals, you should have your own. How will the information from the course help you to enhance your knowledge, improve yourself as a person, achieve your goals?
- **Complete assignments before coming to class.**
- **Listen for the key ideas.** Listen for such phrases as "you need to know . . . ," "the most important thing to consider . . . ," "there are four problems with this approach . . . ," and–a big one–"this will be on the test . . . "; phrases like these should cause you to sit up and take notice. Also, if an instructor says the same thing in several ways, the material being discussed is important.
- **Use short, abbreviated phrases–not full sentences–when taking notes.**
- **Pay attention to PowerPoint slides or what is displayed in class on overhead projectors, whiteboards, or chalk boards. Remember these tips:**
  - Listening is more important than seeing.
  - Don't copy everything that is on every slide.
  - Remember that key points on slides are . . . key points.
  - Check to see if the presentation slides are available online.
  - Remember that presentation slides are not the same as good notes for a class.

Memorize Efficiently

Here's a key principle of effective memorization: Memorize what you need to memorize. *Forget about the rest.*

You have your choice of dozens of techniques of memorization. Also, feel free to devise your own strategies or add those that have worked for you in the past.

REHEARSAL. Say it aloud: rehearsal. Think of this word in terms of its three syllables: re–hear–sal. If you're scratching your head about why you should do this, it's to illustrate the point of *rehearsal:* to transfer material that you encounter into long-term memory.

MNEMONICS. This odd word (pronounced with the "m" silent–"neh MON ix") describes formal techniques used to make material more readily remembered.

©Photodisc/PunchStock

Among the most common mnemonics are the following:

- **Acronyms.** *Acronyms* are words or phrases formed by the first letters of a series of terms.

    For example, Roy G. Biv helps people to remember the colors of the spectrum (red, orange, yellow, green, blue, indigo, and violet).

- **Acrostics.** *Acrostics* are sentences in which the first letters spell out something that needs to be recalled. The benefits of acrostics are similar to those of acronyms.

- **Rhymes and jingles.** "Thirty days hath September, April, June, and November." If you know the rest of the rhyme, you're familiar with one of the most commonly used mnemonic jingles in the English language.

USE OF MULTIPLE SENSES. Every time we encounter new information, all of our senses are potentially at work. Each piece of sensory information is stored in a separate location in the brain, and yet all the pieces are linked in extraordinarily intricate ways.

- **When you learn something, use your body.** Move around. Stand up; sit down. Touch the page. Trace figures with your fingers. Talk to yourself. Think out loud. By involving every part of your body, you've increased the number of potential ways to trigger a relevant memory later, when you need to recall it.

- **Draw and diagram the material.** Structuring written material by graphically grouping and connecting key ideas and themes is a powerful technique. Creating drawings, sketches, and even cartoons can help us remember better.

- **Visualize.** Visualization is effective because it helps make abstract ideas concrete; it engages multiple senses; it permits us to link different bits of information together; and it provides us with a context for storing information.

- **Overlearning.** *Overlearning* consists of studying and rehearsing material past the point of initial mastery. Through overlearning, you can recall the information without even thinking about it.

©Stockbyte/Getty Images

Study for Tests Strategically

Here are some guidelines that can help you do your best on tests:

KNOW WHAT YOU ARE PREPARING FOR. To find out about an upcoming test, ask if it is a "test," an "exam," a "quiz," or something else. These names imply different things. In addition, each kind of test question requires a somewhat different style of preparation.

- **Essay questions.** The best approach to studying for an essay test involves four steps:

    1. Reread your class notes and any notes you've made on assigned readings that will be covered on the upcoming exam. Also go through the readings themselves, reviewing underlined or highlighted material and marginal notes.

    2. Think of likely exam questions. Some instructors give lists of possible essay topics; if yours does, focus on this list and think of other possibilities.

    3. Answer each potential essay question–aloud. You can also write down the main points that any answer should cover.

4. After you've answered the questions, look at the notes and readings again. If you feel confident that you've answered specific questions adequately, check them off. If you had trouble with some questions, review that material immediately. Then repeat step 3, answering the questions again.

- **Multiple-choice, true-false, and matching questions.** Studying for multiple-choice, true-false, and matching questions requires attention to the details. Write down important facts on index cards: They're portable and available all the time, and the act of creating them helps drive the material into your memory.

- **Short-answer and fill-in questions.** Short-answer and fill-in questions are similar to essays in that they require you to recall key pieces of information, but they don't demand that you integrate or compare different types of information. Consequently, the focus of your study should be on the recall of specific, detailed information.

TEST YOURSELF. When you believe you've mastered the material, test yourself on it. You can create a test for yourself, in writing, making its form as close as possible to what you expect the actual test to be.

DEAL WITH TEST ANXIETY. What does the anticipation of a test do to you? *Test anxiety* is a temporary condition characterized by fears and concerns about test-taking. You'll never eliminate test anxiety completely, nor do you want to. A little bit of nervousness can energize us, making us more attentive and vigilant.

On the other hand, for some students, anxiety can spiral into the kind of paralyzing fear that makes their minds go blank. There are several ways to keep this from happening to you:

- *Prepare thoroughly.*
- *Take a realistic view of the test.*
- *Learn relaxation techniques.*
- *Visualize success.*

FORM A STUDY GROUP. *Study groups* can be extremely powerful tools because they help accomplish several things:

- They help members organize and structure the material to approach their studying in a systematic and logical way.
- They allow students to share different perspectives on the material.
- They make it more likely that students will not overlook any potentially important information.
- They force members to rethink the course material, explaining it in words that other group members will understand. This helps both understanding and recall of the information when it is needed on the test.
- Finally, they help motivate members to do their best. When you're part of a study group, you're no longer working just for yourself; your studying also benefits the other study group members. Not wanting to let down your classmates in a study group may encourage you to put in your best effort.

©Rubberball/Getty Images

©Andrey_Popov/Shutterstock

CHAPTER 1
Introduction to Psychology

LEARNING OUTCOMES FOR CHAPTER 1

MODULE 1

LO 1-1   What is the science of psychology?

LO 1-2   What are the major specialties in the field of psychology?

LO 1-3   Where do psychologists work?

PSYCHOLOGISTS AT WORK

The Subfields of Psychology: Psychology's Family Tree

Working at Psychology

MODULE 2

LO 2-1   What are the origins of psychology?

LO 2-2   What are the major approaches in contemporary psychology?

LO 2-3   What are psychology's key issues and controversies?

LO 2-4   What is the future of psychology likely to hold?

A SCIENCE EVOLVES: THE PAST, THE PRESENT, AND THE FUTURE

The Roots of Psychology

Today's Five Major Perspectives

Applying Psychology in the 21st Century: Psychology Matters

Psychology's Key Issues and Controversies

Psychology's Future

Neuroscience in Your Life: Enhancing Your Mind

MODULE 3

LO 3-1   What is the scientific method?

LO 3-2   What role do theories and hypotheses play in psychological research?

LO 3-3   What research methods do psychologists use?

LO 3-4   How do psychologists establish cause-and-effect relationships in research studies?

RESEARCH IN PSYCHOLOGY

The Scientific Method

Psychological Research

Descriptive Research

Experimental Research

LO 4-1 What major issues confront psychologists conducting research?

PROLOGUE *HIGH SCHOOL MASSACRE*

It started like any other school day on a balmy Wednesday at the Marjory Stoneman Douglas High School campus in Parkland, Florida. But it ended with one of the most horrific school shootings in U.S. history. By the time the shooter, 19-year-old Nikolas Cruz, finished walking the halls with a blazing AR-15 rifle, 17 students and teachers lay dead, and many others were wounded.

In the midst of this carnage, the best of humanity was also on display. Teachers and staff put their own lives at risk in an effort to shield and protect their students, in some cases dying as a result. And despite the danger, first responders rushed to help the wounded, and many students sought to comfort and aid their wounded classmates. As people all around the world expressed their grief, many joined together to work toward legal change that would make such shootings less likely.

©Matt McClain/The Washington Post via Getty Images

LOOKING *Ahead*

The Florida school massacre gives rise to a host of important psychological issues. For example, consider these questions asked by psychologists following the catastrophe:

- What motivated the shooter's rampage? Was he driven by political, social, or religious beliefs, or was he psychologically disturbed?

- What internal, biologically based changes occurred in those fleeing for their lives from the shooter?

- What memories did people have of the massacre afterward? How accurate were they?

- What will be the long-term effects of the massacre on the psychological and physical health of the survivors and witnesses?

- What are the most effective ways to help people cope with the sudden and unexpected loss of friends and loved ones?

- Could this tragedy have been prevented if the shooter had received psychological treatment?

As you'll soon see, the field of psychology addresses questions like these—and many, many more. In this chapter, we begin our examination of psychology, the different types of psychologists, and the various roles that psychologists play.

Module 1
Psychologists at Work

Psychology is the scientific study of behavior and mental processes. The simplicity of this definition is in some ways deceiving, concealing ongoing debates about how broad the scope of psychology should be. Should psychologists limit themselves to the study of outward, observable behavior? Is it possible to scientifically study thinking? Should the field encompass the study of such diverse topics as physical and mental health, perception, dreaming, and motivation? Is it appropriate to focus solely on human behavior, or should the behavior of other species be included?

Most psychologists would argue that the field should be receptive to a variety of viewpoints and approaches. Consequently, the phrase *behavior and mental processes* in the definition of psychology must be understood to mean many things: It encompasses not just what people do but also their thoughts, emotions, perceptions, reasoning processes, memories, and even the biological activities that maintain bodily functioning.

Psychologists try to describe, predict, and explain human behavior and mental processes, as well as help to change and improve the lives of people and the world in which they live. They use scientific methods to find answers that are far more valid and legitimate than those resulting from intuition and speculation, which are often inaccurate (see Figure 1).

LEARNING OUTCOMES

LO 1-1 What is the science of psychology?

LO 1-2 What are the major specialties in the field of psychology?

LO 1-3 Where do psychologists work?

psychology The scientific study of behavior and mental processes. (Module 1)

FIGURE 1 The scientific method is the basis of all psychological research and is used to find valid answers. Test your knowledge of psychology by answering these questions.
Source: Adapted from Lamal, P. A. (1979). College students' common beliefs about psychology. *Teaching of Psychology*, 6, 155–158.

Psychological Truths?
To test your knowledge of psychology, try answering the following questions:

1. Infants love their mothers primarily because their mothers fulfill their basic biological needs, such as providing food. True or false?
2. Geniuses generally have poor social adjustment. True or false?
3. The best way to ensure that a desired behavior will continue after training is completed is to reward that behavior every single time it occurs during training rather than rewarding it only periodically. True or false?
4. People with schizophrenia have at least two distinct personalities. True or false?
5. Parents should do everything they can to ensure their children have high self-esteem and a strong sense that they are highly competent. True or false?
6. Children's IQ scores have little to do with how well they do in school. True or false?
7. Frequent masturbation can lead to mental illness. True or false?
8. Once people reach old age, their leisure activities change radically. True or false?
9. Most people would refuse to give painful electric shocks to other people. True or false?
10. People who talk about suicide are unlikely to actually try to kill themselves. True or false?

Scoring: The truth about each of these items: They are all false. Based on psychological research, each of these "facts" has been proven untrue. You will learn the reasons why as we explore what psychologists have discovered about human behavior.

The Subfields of Psychology: Psychology's Family Tree

As the study of psychology has grown, it has given rise to a number of subfields (described in Figure 2). The subfields of psychology can be likened to an extended family, with assorted nieces and nephews, aunts and uncles, and cousins who, although they may not interact on a day-to-day basis, are related to one another because they share a common goal: understanding behavior. One way to identify the key subfields is to look at some of the basic questions about behavior that they address.

WHAT ARE THE BIOLOGICAL FOUNDATIONS OF BEHAVIOR?

Study Alert

The different subfields of psychology allow psychologists to explain the same behavior in multiple ways. Review Figure 2 for a summary of the subfields.

In the most fundamental sense, people are biological organisms. *Behavioral neuroscience* is the subfield of psychology that focuses on how the brain and the nervous system, as well as other biological aspects of the body, determine behavior.

Thus, neuroscientists consider how our body influences our behavior. For example, they may examine the link between specific sites in the brain and the muscular tremors of people affected by Parkinson's disease or attempt to determine how our emotions are related to physical sensations.

HOW DO PEOPLE SENSE, PERCEIVE, LEARN, AND THINK ABOUT THE WORLD?

PsychTech

We now know we cannot text and drive at the same time. Cognitive psychologists have demonstrated that it is impossible to do both without a serious and potentially deadly decline in driving ability.

If you have ever wondered why you are susceptible to optical illusions, how your body registers pain, or how to make the most of your study time, an experimental psychologist can answer your questions. *Experimental psychology* is the branch of psychology that studies the processes of sensing, perceiving, learning, and thinking about the world. (The term *experimental psychologist* is somewhat misleading: Psychologists in every specialty area use experimental techniques.)

Several subspecialties of experimental psychology have become specialties in their own right. One is *cognitive psychology*, which focuses on higher mental processes, including thinking, memory, reasoning, problem solving, judging, decision making, and language.

WHAT ARE THE SOURCES OF CHANGE AND STABILITY IN BEHAVIOR ACROSS THE LIFE SPAN?

A baby producing her first smile . . . taking his first step . . . saying her first word. These universal milestones in development are also singularly special and unique for each person. *Developmental psychology* studies how people grow and change from the moment of conception through death. *Personality psychology* focuses on the consistency in people's behavior over time and the traits that differentiate one person from another.

HOW DO PSYCHOLOGICAL FACTORS AFFECT PHYSICAL AND MENTAL HEALTH?

Frequent depression, stress, and fears that prevent people from carrying out their normal activities are topics that interest health psychologists, clinical psychologists, and counseling psychologists. *Health psychology* explores the relationship between psychological factors and physical ailments or disease. For example, health psychologists are interested in assessing how long-term stress (a psychological factor) can affect physical health and in identifying ways to promote behavior that brings about good health (Yardley & Moss-Morris, 2009; Proyer et al., 2013; Sauter & Hurell, 2017).

Subfield	Description
Behavioral genetics	*Behavioral genetics* studies the inheritance of traits related to behavior.
Behavioral neuroscience	*Behavioral neuroscience* examines the biological basis of behavior.
Clinical psychology	*Clinical psychology* deals with the study, diagnosis, and treatment of psychological disorders.
Clinical neuropsychology	*Clinical neuropsychology* unites the areas of biopsychology and clinical psychology, focusing on the relationship between biological factors and psychological disorders.
Cognitive psychology	*Cognitive psychology* focuses on the study of higher mental processes.
Counseling psychology	*Counseling psychology* focuses primarily on educational, social, and career adjustment problems.
Cross-cultural psychology	*Cross-cultural psychology* investigates the similarities and differences in psychological functioning in and across various cultures and ethnic groups.
Developmental psychology	*Developmental psychology* examines how people grow and change from the moment of conception through death.
Educational psychology	*Educational psychology* is concerned with teaching and learning processes, such as the relationship between motivation and school performance.
Environmental psychology	*Environmental psychology* considers the relationship between people and their physical environment.
Evolutionary psychology	*Evolutionary psychology* considers how behavior is influenced by our genetic inheritance from our ancestors.
Experimental psychology	*Experimental psychology* studies the processes of sensing, perceiving, learning, and thinking about the world.
Forensic psychology	*Forensic psychology* focuses on legal issues, such as determining the accuracy of witness memories.
Health psychology	*Health psychology* explores the relationship between psychological factors and physical ailments or disease.
Industrial/organizational psychology	*Industrial/organizational psychology* is concerned with the psychology of the workplace.
Personality psychology	*Personality psychology* focuses on the consistency in people's behavior over time and the traits that differentiate one person from another.
Program evaluation	*Program evaluation* focuses on assessing large-scale programs, such as the Head Start preschool program, to determine whether they are effective in meeting their goals.
Psychology of women	*Psychology of women* focuses on issues such as discrimination against women and the causes of violence against women.
School psychology	*School psychology* is devoted to counseling children in elementary and secondary schools who have academic or emotional problems.
Social psychology	*Social psychology* is the study of how people's thoughts, feelings, and actions are affected by others.
Sport psychology	*Sport psychology* applies psychology to athletic activity and exercise.

FIGURE 2 The major subfields of psychology.

Photos: (Top) ©Spencer Grant/Science Source; (Middle) ©Monkey Business Images/Shutterstock; (Bottom) ©Don Hammond/DesignPics

Clinical psychology deals with the study, diagnosis, and treatment of psychological disorders. Clinical psychologists are trained to diagnose and treat problems that range from the crises of everyday life, such as unhappiness over the breakup of a relationship, to more extreme conditions, such as profound, lingering depression. Some clinical psychologists also research and investigate issues that vary from identifying the early signs of psychological disturbance to studying the relationship between family communication patterns and psychological disorders.

Like clinical psychologists, counseling psychologists deal with people's psychological problems, but the problems they deal with are more specific. *Counseling psychology* focuses primarily on educational, social, and career adjustment problems. Almost every college has a center staffed with counseling psychologists. This is where students can get advice on the kinds of jobs they might be best suited for, on methods of studying effectively, and on strategies for resolving everyday difficulties, such as problems with roommates and concerns about a specific professor's grading practices. Many large business organizations also employ counseling psychologists to help employees with work-related problems.

HOW DO OUR SOCIAL NETWORKS AFFECT BEHAVIOR?

Our complex networks of social interrelationships are the focus for many subfields of psychology. For example, *social psychology* is the study of how people's thoughts, feelings, and actions are affected by others. Social psychologists concentrate on such diverse topics as human aggression, liking and loving, persuasion, and conformity.

Cross-cultural psychology investigates the similarities and differences in psychological functioning in and across various cultures and ethnic groups. For example, cross-cultural psychologists examine how cultures differ in their use of punishment during child rearing.

EXPANDING PSYCHOLOGY'S FRONTIERS

The boundaries of the science of psychology are constantly growing. Three newer members of the field's family tree–evolutionary psychology, behavioral genetics, and clinical neuropsychology–have sparked particular excitement and debate within psychology.

Evolutionary Psychology *Evolutionary psychology* considers how behavior is influenced by our genetic inheritance from our ancestors. The evolutionary approach suggests that the chemical coding of information in our cells not only determines traits such as hair color and race but also holds the key to understanding a broad variety of behaviors that helped our ancestors survive and reproduce.

Evolutionary psychology stems from Charles Darwin's arguments in his groundbreaking 1859 book, *On the Origin of Species.* Darwin suggested that a process of natural selection leads to the survival of the fittest and the development of traits that enable a species to adapt to its environment.

Evolutionary psychologists take Darwin's arguments a step further. They argue that our genetic inheritance determines not only physical traits such as skin and eye color but certain personality traits and social behaviors as well. For example, evolutionary psychologists suggest that behavior such as shyness, jealousy, and cross-cultural similarities in qualities desired in potential mates are at least partially determined by genetics, presumably because such behavior helped increase the survival rate of humans' ancient relatives (Sefcek, Brumbach, & Vasquez, 2007; Fost, 2015; Lewis et al., 2017).

Although they are increasingly popular, evolutionary explanations of behavior have stirred controversy. By suggesting that many significant behaviors unfold automatically because they are wired into the human species, evolutionary approaches minimize the role of environmental and social forces. Still, the evolutionary approach has stimulated a significant amount of research on how our biological inheritance influences our traits and behaviors (Neher, 2006; Mesoudi, 2011; Flannelly, 2017).

Behavioral Genetics Another rapidly growing area in psychology focuses on the biological mechanisms, such as genes and chromosomes, that enable inherited behavior to unfold. *Behavioral genetics* seeks to understand how we might inherit certain behavioral traits and how the environment influences whether we actually display such traits (Maxson, 2013; Vukasović & Bratko, 2015; Krüger, Korsten, & Hoffman, 2017).

Clinical Neuropsychology *Clinical neuropsychology* unites the areas of neuroscience and clinical psychology: It focuses on the origin of psychological disorders in biological factors. Building on advances in our understanding of the structure and chemistry of the brain, this specialty has already led to promising new treatments for psychological disorders as well as debates over the use of medication to control behavior (Boake, 2008; Holtz, 2011; Craig, 2017).

Working at Psychology

Help Wanted: Assistant professor at a small liberal arts college. Teach undergraduate courses in introductory psychology and courses in specialty areas of cognitive psychology, perception, and learning. Strong commitment to quality teaching, as well as evidence of scholarship and research productivity, necessary.

Help Wanted: Industrial-organizational consulting psychologist. International firm seeks psychologists for full-time career positions as consultants to management. Candidates must have the ability to establish a rapport with senior business executives and help them find innovative and practical solutions to problems concerning people and organizations.

Help Wanted: Clinical psychologist. PhD, internship experience, and license required. Comprehensive clinic seeks psychologist to work with children and adults providing individual and group therapy, psychological evaluations, crisis intervention, and development of behavior treatment plans on multidisciplinary team.

As these job ads suggest, psychologists are employed in a variety of settings. Many doctoral-level psychologists are employed by institutions of higher learning (universities and colleges) or are self-employed, usually working as private practitioners treating clients (see Figure 3). Other work sites include hospitals, clinics, mental health centers,

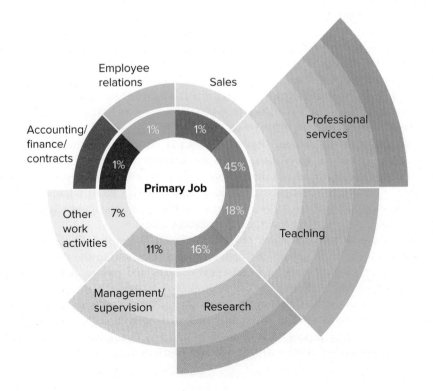

FIGURE 3 The breakdown of where U.S. psychologists (who have a PhD or PsyD) work.

Source: Stamm, K., Lin, Luona, and Cristidis, P. Datapoint, *Monitor on Psychology,* June 2016, 12.

counseling centers, government human-services organizations, businesses, schools, and even prisons. Psychologists are employed in the military, working with soldiers, veterans, and their families, and they work for the federal government in the Department of Homeland Security, fighting terrorism. Psychologists who specialize in program evaluation are increasingly employed by foundations that want to assess the value of programs they fund (DeAngelis & Monahan, 2008; Moscoso et al., 2013; American Psychological Association, 2016).

Most psychologists, though, work in academic settings, allowing them to combine the three major roles played by psychologists in society: teacher, scientist, and clinical practitioner. Many psychology professors are also actively involved in research or in serving clients. Whatever the particular job site, however, psychologists share a commitment to improving individual lives as well as society in general.

Keep in mind that professionals from a variety of occupations use the findings of psychologists. To understand how nonpsychologists use psychology, see the feature titled "From the Perspective of . . ." throughout the text.

From the perspective of...

An Educator Imagine that a classroom teacher wants to improve the performance of a 10-year-old boy who is not doing well in math. What branches of psychology might she draw on to get ideas about how to help him?

©Andersen Ross/Blend Images/Getty Images

PSYCHOLOGISTS: A PORTRAIT

Although there is no "average" psychologist in terms of personal characteristics, we can draw a statistical portrait of the field. There are nearly 200,000 active psychologists working today in the United States, but they are outnumbered by psychologists in other countries. Europe has more than 290,000 psychologists, and in Brazil alone, there are 140,000 licensed psychologists. Although most research is conducted in the United States, psychologists in other countries are increasingly influential in adding to the knowledge base and practices of psychology (Rees & Seaton, 2011; American Psychological Association, 2015; Takooshian et al., 2016).

In the United States, women outnumber men in the field, a big change from earlier years when women faced bias and were actively discouraged from becoming psychologists. Today, women far outnumber male psychologists: for every one male, there are 2.1 female psychologists. There is an active debate about whether and how to seek balance in the percentage of men and women in the field (Cynkar, 2007; Willyard, 2011; American Psychological Association, 2015).

Furthermore, despite the higher proportion of women in the field, women still lag behind when it comes to salaries and high-status positions within the field. For example, female psychologists working in four-year colleges and medical schools earn, on average, 82.7% of what males make (Clay, 2017).

The majority of psychologists in the United States are white, limiting the diversity of the field. Only around 16% of all professionally active psychologists are members of racial minority groups. Although the numbers of minority individuals entering the field are far greater than they were a decade ago and continue to grow, the numbers have not kept up with the dramatic growth of the minority population at large (Maton et al., 2006; Chandler, 2011; American Psychological Association, 2015).

The underrepresentation of racial and ethnic minorities among psychologists is significant for several reasons. First, the field of psychology is diminished by a lack of the diverse perspectives and talents that minority-group members can provide. Furthermore, minority-group psychologists serve as role models for members of minority communities, and their underrepresentation in the profession might deter other minority-group members from entering the field. Finally, because members of minority groups often prefer to receive psychological therapy from treatment providers of their own race or ethnic group, the rarity of minority psychologists can discourage some members of minority groups from seeking treatment (Bryant et al., 2005; Stevens, 2015; Stewart et al., 2017).

THE EDUCATION OF A PSYCHOLOGIST

How do people become psychologists? The most common route is a long one. Most psychologists have a doctorate, either a *PhD* (doctor of philosophy) or, less frequently, a *PsyD* (doctor of psychology). The PhD is a research degree that requires a dissertation based on an original investigation. The PsyD is obtained by psychologists who want to focus on the treatment of psychological disorders. Note that psychologists are distinct from psychiatrists, who have a medical degree and specialize in the diagnosis and treatment of psychological disorders, often using treatments that involve the prescription of drugs.

Both the PhD and the PsyD typically take four or five years of work past the bachelor's level. Some fields of psychology involve education beyond the doctorate. For instance, doctoral-level clinical psychologists, who deal with people with psychological disorders, typically spend an additional year doing an internship.

About a third of people working in the field of psychology have a master's degree as their highest degree, which they earn after two or three years of graduate work. These psychologists teach, provide therapy, conduct research, or work in specialized programs dealing with drug abuse or crisis intervention. Some work in universities, government, and business, collecting and analyzing data.

CAREERS FOR PSYCHOLOGY MAJORS

Although some psychology majors head for graduate school in psychology or an unrelated field, the majority join the workforce immediately after graduation. Most report that the jobs they take after graduation are related to their psychology background.

An undergraduate major in psychology provides excellent preparation for a variety of occupations. Because undergraduates who specialize in psychology develop good analytical skills, are trained to think critically, and are able to synthesize and evaluate information well, employers in business, industry, and the government value their preparation (Kuther, 2003).

The most common areas of employment for psychology majors are in the social services, including working as administrators, serving as counselors, and providing direct care. Some 20% of recipients of bachelor's degrees in psychology work in the social services or in some other form of public affairs. In addition, psychology majors often enter the fields of education or business or work for federal, state, and local governments (see Figure 4; Murray, 2002; Rajecki & Borden, 2011; Sternberg, 2017).

Study Alert
Be sure you can differentiate between a PhD (doctor of philosophy) and a PsyD (doctor of psychology), as well as between psychologists and psychiatrists.

FIGURE 4 Although many psychology majors pursue employment in social services, a background in psychology can prepare one for many professions outside the social services field. What is it about the science and art of psychology that make it such a versatile field?

Source: Adapted from Kuther, T. L. (2003). *Your career in psychology: Psychology and the law.* New York: Wadsworth.

Positions Obtained by Psychology Majors		
Business Field	**Education/ Academic Field**	**Social Field**
Administrative assistant	Administration	Activities coordinator
Advertising trainee	Child-care provider	Behavioral specialist
Affirmative action officer	Child-care worker/	Career counselor
Benefits manager	supervisor	Case worker
Claims specialist	Data management	Child protection worker
Community relations officer	Laboratory assistant	Clinical coordinator
Customer relations	Parent/family education	Community outreach worker
Data management	Preschool teacher	Corrections officer
Employee counselor	Public opinion surveyor	Counselor assistant
Employee recruitment	Research assistant	Crisis intervention counselor
Human resources	Teaching assistant	Employment counselor
coordinator/manager/		Group home attendant
specialist		Mental health assistant
Labor relations manager/		Occupational therapist
specialist		Probation officer
Loan officer		Program manager
Management trainee		Rehabilitation counselor
Marketing		Residence counselor
Personnel manager/officer		Social service assistant
Product and services		Social worker
research		Substance abuse counselor
Programs/events		Youth counselor
coordination		
Public relations		
Retail sales management		
Sales representative		
Special features writing/		
reporting		
Staff training and		
development		
Trainer/training office		

RECAP/EVALUATE/RETHINK

RECAP

LO 1-1 What is the science of psychology?

- Psychology is the scientific study of behavior and mental processes, encompassing not just what people do but also their biological activities, feelings, perceptions, memory, reasoning, and thoughts.

LO 1-2 What are the major specialties in the field of psychology?

- Behavioral neuroscientists focus on the biological basis of behavior, and experimental psychologists study the processes of sensing, perceiving, learning, and thinking about the world.

- Cognitive psychology, an outgrowth of experimental psychology, studies higher mental processes, including memory, knowing, thinking, reasoning, problem solving, judging, decision making, and language.
- Developmental psychologists study how people grow and change throughout the life span.
- Personality psychologists consider the consistency and change in an individual's behavior, as well as the individual differences that distinguish one person's behavior from another's.
- Health psychologists study psychological factors that affect physical disease, whereas clinical psychologists consider the study, diagnosis, and treatment of

abnormal behavior. Counseling psychologists focus on educational, social, and career adjustment problems.
- Social psychology is the study of how people's thoughts, feelings, and actions are affected by others.
- Cross-cultural psychology examines the similarities and differences in psychological functioning among various cultures.
- Other increasingly important fields are evolutionary psychology, behavioral genetics, and clinical neuropsychology.

LO 1-3 Where do psychologists work?

- Psychologists are employed in a variety of settings. Although the primary sites of employment are private practice and colleges, many psychologists are found in hospitals, clinics, community mental health centers, and counseling centers.

EVALUATE

Match each subfield of psychology with the issues or questions posed below.

a. Behavioral neuroscience
b. Experimental psychology
c. Cognitive psychology
d. Developmental psychology
e. Personality psychology
f. Health psychology
g. Clinical psychology
h. Counseling psychology
i. Educational psychology
j. School psychology
k. Social psychology
l. Industrial psychology

1. Joan, a college freshman, is worried about her grades. She needs to learn better organizational skills and study habits to cope with the demands of college.
2. At what age do children generally begin to acquire an emotional attachment to their fathers?
3. It is thought that pornographic films that depict violence against women may prompt aggressive behavior in some men.
4. What chemicals are released in the human body as a result of a stressful event? What are their effects on behavior?
5. Luis is unique in his manner of responding to crisis situations, with an even temperament and a positive outlook.
6. The teachers of 8-year-old Jack are concerned that he has recently begun to withdraw socially and to show little interest in schoolwork.
7. Janetta's job is demanding and stressful. She wonders if her lifestyle is making her more prone to certain illnesses, such as cancer and heart disease.
8. A psychologist is intrigued by the fact that some people are much more sensitive to painful stimuli than others are.
9. A strong fear of crowds leads a young man to seek treatment for his problem.
10. What mental strategies are involved in solving complex word problems?
11. What teaching methods most effectively motivate elementary school students to successfully accomplish academic tasks?
12. Jessica is asked to develop a management strategy that will encourage safer work practices in an assembly plant.

RETHINK

Do you think intuition and common sense are sufficient for understanding why people act the way they do? In what ways is a scientific approach appropriate for studying human behavior?

Answers to Evaluate Questions

a-4; b-8; c-10; d-2; e-5; f-7; g-9; h-1; i-11; j-6; k-3; l-12

KEY TERM

KEY TERM

psychology

Module 2
A Science Evolves: The Past, the Present, and the Future

LEARNING OUTCOMES

LO 2-1 What are the origins of psychology?

LO 2-2 What are the major approaches in contemporary psychology?

LO 2-3 What are psychology's key issues and controversies?

LO 2-4 What is the future of psychology likely to hold?

Seven thousand years ago, people assumed that psychological problems were caused by evil spirits. To allow those spirits to escape from a person's body, ancient healers chipped a hole in a patient's skull with crude instruments–a procedure called *trephining.*

According to the 17th-century philosopher René Descartes, nerves were hollow tubes through which "animal spirits" conducted impulses in the same way that water is transmitted through a pipe. When a person put a finger too close to a fire, heat was transmitted to the brain through the tubes.

Franz Josef Gall, an 18th-century physician, argued that a trained observer could discern intelligence, moral character, and other basic personality characteristics from the shape and number of bumps on a person's skull. His theory gave rise to the field of phrenology, employed by hundreds of practitioners in the 19th century.

Although these explanations might sound far-fetched, in their own times they represented the most advanced thinking about what might be called the psychology of the era. Our understanding of behavior has progressed tremendously since the 18th century, but most of the advances have been recent. As sciences go, psychology is one of the new kids on the block. (For highlights in the development of the field, see Figure 1.)

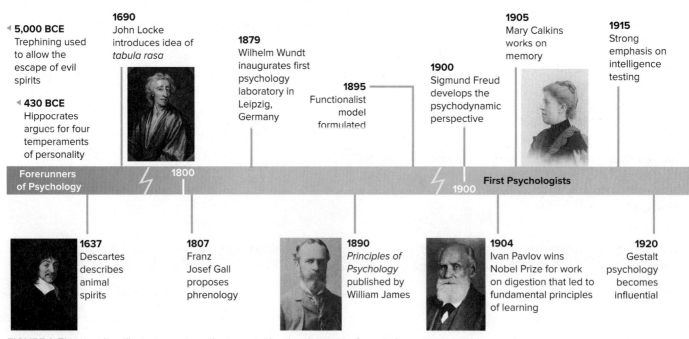

FIGURE 1 This time line illustrates major milestones in the development of psychology.

Sources: (Rene Descartes): ©Everett - Art/Shutterstock; (John Locke): Source: National Gallery of Art; (William James): ©Paul Thompson/FPG/Getty Images; (Ivan Pavlov): ©Bettmann/Getty Images; (Mary Whiton Calkins): Source: Wellesley College Archives; (John B. Watson): ©George Rinhart/Corbis via Getty Images; (Abraham Maslow and Jean Piaget): ©Bettmann/Getty Images; (Dr. Elizabeth Loftus): ©Elizabeth Loftus

The Roots of Psychology

We can trace psychology's roots back to the ancient Greeks, who considered the mind to be a suitable topic for scholarly contemplation. Later philosophers argued for hundreds of years about some of the questions psychologists grapple with today. For example, the 17th-century British philosopher John Locke believed that children were born into the world with minds like "blank slates" (*tabula rasa* in Latin) and that their experiences determined what kind of adults they would become. His views contrasted with those of Plato and Descartes, who argued that some knowledge was inborn in humans.

However, the formal beginning of psychology as a scientific discipline is generally considered to be in the late 19th century, when Wilhelm Wundt, in Leipzig, Germany, established the first experimental laboratory devoted to psychological phenomena. At about the same time, William James was setting up his laboratory in Cambridge, Massachusetts.

When Wundt set up his laboratory in 1879, his aim was to study the building blocks of the mind. He considered psychology to be the study of conscious experience. His perspective, which came to be known as **structuralism,** focused on uncovering the fundamental mental components of perception, consciousness, thinking, emotions, and other kinds of mental states and activities.

To determine how basic sensory processes shape our understanding of the world, Wundt and other structuralists used a procedure called introspection. **Introspection** is a procedure in which people are presented with a stimulus–such as an image or sentence–and asked to describe, in their own words and in as much detail as they could, what they were experiencing. Wundt argued that by analyzing people's reports, psychologists could come to a better understanding of the structure of the mind.

Over time, psychologists challenged Wundt's approach. They became increasingly dissatisfied with the assumption that introspection could reveal the structure of the mind. Introspection was not a truly scientific technique because there were few ways an outside observer could confirm the accuracy of others' introspections. Moreover, people had difficulty describing some kinds of inner experiences, such as emotional

Wilhelm Wundt
©Bettmann/Getty Images

structuralism Wundt's approach, which focuses on uncovering the fundamental mental components of consciousness, thinking, and other kinds of mental states and activities. (Module 2)

introspection A procedure in which people are presented with a stimulus–such as an image or sentence–and asked to describe, in their own words and in as much detail as they can, what they were experiencing. (Module 2)

1924
John B. Watson, an early behaviorist, publishes *Behaviorism*

1951
Carl Rogers publishes *Client-Centered Therapy,* helping to establish the humanistic perspective

1957
Leon Festinger publishes *A Theory of Cognitive Dissonance,* producing a major impact on social psychology

1980
Jean Piaget, an influential developmental psychologist, dies

1985
Increasing emphasis on cognitive perspective

2010
New subfields develop such as clinical neuropsychology and evolutionary psychology

Modern Psychology

2000

1928
Leta Stetter Hollingworth publishes work on adolescence

1953
B. F. Skinner publishes *Science and Human Behavior,* advocating the behavioral perspective

1954
Abraham Maslow publishes *Motivation and Personality,* developing the concept of self-actualization

1969
Arguments regarding the genetic basis of IQ fuel lingering controversies

1981 David Hubel and Torsten Wiesel win Nobel Prize for work on vision cells in the brain

2000
Elizabeth Loftus does pioneering work on false memory and eyewitness testimony

2015 Increasing understanding of role of neuroscience on social behavior, and effects of technology on behavior

William James
©Paul Thompson/FPG/Getty Images

functionalism An early approach to psychology that concentrated on what the mind does–the functions of mental activity–and the role of behavior in allowing people to adapt to their environments. (Module 2)

Gestalt psychology An approach to psychology that focuses on the organization of perception and thinking in a "whole" sense rather than on the individual elements of perception. (Module 2)

Study Alert
Knowing the basic outlines of the history of the field will help you understand how today's major perspectives have evolved.

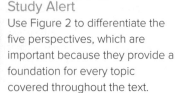

Study Alert
Use Figure 2 to differentiate the five perspectives, which are important because they provide a foundation for every topic covered throughout the text.

responses. Those drawbacks led to the development of new approaches, which largely replaced structuralism.

The perspective that replaced structuralism is known as functionalism. Rather than focusing on the mind's structure, **functionalism** concentrated on what the mind *does* and how behavior *functions*. Functionalists, whose perspective became prominent in the early 1900s, asked what role behavior plays in allowing people to adapt to their environments. For example, a functionalist might examine the function of the emotion of fear in preparing us to deal with emergency situations.

William James, an American psychologist, led the functionalist movement. Functionalists examined how people satisfy their needs through their behavior. The functionalists also discussed how our stream of consciousness–the flow of thoughts in our conscious minds–permits us to adapt to our environment. The American educator John Dewey drew on functionalism to develop the field of school psychology, proposing ways to best meet students' educational needs.

Another important reaction to structuralism was the development of Gestalt psychology in the early 1900s. **Gestalt (geh-SHTALLT) psychology** emphasizes how perception is organized. Instead of considering the individual parts that make up thinking, Gestalt psychologists took the opposite tack, studying how people consider individual elements together as units or wholes. Led by German scientists such as Hermann Ebbinghaus and Max Wertheimer, Gestalt psychologists proposed that "The whole is different from the sum of its parts," meaning that our perception, or understanding, of objects is greater and more meaningful than the individual elements that make up our perceptions. Gestalt psychologists have made substantial contributions to our understanding of perception.

WOMEN IN PSYCHOLOGY: FOUNDING MOTHERS

As in many scientific fields, social prejudices hindered women's participation in the early development of psychology. For example, many universities would not admit women to their graduate psychology programs in the early 1900s.

Despite the hurdles they faced, women made notable contributions to psychology, although their impact on the field was largely overlooked until recently. For example, Margaret Floy Washburn (1871-1939) was the first woman to receive a doctorate in psychology, and she did important work on animal behavior. Leta Stetter Hollingworth (1886-1939) was one of the first psychologists to focus on child development and on women's issues. She collected data to refute the view, popular in the early 1900s, that women's abilities periodically declined during parts of the menstrual cycle (Hollingworth, 1943/1990; Denmark & Fernandez, 1993; Furumoto & Scarborough, 2002).

Mary Calkins (1863-1930), who studied memory in the early part of the 20th century, became the first female president of the American Psychological Association. Karen Horney (pronounced "HORN-eye") (1885-1952) focused on the social and cultural factors behind personality, and she also founded the *American Journal of Psychoanalysis*. June Etta Downey (1875-1932) spearheaded the study of personality traits and became the first woman to head a psychology department at a state university. Anna Freud (1895-1982), the daughter of Sigmund Freud, also made notable contributions to the treatment of abnormal behavior, and Mamie Phipps Clark (1917-1983) carried out pioneering work on how children of color grew to recognize racial differences (Lal, 2002; Galdi, 2015).

Today's Five Major Perspectives

The men and women who laid the foundations of psychology shared a common goal: to explain and understand behavior using scientific methods. Seeking to achieve the same goal, the tens of thousands of psychologists who followed those early pioneers embraced–and often rejected–a variety of broad perspectives.

Neuroscience
Views behavior from the perspective of biological functioning

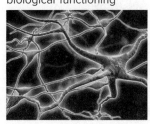

Behavioral Focuses on observable behavior

Psychodynamic
Believes behavior is motivated by inner, unconscious forces over which a person has little control

Cognitive
Examines how people understand and think about the world

Humanistic
Contends that people can control their behavior and that they naturally try to reach their full potential

FIGURE 2 The major perspectives of psychology.

(Neuroscience): ©Science Photo Library/Alamy Stock Photo; (Cognitive): ©David Sanger/The Image Bank/Getty Images; (Behavioral): ©Ariel Skelley/Blend Images; (Humanistic): ©White Packert/The Image Bank/Getty Images; (Psychodynamic): ©Athanasia Nomikou/Shutterstock

The perspectives of psychology offer distinct outlooks and emphasize different factors. Just as we can use more than one map to find our way around a particular region—for instance, a map that shows roads and highways and another map that shows major landmarks—psychologists developed a variety of approaches to understanding behavior. When considered jointly, the different perspectives provide the means to explain behavior in its amazing variety.

Today, the field of psychology includes five major perspectives (summarized in Figure 2). These broad perspectives emphasize different aspects of behavior and mental processes, and each takes our understanding of behavior in a somewhat different direction.

neuroscience perspective The approach that views behavior from the perspective of the brain, the nervous system, and other biological functions. (Module 2)

THE NEUROSCIENCE PERSPECTIVE: BLOOD, SWEAT, AND FEARS

When we get down to the basics, humans are animals made of skin and bones. The **neuroscience perspective** considers how people and nonhumans function biologically: how individual nerve cells are joined together, how the inheritance of certain characteristics from parents and other ancestors influences behavior, how the functioning of the body affects hopes and fears, which behaviors are instinctual, and so forth. Even more complex kinds of behaviors, such as a baby's response to strangers, are viewed as having critical biological components by psychologists who embrace the neuroscience perspective. This perspective includes the study of heredity and evolution, which considers how heredity may influence behavior, and behavioral neuroscience, which examines how the brain and the nervous system affect behavior.

Because every behavior ultimately can be broken down into its biological components, the neuroscience perspective has broad appeal. Psychologists who subscribe to this perspective have made major contributions to the understanding and betterment of human life, ranging from cures for certain types of deafness to drug treatments for people with severe mental disorders. Furthermore, advances in methods for examining the anatomy and functioning of the brain have permitted the neuroscientific perspective to extend its influence across a broad range of subfields

Sigmund Freud
©Ingram Publishing

psychodynamic perspective The approach based on the view that behavior is motivated by unconscious inner forces over which the individual has little control. (Module 2)

behavioral perspective The approach that suggests that observable, external behavior, which can be objectively measured, should be the focus of study. (Module 2)

in psychology. (We'll see examples of these methods throughout this book in *Neuroscience in Your Life*.)

THE PSYCHODYNAMIC PERSPECTIVE: UNDERSTANDING THE INNER PERSON

To many people who have never taken a psychology course, psychology begins and ends with the psychodynamic perspective. Proponents of the **psychodynamic perspective** argue that behavior is motivated by inner forces and conflicts about which we have little awareness or control. They view dreams and slips of the tongue as indications of what a person is truly feeling within a seething cauldron of unconscious psychic activity.

The origins of the psychodynamic view are linked to one person: Sigmund Freud. Freud was an Austrian physician in the early 1900s whose ideas about unconscious determinants of behavior had a revolutionary effect on 20th-century thinking, not just in psychology but in related fields as well. Although some of the original Freudian principles have been roundly criticized, the contemporary psychodynamic perspective has provided a means not only to understand and treat some kinds of psychological disorders but also to understand everyday phenomena such as prejudice and aggression.

THE BEHAVIORAL PERSPECTIVE: OBSERVING THE OUTER PERSON

Whereas the neuroscience and psychodynamic approaches look inside the organism to determine the causes of its behavior, the behavioral perspective takes a different approach. Proponents of the behavioral perspective rejected psychology's early emphasis on the internal workings of the mind. Instead, the **behavioral perspective** suggests that the focus should be on external behavior that can be observed and measured objectively.

John B. Watson was the first major American psychologist to use a behavioral approach. Working in the 1920s, Watson believed that one could gain a complete understanding of behavior by studying the environment in which a person operated.

In fact, Watson believed rather optimistically that it was possible to bring about any desired type of behavior by controlling a person's environment. This philosophy is clear in his own words: "Give me a dozen healthy infants, well-formed, and my own specified world to bring them up in and I'll guarantee to take any one at random and train him to become any type of specialist I might select—doctor, lawyer, artist, merchant-chief, and yes, even beggar-man and thief, regardless of his talents, penchants, tendencies, abilities, vocations and race of his ancestors" (Watson, 1924).

The behavioral perspective was championed by B. F. Skinner, a pioneer in the field. Much of our understanding of how people learn new behaviors is based on the behavioral perspective. As we will see, the behavioral perspective crops up along every byway of psychology. Along with its influence in the area of learning processes, this perspective has made contributions in such diverse areas as treating mental disorders, curbing aggression, resolving sexual problems, and ending drug addiction (Schlinger, 2011; Ruiz, 2015; Fryling, 2017).

THE COGNITIVE PERSPECTIVE: IDENTIFYING THE ROOTS OF UNDERSTANDING

Efforts to understand behavior lead some psychologists straight into the mind. Evolving in part from structuralism and in part as a reaction to behaviorism, which focused so heavily on observable behavior and the environment, the **cognitive perspective**

cognitive perspective The approach that focuses on how people think, understand, and know about the world. (Module 2)

focuses on how people think, understand, and know about the world. The emphasis is on learning how people comprehend and represent the outside world within themselves and how our ways of thinking about the world influence our behavior.

Many psychologists who adhere to the cognitive perspective compare human thinking to the workings of a computer, which takes in information and transforms, stores, and retrieves it. In their view, thinking is *information processing*.

Psychologists who rely on the cognitive perspective ask questions on subjects ranging from how people make decisions to whether a person can watch television and study at the same time. The common elements that link cognitive approaches are an emphasis on how people understand and think about the world and an interest in describing the patterns and irregularities in the operation of our minds.

From the perspective of...

A Health-Care Provider How can a basic understanding of psychology improve your job performance in the health-care industry?

©Tetra Images/Getty Images

THE HUMANISTIC PERSPECTIVE: THE UNIQUE QUALITIES OF THE HUMAN SPECIES

The humanistic perspective rejects the view that behavior is determined largely by automatically unfolding biological forces, unconscious processes, or the environment. Instead, the **humanistic perspective** suggests that all individuals naturally strive to grow, develop, and be in control of their lives and behavior. Humanistic psychologists maintain that each of us has the capacity to seek and reach fulfillment.

According to Carl Rogers and Abraham Maslow, who were central figures in the development of the humanistic perspective, people strive to reach their full potential if they are given the opportunity. The emphasis of the humanistic perspective is on *free will*, the ability to freely make decisions about one's own behavior and life. The notion of free will stands in contrast to *determinism*, which sees behavior as caused, or determined, by things beyond a person's control.

The humanistic perspective assumes that people have the ability to make their own choices about their behavior rather than relying on societal standards. More than any other approach, it stresses the role of psychology in enriching people's lives and helping them achieve self-fulfillment. By reminding psychologists of their commitment to the individual person in society, the humanistic perspective has been an important influence (Nichols, 2011; Linley, 2013; Hayes, 2015).

Don't let the abstract qualities of the broad approaches we have discussed lull you into thinking that they are purely theoretical: These perspectives underlie ongoing work of a practical nature, as we discuss throughout this book. To start seeing how psychology can improve everyday life, read *Applying Psychology in the 21st Century*.

humanistic perspective The approach that suggests that all individuals naturally strive to grow, develop, and be in control of their lives and behavior. (Module 2)

APPLYING PSYCHOLOGY IN THE 21ST CENTURY

PSYCHOLOGY MATTERS

"Investigators search for clues at site of suicide bombing."

"Good jobs for college graduates remain hard to find."

"Eyewitness to killing proves unable to provide reliable clues."

"Social media like Facebook, Twitter, Snapchat, and Instagram change how people interact with others."

"Childhood obesity rates surge."

"Black suspect in robbery dies after scuffle with police."

A quick review of any day's news headlines reminds us that the world is beset by a variety of stubborn problems that resist easy solutions. At the same time, a considerable number of psychologists are devoting their energies and expertise to addressing these problems and improving the human condition. Let's consider some of the ways in which psychology has addressed and helped work toward solutions to major societal problems:

- What are the causes of terrorism? What motivates suicide bombers? Are they psychologically disordered, or can their behavior be seen as a rational response to a particular system of beliefs? As we'll see when we discuss psychological disorders, psychologists are gaining an understanding of the factors that lead people to embrace suicide and to engage in terrorism to further a cause in which they deeply believe (Post, 2015; Theriault, Krause, & Young, 2017; Choma et al., 2018).

- How are social media changing the way we live? Social networking media such as Facebook and Twitter have changed the way people communicate and the way news spreads around the world. How do social media affect the way people relate to each other? How do they affect our perceptions of world events? Psychologists are examining the motivations behind social networking, its influence on individuals and social institutions, and possible beneficial applications of the technology (Kosinski et al., 2015; Young et al., 2017; Zyoud et al., 2018).

- What are the roots of autism spectrum disorder, and why is it on the rise?

What psychological forces led some to embrace the Black Lives Matter movement?
©Rena Schild/Shutterstock

Autism spectrum disorder is a severe developmental disability that impairs one's ability to communicate and relate to others. It exists on a continuum from mild symptoms, such as social awkwardness, to profound dysfunction, such as a complete inability to communicate or care for oneself. Psychologists are rapidly gaining insights into the hereditary and environmental factors that influence autism; the need for this understanding is urgent because the incidence of autism has been growing sharply in recent years and it's unclear why (Pelphrey & Shultz, 2013; Gillespie-Lynch et al., 2015; Commons et al., 2017).

- Why do eyewitnesses to crimes often remember the events inaccurately, and how can we increase the precision of eyewitness accounts? Psychologists' research has come to an important conclusion: Eyewitness testimony in criminal cases is often inaccurate and biased. Memories of crimes are often clouded by emotion, and the questions asked by police investigators often elicit inaccurate responses. Work by psychologists has been used to provide national guidelines for obtaining more accurate memories during criminal investigations (Beaudry et al., 2015; Wixted et al., 2015; Kassin et al., 2018).

- What are the roots of obesity, and how can healthier eating and better physical fitness

be encouraged? Why are some people more predisposed to obesity than others are? What social factors might be at play in the rising rate of obesity in childhood? As is becoming increasingly clear, obesity is a complex problem with biological, psychological, and social underpinnings. Therefore, to be successful, approaches to treating obesity must take many factors into account. There is no magic bullet providing a quick fix, but psychologists recommend a number of strategies that help make weight-loss goals more achievable (MacLean et al., 2009; Neumark-Sztainer, 2009; Puhl & Liu, 2015).

- What are the roots of racism in the United States? Psychologists have discovered that even subtle forms of prejudice and discrimination can cause significant harm in recipients. Furthermore, they have learned that people who sincerely believe themselves to not be racist still harbor unconscious racist thoughts that can translate into discriminatory behavior. On the positive side, they are developing strategies that break down racial barriers and heal the hurt and stigma of decades of racism (Fisher et al., 2017; Mason et al., 2017; David & Derthick, 2018).

- What gives people satisfaction with life and a sense of well being? Research has found that during difficult economic times, it's important to understand that wealth and possessions don't make people happy. Instead, happiness comes from enjoying life's little moments and finding purpose and meaning in what you do (Pavot & Diener, 2013; Crespo & Mesurado, 2015; Jin & Kim, 2017).

These topics represent just a few of the issues that psychologists address daily. To further explore the many ways that psychology has an impact on everyday life, check out the American Psychological Association (APA) website, at www.apa.org, which features psychological applications in everyday life.

RETHINK

- What do *you* think are the major problems affecting society today?
- What are the psychological issues involved in these problems, and how might psychologists help find solutions to them?

Psychology's Key Issues and Controversies

As you consider the many topics and perspectives that make up psychology, ranging from a narrow focus on minute biochemical influences on behavior to a broad focus on social behaviors, you might find yourself thinking that the discipline lacks cohesion. However, the field is more unified than a first glimpse might suggest. For one thing, no matter what topical area a psychologist specializes in, he or she relies primarily on one of the five major perspectives. For example, a developmental psychologist who specializes in the study of children could make use of the cognitive perspective or the psychodynamic perspective or any of the other major perspectives.

Psychologists also agree on what the key issues of the field are (see Figure 3). Although there are major arguments regarding how best to address and resolve the key issues, psychology is a unified science because psychologists of all perspectives agree that the issues must be addressed if the field is going to advance. As you contemplate these key issues, try not to think of them in "either/or" terms. Instead, consider the opposing viewpoints on each issue as the opposite ends of a continuum, with the positions of individual psychologists typically falling somewhere between the two ends.

Issue 1: *Nature (heredity) versus nurture (environment).* How much of people's behavior is due to their genetically determined nature (heredity), and how much is due to nurture, the influences of the physical and social environment in which a child is raised? Furthermore, what is the interplay between heredity and environment? These questions have deep philosophical and historical roots, and they are involved in many topics in psychology.

A psychologist's take on this issue depends partly on which major perspective he or she subscribes to. For example, developmental psychologists whose focus is on how

Study Alert
Use Figure 3 to learn the key issues that underlie every subfield of psychology.

Issue	Neuroscience	Cognitive	Behavioral	Humanistic	Psychodynamic
Nature (heredity) vs. nurture (environment)	Nature (heredity)	Both	Nurture (environment)	Nurture (environment)	Nature (heredity)
Conscious vs. unconscious determinants of behavior	Unconscious	Both	Conscious	Conscious	Unconscious
Observable behavior vs internal mental processes	Internal emphasis	Internal emphasis	Observable emphasis	Internal emphasis	Internal emphasis
Free will vs. determinism	Determinism	Free will	Determinism	Free will	Determinism
Individual differences vs. universal principles	Universal emphasis	Individual emphasis	Both	Individual emphasis	Universal emphasis

FIGURE 3 Key issues in psychology and the positions taken by psychologists subscribing to the five major perspectives of psychology.
(Neuroscience): ©Science Photo Library/Alamy Stock Photo; (Cognitive): ©David Sanger/The Image Bank/Getty Images; (Behavioral): ©Ariel Skelley/Blend Images; (Humanistic): ©White Packert/The Image Bank/Getty Images; (Psychodynamic): ©Athanasia Nomikou/Shutterstock

people grow and change throughout the course of their lives may be most interested in learning more about hereditary influences if they follow a neuroscience perspective. In contrast, developmental psychologists who are proponents of the behavioral perspective are more likely to focus on environment (Rutter, 2002; Moffitt, Caspi, & Rutter, 2006; Barrett, 2011).

However, every psychologist would agree that neither nature nor nurture alone is the sole determinant of behavior; rather, it is a combination of the two. In a sense, then, the real controversy involves how much of our behavior is caused by heredity and how much is caused by environmental influences.

Issue 2: Conscious versus unconscious causes of behavior. How much of our behavior is produced by forces of which we are fully aware, and how much is due to unconscious activity–mental processes that are not accessible to the conscious mind? This question represents one of the great controversies in the field of psychology. For example, clinical psychologists adopting a psychodynamic perspective argue that psychological disorders are brought about by unconscious factors, whereas psychologists employing the cognitive perspective suggest that psychological disorders largely are the result of faulty thinking processes.

Issue 3: Observable behavior versus internal mental processes. Should psychology concentrate solely on behavior that can be seen by outside observers, or should it focus on unseen thinking processes? Some psychologists, particularly those relying on the behavioral perspective, contend that the only legitimate source of information for psychologists is behavior that can be observed directly. Other psychologists, building on the cognitive perspective, argue that what goes on inside a person's mind is critical to understanding behavior, and so we must concern ourselves with mental processes.

free will The idea that behavior is caused primarily by choices that are made freely by the individual. (Module 2)

determinism The idea that people's behavior is produced primarily by factors outside of their willful control. (Module 2)

Issue 4: Free will versus determinism. How much of our behavior is a matter of **free will** (choices made freely by an individual), and how much is subject to **determinism,** the notion that behavior is largely produced by factors beyond people's willful control? An issue long debated by philosophers, the free-will/determinism argument is also central to the field of psychology (Goto et al., 2015; Moynihan, Igou, & van Tilburg, 2017).

For example, some psychologists who specialize in psychological disorders argue that people make intentional choices and that those who display so-called abnormal behavior should be considered responsible for their actions. Other psychologists disagree and contend that such individuals are the victims of forces beyond their control. The position psychologists take on this issue has important implications for the way they treat psychological disorders, especially in deciding whether treatment should be forced on people who don't want it.

Issue 5: Individual differences versus universal principles. Specifically, how much of our behavior is a consequence of our unique and special qualities, the individual differences that differentiate us from other people? Conversely, how much reflects the culture and society in which we live, stemming from universal principles that underlie the behavior of all humans? Psychologists who rely on the neuroscience perspective tend to look for universal principles of behavior, such as how the nervous system operates or the way certain hormones automatically prime us for sexual activity. Such psychologists concentrate on the similarities in our behavioral destinies despite vast differences in our upbringing. In contrast, psychologists who employ the humanistic perspective focus more on the uniqueness of every individual. They consider every person's behavior a reflection of distinct and special individual qualities.

The question of the degree to which psychologists can identify universal principles that apply to all people has taken on new significance in light of the tremendous demographic changes now occurring in the United States and around the world. As we discuss next, these changes raise new and critical issues for the discipline of psychology in the 21st century.

From the perspective of...

A Social Worker Imagine that you have a caseload of clients who come from diverse cultures, ethnicities, and races. How might you consider their diverse backgrounds when assisting them?

©Sam Edwards/age fotostock

Psychology's Future

We have examined psychology's foundations, but what does the future hold for the discipline? Although the course of scientific development is notoriously difficult to predict, several trends seem likely:

- As its knowledge base grows, psychology will become increasingly specialized, and new perspectives will evolve. For example, our growing understanding of the brain and the nervous system, combined with scientific advances in genetics and gene therapy, will allow psychologists to focus on *prevention* of psychological disorders rather than only on their treatment (Cuijpers et al., 2008).

- The evolving sophistication of neuroscientific approaches is likely to have an increasing influence over other branches of psychology. For instance, social psychologists already are increasing their understanding of social behaviors such as persuasion by using brain scans as part of an evolving field known as *social neuroscience*. Furthermore, as neuroscientific techniques become more sophisticated, there will be new ways of applying that knowledge, as we discuss in *Neuroscience in Your Life* (Cacioppo & Decety, 2009; Di Ieva et al., 2015; Mattan, Kubota, & Cloutier, 2017).

- Psychology's influence on issues of public interest also will grow. The major problems of our time–such as violence, terrorism, racial and ethnic prejudice, poverty, and environmental changes, and technological disasters–have important psychological components Already, psychology has had significant influences on social policy, informing lawmakers' decision-making, a trend that is likely to increase (Zimbardo, 2004; Dweck, 2017; Fiske, 2017).

- Psychologists will follow increasingly strict ethical and moral guidelines. When it was revealed in 2015 that several psychologists participated in the interrogation and torture of military prisoners in the aftermath of the 9/11 terrorist attacks and that some of the leaders of the American Psychological Association (APA) were aware of these activities, a national scandal ensued. As a consequence, the APA adopted strict new guidelines that prohibit psychologists from participating in national security interrogations. In addition, psychologists are barred from working at the Guantánamo base in Cuba and at CIA black sites (Risen, 2015; Fink, 2017).

- The public's view of psychology will become more informed. Surveys show that the public at large does not fully understand the scientific underpinnings of the field. However, as the field itself embraces such practices as using scientific evidence to choose the best treatments for psychological disorders, psychology's reputation will grow (Lilienfeld, 2012; Ferguson, 2015).

- Finally, as the population becomes more diverse, issues of diversity–embodied in the study of racial, ethnic, linguistic, and cultural factors–will become more important to psychologists providing services and doing research. The result will be a field that can provide an understanding of *human* behavior in its broadest sense (Quintana et al., 2006; Richmond et al., 2015).

NEUROSCIENCE IN YOUR LIFE: ENHANCING YOUR MIND

Neuroscientists have strived to understand how the normal brain works, as well as what happens to it following injury or disease. Recently, they have begun to use technologies to enhance people's typical existing abilities. For example, researchers are exploring how repetitive transcranial magnetic stimulation (TMS), a form of noninvasive brain stimulation, can enhance cognitive abilities. In one study, researchers used repetitive TMS to stimulate the hippocampus, a brain region involved in memory (see the image below of the area targeted for stimulation). Stimulation over the course of a week led to increased brain connectivity and improved memory (Wang et al., 2014).

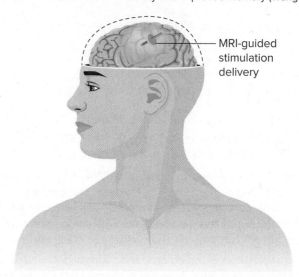

MRI-guided stimulation delivery

Source: Adapted from Wang, J. X., Rogers, L. M., Gross, E. Z., Ryals, A. J., Dokucu, M. E., Brandstatt, K. L., . . . Voss, J. L. "Targeted enhancement of cortical-hippocampal brain networks and associative memory." *Science,* 345(6200), 2014, 1054–1057.

RECAP/EVALUATE/RETHINK

RECAP

LO 2-1 What are the origins of psychology?

- Wilhelm Wundt laid the foundation of psychology in 1879, when he opened his laboratory in Germany.
- Early perspectives that guided the work of psychologists were structuralism, functionalism, and Gestalt theory.

LO 2-2 What are the major approaches in contemporary psychology?

- The neuroscience approach focuses on the biological components of the behavior of people and animals.
- The psychodynamic perspective suggests that powerful, unconscious inner forces and conflicts about which people have little or no awareness are the primary determinants of behavior.
- The behavioral perspective deemphasizes internal processes and concentrates instead on observable, measurable behavior, suggesting that understanding and control of a person's environment are sufficient to fully explain and modify behavior.

- Cognitive approaches to behavior consider how people know, understand, and think about the world.
- The humanistic perspective emphasizes that people are uniquely inclined toward psychological growth and higher levels of functioning and that they will strive to reach their full potential.

LO 2-3 What are psychology's key issues and controversies?

- Psychology's key issues and controversies center on how much of human behavior is a product of nature or nurture, conscious or unconscious thoughts, observable actions or internal mental processes, free will or determinism, and individual differences or universal principles.

LO 2-4 What is the future of psychology likely to hold?

- Psychology will become increasingly specialized, will pay greater attention to prevention instead of just treatment, will become more and more concerned with the public interest, and will take the growing diversity of the country's population into account more fully.

EVALUATE

1. Wundt described psychology as the study of conscious experience, a perspective he called _____.
2. Early psychologists studied the mind by asking people to describe what they were experiencing when exposed to various stimuli. This procedure was known as _____.
3. The statement "In order to study human behavior, we must consider the whole of perception rather than its component parts" might be made by a person subscribing to which perspective of psychology?
4. Jeanne's therapist asks her to recount a violent dream she recently experienced in order to gain insight into the unconscious forces affecting her behavior. Jeanne's therapist is working from a _____ perspective.
5. "It is behavior that can be observed that should be studied, not the suspected inner workings of the mind." This statement was most likely made by someone with which perspective?
   a. Cognitive perspective
   b. Neuroscience perspective
   c. Humanistic perspective
   d. Behavioral perspective

6. "My therapist is wonderful! He always points out my positive traits. He dwells on my uniqueness and strength as an individual. I feel much more confident about myself—as if I'm really growing and reaching my potential." The therapist being described most likely follows a _____ perspective.
7. In the nature-nurture issue, nature refers to heredity, and nurture refers to the _____.
8. Race is a biological concept, not a psychological one. True or false?

RETHINK

Focusing on one of the five major perspectives in use today (that is, neuroscience, psychodynamic, behavioral, cognitive, and humanistic), can you describe the kinds of research questions and studies that researchers using that perspective might pursue?

Answers to Evaluate Questions

1. structuralism; 2. introspection; 3. Gestalt; 4. psychodynamic; 5. d; 6. humanistic; 7. environment; 8. true

KEY TERMS

structuralism	Gestalt (geh-SHTALLT)	psychodynamic perspective	humanistic perspective
introspection	psychology	behavioral perspective	free will
functionalism	neuroscience perspective	cognitive perspective	determinism

Module 3
Research in Psychology

LO 3-1 What is the scientific method?

LO 3-2 What role do theories and hypotheses play in psychological research?

LO 3-3 What research methods do psychologists use?

LO 3-4 How do psychologists establish cause-and-effect relationships in research studies?

Study Alert
Use Figure 1 to remember the four steps of the scientific method (identifying questions, formulating an explanation, carrying out research, and communicating the findings).

scientific method The approach through which psychologists systematically acquire knowledge and understanding about behavior and other phenomena of interest. (Module 3)

The Scientific Method

"Birds of a feather flock together". . . or "Opposites attract"? "Two heads are better than one". . . or "If you want a thing done well, do it yourself"? "The more the merrier". . . or "Two's company, three's a crowd"?

If we were to rely on common sense to understand behavior, we'd have considerable difficulty–especially because commonsense views are often contradictory. In fact, one of the major undertakings for the field of psychology is to develop suppositions about behavior and to determine which of those suppositions are accurate (Ferguson, 2015).

Psychologists–as well as scientists in other disciplines–meet the challenge of posing appropriate questions and properly answering them by relying on the scientific method. The **scientific method** is the approach used by psychologists to systematically acquire knowledge and understanding about behavior and other phenomena of interest. As illustrated in Figure 1, it consists of four main steps: (1) identifying questions of interest, (2) formulating an explanation, (3) carrying out research designed to support or refute the explanation, and (4) communicating the findings.

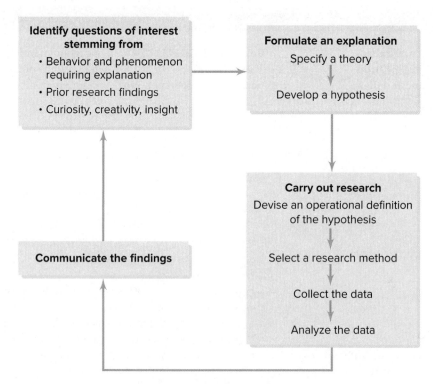

FIGURE 1 The scientific method, which encompasses the process of identifying, asking, and answering questions, is used by psychologists and by researchers from every other scientific discipline to come to an understanding about the world. What do you think are the advantages of this method?

THEORIES: SPECIFYING BROAD EXPLANATIONS

In using the scientific method, psychologists start by identifying questions of interest. We have all been curious at some time about our observations of everyday behavior. If you have ever asked yourself why a particular teacher is so easily annoyed, why a friend is always late for appointments, or how your dog understands your commands, you have been formulating questions about behavior.

Psychologists, too, ask questions about the nature and causes of behavior. They may want to explore explanations for everyday behaviors or for various phenomena. They may also pose questions that build on findings from their previous research or from research carried out by other psychologists. Or they may produce new questions that are based on curiosity, creativity, or insight.

After a question has been identified, the next step in the scientific method is to develop a theory to explain the observed phenomenon. **Theories** are broad explanations and predictions concerning observations of interest. They provide a framework for understanding the relationships among a set of otherwise unorganized facts or principles.

All of us have developed our own informal theories of human behavior, such as "People are basically good" or "People's behavior is usually motivated by self-interest." However, psychologists' theories are more formal and focused. They are established on the basis of a careful study of the psychological literature to identify earlier relevant research and previously formulated theories, as well as psychologists' general knowledge of the field.

Growing out of the diverse approaches employed by psychologists, theories vary both in their breadth and in their level of detail. For example, one theory might seek to explain and predict a phenomenon as broad as emotional experience. A narrower theory might attempt to explain why people display the emotion of fear nonverbally after receiving a threat (Anker & Feeley, 2011; Croom, 2015; Smith et al., 2017).

Psychologists Bibb Latané and John Darley, responding to the failure of bystanders to intervene when Kitty Genovese was murdered in New York, developed what they called a theory of *diffusion of responsibility* (Latané & Darley, 1970). According to their theory, the greater the number of bystanders or witnesses to an event that calls for helping behavior, the more the responsibility for helping is perceived to be shared by all the bystanders. Thus, the greater the number of bystanders in an emergency situation, the smaller the share of the responsibility each person feels–and the less likely that any single person will come forward to help.

theories Broad explanations and predictions concerning observations of interest. (Module 3)

HYPOTHESES: CRAFTING TESTABLE PREDICTIONS

Although the diffusion of responsibility theory seems to make sense, it represented only the beginning phase of Latané and Darley's investigative process. Their next step was to devise a way to test their theory. To do this, they needed to create a hypothesis. A **hypothesis** is a prediction stated in a way that allows it to be tested. Hypotheses stem from theories; they help test the underlying soundness of theories.

In the same way that we develop our own broad theories about the world, we also construct hypotheses about events and behavior. Those hypotheses can range from trivialities (such as why our English instructor wears those weird shirts) to more meaningful matters (such as what is the best way to study for a test). Although we rarely test these hypotheses systematically, we do try to determine whether they are right. Perhaps we try comparing two strategies: cramming the night before an exam versus spreading out our study over several nights. By assessing which approach yields better test performance, we have created a way to compare the two strategies.

A hypothesis must be stated in a way that will allow it to be tested, which involves creating an operational definition. An **operational definition** is the translation of a hypothesis into specific, testable procedures that can be measured and observed in an experiment.

hypothesis A prediction, stemming from a theory, stated in a way that allows it to be tested. (Module 3)

operational definition The translation of a hypothesis into specific, testable procedures that can be measured and observed. (Module 3)

There is no single way to go about devising an operational definition for a hypothesis; it depends on logic, the equipment and facilities available, the psychological perspective being employed, and ultimately the creativity of the researcher. For example, one researcher might develop a hypothesis that uses as an operational definition of "fear" an increase in heart rate. In contrast, another psychologist might use as an operational definition of "fear" a written response to the question "How much fear are you experiencing at this moment?"

Latané and Darley's hypothesis was a straightforward prediction from their more general theory of diffusion of responsibility: The more people who witness an emergency situation, the less likely it is that help will be given to a victim. They could, of course, have chosen another hypothesis (try to think of one!), but their initial formulation seemed to offer the most direct test of the theory.

Psychologists rely on formal theories and hypotheses for many reasons. For one thing, theories and hypotheses allow them to make sense of unorganized, separate observations and bits of data. They permit them to place observations and data within a coherent framework. In addition, theories and hypotheses allow psychologists to move beyond known facts and make deductions about unexplained phenomena and develop ideas for future investigation (van Wesel, Boeije, & Hoijtink, 2013; Barrett & Russell, 2015).

In short, the scientific method, with its emphasis on theories and hypotheses, helps psychologists pose appropriate questions. With properly stated questions in hand, psychologists then can choose from a variety of research methods to find answers.

Study Alert

Remember that a theory is a broad explanation, whereas a hypothesis is a more narrow prediction.

Psychological Research

Research—systematic inquiry aimed at the discovery of new knowledge—is a central ingredient of the scientific method in psychology. It provides the key to understanding the degree to which hypotheses (and the theories behind them) are accurate.

Just as we can apply different theories and hypotheses to explain the same phenomena, we can use a number of alternative methods to conduct research. As we consider the major tools that psychologists use to conduct research, keep in mind that their relevance extends beyond testing and evaluating hypotheses in psychology. All of us carry out elementary forms of research on our own. For instance, a supervisor might evaluate an employee's performance; a physician might systematically test the effects of different doses of a drug on a patient; a salesperson might compare different persuasive strategies. Each of these situations draws on the research practices we are about to discuss.

Descriptive Research

Let's begin by considering several types of *descriptive research* designed to systematically investigate a person, group, or patterns of behavior. These methods include archival research, naturalistic observation, survey research, and case studies.

ARCHIVAL RESEARCH

Suppose that, like the psychologists Latané and Darley (1970), you were interested in finding out more about emergency situations in which bystanders did not provide help. One of the first places you might turn to would be historical accounts. By searching newspaper records, for example, you might find support for the notion that a decrease in helping behavior historically has accompanied an increase in the number of bystanders.

Using newspaper articles is an example of archival research. In **archival research,** existing data, such as census documents, college records, online databases, and newspaper articles, are examined to test a hypothesis. For example, college transcripts may be used to determine if there are gender differences in academic performance. Similarly,

archival research Research in which existing data, such as census documents, college records, and newspaper articles, are examined to test a hypothesis. (Module 3)

Facebook provides a huge pool of data from millions of users that can be used to collect data (Sullivan, Riccio, & Reynolds, 2008; Fisher & Barnes-Farrell, 2013; Kosinski et al., 2015).

Archival research is a relatively inexpensive means of testing a hypothesis because someone else has already collected the basic data. Of course, the use of existing data has several drawbacks. For one thing, the data may not be in a form that allows the researcher to test a hypothesis fully. The information could be incomplete, or it could have been collected haphazardly (Riniolo et al., 2003; Vega, 2006; Zickar, 2015).

Most attempts at archival research are hampered by the simple fact that records with the necessary information often do not exist. In these instances, researchers often turn to another research method: naturalistic observation.

NATURALISTIC OBSERVATION

In **naturalistic observation,** the investigator observes some naturally occurring behavior and does not make a change in the situation. For example, a researcher investigating helping behavior might observe the kind of help given to victims in a high-crime area of a city. The important point to remember about naturalistic observation is that the researcher simply records what occurs, making no modification in the situation that is being observed (Kennison & Bowers, 2011; Haas et al., 2015; Wilson & Joye, 2017).

Although the advantage of naturalistic observation is obvious—we get a sample of what people do in their "natural habitat"—there is also an important drawback: the inability to control any of the factors of interest. For example, we might find so few naturally occurring instances of helping behavior that we would be unable to draw any conclusions. Because naturalistic observation prevents researchers from making changes in a situation, they must wait until the appropriate conditions occur. Furthermore, if people know they are being watched, they may alter their reactions and produce behavior that is not truly representative.

SURVEY RESEARCH

There is no more straightforward way of finding out what people think, feel, and do than asking them directly. For this reason, surveys are an important research method. In **survey research,** a *sample* of people chosen to represent a larger group of interest (a *population*) is asked a series of questions about their behavior, thoughts, or attitudes. Survey methods have become so sophisticated that even with a very small sample researchers are able to infer with great accuracy how a larger group would respond. For instance, a sample of just a few thousand voters is sufficient to predict within one or two percentage points who will win a presidential election—if the representative sample is chosen with care (Sommer & Sommer, 2001; Groves et al., 2004; Igo, 2006).

Researchers investigating helping behavior might conduct a survey by asking people to complete a questionnaire in which they indicate their reluctance for giving aid to someone. Similarly, researchers interested in learning about sexual practices have carried out surveys to learn which practices are common and which are not and to chart changing notions of sexual morality over the last several decades (Reece et al., 2009; Santelli et al., 2009).

However, survey research has several potential pitfalls. For one thing, if the sample of people who are surveyed is not representative of the broader population of interest, the results of the survey will have little meaning. For instance, if a sample of voters in a town includes only Republicans, it would hardly be useful for predicting the results of an election in which both Republicans and Democrats are voting. Consequently, researchers using surveys strive to obtain a *random sample* of the population in question in which every voter in the town has an equal chance of being included in the sample receiving the survey (Davern, 2013; Engel et al., 2015; Nedelec, 2017).

naturalistic observation Research in which an investigator simply observes some naturally occurring behavior and does not make a change in the situation. (Module 3)

In an example of naturalistic observation, researchers observe primates in their natural habitat.
©Suzanne Long/Alamy Stock Photo

survey research Research in which people chosen to represent a larger population are asked a series of questions about their behavior, thoughts, or attitudes. (Module 3)

PsychTech
One of the most efficient ways to conduct surveys is via the web. But web surveys may have sampling problems, given that not everyone has easy access to the web, such as people living in poverty. Consequently, web surveys may not be representative of the broader population.

In addition, survey respondents may not want to admit to holding socially undesirable attitudes. (Most racists know they are racists and might not want to admit it.) Furthermore, people may not want to admit they engage in behaviors that they feel are somehow abnormal–a problem that plagues surveys of sexual behavior because people are often reluctant to admit what they really do in private. Finally, in some cases, people may not even be consciously aware of what their true attitudes are or why they hold them.

From the perspective of...

A Marketing Manager How would you design a survey that targets the customers in which you are most interested?

©Jack Hollingsworth/Getty Images

THE CASE STUDY

case study An in-depth, intensive investigation of an individual or small group of people. (Module 3)

When they read of a suicide bomber in the Middle East, many people wonder what it is about the terrorist's personality or background that leads to such behavior. To answer this question, psychologists might conduct a case study. In contrast to a survey, in which many people are studied, a **case study** is an in-depth, intensive investigation of a single individual or a small group. Case studies often include *psychological testing*, a procedure in which a carefully designed set of questions is used to gain some insight into the personality of the individual or group (Gass et al., 2000; Addus, Chen, & Khan, 2007).

When case studies are used as a research technique, the goal is to use the insights gained from the study of a few individuals to improve our understanding of people in general. Sigmund Freud developed his theories through case studies of individual patients. Similarly, case studies of terrorists might help identify others who are prone to violence.

The drawback to case studies? If the individuals examined are unique in certain ways, it is impossible to make valid generalizations to a larger population. Still, case studies sometimes lead the way to new theories and treatments for psychological disorders.

CORRELATIONAL RESEARCH

variables Behaviors, events, or other characteristics that can change, or vary, in some way. (Module 3)

In using the descriptive research methods we have discussed, researchers often wish to determine the relationship between two variables. **Variables** are behaviors, events, or other characteristics that can change, or vary, in some way. For example, in a study to determine whether the amount of studying makes a difference in test scores, the variables would be study time and test scores.

correlational research Research in which the relationship between two sets of variables is examined to determine whether they are associated, or "correlated." (Module 3)

In **correlational research,** two sets of variables are examined to determine whether they are associated, or "correlated." The strength and direction of the relationship between the two variables are represented by a mathematical statistic known as a *correlation* (or, more formally, a *correlation coefficient*), which can range from +1.0 to −1.0.

A *positive correlation* indicates that as the value of one variable increases, we can predict that the value of the other variable will also increase. For example, if we predict that the more time students spend studying for a test, the higher their grades on the test will be and that the less they study, the lower their test scores will be, we are expecting to find a positive correlation. (Higher values of the variable "amount of study time" would be associated with higher values of the variable "test score," and lower values of "amount of study time" would be associated with lower values of "test score.") The correlation, then, would be indicated by a positive number, and the stronger the association was between studying and test scores, the closer the number would be to +1.0. For example, we might find a correlation of +.85 between test scores and amount of study time, indicating a strong positive association.

In contrast, a *negative correlation* tells us that as the value of one variable increases, the value of the other decreases. For instance, we might predict that as the number of hours spent studying increases, the number of hours spent partying decreases. Here we are expecting a negative correlation, ranging between 0 and −1.0. More studying is associated with less partying, and less studying is associated with more partying. The stronger the association between studying and partying is, the closer the correlation will be to −1.0. For instance, a correlation of −.85 would indicate a strong negative association between partying and studying.

Of course, it's quite possible that little or no relationship exists between two variables. For instance, we would probably not expect to find a relationship between number of study hours and height. Lack of a relationship would be indicated by a correlation close to 0. For example, if we found a correlation of −.02 or +.03, it would indicate that there is virtually no association between the two variables; knowing how much someone studies does not tell us anything about how tall he or she is.

When two variables are strongly correlated with each other, it is tempting to assume that one variable causes changes in the other variable. For example, if we find that more study time is associated with higher grades, we might guess that more studying *causes* higher grades. Although this is not a bad guess, it remains just a guess—because finding that two variables are correlated does not mean that there is a causal relationship between them. The strong correlation suggests that knowing how much a person studies can help us predict how that person will do on a test, but it does not mean that the studying *causes* the test performance. Instead, for instance, people who are more interested in the subject matter might study more than do those who are less interested, and so the amount of interest, not the number of hours spent studying, would predict test performance. The mere fact that two variables occur together does not mean that one causes the other.

Similarly, suppose you learned that the number of houses of worship in a large sample of cities was positively correlated with the number of people arrested, meaning that the more houses of worship, the more arrests there were in a city. Does this mean that the presence of more houses of worship caused the greater number of arrests? Almost surely not, of course. In this case, the underlying cause is probably the size of the city: In bigger cities, there are both more houses of worship *and* more arrests.

One more example illustrates the critical point that correlations tell us nothing about cause and effect but only provide a measure of the strength of a relationship between two variables. We might find that children who watch a lot of television programs featuring high levels of aggression are likely to demonstrate a relatively high degree of aggressive behavior and that those who watch few television shows that portray aggression are apt to exhibit a relatively low degree of such behavior (see Figure 2). But we cannot say that the aggression is *caused* by the TV viewing because many other explanations are possible.

For instance, it could be that children who have an unusually high level of energy seek out programs with aggressive content *and* are more aggressive. The children's energy level, then, could be the true cause of the children's higher incidence of aggression. Also, people who are already highly aggressive might choose to watch shows with a high aggressive content *because* they are aggressive. Clearly, then, any number of causal sequences are possible—none of which can be ruled out by correlational research (Feshbach & Tangney, 2008; Grimes & Bergen, 2008).

The inability of correlational research to demonstrate cause-and-effect relationships is a crucial drawback to its use. There is, however, an alternative technique that does establish causality: the experiment.

Study Alert

The concept that "correlation does not imply causation" is a key principle.

Many studies show that the observation of violence in the media is associated with aggression in viewers. Can we conclude that the observations of violence cause aggression?
©Andrey_Popov/Shutterstock

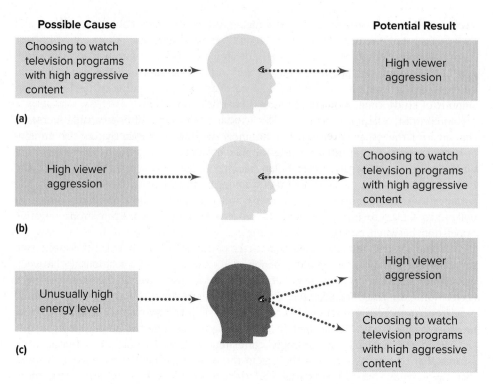

Possible Cause

Potential Result

(a) Choosing to watch television programs with high aggressive content → High viewer aggression

(b) High viewer aggression → Choosing to watch television programs with high aggressive content

(c) Unusually high energy level → High viewer aggression / Choosing to watch television programs with high aggressive content

FIGURE 2 If we find that frequent viewing of television programs with aggressive content is associated with high levels of aggressive behavior, we might cite several plausible causes, as suggested in this figure. For example, (a) choosing to watch shows with aggressive content could produce aggression; or (b) being a highly aggressive person might cause one to choose to watch televised aggression; or (c) having a high energy level might cause a person to both choose to watch aggressive shows and to act aggressively. Correlational findings, then, do not permit us to determine causality. Can you think of a way to study the effects of televised aggression on aggressive behavior that is not correlational?

Experimental Research

Carrying out experiments is the *only* way psychologists can establish cause-and-effect relationships. In a formal **experiment,** the researcher investigates the relationship between two (or more) variables by deliberately changing one variable in a controlled situation and observing the effects of that change on other aspects of the situation. In an experiment, then, the conditions are created and controlled by the researcher, who deliberately makes a change in those conditions in order to observe the effects of that change.

The **experimental manipulation** is the change that a researcher deliberately makes in an experiment. Experimental manipulations are used to detect relationships between different variables (Salazar, Crosby, & DiClemente, 2015).

Several steps are involved in carrying out an experiment, but the process typically begins with the development of one or more hypotheses for the experiment to test. For example, Latané and Darley, in testing their theory of the diffusion of responsibility in bystander behavior, developed this hypothesis: The higher the number of people who witness an emergency situation is, the less likely it is that any of them will help the victim. They then designed an experiment to test this hypothesis.

Their first step was to formulate an operational definition of the hypothesis by conceptualizing it in a way that could be tested. Latané and Darley had to take into account the fundamental principle of experimental research mentioned earlier: Experimenters must manipulate at least one variable in order to observe the effects of the manipulation on another variable while keeping other factors in the situation constant. However, the manipulation cannot be viewed by itself, in isolation; if a cause-and-effect

experiment The investigation of the relationship between two (or more) variables by deliberately producing a change in one variable in a situation and observing the effects of that change on other aspects of the situation. (Module 3)

experimental manipulation The change that an experimenter deliberately produces in a situation. (Module 3)

relationship is to be established, the effects of the manipulation must be compared with the effects of no manipulation or a different kind of manipulation.

EXPERIMENTAL GROUPS AND CONTROL GROUPS

Experimental research requires, then, that the responses of at least two groups be compared. One group will receive some special **treatment**–the manipulation implemented by the experimenter–and another group will receive either no treatment or a different treatment. Any group that receives a treatment is called an **experimental group;** a group that receives no treatment is called a **control group.** (In some experiments, there are multiple experimental and control groups, each of which is compared with another group.)

treatment The manipulation implemented by the experimenter. (Module 3)

experimental group Any group participating in an experiment that receives a treatment. (Module 3)

By employing both experimental and control groups in an experiment, researchers are able to rule out the possibility that something other than the experimental manipulation produced the results observed in the experiment. Without a control group, we couldn't be sure that some other variable, such as the temperature at the time we were running the experiment, the color of the experimenter's hair, or even the mere passage of time, wasn't causing the changes observed.

control group A group participating in an experiment that receives no treatment. (Module 3)

For example, consider a medical researcher who thinks he has invented a medicine that cures the common cold. To test his claim, he gives the medicine one day to a group of 20 people who have colds and finds that 10 days later all of them are cured.

Eureka? Not so fast. An observer viewing this flawed study might reasonably argue that the people would have gotten better even without the medicine. What the researcher obviously needed was a control group consisting of people with colds who *don't* get the medicine and whose health is also checked 10 days later. Only if there is a significant difference between experimental and control groups can the effectiveness of the medicine be assessed. Through the use of control groups, then, researchers can isolate specific causes for their findings–and draw cause-and-effect inferences.

Returning to Latané and Darley's experiment, we see that the researchers needed to translate their hypothesis into something testable. To do this, they decided to create a false emergency situation that would appear to require the aid of a bystander. As their experimental manipulation, they decided to vary the number of bystanders present. They could have had just one experimental group with, say, two people present and a control group for comparison purposes with just one person present. Instead, they settled on a more complex procedure involving the creation of groups of three sizes–consisting of two, three, and six people–that could be compared with one another.

In this experiment, preschoolers' reactions to the puppet are monitored. Can you think of a hypothesis that might be tested in this way?
©Thierry Berrod, Mona Lisa Production/Science Source

INDEPENDENT AND DEPENDENT VARIABLES

Latané and Darley's experimental design now included an operational definition of what is called the **independent variable.** The independent variable is the condition that is manipulated by an experimenter. (You can think of the independent variable as being independent of the actions of those taking part in an experiment; it is controlled by the experimenter.) In the case of the Latané and Darley experiment, the independent variable was the number of people present, which was manipulated by the experimenters.

independent variable The variable that is manipulated by an experimenter. (Module 3)

The next step was to decide how they were going to determine the effect that varying the number of bystanders had on behavior of those in the experiment. Crucial to every experiment is the **dependent variable.** The dependent variable is the variable that is measured in a study. The dependent variable is expected to change as a result of the experimenter's manipulation of the independent variable. The dependent

dependent variable The variable that is measured in an experiment. It is expected to change as a result of the experimenter's manipulation of the independent variable. (Module 3)

variable is dependent on the actions of the *participants* or *subjects*–the people taking part in the experiment.

Latané and Darley had several possible choices for their dependent measure. One might have been a simple yes/no measure of the participants' helping behavior. But the investigators also wanted a more precise analysis of helping behavior. Consequently, they also measured the amount of time it took for a participant to provide help.

Latané and Darley now had all the necessary components of an experiment. The independent variable, manipulated by them, was the number of bystanders present in an emergency situation. The dependent variable was the measure of whether bystanders in each of the groups provided help and the amount of time it took them to do so. Consequently, like all experiments, this one had both an independent variable and a dependent variable. *All* true experiments in psychology fit this straightforward model.

RANDOM ASSIGNMENT OF PARTICIPANTS

To make the experiment a valid test of the hypothesis, Latané and Darley needed to add a final step to the design: properly assigning participants to a particular experimental group.

The significance of this step becomes clear when we examine various alternative procedures. For example, the experimenters might have assigned just males to the group with two bystanders, just females to the group with three bystanders, and both males and females to the group with six bystanders. If they had done this, however, any differences they found in helping behavior could not be attributed with any certainty solely to group size because the differences might just as well have been due to the composition of the group. A more reasonable procedure would be to ensure that each group had the same composition in terms of gender; then the researchers would be able to make comparisons across groups with considerably more accuracy.

Participants in each of the experimental groups ought to be comparable, and it is easy enough to create groups that are similar in terms of gender. The problem becomes a bit more tricky, though, when we consider other participant characteristics. How can we ensure that participants in each experimental group will be equally intelligent, extroverted, cooperative, and so forth, when the list of characteristics–any one of which could be important–is potentially endless?

The solution is a simple but elegant procedure called **random assignment to condition.** Participants are assigned to different experimental groups, or "conditions," on the basis of chance and chance alone. The experimenter might, for instance, flip a coin for each participant and assign a participant to one group when "heads" came up and to the other group when "tails" came up. The advantage of this technique is that there is an equal chance that participant characteristics will be distributed across the various groups. When a researcher uses random assignment–which in practice is usually carried out using computer-generated random numbers–chances are that each of the groups will have approximately the same proportion of intelligent people, cooperative people, extroverted people, males and females, and so on.

Figure 3 provides another example of an experiment. Like all experiments, it includes the following set of key elements, which you should keep in mind as you consider whether a research study is truly an experiment:

- An independent variable, the variable that is manipulated by the experimenter
- A dependent variable, the variable that is measured by the experimenter and that is expected to change as a result of the manipulation of the independent variable
- A procedure that randomly assigns participants to different experimental groups, or "conditions," of the independent variable
- A hypothesis that predicts the effect the independent variable will have on the dependent variable

Study Alert

To remember the difference between dependent and independent variables, recall that a hypothesis predicts how a dependent variable *depends* on the manipulation of the independent variable.

random assignment to condition A procedure in which participants are assigned to different experimental groups or "conditions" on the basis of chance and chance alone. (Module 3)

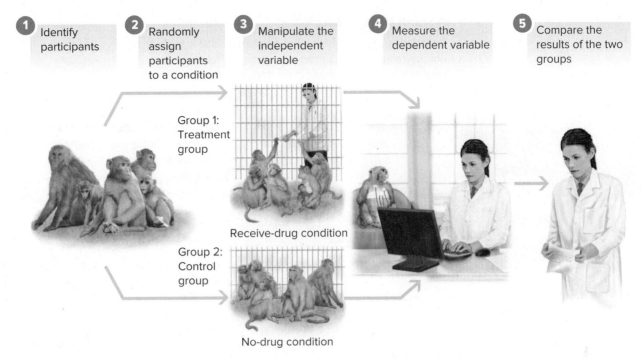

① Identify participants

② Randomly assign participants to a condition

③ Manipulate the independent variable

④ Measure the dependent variable

⑤ Compare the results of the two groups

Group 1: Treatment group

Receive-drug condition

Group 2: Control group

No-drug condition

FIGURE 3 In this depiction of a study investigating the effects of the drug propranolol on heart disease, we can see the basic elements of all true experiments. The participants in the experiment were monkeys that were randomly assigned to one of two groups. Monkeys assigned to the treatment group were given propranolol, hypothesized to prevent heart disease, whereas those in the control group were not given the drug. Administration of the drugs, then, was the independent variable.

All the monkeys were given a high-fat diet that was the human equivalent of two eggs with bacon every morning, and they occasionally were reassigned to different cages to increase their stress. To determine the effects of the drug, the monkeys' heart rates and other measures of heart disease were assessed after 26 months. These measures constituted the dependent variable. The results? As hypothesized, monkeys that received the drug showed slower heart rates and fewer symptoms of heart disease than those that did not.

Source: Based on Kaplan, J. R., & Manuck, S. B. (1989). The effect of propranolol on behavioral interactions among adult male cynomolgus monkeys *(Macaca-fascicularis)* housed in disrupted social groupings. *Psychosomatic Medicine, 51,* 449–462.

Only if each of these elements is present can a research study be considered a true experiment in which cause-and-effect relationships can be determined. (For a summary of the different types of research that we've discussed, see Figure 4.)

WERE LATANÉ AND DARLEY RIGHT?

To test their hypothesis that increasing the number of bystanders in an emergency situation would lower the degree of helping behavior, Latané and Darley placed the participants in a room and told them that the purpose of the experiment was to talk about personal problems associated with college. The discussion was to be held over an intercom, supposedly to avoid the potential embarrassment of face-to-face contact. Chatting about personal problems was not, of course, the true purpose of the experiment, but telling the participants that it was provided a way of keeping their expectations from biasing their behavior. (Consider how they would have been affected if they had been told that their helping behavior in emergencies was being tested. The experimenters could never have gotten an accurate assessment of what the participants would actually do in an emergency. By definition, emergencies are rarely announced in advance.)

The sizes of the discussion groups were two, three, and six people, which constituted the manipulation of the independent variable of group size. Participants were randomly assigned to these groups upon their arrival at the laboratory. Each group included one trained confederate of the experimenters. A *confederate* is an actor employed by a researcher who participates in a psychological experiment, pretending

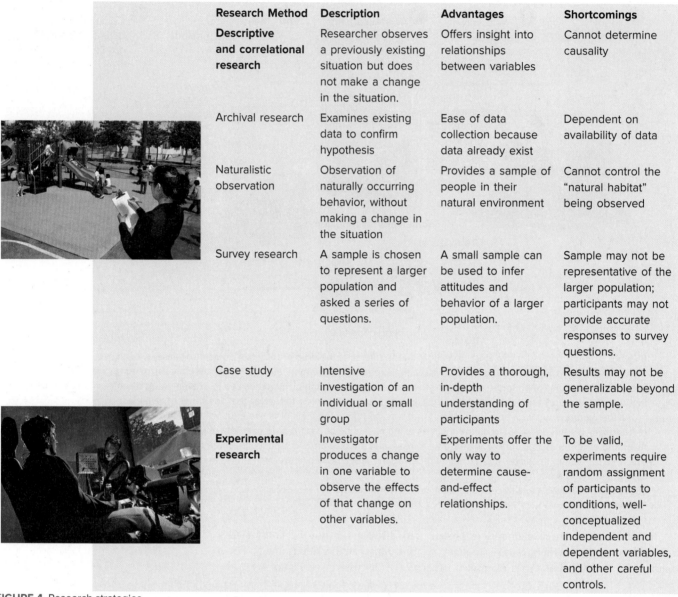

Research Method	Description	Advantages	Shortcomings
Descriptive and correlational research	Researcher observes a previously existing situation but does not make a change in the situation.	Offers insight into relationships between variables	Cannot determine causality
Archival research	Examines existing data to confirm hypothesis	Ease of data collection because data already exist	Dependent on availability of data
Naturalistic observation	Observation of naturally occurring behavior, without making a change in the situation	Provides a sample of people in their natural environment	Cannot control the "natural habitat" being observed
Survey research	A sample is chosen to represent a larger population and asked a series of questions.	A small sample can be used to infer attitudes and behavior of a larger population.	Sample may not be representative of the larger population; participants may not provide accurate responses to survey questions.
Case study	Intensive investigation of an individual or small group	Provides a thorough, in-depth understanding of participants	Results may not be generalizable beyond the sample.
Experimental research	Investigator produces a change in one variable to observe the effects of that change on other variables.	Experiments offer the only way to determine cause-and-effect relationships.	To be valid, experiments require random assignment of participants to conditions, well-conceptualized independent and dependent variables, and other careful controls.

FIGURE 4 Research strategies.

(top): ©Bill Aron/PhotoEdit; (bottom): ©Marc Steinmetz/Visum/The Image Works

to be a participant. The researcher trains the confederate to act in a particular way during the experiment.

As the participants in each group were holding their discussion, they suddenly heard through the intercom one of the other participants–but who in reality was the confederate–having what sounded like an epileptic seizure. The confederate then called for help.

The actual participants' behavior was now what counted. The dependent variable was the time that elapsed from the start of the "seizure" to the time a participant began trying to help the "victim." If 6 minutes went by without a participant offering help, the experiment was ended.

As predicted by the hypothesis, the size of the group had a significant effect on whether a participant provided help. The more people who were present, the less likely it was that someone would supply help, as you can see in Figure 5 (Latané & Darley, 1970).

Because these results are straightforward, it seems clear that the experiment confirmed the original hypothesis. However, Latané and Darley could not be sure that the

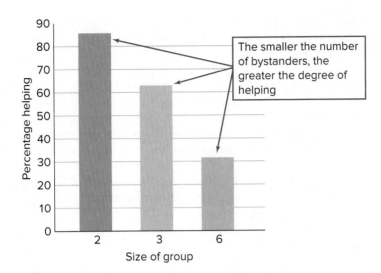

The smaller the number of bystanders, the greater the degree of helping

FIGURE 5 The Latané and Darley experiment showed that as the size of the group witnessing an emergency increased, helping behavior decreased.
Source: Adapted from Darley, J. M., & Latané, B. (1968). Bystanders' intervention in emergencies: Diffusion of responsibility. *Journal of Personality and Social Psychology, 8,* 377–383.

results were truly meaningful until they determined whether the results represented what statisticians call a significant outcome. A **significant outcome** indicates that the findings are statistically meaningful, making it possible for researchers to feel confident that they have confirmed their hypotheses. Using statistical analysis, researchers can determine whether a numeric difference is a real difference or is due merely to chance. Only when differences between groups are large enough that statistical tests show them to be significant is it possible for researchers to confirm a hypothesis (Cwikel, Behar, & Rabson-Hare, 2000; Cohen, 2002).

significant outcome Meaningful results that make it possible for researchers to feel confident that they have confirmed their hypotheses. (Module 3)

MOVING BEYOND THE STUDY

The Latané and Darley study contains all the elements of an experiment: an independent variable, a dependent variable, random assignment to conditions, and multiple experimental groups. Consequently, we can say with some confidence that group size *caused* changes in the degree of helping behavior.

Of course, one experiment alone does not forever resolve the question of bystander intervention in emergencies. Psychologists–like other scientists–require that findings be **replicated,** or repeated, sometimes using other procedures, in other settings, with other groups of participants, before full confidence can be placed in the results of any single experiment. For example, follow-up research shows that college students aren't the only ones who show the bystander effect; young children do as well. Furthermore, a procedure called *meta-analysis* permits psychologists to combine the results of many separate studies into one overall conclusion (Kisely et al., 2015; Plotner et al., 2015; Stone & Rosopa, 2017).

replicated research Research that is repeated, sometimes using other procedures, settings, and groups of participants, to increase confidence in prior findings. (Module 3)

Replication is a critical activity, and many researchers believe that psychologists need to increase the number of studies that are replications of earlier research in order to have greater confidence in their findings. They point to an influential study that attempted to replicate 100 previous findings but that found that only 36% of the replications yielded similarly significant findings as in the original studies. The takeaway message: in order to be fully confident about the meaning of research studies, they need to be replicated (Maxwell, Lau, & Howard, 2015; Open Science Collaboration, 2015; Card, 2017).

In addition to replicating experimental results, psychologists need to test the limitations of their theories and hypotheses to determine under which specific circumstances they do and do not apply. It seems unlikely, for instance, that increasing the number of bystanders *always* results in less helping. In fact, follow-up research shows that bystander intervention is more likely to occur in situations viewed as clear-cut and dangerous because bystanders are more likely to perceive that the presence of others will provide resources for helping. In short, it is critical to continue carrying out experiments to understand the conditions in which exceptions to this general rule occur and other circumstances in which the rule holds (Garcia-Palacios, Hoffman, & Carlin, 2002; Fischer et al., 2011).

Before leaving the Latané and Darley study, note that it represents a good illustration of the basic principles of the scientific method. The two psychologists began with a *question of interest*, in this case stemming from a real-world incident in which bystanders in an emergency did not offer help. They then *formulated an explanation* by specifying a theory of diffusion of responsibility and from that formulated the specific hypothesis that increasing the number of bystanders in an emergency situation would lower the degree of helping behavior. Finally, they *carried out research* to confirm their hypothesis, and they eventually *communicated their findings* by publishing their results. This four-step process embodied in the scientific method underlies all scientific inquiry, allowing us to develop a valid understanding of others'–and our own–behavior.

RECAP/EVALUATE/RETHINK

RECAP

LO 3-1 What is the scientific method?

- The scientific method is the approach psychologists use to understand behavior. It consists of four steps: identifying questions of interest, formulating an explanation, carrying out research that is designed to support or refute the explanation, and communicating the findings.
- To test a hypothesis, researchers must formulate an operational definition, which translates the abstract concepts of the hypothesis into the actual procedures used in the study.

LO 3-2 What role do theories and hypotheses play in psychological research?

- Research in psychology is guided by theories (broad explanations and predictions regarding phenomena of interest) and hypotheses (theory-based predictions stated in a way that allows them to be tested).

LO 3-3 What research methods do psychologists use?

- Archival research uses existing records, such as old newspapers, online databases, or other documents, to test a hypothesis. In naturalistic observation, the investigator acts mainly as an observer, making no change in a naturally occurring situation. In survey research, people are asked a series of questions about their behavior, thoughts, or attitudes. The case study is an in-depth interview and examination of one person or group.
- These descriptive research methods rely on correlational techniques, which describe associations between variables but cannot determine cause-and-effect relationships.

LO 3-4 How do psychologists establish cause-and-effect relationships in research studies?

- In a formal experiment, the relationship between variables is investigated by deliberately producing a change–called the experimental manipulation–in one variable and observing changes in the other variable.
- In an experiment, at least two groups must be compared to assess cause-and-effect relationships. The group receiving the treatment (the special procedure devised by the experimenter) is the experimental group; the second group (which receives no treatment) is the control group. There also may be multiple experimental groups, each of which is subjected to a different procedure and then compared with the others.
- The variable that experimenters manipulate is the independent variable. The variable that they measure and expect to change as a result of manipulation of the independent variable is called the dependent variable.
- In a formal experiment, participants must be assigned randomly to treatment conditions, so that participant characteristics are distributed evenly across the different conditions.
- Psychologists use statistical tests to determine whether research findings are significant.

EVALUATE

1. An explanation for a phenomenon of interest is known as a _____.
2. To test this explanation, a researcher must state it in terms of a testable question known as a _____.
3. An experimenter is interested in studying the relationship between hunger and aggression. She decides that she will measure aggression by counting the number of times a participant will hit a punching bag. In this case, her _____ definition of aggression is the number of times the participant hits the bag.

4. Match the following forms of research to their definitions:

1. Archival research
2. Naturalistic observation
3. Survey research
4. Case study

    a. Directly asking a sample of people questions about their behavior
    b. Examining existing records to test a hypothesis
    c. Looking at behavior in its true setting without intervening in the setting
    d. Doing an in-depth investigation of a person or small group

5. Match each of the following research methods with its primary disadvantage:

1. Archival research
2. Naturalistic observation
3. Survey research
4. Case study

    a. The researcher may not be able to generalize to the population at large.
    b. People's behavior can change if they know they are being watched.
    c. The data may not exist or may be unusable.
    d. People may lie in order to present a good image.

6. A psychologist wants to study the effect of attractiveness on willingness to help a person with a math problem. Attractiveness would be the _____ variable, and the amount of helping would be the _____ variable.

7. The group in an experiment that receives no treatment is called the _____ group.

RETHINK

Starting with the theory that diffusion of responsibility causes responsibility for helping to be shared among bystanders, Latané and Darley derived the hypothesis that the more people who witness an emergency situation, the less likely it is that help will be given to a victim. Can you think of other hypotheses that are based on the same theory of diffusion of responsibility?

Answers to Evaluate Questions

1. theory; 2. hypothesis; 3. operational; 4. 1. b, 2. c, 3. a, 4. d 5. 1. c, 2. b, 3. d, 4. a 6. independent, dependent; 7. control

Module 4
Critical Research Issues

LEARNING OUTCOME

LO 4-1 What major issues confront psychologists conducting research?

Study Alert

Because the protection of experiment participants is essential, remember the key ethical guideline of informed consent.

informed consent A document signed by participants affirming that they have been told the basic outlines of the study and are aware of what their participation will involve. (Module 4)

You probably realize by now that there are few simple formulas for psychological research. Psychologists must make choices about the type of study to conduct, the measures to take, and the most effective way to analyze the results. Even after they have made these essential decisions, they must still consider several critical issues. We turn first to the most fundamental of these issues: ethics.

The Ethics of Research

Put yourself in the place of one of the participants in the experiment conducted by Latané and Darley to examine the helping behavior of bystanders, in which another "bystander" simulating a seizure turned out to be a confederate of the experimenters (Latané & Darley, 1970). How would you feel when you learned that the supposed victim was in reality a paid accomplice?

Although you might at first experience relief that there had been no real emergency, you might also feel some resentment that you had been deceived by the experimenter. You might also experience concern that you had been placed in an embarrassing or compromising situation—one that might have dealt a blow to your self-esteem, depending on how you had behaved.

Most psychologists argue that deception is sometimes necessary to prevent participants from being influenced by what they think a study's true purpose is. (If you knew that Latané and Darley were actually studying your helping behavior, wouldn't you automatically have been tempted to intervene in the emergency?) To avoid such outcomes, a small proportion of research involves deception.

Nonetheless, because research has the potential to violate the rights of participants, psychologists are expected to adhere to a strict set of ethical guidelines aimed at protecting participants (American Psychological Association, 2002). Those guidelines involve the following safeguards:

- Protection of participants from physical and mental harm
- The right of participants to privacy regarding their behavior
- The assurance that participation in research is completely voluntary
- The necessity of informing participants about the nature of procedures before their participation in the experiment
- All experiments must be reviewed by an independent panel before being conducted (Fisher, 2003; Coventry et al., 2003; Crano, Brewer, & Lac, 2015).

One of psychologists' key ethical principles is **informed consent.** Before participating in an experiment, the participants must sign a document affirming that they have been told the basic outlines of the study and are aware of what their participation will involve, what risks the experiment may hold, and the fact that their participation is purely voluntary and they may terminate it at any time. Furthermore, after participation in a study, they must be given a debriefing in which they receive an explanation of the study and the procedures that were involved. The only time informed consent and a debriefing can be eliminated is in experiments in which the risks are minimal, as in a purely observational study in a public place (Barnett, Wise, & Johnson-Greene, 2007; Nagy, 2011; Hetzel-Riggin, 2017).

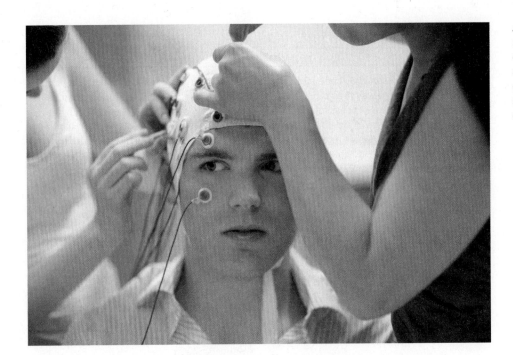

Although readily available and widely used as research subjects, college students may not represent the population at large. What are some advantages and drawbacks of using college students as subjects?
©annedde/Getty Images

 # Exploring Diversity

Choosing Participants Who Represent the Scope of Human Behavior

When Latané and Darley, both college professors, decided who would participate in their experiment, they turned to the people most easily available: college students. Using college students as participants has advantages as well as drawbacks. The big benefit is that because most research occurs in university settings, college students are readily available. Typically, they cost the researcher very little: They participate for either extra course credit or a relatively small payment.

The problem is that college students may not represent the general population adequately. In fact, undergraduate research participants are typically a special group of people: Relative to the general population, college students tend to be from **W**estern, **e**ducated, **i**ndustrialized, **r**ich, and **d**emocratic cultures. That description forms the acronym WEIRD, which led one researcher to apply the nickname to research participants (Jones, 2010; Lancy, 2015).

It's not that there's anything particularly wrong with WEIRD participants. It's just that they may be different from most other people—those who don't go to college or who didn't grow up in a democratic Western culture, who are less affluent, and so forth. All these characteristics could be psychologically relevant. Yet one review found that most research participants do come from the United States, and about the same proportion of those are psychology majors (Arnett, 2008; Henrich, Heine, & Norenzayan, 2010; Kaiser, Thomas, & Bowers, 2017).

Because psychology is a science whose goal is to explain *all* human behavior generally, its studies must use participants who are fully representative of the general population in terms of gender, age, race, ethnicity, socioeconomic status, and educational level (see *Neuroscience in Your Life*). To encourage a wider range of participants, the National Institute of Mental Health and the National Science Foundation—the primary U.S. funding sources for psychological research—now require that experiments address issues of diverse populations (Carpenter, 2002; Lindley, 2006).

NEUROSCIENCE IN YOUR LIFE: THE IMPORTANCE OF USING REPRESENTATIVE PARTICIPANTS

Most neuroscience research is conducted to understand the brains of all individuals. But people differ significantly in the way they process information. For example, culture and experiences shape the way our brains process information. A recent review of seven studies showed that individuals raised in Eastern countries, such as Japan, and individuals raised in Western countries, such as the United States, process information differently during cognitive tasks. In the images below, each brain indicates a different area in which differences were seen. The key indicates within a brain whether Easterners showed greater activation (yellow) or vice versa (green). Overall, Easterners show more activity in the left hemisphere (yellow), whereas Westerners show more activity in the right hemisphere (green). Therefore, to understand the brains of all people, researchers must include participants who represent the rich diversity of the humanity (Han & Ma, 2014).

The areas of the brain in which differences between Easterners and Westerners were seen. Yellow areas indicate that Easterners showed greater activation than Westerners, and green areas indicate that Westerners showed greater activation than Easterners.

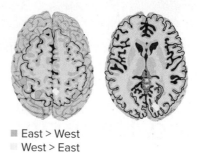

■ East > West
▨ West > East

Source: Adapted from Han, S., & Ma, Y. "Cultural differences in human brain activity: a quantitative meta-analysis." *Neuroimage, 99*, 2014, 293–300.

Should Animals Be Used in Research?

Like those who work with humans, researchers who use nonhuman animals in experiments have their own set of exacting guidelines to ensure that the animals do not suffer. Specifically, researchers must make every effort to minimize discomfort, illness, and pain. Procedures that subject animals to distress are permitted only when an alternative procedure is unavailable and when the research is justified by its prospective value. Moreover, researchers strive to avoid causing physical discomfort, but they are also required to promote the *psychological* well-being of some species of research animals, such as primates (Lutz & Novak, 2005; Miller & Williams, 2011; Herzog, 2017).

But why should animals be used for research in the first place? Can we really learn about human behavior from the results of research employing rats, gerbils, and pigeons?

The answer is that psychological research that does employ nonhumans is designed to answer questions different from those posed in research with humans. For example, the shorter life span of animals (rats live an average of 2 years) allows researchers to learn about the effects of aging in a relatively short time frame. Researchers can also provide greater experimental control over nonhumans and carry out procedures that might not be possible with people. For example, some studies require large numbers of participants that share similar backgrounds or have been exposed to particular environments—conditions that could not practically be met with human beings.

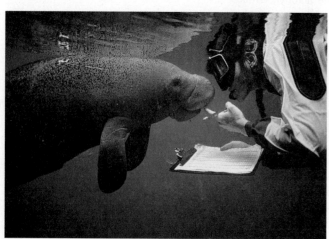

Research involving animals is controversial but when conducted within ethical guidelines yields significant benefits for humans.

©Douglas Faulkner/Science Source

Research with animals has provided psychologists with information that has profoundly benefited humans. For instance, it furnished the keys to detecting eye disorders in children early enough to prevent permanent damage, to communicating more effectively with children with severe intellectual disability, and to reducing chronic pain in people. Still, the use of research using nonhumans is controversial, involving complex moral and philosophical concerns. Consequently, all research involving nonhumans must be carefully reviewed beforehand to ensure that it is conducted ethically (Baker & Serdikoff, 2013; Grundy, 2015; Guidelines for the Treatment of Animals, 2017).

Threats to Experimental Validity: Avoiding Experimental Bias

Even the best-laid experimental plans are susceptible to experimental bias. **Experimental bias** refers to factors that distort the way the independent variable affects the dependent variable in an experiment.

One of the most common forms of experimenter bias relates to the unintentional transmission of expectations to participants by the experimenter, thereby affecting the results. When *experimenter expectations* occur, an experimenter unintentionally transmits cues to participants about the way the experimenter expects them to behave. The danger is that those expectations actually cause the expected result to happen—results that otherwise might not have occurred (Rosenthal, 2003).

A related problem is participant expectations. If you have ever been a participant in an experiment, you probably developed *participant expectations*, guesses about what was expected of you. In fact, participants often develop their own hypotheses about what the experimenter hopes to learn from the study. If participants form their own hypotheses and then act on their hunches, it may be their expectations, rather than the experimental manipulation, that produce the results (Rutherford et al., 2009).

To guard against participant expectations biasing the results of an experiment, the experimenter may try to disguise the true purpose of the experiment. Participants who do not know that helping behavior is being studied, for example, are more apt to act in a "natural" way than they would if they knew.

Sometimes it is impossible to hide the actual purpose of research; when that is the case, other techniques are available to prevent bias. Suppose you were interested in testing the ability of a new drug to alleviate the symptoms of severe depression. If you simply gave the drug to half your participants and not to the other half, the participants who were given the drug might report feeling less depressed merely because they knew they were getting a drug. Similarly, the participants who got nothing might report feeling no better because they knew that they were in a no-treatment control group.

To solve this problem, psychologists typically use a procedure in which all the participants receive a treatment, but those in the control group receive only a **placebo**—a false treatment, such as a pill, "drug," or other substance that has no significant chemical properties or active ingredient. Because members of both groups are kept in the dark about whether they are getting a real or a false treatment, any differences in outcome can be attributed to the quality of the drug and not to the possible psychological effects of being administered a pill or other substance (Justman, 2011; Keränen et al., 2015).

However, a careful researcher must apply one more safeguard in an experiment such as this. To overcome the possibility that *experimenter* expectations will affect the participant, the person who administers the drug shouldn't know whether it is actually the true drug or the placebo. By keeping both the participant and the experimenter who interacts with the participant "blind" to the nature of the drug that is being administered, researchers can more accurately assess the effects of the drug. This method is known as the *double-blind procedure*.

experimental bias Factors that distort how the independent variable affects the dependent variable in an experiment. (Module 4)

Study Alert

Learn the main types of potential bias in experiments: experimenter expectations, participant expectations, and placebo effects.

placebo A false treatment, such as a pill, "drug," or other substance, without any significant chemical properties or active ingredient. (Module 4)

BECOMING AN INFORMED CONSUMER
of Psychology

Thinking Critically About Research

If you were about to purchase an automobile, you would not likely stop at the nearest car dealership and drive off with the first car a salesperson recommended. Instead, you would probably mull over the purchase, read about automobiles, consider the alternatives, talk to others about their experiences, and ultimately put in a fair amount of thought before you made such a major purchase.

In contrast, many of us are considerably less conscientious when we hear about research findings. People often jump to conclusions on the basis of incomplete and inaccurate information, and only rarely do they take the time to critically evaluate the research and data to which they are exposed.

Because the field of psychology is based on an accumulated body of research, we must scrutinize thoroughly the methods, results, and claims of researchers. Several basic questions can help us sort through what is valid and what is not. Among the most important questions to ask are these:

- *What was the purpose of the research?* Research studies should evolve from a clearly specified theory. Furthermore, we must take into account the specific hypothesis that is being tested. Unless we know what hypothesis is being examined, we cannot judge how successful a study has been.
- *How well was the study conducted?* Consider who the participants were, how many were involved, what methods were employed, and what problems the researcher encountered in collecting the data. There are important differences, for example, between a case study that reports the anecdotes of a handful of respondents and a survey that collects data from several thousand people.
- *Are the results presented fairly?* Statements must be assessed on the basis of the actual data they reflect and their logic. For instance, when the manufacturer of car X boasts that "no other car has a better safety record than car X," this does not mean that car X is safer than every other car. It just means that no other car has been proved safer, though many other cars could be just as safe as car X. Expressed in the latter fashion, the finding doesn't seem worth bragging about.

These three basic questions can help you assess the validity of research findings you come across—both within and outside the field of psychology. The more you know how to evaluate research, the better you will be able to assess what the field of psychology has to offer.

RECAP/EVALUATE/RETHINK

RECAP

LO 4-1 What major issues confront psychologists conducting research?

- One of the key ethical principles followed by psychologists is that of informed consent. Participants must be informed, before participation, about the basic outline of the experiment and the risks and potential benefits of their participation.
- Although the use of college students as participants has the advantage of easy availability, there are drawbacks, too. For instance, students do not necessarily represent the population as a whole. The use of nonhuman animals as participants may also have costs in terms of the ability to generalize to humans, although the benefits of using animals in research have been profound.
- Experiments are subject to a number of biases, or threats. Experimenter expectations can produce bias when an experimenter unintentionally transmits cues to participants about her or his expectations regarding their behavior in a given experimental condition. Participant expectations can also bias an experiment. Among the tools experimenters use to help eliminate bias are placebos and double-blind procedures.

EVALUATE

1. Ethical research begins with the concept of informed consent. Before signing up to participate in an experiment, participants should be informed of:
   a. the procedure of the study, stated generally.
   b. the risks that may be involved.
   c. their right to withdraw at any time.
   d. all of these.
2. List three benefits of using animals in psychological research.
3. Deception is one means experimenters can use to try to eliminate participants' expectations. True or false?
4. A false treatment, such as a pill that has no significant chemical properties or active ingredient, is known as a _____.
5. A study has shown that men differ from women in their preference for ice cream flavors. This study was based on a sample of two men and three women. What might be wrong with this study?

RETHINK

A researcher strongly believes that college professors tend to show female students less attention and respect in the classroom than they show male students. He sets up an experimental study involving observations of classrooms in different conditions. In explaining the study to the professors and the students who will participate, what steps should the researcher take to eliminate experimental bias based on both experimenter expectations and participant expectations?

Answers to Evaluate Questions

1. d; 2. (1) We can study some phenomena in animals more easily than we can in people, because with animal subjects we have greater control over environmental and genetic factors. (2) Large numbers of similar participants can be easily obtained. (3) We can look at generational effects much more easily in animals, because of their shorter life span, than we can with people; 3. true; 4. placebo; 5. There are far too few participants. Without a larger sample, no valid conclusions can be drawn about ice cream preferences based on gender.

KEY TERMS

informed consent   experimental bias   placebo

LOOKING Back

EPILOGUE

The field of psychology, as you have seen, is broad and diverse. It encompasses many different subfields and specialties practiced in a variety of settings, with new subfields continually arising. You have also seen that even within the various subfields of the field, it is possible to adopt several different approaches, including the neuroscience, psychodynamic, behavioral, cognitive, and humanistic perspectives.

For all its diversity, though, psychology focuses on certain key issues that serve to unify the field along common lines and shared findings. These issues will reappear as themes throughout this course as you learn about the work and accomplishments of psychologists in the many subfields of the discipline.

In light of what you've already learned about the field of psychology, reconsider the Florida high school massacre described in the prologue of the chapter and answer the following questions:

1. If they were using the neuroscience perspective, how might psychologists explain people's fear responses to the shooter?
2. How would a psychologist using the psychodynamic perspective explain the shooter's behavior differently from a psychologist using the cognitive perspective?
3. What aspects of the shooting would most interest a clinical psychologist? A social psychologist? A forensic psychologist?
4. What might be some ways in which both nature and nurture could have contributed to the shooter's behavior?

Design Elements: Yellow highlighter: ©luckyraccoon/Shutterstock.com; Smartphone: ©and4me/Shutterstock.com; Group of diverse hands: ©MR. Nattanon Kanchak/Shutterstock.com; Woman working on laptop: ©Dragon Images/Shutterstock.com.

VISUAL SUMMARY 1 Introduction to Psychology

MODULE 1 Psychologists at Work

Subfields of Psychology

- Biological foundations
  - Behavioral neuroscience
- Sensing, perceiving, learning, and thinking
  - Experimental and cognitive psychology
- Sources of change and stability
  - Development and personality psychology
- Physical and mental health
  - Health, clinical, and counseling psychology
- Social networks
  - Social and cross-cultural psychology
- Expanding frontiers
  - Evolutionary psychology
  - Behavioral genetics
  - Clinical neuropsychology

Working at Psychology

- Where U.S. psychologists work

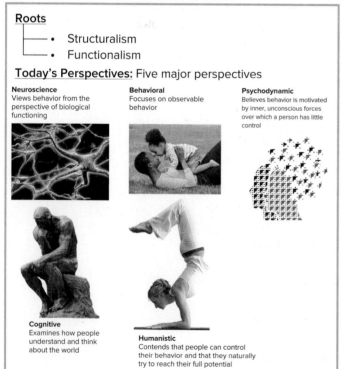

Business/nonprofit, 11%
University/4-year college, 26%
Government/VA medical center, 17%
Medical school/other academic, 7%
Hospital/other health service, 25%
School/other educational, 8%
Independent practice, 6%

MODULE 2 A Science Evolves

Roots

- Structuralism
- Functionalism

Today's Perspectives: Five major perspectives

Neuroscience
Views behavior from the perspective of biological functioning

Behavioral
Focuses on observable behavior

Psychodynamic
Believes behavior is motivated by inner, unconscious forces over which a person has little control

Cognitive
Examines how people understand and think about the world

Humanistic
Contends that people can control their behavior and that they naturally try to reach their full potential

MODULE 3 Research in Psychology

Scientific Method

- Theories: Broad explanations
- Hypotheses: Testable predictions

Descriptive Research: Describes variables and does not explain causality

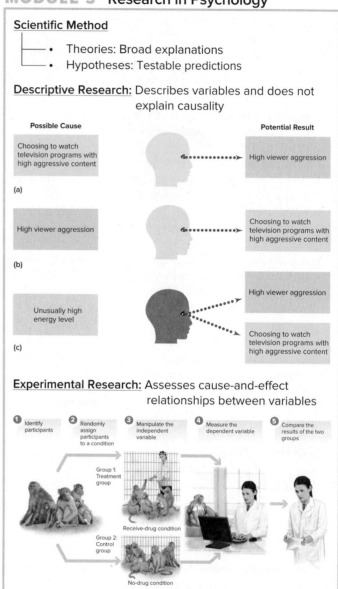

Possible Cause | Potential Result

Choosing to watch television programs with high aggressive content → High viewer aggression
(a)

High viewer aggression → Choosing to watch television programs with high aggressive content
(b)

Unusually high energy level → High viewer aggression / Choosing to watch television programs with high aggressive content
(c)

Experimental Research: Assesses cause-and-effect relationships between variables

1. Identify participants
2. Randomly assign participants to a condition
3. Manipulate the independent variable
4. Measure the dependent variable
5. Compare the results of the two groups

Group 1: Treatment group
Receive-drug condition

Group 2: Control group
No-drug condition

MODULE 4 Critical Research Issues

Ethics of Research
Informed consent

Animal Research
Has significantly benefited humans

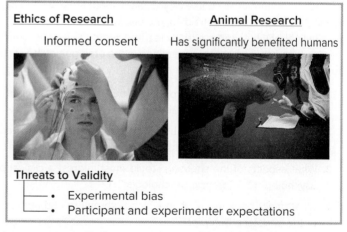

Threats to Validity

- Experimental bias
- Participant and experimenter expectations

(MODULE 1): Source: Stamm, K., Lin, Luona, and Cristidis, P. Datapoint, *Monitor on Psychology,* June 2016, 12. (MODULE 2): (Neuroscience): ©Science Photo Library/Alamy Stock Photo; (Cognitive): ©David Sanger/The Image Bank/Getty Images; (Behavioral): ©Ariel Skelley/Blend Images; (Humanistic): ©White Packert/The Image Bank/Getty Images; (Psychodynamic): ©Athanasia Nomikou/Shutterstock; (MODULE 4): ©annedde/Getty Images

©DGLimages/Shutterstock

CHAPTER 2
Neuroscience and Behavior

LEARNING OUTCOMES FOR CHAPTER 3

MODULE 5

LO 5-1 Why do psychologists study the brain and the nervous system?

LO 5-2 What are the basic elements of the nervous system?

LO 5-3 How does the nervous system communicate electrical and chemical messages from one part to another?

NEURONS: THE BASIC ELEMENTS OF BEHAVIOR

The Structure of the Neuron

How Neurons Fire

Where Neurons Meet: Bridging the Gap

Neurotransmitters: Multitalented Chemical Couriers

MODULE 6

LO 6-1 How are the structures of the nervous system linked?

LO 6-2 How does the endocrine system affect behavior?

THE NERVOUS SYSTEM AND THE ENDOCRINE SYSTEM: COMMUNICATING WITHIN THE BODY

The Nervous System: Linking Neurons

The Evolutionary Foundations of the Nervous System

The Endocrine System: Of Chemicals and Glands

LO 7-1   How do researchers identify the major parts and functions of the brain?

LO 7-2   What are the major parts of the brain, and for what behaviors is each part responsible?

LO 7-3   How do the halves of the brain operate interdependently?

LO 7-4   How can an understanding of the nervous system help us find ways to alleviate disease and pain?

PROLOGUE *THE POWER OF THOUGHT*

One rainy day Dennis Degray was taking out the trash when he slipped on a patch of wet grass and landed chin first. The fall severely injured his spinal cord, leaving Degray a quadriplegic, all communication severed between his brain and the musculature below his head.

But thanks to recent advances in brain-computer interface (BCI) research, Degray, 64, can now type about eight words a minute. That's almost as fast as you can type a text on your cellphone. By merely visualizing his own arm, hand, and finger movements, he can control a computer cursor to spell out words.

One of three test subjects used in the pilot experiment at Stanford University, Degray had two silicon chips, each measuring 1/6-inch square, implanted in his brain. These chips record signals from the motor cortex and send them through a cable to a computer where algorithms translate them into point-and click commands (Goldman, 2017).

LOOKING *Ahead*

It's hard to believe that someone can write words on a computer just by imagining the motions of their hand pressing the keys of an online keyboard. But that's just one way neuroscience is harnessing the remarkable capacity of the brain to improve life for people who suffer severe motor impairment due to disease or injury.

An organ roughly half the size of a loaf of bread, the brain controls our physical, emotional, and intellectual behavior through every waking and sleeping moment. Our movements, thoughts, hopes, aspirations, dreams—our very awareness that we are human—all depend on the brain and the nerves that extend throughout the body, constituting the nervous system.

Because of the importance of the nervous system in controlling behavior and because humans at their most basic level are biological beings, many researchers in psychology and other fields as diverse as computer science, zoology, and medicine have made the biological underpinnings of behavior their specialty. These experts collectively are called *neuroscientists* (Gazzaniga, Ivry, & Mangun, 2002; Cartwright, 2006; Kasemsap, 2017).

Psychologists who specialize in considering the ways in which the biological structures and functions of the body affect behavior are known as **behavioral neuroscientists** (or *biopsychologists*). They seek to answer several key questions: How does the brain control the voluntary and involuntary functioning of the body? How does the brain communicate with other parts of the body? What is the physical structure of the brain, and how does this structure affect behavior? Are psychological disorders caused by biological factors, and how can such disorders be treated?

As you consider the biological processes that we discuss in this chapter, keep in mind the reason why behavioral neuroscience is an essential part of psychology: Our understanding of human behavior requires knowledge of the brain and other parts of the nervous system. Biological factors are central to our sensory experiences, states of consciousness, motivation and emotion, development throughout the life span, and physical and psychological health. Furthermore, advances in behavioral neuroscience have led to the creation of drugs and other treatments for psychological and physical disorders. In short, we cannot understand behavior without understanding our biological makeup (Plomin, 2003; Compagni & Manderscheid, 2006; Schlinger, 2015).

behavioral neuroscientists (or biopsychologists) Psychologists who specialize in considering the ways in which the biological structures and functions of the body affect behavior. (Module 5)

Module 5

Neurons: The Basic Elements of Behavior

Watching Serena Williams hit a stinging backhand, Dario Vaccaro dance a complex ballet routine, or Derek Jeter swing at a baseball, you may have marveled at the complexity—and wondrous abilities—of the human body. But even the most everyday tasks, such as pouring a cup of coffee or humming a tune, depend on a sophisticated sequence of events in the body that is itself truly impressive.

The nervous system is the pathway for the instructions that permit our bodies to carry out such precise activities. Here, we look at the structure and function of neurons, the cells that make up the nervous system, including the brain.

The Structure of the Neuron

Playing the piano, driving a car, or hitting a tennis ball depends, at one level, on exact muscle coordination. But if we consider *how* the muscles can be activated so precisely, we see that more fundamental processes are involved. For the muscles to produce the complex movements that make up any meaningful physical activity, the brain has to provide the right messages to them and coordinate those messages.

Such messages—as well as those that enable us to think, remember, and experience emotion—are passed through specialized cells called neurons. **Neurons,** or nerve cells, are the basic elements of the nervous system. Their quantity is staggering—perhaps as many as 1 *trillion* neurons throughout the body are involved in the control of behavior (Boahen, 2005).

Although there are several types of neurons, they all have a similar structure, as illustrated in Figure 1. Like most cells in the body, neurons have a cell body that con-

LEARNING OUTCOMES

LO 5-1 Why do psychologists study the brain and the nervous system?

LO 5-2 What are the basic elements of the nervous system?

LO 5-3 How does the nervous system communicate electrical and chemical messages from one part to another?

neurons Nerve cells, the basic elements of the nervous system. (Module 5)

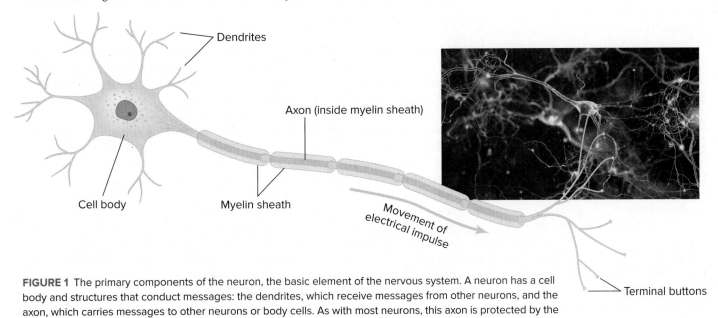

FIGURE 1 The primary components of the neuron, the basic element of the nervous system. A neuron has a cell body and structures that conduct messages: the dendrites, which receive messages from other neurons, and the axon, which carries messages to other neurons or body cells. As with most neurons, this axon is protected by the sausagelike myelin sheath. What advantages does the treelike structure of the neuron provide?

©McGraw-Hill Global Education Holdings LLC, 2000; (Photo): ©whitehoune/Shutterstock

Dendrites

Axon (inside myelin sheath)

Cell body

Myelin sheath

Movement of electrical impulse

Terminal buttons

tains a nucleus. The nucleus incorporates the hereditary material that determines how a cell will function. Neurons are physically held in place by *glial cells*. Glial cells provide nourishment to neurons, insulate them, help repair damage, and generally support neural functioning (Bassotti & Villanacci, 2011; Toft et al., 2013; Keshavarz, 2017).

In contrast to most other cells, however, neurons have a distinctive feature: the ability to communicate with other cells and transmit information across relatively long distances. Many of the body's neurons receive signals from the environment or relay the nervous system's messages to muscles and other target cells, but the vast majority of neurons communicate only with other neurons in the elaborate information system that regulates behavior.

As shown in Figure 1, there's a cluster of fibers at the end of every neuron that are called dendrites. **Dendrites** are the part of the neuron that receives messages from other neurons. They look like the twisted branches of a tree.

On the opposite side of every neuron is a long, slim, tube-like extension called an axon. The **axon** carries messages received by the dendrites to other neurons. The axon is considerably longer than the rest of the neuron. Although most axons are several millimeters in length, some are as long as 3 feet. Axons end in small bulges called terminal buttons. **Terminal buttons** send messages to other neurons. They look like a small bulge at the end of the axon.

The messages that travel through a neuron are electrical in nature. Although there are exceptions, those electrical messages, or *impulses*, generally move across neurons in one direction only, as if they were traveling on a one-way street. Impulses follow a route that begins with the dendrites, continues into the cell body, and leads ultimately along the tube-like extension, the axon, to adjacent neurons.

To prevent messages from short-circuiting one another, axons must be insulated in some fashion (just as electrical wires must be insulated). Most axons are insulated by a **myelin sheath,** a protective coating of fat and protein that wraps around the axon like the casing on links of sausage.

The myelin sheath also serves to increase the velocity with which electrical impulses travel through axons. Those axons that carry the most important and most urgently required information have the greatest concentrations of myelin. If your hand touches a painfully hot stove, for example, the information regarding the pain is passed through axons in the hand and arm that have a relatively thick coating of myelin, speeding the message of pain to the brain so that you can react instantly.

How Neurons Fire

Like a gun, neurons either fire—that is, transmit an electrical impulse along the axon—or don't fire. There is no in-between stage, just as pulling harder on a gun trigger doesn't make the bullet travel faster. Similarly, neurons follow an **all-or-none law:** They are either on or off, with nothing in between the on state and the off state. When there is enough force to pull the trigger, a neuron fires.

Before a neuron is triggered—that is, when it is in a **resting state**—it has a negative electrical charge of about −70 millivolts (a millivolt is one $\frac{1}{1,000}$ of a volt). This charge is caused by the presence of more negatively charged ions within the neuron than outside it. (An ion is an atom that is electrically charged.) You might think of the neuron as a miniature battery in which the inside of the neuron represents the negative pole and the outside represents the positive pole.

When a message arrives at a neuron, gates along the cell membrane open briefly to allow positively charged ions to rush in at rates as high as 100 million ions per second. The sudden arrival of these positive ions causes the charge within the nearby part of the cell to change momentarily from negative to positive. When the positive charge reaches a critical level, the "trigger" is pulled, and an electrical impulse, known as an *action potential*, travels along the axon of the neuron (see Figure 2).

The **action potential** moves from one end of the axon to the other like a flame moving along a fuse. As the impulse travels along the axon, the movement of ions

dendrite A cluster of fibers at one end of a neuron that receives messages from other neurons. (Module 5)

axon The part of the neuron that carries messages destined for other neurons. (Module 5)

terminal buttons Small bulges at the end of axons that send messages to other neurons. (Module 5)

 Study Alert
Remember that *d*endrites *d*etect messages from other neurons; *a*xons carry signals *a*way from the neuron.

myelin sheath A protective coat of fat and protein that wraps around the axon. (Module 5)

all-or-none law The rule that neurons are either on or off. (Module 5)

resting state The state in which there is a negative electrical charge of about −70 millivolts within a neuron. (Module 5)

action potential An electric nerve impulse that travels through a neuron's axon when it is set off by a "trigger," changing the neuron's charge from negative to positive. (Module 5)

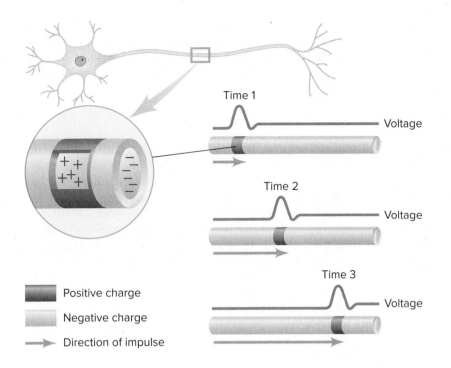

FIGURE 2 Movement of an action potential along an axon. Just before Time 1, positively charged ions enter the cell membrane, changing the charge in the nearby part of the axon from negative to positive and triggering an action potential. The action potential travels along the axon, as illustrated in the changes occurring from Time 1 to Time 3 (from top to bottom in this drawing). Immediately after the action potential has passed through a section of the axon, positive ions are pumped out, restoring the charge in that section to negative. The change in voltage illustrated by the blue line above the axon can be seen in greater detail in Figure 3.

causes a change in charge from negative to positive in successive sections of the axon (see Figure 3). After the impulse has passed through a particular section of the axon, positive ions are pumped out of that section, and its charge returns to negative while the action potential continues to move along the axon.

Just after an action potential has passed through a section of the axon, the cell membrane in that region cannot admit positive ions again for a few milliseconds, and

FIGURE 3 Changes in the voltage in a neuron during the passage of an action potential. In its normal resting state, a neuron has a negative charge of about −70 millivolts. When an action potential is triggered, however, the charge becomes positive, increasing from about −70 millivolts to about +40 millivolts. Immediately following the passage of the action potential, the charge becomes even more negative than it is in its typical resting state. After the charge returns to its normal resting state, the neuron will be fully ready to be triggered once again.

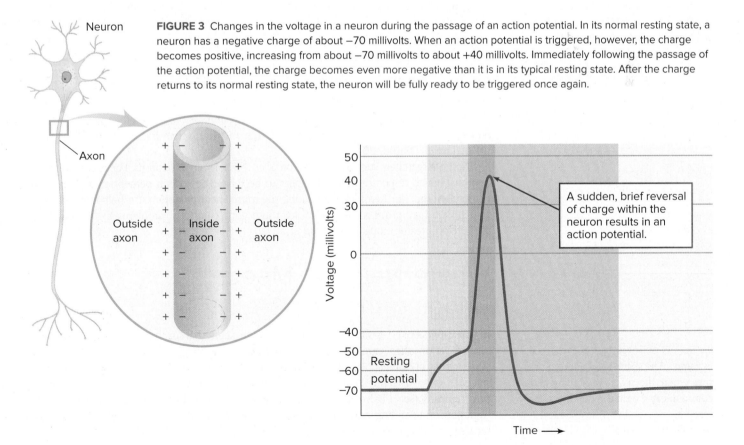

so a neuron cannot fire again immediately no matter how much stimulation it receives. It is as if the gun has to be reloaded after each shot. There then follows a period in which, though it is possible for the neuron to fire, a stronger stimulus is needed than would be if the neuron had reached its normal resting state. Eventually, though, the neuron is ready to fire again.

SPEED OF TRANSMISSION

These complex events can occur at dizzying speeds, although there is great variation among different neurons. The particular speed at which an action potential travels along an axon is determined by the axon's size and the thickness of its myelin sheath. Axons with small diameters carry impulses at about 2 miles per hour; longer and thicker ones can average speeds of more than 225 miles per hour.

Neurons differ not only in terms of how quickly an impulse moves along the axon but also in their potential rate of firing. Some neurons are capable of firing as many as 1,000 times per second; others fire at much slower rates. The intensity of a stimulus determines how much of a neuron's potential firing rate is reached. A strong stimulus, such as a bright light or a loud sound, leads to a higher rate of firing than a less intense stimulus does. Thus, even though all impulses move at the same strength or speed through a particular axon–because of the all-or-none law–there is variation in the frequency of impulses, providing a mechanism by which we can distinguish the tickle of a feather from the weight of someone standing on our toes.

MIRROR NEURONS

mirror neurons Specialized neurons that fire not only when a person enacts a particular behavior, but also when a person simply observes *another* individual carrying out the same behavior. (Module 5)

Although all neurons operate through the firing of action potentials, there is significant specialization among different types of neurons. For example, neuroscientists have discovered the existence of **mirror neurons,** neurons that fire not only when a person enacts a particular behavior but also when a person simply observes *another* individual carrying out the same behavior (Spaulding, 2013; Brucker et al., 2015; Bonini, 2017).

Mirror neurons may help explain how (and why) humans have the capacity to understand others' intentions. Specifically, mirror neurons may fire when we view someone doing something, helping us to predict what their goals are and what they may do next.

The discovery of mirror neurons suggests that the capacity of even young children to imitate others may be an inborn behavior. Furthermore, mirror neurons may be at the root of empathy–those feelings of concern, compassion, and sympathy for others– and even the development of language in humans (Ramachandra, 2009; Rogalsky et al., 2011; Lim & Okuno, 2015).

Some researchers suggest an even broader role for mirror neurons. For example, mirror neurons, which respond to sound, appear to be related to speech perception and language comprehension. Furthermore, stimulating the mirror neuron system can help stroke victims as well and may prove to be helpful for those with emotional problems by helping them to develop greater empathy (Gallese et al., 2011; Hoenen, Lübke, & Pause, 2017).

Where Neurons Meet: Bridging the Gap

synapse The space between two neurons where the axon of a sending neuron communicates with the dendrites of a receiving neuron by using chemical messages. (Module 5)

If you have looked inside a computer, you've seen that each part is physically connected to another part. In contrast, evolution has produced a neural transmission system that at some points has no need for a structural connection between its components. Instead, a chemical connection bridges the gap, known as a synapse, between two neurons (see Figure 4). The **synapse** is the space between two neurons where the axon of a sending neuron communicates with the dendrites of a receiving neuron by using chemical messages.

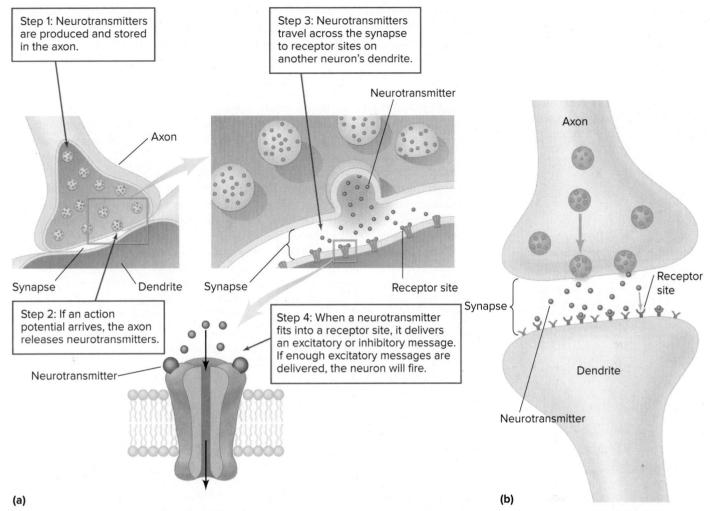

Step 1: Neurotransmitters are produced and stored in the axon.

Step 3: Neurotransmitters travel across the synapse to receptor sites on another neuron's dendrite.

Neurotransmitter

Axon

Synapse

Dendrite

Synapse

Receptor site

Step 2: If an action potential arrives, the axon releases neurotransmitters.

Step 4: When a neurotransmitter fits into a receptor site, it delivers an excitatory or inhibitory message. If enough excitatory messages are delivered, the neuron will fire.

Neurotransmitter

Axon

Receptor site

Synapse

Dendrite

Neurotransmitter

(a)

(b)

FIGURE 4 A synapse is the junction between an axon and a dendrite. Chemical neurotransmitters bridge the synaptic gap between the axon and the dendrite (Mader, 2000). (a) Read Step 1 through Step 4 to follow this chemical process. (b) Just as the pieces of a jigsaw puzzle can fit in only one specific location in a puzzle, each kind of neurotransmitter has a distinctive configuration that allows it to fit into a specific type of receptor cell (Johnson, 2000). Why is it advantageous for axons and dendrites to be linked by temporary chemical bridges rather than by the hard wiring typical of a radio connection or telephone hookup?

(a and b): ©McGraw-Hill Global Education Holdings LLC, 2000.

When a nerve impulse comes to the end of the axon and reaches a terminal button, the terminal button releases a chemical messenger called a neurotransmitter. **Neurotransmitters** carry messages from one neuron to another neuron. Like a boat that ferries passengers across a river, these chemical messengers move from the axon of one neuron to the dendrite of a receiving neurons.

Keep in mind that the chemical mode of message transmission that occurs between neurons differs strikingly from the means by which communication occurs inside neurons: Although messages travel in electrical form *within* a neuron, they move *between* neurons through a chemical transmission system.

There are several types of neurotransmitters, and not all neurons are capable of receiving the chemical message carried by a particular neurotransmitter. In the same way that a jigsaw puzzle piece can fit in only one specific location in a puzzle, each kind of neurotransmitter has a distinctive configuration that allows it to fit into a specific type of receptor site on the receiving neuron (see Figure 4b). It is only when a neurotransmitter fits precisely into a receptor site that successful chemical communication is possible.

If a neurotransmitter does fit into a site on the receiving neuron, the chemical message it delivers is basically one of two types: excitatory or inhibitory.

neurotransmitters Chemicals that carry messages across the synapse to the dendrite (and sometimes the cell body) of a receiver neuron. (Module 5)

 Study Alert

Remember this key fact: Messages inside neurons are transmitted in electrical form, whereas messages traveling between neurons travel via chemical means.

excitatory message A chemical message that makes it more likely that a receiving neuron will fire and an action potential will travel down its axon. (Module 5)

inhibitory message A chemical message that prevents or decreases the likelihood that a receiving neuron will fire. (Module 5)

reuptake The reabsorption of neurotransmitters by a terminal button. (Module 5)

Excitatory messages are chemical messages that make it more likely that a receiving neuron will fire and an action potential will travel down its axon. In contrast, inhibitory messages do just the opposite: **inhibitory messages** provide chemical information that prevents or decreases the likelihood that the receiving neuron will fire.

Because the dendrites of a neuron receive both excitatory and inhibitory messages simultaneously, the neuron must integrate the messages by using a kind of chemical calculator. Put simply, if the excitatory messages ("Fire!") outnumber the inhibitory ones ("Don't fire!"), the neuron fires. In contrast, if the inhibitory messages outnumber the excitatory ones, nothing happens, and the neuron remains in its resting state.

If neurotransmitters remained at the site of the synapse, receiving neurons would be awash in a continual chemical bath, producing constant stimulation or constant inhibition of the receiving neurons. This would make effective communication across the synapse impossible. To avoid this problem, enzymes deactivate the neurotransmitters, or—more commonly—the terminal button sucks them back up in an example of chemical recycling called reuptake.

Reuptake is the process in which a neurotransmitter produced by a terminal button is reabsorbed by the terminal button. Like a vacuum cleaner sucking up dust, neurons reabsorb the neurotransmitters that are now clogging the synapse. All this activity occurs at lightning speed, with the process taking just several milliseconds (Gingrich et al., 2017).

Our understanding of the process of reuptake has permitted the development of a number of drugs used in the treatment of psychological disorders. Some antidepressant drugs, called *SSRIs*, or *selective serotonin reuptake inhibitors*, permit certain neurotransmitters to remain active for a longer period at certain synapses in the brain, thereby reducing the symptoms of depression (Guiard et al., 2011; Hilton et al., 2013; Leong et al., 2017).

Neurotransmitters: Multitalented Chemical Couriers

Neurotransmitters are a particularly important link between the nervous system and behavior. Not only are they important for maintaining vital brain and body functions, but a deficiency or an excess of a neurotransmitter can produce severe behavior disorders. More than a hundred chemicals have been found to act as neurotransmitters, and neuroscientists believe that more may ultimately be identified. The major neurotransmitters and their effects are described in Figure 5 (Schmidt, 2006).

One of the most common neurotransmitters is *acetylcholine* (or *ACh*, its chemical symbol), which is found throughout the nervous system. ACh is involved in our every physical move because—among other things—it transmits messages relating to our skeletal muscles. ACh also aids in memory capabilities. In fact, diminished production of ACh may be related to Alzheimer's disease (Bazalakova et al., 2007; Van der Zee, Platt, & Riedel, 2011; Betterton et al., 2017).

Another common excitatory neurotransmitter, *glutamate*, plays a role in memory. Memories appear to be produced by specific biochemical changes at particular synapses, and glutamate, along with other neurotransmitters, plays an important role in this process (Winters & Bussey, 2005; Micheau & Marighetto, 2011; Solomonia & McCabe, 2015).

Gamma-amino butyric acid (GABA), which is found in both the brain and the spinal cord, appears to be the nervous system's primary inhibitory neurotransmitter. It moderates a variety of behaviors, ranging from eating to aggression. Several common substances, such as the tranquilizer Valium and alcohol, are effective because they permit GABA to operate more efficiently (Ball, 2004; Criswell et al., 2008; Lobo & Harris, 2008).

Another major neurotransmitter is *dopamine (DA)*, which is involved in movement, attention, and learning. The discovery that certain drugs can have a significant effect on dopamine release has led to the development of effective treatments for a wide variety of physical and mental ailments. For instance, Parkinson's disease, from which actor Michael J. Fox suffers, is caused by a deficiency of dopamine in the brain. Techniques for increasing the production of dopamine in Parkinson's patients are proving effective (Iversen & Iversen, 2007; Antonini & Barone, 2008; Hanna-Pladdy, Pahwa, & Lyons, 2015).

Michael J. Fox suffers from Parkinson's disease, and he has become a strong advocate for research into the disorder.
©Theo Wargo/Getty Images

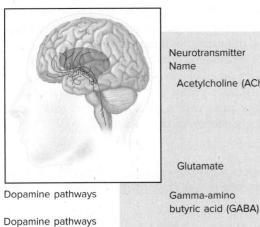

Dopamine pathways

Dopamine pathways

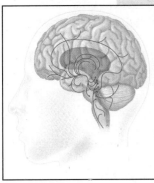

Neurotransmitter Name	Location	Eect	Function
Acetylcholine (ACh)	Brain, spinal cord, peripheral nervous system, especially some organs of the parasympathetic nervous system	Excitatory in brain and autonomic nervous system; inhibitory elsewhere	Muscle movement, cognitive functioning
Glutamate	Brain, spinal cord	Excitatory	Memory
Gamma-amino butyric acid (GABA)	Brain, spinal cord	Main inhibitory neurotransmitter	Eating, aggression, sleeping
Dopamine (DA)	Brain	Inhibitory or excitatory	Movement control, pleasure and reward, attention
Serotonin	Brain, spinal cord	Inhibitory	Sleeping, eating, mood, pain, depression
Endorphins	Brain, spinal cord	Primarily inhibitory, except in hippocampus	Pain suppression, pleasurable feelings, appetites, placebos

FIGURE 5 Major neurotransmitters.

In other instances, overproduction of dopamine produces negative consequences. For example, researchers have hypothesized that schizophrenia and some other severe mental disturbances are affected or perhaps even caused by the presence of unusually high levels of dopamine. Drugs that block the reception of dopamine reduce the symptoms displayed by some people diagnosed with schizophrenia (Howes & Kapur, 2009; Seeman, 2011; Howes et al., 2017).

From the perspective of...

A Health-Care Provider How might your understanding of the nervous system help you explain the symptoms of Parkinson's disease to a patient with the disorder?

©Tetra Images/Getty Images

PsychTech

A team of Swedish researchers has discovered a way to stimulate specific neurons via chemical neurotransmitters, rather than using earlier technologies involving electrical signals to stimulate them. This discovery opens a novel path to treat those who suffer from severe psychological disorders produced by brain dysfunction.

Another neurotransmitter, *serotonin,* is associated with the regulation of sleep, eating, mood, and pain. A growing body of research points toward a broader role for serotonin, suggesting its involvement in such diverse behaviors as alcoholism, depression, suicide, impulsivity, aggression, and coping with stress (Murray et al., 2008; Popa et al., 2008; Carrillo et al., 2009).

Endorphins, another class of neurotransmitters, are a family of chemicals produced by the brain that are similar in structure to painkilling drugs such as morphine. The production of endorphins reflects the brain's effort to deal with pain as well as to elevate mood.

Endorphins also may produce the euphoric feelings that runners sometimes experience after long runs. The exertion and perhaps the pain involved in a long run may stimulate the production of endorphins, ultimately resulting in what has been called "runner's high" (Kolata, 2002; Pert, 2002; Stanojevic, Mitic, & Vujic, 2007).

Endorphin release might also explain other phenomena that have long puzzled psychologists. For example, the act of taking placebos (pills or other substances that contain no actual drugs but that patients *believe* will make them better) may induce the release of endorphins, leading to the reduction of pain (Rajagopal, 2006; Crum & Langer, 2007; Bruehl et al., 2017).

RECAP/EVALUATE/RETHINK

RECAP

LO 5-1 Why do psychologists study the brain and nervous system?

- A full understanding of human behavior requires knowledge of the biological influences underlying that behavior, especially those originating in the nervous system. Psychologists who specialize in studying the effects of biological structures and functions on behavior are known as behavioral neuroscientists.

LO 5-2 What are the basic elements of the nervous system?

- Neurons, the most basic elements of the nervous system, carry nerve impulses from one part of the body to another. Information in a neuron generally follows a route that begins with the dendrites, continues into the cell body, and leads ultimately down the tube-like extension, the axon.

LO 5-3 How does the nervous system communicate electrical and chemical messages from one part to another?

- Most axons are insulated by a coating called the myelin sheath. When a neuron receives a message to fire, it releases an action potential, an electric charge that travels through the axon. Neurons operate according to an all-or-none law: Either they are at rest, or an action potential is moving through them. There is no in-between state.
- When a neuron fires, nerve impulses are carried to other neurons through the production of chemical substances called neurotransmitters that bridge the gaps—known as synapses—between neurons. Neurotransmitters may be either excitatory, telling other neurons to fire, or inhibitory, preventing or decreasing the likelihood of other neurons firing.
- Endorphins, another type of neurotransmitter, are related to the reduction of pain. Endorphins aid in the production of a natural painkiller and are probably responsible for creating the kind of euphoria that joggers sometimes experience after running.

EVALUATE

1. The _____ is the fundamental element of the nervous system.
2. Neurons receive information through their _____ and send messages through their _____.
3. Just as electrical wires have an outer coating, axons are insulated by a coating called the _____ _____.
4. The gap between two neurons is bridged by a chemical connection called a _____.
5. Endorphins are one kind of _____, the chemical "messengers" between neurons.

RETHINK

1. How might psychologists use drugs that mimic the effects of neurotransmitters to treat psychological disorders?
2. In what ways might endorphins help to produce the placebo effect? Is there a difference between *believing* that one's pain is reduced and actually *experiencing* reduced pain? Why or why not?

Answers to Evaluate Questions

1. neuron; 2. dendrites, axons; 3. myelin sheath; 4. synapse; 5. neurotransmitter

KEY TERMS

behavioral neuroscientists (or biopsychologists)	axon	resting state	neurotransmitters
	terminal buttons	action potential	excitatory message
neurons	myelin sheath	mirror neurons	inhibitory message
dendrite	all-or-none law	synapse	reuptake

Module 6

The Nervous System and the Endocrine System: Communicating Within the Body

In light of the complexity of individual neurons and the neurotransmission process, it should come as no surprise that the connections and structures formed by the neurons are complicated. Because each neuron can be connected to 80,000 other neurons, the total number of possible connections is astonishing. For instance, estimates of the number of neural connections within the brain fall in the neighborhood of 10 quadrillion—a 1 followed by 16 zeros—and some experts put the number even higher. However, connections among neurons are not the only means of communication within the body; as we'll see, the endocrine system, which secretes chemical messages that circulate through the blood, also communicates messages that influence behavior and many aspects of biological functioning (Boahen, 2005; Heintz, Brander, & White, 2015).

LEARNING OUTCOMES

LO 6-1 How are the structures of the nervous system linked?

LO 6-2 How does the endocrine system affect behavior?

The Nervous System: Linking Neurons

Whatever the actual number of neural connections, the human nervous system has both logic and elegance. We turn now to a discussion of its basic structures.

CENTRAL AND PERIPHERAL NERVOUS SYSTEMS

As you can see from the schematic representation in Figure 1, the nervous system is divided into two main parts: the central nervous system and the peripheral nervous system. The **central nervous system (CNS)** is composed of the brain and spinal cord. The **spinal cord,** which is about the thickness of a pencil, contains a bundle of neurons that leaves the brain and runs down the length of the back (see Figure 2). As you can see in Figure 2, the spinal cord is the primary means for transmitting messages between the brain and the rest of the body.

However, the spinal cord is not just a communication channel. It also controls some simple behaviors on its own, without any help from the brain. An example is the way the knee jerks forward when it is tapped with a rubber hammer. This behavior is a type of **reflex,** an automatic, involuntary response to an incoming stimulus. A reflex is also at work when you touch a hot stove and immediately withdraw your hand. Although the brain eventually analyzes and reacts to the situation ("Ouch–hot stove–pull away!"), the initial withdrawal is directed only by neurons in the spinal cord.

Several kinds of neurons are involved in reflexes. **Sensory (afferent) neurons** transmit information from the perimeter of the body to the central nervous system and the brain. For example, touching a hot stove sends a message to the brain (hot!) via sensory neurons. **Motor (efferent) neurons** communicate information in the opposite direction, sending messages from the brain and nervous system to the muscles

central nervous system (CNS) The part of the nervous system that includes the brain and spinal cord. (Module 6)

spinal cord A bundle of neurons that leaves the brain and runs down the length of the back and is the main means for transmitting messages between the brain and the body. (Module 6)

reflex An automatic, involuntary response to an incoming stimulus. (Module 6)

sensory (afferent) neurons Neurons that transmit information from the perimeter of the body to the nervous system and brain. (Module 6)

motor (efferent) neurons Neurons that communicate information from the brain and nervous system to muscles and glands. (Module 6)

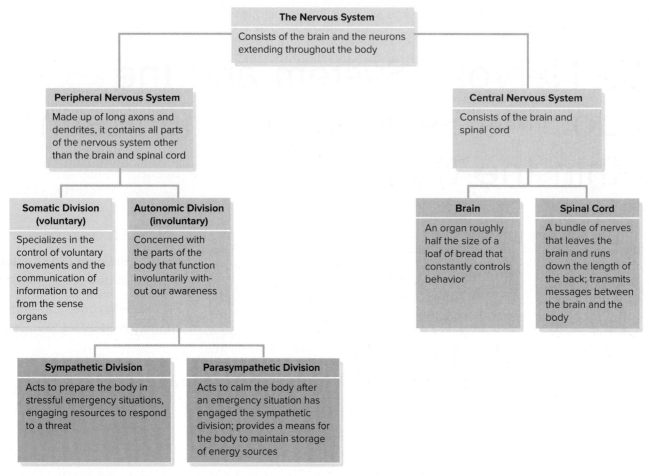

The Nervous System

Consists of the brain and the neurons extending throughout the body

Peripheral Nervous System

Made up of long axons and dendrites, it contains all parts of the nervous system other than the brain and spinal cord

Central Nervous System

Consists of the brain and spinal cord

Somatic Division (voluntary)

Specializes in the control of voluntary movements and the communication of information to and from the sense organs

Autonomic Division (involuntary)

Concerned with the parts of the body that function involuntarily without our awareness

Brain

An organ roughly half the size of a loaf of bread that constantly controls behavior

Spinal Cord

A bundle of nerves that leaves the brain and runs down the length of the back; transmits messages between the brain and the body

Sympathetic Division

Acts to prepare the body in stressful emergency situations, engaging resources to respond to a threat

Parasympathetic Division

Acts to calm the body after an emergency situation has engaged the sympathetic division; provides a means for the body to maintain storage of energy sources

FIGURE 1 A schematic diagram of the relationship of the parts of the nervous system.

FIGURE 2 The central nervous system consists of the brain and spinal cord, and the peripheral nervous system encompasses the network of nerves connecting the brain and spinal cord to other parts of the body.

©Larry Williams/Blend Images/Corbis

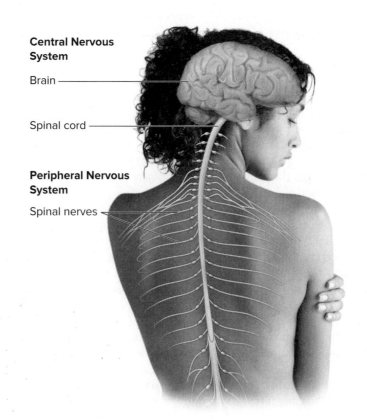

Central Nervous System

Brain

Spinal cord

Peripheral Nervous System

Spinal nerves

Study Alert

Use Figures 1 and 2 to learn the components of the central and peripheral nervous systems.

and glands. When the brain sends a message to the muscles of the hand (hot–move away!), the message travels via motor neurons.

The importance of the spinal cord and reflexes is illustrated by the outcome of accidents in which the cord is injured or severed. In some cases, injury results in *quadriplegia*, a condition in which people lose voluntary muscle movement below the neck. In a less severe but still disabling condition, *paraplegia*, people are unable to voluntarily move any muscles in the lower half of the body.

As suggested by its name, the **peripheral nervous system** branches out from the spinal cord and brain and reaches the extremities of the body. Made up of neurons with long axons and dendrites, the peripheral nervous system encompasses all the parts of the nervous system other than the brain and spinal cord. There are two major divisions of the peripheral nervous system–the somatic division and the autonomic division–both of which connect the central nervous system with the sense organs, muscles, glands, and other organs.

The **somatic division** of the peripheral nervous system specializes in the control of voluntary movements, such as the motion of the eyes to read this sentence or those of the hand to scroll down a page. The somatic division also communicates information to and from the sense organs.

The **autonomic division** of the peripheral nervous system controls the parts of the body that keep us alive–the heart, blood vessels, glands, lungs, and other organs that function involuntarily without our awareness. As you are reading at this moment, the autonomic division of the peripheral nervous system is pumping blood through your body, pushing your lungs in and out, and overseeing the digestion of your last meal.

peripheral nervous system The part of the nervous system that includes the autonomic and somatic subdivisions; made up of neurons with long axons and dendrites, it branches out from the spinal cord and brain and reaches the extremities of the body. (Module 6)

somatic division The part of the peripheral nervous system that specializes in the control of voluntary movements and the communication of information to and from the sense organs. (Module 6)

autonomic division The part of the peripheral nervous system that controls involuntary movement of the heart, glands, lungs, and other organs. (Module 6)

ACTIVATING THE DIVISIONS OF THE AUTONOMIC NERVOUS SYSTEM

The autonomic division plays a particularly crucial role during emergencies. Suppose that as you are reading, you suddenly sense that a stranger is watching you through the window. As you look up, you see the glint of something that might be a knife. As confusion clouds your mind and fear overcomes your attempts to think rationally, what happens to your body? If you are like most people, you react immediately on a physiological level. Your heart rate increases, you begin to sweat, and you develop goose bumps all over your body.

The physiological changes that occur during a crisis result from the activation of one of the two parts of the autonomic nervous system: the **sympathetic division.** The sympathetic division acts to prepare the body for action in stressful situations by engaging all of the organism's resources to run away or to confront the threat. This is often called the "fight-or-flight" response.

In contrast, the **parasympathetic division** acts to calm the body after the emergency has ended. When you find, for instance, that the stranger at the window is actually your roommate, who has lost his keys and is climbing in the window to avoid waking you, your parasympathetic division begins to take over, lowering your heart rate, stopping your sweating, and returning your body to the state it was in before you became alarmed. The parasympathetic division also directs the body to store energy for use in emergencies.

The sympathetic and parasympathetic divisions work together to regulate many functions of the body (see Figure 3). For instance, sexual arousal is controlled by the parasympathetic division, but sexual orgasm is a function of the sympathetic division. The sympathetic and parasympathetic divisions also are involved in a number of disorders. For example, one explanation of documented examples of "voodoo death"–in which a person is literally scared to death resulting from a voodoo curse–may be produced by overstimulation of the sympathetic division due to extreme fear.

sympathetic division The part of the autonomic division of the nervous system that acts to prepare the body for action in stressful situations, engaging all the organism's resources to respond to a threat. (Module 6)

parasympathetic division The part of the autonomic division of the nervous system that acts to calm the body after an emergency has ended. (Module 6)

FIGURE 3 The major functions of the autonomic nervous system. The sympathetic division acts to prepare certain organs of the body for stressful situations, and the parasympathetic division acts to calm the body after the emergency has passed. Can you explain why each response of the sympathetic division might be useful in an emergency?
©McGraw-Hill Global Education Holdings LLC, 2001.

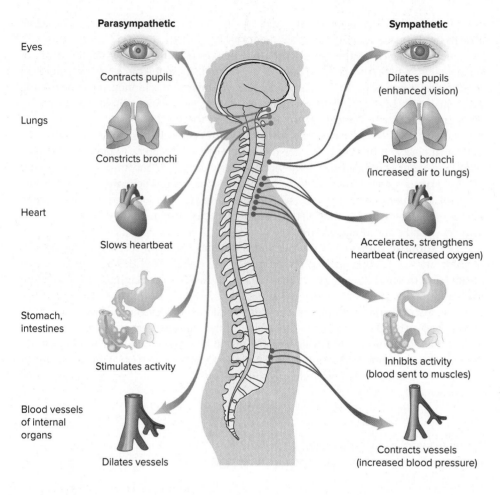

Parasympathetic

Eyes — Contracts pupils

Lungs — Constricts bronchi

Heart — Slows heartbeat

Stomach, intestines — Stimulates activity

Blood vessels of internal organs — Dilates vessels

Sympathetic

Dilates pupils (enhanced vision)

Relaxes bronchi (increased air to lungs)

Accelerates, strengthens heartbeat (increased oxygen)

Inhibits activity (blood sent to muscles)

Contracts vessels (increased blood pressure)

PsychTech
Rob Summers, who was paralyzed when hit by a car at age 20, took his first steps 5 years later after he received an experimental treatment in which electrodes were implanted into his back to stimulate his spinal cord.

From the perspective of...

A Health-Care Provider How would an understanding of the nervous system be valuable in your job as a medical care provider?

©Rubberball Productions/Getty Images

The Evolutionary Foundations of the Nervous System

The complexities of the nervous system can be better understood if we take the course of evolution into consideration. The forerunner of the human nervous system is found in the earliest simple organisms to have a spinal cord. Basically, those organisms were simple input-output devices: When the upper side of the spinal cord was stimulated by, for instance, being touched, the organism reacted with a simple response, such as jerking away. Such responses were completely a consequence of the organism's genetic makeup.

Over millions of years, the spinal cord became more specialized, and organisms became capable of distinguishing between different kinds of stimuli and responding appropriately to them. Ultimately, a portion of the spinal cord evolved into what we would consider a primitive brain.

Today, the nervous system is *hierarchically organized,* meaning that relatively newer (from an evolutionary point of view) and more sophisticated regions of the brain regulate the older, and more primitive, parts of the nervous system. As we move up along the spinal cord and continue upward into the brain then, the functions controlled by the various regions become progressively more advanced.

Why should we care about the evolutionary background of the human nervous system? The answer comes from researchers working in the area of **evolutionary psychology,** the branch of psychology that seeks to identify how behavior is influenced and produced by our genetic inheritance from our ancestors.

Evolutionary psychologists argue that the course of evolution is reflected in the structure and functioning of the nervous system and that evolutionary factors consequently have a significant influence on our everyday behavior. Their work, in conjunction with the research of scientists studying genetics, biochemistry, and medicine, has led to an understanding of how our behavior is affected by heredity, our genetically determined heritage.

Evolutionary psychologists have spawned a new and increasingly influential field: behavioral genetics. As we will discuss further in the chapter on development, **behavioral genetics** is the study of the effects of heredity on behavior. Consistent with the evolutionary perspective, behavioral genetics researchers are finding increasing evidence that cognitive abilities, personality traits, sexual orientation, and psychological disorders are determined to some extent by genetic factors (Maxson, 2013; Appelbaum, Scurich, & Raad, 2015; Barbaro et al., 2017).

The Endocrine System: Of Chemicals and Glands

Another of the body's communication systems, the **endocrine system** is a chemical communication network that sends messages throughout the body via the bloodstream. Its job is to secrete **hormones,** chemicals that circulate through the blood and regulate the functioning or growth of the body. It also influences–and is influenced by–the functioning of the nervous system. Although the endocrine system is not part of the brain, it is closely linked to the hypothalamus.

As chemical messengers, hormones are like neurotransmitters, although their speed and mode of transmission are quite different. Whereas neural messages are measured in thousandths of a second, hormonal communications may take minutes to reach their destination. Furthermore, neural messages move through neurons in specific lines (like a signal carried by wires strung along telephone poles), whereas hormones travel throughout the body, similar to the way radio waves are transmitted across the entire landscape. Just as radio waves evoke a response only when a radio is tuned to the correct station, hormones flowing through the bloodstream activate only those cells that are receptive and "tuned" to the appropriate hormonal message.

A key component of the endocrine system is the tiny **pituitary gland,** which is found near–and regulated by–the hypothalamus in the brain. The pituitary gland has sometimes been called the "master gland" because it controls the functioning of the rest of the endocrine system. But the pituitary gland is more than just the taskmaster of other glands; it has important functions in its own right. For instance, hormones secreted by the pituitary gland control growth. Extremely short people and unusually tall ones usually have pituitary gland abnormalities. Other endocrine glands, shown in Figure 4, affect emotional reactions, sexual urges, and energy levels.

evolutionary psychology The branch of psychology that seeks to identify behavior patterns that are a result of our genetic inheritance from our ancestors. (Module 6)

behavioral genetics The study of the effects of heredity on behavior. (Module 6)

endocrine system A chemical communication network that sends messages throughout the body via the bloodstream. (Module 6)

hormones Chemicals that circulate through the blood and regulate the functioning or growth of the body. (Module 6)

pituitary gland The major component of the endocrine system, or "master gland," which secretes hormones that control growth and other parts of the endocrine system. (Module 6)

©Laurence Mouton/Getty Images

FIGURE 4 Location and function of the major endocrine glands. The pituitary gland controls the functioning of the other endocrine glands and, in turn, is regulated by the hypothalamus.

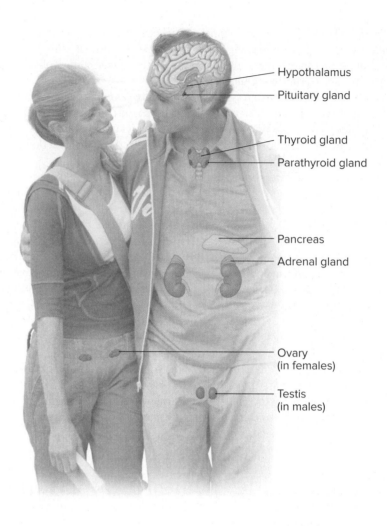

- Hypothalamus
- Pituitary gland
- Thyroid gland
- Parathyroid gland
- Pancreas
- Adrenal gland
- Ovary (in females)
- Testis (in males)

Study Alert

The endocrine system produces hormones, chemicals that circulate through the body via the bloodstream.

Despite its designation as the "master gland," the pituitary is actually a servant of the brain because the brain is ultimately responsible for the endocrine system's functioning. The brain maintains the internal balance of the body through the hypothalamus.

Individual hormones can wear many hats, depending on circumstances. For example, the hormone oxytocin is at the root of many of life's satisfactions and pleasures. In new mothers, oxytocin produces an urge to nurse newborn offspring. The same hormone also seems to stimulate cuddling between species members. And–at least in rats–it encourages sexually active males to seek out females more passionately and females to be more receptive to males' sexual advances. There's even evidence that oxytocin is related to the development of trust in others, helping to grease the wheels of effective social interaction (Guastella, Mitchell, & Dadds, 2008; De Dreu et al., 2011; de Visser et al., 2017).

Although hormones are produced naturally by the endocrine system, the ingestion of artificial hormones has proved to be both beneficial and potentially dangerous. For example, before the early 2000s, physicians frequently prescribed hormone replacement therapy to treat symptoms of menopause in older women. However, because recent research suggests that the treatment has potentially dangerous side effects, health experts now warn that in many cases, the dangers outweigh the benefits (Alexandersen, Karsdal, & Christiansen, 2009; Jacobs et al., 2013; Doty et al., 2015).

The use of testosterone, a male hormone, and drugs known as *steroids*, which act like testosterone, is increasingly common. For athletes and others who want to bulk up their appearance, steroids provide a way to add muscle weight and increase strength.

Steroids can provide added muscle and strength, but they have dangerous side effects. A number of well-known athletes in a variety of sports, such as baseball player Alex Rodriguez, pictured here, have been accused of using the drugs illegally. In fact, a number of them have publicly said they have used them.
©Corey Sipkin/NY Daily News Archive/Getty Images

However, these drugs can lead to stunted growth, shrinking of the testicles, heart attacks, strokes, and cancer, making them extremely dangerous. Furthermore, they can even produce violent behavior. For example, in one tragic case, professional wrestler Chris Benoit strangled his wife, suffocated his son, and later hanged himself—acts that were attributed to his use of steroids (Pagonis, Angelopoulos, & Koukoulis, 2006; Sandomir, 2007; Zahnow et al., 2017).

RECAP/EVALUATE/RETHINK

RECAP

LO 6-1 How are the structures of the nervous system linked?

- The nervous system is made up of the central nervous system (the brain and spinal cord) and the peripheral nervous system. The peripheral nervous system is made up of the somatic division, which controls voluntary movements and the communication of information to and from the sense organs, and the autonomic division, which controls involuntary functions such as those of the heart, blood vessels, and lungs.
- The autonomic division of the peripheral nervous system is further subdivided into the sympathetic and parasympathetic divisions. The sympathetic division prepares the body in emergency situations, and the parasympathetic division helps the body return to its typical resting state.
- Evolutionary psychology, the branch of psychology that seeks to identify behavior patterns that are a result of our genetic inheritance, has led to increased understanding of the evolutionary basis of the structure and organization of the human nervous system.

LO 6-2 How does the endocrine system affect behavior?

- The endocrine system secretes hormones, chemicals that regulate the functioning of the body, via the bloodstream. The pituitary gland secretes growth hormones and influences the release of hormones by other endocrine glands and in turn is regulated by the hypothalamus.

EVALUATE

1. If you put your hand on a red-hot piece of metal, the immediate response of pulling it away would be an example of a(n) _____.
2. The central nervous system is composed of the _____ and the _____.
3. In the peripheral nervous system, the _____ division controls voluntary movements, whereas the _____ division controls organs that keep us alive and function without our awareness.
4. Maria saw a young boy run into the street and get hit by a car. When she got to the fallen child, she was in a state of panic. She was sweating, and her heart was racing. Her biological state resulted from the activation of what division of the nervous system?
   a. parasympathetic
   b. central
   c. sympathetic

5. The emerging field of _____ studies ways in which our genetic inheritance predisposes us to behave in certain ways.

RETHINK

1. In what ways is the "fight-or-flight" response helpful to humans in emergency situations?
2. How might communication within the nervous system result in human consciousness?

Answers to Evaluate Questions

1. reflex; 2. brain, spinal cord; 3. somatic, autonomic; 4. c. sympathetic; 5. evolutionary psychology

KEY TERMS

central nervous system (CNS)	sensory (afferent) neurons	autonomic division	behavioral genetics
spinal cord	motor (efferent) neurons	sympathetic division	endocrine system
reflex	peripheral nervous system	parasympathetic division	hormones
	somatic division	evolutionary psychology	pituitary gland

Module 7
The Brain

It is not much to look at. Soft, spongy, mottled, and pinkish-gray in color, it hardly can be said to possess much in the way of physical beauty. Despite its physical appearance, however, it ranks as the greatest natural marvel that we know and has a beauty and sophistication all its own.

The object to which this description applies: the brain. The brain is responsible for our loftiest thoughts–and our most primitive urges. It is the overseer of the intricate workings of the human body. If one were to attempt to design a computer to mimic the range of capabilities of the brain, the task would be nearly impossible; in fact, it has proved difficult even to come close. The sheer quantity of nerve cells in the brain is enough to daunt even the most ambitious computer engineer. Many billions of neurons make up a structure weighing just 3 pounds in the average adult. However, it is not the number of cells that is the most astounding thing about the brain but its ability to allow the human intellect to flourish by guiding our behavior and thoughts.

We turn now to a consideration of the particular structures of the brain and the primary functions to which they are related. However, a caution is in order. Although we'll discuss specific areas of the brain in relation to specific behaviors, this approach is an oversimplification. No straightforward one-to-one correspondence exists between a distinct part of the brain and a particular behavior. Instead, behavior is produced by complex interconnections among sets of neurons in many areas of the brain: Our behavior, emotions, thoughts, hopes, and dreams are produced by a variety of neurons throughout the nervous system working in concert.

LEARNING OUTCOMES

LO 7-1 How do researchers identify the major parts and functions of the brain?

LO 7-2 What are the major parts of the brain, and for what behaviors is each part responsible?

LO 7-3 How do the two halves of the brain operate interdependently?

LO 7-4 How can an understanding of the nervous system help us find ways to alleviate disease and pain?

Studying the Brain's Structure and Functions: Spying on the Brain

The brain has posed a continual challenge to those who would study it. For most of history, its examination was possible only after an individual had died. Only then could the skull be opened and the brain cut into without serious injury. Although informative, this procedure could hardly tell us much about the functioning of the healthy brain.

Today, however, brain-scanning techniques provide a window into the living brain. Using these techniques, investigators can take a "snapshot" of the internal workings of the brain without having to cut open a person's skull. The most important scanning techniques, illustrated in Figure 1, are the electroencephalogram (EEG), positron emission tomography (PET), functional magnetic resonance imaging (fMRI), and transcranial magnetic stimulation imaging (TMS).

The *electroencephalogram (EEG)* records electrical activity in the brain through electrodes placed on the outside of the skull. Although traditionally the EEG could produce only a graph of electrical wave patterns, new techniques are now used to transform the brain's electrical activity into a pictorial representation of the brain that allows more precise diagnosis of disorders such as epilepsy and learning disabilities.

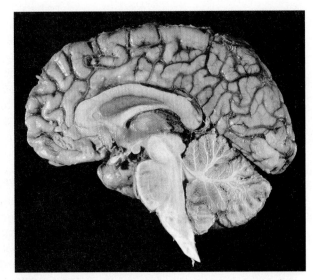

The brain (shown here in cross-section) may not be much to look at, but it represents one of the great marvels of human development. Why do most scientists believe that it will be difficult, if not impossible, to duplicate the brain's abilities?
©Martin M. Rotker/Science Source

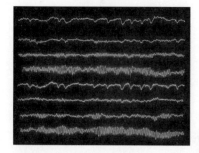

(a) EEG

(b) fMRI

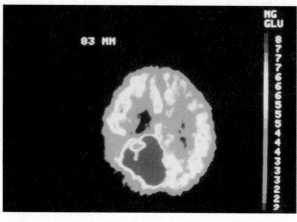

(c) PET scan

(d) TMS Apparatus

FIGURE 1 Brain scans produced by different techniques. (a) A computer-produced EEG image. (b) The fMRI scan uses a magnetic field to provide a detailed view of brain activity on a moment-by-moment basis. (c) The PET scan displays the functioning of the brain at a given moment. (d) Transcranial magnetic stimulation (TMS), the newest type of scan, produces a momentary disruption in an area of the brain, allowing researchers to see what activities are controlled by that area. TMS also has the potential to treat some psychological disorders.

(a) ©SPL/Science Source; (b) ©Steger Photo/Photolibrary/Getty Images; (c) ©Science History Images/Alamy Stock Photo; (d) ©Garo/Phanie/Science Source

Study Alert
Remember how EEG, fMRI, PET, and TMS scans differ in the ways that they produce an image of the brain.

Functional magnetic resonance imaging (fMRI) scans provide a detailed, three-dimensional computer-generated image of brain structures and activity by aiming a powerful magnetic field at the body. With fMRI scanning, it is possible to produce vivid, detailed images of the functioning of the brain.

Using fMRI scans, researchers are able to view features of less than a millimeter in size and view changes occurring in intervals of $1/10$ of a second. For example, fMRI scans can show the operation of individual bundles of nerves by tracing the flow of blood, opening the way for improved diagnosis of ailments ranging from chronic back pain to nervous system disorders such as strokes, multiple sclerosis, and Alzheimer's. Scans using fMRI are routinely used in planning brain surgery because they can help surgeons distinguish areas of the brain involved in normal and disturbed functioning (Loitfelder et al., 2011; Hurschler et al., 2015).

Positron emission tomography (PET) scans show biochemical activity within the brain at a given moment. PET scans begin with the injection of a radioactive (but safe) liquid into the bloodstream, which makes its way to the brain. By locating radiation within the brain, a computer can determine which are the more active regions, providing a striking picture of the brain at work. For example, PET scans may be used in cases of memory problems, seeking to identify the presence of brain tumors (Gronholm et al., 2005; McMurtray et al., 2007).

Transcranial magnetic stimulation (TMS) uses magnetic fields to produce an understanding of the functioning of the brain. In TMS, a tiny region of the brain is bombarded by a strong magnetic field that causes a momentary interruption of electrical activity. Researchers then are able to note the effects of this interruption on normal brain functioning.

One of the newest procedures used to study the brain, TMS is sometimes called a "virtual lesion" because it produces effects similar to what would occur if areas of the brain were physically cut. The enormous advantage of TMS, of course, is that the virtual cut is only temporary. In addition to identifying areas of the brain that are responsible for particular functions, TMS has the potential to treat certain kinds of psychological disorders, such as depression and schizophrenia, by shooting brief magnetic pulses through the brain (Pallanti & Bernardi, 2009; Prasser et al., 2015).

Future discoveries may yield even more sophisticated methods of examining the brain. For example, the emerging field of *optogenetics* involves genetic engineering and the use of special types of light to view individual circuits of neurons. In addition, researchers are developing *hydrogel-embedding* methods. which allow observation of individual brain cells and the wiring of brain circuitry (Deisseroth, 2016; Shirai & Hayashi-Takagi, 2017; Yang, Song, & Qing, 2017).

Advances in our understanding of the brain also are paving the way for the development of new methods for harnessing the brain's neural signals. We consider some of these intriguing findings in *Applying Psychology in the 21st Century.*

APPLYING PSYCHOLOGY IN THE 21ST CENTURY

BYPASSING BROKEN NEURAL PATHWAYS WITH A CHIP IN THE BRAIN

Ian Burkhart was a typical college freshman who was just enjoying a fun, leisurely day with his family at a beach in North Carolina when his whole life changed forever. Ian jumped headfirst into an approaching wave and struck his head on the soft sand of the ocean floor, breaking his neck. From that moment on, Ian permanently lost the feeling and movement in his hands, legs, and feet. He would never walk again or be able to complete even the simplest task with his hands, such as buttoning his shirt or stirring his coffee (Carey, 2016).

But advancements in neural engineering gave Ian a seemingly miraculous opportunity to use his hands again, albeit only for a limited time. To begin, in a delicate brain surgery, doctors implanted a chip in Ian's skull that comprises many tiny electrodes. Each electrode can detect the firing of an individual neuron within a very specific region of Ian's motor cortex–the region responsible for hand movements. Doctors identified this region with brain imaging before the surgery and then further refined their placement of the electrodes during the surgery to isolate nearly 100 specific neurons. The chip sends signals to a port in Ian's skull, which can be connected to computer equipment in the researchers' lab (Bouton et al., 2016).

After Ian healed from the surgery, the next step was to train both Ian and the computer software. Ian spent many hours watching video simulations of specific

©Lee Powell/The Washington Post via Getty Images

hand and finger movements. As Ian watched, he was instructed to imagine himself making those movements. The neurons in his motor cortex responsible for hand movement would fire, attempting to send a signal to Ian's paralyzed hand to move in the way Ian was imagining. Computer software read and analyzed the specific pattern of firing in the neurons monitored by the chip in Ian's skull, learning what patterns corresponded to specific movements. The computer then sent instructions to a device attached to Ian's forearm that could stimulate specific muscles controlling Ian's hand and fingers. So instead of the signal being sent directly from Ian's brain to his hand via motor pathways in the spinal cord, as would happen in a nonparalyzed person, the signal was instead being relayed from the brain to the muscles by an external computer. In this

way, the technology bypassed the blockage caused by Ian's damaged spinal cord.

It took a great deal of effort and months of training, but Ian first regained the ability to close and open his hand just by thinking about it. Eventually, he became able to grasp and lift items with his whole hand and with his fingers, allowing him to lift and pour from a bottle and then pick up a small stirrer and use it. He even learned to manipulate a video game controller. Such reanimation, as it's called, of a paralyzed limb was until recently the stuff of science fiction only. It became a reality for Ian, who is the first person to successfully control his muscles using his own neural signals relayed by computer.

Sadly, the success Ian experienced in the lab will not reverse his paralysis or help him function better in real life. The neural bypass only works when connected to bulky computers and other devices in the researchers' lab, which are not portable at all. At the conclusion of the research, Ian returned to his new normal life of dependence on others for care. Still, the research represented a major advancement toward a day when such technology could be put to more practical use, and Ian is gratified to have played a part in bringing a successful treatment for paralysis one step closer to fruition (Bouton et al., 2016).

RETHINK

- Why do you think Ian volunteered to undergo brain surgery and put in many months of hard work to help develop a technology that he knew would not benefit him?
- How would you explain this research on limb reanimation to a friend who recently became paralyzed?

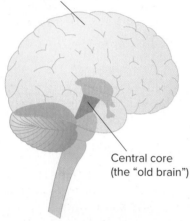

Cerebral cortex
(the "new brain")

Central core
(the "old brain")

FIGURE 2 The major divisions of the brain: the cerebral cortex and the central core. ©McGraw-Hill Global Education Holdings LLC, 2000.

central core The "old brain," which controls basic functions such as eating and sleeping and is common to all vertebrates. (Module 7)

cerebellum (ser-uh-BELL-um) The part of the brain that controls bodily balance. (Module 7)

The Central Core: Our "Old Brain"

Although the capabilities of the human brain far exceed those of the brain of any other species, humans share some basic functions, such as breathing, eating, and sleeping, with more primitive animals. Not surprisingly, those activities are directed by a relatively primitive part of the brain. A portion of the brain known as the **central core** (see Figure 2) is quite similar in all vertebrates (species with backbones). The central core is sometimes referred to as the "old brain" because its evolution can be traced back some 500 million years to primitive structures found in nonhuman species.

If we were to move up the spinal cord from the base of the skull to locate the structures of the central core of the brain, the first part we would come to would be the *hindbrain*, which contains the medulla, pons, and cerebellum (see Figure 3). The *medulla* controls a number of critical body functions, the most important of which are breathing and heartbeat. The *pons* is a bridge in the hindbrain. Containing large bundles of nerves, the pons acts as a transmitter of motor information, coordinating muscles and integrating movement between the right and left halves of the body. It is also involved in regulating sleep.

The **cerebellum** extends from the rear of the hindbrain. Without the help of the cerebellum, we would be unable to walk a straight line without staggering and lurching forward, for it is the job of the cerebellum to control bodily balance. It constantly monitors feedback from the muscles to coordinate their placement, movement, and tension. In fact, drinking too much alcohol seems to depress the activity of the cerebellum, leading to the unsteady gait and movement characteristic of drunkenness. The cerebellum is also involved in several intellectual functions, ranging from the analysis and coordination of sensory information to problem solving (Vandervert, Schimpf, & Liu, 2007; Swain, Kerr, & Thompson, 2011; Ronconi et al., 2017).

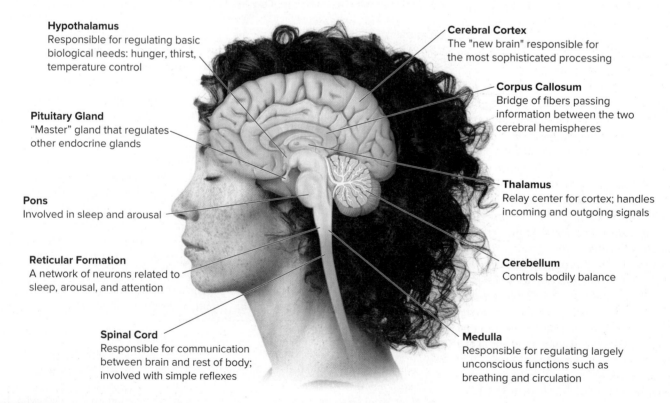

Hypothalamus
Responsible for regulating basic biological needs: hunger, thirst, temperature control

Pituitary Gland
"Master" gland that regulates other endocrine glands

Pons
Involved in sleep and arousal

Reticular Formation
A network of neurons related to sleep, arousal, and attention

Spinal Cord
Responsible for communication between brain and rest of body; involved with simple reflexes

Cerebral Cortex
The "new brain" responsible for the most sophisticated processing

Corpus Callosum
Bridge of fibers passing information between the two cerebral hemispheres

Thalamus
Relay center for cortex; handles incoming and outgoing signals

Cerebellum
Controls bodily balance

Medulla
Responsible for regulating largely unconscious functions such as breathing and circulation

FIGURE 3 The major structures in the brain.
Source: Adapted from Bloom, F. (1975). *Brain, mind, and behavior,* New York: Educational Broadcasting Corp.; (Photo): ©Dana Neely/Taxi/Getty Images

The **reticular formation** is a nerve network in the brain that extends from the medulla through the pons, passing through the middle section of the brain, called the *midbrain,* and into the front-most part of the brain, called the *forebrain.* Like an ever-vigilant guard, the reticular formation produces general arousal of our body. If, for example, we are startled by a loud noise, the reticular formation can prompt a heightened state of awareness to determine whether a response is necessary. The reticular formation also helps regulate our sleep-wake cycle by filtering out background stimuli to allow us to sleep undisturbed.

reticular formation The part of the brain extending from the medulla through the pons; it is related to changes in the level of arousal of the body. (Module 7)

The **thalamus,** which is hidden within the forebrain, acts primarily as a relay station for information about the senses. Messages from the eyes, ears, and skin travel to the thalamus to be communicated upward to higher parts of the brain. The thalamus also integrates information from higher parts of the brain, sorting it out so that it can be sent to the cerebellum and medulla.

thalamus The part of the brain located in the middle of the central core that acts primarily to relay information about the senses. (Module 7)

The **hypothalamus** is located just below the thalamus. Although tiny—about the size of a fingertip—the hypothalamus plays an extremely important role. One of its major functions is to maintain *homeostasis,* a steady internal environment for the body. The hypothalamus helps provide a constant body temperature and monitors the amount of nutrients stored in the cells. A second major function is equally important: the hypothalamus produces and regulates behavior that is critical to the basic survival of the species, such as eating, self-protection, and sex.

hypothalamus A tiny part of the brain, located below the thalamus, that maintains homeostasis and produces and regulates vital behavior, such as eating, drinking, and sexual behavior. (Module 7)

The Limbic System: Beyond the Central Core

In an eerie view of the future, science fiction writers have suggested that people someday will routinely have electrodes implanted in their brains. Those electrodes will permit them to receive tiny shocks that will produce the sensation of pleasure by stimulating certain centers of the brain. When they feel upset, people will simply activate their electrodes to achieve an immediate high.

Although far-fetched—and ultimately improbable—such a futuristic fantasy is based on fact. The brain does have pleasure centers in several areas, including some in the **limbic system.** Consisting of a series of doughnut-shaped structures that include the *amygdala* and *hippocampus,* the limbic system borders the top of the central core and has connections with the cerebral cortex (see Figure 4).

limbic system The part of the brain that controls eating, aggression, and reproduction. (Module 7)

The structures of the limbic system jointly control a variety of basic functions relating to emotions and self-preservation, such as eating, aggression, and reproduction. Injury to the limbic system can produce striking changes in behavior. For example, injury to the amygdala, which is involved in fear and aggression, can turn animals that are usually docile and tame into belligerent savages. Conversely, animals that are usually wild and uncontrollable may become meek and obedient following injury to the amygdala (Gontkovsky, 2005; Smith et al., 2013; Reznikova et al., 2015).

Research examining the effects of mild electric shocks to parts of the limbic system and other parts of the brain has produced some thought-provoking findings. In one classic experiment, rats that pressed a bar received mild electric stimulation through an electrode implanted in their brains, which produced pleasurable feelings. Even starving rats on their way to food would stop to press the bar as many times as they could. Some rats would actually stimulate themselves literally thousands of times an hour—until they collapsed with fatigue (Routtenberg & Lindy, 1965; Fountas & Smith, 2007).

Some humans have also experienced the extraordinarily pleasurable quality of certain kinds of stimulation: As part of the treatment for certain

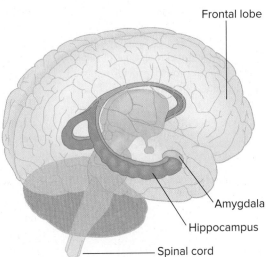

FIGURE 4 The limbic system is involved in self-preservation, learning, memory, and the experience of pleasure.
©McGraw-Hill Global Education Holdings LLC, 1995.

kinds of brain disorders, some people have received electrical stimulation to certain areas of the limbic system. Although at a loss to describe just what it feels like, these people report the experience to be intensely pleasurable, similar in some respects to sexual orgasm.

The limbic system and hippocampus, in particular, play an important role in learning and memory. Their importance is demonstrated in certain patients with epilepsy, who, in an effort to stop their seizures, have had portions of the limbic system removed. One unintended consequence of the surgery is that individuals sometimes have difficulty learning and remembering new information. In one case, a patient who had undergone surgery was unable to remember where he lived, although he had resided at the same address for 8 years. Further, even though the patient was able to carry on animated conversations, he was unable, a few minutes later, to recall what had been discussed (Milner, 1966; Grimm, 2011; de Voogd et al., 2017).

The limbic system, then, is involved in several important functions, including self-preservation, learning, memory, and the experience of pleasure. These functions are hardly unique to humans; in fact, the limbic system is sometimes referred to as the "animal brain" because its structures and functions are so similar to those of other mammals. To identify the part of the brain that provides the complex and subtle capabilities that are uniquely human, we need to turn to another structure–the cerebral cortex.

The Cerebral Cortex: Our "New Brain"

As we have proceeded up the spinal cord and into the brain, our discussion has centered on areas of the brain that control functions similar to those found in less sophisticated organisms. But where, you may be asking, are the portions of the brain that enable humans to do what they do best and that distinguish humans from all other animals? Those unique features of the human brain–indeed, the very capabilities that allow you to come up with such a question in the first place–are embodied in the ability to think, evaluate, and make complex judgments. The principal location of these abilities, along with many others, is the **cerebral cortex.**

cerebral cortex The "new brain," responsible for the most sophisticated information processing in the brain; contains four lobes. (Module 7)

The cerebral cortex is referred to as the "new brain" because of its relatively recent evolution. It consists of a mass of deeply folded, rippled, convoluted tissue. Although only about $\frac{1}{12}$ of an inch thick, it would, if flattened out, cover an area more than 2 feet square. This configuration allows the surface area of the cortex to be considerably greater than it would be if it were smoother and more uniformly packed into the skull. The uneven shape also permits a high level of integration of neurons, allowing sophisticated information processing.

lobes The four major sections of the cerebral cortex: frontal, parietal, temporal, and occipital. (Module 7)

The cerebral cortex consists of four major sections called **lobes.** Each lobe has specialized areas that relate to particular functions. If we take a side view of the brain, the *frontal lobes* lie at the front center of the cortex and the *parietal lobes* lie behind them. The *temporal lobes* are found in the lower-center portion of the cortex, with the *occipital lobes* lying behind them. These four sets of lobes are physically separated by deep grooves called *sulci*. Figure 5 shows the four areas.

Another way to describe the brain is in terms of the functions associated with a particular area. Figure 5 also shows the specialized regions within the lobes related to specific functions and areas of the body. Three major areas are known: the motor areas, the sensory areas, and the association areas. Although we will discuss these areas as though they were separate and independent, keep in mind that this is an oversimplification. In most instances, behavior is influenced simultaneously by several structures and areas within the brain, operating interdependently. To give one example, people use different areas of the brain when they create sentences (a verbal task) compared with when they improvise musical tunes. Furthermore, when people suffer brain injury, uninjured portions of the brain can sometimes take over the functions that were previously handled by the damaged area. In short, the brain is extraordinarily adaptable (Sacks, 2003; Boller, 2004; Brown, Martinez, & Parsons, 2006).

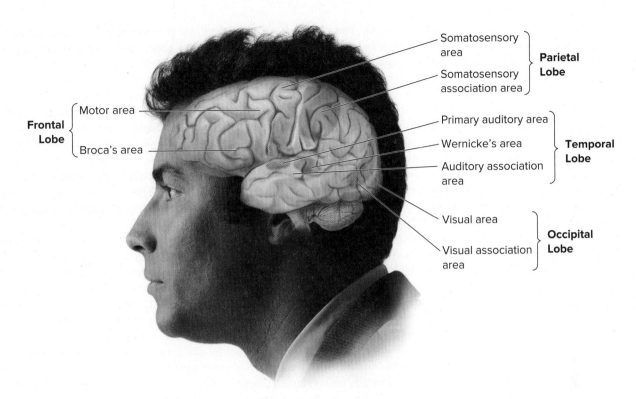

FIGURE 5 The cerebral cortex of the brain. The major physical structures of the cerebral cortex are called lobes. This figure also illustrates the functions associated with particular areas of the cerebral cortex. Are any areas of the cerebral cortex present in nonhuman animals?
©Ron Krisel/Getty Images

THE MOTOR AREA OF THE CORTEX

If you look at the frontal lobe in Figure 5, you will see a shaded portion labeled **motor area.** This part of the cortex is largely responsible for the body's voluntary movement. Every portion of the motor area corresponds to a specific locale within the body. If we were to insert an electrode into a particular part of the motor area of the cortex and apply mild electrical stimulation, there would be involuntary movement in the corresponding part of the body. If we moved to another part of the motor area and stimulated it, a different part of the body would move.

The motor area is so well mapped that researchers have identified the amount and relative location of cortical tissue used to produce movement in specific parts of the human body. For example, the control of movements that are relatively large scale and require little precision, such as the movement of a knee or a hip, is centered in a very small space in the motor area. In contrast, movements that must be precise and delicate, such as facial expressions and finger movements, are controlled by a considerably larger portion of the motor area (Schwenkreis et al., 2007).

In short, the motor area of the cortex provides a guide to the degree of complexity and the importance of the motor capabilities of specific parts of the body. In fact, it may do even more: Increasing evidence shows that not only does the motor cortex control different parts of the body, but it may also direct body parts into complex postures, such as the stance of a football center just before the ball is snapped to the quarterback or a swimmer standing at the edge of a diving board (Pool et al., 2013; Massé-Alarie et al., 2017).

Ultimately, movement, like other behavior, is produced through the coordinated firing of a complex variety of neurons in the nervous system. The neurons that produce movement are linked in elaborate ways and work closely together.

motor area The part of the cortex that is largely responsible for the body's voluntary movement. (Module 7)

THE SENSORY AREA OF THE CORTEX

Given the one-to-one correspondence between the motor area and body location, it is not surprising to find a similar relationship between specific portions of the cortex and

sensory area The site in the brain of the tissue that corresponds to each of the senses, with the degree of sensitivity related to the amount of tissue. (Module 7)

specific senses. The **sensory area** of the cortex includes three regions: one that corresponds primarily to body sensations (including touch and pressure), one relating to sight, and a third relating to sound.

For instance, the *somatosensory area* in the parietal lobe encompasses specific locations associated with the ability to perceive touch and pressure in a particular area of the body. As with the motor area, the amount of brain tissue related to a particular location on the body determines the degree of sensitivity of that location. Specifically, the greater the area devoted to a specific area of the body within the cortex, the more sensitive is that area of the body.

For example, our fingers are related to a larger portion of the somatosensory area in the brain and are the most sensitive to touch. The weird-looking individual in Figure 6 shows what we would look like if the size of every external part of our body corresponded to the amount of brain tissue related to touch sensitivity.

The senses of sound and sight are also represented in specific areas of the cerebral cortex. An *auditory area* located in the temporal lobe is responsible for the sense of hearing. If the auditory area is stimulated electrically, a person will hear sounds such as clicks or hums. It also appears that particular locations within the auditory area respond to specific pitches (Tsuchida, Ueno, & Shimada, 2015; Anderson, Lazard, & Hartley, 2017).

The visual area in the cortex, located in the occipital lobe, responds in the same way to electrical stimulation. Stimulation by electrodes produces the experience of flashes of light or colors, suggesting that the raw sensory input of images from the eyes is received in this area of the brain and transformed into meaningful stimuli. The visual area provides another example of how areas of the brain are intimately related to specific areas of the body: Specific structures in the eye are related to a particular part of the cortex–with, as you might guess, more area of the brain given to the most sensitive portions of the retina (Stenbacka & Vanni, 2007; Libedinsky & Livingstone, 2011).

THE ASSOCIATION AREAS OF THE CORTEX

association areas One of the major regions of the cerebral cortex; the site of the higher mental processes, such as thought, language, memory, and speech. (Module 7)

In a freak accident in 1848, an explosion drove a 3-foot-long iron bar completely through the skull of railroad worker Phineas Gage, where it remained after the accident. Amazingly, Gage survived and, despite the rod lodged through his head, a few minutes later seemed to be fine.

But he wasn't. Before the accident, Gage was hardworking and cautious. Afterward, he became irresponsible, drank heavily, and drifted from one wild scheme to another. In the words of one of his physicians, "He was 'no longer Gage'" (Harlow, 1869).

What had happened to the old Gage? Although there is no way of knowing for sure, we can speculate that the accident injured the region of Gage's cerebral cortex known as the association areas. The **association areas** are the site of higher mental processes such as thinking, language, memory, and speech.

The association areas make up a large portion of the cerebral cortex. The association areas control *executive functions*, which are abilities that are related to planning, goal setting, judgment, and impulse control.

Much of our understanding of the association areas comes from patients who, like Phineas Gage, have suffered some type of brain injury. For example, when parts of the association areas are damaged, people undergo personality changes that affect their ability to make moral judgments and process emotions. At the same time, people with damage in those areas can still be capable of reasoning logically, performing calculations, and recalling information (Bechara et al., 1994).

Injuries to the association areas of the brain can produce *aphasia*, problems with language. In *Broca's aphasia*, speech

FIGURE 6 The greater the amount of tissue in the somatosensory area of the brain that is related to a specific body part, the more sensitive is that body part. If the size of our body parts reflected the corresponding amount of brain tissue, we would look like this strange creature.
©Natural History Museum, London/Science Source

becomes halting, laborious, and often ungrammatical, and a speaker is unable to find the right words. In contrast, *Wernicke's aphasia* produces difficulties both in understanding others' speech and in the production of language. The disorder is characterized by speech that sounds fluent but makes no sense, as in this example from a Wernicke's patient: "Boy, I'm sweating, I'm awful nervous, you know, once in a while I get caught up, I can't mention the tarripoi, a month ago, quite a little. . ." (Caplan, Waters, & Dede, 2007; Robson et al., 2013; Ardila, 2015).

Neuroplasticity and the Brain

Shortly after he was born, Jacob Stark's arms and legs started jerking every 20 minutes. Weeks later he could not focus his eyes on his mother's face. The diagnosis: uncontrollable epileptic seizures involving his entire brain.

His mother, Sally Stark, recalled: "When Jacob was 2½ months old, they said he would never learn to sit up, would never be able to feed himself. . . . They told us to take him home, love him, and find an institution." (Blakeslee, 1992)

Instead, Jacob had brain surgery when he was 5 months old in which physicians removed 20% of his brain. The operation was a complete success. Three years later, Jacob seemed normal in every way, with no sign of seizures.

The surgery that helped Jacob was based on the premise that the diseased part of his brain was producing seizures throughout the brain. Surgeons reasoned that if they removed the misfiring portion, the remaining parts of the brain, which appeared intact in PET scans, would take over. They correctly bet that Jacob could still lead a normal life after surgery, particularly because the surgery was being done at so young an age.

The success of Jacob's surgery illustrates that the brain has the ability to shift functions to different locations after injury to a specific area or in cases of surgery. But equally encouraging are some new findings about the *regenerative* powers of the brain and nervous system.

Scientists have learned in recent years that the brain continually changes, reorganizes itself, and is far more resilient than they once thought. **Neuroplasticity** refers to the brain's ability to change throughout the life span through the addition of new neurons, new interconnections between neurons, and the reorganization of information-processing areas.

Advances in our understanding of neuroplasticity have changed the earlier view that no new brain cells are created after childhood. The reality is very different: Not only do the interconnections between neurons become more complex throughout life, but it now appears that new neurons are also created in certain areas of the brain during adulthood–a process called *neurogenesis*. Each day, thousands of new neurons are created, especially in areas of the brain related to learning and memory (Shors, 2009; Kempermann, 2011; Apple, Fonseca, & Kokovay, 2017).

The ability of neurons to renew themselves during adulthood has significant implications for the potential treatment of disorders of the nervous system (see *Neuroscience in Your Life*). For example, drugs that trigger the development of new neurons might be used to counter such diseases as Alzheimer's, which are produced when neurons die (Waddell & Shors, 2008; Hamilton et al., 2013; Ekonomou et al., 2015).

Furthermore, specific experiences can modify the way in which information is processed. For example, if you learn to read Braille, the amount of tissue in your cortex related to sensation in the fingertips will expand. Similarly, if you take up the violin, the area of the brain that receives messages from your fingers will grow–but only relating to the fingers that actually move across the violin's strings (Schwartz & Begley, 2002; Kolb, Gibb, & Robinson, 2003).

The future also holds promise for people who suffer from the tremors and loss of motor control produced by Parkinson's disease, although the research is mired in controversy. Because Parkinson's disease is caused by a gradual loss of cells that stimulate the production of dopamine in the brain, many investigators have reasoned that a procedure that would increase the supply of dopamine might be effective. They seem to be on the

neuroplasticity Changes in the brain that occur throughout the life span relating to the addition of new neurons, new interconnections between neurons, and the reorganization of information-processing areas. (Module 7)

NEUROSCIENCE IN YOUR LIFE: THE PLASTIC BRAIN

The brain is highly plastic, meaning that it can change in significant ways over the course of the life span. For example, brain plasticity is apparent in patients who lose a limb due to injury. Many such patients experience pain in their missing limb, called phantom limb pain. In a recent study, brain scans of participants with phantom hand pain showed changes in activity within sensory and motor brain regions. For example, regions involved in processing elbow information migrated into regions that previously processed missing hand information.

The images below show brain activity when participants moved their elbows (left) and hands (right; imagined for amputees). In the column labeled elbows, we see differences between activity during movement and rest (yellow indicates the greatest differences) in the same areas as in the column labeled hands, indicating that activity for elbow movements has migrated into regions for hand movements (Raffin et al., 2016).

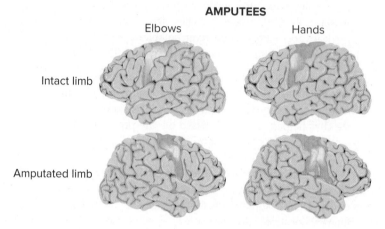

Source: Adapted from Raffin, E., Richard, N., Giraux, P., & Reilly, K. T. (2016). Primary motor cortex changes after amputation correlate with phantom limb pain and the ability to move the phantom limb. *Neuroimage, 130,* 134–144.

right track. When *stem cells*—immature cells from human fetuses that have the potential to develop into a variety of specialized cell types, depending on where they are implanted—are injected directly into the brains of Parkinson's sufferers, they take root and stimulate dopamine production. Preliminary results have been promising, with some patients showing great improvement (Parish & Arenas, 2007; Newman & Bakay, 2008; Wang et al., 2011).

Stem cells thus hold great promise. When a stem cell divides, each newly created cell has the potential to be transformed into more specialized cells that have the potential to repair damaged cells. Because many of the most disabling diseases, ranging from cancer to stroke, result from cell damage, the potential of stem cells to revolutionize medicine is significant.

However, because the source of implanted stem cells typically is aborted fetuses, their use is controversial. Some critics have argued that the use of stem cells in research and treatment should be prohibited, while supporters argue that the potential benefits of the research are so great that stem cell research should be unrestricted. The issue has been politicized, and the question of whether and how stem cell research should be regulated is not clear (Giacomini, Baylis, & Robert, 2007; Holden, 2007; Towns, 2017).

The Specialization of the Hemispheres: Two Brains or One?

The most recent development, at least in evolutionary terms, in the organization and operation of the human brain probably occurred in the last several million years: a specialization of the functions controlled by the left and right sides of the brain (Hopkins & Cantalupo, 2008; MacNeilage, Rogers, & Vallortigara, 2009; Tommasi, 2009).

The brain is divided into two roughly mirror-image halves. Just as we have two arms, two legs, and two lungs, we have a left brain and a right brain. Because of the way nerves in the brain are connected to the rest of the body, these symmetrical left and right halves, called **hemispheres,** control motion in–and receive sensation from– the side of the body opposite their location. The left hemisphere of the brain, then, generally controls the right side of the body, and the right hemisphere controls the left side of the body. Thus, damage to the right side of the brain is typically indicated by functional difficulties in the left side of the body.

Despite the appearance of similarity between the two hemispheres of the brain, they are somewhat different in the functions they control and in the ways they control them. Certain behaviors are more likely to reflect activity in one hemisphere than in the other, or are **lateralized.**

For example, for most people, language processing occurs more in the left side of the brain. In general, the left hemisphere concentrates more on tasks that require verbal competence, such as speaking, reading, thinking, and reasoning. In addition, the left hemisphere tends to process information sequentially, one bit at a time (Hines, 2004).

The right hemisphere has its own strengths, particularly in nonverbal areas such as the understanding of spatial relationships, recognition of patterns and drawings, music, and emotional expression. The right hemisphere tends to process information globally, considering it as a whole (Holowka & Petitto, 2002; Gotts et al., 2013; Longo et al., 2015).

The degree and nature of lateralization vary from one person to another. If, like most people, you are right-handed, the control of language is probably concentrated more in your left hemisphere. By contrast, if you are among the 10% of people who are left-handed or are ambidextrous (you use both hands interchangeably), it is much more likely that the language centers of your brain are located more in the right hemisphere or are divided equally between the left and right hemispheres.

Keep in mind that despite the different strengths of the two hemispheres, the differences in specialization between the hemispheres are not great. Furthermore, the two hemispheres of the brain function in tandem. It is a mistake to think of particular kinds of information as being processed solely in the right or the left hemisphere. The hemispheres work interdependently in deciphering, interpreting, and reacting to the world.

In addition, people who suffer injury to the left side of the brain and lose linguistic capabilities often recover the ability to speak: The right side of the brain often takes over some of the functions of the left side, especially in young children; the extent of recovery increases the earlier the injury occurs (Johnston, 2004).

Furthermore, not every researcher believes that the differences between the two hemispheres of the brain are terribly significant. According to neuroscientist Stephen Kosslyn, a more critical difference occurs in processing between the upper and lower halves of the brain. In his theory, the top-brain system of the brain specializes in planning and goal-setting. In contrast, the bottom-brain system helps classify information coming from our senses, allowing us to understand and classify information. It is still too early to know the accuracy of Kosslyn's theory, but it provides an intriguing alternative to the notion that left-right brain differences are of primary importance (Kosslyn & Miller, 2013).

In any case, evidence continues to grow that the difference between processing in the left and right hemispheres are meaningful. For example, researchers have unearthed evidence that there may be subtle differences in brain lateralization patterns between males and females and members of different cultures, as we see in *Exploring Diversity*.

hemispheres Symmetrical left and right halves of the brain that control the side of the body opposite to their location. (Module 7)

lateralization The dominance of one hemisphere of the brain in specific functions, such as language. (Module 7)

Study Alert

Although the hemispheres of the brain specialize in particular kinds of functions, the degree of specialization is not great, and the two hemispheres work interdependently.

PsychTech

Using a procedure called *hemispherectomy,* in which an entire hemisphere of the brain is removed, surgeons ended Christina Santhouse's seizures, which occurred at the rate of hundreds a day. Despite the removal of the right side of her brain, Christina recently completed a master's degree in speech pathology.

From the perspective of...

An Office Worker Could personal differences in people's specialization of right and left hemispheres be related to occupational success? For example, might a designer who relies on spatial skills have a different pattern of hemispheric specialization than does a lawyer?

©Caia Images/Glow Images

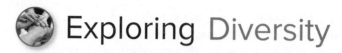

Exploring Diversity

Human Diversity and the Brain

The interplay of biology and environment in behavior is especially clear when we consider evidence suggesting that even in brain structure and function, there are both sex and cultural differences. Let's consider sex differences first. Accumulating evidence seems to show intriguing differences in males' and females' brain lateralization and weight (Boles, 2005; Clements, Rimrodt, & Abel, 2006; Joel & McCarthy, 2017).

For instance, the two sexes show differences in the speed at which their brains develop. Young girls show earlier development in the frontal lobes, which control aggressiveness and language development. On the other hand, boys' brains develop faster in the visual region that facilitates visual and spatial tasks such as geometry (Giedd et al., 2010; Raznahan et al., 2010).

Furthermore, most males tend to show greater lateralization of language in the left hemisphere. For them, language is clearly relegated largely to the left side of the brain. In contrast, women display less lateralization, with language abilities apt to be more evenly divided between the two hemispheres. Such differences in brain lateralization may account, in part, for the superiority often displayed by females on certain measures of verbal skills, such as the onset and fluency of speech (Petersson et al., 2007; Mercadillo et al., 2011).

Other research suggests that men's brains are somewhat bigger than women's brains, even after taking differences in body size into account. In contrast, part of the *corpus callosum,* a bundle of fibers that connects the hemispheres of the brain, is proportionally larger in women than in men (Smith et al., 2007; Taki et al., 2013).

The meaning of such sex differences is far from clear. Consider one possibility related to differences in the proportional size of the corpus callosum: Its greater size in women may permit stronger connections to develop between the parts of the brain that control speech. In turn, this would explain why speech tends to emerge slightly earlier in girls than in boys.

Before we rush to such a conclusion, though, we must consider an alternative hypothesis: The reason verbal abilities emerge earlier in girls may be that infant girls receive greater encouragement to talk than do infant boys. In turn, this greater early experience may foster the growth of certain parts of the brain. Hence, physical brain differences may be a *reflection* of social and environmental influences rather than a *cause* of the differences in men's and women's behavior. At this point, it is impossible to know which of these alternative hypotheses is correct.

Furthermore, newer research suggests that most brains contain elements of male *and* female characteristics. Such findings contradict the notion that a brain is essentially either male or female (Denworth, 2017).

Culture also gives rise to differences in brain size and lateralization. For example, the volume of gray-matter material in the cortex is greater in higher-income adolescents than in low-income adolescents. Furthermore, brain development is related to differences in academic achievement between students of different income levels. Specifically, the brain's cortex is thicker in higher-income students than in lower-income students, and cortex configuration is related to their academic achievement (Mackey et al., 2015).

Clearly, our brains reflect a combination of genetically determined structure and functioning. But they also reflect the impact of the social and cultural experiences to which we are exposed.

The Split Brain: Exploring the Two Hemispheres

When Vicki visited her neurologist, she was desperate: Her frequent and severe epileptic seizures weren't just interfering with her day-to-day life—they were putting her in danger. She never knew when she might just collapse suddenly, making many mundane situations such as climbing stairs potentially life-threatening for her.

Vicki's neurologist had a solution, but a radical and potentially dangerous one: surgically severing the bundle of fibers connecting the two hemispheres of her brain. This procedure would stop the firestorms of electrical impulses that were causing Vicki's seizures, but it would also have its own curious effects on her day-to-day functioning.

In the months after the surgery, Vicki was relieved to be free of the seizures that had taken over her life. But she had new challenges to overcome. Simple tasks such as food shopping or even dressing herself became lengthy ordeals–not because she had difficulty moving or thinking but because the two sides of her brain no longer worked in a coordinated way. Each side directed its half of the body to work independently of the other (Wolman, 2012).

People like Vicki, whose corpus collosums have been cut or injured, are called *split-brain patients.* They offer a rare opportunity for researchers investigating the independent functioning of the two hemispheres of the brain. For example, psychologist Roger Sperry–who won the Nobel Prize for his work–developed a number of ingenious techniques for studying how each hemisphere operates (Sperry, 1982; Savazzi et al., 2007; Bagattini et al., 2015).

In one experimental procedure, patients who were prevented from seeing an object by a screen touched the object with their right hand and were asked to name it (see Figure 7). Because the right side of the body corresponds to the language-oriented left side of the brain, split-brain patients were able to name it. However, if patients touched the object with their left hand, they were unable to name it aloud, even though the information had registered in their brains. When the screen was removed, patients could identify the object they had touched. Information can be learned and remembered, then, using only the right side of the brain. (By the way, unless you've had split-brain surgery, this experiment won't work with you because the bundle of fibers connecting the two hemispheres of a normal brain immediately transfers the information from one hemisphere to the other.)

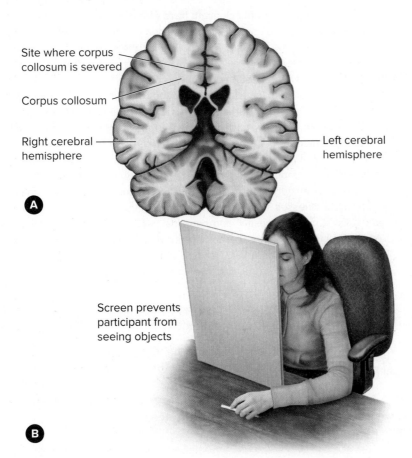

Site where corpus collosum is severed

Corpus collosum

Right cerebral hemisphere

Left cerebral hemisphere

A

Screen prevents participant from seeing objects

B

FIGURE 7 Hemispheres of the brain. (a) The corpus callosum connects the cerebral hemispheres of the brain, as shown in this cross section. (b) A split-brain patient is tested by touching objects behind a screen. Patients could name the objects they touched with their right hand but couldn't name them when they touched them with their left hand. If a split-brain patient with her eyes closed was given a pencil to hold and called it a pencil, what hand was the pencil in? (a and b): ©McGraw-Hill Global Education Holdings LLC, 2008.

It is clear from experiments like this one that the right and left hemispheres of the brain specialize in handling different sorts of information. At the same time, it is important to realize that both hemispheres are capable of understanding, knowing, and being aware of the world, in somewhat different ways. The two hemispheres, then, should be regarded as different in terms of the efficiency with which they process certain kinds of information, rather than as two entirely separate brains. The hemispheres work interdependently to allow the full range and richness of thought of which humans are capable.

BECOMING AN INFORMED CONSUMER
of Psychology

Learning to Control Your Heart—and Mind—Through Biofeedback

When Tammy DeMichael was involved in a horrific car accident that broke her neck and crushed her spinal cord, experts told her that she was doomed to be a quadriplegic for the rest of her life, unable to move from the neck down. But they were wrong. Not only did she regain the use of her arms, but she also was able to walk 60 feet with a cane (Hess, Houg, & Tammaro, 2007).

biofeedback A procedure in which a person learns to control through conscious thought internal physiological processes such as blood pressure, heart and respiration rate, skin temperature, sweating, and the constriction of particular muscles. (Module 7)

The key to DeMichael's astounding recovery: biofeedback. **Biofeedback** is a procedure in which a person learns to control through conscious thought internal physiological processes such as blood pressure, heart and respiration rate, skin temperature, sweating, and the constriction of particular muscles. Although it traditionally had been thought that heart rate, respiration rate, blood pressure, and other bodily functions are under the control of parts of the brain over which we have no influence, psychologists have discovered that these responses are actually susceptible to voluntary control (Cho, Holyoak, & Cannon, 2007; Badke et al., 2011).

In biofeedback, a person is hooked up to electronic devices that provide continuous feedback relating to the physiological response in question. For instance, someone trying to control headaches through biofeedback might have electronic sensors placed on certain muscles on her head and learn to control the constriction and relaxation of those muscles. Later, when she felt a headache starting, she could relax the relevant muscles and abort the pain (Andrasik, 2007; Nestoriuc et al., 2008; Magis & Schoenen, 2011).

DeMichael's treatment was related to a form of biofeedback called *neurofeedback,* in which brain activity is displayed for a patient. Because not all of her nervous system's connections between the brain and her legs were severed, she was able to learn how to send messages to specific muscles, "ordering" them to move. Although it took more than a year, DeMichael was successful in restoring a large degree of her mobility.

Although the control of physiological processes through the use of biofeedback is not easy to learn, it has been employed with success in a variety of ailments, including emotional problems (such as anxiety, depression, phobias, tension headaches, insomnia, and hyperactivity), physical illnesses with a psychological component (such as asthma, high blood pressure, ulcers, muscle spasms, and migraine headaches), and physical problems (such as DeMichael's injuries, strokes, cerebral palsy, and curvature of the spine) (Morone & Greco, 2007; Reiner, 2008; Dias & van Deusen, 2011).

RECAP/EVALUATE/RETHINK

RECAP

LO 7-1 How do researchers identify the major parts and functions of the brain?

- Brain scans take a "snapshot" of the internal workings of the brain without having to cut surgically into a per-

son's skull. Major brain-scanning techniques include the electroencephalogram (EEG), positron emission tomography (PET), functional magnetic resonance imaging (fMRI), and transcranial magnetic stimulation imaging (TMS).

LO 7-2 What are the major parts of the brain, and for what behaviors is each part responsible?

- The central core of the brain is made up of the medulla (which controls functions such as breathing and the heartbeat), the pons (which coordinates the muscles and the two sides of the body), the cerebellum (which controls balance), the reticular formation (which acts to heighten arousal and sudden awareness), the thalamus (which communicates sensory messages to and from the brain), and the hypothalamus (which maintains homeostasis, or body equilibrium, and regulates behavior related to basic survival). The functions of the central core structures are similar to those found in other vertebrates. This central core is sometimes referred to as the "old brain."
- The cerebral cortex–the "new brain"–has areas that control voluntary movement (the motor area); the senses (the sensory area); and thinking, reasoning, speech, and memory (the association areas). The limbic system, found on the border of the "old" and "new" brains, is associated with eating, aggression, reproduction, and the experiences of pleasure and pain.

LO 7-3 How do the two halves of the brain operate interdependently?

- The brain is divided into left and right halves, or hemispheres, each of which generally controls the opposite side of the body. Each hemisphere can be thought of as being specialized in the functions it carries out: The left specializes in verbal tasks, such as logical reasoning, speaking, and reading; the right specializes in nonverbal tasks, such as spatial perception, pattern recognition, and emotional expression.

LO 7-4 How can an understanding of the nervous system help us to find ways to alleviate disease and pain?

- Biofeedback is a procedure by which a person learns to control internal physiological processes. By controlling involuntary responses, people are able to relieve anxiety, tension, migraine headaches, and a wide range of other psychological and physical problems.

EVALUATE

1. Match the name of each brain scan with the appropriate description:

a. EEG	1. By locating radiation within the brain, a computer can provide a striking picture of brain activity.
b. fMRI	2. Electrodes placed around the skull record the electrical signals transmitted through the brain.
c. PET	3. This technique provides a three-dimensional view of the brain by aiming a magnetic field at the body.

2. Match the portion of the brain with its function:

a. medulla	1. Maintains breathing and heartbeat
b. pons	2. Controls bodily balance
c. cerebellum	3. Coordinates and integrates muscle movements
d. reticular formation	4. Activates other parts of the brain to produce general bodily arousal

3. A surgeon places an electrode on a portion of your brain and stimulates it. Immediately, your right wrist involuntarily twitches. The doctor has most likely stimulated a portion of the _____ area of your brain.
4. Each hemisphere controls the _____ side of the body.
5. Nonverbal realms, such as emotions and music, are controlled primarily by the _____ hemisphere of the brain, whereas the _____ hemisphere is more responsible for speaking and reading.

RETHINK

1. Before sophisticated brain-scanning techniques were developed, behavioral neuroscientists' understanding of the brain was based largely on the brains of people who had died. What limitations would this pose, and in what areas would you expect the most significant advances once brain-scanning techniques became possible?
2. Could personal differences in people's specialization of right and left hemispheres be related to occupational success?

Answers to Evaluate Questions

1. a-2, b-3, c-1; 2. a-1, b-3, c-2, d-4; 3. motor; 4. opposite; 5. right, left

KEY TERMS

central core	thalamus	lobes	neuroplasticity
cerebellum (ser-uh-BELL-um)	hypothalamus	motor area	hemispheres
reticular formation	limbic system	sensory area	lateralization
	cerebral cortex	association areas	biofeedback

LOOKING *Back*

EPILOGUE

In our examination of neuroscience, we've traced the ways in which biological structures and functions of the body affect behavior. Starting with neurons, we considered each of the components of the nervous system, culminating in an examination of how the brain permits us to think, reason, speak, recall, and experience emotions—the hallmarks of being human.

Before proceeding, turn back for a moment to the chapter prologue about Dennis Degray, a man paralyzed from the neck down, who is able via a brain-computer interface to move a computer cursor by simply visualizing muscle movements. Consider the following questions:

1. Describe the natural sequence of processes the brain-computer interface (BCI) algorithms duplicate in enabling Dennis Degray to type words on a keyboard?

2. What special challenges might Dennis Degray have faced if his accident had damaged his hippocampus instead of his spine? His amygdala? His Broca's area?

3. Explain how the biofeedback treatment known as neurofeedback works. How does it differ from the BCI used to help Dennis DeGray?

4. Can you think of other potential applications of BCI that could enable people with severe motor impairment to lead more independent lives?

Design Elements: Yellow highlighter: ©luckyraccoon/Shutterstock.com; Smartphone: ©and4me/Shutterstock.com; Group of diverse hands: ©MR. Nattanon Kanchak/Shutterstock.com; Woman working on laptop: ©Dragon Images/Shutterstock.com.

VISUAL SUMMARY 2 Neuroscience and Behavior

Neuron Structure

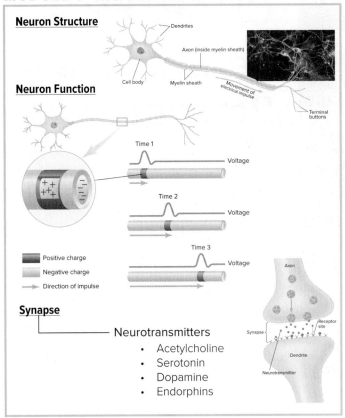

- Dendrites
- Axon (inside myelin sheath)
- Cell body
- Myelin sheath
- Movement of electrical impulse
- Terminal buttons

Neuron Function

- Time 1 — Voltage
- Time 2 — Voltage
- Time 3 — Voltage

■ Positive charge
■ Negative charge
→ Direction of impulse

- Axon
- Synapse
- Receptor site
- Dendrite
- Neurotransmitter

Synapse

Neurotransmitters
- Acetylcholine
- Serotonin
- Dopamine
- Endorphins

Endocrine System

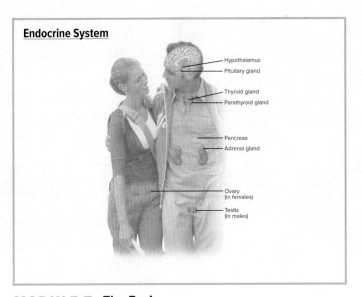

- Hypothalamus
- Pituitary gland
- Thyroid gland
- Parathyroid gland
- Pancreas
- Adrenal gland
- Ovary (in females)
- Testis (in males)

Central Nervous System

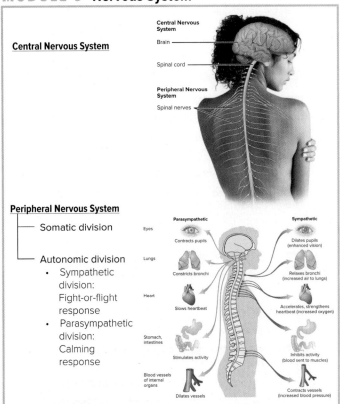

Central Nervous System
- Brain
- Spinal cord

Peripheral Nervous System
- Spinal nerves

Peripheral Nervous System

- Somatic division
- Autonomic division
  - Sympathetic division: Fight-or-flight response
  - Parasympathetic division: Calming response

Parasympathetic / Sympathetic

- Eyes — Contracts pupils / Dilates pupils (enhanced vision)
- Lungs — Constricts bronchi / Relaxes bronchi (increased air to lungs)
- Heart — Slows heartbeat / Accelerates, strengthens heartbeat (increased oxygen)
- Stomach, intestines — Stimulates activity / Inhibits activity (blood sent to muscles)
- Blood vessels of internal organs — Dilates vessels / Contracts vessels (increased blood pressure)

Areas of the Brain

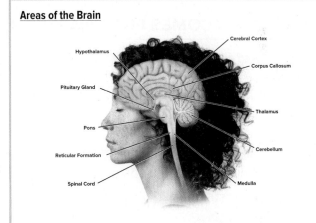

- Hypothalamus
- Pituitary Gland
- Pons
- Reticular Formation
- Spinal Cord
- Cerebral Cortex
- Corpus Callosum
- Thalamus
- Cerebellum
- Medulla

The Central Core: "Old brain"
- Cerebellum
- Reticular formation
- Thalamus
- Hypothalamus

The Cerebral Cortex: "New brain"
- Motor area: Voluntary movement
- Sensory area
  - Somatosensory area
  - Auditory area
  - Visual area
- Association areas
  - Executive functions
  - Personality

The Limbic System
- Emotion
- Self-preservation
- Amygdala
- Hippocampus

Brain Features
- Neuroplasticity
- Lateralization: Two hemispheres with specialized functions
- The Split Brain: Corpus callosum with independent hemispheric functions

(MODULE 5): ©whitehoune/Shutterstock; (a and b): ©McGraw-Hill Global Education Holdings LLC, 2000.; (MODULE 6): (Top): ©Larry Williams/Blend Images/Corbis; (Bottom): ©Laurence Mouton/Getty Images; (Nervous System): ©McGraw-Hill Global Education Holdings LLC, 2001.; (MODULE 7): Source: Adapted from Bloom, F. (1975). *Brain, mind, and behavior.* New York: Educational Broadcasting Corp.,; (Woman): ©Dana Neely/Taxi/Getty Images

©Uppercut/SuperStock

CHAPTER 3
Sensation and Perception

LEARNING OUTCOMES FOR CHAPTER 3

LO 11-1 What principles underlie our organization of the visual world and allow us to make sense of our environment?

LO 11-2 How are we able to perceive the world in three dimensions when our retinas are capable of sensing only two-dimensional images?

LO 11-3 What clues do visual illusions give us about our understanding of general perceptual mechanisms?

PROLOGUE *I FEEL YOUR PAIN, I TASTE YOUR WORDS*

For Sean Day, a college instructor in Charleston, South Carolina, the smell of fresh-cut grass is a dark purple color, and a sip of diet cola produces an unpleasant, sweat-stained yellow. Carol Steen, a New York City-based artist, sees touch, sound, and smell as ranges of colors, an experience that caused her to give up painting and turn to sculpture until she learned to let her color sensations inspire her instead of distract her (Reddy, 2017).

Day and Steen have *synesthesia,* a trait found in about 4.5% of the population in which sensations that are usually experienced separately merge into an amalgam of sensation. Some synesthetes feel pain as colors or feel touch when another person is being touched. Others experience spoken or read words as particular tastes.

LOOKING *Ahead*

Neurologists aren't certain what causes synesthesia, but some research suggests it may result from surviving connections between adjacent sensory brain regions that are normally pruned away as children age. Other studies suggest that synesthetes lack neural controls that usually inhibit connections between sensory areas. In any case, synesthesia isn't considered a condition that needs to be cured, and most of those who experience it consider it a gift rather than a disadvantage.

Phenomena such as synesthesia illustrate how complex and mysterious our senses are and how central they are to normal functioning. Our senses offer a window to the world, not only providing us with an awareness, understanding, and appreciation of the world's beauty but also alerting us to its dangers. Our senses enable us to feel the gentlest of breezes, see flickering lights miles away, and hear the soft murmuring of distant songbirds.

In the upcoming modules, we focus on the field of psychology that is concerned with the ways our bodies take in information through the senses and the ways we interpret that information. We explore both sensation and perception. *Sensation* encompasses the processes by which our sense organs receive information from the environment. *Perception* is the brain's and the sense organs' sorting out, interpretation, analysis, and integration of stimuli.

Although perception clearly represents a step beyond sensation, in practice it is sometimes difficult to find the precise boundary between the two. Indeed, psychologists—and philosophers as well—have argued for years over the distinction. The primary difference is that sensation can be thought of as an organism's first encounter with a raw sensory stimulus, whereas perception is the process by which it interprets, analyzes, and integrates that stimulus with other sensory information.

For example, if we were considering sensation, we might ask about the loudness of a ringing fire alarm. If we were considering perception, we might ask whether someone recognizes the ringing sound as an alarm and identifies its meaning.

To a psychologist interested in understanding the causes of behavior, sensation and perception are fundamental topics because so much of our behavior is a reflection of how we react to and interpret stimuli from the world around us. The areas of sensation and perception deal with a wide range of questions—among them, how we respond to the characteristics of physical stimuli; what processes enable us to see, hear, and experience pain; why visual illusions fool us; and how we distinguish one person from another. As we explore these issues, we'll see how the senses work together to provide us with an integrated view and understanding of the world.

Module 8
Sensing the World Around Us

LO 8-1 What is sensation, and how do psychologists study it?

LO 8-2 What is the relationship between a physical stimulus and the kinds of sensory responses that result from it?

Study Alert

Remember that *sensation* refers to the activation of the sense organs (a physical response), whereas *perception* refers to how stimuli are interpreted (a psychological response).

sensation The activation of the sense organs by a source of physical energy. (Module 8)

perception The sorting out, interpretation, analysis, and integration of stimuli by the sense organs and brain. (Module 8)

stimulus Energy that produces a response in a sense organ. (Module 8)

psychophysics The study of the relationship between the physical aspects of stimuli and our psychological experience of them. (Module 8)

absolute threshold The smallest intensity of a stimulus that must be present for the stimulus to be detected. (Module 8)

As Isabel sat down to Thanksgiving dinner, her father carried the turkey in on a tray and placed it squarely in the center of the table. The noise level, already high from the talking and laughter of family members, grew louder still. As Isabel picked up her fork, the smell of the turkey reached her, and she felt her stomach growl hungrily. The sight and sound of her family around the table, along with the smells and tastes of the holiday meal, made Isabel feel more relaxed than she had since starting school in the fall.

Put yourself in this setting and consider how different it might be if any one of your senses were not functioning. What if you were blind and unable to see the faces of your family members or the welcome shape of the golden-brown turkey? What if you had no sense of hearing and could not listen to the conversations of family members or were unable to feel your stomach growl, smell the dinner, or taste the food? Clearly, you would experience the dinner very differently than someone whose sensory apparatus was intact.

Moreover, the sensations mentioned above barely scratch the surface of sensory experience. Although perhaps you were taught, as I was, that there are just five senses—sight, sound, taste, smell, and touch—that enumeration is too modest. Human sensory capabilities go well beyond the basic five senses. For example, we are sensitive not merely to touch but to a considerably wider set of stimuli—pain, pressure, temperature, and vibration, to name a few. In addition, vision has two subsystems—relating to day and night vision—and the ear is responsive to information that allows us not only to hear but also to keep our balance.

To consider how psychologists understand the senses and, more broadly, sensation and perception, we first need a basic working vocabulary. In formal terms, **sensation** is the activation of the sense organs by a source of physical energy. **Perception** is the sorting out, interpretation, analysis, and integration of stimuli carried out by the sense organs and brain. A **stimulus** is any passing source of physical energy that produces a response in a sense organ.

Stimuli vary in both type and intensity. Different types of stimuli activate different sense organs. For instance, we can differentiate light stimuli (which activate the sense of sight and allow us to see the colors of a tree in autumn) from sound stimuli (which, through the sense of hearing, permit us to hear the sounds of an orchestra). In addition, stimuli differ in intensity, relating to how strong a stimulus needs to be before it can be detected.

Questions of stimulus type and intensity are considered in a branch of psychology known as psychophysics. **Psychophysics** is the study of the relationship between the physical aspects of stimuli and our psychological experience of them. Psychophysics played a central role in the development of the field of psychology. Many of the first psychologists studied issues related to psychophysics, and there is still an active group of psychophysics researchers (Bonezzi, Brendl, & De Angelis, 2011; Acuna et al., 2015; Jack & Schyns, 2017).

Absolute Thresholds: Detecting What's Out There

Just when does a stimulus become strong enough to be detected by our sense organs? The answer to this question requires an understanding of the concept of absolute threshold. An **absolute threshold** is the smallest intensity of a stimulus that must be present for it to be detected (Aazh & Moore, 2007).

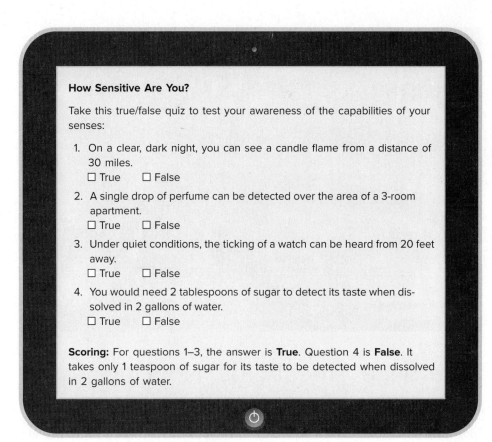

How Sensitive Are You?

Take this true/false quiz to test your awareness of the capabilities of your senses:

1. On a clear, dark night, you can see a candle flame from a distance of 30 miles.
   ☐ True   ☐ False

2. A single drop of perfume can be detected over the area of a 3-room apartment.
   ☐ True   ☐ False

3. Under quiet conditions, the ticking of a watch can be heard from 20 feet away.
   ☐ True   ☐ False

4. You would need 2 tablespoons of sugar to detect its taste when dissolved in 2 gallons of water.
   ☐ True   ☐ False

Scoring: For questions 1–3, the answer is **True**. Question 4 is **False**. It takes only 1 teaspoon of sugar for its taste to be detected when dissolved in 2 gallons of water.

FIGURE 1 This test can shed some light on how sensitive the human senses are.
Source: Galanter, E. (1962). Contemporary psychophysics. In R. Brown, E. Galanter, E. Hess, & G. Maroler (Eds.), *New directions in psychology.* New York: Holt.

Despite the "absolute" in absolute threshold, things are not so cut and dried. As the strength of a stimulus increases, the likelihood that it will be detected increases gradually. Technically, then, an absolute threshold is the stimulus intensity that is detected 50% of the time.

It often takes a very small stimulus to produce a response in our senses. For example, the sense of touch is so sensitive that we can feel a bee's wing falling on our cheeks when it is dropped from a distance of 1 centimeter. Test your knowledge of the absolute thresholds of other senses by completing the questionnaire in Figure 1.

In fact, our senses are so fine-tuned that we might have problems if they were any more sensitive. For instance, if our ears were slightly more acute, we would be able to hear the sound of air molecules in our ears knocking into the eardrum–a phenomenon that would surely prove distracting and might even prevent us from hearing sounds outside our bodies.

Of course, the absolute thresholds we have been discussing are measured under ideal conditions. Normally our senses cannot detect stimulation quite as well because of the presence of noise. *Noise*, as defined by psychophysicists, is background stimulation that interferes with the perception of other stimuli. Hence, noise refers not just to auditory stimuli, as the word suggests, but also to unwanted stimuli that interfere with other senses.

For example, picture a talkative group of people crammed into a small, crowded room at a party. The din of the crowd makes it hard to hear individual voices. In this case, the crowded conditions would be considered "noise," because they are preventing sensation at more discriminating levels. Similarly, we have limited ability to concentrate on several stimuli simultaneously.

PsychTech

Our inability to focus on multiple stimuli simultaneously is the reason why texting while driving is so dangerous. One study mounted video cameras inside trucks and found that truckers were 23 times more likely to be in a collision while texting than while not texting.

Crowded conditions, sounds, and sights can all be considered as noise that interferes with sensation. Can you think of other examples of noise that is not auditory in nature?
©Adam Lubroth/Getty Images

Difference Thresholds: Noticing Distinctions Between Stimuli

Suppose you wanted to choose the six best apples from a supermarket display–the biggest, reddest, and sweetest apples. One approach would be to compare one apple with another systematically until you were left with a few so similar that you could not tell the difference between them. At that point, it wouldn't matter which ones you choose.

Psychologists have discussed this comparison problem in terms of the **difference threshold,** the smallest level of added or reduced stimulation required to sense that a *change* in stimulation has occurred. Thus, the difference threshold is the minimum change in stimulation required to detect the difference between two stimuli, and so it also is called a **just noticeable difference** (Nittrouer & Lowenstein, 2007; Heath & Manzone, 2017).

The size of a stimulus that constitutes a just noticeable difference depends on the initial intensity of the stimulus. The relationship between changes in the original size of a stimulus and the degree to which a change will be noticed forms one of the basic laws of psychophysics: Weber's law. **Weber's law** (*Weber* is pronounced "VAY-ber") states that a just noticeable difference is a *constant proportion* of the intensity of an initial stimulus (rather than a constant amount).

For example, Weber found that the just noticeable difference for weight is 1:50. Consequently, it takes a 1-ounce increase in a 50-ounce weight to produce a noticeable difference, and it would take a 10-ounce increase to produce a noticeable difference if the initial weight were 500 ounces. In both cases, the same proportional increase is necessary to produce a just noticeable difference (1:50 = 10:500). Similarly, the just noticeable difference distinguishing changes in loudness between sounds is larger for sounds that are initially loud than it is for sounds that are initially soft, but the *proportional* increase remains the same.

Weber's law helps explain why a person in a quiet room is more startled by the ringing of a cellphone than is a person in an already noisy room. To produce the same amount of reaction in a noisy room, a cellphone ring would have to be set to a much higher level. Similarly, when the moon is visible during the late afternoon, it appears relatively dim. On the other hand, the moon appears much brighter when it is in the dark night sky.

difference threshold (just noticeable difference) The smallest level of added or reduced stimulation required to sense that a change in stimulation has occurred. (Module 10)

Weber's law A basic law of psychophysics stating that a just noticeable difference is a constant proportion to the intensity of an initial stimulus (rather than a constant amount). (Module 8)

Study Alert

Remember that Weber's law holds for every type of sensory stimuli: vision, sound, taste, and so on.

From the perspective of...

A Software Designer How might you use principles of psychophysics to direct the attention of a software user to a particular part of the computer screen?

©Rubberball/Punchstock

Sensory Adaptation: Turning Down Our Responses

You enter a movie theater, and the smell of popcorn is everywhere. A few minutes later, though, you barely notice the smell. The reason you become accustomed to the odor is sensory adaptation. **Adaptation** is an adjustment in sensory capacity after prolonged exposure to unchanging stimuli. Adaptation occurs as people become accustomed to a stimulus and change their frame of reference. In a sense, our brain mentally turns down the volume of the stimulation that it's experiencing (Carbon & Ditye, 2011; Erb et al., 2013; Nourouzpour et al., 2015).

One example of adaptation is the decrease in sensitivity that occurs after repeated exposure to a strong stimulus. If you were to hear a loud tone over and over, eventually it would begin to sound softer. Similarly, although jumping into a cold lake may be temporarily unpleasant, eventually you probably will get used to the temperature.

This apparent decline in sensitivity to sensory stimuli is due to the inability of the sensory nerve receptors to fire off messages to the brain indefinitely. Because these receptor cells are most responsive to *changes* in stimulation, constant stimulation is not effective in producing a sustained reaction (Wark, Lundstrom, & Fairhall, 2007; Summers et al., 2017).

adaptation An adjustment in sensory capacity after prolonged exposure to unchanging stimuli. (Module 10)

Although initially difficult to tolerate, exposure to cold temperatures eventually becomes less unpleasant due to the phenomenon of adaptation.
©Pashkov Andrey/123RF

Judgments of sensory stimuli are also affected by the context in which the judgments are made. This is the case because judgments are made not in isolation from other stimuli but in terms of preceding sensory experience. You can demonstrate this for yourself by trying a simple experiment:

Take two envelopes, one large and one small, and put 15 nickels in each one. Now lift the large envelope, put it down, and lift the small one. Which seems to weigh more? Most people report that the small one is heavier, although, as you know, the weights are nearly identical. The reason for this misconception is that the visual context of the envelope interferes with the sensory experience of weight. Adaptation to the context of one stimulus (the size of the envelope) alters responses to another stimulus (the weight of the envelope) (Coren, 2004).

RECAP/EVALUATE/RETHINK

RECAP

LO 8-1 What is sensation, and how do psychologists study it?

- Sensation is the activation of the sense organs by any source of physical energy. In contrast, perception is the process by which we sort out, interpret, analyze, and integrate stimuli to which our senses are exposed.

LO 8-2 What is the relationship between a physical stimulus and the kinds of sensory responses that result from it?

- Psychophysics studies the relationship between the physical nature of stimuli and the sensory responses they evoke.
- The absolute threshold is the smallest amount of physical intensity at which a stimulus can be detected. Under ideal conditions, absolute thresholds are extraordinarily sensitive, but the presence of noise (background stimuli that interfere with other stimuli) reduces detection capabilities.
- The difference threshold, or just noticeable difference, is the smallest change in the level of stimulation required to sense that a change has occurred. According to Weber's law, a just noticeable difference is a constant proportion of the intensity of an initial stimulus.
- Sensory adaptation occurs when we become accustomed to a constant stimulus and change our evaluation of it. Repeated exposure to a stimulus results in an apparent decline in sensitivity to it.

EVALUATE

1. _____ is the stimulation of the sense organs; _____ is the sorting out, interpretation, analysis, and integration of stimuli by the sense organs and the brain.
2. The term *absolute threshold* refers to the _____ intensity of a stimulus that must be present for the stimulus to be detected.
3. Weber discovered that for a difference between two stimuli to be perceptible, the stimuli must differ by at least a _____ proportion.
4. After completing a very difficult rock climb in the morning, Carmella found the afternoon climb unexpectedly easy. This example illustrates the phenomenon of _____.

RETHINK

1. How might it be possible to have sensation without perception? Conversely, might it be possible to have perception without sensation?
2. How is sensory adaptation essential for everyday psychological functioning?

Answers to Evaluate Questions

1. Sensation, perception; 2. smallest; 3. constant; 4. adaptation

KEY TERMS

sensation
perception
stimulus

psychophysics
absolute threshold

difference threshold (just noticeable difference)

Weber's law
adaptation

Module 9
Vision: Shedding Light on the Eye

If, as poets say, the eyes provide a window to the soul, they also provide us with a window to the world. Our visual capabilities permit us to admire and to react to scenes ranging from the beauty of a sunset, to the configuration of a lover's face, to the words written on the pages of a book.

Vision starts with *light*, the physical energy that stimulates the eye. Light is a form of electromagnetic radiation waves. Like ocean waves, light is measured in *wavelengths*, the distance between peaks of the lightwaves.

The *visual spectrum* is the range of wavelengths that the human eye can detect. As shown in Figure 1, the visible spectrum that humans can see includes the wavelengths that make up the colors of a rainbow, from the shortest wavelength of violet blue to the longest wavelength of red. Compared to that of nonhumans, the visual spectrum in humans is relatively restricted. For instance, some reptiles and fish sense energies of longer wavelengths than humans do, and certain insects sense energies of shorter wavelengths than humans do.

Light waves coming from some object outside the body (such as the tree in Figure 2) are sensed by the only organ that is capable of responding to the visible spectrum: the eye. Our eyes convert light to a form that can be used by the neurons that serve as messengers to the brain. The neurons themselves take up a relatively small percentage of the total eye. Most of the eye is a mechanical device that is similar in many respects to a nonelectronic camera that uses film, as you can see in Figure 2.

Despite the similarities between the eye and a camera, vision involves processes that are far more complex and sophisticated than those of any camera. Furthermore, once an image reaches the neuronal receptors of the eye, the eye/camera analogy ends, for the processing of the visual image in the brain is more reflective of a computer than it is of a camera.

LEARNING OUTCOMES

LO 9-1 What basic processes underlie the sense of vision?

LO 9-2 How do we see colors?

Illuminating the Structure of the Eye

The ray of light being reflected off the tree in Figure 2 first travels through the *cornea*, a transparent, protective window. The cornea, because of its curvature, bends (or *refracts*) light as it passes through, playing a primary role in focusing the light more sharply. After moving through the cornea, the light traverses the pupil. The *pupil* is a

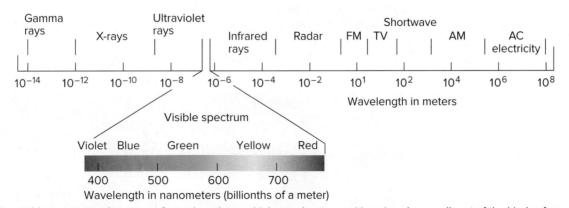

FIGURE 1 The visible spectrum—the range of wavelengths to which people are sensitive—is only a small part of the kinds of wavelengths present in our environment. Is it a benefit or disadvantage to our everyday lives that we aren't more sensitive to a broader range of visual stimuli? Why?

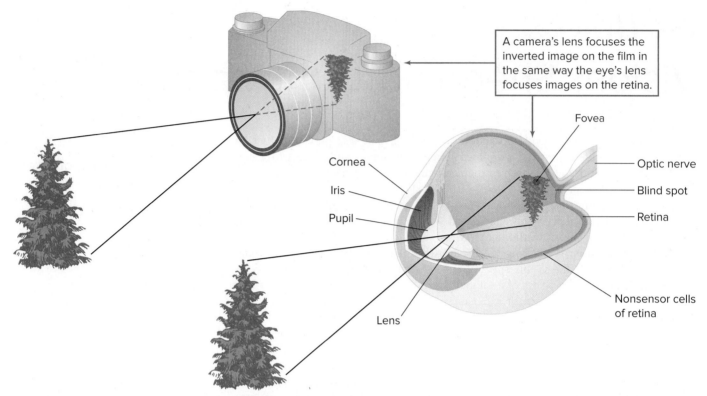

A camera's lens focuses the inverted image on the film in the same way the eye's lens focuses images on the retina.

Fovea

Cornea

Iris

Pupil

Optic nerve

Blind spot

Retina

Nonsensor cells of retina

Lens

FIGURE 2 Although human vision is far more complicated than the most sophisticated camera, in some ways basic visual processes are analogous to those used in photography. Like the automatic lighting system of a traditional, nondigital camera, the human eye dilates to let in more light and contracts to block out light.

dark hole in the center of the *iris,* the colored part of the eye, which in humans ranges from a light blue to a dark brown. The size of the pupil opening depends on the amount of light in the environment. The dimmer the surroundings are, the more the pupil opens to allow more light to enter.

Why shouldn't the pupil be open completely all the time, allowing the greatest amount of light into the eye? The answer relates to the basic physics of light. A small pupil greatly increases the range of distances at which objects are in focus. With a wide-open pupil, the range is relatively small, and details are harder to discern. The eye takes advantage of bright light by decreasing the size of the pupil and thereby becoming more discriminating. In dim light, the pupil expands to enable us to view the situation better–but at the expense of visual detail. (Perhaps one reason candlelight dinners are thought of as romantic is that the dim light prevents one from seeing a partner's physical flaws.)

Once light passes through the pupil, it enters the *lens,* which is directly behind the pupil. The lens acts to bend the rays of light so that they are properly focused on the rear of the eye. The lens focuses light by changing its own thickness, a process

Like the automatic lighting system on a camera, the pupil in the human eye expands to let in more light (left) and contracts to block out light (right). Can humans adjust their ears to let in more or less sound in a similar manner?
(Both): ©Biophoto Associates/Science Source

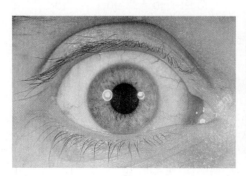
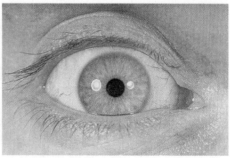

called *accommodation:* It becomes flatter when viewing distant objects and rounder when looking at closer objects.

REACHING THE RETINA

Having traveled through the pupil and lens, the image of the tree finally reaches its ultimate destination in the eye: the retina. The **retina** is the part of the eye that converts the electromagnetic energy of light to electrical impulses for transmission to the brain.

Interestingly, as the image travels through the lens, it has reversed itself. Consequently, the image reaches the retina upside down (relative to its original position). Although it might seem that this reversal would cause difficulties in understanding and moving about the world, this is not the case. The brain automatically interprets the image in terms of its original position.

The retina consists of a thin layer of nerve cells at the back of the eyeball (see Figure 3). There are two kinds of light-sensitive receptor cells in the retina. The names they have been given describe their shapes: rods and cones. **Rods** are thin, cylindrical receptor cells that are highly sensitive to light. **Cones** are typically cone-shaped,

retina The part of the eye that converts the electromagnetic energy of light to electrical impulses for transmission to the brain. (Module 9)

rods Thin, cylindrical receptor cells in the retina that are highly sensitive to light. (Module 9) cones

cones Cone-shaped, light-sensitive receptor cells in the retina that are responsible for sharp focus and color perception, particularly in bright light. (Module 9)

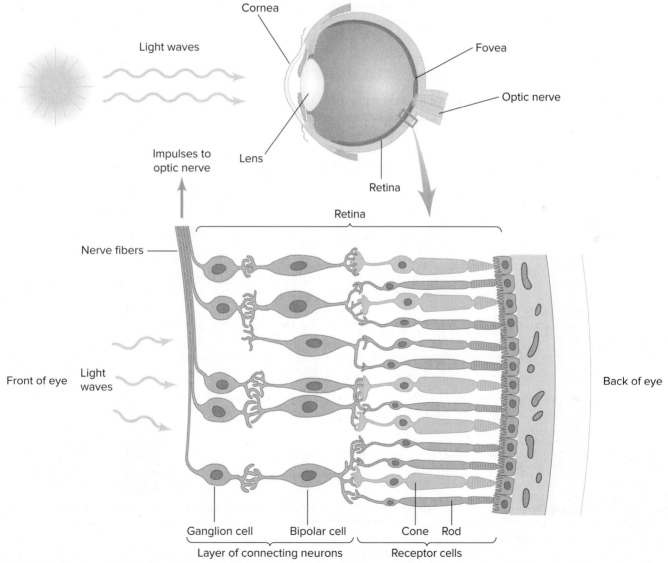

FIGURE 3 The basic cells of the eye. Light entering the eye travels through the ganglion and bipolar cells and strikes the light-sensitive rods and cones located at the back of the eye. The rods and cones then transmit nerve impulses to the brain via the bipolar and ganglion cells.
©McGraw-Hill Global Education Holdings LLC, 2000.

light-sensitive receptor cells that are responsible for sharp focus and color perception, particularly in bright light. The rods and cones are distributed unevenly throughout the retina. Cones are concentrated on the part of the retina called the *fovea*. The fovea is a particularly sensitive region of the retina. If you want to focus on something of particular interest, you will automatically try to center the image on the fovea to see it more sharply.

The rods and cones not only are structurally dissimilar, but they also play distinctly different roles in vision. Cones are primarily responsible for the sharply focused perception of color, particularly in brightly lit situations; rods are related to vision in dimly lit situations and are largely insensitive to color and to details as sharp as those the cones are capable of recognizing. The rods play a key role in *peripheral vision*–seeing objects that are outside the main center of focus–and in night vision.

Rods and cones also are involved in *dark adaptation*, the phenomenon of adjusting to dim light after being in brighter light. (Think of the experience of walking into a dark movie theater and groping your way to a seat but a few minutes later seeing the seats quite clearly.) The speed at which dark adaptation occurs is a result of the rate of change in the chemical composition of the rods and cones. Although the cones reach their greatest level of adaptation in just a few minutes, the rods take 20 to 30 minutes to reach the maximum level. The opposite phenomenon–*light adaptation*, or the process of adjusting to bright light after exposure to dim light–occurs much faster, taking only a minute or so.

SENDING THE MESSAGE FROM THE EYE TO THE BRAIN

When light energy strikes the rods and cones, it starts a chain of events that transforms light into neural impulses that can be communicated to the brain. Even before the neural message reaches the brain, however, some initial coding of the visual information takes place.

What happens when light energy strikes the retina depends in part on whether it encounters a rod or a cone. Rods contain *rhodopsin*, a complex reddish-purple protein whose composition changes chemically when energized by light. The substance in cone receptors is different, but the principles are similar. Stimulation of the nerve cells in the eye triggers a neural response that is transmitted to other nerve cells in the retina called *bipolar cells* and *ganglion cells.*

Bipolar cells receive information directly from the rods and cones and communicate that information to the ganglion cells. The ganglion cells collect and summarize visual information, which is then moved out the back of the eyeball and sent to the brain through a bundle of ganglion axons called the **optic nerve.**

Because the opening for the optic nerve passes through the retina, there are no rods or cones in the area, and that creates a blind spot. Normally, however, this absence of nerve cells does not interfere with vision because you automatically compensate for the missing part of your field of vision. (To find your blind spot, see Figure 4.)

Study Alert
Remember that cones relate to color vision.

optic nerve A bundle of ganglion axons that carry visual information to the brain. (Module 9)

FIGURE 4 To find your blind spot, close your right eye and look at the haunted house with your left eye. You will see the ghost on the periphery of your vision. Now, while staring at the house, move the page toward you. When the page is about a foot from your eye, the ghost will disappear. At this moment, the image of the ghost is falling on your blind spot.

But also notice how, when the page is at that distance, not only does the ghost seem to disappear, but the line also seems to run continuously through the area where the ghost used to be. This simple experiment shows how we automatically compensate for missing information by using nearby material to complete what is unseen. That's the reason you never notice the blind spot. What is missing is replaced by what is seen next to the blind spot. Can you think of any advantages that this tendency to provide missing information gives humans as a species?

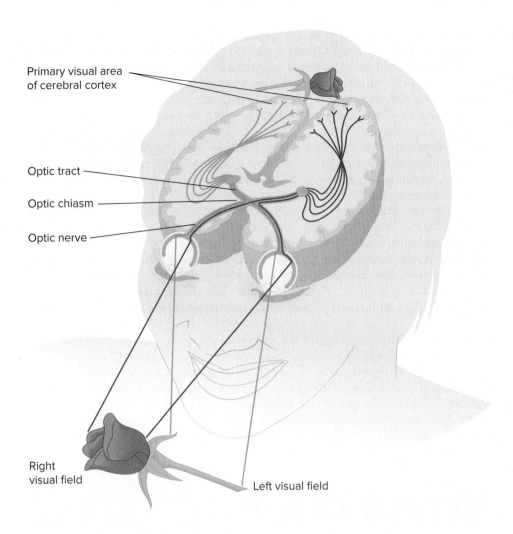

Primary visual area
of cerebral cortex

Optic tract

Optic chiasm

Optic nerve

Right
visual field

Left visual field

FIGURE 5 Because the optic nerve coming from the eye splits at the optic chiasm, the image to a person's right eye is sent to the left side of the brain, and the image to the person's left is transmitted to the right side of the brain.
©McGraw-Hill Global Education Holdings LLC, 2000.

Once beyond the eye itself, the neural impulses relating to the image move through the optic nerve. As the optic nerve leaves the eyeball, its path does not take the most direct route to the part of the brain right behind the eye. Instead, the optic nerves from each eye meet at a point roughly between the two eyes–called the *optic chiasm* (pronounced KI-asm)–where each optic nerve then splits.

When the optic nerves split, the nerve impulses coming from the right half of each retina are sent to the right side of the brain, and the impulses arriving from the left half of each retina are sent to the left side of the brain. Because the image on the retinas is reversed and upside down, however, those images coming from the right half of each retina actually originated in the field of vision to the person's left, and the images coming from the left half of each retina originated in the field of vision to the person's right (see Figure 5).

PROCESSING THE VISUAL MESSAGE

By the time a visual message reaches the brain, it has passed through several stages of processing. One of the initial sites is the ganglion cells. Each ganglion cell gathers information from a group of rods and cones in a particular area of the eye and compares the amount of light entering the center of that area with the amount of light in the area around it. Some ganglion cells are activated by light in the center (and darkness in the surrounding area). Other ganglion cells are activated when there is darkness in the center and light in the surrounding areas. The outcome of this process is to maximize the detection of variations in light and darkness. The image that is passed on to

PsychTech

New technologies are helping the blind to see. For example, by surgically implanting electrodes into the eyes and using a nose-mounted camera and a video processor strapped to the waist, previously totally blind individuals can differentiate plates from cups and can identify large letters.

feature detector Specialized neurons that are activated only by visual stimuli having specific features, such as a particular shape or pattern. (Module 9)

the brain, then, is an enhanced version of the actual visual stimulus outside the body (Lascaratos, Ji, & Wood, 2007; Grünert et al., 2011; Sanes & Masland, 2015).

The ultimate processing of visual images takes place in the visual cortex of the brain, and it is here that the most complex kinds of processing occur. Psychologists David Hubel and Torsten Wiesel won the Nobel Prize in 1981 for their discovery of feature detectors. **Feature detectors** are specialized neurons that are activated only by visual stimuli having certain features, such as a particular shape or pattern. For instance, some feature detectors are activated only by lines of a particular width, shape, or orientation. Other feature detectors are activated only by moving, as opposed to stationary, stimuli (Hubel & Wiesel, 2004; Sebastiani, Castellani, & D'Alessandro, 2011; Jacoby & Schwartz, 2017).

Visual information coming from individual neurons is combined and processed in extraordinarily specialized ways, and different parts of the brain jointly process nerve impulses according to the attributes of an image. For instance, one brain system processes shapes, one processes colors, and others process movement, location, and depth. The specialization goes further: specific parts of the brain are involved in the perception of certain *kinds* of stimuli, such as reacting to human faces, nonhuman animal faces, and inanimate stimuli (Zvyagintsev et al., 2013; Stevens, 2015).

If separate neural systems exist for processing information about specific aspects of the visual world, how are all these data integrated by the brain? The brain makes use of information regarding the frequency, rhythm, and timing of the firing of particular sets of neural cells. Furthermore, the brain's integration of visual information does not occur in any single step or location in the brain but rather is a process that occurs on several levels simultaneously. The ultimate outcome, though, is indisputable: a vision of the world around us (Macaluso, Frith, & Driver, 2000; Werner, Pinna, & Spillmann, 2007).

NEUROSCIENCE IN YOUR LIFE: RECOGNIZING FACES

The ability to recognize faces is important for social bonding in humans as well as other animals. Although it has long been believed that face processing in the brain is genetically determined, recent evidence shows that experience plays an important role as well. To examine whether innate face-processing regions of the brain exist, researchers kept one group of monkeys from seeing faces during development. When the monkeys were approximately 200 days old, the researchers measured their brain activity while they viewed faces and other common objects. Compared to normal monkeys (labeled the controls), those that were face-deprived show less activity for faces (red/yellow areas) compared to objects (purple areas) in visual regions of the brain (the circled regions in the images below). These results show that early sensory experience is important for the development of face recognition and has important implications for those who suffer from prosopagnosia, an inability to recognize faces (Arcaro et al., 2017).

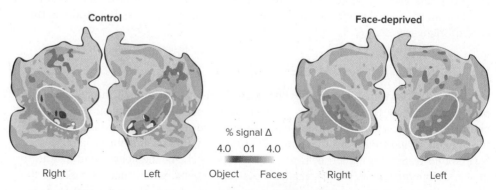

Source: Adapted from Arcaro, M. J., Schade, P. F., Vincent, J. L., Ponce, C. R., & Livingstone, M. S. (2017). Seeing faces is necessary for face-domain formation. *Nature Neuroscience, 20*(10), 1404-1412.

Color Vision and Color Blindness: The 7-Million-Color Spectrum

Although the range of wavelengths to which humans are sensitive is relatively narrow, at least in comparison with the entire electromagnetic spectrum, the portion to which we are capable of responding allows us great flexibility in sensing the world. Nowhere is this clearer than in terms of the number of colors we can discern. A person with normal color vision is capable of distinguishing no less than 7 million different colors (Rabin, 2004).

Although the variety of colors that people are generally able to distinguish is vast, there are certain individuals whose ability to perceive color is quite limited–the color blind. Interestingly, the condition of these individuals has provided some of the most important clues to understanding how color vision operates (Nijboer, te Pas, & van der Smagt, 2011; Alfaro et al., 2015).

From the perspective of...

A Graphic Designer How might you market your products to those who are color blind versus those who have normal color vision?

©Zoonar GmbH/Alamy Stock Photo

Approximately 7% of men and 0.4% of women are color blind. For most people with color-blindness, the world looks dull and lacks contrast (see Figure 6). Red fire engines appear yellow, green grass seems yellow, and the three colors of a traffic light all look yellow. In fact, in the most common form of color-blindness, all red and green objects are seen as yellow. In other forms of color-blindness, people are unable to tell the difference between yellow and blue. In the most extreme cases of color-blindness, which are quite rare, people perceive no color at all. To such individuals, the world looks something like the picture on an old black-and-white TV.

EXPLAINING COLOR VISION

To understand why some people are color blind, we need to consider the basics of color vision. Two processes are involved. The first process is explained by the **trichromatic theory of color vision,** which was first proposed by Thomas Young and extended by

trichromatic theory of color vision The theory that there are three kinds of cones in the retina, each of which responds primarily to a specific range of wavelengths. (Module 9)

FIGURE 6 Those with color blindness see a very different view of the world (left) compared to those who have normal vision (right).
(Both): ©Ralph C. Eagle Jr./Science Source

FIGURE 7 Stare at the dot in this flag for about a minute and then look at a piece of plain white paper. What do you see? Most people see an afterimage that converts the colors in the figure into the traditional red, white, and blue U.S. flag. If you have trouble seeing it the first time, blink once and try again.

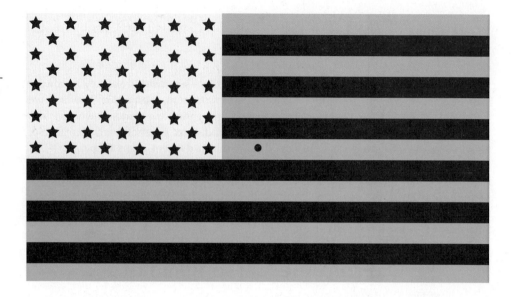

Hermann von Helmholtz in the first half of the 1800s. This theory suggests that there are three kinds of cones in the retina, each of which responds primarily to a specific range of wavelengths. One is most responsive to blue-violet colors, one to green, and the third to yellow-red (Brown & Wald, 1964). According to trichromatic theory, perception of color is influenced by the relative strength with which each of the three kinds of cones is activated. If we see a blue sky, the blue-violet cones are primarily triggered, and the others show less activity.

However, there are aspects of color vision that the trichromatic theory is less successful at explaining. For example, the theory does not explain what happens after you stare at something like the flag shown in Figure 7 for about a minute. Try this yourself and then look at a blank white page: You'll see an image of the traditional red, white, and blue U.S. flag. Where there was yellow, you'll see blue, and where there were green and black, you'll see red and white.

The phenomenon you have just experienced is called an *afterimage*. It occurs because activity in the retina continues even when you are no longer staring at the original picture.

However, the fact that the colors perceived in the afterimage differ from those in the original image calls into question the validity of the trichromatic theory. To explain this failure of the trichromatic theory, alternative explanations for color vision have been developed. One alternative is the opponent-process theory.

According to the **opponent-process theory of color vision,** first proposed by German physiologist Ewald Hering in the 19th century, receptor cells are linked in pairs, working in opposition to each other. Specifically, there are a blue-yellow pairing, a red-green pairing, and a black-white pairing. If an object reflects light that contains more blue than yellow, it will stimulate the firing of the cells sensitive to blue, simultaneously discouraging or inhibiting the firing of receptor cells sensitive to yellow—and the object will appear blue. If, in contrast, a light contains more yellow than blue, the cells that respond to yellow will be stimulated to fire while the blue ones are inhibited, and the object will appear yellow (Robinson, 2007).

The opponent-process theory provides a good explanation for afterimages. When we stare at the yellow in the figure, for instance, our receptor cells for the yellow component of the yellow-blue pairing become fatigued and are less able to respond to yellow stimuli. In contrast, the receptor cells for the blue part of the pair are not tired because they are not being stimulated. When we look at a white surface, the light reflected off it would normally stimulate both the yellow and the blue receptors equally. But the fatigue of the yellow receptors prevents this from happening. They temporarily do not respond to the yellow, which makes the white light appear to be blue. Because the other colors in the figure do the same thing relative to their specific

opponent-process theory of color vision The theory that receptor cells for color are linked in pairs, working in opposition to each other. (Module 9)

Study Alert

Keep in mind that there are two explanations for color vision: trichromatic and opponent-process theories.

opponents, the afterimage produces the opponent colors–for a while. The afterimage lasts only a short time because the fatigue of the yellow receptors is soon overcome, and the white light begins to be perceived more accurately.

We now know that both opponent processes and trichromatic mechanisms are at work in producing the perception of color vision but in different parts of the visual sensing system. Trichromatic processes work within the retina itself, whereas opponent mechanisms operate both in the retina and at later stages of neuronal processing (Horiguchi et al., 2013; Bunce, 2015).

RECAP/EVALUATE/RETHINK

RECAP

LO 9-1 What basic processes underlie the sense of vision?

- Vision depends on sensitivity to light, electromagnetic waves in the visible part of the spectrum that are either reflected off objects or produced by an energy source. The eye shapes the light into an image that is transformed into nerve impulses and interpreted by the brain.
- As light enters the eye, it passes through the cornea, pupil, and lens and ultimately reaches the retina, where the electromagnetic energy of light is converted to nerve impulses for transmission to the brain. These impulses leave the eye via the optic nerve.
- The visual information gathered by the rods and cones is transferred via bipolar and ganglion cells through the optic nerve, which leads to the optic chiasm–the point where the optic nerve splits.

LO 9-2 How do we see colors?

- Color vision seems to be based on two processes described by the trichromatic theory and the opponent-process theory.
- The trichromatic theory suggests that there are three kinds of cones in the retina, each of which is responsive to a certain range of colors. The opponent-process theory presumes pairs of different types of cells in the eye that work in opposition to each other.

EVALUATE

1. Light entering the eye first passes through the _____, a protective window.

2. The structure that converts light into usable neural messages is called the _____.
3. A woman with blue eyes could be described as having blue pigment in her _____.
4. What is the process by which the thickness of the lens is changed in order to focus light properly?
5. The proper sequence of structures that light passes through in the eye is the _____, _____, _____, and _____.
6. Match each type of visual receptor with its function.
   - **a.** rods
   - **b.** cones
   - 1. used for dim light, largely insensitive to color
   - 2. detect color, good in bright light
7. _____ theory states that there are three types of cones in the retina, each of which responds primarily to a different color.

RETHINK

1. If the eye had a second lens that "unreversed" the image hitting the retina, do you think there would be changes in the way people perceive the world?
2. From an evolutionary standpoint, why might the eye have evolved so that the rods, which we rely on in low light, do not provide sharp images? Are there any advantages to this system?

Answers to Evaluate Questions

1. cornea; 2. retina; 3. iris; 4. accommodation; 5. cornea, pupil, lens, retina; 6. a-1, b-2; 7. Trichromatic

KEY TERMS

retina	optic nerve	trichromatic theory of	opponent-process theory
rods	feature detector	color vision	of color vision
cones			

Module 10
Hearing and the Other Senses

LO 10-1 What role does the ear play in the senses of sound, motion, and balance?

LO 10-2 How do smell and taste function?

LO 10-3 What are the skin senses, and how do they relate to the experience of pain?

The blast-off was easy compared with what the astronaut was experiencing now: space sickness. The constant nausea and vomiting were enough to make him wonder why he had worked so hard to become an astronaut. Even though he had been warned that there was a two-thirds chance that his first experience in space would cause these symptoms, he wasn't prepared for how terribly sick he really felt.

Whether or not the astronaut wishes he could head right back to Earth, his experience, a major problem for space travelers, is related to a basic sensory process: the sense of motion and balance. This sense allows people to navigate their bodies through the world and keep themselves upright without falling. Along with hearing–the process by which sound waves are translated into understandable and meaningful forms–the sense of motion and balance resides in the ear.

Sensing Sound

Although many of us think primarily of the outer ear when we speak of the ear, that structure is only one simple part of the whole. The outer ear acts as a reverse megaphone, designed to collect and bring sounds into the internal portions of the ear (see Figure 1). The location of the outer ears on different sides of the head helps with *sound localization,* the process by which we identify the direction from which a sound is coming. Wave patterns in the air enter each ear at a slightly different time, and the brain uses the discrepancy as a clue to the sound's point of origin. In addition, the two outer ears delay or amplify sounds of particular frequencies to different degrees (Schnupp, Nelken, & King, 2011; Tolnai, Beutelmann & Klump, 2017).

sound The movement of air molecules brought about by a source of vibration. (Module 10)

Sound is the movement of air molecules brought about by a source of vibration. Sounds travel through the air in wave patterns similar in shape to those made in water when a stone is thrown into a still pond. Sounds, arriving at the outer ear in the form of wavelike vibrations, are funneled into the *auditory canal,* a tube-like passage that leads to the eardrum. The **eardrum** is the part of the ear that vibrates when sound waves hit it. The more intense the sound, the more the eardrum vibrates. These vibrations are then transferred into the *middle ear,* a tiny chamber containing three bones (the *hammer,* the *anvil,* and the *stirrup*) that transmit vibrations to the oval window, a thin membrane leading to the inner ear. Because the hammer, anvil, and stirrup act as a set of levers, they not only transmit vibrations but also increase their strength. Moreover, because the opening into the middle ear (the eardrum) is considerably larger than the opening out of it (the *oval window*), the force of sound waves on the oval window becomes amplified. The middle ear, then, acts as a tiny mechanical amplifier.

eardrum The part of the ear that vibrates when sound waves hit it. (Module 10)

The *inner ear* is the portion of the ear that changes the sound vibrations into a form in which they can be transmitted to the brain. (As you will see, it also contains the organs that allow us to locate our position and determine how we are moving through space.) When sound enters the inner ear through the oval window, it moves into the **cochlea,** a coiled tube that looks something like a snail and is filled with fluid that vibrates in response to sound. Inside the cochlea is the **basilar membrane,** a structure that runs through the center of the cochlea, dividing it into an upper chamber and a lower chamber. The basilar membrane is covered with **hair cells.** When the hair cells are bent by the vibrations entering the cochlea, the cells send a neural message to the brain (Zhou, Liu, & Davis, 2005; Møller, 2011; Curthoys, 2017).

cochlea (KOKE-lee-uh) A coiled tube in the ear filled with fluid that vibrates in response to sound. (Module 10)

basilar membrane A vibrating structure that runs through the center of the cochlea, dividing it into an upper chamber and a lower chamber and containing sense receptors for sound. (Module 10)

hair cells Tiny cells covering the basilar membrane that, when bent by vibrations entering the cochlea, transmit neural messages to the brain. (Module 10)

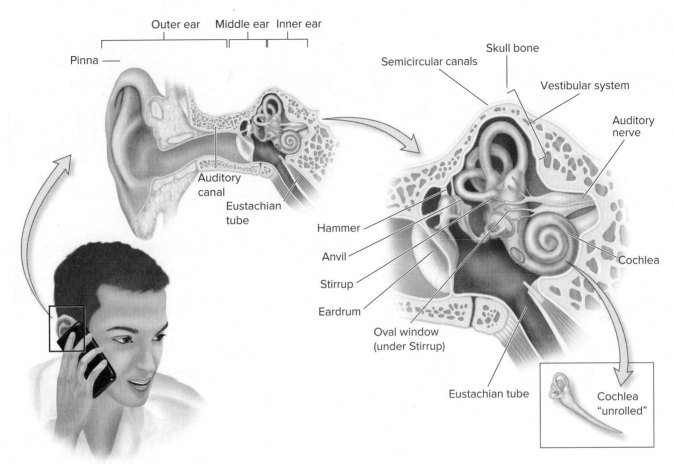

FIGURE 1 The major parts of the ear.
©McGraw-Hill Global Education Holdings LLC, 2008.

THE PHYSICAL ASPECTS OF SOUND

As we mentioned earlier, what we refer to as sound is actually the physical movement of air molecules in regular, wavelike patterns caused by a vibrating source. Sometimes it is even possible to see these vibrations: If you have ever seen an audio speaker that has no enclosure, you know that, at least when the lowest notes are playing, you can see the speaker moving in and out. Less obvious is what happens next: The speaker pushes air molecules into waves with the same pattern as its movement. Those wave patterns soon reach your ear, although their strength has been weakened considerably during their travels. All other sources that produce sound work in essentially the same fashion, setting off wave patterns that move through the air to the ear. Air—or some other medium, such as water—is necessary to make the vibrations of objects reach us. This explains why there can be no sound in a vacuum.

We are able to see the audio speaker moving when low notes are played because of a primary characteristic of sound called frequency. *Frequency* is the number of wave cycles that occur in a second. At very low frequencies, there are relatively few wave cycles per second (see Figure 2). These cycles are visible to the naked eye as vibrations in the speaker. Low frequencies are translated into a sound that is very low in pitch. (*Pitch* is the characteristic that makes sound seem "high" or "low.") For example, the lowest frequency that humans are capable of hearing is 20 cycles per second. Higher frequencies are heard as sounds of higher pitch. At the upper end of the sound spectrum, people can detect sounds with frequencies as high as 20,000 cycles per second.

Amplitude is a feature of wave patterns that allows us to distinguish between loud and soft sounds. Amplitude is the spread between the up-and-down peaks and valleys of air pressure in a sound wave as it travels through the air. Waves with small peaks

FIGURE 2 The sound waves produced by different stimuli are transmitted—usually through the air—in different patterns, with lower frequencies indicated by fewer peaks and valleys per second.
©McGraw-Hill Global Education Holdings LLC, 2000.

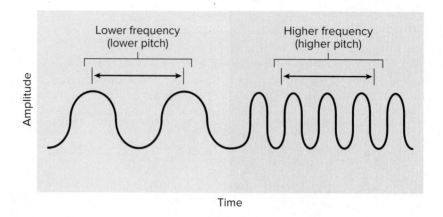

and valleys produce soft sounds; those with relatively large peaks and valleys produce loud sounds.

We are sensitive to broad variations in sound amplitudes. The strongest sounds we are capable of hearing are over a trillion times as intense as the very weakest sound we can hear. This range is measured in *decibels*. When sounds get higher than 120 decibels, they become painful to the human ear.

Our sensitivity to different frequencies changes as we age. For instance, as we get older, the range of frequencies we can detect declines, particularly for high-pitched sounds. This is why high school students sometimes choose high-pitched ring tones for their cell phones in settings where cell phone use is forbidden: the ringing sound goes undetected by their aging teachers (Vitello, 2006; Moreno-Gómez et al., 2017) (see Figure 3).

Explaining Hearing: Listen to the Theories of Sound How are our brains able to sort out wavelengths of different frequencies and intensities? One important clue comes from studies of the basilar membrane, the area in the cochlea that translates physical vibrations into nerve impulses. It turns out that sounds affect different areas of the basilar

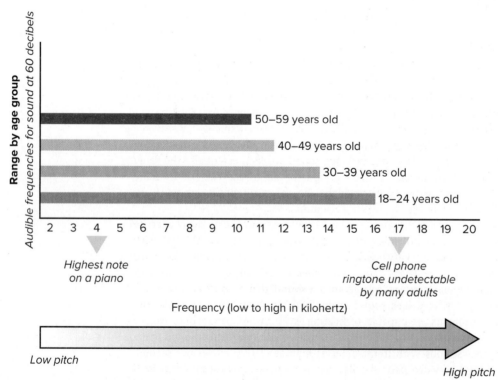

FIGURE 3 Some teenagers set their text-message ring tone to a frequency too high for most adults to hear, allowing them to use cell phones where they are prohibited.

Source: Adapted from Vitello, P. (2006, June 12). A ring tone meant to fall on deaf ears. *The New York Times*, A1.

membrane according to the frequency of the sound wave reaching it. The part of the basilar membrane nearest to the oval window is most sensitive to high-frequency sounds. In contrast, the part of the basilar membrane nearest to the cochlea's inner end is most sensitive to low-frequency sounds. This finding has led to the **place theory of hearing,** which states that different areas of the basilar membrane are specialized to respond to different sound frequencies.

However, place theory does not tell the full story of hearing because of a significant fact: very low frequency sounds trigger neurons across such a wide area of the basilar membrane that no single site is involved. Consequently, an additional explanation for hearing has been proposed: frequency theory. The **frequency theory of hearing** suggests that the entire basilar membrane acts as a microphone, vibrating as a whole in response to a sound. According to this explanation, the nerve receptors send out signals that are tied directly to the frequency (the number of wave crests per second) of the sounds to which we are exposed, with the number of nerve impulses being a direct function of a sound's frequency. Thus, the higher the pitch of a sound (and therefore the greater the frequency of its wave crests), the greater the number of nerve impulses that are transmitted up the auditory nerve to the brain.

Ultimately, it seems that we need both place theory and frequency theory to understand the process of hearing. Specifically, place theory provides a better explanation for the sensing of high-frequency sounds, whereas frequency theory explains what happens when low-frequency sounds are encountered. Medium-frequency sounds incorporate both processes (Hirsh & Watson, 1996; Hudspeth, 2000).

Regardless of whether we employ place theory or frequency theory, we know that after an auditory message leaves the ear, it is transmitted to the auditory cortex of the brain through a complex series of nerve interconnections. And similar to visual nerve cells in the brain that respond to specific kinds of stimuli, auditory neurons respond to specific types of sounds. For example, certain neurons respond selectively to clicks and whistles. Other neurons respond only to a specific sound pattern, such as a steady tone but not an intermittent one. Furthermore, specific neurons transfer information about a sound's location through their particular pattern of firing (Wang et al., 2005; Alho et al., 2006; Romero-Guevara et al., 2015).

If we were to analyze the configuration of the cells in the auditory cortex, we would find that neighboring cells are responsive to similar frequencies. The auditory cortex, then, provides us with a "map" of sound frequencies, just as the visual cortex furnishes a representation of the visual field. In addition, because of the asymmetry in the two hemispheres of the brain, the left and right ears process sound differently. The right ear reacts more to speech, whereas the left ear responds more to music (Sininger & Cone-Wesson, 2004, 2006; McCulloch et al., 2017).

Speech perception requires that we make fine discriminations among sounds that are quite similar in terms of their physical properties. Furthermore, not only are we able to understand *what* is being said from speech, we also can use vocal cues to determine who is speaking, whether they have an accent and where they may be from, and even their emotional state. Such capabilities illustrate the sophistication of our sense of hearing (Pell et al., 2009; Ross et al., 2011; Mattys et al., 2013).

Scientists are also beginning to investigate how we use sound to navigate through our environment. *Echolocation* is the use of sound waves and echoes to determine where objects are. It is the navigational technique that bats use, and some people with impaired vision have learned to use echolocation by generating sounds (such as snapping their fingers or making clicking noises) and using the echoes that bounce off objects to navigate. Although psychologists are early in their research on the phenomenon, it may provide a window into sensory processes and ultimately improve the lives of those with sensory impairments (Thaler, 2015).

Balance: The Ups and Downs of Life Several structures of the ear are related more to our sense of balance than to our hearing. Collectively, these structures are known as the *vestibular system*, which responds to the pull of gravity and allows us to maintain our balance, even when standing in a bus in stop-and-go traffic.

place theory of hearing The theory that different areas of the basilar membrane respond to different frequencies. (Module 10)

frequency theory of hearing The theory that the entire basilar membrane acts like a microphone, vibrating as a whole in response to a sound. (Module 10)

Study Alert
Be sure to understand the differences between the place and frequency theories of hearing.

Zero gravity presents numerous challenges, some of which were depicted in the film *The Martian* with Matt Damon. For example, the weightlessness of the ear's otoliths produces space sickness in most astronauts.
©GENRE FILMS/INTERNATIONAL TRADERS/MID ATLACTIC FILD/20TH CEN/Album/Newscom

semicircular canals Three tube-like structures of the inner ear containing fluid that sloshes through them when the head moves, signaling rotational or angular movement to the brain. (Module 10)

The main structure of the vestibular system is formed by the **semicircular canals** of the inner ear (refer to Figure 1), which consist of three tubes containing fluid that sloshes through them when the head moves, signaling rotational or angular movement to the brain. The pull on our bodies caused by the acceleration of forward, backward, or up-and-down motion, as well as the constant pull of gravity, is sensed by the *otoliths*, tiny, motion-sensitive crystals in the semicircular canals. When we move, these crystals shift as sands do on a windy beach, contacting the specialized receptor *hair cells* in the semicircular canals. The brain's inexperience in interpreting messages from the weightless otoliths is the cause of the space sickness commonly experienced by two-thirds of all space travelers, mentioned at the start of this module (Yoder et al., 2015).

Smell and Taste

Until he bit into a piece of raw cabbage on that February evening . . ., Raymond Fowler had not thought much about the sense of taste. The cabbage, part of a pasta dish he was preparing for his family's dinner, had an odd, burning taste, but he did not pay it much attention. Then a few minutes later, his daughter handed him a glass of cola, and he took a swallow. "It was like sulfuric acid," he said. "It was like the hottest thing you could imagine boring into your mouth." (Goode, 1999)

It was evident that something was very wrong with Fowler's sense of taste. After extensive testing, it became clear that the nerves involved in his sense of taste had been damaged, probably because of a viral infection or a medicine he was taking. (Luckily for him, a few months later, his sense of taste returned to normal.)

Even without disruptions in our ability to perceive the world such as those experienced by Fowler, we all know the important roles that taste and smell play. We'll consider these two senses next.

SMELL

Although many animals have keener abilities to detect odors than we do, the human sense of smell (*olfaction*) permits us to detect more than 10,000 separate smells. We also have a good memory for smells, and long-forgotten events and memories—good

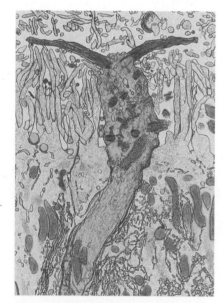

More than 1,000 olfactory receptor cells, like this one in the center of the scan, are spread across the nasal cavity. The cells are specialized to react to particular odors. Do you think it is possible to "train" the nose to pick up a greater number of odors?
©Prof. P. Motta/Dept. of Anatomy/University "La Sapienza", Rome/SPL/Science Source

and bad–can be brought back with the mere whiff of an odor associated with a memory (Willander & Larsson, 2006; Schroers, Prigot, & Fagen, 2007; Arshamian et al., 2013).

Results of "sniff tests" have shown that women generally have a better sense of smell than men do (Engen, 1987). People also have the ability to distinguish males from females on the basis of smell alone. In one experiment, blindfolded students who were asked to sniff the breath of a female or male volunteer who was hidden from view were able to distinguish the sex of the donor at better-than-chance levels. People can also distinguish happy from sad emotions by sniffing underarm smells, and women are able to identify their babies solely on the basis of smell just a few hours after birth (Doty et al., 1982; Fusari & Ballesteros, 2008; Flohr et al., 2017).

The sense of smell is sparked when the molecules of a substance enter the nasal passages and meet *olfactory cells*, the receptor neurons of the nose, which are spread across the nasal cavity. More than 1,000 separate types of receptors have been identified on those cells so far. Each of these receptors is so specialized that it responds only to a small band of different odors. The responses of the separate olfactory cells are then transmitted to the brain, where they are combined into recognition of a particular smell (Marshall, Laing, & Jinks, 2006; Zhou & Buck, 2006; Jia & Hegg, 2015).

Smell may also act as a hidden means of communication for humans. It has long been known that nonhumans release *pheromones*, chemicals they secrete into the environment that produce a social response in other members of the same species. Pheromones transmit messages such as alarm ("danger–predators are close by!") or sexual availability ("I'm interested in sex"). For instance, the vaginal secretions of female monkeys contain pheromones that stimulate the sexual interest of male monkeys (Touhara, 2007; Brennan, 2011; Zizzari et al., 2017).

The degree to which pheromones are part of the human experience remains an open question. Some psychologists believe that human pheromones affect emotional responses, although the evidence is inconclusive. For one thing, it is not clear what specific sense organ is receptive to pheromones. In nonhumans, it is the *vomeronasal organ* in the nose, but in humans, the organ appears to recede during fetal development (Haviland-Jones & Wilson, 2008; Hummer & McClintock, 2009; Gelstein et al., 2011); also see *Applying Psychology in the 21st Century*.

PsychTech

When male participants in a study sniffed women's tears, fMRI brain scans showed reduced activity in the parts of the brain associated with sexual arousal. Apparently, tears contain a chemical signal.

TASTE

The sense of taste (*gustation*) involves receptor cells that respond to four basic stimulus qualities: sweet, sour, salty, and bitter. A fifth category also exists, a flavor called *umami*, although there is controversy about whether it qualifies as a fundamental taste. *Umami* is a hard-to-translate Japanese word, although the English "meaty" or "savory" comes close. Chemically, umami involves food stimuli that contain amino acids (the substances that make up proteins) (McCabe & Rolls, 2007; Erickson, 2008; Nakamura et al., 2011).

Although the specialization of the receptor cells leads them to respond most strongly to a particular type of taste, they are capable of responding to other tastes as well. Ultimately, every taste is simply a combination of the basic flavor qualities, in the same way that the primary colors blend into a vast variety of shades and hues (Yeomans, Tepper, & Ritezschel, 2007; Spence, Auvray, & Smith, 2015).

The receptor cells for taste are located in roughly 10,000 *taste buds*, which are distributed across the tongue and other parts of the mouth and throat. The taste buds wear out and are replaced every 10 days or so. That's a good thing because if our taste buds weren't constantly reproducing, we'd lose the ability to taste after we'd accidentally burned our tongues.

The sense of taste differs significantly from one person to another, largely as a result of genetic factors. Some people, dubbed "supertasters," are

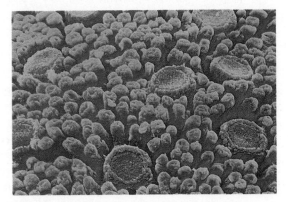

There are 10,000 taste buds on the tongue and on other parts of the mouth. Taste buds wear out and are replaced every 10 days. What would happen if taste buds were not regenerated?
©Science Source

APPLYING PSYCHOLOGY IN THE 21ST CENTURY

SNIFFING OUT FLASH DRIVES

Sensation and perception tell us everything we know about the world around us. But as amazing as these processes are, they do have their limits. We can't see microbes or ultraviolet light, for example, nor can we detect radiation at all. Our ability to apprehend and respond to our environment diminishes greatly beyond the limits of our senses. Indeed, our very understanding of reality is largely bound by our limited sensory and perceptual abilities.

The sense of smell in dogs is much better than that of humans, and their skill can even help detect illegal electronic equipment.
©Tengku Bahar/AFP/Getty Images

Many nonhuman animals have different or greater sensory abilities than we do. Some insects can see ultraviolet light. Bats can hear sounds at much higher frequencies than we can. And dogs can detect much fainter scents. We have a long history of using our canine companions' remarkable sense of smell to help us navigate the world, from hunting foxes to detecting illicit drugs. Enter Iris, an 18-month-old Labrador retriever with an amazingly skillful nose (Polgár et al., 2016).

Iris is a police dog trained by the U.S. Federal Bureau of Investigation with a unique ability: she can sniff out electronics. Iris is one of only four dogs in the United States that have been successfully trained to detect a chemical commonly used on memory chips and present in most electronic storage devices such as flash drives, hard drives, or SD cards. Certain kinds of serious criminal activity such as data theft, espionage, or child pornography typically entail the use of such storage devices, and investigators often need to find these devices to stop the criminal activity or to use them as evidence in court. The problem, though, is that these devices are now small enough to easily conceal in what would seem to be unlikely places—inside jewelry, in hollowed-out hiding spaces within walls or furnishings, or even inside more innocuous kinds of electronic devices. Finding these devices has become all but impossible for human investigators (Dienst, Schreiber, & Valiquette, 2016).

But not for Iris. Deception doesn't work on a dog. Not even the cleverest hiding spaces escape her outstanding canine senses. Her nose leads her right to them. A person would be hard pressed to detect the unique scent of a memory chip right under her own nose, but Iris can detect it at a distance—and quickly, too. She follows the scent trail to the hiding spot and then sits passively as officers retrieve the evidence and reward Iris for a job well done (Merrill, 2016).

We may be just scratching the surface of the capabilities of dogs such as Iris. So if you are passing through airport security, consider that you may be safer because of the extraordinary sensory capabilities of nonhumans.

RETHINK

- Why do you think electronics-sniffing dogs are so rare?
- How might your understanding of the world be different if you had a typical dog's sense of smell?

highly sensitive to taste; they have twice as many taste receptors as "nontasters," who are relatively insensitive to taste. Supertasters (who, for unknown reasons, are more likely to be female than male) find sweets sweeter, cream creamier, and spicy dishes spicier, and weaker concentrations of flavor are enough to satisfy any cravings they may have (Pickering & Gordon, 2006; Cornelis et al., 2017).

Supertasters—who make up about 15% of the U.S. population—may even be healthier than nontasters. Because supertasters find fatty foods distasteful, they are thinner than the general population. In contrast, because they aren't so sensitive to taste, nontasters may seek out relatively sweeter and fattier foods in order to maximize the taste. As a consequence, they may be prone to obesity (Reddy, 2013).

Are you a supertaster? To find out, complete the questionnaire in Figure 4.

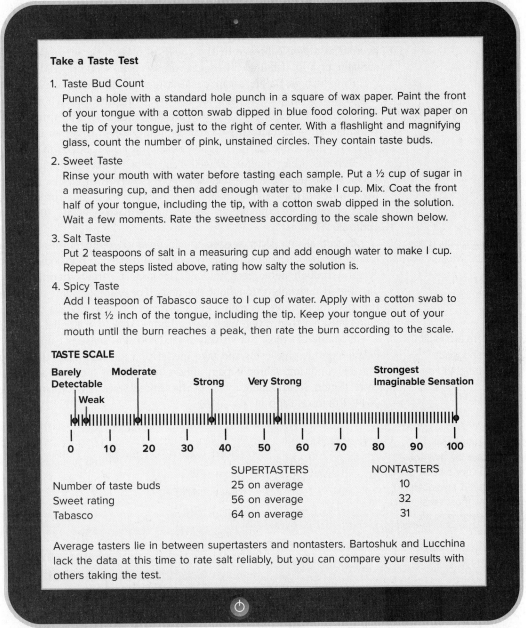

Take a Taste Test

1. Taste Bud Count
   Punch a hole with a standard hole punch in a square of wax paper. Paint the front of your tongue with a cotton swab dipped in blue food coloring. Put wax paper on the tip of your tongue, just to the right of center. With a flashlight and magnifying glass, count the number of pink, unstained circles. They contain taste buds.

2. Sweet Taste
   Rinse your mouth with water before tasting each sample. Put a ½ cup of sugar in a measuring cup, and then add enough water to make I cup. Mix. Coat the front half of your tongue, including the tip, with a cotton swab dipped in the solution. Wait a few moments. Rate the sweetness according to the scale shown below.

3. Salt Taste
   Put 2 teaspoons of salt in a measuring cup and add enough water to make I cup. Repeat the steps listed above, rating how salty the solution is.

4. Spicy Taste
   Add I teaspoon of Tabasco sauce to I cup of water. Apply with a cotton swab to the first ½ inch of the tongue, including the tip. Keep your tongue out of your mouth until the burn reaches a peak, then rate the burn according to the scale.

TASTE SCALE

Barely Detectable   Weak   Moderate   Strong   Very Strong   Strongest Imaginable Sensation

0   10   20   30   40   50   60   70   80   90   100

	SUPERTASTERS	NONTASTERS
Number of taste buds	25 on average	10
Sweet rating	56 on average	32
Tabasco	64 on average	31

Average tasters lie in between supertasters and nontasters. Bartoshuk and Lucchina lack the data at this time to rate salt reliably, but you can compare your results with others taking the test.

FIGURE 4 All tongues are not created equal, according to taste researchers Linda Bartoshuk and Laurie Lucchina. Instead, they suggest that the intensity of a flavor experienced by a given person is determined by that person's genetic background. This taste test can help determine if you are a nontaster, average taster, or supertaster.

Source: Bartoshuk, L., & Lucchina, L. (1997, January 13). Are you a supertaster? *U.S. News & World Report,* 58–59.

The Skin Senses: Touch, Pressure, Temperature, and Pain

It started innocently when Jennifer Darling hurt her right wrist during gym class. At first, it seemed like a simple sprain. But even though the initial injury healed, the excruciating, burning pain accompanying it did not go away. Instead, it spread to her other arm and then to her legs. The pain, which Jennifer described as similar to "a hot iron on your arm," was unbearable–and never stopped.

The source of Darling's pain turned out to be a rare condition known as *reflex sympathetic dystrophy syndrome*, or RSDS. RSDS is a disease characterized by constant, intense pain that is out of proportion to any injury. For a victim of RSDS, a stimulus as mild as a gentle breeze or the touch of a feather can produce agony. Even bright sunlight or a loud noise can trigger intense pain (Coderre, 2011; Harden et al., 2013).

Pain such as Darling's can be devastating, yet a lack of pain can be equally bad. If you never experience pain, for instance, you might not notice that your arm had brushed against a hot pan, and you would suffer a severe burn. Similarly, without the warning sign of abdominal pain that typically accompanies an inflamed appendix, your appendix might eventually rupture, spreading a fatal infection throughout your body.

Pain has other benefits, as well. Pain helps us better appreciate pleasurable experiences. It also may lead us to affiliate more closely with others, by arousing their empathy. And pain may lead us to be more vigilant about our surroundings as we seek to avoid or moderate pain we are experiencing (Bastian et al., 2014; Cameron, Spring, & Todd, 2017).

skin senses The senses of touch, pressure, temperature, and pain. (Module 10)

In fact, all our **skin senses**–touch, pressure, temperature, and pain–play a critical role in survival, making us aware of potential danger to our bodies. Most of these senses operate through nerve receptor cells located at various depths throughout the skin, distributed unevenly throughout the body. For example, some areas, such as the fingertips, have many more receptor cells sensitive to touch and as a consequence are notably more sensitive than other areas of the body (Gardner & Kandel, 2000) (see Figure 5).

Probably the most extensively researched skin sense is pain, and with good reason: People consult physicians and take medication for pain more than for any other symptom or condition. Chronic pain afflicts more than 116 million American adults and costs around $600 billion a year in the United States alone (Park, 2011; Jensen & Turk, 2014; Robinson-Papp et al., 2015).

Study Alert

Remember that there are multiple skin senses, including touch, pressure, temperature, and pain.

FIGURE 5 Skin sensitivity in various areas of the body. The lower the average threshold is, the more sensitive a body part is. The fingers and thumb, lips, nose, cheeks, and big toe are the most sensitive. Why do you think certain areas are more sensitive than others?

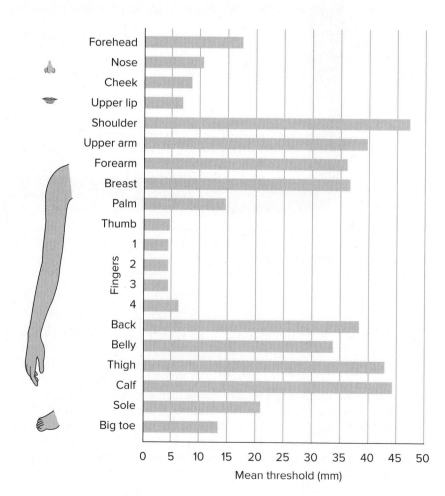

Pain is a response to a great variety of different kinds of stimuli. A light that is too bright can produce pain, and sound that is too loud can be painful. There are also multiple forms of pain; even itching can be considered a form of pain (Papoiu et al., 2013; Bautista, Wilson, & Hoon, 2014; Sutherland, 2016.)

One explanation for pain is that it is an outcome of cell injury; when a cell is damaged, regardless of the source of damage, it releases a chemical called *substance P* that transmits pain messages to the brain.

Some people are more susceptible to pain than others. For example, women experience painful stimuli more intensely than men do. These gender differences are associated with the production of hormones related to menstrual cycles. In addition, certain genes are linked to the experience of pain, so that we may inherit our sensitivity to pain (Kim, Clark, & Dionne, 2009; Park, 2011; Berke et al., 2017).

But the experience of pain is not determined by biological factors alone. For example, women report that the pain experienced in childbirth is moderated to some degree by the joyful nature of the situation. In contrast, even a minor stimulus can produce the perception of strong pain if it is accompanied by anxiety (for example, during a visit to the dentist). Clearly, then, pain is a perceptual response that depends heavily on our emotions and thoughts (Lang, Sorrell, & Rodgers, 2006; Kennedy et al., 2011; Jensen & Turk, 2014).

From the perspective of...

A Medical or Dental Services Provider How would you handle a patient who is anxiously awaiting treatment and complaining that her pain is getting worse?

©Robert Daly/age fotostock

According to the **gate-control theory of pain,** particular nerve receptors in the spinal cord lead to specific areas of the brain related to pain. When these receptors are activated because of an injury or problem with a part of the body, a "gate" to the brain is opened, causing us to experience the sensation of pain (Melzack & Katz, 2004; Vasudeva et al., 2015).

But the gate that produces pain does not necessarily remain open. Specifically, another set of neural receptors can, when stimulated, close the "gate" to the brain, thereby reducing the experience of pain.

The gate can be shut in two different ways. First, other impulses can overwhelm the nerve pathways relating to pain, which are spread throughout the brain. In this case, non-painful stimuli compete with and sometimes displace the neural message of pain, thereby shutting off the painful stimulus. This explains why rubbing the skin around an injury (or even listening to distracting music) helps reduce pain. The competing stimuli can overpower the painful ones (Villemure, Slotnick, & Bushnell, 2003; Somers et al., 2011).

Second, the neural gate producing pain can be shut by psychological factors relating to an individual's current emotions, interpretation of events, and previous experience. Specifically, the brain can close a gate by sending a message down the spinal cord to an injured area, producing a reduction in or relief from pain. Thus, soldiers who are injured in battle may experience no pain—the surprising situation in more than half of all combat injuries. The lack of pain probably occurs because a soldier experiences such relief at still being alive that the brain sends a signal to the injury site to shut down the pain gate (Gatchel & Weisberg, 2000; Pincus & Morley, 2001).

gate-control theory of pain The theory that particular nerve receptors in the spinal cord lead to specific areas of the brain related to pain. (Module 10)

PsychTech
Researcher Sean Mackey exposed participants in a study to a painful stimulus while watching an fMRI scan of their brain. Mackey found that the participants could be trained to exert control over the region of the brain activated by the pain, thereby reducing their experience of pain.

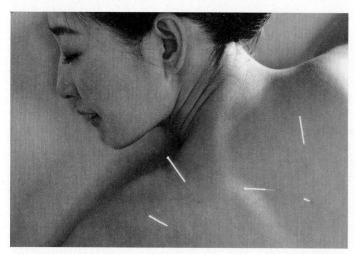

The ancient practice of acupuncture is still used in the 21st century. How does the gate-control theory of pain explain how acupuncture works?
©Fuse/Corbis/Getty Images

Gate-control theory also may explain cultural differences in the experience of pain. Some of these variations are astounding. For example, in India, people who participate in the "hook-swinging" ritual to celebrate the power of the gods have steel hooks embedded under the skin and muscles of their backs. During the ritual, they swing from a pole, suspended by the hooks. What would seem likely to induce excruciating pain instead produces a state of celebration and near euphoria. In fact, when the hooks are later removed, the wounds heal quickly, and after 2 weeks almost no visible marks remain (Kosambi, 1967; Melzack & Katz, 2001).

Gate-control theory suggests that the lack of pain is due to a message from the participant's brain that shuts down the pain pathways. Gate-control theory also may explain the effectiveness of *acupuncture*, an ancient Chinese technique in which sharp needles are inserted into various parts of the body. The sensation from the needles may close the gateway to the brain, reducing the experience of pain. It is also possible that the body's own painkillers–called *endorphins*–as well as positive and negative emotions, play a role in opening and closing the gate (Witt, Jena, & Brinkhaus, 2006; Cabioglu, Ergene, & Tan, 2007; Khedr et al., 2017).

Although the basic ideas behind gate-control theory have been supported by research, other processes are involved in the perception of pain. For instance, it appears that there are multiple neural pathways involved in the experience of pain. Furthermore, the suppression of pain can occur through the natural release of endorphins and other compounds that produce a reduction of discomfort and a sense of well-being. Finally, cognitive factors–such as people's expectations and their prior learning about pain–play a significant role in the perception of pain (Grahek, 2007; Wiech, 2016).

BECOMING AN INFORMED CONSUMER
of Psychology

Managing Pain

Are you one of the more than 116 million people in the United States who suffers from chronic pain? Psychologists and medical specialists have devised several strategies to fight pain. Among the most important approaches are these:

- *Medication.* Painkilling drugs are the most popular treatment in fighting pain. Drugs range from those that directly treat the source of the pain—such as reducing swelling in painful joints—to those that work on the symptoms. Medication can be in the form of pills, patches, injections, or liquids. In a recent innovation, drugs are pumped directly into the spinal cord (Kalb, 2003; Pesmen, 2006; Bagnall, 2010).
- *Nerve and brain stimulation.* Pain can sometimes be relieved when a low-voltage electric current is passed through the specific part of the body that is in pain. For example, in *peripheral-nerve stimulation,* a tiny battery-operated generator is implanted in the lower back. In even more severe cases, electrodes can be implanted surgically directly into the brain, or a handheld battery pack can stimulate nerve cells to provide direct relief (Tugay et al., 2007; Landro, 2010; Tan et al., 2011).
- *Light therapy.* One of the newest forms of pain reduction involves exposure to specific wavelengths of red or infrared light. Certain kinds of light increase the production of enzymes that may promote healing (Underwood, 2005; Evcik et al., 2007).
- *Hypnosis.* For people who can be hypnotized—and not everyone is susceptible—hypnosis can greatly relieve pain. In fact, it can affect the brain and spinal-cord

functioning in injured people, actually improving their physical functioning (Accardi & Milling, 2009; Lee & Raja, 2011; Jensen & Patterson, 2014).

- *Biofeedback and relaxation techniques.* Using *biofeedback,* people learn to control what are usually involuntary functions such as heartbeat, respiration, blood pressure, and muscle tension. Through biofeedback, a person can learn to control the stimulus that is causing the pain. For instance, people with tension headaches or back pain can be trained to relax their bodies to bring themselves relief (Vitiello, Bonello, & Pollard, 2007; Sielski, Rief, & Glombiewski, 2017).

- *Surgery.* In one of the most extreme methods, specific nerve fibers that carry pain messages to the brain can be cut surgically. Still, because of the danger that other bodily functions will be affected, surgery is a treatment of last resort, used most frequently with dying patients (Cullinane, Chu, & Mamelak, 2002; Amid & Chen, 2011).

- *Cognitive restructuring.* Cognitive treatments are effective for people who continually say to themselves, "This pain will never stop," "The pain is ruining my life," or "I can't take it anymore," and are thereby likely to make their pain even worse. By substituting more positive ways of thinking, people can increase their sense of control—and actually reduce the pain they experience (Bogart et al., 2007; Liedl et al., 2011; Ehde, Dillworth, & Turner, 2014).

- *Mirror pain therapy.* One surprising treatment for people who suffer from phantom-limb pain (in which a person with an amputated limb experiences pain where the missing limb used to be) employs mirrors. By using a mirror to make it appear that both limbs are intact, the brain of the amputee stops sending messages perceived as pain (Foell et al., 2014).

How Our Senses Interact

When Matthew Blakeslee shapes hamburger patties with his hands, he experiences a vivid bitter taste in his mouth. Esmerelda Jones (a pseudonym) sees blue when she listens to the note C sharp played on the piano; other notes evoke different hues–so much so that the piano keys are actually color-coded, making it easier for her to remember and play musical scales. (Ramachandran & Hubbard, 2006)

The explanation? Both of these people have an unusual condition known as synesthesia. *Synesthesia* is a perceptual phenomenon in which the stimulation of one sensory system (such as hearing) involuntarily leads a person to experience an additional sensory response in a different sensory system (such as vision).

The origins of synesthesia are a mystery. It is possible that people with synesthesia have unusually dense neural linkages between the different sensory areas of the brain. Another hypothesis is that they lack neural controls that usually inhibit connections between sensory areas (Kadosh, Henik, & Walsh, 2009; Deroy & Spence, 2013; Meier & Rothen, 2015).

Whatever the reason for synesthesia, it is a rare condition. (If you'd like to check out this phenomenon, see Figure 6.) Even so, the senses of all of us do interact and

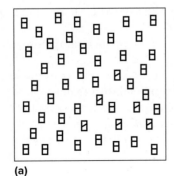

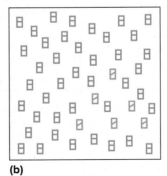

(a)   (b)

FIGURE 6 (a) Try to pick out the 0s in the display. (Note: each 0 appears as a rectangular "ø" with a slash through it.) Most people take several seconds to find them buried among the 8s and to see that the øs form a triangle. For people with certain forms of synesthesia, however, it's easy because they perceive the different numbers in contrasting colors as in (b).

(a and b): Source: Adapted from Ramachandran, V. S., & Hubbard, E. M. (2006). Hearing colors, tasting shapes. *Scientific American, 16,* 76–83.

integrate in a variety of ways. For example, the taste of food is influenced by its texture and temperature. We perceive food that is warmer as sweeter (think of the sweetness of steamy hot chocolate compared with cold chocolate milk). Spicy foods stimulate some of the same pain receptors that are also stimulated by heat–making the use of *hot* as a synonym for *spicy* quite accurate (Balaban, McBurney, & Affeltranger, 2005; Brang et al., 2011; Alfaro et al., 2015).

It's important, then, to think of our senses as interacting with one another. For instance, brain imaging studies show that the senses work in tandem to build our understanding of the world around us. We engage in *multimodal perception*, in which the brain collects the information from the individual sensory systems and integrates and coordinates it (Macaluso & Driver, 2005; Paulmann, Jessen, & Kotz, 2009; Gruber & Block, 2017).

Moreover, despite the fact that very different sorts of stimuli activate our individual senses, they all react according to the same basic principles that we discussed at the start of this chapter. For example, our responses to visual, auditory, and taste stimuli all follow Weber's law involving our sensitivity to changes in the strength of stimuli.

In short, in some ways our senses are more similar to one another than different. Each of them is designed to pick up information from the environment and translate it into useable information. Furthermore, individually and collectively, our senses help us to understand the complexities of the world around us, allowing us to navigate through the world effectively and intelligently.

RECAP/EVALUATE/RETHINK

RECAP

LO 10-1 What role does the ear play in the senses of sound, motion, and balance?

- Sound, motion, and balance are centered in the ear. Sounds, in the form of vibrating air waves, enter through the outer ear and travel through the auditory canal until they reach the eardrum.
- The vibrations of the eardrum are transmitted into the middle ear, which consists of three bones: the hammer, the anvil, and the stirrup. These bones transmit vibrations to the oval window.
- In the inner ear, vibrations move into the cochlea, which encloses the basilar membrane. Hair cells on the basilar membrane change the mechanical energy of sound waves into nerve impulses that are transmitted to the brain. The ear is also involved in the sense of balance and motion.
- Sound has a number of physical characteristics, including frequency and amplitude. The place theory of hearing and the frequency theory of hearing explain the processes by which we distinguish sounds of varying frequency and intensity.

LO 10-2 How do smell and taste function?

- Smell depends on olfactory cells (the receptor cells of the nose), and taste is centered in the taste buds on the tongue and mouth.

LO 10-3 What are the skin senses, and how do they relate to the experience of pain?

- The skin senses are responsible for the experiences of touch, pressure, temperature, and pain. Gate-control theory suggests that particular nerve receptors, when activated, open a "gate" to specific areas of the brain related to pain and that another set of receptors closes the gate when stimulated.
- Among the techniques used frequently to alleviate pain are medication, hypnosis, biofeedback, relaxation techniques, surgery, nerve and brain stimulation, and cognitive therapy.

EVALUATE

1. The tube-like passage leading from the outer ear to the eardrum is known as the _____ _____.
2. The purpose of the eardrum is to protect the sensitive nerves underneath it. It serves no purpose in actual hearing. True or false?
3. The three middle ear bones transmit their sound to the _____ _____.
4. The _____ theory of hearing states that the entire basilar membrane responds to a sound, vibrating more or less, depending on the nature of the sound.
5. The three fluid-filled tubes in the inner ear that are responsible for our sense of balance are known as the _____ _____.

6. The _____ _____ theory states that when certain skin receptors are activated as a result of an injury, a "pathway" to the brain is opened, allowing pain to be experienced.

RETHINK

1. Much research is being conducted on repairing faulty sensory organs through devices such as personal guidance systems and eyeglasses, among others. Do you think that researchers should attempt to improve normal sensory capabilities beyond their "natural" range (for example, make human visual or audio capabilities more sensitive than normal)? What benefits might this ability bring? What problems might it cause?

2. Why might sensitivity to pheromones have evolved differently in humans than in other species? What cultural factors might have played a role?

Answers to Evaluate Questions

1. auditory canal; 2. false: It vibrates when sound waves hit it and transmits the sound.; 3. oval window; 4. frequency; 5. semicircular canals; 6. gate-control

KEY TERMS

sound	basilar membrane	frequency theory of hearing	skin senses
eardrum	hair cells	semicircular canals	gate-control theory of pain
cochlea (KOKE-lee-uh)	place theory of hearing		

Module 11

Perceptual Organization: Constructing Our View of the World

LEARNING OUTCOMES

LO 11-1 What principles underlie our organization of the visual world and allow us to make sense of our environment?

LO 11-2 How are we able to perceive the world in three dimensions when our retinas are capable of sensing only two-dimensional images?

LO 11-3 What clues do visual illusions give us about our understanding of general perceptual mechanisms?

Gestalt (geh-SHTALLT) laws of organization A series of principles that describe how we organize bits and pieces of information into meaningful wholes. (Module 11)

Consider the vase shown in Figure 1a for a moment. Or is it a vase? Take another look, and instead you may see the profiles of two people.

Now that an alternative interpretation has been pointed out, you will probably shift back and forth between the two interpretations. Similarly, if you examine the shapes in Figure 1b long enough, you will probably experience a shift in what you're seeing. The reason for these reversals is this: Because each figure is two-dimensional, the usual means we employ for distinguishing the figure (the object being perceived) from the *ground* (the background or spaces within the object) do not work.

The fact that we can look at the same figure in more than one way illustrates an important point. We do not just passively respond to visual stimuli that happen to fall on our retinas. Rather, we actively try to organize and make sense of what we see.

We turn now from a focus on the initial response to a stimulus (sensation) to what our minds make of that stimulus (perception). Perception is a constructive process by which we go beyond the stimuli that are presented to us and attempt to construct a meaningful situation.

The Gestalt Laws of Organization

Some of the most basic perceptual processes can be described by a series of principles that focus on the ways we organize bits and pieces of information into meaningful wholes. Known as **Gestalt laws of organization,** these principles were set forth in the early 1900s by a group of German psychologists who studied patterns, or *gestalts* (Wertheimer, 1923). Those psychologists discovered a number of important principles that are valid for visual (as well as auditory) stimuli, illustrated in Figure 2: closure, proximity, similarity, and simplicity.

Figure 2a illustrates *closure*: We usually group elements to form enclosed or complete figures rather than open ones. We tend to ignore the breaks in Figure 2a and concentrate on the overall form. Figure 2b demonstrates the principle of *proximity*: We

FIGURE 1 When the usual cues we use to distinguish figure from ground are absent, we may shift back and forth between different views of the same figure. In (a), you can see either a vase or the profiles of two people. In (b), the shaded portion of the figure, called a Necker cube, can appear to be either the front or the back of the cube.

(a)

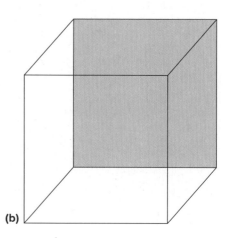

(b)

110

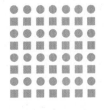

(a) Closure   **(b)** Proximity   **(c)** Similarity   **(d)** Simplicity

FIGURE 2 Organizing these various bits and pieces of information into meaningful wholes constitutes some of the most basic processes of perception, which are summed up in the Gestalt laws of organization. How might we determine if any other species share this organizational tendency?

perceive elements that are closer together as grouped together. As a result, we tend to see pairs of dots rather than a row of single dots in Figure 2b.

Elements that are *similar* in appearance we perceive as grouped together. We see, then, horizontal rows of circles and squares in Figure 2c, rather than vertical mixed columns. Finally, in a general sense, the overriding Gestalt principle is *simplicity*: When we observe a pattern, we perceive it in the most basic, straightforward manner that we can. For example, most of us see Figure 2d as a square with lines on two sides, rather than as the block letter *W* on top of the letter *M*. If we have a choice of interpretations, we generally opt for the simpler one.

Although Gestalt psychology no longer plays a prominent role in contemporary psychology, its legacy endures. One fundamental Gestalt principle that remains influential is that two objects considered together form a whole that is different from the simple combination of the objects. Gestalt psychologists argued that the perception of stimuli in our environment goes well beyond the individual elements that we sense. Instead, it represents an active, constructive process carried out within the brain (Wagemans et al., 2012; Chiu, Lo, & Hsieh, 2017) (see Figure 3).

 Study Alert
The Gestalt laws of organization are classic principles in the field of psychology. Figure 2 can help you remember them.

Top-Down and Bottom-Up Processing

Ca- yo- re-d t-is -en-en-e, w-ic- ha- ev-ry -hi-d l-tt-r m-ss-ng? It probably won't take you too long to figure out that it says: "Can you read this sentence, which has every third letter missing?"

If perception were based primarily on breaking down a stimulus into its most basic elements, understanding the sentence, as well as other ambiguous stimuli, would not

FIGURE 3 Although at first it is difficult to distinguish anything in this drawing, keep looking, and eventually you may see the figure of a dog. The dog represents a Gestalt, or perceptual, whole, which is something greater than the sum of the individual elements.

Republished with permission of the Royal Society, from "The Medawar Lecture 2001 Knowledge for vision: veision for knowledge," Richard L. Gregory, Volume 360, Issue 1458, 2005. Permission conveyed through Copyright Clearance Center, Inc.

FIGURE 4 The power of context is shown
in this figure. Note how the B and the 13
are identical.

Source: Adapted from Coren, S., & Ward, L. M.
(1989). *Sensation and perception* (3rd ed.).
San Diego, CA: Harcourt Brace Jovanovich.

A B C D E F
9 10 11 12 13 14

top-down processing Perception that
is guided by higher-level knowledge,
experience, expectations, and motivations. (Module 11)

be possible. The fact that you were probably able to recognize such an imprecise
stimulus illustrates that perception proceeds along two different avenues, called top-
down processing and bottom-up processing.

In **top-down processing,** perception is guided by higher-level knowledge, experience, expectations, and motivations. You were able to figure out the meaning of the
sentence with the missing letters because of your prior reading experience and because
written English contains redundancies. Not every letter of each word is necessary to
decode its meaning. Moreover, your expectations played a role in your being able to
read the sentence. You were probably expecting a statement that had *something* to do
with psychology, not the lyrics to a Lady Gaga song.

Top-down processing is illustrated by the importance of context in determining
how we perceive objects. Look, for example, at Figure 4. Most of us perceive that the
first row consists of the letters *A* through *F*, while the second contains the numbers
9 through 14. But take a more careful look, and you'll see that the B and the 13 are
identical. Clearly, our perception is affected by our expectations about the two
sequences–even though the two stimuli are exactly the same.

However, top-down processing cannot occur on its own. Even though top-down
processing allows us to fill in the gaps in ambiguous and out-of-context stimuli, we
would be unable to perceive the meaning of such stimuli without bottom-up processing. **Bottom-up processing** consists of the progression of recognizing and processing
information from individual components of a stimuli and moving to the perception of
the whole. We would make no headway in our recognition of the sentence without
being able to perceive the individual shapes that make up the letters. Some perception,
then, occurs at the level of the patterns and features of each of the separate letters.

bottom-up processing Perception
that consists of the progression of recognizing and processing information from
individual components of a stimuli and
moving to the perception of the whole.
(Module 11)

Top-down and bottom-up processing occur simultaneously and interact with each
other in our perception of the world around us. Bottom-up processing permits us to
process the fundamental characteristics of stimuli, whereas top-down processing allows
us to bring our experience to bear on perception. As we learn more about the complex
processes involved in perception, we are developing a better understanding of how
the brain continually interprets information from the senses and permits us to make
responses appropriate to the environment (Folk & Remington, 2008; Westerhausen
et al., 2009; Falasca et al., 2015).

Depth Perception: Translating
2-D to 3-D

As sophisticated as the retina is, the images projected onto it are flat and two-dimensional.
Yet the world around us is three-dimensional, and we perceive it that way. How do
we make the transformation from 2-D to 3-D?

depth perception The ability to view
the world in three dimensions and to
perceive distance. (Module 11)

The ability to view the world in three dimensions and to perceive distance–a skill
known as **depth perception**–is due largely to the fact that we have two eyes. Because
there is a certain distance between the eyes, a slightly different image reaches each
retina. The brain integrates the two images into one view, but it also recognizes the
difference in images and uses this difference to estimate the distance of an object from
us. The difference in the images seen by the left eye and the right eye is known as
binocular disparity (Gillam, Palmisano, & Govan, 2011; Valsecchi et al., 2013; Gao,
Schneider, & Li, 2017).

Railroad tracks that seem to join together in the distance are an example of linear perspective.
©Fuse/Getty Images

To get a sense of binocular disparity, hold a pencil at arm's length and look at it first with one eye and then with the other. There is little difference between the two views relative to the background. Now bring the pencil just 6 inches away from your face, and try the same thing. This time you will perceive a greater difference between the two views.

The difference between the images in the two eyes provides us with a way of determining distance. If we view two objects and one is considerably closer to us than the other is, the retinal disparity will be relatively large. That disparity leads us to have a greater sense of depth between the two. However, if two objects are a similar distance from us, the retinal disparity will be minor. Therefore, we will perceive them as being a similar distance from us.

In some cases, certain cues permit us to obtain a sense of depth and distance with just one eye. These cues are known as *monocular cues.*

For example, *motion parallax* is the monocular cue in which a change in position of an object on the retina allows the perception of movement. For example, suppose you are a passenger in a moving car, and you focus your eye on a stable object such as a tree. Objects that are closer than the tree will appear to move backward, and the nearer the object is, the more quickly it will appear to move. In contrast, objects beyond the tree will seem to move at a slower speed but in the same direction as you are. Your brain is able to use these cues to calculate the relative distances of the tree and other objects.

Similarly, the monocular cue of *relative size* reflects the assumption that if two objects are the same size, the object that makes a smaller image on the retina is farther away than the one that makes a larger image. But it's not just size of an object that provides information about distance; the quality of the image on the retina helps us judge distance. The monocular cue of *texture gradient* provides information about distance because the details of things that are far away are less distinct (Proffitt, 2006).

Finally, anyone who has ever seen railroad tracks that seem to come together in the distance knows that distant objects appear to be closer together than are nearer ones, a phenomenon called linear perspective. *Linear perspective* is a type of perspective in which objects in the distance appear to converge. We use linear perspective as a monocular cue in estimating distance, allowing the two-dimensional image on the retina to record the three-dimensional world (Shimono & Wade, 2002; Bruggeman, Yonas, & Konczak, 2007).

From the perspective of...

A Computer Game Designer What are some techniques you might use to produce the appearance of three-dimensional terrain on a two-dimensional computer screen? What are some techniques you might use to suggest motion?

©Sam Edwards/age fotostock

Perceptual Constancy

Consider what happens as you finish a conversation with a friend and she begins to walk away from you. As you watch her walk down the street, the image on your retina becomes smaller and smaller. Do you wonder why she is shrinking?

Of course not. Despite the very real change in the size of the retinal image, because of perceptual constancy you factor into your thinking the knowledge that your friend is moving farther away from you. **Perceptual constancy** is the recognition that physical objects are consistent and do not vary, even though our sensory input about them changes.

Perceptual constancy allows us to view objects as having an unchanging size, shape, color, and brightness, even if the image on our retina changes. For example, despite the varying size or shape of the images on the retina as an airplane approaches, flies overhead, and then disappears, we do not perceive the airplane as changing shape or size. Experience has taught us that the plane's size remains constant (Wickelgren, 2004; Garrigan & Kellman, 2008; Sachse et al., 2017).

In some cases, though, our application of perceptual constancy can mislead us. One good example of this involves the rising moon. When the moon first appears at night, close to the horizon, it seems to be huge–much larger than when it is high in the sky later in the evening. You may have thought that the apparent change in the size of the moon was caused by the moon's being physically closer to the earth when

perceptual constancy Our understanding that physical objects are unvarying and consistent even though sensory input about them may vary. (Module 11)

Despite the moon appearing very large when it is close to the horizon, perceptual constancy helps us to know that the moon's size has not changed and remains the same.

©Paul Souders/The Image Bank/Getty Images

it first appears. In fact, though, this is not the case at all: the actual image of the moon on our retina is the same, whether it is low or high in the sky.

There are several explanations for the moon illusion. One suggests that the moon appears to be larger when it is close to the horizon primarily because of perceptual constancy. When the moon is near the horizon, the perceptual cues of intervening terrain and objects such as trees on the horizon produce a misleading sense of distance, leading us to misperceive the moon as relatively large.

In contrast, when the moon is high in the sky, we see it by itself, and we don't try to compensate for its distance from us. In this case, then, perceptual constancy leads us to perceive it as relatively small. To experience perceptual constancy, try looking at the moon when it is relatively low on the horizon through a paper-towel tube; the moon suddenly will appear to "shrink" back to normal size (Imamura & Nakamizo, 2006; Kaufman, Johnson, & Liu, 2008; Rogers & Naumenko, 2015).

Perceptual constancy is not the only explanation for the moon illusion, and it remains a puzzle to psychologists. It may be that several different perceptual processes are involved in the illusion (Gregory, 2008; Kim, 2008).

Motion Perception: As the World Turns

When a batter tries to hit a pitched ball, the most important factor is the motion of the ball. How is a batter able to judge the speed and location of a target that is moving at some 90 miles per hour?

The answer rests in part on several cues that provide us with relevant information about the perception of motion. For one thing, the movement of an object across the retina is typically perceived relative to some stable, unmoving background. Moreover, if the stimulus is heading toward us, the image on the retina expands in size, filling more and more of the visual field. In such cases, we assume that the stimulus is approaching—not that it is an expanding stimulus viewed at a constant distance.

It is not, however, just the movement of images across the retina that brings about the perception of motion. If it were, we would perceive the world as moving every time we moved our heads. Instead, one of the critical things we learn about perception is to factor information about our own head and eye movements along with information about changes in the retinal image.

Sometimes we perceive motion when it doesn't occur. Have you ever been on a stationary train that feels as if it is moving because a train on an adjacent track begins to slowly move past? Or have you been in an IMAX movie theater in which you feel as if you were falling as a huge image of a plane moves across the screen? In both cases, the experience of motion is convincing. *Apparent movement* is the perception that a stationary object is moving. It occurs when different areas of the retina are quickly stimulated, leading us to interpret motion (Ekroll & Scherzer, 2009; Lindemann & Bekkering, 2009; Brandon & Saffran, 2011).

Perceptual Illusions: The Deceptions of Perceptions

If you look carefully at the Parthenon, one of the most famous buildings of ancient Greece, still standing at the top of an Athens hill, you'll see that it was built with a bulge on one side. If it didn't have that bulge—and quite a few other architectural "tricks" like it, such as columns that incline inward—it would look as if it were crooked and about to fall down. Instead, it appears to stand completely straight, at right angles to the ground.

The fact that the Parthenon appears to be completely upright is the result of a series of visual illusions. **Visual illusions** are physical stimuli that consistently produce errors in perception. In the case of the Parthenon, the building appears to be completely

visual illusions Physical stimuli that consistently produce errors in perception. (Module 11)

(a)

(b)

(c)

FIGURE 5 (a) In building the Parthenon, the Greeks constructed an architectural wonder that looks perfectly straight, with right angles at every corner. (b) However, if it had been built with completely true right angles, it would have looked as it does here. (c) To compensate for this illusion, the Parthenon was designed to have a slight upward curvature, as shown here.

(Photo): ©Mlenny Photography/E+/Getty Images; (b): Source: Adapted from Luckiesh, M. (1921). *Scientific American Monthly,* 3, 497-501.

Study Alert

The explanation for the Müller-Lyer illusion is complicated. Figure 6 will help you master it.

FIGURE 6 In the Müller-Lyer illusion (a), the vertical line on the left appears shorter than the one on the right, even though they are identical in length. One explanation for the Müller-Lyer illusion suggests that the line on the left (with arrow points directed outward) is perceived as the relatively close corner of a rectangular object, such as the building corner in (b), and the line on the right (with the arrow points directed inward) is interpreted as the inside corner of a rectangular object, such as the room extending away from us (c). Our previous experience with distance cues leads us to assume that the outside corner is closer than the inside corner, and, consequently, the inside corner must be longer.

square, as illustrated in Figure 5a. However, if it had been built that way, it would look to us as it does in Figure 5b. The reason for this is an illusion that makes right angles placed above a line appear as if they were bent. To offset the illusion, the Parthenon was constructed as in Figure 5c, with a slight upward curvature.

The *Müller-Lyer illusion* (illustrated in Figure 6) has fascinated psychologists for decades. Although the two lines are the same length, the one with the arrow tips pointing outward, away from the vertical line (Figure 6a, left) appears to be shorter than the one with the arrow tips pointing inward (Figure 6a, right).

Although all kinds of explanations for visual illusions have been suggested, most concentrate either on the physical operation of the eye or on our misinterpretation of the visual stimulus. For example, one explanation for the Müller-Lyer illusion is that eye movements are greater when the arrow tips point inward, making us perceive the line as longer than it is when the arrow tips face outward. In contrast, a different explanation for the illusion suggests that we unconsciously attribute particular significance to each of the lines (Gregory, 1978). When we see the left line in Figure 6a, we tend to perceive it as if it were the relatively close outside corner of a rectangular object, such as the

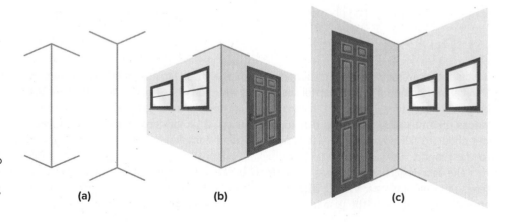

(a)   **(b)**   **(c)**

Optical illusions have been used to slow traffic, as these virtual speed bumps in Iceland illustrate. Although they appear to be hovering above-ground, in fact they are flush to the ground.
©Thorir Ingvarsson/Shutterstock

outside corner of the room illustrated in Figure 6b. In contrast, when we view the line on the right in Figure 6a, we perceive it as the relatively more distant inside corner of a rectangular object, such as the inside room corner in Figure 6c. Because previous experience leads us to assume that the outside corner is closer than the inside corner, we make the further assumption that the inside corner must therefore be longer.

Despite the complexity of the latter explanation, a good deal of evidence supports it. For instance, cross-cultural studies show that people raised in areas where there are few right angles–such as the Zulu in Africa–are much less susceptible to the illusion than are people who grow up where most structures are built using right angles and rectangles (Segall, Campbell, & Herskovits, 1966; Fujita et al., 2017).

 # Exploring DIVERSITY

Culture and Perception

As the example of the Zulu indicates, the culture in which we are raised has clear consequences for how we perceive the world. Consider the drawing in Figure 7. Sometimes called the "devil's tuning fork," it is likely to produce a mind-boggling effect, as the center tine of the fork alternates between appearing and disappearing.

Now try to reproduce the drawing on a piece of paper. Chances are that the task is nearly impossible for you—unless you are a member of an African tribe with little exposure to Western cultures. For such individuals, the task is simple; they have no trouble reproducing the figure. The reason is that Westerners automatically interpret the drawing as something that cannot exist in three dimensions, and they therefore are inhibited from reproducing it. The African tribal members, in contrast, do not make the assumption that the figure is "impossible" and instead view it in two dimensions, a perception that enables them to copy the figure with ease (Deregowski, 1973).

Cultural differences are also reflected in depth perception. A Western viewer of Figure 8 would interpret the hunter in the drawing as aiming for the antelope in the foreground, while an elephant stands under the tree in the background. A member of an isolated African tribe, however, interprets the scene very differently by assuming that the hunter is aiming at the elephant. Westerners use the difference in sizes between the two animals as a cue that the elephant is farther away than the antelope (Hudson, 1960).

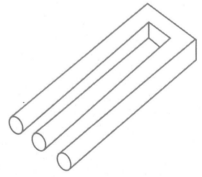

FIGURE 7 The "devil's tuning fork" has three prongs . . . or does it have two?

FIGURE 8 Is the man aiming for the elephant or the antelope? Westerners assume that the difference in size between the two animals indicates that the elephant is farther away, and therefore, the man is aiming for the antelope. In contrast, members of some African tribes, not used to depth cues in two-dimensional drawings, assume that the man is aiming for the elephant. Do you think people who view the picture in three dimensions could explain what they see to someone who views the scene in two dimensions and eventually get that person to view it in three dimensions?

Source: Adapted from Hudson, W. (1960). Pictorial depth perception in subcultural groups in Africa. *Journal of Social Psychology, 52,* 183–208.

Does this mean that basic perceptual processes differ among people of different cultures? No. Variations in learning and experience produce cross-cultural differences in perception, and the underlying psychological processes involved in perception are similar (McCauley & Henrich, 2006).

Although visual illusions may seem like mere psychological curiosities, they actually illustrate something fundamental about perception. There is a basic connection between our prior knowledge, needs, motivations, and expectations about how the world is put together and the way we perceive it. Our view of the world is very much an outcome, then, of fundamental psychological factors. Furthermore, each person perceives the environment in a way that is unique and special (Knoblich & Sebanz, 2006; Repp & Knoblich, 2007).

SUBLIMINAL PERCEPTION

Can stimuli that we're not consciously aware of change our behavior? In some ways, yes.

Subliminal perception refers to the perception of messages about which we have no awareness. The stimulus could be a written word, a sound, or even a smell that activates the sensory system but that is not intense enough for a person to report having experienced it. For example, in some studies, people are exposed to a descriptive label–called a *prime*–about a person (such as the word *smart* or *happy*) so briefly that they cannot report seeing the label. Later, however, they form impressions that are influenced by the content of the prime. Somehow, they have been influenced by the prime that they say they couldn't see, providing some evidence for subliminal perception (Key, 2003; Kawakami & Miura, 2015).

Although subliminal messages (which social psychologists refer to as *priming*) can influence behavior in subtle ways, there's little evidence that they can lead to *major* changes in attitudes or behavior. Most research suggests that they cannot. For example, people who are subliminally exposed to an image of a Coke can and the word *thirst* do later rate themselves as thirstier, and they actually do drink more when given the opportunity. However, they don't particularly care if they drink Coke or some other liquid to quench their thirst (Dijksterhuis, Chartrand, & Aarts, 2007; Parkinson et al., 2017).

In short, although we are able to perceive at least some kinds of information of which we are unaware, there's little evidence that subliminal messages can change our attitudes or behavior in substantial ways. At the same time, subliminal perception does have at least some consequences. If our motivation to carry out a behavior is already high and the appropriate stimuli are presented subliminally, subliminal perception may have at least some effect on our behavior (Pratkanis, Epley, & Savitsky, 2007; Randolph-Seng & Nielsen, 2009; Gafner, 2013).

EXTRASENSORY PERCEPTION (ESP)

Psychologists are highly skeptical of reports of *extrasensory perception*, or ESP–perception that does not involve our known senses. Although almost half of the general population of the United States believes it exists, most psychologists reject the existence of ESP, asserting that there is no sound documentation of the phenomenon (Moore, 2005).

However, a debate in one of the most prestigious psychology journals, *Psychological Bulletin*, heightened interest in ESP in the early 2000s. According to proponents of ESP, reliable evidence existed for an "anomalous process of information transfer," or *psi*. These researchers, who painstakingly reviewed considerable evidence, argued that a cumulative body of research shows reliable support for the existence of psi (Storm & Ertel, 2001; Parra & Argibay, 2007; Storm & Rock, 2015).

Ultimately, their conclusion was challenged and largely discredited for several reasons. For example, critics suggested that the research methodology was inadequate and that the experiments supporting psi are flawed (Kennedy, 2004; Rouder, Morey, & Province, 2013).

Because of questions about the quality of the research, as well as a lack of any credible theoretical explanation for how extrasensory perception might take place, almost no psychologists would claim that there is reliable scientific support for ESP. Still, the topic continues to inspire research, which is the only way the issue will be fully settled (Rose & Blackmore, 2002; Wiseman & Greening, 2002; Bem, 2012).

RECAP/EVALUATE/RETHINK

RECAP

LO 11-1 What principles underlie our organization of the visual world and allow us to make sense of our environment?

- Perception is a constructive process in which people go beyond the stimuli that are physically present and try to construct a meaningful interpretation.
- The Gestalt laws of organization are used to describe the way in which we organize bits and pieces of information into meaningful wholes, known as Gestalts, through closure, proximity, similarity, and simplicity.
- In top-down processing, perception is guided by higher-level knowledge, experience, expectations, and motivations. In bottom-up processing, perception consists of the progression of recognizing and processing information from individual components of a stimuli and moving to the perception of the whole.

LO 11-2 How are we able to perceive the world in three dimensions when our retinas are capable of sensing only two-dimensional images?

- Depth perception is the ability to perceive distance and view the world in three dimensions, even though the images projected on our retinas are two-dimensional. We are able to judge depth and distance as a result of binocular disparity and monocular cues, such as motion parallax, the relative size of images on the retina, and linear perspective.
- Perceptual constancy permits us to perceive stimuli as unvarying in size, shape, and color despite changes in the environment or the appearance of the objects being perceived.
- Motion perception depends on cues such as the perceived movement of an object across the retina and information about how the head and eyes are moving.

LO 11-3 What clues do visual illusions give us about our understanding of general perceptual mechanisms?

- Visual illusions are physical stimuli that consistently produce errors in perception, causing judgments that do not reflect the physical reality of a stimulus accurately. One of the best-known illusions is the Müller-Lyer illusion.
- Visual illusions are usually the result of errors in the brain's interpretation of visual stimuli. Furthermore, culture clearly affects how we perceive the world.
- Subliminal perception refers to the perception of messages about which we have no awareness. The reality of the phenomenon, as well as of ESP, is open to question and debate.

EVALUATE

1. Match each of the following organizational laws with its meaning:

   a. closure
   b. proximity
   c. similarity
   d. simplicity

   1. Elements close together are grouped together.
   2. Patterns are perceived in the most basic, direct manner possible.
   3. Groupings are made in terms of complete figures.
   4. Elements similar in appearance are grouped together.

2. _____ analysis deals with the way in which we break an object down into its component pieces in order to understand it.

3. Processing that involves higher functions such as expectations and motivations is known as _____, whereas processing that recognizes the individual components of a stimulus is known as _____.

4. When a car passes you on the road and appears to shrink as it gets farther away, the phenomenon of _____

_____ permits you to realize that the car is not in fact getting smaller.

5. _____ _____ is the ability to view the world in three dimensions instead of two.

6. The brain makes use of a phenomenon known as _____ _____, or the difference in the images the two eyes see, to give three dimensions to sight.

RETHINK

1. In what ways do painters represent three-dimensional scenes in two dimensions on a canvas? Do you think artists in non-Western cultures use the same or different principles to represent three-dimensionality? Why?

2. Can you think of examples of the combined use of top-down and bottom-up processing in everyday life? Is one type of processing superior to the other?

Answers to Evaluate Questions

1. a-3, b-1, c-4, d-2; 2. Feature; 3. top-down, bottom-up; 4. perceptual constancy; 5. Depth perception; 6. binocular disparity

KEY TERMS

Gestalt (geh-SHTALLT) laws of organization   top-down processing   bottom-up processing   depth perception   perceptual constancy   visual illusions

LOOKING *Back*

EPILOGUE

We have noted the important distinction between sensation and perception, and we have examined the processes that underlie both of them. We've seen how external stimuli evoke sensory responses and how our different senses process the information contained in those responses. We also have focused on the physical structure and internal workings of the individual senses, including vision, hearing, balance, smell, taste, and the skin senses, and we've explored how our brains organize and process sensory information to construct a consistent, integrated picture of the world around us.

Before ending our discussion of sensation and perception, let's reconsider the synesthesia of Sean Day and Carol Steen, whom we met in the prologue. Using your knowledge of sensation and perception, answer these questions:

1. Do you think synesthesia is a matter of sensation (sight, hearing, taste, smell, touch) or of brain processing? Why?

2. One theory is that synesthesia arises in those who retain connections between brain regions that are normally erased as we age. If this is true, do you think many of us could be trained to develop synesthesia? Explain your answer.

3. When you are asked to explain how something tastes or smells, do you ever use words that apply more typically to a different sense, such as vision or hearing? Do you think we all experience synesthesia to some degree?

4. In what ways might synesthesia be a blessing? In what ways might it be a curse? Are there particular occupational areas in which it would be one or the other?

Design Elements: Yellow highlighter: ©luckyraccoon/Shutterstock.com; Smartphone: ©and4me/Shutterstock.com; Group of diverse hands: ©MR. Nattanon Kanchak/Shutterstock.com; Woman working on laptop: ©Dragon Images/Shutterstock.com.

VISUAL SUMMARY 3 Sensation and Perception

MODULE 8 Sensing the World

Absolute thresholds

Difference thresholds

- Just noticeable difference

- Weber's law

Sensory Adaptation

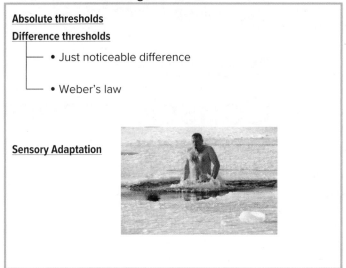

MODULE 9 Vision

Eye Structure

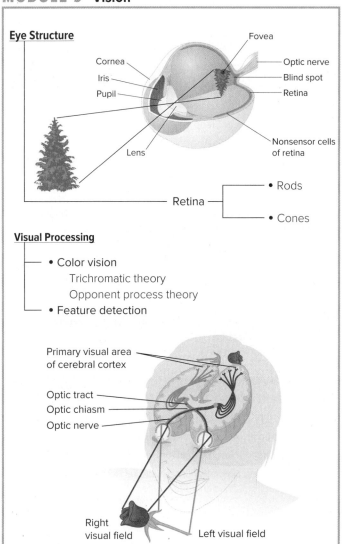

Cornea
Iris
Pupil
Fovea
Optic nerve
Blind spot
Retina
Lens
Nonsensor cells of retina

Retina
- Rods
- Cones

Visual Processing

- Color vision
  Trichromatic theory
  Opponent process theory
- Feature detection

Primary visual area of cerebral cortex
Optic tract
Optic chiasm
Optic nerve
Right visual field
Left visual field

MODULE 10 Hearing and Other Senses

Ear Structure

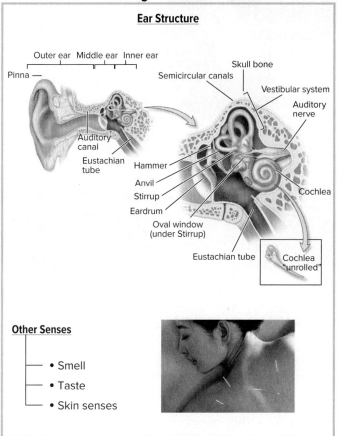

Outer ear Middle ear Inner ear
Pinna
Skull bone
Semicircular canals
Vestibular system
Auditory nerve
Auditory canal
Eustachian tube
Hammer
Anvil
Stirrup
Eardrum
Oval window (under Stirrup)
Cochlea
Eustachian tube
Cochlea "unrolled"

Other Senses

- Smell
- Taste
- Skin senses

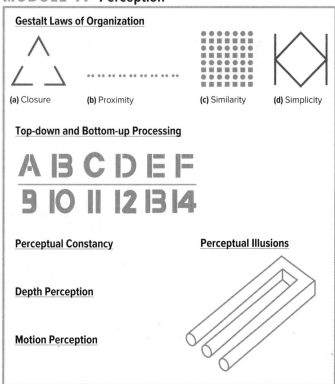

MODULE 11 Perception

Gestalt Laws of Organization

(a) Closure (b) Proximity (c) Similarity (d) Simplicity

Top-down and Bottom-up Processing

A B C D E F
9 10 11 12 13 14

Perceptual Constancy

Depth Perception

Motion Perception

Perceptual Illusions

(MODULE 8): ©Pashkov Andrey/123RF; (MODULE 9): ©McGraw-Hill Global Education Holdings LLC, 2000.; (MODULE 10): ©McGraw-Hill Global Education Holdings LLC, 2008.; (Photo): ©Fuse/Corbis/Getty Images; (MODULE 11): Source: Adapted from Coren, S., & Ward, L. M. (1989). *Sensation and perception* (3rd ed.). San Diego, CA: Harcourt Brace Jovanovich.

©Eugenio Marongiu/Shutterstock

CHAPTER 4
States of Consciousness

LEARNING OUTCOMES FOR CHAPTER 4

	MODULE 12
LO 12-1 What are the states of consciousness?	**SLEEP AND DREAMS**
	The Stages of Sleep
LO 12-2 What happens when we sleep, and what are the meaning and function of dreams?	REM Sleep: The Paradox of Sleep
	Why Do We Sleep, and How Much Sleep Is Necessary?
LO 12-3 What are the major sleep disorders, and how can they be treated?	**Applying Psychology in the 21st Century:** Sleeping to Forget
	Neuroscience in Your Life: Why Are We So Emotional When We Don't Get Enough Sleep?
LO 12-4 How much do we daydream?	The Function and Meaning of Dreaming
	Sleep Disturbances: Slumbering Problems
	Circadian Rhythms: Life Cycles
	Daydreams: Dreams Without Sleep
	Becoming an Informed Consumer of Psychology: Sleeping Better

	MODULE 13
LO 13-1 What is hypnosis, and are hypnotized people in a different state of consciousness?	**HYPNOSIS AND MEDITATION**
	Hypnosis: A Trance-Forming Experience?
LO 13-2 What are the effects of meditation?	Meditation: Regulating Our Own State of Consciousness
	Exploring Diversity: Cross-Cultural Routes to Altered States of Consciousness

DRUG USE: THE HIGHS AND LOWS OF CONSCIOUSNESS

Stimulants: Drug Highs

Depressants: Drug Lows

Narcotics, Opiates, and Opioids: Relieving Pain and Anxiety

Hallucinogens: Psychedelic Drugs

Becoming an Informed Consumer of Psychology: Identifying Drug and Alcohol Problems

LO 14-1 What are the major classifications of drugs, and what are their effects?

PROLOGUE *AN EPIDEMIC HITS CLOSE TO HOME*

Eric Morin's sister described him as a person with a big heart, someone who was cheerful and energetic. His family remembers him as being happy and healthy at their last Thanksgiving celebration. But Eric Morin, father of two children, died a few weeks later, on Christmas Eve of that year, from acute fentanyl poisoning, killed by an overdose of opioids.

Morin had struggled with substance abuse since high school, when he began using marijuana and alcohol. Later, he turned to pills and heroin. It was heroin laced with fentanyl—an opioid so potent that most overdose cases never make it to the emergency room—that killed him.

Morin sought treatment on several occasions. His mother remembers his struggles to get clean—the sweats, the vomiting, the shakes. But despite his best efforts, Morin became one more statistic in the growing list of opioid-related deaths (Hewitt, 2017).

LOOKING *Ahead*

Eric Morin's experience is far from unique. The United States is experiencing a full-blown opiate epidemic, with over 50,000 deaths from drug overdoses in 2016 alone. Drug overdoses are now the most frequent cause of death of those under the age of 50 (Katz, 2017).

Opiates such as heroin and fentanyl promise relief from anxiety and stress. While we don't know exactly what drove Eric Morin to use narcotics, his early experiments with alcohol and marijuana indicate a continual desire for an altered state of consciousness. Why people seek to alter their consciousness, what conscious experience is, and how and why we can alter it are some of the questions we address as we turn our attention to the study of consciousness.

Consciousness is the awareness of the sensations, thoughts, and feelings we experience at a given moment. Consciousness is our subjective understanding of both the environment around us and our private internal world, unobservable to outsiders.

In *waking consciousness,* we are awake and aware of our thoughts, emotions, and perceptions. All other states of consciousness are considered *altered states of consciousness.* Among these, sleeping and dreaming occur naturally; drug use and hypnosis, in contrast, are methods of deliberately altering one's state of consciousness.

In the past, because consciousness is so personal a phenomenon, psychologists were sometimes reluctant to study it. After all, who can say that your consciousness is similar to or, for that matter, different from anyone else's? Although the earliest psychologists, including William James (1890), saw the study of consciousness as central to the field, later psychologists suggested that it was out of bounds for the discipline. They argued that consciousness could be understood only by relying "unscientifically" on what experimental participants said they were experiencing. In this view, it was philosophers—not psychologists—who should speculate on such knotty issues as whether consciousness is separate from the physical body, how people know they exist, and how the body and mind are related to each other (Gennaro, 2004; Barresi, 2007; James, 2015).

Contemporary psychologists reject the view that the study of consciousness is unsuitable for the field of psychology. Instead, they argue that several approaches permit the scientific study of consciousness. For example, behavioral neuroscientists can measure brain-wave patterns under conditions of consciousness ranging from sleep to waking to hypnotic trances. And new understanding of the chemistry of drugs such as marijuana and alcohol has provided insights into the way they produce their pleasurable—as well as adverse—effects (Wells, Phillips, & McCarthy, 2011; Malouff & Rooke, 2013; Liechti, Dolder & Schmid, 2017).

Yet how humans experience consciousness remains an open question. Some psychologists believe that the experience of consciousness is produced by a quantitative increase in neuronal activity that occurs throughout the brain. For example, an alarm clock moves us from sleep to waking consciousness by its loud ringing, which stimulates neurons throughout the brain as a whole (Greenfield, 2002; Koch & Greenfield, 2007; Ward, 2011).

In contrast, others believe that states of consciousness are produced by particular sets of neurons and neuronal pathways that are activated in specific ways. In this view, an alarm clock wakes us from sleep into consciousness because specific neurons related to the auditory nerve are activated; the auditory nerve then sends a message to other neurons to release particular neurotransmitters that produce awareness of the alarm (Tononi & Koch, 2008; Saper, 2013; Schurger et al., 2015).

Although we don't know yet which of these views is correct, it is clear that whatever state of consciousness we are in—be it waking, sleeping, hypnotic, or drug-induced—the complexities of consciousness are profound.

consciousness The awareness of the sensations, thoughts, and feelings being experienced at a given moment. (Module 12)

Module 12
Sleep and Dreams

LEARNING OUTCOMES

LO 12-1 What are the states of consciousness?

LO 12-2 What happens when we sleep, and what are the meaning and function of dreams?

LO 12-3 What are the major sleep disorders, and how can they be treated?

LO 12-4 How much do we daydream?

During a 9-day cross-country bike race, 29-year-old Mike Trevino averaged 1 hour of sleep per day. The first 3 days he didn't sleep at all, and over the next 6, he took completely dream-free naps of at most 90 minutes. His waking thoughts became fuzzy, depicting movielike plots starring himself and his crew. The whole experience was like a serial dream in which he remained conscious, if only barely. He finished in second place.

Trevino's case is unusual–in part because he was able to function with so little sleep for so long–and it raises a host of questions about sleep and dreams. Can we live without sleep? What is the meaning of dreams? More generally, what is sleep?

Although sleeping is a state that we all experience, there are still many unanswered questions about sleep that remain, along with a considerable number of myths. Test your knowledge of sleep and dreams by answering the questionnaire in Figure 1.

Sleep Quiz

Although sleeping is something we all do for a significant part of our lives, myths and misconceptions about the topic abound. Check your knowledge by reading each statement below and check True or False.

1. It is a proven fact that 8 hours of sleep are needed to remain mentally healthy. ☐ True ☐ False	6. The best long-term cure for sleeplessness is regular use of insomnia medications. ☐ True ☐ False
2. Sleep "turns off" most brain activity to promote brain rest and recovery. ☐ True ☐ False	7. Dreams are most often the result of stomach distress caused by what and when we eat. ☐ True ☐ False
3. Sleep deprivation always causes mental imbalance. ☐ True ☐ False	8. When we are asleep and dreaming, our muscles are the most relaxed they can get. ☐ True ☐ False
4. It is impossible to go more than 48 hours without sleep. ☐ True ☐ False	9. If you can't remember your dreams, it's because you want to forget them. ☐ True ☐ False
5. If we lose sleep we can always make it up another night or on the weekend. ☐ True ☐ False	10. Many people never dream. ☐ True ☐ False

Scoring: It is easy to score this quiz because every statement is false. But don't lose any sleep if you missed a few; these are among the most widely held misconceptions about sleeping and dreaming.

FIGURE 1 There are many unanswered questions about sleep. Taking this quiz can help you clear up some of the myths.
Source: Palladino, J. J., & Carducci, B. J., (1984). Students' knowledge of sleep and dreams. *Teaching of Psychology, 11*(3), 189–191.

The Stages of Sleep

Most of us consider sleep a time of tranquility when we set aside the tensions of the day and spend the night in uneventful slumber. However, a closer look at sleep shows that a good deal of activity occurs throughout the night.

Measures of electrical activity in the brain show that the brain is quite active during sleep. It produces electrical discharges with systematic, wavelike patterns that change in height (or amplitude) and speed (or frequency) in regular sequences. There is also significant physical activity in muscle and eye movements.

People progress through a series of distinct stages of sleep during a night's rest—known as *stage 1* through *stage 3* and *REM sleep*—moving through the stages in cycles lasting about 90 minutes. Each of these sleep stages is associated with a unique pattern of brain waves, which you can see in Figure 2.

When people first go to sleep, they move from a waking state in which they are relaxed with their eyes closed into **stage 1 sleep,** which is characterized by relatively rapid, low-amplitude brain waves. This is actually a stage of transition between wakefulness and sleep and lasts only a few minutes. During stage 1, images sometimes appear, as if we were viewing still photos, although this is not true dreaming, which occurs later in the night.

As sleep becomes deeper, people enter **stage 2 sleep,** which makes up about half of the total sleep of those in their early 20s and is characterized by a slower, more regular wave pattern. However, there are also momentary interruptions of sharply pointed, spiky waves that are called, because of their configuration, *sleep spindles*. It becomes increasingly difficult to awaken a person from sleep as stage 2 progresses.

As people drift into **stage 3 sleep,** the deepest stage, the brain waves become slower, with higher peaks and lower valleys in the wave pattern. During stage 3, people are least responsive to outside stimulation.

As you can see in Figure 3, stage 3 sleep is most likely to occur during the early part of the night. In the first half of the night, sleep is dominated by stage 3. The second half is characterized by stages 1 and 2–as well as a fourth stage, REM sleep, during which dreams occur.

stage 1 sleep The state of transition between wakefulness and sleep, characterized by relatively rapid, low-amplitude brain waves. (Module 12)

stage 2 sleep A sleep deeper than that of stage 1, characterized by a slower, more regular wave pattern, along with momentary interruptions of "sleep spindles." (Module 12)

stage 3 sleep The deepest stage of sleep, during which we are least responsive to outside stimulation. (Module 12)

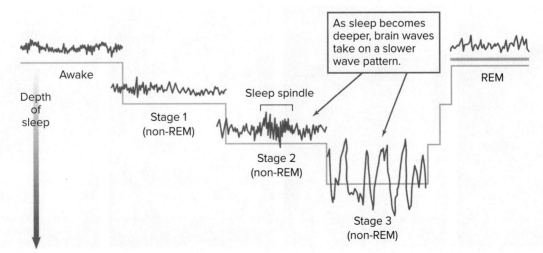

FIGURE 2 Brain-wave patterns (measured by an EEG apparatus) vary significantly during the different stages of sleep (adapted from Hobson, [1989]). As sleep moves from stage 1 through stage 3, brain waves become slower. During REM sleep, however, the fast wave patterns are similar to relaxed wakefulness.

Source: Adapted from Hobson, J. A. (1989). *Sleep.* New York: W. H. Freeman.

FIGURE 3 During the night, the typical sleeper passes through all three stages of sleep and several REM periods.

Source: Adapted from Hartmann, E. (1967). *The biology of dreaming.* Springfield, IL: Charles C. Thomas Publisher.

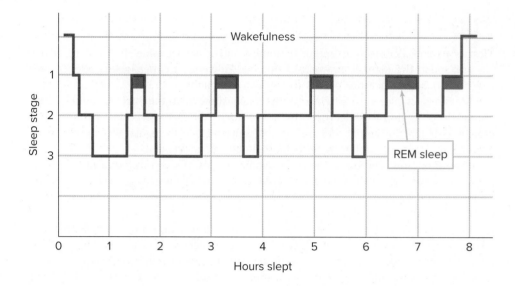

REM Sleep: The Paradox of Sleep

Several times a night, when sleepers have cycled back to a shallower state of sleep, something curious happens. Their heart rate increases and becomes irregular, their blood pressure rises, and their breathing rate increases. Most characteristic of this period is the back-and-forth movement of their eyes, as if they were watching an action-filled movie. This period of sleep is called **rapid eye movement, or REM, sleep,** and it contrasts with stages 1 through 3, which are collectively labeled *non-REM* (or *NREM*) sleep. REM sleep occupies a little more than 20% of adults' total sleeping time.

Paradoxically, while heart rate, blood pressure, and breathing increase during REM sleep, the major muscles of the body appear to be paralyzed. In addition, and most important, REM sleep is usually accompanied by dreams, which—whether or not people remember them—are experienced by *everyone* during some part of their night's sleep. Although some dreaming occurs in non-REM stages of sleep, dreams

rapid eye movement (REM) sleep Sleep occupying 20% of an adult's sleeping time, characterized by increased heart rate, blood pressure, and breathing rate; erections; eye movements; and the experience of dreaming. (Module 12)

 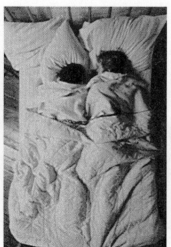  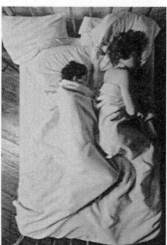

People progress through three distinct stages of sleep during a night's rest spread over cycles lasting about 90 minutes. REM sleep occupies only 20% of adults' sleeping time. These photos, taken at different times of night, show the synchronized patterns of a couple accustomed to sleeping in the same bed.

©Ted Spagna/Science Source

are most likely to occur in the REM period, where they are the most vivid and easily remembered (Leclair-Visonneau et al., 2011; Manni & Terzaghi, 2013; Sikka et al., 2017).

 Study Alert
Differentiate the stages of sleep (stage 1, stage 2, stage 3, and REM sleep), which produce different brain-wave patterns.

There is good reason to believe that REM sleep plays a critical role in everyday human functioning. People deprived of REM sleep–by being awakened every time they begin to display the physiological signs of that stage–show a *rebound effect* when allowed to rest undisturbed. With this rebound effect, REM-deprived sleepers spend significantly more time in REM sleep than they normally would. In addition, REM sleep may play a role in learning and memory, allowing us to rethink and restore information and emotional experiences that we've had during the day (Nishida et al., 2009; Walker & van der Helm, 2009; Nielsen et al., 2015).

From the perspective of...

An Educator How might you use the findings in sleep research to maximize student learning?

©Andersen Ross/Blend Images/Getty Images

Why Do We Sleep, and How Much Sleep Is Necessary?

Sleep is a requirement for normal human functioning, although, surprisingly, the reason why has long baffled scientists. It certainly is reasonable to expect that our bodies would require a tranquil "rest and relaxation" period to revitalize themselves, and experiments with rats show that total sleep deprivation results in death. But why?

One explanation, based on an evolutionary perspective, suggests that sleep permitted our ancestors to conserve energy at night, a time when food was relatively hard to come by. Consequently, they were better able to forage for food when the sun was up.

A second explanation for why we sleep is that sleep restores and replenishes our brains and bodies. For instance, the reduced activity of the brain during non-REM sleep may give neurons in the brain a chance to repair themselves. That reduced activity may also weaken connections among particular nerve cells to conserve energy, which has the effect of aiding memory. Furthermore, the onset of REM sleep stops the release of neurotransmitters called *monoamines* and so permits receptor cells to get some necessary rest and to increase their sensitivity during periods of wakefulness (Steiger, 2007; Bub, Buckhalt, & El-Sheikh, 2011; Tononi & Cirelli, 2013). (Also see *Applying Psychology in the 21st Century*).

Finally, sleep may be essential because it assists physical growth and brain development in children. For example, the release of growth hormones is associated with deep sleep (Peterfi et al., 2010; Grigg-Damberger, 2017).

Still, these explanations remain speculative, and there is no definitive answer as to why sleep is essential. What is increasingly clear is that sleep serves multiple functions and that without sleep, we will eventually die (Stickgold, 2015).

APPLYING PSYCHOLOGY IN THE 21ST CENTURY

SLEEPING TO FORGET

Do we sleep to forget?

An increasing amount of evidence suggests that one primary purpose of sleep may be to help us forget. In this view, sleep allows the brain to eliminate unnecessary information that accumulates throughout the day so that it doesn't become burdensome or confusing, a process called *reverse learning* (Heller et al., 2014).

In support of the reverse-learning view, one study hypothesized that the day's activities trigger increased synaptic growth, which can drown out the strong signal of neural impulses with excessive noise. Our brains must therefore prune back these new connections, the hypothesis goes, which it does while we sleep.

Evidence for this hypothesis comes from research in which investigators examined thin slices of brain tissue taken from mice, some of which had been asleep and some of which had been awake and alert. Looking closely at the size and shape of the synapses, the researchers found an 18% reduction in the size of the synapses in the sleeping mice's brain tissue relative to those of the awake mice (de Vivo et al., 2017).

Another study examined the brains of live mice. The researchers monitored the presence of surface proteins on the mice's

©Stockbyte/Getty Images

brains while they were awake and after they fell asleep and noted a drop in these proteins during sleep, which was consistent with a reduction in synapses (Diering et al., 2017).

To see how synaptic pruning affects what mice remember, the researchers put mice in a cage that delivered a mild but unpleasant electric shock to their feet if they walked on a particular section of the

floor. Some of those mice were then given a chemical known to inhibit synaptic pruning, and then all of the mice were allowed to sleep.

When they were put back in the same cage the next day, all of the mice unsurprisingly acted fearful, refusing to walk across the floor that had previously shocked them. But a difference emerged when the mice were placed in a different cage. The mice that had not been given the chemical explored this new environment curiously, but the mice whose synaptic pruning had been inhibited reacted with fear again, as if they were in the original cage. The researchers concluded that the inhibited mice were unable to focus on the specific attributes of the cage in which they had received shocks. In short, the lack of pruning left them with excessive synapses that produced confused memories (Diering et al., 2017).

While more research needs to be done to fully understand the association of sleep with synaptic pruning, these early findings lend some tentative weight to the process of reverse learning and its role in sleep.

> **RETHINK**
> - Even if synaptic pruning is definitively shown to occur during sleep, would that mean that synaptic pruning is the purpose of sleep? Why or why not?
> - Based on your own experience, how does a good night of sleep affect your memory?

Furthermore, scientists have been unable to establish just how much sleep is absolutely required. Most people today sleep between 7 and 8 hours each night, which is 3 hours a night *less* than people slept a hundred years ago (see Figure 4).

In addition, individuals vary widely, with some people needing as little as 3 hours of sleep. Still, survey data shows that for most people, the more sleep they get, the greater their sense of well-being (McCarthy & Brown, 2015).

Men and women sleep differently. Women typically fall asleep more quickly, they sleep for longer periods and more deeply than men do, and they get up fewer times in the night. On the other hand, men have fewer concerns about the amount of sleep they get than women do, even though they get less sleep. Furthermore, sleep requirements vary over the course of a lifetime: As they age, people generally need less and less sleep (Monk et al., 2011; Petersen, 2011).

People who participate in sleep deprivation experiments, in which they are kept awake for stretches as long as 200 hours, show no lasting effects. It's no fun—they feel weary and irritable, can't concentrate, and show a loss of creativity, even after only minor deprivation. They also show a decline in logical reasoning ability. However, after being allowed to sleep normally, they bounce back quickly and are able to perform at

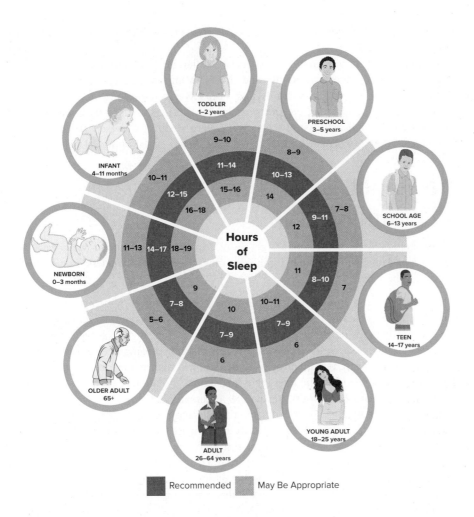

FIGURE 4 Although most people sleep between 7 and 8 hours each night, the amount that individuals need varies a great deal. Where would you place yourself on this graph, and why do you think you need more or less sleep than others?
Source: Adapted from National Sleep Foundation. (2017). How Much Sleep Do We Really Need?

NEUROSCIENCE IN YOUR LIFE: WHY ARE WE SO EMOTIONAL WHEN WE DON'T GET ENOUGH SLEEP?

After a restless night, many people feel increased stress and overreact to events in their lives the next day. Recent research has now identified the neural basis for these reactions. For example, in one study, participants were kept awake all night and then asked to perform an experiment involving exposure to emotional and neutral images. Participants who were sleep deprived reacted to the neutral images as if they were emotional, and they had less connectivity between the amygdala (a region of the brain that processes emotion) and the anterior cingulate cortex (a region of frontal cortex important for emotional regulation). The green in the scan below shows the area of anterior cingulate that has greater connectivity to the amygdala for sleep-rested than sleep-deprived participants. These findings suggest that sleep loss increases emotional reactivity by interfering with our ability to control our emotions (Simon et al., 2015).

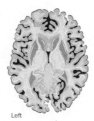

Left

Source: Adapted from Simon, E. B., Oren, N., Sharon, H., Kirschner, A., Goldway, N., Okon-Singer, H., . . . Hendler, T. (2016). Losing neutrality: The neural basis of impaired emotional control without sleep. *Journal of Neuroscience, 35*(38), 13194-13205.

predeprivation levels after just a few days (Mograss et al., 2009; Jackson et al., 2013; Maturana et al., 2015).

In short, as far as we know, most people suffer no permanent consequences of such temporary sleep deprivation. But–and this is an important but–a lack of sleep can make us feel edgy, slow our reaction time, and lower our performance on academic and physical tasks. In addition, we put ourselves and others at risk when we carry out routine activities, such as driving, when we're very sleepy (Anderson & Home, 2006; Morad et al., 2009; Simon et al., 2017). (Also see *Neuroscience in Your Life*.)

The Function and Meaning of Dreaming

I was being chased, and I couldn't get away. My attacker, wearing a mask, was carrying a long knife. He was gaining ground on me. I felt it was hopeless; I knew I was about to be killed.

If you have had a similar dream, you know how utterly convincing are the panic and fear that the events in the dream can bring about. *Nightmares* are unusually frightening dreams. Perhaps surprisingly, they occur fairly often. In one survey, almost half of a group of college students who kept records of their dreams over a 2-week period reported having at least one nightmare. Furthermore, nightmares are associated with negative experiences during the day, including worry and anxiety (Schredl & Reinhard, 2011; Cranston et al., 2017; Reks, Sheaves, & Freeman, 2017).

However, most of the 150,000 dreams the average person experiences by the age of 70 are much less dramatic. They typically encompass everyday events such as going to the supermarket, working at the office, and preparing a meal. Students dream about going to class; professors dream about lecturing. Dental patients dream of getting their teeth drilled; dentists dream of drilling the wrong tooth. The English have tea with the queen in their dreams; in the United States, people go to a bar with the president (Schredl & Piel, 2005; Taylor & Bryant, 2007; Nosek et al., 2015). Figure 5 shows the most common themes found in people's dreams.

But what, if anything, do all these dreams mean? Whether dreams have a specific significance and function is a question that scientists have considered for many years, and they have developed the three alternative theories we discuss below (and summarize in Figure 6).

PSYCHOANALYTIC EXPLANATIONS OF DREAMS: DO DREAMS REPRESENT UNCONSCIOUS WISH FULFILLMENT?

Using psychoanalytic theory, Sigmund Freud viewed dreams as a guide to the unconscious (Freud, 1900). In his **unconscious wish fulfillment theory,** he proposed that dreams represent unconscious wishes that dreamers desire to see fulfilled. To Freud,

Study Alert
Use Figure 6 to learn the differences between the three main explanations of dreaming.

unconscious wish fulfillment theory
Sigmund Freud's theory that dreams represent unconscious wishes that dreamers desire to see fulfilled. (Module 12)

FIGURE 5 Although dreams tend to be subjective to the person having them, common elements frequently occur in everyone's dreams. Why do you think so many common dreams are unpleasant and so few are pleasant? Do you think this tells us anything about the function of dreams?
Source: Adapted from Schneider, A., & Domhoff, G. W. (2015). The quantitative study of dreams.

Thematic Event	Percentage of Dreams Reporting at Least One Event	
	Males	Females
Aggression	47%	44%
Friendliness	38	42
Sexuality	12	4
Misfortune	36	33
Success	15	8
Failure	15	10

Theory	Basic Explanation	Meaning of Dreams	Is Meaning of Dream Disguised?
Unconscious wish fulfillment theory (Freud)	Psychoanalytical explanation in which dreams represent unconscious wishes the dreamer wants to fulfill	Latent content reveals unconscious wishes.	Yes, by manifest content of dreams
Dreams-for-survival theory	Evolutionary explanation in which information relevant to daily survival is reconsidered and reprocessed	Clues to everyday concerns about survival	Not necessarily
Activation-synthesis theory	Neuroscience explanation in which dreams are the result of random activation of various memories, which are tied together in a logical story line	Dream scenario that is constructed is related to dreamer's concerns	Not necessarily

FIGURE 6 Three theories of dreams. As researchers have yet to agree on the fundamental meaning of dreams, several theories about dreaming have emerged.

the *manifest content* of the dream is what we remember and report about the dream—its story line. The manifest content, however, disguises the *latent content,* which includes the actual, underlying wishes that the dream represents. Because the underlying wishes (the latent content) are threatening to the dreamer, they are hidden in the dream's story line (the manifest content).

To Freud, it was important to pierce the armor of a dream's manifest content to understand its true meaning. To do this, Freud tried to get people to discuss their dreams, associating symbols in the dreams with events in the past. He also suggested that certain common symbols with universal meanings appear in dreams. For example, to Freud, dreams in which a person is flying symbolize a wish for sexual intercourse. (See Figure 7 for other common symbols.)

Many psychologists reject Freud's view that dreams typically represent unconscious wishes and that particular objects and events in a dream are symbolic. Rather, they believe that the direct, overt action of a dream is the focal point of its meaning. For example, a dream in which we are walking down a long hallway to take an exam for which we haven't studied does not relate to unconscious, unacceptable wishes. Instead, it simply may mean that we are concerned about an impending test. Even more complex dreams can often be interpreted in terms of everyday concerns and stress (Cartwright, Agargum, & Kirkby, 2006; Boag, 2017).

Moreover, some dreams reflect events occurring in the dreamer's environment as he or she is sleeping. For example, sleeping participants in one experiment were

Symbol (Manifest Content of Dream)	Interpretation (Latent Content)
Climbing up a stairway, crossing a bridge, riding an elevator, flying in an airplane, walking down a long hallway, entering a room, train traveling through a tunnel	Sexual intercourse
Apples, peaches, grapefruits	Breasts
Bullets, fire, snakes, sticks, umbrellas, guns, , hoses knives	Male sex organs
Ovens, boxes, tunnels, closets, caves, bottles, ships	Female sex organs

FIGURE 7 According to Freud, dreams contain common symbols with universal meanings.
©Digital Vision

sprayed with water while they were dreaming. Those unlucky volunteers reported more dreams involving water than did a comparison group of participants who were left to sleep undisturbed (Dement & Wolpert, 1958). Similarly, it is not unusual to wake up to find that the doorbell that was heard ringing in a dream is actually an alarm clock telling us it is time to get up.

However, PET brain scan research does lend a degree of support for the wish fulfillment view. For instance, the limbic and paralimbic regions of the brain, which are associated with emotion and motivation, are particularly active during REM sleep. At the same time, the association areas of the prefrontal cortex, which control logical analysis and attention, are inactive during REM sleep. The high activation of emotional and motivational centers of the brain during dreaming makes it more plausible that dreams may reflect unconscious wishes and instinctual needs, as Freud suggested (Occhionero, 2004; Wehrle et al., 2007; Perogamvros & Schwartz, 2015).

EVOLUTIONARY EXPLANATIONS OF DREAMS: DREAMS-FOR-SURVIVAL THEORY

dreams-for-survival theory The theory suggesting that dreams permit information that is critical for our daily survival to be reconsidered and reprocessed during sleep. (Module 12)

According to the **dreams-for-survival theory,** which is based in the evolutionary perspective, dreams permit us to reconsider and reprocess during sleep information that is critical for our daily survival. Dreaming is considered an inheritance from our animal ancestors, whose small brains were unable to sift sufficient information during waking hours. Consequently, dreaming provided a mechanism that permitted the processing of information 24 hours a day.

In the dreams-for-survival theory, dreams represent concerns about our daily lives, illustrating our uncertainties, indecisions, ideas, and desires. Dreams are seen, then, as consistent with everyday living. Rather than being disguised wishes, as Freud suggested, they represent key concerns growing out of our daily experiences (Ross, 2006; Horton, 2011).

Research supports the dreams-for-survival theory, suggesting that certain dreams permit people to focus on and to consolidate memories, particularly dreams that pertain to "how-to-do-it" memories related to motor skills. For example, rats seem to dream about mazes that they learned to run through during the day, at least according to the patterns of brain activity that appear while they are sleeping (Stickgold et al., 2001; Kuriyama, Stickgold, & Walker, 2004; Smith, 2006).

A similar phenomenon appears to work in humans. For instance, in one experiment, participants learned a visual memory task late in the day. They were then sent to bed but awakened at certain times during the night. When they were awakened at times that did not interrupt dreaming, their performance on the memory task typically improved the next day. But when they were awakened during rapid eye movement (REM) sleep–the stage of sleep when people dream–their performance declined. The implication is that dreaming, at least when it is uninterrupted, can play a role in helping us remember material to which we have been previously exposed (Marshall & Born, 2007; Nishida et al., 2009; Blechner, 2013).

NEUROSCIENCE EXPLANATIONS OF DREAMS: ACTIVATION-SYNTHESIS THEORY

activation-synthesis theory Hobson's theory that the brain produces random electrical energy during REM sleep that stimulates memories stored in the brain. (Module 12

Using the neuroscience perspective, psychiatrist J. Allan Hobson has proposed the activation-synthesis theory of dreams. The **activation-synthesis theory** focuses on the random electrical energy that the brain produces during REM sleep, possibly as a result of changes in the production of particular neurotransmitters. This electrical energy randomly stimulates memories stored in the brain. Because we have a need to make sense of our world even while asleep, the brain takes these chaotic memories and weaves them into a logical story line, filling in the gaps to produce a rational scenario (Hobson, 2005; Hangya et al., 2011).

Activation-synthesis theory has been refined by the *activation information modulation (AIM)* theory. According to AIM, dreams are initiated in the brain's pons, which sends random signals to the cortex. Areas of the cortex that are involved in particular waking behaviors are related to the content of dreams. For example, areas of the brain related to vision are involved in the visual aspects of the dream, whereas areas of the brain related to movement are involved in aspects of the dream related to motion (Hobson, 2007).

Activation-synthesis and AIM theories do not entirely reject the view that dreams reflect unconscious wishes. They suggest that the particular scenario a dreamer produces is not random but instead is a clue to the dreamer's fears, emotions, and concerns. Hence, what starts out as a random process culminates in something meaningful.

Sleep Disturbances: Slumbering Problems

At one time or another, almost all of us have difficulty sleeping–a condition known as insomnia. It could be due to a particular situation, such as the breakup of a relationship, concern about a test score, or the loss of a job. Some cases of insomnia, however, have no obvious cause. Some people are simply unable to fall asleep easily, or they go to sleep readily but wake up frequently during the night. Insomnia is a problem that afflicts as many as one-third of all people. Women and older adults are more likely to suffer from insomnia, as well as people who are unusually thin or are depressed (Henry et al., 2008; Karlson et al., 2013; Ong, 2017).

Some people who *think* they have sleeping problems actually are mistaken. For example, researchers in sleep laboratories have found that some people who report being up all night actually fall asleep in 30 minutes and stay asleep all night. Furthermore, some people with insomnia accurately recall sounds that they heard while they were asleep, which gives them the impression that they were awake during the night (Semler & Harvey, 2005; Yapko, 2006).

Other sleep problems are less common than insomnia, although they are still widespread. For instance, some 20 million people suffer from sleep apnea. *Sleep apnea* is a condition in which a person has difficulty breathing while sleeping. The result is disturbed, fitful sleep and a significant loss of REM sleep, as the person is constantly reawakened when the lack of oxygen becomes great enough to trigger a waking response. Some people with apnea wake as many as 500 times during the course of a night, although they may not even be aware that they have wakened. Not surprisingly, such disturbed sleep results in extreme fatigue the next day. Sleep apnea also may play a role in *sudden infant death syndrome (SIDS)*, a mysterious killer of seemingly normal infants who die while sleeping (Tippin, Sparks, & Rizzo, 2009; Arimoto et al., 2011; Bjornsdottir et al., 2015).

Night terrors are sudden awakenings from non-REM sleep that are accompanied by extreme fear, panic, and strong physiological arousal. Usually occurring in stage 3 sleep, night terrors may be so frightening that a sleeper awakens with a shriek. Although night terrors initially produce great agitation, victims usually can get back to sleep fairly quickly. They are far less frequent than nightmares, and, unlike nightmares, they typically occur during slow-wave, non-REM sleep. They occur most frequently in children between the ages of 3 and 8 (Lowe, Humphreys, & Williams, 2007).

Narcolepsy is uncontrollable sleeping that occurs for short periods while a person is awake. No matter what the activity–holding a heated conversation, exercising, or driving–a narcoleptic will suddenly fall asleep. People with narcolepsy go directly from wakefulness to REM sleep, skipping the other stages. The causes of narcolepsy are not known, although there could be a genetic component, because narcolepsy runs in families (Ervik, Abdelnoor, & Heier, 2006; Nishino, 2007; Billiard, 2008; Zamarian et al., 2015).

PsychTech

Surveys show that use of laptops, tablets, texting, or other technologies in the hour prior to going to bed is associated with sleeping problems.

Sleepwalking and sleeptalking are more common in children than adults, and they both occur during stage 3 of sleep.
©Don Smith/Alamy

We know relatively little about sleeptalking and sleepwalking, two sleep disturbances that are usually harmless. Both occur during stage 3 sleep and are more common in children than in adults. Sleeptalkers and sleepwalkers usually have a vague consciousness of the world around them, and a sleepwalker may be able to walk with agility around obstructions in a crowded room. Unless a sleepwalker wanders into a dangerous environment, sleepwalking typically poses little risk. And the common idea that it's dangerous to wake a sleepwalker? It's just superstition (Lee-Chiong, 2006; Licis et al., 2011; Haridi et al., 2017).

Circadian Rhythms: Life Cycles

circadian rhythms Biological processes that occur regularly on approximately a 24-hour cycle. (Module 12)

The fact that we cycle back and forth between wakefulness and sleep is one example of the body's circadian rhythms. **Circadian rhythms** (from the Latin *circa diem*, or "about a day") are biological processes that occur regularly on approximately a 24-hour cycle. Sleeping and waking, for instance, occur naturally to the beat of an internal pacemaker that works on a cycle of about 24 hours. Several other bodily functions, such as body temperature, hormone production, and blood pressure, also follow circadian rhythms (Beersma & Gordijn, 2007; Blatter & Cajochen, 2007; Labrecque & Cermakian, 2015).

Circadian cycles are complex, and they involve a variety of behaviors. For instance, sleepiness occurs not just in the evening but throughout the day in regular patterns, with most of us getting drowsy in mid-afternoon–regardless of whether or not we have eaten a heavy lunch. By making an afternoon siesta part of their everyday habit, people in several cultures take advantage of the body's natural inclination to sleep at this time (Takahashi et al., 2004; Reilly & Waterhouse, 2007; Egan et al., 2017).

The brain's *suprachiasmatic nucleus (SCN)* controls our circadian rhythms, but there are a number of circadian "clocks" associated with specific parts of the body. For instance, circadian rhythms speed up the heart before dawn to prepare us for the day's challenges. Similarly, the release and retention of various substances in the kidneys are affected by circadian rhythms. Even the processing of information in various areas of the brain may be affected by circadian rhythms and help shape how we perceive the world (Hickok, 2015; Summa & Turek, 2015).

Bright lights may counter some of the symptoms of seasonal affective disorder, which occur during the winter.
©Image Point Fr/Shutterstock

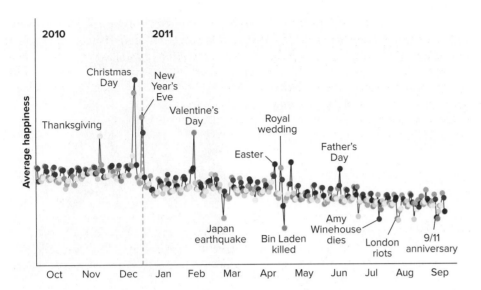

FIGURE 8 A year of tweets shows that Fridays (orange dots), Saturdays (red dots), and Sundays (dark blue dots) are happier than weekdays. The happiest days are holidays, and the unhappiest days are associated with bad news.
Source: Adapted from Dodds, P. & Danforth, C. (2011). in Miller, G. Social scientists wade into the Tweet stream. *Science, 333,* 1814-1815.

Furthermore, the relative amount of light and darkness, which varies with the seasons of the year, also plays a role in regulating circadian rhythms. In fact, some people experience *seasonal affective disorder,* a form of severe depression in which feelings of despair and hopelessness increase during the winter and lift during the rest of the year. The disorder appears to be a result of the brevity and gloom of winter days. Daily exposure to bright lights is sometimes sufficient to improve the mood of those with this disorder (Kasof, 2009; Monteleone, Martiadis, & Maj, 2011; Patten et al., 2017).

People's moods also follow regular patterns. By examining more than 500 million tweets using publicly available Twitter records, a team of psychologists found that words with positive associations (fantastic, super) and negative associations (afraid, mad) followed regular patterns. Across the globe and among different cultures, people were happier in the morning, less so during the day, with a rebound in the evening. Moods are also happier on certain days of the week: we're happier on weekends and holidays. Finally, positive emotions increase from late December to late June as the days get longer, and negative emotions increase as days get shorter (see Figure 8; Golder & Macy, 2011).

Furthermore, there seem to be optimal times for carrying out various tasks. Most adults are at their peak for carrying out cognitive tasks in the late morning. In contrast, focus and concentration on academic tasks declines throughout the afternoon. On the other hand, some research findings show that creativity increases in the evening when people are tired. It may be that fatigue decreases inhibitions, allowing for more creative thought (Matchock & Mordkoff, 2009; Wieth & Zacks, 2011; Shellenbarger, 2012).

Finally, health issues are more apt to appear at certain times of the day. For instance, heart attacks and strokes occur most frequently and are most severe between 6:00 A.M. and noon. Asthma attacks and heartburn are more common during the evening hours (Beck, 2015).

Daydreams: Dreams Without Sleep

It is the stuff of magic: Our past mistakes can be wiped out and the future filled with noteworthy accomplishments. Fame, happiness, and wealth can be ours. In the next moment, though, the most horrible tragedies can occur, leaving us devastated, alone, and penniless.

The source of these scenarios is **daydreams,** fantasies people construct while awake. Unlike dreaming that occurs during sleep, daydreams are more under people's control. Therefore, their content is often related to immediate events in the environment than is the content of the dreams that occur during sleep. Although they may include sexual content, daydreams also pertain to the full gamut of activities or events that are

daydreams Fantasies that people construct while awake. (Module 12)

Daydreams are fantasies that people construct while they are awake. What are the similarities and differences between daydreams and night dreams?
©Aleksandar Mijatovic/Shutterstock

relevant to a person's life. While we are daydreaming, we are still experiencing waking consciousness. However, our awareness of the environment around us declines.

People vary considerably in the amount of daydreaming they do. For example, around 2% to 4% of the population spend at least half their free time fantasizing. Although most people daydream much less frequently, almost everyone fantasizes to some degree. In fact, a study in which experimenters sent texts at random times found that the participants were thinking about something other than what they were doing about half the time (Singer, 2006; Pisarik, Rowell, & Currie, 2013; Reddy, 2016).

The brain is surprisingly active during daydreaming. For example, several areas of the brain that are associated with complex problem solving become activated during daydreaming. In fact, daydreaming may be the only time these areas are activated simultaneously, suggesting that daydreaming may lead to insights about problems that we are grappling with (Fleck et al., 2008; Kounios et al., 2008; Carciofo et al., 2017).

Furthermore, daydreaming may contain elements of *inner speech*, in which people talk to themselves in their heads. Inner speech may help us to plan, be creative, and regulate our emotions (Ren, Wang, & Jarrold, 2016; Alderson-Day et al., 2017; Fernyhough, 2017).

Some scientists see a link between daydreaming and dreams during sleep. The content of daydreams and dreams show many parallels, and the brain areas and processes involved in daydreaming and dreams during sleep are related (Domhoff, 2011).

BECOMING AN INFORMED CONSUMER
of Psychology

Sleeping Better

Do you have trouble sleeping? You're not alone—70 million people in the United States have sleep problems. Half of Americans aged 19 to 29 report they rarely or never get a good night's sleep on weekdays, and nearly a third of working adults get less than 6 hours of sleep a night (Randall, 2012).

For those of us who spend hours tossing and turning in bed, psychologists studying sleep disturbances have a number of suggestions for overcoming insomnia. Here are some ideas (Finley & Cowley, 2005; Buysse et al., 2011; Reddy, 2013):

- *Exercise during the day (at least 6 hours before bedtime).* Not surprisingly, it helps to be tired before going to sleep! Moreover, learning systematic relaxation techniques and biofeedback can help you unwind from the day's stresses and tensions.
- *Avoid long naps—but consider taking short ones.* If you have trouble sleeping at night, it's best to avoid long naps. On the other hand, a short nap lasting 10 to 20 minutes may be ideal to boost energy and increase alertness. In fact, research shows that, at least in preschool children, midday naps improve recall of material learned earlier in the day—although we don't yet know if that applies to older individuals (Kurdziel, Duclos, & Spencer, 2013; Weir, 2016).
- *Choose a regular bedtime and stick to it.* Adhering to a habitual schedule helps your internal timing mechanisms regulate your body more effectively.
- *Avoid drinks with caffeine after lunch.* The effects of beverages such as coffee, tea, and some soft drinks can linger for as long as 8 to 12 hours after they are consumed.
- *Drink a glass of warm milk at bedtime.* Your grandparents were right when they dispensed this advice: Milk contains the chemical tryptophan, which helps people fall asleep.
- *Avoid sleeping pills.* Even though 25% of U.S. adults report having taken medication for sleep in the previous year and some 60 *million* sleeping aid prescriptions are filled annually, in the long run sleep medications can do more harm than good because they disrupt the normal sleep cycle. Rather than sleeping pills, try therapy; it's been proven to work better than drugs (DeAngelis, 2016).
- *Try* not *to sleep.* This approach works because people often have difficulty falling asleep because they are trying so hard. A better strategy is to go to bed only when you feel tired. If you don't get to sleep within 10 minutes, leave the bedroom and do something else, returning to bed only when you feel sleepy. Continue this process all night if necessary. But get up at your usual hour in the morning, and don't take any naps during the day. After 3 or 4 weeks, most people become conditioned to associate their beds with sleep—and fall asleep rapidly at night (Smith & Lazarus, 2001).

For long-term problems with sleep, you might consider visiting a sleep disorders center. For information on accredited clinics, consult the American Academy of Sleep Medicine at www.aasmnet.org.

RECAP/EVALUATE/RETHINK

RECAP

LO 12-1 What are the different states of consciousness?

- Consciousness is a person's awareness of the sensations, thoughts, and feelings at a given moment. Waking consciousness can vary from more active to more passive states.
- Altered states of consciousness include naturally occurring sleep and dreaming, as well as hypnotic and drug-induced states.

LO 12-2 What happens when we sleep, and what are the meaning and function of dreams?

- The brain is active throughout the night, and sleep proceeds through stages 1 through 3, which are identified by unique patterns of brain waves.

- REM (rapid eye movement) sleep is characterized by an increase in heart rate, a rise in blood pressure, an increase in the rate of breathing, and, in males, erections. Dreams most often occur during this stage.
- According to Freud's psychoanalytic approach, dreams have both a manifest content (an apparent story line) and a latent content (a true meaning). He suggested that the latent content provides a guide to a dreamer's unconscious, revealing unfulfilled wishes or desires.
- The dreams-for-survival theory, grounded in an evolutionary perspective, suggests that information relevant to daily survival is reconsidered and reprocessed in dreams.
- Taking a neuroscience approach, the activation-synthesis theory proposes that dreams are a result of random electrical energy that stimulates different memories, which then are woven into a coherent story line.

LO 12-3 What are the major sleep disorders, and how can they be treated?

- Insomnia is a sleep disorder characterized by difficulty sleeping. Sleep apnea is a condition in which people have difficulty sleeping and breathing at the same time. People with narcolepsy have an uncontrollable urge to sleep. Sleepwalking and sleeptalking are relatively harmless.

LO 12-4 How much do we daydream?

- Wide individual differences exist in the amount of time devoted to daydreaming. Almost everyone daydreams or fantasizes to some degree.

EVALUATE

1. _____ is the term used to describe our understanding of the world external to us, as well as our own internal world.
2. A great deal of neural activity goes on during sleep. True or false?
3. Dreams most often occur in _____ sleep.
4. _____ _____ are internal bodily processes that occur on a daily cycle.
5. Freud's theory of unconscious _____ _____ states that the actual wishes an individual expresses in dreams are disguised because they are threatening to the person's conscious awareness.

6. Match the theory of dreaming with its definition.
   1. activation-synthesis theory
   2. dreams-for-survival theory
   3. dreams as wish fulfillment

   a. Dreams permit important information to be reprocessed during sleep.
   b. The manifest content of dreams disguises the latent content of the dreams.
   c. Electrical energy stimulates random memories, which are woven together to produce dreams.

RETHINK

1. Suppose that a new "miracle pill" allows a person to function with only 1 hour of sleep per night. However, because a night's sleep is so short, a person who takes the pill will never dream again. Knowing what you do about the functions of sleep and dreaming, what would be some advantages and drawbacks of such a pill from a personal standpoint? Would you take such a pill?
2. How would studying the sleep patterns of nonhuman species potentially help us figure out which of the theories of dreaming provides the best account of the functions of dreaming?

Answers to Evaluate Questions

1. Consciousness; 2. true; 3. REM; 4. Circadian rhythms; 5. wish fulfillment; 6. 1-c, 2-a, 3-b

KEY TERMS

consciousness	stage 3 sleep	unconscious wish	activation-synthesis theory
stage 1 sleep	rapid eye movement	fulfillment theory	circadian rhythms
stage 2 sleep	(REM) sleep	dreams-for-survival theory	daydreams

Module 13
Hypnosis and Meditation

You are feeling relaxed and drowsy. You are getting sleepier. Your body is becoming limp. Your eyelids are feeling heavier. Your eyes are closing; you can't keep them open anymore. You are totally relaxed. Now, place your hands above your head. But you will find they are getting heavier and heavier–so heavy you can barely keep them up. In fact, although you are straining as hard as you can, you will be unable to hold them up any longer.

An observer watching this scene would notice a curious phenomenon. Many of the people listening to the voice are dropping their arms to their sides. The reason for this strange behavior? Those people have been hypnotized.

LEARNING OUTCOMES

LO 13-1 What is hypnosis, and are hypnotized people in a different state of consciousness?

LO 13-2 What are the effects of meditation?

Hypnosis: A Trance-Forming Experience?

People under **hypnosis** are in a trancelike state of heightened susceptibility to the suggestions of others. In some respects, it appears that they are asleep. Yet other aspects of their behavior contradict this notion, for people are attentive to the hypnotist's suggestions and may carry out bizarre or silly suggestions.

How is someone hypnotized? Typically, the process follows a series of four steps. First, a person is made comfortable in a quiet environment. Second, the hypnotist explains what is going to happen, such as telling the person that he or she will experience a pleasant, relaxed state. Third, the hypnotist tells the person to concentrate on a specific object or image, such as the hypnotist's moving finger or an image of a calm lake. The hypnotist may have the person concentrate on relaxing different parts of the body, such as the arms, legs, and chest. Fourth, once the subject is in a highly relaxed state, the hypnotist may make suggestions that the person interprets as being produced by hypnosis, such as "Your arms are getting heavy" and "Your eyelids are more difficult to open." Because the person begins to experience these sensations, he or she believes they are caused by the hypnotist and becomes susceptible to the suggestions of the hypnotist.

Despite their compliance when hypnotized, people do not lose all will of their own. They will not perform antisocial behaviors, and they will not carry out self-destructive acts. People will not reveal hidden truths about themselves, and they are capable of lying. Moreover, people cannot be hypnotized against their will–despite popular misconceptions (Raz, 2007; Lynn, Laurence, & Kirsch, 2015).

There are wide variations in people's susceptibility to hypnosis. About 5% to 20% of the population cannot be hypnotized at all, and some 15% are very easily hypnotized. Most people fall somewhere in between. Moreover, the ease with which a person is hypnotized is related to a number of other characteristics. People who are readily hypnotized are also easily absorbed while reading books or listening to music, becoming unaware of what is happening around them, and they often spend an unusual amount of time daydreaming. In sum, then, they show a high ability to concentrate and to become completely absorbed in what they are doing (Rubichi et al., 2005; Benham, Woody, & Wilson, 2006; Parris, 2017).

hypnosis A trancelike state of heightened susceptibility to the suggestions of others. (Module 13)

Despite common misconceptions, people cannot be hypnotized against their will, nor do they lose all will of their own when they are hypnotized. Why, then, do people sometimes behave so unusually when asked to by a hypnotist?
©Erin Painter/Midland Daily News/AP Images

Study Alert

The question of whether hypnosis represents a different state of consciousness or is similar to normal waking consciousness is a key issue.

A DIFFERENT STATE OF CONSCIOUSNESS?

The question of whether hypnosis is a state of consciousness that differs qualitatively from normal waking consciousness is controversial. Some psychologists believe hypnosis represents a state of consciousness that differs significantly from other states. In this view, high suggestibility, increased ability to recall and construct images, and acceptance of suggestions that clearly contradict reality characterize it as a different state. Moreover, people who are hypnotized show certain kinds of changes in electrical activity in the brain. Such electrical changes support the position that hypnosis is a state of consciousness different from normal waking (Fingelkurts, Fingelkurts, & Kallio, 2007; Hinterberger, Schöner, & Halsband, 2011; Keppler, 2017).

In this view, hypnosis represents a state of *divided consciousness*. According to famed hypnosis researcher Ernest Hilgard, hypnosis brings about a *dissociation*, or division, of consciousness into two simultaneous components. In one stream of consciousness, hypnotized people are following the commands of the hypnotist. Yet on another level of consciousness, they are acting as "hidden observers," aware of what is happening to them. For instance, hypnotic subjects may appear to be following the hypnotist's suggestion about feeling no pain, yet in another stream of consciousness, they may be actually aware of the pain.

On the other side of the controversy are psychologists who reject the notion that hypnosis is a state significantly different from normal waking consciousness. They argue that altered brain-wave patterns are not sufficient to demonstrate a qualitative difference because no other specific physiological changes occur when people are in trances. Furthermore, little support exists for the contention that adults can recall memories of childhood events accurately while hypnotized. That lack of evidence suggests that there is nothing qualitatively special about the hypnotic trance (Hongchun & Ming, 2006; Wagstaff, 2009; Wagstaff, Wheatcroft, & Jones, 2011).

The controversy over the nature of hypnosis has led to extreme positions on both sides of the issue. In contrast, more recent approaches suggest that the hypnotic state may best be viewed as lying along a continuum. In this view, hypnosis is neither a totally different state of consciousness nor totally similar to normal waking consciousness (Lynn et al., 2000; Kihlstrom, 2005b; Jamieson, 2007).

THE VALUE OF HYPNOSIS

As arguments about the true nature of hypnosis continue, though, one thing is clear: Hypnosis has been used successfully to solve practical human problems. In fact, psychologists working in many different areas have found hypnosis to be a reliable, effective tool. It has been applied to a number of areas, including the following:

- *Controlling pain.* Patients have had chronic pain reduced through hypnotic suggestion. In addition, people can be taught to hypnotize themselves to relieve pain or gain a sense of control over their symptoms. Hypnosis has proved to be particularly useful during childbirth and dental procedures (Hammond, 2007; Accardi & Milling, 2009; Spiegel, 2015).

- *Reducing smoking.* Although it hasn't been successful in stopping drug and alcohol abuse, hypnosis more frequently helps people stop smoking through hypnotic suggestions that the taste and smell of cigarettes are unpleasant (Elkins et al., 2006; Fuller, 2006; Green, Lynn, & Montgomery, 2008).

- *Treating psychological disorders.* Hypnosis sometimes is used during treatment for psychological disorders. For example, it may be employed to heighten relaxation, reduce anxiety, increase expectations of success, or modify self-defeating thoughts (Iglesias, 2005; Golden, 2006; Etzrodt, 2013).

- *Assisting in law enforcement.* Witnesses and victims are sometimes better able to recall the details of a crime when hypnotized. In one case, a witness to the kidnapping of a group of California schoolchildren was placed under hypnosis and was able to recall all but one digit of the license number on the kidnapper's vehicle. On the other hand, hypnotic recollections may also be inaccurate. Consequently, the legal status of hypnosis is unresolved (Whitehouse et al., 2005; Kazar, 2006; Knight & Meyer, 2007).

- *Improving athletic performance.* Athletes sometimes turn to hypnosis to improve their performance. For example, some baseball players have used hypnotism to increase their concentration when batting, with considerable success (Barker & Jones, 2008; Tramontana, 2011; Carlstedt, 2017).

Meditation: Regulating Our Own State of Consciousness

When traditional practitioners of the ancient Eastern religion of Zen Buddhism want to achieve greater spiritual insight, they turn to a technique that has been used for centuries to alter their state of consciousness. This technique is called meditation.

Meditation is a learned technique for refocusing attention that brings about an altered state of consciousness. Meditation typically consists of the repetition of a *mantra*–a sound, word, or syllable–over and over. In some forms of meditation, the focus is on a picture, flame, or specific part of the body. Regardless of the nature of the particular initial stimulus, the key to the procedure is concentrating on it so thoroughly that the meditator becomes unaware of any outside stimulation and reaches a different state of consciousness.

After meditation, people report feeling thoroughly relaxed. They sometimes relate that they have gained new insights into themselves and the problems they are facing. The long-term practice of meditation may even improve health because of the biological changes it produces. For example, during meditation, oxygen usage decreases, heart rate and blood pressure decline, and brain-wave patterns change (Lee, Kleinman, & Kleinman, 2007; Travis et al., 2009; Steinhubl et al., 2015).

meditation A learned technique for refocusing attention that brings about an altered state of consciousness. (Module 13)

Meditation leads to short-term changes in a person's physiological state, as well as longer-term health benefits.
©Liquidlibrary/Getty Images

Anyone can meditate by following a few simple procedures. The fundamentals include sitting in a quiet room with the eyes closed, breathing deeply and rhythmically, and repeating a word or sound–such as the word *one*–over and over. Practiced twice a day for 20 minutes, the technique is effective in bringing about greater relaxation not only during meditation but afterward. Evidence even supports long-term positive effects of some kinds of meditation, such as in the reduction of heart disease (Mohan, Sharma, & Bijlani, 2011; Shaner et al., 2017; Yadav et al., 2017).

From the perspective of...

A Human Resources Specialist Would you allow (or even encourage) employees to engage in meditation during the workday? Why or why not?

©Dex Image/Getty Images

Many cultures use meditation to alter consciousness, though it can take different forms and serve different purposes, depending on the culture. In fact, one reason psychologists study consciousness is the realization that people in many cultures routinely seek ways to alter their states of consciousness (Walsh & Shapiro, 2006).

Exploring Diversity

Cross-Cultural Routes to Altered States of Consciousness

A group of Native-American Sioux men sit naked in a steaming sweat lodge as a medicine man throws water on sizzling rocks to send billows of scalding steam into the air.

Aztec priests smear themselves with a mixture of crushed poisonous herbs, hairy black worms, scorpions, and lizards. Sometimes they drink the potion.

During the 16th century, a devout Hasidic Jew lies across the tombstone of a celebrated scholar. As he murmurs the name of God repeatedly, he seeks to be possessed by the soul of the dead wise man's spirit. If successful, he will attain a mystical state, and the deceased's words will flow out of his mouth.

Each of these rituals has a common goal: suspension from the bonds of everyday awareness and access to an altered state of consciousness. Although they may seem exotic from the vantage point of many Western cultures, these rituals represent an apparently universal effort to alter consciousness (Bartocci, 2004; Irwin, 2006).

Some scholars suggest that the quest to alter consciousness represents a basic human desire. Whether or not we accept such an extreme view, variations in states of consciousness clearly share some basic characteristics across a variety of cultures. One is an alteration in thinking, which may become shallow, illogical, or otherwise different from normal. In addition, people's sense of time can become disturbed, and their perceptions of the physical world and of themselves may change. They may lose self-control, doing things that they would never otherwise do. Finally, they may feel a sense of *ineffability*—the inability to understand an experience rationally or describe it in words (Finkler, 2004; Travis, 2006).

Of course, realizing that efforts to produce altered states of consciousness are widespread throughout the world's societies does not answer a fundamental question: Is the experience of unaltered states of consciousness similar across different cultures?

Because humans share basic biological commonalities in the ways their brains and bodies are wired, we might assume that the fundamental experience of consciousness is similar across cultures. As a result, we could suppose that consciousness shows some basic similarities across cultures. However, the ways in which certain aspects of consciousness are interpreted and viewed show substantial differences from culture to culture. For example, people in disparate cultures view the experience of the passage of time in varying ways. For instance, Arabs appear to perceive the passage of time more slowly than North Americans do (Alon & Brett, 2007).

Study Alert
Remember that although there are alternate techniques used in meditation, they are all designed to bring about an altered state of consciousness in which attention is refocused.

RECAP/EVALUATE/RETHINK

RECAP

LO 13-1 What is hypnosis, and are hypnotized people in a different state of consciousness?

- Hypnosis produces a state of heightened susceptibility to the suggestions of the hypnotist. Under hypnosis, significant behavioral changes occur, including increased concentration and suggestibility, heightened ability to recall and construct images, lack of initiative, and acceptance of suggestions that clearly contradict reality.

LO 13-2 What are the effects of meditation?

- Meditation is a learned technique for refocusing attention that brings about an altered state of consciousness.
- Different cultures have developed their own unique ways to alter states of consciousness.

EVALUATE

1. _____ is a state of heightened susceptibility to the suggestions of others.

2. A friend tells you, "I once heard of a person who was murdered by being hypnotized and then told to jump from the Golden Gate Bridge!" Could such a thing have happened? Why or why not?

3. _____ is a learned technique for refocusing attention to bring about an altered state of consciousness.

4. Leslie repeats a unique sound, known as a _____ when she engages in meditation.

RETHINK

1. Why do you think people in almost every culture seek ways of altering their states of consciousness?

2. Meditation produces several physical and psychological benefits. Does this suggest that we are physically and mentally burdened in our normal state of waking consciousness? Why?

Answers to Evaluate Questions

1. Hypnosis; 2. no; people who are hypnotized cannot be made to perform self-destructive acts; 3. Meditation; 4. mantra

KEY TERMS

hypnosis
meditation

Module 14
Drug Use: The Highs and Lows of Consciousness

Brittany was desperate. As the rest of her family were grieving over the loss of her grandmother, whose funeral they had just attended, she was searching for cash. She finally found a $5 bill in the purse belonging to her 6-year-old cousin. How low was it to steal from a 6-year-old to buy drugs? she wondered. But it didn't matter. Her head was aching, and her mouth was dry, and she would do anything to buy the drugs she needed to get high.

Like many others caught up in the opioid crisis facing the United States, Brittany's descent into addiction started with a legal drug, Percocet, that she was prescribed to deal with pain following the removal of her wisdom teeth. She didn't know that it was highly addictive, and even after the pain was gone, Brittany kept on craving the drug. It turned her from an honors student to an addict desperate for drugs. (Larsen, 2014)

Drugs of one sort or another are a part of almost everyone's life. From infancy on, most people take vitamins, aspirin, cold-relief medicine. However, these drugs rarely produce an altered state of consciousness.

In contrast, some substances, known as psychoactive drugs, lead to an altered state of consciousness. **Psychoactive drugs** influence a person's emotions, perceptions, and behavior. Yet even this category of drugs is common in most of our lives. If you have ever had a cup of coffee or sipped a beer, you have taken a psychoactive drug. A large number of individuals have used more potent–and more dangerous–psychoactive drugs than coffee and beer (see Figure 1); for instance, surveys find that 41% of high school seniors have used an illegal drug in the last year. In addition, 30% report having been drunk on alcohol. The figures for the adult population are even higher (Johnston et al., 2016).

Of course, drugs vary widely in the effects they have on users, in part because they affect the nervous system in very different ways. Some drugs alter the limbic system, and others affect the operation of specific neurotransmitters across the synapses of neurons. For example, some drugs block or enhance the release of neurotransmitters, others block the receipt or the removal of a neurotransmitter, and still others mimic the effects of a particular neurotransmitter (see Figure 2).

Addictive drugs produce a physiological or psychological dependence (or both) on a drug in the user. When a drug is addictive, withdrawal from the drug leads to a craving for it that may be overpowering and nearly irresistible. In *physiological drug dependence*, the body becomes so accustomed to functioning in the presence of a drug that it cannot function without it. In *psychological drug dependence*, people believe that they need the drug to respond to the stresses of daily living. Although we generally associate addiction with drugs such as heroin, everyday sorts of drugs, such as caffeine (found in coffee) and nicotine (found in cigarettes), have addictive aspects as well (Li, Volkow, & Baler, 2007).

We know surprisingly little about the underlying causes of addiction. One of the problems in identifying those causes is that different drugs (such as alcohol and cocaine) affect the brain in very different ways–yet they may be equally addicting. Furthermore, it takes longer to become addicted to some drugs than to others, even though the ultimate consequences of addiction may be equally grave (Nestler & Malenka, 2004; Smart, 2007; Holmes, 2017).

LEARNING OUTCOME

LO 14-1 What are the major classifications of drugs, and what are their effects?

psychoactive drugs Drugs that influence a person's emotions, perceptions, and behavior. (Module 14)

addictive drugs Drugs that produce a biological or psychological dependence in the user so that withdrawal from them leads to a craving for the drug that, in some cases, may be nearly irresistible. (Module 14)

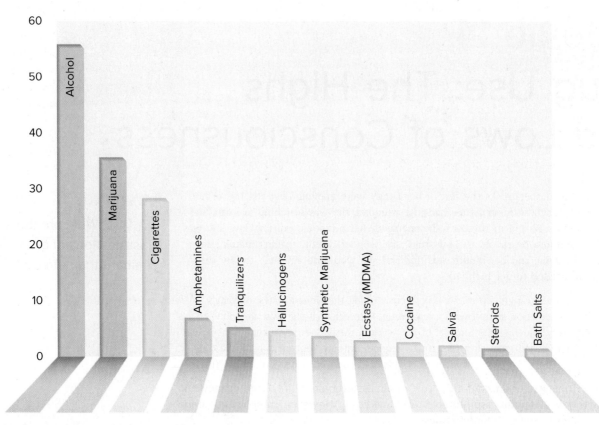

FIGURE 1 How many teenagers use drugs? The results of the most recent comprehensive survey of 14,000 high school seniors across the United States show the percentage of respondents who have used various substances for nonmedical purposes at least once. Can you think of any reasons why teenagers—as opposed to older people—might be particularly likely to use drugs?

Source: Adapted from Johnston, L. D., Miech, R. A., O'Malley, P. M., Bachman, J. G., & Schulenberg, J. E. (2016, December 13). Teen use of any illicit drug other than marijuana at new low, same true for alcohol. University of Michigan News Service: Ann Arbor, MI.

FIGURE 2 Different drugs affect different parts of the nervous system and brain, and each drug functions in one of these specific ways.

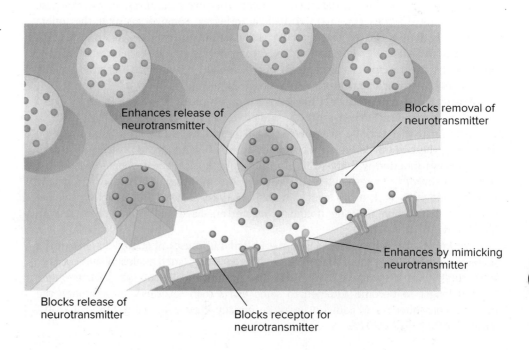

Why do people take drugs in the first place? They do so for many reasons, including the perceived pleasure of the experience. In other words, it simply feels good.

In addition, though, a drug-induced high allows people to escape, at least temporarily, from the everyday pressures of life. And in some cases, people use drugs to attempt to achieve a religious or spiritual state (Korcha et al., 2011; Chapman & Wu, 2015).

In addition, people may be influenced to use drugs by the highly publicized drug use of role models such as movie stars and professional athletes, the easy availability of some illegal drugs, or peer pressure. In some cases, the motive is simply the thrill of trying something new.

Finally, genetic factors may predispose some people to be more susceptible to drugs and to become addicted to them. Regardless of the forces that lead a person to begin using drugs, drug addiction is among the most difficult of all behaviors to modify, even with extensive treatment (Ray & Hutchison, 2007; Vrieze et al., 2013; Reilly et al., 2017).

Because of the difficulty in treating drug problems, most experts believe that the best hope for dealing with the overall societal problem of substance abuse is to prevent people from becoming involved with addictive drugs in the first place. However, there is little accord on how to accomplish this goal.

Even widely employed drug reduction programs–such as D.A.R.E. (Drug Abuse Resistance Education)–are of questionable effectiveness. Used in more than 80% of school districts in the United States, D.A.R.E. consists of a 10-week series of lessons on the dangers of drugs, alcohol, and gangs taught to 5th- and 6th-graders by a police officer. The program is highly popular with school officials, parents, and politicians.

The problem with D.A.R.E.? Repeated careful evaluations have been unable to demonstrate that the D.A.R.E. program is effective in reducing drug use over the long term. In fact, one study even showed that D.A.R.E. graduates were more likely to use marijuana than was a comparison group of nongraduates. On the other hand, D.A.R.E. has updated its curriculum, and some preliminary evidence suggests it may be more successful than the previous version. But the jury is still out on its effectiveness (Lucas, 2008; Vincus et al., 2010; Singh et al., 2011).

PsychTech

Drugs are not the only source of addiction. Increasing evidence suggests that people can develop psychological dependence on the use of technologies, such as social networking sites like Facebook or e-mail.

Study Alert

Use Figure 2 to learn the different ways that drugs produce their effects on a neurological level.

Stimulants: Drug Highs

It's 1:00 A.M., and you still haven't finished reading the last chapter of the text on which you will be tested later in the morning. Feeling exhausted, you turn to the one thing that may help you stay awake for the next 2 hours: a cup of strong black coffee.

If you have ever found yourself in such a position, you have resorted to a major *stimulant,* caffeine, to stay awake. *Caffeine* is one of a number of **stimulants,** drugs whose effect on the central nervous system causes a rise in heart rate, blood pressure, and muscular tension. Caffeine is present not only in coffee; it is an important ingredient in tea, soft drinks, and chocolate as well (see Figure 3).

Caffeine produces several reactions. The major behavioral effects are an increase in attentiveness and a decrease in reaction time. Caffeine can also bring about an improvement in mood, most likely by mimicking the effects of a natural brain chemical, adenosine. Too much caffeine, however, can result in nervousness and insomnia. People can build up a biological dependence on the drug. Regular users who suddenly stop drinking coffee may experience headaches or depression. Many people who drink large amounts of coffee on weekdays have headaches on weekends because of the sudden drop in the amount of caffeine they are consuming (Kennedy & Haskell, 2011; Kamimori et al., 2015).

Nicotine, found in cigarettes, is another common stimulant. The soothing effects of nicotine help explain why cigarette smoking is addictive. Smokers develop a dependence on nicotine, and those who suddenly stop smoking develop a strong craving for the drug. This is not surprising: Nicotine activates neural mechanisms similar to those activated by cocaine, which, as we see in the section on cocaine, is also highly addictive (Haberstick et al., 2005; Ray et al., 2008; Wilcox et al., 2017).

stimulants Drugs that have an arousal effect on the central nervous system, causing a rise in heart rate, blood pressure, and muscular tension. (Module 14)

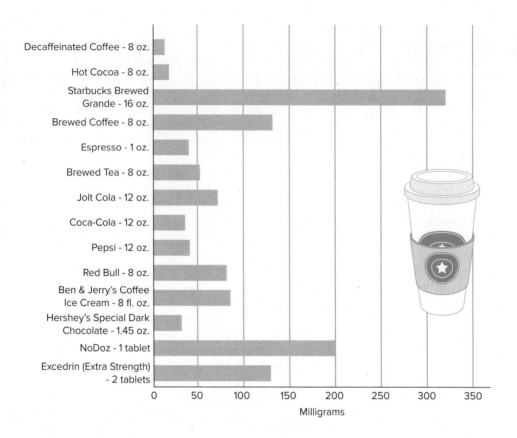

FIGURE 3 How much caffeine do you consume? This chart shows the range of caffeine found in common foods, drinks, and legal drugs.

Source: Adapted from Center for Science in the Public Interest. (2007). *Caffeine content of food & drugs.* Washington, DC: Center for Science in the Public Interest.

AMPHETAMINES

Amphetamines such as dexedrine and benzedrine, popularly known as speed, are strong stimulants. In small quantities, amphetamines–which stimulate the central nervous system–bring about a sense of energy and alertness, talkativeness, heightened confidence, and a mood "high." They increase concentration and reduce fatigue.

But not all the effects of amphetamines are positive: They also cause a loss of appetite, increased anxiety, and irritability. When taken over long periods of time, amphetamines can cause feelings of being persecuted by others, as well as a general sense of suspiciousness. People taking amphetamines may lose interest in sex. If taken in too large a quantity, amphetamines overstimulate the central nervous system to such an extent that convulsions and death can occur (Carhart-Harris, 2007).

Methamphetamine is a white, crystalline drug that U.S. police now say is the most dangerous street drug. "Meth" is highly addictive and relatively cheap, and it produces a strong, lingering high. It has made addicts of people across the social spectrum, ranging from soccer moms to urban professionals to poverty-stricken inner-city residents. After becoming addicted, users take it more and more frequently and in increasing doses. Long-term use of the drug can lead to brain damage (Halkitis, 2009; Kish et al., 2009; Rindone, 2015).

More than 1.5 million people in the United States are regular methamphetamine users. Because it can be made from nonprescription cold pills, retailers such as Walmart and Target have removed these medications from the shelves and keep them behind the pharmacy counter. Illicit labs devoted to the manufacture of methamphetamine have sprung up in many locations around the United States.

Adderall is an amphetamine college students often abuse. It was developed to help those who suffer from ADHD, or attention-deficit hyperactivity disorder. However, many college students use the drug illegally, believing that it increases their focus and the ability to study for long hours. Unfortunately, Adderall is addictive, and users need higher and higher doses to achieve the drug's supposed benefits (Diller, 2017).

Figure 4 provides a summary of the effects of amphetamines and other illegal drugs.

Drugs	Street Name	Effects	Withdrawal Symptoms	Adverse/Overdose Reactions
Stimulants				
Amphetamines		Increased confidence, mood elevation, sense of energy and alertness, decreased appetite, anxiety, irritability, insomnia, transient drowsiness, delayed orgasm	Apathy, general fatigue, prolonged sleep, depression, disorientation, suicidal thoughts, agitated motor activity, irritability, bizarre dreams	Elevated blood pressure, increase in body temperature, face picking, suspiciousness, bizarre and repetitious behavior, vivid hallucinations, convulsions, possible death
Benzedrine	Speed			
Dexedrine	Speed			
Cocaine	Coke, blow, snow, lady, crack			
Cathinone	Bath salts			
Depressants				
Alcohol	Booze	Anxiety reduction, impulsiveness, dramatic mood swings, bizarre thoughts, suicidal behavior, slurred speech, disorientation, slowed mental and physical functioning, limited attention span	Weakness, restlessness, nausea and vomiting, headaches, nightmares, irritability, depression, acute anxiety, hallucinations, seizures, possible death	Confusion, decreased response to pain, shallow respiration, dilated pupils, weak and rapid pulse, coma, possible death
Barbiturates				
Nembutal	Yellowjackets			
Seconal	Reds			
Phenobarbital				
Rohypnol	Roofies, rope, "date-rape drug"	Muscle relaxation, amnesia, sleep	Seizures	Seizures, coma, incapacitation, inability to resist sexual assault
Narcotics				
Heroin	H, Hombre, junk, smack	Reduction of anxiety and pain, difficulty in concentration, slowed speech, decreased physical activity, euphoria	Anxiety, vomiting, sneezing, diarrhea, lower back pain, watery eyes, runny nose, yawning, irritability, tremors, panic, chills and sweating, cramps	Depressed levels of consciousness, low blood pressure, rapid heart rate, shallow breathing, convulsions, coma, possible death
Morphine	Drugstore dope, cube, first line, mud			
Opioids (synthetic drugs such as Vicodin, Percocet, fentanyl, OxyContin)	Oxy, OC, Percs	Pain reduction, shallow breathing, slow heartbeat, seizure (convulsions); cold, clammy skin; confusion	Sweating, chills, abdominal cramps, insomnia, vomiting, diarrhea	Extreme drowsiness, muscle weakness, confusion, cold and clammy skin, pinpoint pupils, shallow breathing, slow heart rate, fainting, or coma
Hallucinogens				
Cannabis	Bhang, kif, ganja, dope, grass, pot, hemp, joint, weed, bone, Mary Jane, reefer	Euphoria, relaxed inhibitions, increased appetite, disoriented behavior	Hyperactivity, insomnia, decreased appetite, anxiety	Severe reactions rare but include panic, paranoia, fatigue, bizarre and dangerous behavior, decreased testosterone over long-term; immune-system effects
Marijuana				
Hashish				
Hash oil				
MDMA	Ecstasy, Molly	Heightened sense of oneself and insight, feelings of peace, empathy, energy	Depression, anxiety, sleeplessness	Increase in body temperature, memory difficulties
LSD	Acid, quasey, microdot, white lightning	Heightened aesthetic responses; vision and depth distortion; heightened sensitivity to faces and gestures; magnified feelings; paranoia, panic, euphoria	Not reported	Nausea and chills; increased pulse, temperature, and blood pressure; slow, deep breathing; loss of appetite; insomnia; bizarre, dangerous behavior
Steroids				
	Rhoids, juice	Aggression, depression, acne, mood swings, masculine traits in women and feminine traits in men	Symptoms can mimic other medical problems and include weakness, fatigue, decreased appetite, weight loss; women may note menstrual changes	Long-term, high-dose effects of steroid use are largely unknown but can lead to swelling and weight gain

FIGURE 4 Drugs and their effects. A comprehensive breakdown of effects of the most commonly used drugs.

Bath salts are an amphetamine-like stimulant containing chemicals related to cathinone. They can produce euphoria and a rise in sociability and sex drive, but the side effects can be severe, including paranoia and agitation (Cottencin, Rolland, & Karila, 2013; Airuehia, Walker, & Nittler, 2015).

COCAINE

The stimulant *cocaine*, and its derivative *crack*, represent a serious concern, although the scope of the problem has declined in recent years. Cocaine is inhaled or "snorted" through the nose, smoked, or injected directly into the bloodstream. It is rapidly absorbed into the body and takes effect almost immediately.

When used in relatively small quantities, cocaine produces feelings of profound psychological well-being, increased confidence, and alertness. Cocaine produces this "high" through the neurotransmitter dopamine. Dopamine is one of the chemicals that transmit between neurons messages that are related to ordinary feelings of pleasure. Normally, when dopamine is released, excess amounts of the neurotransmitter are reabsorbed by the releasing neuron. However, when cocaine enters the brain, it blocks reabsorption of leftover dopamine. As a result, the brain is flooded with dopamine-produced pleasurable sensations (Redish, 2004; Jarlais, Arasteh, & Perlis, 2007; Singer et al., 2017).

However, there is a steep price to be paid for the pleasurable effects of cocaine. The brain may become permanently rewired, triggering a psychological and physical addiction in which users grow obsessed with obtaining the drug. Over time, users deteriorate mentally and physically. In extreme cases, cocaine can cause hallucinations—a common one is of insects crawling over one's body. Ultimately, an overdose of cocaine can lead to death (Little et al., 2009; Roncero et al., 2013; Li et al., 2015).

Almost 2.5 million people in the United States are occasional cocaine users, and as many as 1.5 million people use the drug regularly. Given the strength of cocaine, withdrawal from the drug is difficult. Although the use of cocaine among high school students has declined in recent years, the drug still represents a major problem (Johnston et al., 2009; National Institute on Drug Abuse, 2018).

Study Alert

Figure 4, which summarizes the different categories of drugs (stimulants, depressants, narcotics, and hallucinogens), will help you learn the effects of particular drugs.

Depressants: Drug Lows

In contrast to the initial effect of stimulants, which is an increase in arousal of the central nervous system, the effect of **depressants** is to impede the nervous system by causing neurons to fire more slowly. Small doses result in at least temporary feelings of *intoxication*—drunkenness—along with a sense of euphoria and joy. When large amounts are taken, however, speech becomes slurred and muscle control becomes disjointed, making motion difficult. Ultimately, heavy users may lose consciousness entirely.

depressants Drugs that slow down the nervous system. (Module 14)

ALCOHOL

The most common depressant is alcohol, which is used by more people than is any other drug. Based on liquor sales, the average person over the age of 14 drinks 2½ gallons of pure alcohol over the course of a year. This works out to more than 200 drinks per person. Although alcohol consumption has declined steadily over the last decade, surveys show that more than three-fourths of college students indicate that they have had a drink within the last 30 days (Jung, 2002; Midanik, Tam, & Weisner, 2007).

One of the more disturbing trends is the high frequency of binge drinking among college students. For men, *binge drinking* is defined as having five or more drinks in one sitting; for women, who generally weigh less than men and whose bodies absorb alcohol less efficiently, binge drinking is defined as having four or more drinks at one sitting (Mokdad, Brewer, & Naimi, 2007; Rooke & Hine, 2011).

In Figure 5, people of different ages reported binge drinking in the last 30 days. Note that the highest percentage is that of college-age people. Furthermore, even light

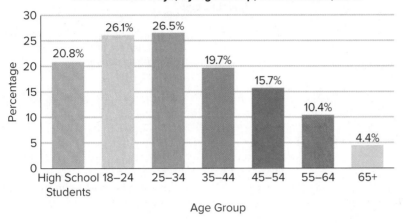

Percentage of People Who Reported Binge Drinking in the Past 30 Days, by Age Group, United States, 2013

High School Students: 20.8%
18–24: 26.1%
25–34: 26.5%
35–44: 19.7%
45–54: 15.7%
55–64: 10.4%
65+: 4.4%

(Y-axis: Percentage; X-axis: Age Group)

FIGURE 5 Self-reported binge drinking at different ages. For men, binge drinking was defined as consuming five or more drinks in one sitting; for women, the total was four or more.

Note: High school students are defined as those in grades 9–12.

Source: Adapted from Centers for Disease Control and Prevention. (2013). *Youth risk behavior surveillance system—2013. Surveillance Summaries.* WR 2010; 59.

drinkers were affected by the high rate of alcohol use: Two-thirds of lighter drinkers said that they had had their studying or sleep disturbed by drunk students, and a quarter of the women said they had been targets of unwanted sexual advances by drunk classmates (Wechsler et al., 2002; CDC Vitalsigns, 2010; Greene & Maggs, 2017).

Women are typically somewhat lighter drinkers than men–although the gap between the sexes is narrowing for older women and has closed completely for teenagers. Women are more susceptible to the effects of alcohol, and alcohol abuse may harm the brains of women more than it harms the brains of men (Mancinelli, Binetti, & Ceccanti, 2007; Chavez et al., 2011; Holzhauer, Wemm & Wulfert, 2017).

There are also cultural and ethnic differences in alcohol consumption. For example, teenagers in Europe drink more than teenagers in the United States do. Furthermore, people of East Asian backgrounds who live in the United States tend to drink significantly less than do Caucasians and African Americans, and their incidence of alcohol-related problems is lower. It may be that physical reactions to drinking, which may include sweating, a quickened heartbeat, and flushing, are more unpleasant for East Asians than for other groups (Garlow, Purselle, & Heninger, 2007; Kantrowitz & Underwood, 2007).

Although alcohol is a depressant, most people believe that it increases their sense of sociability and well-being. This belief is caused because initially alcohol may lead to a reduction in tension and stress, feelings of happiness, and loss of inhibitions.

The effects of alcohol vary significantly, depending on who is drinking it and the setting in which people drink. If alcohol were a newly discovered drug, do you think its sale would be legal?

(Left): ©Exactostock/SuperStock; (Right): ©Jim Arbogast/Getty Images

FIGURE 6 The effects of alcohol. The quantities represent only rough benchmarks; the effects vary significantly depending on an individual's weight, height, recent food intake, genetic factors, and even psychological state. *Note:* A drink refers to a typical 12-ounce bottle of beer, a 1.5-ounce shot of hard liquor, or a 5-ounce glass of wine.

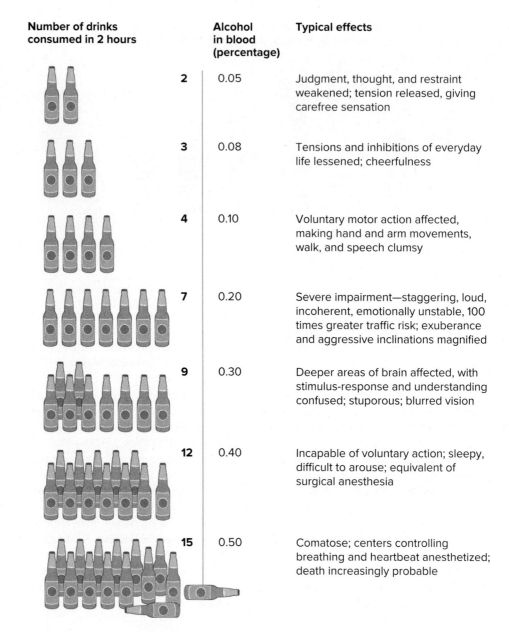

Number of drinks consumed in 2 hours		Alcohol in blood (percentage)	Typical effects
	2	0.05	Judgment, thought, and restraint weakened; tension released, giving carefree sensation
	3	0.08	Tensions and inhibitions of everyday life lessened; cheerfulness
	4	0.10	Voluntary motor action affected, making hand and arm movements, walk, and speech clumsy
	7	0.20	Severe impairment—staggering, loud, incoherent, emotionally unstable, 100 times greater traffic risk; exuberance and aggressive inclinations magnified
	9	0.30	Deeper areas of brain affected, with stimulus-response and understanding confused; stuporous; blurred vision
	12	0.40	Incapable of voluntary action; sleepy, difficult to arouse; equivalent of surgical anesthesia
	15	0.50	Comatose; centers controlling breathing and heartbeat anesthetized; death increasingly probable

However, as the dose of alcohol increases, the depressive effects become more pronounced (see Figure 6). People may feel emotionally and physically unstable. They also show poor judgment and may act aggressively. Moreover, memory is impaired, brain processing of spatial information is diminished, and speech becomes slurred and incoherent. Eventually, they may fall into a stupor and pass out. If they drink enough alcohol in a short time, they may die of alcohol poisoning (Zeigler et al., 2005; Thatcher & Clark, 2006).

Although most people fall into the category of casual users, 14 million people in the United States–1 in every 13 adults–have a drinking problem. *Alcoholics,* people with alcohol-abuse problems, come to rely on alcohol and continue to drink even though it causes serious difficulties. In addition, they become increasingly immune to the effects of alcohol. Consequently, alcoholics must drink progressively more to experience the initial positive feelings that alcohol produces.

In some cases of alcoholism, people must drink constantly in order to feel well enough to function in their daily lives. In other cases, though, people drink inconsistently but occasionally go on binges in which they consume large quantities of alcohol.

It is not clear why certain people become alcoholics and develop a tolerance for alcohol, whereas others do not. There may be a genetic cause, although the question of whether there is a specific inherited gene that produces alcoholism is controversial. What is clear is that the chances of becoming an alcoholic are considerably higher if alcoholics are present in earlier generations of a person's family. However, not all alcoholics have close relatives who are alcoholics. In these cases, environmental stressors are suspected of playing a larger role (Nurnberger & Bierut, 2007; Gizer et al., 2011; Buckner & Shah, 2015).

BARBITURATES

Barbiturates are another form of depressant. They include drugs such as Nembutal, Seconal, and phenobarbital. Barbiturates produce a sense of relaxation and are frequently prescribed by physicians to induce sleep or reduce stress. At larger doses, they produce altered thinking, faulty judgment, and sluggishness.

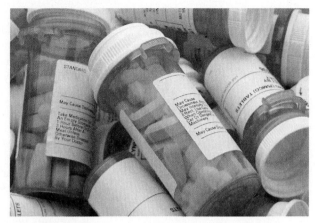

Even legal drugs, when used improperly, lead to addiction.
©David Smart/Shutterstock

Barbiturates are psychologically and physically addictive. When combined with alcohol, they can be deadly because such a combination relaxes the muscles of the diaphragm to such an extent that the user stops breathing.

ROHYPNOL

Rohypnol is sometimes called the "date rape drug" because when it is mixed with alcohol, it can prevent victims from resisting sexual assault. Sometimes people who are unknowingly given the drug are so incapacitated that they have no memory of the assault.

Narcotics, Opiates, and Opioids: Relieving Pain and Anxiety

Narcotics are drugs that increase relaxation and relieve pain and anxiety. Two of the most powerful narcotics, *morphine* and *heroin,* are derived from the poppy seed pod. Although morphine is used medically to control severe pain, heroin is illegal in the United States. This status has not prevented its widespread abuse.

Heroin users usually inject the drug directly into their veins with a hypodermic needle. The immediate effect has been described as a "rush" of positive feeling, similar in some respects to a sexual orgasm—and just as difficult to describe. After the rush, a heroin user experiences a sense of well-being and peacefulness that lasts 3 to 5 hours.

However, when the effects of heroin wear off, users feel extreme anxiety and a desperate desire to repeat the experience. Moreover, larger amounts of heroin are needed each time to produce the same pleasurable effect. These last two properties are all the ingredients necessary for physiological and psychological dependence: The user is constantly either shooting up or attempting to obtain ever-increasing amounts of the drug. Eventually, the life of the addict revolves around heroin.

Heroin is part of a class of drugs called opiates. *Opiates* are narcotics that are derived from natural substances, and they include such drugs as morphine and codeine in addition to heroin. In contrast, *opioids* are synthetic narcotics such as Vicodin, Percocet, fentanyl, and OxyContin, all of which are created in laboratories and are often prescribed to alleviate pain. (The terms *opiates* and *opioids* are often used interchangeably, and when people speak of the "opioid crisis," it typically refers to both categories.)

Opiate and opioid use has reached epidemic proportions. For example, heroin use has more than doubled among young adults 18 to 25 years old from 2002-2004 to 2011-2013. Furthermore, the rate of overdose deaths related to heroin increased 500% between 2000 and 2016 (Cook, 2015; Katz, 2017).

narcotics Drugs that increase relaxation and relieve pain and anxiety. (Module 14)

Although it's not totally clear why use of opioids has increased so rapidly, one reason is that the cost of the drugs has plummeted at the same time the supply has increased substantially Furthermore, some of the newest opioids are 100 times as potent as natural heroin. And that means drugs bought on the street, which could contain virtually anything, are particularly dangerous and can easily lead to overdoses.

Because of the powerful positive feelings opioids produce, addiction to them is particularly difficult to cure. In one treatment that has shown some success, users are given alternative drugs that reduce dependence on heroin and other addictive opiates. For example, *methadone* is a synthetic chemical that satisfies a heroin user's physiological cravings for the drug without providing the "high" that accompanies heroin. Similarly, *Suboxone* is a painkiller that reduces the withdrawal symptoms from heroin. Suboxone comes in tablet form as well as small film strips, both of which are put under the tongue to dissolve quickly. Another treatment is *Vivitrol*, an injection that lasts about a month. It prevents withdrawal symptoms, and it also prevents heroin from producing the positive effects that users crave if heroin is used (Shah, Young, & Vieira, 2014).

Methadone, Suboxone, and Vivitrol allow heroin users to function relatively normally and without the drug cravings. However, although such drugs remove the psychological dependence on heroin, they replace the physiological dependence on heroin with a physiological dependence on the alternative drugs. Consequently, researchers are attempting to identify nonaddictive chemical substitutes that do not produce a physiological craving (Verdejo, Toribio, & Orozco, 2005; Joe, Flynn, & Broome, 2007; Oviedo-Joekes et al., 2009).

Hallucinogens: Psychedelic Drugs

hallucinogen Drugs that are capable of producing alterations in perception, thoughts, and feelings. (Module 14)

Hallucinogens are drugs that alter perceptions, thoughts, and feelings. They can even produce *hallucinations*, the experience of sensing things such as sights, sounds, or smells that seem real but are not.

MARIJUANA

The most common hallucinogen in widespread use today is *marijuana*, whose active ingredient–tetrahydrocannabinol (THC)–is found in a common weed, cannabis. Marijuana is typically smoked in cigarettes or pipes, although it can be cooked and eaten. Close to 40% of high school seniors and around 15% of 8th-graders report having used marijuana in the last year (Johnston et al., 2016; see Figure 7).

FIGURE 7 Although the level of marijuana use has declined slightly in recent years, overall the absolute number of teenagers who have used the drug in the past year remains relatively high.

Source: Adapted from Johnston, L. D., Miech, R. A., O'Malley, P. M., Bachman, J. G., & Schulenberg, J. E. (2016, December 13). Teen use of any illicit drug other than marijuana at new low, same true for alcohol. University of Michigan News Service: Ann Arbor, MI.

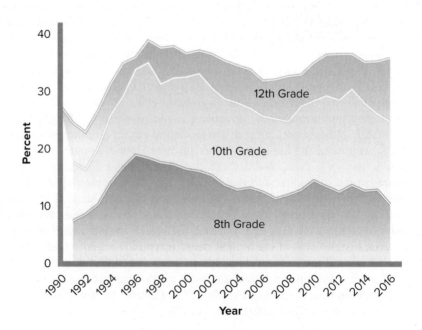

The effects of marijuana vary from person to person, but they typically consist of feelings of euphoria and general well-being. Sensory experiences seem more vivid and intense, and a person's sense of self-importance seems to grow. Memory may be impaired, causing users to feel pleasantly "spaced out."

Marijuana does not seem to produce addiction except for a small number of heavy users. Furthermore, there is little scientific evidence for the popular belief that users "graduate" from marijuana to more dangerous drugs. Overall, most research suggests its use is less harmful than the use of tobacco and alcohol (Barcott & Scherer, 2015).

On the other hand, some research suggests that there are similarities in the way marijuana and drugs such as cocaine and heroin affect the brain, as well as evidence that heavy use may impact negatively on cognitive ability in the long run. Furthermore, heavy use may at least temporarily decrease the production of the male sex hormone testosterone, potentially affecting sexual activity and sperm count (Lane, Cherek, & Tcheremissine, 2007; Rossato, Pagano, & Vettor, 2008; Pardini et al., 2015).

In addition, marijuana smoked during pregnancy may have lasting effects on children who are exposed prenatally, although the research results are inconsistent. Heavy use also affects the ability of the immune system to fight off germs and increases stress on the heart, although it is unclear how strong these effects are. Finally, there is one unquestionably negative consequence of smoking marijuana: The smoke damages the lungs much the way cigarette smoke does, producing an increased likelihood of developing cancer and other lung diseases (Julien, 2001; Reid, MacLeod, & Robertson, 2010).

Despite the possible dangers of marijuana, its use is increasingly accepted. It clearly has several medical uses: it can prevent nausea from chemotherapy, treat some AIDS symptoms, and relieve muscle spasms for people with spinal cord injuries. Furthermore, it may be helpful in the treatment of Alzheimer's disease (Barcott & Scherer, 2015; Finn, 2015).

Many states have made the use of the drug legal if it is prescribed by a health care provider—although it remains illegal under U.S. federal law. And a handful of states, including Alaska, California, Colorado, Massachusetts, Nevada, Oregon, and Washington, have made its use and sale legal, even for recreational use, with no prescription required (Baumrucker et al., 2011; Roffman, 2013; Bradford & Bradford, 2017).

MDMA (ECSTASY OR MOLLY) AND LSD

MDMA (*Ecstasy* or *Molly*) and *lysergic acid diethylamide* (*LSD* or *acid*) fall into the category of hallucinogens. Both drugs affect the operation of the neurotransmitter serotonin in the brain, causing an alteration in brain-cell activity and perception (Buchert et al., 2004; Aleksander, 2013).

MDMA produces feelings of increased energy and euphoria, and users report feeling increased empathy and connection with others. A form of MDMA known as *Molly* is often used at raves and music festivals, and it has led to a rising number of overdoses and even deaths. Furthermore, those who use MDMA may experience declines in memory and performance on intellectual tasks. Such findings suggest that MDMA use may lead to long-term changes in serotonin receptors in the brain (McKinley, 2013; Ebrahimian et al., 2017; Parrott et al., 2017).

LSD, which is structurally similar to serotonin, produces vivid hallucinations. Perceptions of colors, sounds, and shapes are altered so much that even the most mundane experience—such as looking at the knots in a wooden table—can seem moving and exciting. Time perception is distorted, and objects and people may be viewed in a new way, with some users reporting that LSD increases their understanding of the world. For others, however, the experience brought on by LSD can be terrifying, particularly if users have had emotional difficulties in the past. Furthermore, people occasionally experience flashbacks, in which they hallucinate long after they initially used the drug (Baruss, 2003; Wu, Schlenger, & Galvin, 2006).

This drawing, made by someone taking LSD, suggests the effects of hallucinogens on thinking.
©Omikron/Science Source/Getty Images

BECOMING AN INFORMED CONSUMER
of Psychology

Identifying Drug and Alcohol Problems

In a society bombarded with commercials for drugs that are guaranteed to cure everything from restless leg syndrome to erectile dysfunction, it is no wonder that drug-related problems are a major social issue. Yet many people with drug and alcohol problems deny that they have them, and even close friends and family members may fail to realize when occasional social use of drugs or alcohol has turned into abuse.

Certain signs, however, indicate when use becomes abuse (National Institute on Drug Abuse, 2000). Among them are the following:

- Always getting high to have a good time
- Being high more often than not
- Getting high to get oneself going
- Going to work or class while high
- Missing or being unprepared for class or work because you were high
- Feeling bad later about something you said or did while high
- Driving a car while high
- Coming in conflict with the law because of drugs
- Doing something while high that you wouldn't do otherwise
- Being high in nonsocial, solitary situations
- Being unable to stop getting high
- Feeling a need for a drink or a drug to get through the day
- Becoming physically unhealthy
- Failing at school or on the job
- Thinking about liquor or drugs all the time
- Avoiding family or friends while using liquor or drugs

Any combination of these symptoms should be sufficient to alert you to the potential of a serious drug problem. Because drug and alcohol dependence are almost impossible to cure on one's own, people who suspect that they have a problem should seek immediate attention from a psychologist, physician, or counselor.

You can also get help from national hotlines. For alcohol difficulties, call the National Council on Alcoholism at (800) 622-2255. For drug problems, call the National Institute on Drug Abuse at (800) 662-4357. You can also check the Web for a local listing of Alcoholics Anonymous or Narcotics Anonymous. In addition, you can check out the websites of the National Institute on Alcohol Abuse and Alcoholism (www.niaaa.nih.gov) and the National Institute on Drug Abuse (www.nida.nih.gov).

From the perspective of...

A Substance Abuse Counselor How would you explain why people start using drugs to the family members of someone who was addicted? What types of drug prevention programs would you advocate?

©Uppercut/Getty Images

RECAP/EVALUATE/RETHINK

RECAP

LO 14-1 What are the major classifications of drugs, and what are their effects?

- Drugs can produce an altered state of consciousness. However, they vary in how dangerous they are and in whether they are addictive.
- Stimulants cause arousal in the central nervous system. Two common stimulants are caffeine and nicotine. More dangerous are cocaine and amphetamines, which in large quantities can lead to convulsions and death.
- Depressants decrease arousal in the central nervous system. They can cause intoxication along with feelings of euphoria. The most common depressants are alcohol and barbiturates.
- Alcohol is the most frequently used depressant. Its initial effects of released tension and positive feelings yield to depressive effects as the dose of alcohol increases. Both heredity and environmental stressors can lead to alcoholism.
- Morphine and heroin are narcotics, drugs that produce relaxation and relieve pain and anxiety. Because of their addictive qualities, morphine and heroin are particularly dangerous.
- Hallucinogens are drugs that produce hallucinations or other changes in perception. The most frequently used hallucinogen is marijuana, which has several long-term risks. Two other hallucinogens are LSD and Ecstasy.
- A number of signals indicate when drug use becomes drug abuse. A person who suspects that he or she has a drug problem should get professional help. People are almost never capable of solving drug problems on their own.

EVALUATE

1. Drugs that affect a person's consciousness are referred to as _____.

2. Match the type of drug to an example of that type.
   1. narcotic–a pain reliever
   2. amphetamine–a strong stimulant
   3. hallucinogen–capable of producing hallucinations

   a. LSD
   b. heroin
   c. dexedrine, or speed

3. Classify each drug listed as a stimulant (S), depressant (D), hallucinogen (H), or narcotic (N).
   1. nicotine
   2. cocaine
   3. alcohol
   4. morphine
   5. marijuana

4. The effects of LSD can recur long after the drug has been taken. True or false?

5. _____ is a drug that has been used to treat people with heroin addiction.

RETHINK

1. Why have drug education campaigns largely been ineffective in stemming the use of illegal drugs? Should the use of certain now-illegal drugs be made legal? Would stressing reduction of drug use be more effective than completely prohibiting drug use?

2. People often use the word *addiction* loosely, speaking of an addiction to candy or a television show. Can you explain the difference between this type of "addiction" and a true physiological addiction? Is there a difference between this type of "addiction" and a psychological addiction?

Answers to Evaluate Questions

1. psychoactive; **2.** 1-b, 2-c, 3-a; **3.** 1-S, 2-S, 3-D, 4-N, 5-H; **4.** true; **5.** Methadone

KEY TERMS

psychoactive drugs   stimulants   narcotics
addictive drugs   depressants   hallucinogens

LOOKING *Back*

EPILOGUE

Our examination of states of consciousness has ranged widely. It focuses both on natural factors, such as sleep, dreaming, and daydreaming, and on more intentional modes of altering consciousness, including hypnosis, meditation, and drugs. As we consider why people seek to alter their consciousness, we need to reflect on the uses and abuses of the various consciousness-altering strategies in which people engage.

Return briefly to the prologue of this chapter about Eric Morin, who died from acute fentanyl poisoning, and answer the following questions in light of your understanding of addictive drugs:

1. Why do you think Eric Morin found it difficult to stop using heroin despite numerous attempts to do so?
2. Explain the difference between a psychological and a physiological addiction. Can one kind of addiction become the other kind over time?
3. Do you think the fact that Eric started drinking in high school made him more susceptible to a heroin addiction? Is alcohol a gateway drug for more serious drugs? Explain.
4. What healthy activities and practices could you suggest to someone with an opioid addiction to relieve daily stress and prevent depression without the use of narcotic stimulants?

Design Elements: Yellow highlighter: ©luckyraccoon/Shutterstock.com; Smartphone: ©and4me/Shutterstock.com; Group of diverse hands: ©MR. Nattanon Kanchak/Shutterstock.com; Woman working on laptop: ©Dragon Images/Shutterstock.com.

VISUAL SUMMARY 4 States of Consciousness

MODULE 12 Sleep and Dreams

Stages of Sleep: Three stages of sleep, plus REM sleep

As sleep becomes deeper, brain waves take on a slower wave pattern.

Awake
Stage 1 (non-REM)
Sleep spindle
Stage 2 (non-REM)
Stage 3 (non-REM)
REM

- Stage 1
  - Transition from wakefulness to sleep
  - Rapid brain waves
- Stage 2
  - Slower, more regular brain waves
  - Sleep spindles
- Stages 3
  - Slow, high-peaked waves
  - Least responsive to stimulation
- REM sleep
  - Rebound effect
  - Dreaming

Function and Meaning of Dreams: Dreams typically encompass everyday events

- Unconscious wish fulfillment theory
- Dreams-for-survival theory
- Activation-synthesis theory

Sleep Disturbances

- Insomnia
- Sleep apnea
- SIDS
- Night terrors
- Narcolepsy

Circadian Rhythms: 24-hour cycle

MODULE 13 Hypnosis and Meditation

Hypnosis: A trancelike state of heightened suggestibility

Meditation: Learned technique for refocusing attention

MODULE 14 Drug Use

Stimulants: Increase arousal in the nervous system

- Caffeine
- Cocaine
- Amphetamines

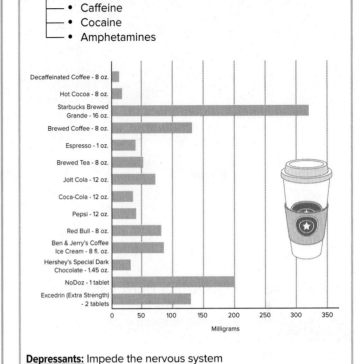

Decaffeinated Coffee - 8 oz.
Hot Cocoa - 8 oz.
Starbucks Brewed Grande - 16 oz.
Brewed Coffee - 8 oz.
Espresso - 1 oz.
Brewed Tea - 8 oz.
Jolt Cola - 12 oz.
Coca-Cola - 12 oz.
Pepsi - 12 oz.
Red Bull - 8 oz.
Ben & Jerry's Coffee Ice Cream - 8 fl. oz.
Hershey's Special Dark Chocolate - 1.45 oz.
NoDoz - 1 tablet
Excedrin (Extra Strength) - 2 tablets

0   50   100   150   200   250   300   350
Milligrams

Depressants: Impede the nervous system

- Alcohol
- Barbiturates
- Rohypnol: "Date-rape" drug

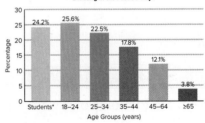

Percentage of People Who Reported Binge Drinking in the Past 30 Days

Students*: 24.2%
18–24: 25.6%
25–34: 22.5%
35–44: 17.8%
45–64: 12.1%
≥65: 3.8%

Age Groups (years)

* High school students
Sources: CDC, Youth Risk Behavior Surveillance System and Behavioral Risk Factor Surveillance System, 2009.

Narcotics: Reduce pain and anxiety

- Heroin
- Morphine

Hallucinogens: Produce changes in perceptual processes

- Marijuana
- MDMA
- LSD

(MODULE 12): (Photo): ©Don Smith/Alamy Stock Photo; Source: Adapted from Hobson, J. A. (1989). *Sleep.* New York: W. H. Freeman.; (MODULE 13): (Hypnosis): ©Erin Painter/Midland Daily News/AP Images; (Meditation): ©Liquidlibrary/Getty Images; (MODULE 14): Source: Adapted from Center for Science in the Public Interest. (2007). *Caffeine content of food & drugs.* Washington, DC: Center for Science in the Public Interest; Adapted from Centers for Disease Control and Prevention. (2013). *Youth risk behavior surveillance system—2013. Surveillance Summaries.* WR 2010; 59.

©MJTH/Shutterstock

CHAPTER 5
Learning

LEARNING OUTCOMES FOR CHAPTER 5

LO 17-1 What are the roles of cognition and thought in learning?

PROLOGUE *NOSING OUT DISEASE*

Seven-year-old Luke Nuttall has Type 1 diabetes. One night his blood sugar levels dropped suddenly while he was sleeping, but his glucose monitor—that is, his *mechanical* glucose monitor—didn't detect the drop. However, his *canine* monitor, a black Labrador named Jedi, picked up the change and immediately woke Luke's mother, as he was trained to do.

Jedi is a diabetes alert dog—a DAD—carefully trained, through procedures developed by psychologists specializing in learning, to detect changes in the bodies of diabetics. Because of their supersensitive noses, dogs are famous for sniffing out bombs and drugs, but they can also learn to detect cancers, urinary tract infections, and diabetic glucose levels.

So add another job title to the services dogs routinely provide to humans in exchange for room and board and a little cuddling (Langley, 2016).

LOOKING *Ahead*

Luke Nuttall may well owe his life to the fact that dogs can learn so effectively. Not only did Jedi learn to detect changes in glucose levels in a diabetic, he also learned what to do when he discovered a change. He didn't try to wake Luke; he ran to Luke's mother, who could provide further help.

Learning is a fundamental topic for psychologists and plays a central role in almost every specialty area of psychology. For example, a psychologist studying perception might ask, "How do we learn that people who look small from a distance are far away and not simply tiny?" A developmental psychologist might inquire, "How do babies learn to distinguish their mothers from other people?" A clinical psychologist might wonder, "Why do some people learn to be afraid when they see a spider?" A social psychologist might ask, "How do we learn to believe that we've fallen in love?"

Each of these questions, although drawn from very different branches of psychology, can be answered only through an understanding of basic learning processes. In each case, a skill or a behavior is acquired, altered, or refined through experience.

In this chapter, we will explore several ways in which learning occurs, including through classical and operant conditioning approaches, which focus on outward, behavioral processes, as well as through cognitive approaches, which focus on mental processes. We will discuss cultural differences in learning and individual differences in learning styles that influence learning effectiveness, and we will examine practical learning programs, such as behavior modification, which are based on these learning approaches.

Module 15
Classical Conditioning

learning A relatively permanent change in behavior brought about by experience. (Module 15)

Does the mere sight of the golden arches in front of McDonald's make you feel pangs of hunger and think about hamburgers? If it does, you are displaying an elementary form of learning called classical conditioning. *Classical conditioning* helps explain such diverse phenomena as crying at the sight of a bride walking down the aisle, fearing the dark, and falling in love.

Classical conditioning is one of a number of different types of learning that psychologists have identified, but a general definition encompasses them all: **Learning** is a relatively permanent change in behavior that is brought about by experience.

How do we know when a behavior has been influenced by learning—or even is a result of learning? Part of the answer relates to the nature-nurture question, one of the fundamental issues underlying the field of psychology. In the acquisition of behaviors, experience—which is essential to the definition of learning—is the "nurture" part of the nature-nurture question.

However, it's not always easy to identify whether a change in behavior is due to nature or nurture because some changes in behavior or performance come about through maturation alone and don't involve experience. For instance, children become better tennis players as they grow older partly because their strength increases with their size—a maturational phenomenon. To understand when learning has occurred, we must differentiate maturational changes from improvements resulting from practice, which indicate that learning actually has occurred.

Similarly, short-term changes in behavior that are due to factors other than learning, such as declines in performance resulting from fatigue or lack of effort, are different from performance changes that are due to actual learning. If Serena Williams has a bad day on the tennis court because of tension or fatigue, this does not mean that she has not learned to play correctly or has "unlearned" how to play well. Because there is not always a one-to-one correspondence between learning and performance, understanding when true learning has occurred is difficult.

It is clear that we are primed for learning from the beginning of life. Infants exhibit a simple type of learning called habituation. *Habituation* is the decrease in response to a stimulus that occurs after repeated presentations of the same stimulus. For example, young infants may initially show interest in a novel stimulus, such as a brightly colored toy, but they will soon lose interest if they see the same toy over and over. (Adults exhibit habituation, too: Newlyweds soon stop noticing that they are wearing a wedding ring.) Habituation permits us to ignore things that have stopped providing new information.

Most learning is considerably more complex than habituation, and the study of learning has been at the core of the field of psychology. Although philosophers since the time of Aristotle have speculated on the foundations of learning, the first systematic research on learning was done at the beginning of the 20th century, when Ivan Pavlov (does the name ring a bell?) developed the framework for learning called classical conditioning.

The Basics of Classical Conditioning

Ivan Pavlov, a Russian physiologist, never intended to do psychological research. In 1904 he won the Nobel Prize for his work on digestion, testimony to his contribution to that field. Yet Pavlov is remembered not for his physiological research but for his experiments on basic learning processes–work that he began quite accidentally (Marks, 2004; Samoilov & Zayas, 2007; Grant & Wingate, 2011).

Pavlov had been studying the secretion of stomach acids and salivation in dogs in response to eating varying amounts and kinds of food. While doing his research, he observed a curious phenomenon: Sometimes salivation would begin in the dogs when they had not yet eaten any food. Just the sight of the experimenter who normally brought the food or even the sound of the experimenter's footsteps was enough to produce salivation in the dogs.

Pavlov's genius lay in his ability to recognize the implications of this discovery. He saw that the dogs were responding not only on the basis of a biological need (hunger) but also as a result of learning–or, as it came to be called, classical conditioning. **Classical conditioning** is a type of learning in which a neutral stimulus (such as the experimenter's footsteps) comes to elicit a response after being paired with a stimulus (such as food) that naturally brings about that response.

Ivan Pavlov (center) developed the principles of classical conditioning.
©Sovfoto/UIG/Getty Images

To demonstrate classical conditioning, Pavlov (1927) attached a tube to the salivary gland of a dog, allowing him to measure precisely the dog's salivation. He then rang a bell and, just a few seconds later, presented the dog with meat. This pairing occurred repeatedly and was carefully planned so that, each time, exactly the same amount of time elapsed between the presentation of the bell and the meat. At first the dog would salivate only when the meat was presented, but soon it began to salivate at the sound of the bell. In fact, even when Pavlov stopped presenting the meat, the dog still salivated after hearing the sound. The dog had been classically conditioned to salivate to the bell.

As you can see in Figure 1, the basic processes of classical conditioning that underlie Pavlov's discovery are straightforward. However, the terminology he chose is not simple.

First, consider the diagram in Figure 1a. Before conditioning, there are two unrelated stimuli: the ringing of a bell and meat. We know that normally the sound of a bell does not lead to salivation but instead to some irrelevant response, such as pricking up the ears or perhaps a startle reaction. The bell is therefore called the neutral stimulus. A **neutral stimulus** is a stimulus that, before conditioning, does not naturally bring about the response in which we are interested.

Prior to conditioning, we also know that meat naturally causes a dog to salivate. Because food placed in a dog's mouth automatically causes salivation to occur, it is known as an unconditioned stimulus. An **unconditioned stimulus (UCS)** is a stimulus that naturally brings about a particular response without having been learned.

The response that the meat elicits (salivation) is called an unconditioned response. An **unconditioned response (UCR)** is a natural, innate response that occurs automatically and needs no training. Unconditioned responses are always brought about by the presence of unconditioned stimuli.

Figure 1b illustrates what happens during conditioning. The bell is rung just before each presentation of the meat. The goal of conditioning is for the dog to associate the bell with the unconditioned stimulus (meat) and therefore to bring about the same sort of response as the unconditioned stimulus.

After a number of pairings of the bell and meat, the bell alone causes the dog to salivate (as in Figure 1c). When conditioning is complete, the bell has changed from a neutral stimulus to what is called a conditioned stimulus. A **conditioned stimulus (CS)** is a once-neutral stimulus that has been paired with an unconditioned stimulus to bring about a response formerly caused only by the unconditioned stimulus. This time, salivation that occurs as a response to the conditioned stimulus (bell) is called a **conditioned response (CR).** After conditioning, then, the conditioned stimulus brings about the conditioned response.

The sequence and timing of the presentation of the unconditioned stimulus and the conditioned stimulus are particularly important. Like a malfunctioning warning

classical conditioning A type of learning in which a neutral stimulus comes to bring about a response after it is paired with a stimulus that naturally brings about that response. (Module 15)

neutral stimulus A stimulus that, before conditioning, does not naturally bring about the response of interest. (Module 15)

unconditioned stimulus (UCS) A stimulus that naturally brings about a particular response without having been learned. (Module 15)

unconditioned response (UCR) A response that is natural and needs no training (e.g., salivation at the smell of food). (Module 15)

conditioned stimulus (CS) A once-neutral stimulus that has been paired with an unconditioned stimulus to bring about a response formerly caused only by the unconditioned stimulus. (Module 15)

conditioned response (CR) A response that, after conditioning, follows a previously neutral stimulus (e.g., salivation at the ringing of a bell). (Module 15)

FIGURE 1 The basic process of classical conditioning. (a) *Before conditioning:* The sound of a bell does *not* produce salivation, meaning that the bell is a neutral stimulus. In contrast, meat naturally brings about salivation, making the meat an unconditioned stimulus (UCS) and salivation an unconditioned response (UCR). (b) *During conditioning:* The bell rings just before the presentation of the meat. (c) *After conditioning:* Eventually, the sound of the bell alone produces salivation. We now can say that conditioning has been accomplished: The previously neutral stimulus of the bell is now considered a conditioned stimulus (CS) that brings about the conditioned response of salivation (CR).

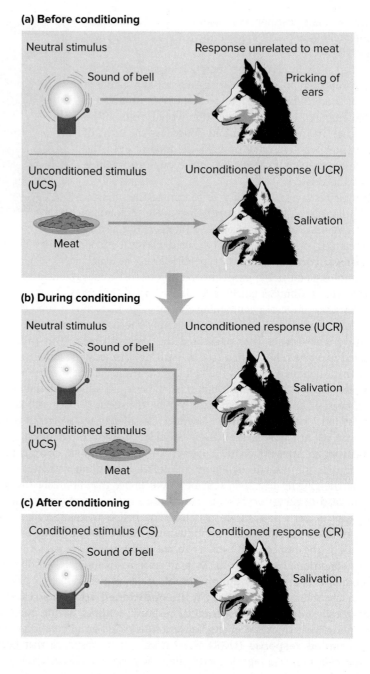

(a) Before conditioning

Neutral stimulus — Sound of bell

Response unrelated to meat — Pricking of ears

Unconditioned stimulus (UCS) — Meat

Unconditioned response (UCR) — Salivation

(b) During conditioning

Neutral stimulus — Sound of bell

Unconditioned response (UCR) — Salivation

Unconditioned stimulus (UCS) — Meat

(c) After conditioning

Conditioned stimulus (CS) — Sound of bell

Conditioned response (CR) — Salivation

Study Alert

Figure 1 can help you to learn and understand the process (and terminology) of classical conditioning, which can be confusing.

light at a railroad crossing that goes on after the train has passed by, a neutral stimulus that *follows* an unconditioned stimulus has little chance of becoming a conditioned stimulus. However, just as a warning light works best if it goes on right before a train passes, a neutral stimulus that is presented *just before* the unconditioned stimulus is most apt to result in successful conditioning. More specifically, conditioning is most effective if the neutral stimulus (which will become a conditioned stimulus) precedes the unconditioned stimulus by between a half second and several seconds, depending on what kind of response is being conditioned (Bitterman, 2006; Jennings et al., 2013; Harvie, Moseley, & Hillier, 2017).

Although the terminology Pavlov used to describe classical conditioning may seem confusing, the following summary can help make the relationships between stimuli and responses easier to understand and remember:

- Conditioned = learned
- Unconditioned = not learned

- An *unconditioned stimulus* (UCS) leads to an *unconditioned response* (UCR).
- *Unconditioned stimulus-unconditioned response* pairings are *not* learned and *not* trained: They are naturally occurring.
- During conditioning, a previously neutral stimulus is transformed into the conditioned stimulus.
- A conditioned stimulus (CS) leads to a conditioned response (CR), and a conditioned stimulus-conditioned response pairing is a consequence of learning and training.
- An *unconditioned response* and a conditioned response are similar (such as salivation in Pavlov's experiment). But the *unconditioned response* occurs naturally, whereas the conditioned response is learned.

Applying Conditioning Principles to Human Behavior

Although the initial conditioning experiments were carried out with animals, classical conditioning principles were soon found to explain many aspects of everyday human behavior. Recall, for instance, the earlier illustration of how people may experience hunger pangs at the sight of McDonald's golden arches. The cause of this reaction is classical conditioning: The previously neutral arches have become associated with the food inside the restaurant (the unconditioned stimulus), causing the arches to become a conditioned stimulus that brings about the conditioned response of hunger.

Many emotional responses are learned through classical conditioning processes. For instance, how do some of us develop fears of mice, spiders, and other creatures that are typically harmless? In a now infamous case study, psychologist John B. Watson and colleague Rosalie Rayner (1920) showed that classical conditioning was at the root of such fears by conditioning an 11-month-old infant named Albert to be afraid of rats. "Little Albert," like most infants, initially was frightened by loud noises but had no fear of rats.

In the study, the experimenters sounded a loud noise whenever Little Albert touched a white, furry rat. The noise (the unconditioned stimulus) evoked fear (the unconditioned response). After just a few pairings of noise and rat, Albert began to show fear of the rat by itself, bursting into tears when he saw it. The rat, then, had become a CS that brought about the CR, fear. Furthermore, the effects of the conditioning lingered: five days later, Albert reacted with some degree of fear not only when shown a rat but also when shown objects that looked similar to the white, furry rat, including a white rabbit, a white sealskin coat, and even a white Santa Claus mask. (By the way, we don't know for certain what happened to Little Albert, and his fate remains a source of considerable speculation. In any case, Watson, the experimenter, has been condemned for using ethically questionable procedures that could never be conducted today [Powell et al., 2014; Griggs, 2015; Digdon, 2017]).

Learning by means of classical conditioning also occurs during adulthood. For example, you may not go to a dentist as often as you should because of previous associations of dentists with pain. In more extreme cases, classical conditioning can lead to the development of *phobias*, which are intense, irrational fears. For example, an insect phobia might develop in someone who is stung by a bee. The insect phobia might be so severe that the person refrains from leaving home.

Posttraumatic stress disorder (PTSD), suffered by some war veterans and others who have had traumatic experiences, can also be produced by classical conditioning. Even years after their battlefield experiences, veterans may feel a rush of fear and anxiety at a stimulus such as a loud noise (Roberts, Moore, & Beckham, 2007; Schreurs, Smith-Bell, & Burhans, 2011; Rosellini et al., 2015).

On the other hand, classical conditioning also relates to pleasant experiences. For instance, you may have a particular fondness for the smell of a certain perfume or aftershave lotion because thoughts of an early love come rushing back whenever you encounter it. Or hearing a certain song can bring back happy or bittersweet emotions due to associations that you have developed in the past.

Classical conditioning also explains why drug addictions are so difficult to treat. Drug addicts learn to associate certain stimuli–such as drug paraphernalia such as a syringe or a room where they use drugs–with the pleasant feelings produced by the drugs. So simply seeing a syringe or entering a certain room can produce reactions associated with the drug and continued cravings for it (Saunders, Yager, & Robinson, 2013; Valyear, Villaruel, & Chaudhri, 2017).

From the perspective of...

An Advertising Executive How might knowledge of classical conditioning be useful in creating an advertising campaign? What, if any, ethical issues arise from this use?

©Image Source/Getty Images

Extinction

What do you think would happen if a dog that had become classically conditioned to salivate at the ringing of a bell never again received food when the bell was rung? The answer lies in one of the basic phenomena of learning: extinction. **Extinction** occurs when a previously conditioned response decreases in frequency and eventually disappears.

To produce extinction, one needs to end the association between conditioned stimuli and unconditioned stimuli. For instance, if we had trained a dog to salivate (the conditioned response) at the ringing of a bell (the conditioned stimulus), we could produce extinction by repeatedly ringing the bell but *not* providing meat (the unconditioned stimulus; see Figure 2). At first the dog would continue to salivate when it

extinction A basic phenomenon of learning that occurs when a previously conditioned response decreases in frequency and eventually disappears. (Module 15)

FIGURE 2 Acquisition, extinction, and spontaneous recovery of a classically conditioned response. (a) A conditioned response (CR) gradually increases in strength during training. (b) However, if the conditioned stimulus (CS) is presented by itself enough times, the conditioned response gradually fades, and extinction occurs. (c) After a pause (d) in which the conditioned stimulus is not presented, spontaneous recovery can occur. However, extinction typically reoccurs soon after.

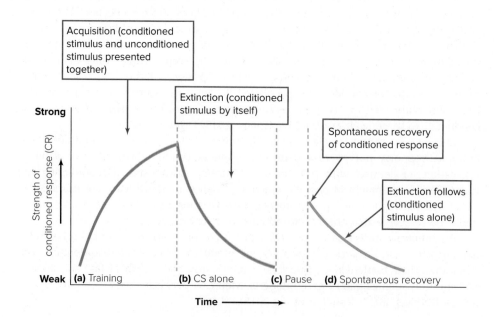

heard the bell, but after a few such instances, the amount of salivation would probably decline, and the dog would eventually stop responding to the bell altogether. At that point, we could say that the response had been extinguished. In sum, extinction occurs when the conditioned stimulus is presented repeatedly without the unconditioned stimulus.

We should keep in mind that extinction can be a helpful phenomenon. Consider, for instance, what it would be like if the fear you experienced while watching the shower murder scene in the classic movie *Psycho* never was extinguished. You might well tremble with fright every time you took a shower.

Once a conditioned response has been extinguished, has it vanished forever? Not necessarily. Pavlov discovered this phenomenon when he returned to his dog a few days after the conditioned behavior had seemingly been extinguished. If he rang a bell, the dog once again salivated–an effect known as **spontaneous recovery,** or the reemergence of an extinguished conditioned response after a period of time and with no further conditioning.

Spontaneous recovery also helps explain why it is so hard to overcome drug addictions. For example, cocaine addicts who are thought to be "cured" can experience an irresistible impulse to use the drug again if they are subsequently confronted by a stimulus with strong connections to the drug, such as a white powder (Diaz & De la Casa, 2011; Tunstall, Verendeev, & Kearns, 2013; Santos, Carey, & Carrera, 2017).

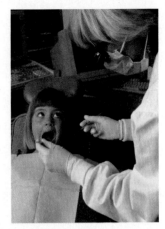

Because of a previous unpleasant experience, a person may expect a similar occurrence when faced with a comparable situation in the future, a process known as stimulus generalization. Can you think of ways that this process occurs in everyday life?

©Scott T. Baxter/Stockbyte/Getty Images

Generalization and Discrimination

Despite differences in color and shape, to most of us a rose is a rose is a rose. The pleasure we experience at the beauty, smell, and grace of the flower is similar for different types of roses. Pavlov noticed a similar phenomenon. His dogs often salivated not only at the ringing of the bell that was used during their original conditioning but at the sound of a buzzer as well.

Such behavior is the result of stimulus generalization. **Stimulus generalization** is a process in which after a stimulus has been conditioned to produce a particular response, other stimuli that are similar to the original stimulus produce the same response. The greater the similarity between two stimuli, the greater the likelihood of stimulus generalization. Little Albert, who, as we mentioned earlier, was conditioned to be fearful of white rats, grew afraid of other furry white things as well. However, according to the principle of stimulus generalization, it is unlikely that he would have been afraid of a black dog because its color would have differentiated it sufficiently from the original fear-evoking stimulus.

The conditioned response elicited by the new stimulus is usually not as intense as the original conditioned response, although the more similar the new stimulus is to the old one, the more similar the new response will be. It is unlikely, then, that Little Albert's fear of the Santa Claus mask was as great as his learned fear of a rat. Still, stimulus generalization permits us to know, for example, that we ought to brake at all red lights, even if there are minor variations in size, shape, and shade.

In contrast, **stimulus discrimination** occurs if two stimuli are sufficiently distinct from each other such that one evokes a conditioned response but the other does not. Stimulus discrimination provides the ability to differentiate between stimuli. For example, my dog Cleo comes running into the kitchen when she hears the sound of the electric can opener, which she has learned is used to open her dog food when her dinner is about to be served. She does not bound into the kitchen at the sound of the food processor, although it sounds similar. In other words, she discriminates between the stimuli of can opener and food processor. Similarly, our ability to discriminate between the behavior of a growling dog and that of one whose tail is wagging can lead to adaptive behavior–avoiding the growling dog and petting the friendly one.

spontaneous recovery The reemergence of an extinguished conditioned response after a period of rest and with no further conditioning. (Module 15)

Study Alert

Remember that stimulus generalization relates to stimuli that are similar to one another, whereas stimulus discrimination relates to stimuli that are different from one another.

stimulus generalization A process in which, after a stimulus has been conditioned to produce a particular response, stimuli that are similar to the original stimulus produce the same response. (Module 15)

stimulus discrimination The process that occurs if two stimuli are sufficiently distinct from one another that one evokes a conditioned response but the other does not; the ability to differentiate between stimuli. (Module 15)

Beyond Traditional Classical Conditioning: Challenging Basic Assumptions

Although Pavlov hypothesized that all learning is nothing more than long strings of conditioned responses, this notion has not been supported by subsequent research. It turns out that classical conditioning provides us with only a partial explanation of how people and animals learn; indeed, Pavlov was wrong in some of his basic assumptions.

For example, according to Pavlov, the process of linking stimuli and responses occurs in a mechanistic, unthinking way. In contrast to this perspective, learning theorists influenced by cognitive psychology have argued that learners actively develop an understanding and expectancy about which particular unconditioned stimuli are matched with specific conditioned stimuli. A ringing bell, for instance, gives a dog something to think about: the impending arrival of food (Kirsch et al., 2004).

Traditional explanations of how classical conditioning operates have also been challenged by John Garcia, a learning psychologist. He found that some organisms–including humans–were *biologically prepared* to quickly learn to avoid foods that smelled or tasted like something that made them sick. For instance, a dog quickly learns to avoid rotting food that in the past made it sick. Similarly, if every time you ate peanuts you had an upset stomach several hours later, eventually you would learn to avoid peanuts. In fact, you might develop a learned *taste aversion,* when the taste of a particular food is associated with unpleasant symptoms such as nausea or vomiting. If you developed a taste aversion to peanuts, merely tasting (or even smelling or in more extreme cases seeing a peanut) could produce such disagreeable symptoms (Garcia, 2003; Masi et al., 2013; Lin, Arthurs, & Reilly, 2017).

The surprising part of Garcia's discovery was his demonstration that conditioning could occur even when the interval between exposure to the conditioned stimulus of tainted food and the response of sickness was as long as 8 hours. Furthermore, the conditioning persisted over very long periods and sometimes occurred after just one exposure.

These findings have had important practical implications. For example, to keep crows from stealing eggs, dairy farmers may lace an egg with a chemical and leave it in a place where crows will find it. The drug temporarily makes the crows ill, but it does not harm them permanently. After exposure to a chemical-laden egg, crows no longer find the eggs appetizing (Cox et al., 2004; Baker, Johnson, & Slater, 2007; Bouton et al., 2011).

RECAP/EVALUATE/RETHINK

RECAP

LO 15-1 What is learning?

- Learning is a relatively permanent change in behavior resulting from experience.

LO 15-2 How do we learn to form associations between stimuli and responses?

- One major form of learning is classical conditioning, which occurs when a neutral stimulus–one that normally brings about no relevant response–is repeatedly paired with a stimulus (called an unconditioned stimulus) that brings about a natural, untrained response.
- Conditioning occurs when the neutral stimulus is repeatedly presented just before the unconditioned stimulus.

After repeated pairings, the neutral stimulus elicits the same response that the unconditioned stimulus brings about. When this occurs, the neutral stimulus has become a conditioned stimulus, and the response a conditioned response.

- Learning is not always permanent. Extinction occurs when a previously learned response decreases in frequency and eventually disappears.
- Stimulus generalization is the tendency for a conditioned response to follow a stimulus that is similar to, but not the same as, the original conditioned stimulus. The opposite phenomenon, stimulus discrimination, occurs when an organism learns to distinguish between stimuli.

EVALUATE

1. _____ involves changes brought about by experience, whereas maturation describes changes resulting from biological development.

2. _____ is the name of the scientist responsible for discovering the learning phenomenon known as _____ conditioning, whereby an organism learns a response to a stimulus to which it normally would not respond.

Refer to the passage below to answer questions 3 through 5:

The last three times little Theresa visited Dr. Lopez for checkups, he administered a painful preventive immunization shot that left her in tears. Today, when her mother takes her for another checkup, Theresa begins to sob as soon as she comes face to face with Dr. Lopez, even before he has had a chance to say hello.

3. The painful shot that Theresa received during each visit was a(n) _____ _____ that elicited the _____ _____, her tears.

4. Dr. Lopez is upset because his presence has become a _____ _____ for Theresa's crying.

5. Fortunately, Dr. Lopez gave Theresa no more shots for quite some time. Over that period, she gradually stopped crying and even came to like him. _____ had occurred.

RETHINK

1. How likely is it that Little Albert, Watson's experimental subject, might have gone through life afraid of Santa Claus? Describe what could have happened to prevent his continual dread of Santa.

2. Can you think of ways that classical conditioning is used by politicians? Advertisers? Moviemakers? Do ethical issues arise from any of these uses?

Answers to Evaluate Questions

1. Learning; 2. Pavlov, classical; 3. unconditioned stimulus, unconditioned response; 4. conditioned stimulus; 5. Extinction

KEY TERMS

learning
classical conditioning
neutral stimulus

unconditioned stimulus (UCS)
unconditioned response (UCR)

conditioned stimulus (CS)
conditioned response (CR)
extinction

spontaneous recovery
stimulus generalization
stimulus discrimination

Module 16
Operant Conditioning

operant conditioning Learning in which a voluntary response is strengthened or weakened, depending on the response's favorable or unfavorable consequences. (Module 18)

Very good . . . What a clever idea . . . Fantastic . . . I agree . . . Thank you . . . Excellent . . . Super . . . Right on . . . This is the best paper you've ever written; you get an A . . . You are really getting the hang of it . . . I'm impressed . . . You're getting a raise . . . Have a cookie . . . You look great . . . I love you . . . .

Few of us mind being the recipient of any of these comments. But what is especially noteworthy about them is that each of these simple statements can be used, through a process known as operant conditioning, to bring about powerful changes in behavior and to teach the most complex tasks. Operant conditioning is the basis for many of the most important kinds of human and animal learning.

Operant conditioning is learning in which a voluntary response is strengthened or weakened, depending on the response's favorable or unfavorable consequences. When we say that a response has been strengthened or weakened, we mean that it has been made more or less likely to recur regularly.

Unlike classical conditioning, in which the original behaviors are the natural, biological responses to the presence of a stimulus such as food, water, or pain, operant conditioning applies to voluntary responses that an organism performs deliberately to produce a desirable outcome. The term *operant* emphasizes this point: The organism *operates* on its environment to produce a desirable result. Operant conditioning is at work when we learn that toiling industriously can bring about a raise or that studying hard results in good grades.

As with classical conditioning, the basis for understanding operant conditioning was laid by work with animals. We turn now to some of that early research, which began with a simple inquiry into the behavior of cats.

Thorndike's Law of Effect

If you placed a hungry cat in a cage and then put a small piece of food outside the cage, just beyond the cat's reach, chances are that the cat would eagerly search for a way out of the cage. The cat might first claw at the sides or push against an opening. Suppose, though, you had rigged things so that the cat could escape by stepping on a small paddle that released the latch to the door of the cage (see Figure 1).

FIGURE 1 Edward L. Thorndike devised this puzzle box to study the process by which a cat learns to press a paddle to escape from the box and receive food. Do you think Thorndike's work has relevance to the question of why people voluntarily work on puzzles and play games, such as sudoku, Angry Birds, and jigsaw puzzles? Do they receive any rewards?

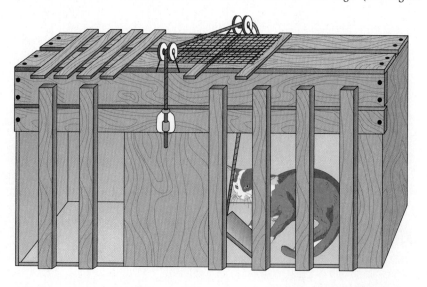

Eventually, as it moved around the cage, the cat would happen to step on the paddle, the door would open, and the cat would eat the food.

What would happen if you then returned the cat to the box? The next time, it would probably take a little less time for the cat to step on the paddle and escape. After a few trials, the cat would deliberately step on the paddle as soon as it was placed in the cage. What would have occurred, according to Edward L. Thorndike (1932), who studied this situation extensively, was that the cat would have learned that pressing the paddle was associated with the desirable consequence of getting food. To summarize that relationship, Thorndike formulated the *law of effect*, which states that *r*esponses that lead to satisfying consequences are more likely to be repeated.

Thorndike believed that the law of effect operates as automatically as leaves fall off a tree in autumn. It was not necessary for an organism to understand that there was a link between a response and a reward. Instead, Thorndike believed, over time and through experience, the organism would make a direct connection between the stimulus and the response without any awareness that the connection existed.

The Basics of Operant Conditioning

Thorndike's early research served as the foundation for the work of one of the 20th century's most influential psychologists, B. F. Skinner (1904-1990). You may have heard of the Skinner box (shown in Figure 2), a chamber with a highly controlled environment that was used to study operant conditioning processes with laboratory animals. Whereas Thorndike's goal was to get his cats to learn to obtain food by leaving the box, animals in a Skinner box learn to obtain food by operating on their environment within the box. Skinner became interested in specifying how behavior varies as a result of alterations in the environment.

Skinner, whose work went far beyond perfecting Thorndike's earlier apparatus, is considered the inspiration for a whole generation of psychologists studying operant conditioning. To illustrate Skinner's contribution, let's consider what happens to a rat in the typical Skinner box (Soorya, Carpenter, & Romanczyk, 2011; Huston et al., 2013).

Suppose you want to teach a hungry rat to press a lever that is in its box. At first, the rat will wander around the box, exploring the environment in a relatively

FIGURE 2 B. F. Skinner with a Skinner box used to study operant conditioning. Laboratory rats learn to press the lever in order to obtain food, which is delivered in the tray.

(Right): ©Nina Leen/Time Life Pictures/Getty Images

random fashion. At some point, however, it will probably press the lever by chance, and when it does, it will receive a food pellet. The first time this happens, the rat will not learn the connection between pressing a lever and receiving food and will continue to explore the box. Sooner or later, the rat will press the lever again and receive a pellet, and in time the frequency of the pressing response will increase. Eventually, the rat will press the lever continually until it satisfies its hunger, thereby demonstrating that it has learned that the receipt of food is contingent on pressing the lever.

REINFORCEMENT: THE CENTRAL CONCEPT OF OPERANT CONDITIONING

Skinner called the process that leads the rat to continue pressing the key "reinforcement." **Reinforcement** is the process by which a stimulus increases the probability that a preceding behavior will be repeated. In other words, pressing the lever is more likely to occur again because of the stimulus of food.

In a situation such as this one, the food is called a reinforcer. A **reinforcer** is any stimulus that increases the probability that a preceding behavior will occur again. Hence, food is a reinforcer because it increases the probability that the behavior of pressing (formally referred to as the *response* of pressing) will take place.

What kind of stimuli can act as reinforcers? Bonuses, toys, and good grades can serve as reinforcers–if they strengthen the probability of the response that occurred before their introduction. What makes something a reinforcer depends on individual preferences. Although a Hershey's bar can act as a reinforcer for one person, an individual who dislikes chocolate may find one dollar more desirable. The only way we can know if a stimulus is a reinforcer for a particular organism is to observe whether the frequency of a previously occurring behavior increases after the presentation of the stimulus.

Of course, we are not born knowing that one dollar can buy us a candy bar. Rather, through experience we learn that money is a valuable commodity because of its association with stimuli, such as food and drink, that are naturally reinforcing. This fact suggests a distinction between primary reinforcers and secondary reinforcers. A *primary reinforcer* satisfies some biological need and works naturally, regardless of a person's previous experience. Food for a hungry person, warmth for a cold person, and relief for a person in pain all would be classified as primary reinforcers.

In contrast, a *secondary reinforcer* is a stimulus that becomes reinforcing because of its association with a primary reinforcer. For instance, we know that money is valuable because we have learned that it allows us to obtain other desirable objects, including primary reinforcers such as food and shelter. Money thus becomes a secondary reinforcer (Moher et al., 2008; Qu, Zhang, & Chen, 2013; Thrailkill & Bouton, 2017).

Secondary reinforcers make up the heart of *token systems* sometimes used in the treatment of some psychological disorders for those who are in institutions. In a token system, a patient is rewarded for showing desired behavior with a token such as a poker chip. The token–an example of a secondary reinforcer–can then be redeemed for something desirable, such as snacks, games, or money.

Neuroscientists are beginning to explore the biological underpinnings of reinforcers. For example, we now know that the neurotransmitter *dopamine* plays a key role in the reinforcement of behavior. When we are exposed to certain kinds of stimuli, a flood of dopamine cascades through parts of the brain, leading to feelings of pleasure that are reinforcing (Trujillo-Pisanty et al., 2011; Thompson & Wolpaw, 2015).

POSITIVE REINFORCERS, NEGATIVE REINFORCERS, AND PUNISHMENT

In many respects, reinforcers can be thought of in terms of rewards; both a reinforcer and a reward increase the probability that a preceding response will occur again. But the term *reward* is limited to *positive* occurrences, and this is where it differs from a reinforcer–for it turns out that reinforcers can be positive or negative.

reinforcement The process by which a stimulus increases the probability that a preceding behavior will be repeated. (Module 16)

reinforcer Any stimulus that increases the probability that a preceding behavior will occur again. (Module 16)

Study Alert
Remember that primary reinforcers satisfy a biological need; secondary reinforcers are effective due to previous association with a primary reinforcer.

A **positive reinforcer** is a stimulus *added* to the environment that brings about an increase in a preceding response. If food, water, money, or praise is provided after a response, it is more likely that that response will occur again in the future. The paychecks that workers get at the end of the week, for example, increase the likelihood that they will return to their jobs the following week.

In contrast, a **negative reinforcer** refers to an unpleasant stimulus whose removal leads to an increase in the probability that a preceding response will be repeated in the future. For example, if you have an itchy rash (an unpleasant stimulus) that is relieved when you apply a certain brand of ointment, you are more likely to use that ointment the next time you have an itchy rash. Using the ointment, then, is negatively reinforcing because it removes the unpleasant itch. Similarly, if your iPod volume is so loud that it hurts your ears when you first turn it on, you are likely to reduce the volume level. Lowering the volume is negatively reinforcing, and you are more apt to repeat the action in the future when you first turn it on. Negative reinforcement, then, teaches the individual that taking an action removes a negative condition that exists in the environment. Like positive reinforcers, negative reinforcers increase the likelihood that preceding behaviors will be repeated (Magoon & Critchfield, 2008).

Note that negative reinforcement is not the same as punishment. **Punishment** refers to a stimulus that *decreases* the probability that a prior behavior will occur again. Unlike negative reinforcement, which produces an *increase* in behavior, punishment reduces the likelihood of a prior response. If we receive a shock that is meant to decrease a certain behavior, then we are receiving punishment, but if we are already receiving a shock and do something to stop that shock, the behavior that stops the shock is considered to be negatively reinforced. In the first case, the specific behavior is apt to decrease because of the punishment; in the second, it is likely to increase because of the negative reinforcement.

There are two types of punishment: positive punishment and negative punishment, just as there are positive reinforcement and negative reinforcement. In both cases, "positive" means adding something, and "negative" means removing something. *Positive punishment* weakens a response by applying an unpleasant stimulus. For instance, spanking a child for misbehaving or sending someone to jail for 10 years for committing a crime are examples of positive punishment. (In both cases, an unpleasant stimulus has been applied.)

In contrast, *negative punishment* consists of the removal of something pleasant. For instance, when a teenager is told she can no longer use her cell phone because she stayed out past her curfew or when an employee is informed that he will have a cut in pay because of a poor job evaluation, negative punishment is being administered. (In both cases, something pleasant–cell phone use or more pay–is being removed.)

Both positive and negative punishment result in a decrease in the likelihood that a prior behavior will be repeated. So a jail term is meant to lead to a reduction in criminal behavior, and loss of a teenager's cell phone is meant to reduce the likelihood of staying out past curfew.

The following rules (and the summary in Figure 3) can help you distinguish these concepts from one another:

- Reinforcement *increases* the frequency of the behavior preceding it; punishment *decreases* the frequency of the behavior preceding it.

- The *application* of a *positive* stimulus brings about an increase in the frequency of behavior and is referred to as positive reinforcement; the *application* of a *negative* stimulus decreases or reduces the frequency of behavior and is called positive punishment.

- The *removal* of a *negative* stimulus that results in an increase in the frequency of behavior is negative reinforcement; the *removal* of a *positive* stimulus that decreases the frequency of behavior is negative punishment.

positive reinforcer A stimulus added to the environment that brings about an increase in a preceding response. (Module 16)

negative reinforcer An unpleasant stimulus whose removal leads to an increase in the probability that a preceding response will be repeated in the future. (Module 16)

punishment A stimulus that decreases the probability that a previous behavior will occur again. (Module 16)

Study Alert

The differences between positive reinforcement, negative reinforcement, positive punishment, and negative punishment are tricky, so pay special attention to Figure 3 and the definitions in the text.

Intended Result	When stimulus is added, the result is . . .	When stimulus is removed or terminated, the result is . . .
Increase in behavior (reinforcement)	**Positive reinforcement** Example: Giving a raise for good performance Result: *Increase* in response of good performance 	**Negative reinforcement** Example: Applying ointment to relieve an itchy rash leads to a higher future likelihood of applying the ointment Result: *Increase* in response of using ointment 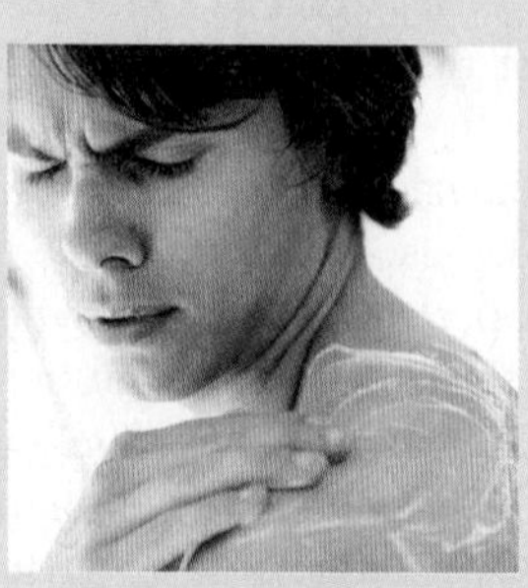
Decrease in behavior (punishment)	**Positive punishment** Example: Yelling at a teenager when she steals a bracelet Result: *Decrease* in frequency of response of stealing 	**Negative punishment** Example: Restricting teenager's access to car due to breaking curfew Result: *Decrease* in response of breaking curfew 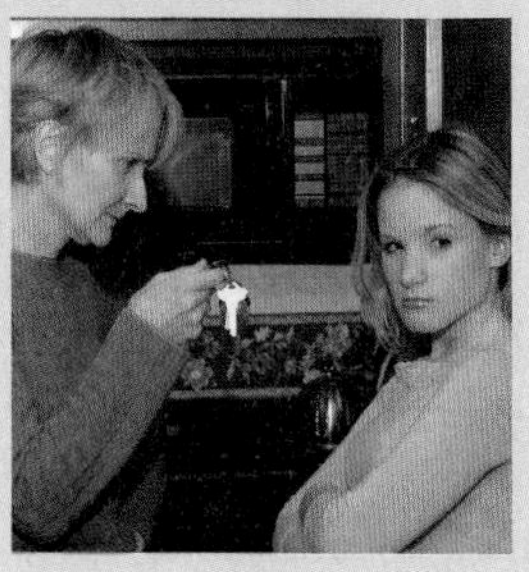

FIGURE 3 Types of reinforcement and punishment.
(Top, Left): ©Andrey_Popov/Shutterstock; (Top, Right): ©Stockbyte/Getty Images; (Bottom, Left): ©Agnieszka Marcinska/Shutterstock; (Bottom, Right): ©Amy Etra/PhotoEdit

THE PROS AND CONS OF PUNISHMENT: WHY REINFORCEMENT BEATS PUNISHMENT

Is punishment an effective way to modify behavior? Punishment often presents the quickest route to changing behavior that, if allowed to continue, might be dangerous to an individual. For instance, a parent may not have a second chance to warn a child not to run into a busy street, and so punishing the first incidence of this behavior may prove to be wise. Moreover, the use of punishment to suppress behavior, even temporarily, provides an opportunity to reinforce a person for subsequently behaving in a more desirable way (Bruno, 2016).

However, punishment has several disadvantages that make its routine use questionable. For one thing, punishment is frequently ineffective, particularly if it is not delivered shortly after the undesired behavior or if the individual is able to leave the setting in which the punishment is being given. An employee who is reprimanded by the boss may quit; a teenager who loses the use of the family car may borrow a friend's car instead. In such instances, the initial behavior that is being punished may be replaced by one that is even less desirable.

Even worse, physical punishment can convey to the recipient the idea that physical aggression is permissible and perhaps even desirable. A father who yells at and hits his son for misbehaving teaches the son that aggression is an appropriate, adult response. The son soon may copy his father's behavior by acting aggressively toward others. In addition, physical punishment is often administered by people who are themselves angry or enraged. It is unlikely that individuals in such an emotional state will be able to think through what they are doing or control carefully the degree of punishment they are inflicting. Ultimately, those who resort to physical punishment run the risk that they will grow to be feared. Punishment can also reduce the self-esteem of recipients unless they can understand the reasons for it (Miller-Perrin, Perrin, & Kocur, 2009; Smith, Springer, & Barrett, 2011; Alampay et al., 2017).

Finally, punishment does not convey any information about what an alternative, more appropriate behavior might be. To be useful in bringing about more desirable behavior in the future, punishment must be accompanied by specific information about the behavior that is being punished, along with specific suggestions concerning a more desirable behavior. Punishing a child for staring out the window in school could merely lead her to stare at the floor instead. Unless we teach her appropriate ways to respond, we have merely managed to substitute one undesirable behavior for another. If punishment is not followed up with reinforcement for subsequent behavior that is more appropriate, little will be accomplished. That's why the scientific research is clear: spanking is both ineffective and ultimately harmful to children. Even punishment in the form of yelling is damaging (Wang & Kenny, 2013; Kubanek, Snyder, & Abrams, 2015).

In short, reinforcing desired behavior is a more appropriate technique for modifying behavior than is using punishment. Both in and out of the scientific arena, then, reinforcement usually beats punishment (Sidman, 2006; Hall et al., 2011; Bruno, 2016).

SCHEDULES OF REINFORCEMENT: TIMING LIFE'S REWARDS

The world would be a different place if poker players never played cards again after the first losing hand, fishermen returned to shore as soon as they missed a catch, or telemarketers never made another phone call after their first hang-up. The fact that such unreinforced behaviors continue, often with great frequency and persistence, illustrates that reinforcement need not be received continually for behavior to be learned and maintained. In fact, behavior that is reinforced only occasionally can ultimately be learned better than can behavior that is always reinforced.

The pattern of the frequency and timing of reinforcement that follow desired behavior is known as the **schedule of reinforcement.** Behavior that is reinforced every time it occurs is on a **continuous reinforcement schedule.** In contrast, behavior that is reinforced some but not all of the time is on a **partial (or intermittent) reinforcement schedule.** Although learning occurs more rapidly under a continuous reinforcement schedule, behavior lasts longer after reinforcement stops when it was learned under a partial reinforcement schedule (Reed, 2007; Holtyn & Lattal, 2013; Mullane et al., 2017).

Why should intermittent reinforcement result in stronger, longer-lasting learning than with continuous reinforcement? We can answer the question by examining how we might behave when using a candy vending machine compared with a Las Vegas slot machine. When we use a vending machine, previous experience has taught us that every time we put in the appropriate amount of money, the reinforcement, a candy bar, ought to be delivered. In other words, the schedule of reinforcement is continuous. In comparison, a slot machine offers intermittent reinforcement. We have learned that after putting in our cash, most of the time we will not receive anything in return. At the same time, though, we know that we will occasionally win something.

Now suppose that, unknown to us, both the candy vending machine and the slot machine are broken, and so neither one is able to dispense anything. It would not be very long before we stopped depositing coins into the broken candy machine. Probably at most we would try only two or three times before leaving the machine in disgust. But the story would be quite different with the broken slot machine. Here, we would drop in money for a considerably longer time, even though there would be no payoff.

In formal terms, we can see the difference between the two reinforcement schedules: Partial reinforcement schedules (such as those provided by slot machines) maintain performance longer than do continuous reinforcement schedules (such as those established in candy vending machines) before *extinction*–the disappearance of the conditioned response–occurs.

schedules of reinforcement Different patterns of frequency and timing of reinforcement following desired behavior. (Module 16)

continuous reinforcement schedule A schedule in which behavior is reinforced every time the behavior occurs. (Module 16)

partial (or intermittent) reinforcement schedule Reinforcing of a behavior some but not all of the time. (Module 16)

Fixed- and Variable-Ratio Schedules   Certain kinds of partial reinforcement schedules produce stronger and lengthier responding before extinction than do others. Some schedules are related to the *number of responses* made before reinforcement is given, and others are related to the *amount of time* that elapses before reinforcement is provided (Reed & Morgan, 2008; Miguez, Witnauer, & Miller, 2011; Manzo et al., 2015).

fixed-ratio schedule A schedule in which reinforcement is given only after a specific number of responses are made. (Module 16)

In a **fixed-ratio schedule,** reinforcement is given only after a specific number of responses. For instance, a rat might receive a food pellet every 10th time it pressed a lever; here, the ratio would be 1:10. Similarly, garment workers are generally paid on fixed-ratio schedules: They receive a specific number of dollars for every blouse they sew. Because a greater rate of production means more reinforcement, people on fixed-ratio schedules are apt to work as quickly as possible (see Figure 4).

variable-ratio schedule A schedule by which reinforcement occurs after a varying number of responses rather than after a fixed number. (Module 16)

In a **variable-ratio schedule,** behaviors are reinforced after an average number of responses, but exactly when reinforcement will occur is unpredictable. A good example of a variable-ratio schedule is a telephone salesperson's job. He might make a sale during the 3rd, 8th, 9th, and 20th calls without being successful during any call in between. Although the number of responses he must make before closing a sale varies, it averages out to a 20% success rate. Under these circumstances, you might expect that the salesperson would try to make as many calls as possible in as short a time as possible. This is the case with all variable-ratio schedules, which lead to a high rate of response and resistance to extinction.

Study Alert

Remember that the different schedules of reinforcement affect the rapidity with which a response is learned and how long it lasts after reinforcement is no longer provided.

Fixed- and Variable-Interval Schedules: The Passage of Time   In contrast to fixed and variable-ratio schedules, in which the crucial factor is the number of responses,

FIGURE 4 Typical outcomes of different reinforcement schedules. (a) In a fixed-ratio schedule, reinforcement is provided after a specific number of responses are made. Because the more responses lead to more reinforcement, fixed-ratio schedules produce a high rate of responding. (b) In a variable-ratio schedule, responding also occurs at a high rate. (c) A fixed-interval schedule produces lower rates of responding, especially just after reinforcement has been presented, because the organism learns that a specified time period must elapse between reinforcements. (d) A variable-interval schedule produces a fairly steady stream of responses.

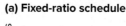

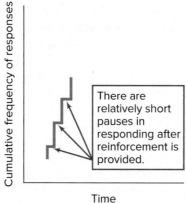

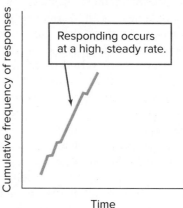

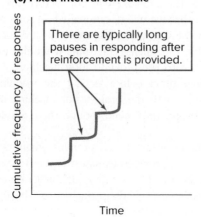

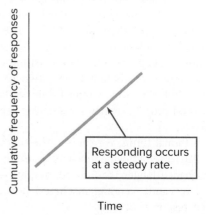

fixed-*interval* and variable-*interval* schedules focus on the amount of time that has elapsed since a person or animal was rewarded. One example of a fixed-interval schedule is a weekly paycheck. For people who receive regular, weekly paychecks, it typically makes relatively little difference exactly how much they produce in a given week.

Because a **fixed-interval schedule** provides reinforcement for a response only if a fixed time period has elapsed, overall rates of response are relatively low. This is especially true in the period just after reinforcement, when the time before another reinforcement is relatively great. Students' study habits often exemplify this reality. If the periods between exams are relatively long (meaning that the opportunity for reinforcement for good performance is given fairly infrequently), students often study minimally or not at all until the day of the exam draws near. Just before the exam, however, students begin to cram for it, signaling a rapid increase in the rate of their studying response. As you might expect, immediately after the exam there is a rapid decline in the rate of responding, with few people opening a book the day after a test. Fixed-interval schedules produce the kind of "scalloping effect" shown in Figure 4 (Saville, 2009; Daniels & Sanabria, 2017).

fixed-interval schedule A schedule in which reinforcement is provided for a response only after a fixed time period has elapsed. (Module 16)

One way to decrease the delay in responding that occurs just after reinforcement and to maintain the desired behavior more consistently throughout an interval is to use a variable-interval schedule. In a **variable-interval schedule,** the time between reinforcements varies around some average rather than being fixed. For example, a professor who gives surprise quizzes that vary from one every 3 days to one every 3 weeks, averaging one every 2 weeks, is using a variable-interval schedule. Compared to the study habits we observed with a fixed-interval schedule, students' study habits under such a variable-interval schedule would most likely be very different. Students would be apt to study more regularly because they would never know when the next surprise quiz was coming. Variable-interval schedules, in general, are more likely to produce relatively steady rates of responding than are fixed-interval schedules, with responses that take longer to extinguish after reinforcement ends.

variable-interval schedule A schedule by which the time between reinforcements varies around some average rather than being fixed. (Module 16)

From the perspective of...

An Educator How would you use your knowledge of operant conditioning to set up a program to increase the likelihood that students will complete their homework more frequently?

©Andersen Ross/Blend Images/Getty Images

DISCRIMINATION AND GENERALIZATION IN OPERANT CONDITIONING

It does not take a child long to learn that a red light at an intersection means stop and a green light indicates that it is permissible to continue, in the same way that a pigeon can learn to peck a key when a green light goes on but not when a red light appears. Just as in classical conditioning, then, operant learning involves the phenomena of discrimination and generalization.

The process by which people learn to discriminate stimuli is known as stimulus control training. In *stimulus control training*, a behavior is reinforced in the presence of a specific stimulus but not in its absence. For example, one of the most difficult discriminations many people face is determining when someone's friendliness is not mere friendliness but a signal of romantic interest. People learn to make the discrimination by observing the presence of certain nonverbal cues–such as increased eye contact and touching–that indicate romantic interest. When such cues are absent, people learn that

PsychTech

Computer-based *adaptive learning* techniques—based on the principles of shaping—present students with new material and then quiz them on it online. Presentation of subsequent material is based on students' previous performance on the quiz, so that the level and difficulty of new material are personalized, leading to great student success.

shaping The process of teaching a complex behavior by rewarding closer and closer approximations of the desired behavior. (Module 16)

no romantic interest is indicated. In this case, the nonverbal cue acts as a discriminative stimulus, one to which an organism learns to respond during stimulus control training. A *discriminative stimulus* signals the likelihood that reinforcement will follow a response. For example, if you wait until your roommate is in a good mood before you ask to borrow her favorite CD, your behavior can be said to be under stimulus control because you can discriminate between her moods.

Just as in classical conditioning, the phenomenon of stimulus generalization, in which an organism learns a response to one stimulus and then exhibits the same response to slightly different stimuli, occurs in operant conditioning. If you have learned that being polite helps you to get your way in a certain situation (reinforcing your politeness), you are likely to generalize your response to other situations. Sometimes, though, generalization can have unfortunate consequences, as when people behave negatively toward all members of a racial group because they have had an unpleasant experience with one member of that group.

SHAPING: REINFORCING WHAT DOESN'T COME NATURALLY

Consider the difficulty of using operant conditioning to teach people to repair an automobile transmission. If you had to wait until they chanced to fix a transmission perfectly before you provided them with reinforcement, the Model T Ford might be back in style long before they mastered the repair process.

There are many complex behaviors, ranging from auto repair to zoo management, that we would not expect to occur naturally as part of anyone's spontaneous behavior. For such behaviors, for which there might otherwise be no opportunity to provide reinforcement (because the behavior would never occur in the first place), a procedure known as shaping is used. **Shaping** is the process of teaching a complex behavior by rewarding closer and closer approximations of the desired behavior. In shaping, you start by reinforcing any behavior that is at all similar to the behavior you want the person to learn. Later, you reinforce only responses that are closer to the behavior you ultimately want to teach. Finally, you reinforce only the desired response. Each step in shaping, then, moves only slightly beyond the previously learned behavior, permitting the person to link the new step to the behavior learned earlier (Krueger & Dayan, 2009; Egervari et al., 2017).

Shaping allows even lower animals to learn complex responses that would never occur naturally, ranging from lions jumping through hoops, dolphins rescuing divers lost at sea, or rodents finding hidden land mines. Shaping also underlies the learning of many complex human skills. For instance, the organization of most textbooks is based on the principles of shaping. Typically, information is presented so that new material builds on previously learned concepts or skills. Thus, the concept of shaping could not be presented until we had discussed the more basic principles of operant learning; also see *Applying Psychology in the 21st Century*.

BIOLOGICAL CONSTRAINTS ON LEARNING: YOU CAN'T TEACH AN OLD DOG JUST ANY TRICK

Not all behaviors can be trained in all species equally well. Instead, there are *biological constraints*, built-in limitations in the ability of animals to learn particular behaviors. In some cases, an organism has a special predisposition that will aid in its learning a behavior (such as pecking behaviors in pigeons). In other cases, biological constraints act to prevent or inhibit an organism from learning a behavior.

For example, it's impossible to train pigs to pick up a disk because they are biologically programmed to push objects like it along the ground. Similarly, although a raccoon can be conditioned to drop a single coin into a piggy bank, it will do so only after rubbing the coin against the outside of the bank. The reason? After catching a fish, raccoons instinctively rub them against the ground to remove their outer covering (Breland & Breland, 1966; Stevens & Pashler, 2002; Thurman & Lu, 2013).

APPLYING PSYCHOLOGY IN THE 21ST CENTURY

HOW UBER AND LYFT PUT THEMSELVES IN THE DRIVER'S SEAT

Uber and Lyft, the transportation companies that use smartphone apps to connect users with drivers, don't actually employ drivers. Instead they operate on an independent-contractor model. That is, drivers work whenever and wherever they like, for as long as they like, and share their profits with the company. Although drivers have challenged the position that they are independent contractors, the arrangement gives Uber and Lyft certain important tax advantages, but one big disadvantage: they can't manage the availability of their drivers. So both companies have turned to the principles of learning to gain better control over when, where, and how long drivers work.

One such tactic is simply telling drivers how close they are to an earnings goal, even alerting them to their next earning opportunity before their current ride is over. For example, a driver who has earned $180 for the night and is trying to sign off might get a message saying "You're $20 away from $200. Are you sure you want to go offline?" The option to "go offline" would be presented, but the button to "keep driving" would be the highlighted one. It's a subtle but effective way to push drivers to go just a little longer than they otherwise would.

Another tactic uses deceptively simple messages to encourage drivers to adopt corporate goals. For example, company research showed that new drivers are much less likely to abandon Uber after they reach the 25-ride threshold. So Uber

©MikeDotta/Shutterstock

gives drivers a signing bonus when they achieve that threshold and sends them encouraging messages along the way, such as "Congratulations, you're halfway there!"

These strategies work by giving people concrete behavioral goals, whether it's to reach a particular earning level for the night, to match that of their previous night, or to exceed their maximum from the week before. People will push themselves to obtain specific targets, much like a video-game player who wants to exceed her prior high score or a runner who wants to get his mile time under 6 minutes. The goal doesn't have to be a defined one, though; the feeling of making progress toward a goal

that is always just out of reach can be powerful reinforcement. Uber is happy to exploit this motivation by showing drivers an array of performance statistics such as trips completed, dollars earned, and time spent online, making driving feel a bit like playing a video game and triggering a compulsion to level up. Drivers can even earn achievement badges (Camerer et al., 1997; Alter, 2017).

One of the most successful tactics Uber uses to keep drivers on the road is showing them the next potential fare while the current passenger is still in the driver's car, much as Netflix cues up the next episode in a series at the end of the current episode. In both cases, control is taken away from the user, as the potential next fare acts as a powerful potential reinforcer.

By applying these simple behavioral principles, Uber and Lyft teach their drivers to choose work schedules that are consistent with the companies' own goals. And drivers learn that lesson well (Rosenblat & Stark, 2016; Ahrens, Pirschel, & Snower, 2017).

> **RETHINK**
>
> - Do you believe it is ethical for companies such as Uber and Lyft to use principles of learning to manipulate when, where, and how long their drivers work? Why or why not?
> - What other tactics based on learning principles might Uber and Lyft use to motivate drivers?

The existence of biological constraints is consistent with evolutionary explanations of behavior. Clearly, there are adaptive benefits that promote survival for organisms that quickly learn–or avoid–certain behaviors. For example, our ability to rapidly learn to avoid touching hot surfaces increases our chances of survival. Additional support for the evolutionary interpretation of biological constraints lies in the fact the associations that animals learn most readily involve stimuli that are most relevant to the specific environment in which they live (Cosmides & Tooby, 2004; Davis, 2007; Behrendt, 2011).

Furthermore, psychologists taking an evolutionary perspective have suggested that we may be genetically predisposed to be fearful of certain stimuli, such as snakes or

Biological constraints make it nearly impossible for animals to learn certain behaviors. Here, psychologist Marian Breland Bailey attempts to overcome the natural limitations that inhibit the success of conditioning this rooster.

©Dr. Marian Breland Bailey

even threatening faces. For example, people in experiments learn associations relatively quickly between photos of faces with threatening expressions and neutral stimuli (such as an umbrella). In contrast, they are slower to learn associations between faces that have pleasant expressions and neutral stimuli. Stimuli that pose potential threats, like snakes or people with hostile facial expressions, posed a potential danger to early humans, and there may be an evolved "fear module" in the brain that is sensitized to such threats (DeLoache & LoBue, 2009; Gerdes, Uhl, & Alpers, 2009; Lester et al., 2017).

COMPARING CLASSICAL AND OPERANT CONDITIONING

We've considered classical conditioning and operant conditioning as two completely different processes. And, as summarized in Figure 5, there are a number of key distinctions between the two forms of learning. For example, the key concept in classical conditioning is the association between stimuli, whereas in operant conditioning it is reinforcement. Furthermore, classical conditioning involves an involuntary, natural, innate behavior, but operant conditioning is based on voluntary responses made by an organism.

Concept	Classical Conditioning	Operant Conditioning
Basic principle	Building associations between a conditioned stimulus and conditioned response.	Reinforcement *increases* the frequency of the behavior preceding it; punishment *decreases* the frequency of the behavior preceding it.
Nature of behavior	Based on involuntary, natural, innate behavior. Behavior is elicited by the unconditioned or conditioned stimulus.	Organism voluntarily operates on its environment to produce a desirable result. After behavior occurs, the likelihood of the behavior occurring again is increased or decreased by the behavior's consequences.
Order of events	Before conditioning, an unconditioned stimulus leads to an unconditioned response. After conditioning, a conditioned stimulus leads to a conditioned response.	Reinforcement leads to an increase in behavior; punishment leads to a decrease in behavior.
Example	After a physician gives a child a series of painful injections (an unconditioned stimulus) that produce an emotional reaction (an unconditioned response), the child develops an emotional reaction (a conditioned response) whenever he sees the physician (the conditioned stimulus).	A student who, after studying hard for a test, earns an A (the positive reinforcer), is more likely to study hard in the future. A student who, after going out drinking the night before a test, fails the test (punishment) is less likely to go out drinking the night before the next test.

FIGURE 5 Comparing key concepts in classical conditioning and operant conditioning.

(Left): ©McGraw-Hill Education/Jill Braaten, photographer; (Right): ©Robin Nelson/PhotoEdit

Some researchers are asking if, in fact, the two types of learning are so different after all. Some learning psychologists have suggested that classical and operant conditioning might share some underlying processes. Arguing from an evolutionary viewpoint, they contend that it is unlikely that two completely separate basic processes would evolve. Instead, one process–albeit with considerable complexity in the way it operates–might better explain behavior. Although it's too early to know if this point of view will be supported, it is clear that there are a number of processes that operate both in classical and operant conditioning, including extinction, stimulus generalization, and stimulus discrimination (Donahoe & Vegas, 2004; Silva, Gonçalves, & Garcia-Mijares, 2007; Lattal et al., 2017).

BECOMING AN INFORMED CONSUMER
of Psychology

Using Behavior Analysis and Behavior Modification

A couple who had been living together for 3 years began to fight frequently. The issues of disagreement ranged from who was going to do the dishes to the quality of their love life.

Disturbed, the couple went to a *behavior analyst,* a psychologist who specialized in behavior-modification techniques. He asked them to keep a detailed written record of their interactions over the next 2 weeks.

When they returned with the data, he carefully reviewed the records with them. In doing so, he noticed a pattern: Each of their arguments had occurred just after one or the other had left a household chore undone, such as leaving dirty dishes in the sink or draping clothes on the only chair in the bedroom.

Using the data the couple had collected, the behavior analyst asked them to list all the chores that could possibly arise and assign each one a point value depending on how long it took to complete. Then he had them divide the chores equally and agree in a written contract to fulfill the ones assigned to them. If either failed to carry out one of the assigned chores, he or she would have to place $1 per point in a fund for the other to spend. They also agreed to a program of verbal praise, promising to reward each other verbally for completing a chore.

The couple agreed to try it for a month and to keep careful records of the number of arguments they had during that period. To their surprise, the number declined rapidly.

The case just presented provides an illustration of behavior modification. **Behavior modification** is a technique for increasing the frequency of desirable behaviors and decreasing the incidence of unwanted ones.

Using the basic principles of learning theory, behavior-modification techniques have proved to be helpful in a variety of situations. People with severe intellectual disability have been taught to dress and feed themselves for the first time in their lives. Behavior modification has also helped people lose weight, give up smoking, behave more safely, and study more effectively (Carels et al., 2011; Geller, 2011; Etienne, 2013; Warmbold-Brann et al., 2017).

The techniques used by behavior analysts are as varied as the list of processes that modify behavior. They include reinforcement scheduling, shaping, generalization training, discrimination training, and extinction. Participants in a behavior-change program do, however, typically follow a series of similar basic steps that include the following:

- *Identifying goals and target behaviors.* The first step is to define desired behavior. Is it an increase in time spent studying? A decrease in weight? An increase in the use of language? A reduction in the amount of aggression displayed by a child? The goals must be stated in observable terms and must lead to specific targets. For instance, a goal might be "to increase study time," whereas the

behavior modification A technique whose goal is to increase the frequency of desirable behaviors and decrease the incidence of unwanted ones. (Module 18)

target behavior would be "to study at least 2 hours per day on weekdays and an hour on Saturdays."

- *Designing a data-recording system and recording preliminary data.* To determine whether behavior has changed, it is necessary to collect data before any changes are made in the situation. This information provides a baseline against which future changes can be measured.
- *Selecting a behavior-change strategy.* The crucial step is to choose an appropriate strategy. Typically, a variety of treatments is used. This might include the systematic use of positive reinforcement for desired behavior (verbal praise or something more tangible, such as food), as well as a program of extinction for undesirable behavior (ignoring a child who throws a tantrum). Selecting the right reinforcers is critical, and it may be necessary to experiment a bit to find out what is important to a particular individual.
- *Implementing the program.* Probably the most important aspect of program implementation is consistency. It is also important to reinforce the intended behavior. For example, suppose a mother wants her son to spend more time on his homework, but as soon as he sits down to study, he asks for a snack. If the mother gets a snack for him, she is likely to be reinforcing her son's delaying tactic, not his studying.
- *Keeping careful records after the program is implemented.* Another crucial task is record keeping. If the target behaviors are not monitored, there is no way of knowing whether the program has actually been successful.
- *Evaluating and altering the ongoing program.* Finally, the results of the program should be compared with baseline, preimplementation data to determine its effectiveness. If the program has been successful, the procedures employed can be phased out gradually. For instance, if the program called for reinforcing every instance of picking up one's clothes from the bedroom floor, the reinforcement schedule could be modified to a fixed-ratio schedule in which every third instance was reinforced. However, if the program has not been successful in bringing about the desired behavior change, consideration of other approaches might be advisable.

Behavior-change techniques based on these general principles have enjoyed wide success and have proved to be one of the most powerful means of modifying behavior. Clearly, it is possible to employ the basic notions of learning theory to improve our lives.

RECAP/EVALUATE/RETHINK

RECAP

LO 16-1 What are the roles of reward and punishment in learning?

- Operant conditioning is a form of learning in which a voluntary behavior is strengthened or weakened. According to B. F. Skinner, the major mechanism underlying learning is reinforcement, the process by which a stimulus increases the probability that a preceding behavior will be repeated.
- Primary reinforcers are rewards that are naturally effective without previous experience because they satisfy a biological need. Secondary reinforcers begin to act as if they were primary reinforcers through association with a primary reinforcer.
- Positive reinforcers are stimuli that are added to the environment and lead to an increase in a preceding

response. Negative reinforcers are stimuli that remove something unpleasant from the environment, also leading to an increase in the preceding response.

- Punishment decreases the probability that a prior behavior will occur. Positive punishment weakens a response through the application of an unpleasant stimulus, whereas negative punishment weakens a response by the removal of something positive. In contrast to reinforcement, in which the goal is to increase the incidence of behavior, punishment is meant to decrease or suppress behavior.
- Schedules and patterns of reinforcement affect the strength and duration of learning. Generally, partial reinforcement schedules–in which reinforcers are not delivered on every trial–produce stronger and longer-lasting learning than do continuous reinforcement schedules.

- Among the major categories of reinforcement schedules are fixed- and variable-ratio schedules, which are based on the number of responses made, and fixed- and variable-interval schedules, which are based on the time interval that elapses before reinforcement is provided.
- Stimulus control training (similar to stimulus discrimination in classical conditioning) is reinforcement of a behavior in the presence of a specific stimulus but not in its absence. In stimulus generalization, an organism learns a response to one stimulus and then exhibits the same response to slightly different stimuli.
- Shaping is a process for teaching complex behaviors by rewarding closer and closer approximations of the desired final behavior.
- There are biological constraints, or built-in limitations, on the ability of an organism to learn: Certain behaviors will be relatively easy for individuals of a species to learn, whereas other behaviors will be either difficult or impossible for them to learn.

LO 16-2 What are some practical methods for bringing about behavior change, both in ourselves and in others?

- Behavior modification is a method for formally using the principles of learning theory to promote the frequency of desired behaviors and to decrease or eliminate unwanted ones.

EVALUATE

1. _____ conditioning describes learning that occurs as a result of reinforcement.
2. Match the type of operant learning with its definition:

1. An unpleasant stimulus is presented to decrease behavior.
2. An unpleasant stimulus is removed to increase behavior.
3. A pleasant stimulus is presented to increase behavior.
4. A pleasant stimulus is removed to decrease behavior.

a. positive reinforcement
b. negative reinforcement
c. positive punishment
d. negative punishment

3. Sandy had had a rough day, and his son's noisemaking was not helping him relax. Not wanting to resort to scolding, Sandy told his son in a serious manner that he was very tired and would like the boy to play quietly for an hour. This approach worked. For Sandy, the change in his son's behavior was
   a. positively reinforcing.
   b. negatively reinforcing.
4. In a _____ reinforcement schedule, behavior is reinforced some of the time, whereas in a _____ reinforcement schedule, behavior is reinforced all the time.
5. Match the type of reinforcement schedule with its definition.

1. Reinforcement occurs after a set time period.
2. Reinforcement occurs after a set number of responses.
3. Reinforcement occurs after a varying time period.
4. Reinforcement occurs after a varying number of responses.

a. fixed-ratio
b. variable-interval
c. fixed-interval
d. variable-ratio

RETHINK

1. Using the scientific literature as a guide, what would you tell parents who want to know if the routine use of physical punishment is a necessary and acceptable form of child rearing?
2. How might operant conditioning be used to address serious personal concerns, such as smoking and unhealthy eating?

Answers to Evaluate Questions

1. Operant; **2.** 1-c, 2-b, 3-a, 4-d; **3.** b; **4.** partial (or intermittent), continuous; **5.** 1-c, 2-a, 3-b, 4-d

KEY TERMS

operant conditioning
reinforcement
reinforcer
positive reinforcer
negative reinforcer

punishment
schedule of reinforcement
continuous reinforcement schedule

partial (or intermittent) reinforcement schedule
fixed-ratio schedule
variable-ratio schedule
fixed-interval schedule

variable-interval schedule
shaping
behavior modification

Module 17

Cognitive Approaches to Learning

LEARNING OUTCOMES

LO 17-1 What are the roles of cognition and thought in learning?

cognitive learning theory An approach to the study of learning that focuses on the thought processes that underlie learning. (Module 17)

Study Alert

Remember that the cognitive learning approach focuses on the *internal* thoughts and expectations of learners, whereas classical and operant conditioning approaches focus on *external* stimuli, responses, and reinforcement.

latent learning Learning in which a new behavior is acquired but is not demonstrated until some incentive is provided for displaying it. (Module 17)

Consider what happens when people learn to drive a car. They don't just get behind the wheel and stumble around until they randomly put the key into the ignition and, later, after many false starts, accidentally manage to get the car to move forward, thereby receiving positive reinforcement. Rather, they already know the basic elements of driving from previous experience as passengers, when they more than likely noticed how the key was inserted into the ignition, the car was put in drive, and the gas pedal was pressed to make the car go forward.

Clearly, not all learning is due to operant and classical conditioning. In fact, such activities as learning to drive a car imply that some kinds of learning must involve higher-order processes in which people's thoughts and memories and the way they process information account for their responses. Such situations argue against regarding learning as the unthinking, mechanical, and automatic acquisition of associations between stimuli and responses, as in classical conditioning, or the presentation of reinforcement, as in operant conditioning.

Some psychologists view learning in terms of the thought processes, or cognitions, that underlie it–an approach known as **cognitive learning theory.** Although psychologists working from the cognitive learning perspective do not deny the importance of classical and operant conditioning, they have developed approaches that focus on the unseen mental processes that occur during learning, rather than concentrating solely on external stimuli, responses, and reinforcements.

In its most basic formulation, cognitive learning theory suggests that it is not enough to say that people make responses because there is an assumed link between a stimulus and a response–a link that is the result of a past history of reinforcement for a response. Instead, according to this point of view, people and even lower animals develop an *expectation* that they will receive a reinforcer after making a response. Two types of learning in which no obvious prior reinforcement is present are latent learning and observational learning.

Latent Learning

Evidence for the importance of cognitive processes comes from a series of animal experiments that revealed a type of cognitive learning called latent learning. In **latent learning,** a new behavior is learned but not demonstrated until some incentive is provided for displaying it (Tolman & Honzik, 1930). In short, latent learning occurs without reinforcement.

In the studies demonstrating latent learning, psychologists examined the behavior of rats in a maze such as the one shown in Figure 1a. In one experiment, a group of rats was allowed to wander around the maze once a day for 17 days without ever receiving a reward (called the unrewarded group). Understandably, those rats made many errors and spent a relatively long time reaching the end of the maze. A second group, however, was always given food at the end of the maze (the rewarded group). Not surprisingly, those rats learned to run quickly and directly to the food box, making few errors.

A third group of rats (the experimental group) started out in the same situation as the unrewarded rats but only for the first 10 days. On the 11th day, a critical experimental manipulation was introduced: From that point on, the rats in this group were given food for completing the maze. The results of this manipulation were

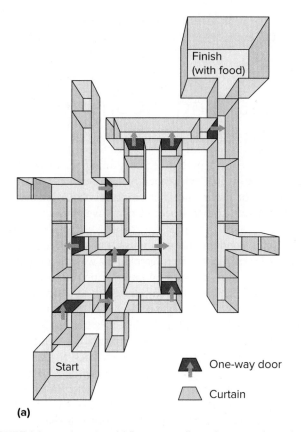

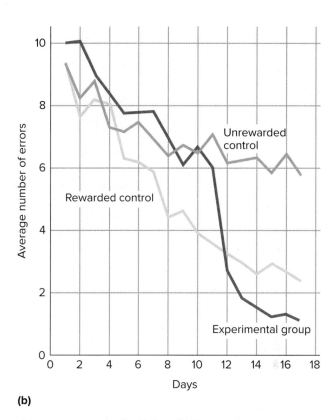

(a)   **(b)**

FIGURE 1 Latent learning. (a) Rats were allowed to roam through a maze of this sort once a day for 17 days. (b) The rats that were never rewarded (the unrewarded control condition) consistently made the most errors, whereas those that received food at the finish every day (the rewarded control condition) consistently made far fewer errors. But the results also showed latent learning: Rats that were rewarded only after the 10th day (the experimental group) showed an immediate reduction in errors and soon became similar in error rate to the rats that had been rewarded consistently. According to cognitive learning theorists, the reduction in errors indicates that the rats had developed a cognitive map—a mental representation—of the maze. Can you think of other examples of latent learning?

(a and b): Source: Adapted from Tolman, E. C., & Honzik, C. H. (1930). Introduction and removal of reward and maze performance in rats. *University of California Publications in Psychology, 4*, 257–275.

dramatic, as you can see from the graph in Figure 1b. The previously unrewarded rats, which had earlier seemed to wander about aimlessly, showed such reductions in running time and declines in error rates that their performance almost immediately matched that of the group that had received rewards from the start.

To cognitive theorists, it seemed clear that the unrewarded rats had learned the layout of the maze early in their explorations; they just never displayed their latent learning until the reinforcement was offered. Instead, those rats seemed to develop a *cognitive map* of the maze—a mental representation of spatial locations and directions.

People, too, develop cognitive maps of their surroundings. For example, latent learning may permit you to know the location of a kitchenware store at a local mall you've frequently visited, even though you've never entered the store and don't even like to cook.

The possibility that we develop our cognitive maps through latent learning presents something of a problem for strict operant conditioning theorists. If we consider the results of the maze-learning experiment, for instance, it is unclear what reinforcement permitted the rats that initially received no reward to learn the layout of the maze because there was no obvious reinforcer present. Instead,

Albert Bandura examined the principles of observational learning.
©Jon Brenneis/Life Magazine/The LIFE Images Collection/Getty Images

the results support a cognitive view of learning, in which changes occurred in unobservable mental processes (Lin et al., 2011; Malin et al., 2015; Forbus, Liang, & Rabkina, 2017).

Observational Learning: Learning Through Imitation

Let's return for a moment to the case of a person learning to drive. How can we account for instances in which an individual with no direct experience in carrying out a particular behavior learns the behavior and then performs it? To answer this question, psychologists have focused on another aspect of cognitive learning: observational learning.

According to psychologist Albert Bandura and colleagues, a major part of human learning consists of **observational learning,** which is learning by watching the behavior of another person, or *model.* Because of its reliance on observation of others—a social phenomenon—the perspective taken by Bandura is often referred to as a *social cognitive* approach to learning (Bandura, 2004, 2009; Waismeyer & Meltzoff, 2017).

Bandura dramatically demonstrated the ability of models to stimulate learning in a classic experiment. In the study, young children saw a film of an adult wildly hitting a 5-foot-tall inflatable punching toy called a Bobo doll (Bandura, Ross, & Ross, 1963a, 1963b). Later the children were given the opportunity to play with the Bobo doll themselves, and, sure enough, most displayed the same kind of behavior, in some cases mimicking the aggressive behavior almost identically.

Not only negative behaviors are acquired through observational learning. In one experiment, for example, children who were afraid of dogs were exposed to a model—dubbed the Fearless Peer—playing with a dog (Bandura, Grusec, & Menlove, 1967). After exposure, observers were considerably more likely to approach a strange dog than were children who had not viewed the Fearless Peer.

Observational learning is particularly important in acquiring skills in which the operant conditioning technique of shaping is inappropriate. Piloting an airplane and performing brain surgery, for example, are behaviors that could hardly be learned by using trial-and-error methods without grave cost—literally—to those involved in the learning process.

Observational learning may have a genetic basis. For example, we find observational learning at work with mother animals teaching their young such activities as hunting. In addition, the discovery of *mirror neurons* that fire when we observe another person carrying out a behavior suggests that the capacity to imitate others may be innate (Huesmann, Dubow, & Boxer, 2011; McElreath, Wallin, & Fasolo, 2013; Fernald, 2015); also see *Neuroscience in Your Life.*

Not all behavior that we witness is learned or carried out, of course. One crucial factor that determines whether we later imitate a model is whether the model is rewarded for his or her behavior. If we observe a friend being rewarded for putting more time into his studies by receiving higher grades, we are more likely to imitate his behavior than we would if his behavior resulted only in being stressed and tired. Models who are rewarded for behaving in a particular way are more apt to be mimicked than are models who receive punishment. Observing the punishment of a model, however, does not necessarily stop observers from learning the behavior. Observers can still describe the model's behavior—they are just less apt to perform it (Bandura, 1994).

Observational learning is central to a number of important issues relating to the extent to which people learn simply by watching the behavior of others. For instance, the degree to which observation of media aggression produces subsequent aggression on the part of viewers is a crucial—and controversial—question, as we discuss next.

observational learning Learning by observing the behavior of another person, or model. (Module 17)

Study Alert

A key point of observational learning approaches: Behavior of models who are rewarded for a given behavior is more likely to be imitated than that of models who are punished for the behavior.

This boy is displaying observational learning based on previous observation of his father. How does observational learning contribute to learning gender roles?
©Ty Milford/Getty Images

NEUROSCIENCE IN YOUR LIFE: LEARNING THROUGH IMITATION

Infants often learn by imitating adults. But what is the neural mechanism for this ability to imitate? Previous research with adults has focused on decreases in *mu activity,* a neural indicator of motor activity in the brain, when subjects are watching and producing actions. But until now this neural marker of imitative behavior has not been tested in infants. A recent study showed that imitation by 7-month-old infants was also related to decreases in mu activity. Specifically, trials in which the infants imitated the experimenter showed a greater decrease in mu activity (shown in green; left image) compared with mu activity on trials in which the infants did not imitate the experimenter (shown in green; image on the right) (Filippi et al., 2016).

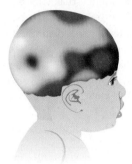

Source: Adapted from Filippi, C. A., Cannon, E. N., Fox, N. A., Thorpe, S. G., Ferrari, P. F., & Woodward, A. L. (2016). Motor system activation predicts goal imitation in 7-month-old infants. *Psychological Science* 27(5), 675-684.

VIOLENCE IN TELEVISION AND VIDEO GAMES: DO THE MEDIA'S MESSAGES MATTER?

In an episode of *The Sopranos,* the famous television series, fictional mobster Tony Soprano murdered one of his associates. To make identification of the victim's body difficult, Soprano and one of his henchmen dismembered the body and dumped the body parts.

A few months later, in real life, two half brothers in Riverside, California, strangled their mother and then cut her head and hands from her body. Victor Bautista, 20, and Matthew Montejo, 15, were caught by police after a security guard noticed that the bundle they were attempting to throw in a Dumpster had a foot sticking out of it. They told police that the plan to dismember their mother was inspired by the *Sopranos* episode (Martelle, Hanley, & Yoshino, 2003).

Like other "media copycat" killings, the brothers' cold-blooded brutality raises a critical issue: Does observing violent, antisocial acts in the media lead viewers to behave in similar ways? Because research on modeling shows that people frequently learn and imitate the aggression that they observe, this question is among the most important issues being addressed by psychologists.

Certainly, the amount of violence in the mass media is enormous. By the time of elementary school graduation, the average child in the United States will have viewed more than 8,000 murders and more than 800,000 violent acts on network television (Mifflin, 1998).

Most psychologists agree that watching high levels of media violence makes viewers more susceptible to acting aggressively. For example, one survey showed that one-fourth of violent young male offenders incarcerated in Florida had attempted to commit a media-inspired copycat crime. A significant proportion of those teenage offenders noted that they paid close attention to the media (Savage & Yancey, 2008; Boxer et al., 2009; Ferguson, 2015).

Violent video games have also been linked with actual aggression. In one of a series of studies by psychologist Craig Anderson and his colleagues, college students who frequently played violent video games, such as *Postal* or *Doom,* were more likely

PsychTech
Video gaming can also have positive consequences: Playing video games with positive, prosocial themes increases empathy and thoughts about helping others.

to have been involved in delinquent behavior and aggression. Frequent players also had lower academic achievement.

On the other hand, there are a few contrary research findings. For example, one meta-analysis of video game influences finds minimal effects on aggression. Furthermore, some researchers argue that violent video games may produce certain positive results—such as a rise in social networking among players (Ferguson, 2011, 2015b; Ferguson & Beresin, 2017).

However, most experts agree that the clear preponderance of evidence points to negative outcomes from violent video games. In fact, a recent task force of the American Psychological Association found substantial evidence that violent video game exposure was associated with higher levels of aggressive behavior, increased thoughts about aggression, higher levels of desensitization to violence, and decreased empathy relating to exposure to violence. Furthermore, the American Pediatric Association has urged parents to minimize their children's exposure to violent media of any sort (Anderson et al., 2015; Groves & Anderson, 2015; American Academy of Pediatrics Council on Communications and Media, 2016; Calvert et al., 2017).

From the perspective of...

A Social Worker What advice would you give to families about children's exposure to violent media and video games?

©Sam Edwards/age fotostock

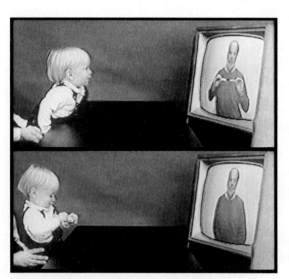

Illustrating observational learning, this infant observes an adult on television and then is able to imitate his behavior. Learning has obviously occurred through the mere observation of the television model.

From: A.N. Meltzoff, Imitation of televised models by infants. (1988). *Child Development, 59,* 1221–1229. Copyright © 1988 Andrew Meltzoff and M. Hanak.

Several aspects of media violence may contribute to real-life aggressive behavior. First, viewing violent media may lower inhibitions against behaving aggressively. In other words, watching television portrayals of violence or using violence to win a video game makes aggression seem a legitimate response to particular situations.

Second, exposure to media violence may distort our understanding of the meaning of others' behavior, predisposing us to view even nonaggressive acts by others as aggressive. For example, a teenager who watches considerable media violence may be predisposed to think that a person who accidentally bumps into him as he walks down the street is being purposely aggressive, even if the reality is that it is truly an accident.

Third, a continuous diet of media aggression may leave us desensitized to violence, and what previously would have repelled us now produces little emotional response. Our sense of the pain and suffering brought about by aggression consequently may be diminished (Carnagey, Anderson, & Bushman, 2007; Ramos et al., 2013).

What about real-life exposure to *actual* violence? Does it also lead to increases in aggression? The answer is yes. Exposure to actual firearm violence (being shot or being shot at) doubles the probability that an adolescent will commit serious violence over the next 2 years. In short, whether the violence is real or fictionalized, observing violent behavior leads to increases in aggressive behavior (Bingenheimer, Brennan, & Earls, 2005; Allwood, 2007; Quinn et al., 2017).

Exploring Diversity

Does Culture Influence How We Learn?

> When a member of the Chilcotin Indian tribe teaches her daughter to prepare salmon, at first she allows the daughter only to observe the entire process. A little later, she permits her child to try out some basic parts of the task. Her response to questions is noteworthy. For example, when the daughter asks about how to do "the backbone part," the mother's response is to repeat the entire process with another salmon. The reason? The mother feels that one cannot learn the individual parts of the task apart from the context of preparing the whole fish. (Tharp, 1989)

It should not be surprising that children raised in the Chilcotin tradition, which stresses instruction that starts by communicating the entire task, may have difficulty with traditional Western schooling. In the approach to teaching most characteristic of Western culture, tasks are broken down into their component parts. Only after each small step is learned is it thought possible to master the complete task.

Do the differences in teaching approaches between cultures affect how people learn? Some psychologists, taking a cognitive perspective on learning, suggest that people develop particular *learning styles,* characteristic ways of approaching material, based on their cultural background and unique pattern of abilities (Barmeyer, 2004; Wilkinson & Olliver-Gray, 2006; Sternberg, 2011).

Learning styles differ along several dimensions. For example, one central dimension is relational versus analytical approaches to learning. As illustrated in Figure 2, people with a *relational learning style* master material best through understanding the "big picture" about something. They need to understand the complete picture of what they're studying before they understand its component parts. For example, students with a relational learning style might learn about the brain by first focusing on the brain as a whole and how it

Relational Style	Analytical Style
• Perceive information as part of total picture	• Focus on detail
• Show intuitive thinking	• Show sequential and structured thinking
• More easily learn materials that have a human, social content	• More easily learn materials that are impersonal
• Have a good memory for verbally presented ideas and information	• Have a good memory for abstract ideas
• Are influenced by others' opinions	• Are not greatly affected by the opinions of others
• Style conflicts with the traditional school environment	• Style matches traditional school environments

FIGURE 2 A comparison of relational versus analytical approaches to learning offers one example of how learning styles differ along several dimensions.

(Photo): ©Fuse/Corbis/Getty Images; Source: Adams et al. *Teaching for diversity and social justice* (2nd ed.). New York: Routledge/Taylor & Francis Group, 2017.

functions. Only after doing that would they then focus on the specific functions of separate areas of the brain.

In contrast, those with an *analytical learning style* do best when they first analyze the the various components underlying an object, phenomenon, or situation. By developing an understanding of the individual parts, they are best able to grasp the full picture. So students with an analytic learning style might learn about the brain most easily by first considering its component parts (neurons, specific areas, lobes) and then by focusing on how they fit together to form the brain.

According to educator Maurianne Adams, certain minority groups in Western societies display characteristic learning styles. For instance, she argues that Caucasian females and African-American, Native-American, and Hispanic-American males and females are more apt to use a relational style of learning than are Caucasian and Asian-American males, who are more likely to employ an analytical style (Adams, Bell, & Griffin, 2007; Chin, 2013).

The conclusion that members of particular ethnic and gender groups have similar learning styles is controversial. Because there is so much diversity within each particular racial and ethnic group, critics argue that generalizations about learning styles cannot be used to predict the style of any single individual, regardless of group membership.

Still, it is clear that values about learning, which are communicated through a person's family and cultural background, have an impact on how successful students are in school. One theory suggests that members of minority groups who were voluntary immigrants are more apt to be successful in school than those who were brought into a majority culture against their will. For example, Korean children in the United States—the sons and daughters of voluntary immigrants—perform quite well, as a group, in school. In contrast, Korean children in Japan, who were often the sons and daughters of people who were forced to immigrate during World War II, essentially as forced laborers, do less well in school. The theory suggests that the motivation to succeed is lower for children in forced immigration groups (Ogbu, 2003; Foster, 2005).

RECAP/EVALUATE/RETHINK

RECAP

LO 17-1 What are the roles of cognition and thought in learning?

- Cognitive approaches to learning consider learning in terms of thought processes, or cognition. Phenomena such as latent learning–in which a new behavior is learned but not performed until some incentive is provided for its performance–and the apparent development of cognitive maps support cognitive approaches.
- Learning also occurs from observing the behavior of others. The major factor that determines whether an observed behavior will actually be performed is the nature of the reinforcement or punishment a model receives.
- Observation of violence is linked to a greater likelihood of subsequently acting aggressively.
- Learning styles are characteristic ways of approaching learning, based on a person's cultural background and unique pattern of abilities. Whether an individual has an analytical or a relational style of learning, for example, may reflect family background or culture.

EVALUATE

1. Cognitive learning theorists are concerned only with overt behavior, not with its internal causes. True or false?

2. In cognitive learning theory, it is assumed that people develop a(n) _____ about receiving a reinforcer when they behave a certain way.
3. In _____ learning, a new behavior is learned but is not shown until appropriate reinforcement is presented.
4. Bandura's _____ theory of learning states that people learn through watching a(n) _____ (another person displaying the behavior of interest).

RETHINK

1. The relational style of learning sometimes conflicts with the traditional school environment. Could a school be created that takes advantage of the characteristics of the relational style? How? Are there types of learning for which the analytical style is clearly superior?
2. What is the relationship between a model (in Bandura's sense) and a role model (as the term is used popularly)? Celebrities often complain that their actions should not be scrutinized closely because they do not want to be role models. How would you respond?

Answers to Evaluate Questions

1. False; cognitive learning theorists are primarily concerned with mental processes; 2. expectation; 3. latent; 4. observational, model

cognitive learning theory   latent learning   observational learning

LOOKING *Back*

EPILOGUE

In this chapter, we discussed several kinds of learning, ranging from classical conditioning, which depends on the existence of natural stimulus–response pairings, to operant conditioning, in which reinforcement is used to increase desired behavior. These approaches to learning focus on outward, behavioral learning processes. Cognitive approaches to learning focus on mental processes that enable learning.

We have also noted that learning is affected by culture and individual differences, with individual learning styles potentially affecting the ways in which people learn most effectively. And we saw some ways in which our learning about learning can be put to practical use through such means as behavior-modification programs designed to decrease negative behaviors and increase positive ones.

Return to the prologue of this chapter and consider the following questions about Luke Nuttall and his dog Jedi:

1. Do you think Jedi learned to detect glucose-level changes in humans through classical conditioning, operant conditioning, or a combination of both?
2. Sketch a basic training program that would teach Jedi to detect the right smells and ignore the wealth of other smells that his nose is capable of detecting. How would you reinforce his correct performance as a glucose detector?
3. If Luke remains healthy and his glucose levels hold steady for a few years, do you think Jedi will forget how to detect glucose changes? Do you think his skills need regular refreshment?

Design Elements: Yellow highlighter: ©luckyraccoon/Shutterstock.com; Smartphone: ©and4me/Shutterstock.com; Group of diverse hands: ©MR. Nattanon Kanchak/Shutterstock.com; Woman working on laptop: ©Dragon Images/Shutterstock.com.

MODULE 15 Classical Conditioning

Ivan Pavlov: Basic principles of classical conditioning

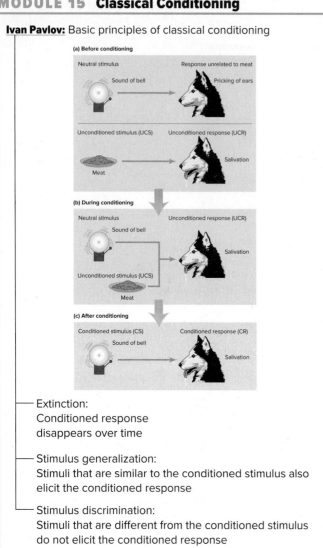

— Extinction:
Conditioned response
disappears over time

— Stimulus generalization:
Stimuli that are similar to the conditioned stimulus also
elicit the conditioned response

— Stimulus discrimination:
Stimuli that are different from the conditioned stimulus
do not elicit the conditioned response

MODULE 16 Operant Conditioning

Basic Principle: Behavior changes in frequency according
to its consequences

— Reinforcement: A stimulus that increases the
probability that a preceding behavior will be repeated

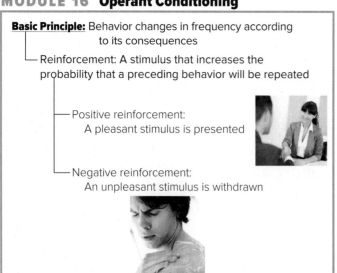

— Positive reinforcement:
A pleasant stimulus is presented

— Negative reinforcement:
An unpleasant stimulus is withdrawn

Basic Principle: Behavior changes in frequency according
to its consequences *(continued)*

— Punishment : A stimulus that decreases the probability
that a preceding behavior will be repeated

— Positive punishment:
An unpleasant stimulus is presented

— Negative punishment:
A pleasant stimulus
is withdrawn

— Schedules of reinforcement

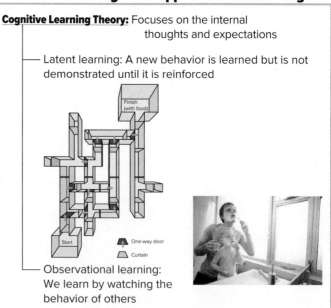

— Shaping: Reinforcing successive
approximations of behavior

MODULE 17 Cognitive Approaches to Learning

Cognitive Learning Theory: Focuses on the internal
thoughts and expectations

— Latent learning: A new behavior is learned but is not
demonstrated until it is reinforced

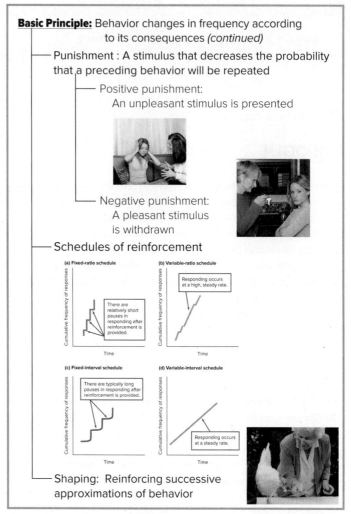

— Observational learning:
We learn by watching the
behavior of others

(MODULE 15): Source: Adapted from Tolman, E. C., & Honzik, C. H. (1930). Introduction and removal of reward and maze performance in rats. *University of California Publications in Psychology, 4,* 257–275.; (MODULE 16): (Interview): ©Andrey_Popov/Shutterstock; (Dr. Marian Breland Bailey): ©Dr. Marian Breland Bailey; (MODULE 17): (Photo): ©Ty Milford/Getty Images

©Eugenio Marongiu/Shutterstock

CHAPTER 6
Memory

LEARNING OUTCOMES FOR CHAPTER 6

MODULE 18

LO 18-1 What is memory?

LO 18-2 Are there different kinds of memory?

LO 18-3 What are the biological bases of memory?

THE FOUNDATIONS OF MEMORY

Sensory Memory

Short-Term Memory

Working Memory

Long-Term Memory

Neuroscience in Your Life: Superior Memory

MODULE 19

LO 19-1 What causes difficulties and failures in remembering?

RECALLING LONG-TERM MEMORIES

Retrieval Cues

Levels of Processing

Explicit and Implicit Memory

Flashbulb Memories

Constructive Processes in Memory: Rebuilding the Past

Applying Psychology in the 21st Century: Memories Are Made to Be Meaningful

Exploring Diversity: Are There Cross-Cultural Differences in Memory?

PROLOGUE *SHE CAN NEVER FORGET*

Jill Price, 51, is a walking diary of everything that has happened in her life since adolescence. Although she has kept a daily journal since 1980, Price doesn't need to check it to recall the events of any given day. Ask her when she first heard the Rick Springfield song "Jessie's Girl," and she'll tell you it was March 7, 1981. She was 16 years and 2 months old. She was in the car with her mom, who was yelling at her. Jill Price *never* forgets.

A New York City native, Price moved twice in her childhood, first to New Jersey, then California. The second move was difficult for her. So in an attempt to memorize all she was leaving, she made lists, took photos, and collected artifacts. After the move, she recalls that she suddenly felt something change dramatically in her brain, and her recall improved drastically. The date was July 1, 1974. Jill was 8 years old.

Intriguingly, Price's perfect recall works only with details that relate to her personally. She remembers lots of '60s and '70s television trivia but finds it more difficult to recall facts and figures from her studies.

Having total recall may seem like a wonderful ability, but Price often finds it maddening and likens it to living with a split-screen view: On one side is the present and on the other, a continually rolling reel of memories of the past (McRobbie, 2017).

LOOKING *Ahead*

Jill Price was the first person to be diagnosed with what scientists now term *highly superior autobiographical memory (HSAM),* a condition affecting the part of memory that stores experiences related to life events. Researchers have discovered that people with HSAM process short-term memories the same way most of us do. The difference is the accuracy and detail of their memories actually *improve* over time. (By the way, if you are wondering if people with HSAM have accurate recall, it appears so: every time they say something that can be corroborated by evidence, they have been proven to be accurate; McGaugh & LePort, 2014; Morris, 2017; Wolk et al., 2017.)

Price's extraordinary memory illustrates the complexity and the mystery of the phenomenon we call memory. Memory allows us to retrieve a vast amount of information. We are able to remember the name of a friend we haven't talked with for years and recall the details of a picture that hung in our childhood bedroom. At the same time, though, memory failures are common. We forget where we left the keys to the car and fail to answer an exam question about material we studied only a few hours earlier. Why?

We turn now to the nature of memory, considering the ways in which information is stored and retrieved. We examine the problems of retrieving information from memory, the accuracy of memories, and the reasons information is sometimes forgotten. We also consider the biological foundations of memory and discuss some practical means of increasing memory capacity.

Module 18
The Foundations of Memory

You are playing a game of Trivial Pursuit, and winning the game comes down to one question: On what body of water is Mumbai located? As you rack your brain for the answer, several fundamental processes relating to memory come into play. You may never, for instance, have been exposed to information regarding Mumbai's location. Or if you have been exposed to it, it may simply not have registered in a meaningful way. In other words, the information might not have been recorded properly in your memory. The initial process of recording information in a form usable to memory, a process called *encoding*, is the first stage in remembering something.

Even if you had been exposed to the information and originally knew the name of the body of water, you may still be unable to recall it during the game because of a failure to retain it. Memory specialists speak of *storage*, the maintenance of material saved in memory. If the material is not stored adequately, it cannot be recalled later.

Memory also depends on one last process—*retrieval:* Material in memory storage has to be located and brought into awareness to be useful. Your failure to recall Mumbai's location, then, may rest on your inability to retrieve information that you learned earlier.

In sum, psychologists consider **memory** to be the process by which we encode, store, and retrieve information (see Figure 1). Each of the three parts of this definition—encoding, storage, and retrieval—represents a different process. You can think of these processes as being analogous to a computer's keyboard (encoding), hard drive (storage), and software that accesses the information for display on the screen (retrieval). Only if all three processes have operated will you experience success and be able to recall the body of water on which Mumbai is located: the Arabian Sea.

Recognizing that memory involves encoding, storage, and retrieval gives us a start in understanding the concept. But how does memory actually function? How do we explain what information is initially encoded, what gets stored, and how it is retrieved?

According to the *three-system approach to memory* that dominated memory research for several decades, there are different memory storage systems or stages through which information must travel if it is to be remembered (Atkinson & Shiffrin, 1968). Historically, the approach has been extremely influential in the development of our understanding of memory, and—although new theories have augmented it—it still provides a useful framework for understanding how information is recalled.

LEARNING OUTCOMES

LO 18-1 What is memory?

LO 18-2 Are there different kinds of memory?

LO 18-3 What are the biological bases of memory?

memory The process by which we encode, store, and retrieve information. (Module 18)

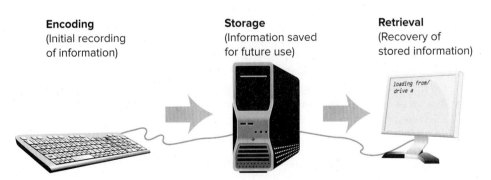

Encoding (Initial recording of information)

Storage (Information saved for future use)

Retrieval (Recovery of stored information)

FIGURE 1 Memory is built on three basic processes—encoding, storage, and retrieval—that are analogous to a computer's keyboard, hard drive, and software to access the information for display on the screen. The analogy is not perfect, however, because human memory is less precise than a computer. How might you modify the analogy to make it more accurate?

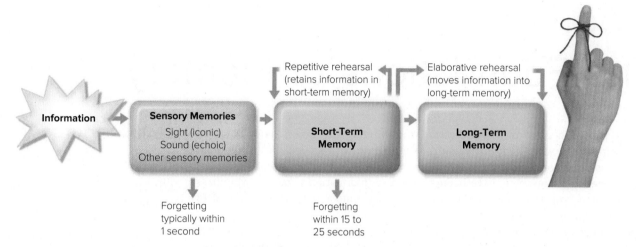

FIGURE 2 In this three-stage model of memory, information initially recorded by the person's sensory system enters sensory memory, which momentarily holds the information. The information then moves to short-term memory, which stores it for 15 to 25 seconds. Finally, the information can move into long-term memory, which is relatively permanent. Whether the information moves from short-term to long-term memory depends on the kind and amount of rehearsal of the material that is performed.

Source: Adapted from Baddeley, A., Chincotta, D., & Adlam, A. (2001). Working memory and the control of action: Evidence from task switching. *Journal of Experimental Psychology: General, 130*, 641–657.

sensory memory The initial, momentary storage of information, lasting only an instant. (Module 18)

short-term memory Memory that holds information for 15 to 25 seconds. (Module 18)

long-term memory Memory that stores information on a relatively permanent basis, although it may be difficult to retrieve. (Module 18)

Study Alert

Although the three types of memory are discussed as separate memory stores, these are not mini-warehouses located in specific areas of the brain. Instead, they represent three different types of memory systems with different characteristics.

A momentary flash of lightning leaves a sensory visual memory, a fleeting but exact replica of the stimulus, which then fades away.

©Brand X Pictures

The three-system memory theory proposes the existence of the three separate memory stores shown in Figure 2. **Sensory memory** refers to the initial, momentary storage of information that lasts only an instant. Here, an exact replica of the stimulus recorded by a person's sensory system is stored very briefly. In a second stage, **short-term memory** holds information for 15 to 25 seconds and stores it according to its meaning, rather than as mere sensory stimulation. The third type of storage system is **long-term memory.** Information is stored in long-term memory on a relatively permanent basis, although it may be difficult to retrieve.

Sensory Memory

A momentary flash of lightning, the sound of a twig snapping, and the sting of a pin-prick all represent stimulation of exceedingly brief duration, but they may nonetheless provide important information that can require a response. Such stimuli are initially–and fleetingly–stored in sensory memory.

Sensory memory is the first storehouse of the information the world presents to us. Actually, we have several types of sensory memories, each related to a different source of sensory information. For instance, *iconic memory* reflects information from the visual system. *Echoic memory* stores auditory information coming from the ears. In addition, there are corresponding memories for each of the other senses.

Sensory memory can store information for only a very short time. If information does not pass into short-term memory, it is lost for good. For instance, iconic memory seems to last less than a second, and echoic memory typically fades within 2 or 3 seconds. However, despite the brief duration of sensory memory, its precision is high: Sensory memory can store an almost exact replica of each stimulus to which it is exposed (Vlassova & Pearson, 2013; Rimmele, Sussman, & Poeppel, 2015).

Psychologist George Sperling (1960) demonstrated the existence of sensory memory in a series of clever and now-classic studies. He briefly exposed people to a series of 12 letters arranged in the following pattern:

F	T	Y	C
K	D	N	L
Y	W	B	M

When exposed to this pattern of letters for just one twentieth of a second, most people could recall only four or five of the letters accurately. Although they knew that they had seen more, the memory of those letters had faded by the time they reported the first few letters. It was possible, then, that the information had initially been accurately stored in sensory memory. But during the time it took to verbalize the first four or five letters, the memory of the other letters faded.

To test that possibility, Sperling conducted an experiment in which a high, medium, or low tone sounded just after a person had been exposed to the full pattern of letters. People were told to report the letters in the highest line if a high tone was sounded, the middle line if the medium tone occurred, or the lowest line at the sound of the low tone. Because the tone occurred after the exposure, people had to rely on their memories to report the correct row.

The results of the study clearly showed that people had been storing the complete pattern in memory. They accurately recalled the letters in the line that had been indicated by the tone regardless of whether it was the top, middle, or bottom line. Obviously, *all* the lines they had seen had been stored in sensory memory. Despite its rapid loss, then, the information in sensory memory was an accurate representation of what people had seen.

By gradually lengthening the time between the presentation of the visual pattern and the tone, Sperling was able to determine with some accuracy the length of time that information was stored in sensory memory. The ability to recall a particular row of the pattern when a tone was sounded declined progressively as the period between the visual exposure and the tone increased. This decline continued until the period reached about 1 second in duration, at which point the row could not be recalled accurately at all. Sperling concluded that the entire visual image was stored in sensory memory for less than a second.

In sum, sensory memory operates as a kind of snapshot that stores information—which may be of a visual, auditory, or other sensory nature—for a brief moment in time. But it is as if each snapshot, immediately after being taken, is destroyed and replaced with a new one. Unless the information in the snapshot is transferred to some other type of memory, it is lost.

Short-Term Memory

Because the information that is stored briefly in sensory memory consists of representations of raw sensory stimuli, it is not meaningful to us. If we are to make sense of it and possibly retain it, the information must be transferred to the next stage of memory: short-term memory. Short-term memory is the memory store in which information first has meaning, although the maximum length of retention there is relatively short (Hamilton & Martin, 2007; Cao, Nosofsky, & Shiffrin, 2017).

The specific process by which sensory memories are transformed into short-term memories is not clear. Some theorists suggest that the information is first translated into graphical representations or images, and others hypothesize that the transfer occurs when the sensory stimuli are changed to words (Baddeley & Wilson, 1985). What is clear, however, is that unlike sensory memory, which holds a relatively full and detailed—if short-lived—representation of the world, short-term memory has incomplete representational capabilities.

In fact, researchers have identified the specific amount of information we can hold in short-term memory: 7 items, or "chunks," of information, with variations up to plus or minus 2 chunks (remember it this way: 7 ± 2). A **chunk** is a group of separate pieces of information stored as a single unit in short-term memory. For example, telephone numbers are typically depicted in three chunks of information in order to make them easier to remember: (201) 226-4610, rather than a string of the separate numbers 2012264610.

Chunks also may consist of categories as words or other meaningful units. For example, consider the following list of 21 letters:

chunk A group of familiar stimuli stored as a single unit in short-term memory. (Module 20)

P B S F O X C N N A B C C B S M T V N B C

Because the list of individual letters exceeds seven items, it is difficult to recall the letters after one exposure. But suppose they were presented as follows:

PBS FOX CNN ABC CBS MTV NBC

In this case, even though there are still 21 letters, you'd be able to store them in short-term memory since they represent only seven chunks.

Chunks can vary in size from single letters or numbers to categories that are far more complicated. The specific nature of what constitutes a chunk varies according to one's past experience. You can see this for yourself by trying an experiment that was first carried out as a comparison between expert and inexperienced chess players and is illustrated in Figure 3 (deGroot, 1978; Grossberg, 2013; Schneider & Logan, 2015).

The chunks of information in short-term memory do not last very long. Just how brief is short-term memory? If you've ever looked up a telephone number, repeated the number to yourself, and then forgotten the number after you've tapped the first three numbers into your phone, you know that information does not remain in short-term memory very long. Most psychologists believe that information in short-term memory is lost after 15 to 25 seconds—unless it is transferred to long-term memory.

REHEARSAL

rehearsal The repetition of information that has entered short-term memory. (Module 18)

The transfer of material from short- to long-term memory proceeds largely on the basis of **rehearsal,** the repetition of information that has entered short-term memory. Rehearsal accomplishes two things. First, as long as the information is repeated, it is maintained in short-term memory. More important, however, rehearsal allows us to

FIGURE 3 Examine the chessboard on the left for about 5 seconds. Then cover up the board and draw the position of the pieces on the blank chessboard. (You could also use your own chessboard and place the pieces in the same positions.) Unless you are an experienced chess player, you are likely to have great difficulty carrying out such a task. Yet chess masters—those who win tournaments—do this quite well (deGroot, 1966). They are able to reproduce correctly 90% of the pieces on the board. In comparison, inexperienced chess players are typically able to reproduce only 40% of the board properly. The chess masters do not have superior memories in other respects; they generally test normally on other measures of memory. What they can do better than others is see the board in terms of chunks or meaningful units and reproduce the position of the chess pieces by using those units.

transfer the information into long-term memory (Jarrold & Tam, 2011; Grenfell-Essam, Ward, & Tan, 2013; Festini & Reuter-Lorenz, 2017).

Whether the transfer is made from short- to long-term memory seems to depend largely on the kind of rehearsal that is carried out. If the information is simply repeated over and over again—as we might do with a telephone number someone tells us as we rush to store it in our phone—it is kept current in short-term memory, but it will not necessarily be placed in long-term memory. Instead, as soon as we stop punching in the phone numbers, the number is likely to be replaced by other information and will be completely forgotten.

In contrast, if the information in short-term memory is rehearsed using a process called elaborative rehearsal, it is much more likely to be transferred into long-term memory. *Elaborative rehearsal* occurs when the information is considered and organized in some fashion. The organization might include expanding the information to make it fit into a logical framework, linking it to another memory, turning it into an image, or transforming it in some other way. For example, a list of vegetables to be purchased at a store could be woven together in memory as items being used to prepare an elaborate salad, could be linked to the items bought on an earlier shopping trip, or could be thought of in terms of the image of a farm with rows of each item.

We can vastly improve our retention of information using such organizational strategies, which are known as mnemonics. *Mnemonics* (pronounced "neh MON ix") are strategies for organizing information in a way that makes the information more likely to be remembered. For instance, when a beginning musician learns that the spaces on the music staff spell the word *FACE*, or when we learn the rhyme "Thirty days hath September, April, June, and November . . . ," we are using mnemonics (Stålhammar, Nordlund, & Wallin, 2015; Choi, Kensinger, & Rajaram, 2017).

Working Memory

Rather than seeing short-term memory as an independent way station into which memories arrive, either to fade or to be passed on to long-term memory, most contemporary memory theorists conceive of short-term memory as far more active. In this view, short-term memory is like an information-processing system that manages both new material gathered from sensory memory and older material that has been pulled from long-term storage. In this increasingly influential view, short-term memory is referred to as working memory.

Working memory is the memory system that holds information temporarily while actively manipulating and rehearsing that information. If you use the analogy of a computer, working memory is the processing that occurs in an open window on your desktop, as compared with the long-term storage of information in the computer's hard drive (Unsworth & Engle, 2005; Vandierendonck & Szmalec, 2011).

Researchers now assume that working memory is made up of several parts. First, it contains a *central executive* processor that is involved in reasoning, decision making, and planning. The central executive integrates and coordinates information from three distinct subsystems, and it determines what we pay attention to and what we ignore.

The three subsystems of working memory serve as storage-and-rehearsal systems: the visual store, the verbal store, and the episodic buffer. The *visual store* specializes in visual and spatial information. In contrast, the *verbal store* holds and manipulates material relating to language, including speech, words, and numbers. Finally, the *episodic buffer* contains information that represents events and occurrences—things that happen to us (see Figure 4; Baddeley, Allen, & Hitch, 2011; Kuncel & Beatty, 2013; Hilbert et al., 2017).

Working memory permits us to keep information in an active state briefly so that we can do something with the information. For instance, we use working memory when we're doing a multistep arithmetic problem in our heads, storing the result of

working memory A memory system that holds information temporarily while actively manipulating and rehearsing that information. (Module 18)

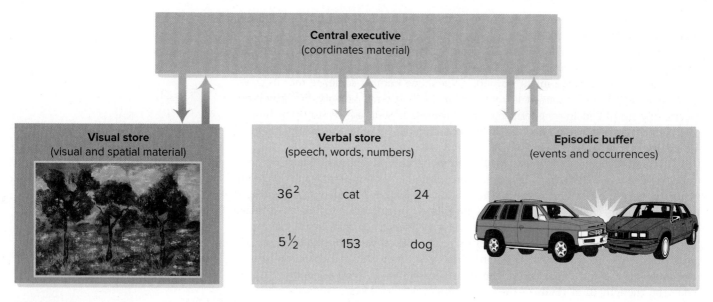

FIGURE 4 Working memory is an active "workspace" in which information is retrieved and manipulated and in which information is held through rehearsal.

Source: Adapted from Baddeley, A., Chincotta, D., & Adlam, A. (2001). Working memory and the control of action: Evidence from task switching. *Journal of Experimental Psychology: General, 130,* 641–657.

one calculation while getting ready to move to the next stage. (I make use of my working memory when I figure a 20% tip in a restaurant by first calculating 10% of the total bill and then doubling it.)

As working memory processes information, it uses a significant amount of cognitive resources during its operation. Furthermore, the amount of information that can be held and processed in working memory seems to be just three to four chunks, depending on the nature of the chunks (Cowan, 2001; Beam, 2014; Heathcoate et al., 2015).

The cognitive effort in the processing of information in working memory also can make us less aware of our surroundings–something that has implications for why it's unsafe to use cell phones while driving. If a phone conversation requires thinking, it will burden working memory and leave drivers less aware of their surroundings, an obviously dangerous state of affairs (Sifrit, 2006; Strayer & Drews, 2007).

Furthermore, stress can reduce the effectiveness of working memory by reducing its capacity. In fact, one study found that students with the highest working memory capacity and greatest math ability were the ones who were most vulnerable to pressure to perform well. Those who should have performed best, then, were the ones most apt to choke on the test because their working memory capacities were reduced by the stress (Schoofs et al., 2013; Edwards et al., 2015; Banks & Boals, 2017).

Long-Term Memory

Material that makes its way from short-term memory to long-term memory enters a storehouse of almost unlimited capacity. Like a new file we save on a hard drive, the information in long-term memory is filed and coded so that we can retrieve it when we need it.

Evidence of the existence of long-term memory, as distinct from short-term memory, comes from a number of sources. For example, people with certain kinds of brain damage have no lasting recall of new information received after the damage occurred, although people and events stored in memory before the injury remain intact (Milner, 1966). Because information that was encoded and stored before the injury can be recalled and because short-term memory after the injury appears to be operational–new

PsychTech

Research shows that when we are faced with complicated questions and material, we are primed to think of computers and search engines such as Google. In what is called the *Google effect,* we are then less likely to store the information in short-term memory and less likely to recall it—but have a better memory for where we can find it on the web (Sparrow, Liu, & Wegner, 2011).

material can be recalled for a very brief period—we can infer that there are two distinct types of memory: one for short-term and one for long-term storage.

Results from laboratory experiments are also consistent with the notion of separate short-term and long-term memory. For example, in one set of studies, people were asked to recall a relatively small amount of information (such as a set of three letters). Then, to prevent practice of the initial information, participants were required to recite some extraneous material aloud, such as counting backward by threes (Brown, 1958; Peterson & Peterson, 1959). By varying the amount of time between the presentation of the initial material and the need for its recall, investigators found that recall was quite good when the interval was very short, but recall declined rapidly thereafter. After 15 seconds had gone by, recall hovered at around 10% of the material initially presented.

Apparently, the distraction of counting backward prevented almost all the initial material from reaching long-term memory. Initial recall was good because it was coming from short-term memory, but those memories were lost at a rapid rate. Eventually, all that could be recalled was the small amount of material that had made its way into long-term storage despite the distraction of counting backward.

The distinction between short- and long-term memory is also demonstrated by the fact that ability to recall information in a list depends on where in the list an item appears. For instance, in some cases, a *primacy effect* occurs, in which items presented early in a list are remembered better. In other cases, a *recency effect* is seen, in which items presented late in a list are remembered best (Tydgat & Grainger, 2009; Jacoby & Wahlheim, 2013; Tam, Bonardi, & Robinson, 2015).

LONG-TERM MEMORY MODULES

Just as short-term memory is often conceptualized in terms of working memory, many contemporary researchers now regard long-term memory as having several components, or *memory modules.* Each of these modules represents a separate memory system in the brain.

One major distinction within long-term memory is that between declarative and procedural memory. **Declarative memory** is memory for factual information: names, faces, dates, and facts, such as "a bike has two wheels." The information stored in declarative memory can be verbally communicated to others and is sometimes called "explicit memory."

In contrast, **procedural memory** (sometimes called *nondeclarative memory* or *implicit memory*) refers to memory for skills and habits, such as how to ride a bike or hit a baseball. For example, procedural memory allows us to ice skate, even if we haven't done it for a long time. (Try to explain how you know how to balance on a bike or catch a ball; it's nearly impossible. Yet you're able to do so because the information is stored in procedural memory.)

You can remember the difference between declarative and procedural memory this way: Information about *things* is stored in declarative memory; information about *how to do things* (procedures) is stored in procedural memory (Bauer, 2008; Freedberg, 2011; Gade et al., 2017).

Declarative memory can be subdivided into semantic memory and episodic memory. **Semantic memory** is memory for general knowledge and facts about the world, as well as memory for the rules of logic that are used to deduce other facts. Because of semantic memory, we remember that the ZIP code for Beverly Hills is 90210, that Mumbai is on the Arabian Sea, and that *memoree* is the incorrect spelling of *memory.* Thus, semantic memory is somewhat like a mental almanac of facts (Tulving, 2002; McNamara, 2013; Grady, St-Laurent, & Burianová, 2015).

In contrast, **episodic memory** is memory for events that occur in a particular time, place, or context. For example, recall of learning to hit a baseball, our first kiss, or arranging a surprise 21st birthday party for our brother is based on episodic memories. Episodic memories relate to particular contexts. For example, remembering *when* and *how* we learned that 2 × 2 = 4 would be an episodic memory; the fact itself (that 2 × 2 = 4) is a semantic memory. (Also see Figure 5.)

declarative memory Memory for factual information: names, faces, dates, and the like. (Module 18)

procedural memory Memory for skills and habits, such as riding a bike or hitting a baseball; sometimes referred to as *nondeclarative memory.* (Module 18)

semantic memory Memory for general knowledge and facts about the world, as well as memory for the rules of logic that are used to deduce other facts. (Module 18)

episodic memory Memory for events that occur in a particular time, place, or context. (Module 18)

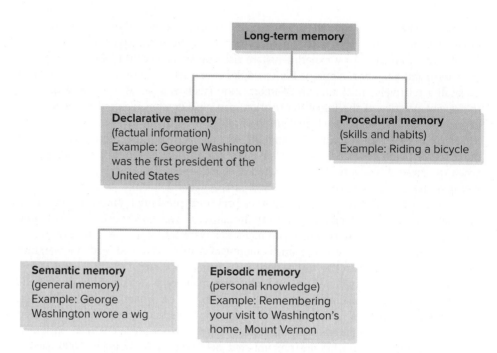

FIGURE 5 Long-term memory can be subdivided into several different types. What type of long-term memory is involved in your recollection of the moment you first arrived on your campus at the start of college? What type of long-term memory is involved in remembering the lyrics to a song, compared with the tune of a song?

Study Alert

Use Figure 5 to help clarify the distinctions between the different types of long-term memory.

Episodic memories can be surprisingly detailed. Consider, for instance, how you'd respond if you were asked to identify what you were doing on a specific day 2 years ago. Impossible? You may think otherwise as you read the following exchange between a researcher and a participant in a study who was asked, in a memory experiment, what he was doing "on Monday afternoon in the third week of September two years ago."

PARTICIPANT: Come on. How should I know?

EXPERIMENTER: Just try it anyhow.

PARTICIPANT: OK. Let's see: Two years ago . . . I would be in high school in Pittsburgh. . . . That would be my senior year. Third week in September—that's just after summer—that would be the fall term. . . . Let me see. I think I had chemistry lab on Mondays. I don't know. I was probably in chemistry lab. Wait a minute—that would be the second week of school. I remember he started off with the atomic table—a big fancy chart. I thought he was crazy trying to make us memorize that thing. You know, I think I can remember sitting . . . . (Lindsay & Norman, 1977)

Episodic memory, then, can provide information about events that happened long in the past. But semantic memory is no less impressive, permitting us to dredge up tens of thousands of facts ranging from the date of our birthday to the knowledge that $1 is less than $5.

SEMANTIC NETWORKS

Try to recall, for a moment, as many things as you can think of that are the color red. Now pull from your memory the names of as many fruits as you can recall.

Did the same item appear when you did both tasks? For many people, an apple comes to mind in both cases since it fits equally well in each category. And the fact that you might have thought of an apple when doing the first task makes it even more likely that you'll think of it when doing the second task.

It's actually quite amazing that we're able to retrieve specific material from the vast store of information in our long-term memories. According to some memory researchers, one key organizational tool that allows us to recall detailed information from long-term memory is the associations that we build between different pieces of information. In this view, knowledge is stored in **semantic networks,** mental representations of clusters of interconnected information (Cummings, Ceponiene, & Koyama, 2006; Poirier et al., 2015).

semantic networks Mental representations of clusters of interconnected information. (Module 18)

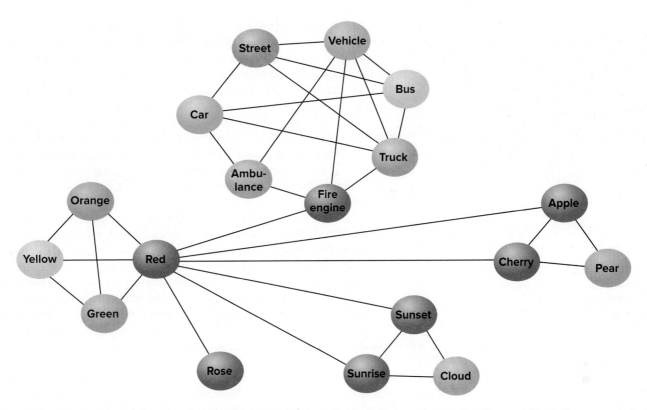

FIGURE 6 Semantic networks in memory consist of relationships between pieces of information, such as those relating to the concept of a fire engine. The lines suggest the connections that indicate how the information is organized within memory. The closer together two concepts are, the greater the strength of the association.

Source: Baddeley, A., Chincotta, D., & Adlam, A. (2001). Working memory and the control of action: Evidence from task switching. *Journal of Experimental Psychology: General,* *130*, 641–657.

Consider, for example, Figure 6, which shows some of the relationships in memory relating to fire engines, the color red, and a variety of other semantic concepts. Thinking about a particular concept leads to recall of related concepts. For example, seeing a fire engine may activate our recollections of other kinds of emergency vehicles, such as an ambulance, which in turn may activate recall of the related concept of a vehicle. And thinking of a vehicle may lead us to think about a bus that we've seen in the past. Activating one memory triggers the activation of related memories in a process known as *spreading activation* (Kreher et al., 2008; Nelson et al., 2013; Kenett et al., 2017).

From the perspective of...

A Marketing Specialist How might advertisers use ways of enhancing memory to promote their products? What ethical principles are involved?

©McGraw-Hill Education

THE NEUROSCIENCE OF MEMORY

Can we pinpoint a location in the brain where long-term memories reside? Is there a single site that corresponds to a particular memory, or is memory distributed in different regions across the brain? Do memories leave an actual physical trace that scientists can view?

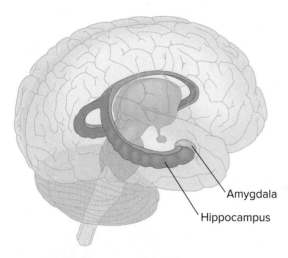

Amygdala

Hippocampus

FIGURE 7 The hippocampus and amygdala, parts of the brain's limbic system, play a central role in the consolidation of memories.

Source: Adapted from Van De Graaff, K. (2000). *Human anatomy* (5th ed.). Boston: McGraw-Hill.

The *engram* is the term for the physical memory trace in the brain that corresponds to a memory. Locating the engram has proved to be a major challenge to psychologists and neuroscientists interested in memory. But by using advanced brain scanning procedures, investigators have learned that certain brain areas and structures specialize in different types of memory-related activities.

The *hippocampus*, a part of the brain's limbic system (see Figure 7), helps to consolidate memories, stabilizing them after they are initially acquired. The hippocampus acts as a kind of neurological e-mail system. That information is subsequently passed along to the cerebral cortex of the brain, where it is actually stored (Peters et al., 2007; Lavenex & Lavenex, 2009; Dudai, 2011).

The significance of the hippocampus is exemplified by studies of individuals who have particularly good, yet specialized, types of memories. For instance, taxi drivers in London, England, must have accurate, complete recall of the location of the maze of streets and alleys within a 6-mile radius of the center of the city. It takes years of study to memorize the material.

It turns out that MRI brain scans of taxi drivers show differences in the shape of the hippocampus compared to non-taxi drivers. The differences are consistent with the idea that particular areas of the hippocampus are involved in the consolidation of spatial memories (Woollett & Maguire, 2009; Jiang, Miao, & Chen, 2017).

The *amygdala*, another part of the limbic system, also plays an important role in memory. The amygdala is especially involved with memories involving emotion. For example, if you are frightened by a large, growling pit bull dog, you're likely to remember the event vividly–an outcome related to the functioning of the amygdala. Encountering the pit bull or any large dog in the future is likely to reactivate the amygdala and bring back the unpleasant memory (Talmi et al., 2008; Pendyam et al., 2013; Kochli et al., 2015).

Memory at the Level of Neurons Although it is clear that the hippocampus and amygdala play a central role in memory formation, how is the transformation of information into a memory reflected at the level of neurons?

One answer is *long-term potentiation*, which shows that certain neural pathways become easily excited while a new response is being learned. At the same time, the number of synapses between neurons increases as the dendrites branch out to receive messages. These changes reflect a process called *consolidation*, in which memories become fixed and stable in long-term memory. Long-term memories take some time to stabilize; this explains why events and other stimuli are not suddenly fixed in memory. Instead, consolidation may continue for days and even years (Meeter & Murre, 2004; Kawashima, Izaki, & Grace, 2006; Hwang et al., 2017).

Because a stimulus may contain different sensory aspects, visual, auditory, and other areas of the brain may be simultaneously processing information about that stimulus. Information storage appears to be linked to the sites where this processing occurs, and it is therefore located in the particular areas that initially processed the information in terms of its visual, auditory, and other sensory stimuli. For this reason, memory traces are distributed throughout the brain. For example, when you recall a beautiful beach sunset, your recollection draws on memory stores located in visual areas of the brain (the view of the sunset), auditory areas (the sounds of the ocean), and tactile areas (the feel of the wind) (Squire, Clark, & Bayley, 2004; Murayama & Kitagami, 2013).

In short, the physical stuff of memory–the engram–is produced by a complex of biochemical and neural processes. Scientists are just beginning to understand how the brain compiles the individual neural components into a single, coherent memory. It may be that the same neurons that fire when we are initially exposed to material are reactivated during efforts to recall that information.

In addition to increasingly understanding the biological basis of how memories are formed and recalled, memory specialists are also beginning to understand how to help people *forget* information through biological treatment. Specifically, they are seeking to understand how to help people forget traumatic events, persistent fears, or even annoying habits. And they are making advances in that direction, learning how to reliably alter memories in mice through a combination of a drug called HDAC inhibitor and training. In humans, such drugs might be used to disrupt the initial encoding of memories, such as treating rape victims soon after the rape to reduce the long-term trauma of the event (Johnson, 2014; Lu, 2015).

Still, although memory researchers have made considerable strides in understanding the neuroscience behind memory, more remains to be learned–and remembered (Gelbard-Sagiv et al., 2008; Brown & Banks, 2015). (For more on the biological basis of memory, see *Neuroscience in Your Life*.)

NEUROSCIENCE IN YOUR LIFE: SUPERIOR MEMORY

Some people have astounding memory and can memorize as many as 100 words in just 5 minutes. But can anyone have superior memory with the appropriate training? Apparently, the answer is yes, for recent research has shown that people's memory can be trained to show significant changes in capacity, and these changes are reflected in changes in the brain. For example, participants in one study spent 30 minutes a day for 6 weeks practicing to improve their memory. Following training, participants were given 10 minutes to remember as many words as they could, and their memory capacity increased from 26 words to 62 words. This improvement was paralleled by increased connectivity between areas of the *medial temporal lobe,* including the hippocampus, and the frontal cortex, similar to what is found in those with strongly superior memories (memory athletes).

In the view of the brain below, the lines show the difference between nonathletes and athletes, with the blue lines showing more connectivity for nonathletes and the red lines showing more connectivity for athletes. The balls indicate major hubs for these connections, with the largest hubs in the frontal cortex. This research demonstrates that even after our ability to remember information is established, practice can enhance it, and that practice results in lasting effects on the way our brains are wired (Dresler et al., 2017).

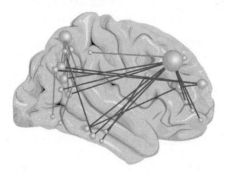

Source: Adapted from Dresler, M., Shirer, W. R., Konrad, B. N., Muller, N. C., Wagner, I. C., Fernandez, G., . . . Greicius, M. D. (2017). Mnemonic training reshapes brain networks to support superior memory. *Neuron, 93*(5), 1227–1235 e1226. doi: 10.1016/j.neuron.2017.02.003.

RECAP/EVALUATE/RETHINK

RECAP

LO 18-1 What is memory?

- Memory is the process by which we encode, store, and retrieve information.

LO 18-2 Are there different kinds of memory?

- Sensory memory, corresponding to each of the sensory systems, is the first place where information is saved. Sensory memories are very brief, but they are precise, storing a nearly exact replica of a stimulus.
- Roughly seven (plus or minus two) chunks of information can be transferred and held in short-term memory. Information in short-term memory is held from 15 to 25 seconds and then, if not transferred to long-term memory, is lost.
- Memories are transferred into long-term storage through rehearsal. If memories are transferred into long-term memory, they become relatively permanent.
- Some theorists view short-term memory as a working memory in which information is retrieved, manipulated, and held through rehearsal. In this view, it is a central executive processor involved in reasoning and decision making; it coordinates a visual store, a verbal store, and an episodic buffer.
- Long-term memory can be viewed in terms of memory modules, each of which is related to separate memory systems in the brain. For instance, we can distinguish between declarative memory and procedural memory. Declarative memory is further divided into episodic memory and semantic memory.
- Semantic networks suggest that knowledge is stored in long-term memory as mental representations of clusters of interconnected information.

LO 18-3 What are the biological bases of memory?

- The hippocampus and amygdala are especially important in the establishment of memory.

- Memories are distributed across the brain, relating to the different sensory information-processing systems involved during the initial exposure to a stimulus.

EVALUATE

1. Match the type of memory with its definition:

   1. Long-term memory
   2. Short-term memory
   3. Sensory memory

   a. Holds information 15 to 25 seconds
   b. Stores information on a relatively permanent basis
   c. Direct representation of a stimulus

2. A(n) _____ is a meaningful group of stimuli that can be stored together in short-term memory.

3. There appear to be two types of declarative memory: _____ memory for knowledge and facts and _____ memory for personal experiences.

4. Some memory researchers believe that long-term memory is stored as associations between pieces of information in _____ networks.

RETHINK

1. It is a truism that "you never forget how to ride a bicycle." Why might this be so? In what type of memory is information about bicycle riding stored?

2. The ability to remember specific skills and the order in which they are used is known as procedural memory. Because driving involves procedural memory, why is it so unsafe to use a cell phone while driving?

Answers to Evaluate Questions

1. 1-b, 2-a, 3-c; 2. chunk; 3. semantic, episodic; 4. semantic

KEY TERMS

memory	long-term memory	working memory	semantic memory
sensory memory	chunk	declarative memory	episodic memory
short-term memory	rehearsal	procedural memory	semantic networks

Module 19
Recalling Long-Term Memories

An hour after his job interview, Ricardo was sitting in a coffee shop, telling his friend Laura how well it had gone, when the woman who had interviewed him walked in. "Well, hello, Ricardo. How are you doing?" Trying to make a good impression, Ricardo began to make introductions but suddenly realized he could not remember the interviewer's name. Stammering, he desperately searched his memory but to no avail. "I *know* her name," he thought to himself, "but here I am, looking like a fool. I can kiss this job good-bye."

Have you ever tried to remember someone's name, convinced that you knew it but unable to recall it no matter how hard you tried? This common occurrence–known as the **tip-of-the-tongue phenomenon**–exemplifies how difficult it can be to retrieve information stored in long-term memory (Brennen, Vikan, & Dybdahl, 2007; Schwartz, 2008; Schwartz & Metcalfe, 2011).

Retrieval Cues

Perhaps recall of names and other memories is not perfect because there is so much information stored in long-term memory. Because the material that makes its way to long-term memory is relatively permanent, the capacity of long-term memory is vast. For instance, if you are like the average college student, your vocabulary includes some 50,000 words, you know hundreds of mathematical "facts," and you are able to conjure up images–such as the way your childhood home looked–with no trouble at all. In fact, simply cataloging all your memories would probably take years of work.

How do we sort through this vast array of material and retrieve specific information at the appropriate time? One way is through retrieval cues. A *retrieval cue* is a stimulus that allows us to recall more easily information that is in long-term memory. It may be a word, an emotion, or a sound; whatever the specific cue, a memory will suddenly come to mind when the retrieval cue is present. For example, the smell of roasting turkey may evoke memories of Thanksgiving or family gatherings.

Retrieval cues guide people through the information stored in long-term memory in much the same way that a search engine such as Google guides people through the Internet. They are particularly important when we are making an effort to *recall* information, as opposed to being asked to *recognize* material stored in memory. In **recall,** a specific piece of information must be retrieved–such as that needed to answer a fill-in-the-blank question or to write an essay on a test. In contrast, **recognition** occurs when people are presented with a stimulus and asked whether they have been exposed to it previously or are asked to identify it from a list of alternatives.

As you might guess, recognition is generally a much easier task than recall (see Figures 1 and 2). Recall is more difficult because it consists of a series of processes: a search through memory, retrieval of potentially relevant information, and then a decision regarding whether the information you have found is accurate. If the information appears to be correct, the search is over, but if it is not, the search must continue. In contrast, recognition is simpler because it involves fewer steps (Leigh, Zinkhan, & Swaminathan, 2006; Moen, Miller, & Lloyd, 2017).

LEARNING OUTCOMES

LO 19-1 What causes difficulties and failures in remembering?

tip-of-the-tongue phenomenon The inability to recall information that one realizes one knows–a result of the difficulty of retrieving information from long-term memory. (Module 19)

recall Memory task in which specific information must be retrieved. (Module 19)

recognition Memory task in which individuals are presented with a stimulus and asked whether they have been exposed to it in the past or to identify it from a list of alternatives. (Module 19)

Study Alert
Remember the distinction between recall (in which specific information must be retrieved) and recognition (in which information is presented and must be identified or distinguished from other material).

FIGURE 1 Try to recall the names of these characters. Because this is a recall task, it is relatively difficult.
©WALT DISNEY PRODUCTIONS/Album/Newscom

FIGURE 2 Naming the characters in Figure 1 (a recall task) is more difficult than solving the recognition problem posed in this list.

Answer this recognition question: Which of the following are the names of the seven dwarfs in the Disney movie *Snow White and the Seven Dwarfs?*	
Goofy	Bashful
Sleepy	Meanie
Smarty	Doc
Scaredy	Happy
Dopey	Angry
Grumpy	Sneezy
Wheezy	Crazy

(The correct answers are Bashful, Doc, Dopey, Grumpy, Happy, Sleepy, and Sneezy.)

levels-of-processing theory The theory of memory that emphasizes the degree to which new material is mentally analyzed. (Module 19)

Levels of Processing

One determinant of how well memories are recalled is the way in which material is first perceived, processed, and understood. The **levels-of-processing theory** emphasizes the degree to which new material is mentally analyzed. It suggests that the amount of information processing that occurs when material is initially encountered is central in determining how much of the information is ultimately remembered. According to this approach, the depth of information processing during exposure to material–meaning the degree to which it is analyzed and considered–is critical; the greater the intensity of its initial processing, the more likely we are to remember it (Craik & Lockhart, 2008; Mungan, Peynircioğlu, & Halpern, 2011).

Because we do not pay close attention to much of the information to which we are exposed, very little mental processing typically takes place, and we forget new material almost immediately. However, information to which we pay greater attention is processed more thoroughly. Therefore, it enters memory at a deeper level–and is less apt to be forgotten than is information processed at shallower levels.

The theory goes on to suggest that there are considerable differences in the ways in which information is processed at various levels of memory. At shallow levels, information is processed merely in terms of its physical and sensory aspects. For example, we may pay attention only to the shapes that make up the letters in the word *dog.* At an intermediate level of processing, the shapes are translated into meaningful units–in this case, letters of the alphabet. Those letters are considered in the context of words, and specific phonetic sounds may be attached to the letters.

At the deepest level of processing, information is analyzed in terms of its meaning. We may see it in a wider context and draw associations between the meaning of the information and broader networks of knowledge. For instance, we may think of dogs not merely as animals with four legs and a tail but also in terms of their relationship to cats and other mammals. We may form an image of our own dog, thereby relating the concept to our own lives. According to the levels-of-processing approach, the deeper the initial level of processing of specific information, the longer the information will be retained.

There are considerable practical implications to the notion that recall depends on the degree to which information is initially processed. For example, the depth of information processing is critical when learning and studying course material. Rote memorization of a list of key terms for a test is unlikely to produce long-term recollection of information because processing occurs at a shallow level. In contrast, thinking about the meaning of the terms and reflecting on how they relate to information that one currently knows results in far more effective long-term retention (Conway, 2002; Wenzel, Zetocha, & Ferraro, 2007; Albanese & Case, 2015).

Explicit and Implicit Memory

If you've ever had surgery, you probably hoped that the surgeons were focused completely on the surgery and gave you their undivided attention while slicing into your body. The reality in most operating rooms is quite different, though. Surgeons may be chatting with nurses about a new restaurant as soon as they sew you up.

If you are like most patients, you are left with no recollection of the conversation that occurred while you were under anesthesia. However, it is very possible that although you had no conscious memories of the discussions on the merits of the restaurant, on some level you probably did recall at least some information. In fact, careful studies have found that people who are anesthetized during surgery can sometimes recall snippets of conversations they heard during surgery–even though they have no conscious recollection of the information (Sebel, Bonke, & Winograd, 1993).

The discovery that people have memories about which they are unaware has been an important one. It has led to speculation that two forms of memory, explicit and implicit, may exist side by side. **Explicit memory** refers to intentional or conscious recollection of information. When we try to remember a name or date we have encountered or learned about previously, we are searching our explicit memory.

In contrast, **implicit memory** refers to memories of which people are not consciously aware but that can affect subsequent performance and behavior. Skills that operate automatically and without thinking, such as jumping out of the path of an automobile coming toward us as we walk down the side of a road, are stored in implicit memory. Similarly, a feeling of vague dislike for an acquaintance, without knowing why we have that feeling, may be a reflection of implicit memories. Perhaps the person reminds us of someone else in our past that we didn't like, even though we are not aware of the memory of that other individual (Gopie, Craik, & Hasher, 2011; Wu, 2013; Vöhringer et al., 2017).

Implicit memory is closely related to the prejudice and discrimination people exhibit toward members of minority groups. Although people may say and even believe they harbor no prejudice, assessment of their implicit memories may reveal that they have negative associations about members of minority groups. Such associations can influence people's behavior without their being aware of their underlying beliefs (Greenwald, Nosek, & Sriram, 2006; Hofmann et al., 2008; Enge, Lupo, & Zárate, 2015).

One way that memory specialists study implicit memory is through experiments that use priming. **Priming** occurs when exposure to a word or concept (called a *prime*) later makes it easier to recall information related to the prime. Priming allows us to remember new information better and faster because of material we already have stored in memory. Priming effects occur even when people have no conscious memory of the original word or concept (Toth & Daniels, 2002; Schacter, Dobbins, & Schnyer, 2004; Geyer, Gokce, & Müller, 2011).

The typical experiment designed to illustrate priming helps clarify the phenomenon. In priming experiments, participants are rapidly exposed to a stimulus such as a word, an object, or perhaps a drawing of a face. The second phase of the experiment is done after an interval ranging from several seconds to several months. At that point, participants are exposed to incomplete perceptual information that is related to the first stimulus, and they are asked whether they recognize it. For example, the new material may consist of the first letter of a word that had been presented earlier or a part of a face that had been shown earlier. If participants are able to identify the stimulus more readily than they identify stimuli that have not been presented earlier, priming has taken place. Clearly, the earlier stimulus has been remembered–although the material resides in implicit memory, not explicit memory.

The same thing happens to us in our everyday lives. Suppose several months ago you watched a documentary on the planets, and the narrator described the moons of Mars, focusing on its moon named Phobos. You promptly forget the name of the moon, at least consciously. Then, several months later, you're completing a crossword puzzle

explicit memory Intentional or conscious recollection of information. (Module 19)

implicit memory Memories of which people are not consciously aware but that can affect subsequent performance and behavior. (Module 19)

priming A phenomenon that occurs when exposure to a word or concept (called a prime) later makes it easier to recall information related to the prime. (Module 21)

that you have partially filled in, and it includes the letters *obos*. As soon as you look at the set of letters, you think of Phobos, and suddenly you recall for the first time since your initial exposure to the information that it is one of the moons of Mars. The sudden recollection occurred because your memory was primed by the letters *obos*.

In short, when information that we are unable to consciously recall affects our behavior, implicit memory is at work. Our behavior may be influenced by experiences of which we are unaware–an example of what has been called "retention without remembering" (Horton et al., 2005; White, 2013; Rossi-Arnaud et al, 2017).

Flashbulb Memories

Ask anyone old enough to recall the day terrorist attacks brought down the Twin Towers in New York City on September 11, 2001. They will likely recall exactly where they were when they heard the news, even though the incident happened years ago.

flashbulb memories Memories of a specific, important, or surprising emotionally significant event that are recalled easily and with vivid imagery. (Module 19)

Their ability to remember details about this fatal event illustrates a phenomenon known as flashbulb memory. **Flashbulb memories** are memories related to a specific, important, or surprising event that are so vivid they represent a virtual snapshot of the event. Several types of flashbulb memories are common among college students. For example, involvement in a car accident, meeting one's roommate for the first time, and the night of high school graduation are all typical flashbulb memories (see Figure 3; Bohn & Berntsen, 2007; Talarico, 2009; Lanciano et al., 2013).

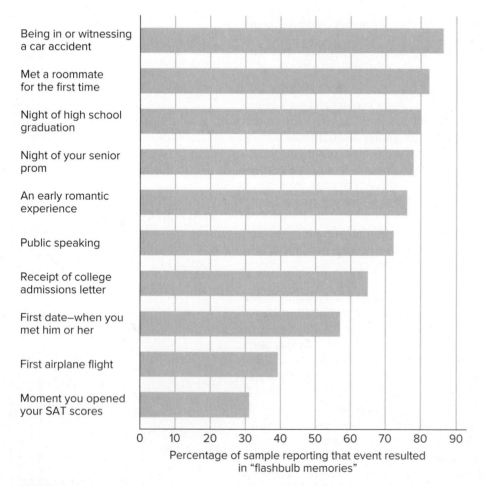

FIGURE 3 These are the most common flashbulb memory events, based on a survey of college students. What are some of your flashbulb memories?

(Right, top): ©Image Source/Getty Images; (Right, middle): ©Digital Vision/SuperStock; (Right, bottom): ©DreamPictures/VStock/Getty Images; (Graph): Source: Adapted from Rubin, D. C. (1986, September). The subtle deceiver: Recalling our past. *Psychology Today*, pp. 39–46.

Of course, flashbulb memories do not contain every detail of an original scene. I remember vividly that decades ago I was sitting in Mr. Sharp's 10th-grade geometry class when I heard that President John Kennedy had been shot. However, although I recall where I was sitting and how my classmates reacted to the news, I do not recollect what I was wearing or what I had for lunch that day.

Furthermore, the details recalled in flashbulb memories are often inaccurate, particularly when they involve highly emotional events. For example, those old enough to remember the day when the World Trade Center in New York was attacked by terrorists typically remember watching television that morning and seeing images of the first plane and then the second plane striking the towers. However, that recollection is wrong: In fact, television broadcasts showed images only of the second plane on September 11. No video of the first plane was available until early the following morning, September 12, when it was shown on television (Schaefer, Halldorson, & Dizon-Reynante, 2011; Hirst et al., 2015).

Flashbulb memories illustrate a more general phenomenon about memory: Memories that are exceptional are more easily retrieved (although not necessarily accurately) than are those relating to events that are commonplace. The more distinctive a stimulus is and the more personal relevance the event has, the more likely we are to recall it later (Talarico & Rubin, 2007; Schaefer, Halldorson, & Dizon-Reynante, 2011; Gandolphe & El Haj, 2017).

Even with a distinctive stimulus, however, we may not remember where the information came from. *Source amnesia* occurs when an individual has a memory for some material but cannot recall where he or she encountered it. For example, source amnesia can explain situations in which you meet someone you know but can't remember where you met that person initially.

Similarly, our motivation to remember material when we are exposed to it initially affects how well we can later recall it. If we know we are going to need to recall material later, we are going to be more attentive to it. In contrast, if we don't expect to need to recall material later, then we are less likely to remember it (Naveh-Benjamin, Guez, & Sorek, 2007; Kassam et al., 2009).

Constructive Processes in Memory: Rebuilding the Past

As we have seen, although it is clear that we can have detailed recollections of significant and distinctive events, it is difficult to gauge the accuracy of such memories. In fact, it is apparent that our memories reflect, at least in part, **constructive processes,** processes in which memories are influenced by the meaning we give to events. When we retrieve information, then, the memory that is produced is affected not just by the direct prior experience we have had with the stimulus but also by our guesses and inferences about its meaning.

The notion that memory is based on constructive processes was first put forward by Frederic Bartlett, a British psychologist. He suggested that people tend to remember information in terms of **schemas,** organized bodies of information stored in memory that bias the way new information is interpreted, stored, and recalled (Bartlett, 1932). Because we use schemas to organize information, our memories often consist of a reconstruction of previous experience. Consequently, schemas are based not only on the actual material to which people are exposed but also on their understanding of the situation, their expectations about the situation, and their awareness of the motivations underlying the behavior of others.

One of the earliest demonstrations of schemas came from a classic study that involved a procedure similar to the children's game of "telephone," in which information from memory is passed sequentially from one person to another. In the study, a participant viewed a drawing in which there were a variety of people of differing racial and ethnic backgrounds on a subway car, one of whom—a white person—was shown

constructive processes Processes in which memories are influenced by the meaning we give to events. (Module 19)

schemas Organized bodies of information stored in memory that bias the way new information is interpreted, stored, and recalled. (Modules 21, 52)

Study Alert
A key fact about memory is that it is a constructive process in which memories are influenced by the meaning given to what is being recalled.

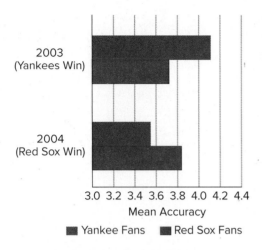

FIGURE 4 Yankee and Red Sox fans were more accurate recalling details of a championship game their team won than they were of a championship game that their team lost.

Source: Adapted from Breslin, C. W., & Safer, M. A. (2011). Effects of event valence on long-term memory for two baseball championship games. *Psychological Science, 20,* 1–5.

with a razor in his hand (Allport & Postman, 1958). The first participant was asked to describe the drawing to someone else without looking back at it. Then that person was asked to describe it to another person (without looking at the drawing), and then the process was repeated with still one more participant.

The report of the last person differed in significant, yet systematic, ways from the initial drawing. Specifically, many people described the drawing as depicting an African American with a knife–an incorrect recollection, given that the drawing showed a razor in the hand of a Caucasian person. The transformation of the Caucasian's razor into an African American's knife clearly indicates that the participants held a schema that included the unwarranted prejudice that African Americans are more violent than Caucasians and thus more apt to be holding a knife. In short, our expectations and knowledge–and prejudices–affect the reliability of our memories (McDonald & Hirt, 1997; Newby-Clark & Ross, 2003; De Brigard et al., 2017).

Although the constructive nature of memory can result in memories that are partially or completely false, they also may be beneficial in some ways. For example, false memories may allow us to keep hold of positive self-images. In addition, they may help us maintain positive relationships with others as we construct overly positive views of them (Howe, 2011).

Similarly, memory is affected by the emotional meaning of experiences. For example, in one experiment, researchers asked devoted Yankee or Red Sox fans about details of two decisive baseball championship games between the teams, one won by the Yankees and the other won by the Red Sox. Fans recalled details of the game their team won significantly more accurately than the game their team lost (see Figure 4; Breslin & Safer, 2011; Guida et al., 2013).

MEMORY IN THE COURTROOM: THE EYEWITNESS ON TRIAL

For Calvin Willis, the inadequate memories of two people cost him more than two decades of his life. Willis was the victim of mistaken identity when a young rape victim picked out his photo as the perpetrator of the rape. On that basis, he was tried, convicted, and sentenced to life in prison. Twenty-one years later, DNA testing showed that Willis was innocent and the victim's identification wrong. (Corsello, 2005)

Unfortunately, Willis is not the only victim to whom apologies have had to be made; many cases of mistaken identity have led to unjustified legal actions. Research on eyewitness identification of suspects, as well as on memory for other details of crimes, has shown that eyewitnesses are apt to make significant errors when they try to recall details of criminal activity–even if they are highly confident about their recollections. Because more than 75,000 prosecutions a year are totally based on eyewitness recollections, the problem is significant (Paterson, Kemp, & Ng, 2011; Lehrer, 2012; McCann et al., 2015).

One reason eyewitnesses tend to make significant errors is the impact of the weapons used in crimes. When a criminal perpetrator displays a gun or knife, it acts like a perceptual magnet, attracting the eyes of the witnesses. As a consequence, witnesses pay less attention to other details of the crime and are less able to recall what actually occurred (Zaitsu, 2007; Pickel, 2009; Sheahan et al., 2017).

The specific wording of questions posed to eyewitnesses by police officers or attorneys also can lead to memory errors. For example, in one experiment, the participants were shown a film of two cars crashing into each other. Some were then asked the question, "About how fast were the cars going when they *smashed* into each other?" On average, they estimated the speed to be 40.8 miles per hour. In contrast, when another group of participants was asked, "About how fast were the cars going when they *contacted* each other?" the average estimated speed was only 31.8 miles per hour (see Figure 5; Loftus & Palmer, 1974).

Although eyewitnesses are often confident in their recollections, in many cases, their confidence is misplaced. In fact, the relationship between confidence and accuracy

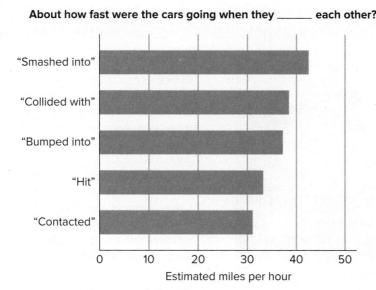

About how fast were the cars going when they _____ each other?

"Smashed into"

"Collided with"

"Bumped into"

"Hit"

"Contacted"

Estimated miles per hour

FIGURE 5 After viewing an accident involving two cars, the participants in a study were asked to estimate the speed of the two cars involved in the collision. Estimates varied substantially, depending on the way the question was worded.
Source: Adapted from Loftus, E. F., & Palmer, J. C. (1974). Reconstruction of automobile destruction: An example of the interface between language and memory. *Journal of Verbal Learning and Verbal Behavior, 13,* 585–589.

is often small and sometimes even negative; in some cases, the more confident a witness, the less accurate are their recollections. On the other hand, several conditions affect the relationship between eyewitness confidence and better accuracy. Specifically, accuracy improves when witnesses see only one suspect at a time; when the suspects don't look conspicuous in the lineup due to their clothing or ethnicity or race; and when the witness is told the offender is not necessarily in the lineup (Wixted & Wells, 2017).

Children's Reliability The problem of memory reliability becomes even more acute when children are witnesses because increasing evidence suggests that children's memories are highly vulnerable to the influence of others. For instance, in one experiment, 5- to 7-year-old girls who had just had routine physical examinations were shown an anatomically explicit doll. The girls were shown the doll's genital area and asked, "Did the doctor touch you here?" Three of the girls who did not have a vaginal or anal exam said that the doctor had in fact touched them in the genital area, and one of those three made up the detail "The doctor did it with a stick" (Brown, Goldstein, & Bjorklund, 2000).

Children's memories are especially susceptible to influence when the situation is highly emotional or stressful. For example, in trials in which there is significant pretrial publicity or in which alleged victims are questioned repeatedly, often by untrained interviewers, the memories of the alleged victims may be influenced by the types of questions they are asked (Goodman & Quas, 2008; Wright, Nash, & Wade, 2015).

Repressed and False Memories: Separating Truth from Fiction Consider the case of Paul Shanley, a Catholic priest. He was convicted and jailed for 12 years for sexual abuse of a victim who claimed he had no memory until adulthood of being abused as a child over a 6-year period. It was not until adulthood that he claimed his repressed memories gradually moved into consciousness. At that point, he reported clearly recalling his years of abuse, and on the basis of those previously repressed memories, the priest was convicted (Wolf, Guyer, & Sharpe, 2010; Otgaar, Howe, & Muris, 2017).

Repressed memories are apparent recollections of events that are initially so shocking that the mind responds by pushing them into the unconscious. Supporters of the notion of repressed memory (based on Freud's psychoanalytic theory) suggest that traumatic memories may remain hidden, possibly throughout a person's lifetime, unless they are triggered by some current circumstance, such as the probing that occurs during psychological therapy.

However, memory researcher Elizabeth Loftus, and many others, maintain that there is little evidence for the phenomenon of repressed memories. They believe that so-called repressed memories may well be inaccurate or even wholly false–representing *false memory*. For example, false memories develop when people are unable to recall

Paul Shanley, a Catholic priest, spent 12 years in jail for the purported sexual abuse of a child over a 6-year period. The victim only recalled the abuse years later when he was an adult.
©Charles Krupa-Pool/Getty Images

MEMORIES ARE MADE TO BE MEANINGFUL

One of Giacomo Regaldi's earliest memories is the day his dad took a day off from work to attend his third-grade clarinet recital and then took the whole family out for dinner to celebrate. Now a professional musician, Giacomo has long cherished this memory as evidence not only of his father's love but also of his approval of Giacomo's musical talents and aspirations.

The problem, though, is that it never happened–Giacomo had no clarinet recital in the third grade. He didn't even take up clarinet until 2 years after that. His father did attend a number of Giacomo's concerts and recitals, and he also did take the family out for dinner many times, but those events never happened together on the same day. Giacomo has taken fragmented memories of different events at different times and woven them together to form a single, cherished memory–although a false one.

This sort of memory error happens to people all the time. The reconstructive nature of memory means that we piece together facts and details of an event with our own interpretations, inferences, and assumptions about it. That memory can then become further contaminated with bits of information we learned later on, with fragments of memories of similar events or even with details that we merely imagined. Indeed, we may even sometimes

©Nicholas Burningham/Alamy Stock Photo

confuse entirely imaginary events with real memories (Pickrell et al., 2017).

These kinds of memory errors would seem to be problematic, and they can be in certain circumstances, such as when the memory of an eyewitness is a key piece of evidence in a criminal trial. But most of the time, they are harmless, and researchers are now learning that in fact, they may serve a useful purpose by reinforcing important parts of our identities. Certain memories take on a special importance because we incorporate them into a narrative; they become part of "the story of my life" and reveal something we value about ourselves,

such as a formative experience we believe shaped us into the person we are today.

In these cases, the accuracy of the memory matters less than what the memory means to us. We might, in our reimagining of the event, exaggerate its drama, minimize details that contradict our interpretation, and in other similar ways unintentionally mold the memory into a form that best fits our favored narrative. In the telling and retelling of a meaningful memory, we may embellish for effect, shift the emphasis to appeal to different listeners, add newly learned details, or incorporate reactions of people we told it to previously. Such alterations and embellishments often endear the memory to us even more strongly (Schacter, Guerin, & St. Jacques, 2011; Dunlop, Guo, & McAdams, 2016).

In one study illustrating false memories, students who opposed a tuition increase at their school were asked to write an essay in support of the tuition increase. Having taken that position and defended it, these students later tended to misremember their initial attitudes and recall that they were more in favor of an increase than they actually had been (Rodriguez & Strange, 2015).

At least sometimes, the value of memory may not lie in its accuracy as much as in the meaning it gives our lives.

> **RETHINK**
>
> - Do you think you are able to tell whether any of your own long-term memories are accurate or contaminated? Why or why not?
> - Do you think it's more important for your autobiographical memories to be accurate or to be personally meaningful? Why do you think so?

the source of a memory of a particular event about which they have only vague recollections. When the source of the memory becomes unclear or ambiguous, people may become confused about whether they actually experienced the event or whether it was imagined. Ultimately, people come to believe that the event actually occurred (Bernstein & Loftus, 2009a; Choi, Kensinger, & Rajaram, 2013; Lynn et al., 2015).

There is great controversy regarding the legitimacy of repressed memories. Many therapists give great weight to authenticity of repressed memories, and their views are supported by research showing that there are specific regions of the brain that help keep unwanted memories out of awareness. On the other side of the issue are researchers who maintain that there is insufficient scientific support for the existence of such memories. There is also a middle ground: memory researchers who suggest that false memories are a result of normal information processing. The challenge for those on all sides of the issue is to distinguish truth from fiction (Strange, Clifasefi, & Garry, 2007; Bernstein & Loftus, 2009b; also see *Applying Psychology in the 21st Century*).

AUTOBIOGRAPHICAL MEMORY: WHERE PAST MEETS PRESENT

Your memory of experiences in your own past may well be a fiction–or at least a distortion of what actually occurred. The same constructive processes that make us inaccurately recall the behavior of others also reduce the accuracy of autobiographical memories. **Autobiographical memory** is our recollections of our own life experiences. Autobiographical memories encompass the episodic memories we hold about ourselves (Sutin & Robins, 2007; Nalbantian, 2011).

For example, we tend to forget information about our past that is incompatible with the way in which we currently see ourselves. One study found that adults who were well adjusted but who had been treated for emotional problems during the early years of their lives tended to forget important but troubling childhood events, such as being in foster care. College students misremember their bad grades–but remember their good ones (see Figure 6; Walker, Skowronski, & Thompson, 2003; Kemps & Tiggemann, 2007; Stanley et al., 2017).

Similarly, when a group of 48-year-olds was asked to recall how they had responded on a questionnaire they had completed when they were high school freshmen, their accuracy was no better than chance. For example, although 61% of the questionnaire respondents said that playing sports and other physical activities was their favorite pastime, only 23% of the adults recalled it accurately (Offer et al., 2000).

It is not just certain kinds of events that are distorted; particular periods of life are remembered more easily than others. For example, when people reach late adulthood, they remember periods of life in which they experienced major transitions, such as attending college and working at their first jobs, better than they remember their middle-age years. Similarly, although most adults' earliest memories of their own lives are of events that occurred when they were toddlers, toddlers show evidence of recall of events that occurred when they were as young as 6 months old (Cordnoldi, De Beni, & Helstrup, 2007; Mace, Bernas, & Clevinger, 2015).

autobiographical memory Our recollections of our own life experiences. (Module 19)

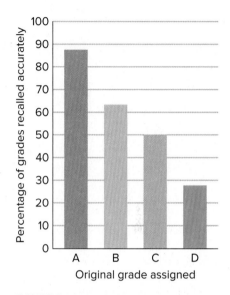

FIGURE 6 We tend to distort memories of unpleasant events. For example, college students are much more likely to accurately recall their good grades while inaccurately recalling their poor ones. Now that you know this, how well do you think you can recall your high school grades?

Source: Adapted from Bahrick, H. P., Hall, L. K., & Berger, S. A. (1996). Accuracy and distortion in memory for high school grades. *Psychological Science, 7,* 265–269.

 # Exploring Diversity

Are There Cross-Cultural Differences in Memory?

Explorers who have visited parts of the world in which there is no written language sometimes return with tales of individuals with phenomenal memories. For instance, storytellers in some preliterate cultures recount long chronicles that include the names and activities of people over multiple generations.

Such feats of memory initially led experts to believe that people in preliterate societies develop a different, and perhaps better, type of memory than do those in cultures that employ a written language. They suggested that in a society that lacks writing, people are motivated to recall information with accuracy, especially information relating to tribal histories and traditions that would be lost if they were not passed down orally from one generation to another (Daftary & Meri, 2002; Berntsen & Rubin, 2004).

Today, however, memory researchers dismiss that view. For one thing, preliterate peoples don't have an exclusive claim to amazing memory feats. Some Hebrew scholars memorize thousands of pages of text and can recall the locations of particular words on the page. Similarly, poetry singers in the Balkans can recall thousands of lines of poetry. Even in cultures in which written language exists, then, astounding feats of memory are possible (Strathern & Stewart, 2003; Rubin et al., 2007).

Memory researchers now believe that there are both similarities and differences in memory across cultures. Basic memory processes seem to be similar. For example, short-term memory capacity, working memory, and the structure of long-term memory—the "hardware"—are universal and operate similarly in people in all cultures.

Storytellers in many cultures can recount hundreds of years of history in vivid detail. Research has found that this amazing ability is due less to basic memory processes than to the ways in which they acquire and retain information.
©Albert Moldvay/National Geographic/Getty Images

In contrast, the way information is acquired and the degree to which it is rehearsed—the "software" of memory—do differ from culture to culture. Culture determines how people frame information initially, how much they practice learning it, and which strategies they use to recall it (Mack, 2003; Wang & Conway, 2006; Rubin et al., 2007).

RECAP/EVALUATE/RETHINK

RECAP

LO 19-1 What causes difficulties and failures in remembering?

- The tip-of-the-tongue phenomenon is the temporary inability to remember information that one is certain one knows. Retrieval cues are a major strategy for recalling information successfully.
- The levels-of-processing approach to memory suggests that the way in which information is initially perceived and analyzed determines the success with which it is recalled. The deeper the initial processing, the greater the recall.

- Explicit memory refers to intentional or conscious recollection of information. In contrast, implicit memory refers to memories of which people are not consciously aware but that can affect subsequent performance and behavior.
- Flashbulb memories are memories centered on a specific, emotionally significant event. The more distinctive a memory is, the more easily it can be retrieved.
- Memory is a constructive process: We relate memories to the meaning, guesses, and expectations we give to events. Specific information is recalled in terms of schemas, organized bodies of information stored in memory

that bias the way new information is interpreted, stored, and recalled.

- Eyewitnesses are apt to make substantial errors when they try to recall the details of crimes. The problem of memory reliability becomes even more acute when the witnesses are children.
- Autobiographical memory is influenced by constructive processes.

EVALUATE

1. While with a group of friends at a dance, Eva bumps into a man she dated last month. But when she tries to introduce him to her friends, she cannot remember his name. What is the term for this occurrence?
2. _____ is the process of retrieving a specific item from memory.
3. A friend tells you, "I know exactly where I was and what I was doing when I heard that Michael Jackson died." What is this type of memory phenomenon called?

4. _____ _____ _____ theory states that the more a person analyzes a statement, the more likely he or she is to remember it later.

RETHINK

1. Research shows that an eyewitness's memory for details of crimes can contain significant errors. How might a lawyer use this information when evaluating an eyewitness's testimony? Should eyewitness accounts be permissible in a court of law?
2. How do schemas help people process information during encoding, storage, and retrieval? In what ways are they helpful? How can they contribute to inaccurate autobiographical memories?

Answers to Evaluate Questions

1. tip-of-the-tongue phenomenon; 2. Recall; 3. flashbulb memory; 4. Levels-of-processing

KEY TERMS

tip-of-the-tongue phenomenon	recognition	implicit memory	constructive processes
recall	levels-of-processing theory	priming	schemas
	explicit memory	flashbulb memories	autobiographical memory

Module 20

Forgetting: When Memory Fails

He could not remember his childhood friends, the house he grew up in, or what he had eaten for breakfast that morning. H. M., as he is referred to in the scientific literature, had lost his ability to remember anything beyond a few minutes, the result of experimental surgery intended to minimize his epileptic seizures. But the removal of his brain's hippocampus and the loss of his temporal lobes quite literally erased H. M.'s past. He had enjoyed a normal memory until he underwent the operation at age 27. After that, H. M. said, every moment felt like waking from a dream. He never knew where he was or the identities of the people around him (Milner, 2005).

As the case of H. M. illustrates, a person without a normal memory faces severe difficulties. All of us who have experienced even routine instances of forgetting–such as not remembering an acquaintance's name or a fact on a test–understand the very real consequences of memory failure.

Of course, memory failure is also essential to remembering important information. The ability to forget inconsequential details about experiences, people, and objects helps us avoid being burdened and distracted by trivial stores of meaningless data. Forgetting helps keep unwanted and unnecessary information from interfering with retrieving information that is wanted and necessary (Schooler & Hertwig, 2012).

Forgetting also permits us to form general impressions and recollections. For example, the reason our friends consistently look familiar to us is because we're able to forget their clothing, facial blemishes, and other transient features that change from one occasion to the next. Instead, our memories are based on a summary of various critical features–a far more economical use of our memory capabilities.

Finally, forgetting provides a practical educational benefit: When we have forgotten something and then are forced to relearn it, we're more likely to remember it better in the future (Bjork, 2015; Boser, 2017).

The first attempts to study forgetting were made by German psychologist Hermann Ebbinghaus about 100 years ago. Using himself as the only participant in his study, Ebbinghaus memorized lists of three-letter nonsense syllables–meaningless sets of two consonants with a vowel in between, such as FIW and BOZ. By measuring how easy it was to relearn a given list of words after varying periods of time had passed since the initial learning, he found that forgetting occurred systematically, as shown in Figure 1. As the figure indicates, the most rapid forgetting occurs in the first 9 hours, particularly in the first hour. After 9 hours, the rate of forgetting slows and declines little, even after the passage of many days.

Despite his primitive methods, Ebbinghaus's study had an important influence on subsequent research, and his basic conclusions have been upheld. There is almost always a strong initial decline in memory, followed by a more gradual drop over time. Furthermore, relearning of previously mastered material is almost always faster than starting from scratch, whether the material is academic information or a motor skill such as serving a tennis ball (Wixted & Carpenter, 2007; Radvansky, Pettijohn, & Kim, 2015).

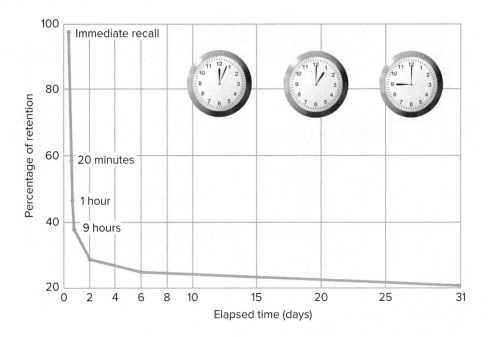

FIGURE 1 In his classic work, Ebbinghaus found that the most rapid forgetting occurs in the first 9 hours after exposure to new material. However, the rate of forgetting then slows down and declines very little even after many days have passed. Check your own memory: What were you doing exactly 2 hours ago? What were you doing last Tuesday at 5 p.m.? Which information is easier to retrieve?

Source: Adapted from Ebbinghaus, H. (1885/1913). *Memory: A contribution to experimental psychology* (H. A. Roger & C. E. Bussenius, Trans.). New York: Columbia University Press.

Why We Forget

Why do we forget? One reason is that we may not have paid attention to the material in the first place–a failure of *encoding*. For example, if you live in the United States, you probably have been exposed to thousands of pennies during your life. Despite this experience, you probably don't have a clear sense of the details of the coin. (See this for yourself by looking at Figure 2.) Consequently, the reason for your memory failure is that you probably never encoded the information into long-term memory initially. Obviously, if information was not placed in memory to start with, there is no way the information can be recalled.

But what about material that has been encoded into memory and that can't later be remembered? Several processes account for memory failures, including decay, interference, and cue-dependent forgetting.

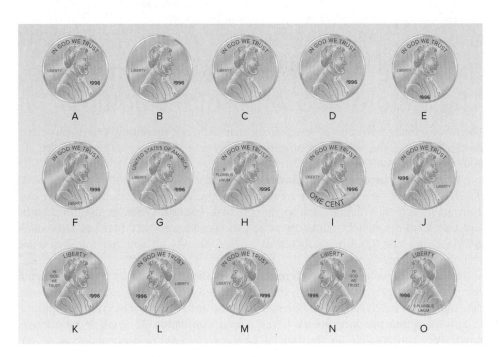

FIGURE 2 One of these pennies is the real thing. Can you find it? Why is this task harder than it seems at first?

Source: Adapted from Nickerson, R. S., & Adams, M. J. (1979). Long-term memory for a common object. *Cognitive Psychology, 11,* 297.

decay The loss of information in memory through its nonuse. (Module 20)

Decay is the loss of information in memory through nonuse. This explanation for forgetting assumes that *memory traces,* the physical changes that take place in the brain when new material is learned, simply fade away or disintegrate over time (Grann, 2007).

Although there is evidence that decay does occur, this does not seem to be the complete explanation for forgetting. Often there is no relationship between how long ago a person was exposed to information and how well that information is recalled. If decay explained all forgetting, we would expect that the more time that has elapsed between the initial learning of information and our attempt to recall it, the harder it would be to remember it because there would be more time for the memory trace to decay. Yet people who take several consecutive tests on the same material often recall more of the initial information when taking later tests than they did on earlier tests. If decay were operating, we would expect the opposite to occur (Hardt, Nader, & Nadel, 2013; Sachser et al., 2017).

interference The phenomenon by which information in memory disrupts the recall of other information. (Module 20)

Because decay does not fully account for forgetting, memory specialists have proposed an additional mechanism: interference. In **interference,** information stored in memory disrupts the recall of other information stored in memory. For example, if I'm trying to recall my college classmate Jake's name and all I can remember is the name of another classmate, James, interference may be at work (Solesio-Jofre et al., 2011; Ecker, Tay, & Brown, 2015).

To distinguish between decay and interference, think of the two processes in terms of a row of books on a library shelf. In decay, the old books are constantly crumbling and rotting away, leaving room for new arrivals. Interference processes suggest that new books knock the old ones off the shelf, where they become hard to find or even totally inaccessible.

cue-dependent forgetting Forgetting that occurs when there are insufficient retrieval cues to rekindle information that is in memory. (Module 20)

Finally, forgetting may occur because of **cue-dependent forgetting,** forgetting that occurs when there are insufficient retrieval cues to rekindle information that is in memory. For example, you may not be able to remember where you lost a set of keys until you mentally walk through your day, thinking of each place you visited. When you think of the place where you lost the keys–say, the library–the retrieval cue of the library may be sufficient to help you recall that you left them on the desk in the library. Without that retrieval cue, you may be unable to recall the location of the keys (Weller et al., 2013).

Study Alert

Memory loss through decay comes from nonuse of the memory; memory loss through interference is due to the presence of other information in memory.

Most research suggests that interference and cue-dependent forgetting are key processes in forgetting. We forget things mainly because new memories interfere with the retrieval of old ones or because appropriate retrieval cues are unavailable, not because the memory trace has decayed (Radvansky, 2010).

Proactive and Retroactive Interference: The Before and After of Forgetting

There are actually two sorts of interference that influence forgetting. One is proactive interference, and the other is retroactive interference (Bunting, 2006; Jacoby et al., 2007; Oberauer, Awh, & Sutterer, 2017).

proactive interference Interference in which information learned earlier disrupts the recall of material learned later. (Module 20)

In **proactive interference,** information learned earlier disrupts the recall of newer material. Suppose, as a student of foreign languages, you first learned French in the 10th grade, and then in the 11th grade you took Spanish. When in the 12th grade you take a college subject achievement test in Spanish, you may find you have difficulty recalling the Spanish translation of a word because all you can think of is its French equivalent.

retroactive interference Interference in which material that was learned later disrupts the retrieval of information that was learned earlier. (Module 20)

In contrast, **retroactive interference** occurs when material that was learned later disrupts the retrieval of information that was learned earlier. If, for example, you have difficulty on a French subject achievement test because of your more recent exposure to Spanish, retroactive interference is the culprit (see Figure 3). Similarly, retroactive interference can account for the lack of accuracy of eyewitness memories, as newer

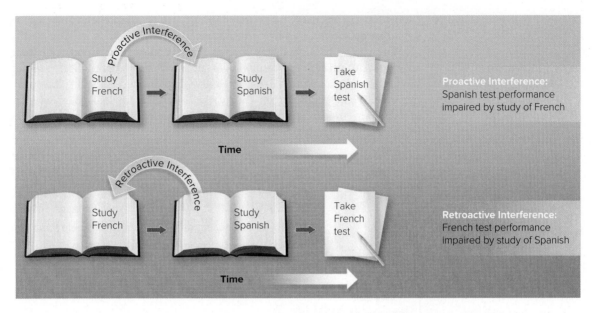

FIGURE 3 Proactive interference occurs when material learned earlier interferes with the recall of newer material. In this example, studying French before studying Spanish interferes with performance on a Spanish test. In contrast, retroactive interference exists when material learned after initial exposure to other material interferes with the recall of the first material. In this case, retroactive interference occurs when recall of French is impaired because of later exposure to Spanish.

information about a crime obtained from newspaper accounts may disrupt the initial memory of the observation of the crime.

One way to remember the difference between proactive and retroactive interference is to keep in mind that *pro*active interference progresses in time—the past interferes with the present. In contrast, *retro*active interference retrogresses in time, working backward as the present interferes with the past.

Although the concepts of proactive and retroactive interference illustrate how material may be forgotten, they still do not explain whether forgetting is caused by the actual loss or modification of information or by problems in the retrieval of information. Most research suggests that material that has apparently been lost because of interference can eventually be recalled if appropriate stimuli are presented, but the question has not been fully answered (Radvansky, 2010).

Memory Dysfunctions: Afflictions of Forgetting

Memory loss creeps up on its victims. It starts with little things such as misplacing keys or glasses. Then, you forget the names of common household items, and you miss appointments. Next, you can't drive in traffic without becoming confused and anxious. You try to hide what's happening, but everybody knows. Finally, your lapses become more consequential: You nearly get run over; you have a traffic accident. When you can no longer do the things you rely on for everyday living, such as getting dressed or making coffee, you know what's going on, though you're helpless to change it.

These memory problems are symptomatic of **Alzheimer's disease,** a progressive brain disorder that leads to a gradual and irreversible decline in cognitive abilities. Alzheimer's is the fourth-leading cause of death among adults in the United States, affecting an estimated 5 million people.

In the beginning, Alzheimer's symptoms appear as simple forgetfulness of things such as appointments and birthdays. As the disease progresses, memory loss becomes more profound, and even the simplest tasks—such as using a telephone—are forgotten.

PsychTech

Having trouble remembering something on your computer screen? According to research by Connor Diemand-Yauman (2010) and colleagues, changing the font into something *harder* to read may make it easier to remember. The explanation is that the unusual font forces us to concentrate more intently on the information, making it more memorable.

Alzheimer's disease A progressive brain disorder that leads to a gradual and irreversible decline in cognitive abilities. (Modules 20, 30)

Ultimately, victims may lose their ability to speak or comprehend language, and physical deterioration sets in, leading to death.

The causes of Alzheimer's disease are not fully understood. Increasing evidence suggests that Alzheimer's results from an inherited susceptibility to a defect in the production of the protein beta amyloid, which is necessary for the maintenance of nerve cell connections. When the synthesis of beta amyloid goes awry, large clumps of cells form, triggering inflammation and the deterioration of nerve cells in the brain (Hyman, 2011; Tan, Yu, & Tan, 2015).

From the perspective of...

A Health-Care Provider What sorts of activities might health-care providers offer their patients to help them combat the memory loss of Alzheimer's disease?

©Rubberball/Getty Images

amnesia Memory loss that occurs without other mental difficulties. (Module 20)

retrograde amnesia Amnesia in which memory is lost for occurrences prior to a certain event, but not for new events. (Module 20)

anterograde amnesia Amnesia in which memory is lost for events that follow an injury. (Module 20)

Korsakoff's syndrome A disease that afflicts long-term alcoholics, leaving some abilities intact but including hallucinations and a tendency to repeat the same story. (Module 20)

Alzheimer's disease is one of a number of memory dysfunctions. Another is **amnesia,** memory loss that occurs without other mental difficulties. The type of amnesia immortalized in countless Hollywood films involves a victim who receives a blow to the head and is unable to remember anything from his or her past. In reality, amnesia of this type, known as retrograde amnesia, is quite rare. In **retrograde amnesia,** memory is lost for occurrences prior to a certain event but not for new events. Usually, lost memories gradually reappear, although full restoration may take as long as several years. In certain cases, some memories are lost forever. But even in cases of severe memory loss, the loss is generally selective. For example, although people suffering from retrograde amnesia may be unable to recall friends and family members, they still may be able to play complicated card games or knit a sweater quite well (Verfaellie & Keane, 2002; Bright, Buckman, & Fradera, 2006).

A second type of amnesia is exemplified by people who remember nothing of their current activities. In **anterograde amnesia,** loss of memory occurs for events that follow an injury. Information cannot be transferred from short-term to long-term memory, resulting in the inability to remember anything other than what was in long-term storage before the injury (Gilboa, Winocur, & Rosenbaum, 2006).

Amnesia is also a result of **Korsakoff's syndrome,** a disease that afflicts long-term alcoholics. Although many of their intellectual abilities may be intact, Korsakoff's sufferers display a strange array of symptoms, including hallucinations and a tendency to repeat the same story over and over (Wester et al., 2013; Scalzo, Bowden, & Hillborn, 2015).

Fortunately, most of us have intact memory, and the occasional failures we suffer may actually be preferable to having a perfect memory. Consider, for instance, the case of a man who had total recall. After reading passages of Dante's *The Divine Comedy* in Italian—a language he did not speak—he was able to repeat them from memory some 15 years later. He could memorize lists of 50 unrelated words and recall them at will more than a decade later. He could even repeat the same list of words backward, if asked (Luria, 1968).

Such a skill at first may seem to be enviable, but it actually presented quite a problem. The man's memory became a jumble of lists of words, numbers, and names; when he tried to relax, his mind was filled with images. Even reading was difficult because every word evoked a flood of thoughts from the past that interfered with his ability to understand the meaning of what he was reading. Partially as a consequence of the man's unusual memory, psychologist A. R. Luria, who studied his case, found him to be a "disorganized and rather dull-witted person" (Luria, 1968). We might be grateful, then, that forgetfulness plays a role in our lives.

Study Alert
Except for Alzheimer's disease, memory disorders are relatively rare.

of Psychology

Improving Your Memory

Apart from the advantages of forgetting, say, a bad date, most of us would like to find ways to improve our memories. Among the effective strategies for studying and remembering course material are:

- *Rely on organization cues.* Recall material you read in textbooks or online by organizing the material in memory the first time you read it. For example, use cues such as chapter outlines or learning objectives. If you take advantage of these "advance organizers," you can make connections, see relationships among the various facts, and process the material at a deeper level, which in turn will later aid recall (Korur, Toker, & Eryilmaz, 2016).

- *Take effective notes.* "Less is more" is perhaps the best advice for taking lecture notes that facilitate recall. Rather than trying to jot down every detail of a lecture, it is better to listen and think about the material, and take down the main points. In effective note taking, thinking about the material when you first hear it is more important than writing it down. This is one reason that borrowing someone else's notes is a bad idea; you will have no framework in memory that you can use to understand them (Feldman, 2017).

- *Practice, practice, practice.* Although practice does not necessarily make perfect, it helps. Use *overlearning,* the process of studying and rehearsing material well beyond your initial mastery of it. Lots of research shows that people demonstrate better long-term recall when they overlearn rather than when they stop practicing just after they initially learn the material (Shibata et al., 2017).

- *Use the keyword technique.* If you are studying a foreign language, try pairing a foreign word with a common English word that has a similar sound. This English word is known as the *keyword.* For example, to learn the Spanish word for duck (*pato,* pronounced *pot-o*), you might choose the keyword *pot.* Once you have thought of a keyword, think of an image in which the the Spanish word *pato* is interacting with the English keyword. For example, you might envision a duck being cooked in a pot to remember the word *pato* (Wyra, Lawson, & Hungi, 2007).

- *Talk to yourself.* If you have trouble remembering names of people who you have recently met, one way to help yourself is to say their names out loud when you are first introduced. It will make it easier to retrieve the information later because the information is stored in additional ways in your brain.

- *Be skeptical about claims that certain drugs improve memory.* Advertisements for vitamins with ginkgo biloba or a "Mental Sharpness Product" would have you believe that taking a drug or supplement can improve your memory. Not so, according to the results of numerous studies. No research has shown that commercial memory enhancers are effective (McDaniel, Maier, & Einstein, 2002; Burns, Bryan, & Nettelbeck, 2006).

RECAP/EVALUATE/RETHINK

RECAP

LO 20-1 Why do we forget information?

- Several processes account for memory failure, including decay, interference (both proactive and retroactive), and cue-dependent forgetting.

LO 20-2 What are the major memory impairments?

- Among the memory dysfunctions are Alzheimer's disease, which leads to a progressive loss of memory, and amnesia, a memory loss that occurs without other mental difficulties and can take the forms of retrograde amnesia and anterograde amnesia. Korsakoff's syndrome is a disease that afflicts long-term alcoholics, resulting in memory impairment.

- Techniques for improving memory include the keyword technique to memorize foreign language vocabulary; organizing text material and lecture notes; talking to yourself; and practice and rehearsal, leading to overlearning.

EVALUATE

1. If, after learning the history of the Middle East for a class 2 years ago, you now find yourself unable to recall what you learned, you are experiencing memory _____, caused by nonuse.

2. Difficulty in accessing a memory because of the presence of other information is known as _____.

3. _____ interference occurs when material is difficult to retrieve because of subsequent exposure to other material; _____ interference refers to difficulty in retrieving material as a result of the interference of previously learned material.

4. Match the following memory disorders with the correct information:
   1. Affects alcoholics; may result in hallucinations
   2. Memory loss occurring without other mental problems
   3. Beta amyloid defect; progressive forgetting and physical deterioration
   a. Alzheimer's disease
   b. Korsakoff's syndrome
   c. Amnesia

RETHINK

1. What are the implications of proactive and retroactive interference for learning multiple foreign languages? Would earlier language training in a different language help or hinder learning a new language?

2. Does the phenomenon of interference help to explain the unreliability of autobiographical memory? Why?

Answers to Evaluate Questions

1. decay; 2. interference; 3. Retroactive, proactive; 4. 1-b, 2-c, 3-a

---

KEY TERMS

decay	proactive	Alzheimer's disease	anterograde amnesia
interference	interference	amnesia	Korsakoff's syndrome
cue-dependent forgetting	retroactive interference	retrograde amnesia	

LOOKING *Back*

EPILOGUE

Our examination of memory has highlighted the processes of encoding, storage, and retrieval, and theories about how these processes occur. We also encountered several phenomena relating to memory, including the tip-of-the-tongue phenomenon and flashbulb memories. Above all, we observed that memory is a constructive process by which interpretations, expectations, and guesses contribute to the nature of our memories.

Before moving on to chapter 8, return to the prologue of this chapter on Jill Price's perfect memory of the events in her life. Consider the following questions in light of what you now know about memory.

1. Which of Jill Price's memory functions—encoding, storage, or retrieval—is apparently most affected by highly superior autobiographical memory (HSAM)?

2. Why do you think Jill Price had more trouble remembering facts and figures in school than she does recalling TV trivia from her childhood?

3. Researchers report that most people with HSAM show obsessive-compulsive behaviors. Jill Price, for example, keeps a storage space packed with personal artifacts, all neatly organized. How might her perfect recall be related to this behavior?

4. From a researcher's perspective, how might you determine whether the memory of a person with HSAM is truly accurate?

Design Elements: Yellow highlighter: ©luckyraccoon/Shutterstock.com; Smartphone: ©and4me/Shutterstock.com; Group of diverse hands: ©MR. Nattanon Kanchak/Shutterstock.com; Woman working on laptop: ©Dragon Images/Shutterstock.com.

VISUAL SUMMARY 6 Memory

MODULE 18 The Foundations of Memory

Memory: Encoding, storing, and retrieving information

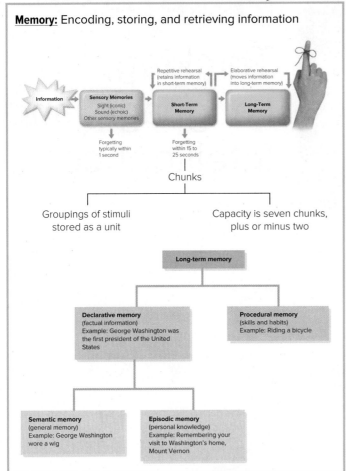

Chunks

Groupings of stimuli stored as a unit

Capacity is seven chunks, plus or minus two

Long-term memory

Declarative memory
(factual information)
Example: George Washington was the first president of the United States

Procedural memory
(skills and habits)
Example: Riding a bicycle

Semantic memory
(general memory)
Example: George Washington wore a wig

Episodic memory
(personal knowledge)
Example: Remembering your visit to Washington's home, Mount Vernon

MODULE 19 Recalling Long-Term Memories

Retrieval Cues: Stimuli that allow recall of information stored in long-term memory
- Recall: Remembering specific information
- Recognition: Knowing whether one has been previously exposed to given information

Levels of Processing Theory: Recall depends on how much the information was processed when it was first encountered

Explicit Memories: Conscious recall of information

Implicit Memories: Memories of which people are not consciously aware

Flashbulb Memories:
Memories of a specific, important, or surprising emotionally significant event that are recalled easily and with vivid imagery

Constructive Processes: Processes in which memories are influenced by the meaning we give to events

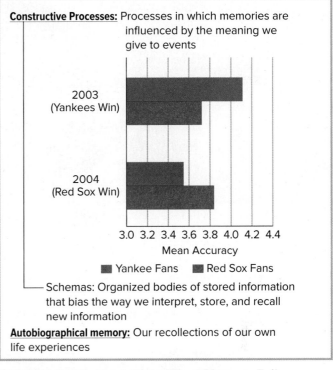

Schemas: Organized bodies of stored information that bias the way we interpret, store, and recall new information

Autobiographical memory: Our recollections of our own life experiences

MODULE 20 Forgetting: When Memory Fails

Decay: Loss of information through nonuse

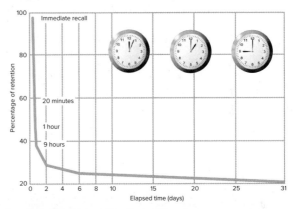

Cue-dependent forgetting: Forgetting that occurs when insufficient retrieval cues are available

Interference: Information in memory disrupts the recall of other information

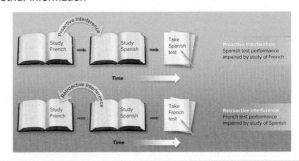

(MODULE 18): (Photo): ©C Squared Studios/Getty Images; Source: Adapted from Baddeley, A., Chincotta, D., & Adlam, A. (2001). Working memory and the control of action: Evidence from task switching. *Journal of Experimental Psychology: General, 130,* 641–657.; (MODULE 19): (Photo): ©Digital Vision/SuperStock; Source: Adapted from Breslin, C. W., & Safer, M. A. (2011). Effects of event valence on long-term memory for two baseball championship games. *Psychological Science, 20,* 1–5.; (MODULE 20): Source: Adapted from Ebbinghaus, H. (1885/1913). *Memory: A contribution to experimental psychology* (H. A. Roger & C. E. Bussenius, Trans.). New York: Columbia University Press.

©Chris Robbins/Moodboard/Glow Images

CHAPTER 7
Thinking, Language, and Intelligence

LEARNING OUTCOMES FOR CHAPTER 7

PROLOGUE *MIND GAMES*

Shawn Green, a research assistant in a psychology lab at the University of Rochester, was designing a computerized test to study neuroplasticity—the brain's ability to rewire itself in response to new experiences. The test would measure the ability to find particular shapes in a busy visual scene. To try out the test, he took it himself. He discovered what he felt must be an error in the test: he consistently achieved perfect scores, a result not at all in keeping with the results from similar tests at other labs.

Green decided to administer the test to other people. He recruited some of his friends, and astonishingly, they too achieved perfect scores. He tried the test one more time, this time on his supervisor. In contrast to Green and his friends, her performance wasn't exceptional; she had an average score.

What was going on? Eventually, Green and his supervisor realized that he and his friends shared one key trait that enabled them to overachieve on the neuroplasticity test: they were all avid video-game players, spending hours each week online, subduing zombies and other villains (Bavelier & Green, 2016).

LOOKING *Ahead*

It turns out that video games, often criticized for producing such negative traits as aggression and mindless addiction, can under the right circumstances positively affect some kinds of cognitive abilities. Certain types of games can improve reaction times, decision-making under pressure, fine-motor control, task-switching, spatial sense, and, especially, attention focusing and distribution. Results like these have led researchers to consider developing games for therapeutic uses to address targeted types of cognitive deficits induced by aging or trauma (Granic. Lobel, & Engels, 2014; Gabbiandini & Greitemeyer, 2017).

Adapting to new experiences and honing new or existing cognitive skills are just two of the many tasks that our own amazing human computer—the brain—can accomplish in the course of our daily lives, even though we may have little or no idea how it does so. The mystery of how the brain processes language and all its nuances—as well as how it uses information to solve problems and make decisions—is the subject to which we now turn.

Answers to these questions come from **cognitive psychology,** the branch of psychology that focuses on the study of higher mental processes, including thinking, language, memory, problem solving, knowing, reasoning, judging, and decision making. Clearly, the realm of cognitive psychology is broad.

We begin by considering concepts, the building blocks of thinking. We examine different strategies for approaching problems, means of generating solutions, and ways of making judgments about the usefulness and accuracy of solutions.

Next, we turn to the way we communicate with others: language. We consider how language is developed and acquired, its basic characteristics, and the relationship between language and thought.

Finally, we examine intelligence. We consider the challenges involved in defining and measuring intelligence and then examine the two groups displaying extremes of intelligence: people with intellectual disabilities and the gifted. We explore what are probably the two most controversial issues surrounding intelligence: the degree to which intelligence is influenced by heredity and by the environment and whether traditional tests of intelligence are biased toward the dominant cultural groups in society—a difficult issue that has both psychological and social significance.

cognitive psychology The branch of psychology that focuses on the study of higher mental processes, including thinking, language, memory, problem solving, knowing, reasoning, judging, and decision making. (Module 21)

Module 21
Thinking

LEARNING OUTCOMES

LO 21-1 What is thinking?

LO 21-2 What processes underlie decision making?

LO 21-3 How do people approach and solve problems?

LO 21-4 What are the major obstacles to problem solving?

thinking Brain activity in which people mentally manipulate information, including words, visual images, sounds, or other data. (Module 21)

mental images Representations in the mind of an object or event. (Module 21)

What are you thinking about at this moment?

The mere ability to pose such a question underscores the distinctive nature of the human ability to think. No other species contemplates, analyzes, recollects, or plans the way humans do. Understanding what thinking is, however, goes beyond knowing that we think. Philosophers, for example, have argued for generations about the meaning of thinking, with some placing it at the core of human beings' understanding of their own existence.

Psychologists define **thinking** as brain activity in which people mentally manipulate information, including words, visual images, sounds, or other data. Thinking transforms information into new and different forms, allowing us to answer questions, make decisions, solve problems, and make plans.

Although a clear sense of what specifically occurs when we think remains elusive, our understanding of the nature of the fundamental elements involved in thinking is growing. We begin by considering our use of mental images and concepts, the building blocks of thought.

Mental Images: Examining the Mind's Eye

Think of your best friend.

Chances are that you "see" some kind of visual image when asked to think of her or him, or any other person or object for that matter. To some cognitive psychologists, such mental images constitute a major part of thinking.

Mental images are representations in the mind of an object or event. They are not just visual representations; our ability to "hear" a tune in our heads also

Athletes use mental imagery to focus on a task, a process they call "getting in the zone." What other occupations might require the use of strong mental imagery?
©Echo/Getty Images

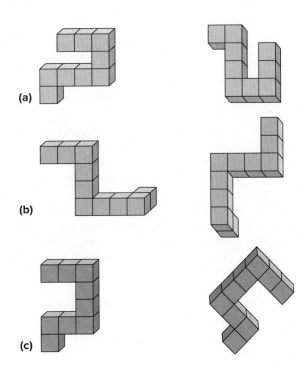

(a)

(b)

(c)

FIGURE 1 Try to mentally rotate one of each pair of patterns to see if it is the same as the other member of that pair. The more you have to mentally rotate a pattern, the longer it will likely take to decide if the patterns match one another. Does this mean that it will take you longer to visualize a map of the world than a map of the United States? Why or why not? Source: Adapted from Shepard, R. N., & Metzler, J. (1971). Mental rotation of three-dimensional objects. *Science, 171*(3972), 701–703.

relies on a mental image. In fact, every sensory modality may produce corresponding mental images (De Beni, Pazzaglia, & Gardini, 2007; Gardini et al., 2009; Koçak et al., 2011).

Research has found that our mental images have many of the properties of the actual stimuli they represent. For example, it takes the mind longer to scan mental images of large objects than small ones, just as the eye takes longer to scan an actual large object than to scan an actual small one. Similarly, we are able to manipulate and rotate mental images of objects, just as we are able to manipulate and rotate them in the real world (see Figure 1; Mast & Kosslyn, 2002; Zacks, 2008; Reisberg, 2013).

Some experts see the production of mental images as a way to improve various skills. For instance, many athletes use mental imagery in their training. Basketball players may try to produce vivid and detailed images of the court, the basket, the ball, and the noisy crowd. They may visualize themselves taking a foul shot, watching the ball, and hearing the swish as it goes through the net. And it works: The use of mental imagery can lead to improved performance in sports (Moran, 2009; Velentzas, Heinen, & Schack, 2011; Wimmer et al., 2017).

PsychTech
Researcher Adam Wilson has developed a method of tweeting by thinking. The process involves being outfitted with electrodes that react to changes in brain activity. It's slow going, though: the fastest tweeters are able to create tweets at only eight characters per minute.

From the perspective of...

A Human Resources Specialist How might you use the research on mental imagery to improve employees' performance?

©Dex Image/Getty Images

Concepts: Categorizing the World

If someone asks you what is in your kitchen cabinet, you might answer with a detailed list of items (a jar of peanut butter, three boxes of macaroni and cheese, six unmatched dinner plates, and so forth). More likely, though, you would respond by naming some broader categories, such as "food" and "dishes."

concept A mental grouping of similar objects, events, or people. (Module 21)

Using such categories reflects the operation of concepts. **Concepts** are mental groupings of similar objects, events, or people. Concepts enable us to organize complex phenomena into cognitive categories that are easier to understand and remember (Connolly, 2007; Kreppner et al., 2011; Mack, Love & Preston, 2017).

Concepts help us classify newly encountered objects on the basis of our past ex perience. For example, we can surmise that someone tapping a handheld screen is probably using some kind of computer or tablet, even if we have never encountered that specific model before. Ultimately, concepts influence behavior. We would assume, for instance, that it might be appropriate to pet an animal after determining that it is a dog, whereas we would behave differently after classifying the animal as a wolf.

When cognitive psychologists first studied concepts, they focused on those that were clearly defined by a unique set of properties or features. For example, an equilateral triangle is a closed shape that has three sides of equal length. If an object has these characteristics, it is an equilateral triangle; if it does not, it is not an equilateral triangle.

Other concepts–often those with the most relevance to our everyday lives–are more ambiguous and difficult to define. For instance, broader concepts such as "table" and "bird" have a set of general, relatively loose characteristic features rather than unique, clearly defined properties that distinguish an example of the concept from a nonexample.

prototypes Typical, highly representative examples of a concept. (Module 21)

When we consider these more ambiguous concepts, we usually think of examples called prototypes. **Prototypes** are typical, highly representative examples of a concept that correspond to our mental image or best example of the concept.

For instance, for most people, the prototype of a dog is something like the common beagle, rather than the relatively rare shih tzu, Finnish spitz, otterhound, or mudi (breeds you've probably never heard of). Similarly, although a robin and an ostrich are both examples of birds, the robin is an example that comes to most people's minds far more readily. Consequently, robin is a prototype of the concept "bird."

Relatively high agreement exists among people in a particular culture about which examples of a concept are prototypes as well as which examples are not. For instance, most people in Western cultures consider cars and trucks good examples of vehicles, whereas elevators and wheelbarrows are not considered very good examples. Consequently, cars and trucks are prototypes of the concept of a vehicle.

Concepts enable us to think about and understand more readily the complex world in which we live. For example, the suppositions we make about the reasons for other people's behavior are based on the ways in which we classify behavior. Hence, our conclusion about a person who washes her hands 20 times a day could vary, depending on whether we place her behavior within the conceptual framework of a health-care worker or a mental patient. Similarly, physicians make diagnoses by drawing on concepts and prototypes of symptoms that they learned about in medical school. Finally, concepts and prototypes facilitate our efforts to draw suitable conclusions through the cognitive process we turn to next.

Algorithms and Heuristics

algorithm A rule that, if applied appropriately, guarantees a solution to a problem. (Module 21)

When faced with making a decision, we often turn to various kinds of cognitive shortcuts, known as algorithms and heuristics, to help us. An **algorithm** is a rule that, if applied appropriately, guarantees a solution to a problem. We can use an algorithm even if we cannot understand why it works. For example, you may know that you can find the length of the third side of a right triangle by using the formula $a^2 + b^2 = c^2$, although you may not have the foggiest notion of the mathematical principles behind the formula.

For many problems and decisions, however, no algorithm is available. In those instances, we may be able to use heuristics to help us. A **heuristic** is a thinking strategy that may lead us to a solution to a problem or decision but–unlike algorithms–may sometimes lead to errors. Heuristics increase the likelihood of success in coming to a solution, but unlike algorithms, they cannot ensure it. For example, when I play tic-tac-toe, I follow the heuristic of placing an X in the center square when I start the game. This tactic doesn't guarantee that I will win, but experience has taught me that it will increase my chances of success. Similarly, some students follow the heuristic of preparing for a test by ignoring the assigned textbook reading and only studying their lecture notes–a strategy that may or may not pay off.

Although heuristics often help people solve problems and make decisions, certain kinds of heuristics may lead to inaccurate conclusions. For example, the *availability heuristic* involves judging the likelihood of an event occurring on the basis of how easy it is to think of examples. According to this heuristic, we assume that events we remember easily are likely to have occurred more frequently in the past–and are more likely to occur in the future–than events that are harder to remember.

For instance, the availability heuristic makes us more afraid of dying in a plane crash than in an auto accident, despite statistics clearly showing that airplane travel is much safer than auto travel. Similarly, although 10 times as many people die from falling out of bed than from lightning strikes, we're more afraid of being hit by lightning. The reason is that plane crashes and lightning strikes receive far more publicity, and they are therefore more easily remembered (Kluger, 2006; Caruso, 2008; Geurten et al., 2015).

We also make use of a familiarity heuristic. The *familiarity heuristic* leads us to prefer familiar objects, people, and things to those that are unfamiliar or strange to us. For example, we might purchase a book written by a familiar author rather than one written by an author we never heard of, even if the topic of the book by the unfamiliar author sounds more appealing.

The familiarity heuristic typically saves us a great deal of time when we are making decisions, since we often just go with what seems most familiar. On the other hand, it's not so good if you are an emergency room physician susceptible to the familiarity heuristic. If you simply settle on the first, most obvious diagnosis for a patient presenting particular symptoms (the ones that are most familiar to you), you may miss making a more accurate diagnosis (Herbert, 2011).

Algorithms and heuristics may be characteristic of human thinking, but scientists are now programming computers to mimic human thinking and problem solving. In fact, they are making significant inroads with computers in terms of the ability to solve problems and carry out some forms of intellectual activities. According to experts who study *artificial intelligence*, the field that examines how to use technology to imitate the outcome of human thinking, problem solving, and creative activities, computers can show rudiments of humanlike thinking because of their knowledge of where to look–and where not to look–for an answer to a problem. They suggest that the capacity of computer programs, such as those that play chess, to evaluate potential moves and to ignore unimportant possibilities gives them thinking ability (Megill, 2013; Ghahramani, 2015; Hernández-Orallo, 2017).

Solving Problems

According to an old legend, a group of Vietnamese monks guard three towers on which sit 64 golden rings. The monks believe that if they succeed in moving the rings from the first tower to the third according to a series of rigid rules, the world as we know it will come to an end. (Should you prefer that the world remain in its present state, there's no need for immediate concern: The puzzle is so complex that it will take the monks about a trillion years to solve it.)

In the Tower of Hanoi puzzle, a simpler version of the task facing the monks, three disks are placed on three posts in the order shown in Figure 2. The goal of the

heuristic A thinking strategy that may lead us to a solution to a problem or decision but–unlike algorithms–may sometimes lead to errors. (Module 21)

Study Alert
Remember that algorithms are rules that *always* provide a solution, whereas heuristics are shortcuts that *may* provide a solution.

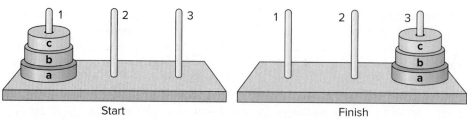

FIGURE 2 The goal of the Tower of Hanoi puzzle is to move all three disks from the first post to the third and still preserve the original order of the disks, using the fewest number of moves possible while following the rules that only one disk at a time can be moved and no disk can cover a smaller one during a move. Try it yourself before you look at the solution, which is listed according to the sequence of moves.

(Solution: Move C to 3, B to 2, C to 2, A to 3, C to 1, B to 3, and C to 3.)

Study Alert

Use the three steps of problem solving to organize your studying: Preparation, Production, and Judgment (PPJ).

puzzle is to move all three disks to the third post, arranged in the same order, by using as few moves as possible. There are two restrictions: Only one disk can be moved at a time, and no disk can ever cover a smaller one during a move.

Why are cognitive psychologists interested in the Tower of Hanoi problem? Because the way people go about solving such puzzles helps illuminate how people solve complex, real-life problems. Psychologists have found that problem solving typically involves the three steps illustrated in Figure 3: preparing to create solutions, producing solutions, and evaluating the solutions that have been generated.

PREPARATION: UNDERSTANDING AND DIAGNOSING PROBLEMS

When approaching a problem like the Tower of Hanoi, most people begin by trying to understand the problem thoroughly. If the problem is a novel one, they probably will pay particular attention to any restrictions placed on coming up with a solution—such as the rule for moving only one disk at a time in the Tower of Hanoi problem. If, by contrast, the problem is a familiar one, they are apt to spend considerably less time in this preparation stage.

Problems vary from well defined to ill defined. In a *well-defined problem*—such as a mathematical equation or the solution to a jigsaw puzzle—both the nature of the problem itself and the information needed to solve it are available and clear. Thus, we can make straightforward judgments about whether a potential solution is appropriate. With an *ill-defined problem,* such as how to increase morale on an assembly line or to bring peace to the Middle East, not only may the specific nature of the problem be unclear, the information required to solve the problem may be even less obvious (Newman, Willoughby, & Pruce, 2011; Mayer, 2013; Tschentscher & Hauk, 2017).

Kinds of Problems Typically, a problem falls into one of the three categories shown in Figure 4: arrangement, inducing structure, and transformation. Solving each type requires somewhat different kinds of psychological skills and knowledge. (See Figure 5 for solutions to these problems.)

Arrangement problems require the problem solver to rearrange or recombine elements of the problem in a way that will satisfy specific criteria. Usually, several different arrangements can be made, but only one or a few of the arrangements will produce a solution. Anagram problems and jigsaw puzzles are examples of arrangement problems (Coventry et al., 2003; Reed, 2017).

In *problems of inducing structure*, a person must identify the existing relationships among the elements presented in the problem and then construct a new relationship among them. In such a problem, the problem solver must determine not only the relationships among the elements but also the structure and size of the elements involved. In the example shown in Figure 4b, a person must first determine that the solution requires the numbers to be considered in pairs (14-24-34-44-54-64). Only after

Preparation
Understanding and diagnosing problems

Production
Generating solutions

Judgment
Evaluating solutions

FIGURE 3 Steps in problem solving.

a. **Arrangement problems**

1. Anagrams: Rearrange the letters in each set to make an English word:

2. Two strings hang from a ceiling but are too far apart to allow a person to hold one and walk to the other. On the floor are a book of matches, a screwdriver, and a few pieces of cotton. How could the strings be tied together?

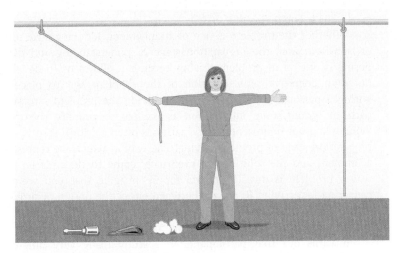

b. **Problems of inducing structure**

1. What number comes next in the series?
   1 4 2 4 3 4 4 4 5 4 6 4

2. Complete these analogies:
   baseball is to bat as tennis is to _____

   merchant is to sell as customer is to _____

c. **Transformation problems**

1. Water jars: A person has three jars with the following capacities:

Jar A:
28 ounces

Jar B:
7 ounces

Jar C:
5 ounces

How can the person measure exactly 11 ounces of water?

2. Ten coins are arranged in the following way. By moving only *two* of the coins, make two rows that each contains six coins.

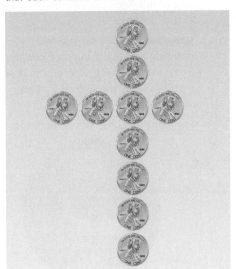

FIGURE 4 The three major categories of problems: (a) arrangement, (b) inducing structure, and (c) transformation. Solutions appear in Figure 5.

Source: Adapted from Bourne, L. E., Dominowski, R. L., Loftus, E. F., & Healy, A. F. (1986). *Cognitive processes* (2nd ed.). Englewood Cliffs, NJ: Prentice Hall.

a. Arrangement problems

  1. FACET, DOUBT, THICK, NAIVE, ANVIL

  2. The screwdriver is tied to one of the strings. This makes a pendulum that can be swung to reach the other string.

b. Problems of inducing structure

  1. 7

  2. racket; buy

c. Transformation problems

  1. Fill jar A; empty into jar B once and into jar C twice. What remains in jar A is 11 ounces.

  2.

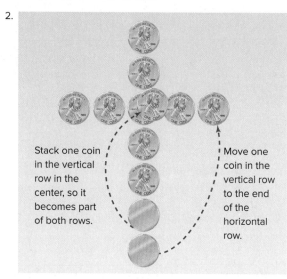

Stack one coin in the vertical row in the center, so it becomes part of both rows.

Move one coin in the vertical row to the end of the horizontal row.

FIGURE 5 Solutions to the problems in Figure 4.

Source: Adapted from Bourne, L. E., Dominowski, R. L., Loftus, E. F., & Healy, A. F. (1986). *Cognitive processes* (2nd ed.). Englewood Cliffs, NJ: Prentice Hall.

identifying that part of the problem can a person determine the solution rule (the first number of each pair increases by one, whereas the second number remains the same).

The Tower of Hanoi puzzle represents the third kind of problem—the *transformation problem*—that consists of an initial state, a goal state, and a method for changing the initial state into the goal state. In the Tower of Hanoi problem, the initial state is the original configuration, the goal state is to have the three disks on the third peg, and the method is the rules for moving the disks (Majeres, 2007; Van Belle et al., 2011; Schiff & Vakil, 2015).

Whether the problem is one of arrangement, inducing structure, or transformation, the preparation stage of understanding and diagnosing is critical in problem solving because it allows us to develop our own cognitive representation of the problem and to place it within a personal framework. We may divide the problem into subparts or ignore some information as we try to simplify the task. Winnowing out nonessential information is often a critical step in the preparation stage of problem solving. The way in which we represent a problem—and the solution we eventually come to—depends on the way a problem is initially framed for us. Imagine that you were a cancer patient having to choose between either the option of surgery or of radiation, as shown in Figure 6, and you were given some statistical information about the options. What would you choose?

It turns out that participants in a study made very different choices depending on how the problem was framed. When their choices were framed in terms of the likelihood of *survival*, only 18% of participants chose radiation over surgery. However, when the choice was framed in terms of the likelihood of *dying*, 44% chose radiation over surgery—even though the outcomes are similar with either treatment option (Tversky & Kahneman, 1987; Chandran & Menon, 2004).

Problem: Surgery or radiation?

Survival Frame	Mortality Frame
Surgery: Of 100 people having surgery, 90 live through the postoperative period, 68 are alive at the end of the first year, and 34 are alive at the end of 5 years.	**Surgery:** Of 100 people having surgery, 10 die during surgery, 32 die by the end of the first year, and 66 die by the end of 5 years.
Radiation: Of 100 people having radiation therapy, all live through the treatment, 77 are alive at the end of 1 year, and 22 are alive at the end of 5 years.	**Radiation:** Of 100 people having radiation therapy, none dies during the treatment, 23 die by the end of 1 year, and 78 die by the end of 5 years.
Far more patients choose surgery.	Far more patients choose radiation.

FIGURE 6 A decision often is affected by the way a problem is framed. In this case, most would choose radiation over surgery, despite similar results.

(Left) ©Hoby Finn/Photodisc/Getty Images;
(Right) ©Stockbyte/Getty Images

PRODUCTION: GENERATING SOLUTIONS

After preparation, the next stage in problem solving is the production of possible solutions. If a problem is relatively simple, we may already have a direct solution stored in long-term memory, and all we need to do is retrieve the appropriate information. If we cannot retrieve or do not know the solution, we must generate possible solutions and compare them with information in long- and short-term memory.

At the most basic level, we can solve problems through trial and error. Thomas Edison invented the lightbulb only because he tried thousands of different kinds of materials for a filament before he found one that worked (carbon). The difficulty with trial and error, of course, is that some problems are so complicated that it would take a lifetime to try out every possibility. For example, according to some estimates, there are some 10^{120} possible sequences of chess moves (Fine & Fine, 2003).

In place of trial and error, complex problem solving often involves the use of heuristics, cognitive shortcuts that can generate solutions. Probably the most frequently applied heuristic in problem solving is a **means-ends analysis,** which involves repeated tests for differences between the desired outcome and what currently exists. Consider this simple example (Bosse, Gerritsen, & Treur, 2011; Bieberstein & Roosen, 2015):

> I want to take my son to preschool. What's the difference between what I have and what I want? One of distance. What changes distance? My automobile. My automobile won't work. What is needed to make it work? A new battery. What has new batteries? An auto repair shop....

In a means-end analysis, each step brings the problem solver closer to a resolution. Although this approach is often effective, if the problem requires indirect steps that temporarily *increase* the discrepancy between a current state and the solution, means-ends analysis can be counterproductive. For example, sometimes the fastest route to the summit of a mountain requires a mountain climber to backtrack temporarily; a means-end approach–which implies that the mountain climber should always forge ahead and upward–will be ineffective in such instances.

For other problems, the best approach is to work backward by focusing on the goal, rather than the starting point, of the problem. Consider, for example, the water lily problem:

> Water lilies are growing on Blue Lake. The water lilies grow rapidly, so that the amount of water surface covered by lilies doubles every 24 hours. On the first day of summer, there was just one water lily. On the 90th day of the summer, the lake was entirely covered. On what day was the lake half covered? (Reisberg, 1997)

If you start searching for a solution to the problem by thinking about the initial state on day 1 (one water lily) and move forward from there, you're facing a daunting task of trial-and-error estimation. But try taking a different approach: Start with day 90, when the entire lake was covered with lilies. Given that the lilies double their coverage daily, on the prior day only half the lake was covered. The answer, then, is day 89, a solution found by working backward (Bourne et al., 1986; Hunt, 1994; Shogren & Wehrmeyer, 2017).

Forming Subgoals: Dividing Problems into Their Parts Another heuristic commonly used to generate solutions is to divide a problem into intermediate steps, or *subgoals*, and solve each of those steps. For instance, in our modified Tower of Hanoi problem, we could choose several obvious subgoals, such as moving the largest disk to the third post.

Insight: Sudden Awareness Some approaches to generating possible solutions focus less on step-by-step heuristics than on the sudden bursts of comprehension that one may experience during efforts to solve a problem. In a classic study, the German psychologist Wolfgang Köhler examined learning and problem-solving processes in chimpanzees (Köhler, 1927). In his studies, Köhler exposed chimps to challenging situations

means-ends analysis Involves repeated tests for differences between the desired outcome and what currently exists. (Module 21)

PsychTech

Research comparing people working together to solve problems face-to-face versus communicating via e-mail finds that those using e-mail are more satisfied with the process and believe they find better solutions.

insight A sudden awareness of the relationships among various elements that had previously appeared to be independent of one another. (Module 21)

in which the elements of the solution were all present; all the chimps needed to do was put them together.

In one of Köhler's studies, chimps were kept in a cage in which boxes and sticks were strewn about and a bunch of tantalizing bananas hung from the ceiling, out of reach. Initially, the chimps made trial-and-error attempts to get to the bananas: They would throw the sticks at the bananas, jump from one of the boxes, or leap wildly from the ground. Frequently, they would seem to give up in frustration, leaving the bananas dangling temptingly overhead. But then, in what seemed like a sudden revelation, they would stop whatever they were doing and stand on a box to reach the bananas with a stick (see Figure 7). Köhler called the cognitive process underlying the chimps' new behavior **insight,** a sudden awareness of the relationships among various elements that had previously appeared to be unrelated.

Although Köhler emphasized the apparent suddenness of insightful solutions, subsequent research has shown that prior experience and trial-and-error practice in problem solving must precede "insight." Consequently, the chimps' behavior may simply represent the chaining together of previously learned responses, no different from the way a pigeon learns, by trial and error, to peck a key (Wen, Butler, & Koutstaal, 2013; Kizilirmak et al., 2015).

Can we help people achieve insight when they are seeking to solve problems? The answer is yes. One way is to directly train them, giving them practice in generating solutions that require out-of-the-box thinking. Another way is to provide cross-cultural experiences that show people that their traditional ways of thinking may be inadequate when applied to the problems faced by those living in other cultures (Leung & Chiu, 2010; Wen, Butler, & Koutstaal, 2013).

JUDGMENT: EVALUATING SOLUTIONS

The final stage in problem solving is judging the adequacy of a solution. Often this is a simple matter: If the solution is clear—as in the Tower of Hanoi problem—we will know immediately whether we have been successful (Varma, 2007).

(a)

(b)

(c)

FIGURE 7 (a) In an impressive display of insight, Sultan, one of the chimpanzees in Köhler's experiments in problem solving, sees a bunch of bananas that is out of reach. (b) He then carries over several crates, stacks them, and (c) stands on them to reach the bananas.
©Superstock

APPLYING PSYCHOLOGY IN THE 21ST CENTURY

ARE OUR ATTENTION SPANS BECOMING SHORTER?

Do you have a low tolerance for down time? When you find you have a few minutes to spare, such as while waiting in line at a store checkout or riding an elevator, do you feel a compulsion to pull out your smartphone and check your e-mail or social media?

If you answered yes, you're not alone; many people report they multitask more than ever. This increase in multitasking has led researchers to ask if the vast and ever-increasing amount of media vying for our attention has had an impact on our attention spans.

To address the issue, software giant Microsoft conducted research involving surveys and brain scans of 2,000 Canadians. The findings showed that attention span, which was defined as the duration of concentrated effort on a task without becoming distracted, had fallen from an average of 12 seconds in 2000 (around the time when mobile devices were taking off) to 8 seconds 15 years later. Attention was worst for participants who were heavier consumers of media, particularly social media, and who were early adopters of new technology or frequently used multiple media devices, such as using a tablet or smartphone while watching television (McSpadden, 2015).

©Jetta Productions/Blend Images

The researchers suggested that digital media enthusiasts might have simply become very good at quickly determining whether a new task is interesting enough to merit their continued attention. When they become bored, they quickly look elsewhere. However, they also show bursts of high attention, suggesting they are capable of focusing intently when they want to do so.

But this research is not without its critics, who rightly point out that attention span likely varies according to the task we are carrying out. Some tasks are simply more interesting to us than others, and our attention span will likely be lengthier for more engaging activities than less interesting ones.

Furthermore, attention span reflects the fact that the brain is simply good at adapting to its environment and picking out the stimuli that are the most useful. For example, other research shows that people who play a lot of video games have an enhanced ability to track moving objects, mentally rotate objects, and notice changes–that is, in many ways, their attention to detail is actually better than that of nongamers. Perhaps it's not all that surprising that given the choice between staring at the walls in a waiting room or reading something engaging on a screen in your hand, most people would choose the latter (Boot et al., 2008; Maybin, 2017).

RETHINK

- Are there tasks on which you can focus your attention for more than a few seconds? What seems to determine whether your attention remains focused or drifts?
- If people who like to play video games tend to have better ability than others to track moving objects, does that mean that they improved that skill by playing video games? Why or why not?

If the solution is less concrete or if there is no single correct solution, evaluating solutions becomes more difficult. In such instances, we must decide which alternative solution is best. Unfortunately, we often quite inaccurately estimate the quality of our own ideas. For instance, a team of drug researchers working for a particular company may consider their remedy for an illness to be superior to all others, overestimating the likelihood of their success and downplaying the approaches of competing drug companies (Eizenberg & Zaslavsky, 2004; Mihalca, Mengelkamp, & Schnotz, 2017).

Theoretically, if we rely on appropriate heuristics and valid information, we can make accurate choices among alternative solutions. However, several kinds of obstacles to problem solving act to bias the decisions and judgments we make. In fact, a wide range of behaviors are affected by these biases, ranging from the judgments we form of others to the choices we make about financial investments. Examining biases in decision making has influenced the development of an influential new field known as *behavioral economics,* which examines how psychological factors can explain economic decision making (Peters et al., 2017).

FIGURE 8 The problem here is to place three candles at eye level on a nearby door so that the wax will not drip on the floor as the candles burn—using only material in the figure. For a solution, see Figure 9.

Source: Adapted from Duncker, K. On problem solving. *Psychological Monographs,* 1945, 58 (5, whole no. 270)

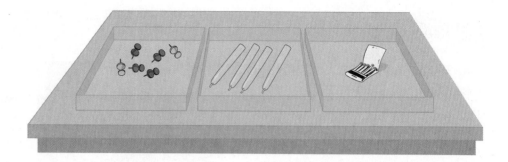

IMPEDIMENTS TO SOLUTIONS: WHY IS PROBLEM SOLVING SUCH A PROBLEM?

Consider the following problem-solving test illustrated in Figure 8 (Duncker, 1945):

> You are given a set of tacks, candles, and matches, each in a small box, and told your goal is to place three candles at eye level on a nearby door so that wax will not drip on the floor as the candles burn. How would you approach this challenge?

If you have difficulty solving the problem, you are not alone. Most people cannot solve it when it is presented in the manner illustrated in the figure, in which the objects are *inside* the boxes. However, if the objects were presented *beside* the boxes, just resting on the table, chances are that you would solve the problem much more readily–which, in case you are wondering, requires tacking the boxes to the door and then placing the candles inside them (see Figure 9).

The difficulty you probably encountered in solving this problem stems from its presentation, which misled you at the initial preparation stage. Actually, significant obstacles to problem solving can exist at each of the three major stages. Although cognitive approaches to problem solving suggest that thinking proceeds along fairly rational, logical lines as a person confronts a problem and considers various solutions, several factors can hinder the development of creative, appropriate, and accurate solutions.

functional fixedness The tendency to think of an object only in terms of its typical use. (Module 21)

Functional Fixedness The difficulty most people experience with the candle problem is caused by functional fixedness. **Functional fixedness** is the tendency to think of an object only in terms of its typical use. For instance, functional fixedness probably leads you to think of a book as something to read instead of its other potential uses–for example, as a doorstop or as kindling for a fire. In the candle problem, because the objects are first presented inside the boxes, functional fixedness leads most people to see the boxes simply as containers for the objects they hold rather than as a potential part of the solution. They cannot envision another function for the boxes.

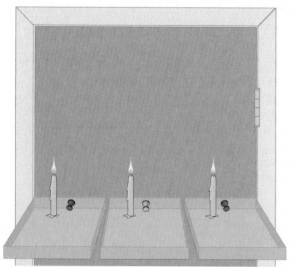

FIGURE 9 A solution to the problem in Figure 8 involves tacking the boxes to the door and placing the candles in the boxes.

A classic experiment (Luchins, 1946) demonstrated functional fixedness. As you can see in Figure 10, the object of the task is to use the jars in each row to measure out the designated amount of liquid. (Try it yourself to get a sense of the power of functional fixedness before moving on.)

If you have tried to solve the problem, you know that the first five rows are all solved in the same way: First fill the largest jar (B) and then from it fill the middle-size jar (A) once and the smallest jar (C) two times. What is left in B is the designated amount. (Stated as a formula, the designated amount is B–A–2C.) The demonstration of mental set comes in the sixth row of the problem, a point at which you probably encountered some difficulty. If you are like most people, you tried the formula and were perplexed when it failed. Chances are, in fact, that you missed the simple (but different) solution to the problem, which involves merely subtracting C from A. Interestingly, people who were given the problem in row 6 *first* had no difficulty with it at all.

Inaccurate Evaluation of Solutions When the United States invaded Iraq in 2003, it did so because governmental leaders believed that the country secretly had weapons of mass destruction that posed a danger to the United States. But later evidence showed that the belief was false. Still, government leaders had made up their minds early that there were such weapons, and they ignored contradictory evidence and focused more on information that supported their view (U.S. Senate Select Committee on Intelligence, 2004).

The mistake made by governmental leaders exemplifies **confirmation bias,** in which problem solvers prefer their first hypothesis and ignore contradictory information that supports alternative hypotheses or solutions. Even when we find evidence that contradicts a solution we have chosen, we are apt to stick with our original hypothesis.

Confirmation bias occurs for several reasons. For one thing, because rethinking a problem that appears to be solved already takes extra cognitive effort, we are apt to stick with our first solution. For another, we give greater weight to subsequent information that supports our initial position than to information that is not supportive of it (Koslowski, 2013; Rajsic, Wilson, & Pratt, 2015; Mercier, 2017).

Given jars with these capacities (in ounces):

	A	B	C	Obtain:
1.	21	127	3	100
2.	14	163	25	99
3.	18	43	10	5
4.	9	42	6	21
5.	20	59	4	31
6.	28	76	3	25

FIGURE 10 Try this classic demonstration, which illustrates the importance of mental set in problem solving. The object is to use the jars in each row to obtain the designated amount of liquid.

Creativity and Problem Solving

Despite obstacles to problem solving, many people adeptly discover creative solutions to problems. One enduring question that cognitive psychologists have sought to answer is what factors underlie **creativity,** the ability to generate original ideas or solve problems in novel ways.

Understanding the stages people go through as they approach and solve problems still leaves us with the question: Why are some people better at finding good solutions than other people are? Even the simplest situations reveal a wide range of abilities in problem solving. To explore this for yourself, make a list of all the uses you can think of for a glass jar. When you feel you have run out of possibilities, compare your list to this one compiled by a 12-year-old girl:

> You can keep seashells from your vacation in it to decorate your room. You can put sand on the bottom of it and pour melted wax over the sand and stick a wick in it to make a candle. You can use it as a drinking glass. You can keep rubber bands or paper clips or colored marbles in it. You can make a granola mix and store it for months if the jar has a tight lid. You can put water in the bottom and start an avocado tree from a pit. You can store bacon grease in a jar, or fill it with hand soaps and place it by the bathroom sink. You can use it as a flower vase or a "candy dish" for wrapped candies. If you punch holes in the lid, a jar can be a salt or sugar shaker. You can layer pudding and berries and whipped cream in it for a fancy dessert. You can keep your loose change in a jar or use it as a cocktail shaker. You can keep your goldfish in it while you clean the tank. You can organize shelves in the garage or basement by putting small things like nails and screws and bolts with others of the same size, each in their own jar. You can organize your pantry, too: a jar for white rice, one for wild rice, another for black beans, and so on. You can measure rainfall for a month with a jar. Or place it beneath a leaky sink pipe.

This list shows extraordinary creativity. Unfortunately, it is much easier to identify *examples* of creativity than to determine its causes. Similarly, it's not clear that the kind of creativity shown by highly creative people in the arts, such as singer Lady Gaga, is the same kind of creativity shown by highly creative people in the sciences, such as Steven Hawking (Simonton, 2009; Lavazza & Manzotti, 2013; Yi, Plucker, & Guo, 2015).

confirmation bias The tendency to seek out and weight more heavily information that supports one's initial hypothesis and to ignore contradictory information that supports alternative hypotheses or solutions. (Module 21)

creativity The ability to generate original ideas or solve problems in novel ways. (Module 21)

divergent thinking Thinking that generates unusual, yet nonetheless appropriate, responses to problems or questions. (Module 21)

convergent thinking Thinking in which a problem is viewed as having a single answer and which produces responses that are based primarily on knowledge and logic. (Module 21)

Singer-songwriter, Lady Gaga has been a trailblazer in both music and fashion. Do you think she relies more on convergent or divergent thinking in her work?
©vipflash/Shutterstock

Study Alert

Remember *d*ivergent thinking produces *d*ifferent and *d*iverse kinds of responses, whereas convergent thinking produces more commonsense kinds of responses.

From the perspective of...

A Manufacturer How might you encourage your employees to develop creative ways to improve the products that you produce?

©Kali Nine LLC/Getty Images

However, we do know that several characteristics are associated with creativity. For one thing, highly creative individuals show divergent thinking. **Divergent thinking** is thinking that generates multiple and unusual, although appropriate, responses to problems or questions. When we use "out-of-the-box" thinking, we're showing divergent thinking.

Divergent thinking contrasts with convergent thinking. **Convergent thinking** is thinking in which a problem is viewed as having a single answer and which produces a solution that is based primarily on knowledge and logic. For instance, someone relying on convergent thinking would answer "You read it" to the query "What can you do with a newspaper?" In contrast, "You can use it as a dustpan" is a more divergent—and creative—response (Schepers & van den Berg, 2007; Zeng, Proctor, & Salvendy, 2011; Haas, 2017).

Creative people also show cognitive complexity in their thinking. *Cognitive complexity* is the preference for elaborate, intricate, and complex thoughts and solutions to problems. For instance, creative people often have a wider range of interests and are more independent and more interested in philosophical or abstract problems than are less creative individuals (Richards, 2006; Kaufman & Plucker, 2011).

One factor that is *not* closely related to creativity is intelligence. Traditional intelligence tests, which ask focused questions that have only one acceptable answer, tap convergent thinking skills. Highly creative people may therefore find that such tests penalize their divergent thinking. This may explain why researchers consistently find that creativity is only slightly related to school grades and intelligence when intelligence is measured using traditional intelligence tests (Heilman, 2005; Norton, Heath, & Ventura, 2013; Jung & Chang, 2017).

Does creativity change as we age? Research suggests that we actually become *less* creative the older we get. One reason may be that as we get older, we know more. Although this increased knowledge is generally advantageous, it may hinder creativity because we are more apt to ignore evidence that contradicts what we believe to be true. In a sense, we get stuck in our ways. Furthermore, when we get older, we already have developed a set of solutions to common problems, and we are more likely to turn to them and avoid exploring more creative ideas. In short, getting older is not helpful in finding creative solutions to problems (Gopnik, Griffiths, & Lucas, 2015; Gopnik & Griffiths, 2017).

BECOMING AN INFORMED CONSUMER
of Psychology

Thinking Critically and Creatively

Can we learn to be better and more creative thinkers?

Cognitive researchers have found that people can learn the abstract rules of logic and that such knowledge can improve our reasoning about the underlying causes of everyday events in our lives. Research suggests that critical and creative thinkers are made, not born. Consider, for instance, the following suggestions for increasing critical thinking and creativity (Burbach, Matkin, & Fritz, 2004; Kaufman & Baer, 2006).

- *Redefine problems.* We can modify boundaries and assumptions by rephrasing a problem at either a more abstract or a more concrete level.
- *Use subgoals.* By developing subgoals, we can divide a problem into intermediate steps. This process, known as *fractionation*, allows us to examine each part for new possibilities and approaches, leading to a novel solution for the problem as a whole.
- *Adopt a critical perspective.* Rather than passively accepting assumptions or arguments, we can evaluate material critically, consider its implications, and think about possible exceptions and contradictions.
- *Consider the opposite.* By considering the opposite of a concept we're seeking to understand, we can sometimes make progress. For example, to define "good mental health," it may be useful to consider what "bad mental health" means.
- *Use analogies.* Analogies provide alternative frameworks for the interpretation of facts and help us uncover new understanding. One particularly effective means of coming up with analogies is to look for examples in the natural world. For instance, architects discovered how to construct the earliest skyscrapers by noting how lily pads on a pond could support the weight of a person (Bearman, Ball, & Ormerod, 2007; Cho, Holyoak, & Cannon, 2007).
- *Think divergently.* Instead of the most logical or common use for an object, consider how you might use the object if you were forbidden to use it in the usual way.
- *Think convergently.* Although it sounds counterintuitive, researchers have found that a combination of divergent *and* convergent thinking can lead to greater creativity. Programs that attempt to teach children to be more creative train participants to alternate periods of divergent thinking with intense convergent thinking (Beghetto & Kaufman, 2010).
- *Use heuristics.* Heuristics are cognitive shortcuts that can help bring about a solution to a problem. If the problem has a single correct answer and you can use or construct a heuristic, you can often find the solution more rapidly and effectively.
- *Experiment with various solutions.* Don't be afraid to use different routes to find solutions for problems (verbal, mathematical, graphic, even dramatic). For instance, try to come up with every conceivable idea you can, no matter how wild or bizarre it may seem at first. After you've come up with a list of solutions, review each one and try to think of ways to make what at first appeared impractical seem more feasible.
- *Walk away.* Sometimes just taking a step back from a problem you're trying to solve and doing something routine and even thoughtless can help bring about creativity. Watching TV, taking a shower, or having a snack may free our minds to come up with innovative solutions (Wiley & Jarosz, 2012; Shellenbarger, 2013).

RECAP/EVALUATE/RETHINK

RECAP

LO 21-1 What is thinking?

- Cognitive psychology encompasses the higher mental processes, including the way people know and understand the world, process information, make decisions and judgments, and describe their knowledge and understanding to others.
- Thinking is the manipulation of mental representations of information. Thinking transforms such representations into novel and different forms, permitting

people to answer questions, solve problems, and reach goals.

- Mental images are representations in the mind of an object or event.
- Concepts are categorizations of objects, events, or people that share common properties.

LO 21-2 What processes underlie reasoning and decision making?

- Decisions sometimes (but not always) may be improved through the use of algorithms and heuristics. An algorithm is a rule that, if applied appropriately, guarantees a solution; a heuristic is a cognitive shortcut that may lead to a solution but is not guaranteed to do so.

LO 21-3 How do people approach and solve problems?

- Problem solving typically involves three major stages: preparation, production of solutions, and evaluation of solutions that have been generated.
- Preparation involves placing the problem in one of three categories. In arrangement problems, a group of elements must be rearranged or recombined in a way that will satisfy a certain criterion. In problems of inducing structure, a person first must identify the existing relationships among the elements presented and then construct a new relationship among them. Finally, transformation problems consist of an initial state, a goal state, and a method for changing the initial state into the goal state.
- In the production stage, people try to generate solutions. They may find solutions to some problems in long-term memory. Alternatively, they may solve some problems through simple trial and error and use algorithms and heuristics to solve more complex problems.
- Using the heuristic of a means-ends analysis, a person will repeatedly test for differences between the desired outcome and what currently exists, trying each time to come closer to the goal.
- Köhler's research with chimpanzees illustrates insight, a sudden awareness of the relationships among elements that had previously seemed unrelated.

LO 21-4 What are the major obstacles to problem solving?

- Several factors hinder effective problem solving. Mental set, of which functional fixedness is an example, is the tendency for old patterns of problem solving to persist. Inappropriate use of algorithms and heuristics can also act as an obstacle to the production of solutions. Confirmation bias, in which initial hypotheses are favored, can hinder the accurate evaluation of solutions to problems.

- Creativity is the ability to combine responses or ideas in novel ways. Creativity is related to divergent thinking (the ability to generate unusual, but still appropriate, responses to problems or questions) and cognitive complexity.

EVALUATE

1. _____ _____ are representations in the mind of an object or event.
2. _____ are categorizations of objects that share common properties.
3. Solving a problem by trying to reduce the difference between the current state and the goal state is known as a _____ _____.
4. _____ is the term used to describe the sudden "flash" of revelation that often accompanies the solution to a problem.
5. Thinking of an object only in terms of its typical use is known as _____ _____. A broader, related tendency to approach a problem in a certain way because that method worked previously is known as a _____ _____.
6. Generating unusual but appropriate approaches to a question is known as _____ _____.

RETHINK

1. How might the availability heuristic contribute to prejudices based on race, age, and gender? Can awareness of this heuristic prevent this from happening?
2. Why do you think people use algorithms and heuristics? How can we avoid coming to poor solutions based on their use?

Answers to Evaluate Questions

1. Mental images; 2. Concepts; 3. means-end analysis; 4. Insight
5. functional fixedness; mental set; 6. divergent thinking

KEY TERMS

cognitive psychology	prototypes	insight	creativity
thinking	algorithm	functional fixedness	divergent thinking
mental images	heuristic	mental set	convergent thinking
concept	means-ends analysis	confirmation bias	

Module 22
Language

'Twas brillig, and the slithy toves
Did gyre and gimble in the wabe:
All mimsy were the borogoves,
And the mome raths outgrabe.

Although few of us have ever come face to face with a tove, we have little difficulty in discerning that in Lewis Carroll's (1872) poem "Jabberwocky," the expression *slithy toves* contains an adjective, *slithy,* and the noun it modifies, *toves.*

Our ability to make sense out of nonsense, if the nonsense follows typical rules of language, illustrates the complexity of both human language and the cognitive processes that underlie its development and use. The use of **language**–the communication of information through symbols arranged according to systematic rules–is a central cognitive ability, one that is indispensable for us to communicate with one another. Not only is language central to communication, it is also closely tied to the very way in which we think about and understand the world. Without language, our ability to transmit information, acquire knowledge, and cooperate with others would be tremendously hindered. No wonder psychologists have devoted considerable attention to studying language (Hoff, 2008; Reisberg, 2009; LaPointe, 2013; Carnevale, Luna & Lerman, 2017).

Grammar: Language's Language

To understand how language develops and relates to thought, we first need to review some of the formal elements of language. The basic structure of language rests on **grammar,** the system of rules that determine how our thoughts can be expressed.

Grammar deals with three major components of language: phonology, syntax, and semantics. **Phonology** is the study of **phonemes,** the smallest basic units of speech that affect meaning, and of the way we use those sounds to form words and produce meaning. For instance, the *a* sound in *fat* and the *a* sound in *fate* represent two different phonemes in English (Hardison, 2006; Creel & Bregman, 2011).

Linguists have identified more than 800 different phonemes among all the world's languages. Although English speakers use just 52 phonemes to produce words, other languages use as few as 15 to as many as 141. Differences in phonemes are one reason people have difficulty learning other languages. For example, to a Japanese speaker, whose native language does not have an *r* phoneme, pronouncing such English words as *roar* presents some difficulty (Gibbs, 2002; Iverson et al., 2003; Redford, 2017).

Syntax refers to the rules that indicate how words and phrases can be combined to form sentences. Every language has intricate rules that guide the order in which words may be strung together to communicate meaning. English speakers have no difficulty recognizing that "TV down the turn" is not a meaningful sequence, whereas "Turn down the TV" is. To understand the effect of syntax in English, consider the changes in meaning caused by the different word orders in the following three utterances: "John kidnapped the boy," "John, the kidnapped boy," and "The boy kidnapped John" (Robert, 2006; Frank, Goldwater, & Keller, 2013).

Semantics is the third major component of language. **Semantics** refers to the meaning of words and sentences. Every word has particular semantic features. For example, *boy* and *man* share certain semantic features (both refer to males), but they also differ semantically (in terms of age).

LEARNING OUTCOMES

LO 22-1 How do people use language?

LO 22-2 How does language develop?

language The communication of information through symbols arranged according to systematic rules. (Module 22)

grammar The system of rules that determine how our thoughts can be expressed. (Module 22)

phonology The study of the smallest units of speech, called phonemes. (Module 22)

phonemes The smallest units of speech. (Module 22)

syntax Ways in which words and phrases can be combined to form sentences. (Module 22)

semantics The meaning of words and sentences. (Module 22)

Semantic rules allow us to use words to convey subtle nuances in meaning. For instance, we can use slightly different wording–semantics–about an event to convey subtle differences in meaning. If we had just seen a girl named Laura get hit by a truck, we might say, "A truck hit Laura." But if we were answering a question about why Laura was not at a party the night before, we might say, "Laura was hit by a truck" (Pietarinen, 2006; Paciorek & Williams, 2015; Srinivasan et al., 2017).

Despite the complexities of language, most of us acquire the basics of grammar without even being aware that we have learned its rules. Moreover, even though we may have difficulty explicitly stating the rules of grammar, our linguistic abilities are so sophisticated that we can utter an infinite number of different statements. How do we acquire such abilities?

Language Development: Developing a Way with Words

To parents, the sounds of their infant babbling and cooing are music to their ears (except, perhaps, at three o'clock in the morning). These sounds also serve an important function. They mark the first step on the road to the development of language.

BABBLING

babble Meaningless speechlike sounds made by children from around the age of 3 months through 1 year. (Module 22)

Children **babble**–make speechlike but meaningless sounds–from around the age of 3 months through 1 year. While babbling, they may produce, at one time or another, any of the sounds found in all languages, not just the language to which they are exposed. Even deaf children display their own form of babbling; infants who are unable to hear yet who are exposed to sign language from birth "babble" with their hands (Petitto, 1993; Majorano & D'Odorico, 2011; Shehata-Dieler et al., 2013).

An infant's babbling increasingly reflects the specific language being spoken in the infant's environment, initially in terms of pitch and tone and eventually in terms of specific sounds. Young infants can distinguish among all 869 phonemes that have been identified across the world's languages. However, after the age of 6 to 8 months, that ability begins to decline. Infants begin to "specialize" in the language to which they are exposed as neurons in their brains reorganize to respond to the particular phonemes infants routinely hear.

Some theorists argue that a *critical period* exists for language development early in life in which a child is particularly sensitive to language cues and most easily acquires language. In fact, if children are not exposed to language during this critical period, later they will have great difficulty overcoming this deficit (Bates, 2005; Shafer & Garrido-Nag, 2007; Choubsaz & Gheitury, 2017).

Cases in which abused children have been isolated from contact with others support the theory of such critical periods. In one case, for example, a girl named Genie was exposed to virtually no language from the age of 20 months until she was rescued at age 13. She was unable to speak at all. Despite intensive instruction, she learned only some words and was never able to master the complexities of language (Rymer, 1994; Veltman & Browne, 2001).

PRODUCTION OF LANGUAGE

By the time children are approximately 1 year old, they stop producing sounds that are not in the language to which they have been exposed. It is then a short step to the production of actual words. In English, these are typically short words that start with a consonant sound such as *b, d, m, p,* and *t*–this helps explain why *mama* and *dada* are so often among babies' first words. Of course, even before they produce their first words, children can understand a fair amount of the language they hear. Language comprehension precedes language production.

A syllable in signed language, similar to the ones seen in the manual babbling of deaf infants and in the spoken babbling of hearing infants. The similarities in language structure suggest that language has biological roots.

Courtesy, Dr. Laura Ann Petitto @1991. Photo by Robert LaMarche

After the age of 1 year, children begin to learn more complicated forms of language. They produce two-word combinations, the building blocks of sentences, and sharply increase the number of different words they are able to use. By age 2, the average child has a vocabulary of more than 50 words. Just 6 months later, that vocabulary has grown to several hundred words.

Also around the age of 2, children begin to produce short, two-word sentences. However, the sentences children first produce are characterized as telegraphic speech. **Telegraphic speech** consists of sentences in which only essential words are used, usually nouns and verbs only. Rather than saying, "I showed you the book," a child using telegraphic speech may say, "I show book," and "I am drawing a dog" may become "Drawing dog." As children get older, of course, they use less telegraphic speech and produce increasingly complex sentences (Volterra et al., 2003; Pérez-Leroux, Pirvulescu, & Roberge, 2011).

By age 3, children learn to make plurals by adding -s to nouns and to form the past tense by adding -ed to verbs. This skill also leads to errors, since children tend to apply rules inflexibly. In such **overgeneralization,** children employ rules even when doing so results in errors. Thus, although it is correct to say "he walked" for the past tense of *walk*, the -ed rule doesn't work quite so well when children say "he runned" for the past tense of *run* (Gershkoff-Stowe, Connell, & Smith, 2006; Kidd & Lum, 2008; Pozzan & Valian, 2017).

By age 5, children have acquired the basic rules of language. However, they do not attain a full vocabulary and the ability to comprehend and use subtle grammatical rules until later. For example, a 5-year-old boy who sees a blindfolded doll and is asked, "Is the doll easy or hard to see?" would have great trouble answering the question. In fact, if he were asked to make the doll easier to see, he would probably try to remove the doll's blindfold. By the time they are 8 years old, however, children have little difficulty understanding this question because they realize that the doll's blindfold has nothing to do with an observer's ability to see the doll (Hoff, 2003; Dockrell & Marshall, 2015).

telegraphic speech Sentences in which only essential words are used. (Module 22)

overgeneralization The phenomenon by which children overapply a language rule, thereby making linguistic errors. (Module 22)

Understanding Language Acquisition: Identifying the Roots of Language

Anyone who spends even a little time with children will notice the enormous strides that they make in language development throughout childhood. However, the reasons for this rapid growth are far from obvious. Psychologists have offered three major explanations: one based on learning theory, one based on innate processes, and one that involves something of a combination of the two.

LEARNING-THEORY APPROACHES: LANGUAGE AS A LEARNED SKILL

The **learning-theory approach** suggests that language acquisition follows the principles of reinforcement and conditioning discovered by psychologists who study learning. For example, a child who says "mama" receives hugs and praise from her mother, which reinforce the behavior of saying "mama" and make its repetition more likely. This view suggests that children first learn to speak by being rewarded for making sounds that approximate speech. Ultimately, through a process of *shaping*, in which closer approximations of correct speech are rewarded, language becomes more and more like adult speech (Skinner, 1957; Ornat & Gallo, 2004).

In support of the learning-theory approach to language acquisition, the more that parents speak to their young children, the more proficient the children become in language use. In addition, by the time they are 3 years old, children who hear higher levels of linguistic sophistication in their parents' speech show a greater rate of vocabulary growth, vocabulary use, and even general intellectual achievement than do children whose parents' speech is more simple (Hart & Risley, 1997).

learning-theory approach (to language development) The theory that language acquisition follows the principles of reinforcement and conditioning. (Module 22)

The learning-theory approach is less successful in explaining how children acquire language rules. Children are reinforced not only when they use language correctly but also when they use it incorrectly. For example, parents answer a child's query of "Why the dog won't eat?" as readily as they do the correctly phrased question, "Why won't the dog eat?" Listeners understand both sentences equally well. Learning theory, then, has difficulty fully explaining language acquisition.

NATIVIST APPROACHES: LANGUAGE AS AN INNATE SKILL

Pointing to such problems with learning-theory approaches to language acquisition, linguist Noam Chomsky (1978, 1991) provided a groundbreaking alternative. He argued that humans are born with an innate linguistic capability that emerges primarily as a function of maturation.

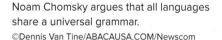

nativist approach (to language development) The theory that humans are biologically prewired to learn language at certain times and in particular ways. (Module 22)

According to Chomsky's **nativist approach,** humans are biologically prewired to learn language at certain periods in their lives and in a particular way. Furthermore, he suggests that all the world's languages share a common underlying structure that is prewired, biologically determined, and universal.

The nativist approach argues that the human brain contains an inherited neural system, which Chomsky calls *universal grammar*, that lets us understand the structure language provides. These inborn capabilities give us strategies and techniques for learning the unique characteristics of our own native language (McGilvray, 2004; White, 2007; Yang et al., 2017).

Evidence collected by neuroscientists supports Chomsky's view. This research suggests that the ability to use language, which was a significant evolutionary advance in human beings, is tied to specific neurological developments. For example, scientists have discovered a gene related to the development of language abilities that may have emerged as recently–in evolutionary terms–as 100,000 years ago.

Furthermore, it is clear that there are specific sites within the brain that are closely tied to language and that the shape of the human mouth and throat are tailored to the production of speech. And there is evidence that features of specific types of languages are tied to particular genes, such as in "tonal" languages in which pitch is used to convey meaning (Grigorenko, 2009; Perovic & Radenovic, 2011; Lieberman, 2015).

However, Chomsky's nativist view is contradicted by some researchers. For instance, learning theorists contend that the apparent ability of certain animals, such as

Noam Chomsky argues that all languages share a universal grammar.
©Dennis Van Tine/ABACAUSA.COM/Newscom

chimpanzees, to learn the fundamentals of human language (as we discuss later in this module) contradicts the innate linguistic capability view. Furthermore, some cognitive psychologists believe that what underlies children's language learning is their use of general cognitive abilities, as well as skills attained through social interaction with others (Ibbotson & Tomasello, 2016).

INTERACTIONIST APPROACHES

To reconcile the differing views of the learning-theory and nativist approaches, many theorists hold a compromise view, known as the interactionist approach to language development. The **interactionist approach** suggests that language development is determined by both genetic and social factors, produced through a combination of genetically determined predispositions *and* the social world in which one is raised.

Specifically, proponents of the interactionist approach suggest that the brain is hardwired for our acquisition of language, in essence providing the "hardware" that allows us to develop language. However, it is the exposure to language from social interactions with others that allows us to develop the appropriate "software" to understand and produce language.

The interactionist approach has many proponents. Still, the issue of how language is acquired remains hotly contested (Pinker & Jackendoff, 2005; Hoff, 2008; Waxman, 2009).

interactionist approach (to language development) The view that language development is produced through a combination of genetically determined predispositions and environmental circumstances that help teach language. (Module 22)

> **Study Alert**
> It's important to be able to compare and contrast the major approaches to language development: learning-theory, nativist, and interactionist approaches.

From the perspective of...

A Child-Care Provider How would you encourage children's language abilities at the different stages of development?

©Rubberball/Getty Images

The Influence of Language on Thinking: Do Eskimos Have More Words for Snow Than Texans Do?

Do Eskimos living in the frigid Arctic have a more expansive vocabulary for discussing snow than people living in warmer climates do?

It makes sense, and arguments that the Eskimo language has many more words than English does for snow have been made since the early 1900s. At that time, linguist Benjamin Lee Whorf contended that because snow is so relevant to Eskimos' lives, their language provides a particularly rich vocabulary to describe it–considerably larger than what we find in other languages, such as English (Martin & Pullum, 1991; Pinker, 1994).

The contention that the Eskimo language is especially abundant in snow-related terms led to the linguistic-relativity hypothesis. According to the **linguistic-relativity hypothesis,** language shapes and helps determine the way people perceive and understand the world. That is, language provides us with categories we use to construct our view of others and events in the world around us. In this way, language shapes and produces thought (Whorf, 1956; Tan et al., 2008; Bylund & Athanasopoulos, 2017).

Let's consider another possibility, however. Suppose that instead of language being the *cause* of certain ways of thinking, thought *produces* language. The only reason to expect that Eskimo language might have more words for snow than English does is that snow is considerably more relevant to Eskimos than it is to people in other cultures.

linguistic-relativity hypothesis The hypothesis that language shapes and may determine the way people perceive and understand the world. (Module 22)

Which view is correct? Most recent research refutes the linguistic-relativity hypothesis and suggests, instead, that thinking produces language. In fact, new analyses of the Eskimo language suggest that Eskimos have no more words for snow than English speakers do. If one examines the English language closely, one sees that it is hardly impoverished when it comes to describing snow (consider, for example, *sleet, slush, blizzard,* and *dusting).*

Still, the linguistic-relativity hypothesis has not been entirely discarded. A newer version of the hypothesis suggests that speech patterns may influence certain aspects of thinking. For example, in some languages, such as English, speakers distinguish between nouns that can be counted (such as "five chairs") and nouns that require a measurement unit to be quantified (such as "a liter of water"). In some other languages, such as the Mayan language called Yucatec, however, all nouns require a measurement unit. In such cultures, people appear to think more closely about what things are made of than do people in cultures in which languages such as English are spoken (Gentner, Goldin, & Goldin-Meadow, 2003; Tsukasaki & Ishii, 2004; Stam, 2015).

Similarly, Russian speakers have more words for light and dark blues and are better able to discriminate shades of blue visually than English speakers. The Icelandic language contains 24 words for different types of waves. Furthermore, some tribes say north, south, east, and west instead of left and right, and they have better spatial orientation. Finally, the Piraha language uses terms such as *few* and *many* rather than specific numbers, and speakers are unable to keep track of exact quantities (Boroditsky, 2010; Fuhrman et al., 2011).

In short, although research does not support the linguistic-relativity hypothesis that language *causes* thought, it is clear that language influences how we think. And, of course, it certainly is the case that thought influences language, suggesting that language and thinking interact in complex ways (Ross, 2004; Thorkildsen, 2006; Proudfoot, 2009).

Study Alert

The linguistic-relativity hypothesis suggests *l*anguage *l*eads to thought.

Do Animals Use Language?

One question that has long puzzled psychologists is whether language is uniquely human or if other animals are able to acquire it as well. Many animals communicate with one another in rudimentary forms. For instance, fiddler crabs wave their claws to signal, bees dance to indicate the direction in which food will be found, and certain birds call "*zick, zick*" during courtship and "*kia*" when they are about to fly away. However, researchers have yet to demonstrate conclusively that these animals use true language, which is characterized in part by the ability to produce and communicate new and unique meanings by following a formal grammar.

Psychologists, however, have been able to teach chimps to communicate at surprisingly high levels. For instance, after 4 years of training, a chimp named Washoe learned to make signs for 132 words and combine those signs into simple sentences. Even more impressively, Kanzi, a bonobo (a kind of small chimpanzee), has linguistic skills that some psychologists claim are close to those of a 2-year-old human being. Kanzi's trainers suggest that he can create grammatically sophisticated sentences and can even invent new rules of syntax (Savage-Rumbaugh, Toth, & Schick, 2007; Slocombe, Waller, & Liebal, 2011).

More generally, researchers have found evidence that nonhuman primates use several basic components of human language. For example, they use vocalizations that they modify based on social and other environmental influences, and they take turns communicating about food resources. Furthermore, they have physical structures that allow them to produce vowel sounds similar to human language (Snowdon, 2017).

Despite the skills primates such as Kanzi display, critics contend that the language such animals use still lacks the grammar and the complex and novel constructions of human language. Instead, they maintain that the chimps are displaying a skill no

Psychologist and primatologist Sue Savage-Rumbaugh with a primate friend, Kanzi. Does the use of sign language by primates indicate true mastery of language?

©Laurentiu Garofeanu/Barcroft USA/Barcoft Media via Getty Images different from that of a dog that learns to lie down on command to get a reward. Furthermore, we lack firm evidence that animals can recognize and respond to the mental states of others of their species, an important aspect of human communication. Consequently, the issue of whether other animals can use language in a way that humans do remains controversial (Beran, Smith, & Perdue, 2013; Crockford, Wittig, & Zuberbühler, 2015; ten Cate, 2017).

 # Exploring Diversity

Teaching with Linguistic Variety: Bilingual Education

In New York City, nearly half of the students speak a language other than English in their homes, with more than 180 languages represented. Furthermore, 1 in 6 of the city's 1.1 million students is enrolled in some form of bilingual or English as a Second Language instruction.

And New York City is far from the only school district with a significant population of nonnative English speakers. From the biggest cities to the most rural areas, the face—and voice—of education in the United States is changing. More and more schoolchildren today have last names like Kim, Valdez, and Karachnicoff. In seven states, including Texas and Colorado, more than one-quarter of the students are not native English speakers. For some 55 million Americans, English is their second language (Holloway, 2000; Shin & Kominski, 2010; see Figure 1).

How to appropriately and effectively teach the increasing number of children who do not speak English is not always clear. Many educators maintain that *bilingual education* is best. With a bilingual approach, students learn some subjects in their native language while simultaneously learning English. Proponents of bilingualism believe that students must develop a sound footing in basic subject areas and that, initially at least, teaching those subjects in their native language is the only way to provide them with that foundation. During the same period, they learn English, with the eventual goal of shifting all instruction into English.

In contrast, other educators insist that all instruction ought to be in English from the moment students, including those who speak no English at all, enroll in school. In *immersion programs,* students are immediately plunged into English instruction in all subjects. The reasoning—endorsed by voters in California in a referendum designed to end bilingual education—is that teaching students in a language other than English simply hinders nonnative English speakers' integration into society and ultimately does them a disservice. Proponents of English immersion programs point as evidence to improvements in standardized test scores that followed the end of bilingual education programs (Wildavsky, 2000).

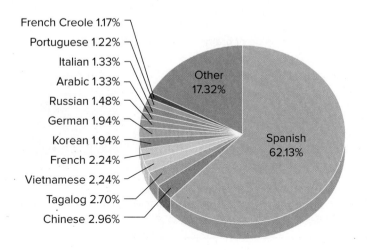

French Creole 1.17%
Portuguese 1.22%
Italian 1.33%
Arabic 1.33%
Russian 1.48%
German 1.94%
Korean 1.94%
French 2.24%
Vietnamese 2.24%
Tagalog 2.70%
Chinese 2.96%
Other 17.32%
Spanish 62.13%

FIGURE 1 The language of diversity. One-fifth of the people in the United States speak a language other than English at home. Spanish is most prevalent; the rest of non-English speakers use an astounding variety of different languages.

Source: Adapted from MLA. (2010). MLA Language Map; all languages other than English combined. (Based on 2000 U.S. Census Bureau figures).

Although the controversial issue of bilingual education versus immersion has strong political undercurrents, evidence shows that the ability to speak two languages provides significant cognitive benefits over speaking only one language. For example, bilingual speakers show more cognitive flexibility and may understand concepts more easily than do those who speak only one language. They have more linguistic tools for thinking because of their multiple-language abilities. In turn, this makes them more creative and flexible in solving problems (Kuo, 2007; Yim & Rudoy, 2013; Christoffels et al., 2015).

In addition, the advantages of bilingualism start early: by the time bilingual children are 3 or 4 years old, their cognitive development is superior to that of children who speak only one language. It's an advantage that lasts into old age. In fact, bilingualism provides protection from the cognitive declines that are typical in late adulthood (Bialystok et al., 2010; Bialystok & Craik, 2011; Bialystok, 2011).

Furthermore, speaking several languages changes the organization of the brain. For example, bilingual speakers who learn their second language as adults show different areas of brain activation compared with those who learn their second language in childhood. And those who are immersed in intensive language instruction show growth in the hippocampus. In addition, brain scans show that people who speak multiple languages have distinct patterns of brain activity according to the language that they are using, and bilingualism produces more efficient processing on some cognitive tasks (Kovacs & Mehler, 2009; Bialystok et al., 2010; Kluger, 2013). Also see *Neuroscience in Your Life*.

Related to questions about bilingual education is the matter of *biculturalism*—that is, being a member of two cultures and its psychological impact. Some psychologists argue that society should promote an *alternation model* of bicultural competence. Such a model supports members of a culture in their efforts to maintain their original cultural identity as well as in their integration into the adopted culture. In this view, a person can belong to two cultures and have two cultural identities without having to choose between them. Whether society will adopt the alternation model remains to be seen (Carter, 2003; Benet-Martínez, Lee, & Leu, 2006; Tadmor, 2007).

NEUROSCIENCE IN YOUR LIFE: BEING BILINGUAL AFFECTS PROCESSING IN THE BRAIN

Because it appears increasingly clear that people who are bilingual have certain cognitive advantages, such as greater cognitive flexibility, researchers are now exploring whether being bilingual affects the structure and functioning of the brain. And they have found, for example, that Spanish-English bilingual adults have more grey matter volume in frontal and parietal brain regions than English monolinguals. This can be seen in the two images of the brain below, where the red indicates the areas that have more grey matter volume for bilinguals. The findings suggest that managing the use of two separate languages affects both the size and structure of the brain, potentially affecting its functioning (Olulade et al., 2016).

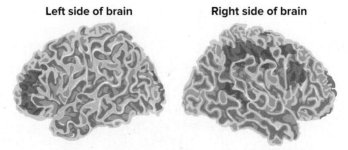

Left side of brain **Right side of brain**

Source: Adapted from Olulade, O. A., Jamal, N. I., Koo, D. S., Perfetti, C. A., LaSasso, C., & Eden, G. F. "Neuroanatomical Evidence in Support of the Bilingual Advantage Theory." *Cerebral Cortex,* 26(7), 2016, 3196-3204. doi: 10.1093/cercor/bhv152

RECAP/EVALUATE/RETHINK

RECAP

LO 22-1 How do people use language?

- Language is the communication of information through symbols arranged according to systematic rules. All languages have a grammar–a system of rules that determines how thoughts can be expressed–that encompasses the three major components of language: phonology, syntax, and semantics.

LO 22-2 How does language develop?

- Language production, which follows language comprehension, develops out of babbling, which then leads to the production of actual words. After 1 year of age, children use two-word combinations, increase their vocabulary, and use telegraphic speech, which drops words not critical to the message. By age 5, acquisition of language rules is relatively complete.
- Learning theorists suggest that language is acquired through reinforcement and conditioning. In contrast, the nativist approach suggests that an innate language-acquisition device guides the development of language. The interactionist approach argues that language development is produced through a combination of genetically determined predispositions and environmental circumstances that help teach language.
- The linguistic-relativity hypothesis suggests that language shapes and may determine the way people think about the world. Most evidence suggests that although language does not determine thought, it does affect the way people store information in memory and how well they can retrieve it.
- The degree to which language is a uniquely human skill remains an open question. Some psychologists contend that even though certain primates communicate at a high level, those animals do not use language. Other psychologists suggest that those primates truly understand and produce language in much the same way as humans do.

- People who speak more than one language may have a cognitive advantage over those who speak only one.

EVALUATE

1. Match the component of grammar with its definition:

   1. Syntax
   2. Phonology
   3. Semantics

   a. Rules showing how words can be combined into sentences.
   b. Rules governing the meaning of words and sentences.
   c. The study of the sound units that affect speech.

2. Language production and language comprehension develop in infants about the same time. True or false?
3. _____ _____ refers to the phenomenon in which young children omit nonessential portions of sentences.
4. A child knows that adding *-ed* to certain words puts the words in the past tense. As a result, instead of saying "He came," the child says "He comed." This is an example of _____.
5. _____ theory assumes that language acquisition is based on principles of conditioning and shaping.
6. In his theory of language acquisition, Chomsky argues that language acquisition is an innate ability tied to the structure of the brain. True or false?

RETHINK

1. Do people who use two languages, one at home and one at school, automatically have two cultures? Why might people who speak two languages have cognitive advantages over those who speak only one?
2. Why is overgeneralization seen as an argument against a strict learning-theory approach to explaining language acquisition?

Answers to Evaluate Questions

1. 1-a, 2-c, 3-b; 2. false; language comprehension precedes language; 3. Telegraphic speech; 4. overgeneralization; 5. Learning; 6. true

KEY TERMS

language	babble	nativist approach (to	linguistic-relativity
grammar	telegraphic speech	language development)	hypothesis
phonology	overgeneralization	interactionist approach (to	
phonemes	learning-theory approach	language development)	
syntax	(to language		
semantics	development)		

Module 23
Intelligence

Native sailors in the Marshall Islands in the South Pacific are capable of traveling 100 miles in open ocean waters. Although their destination may be just a small dot of land less than a mile wide, the sailors are able to navigate precisely toward it without the aid of a compass, chronometer, sextant, or any of the other sailing tools that are used by Western navigators. They are able to sail accurately even when the winds do not allow a direct approach to the island and they must take a zigzag course. (Tingley, 2016)

How do the Marshall Islands sailors navigate so effectively? If you asked them, they could not explain it. They might tell you they use a process that takes into account the rising and setting of the stars and the appearance, sound, and feel of the waves against the side of the boat. But at any given moment as they are sailing along, they could not identify their position or say why they are doing what they are doing. Nor could they explain the navigational theory underlying their sailing technique.

Some people might say that the inability of the Marshall Island sailors to explain in Western terms how their sailing technique works is a sign of primitive or even unintelligent behavior. In fact, if we gave these sailors a Western standardized test of navigational knowledge and theory or, for that matter, a traditional test of intelligence, they might do poorly on it. Yet, as a practical matter, it is not possible to accuse the Marshall Island sailors of being unintelligent: Despite their inability to explain how they do it, they are able to navigate successfully through the open ocean waters.

The navigation used by the Marshall Island sailors points out the difficulty in coming to grips with what is meant by intelligence. To a Westerner, traveling in a straight line along the most direct and quickest route by using a sextant and other navigational tools is likely to represent the most "intelligent" kind of behavior; in contrast, a zigzag course, based on the "feel" of the waves, would not seem very reasonable. To the Marshall Island sailors, who are used to their own system of navigation, however, the use of complicated navigational tools might seem so overly complex and unnecessary that they might think of Western navigators as lacking in intelligence.

It is clear from this example that the term *intelligence* can take on many meanings. If, for instance, you lived in a remote part of the Australian outback, you might differentiate between more intelligent and less intelligent people according to their mastery of hunting skills, whereas to someone living in urban Miami, intelligence might be exemplified by being "streetwise" or achieving success in business.

Each of these conceptions of intelligence is reasonable. Each represents an instance in which more intelligent people are better able to use the resources of their environment than are less intelligent people, a distinction that is presumably basic to any definition of intelligence. Yet it is also clear that these conceptions represent very different views of intelligence.

That two such different sets of behavior can exemplify the same psychological concept has long posed a challenge to psychologists. For years they have grappled with the issue of

Some South Pacific islanders are able to navigate with great accuracy across open seas without the standard navigation tools used by sailors in Western cultures. Their abilities illustrate that people attain their goals in multiple ways and that there is no single route to success.
©Danita Delimont/Galo Images/Getty Images

devising a general definition of intelligence. Ironically, laypersons have fairly clear ideas of what intelligence is, although the nature of their ideas is related to their culture. Westerners view intelligence as the ability to establish categories and debate rationally. In contrast, people in Eastern cultures and some African communities view intelligence more in terms of understanding and relating to one another (Crowne, 2013; Blackwell, Rodriguez, & Guerra-Carrillo, 2015; Chao, Takeuchi, & Farh, 2017).

The definition of intelligence that psychologists employ contains some of the same elements found in the layperson's conception. To psychologists, **intelligence** is the capacity to understand the world, think rationally, and use resources effectively when faced with challenges.

This definition does not lay to rest a key question asked by psychologists: Is intelligence a unitary attribute, or are there different kinds of intelligence? We turn now to various theories of intelligence that address the issue.

intelligence The capacity to understand the world, think rationally, and use resources effectively when faced with challenges. (Module 23)

Theories of Intelligence: Are There Different Kinds of Intelligence?

Perhaps you see yourself as a good writer but as someone who lacks ability in math. Or maybe you view yourself as a "science" person who easily masters physics but has few strengths in interpreting literature. Perhaps you view yourself as generally fairly smart with intelligence that permits you to excel across domains.

The different ways in which people view their own talents mirror a question that psychologists have grappled with. Is intelligence a single, general ability, or is it multifaceted and related to specific abilities? Early psychologists interested in intelligence assumed that there was a single, general factor for mental ability, which they called **g,** or the **g-factor.** This assumption was based on the fact that different types of measures of intelligence, whether they focused on, say, mathematical expertise, verbal competency, or spatial visualization skills, all ranked test-takers in roughly the same order. People who were good on one test generally were good on others; those who did poorly on one test tended to do poorly on others.

Given that there was a correlation between performance on the different types of tests, the assumption was that there was a general, global intellectual ability underlying performance on the various measures–the *g-factor*. This general intelligence factor was thought to underlie performance in every aspect of intelligence, and it was the *g*-factor that was presumably being measured on tests of intelligence (Haier et al., 2009; Major, Johnson, & Bouchard, 2011; Das, 2015).

More recent theories explain intelligence in a different light. Rather than viewing intelligence as a unitary entity, some psychologists consider it to be a multidimensional concept that includes different types of intelligence (Stankov, 2003; Sternberg & Pretz, 2005; Tutwiler, Lin, & Chang, 2013).

g or *g*-factor The single, general factor for mental ability assumed to underlie intelligence in some early theories of intelligence. (Module 23)

FLUID AND CRYSTALLIZED INTELLIGENCE

Some psychologists suggest that there are two kinds of intelligence: fluid intelligence and crystallized intelligence. **Fluid intelligence** is the ability to think logically, reason abstractly, solve problems, and find patterns. We use fluid intelligence when we are applying a strategy to resolve an issue (Di Fabio & Palazzeschi, 2009; Euler et al., 2015; Kyllonen & Kell, 2017).

In contrast, **crystallized intelligence** is the accumulation of information, knowledge, and skills that people have learned through experience and education. It reflects the facts that we have learned and information that resides in our long-term memory. When we learn a new language, we use crystallized intelligence as we acquire new vocabulary words.

The differences between fluid intelligence and crystallized intelligence become especially evident in late adulthood. At that point in the life span, people show declines

fluid intelligence Intelligence that reflects the ability to think logically, reason abstractly, and solve problems. (Module 23)

crystallized intelligence The accumulation of information, knowledge, and skills that people have learned through experience and education. (Module 23)

Piloting a helicopter requires the use of both fluid intelligence and crystallized intelligence. Which of the two kinds of intelligence do you believe is more important for such a task?
©bennymarty/123RF

theory of multiple intelligences
Gardner's intelligence theory that proposes that there are eight distinct spheres of intelligence. (Module 23)

🖊 Study Alert
Remember, Gardner's theory suggests that each individual has every kind of intelligence but in different degrees.

practical intelligence According to Sternberg, intelligence related to overall success in living. (Module 23)

in fluid, but not crystallized, intelligence (Tranter & Koutstaal, 2008; Ackerman, 2011; Pezoulas et al., 2017).

GARDNER'S MULTIPLE INTELLIGENCES: THE MANY WAYS OF SHOWING INTELLIGENCE

Psychologist Howard Gardner has taken an approach very different from traditional thinking about intelligence. Gardner argues that rather than asking "How smart are you?" we should be asking a different question: "How are you smart?" In answering the latter question, Gardner has developed a **theory of multiple intelligences** that has become quite influential (Gardner, 2000; Kaufman, Kaufman, & Plucker, 2013; Jung & Chang, 2017).

Gardner argues that we have a minimum eight different forms of intelligence, each relatively independent of the others: musical, bodily kinesthetic, logical-mathematical, linguistic, spatial, interpersonal, intrapersonal, and naturalist. (Figure 1 describes the eight types of intelligence, with some of Gardner's examples of people who excel in each type.) In Gardner's view, each of the multiple intelligences is linked to an independent system in the brain. Furthermore, he suggests that there may be even more types of intelligence, such as *existential intelligence*, which involves identifying and thinking about the fundamental questions of human existence. For example, the Dalai Lama might exemplify this type of intelligence (Gardner, 1999, 2000).

Although Gardner illustrates his conception of the specific types of intelligence with descriptions of well-known people, each person has the same eight kinds of intelligence—in different degrees. Moreover, although the eight basic types of intelligence are presented individually, Gardner suggests that these separate intelligences do not operate in isolation. Normally, any activity encompasses several kinds of intelligence working together.

The concept of multiple intelligences has led to the development of intelligence tests that include questions in which more than one answer can be correct; these provide an opportunity for test-takers to demonstrate creative thinking. In addition, many educators, embracing the concept of multiple intelligences, have designed classroom curricula that are meant to draw on different aspects of intelligence (Tirri & Nokelainen, 2008; Davis et al., 2011; Sternberg, 2015).

PRACTICAL AND EMOTIONAL INTELLIGENCE: TOWARD A MORE INTELLIGENT VIEW OF INTELLIGENCE

Consider the following situation:

> An employee who reports to one of your subordinates has asked to talk with you about waste, poor management practices, and possible violations of both company policy and the law on the part of your subordinate. You have been in your present position only a year, but in that time you have had no indications of trouble about the subordinate in question. Neither you nor your company has an "open door" policy, so it is expected that employees should take their concerns to their immediate supervisors before bringing a matter to the attention of anyone else. The employee who wishes to meet with you has not discussed this matter with her supervisors because of its delicate nature. (Sternberg, 1998)

Your response to this situation has a lot to do with your future success in a business career, according to psychologist Robert Sternberg. The question is one of a series designed to help give an indication of your intelligence. However, it is not traditional intelligence that the question is designed to tap but rather intelligence of a specific kind: practical intelligence. **Practical intelligence** is intelligence related to overall success in living (Muammar, 2007; Wagner, 2011; Baczyńska & Thornton, 2017).

1. Musical intelligence (skills in tasks involving music). Case example:

When he was 3, Yehudi Menuhin was smuggled into San Francisco Orchestra concerts by his parents. By the time he was 10 years old, Menuhin was an international performer.

©Erich Auerbach/Getty Images

2. Bodily kinesthetic intelligence (skills in using the whole body or various portions of it in the solution of problems or in the construction of products or displays, exemplified by dancers, athletes, actors, and surgeons). Case example:

Known for his athleticism, New York Yankees baseball captain Derek Jeter played baseball, basketball, and ran track in high school.

©Rena Schild/Shutterstock

3. Logical-mathematical intelligence (skills in problem solving and scientific thinking). Case example:

Barbara McClintock, who won the Nobel Prize in medicine, describes one of her breakthroughs, which came after thinking about a problem for half an hour . . . : "Suddenly I jumped and ran back to the (corn) field. At the top of the field (the others were still at the bottom) I shouted, 'Eureka, I have it!'"

©Science Source

4. Linguistic intelligence (skills involved in the production and use of language). Case example:

At the age of 10, T. S. Eliot created a magazine called *Fireside,* to which he was the sole contributor.

©Bettmann/Getty Images

5. Spatial intelligence (skills involving spatial configurations, such as those used by artists and architects). Case example:

Natives of the Truk Islands navigate at sea without instruments. During the actual trip, the navigator must envision mentally a reference island as it passes under a particular star, and from that he computes the number of segments completed, the proportion of the trip remaining, and any corrections in heading.

©Danita Delimont/Galo Images/ Getty Images

6. Interpersonal intelligence (skills in interacting with others, such as sensitivity to the moods, temperaments, motivations, and intentions of others). Case example:

When Anne Sullivan began instructing the deaf and blind Helen Keller, her task was one that had eluded others for years. Yet, just 2 weeks after beginning her work with Keller, Sullivan achieved great success.

©Bettmann/Getty Images

7. Intrapersonal intelligence (knowledge of the internal aspects of oneself; access to one's own feelings and emotions). Case example:

Writer Toni Morrison, who won Pulitzer and Nobel Prizes, began writing as a college student at Howard University. She wrote her first novel while working at a full-time job and raising two children as a single mother, getting up at 4:00 each morning to work on the book.

©Olga Besnard/123RF

8. Naturalist intelligence (ability to identify and classify patterns in nature). Case example:

During prehistoric times, hunter/ gatherers would rely on naturalist intelligence to identify what flora and fauna were edible. People who are adept at distinguishing nuances between large numbers of similar objects may be expressing naturalist intelligence abilities.

©Fernando Tatay/Shutterstock

FIGURE 1 Howard Gardner believes that there are eight major kinds of intelligences, corresponding to abilities in different domains. In what area does your greatest intelligence reside, and why do you think you have particular strengths in that area?

Sources: Adapted from Gardner, H. (2000). The giftedness matrix: A developmental perspective. In R. C. Friedman & B. M. Shore (Eds.), *Talents unfolding: Cognition and development.* Washington, DC: American Psychological Association; (Yehudi Menuhin) ©Harold Holt/Hulton Archive/Getty Images; (Trobriand Islands) ©Danita Delimont/Galo Images/Getty Images; (Baseball player) ©Bettmann/Corbis; (Helen Keller) ©Bettmann/Corbis; (Barbara McClintock, American Cytogenetist) ©Science Source; (Virginia Woolf) ©George C. Beresford/Getty Images; (T.S. Eliot reviews early poetry) ©Bettmann/Corbis; (Forest of redwood trees) ©Corbis RF

Noting that traditional tests were designed to relate to academic success, Sternberg points to evidence showing that most traditional measures of intelligence do not relate especially well to *career* success (McClelland, 1993). Specifically, although successful business executives usually score at least moderately well on intelligence tests, the rate at which they advance and their ultimate business achievements are only minimally associated with traditional measures of their intelligence.

Sternberg argues that career success requires a very different type of intelligence from that required for academic success. Whereas academic success is based on knowledge of a specific information base obtained from reading and listening, practical intelligence is learned mainly through observation of others' behavior. People who are high in practical intelligence are able to learn general norms and principles and apply them appropriately. Consequently, practical intelligence tests, like the one shown in Figure 2, measure the ability to employ broad principles in solving everyday problems (Stemler & Sternberg, 2006; Stemler et al., 2009; Sternberg, 2013).

In addition to practical intelligence, Sternberg argues there are two other basic, interrelated types of intelligence related to life success: analytical and creative. Analytical intelligence focuses on abstract but traditional types of problems measured on IQ tests, whereas creative intelligence involves the generation of novel ideas and products (Benderly, 2004; Sternberg, Kaufman, & Pretz, 2004; Sternberg, Grigorenko, & Kidd, 2005).

Some psychologists broaden the concept of intelligence even further beyond the intellectual realm to include emotions. **Emotional intelligence** is the set of skills that underlie the accurate assessment, evaluation, expression, and regulation of emotions (Mayer, Salovey, & Caruso, 2008; Humphrey, Curran, & Morris, 2007; Anderson, Paul, & Brown, 2017).

emotional intelligence The set of skills that underlie the accurate assessment, evaluation, expression, and regulation of emotions. (Module 23)

FIGURE 2 Most standard tests of intelligence primarily measure analytical skills; more comprehensive tests measure creative and practical abilities as well.

Source: Adapted from Sternberg, R. J. (2000). Intelligence and wisdom. In R. J. Sternberg (Ed.), *Handbook of intelligence.* New York: Cambridge University Press.

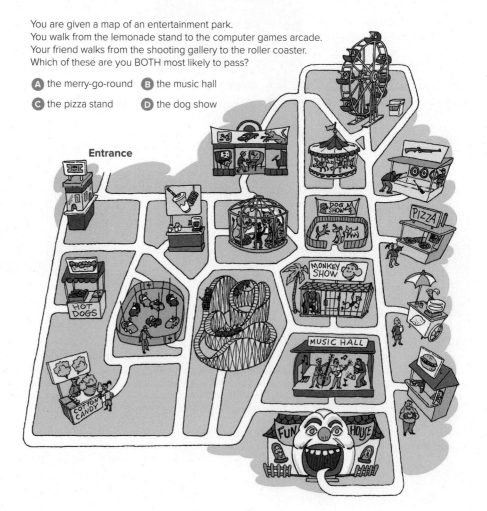

You are given a map of an entertainment park.
You walk from the lemonade stand to the computer games arcade.
Your friend walks from the shooting gallery to the roller coaster.
Which of these are you BOTH most likely to pass?

A the merry-go-round   B the music hall

C the pizza stand   D the dog show

Major Approaches to Intelligence	
Approach	**Characteristics**
Fluid and crystallized intelligence	Fluid intelligence relates to the ability to think logically, reason abstractly, and solve problems; crystallized intelligence relates to information, skills, and strategies learned through experience
Gardner's multiple intelligences	Eight independent forms of intelligence
Practical intelligence	Intelligence in terms of nonacademic, career, and personal success
Emotional intelligence	Intelligence that provides an understanding of what other people are feeling and experiencing and permits us to respond appropriately to others' needs

FIGURE 3 Just as there are many views of the nature of intelligence, there are also numerous ways to demonstrate intelligent behavior. This summary provides an overview of the various approaches used by psychologists.

Emotional intelligence is the basis of empathy for others, self-awareness, and social skills. It encompasses the ability to get along well with others. It provides us with an understanding of what other people are feeling and experiencing, which permits us to respond appropriately to others' needs. These abilities may help explain why people with only modest scores on traditional intelligence tests can be quite successful: the basis of their success may be a high emotional intelligence, which allows them to respond appropriately and quickly to others' feelings.

Although the notion of emotional intelligence makes sense, it has yet to be quantified in a rigorous manner. Furthermore, the view that emotional intelligence is so important that skills related to it should be taught in school has raised concerns among some educators. They suggest that the nurturance of emotional intelligence is best left to students' families, especially because there is no well-specified set of criteria for what constitutes emotional intelligence (Becker, 2003; Vesely, Saklofske, & Leschied, 2013).

Still, the notion of emotional intelligence reminds us that there are many ways to demonstrate intelligent behavior—just as there are multiple views of the nature of intelligence (Fox & Spector, 2000; Barrett & Salovey, 2002; Parke, Seo, & Sherf, 2015). Figure 3 presents a summary of the different approaches used by psychologists.

Study Alert

Traditional intelligence relates to academic performance; practical intelligence relates to success in life; emotional intelligence relates to emotional skills.

Assessing Intelligence

Given the variety of approaches to the components of intelligence, it is not surprising that measuring intelligence has proved challenging. Psychologists who study intelligence have focused much of their attention on the development of **intelligence tests** that quantify a person's level of intelligence. These tests have proved to be of great benefit in identifying students in need of special attention in school, diagnosing specific learning difficulties, and helping people make the best educational and vocational choices. At the same time, their use has proved controversial, raising important social and educational issues.

Historically, the first effort at intelligence testing was based on an uncomplicated but completely wrong assumption: that the size and shape of a person's head could be used as an objective measure of intelligence. The idea was put forward by Sir Francis Galton (1822-1911), an eminent English scientist whose ideas in other domains proved to be considerably better than his notions about intelligence.

Galton's motivation to identify people of high intelligence stemmed from personal prejudices. He sought to demonstrate the natural superiority of people of high social class (including himself) by showing that intelligence is inherited. He hypothesized

intelligence tests Tests devised to quantify a person's level of intelligence. (Module 23)

Alfred Binet.
©Albert Harlingue/Roger-Viollet/The Image Works

mental age The age for which a given level of performance is average or typical. (Module 23)

intelligence quotient (IQ) A score that takes into account an individual's mental and chronological ages. (Module 23)

that head configuration, which is genetically determined, is related to brain size and therefore is related to intelligence.

Galton's theories were proved wrong on virtually every count. Head size and shape are not related to intellectual performance, and subsequent research has found little relationship between brain size and intelligence. However, Galton's work did have at least one desirable result: He was the first person to suggest that intelligence could be quantified and measured in an objective manner (Jensen, 2002).

BINET AND THE DEVELOPMENT OF IQ TESTS

French psychologist Alfred Binet (1857–1911) developed the first real intelligence test. His tests followed from a simple premise: If performance on certain tasks or test items improved with *chronological,* or physical, age, performance could be used to distinguish more intelligent people from less intelligent ones within a particular age group. On the basis of this principle, Binet devised the first formal intelligence test, which was designed to identify the "dullest" students in the Paris school system in order to provide them with remedial aid.

Binet began by presenting tasks to same-age students who had been labeled "bright" or "dull" by their teachers. If a task could be completed by the bright students but not by the dull ones, he retained that task as a proper test item; otherwise, it was discarded. In the end, he came up with a test that distinguished between the bright and dull groups, and—with further work—one that distinguished among children in different age groups (Binet & Simon, 1916; Sternberg & Jarvin, 2003).

On the basis of the Binet test, children were assigned a score relating to their **mental age,** the age for which a given level of performance is average or typical. For example, if the average 8-year-old answered, say, 45 items correctly on a test, anyone who answered 45 items correctly would be assigned a mental age of 8 years. Consequently, whether the person taking the test was 20 years old or 5 years old, he or she would have the same mental age of 8 years (Cornell, 2006).

Assigning a mental age to students provided an indication of their general level of performance. However, it did not allow for adequate comparisons among people of different chronological ages. By using mental age alone, for instance, we might assume that an 18-year-old responding at a 20-year-old's level would be demonstrating the same degree of intelligence as a 5-year-old answering at a 7-year-old's level, when actually the 5-year-old would be displaying a much greater *relative* degree of intelligence.

A solution to the problem came in the form of the **intelligence quotient (IQ),** a measure of intelligence that takes into account an individual's mental *and* chronological (physical) age. Historically, the first IQ scores employed the following formula, in which *MA* stands for mental age and *CA* for chronological age:

$$IQ \text{ score} = \frac{MA}{CA} \times 100$$

Using this formula, we can return to the earlier example of an 18-year-old performing at a mental age of 20 and calculate an IQ score of (20/18) × 100 = 111. In contrast, the 5-year-old performing at a mental age of 7 comes out with a considerably higher IQ score: (7/5) × 100 = 140.

As a bit of trial and error with the formula will show you, anyone who has a mental age equal to his or her chronological age will have an IQ equal to 100. Moreover, people with a mental age that is lower than their chronological age will have IQs that are lower than 100.

Although the basic principles behind the calculation of an IQ score still hold, today IQ scores are determined in a different manner and are known as *deviation IQ scores.* First, the average test score for everyone of the same age who takes the test is determined, and that average score is assigned an IQ of 100. Then, with the aid of statistical techniques that calculate the differences (or "deviations") between each score and the average, IQ scores are assigned.

Study Alert

It's important to know the traditional formula for IQ scores in which IQ is the ratio of mental age divided by chronological age, multiplied by 100. Remember, though, that today, the calculation of IQ scores is done in a more sophisticated manner.

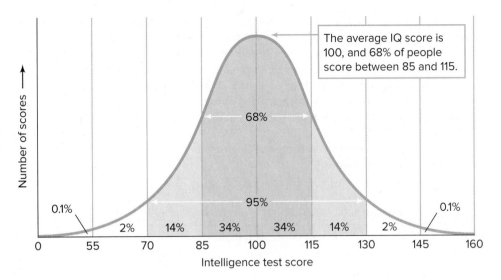

The average IQ score is 100, and 68% of people score between 85 and 115.

FIGURE 4 The average and most common IQ score is 100, and 68% of all people are within a 30-point range centered on 100. Some 95% of the population have scores that are within 30 points above or below 100, and 99.8% have scores that are between 55 and 145.

As you can see in Figure 4, when IQ scores from large numbers of people are plotted on a graph, they form a *bell-shaped distribution* (called "bell-shaped" because it looks like a bell when plotted). Approximately two-thirds of all individuals fall within 15 IQ points of the average score of 100. As scores increase or fall beyond that range, the percentage of people in a category falls considerably.

CONTEMPORARY IQ TESTS: GAUGING INTELLIGENCE

Remnants of Binet's original intelligence test are still with us, although the test has been revised in significant ways. Now in its fifth edition and called the *Stanford-Binet Intelligence Scale*, the test consists of a series of items that vary according to the age of the person being tested (Roid, Nellis, & McClellan, 2003). For example, young children are asked to copy figures or answer questions about everyday activities. Older people are asked to solve analogies, explain proverbs, and describe similarities that underlie sets of words.

The test is administered orally and includes both verbal and nonverbal assessments. An examiner begins by finding a mental age level at which a person is able to answer all the questions correctly and then moves on to successively more difficult problems.

Now in its fifth edition, the Stanford-Binet test consists of a series of items that vary in nature according to the age of the person being tested. What can we learn about a person from a test of this type?
©Lewis J. Merrim/Science Source

When a mental age level is reached at which no items can be answered, the test is over. By studying the pattern of correct and incorrect responses, the examiner is able to compute an IQ score for the person being tested. In addition, the Stanford-Binet test yields separate subscores that provide clues to a test-taker's particular strengths and weaknesses.

The IQ tests most frequently used in the United States were devised by psychologist David Wechsler and are known as the *Wechsler Adult Intelligence Scale-IV*, or, more commonly, the *WAIS-IV* (for adults) and a children's version, the *Wechsler Intelligence Scale for Children-V*, or *WISC-V*. Both the WAIS-IV and the WISC-V measure verbal comprehension, perceptual reasoning, working memory, and processing speed (see sample WAIS-IV items in Figure 5).

Types of Items on WAIS-IV		
Name	**Goal of Item**	**Example**
Information	Assess general information	Who wrote *Tom Sawyer?*
Comprehension	Assess understanding and evaluation of social norms and past experience	Why is copper often used for electrical wires?
Arithmetic	Assess math reasoning through verbal problems	Three women divided 18 golf balls equally among themselves. How many golf balls did each person receive?
Similarities	Test understanding of how objects or concepts are alike, tapping abstract reasoning	In what way are a circle and a triangle alike?
Figure weights	Test perceptual reasoning	Problems require test-taker to determine which possibility balances the final scale. 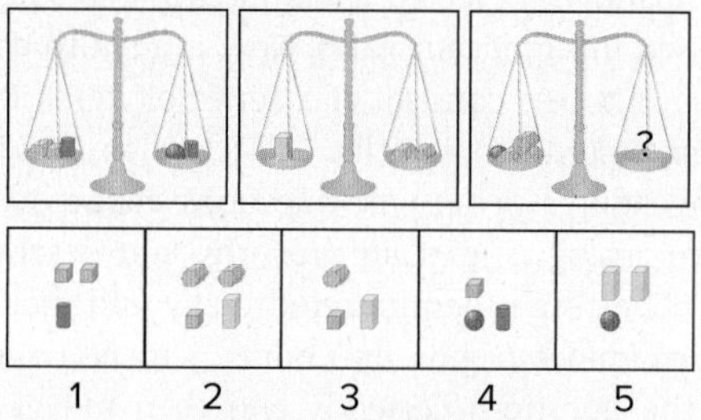
Matrix reasoning	Test spatial reasoning	Test-taker must decide which of the five possibilities replaces the question mark and completes the sequence. 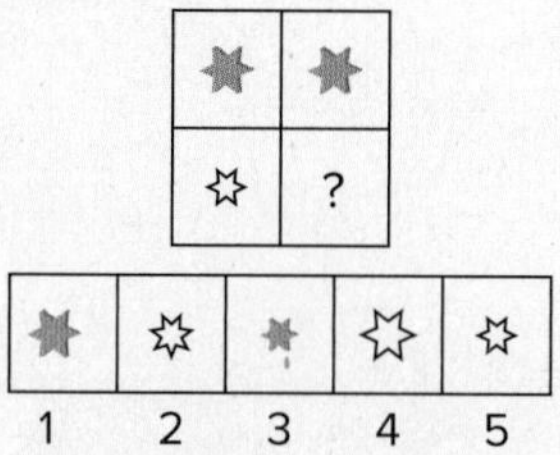
Block design item	Test understanding of relationship of parts to whole	Problems require test-takers to reproduce a design in fixed amount of time. 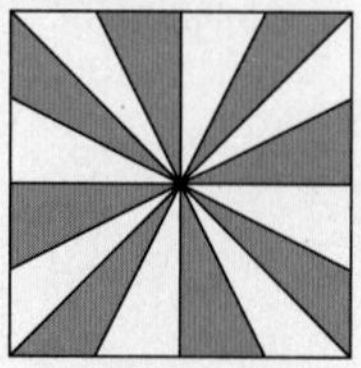

FIGURE 5 Typical kinds of items found on the Wechsler Adult Intelligence Scales (WAIS-IV). Simulated items similar to those in the *Wechsler Adult Intelligence Scale, Fourth Edition (WAIS-IV)*.

Source: Adapted from *Wechsler Adult Intelligence Scale-Fourth Edition* (WAIS-IV). (2008). Pearson Education, Inc.

Because the Stanford-Binet, WAIS-IV, and WISC-V all require individualized, one-on-one administration, they are relatively difficult to administer and score on a large-scale basis. Consequently, there are now a number of IQ tests that allow group administration. Rather than having one examiner ask one person at a time to respond to individual items, group IQ tests are strictly paper-and-pencil tests. The primary advantage of group tests is their ease of administration (Anastasi & Urbina, 1997; Danner et al., 2011).

However, sacrifices are made in group testing that, in some cases, may outweigh the benefits. For instance, group tests generally offer fewer kinds of questions than do tests administered individually. Furthermore, people may be more motivated to perform at their highest ability level when working on a one-to-one basis with a test administrator than they are in a group. Finally, in some cases, it is simply impossible to employ group tests, particularly with young children or people with unusually low IQs.

RELIABILITY AND VALIDITY: TAKING THE MEASURE OF TESTS

When we use a ruler, we expect to find that it measures an inch in the same way it did the last time we used it. When we weigh ourselves on the bathroom scale, we hope that the variations we see on the scale are due to changes in our weight and not to errors on the part of the scale (unless the change in weight is in an unwanted direction!).

In the same way, we hope that psychological tests have reliability. **Reliability** refers to the consistency of a test in measuring what it is trying to measure. We need to be sure that each time we administer a test, a test-taker will achieve the same or nearly similar results, assuming that nothing about the person has changed relevant to what is being measured.

reliability The property by which tests measure consistently what they are trying to measure. (Module 23)

Suppose, for instance, that when you first took the SAT exams, you scored 400 on the verbal section of the test. Then, after taking the test again a few months later, you scored 700. Upon receiving your new score, you might well stop celebrating for a moment to question whether the test is reliable because it is unlikely that your abilities could have changed enough to raise your score by 300 points (Coyle, 2006).

But suppose your score changed hardly at all, and both times you received a score of about 400. You couldn't complain about a lack of reliability. However, if you knew your verbal skills were above average, you might be concerned that the test did not adequately measure what it was supposed to measure. In sum, the question has now become one of validity rather than reliability. A test has **validity** when it actually measures what it is supposed to measure.

validity The property by which tests actually measure what they are supposed to measure. (Module 23)

Knowing that a test is reliable is no guarantee that it is also valid. For instance, Sir Francis Galton assumed that skull size is related to intelligence, and he was able to measure skull size with great reliability. However, the measure of skull size was not valid–it had nothing to do with intelligence. In this case, then, we have reliability without validity.

However, if a test is unreliable, it cannot be valid. Assuming that all other factors–motivation to score well, knowledge of the material, health, and so forth–are similar, if a person scores high the first time he or she takes a specific test and low the second time, the test cannot be measuring what it is supposed to measure. Therefore, the test is both unreliable and not valid.

Test validity and reliability are prerequisites for accurate assessment of intelligence–as well as for any other measurement task carried out by psychologists. Consequently, the measures of personality carried out by personality psychologists, clinical psychologists' assessments of psychological disorders, and social psychologists' measures of attitudes must meet the tests of validity and reliability for the results to be meaningful (Yao, Zhour, & Jiang, 2006; Markus & Borsboom, 2013; Deng & Georgiou, 2015.)

Assuming that a test is both valid and reliable, one further step is necessary in order to interpret the meaning of a particular test-taker's score: the establishment of norms. **Norms** are standards of test performance that permit the comparison of one person's score on a test to the scores of others who have taken the same test. For

norms Standards of test performance that permit the comparison of one person's score on a test with the scores of other individuals who have taken the same test. (Module 23)

example, a norm permits test-takers to know that they have scored, say, in the top 15% of those who have taken the test previously. Tests for which norms have been developed are known as *standardized tests.*

Test designers develop norms by calculating the average score achieved by a specific group of people for whom the test has been designed. Then the test designers can determine the extent to which each person's score differs from the scores of the other individuals who have taken the test in the past and provide future test-takers with a qualitative sense of their performance.

Obviously, the samples of test-takers who are employed in the establishment of norms are critical to the norming process. The people used to determine norms must be representative of the individuals to whom the test is directed.

From the perspective of...

A Human Resource Specialist Job interviews are really a kind of test, but they rely on interviewers' judgments and have no formal validity or reliability. Do you think job interviews can be made to have greater validity and reliability?

©Dex Image/Getty Images

ADAPTIVE TESTING: USING COMPUTERS TO ASSESS PERFORMANCE

Ensuring that tests are reliable, valid, and based on appropriate norms has become more critical with computer-administered testing. In computerized versions of tests such as the Graduate Record Exam, a test used to determine entrance to graduate school, not only are test questions viewed and answered on a computer, but the test itself is individualized. With adaptive testing, not every test-taker receives the same sets of test questions. Instead, the computer first presents a randomly selected question of moderate difficulty. If the test-taker answers it correctly, the computer then presents a randomly chosen item of slightly greater difficulty. If the test-taker answers it incorrectly, the computer presents a slightly easier item. Each question becomes slightly harder or easier than the question preceding it, depending on whether the previous response is correct. Ultimately, the greater the number of difficult questions answered correctly, the higher the score (Barrada, Abad, & Olea, 2011; Liu, Ying, & Zhang, 2015; Cheng, Diao, & Behrens, 2017).

Variations in Intellectual Ability

More than 7 million people in the United States, including around 11 per 1,000 children, have been identified as far enough below average in intelligence that they can be regarded as having serious deficits. Individuals with low IQs (people with intellectual disabilities) as well as those with unusually high IQs (the intellectually gifted) require special attention if they are to reach their full potential.

INTELLECTUAL DISABILITIES

Although sometimes thought of as a rare phenomenon, intellectual disabilities occur in 1-3% of the population. There is wide variation among those labeled intellectually disabled (formerly known as *mentally retarded*), in large part because of the inclusiveness of the definition developed by the American Association on Intellectual and Developmental Disabilities. The association suggests that **intellectual disability** is a disability characterized by significant limitations in both intellectual functioning and in adaptive behavior, which covers many everyday social and practical skills, and originates before the age of 18 (American Association of Intellectual and Developmental Disabilities, 2015).

Although below-average intellectual functioning can be measured in a relatively straightforward manner–using standard IQ tests–it is more difficult to determine how to gauge limitations in adaptive behavior. Consequently, there is a lack of uniformity in how experts apply the term *intellectual disabilities*. People labeled intellectually disabled vary, from those who can be taught to work and function with little special attention to those who cannot be trained and are institutionalized throughout their lives (Detterman, Gabriel, & Ruthsatz, 2000; Greenspan, 2006; American Association of Intellectual and Developmental Disabilities, 2015).

Most people with intellectual disabilities have relatively minor deficits and are classified as having *mild intellectual disability*. These individuals, who have IQ scores ranging from 55 to 69, constitute some 90% of all people with intellectual disabilities. Although their development is typically slower than that of their peers, they can function quite independently by adulthood and are able to hold jobs and have families of their own (Smith, 2006; van Nieuwenhuijzen et al., 2011; Nouwens et al., 2017).

With greater degrees of intellectual deficit, the difficulties are more pronounced. For people with *moderate intellectual disability* (IQs of 40 to 54), deficits are obvious early, with language and motor skills lagging behind those of peers. Although these individuals can hold simple jobs, they need to have some degree of supervision throughout their lives. Individuals with *severe intellectual disability* (IQs of 25 to 39) and *profound intellectual disability* (IQs below 25) are generally unable to function independently and typically require care for their entire lives (Garwick, 2007).

Identifying the Roots of Intellectual Disabilities What produces intellectual disabilities? In nearly one-third of the cases, there is an identifiable cause related to biological or environmental factors. The most common preventable cause of intellectual disabilities is **fetal alcohol syndrome,** produced by a mother's use of alcohol while pregnant. Increasing evidence shows that even small amounts of alcohol intake can produce intellectual deficits. One in every 750 infants is born with fetal alcohol syndrome in the United States (Murthy et al., 2009; Jacobson et al., 2011; Lewis et al., 2015).

Down syndrome represents another major cause of intellectual disabilities. *Down syndrome* results when a person is born with 47 chromosomes instead of the usual 46. In most cases, there is an extra copy of the 21st chromosome, which leads to problems in how the brain and body develop (Sherman et al., 2007; Vicari, Pontillo, & Armando, 2013).

In other cases of intellectual disabilities, an abnormality occurs in the structure of particular chromosomes. Birth complications, such as a temporary lack of oxygen, may also cause intellectual disability. In some cases, intellectual disabilities begin after birth following a head injury, a stroke, or infections such as meningitis (Plomin, 2005; Bittles, Bower, & Hussain, 2007; Fevang et al., 2017).

However, the majority of cases of intellectual disabilities are classified as familial intellectual disability. **Familial intellectual disability** is intellectual disability in which no apparent biological or genetic problems exist, but there is a history of intellectual disability among family members. Whether the family background of intellectual disabilities is caused by environmental factors, such as extreme continuous poverty leading to malnutrition, or by some underlying genetic factor is usually impossible to determine (Zigler et al., 2002; Franklin & Mansuy, 2011).

Integrating Individuals with Intellectual Disabilities Important advances in the care and treatment of those with intellectual disabilities have been made since the Education for All Handicapped Children Act (Public Law 94-142) was passed by Congress in the mid-1970s. In this federal law, Congress stipulated that people with intellectual

intellectual disability A condition characterized by significant limitations both in intellectual functioning and in conceptual, social, and practical adaptive skills. (Module 23)

fetal alcohol syndrome The most common cause of intellectual disability in newborns, occurring when the mother uses alcohol during pregnancy. (Module 23)

familial intellectual disability Intellectual disability in which no apparent biological defect exists but there is a history of intellectual disability in the family. (Module 23)

Study Alert

Remember that in most cases of intellectual disability, there is no apparent biological deficiency, but a history of intellectual disability exists in the family.

disabilities are entitled to a full education and that they must be educated and trained in the least restrictive environment—a process known as mainstreaming. *Mainstreaming* is the practice of educating students with intellectual deficits and other special needs in regular classes during specific time periods (Katsiyannis, Zhang, & Woodruff, 2005; Aussilloux & Bagdadli, 2006; Gibb et al., 2007).

The philosophy behind mainstreaming suggests that the interaction of students with and without intellectual disabilities in regular classrooms will improve educational opportunities for those with intellectual disabilities, increase their social acceptance, and facilitate their integration into society as a whole. In mainstreaming, special education classes still exist; some individuals with intellectual disabilities function at too low of a level to benefit from placement in regular classrooms. Moreover, children with intellectual disabilities who are mainstreamed into regular classes typically attend special classes for at least part of the day (Hastings & Oakford, 2003; Williamson, McLeskey, & Hoppey, 2006; Benitez et al., 2017).

THE INTELLECTUALLY GIFTED

intellectually gifted The 2-4% segment of the population who have IQ scores greater than 130. (Module 23)

Another group of people—the intellectually gifted—differ from those with average intelligence as much as individuals with intellectual disability do, although in a different manner. Accounting for 2-4% of the population, the **intellectually gifted** have IQ scores greater than 130.

Although stereotypes about the gifted suggests that they are awkward, shy, social misfits who don't get along well with peers, most research indicates just the opposite: The intellectually gifted do well across almost every domain. They are most often outgoing, well-adjusted, healthy, popular people who are able to do most things better than the average person can (Mueller, 2009; Sternberg, Jarvin, & Grigorenko, 2011; Strenze, 2015).

For example, in a famous study by psychologist Lewis Terman that started in the early 1920s, 1,500 children who had IQ scores above 140 were followed for the rest of their lives. From the start, the members of this group were more physically, academically, and socially capable than were their nongifted peers. In addition to doing better in school, they also showed better social adjustment than average. All these advantages paid off in terms of career success: As a group, the gifted received more awards and distinctions, earned higher incomes, and made more contributions in art and literature than did typical individuals. Perhaps most important, they reported greater satisfaction in life than did the nongifted (Hegarty, 2007; Warne & Liu, 2017).

Of course, not every member of the group Terman studied was successful. Furthermore, high intelligence is not a homogeneous quality; a person with a high overall IQ is not necessarily gifted in every academic subject but may excel in just one or two. A high IQ is not a universal guarantee of success (Winner, 2003; Clemons, 2006).

Group Differences in Intelligence: Genetic and Environmental Determinants

Kwang is often washed with a pleck tied to a:

a. rundel

b. flink

c. pove

d. quirj

If you found this kind of item on an intelligence test, you would probably complain that the test was totally absurd and had nothing to do with your intelligence or anyone else's–and rightly so. How could anyone be expected to respond to items presented in a language that was so unfamiliar?

Yet to some people, even more reasonable questions may appear just as nonsensical. Consider the example of a child raised in a city who is asked about procedures for milking cows or of someone raised in a rural area who is asked about subway ticketing procedures. Obviously, the previous experience of the test-takers would affect their ability to answer correctly. And if such types of questions were included on an IQ test, a critic could rightly contend that the test had more to do with prior experience than with intelligence.

Although IQ tests do not include questions that are so clearly dependent on prior knowledge as questions about cows and subways, the background and experiences of test-takers do have the potential to affect results. In fact, the issue of devising fair intelligence tests that measure knowledge unrelated to culture and family background and experience is central to explaining an important and persistent finding: Members of certain racial and cultural groups consistently score lower on traditional intelligence tests than do members of other groups. For example, as a group, blacks tend to average 10 to 15 IQ points lower than whites. Does this variation reflect a true difference in intelligence, or are the questions biased with regard to the kinds of knowledge they test? Clearly, if whites perform better because of their greater familiarity with the kind of information that is being tested, their higher IQ scores are not an indication that they are more intelligent than members of other groups (Morgan, Marsiske, & Whitfield, 2008; Suzuki, Short, & Lee, 2011; Loehlin et al., 2015).

There is good reason to believe that some standardized IQ tests contain elements that discriminate against minority-group members whose experiences differ from those of the white majority. Consider the question "What should you do if another child grabbed your hat and ran off with it?" Most middle-class white children answer that they would tell an adult, and this response is scored as correct. However, a reasonable response might be to chase the person and fight to get the hat back, the answer that is chosen by many urban black children–but one that is scored as incorrect (Aiken, 1997; Reynolds & Ramsay, 2003).

 # Exploring Diversity

The Relative Influence of Genetics and Environment: Nature, Nurture, and IQ

In an attempt to produce a **culture-fair IQ test,** one that does not discriminate against the members of any minority group, psychologists have tried to devise test items that assess experiences common to all cultures or emphasize questions that do not require language usage. However, test makers have found this difficult to do because past experiences, attitudes, and values almost always have an impact on respondents' answers (Fagan & Holland, 2009; Rizzi & Posthuma, 2013).

For example, children raised in Western cultures group things on the basis of what they are (such as putting *dog* and *fish* into the category of *animal*). In contrast, members of the Kpelle tribe in Africa see intelligence demonstrated by grouping things according to what they *do* (grouping *fish* with *swim*). Similarly, when asked to memorize the positions on a chessboard of objects typical to a U.S. household, children in the United States performed better than did children living in remote African villages. But if rocks are used instead of household objects, the African children do better. In short, it is difficult to produce a truly culture-fair test (Valencia & Suzuki, 2003; Barnett et al., 2011).

The efforts of psychologists to produce culture-fair measures of intelligence relate to a lingering controversy over differences in intelligence between members of different racial and ethnic groups. In attempting to identify whether there are differences between such

culture-fair IQ test A test trial that does not discriminate against the members of any minority group. (Module 23)

groups, psychologists have had to confront the broader issue of determining the relative contribution to intelligence of genetic factors (heredity) and experience (environment)—the nature-nurture issue that is one of the basic issues of psychology.

Richard Herrnstein, a psychologist, and Charles Murray, a sociologist, fanned the flames of the debate with the publication of their book *The Bell Curve* in the mid-1990s (Herrnstein & Murray, 1994). They argued that an analysis of IQ differences between whites and blacks demonstrated that although environmental factors played a role, there were also basic genetic differences between the two races. They based their argument on a number of findings. For instance, on average, whites score 15 points higher than blacks on traditional IQ tests even when socioeconomic status (SES) is taken into account. According to Herrnstein and Murray, middle- and upper-SES blacks score lower than middle- and upper-SES whites, just as lower-SES blacks score lower on average than lower-SES whites. Intelligence differences between blacks and whites, they concluded, could not be attributed to environmental differences alone. However, this was a conclusion, as we shall see, that was soon refuted.

IQ AND HERITABILITY

heritability The degree to which a characteristic is related to genetic, inherited factors. (Module 23)

There is no doubt that intelligence shows high heritability. **Heritability** is the degree to which a characteristic is related to genetic, inherited factors (e.g., Miller & Penke, 2007; Plomin, 2009; van Soelen et al., 2011).

As can be seen in Figure 6, the closer the genetic link between two related people, the greater the correspondence of IQ scores. Using data such as these, Herrnstein and Murray argued that differences between races in IQ scores were largely caused by genetically based differences in intelligence.

However, many psychologists reacted strongly against the arguments laid out in *The Bell Curve*, refuting several of the book's basic conclusions. One criticism is that even within similar socioeconomic groups, wide variations in IQ remain among individual households. Furthermore, the living conditions of blacks and whites are likely different even when their socioeconomic status (SES) is similar. In addition, as we discussed earlier, there is reason to believe that traditional IQ tests may discriminate against lower-SES urban blacks by asking for information pertaining to experiences they are unlikely to have had (Nisbett, 2007; Levine, 2011).

Moreover, blacks who are raised in economically enriched environments have IQ scores similar to whites in comparable environments. For example, in a study of black

Relationship	Genetic overlap	Rearing	Correlation
Monozygotic (identical) twins	100%	Together	.86
Dizygotic (fraternal) twins	50%	Together	.62
Siblings	50%	Together	.41
Siblings	50%	Apart	.24
Parent-child	50%	Together	.35
Parent-child	50%	Apart	.31
Adoptive parent-child	0%	Together	.16
Unrelated children	0%	Together	.25
Spouses	0%	Apart	.29

The difference between these two correlations shows the impact of the environment

The relatively low correlation for unrelated children raised together shows the importance of genetic factors

FIGURE 6 The relationship between IQ and closeness of genetic relationship. In general, the more similar the genetic and environmental background of two people, the greater the correlation is. Note, for example, that the correlation for spouses, who are genetically unrelated and have been reared apart, is relatively low, whereas the correlation for identical twins reared together is substantial.

Source: Adapted from Henderson, N. D. (1982). Correlations in IQ for pairs of people with varying degrees of genetic relatedness and shared environment. *Annual Review of Psychology, 33*, 219–243.

children who had been adopted at an early age by white middle-class families of above-average intelligence, the IQ scores of those children averaged 106–about 15 points above the average IQ scores of unadopted black children in the study. Other research shows that the racial gap in IQ narrows considerably after a college education, and cross-cultural data demonstrate that when racial gaps exist in other cultures, the economically disadvantaged groups typically have lower scores. In short, the evidence that genetic factors play the major role in determining racial differences in IQ is not compelling (Scarr & Weinberg, 1976; Fagan & Holland, 2007; Nisbett, 2009; Thaler et al., 2015).

Furthermore, drawing comparisons between different races on any dimension, including IQ scores, is an imprecise, potentially misleading, and often fruitless venture. By far, the greatest discrepancies in IQ scores occur when comparing *individuals*, not when comparing mean IQ scores of different *groups*. There are blacks who score high on IQ tests and whites who score low, just as there are whites who score high and blacks who score low. For the concept of intelligence to aid in the betterment of society, we must examine how *individuals* perform and not the groups to which they belong (Fagan & Holland, 2002, 2007).

The more critical question to ask, then, is not whether hereditary or environmental factors primarily underlie intelligence but whether there is anything we can do to maximize the intellectual development of each individual. If we can find ways to do this, we will be able to make changes in the environment–which may take the form of enriched home and school environments–that can lead each person to reach his or her potential.

Study Alert
Remember that the differences in IQ scores are much greater when comparing individuals than when comparing groups.

From the perspective of...

A College Admissions Officer Imagine you notice that students who are members of minority groups systematically receive lower scores on standardized college entrance exams. What suggestions do you have for helping these students improve their scores?

©Flying Colours Ltd/Getty Images

RECAP/EVALUATE/RETHINK

RECAP

LO 23-1 What are the different definitions and conceptions of intelligence?

- Because intelligence can take many forms, defining it is challenging. One commonly accepted view is that intelligence is the capacity to understand the world, think rationally, and use resources effectively when faced with challenges.
- The earliest psychologists assumed that there is a general factor for mental ability called *g*. However, later psychologists disputed the view that intelligence is uni-dimensional.
- Some researchers suggest that intelligence can be broken down into fluid intelligence and crystallized

intelligence. Gardner's theory of multiple intelligences proposes that there are eight spheres of intelligence.
- Information-processing approaches examine the processes underlying intelligent behavior rather than focusing on the structure of intelligence.
- Practical intelligence is intelligence related to overall success in living; emotional intelligence is the set of skills that underlie the accurate assessment, evaluation, expression, and regulation of emotions.

LO 23-2 What are the major approaches to measuring intelligence, and what do intelligence tests measure?

- Intelligence tests have traditionally compared a person's mental age and chronological age to yield an IQ, or intelligence quotient, score.

- Specific tests of intelligence include the Stanford-Binet test, the Wechsler Adult Intelligence Scale–IV (WAIS-IV), and the Wechsler Intelligence Scale for Children-V (WISC-V).
- Tests are expected to be both reliable and valid. Reliability refers to the consistency with which a test measures what it is trying to measure. A test has validity when it actually measures what it is supposed to measure.

LO 23-3 How can the extremes of intelligence be characterized?

- The levels of intellectual disability include mild, moderate, severe, and profound intellectual disability.
- About one-third of the cases of intellectual disability have a known biological cause; fetal alcohol syndrome is the most common. Most cases, however, are classified as familial intellectual disability, for which there is no known biological cause.
- The intellectually gifted are people with IQ scores greater than 130. Intellectually gifted people tend to be healthier and more successful than the nongifted.

LO 23-4 Are traditional IQ tests culturally biased?

- Traditional intelligence tests have frequently been criticized for being biased in favor of the white middle-class population. This controversy has led to attempts to devise culture-fair tests, IQ measures that avoid questions that depend on a particular cultural background.

LO 23-5 To what degree is intelligence influenced by the environment and to what degree by heredity?
- Attempting to distinguish environmental from hereditary factors in intelligence is probably futile and certainly misguided. Because individual IQ scores vary far more than do group IQ scores, it is more critical to ask what can be done to maximize the intellectual development of each individual.

1. _____ is a measure of intelligence that takes into account a person's chronological and mental ages.
2. Some psychologists make the distinction between _____ intelligence, which reflects the ability to think logically, reason abstractly, and solve problems, and _____ intelligence, which is the accumulation of information, knowledge, and skills that people have learned through experience and education.
3. _____ _____ _____ is the most common biological cause of intellectual disability.
4. People with high intelligence are generally shy and socially withdrawn. True or false?
5. A(n) _____ test tries to use only questions appropriate to all the people taking the test.

1. What is the role of emotional intelligence in the classroom? How might emotional intelligence be tested? Should emotional intelligence be a factor in determining academic promotion to the next grade?
2. Why might a test that identifies a disproportionate number of minority group members for special educational services and remedial assistance be considered potentially biased? Isn't the purpose of the test to help persons at risk of falling behind academically? How can a test created for a good purpose be biased?

Answers to Evaluate Questions

1. IQ; 2. fluid; crystallized; 3. Fetal alcohol syndrome; 4. false; the gifted are generally more socially adept than those with lower IQs; 5. culture-fair

---

KEY TERMS

intelligence	practical intelligence	validity	intellectually gifted
g or *g*-factor	emotional intelligence	norms	culture-fair IQ test
fluid intelligence	intelligence tests	intellectual disability	heritability
crystallized intelligence	mental age	fetal alcohol syndrome	
theory of multiple intelligences	intelligence quotient (IQ)	familial intellectual disability	
	reliability		

LOOKING *Back*

EPILOGUE

The topics in this chapter occupy a central place in the field of psychology, encompassing a variety of areas—including thinking, problem solving, decision making, creativity, language, memory, and intelligence. We first examined thinking and problem solving, focusing on the importance of mental images and concepts and identifying the steps commonly involved in solving problems. We discussed language, describing the components of grammar and tracing language development in children. Finally, we considered intelligence. Some of the most heated discussions in all of psychology focus on this topic, engaging educators, policymakers, politicians, and psychologists alike. The issues include the very meaning of intelligence, its measurement, individual extremes of intelligence, and finally, the heredity/environment question.

Before proceeding, turn back to the prologue about the cognitive benefits of certain types of videogames. Answer the following questions in light of what you have learned about thinking, problem solving, and language:

1. How might videogames enhance a person's decision-making ability? Problem-solving skills? Spatial sense? Attention skills?

2. Among the many types of videogames—action games, strategy games, word games, hidden-object games, puzzle games—do you think particular types have targeted benefits for certain types of cognitive skills? Explain.

3. How might mental images, concepts, and logical reasoning play a part in working through a complex videogame? How might gamers use algorithms and heuristics in playing videogames?

4. How would researchers establish that playing videogames causes improved performance and eliminate the possibility that videogames simply attract persons who already have particular kinds of superior cognitive skills? In other words, how would researchers establish cause-and-effect instead of correlational explanations?

Design Elements: Yellow highlighter: ©luckyraccoon/Shutterstock.com; Smartphone: ©and4me/Shutterstock.com; Group of diverse hands: ©MR. Nattanon Kanchak/Shutterstock.com; Woman working on laptop: ©Dragon Images/Shutterstock.com.

Visual Summary

MODULE 21 Thinking and Reasoning

Mental images:
Representations in the mind of an object or event

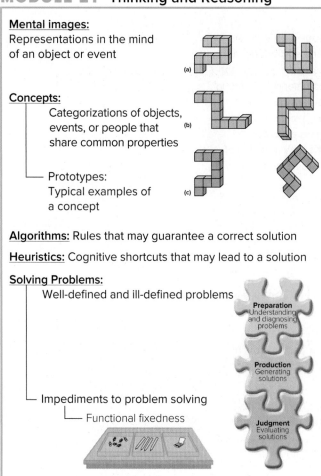

(a)
(b)
(c)

Concepts:
— Categorizations of objects, events, or people that share common properties

— Prototypes: Typical examples of a concept

Algorithms: Rules that may guarantee a correct solution

Heuristics: Cognitive shortcuts that may lead to a solution

Solving Problems:
— Well-defined and ill-defined problems

Preparation
Understanding and diagnosing problems

Production
Generating solutions

Judgment
Evaluating solutions

— Impediments to problem solving
— Functional fixedness

MODULE 22 Language

Language Development
— Babbling: Speech-like sounds that are meaningless
— Telegraphic speech: Sentences in which only essential words are used
— Overgeneralization: The phenomenon in which children over-apply a language rule, thereby making a linguistic error

Approaches to Learning Language
— Learning-theory approach
— Nativist approach
— Interactionist approach

Linguistic-Relativity Hypothesis: The hypothesis that language shapes and may determine the way people perceive and understand the world

MODULE 23 Intelligence

Theories of Intelligence
— *g*-factor: Single factor underlying mental ability

— Fluid intelligence: Information-processing capabilities, reasoning, and memory

— Crystallized intelligence: Accumulation of information, knowledge, and skills learned through experience and education

— Gardner's multiple intelligences

— Practical intelligence: Intelligence related to overall success in living

— Emotional intelligence: Skills that underlie the accurate assessment, evaluation, expression, and regulation of emotions

Assessing Intelligence: Intelligence tests
— Binet developed IQ tests

• Mental age: the average age of individuals who achieve a particular level of performance on a test

• IQ: a score based on an individual's mental and chronological ages

$$\text{IQ score} = \frac{MA}{CA} \times 100$$

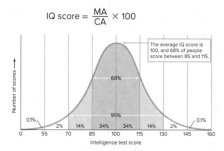

The average IQ score is 100, and 68% of people score between 85 and 115.

— Contemporary IQ tests

• Wechsler Adult Intelligence Scale–IV

• Wechsler Intelligence Scale for Children–IV

Variations in Intellectual Ability
— Intellectual Disability

• A disability characterized by significant limitations both in intellectual functioning and in conceptual, social, and practical adaptive skills

• Fetal alcohol syndrome and familial retardation

— Intellectually Gifted

• IQ scores greater than 130

• Most often outgoing, well adjusted, healthy, popular

(MODULE 21): (a-c): Source: Adapted from Shepard, R. N., & Metzler, J. (1971). Mental rotation of three-dimensional objects. *Science, 171*(3972), 701–703; (MODULE 22): ©Laurentiu Garofeanu/Barcroft USA/Barcoft Media via Getty Images

©Yasuyoshi Chiba/AFP/Getty Images

CHAPTER 8
Motivation and Emotion

LEARNING OUTCOMES FOR CHAPTER 8

PROLOGUE *THE (FALSE) PICTURE OF HEALTH*

Daniella Isaacs, already on a gluten-free diet because of her celiac disease, became fixated on "clean living" and "healthy eating" and entirely cut sugar, dairy, and even gluten-free bread and pasta out of her diet. She liked the results so much that she began posting pictures of her food and her thinning body on Instagram.

Then it got intense. Feeding off the "likes" on Instagram, she restricted her diet even more and added gym work and running to her routine. She avoided eating out because she wanted to control the food on her plate. If she went to a friend's house, she volunteered to cook so she could choose the food.

Daniella's periods stopped, her hair began to fall out, and she felt more and more unwell, but her Instagram following kept growing. "People were giving me compliments about how thin I was," she says, "despite looking borderline anorexic. I got sucked up by Instagram and got sick. Being thinner didn't make me any happier." (Nagesh, 2017).

LOOKING *Ahead*

What explains Daniella Isaacs's obsession with "healthy eating"—an obsession that led to excessive weight loss and dietary deficiencies? Was she driven mainly by concern for her health? Was she motivated by the desire to become more attractive? And considering her craving for approval from her Instagram followers, were her emotional needs and attitude the primary factors driving her behavior?

These questions and many others are addressed by psychologists who study the topics of motivation and emotion. Psychologists who study motivation seek to discover the particular desired goals—the motives—that underlie behavior. Behaviors as basic as drinking to satisfy thirst and as inconsequential as taking a stroll to get exercise exemplify motives. Psychologists specializing in the study of motivation assume that such underlying motives steer our choices of activities.

While motivation concerns the forces that direct future behavior, emotion pertains to the feelings we experience throughout our lives. The study of emotions focuses on our internal experiences at any given moment. All of us feel a variety of emotions: happiness at succeeding at a difficult task, sadness over the death of a loved one, anger at being treated unfairly. Because emotions not only play a role in motivating our behavior but also act as a reflection of our underlying motivation, they play an important role in our lives.

We begin this set of modules by focusing on the major conceptions of motivation, discussing how different motives and needs jointly affect behavior. We consider motives that are biologically based and universal in the animal kingdom, such as hunger, as well as motives that are unique to humans, such as the need for achievement.

We then turn to emotions. We consider the roles and functions that emotions play in people's lives and discuss several approaches that explain how people understand their emotions. Finally, we look at how nonverbal behavior communicates emotions.

Module 24
Explaining Motivation

In just a moment, 27-year-old Aron Ralston's life changed. An 800-pound boulder dislodged where Ralston was hiking in a narrow, isolated Utah canyon, pinning his lower arm to the ground.

For the next five days, Ralston lay trapped, unable to escape. An experienced climber who had search-and-rescue training, he had ample time to consider his options. He tried unsuccessfully to chip away at the rock, and he rigged up ropes and pulleys around the boulder in a vain effort to move it.

Finally, out of water and nearly dehydrated, Ralston reasoned there was only one option left short of dying. In acts of incredible bravery, Ralston broke two bones in his wrist, applied a tourniquet, and used a dull pen knife to amputate his arm beneath the elbow.

Freed from his entrapment, Ralston climbed out from where he had been pinned and then hiked five miles to safety. (Cox, 2003; Lofholm, 2003)

What factors lay behind Ralston's resolve?

To answer this question, psychologists employ the concept of **motivation,** the factors that direct and energize the behavior of humans and other organisms. Motivation has biological, cognitive, and social aspects, and the complexity of the concept has led psychologists to develop a variety of approaches. All seek to explain the energy that guides people's behavior in specific directions.

LEARNING OUTCOMES

LO 24-1 How does motivation direct and energize behavior?

motivation The factors that direct and energize the behavior of humans and other organisms. (Module 24)

What was the motivation behind Aron Ralston's heroic efforts to free himself from the rock that had pinned his arm to the ground?
©Aron Ralston/ZUMA Press/Newscom

Instinct Approaches: Born to Be Motivated

instincts Inborn patterns of behavior that are biologically determined rather than learned. (Module 24)

instinct approaches to motivation The explanation of motivation that suggests people and animals are born preprogrammed with sets of behaviors essential to their survival. (Module 24)

When psychologists first tried to explain motivation, they turned to **instincts,** inborn patterns of behavior that are biologically determined rather than learned. According to **instinct approaches to motivation,** people and animals are born preprogrammed with sets of behaviors essential to their survival. Those instincts provide the energy that channels behavior in appropriate directions. Hence, sexual behavior may be a response to an instinct to reproduce, and exploratory behavior may be motivated by an instinct to examine one's territory.

This instinct approach presents several difficulties, however. For one thing, psychologists do not agree on what, or even how many, primary instincts exist. One early psychologist, William McDougall (1908), suggested that there are 18 instincts. Other theorists came up with even more–with one sociologist (Bernard, 1924) claiming that there are exactly 5,759 distinct instincts!

Furthermore, instinct approaches are unable to explain why certain patterns of behavior and not others have evolved in a given species. In addition, although it is clear that a great deal of animal behavior is based on instincts, much of the variety and complexity of human behavior is learned and thus cannot be seen as instinctual.

As a result of these shortcomings, newer explanations have replaced conceptions of motivation based on instincts. However, instinct approaches still play a role in certain theories, especially those based on evolutionary approaches that focus on our genetic inheritance. Furthermore, Freud's work suggests that instinctual drives of sex and aggression motivate behavior (Katz, 2001).

Drive-Reduction Approaches: Satisfying Our Needs

drive-reduction approaches to motivation Theories suggesting that a lack of some basic biological need produces a drive to push an organism to satisfy that need. (Module 24)

drive Motivational tension, or arousal, that energizes behavior to fulfill a need. (Module 24)

After rejecting instinct theory, psychologists first proposed simple drive-reduction theories of motivation to take its place (Hull, 1943). **Drive-reduction approaches to motivation** suggest that a lack of some basic biological need (such as a lack of water) produces a drive to push an organism to satisfy that need (in this case, seeking water).

To understand this approach, we need to understand the concept of drive. A **drive** is motivational tension, or arousal, that energizes behavior to fulfill a need.

Many basic drives, such as hunger, thirst, sleep, and sex, are related to biological needs of the body or of the species as a whole. These are called *primary drives*. Primary drives contrast with secondary drives in which behavior fulfills no obvious biological need. In *secondary drives*, prior experience and learning bring about needs. For instance, some people have strong needs to achieve academically and professionally. We can say that their achievement need is reflected in a secondary drive that motivates their behavior (Johnson, Stewart, & Bachman, 2015; Huang, Etkin, & Jin, 2017).

We usually try to satisfy a primary drive by reducing the need underlying it. For example, we become hungry after not eating for a few hours and may raid the refrigerator, especially if the next scheduled meal is not imminent. If the weather turns cold, we put on extra clothing or raise the setting on the thermostat to keep warm. If our bodies need liquids to function properly, we experience thirst and seek out water.

HOMEOSTASIS

homeostasis The body's tendency to maintain a steady internal state. (Module 24)

Homeostasis, the body's tendency to maintain a steady internal state, underlies primary drives. Using feedback loops, homeostasis brings deviations in body functioning back to an optimal state, similar to the way a thermostat and a furnace work in a home heating system to maintain a steady temperature. Receptor cells throughout the body constantly monitor factors such as temperature and nutrient levels. When deviations from the ideal state occur, the body adjusts in an effort to return to an optimal state. Many fundamental needs, including the needs for food, water, stable body temperature, and sleep, operate via homeostasis (Porkka-Heiskanen & Kalinchuk, 2011; Porkka-Heiskanen, 2013; Betley et al., 2015).

Although drive-reduction theories provide a good explanation of how primary drives motivate behavior, they cannot fully explain a behavior in which the goal is not to reduce a drive but rather to maintain or even increase the level of excitement or arousal. For instance, some behaviors seem to be motivated by nothing more than curiosity, such as rushing to check e-mail messages. Similarly, many people pursue thrilling activities such as riding a roller coaster or steering a raft down the rapids of a river. Such behaviors certainly don't suggest that people seek to reduce all drives, as drive-reduction approaches would indicate (Begg & Langley, 2001; Rosenbloom & Wolf, 2002; Wishart, Somoray, & Rowland, 2017).

Both curiosity and thrill-seeking behavior, then, cast doubt on drive-reduction approaches as a complete explanation for motivation. In both cases, rather than seeking to reduce an underlying drive, people and animals appear to be motivated to increase their overall level of stimulation and activity. To explain this phenomenon, psychologists have devised an alternative: arousal approaches to motivation.

Study Alert
To remember the concept of homeostasis, keep in mind the analogy of a thermostat that regulates the temperature in a house.

Arousal Approaches: Beyond Drive Reduction

According to **arousal approaches to motivation,** people try to maintain a steady level of stimulation and activity. Similar to drive-reduction explanations of motivation, the arousal approach suggests that if our stimulation and activity levels become uncomfortably high, we try to reduce them. But unlike the drive-reduction perspective, the arousal approach additionally suggests that if levels of stimulation and activity are too *low*, we will try to increase them by seeking stimulation.

People vary widely in the optimal level of arousal they seek out, with some people looking for especially high levels of arousal. For example, people who participate in daredevil sports, high-stakes gamblers, and criminals who pull off high-risk robberies may be exhibiting a particularly high need for arousal (see Figure 1; Roets & Van Hiel, 2011; Lang & Bradley, 2013; Stevens et al., 2015).

arousal approaches to motivation
The belief that we try to maintain certain levels of stimulation and activity. (Module 24)

Incentive Approaches: Motivation's Pull

When a luscious dessert appears on the table after a filling meal, its appeal has little or nothing to do with internal drives or the maintenance of arousal. Rather, if we choose to eat the dessert, such behavior is motivated by the external stimulus of the dessert itself, which acts as an anticipated reward. This reward, in motivational terms, is an *incentive.*

Incentive approaches to motivation suggest that motivation stems from the desire to attain external rewards, known as incentives. In this view, the desirable properties of external stimuli—whether grades, money, affection, food, or sex—account for a person's motivation (Festinger et al., 2009).

Although the theory explains why we may succumb to an incentive (such as a mouth-watering dessert) even though we lack internal cues (such as hunger), it does not provide a complete explanation of motivation because organisms sometimes seek to fulfill needs even when incentives are not apparent. Consequently, many psychologists believe that the internal drives proposed by drive-reduction theory work in tandem with the external incentives of incentive theory to "push" and "pull" behavior,

incentive approaches to motivation
Theories suggesting that motivation stems from the desire to attain external rewards, known as incentives. (Module 24)

FIGURE 1 Some people seek high levels of arousal, whereas others are more easygoing. You can get a sense of your own preferred level of stimulation by completing this questionnaire.

Source: Adapted from Zuckerman, M. (1978, February). The search for high sensation. *Psychology Today,* 30–46.

Are You a Sensation Seeker?

How much do you crave stimulation in your everyday life? Complete the following questionnaire to find out. Circle either A or B in each pair or statements.

1. A My definition of the good life is to be at peace and comfortable in my skin.
   B My definition of the good life is to grab every experience possible.
2. A When I see an unfamiliar ride at an amusement park, I get right in line.
   B When I see a new ride, I need to watch how it works a few times before trying it.
3. A My ideal job would involve travel and a wealth of new experiences.
   B My ideal job would be to do something I like and keep getting better at it.
4. A I am a big fan of a lazy summer day, a beach or backyard, and a good book.
   B I love winter with its brisk days and outdoor activities like skiing and snowboarding.
5. A I look forward to meeting new people and trying new things.
   B I like hanging out with my friends and doing things we know we enjoy.
6. A I think it's foolish to take unnecessary risks just for a sense of adventure.
   B I am attracted to challenges, even if they're a bit dangerous.
7. A I like movies that are funny or where I know the good guys are going to win.
   B I like edgy movies that are unpredictable or explore new ideas.
8. A The best art makes you think or shakes up your old ideas and preconceptions.
   B Good art is beautiful and makes you feel serene.
9. A For vacations I prefer to go places I like and eat at restaurants I know.
   B My ideal vacation is to go somewhere new where I can try different things.
10. A If I lived in frontier days, I would head West to pursue potential opportunities.
    B If I lived in frontier days, I would stay in the East and make a good life there.
11. A The people I'm drawn to are unusual and have kind of wild ideas.
    B I like people who are like me and know who they are.
12. A I would never allow myself to be hypnotized, especially in public.
    B I would probably volunteer to be hypnotized, just to give it a try.
12. A I would love to try things like parachuting, bungee jumping, and hang gliding.
    B It makes no sense to jump out of a perfectly good airplane or off a bridge.

Scoring: Give yourself a point for each of these responses: 1B, 2A, 3A, 4B, 5A, 6B, 7B, 8A, 9B, 10A, 11A, 12B, 13A. Add up the points, and then use the following key to find your sensation-seeking score.

12–13 Very high sensation seeking
10–11 High sensation seeking
 6–9 Average sensation seeking
 4–5 Low sensation seeking
 1–3 Very low sensation seeking

Your results can give you a rough idea of your sensation-seeking tendencies. Understand that this is a short questionnaire based on the responses of a small sample of college students, giving at best an imprecise picture. Understand, too, that as people age, their sensation scores tend to become lower.

respectively. Thus, at the same time that we seek to satisfy our underlying hunger needs (the push of drive-reduction theory), we are drawn to food that appears very appetizing (the pull of incentive theory). Rather than contradicting each other, then, drives and incentives may work together in motivating behavior (Berridge, 2004; Belasen & Fortunato, 2013; Goswami & Urminsky, 2017).

Cognitive Approaches: The Thoughts Behind Motivation

Cognitive approaches to motivation suggest that motivation is the outcome of people's thoughts, beliefs, expectations, and goals. For instance, the degree to which people are motivated to study for a test is based on their expectation of how well studying will pay off in terms of a good grade.

Cognitive theories of motivation draw a key distinction between intrinsic and extrinsic motivation. *Intrinsic motivation* causes us to participate in an activity for our own enjoyment rather than for any actual or concrete reward that it will bring us. In contrast, *extrinsic motivation* causes us to do something for money, a grade, or some other actual, concrete reward (Shaikholeslami & Khayyer, 2006; Finkelstein, 2009; Hofeditz et al., 2017).

For example, when a physician works long hours because she loves medicine, intrinsic motivation is prompting her; if she works hard to make a lot of money, extrinsic motivation underlies her efforts. Similarly, if we study a lot because we love the subject matter, we are being guided by intrinsic motivation. On the other hand, if all we care about is the grade we get in the course, that studying is due to extrinsic motivation (Emmett & McGee, 2013).

We are more apt to persevere, work harder, and produce work of higher quality when motivation for a task is intrinsic rather than extrinsic. In fact, in some cases, providing rewards for desirable behavior (thereby increasing extrinsic motivation) actually may decrease intrinsic motivation (Grant, 2008; Nishimura, Kawamura, & Sakurai, 2011; Bolkan, 2015).

cognitive approaches to motivation Theories suggesting that motivation is a result of people's thoughts, beliefs, expectations, and goals. (Module 24)

From the perspective of...

An Educator Do you think that giving students grades serves as an external reward that may decrease intrinsic motivation for learning about the subject matter? Why or why not?

©Andersen Ross/Blend Images/Getty Images

Maslow's Hierarchy: Ordering Motivational Needs

What do Eleanor Roosevelt, Abraham Lincoln, and Albert Einstein have in common? The common thread, according to a model of motivation devised by psychologist Abraham Maslow, is that each of them fulfilled the highest levels of motivational needs underlying human behavior.

Maslow's model places motivational needs in a hierarchy and suggests that before more sophisticated, higher-order needs can be met, certain primary needs must be satisfied (Maslow, 1970, 1987). A pyramid can represent the model, with the more basic needs at the bottom and the higher-level needs at the top (see Figure 2). To activate a specific higher-order need, thereby guiding behavior, a person must first fulfill the more basic needs in the hierarchy.

The basic needs are primary drives: needs for water, food, sleep, sex, and the like. To move up the hierarchy, a person must first meet these basic physiological needs. Safety needs come next in the hierarchy; Maslow suggests that people need a safe,

FIGURE 2 Maslow's hierarchy shows how our motivation progresses up the pyramid from the broadest, most fundamental biological needs to higher-order ones. Do you agree that lower-order needs must be satisfied before higher-order needs? Do hermits and monks who attempt to fulfill spiritual needs while denying basic physical needs contradict Maslow's hierarchy?

Source: Adapted from Maslow, A. H. (1970). *Motivation and personality*. New York: Harper & Row.

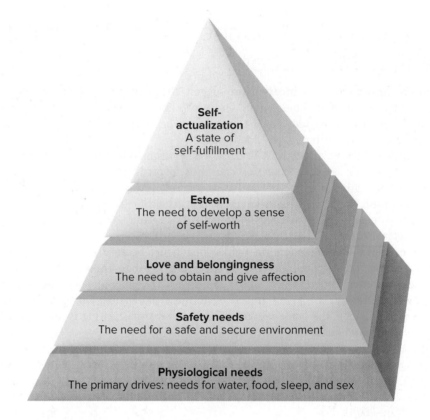

Self-actualization
A state of
self-fulfillment

Esteem
The need to develop a sense
of self-worth

Love and belongingness
The need to obtain and give affection

Safety needs
The need for a safe and secure environment

Physiological needs
The primary drives: needs for water, food, sleep, and sex

self-actualization A state of self-fulfillment in which people realize their highest potential in their own unique way. (Modules 24, 32)

secure environment in order to function effectively. Physiological and safety needs compose the lower-order needs.

Only after meeting the basic lower-order needs can a person consider fulfilling higher-order needs, such as the needs for love and a sense of belonging, esteem, and self-actualization. Love and belongingness needs include the needs to obtain and give affection and to be a contributing member of some group or society. After fulfilling these needs, a person strives for esteem. Esteem is the recognition that others value your competence and worth, and that they admire you for your qualities.

After these four sets of needs (physiological needs, safety needs, love and belongingness, and esteem) are fulfilled—no easy task—a person is able to strive for the highest-level need, self-actualization. **Self-actualization** is a state of self-fulfillment in which people realize their highest potentials in their own unique way. Although Maslow first suggested that self-actualization occurred in only a few famous individuals, he later expanded the concept to encompass everyday people. For example, a parent with excellent nurturing skills who raises a family, a teacher who year after year creates an environment that maximizes students' opportunities for success, and an artist who realizes his creative potential all may be self-actualized. The important thing is that people feel at ease with themselves and satisfied that they are using their talents to the fullest. In a sense, achieving self-actualization reduces the striving and yearning for greater fulfillment that mark most people's lives and instead provides a sense of satisfaction with their current state of affairs (Bauer, Schwab, & McAdams, 2011; Ivtzan et al., 2013; Winston, Maher, & Easvaradoss, 2017).

Although research has been unable to validate the specific ordering of Maslow's stages and it is difficult to measure self-actualization objectively, Maslow's hierarchy of needs is important for two reasons: It highlights the complexity of human needs, and it emphasizes the idea that until more basic biological needs are met, people will be relatively unconcerned with higher-order needs. For example, if people are hungry, their first interest will be in obtaining food; they will not be concerned with needs such as love and self-esteem (Ojha & Pramanick, 2009; LaLumiere & Kalivas, 2013; Beitel et al., 2015).

Maslow's hierarchy of needs has also spawned other approaches to motivation. For example, Edward Deci and Richard Ryan have considered human needs in terms of psychological well-being. They suggest in their *self-determination theory* that people have the need for these three basic states: (1) competence, (2) autonomy, and (3) relatedness. Competence is the need to produce desirable outcomes, whereas autonomy is the need to feel control over our own lives. Finally, relatedness is the need to be involved in close, warm relationships with others. In the view of self-determination theory, these three psychological needs are genetically determined and universal across cultures, and they are as essential as basic biological needs (Jang et al., 2009; Ryan & Deci, 2011; Ryan & Deci, 2017).

Applying the Different Approaches to Motivation

The various theories of motivation (summarized in Figure 3) give several perspectives on it. Which provides the fullest account of motivation? Actually, many of the approaches are complementary rather than contradictory. In fact, employing more than one approach can help us understand motivation in a particular instance.

Consider, for example, Aron Ralston's accident while hiking (described earlier). His interest in climbing in an isolated and potentially dangerous area may be explained by arousal approaches to motivation. From the perspective of instinct approaches, we

Study Alert
Review the distinctions among the different explanations for motivation (instinct, drive reduction, arousal, incentive, cognitive, and Maslow's hierarchy of needs).

Instinct
People and animals are born with preprogrammed sets of behaviors essential to their survival.

Drive reduction
When some basic biological requirement is lacking, a drive is produced.

Arousal
People seek an optimal level of stimulation. If the level of stimulation is too high, they act to reduce it; if it is too low, they act to increase it.

Incentive
External rewards direct and energize behavior.

Cognitive
Thoughts, beliefs, expectations, and goals direct motivation.

Hierarchy of needs
Needs form a hierarchy; before higher-order needs are met, lower-order needs must be fulfilled.

FIGURE 3 The major approaches to motivation.

(Top, Left) ©Blend Images/Getty Images; (Top, Middle) ©Digital Vision/Getty Images; (Top, Right) ©wavebreakmedia/Shutterstock; (Bottom, Left) Source: LCPL Casey N. Thurston, USMC/DoD Media; (Bottom, Middle) ©Corbis/VCG/Getty Images

realize that Ralston had an overwhelming instinct to preserve his life at all costs. From a cognitive perspective, we see his careful consideration of various strategies to extricate himself from the boulder.

In short, applying multiple approaches to motivation in a given situation provides a broader understanding than we might obtain by employing only a single approach. We'll see this again when we consider specific motives–such as the needs for food, achievement, affiliation, and power–and draw on several of the theories for the fullest account of what motivates our behavior.

RECAP/EVALUATE/RETHINK

RECAP

LO 24-1 How does motivation direct and energize behavior?

- Motivation relates to the factors that direct and energize behavior.
- Drive is the motivational tension that energizes behavior to fulfill a need.
- Homeostasis, the maintenance of a steady internal state, often underlies motivational drives.
- Arousal approaches suggest that we try to maintain a particular level of stimulation and activity.
- Incentive approaches focus on the positive aspects of the environment that direct and energize behavior.
- Cognitive approaches focus on the role of thoughts, expectations, and understanding of the world in producing motivation.
- Maslow's hierarchy suggests that there are five basic needs: physiological, safety, love and belongingness, esteem, and self-actualization. Only after the more basic needs are fulfilled can a person move toward meeting higher-order needs.

EVALUATE

1. _____ are forces that guide a person's behavior in a certain direction.
2. Biologically determined, inborn patterns of behavior are known as _____.
3. Your psychology professor tells you, "Explaining behavior is easy! When we lack something, we are motivated to get it." Which approach to motivation does your professor subscribe to?

4. By drinking water after running a marathon, a runner tries to keep his or her body at an optimal level of functioning. This process is called _____.
5. I help an elderly person cross the street because doing a good deed makes me feel good. What type of motivation is at work here? What type of motivation would be at work if I were to help an elderly man across the street because he paid me $20?
6. According to Maslow, a person with no job, no home, and no friends can become self-actualized. True or false?

RETHINK

1. Which approaches to motivation are more commonly used in the workplace? How might each approach be used to design employment policies that can sustain or increase motivation?
2. A writer who works all day composing copy for an advertising firm has a hard time keeping her mind on her work and continually watches the clock. After work she turns to a collection of stories she is creating and writes long into the night, completely forgetful of the clock. What ideas from your reading on motivation help to explain this phenomenon?

Answers to Evaluate Questions

1. Motives; 2. instincts; 3. drive reduction; 4. homeostasis; 5. intrinsic; extrinsic; 6. false; lower-order needs must be fulfilled before self-actualization can occur.

KEY TERMS

motivation	drive-reduction approaches to motivation	arousal approaches to motivation	cognitive approaches to motivation
instincts	drive	incentive approaches to motivation	self-actualization
instinct approaches to motivation	homeostasis		

Module 25

Human Needs and Motivation: Eat, Drink, and Be Daring

As a sophomore at the University of California, Santa Cruz, Lisa Arndt followed a menu of her own making: For breakfast she ate cereal or fruit with 10 diet pills and 50 chocolate-flavored laxatives. Lunch was a salad or sandwich; dinner: chicken and rice. But it was the feast that followed that Arndt relished most. Almost every night at about 9 P.M., she would retreat to her room and eat an entire small pizza and a whole batch of cookies. Then she'd wait for the day's laxatives to take effect. "It was extremely painful," says Arndt of those days. . . . "But I was that desperate to make up for my bingeing. I was terrified of fat the way other people are afraid of lions or guns." (Hubbard, O'Neill, & Cheakalos, 1999)

Lisa was one of the estimated 10 million women and 1 million men who suffer from eating disorders. These disorders, which usually appear during adolescence, can bring about extraordinary weight loss and other forms of physical deterioration. Extremely dangerous, they sometimes result in death.

Why are Lisa and others like her subject to such disordered eating, which revolves around the motivation to avoid weight gain at all costs? And why do so many other people engage in overeating, which leads to obesity?

To answer these questions, we must consider some of the specific needs that underlie behavior. In this module, we examine several of the most important human needs. We begin with hunger, the primary drive that has received the most attention from researchers, and then we turn to secondary drives–those uniquely human endeavors based on learned needs and past experience that help explain why people strive to achieve, to affiliate with others, and to seek power over others.

The Motivation Behind Hunger and Eating

Two hundred million people in the United States–some two-thirds of the population–are overweight. More than one-third of the U.S. population is so heavy that they have **obesity,** body weight that is more than 20% above the average weight for a person of a particular height (Sharpe, 2013; Ogden et al., 2014).

And the rest of the world is not far behind: A billion people around the globe are overweight or obese. With average weight rising in most countries, the World Health Organization has said that worldwide obesity has reached epidemic proportions, producing increases in heart disease, diabetes, cancer, and premature deaths. Obesity rates have doubled in 73 countries, and that has led to 4 million premature deaths (Fischetti, 2016; Datar, 2017; Jacobs & Richtel, 2017).

The most widely used measure of obesity is *body mass index (BMI),* which is based on a ratio of weight to height. People with a BMI greater than 30 are considered obese, whereas those with a BMI between 25 and 30 are overweight. (Use the formulas in Figure 1 to determine your own BMI.)

Although the definition of obesity is clear from a scientific point of view, people's perceptions of what an ideal body looks like vary significantly across different cultures and within Western cultures from one time period to another. For instance, many

LEARNING OUTCOMES

LO 25-1 What biological and social factors underlie hunger?

LO 25-2 What are the varieties of sexual behavior?

LO 25-3 How are needs relating to achievement, affiliation, and power motivation exhibited?

obesity Body weight that is more than 20% above the average weight for a person of a particular height. (Module 25)

FIGURE 1 Use this procedure to find your body mass index.

To calculate your body mass index, follow these steps:

1. Indicate your weight in pounds: _____ pounds
2. Indicate your height in inches: _____ inches
3. Divide your weight (item 1) by your height (item 2), and write the outcome here: _____.
4. Divide the result above (item 3) by your height (item 2), and write the outcome here: _____.
5. Multiply the number above by 703, and write the product here: _____. This is your body mass index.

Example:

For a person who weights 210 pounds and who is 6 feet tall, divide 210 pounds by 72 inches, which equals 2.917. Then divide 2.917 by 72 inches (item 3), which yields .041. Multiplying .041 (from item 4) by 703 yields a BMI of 28.5.

Interpretation:
- Underweight = less than 18.5
- Normal weight = 18.5–24.9
- Overweight = 25–29.9
- Obesity = BMI of 30 or greater

Keep in mind that a BMI greater than 25 may or may not be due to excess body fat. For example, professional athletes may have little fat but weigh more than the average person because they have greater muscle mass.

contemporary Western cultures stress the importance of slimness in women—a relatively recent view. In 19th-century Hawaii, the most attractive women were those who were the heaviest. Furthermore, for most of the 20th century—except for periods in the 1920s and the most recent decades—the ideal female figure was relatively full. Even today, weight standards differ among different cultural groups. For instance, in some traditional Arab cultures, obese women are so prized as wives that parents force-feed their female children to make them more desirable (Blixen, Singh, & Xu, 2006; Marsh, Hau, & Sung, 2007; Franko & Roehrig, 2011; Lin et al., 2015).

Regardless of cultural standards for appearance and weight, no one doubts that being overweight represents a major health risk. However, controlling weight is complicated because eating behavior involves a variety of mechanisms. In our discussion of what motivates people to eat, we'll start with the biological aspects of eating.

BIOLOGICAL FACTORS IN THE REGULATION OF HUNGER

In contrast to human beings, other species are unlikely to become obese. Internal mechanisms regulate not only the quantity of food they take in but also the kind of food they desire. For example, rats that have been deprived of particular foods seek out alternatives that contain the specific nutrients their diet is lacking, and many species, given the choice of a wide variety of foods, select a well-balanced diet (Woods et al., 2000; Jones & Corp, 2003; Adler, 2013).

Complex biological mechanisms tell organisms whether they require food or should stop eating. It's not just a matter of an empty stomach causing hunger pangs and a full one alleviating those pangs. (Even individuals who have had their stomachs removed still experience the sensation of hunger.) One important factor is changes in the chemical composition of the blood. For instance, changes in levels of *glucose*, a kind of sugar, regulate feelings of hunger. In addition, the hormone *insulin* leads the body to store excess sugar in the blood as fats and carbohydrates. Finally, the hormone *ghrelin* communicates to the brain feelings of hunger. The production of ghrelin increases according to meal schedules as well as the sight or smell of food, producing the feeling that tells us we're hungry and should eat (Kojima & Kangawa, 2008; Langlois et al., 2011; Massadi et al., 2017).

The brain's *hypothalamus* monitors glucose levels. Increasing evidence suggests that the hypothalamus carries the primary responsibility for monitoring food intake. Injury to the hypothalamus has radical consequences for eating behavior, depending on the site of the injury. For example, rats whose *lateral hypothalamus* is damaged may literally starve to death. They refuse food when it is offered; unless they are force-fed, they eventually die. On the other hand, rats with an injury to the *ventromedial hypothalamus* display the opposite problem: extreme overeating. Rats with this injury may increase in weight by as much as 400%. Similar phenomena occur in humans who have tumors on the hypothalamus (Seymour, 2006; Fedeli et al., 2009; Barson, Morganstern, & Leibowitz, 2011).

Although the important role the hypothalamus plays in regulating food intake is clear, the exact way this organ operates is still unclear. One hypothesis suggests that injury to the hypothalamus affects the weight set point. The **weight set point** is a particular level of weight that the body strives to maintain. Acting as a kind of internal weight thermostat, the hypothalamus regulates food intake by calling for either greater or lesser food intake (Berthoud, 2002; Cornier, 2011; Alboni et al., 2017).

In most cases, the hypothalamus does a good job. Even people who are not deliberately monitoring their weight show only minor weight fluctuations in spite of substantial day-to-day variations in how much they eat and exercise. However, injury to the hypothalamus can alter the weight set point, and a person then struggles to meet the internal goal by increasing or decreasing food consumption. Even temporary exposure to certain drugs can alter the weight set point (Khazaal et al., 2008; Sternson, Betley, & Cao, 2013; Palmiter, 2015).

Genetic factors determine the weight set point, at least in part. People seem destined, through heredity, to have a particular **metabolism,** the rate at which food is converted to energy and expended by the body. People with a high metabolic rate can eat virtually as much as they want without gaining weight, whereas others with low metabolism may eat literally half as much yet gain weight readily (Jequier, 2002; Westerterp, 2006).

SOCIAL FACTORS IN EATING

You've just finished a full meal and feel completely stuffed. Suddenly your host announces with great fanfare that he will be serving his "house specialty" dessert, bananas flambé, and that he has spent the better part of the afternoon preparing it. Even though you are full and don't even like bananas, you accept a serving of his dessert and eat it all.

Clearly, internal biological factors do not fully explain our eating behavior. External social factors, based on societal rules and on what we have learned about appropriate eating behavior, also play an important role. Take, for example, the simple fact that people customarily eat breakfast, lunch, and dinner at approximately the same times every day. Because we tend to eat on schedule every day, we feel hungry as the usual hour approaches, sometimes quite independently of what our internal cues are telling us.

Similarly, we put roughly the same amount of food on our plates every day, even though the amount of exercise we may have had (and consequently our need for energy replenishment) varies from day to day. We also tend to prefer particular foods over others. Rats and dogs may be a delicacy in certain Asian cultures, but few people in Western cultures find them appealing despite their potentially high nutritional value. Even the amount of food we eat varies according to cultural norms. For instance,

weight set point The particular level of weight that the body strives to maintain. (Module 25)

metabolism The rate at which food is converted to energy and expended by the body. (Module 25)

Study Alert
A key point: Eating and hunger are influenced both by biological and social factors.

people in the United States eat bigger portions than do people in France. In sum, cultural influences and our individual habits play important roles in determining when, what, and how much we eat (Rozin et al., 2003; Leeman, Fischler, & Rozin, 2011; Gu et al., 2017).

Other social factors relate to our eating behavior as well. Some of us head toward the refrigerator after a difficult day, seeking solace in a pint of Heath Bar Crunch ice cream. Why? Perhaps when we were children, our parents gave us food when we were upset. Eventually, we may have learned through the basic mechanisms of classical and operant conditioning to associate food with comfort and consolation. Similarly, we may learn that eating, which focuses our attention on immediate pleasures, provides an escape from unpleasant thoughts. Consequently, we may eat when we feel distressed (Elfhag, Tynelius, & Rasmussen, 2007; Tsenkova, Boylan, & Ryff, 2013; Higgs, 2015).

THE ROOTS OF OBESITY

Given that biological as well as social factors influence eating behavior, determining the causes of obesity has proved to be a challenging task. Researchers have followed several paths.

Some psychologists suggest that oversensitivity to external eating cues based on social factors, coupled with insensitivity to internal hunger cues, produce obesity. Others argue that overweight people have higher weight set points than other people do. Because their set points are unusually high, their attempts to lose weight by eating less may make them especially sensitive to external, food-related cues and therefore more apt to overeat and perpetuate their obesity (West, Harvey-Berino, & Raczynski, 2004; Tremblay, 2004; Kanoski et al., 2011).

But why may some people's weight set points be higher than those of others? One biological explanation is that obese individuals have higher levels of the hormone *leptin*, which appears to be designed, from an evolutionary standpoint, to "protect" the body against weight loss. The body's weight-regulation system thus appears to be designed more to protect against losing weight than to protect against gaining it. Therefore, it's easier to gain weight than to lose it (Thanos et al., 2013; Wabitsch et al., 2015; Pontzer, 2017).

Although obesity is reaching epidemic proportions in the United States, its exact causes remain unclear.
©Roberto Michel/Shutterstock

Another biologically based explanation for obesity relates to fat cells in the body. Starting at birth, the body stores fat either by increasing the number of fat cells or by increasing the size of existing fat cells. Furthermore, any loss of weight past infancy does not decrease the number of fat cells; it only affects their size. Consequently, people are stuck with the number of fat cells they inherit from an early age, and the rate of weight gain during the first 4 months of life is related to being overweight during later childhood (Stettler et al., 2005; Moore, Wilkie, & Desrochers, 2017).

According to the *weight-set-point hypothesis*, the presence of too many fat cells from earlier weight gain may result in the set point's becoming "stuck" at a higher level than desirable. In such circumstances, losing weight becomes a difficult proposition because one is constantly at odds with one's own internal set point when dieting (Freedman, 1995; Leibel, Rosenbaum, & Hirsch, 1995).

Not everyone agrees with the set-point explanation for obesity. For example, it's hard to see how the set-point explanation could explain the rapid rise in obesity that has occurred over the last several decades in the United States. Why would so many people's weight set points simultaneously increase?

Consequently, some researchers argue that the body does not try to maintain a fixed weight set point. Instead, they suggest, the body has a *settling point*, determined by a combination of our genetic heritage and the nature of the environment in which we live. If high-fat foods are prevalent in our environment and we are genetically predisposed to obesity, we settle into an equilibrium that maintains relatively high weight. In contrast, if our environment is nutritionally healthier, a genetic predisposition to obesity will not be triggered, and we will settle into an equilibrium in which our weight is lower (also see *Applying Psychology in the 21st Century*; Pi-Sunyer, 2003; Sullivan, Smith, & Grove, 2011).

EATING DISORDERS

Eating disorders are among the 10 most frequent causes of disability in young women. One devastating weight-related disorder is **anorexia nervosa.** In this severe eating disorder, people may refuse to eat while denying that their behavior and appearance—which can become skeleton-like—are unusual. Some 10% of people with anorexia literally starve themselves to death (Striegel-Moore & Bulik, 2007; Arcelus et al., 2011).

Anorexia nervosa mainly afflicts females between the ages of 12 and 40, although both men and women of any age may develop it. People with the disorder are often successful, attractive, and relatively affluent. The disorder often begins after serious dieting, which somehow gets out of control. Life begins to revolve around food: Although people with the disorder eat little, they may cook for others, go shopping for food frequently, or collect cookbooks (Boivin, 2005; Myers, 2007; Jacobs et al., 2009).

A related problem, **bulimia,** from which Lisa Arndt (described earlier) suffered, is a disorder in which people binge on large quantities of food. For instance, they may consume an entire gallon of ice cream and a whole pie in a single sitting. After such a binge, sufferers feel guilt and depression and often induce vomiting or take laxatives to rid themselves of the food—behavior known as purging. Constant bingeing-and-purging cycles and the use of drugs to induce vomiting or diarrhea can lead to heart failure. Often, though, the weight of a person with bulimia remains normal (Mora-Giral et al., 2004; Couturier & Lock, 2006; Lampard et al., 2011).

Eating disorders represent a growing problem: Estimates show that between 1-4% of high school-age and college-age women have either anorexia nervosa or bulimia. As many as 10% of women suffer from bulimia at some point in their lives. Furthermore, an increasing amount of research shows that almost as many men suffer from binge eating as do women (Swain, 2006; Park, 2007; Striegel et al., 2011).

What are the causes of anorexia nervosa and bulimia? Some researchers suspect a biological cause such as a chemical imbalance in the hypothalamus or pituitary gland, perhaps brought on by genetic factors. Furthermore, brain scans of people with eating

anorexia nervosa A severe eating disorder in which people may refuse to eat while denying that their behavior and appearance—which can become skeleton-like—are unusual. (Module 25)

bulimia A disorder in which a person binges on large quantities of food, followed by efforts to purge the food through vomiting or other means. (Module 25)

APPLYING PSYCHOLOGY IN THE 21ST CENTURY

A LOSING BATTLE FOR THE BIGGEST LOSERS

Losing weight is challenging, but keeping the weight off over the long term may be even a greater challenge. Many successful dieters struggle to maintain their new weight, and many end up gaining much of their original weight back. To find out why, a recent study looked at what happens to some of the most successful dieters: contestants on the eighth season of the reality television show *The Biggest Loser* in the 6 years after they finished their remarkable weight loss. The news wasn't good. Of the 14 contestants studied, all of whom had lost substantial weight during the show, all but one regained much of that weight in the subsequent 6 years. Four of them not only regained all the weight they had lost but gained more (Fothergill et al., 2016).

The researchers discovered that the dieters were locked in a chronic battle against their own biology: their bodies were fighting hard to resume their original weight, and their bodies had powerful biological tools for doing so. One of these is called *resting metabolism*, the rate at which food is converted to energy and expended by the body while one is not physically active. When the dieters began their weight-loss journey, they showed normal metabolic rates for their size (burning 2,600 calories per day, on average). By the end of the season, the contestants had all

©Stockbyte/Getty Images

lost substantial weight, but their metabolisms also slowed markedly. The rate was too slow for them to burn enough calories each day (2,000 on average) to stay at their new weights.

That wasn't the surprise, though–researchers already knew that decreased metabolism accompanies weight loss. What was new and surprising about this research was the finding that the depressed metabolism didn't rise over time. Even at the 6-year follow up, the

average metabolic rate had gone even further down, to 1,900 calories burned per day. This is despite the fact that the physical activity level of the former contestants, which nearly doubled from the start to the end of the competition, remained at its new heightened level at the 6-year follow up. In essence, the contestants' bodies were playing a cruel trick on them: even though they stayed physically active, they were burning far fewer calories than before. Maintaining their new weight was impossible without continuing their restrictive diet. Essentially, they were doomed to either gain the weight back or stay perpetually hungry and feel deprived.

The news isn't entirely hopeless, though. What about that one contestant who maintained her weight loss for 6 years after the season ended? She wasn't immune to the effect, as she now burns nearly 600 calories less per day than before. But she maintained her weight loss by constantly watching her diet and staying active. So losing weight remains a constant battle, one that entails a state of constant dieting (Fothergill et al., 2016; Hao et al., 2016).

> **RETHINK**
> - Some people argue that gaining weight indicates a lack of will power. How would you use these research findings to rebut that argument?
> - Based on this research, what advice would you give to a friend who is struggling to lose weight?

disorders show that they process information about food differently from healthy individuals (Mohr & Messina, 2015; Weir, 2016; de Abreu & Filho, 2017).

Others believe that the cause has roots in society's valuation of slenderness and the parallel notion that obesity is undesirable. These researchers maintain that people with anorexia nervosa and bulimia become preoccupied with their weight and take to heart the cliché that one can never be too thin. This may explain why eating disorders increase as countries become more developed and Westernized and dieting becomes more popular. Finally, some psychologists suggest that the disorders result from overly demanding parents or other family problems (Kluck, 2008; Cook-Cottone & Smith, 2013; Milos et al., 2017).

Complete explanations for anorexia nervosa and bulimia remain elusive. These disorders most likely stem from both biological and social causes, and successful treatment probably encompasses several strategies, including therapy and dietary changes (O'Brien & LeBow, 2007; Wilson, Grilo, & Vitousek, 2007; Cooper & Shafran, 2008).

If you or a family member needs advice or help with an eating problem, contact the American Anorexia Bulimia Association at www.aabainc.org or call (212) 575-6200. You can get more information at www.nlm.nih.gov/medlineplus/eatingdisorders.html.

BECOMING AN INFORMED CONSUMER
of Psychology

Dieting and Losing Weight Successfully

Although 60% of the people in the United States say they want to lose weight, it's a losing battle for most of them. Most people who diet eventually regain the weight they lost, so they try again and get caught in a seemingly endless cycle of weight loss and gain (Parker-Pope, 2003; Cachelin & Regan, 2006).

You should keep several things in mind when trying to lose weight (Heshka et al., 2003; Freedman & Waldrop, 2011):

Despite looking skeletonlike to others, people with the eating disorder anorexia nervosa see themselves as overweight.
©Denis Putilov/Alamy Stock Photo

- *There is no easy route to weight control.* You will have to make permanent changes in your life to lose weight without gaining it back. The most obvious strategy—cutting down on the amount of food you eat—is just the first step toward a lifetime commitment to changing your eating habits.
- *Keep track of what you eat and what you weigh.* Unless you keep careful records, you won't really know how much you are eating and whether any diet is working.
- *Eat "big" foods.* Eat fiber and foods that are bulky and heavy but low in calories, such as grapes and soup. Such foods trick your body into thinking you've eaten more and thus decrease hunger.
- *Cut out television.* One reason for the epidemic of obesity is the number of hours people in the United States spend viewing television. Not only does watching television preclude other activities that burn calories (even walking around the house is helpful), people often gorge on junk food while watching TV (Hu et al., 2003).
- *Exercise.* Exercise at least 30 consecutive minutes three times each week. When you exercise, you use up fat stored in your body as fuel for muscles, which is measured in calories. As you use up this fat, you will probably lose weight. Almost any activity helps burn calories.
- *Decrease the influence of external social stimuli on your eating behavior.* Serve yourself smaller portions of food, and leave the table before you see what is being served for dessert. Don't even buy snack foods such as nachos and potato chips; if they're not readily available in the kitchen cupboard, you're not apt to eat them. Wrap refrigerated foods in aluminum foil so that you cannot see the contents and be tempted every time you open the refrigerator.
- *Avoid fad diets.* No matter how popular they are at a particular time, extreme diets, including liquid diets, usually don't work in the long run and can be dangerous to your health.
- *Avoid taking any of the numerous diet pills advertised on television that promise quick and easy results.* They don't work.
- *Lose weight with others by joining a support group.* Being part of a group that is working to lose weight will encourage you to keep to your diet.

PsychTech

Wireless monitoring systems that track what dieters eat and how much they exercise help them to increase self-monitoring, one of the keys to effective weight loss.

- *Maintain good eating habits.* When you have reached your desired weight, maintain the new habits you learned while dieting to avoid gaining back the weight you have lost.
- *Set reasonable goals.* Know how much weight you want to lose before you start to diet. Don't try to lose too much weight too quickly, or you may doom yourself to failure. Even small changes in behavior—such as walking 15 minutes a day or eating a few less bites at each meal—can prevent weight gain (Kirk et al., 2003; Freedman & Waldrop, 2011).

Sexual Motivation

Anyone who has seen two dogs mating knows that sexual behavior has a biological basis. Their sexual behavior appears to occur naturally without much prompting on the part of others. A number of genetically controlled factors influence the sexual behavior of nonhuman animals. For instance, animal behavior is affected by the presence of certain hormones in the blood. Moreover, female animals are receptive to sexual advances only during certain relatively limited periods of the year.

Human sexual behavior, by comparison, is more complicated, although the underlying biology is not all that different from that of related species. In males, for example, the *testes* begin to secrete **androgens,** male sex hormones, at puberty. (See Figure 2 for the basic anatomy of the male and female **genitals,** or sex organs.) Not only do androgens produce secondary sex characteristics, such as the growth of body hair and a deepening of the voice, but they also increase the sex drive. Because the level of androgen production by the testes is fairly constant, men are capable of (and interested in) sexual activities without any regard to biological cycles. Given the proper stimuli leading to arousal, male sexual behavior can occur at any time (Goldstein, 2000).

Women show a different pattern. When they reach maturity at puberty, the two *ovaries* begin to produce **estrogens,** female sex hormones. However, those hormones are not produced consistently; instead, their production follows a cyclical pattern. The greatest output occurs during **ovulation,** when an egg is released from the ovaries, making the chances of fertilization by a sperm cell highest. While in nonhumans the period around ovulation is the only time the female is receptive to sex, people are different. Although there are variations in reported sex drive, women are receptive to sex throughout their cycles (Leiblum & Chivers, 2007).

In addition, some evidence suggests that males have a stronger sex drive than females do. For instance, men think about sex more than women do. Specifically, whereas 54% of men report thinking about sex every day, only 19% of women report thinking about it on a daily basis (Gangestad et al., 2004; Baumeister & Stillman, 2006; Carvalho & Nobre, 2011).

Though biological factors "prime" people for sex, it takes more than hormones to motivate and produce sexual behavior. In animals, the presence of a partner who provides arousing stimuli leads to sexual activity. Humans are considerably more versatile; not only other people but nearly any object, sight, smell, sound, or other stimulus can lead to sexual excitement. Because of prior associations, then, people may be turned on sexually by the smell of perfume or the sound of a favorite song hummed softly in their ears. The reaction to a specific, potentially arousing stimulus, as we shall see, is highly individual—what turns one person on may do just the opposite for another (Benson, 2003).

MASTURBATION: SOLITARY SEX

If you listened to physicians 100 years ago, you would have been told that **masturbation,** sexual self-stimulation often using the hand to rub the genitals, would lead to a wide variety of physical and mental disorders, ranging from hairy palms to insanity. If those

androgens Male sex hormones secreted by the testes. (Module 25)

genitals The male and female sex organs. (Module 25)

estrogens Class of female sex hormones. (Module 25)

ovulation The point at which an egg is released from the ovaries. (Module 25)

masturbation Sexual self-stimulation. (Module 25)

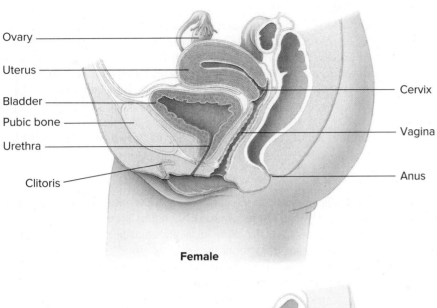

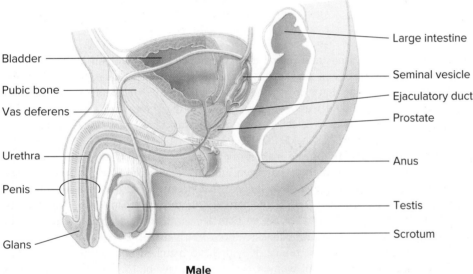

FIGURE 2 Cutaway side views of the female and male sex organs.

physicians had been correct, however, most of us would be wearing gloves to hide the sight of our hair-covered palms because masturbation is one of the most frequently practiced sexual activities. Some 94% of all males and 63% of all females have masturbated at least once; among college students, the frequency ranges from "never" to "several times a day" (Hunt, 1974; Michael et al., 1994; Polonsky, 2006; Buerkle, 2011).

Men and women typically begin to masturbate for the first time at different ages. Furthermore, men masturbate considerably more often than women do, although there are differences in frequency according to age. Male masturbation is most common in the early teens and then declines; females both begin and reach a maximum frequency later. There are also some racial differences: African-American men and women masturbate less than whites do (Oliver & Hyde, 1993; Pinkerton et al., 2002; Das, Parish, & Laumann, 2009).

Although masturbation is often considered an activity to engage in only if no other sexual outlets are available, this view bears little relationship to reality. Close to three-fourths of married men age 20 to 40 report masturbating an average of 24 times a year, and 68% of the married women in the same age group masturbate an average of 10 times a year (Michael et al., 1994; Das, 2007; Regnerus, Price, & Gordon, 2017).

Despite the high incidence of masturbation, attitudes toward it still reflect some of the negative views of yesteryear. For instance, one survey found that around 10% of people who masturbated experienced feelings of guilt; 5% of the males and 1% of the females considered their behavior perverted (Arafat & Cotton, 1974). Despite these negative attitudes, however, most experts on sex view masturbation as a healthy and legitimate–and harmless–sexual activity. In addition, masturbation is seen as providing a means of learning about one's own sexuality and a way of discovering changes in one's body such as the emergence of precancerous lumps (Coleman, 2002; Levin, 2007; Herbenick et al., 2009).

HETEROSEXUALITY

heterosexuality Sexual attraction and behavior directed to the other sex. (Module 25)

For heterosexuals, engaging in sexual intercourse often is perceived as achieving one of life's major milestones. However, **heterosexuality,** sexual attraction and behavior directed to the other sex, consists of far more than male-female intercourse. Kissing, petting, caressing, massaging, and other forms of sex play are all components of heterosexual behavior. Still, sex researchers' focus has been on the act of intercourse, especially in terms of its first occurrence and its frequency.

PREMARITAL SEX

Until fairly recently, premarital sexual intercourse, at least for women, was considered one of the major taboos in our society. Traditionally, women have been warned by society that "nice girls don't do it"; men have been told that premarital sex is okay for them, but they should marry virgins. This view that premarital sex is permissible for males but not for females is called the **double standard** (Liang, 2007; Lyons et al., 2011; Penhollow, Young, & Nnaka, 2017).

double standard The view that premarital sex is permissible for males but not for females. (Module 25)

As recently as the 1970s, the majority of adult Americans believed that premarital sex was always wrong. But there has been a dramatic change in public opinion since then. The percentage of people who believe that premarital sex is "not wrong at all" has increased from just over 25% in the early 1970s to more than 55% in 2012. More than half say that living together before marriage is morally acceptable (Thornton & Young-DeMarco, 2001; Harding & Jencks, 2003; Smith & Son, 2013).

Actual rates of premarital sexual activity have matched changes in attitude. For instance, more than one-half of women between the ages of 15 and 19 have had premarital sexual intercourse. These figures are close to double the number of women in the same age range who reported having intercourse in 1970. Clearly, the trend over the last several decades has been toward more women engaging in premarital sexual activity (Jones, Darroch, & Singh, 2005; Sprecher, Treger, & Sakaluk, 2013; Elias, Fullerton, & Simpson, 2015).

Males, too, have shown an increase in the incidence of premarital sexual intercourse, although the increase has not been as dramatic as it has been for females–probably because the rates for males were higher to begin with. For instance, the first surveys of premarital intercourse carried out in the 1940s showed an incidence of 84% across males of all ages; recent figures are closer to 95%. Moreover, the average age of males' first sexual experience has been declining steadily. Almost half of males have had sexual intercourse by the age of 18; by the time they reach age 20, 88% have had intercourse. Overall, 70% of all teens have had intercourse by their 19th birthday (Hyde, Mezulis, & Abramson, 2008; Guttmacher Institute, 2012).

MARITAL SEX

To judge by the number of articles about sex in heterosexual marriages, one would think that sexual behavior was the number one standard by which marital bliss is measured. Married couples are often concerned that they are having too little sex, too much sex, or the wrong kind of sex (Harvey, Wenzel, & Sprecher, 2004).

Although sex in marriage is measured along many dimensions, one is certainly the frequency of sexual intercourse. What is typical? As with most other types of sexual activities, we have no easy answer to the question because individuals vary so widely in their patterns. We do know that 43% of married couples have sexual intercourse a few times a month, and 36% of couples have it two or three times a week. With increasing age and length of marriage, the frequency of intercourse declines. Still, sex continues into late adulthood with almost half of people reporting that they engage in high-quality sexual activity at least once a month (Michael et al., 1994; Powell, 2006).

Furthermore, sexual activity provides benefits beyond the immediate pleasure. It generates a kind of sexual afterglow that cements relationships and increases marital satisfaction. Moreover, the frequency of sexual intercourse may be related to relationship satisfaction (Brody & Costa, 2017; Meltzer et al., 2017).

Although early research found **extramarital sex** to be widespread, the current reality appears to be otherwise. According to surveys, 85% of married women and more than 75% of married men report having no sexual partners other than their spouses. Furthermore, the median number of sex partners inside and outside of marriage since the age of 18 was six for men and two for women. Accompanying these numbers is a high, consistent degree of disapproval of extramarital sex, with 9 of 10 people saying that it is "always" or "almost always" wrong (Whisman & Snyder, 2007; DeMaris, 2013; Labrecque & Whisman, 2017).

> **extramarital sex** Sexual activity between a married person and someone who is not his or her spouse. (Module 25)

HOMOSEXUALITY AND BISEXUALITY

Homosexuals are sexually attracted to members of their own sex, whereas **bisexuals** are sexually attracted to people of the same sex and the other sex. Most people now use the terms *gay* and *lesbian* to refer to male and female homosexuals, respectively, in part because the terms *gay* and *lesbian* refer to a broader array of attitudes and lifestyles than the term *homosexual*, which focuses on the sexual act.

The number of people who choose same-sex sexual partners at one time or another is considerable. Estimates suggest that around 20–25% of males and about 15% of females have had at least one gay or lesbian experience during adulthood. The exact number of people who identify themselves as exclusively homosexual has proved difficult to gauge; some estimates are as low as 1.1% and some as high as 10%. Most experts suggest that 4% to 10% of both men and women identify as gay or lesbian (or other non-heterosexual identities) during extended periods of their lives (Sells, 1994; Firestein, 1996; Gates, 2017).

Although people often view homosexuality and heterosexuality as two completely distinct sexual orientations, the issue is not that simple. Pioneering sex researcher Alfred Kinsey acknowledged this when he considered sexual orientation along a scale or continuum with "exclusively homosexual" at one end and "exclusively heterosexual" at the other. In the middle were people who showed both homosexual and heterosexual behavior. Kinsey's approach suggests that sexual orientation is dependent on a person's sexual feelings and behaviors and romantic feelings (Weinberg, Williams, & Pryor, 1991; Jeffery, 2015).

> **homosexuals** Persons who are sexually attracted to members of their own sex. (Module 25)
>
> **bisexuals** Persons who are sexually attracted to people of the same sex and the other sex. (Module 25)

DETERMINING THE CAUSES OF SEXUAL ORIENTATION

What determines people's sexual orientation? Although there are a number of theories, none has proved completely satisfactory.

Considerable research suggests that biological and genetic factors underlie sexual orientation. For example, studies of identical twins provide evidence for a genetic cause of sexual orientation. Studies find that when one twin identified himself or herself as homosexual, the occurrence of homosexuality in the other twin was higher than it was in the general population. Such results occur even for twins who have been separated early in life and who therefore are not necessarily raised in similar social environments. Furthermore, some research suggests that an area on the X chromosome is associated with homosexuality (Gooren, 2006; LeVay, 2011; Servick, 2014).

Hormones also may play a role in determining sexual orientation. For example, research shows that women exposed before birth to DES (diethylstilbestrol), a drug their mothers took to avoid miscarriage, were more likely to be gay or bisexual (Reinisch, Mortensen, & Sanders, 2017).

Further evidence suggests that differences in brain structures may be related to sexual orientation. For instance, the structure of the anterior hypothalamus, an area of the brain that governs sexual behavior, differs in male homosexuals and heterosexuals. Similarly, other research shows that, compared with heterosexual men or women, gay men have a larger anterior commissure, which is a bundle of neurons connecting the right and left hemispheres of the brain (Byne, 1996; Witelson et al., 2008; Rahman & Yusuf, 2015).

In short, considerable research suggests the importance of biological and genetic factors at the roots of homosexuality, but the research is not conclusive in pinpointing the specific cause. Nevertheless, it seems likely that some inherited or biological factor predisposes people toward homosexuality (Teodorov et al., 2002; Rahman, Kumari, & Wilson, 2003; Burri, Spector, & Qazi, 2015).

In contrast, little evidence suggests that sexual orientation is brought about by child-rearing practices or family dynamics. Although proponents of psychoanalytic theories once argued that the nature of the parent-child relationship can produce homosexuality (e.g., Freud, 1922/1959), research evidence does not support such explanations (Isay, 1994; Roughton, 2002).

Another explanation for sexual orientation rests on learning theory (Masters & Johnson, 1979). According to this view, sexual orientation is learned through rewards and punishments in much the same way that we may learn to prefer swimming over tennis. For example, a young adolescent who had an unpleasant heterosexual experience might develop disagreeable associations with the other sex. If the same person had a rewarding, pleasant gay or lesbian experience, homosexuality might be incorporated into his or her sexual fantasies. If such fantasies are used during later sexual activities–such as masturbation–they may be positively reinforced through orgasm, and the association of homosexual behavior and sexual pleasure eventually may cause homosexuality to become the preferred form of sexual behavior.

Although the learning-theory explanation is plausible, several difficulties rule it out as a definitive explanation. Because our society has traditionally held homosexuality in low esteem, one ought to expect that the negative treatment of homosexual behavior would outweigh the rewards attached to it. Furthermore, children growing up with a gay or lesbian parent are statistically unlikely to become homosexual, which thus contradicts the notion that homosexual behavior may be learned from others (Tasker, 2005).

Because of the difficulty in finding a consistent explanation for sexual orientation, we can't definitively answer the question of what determines it. No one single factor likely orients a person toward homosexuality or heterosexuality. Instead, it seems reasonable to assume that a combination of biological and environmental factors is involved (Hyde, Mezulis, & Abramson, 2008; Bailey et al, 2016).

Although we don't know exactly why people develop a certain sexual orientation, one thing is clear: Despite increasingly positive attitudes toward homosexuality, many gays and lesbians face antigay attitudes and discrimination, and it can take a toll. Lesbians and gays have higher rates of depression and suicide than do their straight counterparts. There are even physical health disparities due to prejudice that gays and lesbians may experience. Because of this, the American Psychological Association and other major mental health organizations have endorsed efforts to eliminate discrimination against gays and lesbians (Kwon, 2013; Lick, Durso, & Johnson, 2013; Moody et al., 2017).

However, attitudes toward homosexuality have changed dramatically in the past two decades, with younger generations in particular becoming more positive. For example, 64% of those under 30 support same-sex marriage. Overall, tolerance for gays and lesbians has grown substantially in the United States (Smith & Son, 2013).

Study Alert

The determinants of sexual orientation have proven difficult to pinpoint. It is important to know the variety of explanations that have been put forward.

Extensive research has found that bisexuals and homosexuals enjoy the same overall degree of mental and physical health as heterosexuals do.
©Rachel Epstein/The Image Works

TRANSGENDER INDIVIDUALS

An increasing number of individuals consider themselves transgender. **Transgender** is a general term encompassing people whose gender identity, gender expression, or behavior is not consistent with the sex to which they were assigned at birth.

Transgender people may have male bodies but view their gender identity as female, or they may have female bodies and have a male gender identity. In other cases, transgender individuals may view themselves as a third gender (neither male nor female). They also may wish to be referred to not as "she" or "he" but rather some other, more neutral pronoun, such as "ze" or "they" (Prince, 2005; Hyde, Mezulis, & Abramson, 2008; Scelfo, 2015).

In some cases, transgender individuals may seek sex-change operations in which their existing genitals are surgically removed and the genitals of the desired sex are fashioned. Several steps, including intensive counseling, hormone injections, and living as a member of the desired sex for several years, precede surgery, which is, not surprisingly, highly complicated. The outcome, though, can be quite positive (Lobato, Koff, & Manenti, 2006; Richards, 2011; Gorton & Erickson-Schroth, 2017).

Transgender issues have become increasingly prominent in recent years. For instance, college campuses have struggled with how to best provide restrooms that address the needs of the transgender community. Do individuals who have the genitals of a male but who identify as females use traditional men's rooms or women's rooms? One solution has been the establishment of unisex or all-gender restrooms (Steinmetz, 2015).

Whereas the term transgender centers on gender identity concerns, the term *intersex* refers to the small number of people who are born with genitals that makes their sexual identity ambiguous. An *intersex person* has an atypical combination of sexual organs or chromosomal or gene patterns. In some cases, they are born with both male and female sexual organs, or the organs are ambiguous. It is an extremely rare condition, found in 1 in 4,500 births. Intersexism involves a complex mix of physiological and psychological issues (Lehrman, 2007; Diamond, 2009).

transgender An umbrella term for persons whose gender identity, gender expression, or behavior does not conform to that typically associated with the sex to which they were assigned at birth. (Module 25)

RESTROOM for ALL GENDERS
You can use this restroom regardless of gender, identity or expression.

©TheChoperPilot/Shutterstock

The Needs for Achievement, Affiliation, and Power

Although hunger may be one of the more potent primary drives in our day-to-day lives, powerful secondary drives that have no clear biological basis also motivate us. Among the more prominent of these are the needs for achievement, affiliation, and power.

THE NEED FOR ACHIEVEMENT: STRIVING FOR EXCELLENCE

need for achievement A stable, learned characteristic in which a person obtains satisfaction by striving for and achieving challenging goals. (Module 25)

Study Alert
A key feature of people with a high need for achievement is that they prefer tasks of *moderate* difficulty.

need for affiliation An interest in establishing and maintaining relationships with other people. (Module 25)

The **need for achievement** refers to a person's desire to strive for and achieve challenging accomplishments (McClelland et al., 1953). People with a high need for achievement seek out situations in which they can compete against some objective standard–such as grades, money, or winning a game–and prove themselves successful.

But people who have a high need for achievement are selective about their challenges: They tend to avoid situations in which success will come too easily (which would be unchallenging) or situations in which success is highly unlikely. Instead, people high in achievement motivation generally choose tasks that are of intermediate difficulty (Speirs-Neumeister & Finch, 2006; Mills, 2011).

In contrast, people with low achievement motivation tend to be motivated primarily by a desire to avoid failure. As a result, they seek out easy tasks so they are sure to avoid failure, or they seek out very difficult tasks for which failure has no negative implications because almost anyone would fail at them. People with a high fear of failure will stay away from tasks of intermediate difficulty because they may fail where others have been successful (Puca, 2005; Morrone & Pintrich, 2006; Pekrun, 2017).

A high need for achievement generally produces positive outcomes, at least in a success-oriented culture such as Western society. For instance, people motivated by a high need for achievement are more likely to attend college than are their low-achievement counterparts. And once they are in college, they tend to receive higher grades in classes that are related to their future careers. Furthermore, high achievement motivation is related to future economic and occupational success (McClelland, 1985; Thrash & Elliot, 2002; Liem, 2015).

How can we measure a person's need for achievement? Most frequently, psychologists employ the *Thematic Apperception Test (TAT)*. Using the TAT, an examiner shows a series of ambiguous pictures, such as the one in Figure 3. The examiner tells participants to write a story that describes what is happening, who the people are, what led to the situation, what the people are thinking or wanting, and what will happen next. Researchers then use a standard scoring system to determine the amount of achievement imagery in people's stories. For example, someone who writes a story in which the main character strives to beat an opponent, studies in order to do well at some task, or works hard in order to get a promotion shows clear signs of an achievement orientation. The inclusion of such achievement-related imagery in the participants' stories is assumed to indicate an unusually high degree of concern with–and therefore a relatively strong need for–achievement (Tuerlinckx, De Boeck, & Lens, 2002; Verdon, 2011).

THE NEED FOR AFFILIATION: STRIVING FOR FRIENDSHIP

Few of us choose to lead our lives as hermits. Why?

One main reason is that most people have a **need for affiliation,** an interest in establishing and maintaining relationships with other people. Individuals with a high need for affiliation write TAT stories that emphasize the desire to maintain or reinstate friendships and show concern over being rejected by friends.

People who have higher affiliation needs are particularly sensitive to relationships with others. They desire to be with their friends more of the time and alone less often, compared with people who are lower in the need for affiliation. However, gender is a greater determinant of how much time is actually spent with friends: Regardless of

FIGURE 3 This ambiguous picture is similar to those used in the Thematic Apperception Test to determine people's underlying motivation. What do you see? Do you think your response is related to your motivation?
©Science Source

their affiliative orientation, female students spend significantly more time with their friends and less time alone than male students do (Johnson, 2004; Semykina & Linz, 2007; Hofer et al., 2017).

THE NEED FOR POWER: STRIVING FOR IMPACT ON OTHERS

If your fantasies include becoming president of the United States or running Microsoft, your dreams may reflect a high need for power. The **need for power,** a tendency to seek impact, control, or influence over others and to be seen as a powerful individual, is an additional type of motivation (Winter, 2007; Pratto et al., 2011; Winter, 2016).

As you might expect, people with strong needs for power are more apt to belong to organizations and seek office than are those low in the need for power. They also tend to work in professions in which their power needs may be fulfilled, such as business management and—you may or may not be surprised—teaching (Jenkins, 1994). In addition, they seek to display the trappings of power. Even in college, they are more likely to collect prestigious possessions, such as electronic equipment and sports cars.

Some significant gender differences exist in the display of need for power. Men with high power needs tend to show unusually high levels of aggression, drink heavily, act in a sexually exploitative manner, and participate more frequently in competitive sports—behaviors that collectively represent somewhat extravagant, flamboyant behavior. In contrast, women display their power needs with more restraint; this is congruent with traditional societal constraints on women's behavior. Women with high power needs are more apt than men to channel those needs in a socially responsible manner, such as by showing concern for others or displaying highly nurturing behavior (Winter, 2007; Schultheiss & Schiepe-Tiska, 2013; Sibunruang, Capezio, & Restubog, 2015).

need for power A tendency to seek impact, control, or influence over others and to be seen as a powerful individual. (Module 25)

From the perspective of...

A Human Resources Specialist How might you use characteristics such as need for achievement, need for affiliation, and need for power to select workers for jobs?

©Dex Image/Getty Images

RECAP/EVALUATE/RETHINK

RECAP

LO 25-1 What biological and social factors underlie hunger?

- Eating behavior is subject to homeostasis, as most people's weight stays within a relatively stable range. The hypothalamus in the brain is central to the regulation of food intake.
- Social factors, such as mealtimes, cultural food preferences, and other learned habits, also play a role in the regulation of eating by determining when, what, and how much one eats. An oversensitivity to social cues

and an insensitivity to internal cues may also be related to obesity. In addition, obesity may be caused by an unusually high weight set point—the weight the body attempts to maintain—and genetic factors.

LO 25-2 What are the varieties of sexual behavior?

- Although biological factors, such as the presence of androgens (male sex hormones) and estrogens (female sex hormones), prime people for sex, almost any kind of stimulus can produce sexual arousal depending on a person's prior sexual experience.

- The frequency of masturbation is high, particularly for males. Although attitudes toward masturbation are increasingly liberal, they have traditionally been negative even though no negative consequences have been detected.
- Heterosexuality, or sexual attraction to members of the other sex, is the most common sexual orientation.
- The double standard by which premarital sex is thought to be more permissible for men than for women has declined, particularly among young people.
- Homosexuals are sexually attracted to members of their own sex; bisexuals are sexually attracted to people of the same sex and the other sex. No explanation for why people become homosexual has been confirmed; among the possibilities are genetic or biological factors, childhood and family influences, and prior learning experiences and conditioning. However, no relationship exists between sexual orientation and psychological adjustment.
- Transgender is a general term encompassing people whose gender identity, gender expression, or behavior is not consistent with the sex to which they were assigned at birth.

LO 25-3 How are needs relating to achievement, affiliation, and power motivation exhibited?

- Need for achievement refers to the stable, learned characteristic in which a person strives to attain a level of excellence. Need for achievement is usually measured through the Thematic Apperception Test (TAT), a series of pictures about which a person writes a story.
- The need for affiliation is a concern with establishing and maintaining relationships with others, whereas the need for power is a tendency to seek to exert an impact on others.

EVALUATE

1. Match the following terms with their definitions:

    1. Hypothalamus
    2. Lateral hypothalamic damage
    3. Ventromedial hypothalamic damage

    a. Leads to refusal of food and starvation
    b. Responsible for monitoring food intake
    c. Causes extreme overeating

2. The _____ _____ _____ is the specific level of weight the body strives to maintain.
3. _____ is the rate at which the body produces and expends energy.
4. Although the incidence of masturbation among young adults is high, once men and women become involved in intimate relationships, they typically cease masturbating. True or false?
5. The increase in premarital sex in recent years has been greater for women than for men. True or false?
6. Julio is the type of person who constantly strives for excellence. He feels intense satisfaction when he is able to master a new task. Julio most likely has a high need for _____.
7. Debbie's Thematic Apperception Test (TAT) story depicts a young girl who is rejected by one of her peers and seeks to regain her friendship. What major type of motivation is Debbie displaying in her story?
    a. Need for achievement
    b. Need for motivation
    c. Need for affiliation
    d. Need for power

RETHINK

1. In what ways do societal expectations, expressed by television shows and commercials, contribute to both obesity and excessive concern about weight loss? How could television contribute to better eating habits and attitudes toward weight? Should it be required to do so?
2. Why do discussions of sexual behavior, which is such a necessary part of human life, have so many negative connotations in Western society?

Answers to Evaluate Questions

1. 1-b, 2-a, 3-c; 2. weight set point; 3. Metabolism; 4. false; 5. true; 6. achievement; 7. c

KEY TERMS

obesity
weight set point
metabolism
anorexia nervosa
bulimia

androgens
genitals
estrogens
ovulation
masturbation

heterosexuality
double standard
extramarital sex
homosexuals
bisexuals

transgender
need for achievement
need for affiliation
need for power

Module 26

Understanding Emotional Experiences

Karl Andrews held in his hands the envelope he had been waiting for. It could be the ticket to his future: an offer of admission to his first-choice college. But what was it going to say? He knew it could go either way. His grades were pretty good, and he had been involved in some extracurricular activities, but his SAT scores had not been terrific. He felt so nervous that his hands shook as he opened the thin envelope (not a good sign, he thought). Here it comes. "Dear Mr. Andrews," it read. "The Trustees of the University are pleased to admit you. . . ." That was all he needed to see. With a whoop of excitement, Karl found himself jumping up and down gleefully. A rush of emotion overcame him as it sank in that he had, in fact, been accepted. He was on his way.

At one time or another, all of us have experienced the strong feelings that accompany both very pleasant and very negative experiences. Perhaps we have felt the thrill of getting a sought-after job, the joy of being in love, the sorrow over someone's death, or the anguish of inadvertently hurting someone. Moreover, we experience such reactions on a less intense level throughout our daily lives with such things as the pleasure of a friendship, the enjoyment of a movie, and the embarrassment of breaking a borrowed item.

Despite the varied nature of these feelings, they all represent emotions. Although everyone has an idea of what an emotion is, formally defining the concept has proved to be an elusive task. Here, we'll use a general definition: **Emotions** are feelings that generally have both physiological and cognitive elements and that influence behavior.

Think, for example, about how it feels to be happy. First, we obviously experience a feeling that we can differentiate from other emotions. It is likely that we also experience some identifiable physical changes in our bodies: Perhaps the heart rate increases, or—as in the example of Karl Andrews—we find ourselves "jumping for joy." Finally, the emotion probably encompasses cognitive elements: Our understanding and evaluation of the meaning of what is happening prompts our feelings of happiness.

It is also possible, however, to experience an emotion without the presence of cognitive elements. For instance, we may react with fear to an unusual or novel situation (such as coming into contact with an erratic, unpredictable individual), or we may experience pleasure over sexual excitation without having cognitive awareness or understanding of just what makes the situation exciting.

Some psychologists argue that one system governs emotional responses to a given situation and another governs cognitive reactions to it. Assuming there are two systems, does one predominate over the other? Some theorists suggest that we first respond to a situation with an emotional reaction and later try to make sense of it cognitively. For example, we may enjoy a complex modern symphony without at first understanding it or knowing why we like it. In contrast, other theorists propose that people first develop cognitions about a situation and then react emotionally. This school of thought suggests that we must think about and understand a stimulus or situation, relating it to what we already know, before we can react on an emotional level (Murphy & Zajonc, 1993; Lazarus, 1995; Martin & Kerns, 2011).

Because proponents of both sides of this debate can cite research to support their viewpoints, the question is far from resolved. Perhaps the sequence varies from situation to situation, with emotions predominating in some instances and cognitive processes

LEARNING OUTCOMES

LO 26-1 What are emotions, and how do we experience them?

LO 26-2 What are the functions of emotions?

LO 26-3 What are the explanations for emotions?

LO 26-4 How does nonverbal behavior relate to the expression of emotions?

emotions Feelings that generally have both physiological and cognitive elements and that influence behavior. (Module 26)

occurring first in others. Both sides agree that we can experience emotions that involve little or no conscious thought. We may not know why we're afraid of mice because we understand objectively that they represent no danger, but we may still be frightened when we see them. Neuroimaging studies of the brain may help resolve this debate as well as others about the nature of emotions (Niedenthal, 2007; Karaszewski, 2008; López-Pérez & Ambrona, 2015).

The Functions of Emotions

Imagine what it would be like if we didn't experience emotion. We would have no depths of despair, no depression, and no remorse, but at the same time we would also have no happiness, joy, or love. Obviously, life would be considerably less satisfying and even dull if we lacked the capacity to sense and express emotion.

But do emotions serve any purpose beyond making life interesting? Indeed they do. Psychologists have identified several important functions that emotions play in our daily lives (Gross, 2006; Siemer, Mauss, & Gross, 2007; Rolls, 2011). Among the most important of those functions are the following:

- *Preparing us for action.* Emotions act as a link between events in our environment and our responses to them. For example, if you saw an angry dog charging toward you, your emotional reaction (fear) would be associated with physiological arousal of the sympathetic division of the autonomic nervous system, the activation of the "fight-or-flight" response.

- *Shaping our future behavior.* Emotions promote learning that will help us make appropriate responses in the future. For instance, your emotional response to unpleasant events teaches you to avoid similar circumstances in the future.

- *Helping us interact more effectively with others.* We often communicate the emotions we experience through our verbal and nonverbal behaviors, making our emotions obvious to observers. These behaviors can act as signals to observers, allowing them to understand better what we are experiencing and to help them predict our future behavior.

Determining the Range of Emotions: Labeling Our Feelings

If we were to list the words in the English language that have been used to describe emotions, we would end up with at least 500 examples (Averill, 1975). The list would range from such obvious emotions as *happiness* and *fear* to less common ones, such as *adventurousness* and *pensiveness*.

One challenge for psychologists has been to sort through this list to identify the most important, fundamental emotions. Theorists have hotly contested the issue of cataloging emotions and have come up with different lists, depending on how they define the concept of emotion. In fact, some reject the question entirely, saying that *no* set of emotions should be singled out as most basic and that emotions are best understood by breaking them down into their component parts. Other researchers argue for looking at emotions in terms of a hierarchy, dividing them into positive and negative categories and then organizing them into increasingly narrower subcategories (see Figure 1; Manstead, Frijda, & Fischer, 2003; Dillard & Shen, 2007; Livingstone et al., 2011).

Still, most researchers suggest that a list of basic emotions would include, at a minimum, happiness, anger, fear, sadness, and disgust. Other lists are broader, including emotions such as surprise, contempt, guilt, and joy (Shweder, 1994; Tracy & Robins, 2004; Greenberg, 2015).

One difficulty in defining a basic set of emotions is that substantial differences exist in descriptions of emotions among various cultures. For instance, Germans report

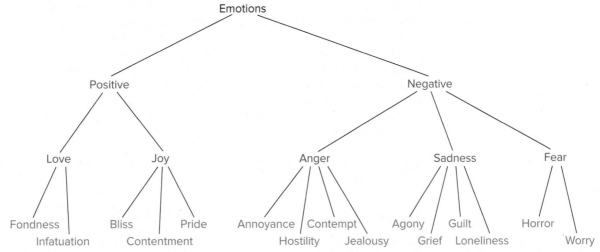

FIGURE 1 One approach to organizing emotions is to use a hierarchy, which divides emotions into increasingly narrow subcategories.

Source: Adapted from Fischer, K. W., Shaver, P. R., & Carnochan, P. (1990). How emotions develop and how they organize development. *Cognition and Emotion, 4,* 81–127.

experiencing *schadenfreude,* a feeling of pleasure over another person's difficulties, and the Japanese experience *hagaii,* a mood of vulnerable heartache colored by frustration. In Tahiti, people experience *musu,* a feeling of reluctance to yield to unreasonable demands made by one's parents.

Finding *schadenfreude, hagaii,* or *musu* in a particular culture doesn't mean that the members of other cultures are incapable of experiencing such emotions, of course. It suggests, though, that fitting a particular emotion into a linguistic category to describe that emotion may make it easier to discuss, contemplate, and perhaps experience (Kuppens et al., 2006; van Dijk et al., 2011; Dasborough & Harvey, 2017).

The Roots of Emotions

I've never been so angry before; I feel my heart pounding, and I'm trembling all over. . . . I don't know how I'll get through the performance. I feel like my stomach is filled with butterflies. . . . That was quite a mistake I made! My face must be incredibly red. . . . When I heard the footsteps in the night, I was so frightened that I couldn't catch my breath.

If you examine our language, you will find that there are literally dozens of ways to describe how we feel when we experience an emotion and that the language we use to describe emotions is, for the most part, based on the physical symptoms that are associated with a particular emotional experience (Kobayashi, Schallert, & Ogren, 2003; Manstead & Wagner, 2004; Spackman, Fujiki, & Brinton, 2006).

Consider, for instance, the experience of fear. Imagine that it is late on New Year's Eve. You are walking down a dark road, and you hear a stranger approaching behind you. He clearly is not trying to hurry by but is coming directly toward you. You think about what you will do if the stranger attempts to rob you or, worse, hurt you in some way.

While these thoughts are running through your head, something dramatic will be happening to your body. The most likely reactions, which are associated with activation of the autonomic nervous system, include an increase in your rate of breathing, an acceleration of your heart rate, a widening of your pupils (to increase visual sensitivity), and a dryness in your mouth as the functioning of your salivary glands and in fact of your entire digestive system ceases. At the same time, though, your sweat glands probably will increase their activity because increased sweating will help you rid yourself of the excess heat developed by any emergency activity in which you engage.

Of course, all these physiological changes are likely to occur without your awareness. At the same time, though, the emotional experience accompanying them will be obvious to you: You most surely would report being fearful.

Although it is easy to describe the general physical reactions that accompany emotions, defining the specific role that those physiological responses play in the experience of emotions has proved to be a major puzzle for psychologists. As we shall see, some theorists suggest that specific physiological reactions *cause* us to experience a particular emotion. For example, when the heart is pounding and we are breathing deeply, we then experience fear. In contrast, other theorists suggest the opposite sequence–that is, we experience an emotion, and that causes us to have a physiological reaction. In this view, then, as a result of experiencing the emotion of fear, our heart pounds and our breathing deepens.

THE JAMES-LANGE THEORY: DO GUT REACTIONS EQUAL EMOTIONS?

To William James and Carl Lange, who were among the first researchers to explore the nature of emotions, emotional experience is, very simply, a reaction to instinctive bodily events that occur as a result of some situation or event in the environment. This view is summarized in James's statement, "We feel sorry because we cry, angry because we strike, afraid because we tremble" (James, 1890).

James and Lange took the view that the instinctive response of crying at a loss leads us to feel sorrow, that striking out at someone who frustrates us results in our feeling anger, that trembling at a menacing threat causes us to feel fear. They suggested that for every major emotion there is an accompanying physiological or "gut" reaction of internal organs–called a *visceral experience*. It is this specific pattern of visceral response that leads us to label the emotional experience.

James-Lange theory of emotion The belief that emotional experience is a reaction to bodily events occurring as a result of an external situation ("I feel sad because I am crying"). (Module 26)

In sum, James and Lange proposed that we experience emotions as a result of physiological changes that produce specific sensations. The brain interprets these sensations as specific kinds of emotional experiences (see the first part of Figure 2). This view has come to be called the **James-Lange theory of emotion** (Cobos et al., 2002; Stolorow & Stolorow, 2013; Šolcová & Lačev, 2017).

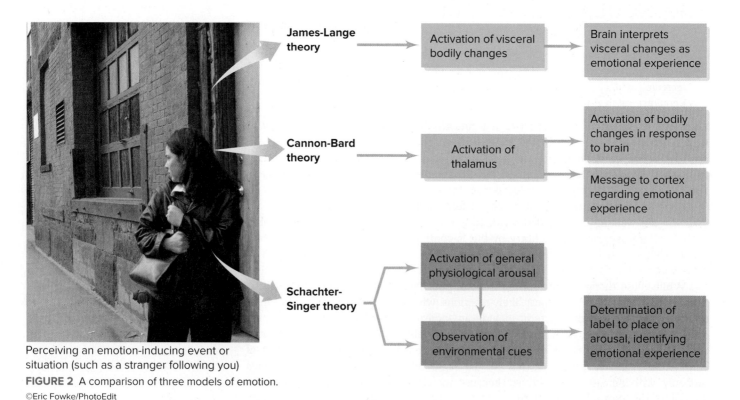

Perceiving an emotion-inducing event or situation (such as a stranger following you)

FIGURE 2 A comparison of three models of emotion.
©Eric Fowke/PhotoEdit

The James-Lange theory, however, has some serious drawbacks. For the theory to be valid, visceral changes would have to occur rapidly because we experience some emotions–such as fear upon hearing a stranger rapidly approaching on a dark night– almost instantaneously. Yet some visceral changes occur slowly. Therefore, it's hard to see how they could be the source of an immediate emotional experience.

The James-Lange theory poses another difficulty: Physiological arousal does not invariably produce emotional experience. For example, a person who is jogging has an increased heartbeat and respiration rate, as well as many of the other physiological changes associated with certain emotions. Yet joggers typically do not think of such changes in terms of emotion. Thus, visceral changes by themselves are not always sufficient to produce emotion.

Finally, our internal organs produce a relatively limited range of sensations. Although some types of physiological changes are associated with specific emotional experiences, it is difficult to imagine how each of the many emotions that people are capable of experiencing could be the result of a unique visceral change. Many emotions actually are associated with relatively similar sorts of visceral changes, a fact that contradicts the James-Lange theory (Cameron, 2002; Rinaman, Banihashemi, & Koehnle, 2011).

THE CANNON-BARD THEORY: PHYSIOLOGICAL REACTIONS AS THE RESULT OF EMOTIONS

In response to the difficulties inherent in the James-Lange theory, Walter Cannon and later Philip Bard suggested an alternative view. In what has come to be known as the **Cannon-Bard theory of emotion,** they proposed the model illustrated in the second part of Figure 2 (Cannon, 1929). This theory rejects the view that physiological arousal alone leads to the perception of emotion. Instead, the theory assumes that both physiological arousal *and* the emotional experience are produced simultaneously by the same nerve stimulus, which Cannon and Bard suggested emanates from the *thalamus* in the brain.

The theory states that after we perceive an emotion-producing stimulus, the thalamus is the initial site of the emotional response. Next, the thalamus sends a signal to the autonomic nervous system, thereby producing a visceral response. At the same time, the thalamus also communicates a message to the cerebral cortex regarding the nature of the emotion being experienced. Hence, it is not necessary for different emotions to have unique physiological patterns associated with them–as long as the message sent to the cerebral cortex differs according to the specific emotion.

The Cannon-Bard theory seems to have been accurate in rejecting the view that physiological arousal alone accounts for emotions. However, more recent research has led to some important modifications of the theory. For one thing, we now understand that the hypothalamus and the limbic system, not the thalamus, play a major role in emotional experience. In addition, the simultaneous occurrence of the physiological and emotional responses, which is a fundamental assumption of the Cannon-Bard theory, has yet to be demonstrated conclusively. This ambiguity has allowed room for yet another theory of emotions: the Schachter-Singer theory.

THE SCHACHTER-SINGER THEORY: EMOTIONS AS LABELS

Suppose that as you are being followed down that dark street on New Year's Eve, you notice a man being followed by another shady figure on the other side of the street. Now assume that instead of reacting with fear, the man begins to laugh and act gleeful. Would the reactions of this other individual be sufficient to lay your fears to rest? Might you, in fact, decide there is nothing to fear and get into the spirit of the evening by beginning to feel happiness and glee yourself?

According to an explanation that focuses on the role of cognition, the **Schachter-Singer theory of emotion,** this might very well happen. This approach to explaining emotions emphasizes that we identify the emotion we are experiencing by observing

Cannon-Bard theory of emotion
The belief that both physiological arousal and emotional experience are produced simultaneously by the same nerve stimulus. (Module 26)

Study Alert
Use Figure 2 to distinguish the three classic theories of emotion (James-Lange, Cannon-Bard, and Schachter-Singer).

Schachter-Singer theory of emotion
The belief that emotions are determined jointly by a nonspecific kind of physiological arousal and its interpretation, based on environmental cues. (Module 26)

our environment and comparing ourselves with others (Schachter & Singer, 1962; Schachter & Singer, 2001; Shaked & Clore, 2017).

Schachter and Singer's classic experiment found evidence for this hypothesis. In the study, participants were told that they would receive an injection of a vitamin. In reality, they were given epinephrine, a drug that causes responses that typically occur during strong emotional reactions, such as an increase in physiological arousal, including higher heart and respiration rates and a reddening of the face. The members of both groups were then placed individually in a situation where a confederate of the experimenter acted in one of two ways. In one condition, he acted angry and hostile; in the other condition, he behaved as if he were exuberantly happy.

The purpose of the experiment was to determine whether participants' emotions would be influenced by the confederate's behavior. And they were: When participants were asked to describe their own emotional state at the end of the experiment, those participants exposed to the angry confederate reported that they felt angry, whereas those participants exposed to the happy confederate reported feeling happy. In sum, the results suggest that participants used the behavior of the confederate to explain the physiological arousal they were experiencing.

The results of the Schachter-Singer experiment, then, supported a cognitive view of emotions in which emotions are determined jointly by a relatively nonspecific kind of physiological arousal *and* the labeling of that arousal on the basis of cues from the environment (refer to the third part of Figure 2). Although later research has found that arousal is more specific than Schachter and Singer believed, they were right in assuming that when the source of physiological arousal is unclear, we may look to our surroundings to determine what we are experiencing.

From the perspective of...

An Advertising Executive How might you use Schachter and Singer's findings on the labeling of arousal to create interest in a product?

©Image Source/Getty Images

CONTEMPORARY PERSPECTIVES ON THE NEUROSCIENCE OF EMOTIONS

When Schachter and Singer carried out their groundbreaking experiment in the early 1960s, the ways in which they could evaluate the physiological changes that accompany emotion were relatively limited. However, advances in the measurement of the nervous system and other parts of the body have allowed researchers to examine more closely the biological responses involved in individual emotions. As a result, evidence is growing that specific patterns of biological arousal are associated with specific emotions (Woodson, 2006; Stifter, Dollar, & Cipriano, 2011; Christensen et al., 2017).

For instance, researchers have found that different emotions produce activation of different portions of the brain. In one study, participants undergoing positron emission tomography (PET) brain scans were asked to recall events that made them sad, such as deaths and funerals, or events that made them feel happy, such as weddings and births. They also looked at photos of faces that appeared to be happy or sad. The results of the PET scans were clear: Happiness was related to a decrease in activity in certain areas of the cerebral cortex, whereas sadness was associated with increases in activity in particular portions of the cortex (Hamann et al., 2002; Prohovnik et al., 2004; Johnston & Olson, 2015).

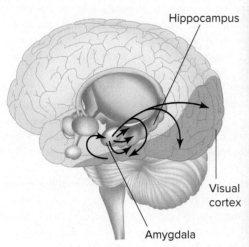

Hippocampus

Visual cortex

Amygdala

FIGURE 3 Connections from the amygdala allow it to mediate many of the autonomic expressions of emotional states through the hippocampus and visual cortex.

Sources: (Left) Adapted from Dolan, R. J. (2002). Emotion, cognition, and behavior. *Science, 298,* 1191–1194; (Right) ©Image Source/Getty Images

In addition, new research shows that the *amygdala,* in the brain's temporal lobe, plays an important role in the experience of emotions. The amygdala provides a link between the perception of an emotion-producing stimulus and the recall of that stimulus later. For example, if we've once been attacked by a vicious pit bull, the amygdala processes that information and leads us to react with fear when we see a pit bull at future times (LaBar, 2007; Pessoa, 2011; Christensen et al., 2017).

Because neural pathways connect the amygdala, the visual cortex, and the *hippocampus* (which plays an important role in the consolidation of memories), some scientists speculate that emotion-related stimuli can be processed and responded to almost instantaneously (see Figure 3). This immediate response occurs so rapidly that higher-order, more rational thinking, which takes more time, seems not to be involved initially. In a slower but more thoughtful response to emotion-evoking stimuli, emotion-related sensory information is first evaluated and then sent on to the amygdala. It appears that the quicker system offers an immediate response to emotion-evoking stimuli, whereas the slower system helps confirm a threat and prepare a more thoughtful response (Dolan, 2002; also see *Neuroscience and Your Life*).

Study Alert

It is important to understand the basic neuroscience of emotional experience.

NEUROSCIENCE AND YOUR LIFE: EMOTION AND THE BRAIN

Our emotions may seem very personal, but neuroscientists are now discovering that they have a distinct neurological basis that is similar across individuals. In an innovative approach to studying the brain, researchers measured brain activity while participants watched movies or imagined six basic emotions (disgust, fear, happiness, sadness, anger, and surprise). The researchers then identified a distributed pattern of activity across the brain for each basic emotion (see images below). Based on the activity pattern for each emotion, the researchers accurately predicted which emotion the participants were experiencing (Saarimäki et al., 2016).

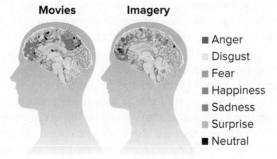

Movies   Imagery

■ Anger
▨ Disgust
■ Fear
■ Happiness
▨ Sadness
▨ Surprise
■ Neutral

Source: Adapted from Saarimaki, H., Gotsopoulos, A., Jaaskelainen, I. P., Lampinen, J., Vuilleumier, P., Hari, R., . . . Nummenmaa, L. (2016). Discrete neural signatures of basic emotions. *Cerebral Cortex, 26*(6), 2563–2573. doi: 10.1093/cercor/bhv086

MAKING SENSE OF THE MULTIPLE PERSPECTIVES ON EMOTION

As new approaches to emotion continue to develop, it is reasonable to ask why so many theories of emotion exist and, perhaps more important, which one provides the most complete explanation. Actually, we have only scratched the surface. There are almost as many explanatory theories of emotion as there are individual emotions (e.g., Frijda, 2005; Prinz, 2007; Herzberg, 2009; Reeve, 2014).

Why are theories of emotion so plentiful? For one thing, emotions are not a simple phenomenon but are intertwined closely with motivation, cognition, neuroscience, and a host of related branches of psychology. For example, evidence from brain imaging studies shows that even when people come to supposedly rational, nonemotional decisions—such as making moral or philosophical judgments—emotions come into play (Greene et al., 2001).

Furthermore, contradictory evidence of one sort or another challenges each approach. Consequently, no theory has proved invariably accurate in its predictions.

This abundance of perspectives on emotion is not a cause for despair—or unhappiness, fear, or any other negative emotion. It simply reflects the fact that psychology is an evolving, developing science. As we gather more evidence, specific answers to questions about the nature of emotions will become clearer.

PsychTech

Because human facial expressions of emotions involve using dozens of muscles, it is only recently that researchers have been able to develop software to read them reasonably accurately.

Exploring Diversity

Do People in All Cultures Express Emotion Similarly?

Consider, for a moment, the six photos displayed in Figure 4. Can you identify the emotions being expressed by the person in each of the photos?

If you are a good judge of facial expressions, you will conclude that these expressions display six of the basic emotions: happiness, anger, sadness, surprise, disgust, and fear. Hundreds of studies of nonverbal behavior show that these emotions are consistently distinct and identifiable even by untrained observers (Ekman, 2007).

Interestingly, these six emotions are not unique to members of Western cultures; rather, they constitute the basic emotions expressed universally by members of the human race, regardless of where individuals have been raised and what learning experiences they have had. Psychologist Paul Ekman convincingly demonstrated this point when he studied members of an isolated New Guinea jungle tribe who had had almost no contact with Westerners (Ekman, 1972). The people of the tribe did not speak or understand English, had never seen a movie, and had very limited experience with Caucasians before Ekman's arrival. Yet their nonverbal responses to emotion-evoking stories, as well as their ability to identify basic emotions, were quite similar to those of Westerners.

Being so isolated, the New Guineans could not have learned from Westerners to recognize or produce similar facial expressions. Instead, their similar abilities and manner of responding emotionally appear to have been present innately. Although one could argue that similar experiences in both cultures led the members of each one to learn similar types of nonverbal behavior, this appears unlikely because the two cultures are so very different. The expression of basic emotions, thus, seems to be universal (Ekman, 1994; Izard, 1994; Matsumoto, 2002).

Why do people across cultures express emotions similarly? A hypothesis known as the **facial-affect program** offers one explanation. The facial-affect program—which is assumed to be universally present at birth—is analogous to a computer software program that is activated when a particular emotion is experienced. When set in motion, the "program" produces a set of nerve impulses that make the face display an appropriate expression. Each primary emotion is related to a unique set of muscular movements, forming the kinds of expressions shown in Figure 4. For example, the emotion of happiness is universally displayed by movement of the zygomatic major, a muscle that raises the corners of the mouth and forms what we would call a smile (Ekman, 2003; Kendler et al., 2008; Krumhuber & Scherer, 2011).

facial-affect program Activation of a set of nerve impulses that make the face display the appropriate expression. (Module 26)

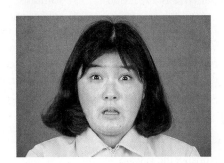

FIGURE 4 These photos demonstrate six of the primary emotions: happiness, anger, sadness, surprise, disgust, and fear.
Source: ©Matsumoto Photos 1988

The importance of facial expressions is illustrated by an intriguing notion known as the **facial-feedback hypothesis.** According to this hypothesis, facial expressions not only *reflect* emotional experience, but they also help *determine* how people experience and label emotions. Basically, "wearing" an emotional expression provides muscular feedback to the brain that helps produce an emotion congruent with that expression (Davis, Senghas, & Ochsner, 2009; Balconi, Bortolotti, & Crivelli, 2013).

For instance, the muscles activated when we smile may send a message to the brain indicating the experience of happiness—even if there is nothing in the environment that would produce that particular emotion. Some theoreticians have gone further by suggesting that facial expressions are *necessary* for an emotion to be experienced (Rinn, 1984, 1991). In this view, if no facial expression is present, the emotion cannot be felt.

Support for this facial-feedback hypothesis comes from a classic experiment carried out by psychologist Paul Ekman and colleagues (Ekman, Levenson, & Friesen, 1983). In the study, professional actors were asked to follow very explicit instructions regarding the movements of muscles in their faces. You might try this example yourself:

- Raise your brows and pull them together.
- Raise your upper eyelids.
- Now stretch your lips horizontally back toward your ears.

After carrying out these directions—which, as you may have guessed, are meant to produce an expression of fear—the actors' heart rates rose and their body temperatures declined, physiological reactions that characterize fear. Overall, facial expressions representing the primary emotions produced physiological effects similar to those accompanying the genuine emotions in other circumstances (Keillor et al., 2002; Soussignan, 2002).

facial-feedback hypothesis The hypothesis that facial expressions not only reflect emotional experience but also help determine how people experience and label emotions. (Module 26)

RECAP/EVALUATE/RETHINK

RECAP

LO 26-1 What are emotions, and how do we experience them?

- Emotions are broadly defined as feelings that may affect behavior and generally have both a physiological component and a cognitive component. Debate continues over whether separate systems govern cognitive and emotional responses and whether one has primacy over the other.

LO 26-2 What are the functions of emotions?

- Emotions prepare us for action, shape future behavior through learning, and help us interact more effectively with others.

LO 26-3 What are the explanations for emotions?

- Several theories explain emotions. The James-Lange theory suggests that emotional experience is a reaction to bodily, or visceral, changes that occur as a response to an environmental event and are interpreted as an emotional response.
- In contrast, the Cannon-Bard theory contends that both physiological arousal and an emotional experience are produced simultaneously by the same nerve stimulus and that the visceral experience does not necessarily differ among differing emotions.
- The Schachter-Singer theory suggests that emotions are determined jointly by a relatively nonspecific physiological arousal and the subsequent labeling of that arousal, using cues from the environment to determine how others are behaving in the same situation.
- The most recent approaches to emotions focus on their biological origins. For instance, it now seems that specific patterns of biological arousal are associated with individual emotions. Furthermore, new scanning techniques have identified the specific parts of the brain that are activated during the experience of particular emotions.

LO 26-4 How does nonverbal behavior relate to the expression of emotions?

- A person's facial expressions can reveal emotions. In fact, members of different cultures understand others'

emotional expressions in similar ways. One explanation for this similarity is that an innate facial-affect program activates a set of muscle movements representing the emotion being experienced.
- The facial-feedback hypothesis suggests that facial expressions not only reflect, but also produce, emotional experiences.

EVALUATE

1. Emotions are always accompanied by a cognitive response. True or false?
2. The _____ _____ theory of emotion states that emotions are a response to instinctive bodily events.
3. According to the _____ _____ theory of emotion, both an emotional response and physiological arousal are produced simultaneously by the same nerve stimulus.
4. Your friend–a psychology major–tells you, "I was at a party last night. During the course of the evening, my general level of arousal increased. Since I was at a party where people were enjoying themselves, I assume I must have felt happy." What theory of emotion does your friend subscribe to?
5. What are the six primary emotions that can be identified from facial expressions?

RETHINK

1. If researchers learned how to control emotional responses so that targeted emotions could be caused or prevented, what ethical concerns m.ight arise? Under what circumstances, if any, should such techniques be used?
2. Many people enjoy watching movies, sporting events, and music performances in crowded theaters and arenas more than they like watching them at home alone. Which theory of emotions may help explain this? How?

Answers to Evaluate Questions

1. false; emotions may occur without a cognitive response; 2. James-Lange; 3. Cannon-Bard; 4. Schachter-Singer; 5. surprise, sadness, happiness, anger, disgust, and fear

KEY TERMS

emotions	Cannon-Bard theory	Schachter-Singer theory	facial-affect program
James-Lange theory	of emotion	of emotion	facial-feedback hypothesis
of emotion			

LOOKING *Back*

EPILOGUE

Motivation and emotions are two interrelated aspects of psychology. In these modules, we first considered the topic of motivation, which has spawned a great deal of theory and research examining primary and secondary drives. We then turned to a discussion of emotions, beginning with their functions and proceeding to a review of three major theories that seek to explain what emotions are and how they and their associated physiological symptoms emerge in the individual. Finally, we looked at cultural differences in the expression and display of emotions and discussed the facial-affect program, which seems to be innate and to regulate the nonverbal expression of the basic emotions.

Return to the prologue of this group of modules, which describes Daniella Isaacs's obsession with her diet, exercise, and appearance. Using your knowledge of motivation and emotion, consider the following questions:

1. How would the "push and pull" of drive-reduction theory and incentive theory explain why Isaacs was motivated to reduce and severely restrict her food intake to the point of illness? In your opinion, do these two theories adequately explain what happened to Isaacs?
2. Do you think Isaacs was primarily displaying intrinsic or extrinsic motivation when she began to pursue her "healthy eating" diet? How did the feedback she received from Instagram change her motivation?
3. Isaacs described herself as being "borderline anorexic." In what ways do her symptoms fit the definition of anorexia nervosa and in what ways do they differ?
4. What role do you think emotions played in Isaacs's situation? How can her emotional responses to her experiences help her regain a truly healthy lifestyle?

Design Elements: Yellow highlighter: ©luckyraccoon/Shutterstock.com; Smartphone: ©and4me/Shutterstock.com; Group of diverse hands: ©MR. Nattanon Kanchak/Shutterstock.com; Woman working on laptop: ©Dragon Images/Shutterstock.com.

VISUAL SUMMARY 8 Motivation and Emotion

MODULE 24 Explaining Motivation

Motivation: The factors that direct and energize the behavior of humans and other organisms

└── The major approaches to motivation

Instinct
People and animals are born with preprogrammed sets of behaviors essential to their survival.

Drive reduction
When some basic biological requirement is lacking, a drive is produced.

Arousal
People seek an optimal level of stimulation. If the level of stimulation is too high, they act to reduce it; if it is too low, they act to increase it.

Incentive
External rewards direct and energize behavior.

Cognitive
Thoughts, beliefs, expectations, and goals direct motivation.

Hierarchy of needs
Needs form a hierarchy; before higher-order needs are met, lower-order needs must be fulfilled.

MODULE 25 Human Needs and Motivation

Motivation Behind Hunger and Eating
Obesity has reached epidemic proportions

├── Factors that affect eating
│   ├── • Biological factors
│   └── • Social factors and learned eating behaviors
└── Eating disorders
    ├── • Anorexia nervosa
    └── • Bulimia

Sexual Motivation

├── Puberty: Hormone secretion begins
├── Men and women differ in hormone production
├── Masturbation: high incidence
├── Heterosexuality: sexual attraction to the other sex
├── Premarital sex: decline in double standard
├── Homosexuality: sexual attraction to one's own sex
├── Bisexuality: sexual attraction to both sexes
└── Transgender: refers to persons whose gender identity, gender expression, or behavior does not conform to that associated with the sex to which they were assigned at birth

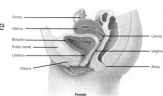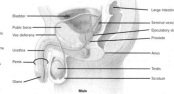

Female

Ovary, Uterus, Bladder, Pubic bone, Urethra, Clitoris, Cervix, Vagina, Anus

Male

Bladder, Pubic bone, Vas deferens, Urethra, Penis, Glans, Large intestine, Seminal vesicle, Ejaculatory duct, Prostate, Anus, Testis, Scrotum

Needs for Achievement, Affiliation, and Power:
Striving for excellence
Maintaining relationships
Influencing others

MODULE 26 Understanding Emotional Experiences

Functions of Emotions

├── Prepare us for action

├── Shape our future behavior

└── Help us to interact more effectively with others

Theories of Emotions

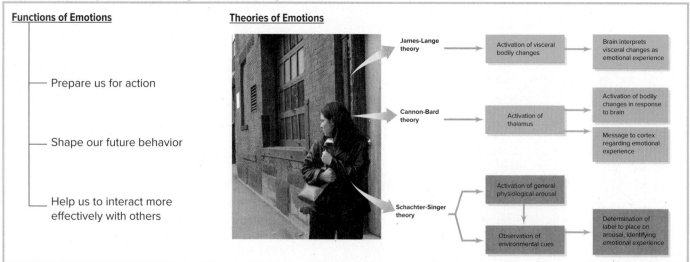

James-Lange theory → Activation of visceral bodily changes → Brain interprets visceral changes as emotional experience

Cannon-Bard theory → Activation of thalamus → Activation of bodily changes in response to brain / Message to cortex regarding emotional experience

Schachter-Singer theory → Activation of general physiological arousal / Observation of environmental cues → Determination of label to place on arousal, identifying emotional experience

(MODULE 24) ©Blend Images/Getty Images; ©Digital Vision/Getty Images; ©wavebreakmedia/Shutterstock; Source: LCPL Casey N. Thurston, USMC/DoD Media; ©Corbis/VCG/Getty Images; (MODULE 25) ©Roberto Michel/Shutterstock; (MODULE 26) ©Eric Fowke/PhotoEdit

©Nancy Mao Smith/Shutterstock

LEARNING OUTCOMES FOR CHAPTER 9

MODULE 27

LO 27-1 How do psychologists study the degree to which development is an interaction of hereditary and environmental factors?

LO 27-2 What is the nature of development before birth?

LO 27-3 What factors affect a child during the mother's pregnancy?

NATURE AND NURTURE: THE ENDURING DEVELOPMENTAL ISSUE
Determining the Relative Influence of Nature and Nurture
Developmental Research Techniques
Prenatal Development: Conception to Birth

MODULE 28

LO 28-1 What are the major competencies of newborns?

LO 28-2 What are the milestones of physical and social development during childhood?

LO 28-3 How does cognitive development proceed during childhood?

INFANCY AND CHILDHOOD
The Extraordinary Newborn
Neuroscience in Your Life: Emotional Responses in Infancy
The Growing Child: Infancy Through Middle Childhood

PROLOGUE *THE LITTLEST PIONEER*

He doesn't know it yet, but Zain Rajani is a pioneer. Zain's parents tried to conceive for 4 years before his birth—at first naturally, next with hormones, and then through *in vitro fertilization* (IVF), in which his mother's eggs were gathered, fertilized outside the body, and returned to her uterus to develop.

When these methods failed, the family moved on to a new technique. Instead of removing eggs from Zain's mother's body, the doctors removed mitochondria—essentially the powerhouse of a cell—from her egg stem cells. Then, they added the mitochondria to her eggs—on the theory that this would "rejuvenate" her existing eggs and stimulate fertilization.

It worked. Zain became one of the first success stories using this technique, and his parents couldn't be happier (Park, 2015).

LOOKING *Ahead*

It used to be simpler. People came into the world in one basic way: a man's sperm fertilized a woman's egg, and the resulting embryo developed over the course of 9 months into an infant. Today, scientists, motivated by the desire to help people for whom the basics aren't working, have developed a range of techniques to give the fertilization and birth process a helping hand.

Developmental psychology is the branch of psychology that studies the patterns of growth and change that occur throughout life. It deals with issues ranging from new ways of conceiving children, to learning how to raise children most sensibly, to understanding the milestones of life that we all face.

Developmental psychologists study the interaction between the unfolding of biologically predetermined patterns of behavior and a constantly changing, dynamic environment. They ask how our genetic background affects our behavior throughout our lives and whether heredity limits our potential. Similarly, they seek to understand the ways in which the environment works with—or against—our genetic capabilities, how the world we live in affects our development, and how we can be encouraged to reach our full potential.

We begin by examining the approaches psychologists use to study development change across the life span. Then we consider the very start of development, beginning with conception and the 9 months of life before birth. We look at genetic as well as environmental influences on the unborn individual and the way they can affect behavior throughout the remainder of the life cycle.

Next, we examine development that occurs after birth: the enormous and rapid growth that takes place during the early stages of life and the physical, social, and cognitive change throughout infancy, toddlerhood, and middle childhood. We then move on to development from adolescence through adulthood and end with a discussion of the ways in which people prepare themselves for death.

Module 27

Nature and Nurture: The Enduring Developmental Issue

How many bald, 6-foot-6, 250-pound volunteer firefighters in New Jersey wear droopy mustaches, aviator-style eyeglasses, and a key ring on the right side of the belt? The answer is two: Gerald Levey and Mark Newman. They are twins who were separated at birth. Neither twin even knew the other existed until they were reunited–in a fire station–by a fellow firefighter who knew Newman and was startled to see his double, Levey, at a firefighters' convention.

The lives of the twins, although separate, took remarkably similar paths. Levey went to college and studied forestry; Newman planned to study forestry in college but instead took a job trimming trees. Both had jobs in supermarkets. One had a job installing sprinkler systems; the other installed fire alarms.

Both men are unmarried and find the same kind of woman–"tall, slender, long hair"–attractive. They share similar hobbies and enjoy hunting, fishing, going to the beach, and watching old John Wayne movies and professional wrestling. Both like Chinese food and drink the same brand of beer. Their mannerisms are also similar– for example, each one throws his head back when he laughs. And, of course, there is one more thing: They share a passion for fighting fires.

The similarities we see in twins Gerald Levey and Mark Newman vividly raise one of the fundamental questions posed by **developmental psychology,** the study of the patterns of growth and change that occur throughout life. The question is this: How can we distinguish between the *environmental* causes of behavior (the influence of parents, siblings, family, friends, schooling, nutrition, and all the other experiences to which a child is exposed) and *hereditary* causes (those based on an individual's genetic makeup that influence growth and development throughout life)? This question embodies the **nature-nurture issue.** In this context, nature refers to hereditary factors, and nurture refers to environmental influences.

LEARNING OUTCOMES

LO 27-1 How do psychologists study the degree to which development is an interaction of hereditary and environmental factors?

LO 27-2 What is the nature of development before birth?

LO 27-3 What factors affect a child during the mother's pregnancy?

developmental psychology The branch of psychology that studies the patterns of growth and change that occur throughout life. (Module 27)

nature-nurture issue The issue of the degree to which environment and heredity influence behavior. (Module 27)

Gerald Levey and Mark Newman.
©Thomas Wanstall/The Image Works

Although the question was first posed as a nature-*versus*-nurture issue, developmental psychologists today agree that *both* nature and nurture interact to produce specific developmental patterns and outcomes. Consequently, the question has evolved into this: *How and to what degree* do environment and heredity both produce their effects? No one develops free of environmental influences or without being affected by his or her inherited *genetic makeup.* However, the debate over the comparative influence of the two factors remains active; different approaches and different theories of development emphasize the environment or heredity to a greater or lesser degree (Perovic & Radenovic, 2011; Gruber, 2013; Limberg, 2015).

For example, some developmental theories rely on basic psychological principles of learning and stress the role learning plays in producing changes in a developing child's behavior. Such theories emphasize the role of the environment in development. In contrast, other developmental theories emphasize the influence of one's physiological makeup and functioning on development. Such theories stress the role of heredity and *maturation*–the unfolding of biologically predetermined patterns of behavior–in producing developmental change. Maturation can be seen, for instance, in the development of sex characteristics (such as breasts and body hair) that occurs at the start of adolescence.

Furthermore, the work of *behavioral geneticists*, who study the effects of heredity on behavior, and the theories of evolutionary psychologists, who identify behavior patterns that result from our genetic inheritance, have influenced developmental psychologists. Behavioral geneticists are finding increasing evidence that cognitive abilities, personality traits, sexual orientation, and psychological disorders are determined to some extent by genetic factors (Vernon et al., 2008; Schermer et al., 2011; Krüger, Korsten, & Hoffman, 2017).

Behavioral genetics lies at the heart of the nature-nurture question. Although no one would argue that our behavior is determined *solely* by inherited factors, evidence collected by behavioral geneticists does suggest that our genetic inheritance predisposes us to respond in particular ways to our environment, and even to seek out particular kinds of environments (Davis, Haworth, & Plomin, 2009; Bienvenu, Davydow, & Kendler, 2011; Barnes & Jacobs, 2013).

Despite their differences over theory, developmental psychologists concur on some points. They agree that genetic factors not only provide the potential for specific behaviors or traits to emerge but also place limitations on the emergence of such behavior or traits. For instance, heredity defines people's general level of intelligence and sets an upper limit that–regardless of the quality of the environment–people cannot exceed. Heredity also places limits on physical abilities; humans simply cannot run at a speed of 60 miles an hour or grow as tall as 10 feet, no matter the quality of their environment (Dodge, 2004; Pinker, 2004; Loehlin et al., 2015).

Figure 1 lists some of the characteristics most affected by heredity. As you consider these items, keep in mind that these characteristics are not *entirely* determined by heredity because environmental factors also play a role.

Developmental psychologists also agree that in most instances environmental factors play a critical role in enabling people to reach the potential capabilities that their genetic background makes possible. If Albert Einstein had received no intellectual stimulation as a child and had not been sent to school, it is unlikely that he would have reached his genetic potential. Similarly, a great athlete such as baseball star Derek Jeter would have been unlikely to display much physical skill if he had not been raised in an environment that nurtured his innate talent and gave him the opportunity to train and perfect his natural abilities.

Clearly, the relationship between heredity and environment is complex. Therefore, developmental psychologists typically take an *interactionist* position on the nature-nurture issue by suggesting that a combination of hereditary and environmental factors influences development. Developmental psychologists face the challenge of identifying the relative strength of each of these influences on the individual as well as that of identifying the specific changes that occur over the course of development (McGregor & Capone, 2004; Moffitt, Caspi, & Rutter, 2006; Steinbeis et al., 2017).

Study Alert

The nature–nurture issue is a key question that is pervasive throughout the field of psychology. It explores how and to what degree environment and heredity produce their joint effects.

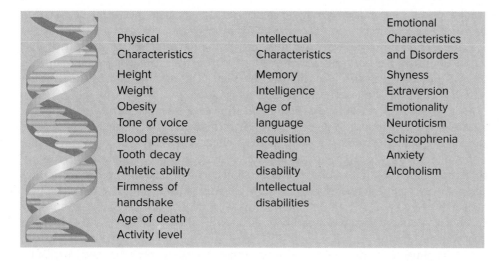

Physical Characteristics	Intellectual Characteristics	Emotional Characteristics and Disorders
Height	Memory	Shyness
Weight	Intelligence	Extraversion
Obesity	Age of	Emotionality
Tone of voice	language	Neuroticism
Blood pressure	acquisition	Schizophrenia
Tooth decay	Reading	Anxiety
Athletic ability	disability	Alcoholism
Firmness of	Intellectual	
handshake	disabilities	
Age of death		
Activity level		

FIGURE 1 Characteristics influenced significantly by genetic factors. Although these characteristics have strong genetic components, they are also affected by environmental factors.

Determining the Relative Influence of Nature and Nurture

Developmental psychologists use several approaches to determine the relative influence of genetic and environmental factors on behavior. In one approach, researchers can experimentally control the genetic makeup of laboratory animals by carefully breeding them for specific traits. For instance, by observing animals with identical genetic backgrounds placed in varied environments, researchers can learn the effects of specific kinds of environmental stimulation. Although researchers must be careful when generalizing the findings of nonhuman research to a human population, findings from animal research provide important information that cannot be obtained for ethical reasons by using human participants.

Human twins serve as another important source of information about the relative effects of genetic and environmental factors. If **identical twins** (those who are genetically identical) display different patterns of development, those differences have to be attributed to variations in the environment in which the twins were raised. The most useful data come from identical twins (such as Gerald Levey and Mark Newman) who are adopted at birth by different sets of adoptive parents and raised apart in differing environments. Studies of nontwin siblings who are raised in totally different environments also shed some light on the issue. Because they have relatively similar genetic backgrounds, siblings who show similarities as adults provide strong evidence for the importance of heredity (Vitaro, Brendgen, & Arseneault, 2009; Sternberg, 2011; Farnsworth, 2015).

Researchers can also take the opposite tack. Instead of concentrating on people with similar genetic backgrounds who are raised in different environments, they may consider people raised in similar environments who have totally dissimilar genetic backgrounds. For example, if they find similar courses of development in two adopted children who have different genetic backgrounds and have been raised in the same family, they have evidence for the importance of environmental influences on development. Moreover, psychologists can carry out research involving animals with dissimilar genetic backgrounds; by experimentally varying the environment in which the animals are raised, they can determine the influence of environmental factors (independent of heredity) on development (Petrill & Deater-Deckard, 2004; Beam & Turkheimer, 2013; Tosto et al., 2017).

identical twins Twins who are genetically identical. (Module 27)

Developmental Research Techniques

Because of the demands of measuring behavioral change across different ages, developmental researchers use several unique methods. The most frequently used, **cross-sectional research,** compares people of different ages at the same point in time. Cross-sectional

cross-sectional research A research method that compares people of different ages at the same point in time. (Module 27)

studies provide information about differences in development between different age groups (Creasey, 2005; Huijie, 2006; Card, 2017).

Suppose, for instance, we were interested in the development of intellectual ability in adulthood. To carry out a cross-sectional study, we might compare a sample of 25-, 45-, and 65-year-olds who all take the same IQ test. We then can determine whether average IQ test scores differ in each age group.

Cross-sectional research has limitations, however. For instance, we cannot be sure that the differences in IQ scores we might find in our example are due to age differences alone. Instead, the scores may reflect differences in the educational attainment of the cohorts represented. A *cohort* is a group of people who grow up at similar times, in similar places, and in similar conditions. In the case of IQ differences, any age differences we find in a cross-sectional study may reflect educational differences among the cohorts studied: People in the older age group may belong to a cohort that was less likely to attend college than were the people in the younger groups.

A longitudinal study, the second major research strategy developmental psychologists use, provides one way around this problem. **Longitudinal research** traces the behavior of one or more participants as the participants age. Longitudinal studies assess *change* in behavior over time, whereas cross-sectional studies assess *differences* among groups of people.

For instance, consider how we might investigate intellectual development during adulthood by using a longitudinal research strategy. First, we might give an IQ test to a group of 25-year-olds. We'd then come back to the same people 20 years later and retest them at age 45. Finally, we'd return to them once more when they were 65 years old and test them again.

By examining changes at several points in time, we can see how individuals develop. Clearly, though, longitudinal research requires a significant expenditure of time as the researcher waits for the participants to get older. In addition, participants who begin a study at an early age may drop out, move away, or even die as the research continues. Moreover, participants who take the same test at several points in time may become "test-wise" and perform better each time they take it because they have become more familiar with the test. Still, longitudinal research is an important technique of developmental researchers.

longitudinal research A research method that investigates behavior as participants get older. (Module 27)

Study Alert

Be sure to be able to distinguish the two different types of developmental research: cross-sectional (comparing people of different ages at the same time) and longitudinal (studying participants as they age).

Prenatal Development: Conception to Birth

Leah and John Howard's joy at learning Leah was pregnant turned to anxiety when Leah's doctor discovered that her brother had died from Duchenne muscular dystrophy (DMD) at age 12. The disease, the doctor explained, was an X-linked inherited disorder. If Leah turned out to be a carrier, there was a 50% chance that the baby would inherit the disease if it were male. The doctor advised them to have an ultrasound to determine the baby's sex. It turned out to be a boy.

The Howards faced two options. The doctor could take a chorion villus sampling now or wait a month and perform an amniocentesis. Both carried a very low risk for miscarriage. Leah chose amniocentesis, but the results were inconclusive. The doctor then suggested a fetal muscle biopsy to confirm the presence or lack of the muscle protein dystrophin. The absence of dystrophin would signal DMD. The risk of miscarriage, however, was not inconsiderable.

Four months pregnant at this point and tired of the worries and tears, Leah and John decided to take their chances and look forward to their baby's birth.

The Howards' case shows the difficult choices that parents may encounter due to our increasing understanding of life spent inside a mother's womb.

Yet, our knowledge of the biology of *conception*–when a male's sperm cell penetrates a female's egg cell–and its aftermath makes the start of life no less of a miracle. Let's consider how an individual is created by looking first at the genetic endowment that a child receives at the moment of conception.

THE BASICS OF GENETICS

The one-cell entity established at conception contains 23 pairs of **chromosomes**, rod-shaped structures that contain all basic hereditary information. One member of each pair is from the mother, and the other is from the father.

Each chromosome contains thousands of **genes**–smaller units through which genetic information is transmitted. Either individually or in combination, genes produce each person's particular characteristics. Composed of sequences of *DNA (deoxyribonucleic acid)* molecules, genes are the biological equivalent of "software" that programs the future development of all parts of the body's hardware. Humans have some 25,000 different genes (see Figure 2).

Some genes control the development of systems common to all members of the human species–the heart, circulatory system, brain, lungs, and so forth; others shape the characteristics that make each human unique, such as facial configuration, height, and eye color. The child's sex is also determined by a particular combination of genes.

Specifically, a child inherits an X chromosome from its mother and either an X or a Y chromosome from its father. When it receives an XX combination, it is a female; with an XY combination, it develops as a male. Male development is triggered by a single gene on the Y chromosome; without the presence of that specific gene, the individual will develop as a female.

As behavioral geneticists have discovered, genes are also at least partially responsible for a wide variety of personal characteristics, including cognitive abilities, personality traits, and psychological disorders. Of course, few of these characteristics are determined by a single gene. Instead, most traits result from a combination of multiple genes that operate together with environmental influences (Ramus, 2006; Armbruster et al., 2011; Kasantseva et al., 2015).

THE HUMAN GENOME PROJECT

Our understanding of genetics took a giant leap forward in 2001, when scientists were able to map the specific location and sequence of every human gene as part of the

chromosomes Rod-shaped structures that contain all basic hereditary information. (Module 27)

genes The parts of the chromosomes through which genetic information is transmitted. (Module 27)

Study Alert
It's important to understand the basic building blocks of genetics: chromosomes, which contain genes, which in turn are composed of sequences of DNA.

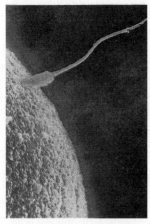
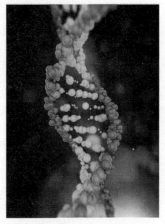

| (a) Conception | (b) 23 pairs of chromosomes | (c) DNA sequence | (d) Genes |

FIGURE 2 Every individual's characteristics are determined by the individual's specific genetic information. (a) At the moment of conception, (b) humans receive 23 pairs of chromosomes, half from the mother and half from the father. (c) These chromosomes are made up of coils of DNA. (d) Each chromosome contains thousands of genes that "program" the future development of the body.

(a) ©D.W. Fawcett/Science Source; (b) ©Willatt, East Anglian Regional Genetics Service/SPL/Science Source; (c) ©Double Brain/Shutterstock; (d) ©Biophoto Associates/Science Source

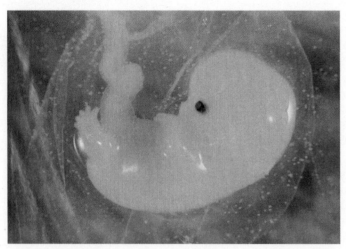 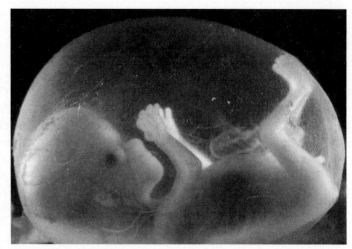

These remarkable photos of live fetuses display the degree of physical development at prenatal ages 4 and 15 weeks.
(Left) ©SPL/Science Source; (Right) ©Petit Format/Science Source

massive *Human Genome Project*. The accomplishment was one of the most important in the history of biology (International Human Genome Sequencing Consortium, 2003; Grigorenko & Dozier, 2013; Özdemir et al., 2017).

The success of the Human Genome Project started a revolution in health care because scientists can identify the particular genes responsible for genetically caused disorders. It is already leading not only to the identification of risk factors in children but also to the development of new treatments for physical and psychological disorders.

THE EARLIEST DEVELOPMENT

zygote The new cell formed by the union of an egg and sperm. (Module 27)

When an egg becomes fertilized by the sperm, the resulting one-celled entity, called a **zygote,** immediately begins to develop. The zygote starts out as a microscopic speck. Three days after fertilization, though, the zygote increases to around 32 cells; within a week, it has grown to 100-150 cells. These first 2 weeks are known as the *germinal period.*

embryo A developed zygote that has a heart, a brain, and other organs. (Module 27)

Two weeks after conception, the developing individual enters the *embryonic period,* which lasts from week 2 through week 8; he or she is now called an **embryo.** As an embryo develops through an intricate, preprogrammed process of cell division, it grows 10,000 times larger by 4 weeks of age and attains a length of about one-fifth of an inch. At this point it has developed a rudimentary beating heart, a brain, an intestinal tract, and a number of other organs. Although all these organs are at a primitive stage of development, they are clearly recognizable. Moreover, by week 8, the embryo is about an inch long and has discernible arms, legs, and a face.

fetus A developing individual from 8 weeks after conception until birth. (Module 27)

From week 8 and continuing until birth, the developing individual enters the *fetal period* and is called a **fetus.** At the start of this period, it begins to respond to touch; it bends its fingers when touched on the hand. At 16 to 18 weeks, its movements become strong enough for the mother to sense them. At the same time, hair may begin to grow on its head, and the facial features become similar to those the child will display at birth. The major organs begin functioning, although the fetus could not be kept alive outside the mother. In addition, a lifetime's worth of brain neurons are produced–although it is unclear whether the brain is capable of thinking at this early stage.

age of viability The point at which a fetus can survive if born prematurely. (Module 27)

Within the womb the fetus continues to develop before birth. It begins to grow fatty deposits under the skin, and it gains weight. The fetus reaches the **age of viability,** the point at which it can survive if born prematurely, at about prenatal age 22 weeks. By week 24, a fetus has many of the characteristics it will display as a newborn. In fact, when an infant is born prematurely at this age, it can open and close its eyes; suck; cry; look up, down, and around; and even grasp objects placed in its hands.

At prenatal age 28 weeks, the fetus weighs less than 3 pounds and is about 16 inches long. It may be capable of learning: One study found that the infants of mothers who had repeatedly read aloud *The Cat in the Hat* by Dr. Seuss before the infants' birth preferred the sound of that particular story to other stories after they were born (Spence & DeCasper, 1982; Del Giudice, 2011; Moon, Lagercrantz, & Kuhl, 2013).

Before birth, a fetus passes through several *sensitive periods.* A sensitive period is the time when organisms are particularly susceptible to certain kinds of stimuli. For example, fetuses are especially affected by their mothers' use of drugs during certain sensitive periods before birth. If they are exposed to a particular drug before or after the sensitive period, it may have relatively little impact; if exposure comes during a sensitive period, the impact will be significant (Werker & Tees, 2005; Uylings, 2006; Sandman, 2015).

Study Alert

Sensitive (or critical) periods, which can occur before or after birth, are important because they indicate the time that organisms are particularly susceptible to damage that may affect them for the rest of their lives.

From the perspective of...

An Educator How would you use your knowledge of sensitive periods in language development to improve students' learning? Would you want to teach children more than one language during this time?

©Andersen Ross/Blend Images/Getty Images

Sensitive periods can also occur after birth. Some language specialists suggest, for instance, that there is a period in which children are particularly receptive to developing language. If children are not exposed to appropriate linguistic stimuli, their language development may be impaired (Sohr-Preston & Scaramella, 2006; Innocenti, 2007; Opendak, Gould, & Sullivan, 2017).

In the final weeks of pregnancy, the fetus continues to gain weight and grow. At the end of the normal 38 weeks of pregnancy, the fetus typically weighs 7 pounds and is about 20 inches in length. However, the story is different for *preterm infants,* who are born before week 38. Because they have not been able to develop fully, they are at higher risk for illness, future problems, and even death. For infants who have been in the womb for more than 30 weeks, the prospects are relatively good. However, for those born before week 30, the story is often less positive. Such newborns, who may weigh as little as 2 pounds at birth, are in grave danger because they have immature organs; they have less than a 50-50 chance of survival. If they do survive—and it takes extraordinarily heroic (and expensive) medical intervention to ensure this—they may later experience significant developmental delays.

GENETIC INFLUENCES ON THE FETUS

The process of fetal growth that we have just described reflects normal development, which occurs in 95-98% of all pregnancies. Some individuals are less fortunate; in the remaining 2-5% of cases, children are born with serious birth defects. A major cause of such defects is faulty genes or chromosomes. Here are some of the more common genetic and chromosomal difficulties.

- *Phenylketonuria (PKU).* A child born with the inherited disease phenylketonuria cannot produce an enzyme that is required for normal development. This deficiency results in an accumulation of poisons that eventually cause profound intellectual disability. The disease is treatable, however, if it is caught early. Most infants today are routinely tested for PKU, and children with the disorder can be placed on a special diet that allows them to develop normally (Christ, Steiner, & Grange, 2006; Widaman, 2009; Romani et al., 2017).

- *Sickle-cell anemia.* About 10% of the African American population has the possibility of passing on sickle-cell anemia, a disease that gets its name from the abnormally shaped red blood cells it causes. Children with the disease may have episodes of pain, yellowish eyes, stunted growth, and vision problems (Selove, 2007; Wills, 2013).

- *Tay-Sachs disease.* Children born with Tay-Sachs disease, a disorder most often found in Jews of Eastern European ancestry, usually die by age 3 or 4 because of the body's inability to break down fat. If both parents carry the genetic defect that produces the fatal illness, their child has a 1 in 4 chance of being born with the disease (Leib et al., 2005; Weinstein, 2007).

- *Down syndrome.* Down syndrome, one of the causes of intellectual disability, occurs when the zygote receives an extra chromosome at the moment of conception. Down syndrome is often related to the mother's age; mothers over 35 and younger than 18 stand a higher risk than do other women of having a child with the syndrome (Roizen & Patterson, 2003; Sherman et al., 2007; Nærland et al., 2017).

PRENATAL ENVIRONMENTAL INFLUENCES

Genetic factors are not the only causes of difficulties in fetal development. Environmental influences—the *nurture* part of the nature–nurture equation—also affect the fetus. Some of the more profound consequences are brought about by **teratogens,** environmental agents such as drugs, chemicals, viruses, or other factors that produce birth defects. Among the major prenatal environmental influences on the fetus are the following:

teratogens Environmental agents such as drugs, chemicals, viruses, or other factors that produce birth defects. (Module 27)

- *Mother's nutrition.* What a mother eats during her pregnancy can have important implications for the health of her baby. Seriously undernourished mothers cannot provide adequate nutrition to a growing fetus, and they are likely to give birth to underweight babies. Poorly nourished babies are also more susceptible to disease, and a lack of nourishment may have an adverse impact on their mental development (Najman et al., 2004; Everette, 2008; Nyaradi et al., 2013).

- *Mother's illness.* Even minor illnesses that a mother catches during the early months of pregnancy can have devastating consequences for a developing fetus. For example, if pregnant women contract rubella (German measles), syphilis, diabetes, or high blood pressure, each disease may produce permanent, lifelong effects on the fetus (Nesheim et al., 2004; Magoni et al., 2005).

- *Mother's emotional state.* A mother's emotional state affects her baby. Mothers who are anxious and tense during the last months of their pregnancies are more apt to have irritable infants who sleep and eat poorly. The reason? The autonomic nervous system of the fetus becomes especially sensitive as a result of chemical changes produced by the mother's emotional state (Hollins, 2007; Kumari & Joshi, 2013).

- *Mother's use of drugs.* Mothers who take illegal, physically addictive drugs such as cocaine run the risk of giving birth to babies who are similarly addicted. Their newborns suffer painful withdrawal symptoms and sometimes show permanent physical and mental impairment. Even legal drugs taken by a pregnant woman (who may not know that she has become pregnant) can have a tragic effect (Schechter, Finkelstein, & Koren, 2005; Singer & Richardson, 2011; Nygaard et al., 2017).

- *Alcohol.* Alcohol is extremely dangerous to fetal development. For example, as many as 1.5 out of every 1,000 infants are born with *fetal alcohol syndrome disorder (FASD)*, a condition resulting in below-average intelligence, growth delays, and facial deformities. FASD is now the primary preventable cause of intellectual disability. Even mothers who use small amounts of alcohol during pregnancy place their child at risk (Ikonomidou et al., 2000; Niccols, 2007; Murthy et al., 2009; Lewis et al., 2015).

Environmental Factor	Possible Effect on Prenatal Development
Rubella (German measles)	Blindness, deafness, heart abnormalities, stillbirth
Syphilis	Intellectual disability, physical deformities, maternal miscarriage
Addictive drugs	Low birth weight, addiction of infant to drug, with possible death after birth from withdrawal
Nicotine	Premature birth, low birth weight and length
Alcohol	Intellectual disability, lower-than-average birth weight, small head, limb deformities
Radiation from X-rays	Physical deformities, intellectual disability
Inadequate diet	Reduction in growth of brain, smaller-than-average weight and length at birth
Mother's age—younger than 18 at birth of child	Premature birth, increased incidence of Down syndrome
Mother's age—older than 35 at birth of child	Increased incidence of Down syndrome
DES (diethylstilbestrol)	Reproductive difficulties and increased incidence of genital cancer in children of mothers who were given DES during pregnancy to prevent miscarriage
AIDS	Possible spread of AIDS virus to infant; facial deformities; growth failure
Accutane	Intellectual disability and physical deformities

FIGURE 3 A variety of environmental factors can play a role in prenatal development.

- *Nicotine use.* Pregnant mothers who smoke put their children at considerable risk. Smoking while pregnant can lead to miscarriage and infant death. For children who do survive, the negative consequences of mother's tobacco use can last a lifetime (Shea & Steiner, 2008; Rogers, 2009; Magee et al., 2013).

Several other environmental factors have an impact on the child before and during birth (see Figure 3). Keep in mind, however, that although we have been discussing the influences of genetics and environment separately, neither factor works alone. Furthermore, despite the emphasis here on some of the ways in which development can go wrong, the vast majority of births occur without difficulty. And in most instances, subsequent development also proceeds normally.

RECAP/EVALUATE/RETHINK

RECAP

LO 27-1 How do psychologists study the degree to which development is an interaction of hereditary and environmental factors?

- Developmental psychology studies growth and change throughout life. One fundamental question is how much developmental change is due to heredity and how much is due to environment—the nature–nurture issue. Heredity seems to define the upper limits of our growth and change, whereas the environment affects the degree to which the upper limits are reached.

- Cross-sectional research compares people of different ages with one another at the same point in time. In contrast, longitudinal research traces the behavior of one or more participants as the participants become older. Finally, sequential research combines the two methods by examining several different age groups at several points in time.

LO 27-2 What is the nature of development before birth?

- At the moment of conception, a male's sperm cell and a female's egg cell unite; each contributes to the new individual's genetic makeup. The union of sperm and egg produces a zygote, which contains 23 pairs of chromosomes; one member of each pair comes from the father and the other comes from the mother.

- Each chromosome contains genes through which genetic information is transmitted. Genes, which are composed of DNA sequences, are the "software" that programs the future development of the body's hardware.
- Genes affect not only physical attributes, but also a wide array of personal characteristics such as cognitive abilities, personality traits, and psychological disorders.
- After two weeks the zygote becomes an embryo. By week 8, the embryo is called a fetus and is responsive to touch and other stimulation. At about week 22 it reaches the age of viability, which means it may survive if born prematurely. A fetus is normally born after 38 weeks of pregnancy; it weighs around 7 pounds and measures about 20 inches.

LO 27-3 What factors can affect a child during the mother's pregnancy?

- Genetic abnormalities produce birth defects such as phenylketonuria (PKU), sickle-cell anemia, Tay-Sachs disease, and Down syndrome.
- Among the environmental influences on fetal growth are the mother's nutrition, illnesses, and drug intake.

EVALUATE

1. Developmental psychologists are interested in the effects of both _____ and _____ on development.

2. Environment and heredity both influence development with genetic potentials generally establishing limits on environmental influences. True or false?
3. By observing genetically similar animals in differing environments, we can increase our understanding of the influences of hereditary and environmental factors in humans. True or false?
4. _____ research studies the same individuals over a period of time, whereas _____-_____ research studies people of different ages at the same time.
5. Match each of the following terms with its definition:

   1. Zygote
   2. Gene
   3. Chromosome

   a. Smallest unit through which genetic information is passed.
   b. Fertilized egg
   c. Rod-shaped structure containing genetic information

6. Specific kinds of growth must take place during a _____ period if the embryo is to develop normally.

RETHINK

1. When researchers find similarities in development between very different cultures, what implications might such findings have for the nature–nurture issue?
2. Consider the factors that might determine when a child learns to walk. What kinds of environmental influences might be involved? What kinds of genetic influences might be involved?

Answers to Evaluate Questions

1. heredity (or nature), environment (or nurture); 2. true; 3. true; 4. Longitudinal, cross-sectional; 5. 1-b, 2-a, 3-c; 6. sensitive (or critical)

KEY TERMS

developmental psychology	cross-sectional research	genes	fetus
nature–nurture issue	longitudinal research	zygote	age of viability
identical twins	chromosomes	embryo	teratogens

Module 28
Infancy and Childhood

His head was molded into a long melon shape and came to a point at the back. . . . He was covered with a thick greasy white material known as "vernix," which made him slippery to hold and also allowed him to slip easily through the birth canal. In addition to a shock of black hair on his head, his body was covered with dark, fine hair known as "lanugo." His ears, his back, his shoulders, and even his cheeks were furry. . . . His skin was wrinkled and quite loose, ready to scale in creased places such as his feet and hands. . . . His ears were pressed to his head in unusual positions—one ear was matted firmly forward on his cheek. His nose was flattened and pushed to one side by the squeeze as he came through the pelvis. (Brazelton, 1969, p. 3)

What kind of creature is this? Although the description hardly fits that of the adorable babies seen in advertisements for baby food, we are in fact talking about a normal, completely developed child just after the moment of birth. Called a **neonate,** a newborn arrives in the world in a form that hardly meets the standards of beauty against which we typically measure babies. Yet ask any parents: Nothing is more beautiful or exciting than the first glimpse of their newborn.

The Extraordinary Newborn

Several factors cause a neonate's strange appearance. The trip through the mother's birth canal may have squeezed the incompletely formed bones of the skull together and squashed the nose into the head. The skin secretes *vernix,* a white greasy covering, for protection before birth, and the baby may have *lanugo,* a soft fuzz, over the entire body for a similar purpose. The infant's eyelids may be puffy with an accumulation of fluids because of the upside-down position during birth.

All these features change during the first 2 weeks of life as the neonate takes on a more familiar appearance. Even more impressive are the capabilities a neonate begins to display from the moment of birth—capabilities that grow at an astounding rate over the ensuing months.

REFLEXES

A neonate is born with a number of **reflexes**—unlearned, involuntary responses that occur automatically in the presence of certain stimuli. Critical for survival, many of those reflexes unfold naturally as part of an infant's ongoing maturation. The *rooting reflex,* for instance, causes neonates to turn their heads toward things that touch their cheeks—such as the mother's nipple or a bottle. Similarly, a *sucking reflex* prompts infants to suck at things that touch their lips. Among other reflexes are a *gag reflex* (to clear the throat), the *startle reflex* (a series of movements in which an infant flings out the arms, fans the fingers, and arches the back in response to a sudden noise), and the *Babinski reflex* (a baby's toes fan out when the outer edge of the sole of the foot is stroked).

Infants lose these primitive reflexes after the first few months of life and replace them with more complex and organized behaviors. Although at birth a neonate is capable of only jerky, limited

LEARNING OUTCOMES

LO 28-1 What are the major competencies of newborns?

LO 28-2 What are the milestones of physical and social development during childhood?

LO 28-3 How does cognitive development proceed during childhood?

neonate A newborn child. (Module 28)

reflexes Unlearned, involuntary responses that occur automatically in the presence of certain stimuli. (Module 28)

Many of the reflexes that a neonate is born with are critical for survival and unfold naturally as a part of the infant's ongoing maturation. Do you think humans have more or fewer reflexes than other animals do?
©Emma Kim/Cultura/Getty Images

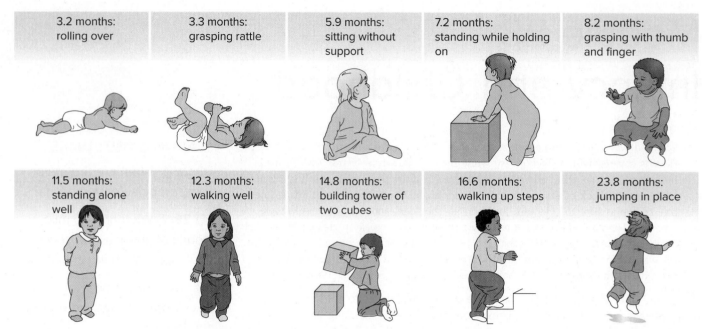

FIGURE 1 Although at birth a neonate can make only jerky, limited voluntary movements, during the first year of life the ability to move independently grows enormously. The ages indicate the time when 50% of children are able to perform each skill. Remember, however, that the time when each skill appears can vary considerably. For example, 25% of children are able to walk well at age 11 months; by 15 months, 90% of children are walking well.

Source: Adapted from Frankenburg, W. K., Dodds, J., Archer, P., Shapiro, H., & Bresnick, B. (1992). The Denver II: A major revision and restandardization of the Denver developmental screening test. *Pediatrics, 89,* 91–97.

Study Alert

The basic reflexes—unlearned, involuntary responses—include the rooting reflex, the sucking reflex, the gag reflex, the startle reflex, and the Babinski reflex.

voluntary movements, the ability to move independently grows enormously during the first year of life. The typical baby rolls over by the age of about 3 months, sits without support at about 6 months, stands alone at about 11 months, and walks at just over a year old. Not only does the ability to make large-scale movements improve during this time, but fine-muscle movements also become increasingly sophisticated (see Figure 1).

DEVELOPMENT OF THE SENSES: TAKING IN THE WORLD

When proud parents peer into the eyes of their neonate, is the child able to return their gaze? Although it was thought for some time that newborns can only see a hazy blur, most current findings indicate that neonates' capabilities are far more impressive. Newborns can see objects reasonably well that are within 7- to 8-inches of their eyes, although they have a limited capacity to see beyond that distance, and can follow moving objects within their field of vision. They also show the beginnings of depth perception as they react by raising their hands when an object appears to be moving rapidly toward the face (Maurer et al., 1999; Craighero et al., 2011).

You might think that it would be hard to figure out just how well neonates can see because their lack of both language and reading ability clearly prevents them from saying what direction the E on a vision chart is facing. However, researchers have devised a number of ingenious methods that rely on the newborn's biological responses and innate reflexes to test perceptual skills.

For instance, infants who see a novel stimulus typically pay close attention to it; as a consequence, their heart rates increase. But if they repeatedly see the same stimulus, their attention to it decreases, as indicated by a return to a slower heart rate. This phenomenon is known as **habituation,** the decrease in the response to a stimulus that occurs after repeated presentations of the same stimulus. By studying habituation, developmental psychologists can tell when a child who is too young to speak can detect and discriminate a stimulus (Hannon & Johnson, 2005; del Rosal, Alonso, & Moreno, 2006; Molina et al., 2015).

habituation The decrease in the response to a stimulus that occurs after repeated presentations of the same stimulus. (Module 28)

Researchers have developed many other methods for measuring neonate and infant perception. One technique, for instance, involves babies sucking on a nipple attached to a computer. A change in the rate and vigor with which the babies suck helps researchers infer that babies can perceive variations in stimuli. Other approaches include examining babies' eye movements and observing which way babies move their heads in response to a visual stimulus (Franklin, Pilling, & Davies, 2005; Bulf, Johnson, & Valenza, 2011).

Through the use of such research techniques, we now know that infants' visual perception is remarkably sophisticated from the start of life. At birth, babies prefer patterns with contours and edges over less distinct patterns, indicating that they can respond to the configuration of stimuli. Furthermore, even newborns are aware of size constancy because they are apparently sensitive to the phenomenon by which objects stay the same size even though the image on the retina may change size as the distance between the object and the retina varies (Norcia et al., 2005; Moore, Goodwin, & George, 2007; Hadad, Maurer, & Lewis, 2017).

In fact, neonates can discriminate facial expressions—and even imitate them. As you can see in Figure 2, newborns can produce a good imitation of an adult's expressions. Even very young infants, then, can respond to the emotions and moods that their caregivers' facial expressions reveal. This capability provides the foundation for social interaction skills in children (Meltzoff, 1996; Grossmann, Striano, & Friederici, 2007; Bahrick, Lickliter, & Castellanos, 2013).

Other visual abilities grow rapidly after birth. By the end of their first month, babies can distinguish some colors from others; after 4 months, they can focus on near or far objects. By the age of 4 or 5 months, they are able to recognize two- and three-dimensional objects, and they can perceive the gestalt organizing principles discovered by psychologists who study perception. By the age of 7 months, neural systems related to the processing of information about facial expressions are highly sophisticated and cause babies to respond differently to specific facial expressions (see *Neuroscience*

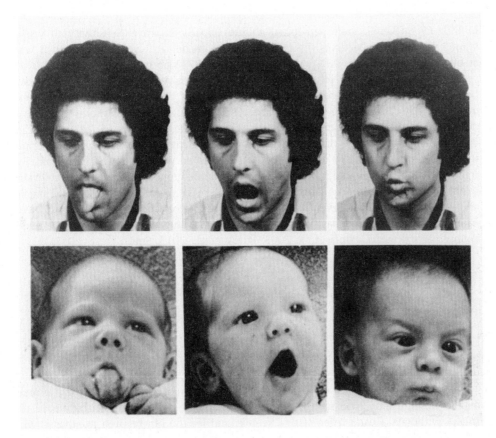

FIGURE 2 This newborn infant is clearly imitating the expressions of the adult model in these amazing photos. How does this ability contribute to social development?

(All) From: A.N. Meltzoff & M.K. Moore, 'Imitation of facial and manual gestures by human neonates.' Science, 1977, 198, 75-78. Copyright ©1977 Andrew Meltzoff

NEUROSCIENCE IN YOUR LIFE: EMOTIONAL RESPONSES IN INFANCY

Particular emotions elicit particular neural responses, even in early infancy. Furthermore, infants differ significantly in their neural responses to different emotions. Are these differences in brain response related to temperament? To answer this question, researchers measured neural activity while 7-month-old infants looked at pictures of happy faces. Compared with those who scored high on negative emotionality, the infants who scored low on negative emotionality—that is, those who had a propensity toward more positive thinking—had a greater neural response to happy faces in the left frontal cortex. The results suggest that neural responses to emotional stimuli are related to an infant's temperament (Ravicz et al., 2015).

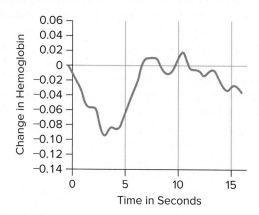

In the image, you can see when brain activity occurred (x-axis) and how much hemoglobin levels changed (y-axis) as blood went to active brain areas.

Source: Adapted from Ravicz, M. M., Perdue, K. L., Westerlund, A., Vanderwert, R. E., & Nelson, C. A. (2015). Infants' neural responses to facial emotion in the prefrontal cortex are correlated with temperament: a functional near-infrared spectroscopy study. *Frontiers in Psychology, 6,* 922.

in Your Life). Overall, their perceptual abilities rapidly improve: Sensitivity to visual stimuli, for instance, becomes three to four times greater at 1 year of age than it was at birth (Striano & Vaish, 2006; Leppänen et al., 2007; Xiao et al., 2015).

In addition to vision, infants display other impressive sensory capabilities. Newborns can distinguish different sounds to the point of being able to recognize their own mothers' voices at the age of 3 days. They can also make the subtle perceptual distinctions that underlie language abilities. For example, at 2 days of age, infants can distinguish between their native tongue and foreign languages, and they can discriminate between such closely related sounds as *ba* and *pa* when they are 4 days old. By 6 months of age, they can discriminate virtually any difference in sound that is relevant to the production of language. Moreover, they can recognize different tastes and smells at a very early age. There even seems to be something of a built-in sweet tooth: Neonates prefer liquids that have been sweetened with sugar over their unsweetened counterparts (Rivera-Gaxiola et al., 2005; Purdy et al., 2013; Smith et al., 2017).

The Growing Child: Infancy Through Middle Childhood

Three-year-old Lisa Palermo always had Cheerios on her breath. Mindy Crowell, Lisa's day care teacher, thought little of it until she noticed that the classroom Cheerios stash was steadily dwindling.

The Cheerios were stored in a plastic bin in the clothes closet. Keeping an eye on the closet, Mindy soon saw Lisa enter it, manipulate the fastener of the bin, reach in and withdraw a hand laden with Cheerios, and let the bin refasten itself, as it was designed to do. Mindy was amazed: Somehow, Lisa, barely able to navigate a crayon, had learned how to undo the supposedly child-proof fastener–a task that Mindy herself found difficult.

Mindy waited to see what would happen next. What she found was that Lisa was an excellent teacher. In the next few days, Paul, Olivia, and Kelly began to frequent the bin and do exactly what Lisa had done.

At 3 years old, Lisa asserted her personality, illustrating the tremendous growth that occurs in a variety of domains during the first year of life. Throughout the remainder of childhood, moving from infancy into middle childhood and the start of adolescence around age 11 or 12, children develop physically, socially, and cognitively in extraordinary ways. In the remainder of this module, we'll consider this development.

PHYSICAL DEVELOPMENT

Children's physical growth provides the most obvious sign of development. During the first year of life, children typically triple their birthweight, and their height increases by about half. This rapid growth slows down as the child gets older–think how gigantic adults would be if that rate of growth was constant. From age 3 to the beginning of adolescence at around age 13, growth averages a gain of about 5 pounds and 3 inches a year (see Figure 3).

The physical changes that occur as children develop are not just a matter of increasing growth; the relationship of the size of the various body parts to one another

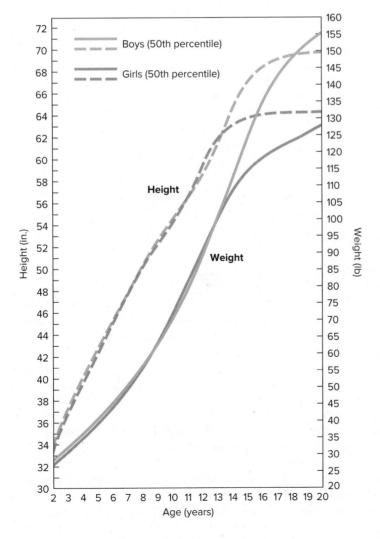

FIGURE 3 The average heights and weights of males and females in the United States from age 2 through age 20. At what ages are girls typically heavier and taller than boys?

Source: Adapted from National Center for Health Statistics. (2000). *Health United States, 2000 with adolescent health chartbook.* Hyattsville, MD: National Center for Health Statistics.

FIGURE 4 As development progresses, the size of the head relative to the rest of the body decreases until the individual reaches adulthood. Why do you think the head starts out so large?

Source: Adapted from Robbins, W. J. (1929). *Growth*. New Haven, CT: Yale University Press.

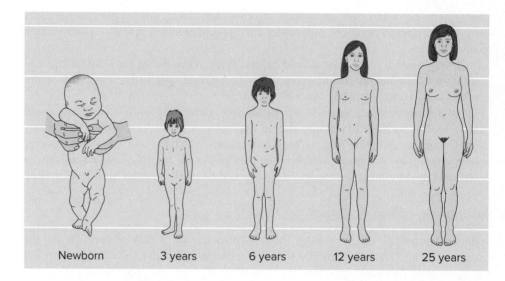

Newborn   3 years   6 years   12 years   25 years

changes dramatically as children age. As you can see in Figure 4, the head of a fetus (and a newborn) is disproportionately large. However, the head soon becomes more proportional in size to the rest of the body as growth occurs mainly in the trunk and legs (Adolph & Berger, 2011).

DEVELOPMENT OF SOCIAL BEHAVIOR: TAKING ON THE WORLD

As anyone who has seen infants smiling at the sight of their mothers can guess, at the same time that infants grow physically and hone their perceptual abilities, they also develop socially. The nature of a child's early social development provides the foundation for social relationships that will last a lifetime.

attachment The positive emotional bond that develops between a child and a particular individual. (Module 28)

Attachment, the positive emotional bond that develops between a child and a particular individual, is the most important form of social development that occurs during infancy. The earliest studies of attachment were carried out by animal ethologist Konrad Lorenz (1966). Lorenz focused on newborn goslings, which under normal circumstances instinctively follow their mother, the first moving object they perceive after birth. Lorenz found that goslings whose eggs were raised in an incubator and that viewed him immediately after hatching would follow his every movement as if he were their mother. He labeled this process *imprinting*, behavior that takes place during a critical period and involves attachment to the first moving object that is observed.

Our understanding of attachment progressed when psychologist Harry Harlow, in a classic study, gave infant monkeys the choice of cuddling a wire "monkey" that provided milk or a soft, terry cloth "monkey" that was warm but did not provide milk. Their choice was clear: They spent most of their time clinging to the warm cloth "monkey," although they made occasional forays to the wire monkey to nurse. Obviously, the cloth monkey provided greater comfort to the infants; milk alone was insufficient to create attachment (see Figure 5; Harlow & Zimmerman, 1959; Blum, 2002; Levine & Munsch, 2011).

FIGURE 5 Although the wire "mother" dispensed milk to the hungry infant monkey, the infant preferred the soft, terry cloth "mother." Do you think human babies would react the same way? What does this experiment tell us about attachment?

©Nina Leen/Time Life Pictures/Getty Images.

Building on this pioneering work, developmental psychologists have suggested that human attachment grows through the responsiveness of infants' caregivers to signals such as crying, smiling, reaching, and clinging. The more that caregivers respond to signals that children give off regarding their emotions, the more likely it is that the child will become securely attached to the caregiver. Full attachment eventually develops as a result of the complex series of interactions between caregiver and child. In the course of these interactions, the infant plays as critical and active of a role as the caregiver does in the formation of the bond between them. Infants who respond positively to a caregiver produce more positive behavior on the caregiver's part, which, in turn, produces an even stronger degree of attachment in the child.

Assessing Attachment Developmental psychologists have devised a quick and direct way to measure attachment. Developed by Mary Ainsworth, the *Ainsworth strange situation* consists of a sequence of events involving a child and (typically) his or her mother. Initially, the mother and baby enter an unfamiliar room, and the mother permits the baby to explore while she sits down. An adult stranger then enters the room; after this the mother leaves. The mother returns, and the stranger leaves. The mother once again leaves the baby alone, and the stranger returns. Finally, the stranger leaves, and the mother returns (Ainsworth et al., 1978; Van Rosmalen, Van Der Veer, & Van Der Horst, 2015; Posada & Trumbell, 2017).

Babies' reactions to the experimental situation vary drastically, depending, according to Ainsworth, on their degree of attachment to the mother:

Study Alert
Attachment—the positive emotional bond that develops between a child and a particular individual—is a key concept in understanding the social development of children.

- *Securely attached children.* Children who are securely attached employ the mother as a kind of home base; they explore independently but return to her occasionally. When she leaves, they exhibit distress, and they go to her when she returns.

- *Avoidant children.* Avoidant children do not cry when the mother leaves, and they seem to avoid her when she returns, as if they were indifferent to her.

- *Ambivalent children.* Ambivalent children display anxiety before they are separated and are upset when the mother leaves, but they may show ambivalent reactions to her return, such as seeking close contact but simultaneously hitting and kicking her.

- *Disorganized-disoriented children.* A fourth reaction is disorganized-disoriented; these children show inconsistent and often contradictory behavior. For example, they may approach their mother but at the same time avoid eye contact or otherwise act in an inappropriate way.

The nature of attachment between children and their mothers has far-reaching consequences for later development. For example, children who are securely attached to their mothers tend to be more socially and emotionally competent than are their less securely attached peers, and others find them more cooperative, capable, and playful. Furthermore, children who are securely attached at age 1 show fewer psychological difficulties when they grow older compared with avoidant and ambivalent youngsters. As adults, children who are securely attached tend to have more successful romantic relationships. On the other hand, being securely attached at an early age does not guarantee good adjustment later; conversely, children who lack secure attachment do not always have difficulties later in life (Hardy, 2007; Redshaw & Martin, 2013; Hennessy & Shair, 2017).

The Father's Role Although early developmental research focused largely on the mother-child relationship, more recent research has highlighted the father's role in parenting—and with good reason: The number of fathers who are primary caregivers for their children has grown significantly, and fathers play an increasingly important role in their children's lives. For example, in almost 13% of families with children, the father is the parent who stays at home to care for preschoolers (Day & Lamb, 2004; Halford, 2006; Kulik & Sadeh, 2015).

When fathers interact with their children, their play often differs from mothers' play. Fathers engage in more physical, rough-and-tumble sorts of activities, whereas mothers play more verbal and traditional games, such as peekaboo. Despite such behavioral differences, the nature of attachment between fathers and children compared with that between mothers and children can be similar. In fact, children can form multiple attachments simultaneously (Pellis & Pellis, 2007; Diener et al., 2008; Bureau et al., 2017).

Social Relationships with Peers By the time they are 2 years old, children become less dependent on their parents, more self-reliant, and increasingly prefer to play with friends. Initially, play is relatively independent: Even though they may be sitting side by side, 2-year-olds pay more attention to toys than to one another when playing. Later, however, children actively interact, modify one another's behavior, and exchange roles during play (Lindsey & Colwell, 2003; Colwell & Lindsey, 2005; Whitney & Green, 2011).

Cultural factors also affect children's styles of play. For example, Korean-American children engage in less pretend play than do their Anglo-American counterparts (Bai, 2005; Drewes, 2005; Suizzo & Bornstein, 2006).

As children reach school age, their social interactions become more frequent, and they begin to follow set patterns of behavior. For example, they may engage in elaborate games involving teams and rigid rules. In addition to providing enjoyment, such play allows children to become increasingly competent in their interactions with others. For instance, during play, they learn to take the perspective of other people. Children also learn to infer others' thoughts and feelings, even when those thoughts and feelings are not directly expressed (Royzman, Cassidy, & Baron, 2003; Yang et al., 2013).

In short, social interaction helps children interpret the meaning of others' behavior and develop the capacity to respond appropriately. Furthermore, children learn physical and emotional self-control: They learn to avoid hitting a playmate who beats them at a game. They learn to be polite and to control their emotional displays and facial expressions (e.g., smiling even when receiving a disappointing gift). Situations that provide children with opportunities for social interaction, then, may enhance their social development (Feldman, 1993; Talukdar & Shastri, 2006; Whitebread et al., 2009).

The Consequences of Child Care Outside the Home Research on the importance of social interaction is corroborated by work that examines the benefits of child care out of the home, which is an important part of an increasing number of children's lives. For instance, almost 30% of preschool children whose mothers work outside the home spend their days in child-care centers. By the age of 6 months, almost two-thirds of infants are cared for by people other than their mothers for part of the day. Most of these infants begin child care before the age of 4 months and are cared for by people other than their mothers almost 30 hours per week (see Figure 6; National Research Council, 2001; NICHD Early Child Care Research Network, 2006).

Do child-care arrangements outside the home benefit children's development? If the programs are of high quality, they can. According to the results of a large study supported by the U.S. National Institute of Child Health and Development, children who attend high-quality child-care centers may not only do as well as children who stay at home with their parents, but in some respects, they may actually do better. Children in child care are generally more considerate and sociable than other children, and they interact

FIGURE 6 According to a study by the National Institute of Child Health and Human Development, children were more likely to spend time in some kind of child care outside the home or family as they got older.

Source: Adapted from National Institute of Child Health and Human Development (NICHD) Early Child Care Research Network. (2006). Child-care effect sizes for the NICHD study of early child care and youth development. *American Psychologist, 61*, 99–116.

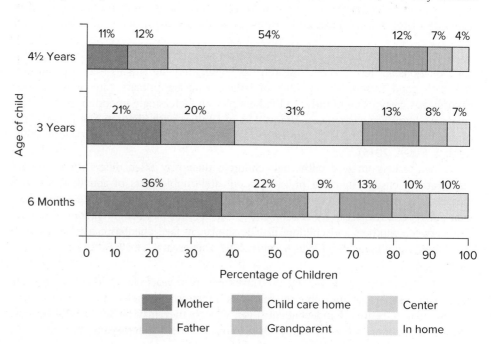

more positively with teachers. They may also be more compliant and regulate their own behavior more effectively (NICHD Early Child Care Research Network, 1999, 2001).

In addition, especially for children from poor or disadvantaged homes, child care in specially enriched environments–those with many toys, books, a variety of children, and high-quality providers–may be more intellectually stimulating than the home environment. Such child care can lead to increased intellectual achievement, demonstrated in higher IQ scores, and better language development. In fact, children in care centers sometimes are found to score higher on tests of cognitive abilities than are those who are cared for by their mothers or by sitters or home day-care providers–effects that last into adulthood (Burchinal, Roberts, & Riggins, 2000; Dearing, McCartney, & Taylor, 2009; Reid, Martin, & Brooks-Gunn, 2017).

However, child care outside the home does not have universally positive outcomes. Children may feel insecure after placement in low-quality child care or in multiple child-care settings. Furthermore, some research suggests that infants who are involved in outside care more than 20 hours a week in the first year show less secure attachment to their mothers than do those who have not been in child care outside the home. Finally, children who spent long hours in child care as infants and preschoolers may have a reduced ability to work independently and to manage their time effectively when they reach elementary school (NICHD Early Child Care Research Network, 2001; Vandell et al., 2005; Pluess & Belsky, 2009).

The key to the success of nonparental child care is its quality. High-quality child care produces benefits; low-quality child care provides little or no gain and may even hinder children's development. In short, significant benefits result from the social interaction and intellectual stimulation provided by high-quality child-care centers–especially for children from impoverished environments (NICHD Early Child Care Research Network, 2002; National Association for the Education of Young Children, 2005; Landry et al., 2013).

Parenting Styles and Social Development Parents' child-rearing practices are critical in shaping their children's social competence. According to classic research by developmental psychologist Diana Baumrind, four main categories describe different parenting styles (see Figure 7; Baumrind, 2005; Lagacé-Séguin & d'Entremont, 2006; Lewis & Lamb, 2011):

- **Authoritarian parents** are rigid and punitive, and they value unquestioning obedience from their children. They have strict standards and discourage expressions of disagreement.
- **Permissive parents** give their children relaxed or inconsistent direction and, although they are warm, require little of them.
- **Authoritative parents** are firm and set limits for their children. As the children get older, these parents try to reason and explain things to them. They also set clear goals and encourage their children's independence.
- **Uninvolved parents** show little interest in their children. Emotionally detached, they view parenting as nothing more than providing food, clothing, and shelter for children. At their most extreme, uninvolved parents are guilty of neglect, a form of child abuse.

As you might expect, the four kinds of child-rearing styles seem to produce very different kinds of behavior in children (with many exceptions, of course). Children of authoritarian parents tend to be unsociable, unfriendly, and relatively withdrawn. In contrast, permissive parents' children show immaturity, moodiness, dependence, and low self-control. The children of authoritative parents fare best: With high social skills, they are likable, self-reliant, independent, and cooperative. Worst off are the children of uninvolved parents; they feel unloved and emotionally detached, and their physical development and cognitive development are impeded (Berk, 2005; Snyder, Cramer, & Afrank, 2005; Llorca-Mestre et al., 2017).

Before we rush to congratulate authoritative parents and condemn authoritarian, permissive, and uninvolved ones, it is important to note that in many cases, nonauthoritative

Study Alert

Know the four major types of child-rearing practices—authoritarian, permissive, authoritative, and uninvolved—and their effects.

authoritarian parents Parents who are rigid and punitive and value unquestioning obedience from their children. (Module 28)

permissive parents Parents who give their children relaxed or inconsistent direction and, although they are warm, require little of them. (Module 28)

authoritative parents Parents who are firm, set clear limits, reason with their children, and explain things to them. (Module 28)

uninvolved parents Parents who show little interest in their children and are emotionally detached. (Module 28)

Parenting Style	Parent Behavior	Type of Behavior Produced in Child
Authoritarian	Rigid, punitive, strict standards (example: "If you don't clean your room, I'm going to take away your iPhone for good and ground you.")	Unsociable, unfriendly, withdrawn
Permissive	Lax, inconsistent, undemanding (example: "It might be good to clean your room, but I guess it can wait.")	Immature, moody, dependent, low self-control
Authoritative	Firm, sets limits and goals, uses reasoning, encourages independence (example: "You'll need to clean your room before we can go out to the restaurant. As soon as you finish, we'll leave.")	Good social skills, likable, self-reliant, independent
Uninvolved	Detached emotionally, sees role only as providing food, clothing, and shelter (example: "I couldn't care less if your room is a pigsty.")	Indifferent, rejecting behavior

FIGURE 7 According to developmental psychologist Diana Baumrind (1971), four main parenting styles characterize child rearing.
©Gary John Norman/Getty Images

temperament A basic, inborn characteristic way of responding and behavioral style. (Module 37)

parents also produce perfectly well-adjusted children. Moreover, children are born with a particular **temperament**–a basic, inborn characteristic way of responding and behavioral style. Some children are naturally easygoing and cheerful, whereas others are irritable and fussy or pensive and quiet. The kind of temperament a baby is born with may in part bring about specific kinds of parental child-rearing styles (Miner & Clarke-Stewart, 2008; Coplan, Reichel, & Rowan, 2009; Costa & Figueiredo, 2011).

In addition, children vary considerably in their degree of *resilience*, the ability to overcome circumstances that place them at high risk for psychological or even physical harm. Highly resilient children have temperaments that evoke positive responses from caregivers. Such children display unusual social skills: outgoingness, intelligence, and a feeling that they have control over their lives. In a sense, resilient children try to shape their own environment rather than being victimized by it (Deater-Deckard, Ivy, & Smith, 2005; Vellacott, 2007; Naglieri, LeBuffe, & Ross, 2013).

We also need to keep in mind that these findings regarding child-rearing styles apply primarily to U.S. society, which highly values children's growing independence and diminishing reliance on their parents. In contrast, Japanese parents encourage dependence to promote the values of cooperation and community life. These differences in cultural values result in very different philosophies of child rearing. For example, Japanese mothers believe it is a punishment to make a young child sleep alone; thus, many children sleep next to their mothers throughout infancy and toddlerhood (Jones, 2007; Pinquart & Kauser, 2017).

In sum, a child's upbringing results from the child-rearing philosophy parents hold, the specific practices they use, and the nature of their own and their child's personalities. As is the case with other aspects of development, then, behavior is a function of a complex interaction of environmental and genetic factors.

Erikson's Theory of Psychosocial Development In tracing the course of social development, some theorists have considered how the challenges of society and culture change as an individual matures. Following this path, psychoanalyst Erik Erikson developed one of the more comprehensive theories of social development. Erikson (1963) viewed the developmental changes that occur throughout life as a series of eight stages of psychosocial development; of these, four occur during childhood. **Psychosocial development** involves changes in our interactions and understanding of one another as well as in our knowledge and understanding of ourselves as members of society.

Erikson suggests that passage through each of the stages necessitates the resolution of a crisis or conflict. Accordingly, Erikson represents each stage as a pairing of the most positive and most negative aspects of the crisis of that period. Although each crisis is never resolved entirely–life becomes increasingly complicated as we grow older–it has to be resolved sufficiently to equip us to deal with demands made during the following stage of development.

The first stage of psychosocial development is the **trust-versus-mistrust stage** (ages birth to 1½ years). During this period, infants develop feelings of trust or mistrust, primarily depending on how well their caregivers meet their needs. If their physical requirements and psychological needs for attachment are consistently met and their interactions with the world are generally positive, they will develop a sense of trust. In contrast, inconsistent care and unpleasant interactions with others can lead to mistrust and a view of the world as a harsh and unfriendly place.

In the second stage, the **autonomy-versus-shame-and-doubt stage** (ages 1½ to 3 years), toddlers develop independence and autonomy if exploration and freedom are encouraged, or they experience shame, self-doubt, and unhappiness if they are overly restricted and protected. According to Erikson, the key to the development of a sense of independence during this period is for the child's caregivers to provide a reasonable amount of control. If parents are overly controlling, children cannot assert themselves and develop their own sense of control over their world; if parents provide too little control, children can become demanding and dictatorial.

Next, children face the crises of the **initiative-versus-guilt stage** (ages 3 to 6). In this stage, children's desire to act independently conflicts with the guilt that comes from the unintended and unexpected consequences of such behavior. Children in this period come to understand that they are persons in their own right, and they begin to make decisions about their behavior. If parents react positively to children's attempts at independence, their children will develop skills in accomplishing tasks and overcoming challenges.

The fourth and last stage of childhood is the **industry-versus-inferiority stage** (ages 6 to 12). During this period, increasing competency in all areas, whether social interactions or academic skills, characterizes successful psychosocial development. In contrast, difficulties in this stage lead to feelings of failure and inadequacy.

Erikson's theory suggests that psychosocial development continues throughout life, and he proposes four more crises that are faced after childhood (described in module 29). Although his theory has been criticized on several grounds–such as the imprecision of the concepts he employs and his greater emphasis on male development than female development–it remains influential and is one of the few theories that encompass the entire life span.

COGNITIVE DEVELOPMENT: CHILDREN'S THINKING ABOUT THE WORLD

Suppose you had two drinking glasses of different shapes–one short and broad and one tall and thin. Now imagine that you filled the short, broad one with soda about halfway and then poured the liquid from that glass into the tall one. The soda would appear to fill about three-quarters of the second glass. If someone asked you whether there was more soda in the second glass than there had been in the first, what would you say?

You might think that such a simple question hardly deserves an answer; of course, there is no difference in the amount of soda in the two glasses. However, most 4-year-olds would be likely to say that there is more soda in the second glass. If you then poured the soda back into the short glass, they would say there is now less soda than there was in the taller glass.

Why are young children confused by this problem? The reason is not immediately obvious. Anyone who has observed preschoolers must be impressed by how far they

psychosocial development Development of individuals' interactions and understanding of each other and of their knowledge and understanding of themselves as members of society. (Module 28)

trust-versus-mistrust stage According to Erikson, the first stage of psychosocial development, occurring from birth to age 1½ years, during which time infants develop feelings of trust or lack of trust. (Module 28)

autonomy-versus-shame-and-doubt stage The period during which, according to Erikson, toddlers (ages 1½ to 3 years) develop independence and autonomy if exploration and freedom are encouraged or shame and self-doubt if they are restricted and overprotected. (Module 28)

initiative-versus-guilt stage According to Erikson, the period during which children ages 3 to 6 years experience conflict between independence of action and the sometimes negative results of that action. (Module 28)

industry-versus-inferiority stage According to Erikson, the last stage of childhood, during which children age 6 to 12 years may develop positive social interactions with others or may feel inadequate and become less sociable. (Module 28)

Study Alert

Four of Erikson's stages of psychosocial development occur during childhood: trust-versus-mistrust, autonomy-versus-shame-and-doubt, initiative-versus-guilt, and industry-versus-inferiority.

have progressed from the early stages of development. They speak with ease, know the alphabet, count, play complex games, use computers, tell stories, and communicate ably. Yet despite this seeming sophistication, there are deep gaps in children's understanding of the world. The gaps in children's understanding relate to their level of cognitive development. **Cognitive development** is the process by which children's understanding of the world changes due to their age and experience. In contrast to the theories of physical and social development discussed earlier (such as those of Erikson), theories of cognitive development seek to explain the quantitative and qualitative intellectual advances that occur during development.

cognitive development The process by which a child's understanding of the world changes due to the child's age and experience. (Module 28)

Piaget's Theory of Cognitive Development No theory of cognitive development has had more impact than that of Swiss psychologist Jean Piaget. Piaget (1970) suggested that children around the world proceed through a series of four stages in a fixed order. He maintained that these stages differ not only in the *quantity* of information acquired at each stage but in the *quality* of knowledge and understanding as well. Taking an interactionist point of view, he suggested that movement from one stage to the next occurs when a child reaches an appropriate level of maturation *and* is exposed to relevant types of experiences. Piaget assumed that, without having such experiences, children cannot reach their highest level of cognitive growth.

Piaget proposed four stages: the sensorimotor, preoperational, concrete operational, and formal operational (see Figure 8). Let's examine each of them and the approximate ages that they span.

Sensorimotor Stage: Birth to 2 Years. During the **sensorimotor stage,** children base their understanding of the world primarily on touching, sucking, chewing, shaking, and manipulating objects. In the initial part of the stage, children have relatively little competence in representing the environment by using images, language, or other kinds of symbols. Consequently, infants lack what Piaget calls **object permanence,** the awareness that objects–and people–continue to exist even if they are out of sight.

Study Alert

Use Figure 8 to help remember Piaget's stages of cognitive development.

sensorimotor stage According to Piaget, the stage from birth to 2 years, during which a child has little competence in representing the environment by using images, language, or other symbols. (Module 28)

object permanence The awareness that objects–and people–continue to exist even if they are out of sight. (Module 28)

preoperational stage According to Piaget, the period from 2 to 7 years of age that is characterized by language development. (Module 28)

How can we know that children lack object permanence? Although we cannot ask infants, we can observe their reactions when a toy they are playing with is hidden under a blanket. Until the age of about 9 months, children will make no attempt to locate the hidden toy. However, soon after that age, they will begin an active search for the missing object, indicating that they have developed a mental representation of the toy. Object permanence, then, is a critical development during the sensorimotor stage.

Preoperational Stage: 2 to 7 Years. During the **preoperational stage,** children develop the use of language. The internal representational systems they develop allow them to describe people, events, and feelings. They even use symbols in play, pretending, for example, that a book pushed across the floor is a car.

Cognitive Stage	Approximate Age Range	Major Characteristics
Sensorimotor	Birth–2 years	Development of object permanence, development of motor skills, little or no capacity for symbolic representation
Preoperational	2–7 years	Development of language and symbolic thinking, egocentric thinking
Concrete operational	7–12 years	Development of conservation, mastery of the concept of reversibility
Formal operational	12 years–adulthood	Development of logical and abstract thinking

FIGURE 8 According to Piaget, all children pass through four stages of cognitive development.
©Farrell Grehan/Corbis via Getty Images

Although children use more advanced thinking in this stage than they did in the earlier sensorimotor stage, their thinking is still qualitatively inferior to that of adults. We see this when we observe a preoperational child using **egocentric thought,** a way of thinking in which the child views the world entirely from his or her own perspective. Preoperational children think that everyone shares their perspective and knowledge. Thus, children's stories and explanations to adults can be maddeningly uninformative because they are delivered without any context. For example, a preoperational child may start a story with, "He wouldn't let me go," neglecting to mention who "he" is or where the storyteller wanted to go. We also see egocentric thinking when children at the preoperational stage play hiding games. For instance, 3-year-olds frequently hide with their faces against a wall and covering their eyes–although they are still in plain view. It seems to them that if *they* cannot see, then no one else will be able to see them because they assume that others share their view.

In addition, preoperational children have not yet developed the ability to comprehend the **principle of conservation,** which is the understanding that quantity is unrelated to the arrangement and physical appearance of objects. Children who can use the principle of conservation have awareness that important attributes of objects (such as amount or volume) do not change despite superficial changes. In contrast, children who have not mastered conservation do not understand that the overall amount or volume of an object does not change when its shape or configuration changes.

The question about the two glasses–one short and broad, and the other tall and thin–with which we began our discussion of cognitive development illustrates this point clearly. Children who do not understand the principle of conservation believe that the amount of liquid changes as it is poured back and forth between glasses of different sizes. They simply are unable to comprehend that a change in appearance does not mean there is a change in amount. Instead, they truly believe that quantity changes as appearance changes (see Figure 9).

Concrete Operational Stage: 7 to 12 Years. Mastery of the principle of conservation marks the beginning of the **concrete operational stage.** However, children do not fully understand some aspects of conservation–such as conservation of weight and volume–for a number of years.

During the concrete operational stage, children develop the ability to think in a more logical manner and begin to overcome some of the egocentrism characteristic of the preoperational period. One of the major principles children learn during this stage is reversibility, the idea that some changes can be undone by reversing an earlier action. For example, they can understand that when someone rolls a ball of clay into a long sausage shape, that person can recreate the original ball by reversing the action. Children can even conceptualize this principle in their heads without having to see the action performed before them.

Although children make important advances in their logical capabilities during the concrete operational stage, their thinking still displays one major limitation: They are largely bound to the concrete, physical reality of the world. For the most part, they have difficulty understanding questions of an abstract or hypothetical nature.

Formal Operational Stage: 12 Years to Adulthood. The **formal operational stage** produces a new kind of thinking that is abstract, formal, and logical. Thinking is no longer tied to events that individuals observe in the environment but makes use of logical techniques to resolve problems.

The way in which children approach the "pendulum problem" devised by Piaget (Piaget & Inhelder, 1958) illustrates the emergence of formal operational thinking. The problem solver is asked to figure out what determines how fast a pendulum swings. Is it the length of the string, the weight of the pendulum, or the force with which the pendulum is pushed? (For the record, the answer is the length of the string.)

Children in the concrete operational stage approach the problem haphazardly without a logical or rational plan of action. For example, they may simultaneously change the length of the string, the weight on the string, and the force with which they push the pendulum. Because they are varying all the factors at once, they cannot

egocentric thought A way of thinking in which a child views the world entirely from his or her own perspective. (Module 28)

Children who have not mastered the principle of conservation assume that the volume of liquid increases when it is poured from a short, wide container to a tall, thin one. What other tasks might a child under age 7 have difficulty comprehending?
©Tony Freeman/PhotoEdit

principle of conservation The knowledge that quantity is unrelated to the arrangement and physical appearance of objects. (Module 28)

concrete operational stage According to Piaget, the period from 7 to 12 years of age that is characterized by logical thought and a loss of egocentrism. (Module 28)

formal operational stage According to Piaget, the period from age 12 to adulthood that is characterized by abstract thought. (Module 28)

FIGURE 9 These tests are frequently used to assess whether children have learned the principle of conservation across a variety of dimensions. Do you think children in the preoperational stage can be taught to avoid conservation mistakes before the typical age of mastery?

Source: Adapted from Schickedanz, J. A., Schickedanz, D. I., Forsyth, P. D., & Forsyth, G. A. (2001). *Understanding Children and Adolescents* (4th ed.). Upper Saddle River, NJ: Pearson Education.

Conservation of ...	Modality	Change in physical appearance	Average age at full mastery
Number	Number of elements in a collection	Rearranging or dislocating elements	6–7 years
Substance (mass)	Amount of a malleable substance (e.g., clay or liquid)	Altering shape	7–8 years
Length	Length of a line or object	Altering shape or configuration	7–8 years
Area	Amount of surface covered by a set of plane figures	Rearranging the figures	8–9 years
Weight	Weight of an object	Altering shape	9–10 years
Volume	Volume of an object (in terms of water displacement)	Altering shape	14–15 years

tell which factor is the critical one. In contrast, people in the formal operational stage approach the problem systematically. Acting as if they were scientists conducting an experiment, they examine the effects of changes in one variable at a time. This ability to rule out competing possibilities characterizes formal operational thought.

Although formal operational thought emerges during the teenage years, some individuals use this type of thinking only infrequently. Moreover, it appears that many individuals never reach this stage at all; most studies show that only 40-60% of college students and adults fully reach it, with some estimates running as low as 25% of the general population. In addition, in certain cultures–particularly those that are less technically oriented than Western societies–almost no one reaches the formal operational stage (Keating & Clark, 1980; Super, 1980; Genovese, 2006).

Evaluating Piaget's Theory. No other theorist has given us as comprehensive a theory of cognitive development as Piaget has. Still, many contemporary theorists suggest that a better explanation of how children develop cognitively can be provided by theories that do not involve a stage approach. For instance, children are not always consistent in their performance of tasks that–if Piaget's theory is accurate–ought to be performed equally well at a particular stage (Feldman, 2003, 2004).

Furthermore, some developmental psychologists suggest that cognitive development proceeds in a more continuous fashion than Piaget's stage theory implies. They propose that cognitive development is primarily quantitative rather than qualitative. They argue that although there are differences in when, how, and to what extent a child can use specific cognitive abilities–reflecting quantitative changes–the underlying cognitive processes change relatively little with age (Gelman & Baillargeon, 1983; Case & Okamoto, 1996).

Piaget also underestimated the age at which infants and children can understand specific concepts and principles; in fact, they seem to be more sophisticated in their cognitive abilities than Piaget believed. For instance, some evidence suggests that infants as young as 5 months have rudimentary mathematical skills (Wynn, Bloom, & Chiang, 2002; McCrink & Wynn, 2007; van Marle & Wynn, 2009).

Despite such criticisms, most developmental psychologists agree that although the processes that underlie changes in cognitive abilities may not unfold in the manner Piaget's theory suggests, he has generally provided us with an accurate account of age-related changes in cognitive development. Moreover, his theory has had an enormous influence in education. For example, Piaget suggests that individuals cannot increase their cognitive performance unless both cognitive readiness brought about by maturation and appropriate environmental stimulation are present. This view has inspired the nature and structure of educational curricula and teaching methods. Researchers have also used Piaget's theory and methods to investigate issues surrounding animal cognition, such as whether primates show object permanence (they seem to) (Egan, 2005; Cunningham, 2006; Jablonka, 2017).

Information-Processing Approaches: Charting Children's Mental Programs If cognitive development does not proceed as a series of stages as Piaget suggested, what does underlie the enormous growth in children's cognitive abilities that even the most untutored eye can observe? To many developmental psychologists, changes in information-processing capabilities account for cognitive development. **Information processing** refers to the way in which people take in, use, and store information (Casasola, 2011; Lillard & Woolley, 2015).

According to the information-processing approach, quantitative changes occur in children's ability to organize and manipulate information. From this perspective, children become increasingly adept at information processing, much as a computer program may become more sophisticated as a programmer modifies it on the basis of experience. Information-processing approaches consider the kinds of "mental programs" that children invoke when approaching problems.

Several significant changes occur in children's information-processing capabilities. For one thing, speed of processing increases with age as some abilities become more automatic. The speed at which children can scan, recognize, and compare stimuli increases with age. As they grow older, children can pay attention to stimuli longer and discriminate between different stimuli more readily, and they are less easily distracted (Van den Wildenberg & Van der Molen, 2004; Diaz & Bell, 2011).

Memory also improves dramatically with age. Preschoolers can hold only two or three chunks of information in short-term memory, 5-year-olds can hold four, and 7-year-olds can hold five. (Adults are able to keep seven, plus or minus two, chunks in short-term memory.) The size of the chunks also grows with age, as does the sophistication and organization of knowledge stored in memory (see Figure 10). Still, memory capabilities are impressive at a very early age: Even before they can speak, infants can remember for months events in which they actively participated (Bayliss et al., 2005; Ślusarczyk & Niedźwieńska, 2013).

Finally, improvement in information processing relates to advances in **metacognition,** an awareness and understanding of one's own cognitive processes. Metacognition involves the planning, monitoring, and revising of cognitive strategies. Younger children, who lack an awareness of their own cognitive processes, often do not realize their incapabilities. Thus, when they misunderstand

information processing The way in which people take in, use, and store information. (Module 28)

metacognition An awareness and understanding of one's own cognitive processes. (Module 28)

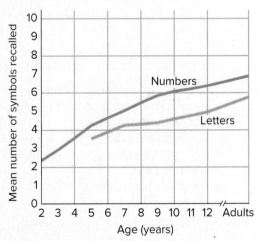

FIGURE 10 Memory span increases with age for both numbers and letters.

Source: Adapted from Dempster, F. N. (1981). Memory span: Sources for individual and developmental differences. *Psychological Bulletin, 89,* 63–100.

others, they may fail to recognize their own errors. It is only later, when metacognitive abilities become more sophisticated, that children are able to know when they *don't* understand. Such increasing sophistication reflects a change in children's *theory of mind*, their knowledge and beliefs about the way the mind operates (Lockl & Schneider, 2007; Sodian, 2011; O'Leary & Sloutsky, 2017).

PsychTech

A quarter of parents with children between the ages of 0 to 5 report that their children use the Internet.

zone of proximal development (ZPD) According to Vygotsky, the gap between what children already are able to accomplish on their own and what they are not quite ready to do by themselves. (Module 28)

Vygotsky's View of Cognitive Development: Considering Culture According to Russian developmental psychologist Lev Vygotsky, the culture in which we are raised significantly affects our cognitive development. In an increasingly influential view, Vygotsky suggests that the focus on individual performance of both Piagetian and information-processing approaches is misplaced. Instead, he holds that we cannot understand cognitive development without taking into account the social and cultural vaspects of learning (Vygotsky, 1926/1997; Maynard & Martini, 2005; Rieber & Robinson, 2006).

Vygotsky argues that cognitive development occurs as a consequence of social interactions in which children work with others to jointly solve problems. Through such interactions, children's cognitive skills increase, and they gain the ability to function intellectually on their own. More specifically, he suggests that children's cognitive abilities increase when they encounter information that falls within their zone of proximal development. The **zone of proximal development (ZPD)** is the gap between what children already are able to accomplish on their own and what they are not quite ready to do by themselves. When children receive information that falls within the ZPD, they can increase their understanding or master a new task. In contrast, if the information lies outside children's ZPD, they will not be able to master it.

In short, cognitive development occurs when parents, teachers, or skilled peers assist a child by presenting new information that resides within the child's ZPD, a process Vygotsky calls scaffolding. *Scaffolding* is support for learning and problem solving that encourages independence and growth. Vygotsky claims that scaffolding not only helps children to solve specific problems but also aids in the development of overall cognitive abilities (Schaller & Crandall, 2004; Coulson & Harvey, 2013).

More than other approaches to cognitive development, Vygotsky's theory considers how an individual's cultural and social background affects intellectual growth. The way in which children understand the world grows out of interactions with parents, peers, and other members of their own, specific culture (John-Steiner & Mahn, 2003; Kozulin et al., 2003).

RECAP/EVALUATE/RETHINK

RECAP

LO 28-1 What are the major competencies of newborns?

- Newborns, or neonates, have reflexes—unlearned, involuntary responses that occur automatically in the presence of certain stimuli.
- Sensory abilities also develop rapidly; infants can distinguish color, depth, sound, tastes, and smells relatively soon after birth.
- After birth, physical development is rapid; children typically triple their birthweight in a year.

LO 28-2 What are the milestones of physical and social development during childhood?

- Attachment—the positive emotional bond between a child and a particular individual—marks social development in infancy. Measured in the laboratory by means of the Ainsworth strange situation, attachment relates to later social and emotional adjustment.
- As children become older, the nature of their social interactions with peers changes. Initially play occurs relatively independently, but it becomes increasingly cooperative.
- The different child-rearing styles include authoritarian, permissive, authoritative, and uninvolved.
- According to Erikson, eight stages of psychosocial development involve people's changing interactions and understanding of themselves and others. During childhood, the four stages are trust-versus-mistrust (birth to 1½ years), autonomy-versus-shame-and-doubt (1½ to 3 years), initiative-versus-guilt (3 to 6 years), and industry-versus-inferiority (6 to 12 years).

LO 28-3 How does cognitive development proceed during childhood?

- Piaget's theory suggests that cognitive development proceeds through four stages in which qualitative changes occur in thinking: the sensorimotor stage (birth to 2 years), the preoperational stage (2 to 7 years), the concrete operational stage (7 to 12 years), and the formal operational stage (12 years to adulthood).
- Information-processing approaches suggest that quantitative changes occur in children's ability to organize and manipulate information about the world, such as significant increases in speed of processing, attention span, and memory. In addition, children advance in metacognition, the awareness and understanding of one's own cognitive processes.
- Vygotsky argued that children's cognitive development occurs as a consequence of social interactions in which children and others work together to solve problems.

EVALUATE

1. Researchers studying newborns use _____, or the decrease in the response to a stimulus that occurs after repeated presentations of the same stimulus, as an indicator of a baby's interest.
2. The emotional bond that develops between a child and its caregiver is known as _____.
3. Match the parenting style with its definition:

1. Permissive
2. Authoritative
3. Authoritarian
4. Uninvolved

a. Rigid; highly punitive; demanding obedience
b. Gives little direction; lax on obedience
c. Firm but fair; tries to explain parental decisions
d. Emotionally detached and unloving

4. Erikson's theory of _____ development involves a series of eight stages, each of which must be resolved for a person to develop optimally.
5. Match the stage of development with the thinking style characteristic of that stage:

1. Egocentric thought
2. Object permanence
3. Abstract reasoning
4. Conservation

a. Sensorimotor
b. Formal operational
c. Preoperational
d. Concrete operational

6. _____-_____ theories of development suggest that the way in which a child handles information is critical to his or her development.
7. According to Vygotsky, information that is within a child's _____ _____ _____ _____ is most likely to result in cognitive development.

RETHINK

1. Do you think the widespread use of IQ testing in the United States contributes to parents' views that their children's academic success is due largely to the children's innate intelligence? Why? Would it be possible (or desirable) to change this view?
2. In what ways might the infant's major reflexes–the rooting, sucking, gagging, and Babinski reflexes–have had survival value, from an evolutionary perspective? Does the infant's ability to mimic the facial expressions of adults have a similar value?

Answers to Evaluate Questions

1. habituation; 2. attachment; 3. 1-b, 2-c, 3-a, 4-d; 4. psychosocial; 5. 1-c, 2-a, 3-b, 4-d; 6. Information-processing; 7. zone of proximal development

KEY TERMS

neonate	uninvolved parents	industry-versus-inferiority stage	principle of conservation
reflexes	temperament	cognitive development	concrete operational stage
habituation	psychosocial development	sensorimotor stage	formal operational stage
attachment	trust-versus-mistrust stage	object permanence	information processing
authoritarian parents	autonomy-versus-shame-and-doubt stage	preoperational stage	metacognition
permissive parents	initiative-versus-guilt stage	egocentric thought	zone of proximal development (ZPD)
authoritative parents			

Module 29
Adolescence: Becoming an Adult

LEARNING OUTCOME

LO 29-1 What major physical, social, and cognitive transitions characterize adolescence?

adolescence The developmental stage between childhood and adulthood. (Module 29)

Joseph Charles, Age 13: "Being 13 is very hard at school. I have to be bad in order to be considered cool. I sometimes do things that aren't good. I have talked back to my teachers and been disrespectful to them. I do want to be good, but it's just too hard." (Gibbs, 2005, p. 51)

Marco Colson, Age 15: "Stay Out" says the sign on Marco's door. Inside, the floor is cluttered with dirty clothes, candy wrappers, and other debris. What color is the carpet on the floor? "I don't think I remember," says Marco with a smile.

Alissa Cruz, Age 17: "I was invited to join the National Honor Society because of my grades. But at the induction, the parents just stared at me. It was like they couldn't believe that someone with a nose stud and pink streaks in her hair could be smart enough to be in the National Honor Society. I'm hoping to be a teacher in the public schools, but do you think they'd hire someone who looks like me?"

Although Joseph, Marco, and Alissa have never met, they share anxieties that are common to adolescence—concerns about friends, parents, appearance, independence, and their futures.

Adolescence, the developmental stage between childhood and adulthood, is a crucial period. It is a time of profound changes and, occasionally, turmoil. Considerable biological change occurs as adolescents attain sexual and physical maturity. At the same time and rivaling these physiological changes, important social, emotional, and cognitive changes occur as adolescents strive for independence and move toward adulthood.

Because many years of schooling precede most people's entry into the workforce in Western societies, the stage of adolescence is fairly long; it begins just before the teenage years and ends just after them. Adolescents are no longer children, yet society doesn't quite consider them adults. They face a period of rapid physical, cognitive, and social change that affects them for the rest of their lives.

Dramatic changes in society also affect adolescents' development. More than half of all children in the United States will spend all or some of their childhood and adolescence in single-parent families. Furthermore, adolescents spend considerably less time with their parents and more with their peers than they did several decades ago. Finally, the ethnic and cultural diversity of adolescents as a group is increasing dramatically. A third of all adolescents today are of non-European descent; by the year 2050, the number of adolescents of Hispanic, African American, Native American, and Asian origin collectively will surpass that of whites (National Adolescent Health Information Center, 2003).

Physical Development: The Changing Adolescent

If you think back to the start of your own adolescence, the most dramatic changes you probably remember are physical. A spurt in height, the growth of breasts in girls, deepening voices in boys, the development of body hair, and intense sexual feelings cause curiosity, interest, and sometimes embarrassment for individuals entering adolescence.

Not since infancy has development been so dramatic. Beginning around age 10 for girls and age 12 for boys, a growth spurt leads to rapid increases in weight and height. Adolescents may grow as much as 5 inches in 1 year. The physical changes that occur at the start of adolescence result largely from a surge in levels of growth hormone, and they affect virtually every aspect of an adolescent's life.

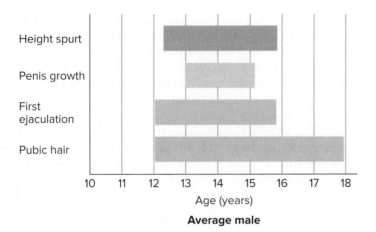

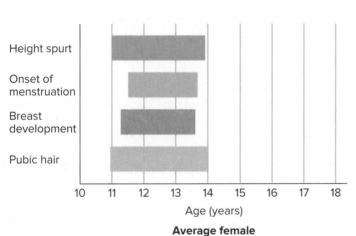

FIGURE 1 The range of ages during which major sexual changes occur during adolescence is shown by the colored bars.

Source: Adapted from Tanner, J. M. (1978). *Education and physical growth* (2nd ed.). New York: International Universities Press.

Puberty is the period at which maturation of the sexual organs occurs. Over the past century in Western cultures, the average age at which adolescents reach sexual maturity has steadily decreased, most likely as a result of improved nutrition and medical care.

For girls, puberty typically begins at about age 11 or 12 for girls, when menstruation starts. However, there are wide variations (see Figure 1). For example, some girls begin to menstruate as early as age 8 or 9 or as late as age 16. Furthermore, sexual attraction to others begins even before the maturation of the sexual organs at around age 10 (see Figure 1; Tanner, 1990; Shanahan et al., 2013; Herting & Sowell, 2017).

For boys, their first ejaculation, formally known as *spermarche*, typically happens at the beginning of puberty. Spermarche usually occurs around the age of 13 (see Figure 1). At first, relatively few sperm are produced during an ejaculation, but the amount increases significantly within a few years.

The age at which puberty begins has significant implications for the way adolescents feel about themselves—as well as the way others treat them. Preadolescents who start puberty considerably earlier than their peers may feel isolated and different, and they are at risk for mental health issues (Mendle et al., 2016; Weir, 2016; Park, Yun, & Walsh, 2017).

In some cases, early maturation is favorable for boys. For example, early-maturing boys do better in athletics, are generally more popular with peers, and have more positive self-concepts. However, the picture differs for girls. Although early-maturing girls are more sought after as dates and have better self-esteem than later-maturing girls do, some consequences of early physical maturation may be less positive. For example, early breast

puberty The period at which maturation of the sexual organs occurs, beginning at about age 11 or 12 for girls and 13 or 14 for boys. (Module 29)

Although puberty begins around 11 or 12 for girls and 13 or 14 for boys, there are wide variations. What are some of the advantages and disadvantages of early puberty?

©Purestock/SuperStock

development may set them apart from their peers and be a source of ridicule (Blumenthal et al., 2011; Mensah et al., 2013; Natsuaki, Samuels, & Leve, 2015).

Late physical maturation may produce certain psychological difficulties for both boys and girls. Boys who are smaller and less coordinated than their more mature peers tend to feel ridiculed and less attractive. Similarly, late-maturing girls are at a disadvantage in middle school and early high school. They hold relatively low social status and may be overlooked in dating (Lanza & Collins, 2002).

Clearly, the rate at which physical changes occur during adolescence can affect the way in which people are viewed by others and the way they view themselves. Just as important as physical changes, however, are the psychological and social changes that unfold during adolescence.

Moral and Cognitive Development: Distinguishing Right from Wrong

In a European country, a woman is near death from a special kind of cancer. The one drug that the doctors think might save her is a medicine that a medical researcher has recently discovered. The drug is expensive to make, and the researcher is charging 10 times the cost, or $5,000, for a small dose. The sick woman's husband, Henry, approaches everyone he knows in hope of borrowing money, but he can get together only about $2,500. He tells the researcher that his wife is dying and asks him to lower the price of the drug or let him pay later. The researcher says, "No, I discovered the drug, and I'm going to make money from it." Henry is desperate and considers stealing the drug for his wife.

What would you tell Henry to do?

KOHLBERG'S THEORY OF MORAL DEVELOPMENT

In the view of psychologist Lawrence Kohlberg, the advice you give Henry reflects your level of moral development. According to Kohlberg, people pass through a series of levels in the evolution of their sense of justice and in the kind of reasoning they use to make moral judgments (Kohlberg, 1984).

Specifically, Kohlberg suggests that changes in moral reasoning can be understood best as the three-level sequence described in Figure 2. Because of their cognitive limitations, preadolescent children who reason at Level 1 morality tend to think in terms of concrete, unvarying rules ("It is always wrong to steal" or "I'll be punished if I steal"). At Level 2 morality, older children tend to focus on the broad rules of society ("Good people don't steal" or "What if everyone stole?"). Those at Level 2 consider moral questions in terms of their own position as good and responsible members of society.

Adolescents, however, can reason on a higher plane and potentially have the ability to reason at Level 3. At Level 3, adolescents consider moral issues in terms of principles that are broader than the rules of individual societies. Because they can comprehend broad, universal moral principles, they understand that morality is not always black and white and that conflict can exist between two sets of socially accepted standards.

Kohlberg's theory assumes that people move through the levels in a fixed order and that they cannot reach the highest level until about age 13–primarily because of limitations in cognitive development before that age. However, many people never reach the highest level of moral reasoning. In fact, Kohlberg found that only a relatively small percentage of adults rise above the second level of his model (Kohlberg & Ryncarz, 1990; Moshman, 2011; Vera-Estay, Dooley, & Beauchamp, 2015).

Although Kohlberg's theory has had a substantial influence on our understanding of moral development, the research support is mixed. One difficulty with the theory

| | Sample Moral Reasoning | |
Level	In Favor of Stealing the Drug	Against Stealing the Drug
Level 1 Preconventional morality: The main considerations at this level are the avoidance of punishment and the desire for rewards.	"You shouldn't just let your wife die. People will blame you for not doing enough, and they'll blame the scientist for not selling you the drug for less money."	"You can't steal the drug because you'll be arrested and go to jail. Even if you aren't caught, you'll feel guilty, and you'll always worry that the police may figure out what you did."
Level 2 Conventional morality: Membership in society becomes important at this level. People behave in ways that will win the approval of others.	"Who will blame you if you steal a life-saving drug? But if you just let your wife die, you won't be able to hold your head up in front of your family or neighbors."	"If you steal the drug, everyone will treat you like a criminal. They will wonder why you couldn't have found some other way to save your wife."
Level 3 Postconventional morality: People accept that there are certain broad principles of morality that should govern our actions. These principles are more critical than the particular laws in a society.	"If you simply follow the law, you will violate the underlying principle of saving your wife's life. If you do steal the drug, society will understand your actions and respect them. You can't let an inadequate, outdated law prevent you from doing the right thing."	"You can't change your standards of honesty whenever it suits your needs. Others may not blame you for stealing the drug, but your conscience will blame you for betraying your own moral code."

FIGURE 2 Developmental psychologist Lawrence Kohlberg theorized that people move through a three-level sequence of moral reasoning in a fixed order. However, he contended that few people ever reach the highest level of moral reasoning.

Sources: Adapted from Kohlberg, L. (1969). Stage and sequence: The cognitive-developmental approach to socialization. In D. Goslin (Ed.), *Handbook of Socialization Theory and Research* (pp. 381–382). Chicago: Rand McNally; (Photo) ©Steven Puetzer/Photographer's Choice/Getty Images

is that it pertains to moral *judgments*, not moral *behavior*. Knowing right from wrong does not mean that we will always act in accordance with our judgments. In addition, the theory applies primarily to Western society and its moral code; cross-cultural research conducted in cultures with different moral systems suggests that Kohlberg's theory is not necessarily applicable (Barandiaran, Pascual, & Samaniego, 2006; Stey, Lapsley, & McKeever, 2013; Buon, Habib, & Frey, 2017).

MORAL DEVELOPMENT IN WOMEN

One glaring shortcoming of Kohlberg's research is that he primarily used male participants. Furthermore, psychologist Carol Gilligan (1996) argues that because of men's and women's distinctive socialization experiences, a fundamental difference exists in the way each gender views moral behavior. According to Gilligan, men view morality primarily in terms of broad principles, such as justice and fairness. In contrast, women see it in terms of responsibility toward individuals and willingness to make sacrifices to help a specific individual within the context of a particular relationship. Compassion for individuals is a more salient factor in moral behavior for women than it is for men.

Because Kohlberg's model defines moral behavior largely in terms of abstract principles such as justice, Gilligan finds that it inadequately describes females' moral development. She suggests that women's morality centers on individual well-being and social relationships–a morality of *caring*. In her view, compassionate concern for the welfare of others represents the highest level of morality.

The fact that Gilligan's conception of morality differs greatly from Kohlberg's suggests that gender plays an important role in determining what a person sees as moral. Although the research evidence is not definitive, it seems plausible that their differing conceptions of what constitutes moral behavior may lead men and women to regard the morality of a specific behavior in different ways (Sherblom, 2008; Walker & Frimer, 2009; Capraro & Sippel, 2017).

Study Alert

The difference between the Kohlberg and Gilligan approaches to moral development is significant. Kohlberg's theory focuses on stages, and Gilligan's rests on gender differences.

Social Development: Finding One's Self in a Social World

"Who am I?" "How do I fit into the world?" "What is life all about?"

Questions such as these assume special significance during the teenage years, as adolescents seek to find their place in the broader social world. As we will see, this quest takes adolescents along several routes.

ERIKSON'S THEORY OF PSYCHOSOCIAL DEVELOPMENT: THE SEARCH FOR IDENTITY

Erikson's theory of psychosocial development emphasizes the search for identity during the adolescent years. As noted earlier, psychosocial development encompasses the way people's understanding of themselves, one another, and the world around them changes during the course of development (Erikson, 1963).

The fifth stage of Erikson's theory (summarized, with the other stages, in Figure 3), the **identity-versus-role-confusion stage,** encompasses adolescence. During this stage, a time of major testing, people try to determine what is unique about themselves. They attempt to discover who they are, what their strengths are, and what kinds of roles they are best suited to play for the rest of their lives—in short, their **identity.** A person confused about the most appropriate role to play in life may lack a stable identity, adopt an unacceptable role such as that of a social deviant, or have difficulty maintaining close personal relationships later in life (Updegraff et al., 2004; Vleioras & Bosma, 2005; Goldstein, 2006).

During the identity-versus-role-confusion period, an adolescent feels pressure to identify what to do with his or her life. Because these pressures come at a time of major physical changes as well as important changes in what society expects of them, adolescents can find the period an especially difficult one. The identity-versus-role-confusion stage has another important characteristic: declining reliance on adults for information with a shift toward using the peer group as a source of social judgments. The peer group becomes increasingly important, enabling adolescents to form close, adultlike

identity-versus-role-confusion stage According to Erikson, a time in adolescence of major testing to determine one's unique qualities. (Module 29)

identity The distinguishing character of the individual: who each of us is, what our roles are, and what we are capable of. (Module 29)

Stage	Approximate Age	Positive Outcomes	Negative Outcomes
1. Trust-vs.-mistrust	Birth–1½ years	Feelings of trust from environmental support	Fear and concern regarding others
2. Autonomy-vs.-shame-and-doubt	1½–3 years	Self-suffciency if exploration is encouraged	Doubts about self, lack of independence
3. Initiative-vs.-guilt	3–6 years	Discovery of ways to initiate actions	Guilt from actions and thoughts
4. Industry-vs.-inferiority	6–12 years	Development of sense of competence	Feelings of inferiority, no sense of mastery
5. Identity-vs.-role-confusion	Adolescence	Awareness of uniqueness of self, knowledge of role to be followed	Inability to identify appropriate roles in life
6. Intimacy-vs.-isolation	Early adulthood	Development of loving, sexual relationships and close friendships	Fear of relationships with others
7. Generativity-vs.-stagnation	Middle adulthood	Sense of contribution to continuity of life	Trivialization of one's activities
8. Ego-integrity-vs.-despair	Late adulthood	Sense of unity in life's accomplishments	Regret over lost opportunities of life

FIGURE 3 Erikson's stages of psychosocial development. According to Erikson, people proceed through eight stages of psychosocial development across their lives. He suggested that each stage requires the resolution of a crisis or conflict and may produce both positive and negative outcomes.
©Jon Erikson/Science Source

relationships and helping them clarify their personal identities. According to Erikson, the identity-versus-role-confusion stage marks a pivotal point in psychosocial development, paving the way for continued growth and the future development of personal relationships.

During early adulthood, people enter the **intimacy-versus-isolation stage.** Spanning the period of early adulthood (from post-adolescence to the early 30s), this stage focuses on developing close relationships with others. Difficulties during this stage result in feelings of loneliness and a fear of such relationships; successful resolution of the crises of this stage results in the possibility of forming relationships that are intimate on a physical, intellectual, and emotional level.

Development continues during middle adulthood as people enter the **generativity-versus-stagnation stage.** Generativity is the ability to contribute to one's family, community, work, and society and to assist the development of the younger generation. Success in this stage results in a person's feeling positive and optimistic about the continuity of life and his or her contribution to humanity. On the other hand, difficulties in this stage lead people to feel that their activities are trivial and unimportant and that their lives are stagnant. They may feel they have made poor career choices.

Finally, the last stage of psychosocial development, the **ego-integrity-versus-despair stage,** spans later adulthood and continues until death. People in this stage ask themselves if they have lived a meaningful life. If they see their lives positively, they feel a sense of accomplishment; if not, they feel regret over a misspent life.

Notably, Erikson's theory suggests that development does not stop at adolescence but continues throughout adulthood. A substantial amount of research now confirms this view. For instance, a 22-year study by psychologist Susan Whitbourne found considerable support for the fundamentals of Erikson's theory; the study determined that psychosocial development continues through adolescence and adulthood. In sum, adolescence is not an end point but rather a way station on the path of psychosocial development (Whitbourne et al., 1992; McAdams et al., 1997).

Although Erikson's theory provides a broad outline of identity development, critics have pointed out that his approach is anchored in male-oriented concepts of individuality and competitiveness. In an alternative conception, psychologist Carol Gilligan suggests that women may develop identity through the establishment of relationships. In her view, a primary component of women's identity is the construction of caring networks among themselves and others (Gilligan, 2004).

STORMY ADOLESCENCE: MYTH OR REALITY?

Does puberty invariably foreshadow a stormy, rebellious period of adolescence?

At one time, psychologists thought that adolescence was a period filled with stress and unhappiness. Today, however, research shows that this characterization is largely a myth. The reality is that most young people pass through adolescence without great turmoil in their lives and that they get along with their parents reasonably well (Granic, Hollenstein, & Dishion, 2003; Steinberg, 2016).

Not that adolescence is completely calm! In most families with adolescents, the amount of arguing and bickering clearly rises. Most young teenagers, as part of their search for identity, experience tension between their attempts to become independent from their parents and their actual dependence on them. They may experiment with a range of behaviors and flirt with a variety of activities that their parents, and even society as a whole, find objectionable. Happily, though, for most families such tensions stabilize during middle adolescence–around age 15 or 16–and eventually decline around age 18 (Smetana, Daddis, & Chuang, 2003; Smetana, 2005; Hadiwijaya et al., 2017).

One reason for the increase in discord during adolescence appears to be the protracted period in which children stay at home with their parents. In prior historical periods–and in some non-Western cultures today–children leave home immediately after puberty and are considered adults. Today, however, sexually mature adolescents

intimacy-versus-isolation stage
According to Erikson, a period during early adulthood that focuses on developing close relationships. (Module 29)

generativity-versus-stagnation stage
According to Erikson, a period in middle adulthood during which we take stock of our contributions to family and society. (Module 29)

ego-integrity-versus-despair stage
According to Erikson, a period from late adulthood until death during which we review life's accomplishments and failures. (Module 29)

Study Alert
The characterization of a stormy adolescence is a myth for most adolescents.

PsychTech
Adolescent use of social media such as Facebook is growing rapidly: 94% of teenagers use Facebook , and a quarter of them access their Facebook pages continuously throughout the day.

may spend as many as 7 or 8 years with their parents. Current social trends even hint at an extension of the conflicts of adolescence beyond the teenage years because a significant number of young adults–known as *boomerang children*–return to live with their parents, typically for economic reasons, after leaving home for some period. Although some parents welcome the return of their children, others are less sympathetic, which opens the way to conflict (Bianchi & Casper, 2000; Lewin, 2003; Otters & Hollander, 2015).

Another source of strife with parents lies in the way adolescents think. Adolescence fosters *adolescent egocentrism,* a state of self-absorption in which a teenager views the world from his or her own point of view. Egocentrism leads adolescents to be highly critical of authority figures, unwilling to accept criticism, and quick to fault others. It also makes them believe that they are the center of everyone else's attention, which leads to self-consciousness.

Furthermore, adolescents develop *personal fables*–the belief that one's experience and beliefs are unique, exceptional, and shared by no one else. Such personal fables may make adolescents feel invulnerable to the risks that threaten others (Alberts, Elkind, & Ginsberg, 2007; Schwartz, Maynard, & Uzelac, 2008; Boeve-de Pauw, Donche, & Van Petegem, 2011).

Finally, parent-adolescent discord occurs because adolescents are much more apt to engage in risky behavior than they are later in life. In part, their riskiness is due to the immaturity of brain systems that regulate impulse control, some of which do not fully develop until people are in their mid-20s. Furthermore, adolescents have a greater tolerance for ambiguity and uncertainty, leading them to tolerate risks that adults would be less likely to accept (Steinberg, 2007, 2016).

ADOLESCENT SUICIDE

Although the vast majority of teenagers pass through adolescence without major psychological difficulties, some experience unusually severe psychological problems. Sometimes those problems become so extreme that adolescents take their own lives. Suicide is the third leading cause of death for adolescents (after accidents and homicide) in the United States. More teenagers and young adults die from suicide than from cancer, heart disease, AIDS, birth defects, stroke, pneumonia and influenza, and chronic lung disease combined (CDC, 2004b).

A teenager commits suicide every 90 minutes. Furthermore, the reported rate of suicide may actually be understated because medical personnel hesitate to report suicide as a cause of death. Instead, they frequently label a death as an accident in an effort to protect the survivors. Overall, as many as 200 adolescents may attempt suicide for every one who actually takes his or her own life (CDC, 2000; Brausch & Gutierrez, 2009).

Male adolescents are five times more likely to commit suicide than females are, although females *attempt* suicide more often than males do. The rate of adolescent suicide is significantly greater among whites than among nonwhites. On the other hand, Native Americans have the highest suicide rate of any ethnic group in the United States, and Asian Americans have the lowest rate (CDC, 2004b; Boden, Fergusson, & Horwood, 2007; Bossarte & Swahn, 2011).

As the rate of suicide has slowly declined, the rates are still higher for adolescents than for any other age group except for the elderly. Some psychologists suggest that the sharp rise in stress that teenagers experience–in terms of academic and social pressure, alcoholism, drug abuse, and family difficulties–provokes the most troubled adolescents to take their own lives. However, that is not the whole story, because the suicide rate for other age groups has remained fairly stable in the past few decades. It is unlikely that stress has increased only for adolescents and not for the rest of the population (Lubell et al., 2004; Valois, Zullig, & Hunter, 2013).

Although the question of why adolescent suicide rates are so high remains unanswered, several factors put adolescents at risk. One factor is depression, characterized by unhappiness, extreme fatigue, and–a variable that seems especially important–a

These young people are mourning the death of a peer who committed suicide. The rate of suicide among teenagers has risen significantly over the past few decades. Can you think of any reasons for this phenomenon?

©RichLegg/E+/Getty Images

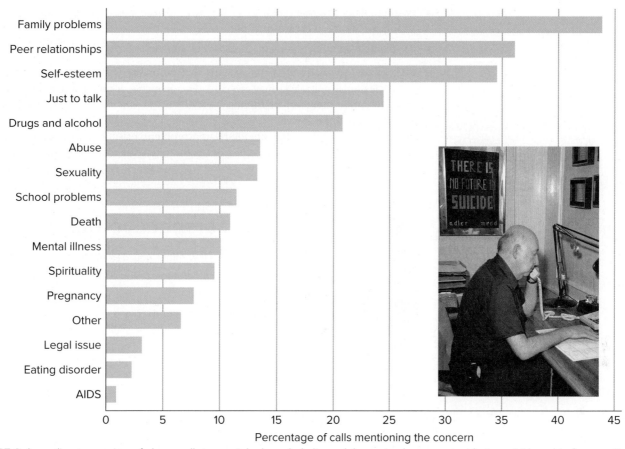

FIGURE 4 According to a review of phone calls to one telephone help line, adolescents who were considering suicide most often mentioned family, peer relationships, and self-esteem problems.

Sources: (Left) Adapted from Boehm, K. E., & Campbell, N. B. (1995). Suicide: A review of calls to an adolescent peer listening phone service. *Child Psychiatry and Human Development, 26,* 61–66; (Right) ©Mary Kate Denny/PhotoEdit.

profound sense of hopelessness. In other cases, adolescents who commit suicide are perfectionists who are inhibited socially and prone to extreme anxiety when they face any social or academic challenge. Furthermore, in some cases, bullying, both in person and cyberbullying, may result in suicide (see Figure 4; Caelian, 2006; Barzilay et al., 2015; Young et al., 2017).

Family background and adjustment difficulties are also related to suicide. A long-standing history of conflicts between parents and children may lead to adolescent behavior problems, such as delinquency, dropping out of school, and aggressive tendencies. In addition, teenage alcoholics and abusers of other drugs have a relatively high rate of suicide (Winstead & Sanchez, 2005; Bagge & Sher, 2008; Hardt et al., 2008).

Several warning signs indicate when a teenager's problems may be severe enough to warrant concern about the possibility of a suicide attempt. They include the following:

- School problems, such as missing classes, truancy, and a sudden change in grades
- Frequent incidents of self-destructive behavior, such as careless accidents
- Loss of appetite or excessive eating
- Withdrawal from friends and peers
- Sleeping problems
- Signs of depression, tearfulness, or overt indications of psychological difficulties, such as hallucinations
- A preoccupation with death, an afterlife, or what would happen "if I died"

- Putting affairs in order, such as giving away prized possessions or making arrangements for the care of a pet
- An explicit announcement of thoughts of suicide

If you know someone who shows signs that he or she is suicidal, urge that person to seek professional help. You may need to take assertive action, such as enlisting the assistance of family members or friends. Talk of suicide is a serious signal for help and not a confidence to be kept.

For immediate help with a suicide-related problem, call (800) 273-8255, a national hotline staffed with trained counselors, or access www.suicidepreventionlifeline.org.

From the perspective of...

A Social Worker How might you determine if an adolescent is at risk for suicide? What strategies would you use to prevent the teen from committing suicide? Would you use different strategies depending on the teenager's gender?

©Sam Edwards/age fotostock

Exploring Diversity

Rites of Passage: Coming of Age Around the World

It is not easy for male members of the Awa tribe in New Guinea to make the transition from childhood to adulthood. First come whippings with sticks and prickly branches both for the boys' own past misdeeds and in honor of those tribesmen who were killed in warfare. In the next phase of the ritual, adults jab sharpened sticks into the boys' nostrils. Then they force a 5-foot length of vine into the boys' throats until they gag and vomit. Finally, tribesmen cut the boys' genitals, causing severe bleeding.

Although the rites that mark the coming of age of boys in the Awa tribe sound horrifying to Westerners, they are comparable to those in other cultures. In some, youths must kneel on hot coals without displaying pain. In others, girls must toss wads of burning cotton from hand to hand and allow themselves to be bitten by hundreds of ants (Selsky, 1997).

Other cultures have less fearsome although equally important ceremonies that mark the passage from childhood to adulthood. For instance, when a girl first menstruates in traditional Apache tribes, the event is marked by dawn-to-dusk chanting. Western religions, too, have several types of celebrations, including bar mitzvahs and bat mitzvahs at age 13 for Jewish boys and girls, respectively, and confirmation ceremonies for children in many Christian denominations (Magida, 2006).

In most societies, males are the focus of coming-of-age ceremonies. The reason for this gender distinction may be that in most cultures, men traditionally have higher status than women, and therefore, those cultures regard boys' transition into adulthood as more important to celebrate.

However, another fact may explain why most cultures place greater emphasis on male rather than female rites. For females, the transition from childhood is marked by a definite biological event: menstruation. For males, in contrast, no single event can be used to pinpoint entry into adulthood. Thus, men are forced to rely on culturally determined rituals to acknowledge their arrival into adulthood.

RECAP/EVALUATE/RETHINK

RECAP

LO 29-1 What major physical, social, and cognitive transitions characterize adolescence?

- Adolescence, the developmental stage between childhood and adulthood, is marked by the onset of puberty, the point at which sexual maturity occurs. The age at which puberty begins has implications for the way people view themselves and the way others see them.
- Moral judgments during adolescence increase in sophistication, according to Kohlberg's three-level model. Although Kohlberg's levels provide an adequate description of males' moral judgments, Gilligan suggests that women view morality in terms of caring for individuals rather than in terms of broad general principles of justice.
- According to Erikson's model of psychosocial development, adolescence may be accompanied by an identity crisis. Adolescence is followed by three more stages of psychosocial development that cover the remainder of the life span.
- Suicide is the third leading cause of death in adolescents.

EVALUATE

1. _____ is the period during which the sexual organs begin to mature.

2. Delayed maturation typically provides both males and females with a social advantage. True or false?

3. _____ proposed a set of three levels of moral development ranging from reasoning based on rewards and punishments to abstract thinking involving concepts of justice.

4. Erikson believed that during adolescence, people must search for _____, whereas during the early adulthood, the major task is _____.

RETHINK

1. In what ways do school cultures help or hurt teenage students who are going through adolescence? What school policies might benefit early-maturing girls and late-maturing boys? Explain how same-sex schools could help students going through adolescence, as some have argued.

2. Many cultures have "rites of passage" through which young people are officially recognized as adults. Do you think such rites can be beneficial? Does the United States have any such rites? Would setting up an official designation that one has achieved "adult" status have benefits?

Answers to Evaluate Questions

1. Puberty; 2. false; both male and female adolescents suffer if they mature late; 3. Kohlberg; 4. identity, intimacy

KEY TERMS

adolescence	identity	generativity-versus-stagnation stage	ego-integrity-versus-despair stage
puberty	intimacy-versus-isolation stage		
identity-versus-role-confusion stage			

Module 30
Adulthood

LEARNING OUTCOMES

LO 30-1 What are the principal kinds of physical, social, and intellectual changes that occur in early and middle adulthood, and what are their causes?

LO 30-2 How does the reality of late adulthood differ from the stereotypes about that period?

LO 30-3 How can we adjust to death?

emerging adulthood The period beginning in the late teenage years and extending into the mid-20s. (Module 30)

I thought I got better as I got older. I found out that wasn't the case in a real hurry last year. After going twelve years in professional football and twelve years before that in amateur football without ever having surgery performed on me, the last two seasons of my career I went under the knife three times. It happened very quickly and without warning, and I began to ask myself, "Is this age? Is this what's happening?" Because up until that moment, I'd never realized that I was getting older. (Brian Sipe, quoted in Kotre & Hall, 1990, pp. 257, 259-260)

As a former professional football player, Brian Sipe intensely felt the changes in his body brought about by aging. But the challenges he experienced are part of a normal process that affects all people as they move through adulthood.

Psychologists generally agree that early adulthood begins around age 20 and lasts until about age 40 to 45, when middle adulthood begins and continues until around age 65. Despite the enormous importance of these periods of life in terms of both the accomplishments that occur in them and their overall length (together they span some 44 years), they have been studied less than has any other stage. For one reason, the physical changes that occur during these periods are less apparent and more gradual than those at other times during the life span. In addition, the diverse social changes that arise during this period defy simple categorization.

The variety of changes that occur in early adulthood have led many developmental psychologists to view the start of the period as a transitional phase called emerging adulthood. **Emerging adulthood** is the period beginning in the late teenage years and extending into the mid-20s.

During emerging adulthood, people are no longer adolescents, although the brain is still growing and modifying its neural pathways. It is typically a period of uncertainty in which postadolescents haven't fully taken on the responsibilities of adulthood. Instead, they are still engaged in determining who they are and what their life and career paths should be. It is a time of uncertainty and instability, as well as self-discovery (Bukobza, 2009; Lamborn & Groh, 2009; Schwartz et al., 2013).

The view that adulthood is preceded by an extended period of emerging adulthood reflects the new reality of the economies of industrialized countries. These economies have shifted away from manufacturing to a focus on technology and information, thus requiring increasing time spent in educational training. Furthermore, the age at which most people marry and have children has risen significantly (Arnett, 2007, 2011).

There's also an increasing ambivalence about reaching adulthood. When people in their late teens and early 20s are asked if they feel they have reached adulthood, most say "yes and no" (see Figure 1). In short, emerging adulthood is an age of identity exploration in which individuals are more self-focused and uncertain than they will be later in early adulthood (Arnett, 2000, 2006; Verschueren et al., 2017).

As we discuss the changes that occur through emerging adulthood, early adulthood, middle adulthood, and ultimately late adulthood, keep in mind the demarcations between the periods are fuzzy. However, the changes are certainly no less profound than they were in earlier periods of development.

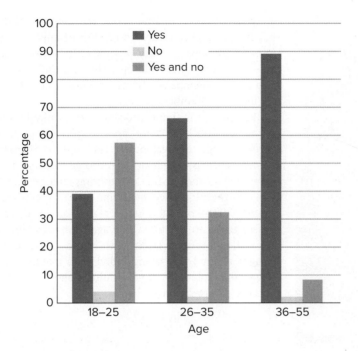

FIGURE 1 Evidence of a period of emerging adulthood is provided by the responses to a questionnaire asking, "Do you feel that you have reached adulthood?" Most people between the ages of 18 and 25 were ambivalent, responding "yes and no." Later, this ambivalence disappeared, with most people 26–35 saying "yes."

Source: Adapted from Arnett, J. J. (2006). *Emerging adulthood: The winding road from the late teens through the twenties.* New York: Oxford University Press.

Physical Development: The Peak of Health

For most people, early adulthood marks the peak of physical health. From about 18 to 25 years of age, people's strength is greatest, their reflexes are quickest, and their chances of dying from disease are quite slim. Moreover, reproductive capabilities are at their highest level.

Around age 25, the body becomes slightly less efficient and more susceptible to disease. Overall, however, ill health remains the exception; most people stay remarkably healthy during early adulthood. (Can you think of any machine other than the body that can operate without pause for so long a period?)

During middle adulthood, people gradually become aware of changes in their bodies. They often experience weight gain (although they can avoid such increases through diet and exercise). Furthermore, the sense organs gradually become less sensitive, and reactions to stimuli are slower. But generally, the physical declines that occur during middle adulthood are minor and often unnoticeable (DiGiovanna, 1994). The major biological change that does occur during middle adulthood pertains to reproductive capabilities. On average, during their late 40s or early 50s, women begin **menopause,** during which they stop menstruating and are no longer fertile. Because menopause is accompanied by a significant reduction in the production of estrogen, a female hormone, women sometimes experience symptoms such as hot flashes, sudden sensations of heat. Many symptoms can be treated through *hormone therapy (HT)* in which menopausal women take the hormones estrogen and progesterone.

However, hormone therapy poses several dangers, such as an increase in the risk of breast cancer, blood clots, and coronary heart disease. These uncertainties make the routine use of HT controversial. Currently, the medical consensus seems to be that younger women with severe menopausal symptoms ought to consider HT on a short-term basis. On the other hand, HT is less appropriate for older women after menopause (Lindh-Astrand, Brynhildsen, & Hoffmann, 2007; MacLennan, 2009; McCarrey & Resnick, 2015).

Menopause was once blamed for a variety of psychological symptoms, including depression and memory loss. However, if such difficulties occur, they may be caused

menopause The period during which women stop menstruating and are no longer fertile. (Module 30)

Women's reactions to menopause vary significantly across cultures. According to one study, the more a society values old age, the less difficulty its women have during menopause. Why do you think this would be the case?

©BananaStock/Alamy Stock Photo

by women's expectations about reaching an "old" age in a society that highly values youth. For example, women's reactions to menopause vary significantly across cultures. The more a society values old age, the less difficulty its women have during menopause (Beyene, Gilliss, & Lee, 2007; Espinola, DeVinney, & Steinberg, 2017).

For men, the aging process during middle adulthood is somewhat subtler. There are no physiological signals of increasing age equivalent to the end of menstruation in women; that is, no male menopause exists. In fact, men remain fertile and capable of fathering children until well into late adulthood. However, some gradual physical decline occurs. Sperm production decreases, and the frequency of orgasm tends to decline. Once again, though, any psychological difficulties associated with these changes are usually brought about by an aging individual's inability to meet the exaggerated standards of youthfulness and not by the person's physical deterioration.

Social Development: Working at Life

Whereas physical changes during adulthood reflect development of a quantitative nature, social developmental transitions are qualitative and more profound. During this period, people typically launch themselves into careers, marriage, and families.

The entry into early adulthood is usually marked by leaving one's childhood home and entering the world of work. People envision life goals and make career choices. Their lives often center on their careers, which form an important part of their identity (Vaillant & Vaillant, 1990; Levinson, 1990, 1992).

In their early 40s, however, people may begin to question their lives as they enter a period called the *midlife transition*. The idea that life will end at some point can become more influential in their thinking, which leads them to question their past accomplishments (Gould, 1978; Boylan & Ryff, 2015).

Although some psychologists—and popular opinion—suggest that physical aging and dissatisfaction with one's life mark a so-called "midlife crisis," there is little evidence for such a "crisis." In fact, the passage into middle age is relatively calm for most people. Most 40-year-olds view their lives and accomplishments positively enough to proceed relatively smoothly through midlife, and the 40s and 50s are often a particularly rewarding period. Rather than looking to the future, people concentrate on the present; their involvement with their families, friends, and other social groups takes on new importance. A major developmental thrust of this period is coming to terms with one's circumstances (Whitbourne, 2010; Dare, 2011; Wojciechowska, 2017).

Finally, during the last stages of adulthood, people become more accepting of others and of their own lives and are less concerned about issues or problems that once bothered them. They come to accept the fact that death is inevitable, and they try to understand their accomplishments in terms of the broader meaning of life. Although people may begin for the first time to label themselves as "old," many also develop a sense of wisdom and feel freer to enjoy life (Miner-Rubino, Winter, & Stewart, 2004; Ward-Baker, 2007; Galambos et al., 2015).

Marriage, Children, and Divorce: Family Ties

In the typical fairy tale, a dashing young man and a beautiful young woman marry, have children, and live happily ever after. However, that scenario does not match the realities of love and marriage in the 21st century. Today, it is just as likely that the man and woman would first live together, then get married and have children, but ultimately get divorced.

The percentage of U.S. households made up of unmarried couples has increased dramatically over the last two decades. At the same time, the average age at which marriage takes place is higher than at any time since the turn of the last century. These changes have been dramatic, and they suggest that the institution of marriage has changed considerably from earlier historical periods.

When people do marry, the probability of divorce is high, especially for younger couples. Even though divorce rates have been declining since they peaked in 1981, about half of all first marriages end in divorce. Before they are 18 years old, two-fifths of children will experience the breakup of their parents' marriages. Moreover, the rise in divorce is not just a U.S. phenomenon: The divorce rate has accelerated over the past several decades in most industrialized countries. In some countries, the increase has been enormous. In South Korea, for example, the divorce rate quadrupled from 11% to 47% in the 12-year period ending in 2002 (Lankov, 2004; Olson & DeFrain, 2005; Park & Raymo, 2013).

Changes in marriage and divorce trends have doubled the number of single-parent households in the United States over the last two decades. Almost 25% of all family households are now headed by one parent, compared with 13% in 1970. If present trends continue, almost three-fourths of American children will spend some portion of their lives in a single-parent family before they turn 18. For children in minority households, the numbers are even higher. Almost 60% of all black children and more than a third of all Hispanic children live in homes with only one parent. Furthermore, in most single-parent families, the children live with the mother rather than the father—a phenomenon that is consistent across racial and

The number of single-parent families has doubled within the past decade, with the mother usually as head of the household. What are some of the challenges facing children in single-parent families?
©Robert Houser/UpperCut Images/Getty Images

ethnic groups throughout the industrialized world (U.S. Bureau of the Census, 2000; Sarsour et al., 2011).

What are the economic and emotional consequences for children living in homes with only one parent? Single-parent families are often economically less well off, and this economic disadvantage has an impact on children's opportunities. More than a third of single-mother families with children have incomes below the poverty line. In addition, good child care at an affordable price is often hard to find. Furthermore, for children of divorce, the parents' separation is often a painful experience that may result in obstacles to establishing close relationships later in life. Children may blame themselves for the breakup or feel pressure to take sides (U.S. Bureau of the Census, 2000; Wallerstein et al., 2000; Liu, He, & Wu, 2007).

Most evidence suggests, however, that children from single-parent families are no less well adjusted than are those from two-parent families. In fact, children may be more successful growing up in a harmonious single-parent family than in a two-parent family that engages in continuous conflict (Kelly, 2000; Olson & DeFrain, 2005; Koh et al., 2017).

Changing Roles of Men and Women

One of the major changes in family life in the last two decades has been the evolution of men's and women's roles. More women than ever before act simultaneously as wives, mothers, and wage earners—in contrast to women in traditional marriages in which the husband is the sole wage earner and the wife assumes primary responsibility for care of the home and children.

Almost three-fourths of all women with children under the age of 18 are employed outside the home, and 65% of mothers with children under age 6 are working. In the mid-1960s, only 17% of mothers of 1-year-olds worked full-time; now, more than half are in the labor force (Bureau of Labor Statistics, 2013).

Most married working women are not free of household responsibilities. Even in marriages in which the spouses hold jobs that have similar status and require similar hours, the distribution of household tasks between husbands and wives has not changed substantially. Working wives are still more likely than husbands to feel responsible for traditional homemaking tasks such as cooking and cleaning. In contrast, husbands still view themselves as responsible primarily for household tasks such as repairing broken appliances and doing yardwork (Juster, Ono, & Stafford, 2002; Damaske, 2011).

WOMEN'S "SECOND SHIFT"

Working mothers can put in a staggering number of hours. One survey, for instance, found that if we add the number of hours worked on the job and in the home, employed mothers of children under 3 years of age put in an average of 90 hours per week! The additional work women perform is sometimes called the "second shift." National surveys show women who are both employed and mothers put in an extra month of 24-hour days during the course of a year. Researchers see similar patterns in many developing societies throughout the world, with women working at full-time jobs and also having primary responsibilities for child care (Hochschild, 2001; Jacobs & Gerson, 2004; Bureau of Labor Statistics, 2007).

Consequently, rather than careers being a substitute for what women do at home, they are often an addition to the role of homemaker. It is not surprising that some wives feel resentment toward husbands who spend less time on child care and housework than the wives had expected before the birth of their children (Kiecolt, 2003; Gerstel, 2005; Fagan & Press, 2008).

Later Years of Life: Growing Old

> I've always enjoyed doing things in the mountains–hiking or, more recently, active cliff-climbing. The more difficult the climb, the more absorbing it is. The climbs I really remember are the ones I had to work on. Maybe a particular section where it took two or three tries before I found the right combination of moves that got me up easily–and, preferably, elegantly. It's a wonderful exhilaration to get to the top and sit down and perhaps have lunch and look out over the landscape and be so grateful that it's still possible for me to do that sort of thing. (Lyman Spitzer, age 74, quoted in Kotre & Hall, 1990, pp. 358-359)

If you can't quite picture a 74-year-old rock-climbing, some rethinking of your view of late adulthood may be in order. In spite of the societal stereotype of "old age" as a time of inactivity and physical and mental decline, gerontologists, specialists who study aging, are beginning to paint a very different portrait of late adulthood.

By focusing on the period of life that starts at around age 65, gerontologists are making important contributions to clarifying the capabilities of older adults. Their work is demonstrating that significant developmental processes continue even during old age. And as people live longer, the absolute number of people within older adulthood will continue to increase. Consequently, developing an understanding of late adulthood has become a critical priority for psychologists (Moody, 2000; Schaie, 2005b; Jia, Zack, & Thompson, 2011).

PHYSICAL CHANGES IN LATE ADULTHOOD: THE AGING BODY

Napping, eating, walking, conversing. It probably doesn't surprise you that these relatively nonstrenuous activities represent the typical pastimes of late adulthood. But it is striking that these activities are identical to the most common leisure activities reported in a survey of college students (Harper, 1978). Although the students cited more active pursuits–such as sailing and playing basketball–as their favorite activities, in actuality they engaged in such sports relatively infrequently and spent most of their free time napping, eating, walking, and conversing.

Although the leisure activities in which older adults engage may not differ all that much from the ones that younger people pursue, many physical changes are, of course, brought about by the aging process. The most obvious are those of appearance–hair thinning and turning gray, skin wrinkling and folding, and sometimes a slight loss of height as the thickness of the disks between vertebrae in the spine decreases. But subtler changes also occur in the body's biological functioning. For example, sensory capabilities decrease as a result of aging: Vision, hearing, smell, and taste become less sensitive. Reaction time slows, and physical stamina changes (Schieber, 2006; Madden, 2007; Schilling & Diehl, 2015).

What are the reasons for these physical declines? **Genetic programming theories of aging** suggest that the DNA genetic code includes a built-in time limit for the reproduction of human cells. These theories suggest that after a certain time cells stop dividing or become harmful to the body–as if a kind of automatic self-destruct button had been pushed. In contrast, **wear-and-tear theories of aging** suggest that the mechanical functions of the body simply work less efficiently as people age. Waste byproducts of energy production eventually accumulate, and mistakes are made when cells divide. Eventually, the body in effect wears out like an old automobile (Miquel, 2006; Hayflick, 2007; Helgeson & Zajdel, 2017).

Evidence supports both the genetic programming and the wear-and-tear views, and it may be that both processes contribute to natural aging. It is clear, however, that physical aging is not a disease but a natural biological process. Many physical functions do not decline with age. For example, sex remains pleasurable well into old age (although the frequency of sexual activity decreases), and some people report that

genetic preprogramming theories of aging Theories that suggest that human cells have a built-in time limit to their reproduction and that they are no longer able to divide after a certain time. (Module 30)

wear-and-tear theories of aging Theories that suggest that the mechanical functions of the body simply stop working efficiently. (Module 30)

Study Alert

Two major theories of aging—the genetic preprogramming and the wear-and-tear views—explain some of the physical changes that take place in older adults.

the pleasure they derive from sex increases during late adulthood (Gelfand, 2000; DeLamater & Sill, 2005; Wilkin & Haddock, 2011).

COGNITIVE CHANGES: THINKING ABOUT— AND DURING—LATE ADULTHOOD

At one time, many gerontologists would have agreed with the popular view that older adults are forgetful and confused. Today, however, most research indicates that this assessment is far from an accurate one of older people's capabilities.

One reason for the change in view is that more sophisticated research techniques exist for studying the cognitive changes that occur in late adulthood. For example, if we were to give a group of older adults an IQ test, we might find that the average score was lower than the score achieved by a group of younger people. We might conclude that this signifies a decline in intelligence. Yet, if we looked a little more closely at the specific test, we might find that the conclusion was unwarranted. For instance, many IQ tests include portions based on physical performance (such as arranging a group of blocks) or on speed. In such cases, poorer performance on the IQ test may be due to gradual decreases in reaction time—a physical decline that accompanies late adulthood and has little or nothing to do with older adults' intellectual capabilities.

Other difficulties hamper research into cognitive functioning during late adulthood. For example, older people are often less healthy than younger ones; when only *healthy* older adults are compared to healthy younger adults, intellectual differences are far less evident. Furthermore, the average number of years in school is often lower in older adults (for historical reasons) than in younger ones, and older adults may be less motivated to perform well on intelligence tests than younger people are. Finally, traditional IQ tests may be inappropriate measures of intelligence in late adulthood. Older adults sometimes perform better on tests of practical intelligence than younger individuals do (Dixon & Cohen, 2003; Johnson & Deary, 2011).

Still, some declines in intellectual functioning during late adulthood do occur, although the pattern of age differences is not uniform for different types of cognitive abilities (see Figure 2). In general, skills relating to *fluid intelligence* (which involves information-processing skills such as memory, calculations, and analogy solving) show declines in late adulthood. In contrast, skills relating to *crystallized intelligence* (intelligence

FIGURE 2 Age-related changes in intellectual skills vary according to the specific cognitive ability in question.

Source: Adapted from Schaie, K. W. (2005a). Longitudinal studies. In *Developmental influences on adult intelligence: The Seattle Longitudinal Study*. New York: Oxford University Press.

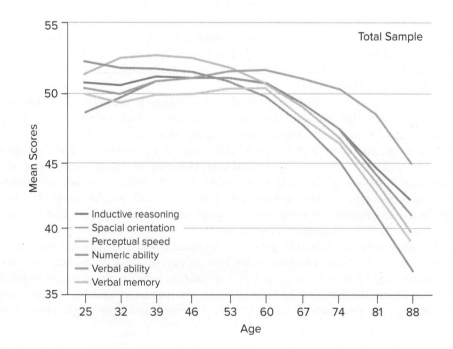

based on the accumulation of information, skills, and strategies learned through experience) remain steady and in some cases actually improve (van Hooren, Valentijn, & Bosma, 2007; Kaufman, Johnson, & Liu, 2008; Dixon et al., 2013).

Even when changes in intellectual functioning occur during later adulthood, people often are able to compensate for any decline. They can still learn what they want to learn; it may just take more time. Furthermore, teaching older adults strategies for dealing with new problems can prevent declines in performance (Cavallini, Pagnin, & Vecchi, 2003; Peters et al., 2007; Finke, Howe, & Huston, 2017).

MEMORY CHANGES IN LATE ADULTHOOD: ARE OLDER ADULTS FORGETFUL?

One of the characteristics most frequently attributed to late adulthood is forgetfulness. How accurate is this assumption?

Most evidence suggests that memory change is not an inevitable part of the aging process. For instance, research shows that older people in cultures in which older adults are held in high esteem, such as mainland China, are less likely to show memory losses than do those living in cultures in which the expectation is that memory will decline. Similarly, when older people in Western societies are reminded of the advantages of age (for example, "age brings wisdom"), they tend to do better on tests of memory (Levy, 1996; Dixon, Rust, & Feltmate, 2007; Pinal, Zurrón, & Díaz, 2015).

Even when people show memory declines during late adulthood, their deficits are limited to certain types of memory. For instance, losses tend to be limited to episodic memories that relate to specific experiences in people's lives. Other types of memories, such as semantic memories (that refer to general knowledge and facts) and implicit memories (memories of which we are not consciously aware), are largely unaffected by age (Mitchell & Schmitt, 2006; St. Jacques & Levine, 2007; Blumen, Rajaram, & Henkel, 2013).

Declines in episodic memories can often be traced to changes in older adults' lives. For instance, it is not surprising that a retired person, who may no longer face the same kind of consistent intellectual challenges encountered on the job, may have less practice in using memory or even be less motivated to remember things, which leads to an apparent decline in memory. Even in cases in which long-term memory declines, older adults can profit from training that targets memory skills (West, Bagwell, & Dark-Freudeman, 2007; Morcom & Friston, 2011; Després et al., 2017).

In the past, older adults with severe cases of memory decline accompanied by other cognitive difficulties were said to suffer from *senility*. Now, most gerontologists

Although fluid intelligence declines in late adulthood, skills relating to crystallized intelligence remain steady and may actually improve.
©icsnaps/Shutterstock

APPLYING PSYCHOLOGY IN THE 21ST CENTURY

HOW DO COGNITIVE ABILITIES RISE AND FALL AS WE AGE?

Common wisdom holds that young adults are quick-witted and that cognitive faculties decline over the life span until old age brings slow-minded confusion. This, however, is largely a myth, as only a moment of thought would suggest. The mind doesn't simply start out strong and weaken with age. A longer lifetime of experience typically means that older adults have a wider and deeper body of knowledge, and indeed, older adults tend to perform better on tests of crystallized intelligence than do younger adults. Younger adults, on the other hand, tend to do better on tests of fluid intelligence. So "what you know" tends to improve with age, but "figuring things out" peaks early.

At least this was the picture until recently. Intriguing new research conducted on nearly 50,000 participants via a battery of online tests of cognitive functioning suggests a more complex and nuanced perspective on changes over the life span. Rather than lumping together multiple tests results into composite scores on fluid intelligence and crystallized intelligence as is often done, the researchers analyzed performance on individual tests

©cwa/Alamy Stock Photo

and found that different cognitive abilities develop in different ways (Hartshorne & Germine, 2015).

For example, the researchers showed that mental manipulation–a measure of fluid intelligence–reaches its peak in the late teen years and then quickly declines, which is consistent with other research. But they found that performance on short-term memory tasks, such as remembering

people's names, peaks in the mid-20s and remains strong until the mid-30s. Working memory capacity, however–the size of the work space in memory–doesn't peak until the 30s. In one particularly novel test included by these researchers, subjects were asked to determine a person's mood from just a photograph of his or her eyes–a vague and difficult judgment to make. Performance on this test didn't peak until around midlife and remained strong thereafter. And one test of crystallized intelligence–a vocabulary test–didn't show that skill peaking until the late 60s.

"At any given age, you're getting better at some things, you're getting worse at some other things, and you're at a plateau at some other things. There's probably not one age at which you're peak on most things, much less all of them," said Joshua Hartshorne, one of the researchers (Trafton, 2015, p. 8).

RETHINK

- Why do you think some cognitive abilities get better with age while others get worse?
- In what way is judging a person's emotional state from his or her eyes an important cognitive ability? How might this ability combine with other cognitive abilities to produce better decision making?

Alzheimer's disease A progressive brain disorder that leads to a gradual and irreversible decline in cognitive abilities. (Modules 20, 30)

view senility as an imprecise label that has outlived its usefulness. Instead, gerontologists explain symptoms of mental deterioration using more precise factors.

For example, rather than use senility to describe memory loss in general, gerontologists now recognize **Alzheimer's disease** as a progressive brain disorder that leads to a gradual and irreversible decline in cognitive abilities. More than 5.5 million Americans have the disease, and 1 in 10 people age 65 and older are afflicted. Unless a cure is found, some 11 million people are expected to have Alzheimer's in 2050 (Rogers, 2007; Alzheimer's Association, 2017).

Alzheimer's occurs when production of the *beta amyloid precursor protein* goes awry, producing large clumps of cells that trigger inflammation and deterioration of nerve cells. The brain shrinks, neurons die, and several areas of the hippocampus and frontal and temporal lobes deteriorate. So far, there is no effective treatment, although preliminary research suggests that diet, exercise, and an active social life can slow the decline in cognitive capabilities brought on by Alzheimer's (Wolfe, 2006; Medeiros et al., 2007; Behrens, Lendon, & Roe, 2009; Kivipelto & Hakansson, 2017).

In other cases, cognitive declines may be caused by temporary anxiety and depression, which can be treated successfully, or may even be due to overmedication. The danger is that people with such symptoms may be left untreated, thereby continuing their decline (Sachs-Ericsson et al., 2005; Diniz et al., 2013).

Study Alert

It's important to be able to describe the nature of intellectual changes during late adulthood.

In sum, declines in cognitive functioning in late adulthood are, for the most part, not inevitable. The key to maintaining cognitive skills may lie in intellectual stimulation. Like the rest of us, older adults need a stimulating environment in order to hone and maintain their skills (Bosma et al., 2003; Glisky, 2007; Hertzog et al., 2008; also see *Applying Psychology in the 21st Century*).

THE SOCIAL WORLD OF LATE ADULTHOOD: OLD BUT NOT ALONE

Just as the view that old age predictably means mental decline has proved to be wrong, so has the view that late adulthood inevitably brings loneliness. People in late adulthood most often see themselves as functioning members of society; only a small number of them report that loneliness is a serious problem (Jylha, 2004; Berkman, Ertel, & Glymour, 2011; Luong, Rauers, & Fingerman, 2015).

Certainly, late adulthood brings significant challenges. People who have spent their adult lives working and then enter retirement bring about a major shift in the roles they play. Moreover, many people must face the death of their spouse. Especially if the marriage has been a long and good one, the death of a partner means the loss of a companion, confidante, and lover. It can also bring about changes in economic well-being.

There is no single way to age successfully, and several theories have been developed to describe the process. According to the **disengagement theory of aging**, aging is characterized by a gradual withdrawal from the world. In this view, as people get older, they separate themselves from others on physical, psychological, and social levels. In this view, such disengagement is appropriate and even beneficial. The reason is that disengagement serves the purpose of providing an opportunity for increased reflectiveness and decreased emotional investment in others at a time of life when social relationships will inevitably be ended by death (Adams, 2004; Wrosch, Bauer, & Scheier, 2005).

However, only a little research supports the disengagement theory of aging, and alternative theories have been suggested. The major alternative is the activity theory of aging. According to the **activity theory of aging**, people who age most successfully are those who maintain the interests, activities, and level of social interaction they experienced during their earlier periods of adulthood. Activity theory argues that people who are aging effectively show a continuation of the activities in which they participated during the earlier part of their lives (Crosnoe & Elder, 2002; Nimrod & Kleiber, 2007; Roos & Zaaiman, 2017).

Most research supports the activity theory of aging. On the other hand, not all people in late adulthood need a life filled with activities and social interaction to be happy. As in every stage of life, some older adults are just as satisfied leading a relatively inactive, solitary existence. What may be more important is how people view the aging process: Evidence shows that positive self-perceptions of aging are associated with increased longevity (Levy et al., 2002; Levy & Myers, 2004).

Regardless of how people age, most engage in a process of **life review** in which they examine and evaluate their lives. Remembering and reconsidering what has occurred in the past, people in late adulthood often come to a better understanding of themselves. They sometimes resolve lingering problems and conflicts and face their lives with greater wisdom and serenity.

Clearly, people in late adulthood are not just marking time until death. Rather, old age is a time of continued growth and development as important as any other period of life.

Maintaining interests and activities one had during middle age can contribute to a more successful late adulthood, according to the activity theory of aging.
©Jupiterimages/Getty Images

disengagement theory of aging The theory that suggests that successful aging is characterized by a gradual withdrawal from the world on physical, psychological, and social levels. (Module 30)

activity theory of aging The theory that suggests that successful aging is characterized by maintaining the interests and activities of earlier stages of life. (Module 30)

life review The process by which people examine and evaluate their lives. (Module 30)

From the perspective of...

A Health-Care Provider What sorts of recommendations would you make to your older patients about how to deal with aging? How would you handle someone who believed that getting older had only negative consequences?

©Tetra Images/Getty Images

BECOMING AN INFORMED CONSUMER
of Psychology

Adjusting to Death

At some time in our lives, we all face death—certainly our own as well as the deaths of friends, loved ones, and even strangers. Although there is nothing more inevitable in life, death remains a frightening, emotion-laden topic. Certainly, little is more stressful than the death of a loved one or the contemplation of our own imminent death, and preparing for death is one of our most crucial developmental tasks (American Psychological Association, 2000).

A few generations ago, talk of death was taboo. The topic was never mentioned to dying people, and gerontologists had little to say about it. That changed, however, with the pioneering work of Elizabeth Kübler-Ross (1969), who brought the subject of death into the open with her observation that those facing impending death tend to move through five broad stages:

- *Denial.* In this stage, people resist the idea that they are dying. Even if told that their chances for survival are small, they refuse to admit that they are facing death.
- *Anger.* After moving beyond the denial stage, dying people become angry—angry at people around them who are in good health, angry at medical professionals for being ineffective, angry at God.
- *Bargaining.* Anger leads to bargaining in which the dying try to think of ways to postpone death. They may decide to dedicate their lives to religion if God saves them. They may say, "If only I can live to see my son married, I will accept death then."
- *Depression.* When dying people come to feel that bargaining is no use, they move to the next stage: depression. They realize that their lives really are coming to an end, which leads to what Kübler-Ross calls "preparatory grief" for their own deaths.
- *Acceptance.* In this stage, people accept impending death. Usually they are unemotional and uncommunicative; it is as if they have made peace with themselves and are expecting death with no bitterness.

Although Kübler-Ross believed that all people go through the stages in a similar fashion, research shows that not everyone experiences each of the stages in the same way. In fact, Kübler-Ross's stages are applicable only to people who are fully aware that they are dying and have the time to evaluate their impending death. Furthermore, vast differences occur in the way individuals react to impending death. The specific cause and duration of dying, as well as the person's sex, age, personality, and the type of support received from family and friends, all have an impact on how people respond to death (Carver & Scheier, 2002; Coyle, 2006).

Few of us enjoy the contemplation of death. Yet awareness of its psychological aspects and consequences can make its inevitable arrival less anxiety producing and perhaps more understandable.

RECAP/EVALUATE/RETHINK

RECAP

LO 30-1 What are the principal kinds of physical, social, and intellectual changes that occur in early and middle adulthood, and what are their causes?

- Early adulthood marks the peak of physical health. Physical changes occur relatively gradually in men and women during adulthood.
- One major physical change occurs at the end of middle adulthood for women: They begin menopause, after which they are no longer fertile.
- During middle adulthood, people typically experience a midlife transition in which the notion that life will end becomes more important. In some cases this may lead to a midlife crisis, although the passage into middle age is typically relatively calm.
- As aging continues during middle adulthood, people realize in their 50s that their lives and accomplishments are fairly well set, and they try to come to terms with them.
- Among the important developmental milestones during adulthood are marriage, family changes, and divorce. Another important determinant of adult development is work.

LO 30-2 How does the reality of late adulthood differ from the stereotypes about that period?

- Old age may bring marked physical declines caused by genetic preprogramming or physical wear and tear. Although the activities of people in late adulthood are not all that different from those of younger people, older adults experience declines in reaction time, sensory abilities, and physical stamina.
- Intellectual declines are not an inevitable part of aging. Fluid intelligence does decline with age, and long-term memory abilities are sometimes impaired. In contrast, crystallized intelligence shows slight increases with age, and short-term memory remains at about the same level.
- Although disengagement theory sees successful aging as a process of gradual withdrawal from the physical, psychological, and social worlds, there is little research supporting this view. Instead, activity theory, which suggests that the maintenance of interests and activities from earlier years leads to successful aging, is a more accurate explanation.

LO 30-3 How can we adjust to death?

- According to Kübler-Ross, dying people move through five stages as they face death: denial, anger, bargaining, depression, and acceptance.

EVALUATE

1. Rob recently turned 40 and surveyed his goals and accomplishments to date. Although he has accomplished a lot, he realized that many of his goals will not be met in his lifetime. This stage is called a _____ _____.
2. In households where both partners have similar jobs, the division of labor that generally occurs is the same as in "traditional" households where the husband works and the wife stays at home. True or false?
3. _____ _____ theories suggest that there is a maximum time span in which cells are able to reproduce. This time limit explains the eventual breakdown of the body.
4. Lower IQ test scores during late adulthood do not necessarily mean a decrease in intelligence. True or false?
5. During old age, a person's _____ intelligence continues to increase, whereas _____ intelligence may decline.
6. In Kübler-Ross's _____ stage, people resist the idea of death. In the _____ stage, they attempt to make deals to avoid death, and in the _____ stage, they passively await death.

RETHINK

1. Is the possibility that life may be extended for several decades a mixed blessing? What societal consequences might an extended life span bring about?
2. Does the finding that people in late adulthood require intellectual stimulation have implications for the societies in which older people live? In what way might stereotypes about older individuals contribute to their isolation and lack of intellectual stimulation?

Answers to Evaluate Questions

1. midlife transition; 2. true; 3. Genetic preprogramming; 4. true; 5. crystallized, fluid; 6. denial, bargaining, acceptance

emerging adulthood	wear-and-tear theories of	disengagement theory of	life review
menopause	aging	aging	
genetic preprogramming	Alzheimer's disease	activity theory of aging	
theories of aging			

LOOKING *Back.*

EPILOGUE

We have traced major events in the development of physical, social, and cognitive growth throughout the life span. Clearly, people change throughout their lives.

As we explored each area of development, we encountered anew the nature–nurture issue, concluding in every significant instance that both nature and nurture contribute to a person's development of skills, personality, and interactions. Specifically, our genetic inheritance—nature—lays down general boundaries within which we can advance and grow; our environment—nurture—helps determine the extent to which we take advantage of our potential.

Before proceeding to the next set of modules, turn to the prologue of this chapter, which discussed Zain Rajani, who was conceived through an experimental technique involving his mother's stem cells. Using your knowledge of human development, consider the following questions.

1. The new stem-cell-enhanced IVF technique has had both successes and failures. How would scientists study whether the new technique is any more successful than traditional IVF?

2. Is the fact that the new technique worked in Zain's mother's case after years of unsuccessful IVF attempts conclusive in establishing the new technique's superiority?

3. Zain Rajani was conceived from a "rejuvenated" egg. How might you think Zain's future physical or cognitive development could be affected by the "helping hand" his mother's egg received from the doctors?

4. Like traditional IVF, the new stem-cell technique is controversial, especially among people who believe that such procedures are akin to "playing God." Do you think Zain's parents should tell him and others how he was born, or should they try to shield him from potential notoriety, kidding from classmates, and abuse from critics? What would you do?

Design Elements: Yellow highlighter: ©luckyraccoon/Shutterstock.com; Smartphone: ©and4me/Shutterstock.com; Group of diverse hands: ©MR. Nattanon Kanchak/Shutterstock.com; Woman working on laptop: ©Dragon Images/Shutterstock.com.

VISUAL SUMMARY 9 Development

MODULES 27 Nature and Nurture: The Enduring Developmental Issue

Developmental Research Techniques
— Cross-sectional, longitudinal, sequential

Basics of Genetics: Chromosomes and genes

Earliest Development

— Zygote: a fertilized egg

— Embryo: between 2 and 8 weeks old after conception

— Fetus: between 8 weeks and birth

— Age of viability: about 22 weeks from conception

Nature and Nurture

— Nature: Refers to hereditary factors

— Nurture: Refers to environmental influences

MODULE 28 Infancy and Childhood

The Extraordinary Newborn

— Reflexes: Rooting, sucking, gag, Babinski

— Development of the senses

Infancy through Middle Childhood, about age 12

— Physical development: rapid growth

— Social development

- Attachment: positive emotional bond between child and caregiver
- Ainsworth strange situation
- Social relationships with peers

— Child care outside the home

— Four parenting styles

— Erikson's theory of psychosocial development

- Trust-versus-mistrust stage: birth to age 1½
- Autonomy-versus-shame-and-doubt stage: ages 1½ to 3
- Initiative-versus-guilt stage: ages 3 to 6
- Industry-versus-inferiority stage: ages 6 to 12

— Cognitive development

— Piaget's theory of cognitive development

Cognitive Stage	Approximate Age Range	Major Characteristics
Sensorimotor	Birth–2 years	Development of object permanence, development of motor skills, little or no capacity for symbolic representation
Preoperational	2–7 years	Development of language and symbolic thinking, egocentric thinking
Concrete operational mastery	7–12 years	Development of conservation, of concept of reversibility
Formal operational	12 years–adulthood	Development of logical and abstract thinking

— Information processing approaches

MODULE 29 Adolescence: Becoming an Adult

Physical Development: Rapid weight and height gains; onset of puberty

Moral Development: Changes in moral reasoning

Sample Moral Reasoning

Level	In Favor of Stealing the Drug	Against Stealing the Drug
Level 1 Preconventional morality: The main considerations at this level are the avoidance of punishment and the desire for rewards.	"You shouldn't just let your wife die. People will blame you for not doing enough, and they'll blame the scientist for not selling you the drug for less money."	"You can't steal the drug because you'll be arrested and go to jail. Even if you aren't caught, you'll feel guilty and you'll always worry that the police may figure out what you did."
Level 2 Conventional morality: Membership in society becomes important at this level. People behave in ways that will win the approval of others.	"Who will blame you if you steal a life-saving drug? But if you just let your wife die, you won't be able to hold your head up in front of your family or neighbors."	"If you steal the drug, everyone will treat you like a criminal. They will wonder why you couldn't have found some other way to save your wife."
Level 3 Post-conventional morality: People accept that there are certain broad principles of morality that should govern our actions. These principles are more critical than the particular laws in a society.	"If you simply follow the law, you will violate the underlying principle of saving your wife's life. If you do steal the drug, society will understand your actions and respect them. You can't let an inadequate, outdated law prevent you from doing the right thing."	"You can't change your standards of honesty whenever it suits your needs. Others may not blame you for stealing the drug, but your conscience will blame you for betraying your own moral code."

Social Development: Erikson's theory of psychosocial development

Stage	Approximate Age	Positive Outcomes	Negative Outcomes
1. Trust-vs-mistrust	Birth–1½ years	Feelings of trust from environmental support	Fear and concern regarding others
2. Autonomy-vs-shame-and-doubt	1½–3 years	Self-sufficiency if exploration is encouraged	Doubts about self, lack of independence
3. Initiative-vs-guilt	3–6 years	Discovery of ways to initiate actions	Guilt from actions and thoughts
4. Industry-vs-inferiority	6–12 years	Development of sense of competence	Feelings of inferiority, no sense of mastery
5. Identity-vs-role-confusion	Adolescence	Awareness of uniqueness of self, knowledge of role to be followed	Inability to identify appropriate roles in life
6. Intimacy-vs-isolation	Early adulthood	Development of loving, sexual relationships and close friendships	Fear of relationships with others
7. Generativity-vs-stagnation	Middle adulthood	Sense of contribution to continuity of life	Trivialization of one's activities
8. Ego-integrity-vs-despair	Late adulthood	Sense of unity in life's accomplishments	Regret over lost opportunities of life

MODULE 30 Adulthood

Physical Development

— Early adulthood: peak of health

— Middle adulthood: menopause for women

Social Development

— Early adulthood: Focus on career, marriage, family

— Midlife transition: Relatively calm, come to terms with one's circumstances

— Late adulthood: Acceptance of others and one's circumstances

Marriage, Children, and Divorce

— People marry later in life than ever before; about half of all first marriages end in divorce

— Many single-parent households

Growing Old: Late adulthood

— Physical changes
- Genetic preprogramming aging theory
- Wear-and-tear aging theory

— Cognitive changes
- Fluid intelligence declines; crystallized intelligence remains steady
- Memory change not inevitable
  — Alzheimer's disease: Gradual, irreversible brain disorder that leads to a decline in cognitive abilities

— Social world
- Disengagement theory of aging
- Activity theory of aging

Module 27) ©D.W. Fawcett/Science Source; ©SPL/Science Source; (Module 28) ©Emma Kim/Cultura/Getty Images; ©Nina Leen/Time Life Pictures/Getty Images; ©Farrell Grehan/Corbis via Getty Sumages (Module 29) Source: Adapted from Kohlberg, L. "Stage and sequence: The cognitive-developmental approach to socialization." In D. Goslin (Ed.), *Handbook of Socialization Theory and Research* (381–382). Chicago: Rand McNally, 1969; ©Steven Puetzer/Photographer's Choice/Getty Images; ©Jon Erikson/Science Source (Module 30) ©BananaStock/Alamy Stock Photo; ©Jupiterimages/Getty Images

©santypan/Shutterstock

CHAPTER 10
Personality

LEARNING OUTCOMES FOR CHAPTER 10

PROLOGUE *GOOD GUY OR GOOD FELLA?*

Racing cyclist Lance Armstrong was an idol to many. He won the prestigious Tour de France road race seven consecutive times—a feat that had been unequaled in his sport. And remarkably, he did all this after having been diagnosed with stage-three testicular cancer that had spread to his lungs and brain. Despite his poor prognosis, Armstrong defeated the disease and made an amazing comeback as a professional athlete. Not only that but he also founded the Lance Armstrong Foundation to support cancer patients and helped to develop other charitable organizations.

But Armstrong had a side that most people never saw. His cycling comeback was haunted by allegations of doping—allegations that Armstrong repeatedly and strenuously denied for years. But in the end, the evidence caught up with him, and he publicly admitted that he had been doping. A federal prosecutor called him "a doper, dealer, and liar." He was stripped of his Tour de France titles, and he is the target of a $100 million suit for committing fraud (Schrotenboer, 2016; Macur, 2017).

LOOKING *Ahead*

Who is the real Lance Armstrong? Is he the disciplined, hardworking athlete-hero who overcame cancer to win the Tour de France seven times and started a foundation to aid cancer patients? Or is he the cheat who used drugs to enhance his athletic performance, lied about it when confronted, and now downplays the role doping played in his success?

Many people, like Armstong, have more than one side to their personalities, appearing one way to some people and quite differently to others. At the same time, you probably know people whose behavior is so consistent that you can easily predict how they are going to behave, no matter what the situation. Determining who a person truly is falls to a branch of psychology that seeks to understand the characteristic ways people behave—personality psychology.

Personality is the pattern of enduring characteristics that produce consistency and individuality in a given person. Personality encompasses the behaviors that make each of us unique and that differentiate us from others. Personality also leads us to act consistently in different situations and over extended periods of time.

We will consider a number of approaches to personality. For historical reasons, we begin with psychodynamic theories of personality, which emphasize the importance of the unconscious. Next, we consider approaches that concentrate on identifying the most fundamental personality traits; theories that view personality as a set of learned behaviors; biological and evolutionary perspectives on personality; and approaches, known as humanistic theories, that highlight the uniquely human aspects of personality. We end our discussion by focusing on how personality is measured and how personality tests can be used.

personality The pattern of enduring characteristics that produce consistency and individuality in a given person. (Module 31)

Module 31
Psychodynamic Approaches to Personality

LEARNING OUTCOMES

LO 31-1 How do psychologists define and use the concept of personality?

LO 31-2 What do the theories of Freud and his successors tell us about the structure and development of personality?

psychodynamic approaches to personality Approaches that assume that personality is primarily unconscious and motivated by inner forces and conflicts about which people have little awareness. (Module 31)

The college student was intent on making a good first impression on an attractive woman he had spotted across a crowded room at a party. As he walked toward her, he mulled over a line he had heard in an old movie the night before: "I don't believe we've been properly introduced yet." To his horror, what came out was a bit different. After threading his way through the crowded room, he finally reached the woman and blurted out, "I don't believe we've been properly seduced yet."

Although this student's error may seem to be merely an embarrassing slip of the tongue, according to some personality theorists, such a mistake is not an error at all (Motley, 1987). Instead, *psychodynamic personality theorists* might argue that the error illustrates one way in which behavior is triggered by inner forces that are beyond our awareness. These hidden drives, shaped by childhood experiences, play an important role in energizing and directing everyday behavior.

Psychodynamic approaches to personality are based on the idea that personality is primarily unconscious and motivated by inner forces and conflicts about which people have little awareness. The most important pioneer of the psychodynamic approach was Sigmund Freud. A number of Freud's followers, including Carl Jung, Karen Horney, and Alfred Adler, refined Freud's theory and developed their own psychodynamic approaches.

Freud's Psychoanalytic Theory: Mapping the Unconscious Mind

psychoanalytic theory Freud's theory that unconscious forces act as determinants of personality. (Module 31)

unconscious A part of the personality that contains the memories, knowledge, beliefs, feelings, urges, drives, and instincts of which the individual is not aware. (Module 31)

Sigmund Freud, an Austrian physician, developed **psychoanalytic theory** in the early 1900s. According to Freud's theory, conscious experience is only a small part of our psychological makeup and experience. He argued that much of our behavior is motivated by the **unconscious,** a part of the personality that contains the memories, knowledge, beliefs, feelings, urges, drives, and instincts of which the individual is not aware.

Like the unseen mass of a floating iceberg, the contents of the unconscious far surpass in quantity the information in our conscious awareness. Freud maintained that to understand personality, it is necessary to expose what is in the unconscious. But because the unconscious disguises the meaning of the material it holds, the content of the unconscious cannot be observed directly. It is therefore necessary to interpret clues to the unconscious–slips of the tongue, fantasies, and dreams–to understand the unconscious processes that direct behavior. A slip of the tongue such as the one quoted earlier (sometimes termed a *Freudian slip*) may be interpreted as revealing the speaker's unconscious sexual desires.

To Freud, much of our personality is determined by our unconscious. Some of the unconscious is made up of the *preconscious*, which contains material that is not threatening and is easily brought to mind, such as the knowledge that 2 + 2 = 4. But deeper in the unconscious are instinctual drives–the wishes, desires, demands, and needs that are hidden from conscious awareness because of the conflicts and pain they would cause if they were part of our everyday lives. The unconscious provides a "safe haven" for our recollections of threatening events.

STRUCTURING PERSONALITY: ID, EGO, AND SUPEREGO

To describe the structure of personality, Freud developed a comprehensive theory that held that personality consists of three separate but interacting components: the id, the ego, and the superego. Freud suggested that the three structures can be diagrammed to show how they relate to the conscious and the unconscious (see Figure 1).

Although the three components of personality Freud described may appear to be actual physical structures in the nervous system, they are not. Instead, they represent abstract conceptions of a general *model* of personality that describes the interaction of forces that motivate behavior.

If personality consisted only of primitive, instinctual cravings and longings, it would have just one component: the id. The **id** is the instinctual and unorganized part of personality. From the time of birth, the id attempts to reduce tension created by primitive drives related to hunger, sex, aggression, and irrational impulses. Those drives are fueled by "psychic energy," which we can think of as a limitless energy source constantly putting pressure on the various parts of the personality.

The id operates according to the *pleasure principle* in which the goal is the immediate reduction of tension and the maximization of satisfaction. However, in most cases, reality prevents the fulfillment of the demands of the pleasure principle: We cannot always eat when we are hungry, and we can discharge our sexual drives only when the time and place are appropriate. To account for this fact of life, Freud suggested a second component of personality, which he called the ego.

The **ego** is the rational and logical part of personality that attempts to balance the desires of the id and the realities of the objective, outside world. It starts to develop soon after birth.

In contrast to the pleasure-seeking id, the ego operates according to the *reality principle* in which instinctual energy is restrained to maintain the individual's safety and to help integrate the person into society. In a sense, then, the ego is the "executive" of personality: It makes decisions, controls actions, and allows thinking and problem solving of a higher order than the id's capabilities permit.

The superego is the final personality structure to develop in childhood. According to Freud, the **superego** is the part of personality that harshly judges the morality of

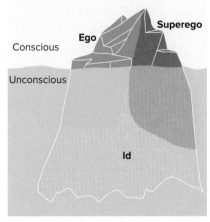

FIGURE 1 In Freud's personality model, there are three major components: the id, the ego, and the superego. As the iceberg analogy shows, only a small portion of personality is conscious. Why do you think that only the ego and superego have conscious components?

id The instinctual and unorganized part of personality whose sole purpose is to reduce tension created by primitive drives related to hunger, sex, aggression, and irrational impulses. (Module 40)

ego The part of personality that attempts to balance the desires of the id and the realities of the objective, outside world. (Module 40)

superego The part of personality that harshly judges the morality of our behavior. (Module 40)

Freud suggests that the superego, the part of the personality that represents the rights and wrongs of society, develops from direct teaching from parents, teachers, and other significant individuals.
©Monkey Business Images/Shutterstock

Study Alert
Remember that the three parts of personality in Freud's theory—the id, the ego, and the superego—are abstract conceptions that don't exist as physical structures in the brain.

our behavior. It represents the rights and wrong of society as taught and modeled by a person's parents, teachers, and other significant individuals.

The superego includes the *conscience*, which prevents us from behaving in a morally improper way by making us feel guilty if we do wrong. The superego helps us control impulses coming from the id, making our behavior less selfish and more virtuous.

Neither the id nor superego parts of personality are realistic, practical, or logical in that they do not consider the realities society imposes. For example, the superego, if left to operate by itself and without restraint, would create perfectionists unable to make the moral compromises that life sometimes requires. On the other hand, an unrestrained id would produce a primitive, pleasure-seeking, thoughtless individual on a mission to fulfill every desire without delay. Consequently, the ego must constrain and negotiate between the conflicting demands of the superego and id.

DEVELOPING PERSONALITY: PSYCHOSEXUAL STAGES

Freud also provided us with a view of how personality develops. He suggests personality development proceeds through a series of five **psychosexual stages** during which children encounter conflicts between the demands of society and their own sexual urges (in which sexuality is more about experiencing pleasure and less about lust).

According to Freud, if we are not able to resolve the conflicts that occur at a particular psychosexual stage, we may become locked in that conflict throughout life—something he called fixation. **Fixations** are conflicts or concerns that persist beyond the developmental period in which they first occur. Such conflicts may be due to having needs ignored, such as ending breast feeding too early or being treated too strictly during toilet training. Alternatively, fixation may occur if children are overindulged during an earlier period, such as when parents are overly attentive to a child or provide lavish rewards during toilet training.

The sequence Freud proposed is noteworthy because it explains how experiences and difficulties during a particular childhood stage may predict specific characteristics in the adult personality. This theory is also unique in associating each stage with a major biological function, which Freud assumed to be the focus of pleasure in a given period. (See Figure 2 for a summary of the stages.)

In the first psychosexual stage of development, called the **oral stage,** the baby's mouth is the focal point of pleasure. During the first 12 to 18 months of life, children suck, eat, mouth, and bite anything they can put into their mouths. To Freud, this behavior suggested that the mouth is the primary site of a kind of sexual pleasure and that weaning (withdrawing the breast or bottle) represents the main conflict during the oral stage. If infants are either overindulged (perhaps by being fed every time they cry) or frustrated in their search for oral gratification, they may become fixated at this stage.

psychosexual stages Developmental periods that children pass through during which they encounter conflicts between the demands of society and their own sexual urges. (Module 31)

fixations Conflicts or concerns that persist beyond the developmental period in which they first occur. (Module 31)

oral stage According to Freud, a stage from birth to age 12 to 18 months, in which an infant's center of pleasure is the mouth. (Module 31)

Study Alert

The five psychosexual stages of personality development in Freud's theory—oral, anal, phallic, latency, and genital—indicate how personality develops as people age.

Stage	Age	Major Characteristics
Oral	Birth to 12–18 months	Interest in oral gratification from sucking, eating, mouthing, biting
Anal	12–18 months to 3 years	Gratification from expelling and withholding feces; coming to terms with society's controls relating to toilet training
Phallic	3 to 5–6 years	Interest in the genitals, coming to terms with Oedipal conflict leading to identification with same-sex parent
Latency	5–6 years to adolescence	Sexual concerns largely unimportant
Genital	Adolescence to adulthood	Reemergence of sexual interests and establishment of mature sexual relationships

FIGURE 2 Freud's theory of personality development suggests several distinct stages.
©Ingram Publishing

For example, fixation might occur if an infant's oral needs were constantly gratified immediately at the first sign of hunger rather than if the infant learned that feeding takes place on a schedule because eating whenever an infant wants to eat is not always realistic. Fixation at the oral stage might produce an adult who was unusually interested in oral activities–eating, talking, smoking–or who showed symbolic sorts of oral interests such as being "bitingly" sarcastic or very gullible ("swallowing" anything).

From around age 12-18 months until 3 years of age–a period in which the emphasis in Western cultures is on toilet training–a child enters the **anal stage.** At this point, the major source of pleasure changes from the mouth to the anal region, and children obtain considerable pleasure from both retention and expulsion of feces. If toilet training is particularly demanding, fixation might occur. Fixation during the anal stage might result in unusual rigidity, orderliness, punctuality–or extreme disorderliness or sloppiness–in adulthood.

At about age 3, the **phallic stage** begins. At this point, there is another major shift in the child's primary source of pleasure. Now interest focuses on the genitals and the pleasures derived from fondling them. During this stage, the child must also negotiate one of the most important hurdles of personality development: the Oedipal conflict.

The **Oedipal conflict** is a child's intense, sexual interest in his or her opposite-sex parent. According to Freudian theory, the Oedipal conflict plays out as children focus attention on their genitals, and the differences between male and female anatomy become more salient.

According to Freud, a male child unconsciously begins to develop a sexual interest in his mother, starts to see his father as a powerful rival, and harbors a wish to replace his father and enjoy the affections of his mother. (The situation mirrors a tragic Greek play in which the son Oedipus kills his father and marries his mother, hence the term "Oedipal conflict.") But because a son views his father as too powerful, he develops a fear that his father may retaliate drastically by removing the source of the threat: his penis.

Also according to Freud, the fear of losing his penis leads to *castration anxiety,* which ultimately becomes so powerful that the child represses his desires for his mother and identifies with his father. **Identification** is the process of wanting to be like another person as much as possible, imitating that person's behavior and adopting similar beliefs and values. By identifying with his father, a son seeks to obtain a woman like his unattainable mother.

Freud argued that the process is different for girls. He suggested that they experience sexual arousal related to their fathers and begin to have penis envy. They wish they had the anatomical part that seems most clearly "missing" from their bodies–that is, girls realize they lack a penis.

Blaming their mothers for this missing piece of anatomy, girls come to believe that their mothers are responsible for their "castration." Like males, though, they find that they can resolve such unacceptable feelings by identifying with the same-sex parent, behaving like her, and adopting her attitudes and values. In this way, a girl's identification with her mother is completed. (We should note that these ideas about the identification process in girls led to considerable criticism that Freud was sexist, favoring males over females.)

Through these complicated–and to many critics, far-fetched–sequences of events, Freud argued that the Oedipal conflict is resolved and that both males and females move on to the next stage of development. If difficulties arise during the resolution of the Oedipal conflict, however, all sorts of problems are thought to occur, including improper sex-role behavior and the failure to develop a conscience.

After the resolution of the Oedipal conflict, typically around age 5 or 6, children move into the **latency period,** which lasts until puberty. During this period, sexual interests become dormant, even in the unconscious. Then, during adolescence, sexual feelings re-emerge, which marks the start of the final period, the **genital stage,** which extends until death. The focus during the genital stage is on mature, adult sexuality, which Freud defined as sexual intercourse.

According to Freud, a child goes through the anal stage from age 12–18 months until 3 years of age. Toilet training is a crucial event at this stage—one that psychoanalytic theory claims directly influences the formation of an individual's personality.

©Miller Margaret/Science Source/Getty Images

anal stage According to Freud, a stage from age 12 to 18 months to 3 years of age, in which a child's pleasure is centered on the anus. (Module 31)

phallic stage According to Freud, a period beginning around age 3 during which a child's pleasure focuses on the genitals. (Module 31)

Oedipal conflict A child's intense, sexual interest in his or her opposite-sex parent. (Module 31)

identification The process of wanting to be like another person as much as possible, imitating that person's behavior and adopting similar beliefs and values. (Module 31)

latency period According to Freud, the period between the phallic stage and puberty during which children's sexual concerns are temporarily put aside. (Module 31)

genital stage According to Freud, the period from puberty until death, marked by mature sexual behavior (that is, sexual intercourse). (Module 31)

DEFENSE MECHANISMS

Freud's efforts to describe and theorize about the underlying dynamics of personality and its development were motivated by very practical problems that his patients faced in dealing with *anxiety,* an intense, negative emotional experience. According to Freud, anxiety is a danger signal to the ego. Although anxiety can arise from realistic fears—such as seeing a poisonous snake about to strike—it can also occur in the form of *neurotic anxiety* in which irrational impulses emanating from the id threaten to burst through and become uncontrollable.

Because anxiety is obviously unpleasant, Freud believed that people develop a range of ways to deal with it, which he called defense mechanisms. **Defense mechanisms** are unconscious strategies that people use to reduce anxiety by distorting reality and concealing the source of the anxiety from themselves.

The primary defense mechanism is repression. **Repression** occurs when the ego pushes unacceptable or unpleasant thoughts and impulses out of consciousness but maintains them in the unconscious.

Repression is the most direct method of dealing with anxiety; instead of handling an anxiety-producing impulse on a conscious level, we simply ignore it. For example, a college student who feels hatred for his mother may repress those personally and socially unacceptable feelings. The feelings remain lodged within the unconscious because acknowledging them would provoke anxiety. Similarly, memories of childhood abuse may be repressed. Although such memories may not be consciously recalled, according to Freud they can affect later behavior, and they may be revealed through dreams or slips of the tongue or symbolically in some other fashion.

If repression is ineffective in keeping anxiety at bay, we might use other defense mechanisms. Freud and later his daughter, Anna Freud (who became a well-known psychoanalyst), formulated an extensive list of potential defense mechanisms. The major defense mechanisms are summarized in Figure 3 (Perry, Presniak, & Olson, 2013; Boag, 2015; Zhang & Guo, 2017).

defense mechanisms In Freudian theory, unconscious strategies that people use to reduce anxiety by distorting reality and concealing the source of the anxiety from themselves. (Module 31)

repression The defense mechanism in which the ego pushes unacceptable or unpleasant thoughts and impulses out of consciousness but maintains them in the unconscious. (Module 40)

Study Alert

Use Figure 3 to remember the most common defense mechanisms (unconscious strategies used to reduce anxiety by concealing its source from ourselves and others).

Freud's Defense Mechanisms		
Defense Mechanism	**Explanation**	**Example**
Repression	Unacceptable or unpleasant impulses are pushed out of awareness and back into the unconscious.	A woman is unable to consciously recall that she was raped.
Regression	People behave as if they were at an earlier stage of development.	A boss has a temper tantrum when an employee makes a mistake.
Displacement	The expression of an unwanted feeling or thought is redirected from a more threatening powerful person to a weaker one.	A brother yells at his younger sister after a teacher gives him a bad grade.
Rationalization	People provide self-justifying explanations in place of the actual, but threatening, reason for their behavior.	A student who goes out drinking the night before a big test rationalizes his behavior by saying the test isn't all that important.
Denial	People refuse to accept or acknowledge an anxiety-producing piece of information.	A student refuses to believe that he has flunked a course.
Projection	People attribute unwanted impulses and feelings to someone else.	A man who is unfaithful to his wife and feels guilty suspects that his wife is unfaithful.
Sublimation	People divert unwanted impulses into socially approved thoughts, feelings, or behaviors.	A person with strong feelings of aggression becomes a soldier.
Reaction formation	Unconscious impulses are expressed as their opposite in consciousness.	A mother who unconsciously resents her child acts in an overly loving way toward the child.

FIGURE 3 According to Freud, people use a wide range of defense mechanisms to cope with anxieties.

Imitating a person's behavior and adopting similar beliefs and values are part of Freud's concept of identification. How can this concept be applied to the definition of gender roles? Is identification similar in all cultures?
©Steve Hix/age fotostock

All of us employ defense mechanisms to some degree, according to Freudian theory, and they can serve a useful purpose by protecting us from unpleasant information. Yet some people fall prey to them to such an extent that they must constantly direct a large amount of psychic energy toward hiding and rechanneling unacceptable impulses. When this occurs, everyday living becomes difficult. In such cases, the result is a mental disorder produced by anxiety–what Freud called "neurosis." (Psychologists rarely use this term today, although it endures in everyday conversation.)

EVALUATING FREUD'S LEGACY

Freud's theory has had a significant impact on the field of psychology–and even more broadly on Western philosophy and literature. The general ideas that we have unconscious thoughts that influence behavior, that we employ defense mechanisms, and that some adult psychological problems have their roots in childhood difficulties are widely accepted (Boag, Brakel, & Tavitie, 2016; Zhang et al., 2016).

However, contemporary personality psychologists have leveled significant criticisms against many foundational explanations of personality development in psychoanalytic theory. Among the most important is the lack of compelling scientific data to support the process of personality development that Freud laid out. Although individual case studies *seem* supportive, we lack conclusive evidence that shows the personality is structured and operates along the lines Freud laid out (Tummala-Nara, 2016).

The lack of research evidence is due, in part, to the fact that Freud's conception of personality is built on unobservable abstract concepts. Moreover, it is not clear that the stages of personality Freud laid out provide an accurate description of personality development. We also know now that important changes in personality can occur in adolescence and adulthood–something that Freud did not believe happened. Instead, he argued that personality largely is set by the time we reach adolescence.

The vague nature of Freud's theory also makes it difficult to predict how an adult will display certain developmental difficulties. For instance, if a person is fixated at the anal stage, according to Freud, he or she may be unusually messy or unusually neat. Freud's theory offers no way to predict how the difficulty will be exhibited. Furthermore, Freud can be faulted for seeming to view women as inferior to men because he argued that women have weaker superegos than men do and in some ways unconsciously yearn to be men (the concept of penis envy).

370 **Chapter 10** Personality

Finally, Freud made his observations and derived his theory from a limited population. His theory was based almost entirely on upper-class Austrian women living in the strict, puritanical era of the early 1900s who had come to him seeking treatment for psychological and physical problems. How far one can generalize beyond this population is a matter of considerable debate. For instance, in some Pacific Island societies, the mother's oldest brother and not the father plays the role of disciplinarian. In such a culture, it is unreasonable to argue that the Oedipal conflict will progress in the same way that it did in Austrian society in which the father typically was the major disciplinarian. In short, a cross-cultural perspective raises questions about the universality of Freud's view of personality development (Doi, 1990; Grünbaum, 2015).

Still, Freud generated an important method of treating psychological disturbances called *psychoanalysis*. As we will see when we discuss treatment approaches to psychological disorders, psychoanalysis remains in use today (Frosch, 2011; Altman & Stile, 2015).

Moreover, Freud's emphasis on the unconscious has been partially supported by current research on dreams and implicit memory. As first noted when we discussed dreaming, advances in neuroscience are consistent with some of Freud's arguments. For example, the fact that some behavior is motivated by occurrences that apparently have been forgotten, as well as the discovery of neural pathways relating to emotional memories, supports the notion of repression.

Furthermore, cognitive and social psychologists have found increasing evidence that unconscious processes help us think about and evaluate our world, set goals, and choose a course of action. Unconscious processes also help determine how we form attitudes toward others (Teague, 2013; Bargh, 2014; Fayek, 2017).

The Neo-Freudian Psychoanalysts: Building on Freud

Freud laid the foundation for important work done by a series of successors who were trained in traditional Freudian theory but later rejected some of its major points. These theorists are known as **neo-Freudian psychoanalysts.**

neo-Freudian psychoanalysts Psychoanalysts who were trained in traditional Freudian theory but who later rejected some of its major points. (Module 31)

The neo-Freudians placed greater emphasis than Freud did on the functions of the ego by suggesting that it has more control than the id does over day-to-day activities. They focused more on the social environment and minimized the importance of sex as a driving force in people's lives. They also paid greater attention to the effects of society and culture on personality development.

JUNG'S COLLECTIVE UNCONSCIOUS

Carl Jung (pronounced "yoong"), one of the most influential neo-Freudians, rejected Freud's view of the primary importance of unconscious sexual urges. Instead, he looked at the primitive urges of the unconscious more positively. He argued that they represented a more general and positive life force that goes back to the dawn of the existence of life, motivating creativity and positive conflict resolution (Cassells, 2007; Wilde, 2011; Addison, 2017).

collective unconscious According to Jung, an inherited set of ideas, feelings, images, and symbols that are shared with all humans because of our common ancestral past. (Module 31)

Jung suggested that we have a universal **collective unconscious**–an inherited set of ideas, feelings, images, and symbols that are shared with all humans because of our common ancestral past. This collective unconscious, which is in the deepest layer of the unconscious, is similar in everyone and is displayed in behavior that is common across diverse cultures–such as love of mother, belief in a supreme being, and even behavior as specific as fear of snakes (Hauke, 2006; Finn, 2011).

archetypes According to Jung, universal symbolic representations of particular types of people, objects, ideas, or experiences. (Module 31)

Jung went on to propose that the collective unconscious contains **archetypes,** universal symbolic representations of particular types of people, objects, ideas, or experiences. For instance, a *mother archetype*, which contains reflections of our ancestors' relationships with mother figures, is suggested by the prevalence of mothers in art,

In terms of Jung's theory, Luke Skywalker and Kylo Ren from the *Star Wars* movies represent the archetypes, or universally recognizable symbols, of good and evil.
(left): ©AF archive/Alamy Stock Photo;
(right): ©Photo 12/Alamy Stock Photo

religion, literature, and mythology. (Think of the Virgin Mary, Earth Mother, wicked stepmothers in fairy tales, Mother's Day, and so forth!) Jung also suggested that men possess an unconscious *feminine archetype* that affects how they behave, and women have an unconscious *male archetype* that colors their behavior (Jung, 1961; Smetana, 2007; Potash, 2015).

To Jung, archetypes play an important role in determining our day-to-day reactions, attitudes, and values. For example, Jung might explain the popularity of the *Star Wars* movies as being due to their use of broad archetypes of good (Luke Skywalker) and evil (Kylo Ren).

Although no reliable research evidence confirms the existence of the collective unconscious—and even Jung acknowledged that such evidence would be difficult to produce—Jung's theory has had significant influence in areas beyond psychology. For example, personality types derived from Jung's personality approach form the basis for the Myers-Briggs personality test, which is widely used in business and industry to provide insights into how employees make decisions and perform on the job (Wilde, 2011; Mills, 2013; Wang et al., 2017).

From the perspective of...

An Advertising Executive How might you use Jung's concept of archetypes in designing your advertisements? Which of the archetypes would you use?

©Image Source/Getty Images

HORNEY'S NEO-FREUDIAN PERSPECTIVE

Karen Horney (pronounced "HORN-eye") was one of the earliest psychologists to champion women's issues and is sometimes called the first feminist psychologist. Horney suggested that personality develops in the context of social relationships and depends particularly on the relationship between parents and child and how well the child's needs are met. She rejected Freud's suggestion that women have penis envy; she asserted that what women envy most in men is not their anatomy but the independence, success, and freedom women often are denied (Horney, 1937; Smith, 2007; Coolidge et al., 2011).

Horney was also one of the first to stress the importance of cultural factors in the determination of personality. For example, she suggested that society's rigid gender

Karen Horney was one of the earliest proponents of women's issues.

©Bettmann/Getty Images

roles for women lead them to experience ambivalence about success because they fear they will make enemies if they are too successful. Her conceptualizations, developed in the 1930s and 1940s, laid the groundwork for many of the central ideas of feminism that emerged decades later (Eckardt, 2005; Jones, 2006).

ADLER AND THE OTHER NEO-FREUDIANS

Alfred Adler, another important neo-Freudian psychoanalyst, also considered Freudian theory's emphasis on sexual needs misplaced. Instead, Adler proposed that the primary human motivation is a striving for superiority, not in terms of superiority over others but in a quest for self-improvement and perfection.

Adler used the term *inferiority complex* to describe adults who have not been able to overcome feelings of inadequacy they developed as children. An *inferiority complex* is a lack of self-worth, a feeling that one is not as good as others. Early social relationships with parents have an important effect on children's ability to outgrow feelings of personal inferiority. If children have positive experiences, they can orient themselves toward attaining socially useful goals.

Other neo-Freudians included Erik Erikson, whose theory of psychosocial development we discussed in other modules, and Freud's daughter, Anna Freud. Like Adler and Horney, they focused less than Freud did on inborn sexual and aggressive drives and more on the social and cultural factors behind personality.

RECAP/EVALUATE/RETHINK

RECAP

LO 31-1 How do psychologists define and use the concept of personality?

- Personality is the pattern of enduring, distinctive characteristics that produce consistency and individuality in a given person.

LO 31-2 What do the theories of Freud and his successors tell us about the structure and development of personality?

- According to psychodynamic approaches to personality, much behavior is caused by parts of personality that are found in the unconscious and of which we are unaware.
- Freud's psychoanalytic theory, one of the psychodynamic approaches, suggests that personality is composed of the id, the ego, and the superego. The id is the unorganized, inborn part of personality whose purpose is to immediately reduce tensions relating to hunger, sex, aggression, and other primitive impulses. The ego restrains instinctual energy to maintain the individual's safety and to help the person be a member of society. The superego represents society's rights and wrongs and includes the conscience.

- Freud's psychoanalytic theory suggests that personality develops through a series of psychosexual stages (oral, anal, phallic, latency, and genital), each of which is associated with a primary biological function.
- Defense mechanisms, according to Freudian theory, are unconscious strategies that people use to reduce anxiety by distorting reality and concealing the true source of the anxiety from themselves.
- Freud's psychoanalytic theory has provoked a number of criticisms, including a lack of supportive scientific data, the theory's inadequacy in making predictions, and its reliance on a highly restricted population. On the other hand, recent neuroscience research has offered some support for the concept of the unconscious.
- Neo-Freudian psychoanalytic theorists built on Freud's work, although they placed greater emphasis on the role of the ego and paid more attention to the role of social factors in determining behavior.

EVALUATE

1. _____ approaches state that behavior is motivated primarily by unconscious forces.

2. Match each section of the personality (according to Freud) with its description:

   1. Ego
   2. Id
   3. Superego

   a. Determines right from wrong on the basis of cultural standards
   b. Operates according to the "reality principle"; energy is redirected to integrate the person into society
   c. Seeks to reduce tension brought on by primitive drives

3. Which of the following represents the proper order of personality development, according to Freud?
   a. Oral, phallic, latency, anal, genital
   b. Anal, oral, phallic, genital, latency
   c. Oral, anal, phallic, latency, genital
   d. Latency, phallic, anal, genital, oral

4. _____ _____ is the term Freud used to describe unconscious strategies used to reduce anxiety by distorting reality and concealing the source of the anxiety from themselves.

RETHINK

1. Can you think of ways in which Freud's theories of unconscious motivations are commonly used in popular culture? How accurately do you think such popular uses of Freudian theories reflect Freud's ideas?
2. What are some examples of archetypes in addition to those mentioned in this module? In what ways are archetypes similar to and different from stereotypes?

Answers to Evaluate Questions

1. Psychodynamic; **2.** 1-b, 2-c, 3-a; **3.** c; **4.** Defense mechanisms

KEY TERMS

personality	id	anal stage	defense mechanisms
psychodynamic approaches to personality	ego	phallic stage	repression
	superego	Oedipal conflict	neo-Freudian psychoanalysts
psychoanalytic theory	psychosexual stages	identification	
unconscious	fixations	latency period	collective unconscious
	oral stage	genital stage	archetypes

Module 32

Trait, Learning, Biological and Evolutionary, and Humanistic Approaches to Personality

LEARNING OUTCOMES

LO 32-1 What are the major aspects of trait, learning, biological and evolutionary, and humanistic approaches to personality?

"Tell me about Nelson," said Johnetta.

"Oh, he's just terrific. He's the friendliest guy I know—goes out of his way to be nice to everyone. He hardly ever gets mad. He's just so even-tempered, no matter what's happening. And he's really smart, too. About the only thing I don't like is that he's always in such a hurry to get things done. He seems to have boundless energy, much more than I have."

"He sounds great to me, especially in comparison to Rico," replied Johnetta. "He is so self-centered and arrogant that it drives me crazy. I sometimes wonder why I ever started going out with him."

Friendly. Even-tempered. Smart. Energetic. Self-centered. Arrogant.

The above exchange is made up of a series of trait characterizations of the speakers' friends. In fact, much of our own understanding of others' behavior is based on the premise that people possess certain traits that are consistent across different situations. For example, we generally assume that if someone is outgoing and sociable in one situation, he or she is outgoing and sociable in other situations (Mischel, 2004; Leising et al., 2014).

Dissatisfaction with the emphasis in psychoanalytic theory on unconscious—and difficult-to-demonstrate—processes in explaining a person's behavior led to the development of alternative approaches to personality, including a number of trait-based approaches. Other theories reflect established psychological perspectives, such as learning theory, biological and evolutionary approaches, and the humanistic approach.

Trait Approaches: Placing Labels on Personality

traits Consistent, habitual personality characteristics and behaviors that are displayed across different situations. (Module 41)

trait theory A model of personality that seeks to identify the basic traits necessary to describe personality. (Module 41)

Study Alert

All trait theories explain personality in terms of traits (consistent personality characteristics and behaviors), but they differ in terms of which and how many traits are seen as fundamental.

If someone asked you to characterize another person, as Johnetta did of her friend, you probably would come up with a list of traits. **Traits** are consistent, habitual personality characteristics and behaviors that are displayed across different situations.

Trait theory is the personality approach that seeks to identify the basic traits necessary to describe personality. Trait theorists do not assume that some people have a particular trait while others do not. Instead, they propose that all people possess a set of traits, but the degree to which a particular trait applies to a specific person varies and can be quantified.

For instance, they might assume that all people have the trait of "friendliness" but in different degrees. You may be relatively friendly, whereas I may be relatively unfriendly. But we both have a "friendliness" trait, although your degree of "friendliness" is higher than mine.

The major challenge for trait theorists taking this approach has been to identify the specific basic traits necessary to describe personality. As we shall see, different theorists have come up with surprisingly different sets of traits.

ALLPORT'S TRAIT THEORY: IDENTIFYING BASIC CHARACTERISTICS

When personality psychologist Gordon Allport systematically pored over an unabridged dictionary in the 1930s, he came up with some 18,000 separate terms that could be used to describe personality. Although he was able to pare down the list to 4,500 descriptors after eliminating words with similar meanings, he was left with a problem crucial to all trait approaches: Which traits are the most important in characterizing personality?

Allport eventually answered this question by suggesting that there are three fundamental categories of traits: cardinal, central, and secondary (Allport, 1966):

- **Cardinal traits.** A *cardinal trait* is a single, overriding characteristic that directs most of a person's behavior. For example, a totally selfless woman may direct all her energy toward humanitarian activities; an intensely power-hungry person may be driven by an all-consuming need for control.

- **Central traits.** Few people have a single, comprehensive cardinal trait. Instead, they possess 5-10 central traits that make up the core of personality. *Central traits,* such as warmth or honesty, describe an individual's major characteristics. Each central trait is assumed to imply the presence of other traits. For example, people who have a central trait of warmth also are likely to be sociable and friendly.

- **Secondary traits.** Finally, *secondary traits* are characteristics that affect behavior in fewer situations and are less influential than central or cardinal traits. For instance, a reluctance to eat meat and a love of modern art would be considered secondary traits (Smrtnik-Vitulić & Zupančič, 2011; Kahn et al., 2013; Zhao & Smillie, 2015).

CATTELL AND EYSENCK: FACTORING OUT PERSONALITY

Later attempts to identify primary personality traits centered on a statistical technique known as factor analysis. *Factor analysis* is a statistical method of identifying patterns among a large number of variables and combining them into more fundamental groupings. For example, a personality researcher might ask a large group of people to rate themselves on a number of specific traits. By using factor analysis and statistically computing which traits are associated with one another, a researcher can identify the fundamental patterns of traits–called *factors*–that cluster together in the same person.

Using factor analysis, personality psychologist Raymond Cattell suggested that 16 pairs of *traits* represent the basic dimensions of personality. Using that set of traits, he developed the Sixteen Personality Factor Questionnaire, or 16 PF, a personality scale that is still in use today (Cattell, Cattell, & Cattell, 2000; Djapo et al., 2011; Wright, 2017).

Another trait theorist, psychologist Hans Eysenck (1995), also used factor analysis to identify patterns of traits, but he came to a very different conclusion about the nature of personality. He found that personality could best be described in terms of just three major dimensions: extraversion, neuroticism, and psychoticism. The *extraversion* dimension describes a person's level of sociability, whereas the *neuroticism* dimension encompasses an individual's emotional stability. Finally, *psychoticism* is the degree to which reality is distorted. By evaluating people along these three dimensions, Eysenck was able to predict behavior accurately in a variety of situations. Figure 1 lists specific traits associated with each of the dimensions.

THE BIG FIVE PERSONALITY TRAITS

For the last two decades, the most influential trait approach contends that five traits or factors–called the "Big Five"–lie at the core of personality. Using factor analytic statistical techniques, a consistent body of research has identified a similar set of five factors that underlie personality. The specific five factors are *openness to experience,*

Extraversion
- Sociable
- Lively
- Active
- Assertive
- Sensation-seeking

Neuroticism
- Anxious
- Depressed
- Guilt feelings
- Low self-esteem
- Tense

Psychoticism
- Aggressive
- Cold
- Egocentric
- Impersonal
- Impulsive

FIGURE 1 Eysenck described personality in terms of three major dimensions: extraversion, neuroticism, and psychoticism. Using these dimensions, he could predict people's behavior in many types of situations.

Source: Eysenck, H. J. (1991). Biological dimensions of personality. In L. A. Pervin (Ed.), *Handbook of personality: Theory and research.* New York: Guilford Press.

Study Alert

You can remember the "Big Five" set of personality traits by using the acronym OCEAN (openness to experience, conscientiousness, extraversion, agreeableness, and neuroticism).

FIGURE 2 Five broad trait factors, referred to as the "Big Five," are considered to be the core of personality.

Sources: Adapted from Pervin, 1990, and McCrae & Costa, 1986.

The Big Five Personality Factors and Dimensions of Sample Traits

Openness to experience	Agreeableness
Independent—Conforming	Sympathetic—Fault-finding
Imaginative—Practical	Kind—Cold
Preference for variety—Preference for routine	Appreciative—Unfriendly
Conscientiousness	**Neuroticism (Emotional stability)**
Careful—Careless	Stable—Tense
Disciplined—Impulsive	Calm—Anxious
Organized—Disorganized	Secure—Insecure
Extraversion	
Talkative—Quiet	
Fun-loving—Sober	
Sociable—Retiring	

conscientiousness, extraversion, agreeableness, and *neuroticism* (emotional stability). They are described in Figure 2.

The Big Five emerge consistently across a number of domains. For example, factor analyses of major personality inventories, self-report measures made by observers of others' personality traits, and checklists of self-descriptions yield similar factors. In addition, the Big Five emerge consistently in different populations of individuals, including children, college students, older adults, and speakers of different languages. Cross-cultural research conducted in areas ranging from Europe to the Middle East to Africa also has been supportive. Finally, studies of brain functioning show that Big Five personality traits are related to the way the brain processes information (Vecchione et al., 2011; Saucier & Srivastava, 2015; Bouvard & Roulin, 2017).

In short, a growing consensus exists that the Big Five represent the best description of personality traits we have today. Still, the debate over the specific number and kinds of traits—and even the usefulness of trait approaches in general—remains a lively one.

EVALUATING TRAIT APPROACHES TO PERSONALITY

Trait approaches have several virtues. They provide a clear, straightforward explanation of people's behavioral consistencies. Furthermore, traits allow us to readily compare one person with another. Because of these advantages, trait approaches to personality have had an important influence on the development of several useful personality measures (Wiggins, 2003; Larsen & Buss, 2006; Cook, 2013).

However, trait approaches also have some drawbacks. For example, we have seen that various trait theories describing personality come to different conclusions about which traits are the most fundamental and descriptive. The difficulty in determining which of the theories is the most accurate has led some personality psychologists to question the validity of trait conceptions of personality in general.

Trait approaches suffer from an even more fundamental difficulty: Even if we identify a set of primary traits, all we have done is provide a set of labels for personality. But labeling personality traits is not an *explanation* of how those traits developed in a person nor of how they function to determine behavior. For example, if we say that someone who donates money to charity has the trait of generosity, we still do not know *why* that person became generous in the first place or why the person displays generosity in a specific situation. In the view of some critics, then, traits do not provide explanations for behavior; they merely label it.

Learning Approaches: We Are What We've Learned

The psychodynamic and trait approaches we've been discussing concentrate on the "inner" person—the fury of a powerful id or a critical set of traits that describes the core of an individual. In contrast, learning approaches to personality focus on the external world in which a person lives and how external influences determine and affect personality.

SKINNER'S BEHAVIORIST APPROACH

According to the most influential learning theorist, B. F. Skinner (who carried out pioneering work on operant conditioning), personality is a collection of learned behavior patterns (Skinner, 1975). Similarities in responses across different situations are caused by similar patterns of reinforcement that have been received in such situations in the past. If I am sociable both at parties and at meetings, it is because I have been reinforced for displaying social behaviors—not because I am fulfilling an unconscious wish based on experiences during my childhood or because I have an internal trait of sociability.

Learning theorists such as Skinner are less interested in the consistencies in behavior across situations than in ways of modifying behavior. To a learning theorist who subscribes to Skinner's view, humans are infinitely changeable through the process of learning new behavior patterns. If we are able to control and modify the patterns of reinforcers in a situation, behavior that other theorists would view as stable and unyielding can be changed and ultimately improved. Learning theorists are optimistic in their attitudes about the potential for resolving personal and societal problems through treatment strategies based on learning theory.

SOCIAL COGNITIVE APPROACHES TO PERSONALITY

Not all learning theories of personality take such a rigid view in rejecting the importance of what is "inside" a person by focusing solely on the "outside." Unlike other learning approaches to personality, **social cognitive approaches to personality** emphasize the influence of cognition—thoughts, feelings, expectations, and values—as well as observation of others' behavior, on personality. According to Albert Bandura, one of the main proponents of this point of view, people can foresee the possible outcomes of certain behaviors in a specific setting without actually having to carry them out. This understanding comes primarily through *observational learning*—viewing the actions of others and observing the consequences (Bandura, 1999).

For instance, children who view a model behaving in, say, an aggressive manner tend to copy the behavior if the consequences of the model's behavior are seen as positive. If, in contrast, the model's aggressive behavior has resulted in no consequences or negative consequences, children are considerably less likely to act aggressively. According to social cognitive approaches, then, personality develops through repeated observation of others' behavior.

Bandura places particular emphasis on the role played by self-efficacy. **Self-efficacy** is the belief that we can master a situation and produce positive outcomes. Self-efficacy underlies people's faith in their ability to successfully carry out a particular task or to produce a desired outcome. People with high self-efficacy have higher aspirations and greater persistence in working to attain goals than those with lower self-efficacy. Furthermore, they ultimately achieve greater success (Bandura & Locke, 2003; Dunlop, Beatty, & Beauchamp, 2011; Sezgin & Erdogan, 2015).

social cognitive approaches to personality Theories that emphasize the influence of a person's cognitions—thoughts, feelings, expectations, and values—as well as observation of others' behavior, in determining personality. (Module 32)

self-efficacy The belief that we can master a situation and produce positive outcomes. (Module 32)

PsychTech
Researchers have been investigating differences in self-efficacy between people in their use of technology. One difference is age: younger adults appear to have more confidence in their technological expertise than older adults do.

Self-efficacy, the belief in one's own capabilities, leads to higher aspirations and greater persistence.

©McGraw-Hill Education/Lars Niki, photographer

self-esteem The component of personality that encompasses our positive and negative self-evaluations. (Module 32)

How do we develop self-efficacy? One way is by paying close attention to our prior successes and failures. If we try snowboarding and experience little success, we'll be less likely to try it again. However, if our initial efforts appear promising, we'll be more likely to attempt it again. Direct reinforcement and encouragement from others also play a role in developing self-efficacy (Buchanan & Selmon, 2008; Artistico et al., 2013; Wright, 2017).

Compared with other learning theories of personality, social cognitive approaches are distinctive in their emphasis on the reciprocity between individuals and their environment. Not only is the environment assumed to affect personality, but people's behavior and personalities are also assumed to "feed back" and modify the environment (Bandura, 1999, 2000).

HOW MUCH CONSISTENCY EXISTS IN PERSONALITY?

Another social cognitive theorist, Walter Mischel, takes a different approach to personality from that of Albert Bandura. He rejects the view that personality consists of broad traits that lead to substantial consistencies in behavior across different situations. Instead, he sees personality as considerably more variable from one situation to another (Mischel, 2009).

In this view, particular situations give rise to particular kinds of behavior. Some situations are especially influential (think of a movie theater, where everyone displays pretty much the same behavior by sitting quietly and watching the film). Other situations permit much variability in behavior (think of a party, for example, where some people may be dancing, while others are eating and drinking).

From this perspective, personality cannot be considered without taking the particular context of the situation into account—a view known as *situationism*. In his *cognitive-affective processing system (CAPS)* theory, Mischel argues that people's thoughts and emotions about themselves and the world determine how they view, and then react, in particular situations. Personality is thus seen as a reflection of how people's prior experiences in different situations affect their behavior (Mischel & Shoda, 2008; McCrae et al., 2011; Huprich & Nelson, 2015).

SELF-ESTEEM

Our behavior also reflects the view we have of ourselves and the way we value the various parts of our personalities. **Self-esteem** is the component of personality that encompasses our positive and negative self-evaluations. Unlike self-efficacy, which focuses on our views of whether we are able to carry out a task, self-esteem relates to how we feel about ourselves.

Although people have a general level of self-esteem, it is not unidimensional. We may see ourselves positively in one domain but negatively in others. For example, a good student may have high self-esteem in academic domains but lower self-esteem in sports (Gentile et al., 2009; Gadbois & Sturgeon, 2011; Mirzairad et al., 2017).

The development of self-esteem is strongly affected by cultural factors. For example, consider the characteristic of *relationship harmony*, which is a sense of success in forming close bonds with others. For people living in Asian cultures, having high relationship harmony is a more important component of self-esteem than it is for those living in more individualistic Western societies (Lun & Bond, 2006; Cheng & Kwan, 2008; Chin, 2015).

Although almost all of us go through periods in which our self-esteem is challenged and temporarily reduced (for instance, after an undeniable failure), some people are chronically low in self-esteem. For them, failure seems to be an inevitable part of life. In fact, low self-esteem may lead to a cycle of failure in which past failure breeds future failure.

For example, consider students with low self-esteem who are studying for a test. Because of their low self-esteem, they expect to do poorly on the test. In turn, this

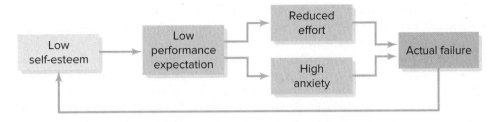

belief raises their anxiety level, which makes it increasingly difficult to study and perhaps even leads them not to work as hard. Because of these attitudes, they do, in fact, perform badly on the test. Ultimately, the failure reinforces their low self-esteem, and the cycle is perpetuated, as illustrated in Figure 3. In short, low self-esteem can lead to a self-destructive cycle of failure.

On the other hand, high levels of self-esteem can also be troublesome if they are unwarranted. According to a growing body of data, an increasing number of college-age students have high levels of *narcissism*, in which people show self-absorption and hold inflated views of themselves. For example, over the past three decades, thousands of American college students participating in a variety of psychological research studies were asked to take the Narcissism Personality Inventory (NPI), a test of narcissistic tendencies. A summary of more than 100 such studies conducted over a 25-year period showed a significant increase in participants' narcissism scores (Dingfelder, 2011; Twenge & Kasser, 2013; Barry et al., 2017).

What might produce the increase in narcissism in young Americans? Research points to social networking media. In recent years, it has become typical for young people to self-promote in carefully edited online profiles. The most mundane aspects of their daily lives are viewed as worthy of broadcasting to the world, whether in Twitter tweets, Facebook postings, or YouTube videos. Another explanation is that parents may increasingly be inflating their children's sense of self-importance by shielding them from situations in which they might fail (Twenge, 2013; Twenge, Campbell, & Gentile, 2013; Kauten et al., 2015).

From the perspective of...

An Educator How might you encourage your students' development of self-esteem and self-efficacy? What steps would you take to ensure that their self-esteem did not become overinflated?

©Andersen Ross/Blend Images/Getty Images

EVALUATING LEARNING APPROACHES TO PERSONALITY

Because they ignore the internal processes, such as thoughts and emotions, traditional learning theorists such as Skinner have been accused of oversimplifying personality far too much. Their critics think that reducing behavior to a series of stimuli and responses and excluding thoughts and feelings from the realm of personality leaves behaviorists practicing an unrealistic and inadequate form of science.

Of course, some of these criticisms are blunted by social cognitive approaches, which explicitly consider the role of cognitive processes in personality. Still, learning approaches tend to share a highly *deterministic* view of human behavior, which maintains that behavior is shaped primarily by forces beyond the individual's control. As in psychoanalytic theory (which suggests that personality is determined by the unconscious forces) and trait approaches (which view personality in part as a mixture of genetically determined traits), learning theory's reliance on deterministic principles de-emphasizes people's ability to pilot their own course through life.

Nonetheless, learning approaches have had a major impact on the study of personality. For one thing, they have helped make personality psychology an objective, scientific venture by focusing on observable behavior and the effects of the environments. In addition, they have produced important, successful means of treating a variety of psychological disorders. The degree of success of these treatments is a testimony to the merits of learning theory approaches to personality.

Biological and Evolutionary Approaches: Are We Born with Personality?

Approaching the question of what determines personality from a different direction, **biological and evolutionary approaches to personality** suggest that important components of personality are inherited. Building on the work of behavioral geneticists, researchers using biological and evolutionary approaches argue that personality is determined at least in part by our genes in much the same way that our height is largely a result of genetic contributions from our ancestors. The evolutionary perspective assumes that personality traits that led to our ancestors' survival and reproductive success are more likely to be preserved and passed on to subsequent generations (Buss, 2001, 2009, 2011; Yarkoni, 2015).

The results of research studies conducted on twins who are genetically identical but raised apart from one another by different caretakers illustrate the importance of genetic factors in personality. Personality tests indicate that in major respects, genetically identical twins raised apart are quite similar in personality, even if they were separated at an early age.

Moreover, certain traits are more heavily influenced by heredity than are others. For example, *social potency* (the degree to which a person assumes mastery and leadership roles in social situations) and *traditionalism* (the tendency to follow authority) had particularly strong genetic components, whereas achievement and social closeness had relatively weak genetic components (see Figure 4; Bouchard et al., 2004).

Study Alert

Remember that biological and evolutionary approaches focus on the ways in which people's genetic heritage affects personality.

biological and evolutionary approaches to personality Theories that suggest that important components of personality are inherited. (Module 32)

Biological and evolutionary approaches to personality seek to explain the consistencies in personality that are found in some families.
©Image Source

Infants are born with particular temperaments—dispositions that are consistent throughout childhood.
©Image Source

Furthermore, it is increasingly clear that the roots of adult personality emerge early in life. Infants are born with a specific **temperament,** an individual's behavioral style and characteristic way of responding. Temperament encompasses several dimensions, including general activity level and mood. For instance, some babies are quite active, whereas others are relatively calm. Similarly, some are relatively easygoing, whereas others are irritable, easily upset, and difficult to soothe. Temperament is quite consistent, with significant stability from infancy well into adolescence (Evans & Rothbart, 2009; Hori et al., 2011; Bates & Pettit, 2015; also see *Applying Psychology in the 21st Century*).

Some researchers contend that specific genes are related to personality. For example, people with a longer dopamine-4 receptor gene are more likely to be thrill-seekers than are those without such a gene. These thrill-seekers tend to be extroverted, impulsive, quick-tempered, and always in search of excitement and novel situations. Furthermore, the structure of their brains may reflect their thrill-seeking tendencies (Golimbet et al., 2007; Ray et al., 2009; Wishart, Somoray, & Rowland, 2017; also see *Neuroscience in Your Life*).

temperament A basic, inborn characteristic way of responding and behavioral style. (Module 37)

NEUROSCIENCE IN YOUR LIFE: THE NEUROLOGICAL UNDERPINNINGS OF PERSONALITY

A large part of what makes us who we are is personality. Although the five-factor model has been influential in describing personality traits, its neurobiological basis has been largely unknown. However, in a recent study with over 500 participants, neuroscientists looked at how the shape of the brain relates to the five basic personality traits of openness to experience, conscientiousness, extraversion, agreeableness, and neuroticism. They found that the shape of certain brain areas relates to each of the five personality traits. For example, high levels of conscientiousness related to thicker cortex in two brain areas (shown in blue in three views of the brain below) (Riccelli et al., 2017).

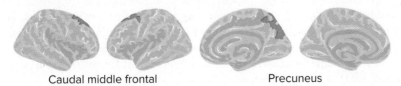

Caudal middle frontal   Precuneus

Source: Adapted from Riccelli, R., Toschi, N., Nigro, S., Terracciano, A., & Passamonti, L. (2017). Surface-based morphometry reveals the neuroanatomical basis of the five-factor model of personality. *Social Cognitive and Affective Neuroscience, 12*(4), 671–684. doi: 10.1093/scan/nsw175

APPLYING PSYCHOLOGY IN THE 21ST CENTURY

DOES PERSONALITY SHIFT FROM GENERATION TO GENERATION?

Research has long shown that personality is largely stable across the lifespan, and this is generally a good thing. It means that the person you hire (or befriend, or marry) today will, for the most part, continue to be that same person tomorrow and next year and 5 years from now. Our social world would be a lot harder to navigate if individual people's personalities drifted substantially over time (McCrae & Costa, 1994; Borghuis et al., 2017).

But are larger-scale changes in personality possible? That is, do average traits of a given population drift over time, from generation to generation? A moment's thought would suggest they do. After all, we might assume that people today are a lot different personality-wise from people in the Middle Ages. More important, compelling research out of Finland confirms this intuition.

Researchers took advantage of Finland's history of compulsory military conscription, which requires all Finnish men to spend time serving their country, mostly in military roles. For many years, those who choose military service—about 80% of all young Finnish men—have been given a standardized personality test at the start of their training. These tests provided an enormous data set for researchers to examine. They chose data from men born between 1962 and 1976, which allowed them to include tax data showing these men's average earnings later in

©Sam Edwards/Glow Images

life (between ages 30 and 34). This data set included over 400,000 Finnish men and allowed researchers to look at personality trends over time and how those trends related to average income (Jokela et al., 2017).

What they found was remarkable: The personality traits of self-confidence, sociability, leadership motivation, activity-energy, achievement striving, dutifulness, and deliberation all increased year after year for each new cohort of soldiers between 1962 and 1978. (A *cohort* is a

group of people sharing a characteristic in common—in this case, membership in a given year's military enrollees.) Of those traits, self-confidence, sociability, and leadership motivation increased the most, followed by activity-energy and achievement striving. Dutifulness and deliberation grew at a slower but still steady rate.

If it appears to you that these traits all seem to be related to career success, you're right. When they examined later income levels, they found that the relatively modest growth in these personality traits predicted substantially greater earnings, with the cohort born in 1976 earning about 12% more than the 1962 cohort. Why this should be the case was unclear. The researchers controlled for obvious factors such as inflation and educational attainment, but the underlying cause for the finding remains elusive.

Explaining why personality changes across generations will be the focus of further research, with likely candidates being changes in health, nutrition, and quality of education. But for the moment, it seems clear that personality can change in subtle yet important ways across generations (Jokela et al., 2017).

> **RETHINK**
>
> - Cohort differences can sometimes be explained by changes in the social, cultural, or economic conditions under which cohorts grew up. What might be some such environmental changes that could explain the personality changes found in this research?
> - In what ways do you think social and cultural shifts that are happening today might be affecting generational personalities?

Does the identification of specific genes linked to personality, coupled with the existence of temperaments from the time of birth, mean that we are destined to have certain types of personalities? Hardly. First, it is unlikely that any single gene is linked to a specific trait. For instance, the dopamine-4 receptor accounts for only around 10% of the variation in novelty seeking between different individuals. The rest of the variation is attributable to other genes and environmental factors (Keltikangas-Järvinen et al., 2004; Lahti et al., 2005; Kandler, Riemann, & Angleitner, 2013).

More important, genes interact with the environment. As we see in discussions of the heritability of intelligence and the nature–nurture issue, it is impossible to completely divorce genetic factors from environmental factors. Although studies of identical twins raised in different environments are helpful, they are not definitive because it is impossible to assess and control environmental factors fully. Furthermore, estimates of the influence of genetics are just that–estimates–and apply to groups, not individuals. Consequently, findings such as those shown in Figure 4 must be regarded as approximations.

Finally, even if more genes are found to be linked to specific personality characteristics, genes still cannot be viewed as the sole cause of personality. For one thing, genetically determined characteristics may not be expressed if they are not "turned on" by particular environmental experiences. Furthermore, behaviors produced by genes may help to create a specific environment. For instance, a cheerful, smiley baby may lead the parents to smile more and be more responsive, thereby creating a supportive, pleasant environment. In contrast, the parents of a cranky, fussy baby may be less inclined to smile at the child; in turn, the environment in which that child is raised will be less supportive and pleasant. In a sense, then, genes not only influence a person's behavior–they also help produce the environment in which a person develops (Kim-Cohen, Caspi, & Moffitt, 2003; Kim-Cohen et al., 2005; Kendler et al., 2017).

Although an increasing number of personality theorists are taking biological and evolutionary factors into account, no comprehensive, unified theory that considers biological and evolutionary factors is widely accepted. Still, it is clear that certain personality traits have substantial genetic components and that heredity and environment interact to determine personality (Bouchard, 2004; South & Krueger, 2008; South et al., 2013).

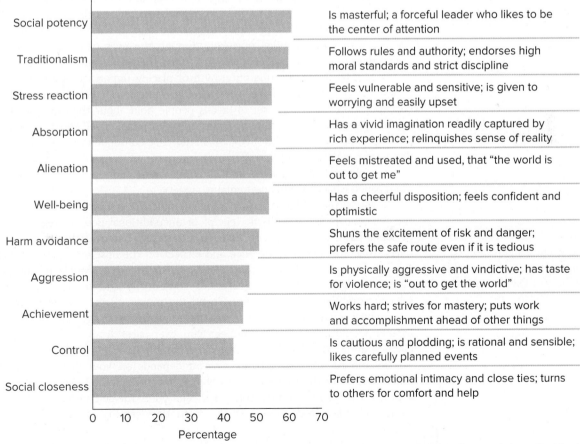

FIGURE 4 The inherited roots of personality. The percentages indicate the degree to which 11 personality characteristics reflect the influence of heredity.

Source: Adapted from Tellegen, A., Lykken, D. T., Bouchard, T. J., Jr., Wilcox, K. J., Segal, N. L., & Rich, S. (1998). Personality similarity in twins reared apart and together. *Journal of Personality and Social Psychology, 54*, 1031–1039.

Humanistic Approaches: The Uniqueness of You

In all the approaches to personality that we have discussed, where is an explanation for the saintliness of a Mother Teresa, the creativity of a Michelangelo, and the brilliance and perseverance of an Einstein? An understanding of such unique individuals—as well as more ordinary sorts of people who have some of the same attributes—comes from humanistic theory.

According to humanistic theorists, all the approaches to personality we have discussed share a fundamental misperception in their views of human nature. Instead of seeing people as controlled by unconscious, unseen forces (psychodynamic approaches), a set of stable traits (trait approaches), situational reinforcements and punishments (learning theory), or inherited factors (biological and evolutionary approaches), **humanistic approaches to personality** emphasize people's inherent goodness and their tendency to move toward higher levels of functioning. It is this conscious, self-motivated ability to change and improve, along with people's unique creative impulses, that humanistic theorists argue make up the core of personality.

humanistic approaches to personality Theories that emphasize people's innate goodness and desire to achieve higher levels of functioning. (Module 32)

ROGERS AND THE NEED FOR SELF-ACTUALIZATION

The major proponent of the humanistic point of view is Carl Rogers (1971). Along with other humanistic theorists, such as Abraham Maslow, Rogers maintains that all people have a fundamental need for **self-actualization,** a state of self-fulfillment in which people realize their highest potential, each in a unique way. He further suggests that people develop a need for positive regard that reflects the desire to be loved and respected. Because others provide this positive regard, we grow dependent on them. We begin to see and judge ourselves through the eyes of other people, relying on their values and being preoccupied with what they think of us.

self-actualization A state of self-fulfillment in which people realize their highest potential in their own unique way. (Modules 24, 32)

According to Rogers, one outgrowth of placing importance on others' opinions is that a conflict may grow between people's actual life experiences and their self-concept. *Self-concept* is the set of beliefs people hold about their own abilities, behavior, and personality. If the discrepancies between people's self-concepts and what they actually experience in their lives are minor, the consequences are minor. But if the discrepancies between one's experience and one's self-concept are great, they will lead to psychological disturbances in daily functioning. For instance, people with large discrepancies may experience frequent anxiety.

Rogers suggests that one way of overcoming the discrepancy between experience and self-concept is through the receipt of unconditional positive regard from another person—a parent, friend, spouse, or even a therapist. **Unconditional positive regard** refers to an attitude of acceptance and respect on the observer's part, no matter what a person says or does. This acceptance, says Rogers, gives people the opportunity to evolve and grow both cognitively and emotionally and to develop more realistic self-concepts. You may have experienced the power of unconditional positive regard when you confided in someone, revealing embarrassing secrets because you knew the listener would still love and respect you even after hearing the worst about you (Snyder, 2002; Marshall, 2007; Patterson & Joseph, 2013).

unconditional positive regard An attitude of acceptance and respect on the part of an observer, no matter what a person says or does. (Module 32)

In contrast, *conditional positive regard* depends on your behavior. In such cases, others withdraw their love and acceptance if you do something of which they don't approve. The result is a discrepancy between your true self and what others wish you would be, which leads to anxiety and frustration (see Figure 5).

EVALUATING HUMANISTIC APPROACHES

Although humanistic theories suggest the value of providing unconditional positive regard toward people, unconditional positive regard toward humanistic theories has

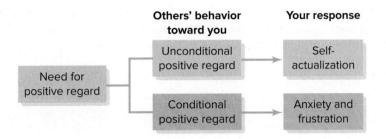

FIGURE 5 According to the humanistic view of Carl Rogers, people have a basic need to be loved and respected. If you receive unconditional positive regard from others, you will develop a more realistic self-concept, but if the response is conditional, it may lead to anxiety and frustration.

been less forthcoming. The criticisms have centered on the difficulty of verifying the basic assumptions of the approach as well as on the question of whether unconditional positive regard does, in fact, lead to greater personality adjustment.

Humanistic approaches have also been criticized for making the assumption that people are basically "good"–a notion that is unverifiable–and, equally important, for using nonscientific values to build supposedly scientific theories. Still, humanistic theories have been important in highlighting the uniqueness of human beings and guiding the development of a significant form of therapy designed to alleviate psychological difficulties (Elkins, 2009; Kogstad, Ekeland, & Hummelvoll, 2011; Hounkatin et al., 2015).

Comparing Approaches to Personality

In light of the multiple approaches we have discussed, you may be wondering which of the theories provides the most accurate description of personality. That question cannot be answered precisely. Each theory is built on different assumptions and focuses on somewhat different aspects of personality (see Figure 6).

Theoretical Approach and Major Theorists	Conscious Versus Unconscious Determinants of Personality	Nature (Hereditary Factors) Versus Nurture (Environmental Factors)	Free Will Versus Determinism	Stability Versus Modifiability
Psychodynamic (Freud, Jung, Horney, Adler)	Emphasizes the unconscious	Stresses innate, inherited structure of personality while emphasizing importance of childhood experience	Stresses determinism, the view that behavior is directed and caused by factors outside one's control	Emphasizes the stability of characteristics throughout a person's life
Trait (Allport, Cattell, Eysenck)	Disregards both conscious and unconscious	Approaches vary	Stresses determinism, the view that behavior is directed and caused by factors outside one's control	Emphasizes the stability of characteristics throughout a person's life
Learning (Skinner, Bandura)	Disregards both conscious and unconscious	Focuses on the environment	Stresses determinism, the view that behavior is directed and caused by factors outside one's control	Stresses that personality remains flexible and resilient throughout one's life
Biological and evolutionary (Tellegen)	Disregards both conscious and unconscious	Stresses the innate, inherited determinants of personality	Stresses determinism, the view that behavior is directed and caused by factors outside one's control	Emphasizes the stability of characteristics throughout a person's life
Humanistic (Rogers, Maslow)	Stresses the conscious more than the unconscious	Stresses the interaction between nature and nurture	Stresses the freedom of individuals to make their own choices	Stresses that personality remains flexible and resilient throughout one's life

FIGURE 6 The multiple perspectives on personality.

Furthermore, there is no clear way to scientifically test the various approaches and their assumptions against one another. Given the complexity of every individual, it seems reasonable that personality can be viewed from a number of perspectives simultaneously (Pervin, 2003).

RECAP/EVALUATE/RETHINK

RECAP

LO 32-1 What are the major aspects of trait, learning, biological and evolutionary, and humanistic approaches to personality?

- Trait approaches have been used to identify relatively enduring dimensions along which people differ from one another–dimensions known as traits.
- Learning approaches to personality concentrate on observable behavior. To a strict learning theorist, personality is the sum of learned responses to the external environment.
- Social cognitive approaches concentrate on the role of cognition in determining personality. Those approaches pay particular attention to self-efficacy and self-esteem in determining behavior.
- Biological and evolutionary approaches to personality focus on the way in which personality characteristics are inherited.
- Humanistic approaches emphasize people's inherent goodness. They consider the core of personality in terms of a person's ability to change and improve.
- The major personality approaches differ substantially from one another; the differences may reflect both their focus on different aspects of personality and the overall complexity of personality.

EVALUATE

1. Carl's determination to succeed is the dominant force in all his activities and relationships. According to Allport's theory, this is an example of a _____ trait. In contrast, Cindy's fondness for old western movies is an example of a _____ trait.

2. Eysenck might describe a person who enjoys activities such as parties and hang gliding as high on what trait?

3. Proponents of which approach to personality would be most likely to agree with the statement, "Personality can be thought of as learned responses to a person's upbringing and environment"?
   a. Humanistic
   b. Biological and evolutionary
   c. Learning
   d. Trait

4. Bandura would rate a person who would make the statement, "I know I can't do it" as low on _____
   _____.

5. Which approach to personality emphasizes the innate goodness of people and their desire to grow?
   a. Humanistic
   b. Psychodynamic
   c. Learning
   d. Biological and evolutionary

RETHINK

1. If personality traits are merely descriptive and not explanatory, what use are they? Can assigning a trait to a person be harmful–or helpful? Why or why not?

2. In what ways are Cattell's 16 source traits, Eysenck's three dimensions, and the "Big Five" factors similar, and in what ways are they different? Which traits seem to appear in all three schemes (under one name or another), and which are unique to one scheme? Why is this significant?

Answers to Evaluate Questions

1. cardinal, secondary; 2. extraversion; 3. c; 4. self-efficacy; 5. a

KEY TERMS

traits	self-efficacy	temperament	self-actualization
trait theory	self-esteem	humanistic approaches to	unconditional positive
social cognitive approaches to personality	biological and evolutionary approaches to personality	personality	regard

Module 33

Assessing Personality: Determining What Makes Us Distinctive

You have a need for other people to like and admire you.

You have a tendency to be critical of yourself.

You have a great deal of unused potential that you have not turned to your advantage.

Although you have some personality weaknesses, you generally are able to compensate for them.

Relating to members of the opposite sex has presented problems for you.

Although you appear to be disciplined and self-controlled to others, you tend to be anxious and insecure inside.

At times you have serious doubts about whether you have made the right decision or done the right thing.

You prefer a certain amount of change and variety and become dissatisfied when hemmed in by restrictions and limitations.

You do not accept others' statements without satisfactory proof.

You have found it unwise to be too frank in revealing yourself to others.

If you think these statements provide a surprisingly accurate account of your personality, you are not alone: Most college students think that these descriptions are tailored just to them. In fact, the statements were designed intentionally to be so vague that they apply to just about anyone (Forer, 1949; Russo, 1981).

The ease with which we can agree with such imprecise statements underscores the difficulty in coming up with accurate and meaningful assessments of people's personalities. Psychologists interested in assessing personality must be able to define the most meaningful ways of discriminating between one person's personality and another's. To do this, they use **psychological tests,** standard measures devised to assess behavior objectively. With the results of such tests, psychologists can help people better understand themselves and make decisions about their lives. Researchers interested in the causes and consequences of personality also employ psychological tests (Hambleton, 2006; Miller, McIntire, & Lovler, 2011; Hambleton & Zenisky, 2013).

Like the assessments that seek to measure intelligence, all psychological tests must have reliability and validity. *Reliability* refers to a test's measurement consistency. If a test is reliable, it yields the same result each time it is administered to a specific person or group. In contrast, unreliable tests give different results each time they are administered.

For meaningful conclusions to be drawn, tests also must be valid. Tests have *validity* when they actually measure what they are designed to measure. If a test is constructed to measure sociability, for instance, we need to know that it actually measures sociability and not some other trait.

Finally, psychological tests are based on *test norms,* the distribution of test scores for a large sample of individuals who have taken a test. Test norms allow us to compare one person's score on a test with the scores of others who have taken the same test. For example, knowing the norms of a test permits test-takers who have received a certain score to know that they have scored in the top 10% of all those who have taken the test.

psychological tests Standard measures devised to assess behavior objectively; used by psychologists to help people make decisions about their lives and understand more about themselves. (Module 33)

Study Alert

The distinction between reliability and validity is important. For instance, a test that measures trustfulness is reliable if it yields the same results each time it is administered, whereas it is valid if it measures trustfulness accurately.

Test norms are established by administering a specific test to a large number of people and determining the typical scores. It is then possible to compare a single person's score with the scores of the group, which provides a comparative measure of test performance against the performance of others who have taken the test.

The establishment of appropriate test norms is not a simple endeavor. For instance, the specific group that is employed to determine test norms has a profound effect on the way an individual's performance is evaluated. In fact, as we discuss next, the process of establishing test norms can take on political overtones.

# Exploring Diversity

Should Race and Ethnicity Be Used to Establish Test Norms?

The passions of politics may confront the objectivity of science when test norms are established, at least in the realm of standardized tests that are meant to predict future job performance. In fact, a national controversy has developed around the question of whether different test norms should be established for members of various racial and ethnic groups (Manly, 2005; Manly & Echemendia, 2007; Pedraza & Mungas, 2008).

The test that sparked the controversy was the U.S. government's General Aptitude Test Battery, a test that measures a broad range of abilities from eye-hand coordination to reading proficiency. The problem was that African Americans and Hispanics tend to score lower on the test, on average, than do members of other groups. The lower scores often are due to a lack of prior relevant experience and job opportunities, which in turn has been due to prejudice and discrimination.

To promote the employment of minority racial groups, the government developed a separate set of test norms for African Americans and Hispanics. Rather than using the pool of all people who took the tests, the scores of African American and Hispanic applicants were compared only with the scores of other African Americans and Hispanics. Consequently, a Hispanic who scored in the top 20% of the Hispanics taking the test was considered to have performed equivalently to a white job applicant who scored in the top 20% of the whites who took the test, even though the absolute score of the Hispanic might be lower than that of the white.

Critics of the adjusted test norming system suggested that such a procedure discriminates in favor of certain racial and ethnic groups at the expense of others, thereby fanning the flames of racial bigotry. The practice was challenged legally; with the passage of the Civil Rights Act in 1991, race-based test norming on the General Aptitude Test Battery was discontinued (Galef, 2001).

However, proponents of race-based test norming continue to argue that test norming procedures that take race into account are an affirmative action tool that simply permits minority job-seekers to be placed on an equal footing with white job-seekers. Furthermore, a panel of the National Academy of Sciences supported the practice of adjusting test norms. It suggested that the unadjusted test norms are not very useful in predicting job performance and that they would tend to screen out otherwise qualified minority group members (Fleming, 2000).

Job testing is not the only area in which issues arise regarding test norms and the meaning of test scores. The issue of how to treat racial differences in IQ scores is also controversial and divisive. Clearly, race-based test norming raises profound and intense feelings that may come into conflict with scientific objectivity (Leiter & Leiter, 2003; Rushton & Jensen, 2006; Davis, 2009).

The issue of establishing test norms is further complicated by the existence of a wide array of personality measures and approaches to assessment. We next consider some of these measures.

From the perspective of...

A Politician Imagine that you had to vote on a law that would require institutions and organizations to perform race-based test norming procedures on standardized tests. Would you support such a law? Why or why not? In addition to race, should test norming procedures take other factors into account? Which ones and why?

©Exactostock/SuperStock

Self-Report Measures of Personality

If someone wanted to assess your personality, one possible approach would be to carry out an extensive interview with you to determine the most important events in your childhood, your social relationships, and your successes and failures. Obviously, though, such a technique would take extraordinary time and effort.

It is also unnecessary. Just as physicians draw only a small sample of your blood to test, psychologists can use self-report measures. In a **self-report measure,** people are asked questions about their own behavior and traits. This sampling of self-report data is then used to infer the presence of particular personality characteristics. For example, a researcher who was interested in assessing a person's orientation to life might administer the questionnaire shown in Figure 1. Although the questionnaire consists of only a few questions, the answers can be used to generalize about personality characteristics. (Try it yourself!)

One of the best examples of a self-report measure, and one of the most frequently used personality tests, is the **Minnesota Multiphasic Personality Inventory-2-Restructured Form (MMPI-2-RF).** Although the original purpose of this measure was to identify people with specific sorts of psychological difficulties, it has been found to predict a variety of other behaviors. For instance, MMPI-2-RF scores have been shown to be good predictors of whether college students will marry within 10 years of graduating and whether they will get advanced degrees. Police departments use the test to measure whether police officers are likely to use their weapons. Psychologists in Russia administer a modified form of the MMPI-2-RF to their astronauts and Olympic athletes (Sellbom, Fischler, & Ben-Porath, 2007; Butcher, 2011; Zahn et al., 2017).

The test consists of a series of 338 items to which a person responds "true," "false," or "cannot say." The questions cover a variety of issues ranging from mood ("I feel useless at times") to opinions ("People should try to understand their dreams") to physical and psychological health ("I am bothered by an upset stomach several times a week" and "I have strange and peculiar thoughts").

There are no right or wrong answers. Instead, interpretation of the results rests on the pattern of responses. The test yields scores on 51 separate scales, including several scales meant to measure the validity of the respondent's answers. For example, there is a "lie scale" that indicates when people are falsifying their responses in order to present themselves more favorably (through items such as, "I can't remember ever having a bad night's sleep") (Stein & Graham, 2005; Bacchiochi, 2006; Anderson et al., 2015).

self-report measures A method of gathering data about people by asking them questions about their own behavior and traits. (Module 33)

Minnesota Multiphasic Personality Inventory-2-Restructured Form (MMPI-2-RF) A widely used self-report test that identifies people with psychological difficulties and is employed to predict some everyday behaviors. (Module 33)

The Life Orientation Test

Use the following scale to answer the items below:

0	1	2	3	4
Strongly Disagree	Disagree	Neutral	Agree	Strongly agree

1. In uncertain times, I usually expect the best.
2. It's easy for me to relax.
3. If something can go wrong for me, it will.
4. I'm always optimistic about my future.
5. I enjoy my friends a lot.
6. It's important for me to keep busy.
7. I hardly ever expect things to go my way.
8. I don't get upset too easily.
9. I rarely count on good things happening to me.
10. Overall, I expect more good things to happen to me than bad.

Scoring: First, reverse your answers to questions 3, 7, and 9. Do this by changing a 0 to a 4, a 1 to a 3, a 3 to a 1, and a 4 to a 0 (answers of 2 stay as 2). Then sum the reversed scores, and add them to the scores you gave to questions 1, 4, and 10. (Ignore questions 2, 5, 6, and 8, which are filler items.)

The total score you get is a measure of a particular orientation to life: your degree of optimism. The higher your scores, the more positive and hopeful you generally are about life. For comparison purposes the average score for college students is 14.3, according to the results of a study by Scheier, Carver, and Bridges (1994). People with a higher degree of optimism generally deal with stress better than do those with lower scores.

FIGURE 1 The Life Orientation Test. Complete this test by indicating the degree to which you agree with each of the 10 statements, using the scale from 0 to 4 for each item. Try to be as accurate as possible. There are no right or wrong answers.

Source: Adapted from Scheier, M. F., Carver, C. S., & Bridges, M. W. (1994). Distinguishing optimism from neuroticism (and trait anxiety, self-mastery, and self-esteem): A reevaluation of the Life Orientation Test. *Journal of Personality and Social Psychology, 67,* 1063–1078.

test standardization A technique used to validate questions in personality tests by studying the responses of people with known diagnoses. (Module 33)

How did the authors of the MMPI-2-RF determine what specific patterns of responses indicate? The procedure they used is typical of personality test construction–a process known as **test standardization.** To create the test, the test authors asked groups of psychiatric patients with a specific diagnosis, such as depression or schizophrenia, to complete a large number of items. They then determined which items best differentiated members of those groups from a comparison group of normal participants and included those specific items in the final version of the test. By systematically carrying out this procedure on groups with different diagnoses, the test authors were able to devise a number of subscales that identified forms of abnormal behavior (see Figure 2).

When the MMPI-2-RF is used for the purpose for which it was devised–identification of personality disorders–it does a good job. However, like other personality tests, it presents an opportunity for abuse. For instance, employers who use it as a screening tool for job applicants may interpret the results improperly by relying too heavily on the results of individual scales instead of taking into account the overall patterns of results, which requires skilled interpretation. Furthermore, critics point out that the individual scales overlap, which makes their interpretation difficult. In sum, although the MMPI-2-RF remains the most widely used personality test and has been translated into more than 100 languages, it must be used with caution (Williams & Butcher, 2011; Ben-Porath, Corey, & Tarescavage, 2017).

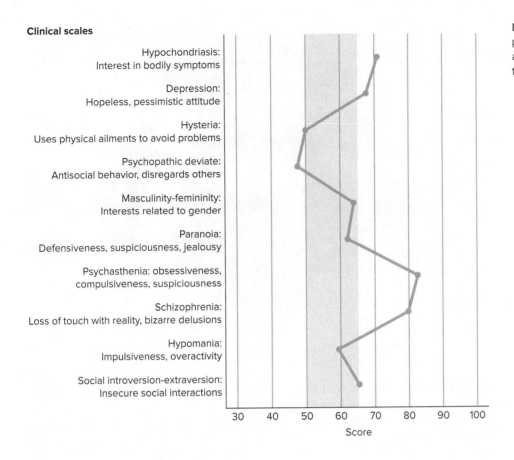

Clinical scales

- Hypochondriasis:
Interest in bodily symptoms
- Depression:
Hopeless, pessimistic attitude
- Hysteria:
Uses physical ailments to avoid problems
- Psychopathic deviate:
Antisocial behavior, disregards others
- Masculinity-femininity:
Interests related to gender
- Paranoia:
Defensiveness, suspiciousness, jealousy
- Psychasthenia: obsessiveness,
compulsiveness, suspiciousness
- Schizophrenia:
Loss of touch with reality, bizarre delusions
- Hypomania:
Impulsiveness, overactivity
- Social introversion-extraversion:
Insecure social interactions

30 40 50 60 70 80 90 100
Score

FIGURE 2 An MMPI-2-RF profile of a person who suffers from obsessional anxiety, social withdrawal, and delusional thinking.

Projective Methods

If you were shown the shape presented in Figure 3 and asked what it represented to you, you might not think that your impressions would mean very much. But to a psychodynamic theoretician, your responses to such an ambiguous figure would provide valuable clues to the state of your unconscious and ultimately to your general personality characteristics.

The shape in the figure is representative of inkblots used in projective personality tests. In **projective personality tests,** people are shown an ambiguous, vague stimulus and asked to describe it or to tell a story about it in order to infer information about their personality. Responses are considered to be "projections" of the test-taker's personality, and they are scored and interpreted using a standardized scoring method.

The best-known projective test is the **Rorschach test.** Devised by Swiss psychiatrist Hermann Rorschach (1924), the test involves showing a series of symmetrical stimuli similar to the one in Figure 3 to people who are then asked what the figures represent to them. Their responses are recorded, and people are classified into personality types requiring a complex set of judgments on the part of the examiner. For instance, individuals who see a bear in one particular Rorschach inkblot are thought to have a strong degree of emotional control, according to the scoring guidelines Rorschach developed (Silverstein, 2007; Searls, 2017).

The **Thematic Apperception Test (TAT)** is another well-known projective test. The TAT consists of a series of pictures about which a person is asked to write a story. The stories are then used to draw inferences about the writer's personality characteristics (Langan-Fox & Grant, 2006; Manjhi & Purty, 2017).

Tests with stimuli as ambiguous as those used in the Rorschach and TAT require a high degree of training, skill, and care in their interpretation—so much so that many psychologists question the validity of projective test results. The Rorschach in particular has been criticized for requiring examiners to make many broad inferences that

projective personality test A test in which a person is shown an ambiguous stimulus and asked to describe it or tell a story about it. (Module 33)

Rorschach test A test that involves showing a series of symmetrical visual stimuli to people who then are asked what the figures represent to them. (Module 33)

Study Alert

In projective tests such as the Rorschach, researchers present an ambiguous stimulus and ask a person to describe or tell a story about it. They then use the responses to make inferences about personality.

Thematic Apperception Test (TAT) A test consisting of a series of pictures about which a person is asked to write a story. (Module 33)

FIGURE 3 This inkblot is similar to the type used in the Rorschach personality test. What do you see in it?
©Spencer Grant/Science Source

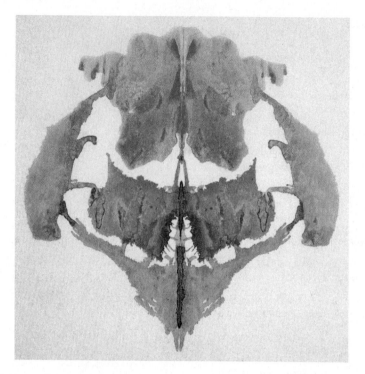

lack an objective basis, at least in the view of critics. Furthermore, attempts to standardize the scoring of the Rorschach have frequently failed.

Despite such problems, both the Rorschach and the TAT are widely used, especially in clinical settings, and their proponents suggest that their reliability and validity are great enough to provide useful inferences about personality (Society for Personality Assessment, 2005; Campos, 2011; Husain, 2015).

Behavioral Assessment

If you were a psychologist subscribing to a *learning* approach to personality, you would be likely to object to the indirect nature of projective tests. Instead, you would be more apt to use **behavioral assessment**–direct measures of an individual's behavior designed to describe characteristics indicative of personality. As with observational research, behavioral assessment may be carried out naturalistically by observing people in their own settings: in the workplace, at home, or in school. In other cases, behavioral assessment occurs in the laboratory under controlled conditions in which a psychologist sets up a situation and observes an individual's behavior (Miller & Leffard, 2007; O'Brien & Young, 2013; Wannez et al., 2017).

Regardless of the setting in which behavior is observed, an effort is made to ensure that behavioral assessment is carried out objectively and quantifies behavior as much as possible. For example, an observer may record the number of social contacts a person initiates, the number of questions asked, or the number of aggressive acts. Another method is to measure the duration of events: the duration of a child's temper tantrum, the length of a conversation, the amount of time spent working, or the time spent in cooperative behavior.

Behavioral assessment is particularly appropriate for observing–and eventually remedying–specific behavioral difficulties, such as shyness in children. It provides a means of assessing the specific nature and incidence of a problem and subsequently allows psychologists to determine whether intervention techniques have been successful.

Behavioral assessment techniques based on learning theories of personality have also made important contributions to the treatment of certain kinds of psychological difficulties. In addition, they are also used to make hiring and personnel decision in the workplace.

behavioral assessment Direct measures of an individual's behavior used to describe personality characteristics. (Module 33)

# of Psychology

Assessing Personality Assessments

Many companies, ranging from General Motors to Microsoft, employ personality tests to help determine who gets hired. In fact, workplace personality testing has become a big business, with companies spending $500 million a year to help identify the best employees (Weber & Dwoskin, 2014).

What kinds of questions are potential workers asked? In one example, potential Microsoft employees have been asked brainteasers such as "If you had to remove one of the 50 U.S. states, which would it be?" (Hint: First define *remove*. If you mean the death of everyone in the state, suggest a low-population state. If you mean quitting the country, then go for an outlying state such as Alaska or Hawaii.) Other employers ask questions that are even more vague ("Describe November"). With such questions, it's not always clear that the tests are reliable or valid (McGinn, 2003).

Before relying too heavily on the results of such personality testing as a potential employee, employer, or consumer of testing services, you should keep several points in mind:

- *Understand what the test claims to measure.* Standard personality measures are accompanied by information that discusses how the test was developed, to whom it is most applicable, and how the results should be interpreted. Read any explanations of the test; they will help you understand the results.
- *Do not base a decision only on the results of any one test.* Test results should be interpreted in the context of other information, such as academic records, social interests, and home and community activities.
- *Remember that test results are not always accurate.* The results may be in error; the test may be unreliable or invalid. For example, you may have had a "bad day" when you took the test, or the person scoring and interpreting the test may have made a mistake. You should not place too much significance on the results of a single administration of any test.

In sum, it is important to keep in mind the complexity of human behavior—particularly your own. No single test can provide an understanding of the intricacies of someone's personality without considering a good deal more information than can be provided in a single testing session (Gladwell, 2004; Paul, 2004; Hogan, Davies, & Hogan, 2007).

RECAP/EVALUATE/RETHINK

RECAP

LO 33-1 How can we most accurately assess personality?

- Psychological tests such as the MMPI-2-RF are standard assessment tools that measure behavior objectively. They must be reliable (measuring what they are trying to measure consistently) and valid (measuring what they are supposed to measure).

LO 33-2 What are the major types of personality measures?

- Self-report measures ask people about a sample range of their behaviors. These reports are used to infer the presence of particular personality characteristics.
- Projective personality tests (such as the Rorschach and the TAT) present an ambiguous stimulus; the test administrator infers information about the test-taker from his or her responses.

- Behavioral assessment is based on the principles of learning theory. It employs direct measurement of an individual's behavior to determine characteristics related to personality.

EVALUATE

1. _____ is the consistency of a personality test; _____ is the ability of a test to actually measure what it is designed to measure.
2. _____ _____ are standards used to compare scores of different people taking the same test.
3. Tests such as the MMPI-2-RF, in which a small sample of behavior is assessed to determine larger patterns, are examples of which of the following?
   a. Cross-sectional tests
   b. Projective tests
   c. Achievement tests
   d. Self-report tests

4. A person shown a picture and asked to make up a story about it would be taking a _____ personality test.

RETHINK

1. Should personality tests be used for personnel decisions? Should they be used for other social purposes, such as identifying individuals at risk for certain types of personality disorders?
2. What do you think are some of the problems that developers and interpreters of self-report personality tests must deal with in their effort to provide useful information about test-takers? Why is a "lie scale" included on such measures?

Answers to Evaluate Questions

1. Reliability, validity; 2. Test norms; 3. d; 4. projective

KEY TERMS

psychological tests
self-report measures
Minnesota Multiphasic
   Personality Inventory-
   2-Restructured Form
   (MMPI-2-RF)

test standardization
projective personality test
Rorschach test
Thematic Apperception
   Test (TAT)
behavioral assessment

LOOKING *Back*

EPILOGUE

We have discussed the different ways in which psychologists have interpreted the development and structure of personality. The perspectives we examined ranged from Freud's analysis of personality based primarily on internal, unconscious factors to the externally based view championed by learning theorists of personality as a learned set of traits and actions. We also noted that there are many ways to interpret personality; by no means does a consensus exist on what the key traits are that are central to personality.

Return to the prologue of this chapter and consider the case of Lance Armstrong, the athlete-hero who beat cancer to win the Tour de France seven times and launched a foundation to help cancer patients while he was also doping and hiding the fact to receive money from his sponsors. Use your understanding of personality to consider the following questions.

1. How might a psychoanalytic approach to personality, using the concepts of id, ego, and superego, explain the contradictions in Lance Armstrong's personality?
2. In talking about his years of doping, does Armstrong appear to employ any of Freud's defense mechanisms to explain his behavior? If so, which ones, and why, according to Freud, might he adopt them?
3. How would a supporter of a social cognitive approach to personality interpret and explain Armstrong's seemingly contradictory behavior? How might the concepts of observational learning and self-efficacy apply to a case like Armstrong's?
4. Would Armstrong be a good candidate for a personality inventory that uses self-report data to infer particular personality characteristics? Explain your answer.

Design Elements: Yellow highlighter: ©luckyraccoon/Shutterstock.com; Smartphone: ©and4me/Shutterstock.com; Group of diverse hands: ©MR. Nattanon Kanchak/Shutterstock.com; Woman working on laptop: ©Dragon Images/Shutterstock.com.

VISUAL SUMMARY 10 Personality

MODULE 31 Psychodynamic Approaches

Freud's Psychoanalytic Theory

— Conscious experience: only part of our psychological experience

— Unconscious: part of the personality of which we are not aware

— Structure of personality

  • Id: Represents the raw, unorganized, inborn part of personality

  • Ego: Strives to balance desires of the id and realities of the outside world

  • Superego: Harshly judges the morality of our behavior

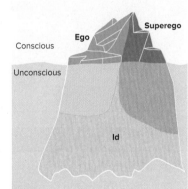

— Psychosexual stages

Stage	Age	Major Characteristics
Oral	Birth to 12–18 months	Interest in oral gratification from sucking, eating, mouthing, biting
Anal	12–18 months to 3 years	Gratification from expelling and withholding feces; coming to terms with society's controls relating to toilet training
Phallic	3 to 5–6 years	Interest in the genitals; coming to terms with Oedipal conflict leading to identification with same-sex parent
Latency	5–6 years to adolescence	Sexual concerns largely unimportant
Genital	Adolescence to adulthood	Reemergence of sexual interests and establishment of mature sexual relationships

— Defense mechanisms: Unconscious strategies people use to reduce anxiety

Neo-Freudian Psychoanalysts: Emphasize the ego more than Freud: Carl Jung, Karen Horney, Alfred Adler

MODULE 32 Trait, Learning, Biological and Evolutionary, and Humanistic Approaches

Trait Approaches: Emphasize consistent personality characteristics and behaviors called traits

— Eysenck: Extraversion, neuroticism, and psychoticism

— The big five personality traits: Openness to experience, conscientiousness, extraversion, agreeableness, neuroticism

Learning Approaches: Emphasize that personality is the sum of learned responses to the external environment

— B. F. Skinner: Personality is a collection of learned behavior patterns that are a result of reinforcement

Learning Approaches (continued)

— Social cognitive approaches: Emphasize the influence of cognition as well as observation of others' behavior on personality

— Self-efficacy and self-esteem

Biological and Evolutionary Approaches:
Suggest that important components of personality are inherited, such as temperament

Humanistic Approaches: Emphasize people's inherent goodness and their tendency to move toward higher levels of functioning

— Carl Rogers

  • Self-actualization

  • Positive regard reflects the desire to be loved and respected

MODULE 33 Assessing Personality

Psychological Tests: Standard measures that assess behavior objectively

  • Reliability
  • Validity
  • Norms

Self-report Measures: A method of gathering data by asking people questions about their own behavior and traits

Projective Methods: People are shown an ambiguous stimulus and asked to describe it or tell a story about it

— Rorschach test

— Thematic Apperception Test (TAT)

Behavioral Assessment: Measures of a person's behavior designed to describe characteristics indicative of personality

(MODULE 31) (photo): ©Ingram Publishing; (MODULE 32) (photo): ©Image Source; (MODULE 33) (photo): ©Spencer Grant/Science Source

©Fancy Collection/SuperStock

CHAPTER 11
Health Psychology: Stress, Coping, and Well-Being

LEARNING OUTCOMES FOR CHAPTER 11

MODULE 34

LO 34-1 How is health psychology a union between medicine and psychology?

LO 34-2 What is stress, how does it affect us, and how can we best cope with it?

STRESS AND COPING

Stress: Reacting to Threat and Challenge

The High Cost of Stress

Coping with Stress

Applying Psychology in the 21st Century: Does Using Facebook Make You Feel Bad?

Neuroscience in Your Life: The Neuroscience of Resilience

Becoming an Informed Consumer of Psychology: Effective Coping Strategies

MODULE 35

LO 35-1 How do psychological factors affect health-related problems such as coronary heart disease, cancer, and smoking?

PSYCHOLOGICAL ASPECTS OF ILLNESS AND WELL-BEING

The As, Bs, and Ds of Coronary Heart Disease

Psychological Aspects of Cancer

Smoking

Exploring Diversity: Hucksters of Death: Promoting Smoking Throughout the World

MODULE 36

LO 36-1 How do our interactions with physicians affect our health and compliance with medical treatment?

LO 36-2 How does a sense of well-being develop?

PROMOTING HEALTH AND WELLNESS

Following Medical Advice

Well-Being and Happiness

PROLOGUE *BREAKING BAD NEWS*

The situation couldn't be more stressful: Dr. Morgan Wilber, an emergency medical resident at Orlando Health, must give a mom and dad the worst possible news: their child is brain-dead.

Thankfully, though, this is just for practice. The "parents" are professional actors in a program called "Breaking Bad News," which trains doctors in how to say these very difficult things to patients and families. According to Anthony Orsini, who developed the program, the only way to learn this skill is through experience. He therefore created scenarios in which a resident delivers bad news to actors while being videotaped and then receives feedback from doctors and real parents.

No communicative act in the doctor–patient relationship is more important. Says Noelle Moore, a mother who lost her baby and now works with the program, "When a child dies, that moment is like a snapshot in your mind. You never forget what the person says to you, how they say it, and the different sights and sounds in that moment" (Miller, 2016).

LOOKING *Ahead*

While the residents in Orsini's program don't look forward to their hour before the camera, they appreciate that their experience during the simulation can minimize the stress they will feel later, when they have to deliver actual bad news.

Stress and how we cope with it have long been central topics of interest for psychologists. However, in recent years, the focus has broadened as psychology has come to view stress in the broader context of one of psychology's newer subfields: health psychology.

Health psychology investigates the psychological factors related to wellness and illness, including the prevention, diagnosis, and treatment of medical problems. Health psychologists investigate the effects of psychological factors such as stress on illness. They examine the psychological principles underlying treatments for disease and illness. They also study prevention: how healthier behavior can help people avoid and reduce health problems such as stress and heart disease.

Health psychologists take a decisive stand on the enduring mind–body issue that philosophers and, later, psychologists have debated since the time of the ancient Greeks. In their view, the mind and the body are clearly linked rather than representing two distinct systems (Sternberg, 2000; Dalal & Misra, 2006; Grosso, 2015).

Health psychologists recognize that good health and the ability to cope with illness are affected by psychological factors such as thoughts, emotions, and the ability to manage stress. They have paid particular attention to the *immune system,* the complex system of organs, glands, and cells that constitutes our bodies' natural line of defense in fighting disease.

In fact, health psychologists are among the primary investigators in a growing field called **psychoneuroimmunology,** or **PNI,** the study of the relationship among psychological factors, the immune system, and the brain. PNI has led to discoveries such as the existence of an association between a person's emotional state and the success of the immune system in fighting disease (Mathews & Janusek, 2011; Sperner-Unterweger & Fuchs, 2015; Ayling et al., 2017).

In sum, health psychologists view the mind and the body as two parts of a whole human being that cannot be considered independently. This more recent view marks a sharp departure from earlier thinking. Previously, disease was seen as a purely biological phenomenon, and psychological factors were of little interest to most health-care workers. In the early 20th century, the primary causes of death were short-term infections from which one either rapidly recovered—or died. Now, however, the major causes of death, such as heart disease, cancer, and diabetes, are chronic illnesses that pose significant psychological issues because they often cannot be cured and may linger for years (Rotan & Ospina-Kammerer, 2007; Berecki-Gisolf et al., 2013; Chen et al., 2017).

Advances in health psychology have had an impact across a variety of disciplines and professions. For instance, health-care professionals such as physicians and nurses, social workers, dietitians, pharmacists, occupational therapists, and even clergy are increasingly likely to receive training in health psychology.

In modules 43 through 45, we discuss the ways in which psychological factors affect health. We first focus on the causes and consequences of stress as well as on the means of coping with it. Next, we explore the psychological aspects of several major health problems, including heart disease, cancer, and ailments resulting from smoking. Finally, we examine the ways in which patient–physician interactions influence our health and offer suggestions for increasing people's compliance with recommendations about behavior that will improve their well-being.

health psychology The branch of psychology that investigates the psychological factors related to wellness and illness, including the prevention, diagnosis, and treatment of medical problems. (Module 34)

psychoneuroimmunology (PNI) The study of the relationship among psychological factors, the immune system, and the brain. (Module 34)

Module 34
Stress and Coping

LEARNING OUTCOMES

LO 34-1 How is health psychology a union between medicine and psychology?

LO 34-2 What is stress, how does it affect us, and how can we best cope with it?

stress A person's response to events that are threatening or challenging. (Module 34)

Study Alert

Remember the distinction between stressors and stress, which can be tricky: stressors (such as an exam) cause stress (the physiological and psychological reaction that comes from the exam).

Sheila Gray remembers the worst moment of her life: The day she heard about the mass shootings at Sandy Hook Elementary School in 2012 in Connecticut. Though Gray lives in Michigan, she immediately jumped in the car and drove to her 7-year-old daughter's school. She brought the girl home. "My heart was pounding. I started crying, and I just couldn't stop," Gray says. Then and there, she decided that her daughter, Merilee, would never return to her school. She began homeschooling the girl. Friends could come over, but Gray found she couldn't let Merilee out of her sight. "So much can happen when you walk away from your child," Gray says. "I was terrified by that loss of control."

Stress: Reacting to Threat and Challenge

Most of us need little introduction to the phenomenon of **stress,** people's response to events that threaten or challenge them. Whether they are a paper or an exam deadline, a family problem, or even the ongoing threat of a terrorist attack, life is full of circumstances and events known as *stressors* that produce threats to our well-being. Even pleasant events–such as planning a party or beginning a sought-after job–can produce stress, although negative events result in greater detrimental consequences than positive ones do.

All of us face stress in our lives. Some health psychologists believe that daily life actually involves a series of repeated sequences of perceiving a threat, considering ways to cope with it, and ultimately adapting to the threat with greater or lesser success. Although adaptation is often minor and occurs without our awareness, adaptation requires a major effort when stress is more severe or long lasting. Ultimately, our attempts to overcome stress may produce biological and psychological responses that result in health problems (Dolbier, Smith, & Steinhardt, 2007; Finan, Zautra, & Wershba, 2011; Dierolf et al., 2017).

THE NATURE OF STRESSORS: MY STRESS IS YOUR PLEASURE

Stress is a very personal thing. Although certain kinds of events, such as the death of a loved one or participation in military combat, are universally stressful, other situations may or may not be stressful to a specific person.

Consider, for instance, bungee jumping. Some people would find jumping off a bridge while attached to a slender rubber tether extremely stressful. However, there are individuals who see such an activity as challenging and fun-filled. Whether bungee jumping is stressful depends in part, then, on a person's perception of the activity.

For people to consider an event stressful, they must perceive it as threatening or challenging and must lack all the resources to deal with it effectively. Consequently, the same event may at some times be stressful and at other times provoke no stressful reaction

Even positive events can produce significant stress.
©Beijing Eastphoto stockimages Co., Ltd/Alamy Stock Photo

at all. A young man experiences stress when he is turned down for a date—if he attributes the refusal to his unattractiveness or unworthiness. But if he attributes it to some factor unrelated to his self-esteem, such as a previous commitment of the woman he asked, the experience of being refused may create no stress at all. Hence, a person's interpretation of events plays an important role in the determination of what is stressful (Giacobbi et al., 2004; Friborg, Hjemdal, & Rosenvinge, 2006; Tuckey et al., 2015).

CATEGORIZING STRESSORS

What kinds of events tend to be seen as stressful? There are three general types of stressors: cataclysmic events, personal stressors, and background stressors.

Cataclysmic events are strong stressors that occur suddenly and typically affect many people simultaneously. Disasters such as tornadoes and plane crashes as well as terrorist attacks are examples of cataclysmic events that can affect hundreds or thousands of people simultaneously.

Although it might seem that cataclysmic events would produce potent, lingering stress, in many cases they do not. In fact, cataclysmic events involving natural disasters may produce less stress in the long run than events that initially are not as devastating. One reason is that natural disasters have a clear resolution. Once they are over, people can look to the future knowing that the worst is behind them. Moreover, others who also experienced the disaster share the stress induced by cataclysmic events. Such sharing permits people to offer one another social support and a firsthand understanding of the difficulties others are going through (Yesilyaprak, Kisac, & Sanlier, 2007; Schwarzer & Luszczynska, 2013).

In contrast, terrorist attacks such as the one on the World Trade Center in 2001 or the Boston Marathon bombings in 2013 are cataclysmic events that produce considerable stress. Terrorist attacks are deliberate, and victims (and observers) know that future attacks are likely. Government warnings in the form of heightened terror alerts may further increase the stress. Furthermore, exposure to repeated events, whether experienced directly or through the media, may lead to increased sensitivity to stress (Laugharne, Janca, & Widiger, 2007; Watson, Brymer, & Bonanno, 2011; Garfin, Holman, & Silver, 2015).

The second major category of stressor is the personal stressor. **Personal stressors** include major life events such as the death of a parent or spouse, the loss of one's job, a major personal failure, or even something positive such as getting married. Typically, personal stressors produce an immediate major reaction that soon tapers off. For example, stress arising from the death of a loved one tends to be greatest just after the time of death, but people begin to feel less stress and are better able to cope with the loss after the passage of time.

Some victims of major catastrophes and severe personal stressors experience **posttraumatic stress disorder,** or **PTSD,** in which a person has experienced a significantly stressful event that has long-lasting effects that may include re-experiencing the event in vivid flashbacks or dreams. An episode of PTSD may be triggered by an otherwise innocent stimulus, such as the sound of a honking horn, that leads a person to re-experience a past event that produced considerable stress.

Symptoms of posttraumatic stress disorder also include emotional numbing, sleep difficulties, interpersonal problems, alcohol and drug abuse, and in some cases suicide. For instance, the suicide rate for military veterans, many of whom participated in the Iraq and Afghanistan wars, is twice as high as for nonveterans (Pole, 2007; Magruder & Yeager, 2009; Munjiza et al., 2017).

Between 10-18% of soldiers returning from Iraq and Afghanistan show symptoms of PTSD, and the United States spends $3 billion a year on treating the disorder in military veterans. Furthermore, those who have experienced child abuse or rape, rescue workers facing overwhelming situations, and victims of sudden natural disasters or accidents that produce feelings of helplessness and shock may suffer from the same disorder (Horesh et al., 2011; Huang & Kashubeck-West, 2015; Thompson, 2015).

cataclysmic events Strong stressors that occur suddenly and typically affect many people at once (e.g., natural disasters). (Module 34)

personal stressors Major life events, such as the death of a family member, that have immediate negative consequences that generally fade with time. (Module 34)

posttraumatic stress disorder (PTSD) A phenomenon in which victims of major catastrophes or strong personal stressors feel long-lasting effects that may include re-experiencing the event in vivid flashbacks or dreams. (Module 34)

FIGURE 1 The closer people lived to the site of the World Trade Center terrorist attack, the greater the rate of posttraumatic stress disorder.

Source: Adapted from Susser, E. S., Herman, D. B., & Aaron, B. (2002). Combating the terror of terrorism. *Scientific American, 287,* 70–77.

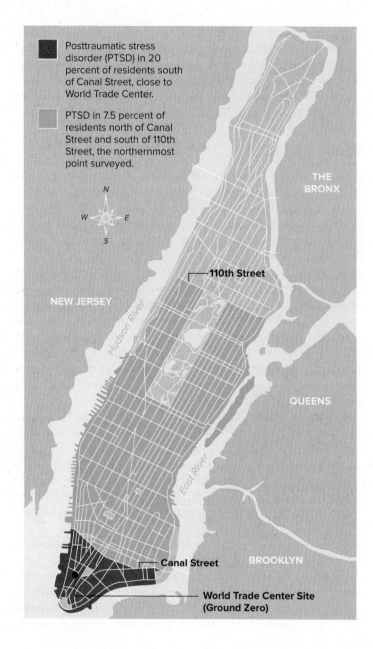

Posttraumatic stress disorder (PTSD) in 20 percent of residents south of Canal Street, close to World Trade Center.

PTSD in 7.5 percent of residents north of Canal Street and south of 110th Street, the northernmost point surveyed.

110th Street

NEW JERSEY

Hudson River

THE BRONX

QUEENS

East River

Canal Street

BROOKLYN

World Trade Center Site (Ground Zero)

background stressors ("daily hassles") Everyday annoyances, such as being stuck in traffic, that cause minor irritations and may have long-term ill effects if they continue or are compounded by other stressful events. (Module 34)

In addition to traditional forms of PTSD, soldiers who have faced multiple tours of duty and who may have actually thrived during years of combat face their own kind of PTSD. After they return home, they may have to unlearn the skills that helped them survive in combat, such as constant vigilance, an intolerance for carelessness, and extreme decisiveness (Carey, 2016).

Terrorist attacks produce high incidences of PTSD. For example, 11% of people in New York City had some form of PTSD in the months after the September 11 terrorist attacks. But the responses varied significantly with a resident's proximity to the attacks, as illustrated in Figure 1; the closer someone lived to the World Trade Center, the greater the likelihood of PTSD. Furthermore, for many people, the effects of PTSD were still evident a decade after the attacks (Lee, Isaac, & Janca, 2007; Marshall et al., 2007; Neria, DiGrande, & Adams, 2011).

Background stressors, or more informally, *daily hassles,* are the third major category of stressors. Exemplified by standing in a long line at a bank and getting stuck in a traffic jam, daily hassles are the minor irritations of life that we all face time and

©mauritius images GmbH/Alamy Stock Photo

time again. Another type of background stressor is a long-term, chronic problem, such as experiencing dissatisfaction with school or a job, being in an unhappy relationship, or living in crowded quarters without privacy (Weinstein et al., 2004; McIntyre, Korn, & Matsuo, 2008; Barke, 2011).

By themselves, daily hassles do not require much coping or even a response on the individual's part, although they certainly produce unpleasant emotions and moods. Yet, daily hassles add up—and ultimately, they may take as great of a toll as a single, more stressful incident. In fact, the *number* of daily hassles people face is associated with psychological symptoms and health problems such as flu, sore throat, and backaches.

The flip side of hassles is *uplifts,* the minor positive events that make us feel good—even if only temporarily. As indicated in Figure 2, uplifts range from relating well to a companion to finding one's surroundings pleasing. What is especially intriguing about uplifts is that they are associated with people's psychological health in just the opposite way that hassles are: The greater the number of uplifts we experience, the fewer the psychological symptoms we report later (Chamberlain & Zika, 1990; Hurley & Kwon, 2013; Schmidt et al., 2017).

PsychTech

An analysis of the emotional content of words sent in text messages during the hours following the 9/11 terrorist attack showed that over the course of the day, sadness and anxiety-related words remained steady but anger-related words increased steadily.

FIGURE 2 The most common everyday hassles and uplifts. How many of these are part of your life, and how do you cope with the hassles?

Sources: Adapted from (hassles) Chamberlain & Zika, 1990; (uplifts) Kanner et al., 1981.

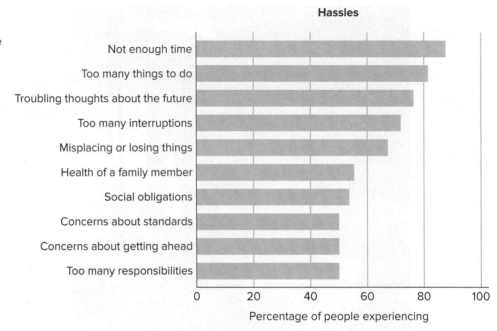

Hassles

- Not enough time
- Too many things to do
- Troubling thoughts about the future
- Too many interruptions
- Misplacing or losing things
- Health of a family member
- Social obligations
- Concerns about standards
- Concerns about getting ahead
- Too many responsibilities

Percentage of people experiencing

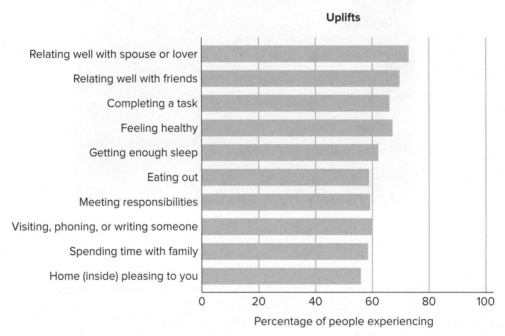

Uplifts

- Relating well with spouse or lover
- Relating well with friends
- Completing a task
- Feeling healthy
- Getting enough sleep
- Eating out
- Meeting responsibilities
- Visiting, phoning, or writing someone
- Spending time with family
- Home (inside) pleasing to you

Percentage of people experiencing

The High Cost of Stress

Study Alert

Remember the three categories of stressors—cataclysmic events, personal stressors, and background stressors—and that they produce different levels of stress.

Stress has both biological and psychological consequences. Some of those consequences begin almost instantaneously, whereas others unfold over time.

Often the most immediate reaction to stress is biological. Specifically, exposure to stressors generates a rise in hormone secretions by the adrenal glands, an increase in heart rate and blood pressure, and changes in how well the skin conducts electrical impulses. On a short-term basis, these responses may be adaptive because they produce an "emergency reaction" in which the body prepares to defend itself through activation of the sympathetic nervous system. Those responses may allow more effective coping with the stressful situation (Akil & Morano, 1996; McEwen, 1998).

However, continued exposure to stress results in a decline in the body's overall level of biological functioning because of the constant secretion of stress-related hormones. Over time, stressful reactions can promote deterioration of body tissues such as blood vessels and the heart. Ultimately, we become more susceptible to disease as our ability to fight off infection is lowered (Ellins et al., 2008; Miller, Chen, & Parker, 2011; Farrell et al., 2017).

Furthermore, stress can produce or worsen physical problems. Specifically, **psychophysiological disorders** are medical problems that are influenced by an interaction of psychological, emotional, and physical difficulties. Common psychophysiological disorders include high blood pressure, headaches, backaches, skin rashes, indigestion, fatigue, and constipation. Stress has even been linked to the common cold (Andrasik, 2006; Gupta, 2013; Gianaros & Wager, 2015).

On a psychological level, high levels of stress prevent people from adequately coping with life. Their view of the environment can become clouded (for example, a minor criticism made by a friend is blown out of proportion). Moreover, at the highest levels of stress, emotional responses may be so extreme that people are unable to act at all. People under a lot of stress also become less able to deal with new stressors.

In short, stress affects us in multiple ways. It may increase the risk that we will become ill, it may directly cause illness, it may make us less able to recover from a disease, and it may reduce our ability to cope with future stress. (See Figure 3 to get a measure of your own level of stress.)

psychophysiological disorders
Medical problems influenced by an interaction of psychological, emotional, and physical difficulties. (Module 34)

How Stressed Are You?

Find out how stressed you are by responding to the following statements in terms of the last month only. Add up the score from each box. The rough scoring guide below will help you get a sense of your stress level.

1. I was convinced that the big things in my life were beyond my control.
   ☐ 0=never, 1=infrequently, 2=sometimes, 3=fairly often, 4=very often

2. I felt that I could at least control the minor irritations in my life.
   ☐ 4=never, 3=infrequently, 2=sometimes, 1=fairly often, 0=very often

3. I became upset at something that I didn't expect to happen.
   ☐ 4=never, 3=infrequently, 2=sometimes, 1=fairly often, 0=very often

4. I felt confident that I could handle my personal problems.
   ☐ 4=never, 3=infrequently, 2=sometimes, 1=fairly often, 0=very often

5. I felt nervous, anxious, and under stress.
   ☐ 0=never, 1=infrequently, 2=sometimes, 3=fairly often, 4=very often

6. I felt myself to be the master of my life.
   ☐ 4=never, 3=infrequently, 2=sometimes, 1=fairly often, 0=very often

7. I realized that I simply couldn't manage or cope with everything I had to do.
   ☐ 0=never, 1=infrequently, 2=sometimes, 3=fairly often, 4=very often

8. I felt that troubles and worries were mounting so high I couldn't get past them.
   ☐ 0=never, 1=infrequently, 2=sometimes, 3=fairly often, 4=very often

9. I felt that, overall, things were heading in the right direction.
   ☐ 4=never, 3=infrequently, 2=sometimes, 1=fairly often, 0=very often

10. I lost my temper because of something that I couldn't control.
    ☐ 0=never, 1=infrequently, 2=sometimes, 3=fairly often, 4=very often

Here's a rough scoring guide:

0–10 low stress
11–20 moderately low stress
21–30 moderately high stress
31–40 high stress

FIGURE 3 To get a sense of the level of stress in your life, complete this questionnaire.

Source: Adapted from Cohen, S., Kamarck, T., & Mermelstein, R. (1983). A global measure of perceived stress. *Journal of Health and Social Behavior, 24*, 385–396.

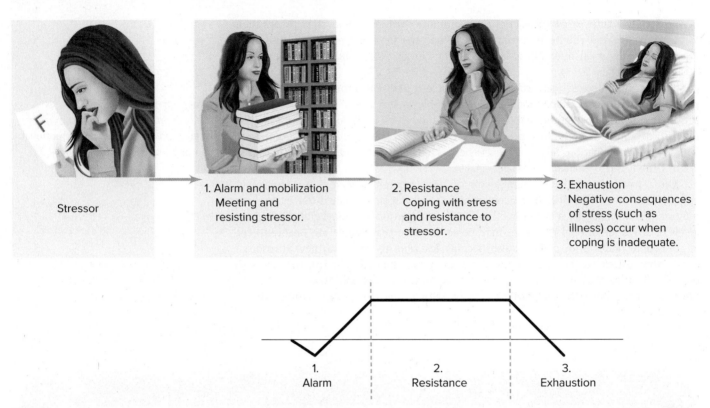

FIGURE 4 According to the general adaptation syndrome (GAS) model, there are three major stages to stress responses: alarm and mobilization; resistance; and exhaustion. The graph below the illustration shows the degree of effort expended to cope with stressors at each of the three stages. ©McGraw-Hill Global Education Holdings LLC, 1978.

THE GENERAL ADAPTATION SYNDROME MODEL: THE COURSE OF STRESS

general adaptation syndrome (GAS) A theory developed by Selye that suggests that a person's response to a stressor consists of three stages: alarm and mobilization, resistance, and exhaustion. (Module 34)

The effects of long-term stress are illustrated in a series of stages proposed by Hans Selye (pronounced "sell-yay"), a pioneering stress theorist (Selye, 1993). This model, the **general adaptation syndrome (GAS),** suggests that the physiological response to stress follows the same set pattern regardless of the cause of stress.

As shown in Figure 4, the GAS has three phases. The first stage—*alarm and mobilization*—occurs when people become aware of the presence of a stressor. On a biological level, the sympathetic nervous system becomes energized, which helps a person cope initially with the stressor.

However, if the stressor persists, people move into the second response stage: *resistance.* During this stage, the body is actively fighting the stressor on a biological level. During resistance, people use a variety of means to cope with the stressor—sometimes successfully but at a cost of some degree of physical or psychological well-being. For example, a student who faces the stress of failing several courses might spend long hours studying, seeking to cope with the stress.

If resistance is inadequate, people enter the last stage of the GAS: *exhaustion.* During the exhaustion stage, a person's ability to fight the stressor declines to the point where negative consequences of stress appear: physical illness and psychological symptoms in the form of an inability to concentrate, heightened irritability, or, in severe cases, disorientation and a loss of touch with reality. In a sense, people wear out, and their physiological resources to fight the stressor are used up.

How do people move out of the third stage after they have entered it? In some cases, exhaustion allows people to escape a stressor. For example, people who become ill from overwork may be excused from their duties for a time, which gives them a temporary respite from their responsibilities. At least for a time, then, the immediate stress is reduced.

Study Alert

Remember the three stages of the general adaptation syndrome with the acronym *ARE* (*A*larm and mobilization; *R*esistance; and *E*xhaustion).

Although the GAS has had a substantial impact on our understanding of stress, critics have challenged Selye's theory. Specifically, the theory suggests that one's biological reaction to stress is similar regardless of the stressor. However, some health psychologists disagree, asserting instead that people's biological responses are specific to the way they appraise a stressful event. Research supporting this perspective has led to an increased focus on psychoneuroimmunology, as we consider next (Gaab et al., 2005; Irwin, 2008; Taylor, 2015).

PSYCHONEUROIMMUNOLOGY AND STRESS

Contemporary health psychologists specializing in **psychoneuroimmunology (PNI)** have taken a broader approach to stress. Focusing on the outcomes of stress, they have identified three main consequences of it (see Figure 5).

First, stress has direct physiological results, including an increase in blood pressure, an increase in hormonal activity, and an overall decline in the functioning of the immune system. Second, stress leads people to engage in behaviors that are harmful to their health, including increased nicotine, drug, and alcohol use; poor eating habits; and decreased sleep. Third, stress produces some indirect consequences that ultimately result in declines in health. For example, high levels of stress reduce the likelihood a person will seek health care. In addition, stress may result in less compliance with medical advice when it is sought. Both the reductions in seeking medical care and decreased compliance can indirectly lead to declines in health (Lindblad, Lindahl, & Theorell, 2006; Stowell, Robles, & Kane, 2013; Douthit & Russotti, 2017).

Why is stress so damaging to the immune system? One reason is that stress likely decreases the ability of the immune system to respond to disease, permitting germs that produce colds to reproduce more easily or allowing cancer cells to spread more rapidly. In normal circumstances, our bodies produce disease-fighting white blood cells called *lymphocytes*. Our bodies normally produce them at an extraordinary rate–some 10 million every few seconds. Stress may decrease this level of production (Zhou et al., 2017).

Another way that stress affects the immune system is by overstimulating it. Rather than fighting invading bacteria, viruses, and other foreign invaders, the immune system may begin to attack the body itself and damage healthy tissue. When that happens, it can lead to disorders such as arthritis and allergic reactions (Baum, Lorduy, & Jenkins, 2011; Marques et al., 2015).

The ability to fight off disease is related to psychological factors. Here a cell from the body's immune system engulfs and destroys disease-producing bacteria.
©Science Source

psychoneuroimmunology (PNI) The study of the relationship among psychological factors, the immune system, and the brain. (Module 34)

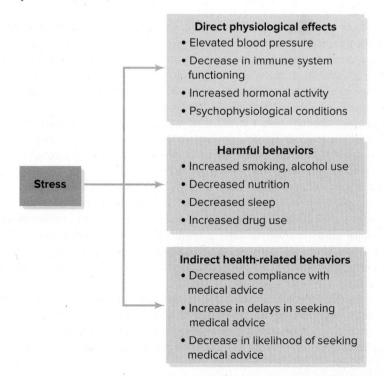

Direct physiological effects
- Elevated blood pressure
- Decrease in immune system functioning
- Increased hormonal activity
- Psychophysiological conditions

Harmful behaviors
- Increased smoking, alcohol use
- Decreased nutrition
- Decreased sleep
- Increased drug use

Indirect health-related behaviors
- Decreased compliance with medical advice
- Increase in delays in seeking medical advice
- Decrease in likelihood of seeking medical advice

Stress

FIGURE 5 Three major types of consequences result from stress: direct physiological effects, harmful behaviors, and indirect health-related behaviors.
Source: Adapted from Baum, A. (1994). Behavioral, biological, and environmental interactions in disease processes. In S. Blumenthal, K. Matthews, & S. Weiss (Eds.), *New research frontiers in behavioral medicine: Proceedings of the National Conference.* Washington, DC: NIH Publications.

Coping with Stress

Stress is a normal part of life—and not necessarily a completely bad part. For example, without stress, we might not be sufficiently motivated to complete the activities we need to accomplish.

However, it is also clear that too much stress can take a toll on physical and psychological health. How do people deal with stress? Is there a way to reduce its negative effects?

Efforts to control, reduce, or learn to tolerate the threats that lead to stress are known as **coping**. We habitually use certain coping responses to deal with stress. Most of the time, we're not aware of these responses—just as we may be unaware of the minor stressors of life until they build up to harmful levels (Wrzesniewski & Chylinska, 2007; Chao, 2011).

We also have other, more direct, and potentially more positive ways of coping with stress, which fall into two main categories (Folkman & Moskowitz, 2004; Baker & Berenbaum, 2007; Pow & Cashwell, 2017).

coping The efforts to control, reduce, or learn to tolerate the threats that lead to stress. (Module 34)

- **Emotion-focused coping.** In *emotion-focused coping*, people try to manage their emotions in the face of stress by seeking to change the way they feel about or perceive a problem. Examples of emotion-focused coping include strategies such as accepting sympathy from others and looking at the bright side of a situation.

- **Problem-focused coping.** *Problem-focused coping* attempts to modify the stressful problem or source of stress. Problem-focused strategies lead to changes in behavior or to the development of a plan of action to deal with stress. Starting a study group to improve poor classroom performance is an example of problem-focused coping. In addition, one might take a time-out from stress by creating positive events. For example, taking a day off from caring for a relative with a serious, chronic illness to go a health club or spa can bring significant relief from stress.

People often employ both emotion-focused and problem-solving coping strategies simultaneously to deal with stress. In other cases, the type of strategy differs according to the situation. For example, they tend to use emotion-focused strategies more frequently when they perceive circumstances as being unchangeable, and they use problem-focused strategies more often in situations they see as relatively modifiable (Stanton et al., 2000; Penley, Tomaka, & Wiebe, 2002).

Some forms of coping are less successful. One of the least effective forms of coping is avoidant coping. In *avoidant coping*, a person may use wishful thinking to reduce stress or use more direct escape routes, such as drug use, alcohol use, and overeating. An example of wishful thinking to avoid a test would be to say to oneself, "Maybe it will snow so hard tomorrow that the test will be canceled." Alternatively, a person might get drunk to avoid a problem. Either way, avoidant coping usually results in a postponement of dealing with a stressful situation, and this often makes the problem even worse (Glass et al., 2009; Sikkema et al., 2013; Dunkley et al., 2017).

Another way of dealing with stress occurs unconsciously through the use of defense mechanisms. *Defense mechanisms* are unconscious strategies that people use to reduce anxiety by concealing the source from themselves and others. Defense mechanisms permit people to avoid stress by acting as if the stress were not even there. For example, one study examined California college students who lived in dormitories close to a geological fault (Lehman & Taylor, 1988). Those who lived in dorms that were known to be unlikely to withstand an earthquake were significantly *more* likely to doubt experts' predictions of an impending earthquake than were those who lived in safer structures.

Another defense mechanism used to cope with stress is *emotional insulation* in which a person stops experiencing any emotions at all and thereby remains unaffected and unmoved by both positive and negative experiences. The problem with defense mechanisms, of course, is that they merely hide the problem and do not deal with reality.

LEARNED HELPLESSNESS

Have you ever faced an intolerable situation that you just couldn't resolve, and you finally simply gave up and accepted things the way they were? This example illustrates one of the possible consequences of being in an environment in which control over a situation is not possible—a state that produces learned helplessness. **Learned helplessness** occurs when people conclude that unpleasant or aversive stimuli cannot be controlled. They develop a view of the world that becomes so ingrained that they cease trying to remedy the aversive circumstances even if they actually can exert some influence on the situation. For example, students who decide they are simply "no good in math" may not work very hard in math classes because they believe that no matter how hard they try, they'll never succeed. Their learned helplessness virtually ensures that they won't do well in math classes (Aujoulat, Luminet, & Deccache, 2007; Seligman, 2007; Filippello et al., 2015).

Victims of learned helplessness have concluded that there is no link between the responses they make and the outcomes that occur. People experience more physical symptoms and depression when they perceive that they have little or no control than they do when they feel a sense of control over a situation (Chou, 2005; Bjornstad, 2006; Figen, 2011).

learned helplessness A state in which people conclude that unpleasant or aversive stimuli cannot be controlled—a view of the world that becomes so ingrained that they cease trying to remedy the aversive circumstances even if they actually can exert some influence on the situation. (Module 34)

COPING STYLES: HARDINESS AND RESILIENCE

Most of us characteristically cope with stress by employing a *coping style* that represents our general tendency to deal with stress in a specific way. For example, you may know people who habitually react to even the smallest amount of stress with hysteria and others who calmly confront even the greatest stress in an unflappable manner. These kinds of people clearly have very different coping styles (Taylor, 2003; Kato & Pedersen, 2005).

Hardiness   Among those who cope with stress most successfully are people who are equipped with **hardiness,** a personality trait characterized by a sense of commitment, the perception of problems as challenges, and a sense of control. People with the hardiness trait have a lower rate of stress-related illness (Baumgartner, 2002; Maddi, 2007; Maddi et al., 2011).

hardiness A personality trait characterized by a sense of commitment, the perception of problems as challenges, and a sense of control. (Module 43)

Specifically, the three components of hardiness operate in different ways:

- *Commitment*. People with a strong level of commitment tend to throw themselves into whatever they are doing. They have a sense that their activities are important and meaningful.

- *Challenge*. Hardy people believe that change, rather than stability, is the standard condition of life. To them, the anticipation of change is something positive, rather than change being seen as a threat to their security.

- *Control*. Hardiness is marked by a sense of control—the perception that people can influence the events in their lives.

Hardy individuals approach stress optimistically and take direct action to learn about and deal with stressors; they thereby change stressful events into less threatening ones. As a consequence, hardiness acts as a defense against stress-related illness (Bartone et al., 2008; Vogt et al., 2008; Stoppelbein, McRae & Greening, 2017).

Resilience   For those who confront the most profound difficulties, such as the death of a loved one or a permanent injury such as paralysis after an accident, a key ingredient in their psychological recovery is their degree of resilience. **Resilience** is the ability to withstand, overcome, and actually thrive after profound adversity (Bonanno, 2004; Norlander, Von Schedvin, & Archer, 2005; Jackson, 2006). (Also see *Neuroscience in Your Life.*)

Resilient people are generally optimistic, good-natured, and have good social skills. They are usually independent, and they have a sense of control over their own

resilience The ability to withstand, overcome, and actually thrive after profound adversity.

NEUROSCIENCE IN YOUR LIFE: THE NEUROSCIENCE OF RESILIENCE

Those who have experienced extreme stress, such as soldiers in combat, may develop psychological disorders such as posttraumatic stress disorder (PTSD). But not everyone who has lived through trauma develops these psychological disorders. What are the neurobiological differences between those who develop such disorders and those who are resilient to stress? Recent evidence suggests that resilience to stress is related to structural differences in certain parts of the brain involved in executive control and emotional arousal (shown in the images below). These brain differences may thus be important markers for understanding who is and is not predisposed to psychological disorders when exposed to high levels of stress (Gupta et al., 2017).

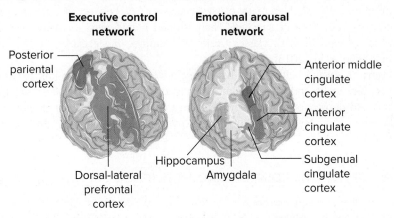

Source: Adapted from Gupta, A., Love, A., Kilpatrick, L. A., Labus, J. S., Bhatt, R., Chang, L., . . . Mayer, E. A. (2017). Morphological brain measures of cortico-limbic inhibition related to resilience. *Journal of Neuroscience Research, 95*(9), 1760-1775. doi: 10.1002/jnr.24007

destiny—even if fate has dealt them a devastating blow. In short, they work with what they have and make the best of whatever situation they find themselves in (Friborg et al., 2005; Deshields et al., 2006; Sinclair et al., 2013).

Resilience may have its origins in a complex series of biological reactions that occur when people confront devastating situations. These reactions involve the release of the hormone cortisol. Although cortisol is helpful in responding to challenges, too much can produce damage. Other chemicals, however, can moderate the effects of cortisol, and it may be that drugs or therapy can stimulate the production of these moderating chemicals. Furthermore, some people may be genetically predisposed to produce these chemicals, making them more resilient (Cole et al., 2010; Stix, 2011).

Resilience sometimes gives rise to *posttraumatic growth*, positive change that people experience as a result of a traumatic event. Rather than bouncing back to the psychological state they were in before the traumatic event, they actually see new opportunities emerge in their lives. Some people form closer connections with others who have also suffered. Finally, they may develop a sense of self-efficacy, the feeling that because they survived a highly stressful, life-altering event, they can live through anything life throws their way. In a sense, then, resilient people may find that a highly traumatic event leads to personal growth (Tedeschi et al., 2017; Wlodarczyk et al., 2017).

SOCIAL SUPPORT: TURNING TO OTHERS

Our relationships with others also help us cope with stress. Researchers have found that having **social support,** being part of a mutual network of caring, interested others, enables us to experience lower levels of stress, better cope with the stress we do undergo, and generally experience better health in general (Bolger & Amarel, 2007; García-Herrero et al., 2013; Pietromonaco & Collins, 2017).

The social and emotional support people provide each other helps in dealing with stress in several ways. For instance, such support demonstrates that a person is an important and valued member of a social network. Similarly, other people can provide

social support A mutual network of caring, interested others. (Module 34)

APPLYING PSYCHOLOGY IN THE 21ST CENTURY

DOES USING FACEBOOK MAKE YOU FEEL BAD?

Research is clear: Social interaction is good for you. Having stronger social ties is associated with a host of beneficial outcomes, such as better health, reduced rates of mental illness, and reduced rates of harmful behaviors such as alcohol abuse. And you even live longer (Uchino, 2006; Pietromonaco & Collins, 2017).

However, the research literature that establishes these benefits is largely based on real-world, face-to-face interaction rather than interactions via online social networks. With the latter type growing in popularity, an important question emerges: Does online social networking provide the same health benefits as real-world social networking?

There are plenty of reasons to think that online social networking operates differently from face-to-face interaction. People often manage their social-networking profiles to display mostly positive events in their lives, which may create an illusion online that most other people are doing better that you are and in turn lead to reduced self-esteem and increased depression. Conversely, it's plausible that people use social media to reinforce existing real-world relationships and facilitate access to social support, producing positive benefits. Research literature has largely produced a confusing and difficult-to-interpret picture, with multiple studies supporting each of these hypotheses (Nabi, Prestin, & So, 2013; Appel, Gerlach, & Crusis, 2016).

One recent study sheds some light on this landscape. It used a large sample size of over 5,000 adults, monitored their Facebook use, and compared it to measures of their real-world social activity over a period of 2 years and self-reports of their mental health (Shakya & Christakis, 2017).

The findings weren't very reassuring for Facebook users. The researchers looked at the frequency with which participants "liked" others' Facebook posts, clicked on posted links, and updated their own status message. Higher levels of these measures were associated with poorer life satisfaction and mental health. On the other hand, having more real-world friends, feeling closer to those real-world friends, and having more frequent interactions with real-world friends were all associated with greater life satisfaction and self-reported mental health.

One possible explanation for such findings is that people who are already feeling bad might be more inclined to take to Facebook, perhaps trying to gain

©Antonio Guillem/Shutterstock

social support or alleviate loneliness or boredom. But the research took into account how participants were feeling at the start, and it was still the case that the more they used Facebook, the worse they felt.

As for why Facebook usage had these ill effects, the researchers weren't sure. The drop in well-being associated with frequent liking of other people's posts seems consistent with the hypothesis that unfavorable comparison to other people's strategically edited lives is driving down self-esteem. But we need more research to fully understand the effects of Facebook use (Shakya & Christakis, 2017).

> **RETHINK**
>
> - In your experience, how does online social interaction differ from real-world social interaction?
> - In what ways might the quality of online social interaction matter as much as, or even more than, the quantity in determining the consequences of Facebook use?

information and advice about appropriate ways of dealing with stress (Day & Livingstone, 2003; Lindorff, 2005; Li et al., 2015; also see *Applying Psychology in the 21st Century*).

Finally, people who are part of a social support network can provide actual, physical aid to help others in stressful situations. For instance, they can supply temporary living quarters to a person whose house has burned down, or they can offer study help to a student who is experiencing stress because of poor academic performance (Takizawa, Kondo, & Sakihara, 2007).

Findings that attendance at religious services (as well as spirituality in general) provides health-related benefits also illustrate the importance of social support. For example, healthy people who regularly attend religious services live longer than those who do not attend regularly (Powell, Shahabi, & Thoresen, 2003; Gilbert, 2007; Hayward & Elliott, 2011).

Recent research is also beginning to identify how social support affects brain processing. For instance, one experiment found that activation of the areas of the brain reflecting stress was reduced when social support–simply being able to hold the hand of another person–was available (Coan, Schaefer, & Davidson, 2006).

From the perspective of...

A Social Worker How would you help people deal with and avoid stress in their everyday lives? How might you encourage people to create social support networks?

©Sam Edwards/age fotostock

BECOMING AN INFORMED CONSUMER
of Psychology

Effective Coping Strategies

How can we deal with the stress in our lives? Although there is no universal solution because effective coping depends on the nature of the stressor and the degree to which it can be controlled, here are some general guidelines (AFolkman & Moskowitz, 2000):

- *Turn a threat into a challenge.* When a stressful situation might be controllable, the best coping strategy is to treat the situation as a challenge and focus on ways to control it. For instance, if you experience stress because your car is always breaking down, you might take a course in auto mechanics and learn to deal directly with the car's problems.
- *Make a threatening situation less threatening.* When a stressful situation seems to be uncontrollable, you need to take a different approach. It is possible to change your appraisal of the situation, view it in a different light, and modify your attitude toward it. Research supports the old truism, "Look for the silver lining in every cloud" (Smith & Lazarus, 2001; Cheng & Cheung, 2005).
- *Change your goals.* If you are faced with an uncontrollable situation, a reasonable strategy is to adopt new goals that are practical in view of the particular situation. For example, a dancer who has been in an automobile accident and has lost full use of her legs may no longer aspire to a career in dance but might modify her goals and try to become a choreographer.
- *Modify your physiological reactions to stress.* Many people don't know that they can directly change their physiological reactions to stress, which can help with coping. For example, biofeedback (in which a person learns to control internal physiological processes through conscious thought) can alter basic physiological reactions to stress and permit the person to reduce blood pressure, heart rate, and other consequences of heightened stress. Exercise can also be effective in reducing stress (Langreth, 2000; Spencer et al., 2003; Hamer, Taylor, & Steptoe, 2006).
- *Change the situations that are likely to cause stress.* In *proactive coping,* you anticipate and try to head off stress *before* you encounter it. For example, if you know your upcoming week is going to be grueling because you must take a number of major tests, rearrange your schedule so you have more time to study or take direct steps to improve your chances for success by attending test review sessions (Bode et al., 2007; Kalka, 2017).

RECAP/EVALUATE/RETHINK

RECAP

LO 34-1 How is health psychology a union between medicine and psychology?

- The field of health psychology considers how psychology can be applied to the prevention, diagnosis, and treatment of medical problems.

LO 34-2 What is stress, how does it affect us, and how can we best cope with it?

- Stress is a response to threatening or challenging environmental conditions. People encounter stressors–the circumstances that produce stress–of both a positive and a negative nature.
- The way an environmental circumstance is interpreted affects whether it will be considered stressful. Still, there are general classes of events that provoke stress: cataclysmic events, personal stressors, and background stressors (daily hassles).
- Stress produces immediate physiological reactions. In the short term, those reactions may be adaptive, but in the long term, they may have negative consequences, including the development of psychophysiological disorders.
- The consequences of stress can be explained in part by Selye's general adaptation syndrome (GAS), which suggests that there are three stages in stress responses: alarm and mobilization, resistance, and exhaustion.
- Coping with stress can take a number of forms, including the unconscious use of defense mechanisms and the use of emotion-focused or problem-focused coping strategies.
- Stress can be reduced by developing a sense of control over one's circumstances. In some cases, however, people develop a state of learned helplessness.

EVALUATE

1. _____ is defined as a response to challenging or threatening events.
2. Match each portion of the GAS with its definition.

   1. Alarm and mobilization
   2. Exhaustion
   3. Resistance

   a. Ability to adapt to stress diminishes; symptoms appear
   b. Activation of sympathetic nervous system
   c. Use of various strategies to cope with a stressor

3. Stressors that affect a single person and produce an immediate major reaction are known as
   a. Personal stressors
   b. Psychic stressors
   c. Cataclysmic stressors
   d. Daily stressors
4. People with the personality characteristic of _____ seem to be better able to successfully combat stressors.

RETHINK

1. Why are cataclysmic stressors less stressful in the long run than other types of stressors? Does the reason relate to the coping phenomenon known as social support? How?
2. Given what you know about coping strategies, how would you train people to avoid stress in their everyday lives? How would you use this information with a group of veterans from the war in Afghanistan suffering from posttraumatic stress disorder?

Answers to Evaluate Questions

1. Stress; 2. 1-b, 2-a, 3-c; 3. a; 4. hardiness.

KEY TERMS

health psychology
stress
cataclysmic events
personal stressors
posttraumatic stress
  disorder (PTSD)

background stressors
  ("daily hassles")
psychophysiological
  disorders
general adaptation
  syndrome (GAS)

psychoneuroimmunology
  (PNI)
coping
learned helplessness
hardiness
resilience

social support

Module 35

Psychological Aspects of Illness and Well-Being

LEARNING OUTCOME

LO 35-1 How do psychological factors affect health-related problems such as coronary heart disease, cancer, and smoking?

Can simply talking with others about your experiences as a patient fighting cancer extend your life?

As recently as three decades ago, most psychologists and health-care providers would have scoffed at the notion that participating in a discussion group could improve a cancer patient's chances of survival. Today, however, such methods have gained increasing acceptance.

Growing evidence suggests that psychological factors have a substantial impact both on major health problems that were once seen in purely physiological terms and on our everyday sense of health, well-being, and happiness. We'll consider the psychological components of three major health problems—heart disease, cancer, and smoking—and then consider the nature of people's well-being and happiness.

The As, Bs, and Ds of Coronary Heart Disease

Tim knew it wasn't going to be his day when he got stuck in traffic behind a slow-moving farm truck. How could the driver dawdle like that? Didn't he have anything of any importance to do? Things didn't get any better when Tim arrived on campus and discovered the library didn't have the books he needed. He could almost feel the tension rising.

"I need that material to finish my paper," he thought to himself.

He knew that meant he wouldn't be able to get his paper done early, and that meant he wouldn't have the time he wanted to revise the paper. He wanted it to be a first-class paper. This time, Tim wanted to get a better grade than his roommate, Luis. Although Luis didn't know it, Tim felt that they were in competition and that Luis was always trying to better him, whether academically or just playing cards.

"In fact," Tim mused to himself, "I feel like I'm in competition with everyone, no matter what I'm doing."

Have you, like Tim, ever seethed impatiently at being caught behind a slow-moving vehicle, felt anger and frustration at not finding material you needed at the library, or experienced a sense of competitiveness with your classmates?

Many of us experience these sorts of feelings at one time or another, but for some people, they represent a pervasive, characteristic set of personality traits known as the Type A behavior pattern. The **Type A behavior pattern** is a cluster of behaviors involving hostility, competitiveness, time urgency, and feeling driven. In contrast, the **Type B behavior pattern** is characterized by a patient, cooperative, noncompetitive, and nonaggressive manner. It's important to keep in mind that Type A and Type B represent the ends of a continuum, and most people fall somewhere in between the two endpoints. Few people are purely a Type A or a Type B.

The importance of the Type A behavior pattern lies in its links to coronary heart disease. Men who display the Type A pattern develop coronary heart disease twice as often and suffer significantly more fatal heart attacks than do those classified as having the Type B pattern. Moreover, the Type A pattern predicts who is going to develop

Type A behavior pattern A cluster of behaviors involving hostility, competitiveness, time urgency, and feeling driven. (Module 35)

Type B behavior pattern A cluster of behaviors characterized by a patient, cooperative, noncompetitive, and nonaggressive manner. (Module 35)

heart disease at least as well as–and independently of–any other single factor, including age, blood pressure, smoking habits, and cholesterol levels in the body (Beresnevaité, Taylor, & Bagby, 2007; Korotkov et al., 2011).

Hostility is the key component of the Type A behavior pattern that is related to heart disease. Although competition, time urgency, and feelings of being driven may produce stress and potentially other health and emotional problems, they aren't linked to coronary heart disease the way that hostility is (Williams et al., 2000; Boyle et al., 2005; Ohira et al., 2007).

Why is hostility so toxic? The key reason is that hostility produces excessive physiological arousal in stressful situations. That arousal, in turn, results in increased production of the hormones epinephrine and norepinephrine as well as increases in heart rate and blood pressure. Such an exaggerated physiological response ultimately produces an increased incidence of coronary heart disease (Demaree & Everhart, 2004; Eaker et al., 2004; Myrtek, 2007).

It's important to keep in mind that not everyone who displays Type A behaviors is destined to have coronary heart disease. For one thing, a firm association between Type A behaviors and coronary heart disease has not been established for women; most findings pertain to males partly because, until recently, most research was done on men. In addition, other types of negative emotions besides the hostility found in Type A behavior appear to be related to heart attacks. For example, psychologist Johan Denollet has found evidence that what he calls *Type D*–for "distressed"–behavior is linked to coronary heart disease. In this view, insecurity, anxiety, and the negative outlook Type Ds display put them at risk for repeated heart attacks (Denollet & Pedersen, 2011; Šmigelskas et al., 2015; Lin et al., 2017).

Study Alert

It's important to distinguish among Type A (hostility, competitiveness), Type B (patience, cooperativeness), and Type D (distressed) behaviors.

From the perspective of...

A Health-Care Provider What type of advice would you give to your patients about the connections between personality and disease? For example, would you encourage Type A people to become "less Type A" to decrease their risk of heart disease?

©Rubberball/Getty Images

Psychological Aspects of Cancer

Hardly any disease is feared more than cancer. Most people think of cancer in terms of lingering pain, and being diagnosed with the disease is typically viewed as receiving a death sentence.

Although a diagnosis of cancer is not as grim as it once was–several kinds of cancer have a high cure rate if detected early enough–cancer remains the second leading cause of death after coronary heart disease. The precise trigger for the disease is not well understood, but the process by which cancer spreads is straightforward. Certain cells in the body become altered and multiply rapidly in an uncontrolled fashion. As those cells grow, they form tumors; if left unchecked, the tumors suck nutrients from healthy cells and body tissue and ultimately destroy the body's ability to function properly.

Although the processes involved in the spread of cancer are basically physiological, some research suggests that the emotional responses of cancer patients to their disease may affect its course. For example, some findings show that a "fighting spirit" leads to better coping. On the other hand, there is little evidence that long-term survival rates are better than for patients with less-positive attitudes (Rom, Miller, & Peluso, 2009; Heitzmann et al., 2011; Brandao et al., 2015).

Despite conflicting evidence, health psychologists believe that patients' emotions may at least partially determine the course of their disease. In the case of cancer, it is possible that positive emotional responses may help generate specialized "killer" cells that help control the size and spread of cancerous tumors. Conversely, negative emotions may suppress the ability of those cells to fight tumors (Noy, 2006; Mosher et al., 2015; Lutgendorf & Andersen, 2015).

Is a particular personality type linked to cancer? Some researchers suggest that cancer patients are less emotionally reactive, suppress anger, and lack outlets for emotional release. However, the data are too tentative and inconsistent to suggest firm conclusions about a link between personality characteristics and cancer. Certainly no conclusive evidence suggests that people who develop cancer would not have done so if their personality had been of a different sort or if their attitudes had been more positive (Holland & Lewis, 2001; Porcerelli et al., 2015).

What is increasingly clear, however, is that certain types of psychological therapy have the potential for improving quality of life and even extending the lives of cancer patients by slowing the progression of the disease. For example, the results of one study showed that women with breast cancer who received psychological treatment lived at least a year and a half longer and experienced less anxiety and pain than did women who did not participate in therapy. Research on patients with other health problems, such as heart disease, also has found that therapy can be both psychologically and medically beneficial (Lemogne et al., 2013; Spiegel, 2014; Perrier & Ginis, 2017).

Smoking

Would you walk into a convenience store and buy an item with a label warning you that its use could kill you? Although most people would probably answer no, millions make such a purchase everyday: a pack of cigarettes. Furthermore, they do this despite clear, well-publicized evidence that smoking is linked to cancer, heart attacks, strokes, bronchitis, emphysema, and a host of other serious illnesses. Smoking is the leading preventable cause of death in the United States; worldwide, 7 million people die each year from the effects of smoking (World Health Organization, 2017).

WHY PEOPLE SMOKE

Why do people smoke despite all the evidence showing that it is bad for their health? It is not that they are somehow unaware of the link between smoking and disease; surveys show that most *smokers* agree with the statement "Cigarette smoking frequently causes disease and death." And almost three-quarters of the 45 million smokers in the United States say they would like to quit (Price, 2008; CDC, 2013).

Genetics seems to determine, in part, whether people will become smokers, how much they will smoke, and how easily they can quit. Genetics also influences how susceptible people are to the harmful effects of smoking. For instance, although African Americans smoke fewer cigarettes than whites, they are more likely to die from smoking-related illnesses than whites. This difference may be due to genetically produced variations in how efficiently enzymes can reduce the effects of the cancer-causing chemicals in tobacco smoke (Li et al., 2003; Li et al., 2008; Minică, 2017).

Although genetics plays a role in smoking, social factors are the primary cause of the habit. Smoking at first may be seen as "cool" or sophisticated, as a rebellious act, or as facilitating calm performance in stressful situations. Exposure to smoking in media such as film also leads to a higher risk of becoming an established smoker. In addition, smoking is sometimes viewed as a "rite of passage" for adolescents, undertaken at the urging of friends and seen as a sign of growing up (Wills et al., 2008; Heatherton & Sargent, 2009; Mayer et al., 2015).

Ultimately, smoking becomes a habit. And it's an easy habit to pick up: Smoking even a single cigarette can lead to a smoker finding that *not* smoking requires an effort or involves discomfort. Subsequently, people begin to label themselves

Although smoking is prohibited in an increasing number of places, it remains a substantial social problem.

©McGraw-Hill Education/Jack Holtel, photographer

smokers, and smoking becomes part of how they view themselves. Moreover, they become dependent physiologically because nicotine, a primary ingredient of tobacco, is highly addictive.

When people become addicted to smoking, a complex relationship develops among smoking, nicotine levels, and a smoker's emotions. When this happens, a certain nicotine level becomes associated with a positive emotional state brought about by smoking. As a result, people smoke in an effort to regulate *both* their emotional states and the nicotine levels in the blood (Kassel et al., 2007; Ursprung, Sanouri, & DiFranza, 2009; Dennis, 2011).

E-cigarettes The newest trend in smoking is the use of *electronic cigarettes*, or *e-cigarettes*, which are battery-powered, cigarette-shaped devices that deliver nicotine that is vaporized to form a mist. They simulate the experience of smoking tobacco.

E-cigarette use is growing: More than a third of high school students have tried e-cigarettes at least once, and the numbers continue to increase. Data from the Centers for Disease Control and Prevention show that e-cigarette use among middle- and high-school age youth rose 900% between 2011 and 2015, surpassing use of every other form of tobacco among those age groups. Some 16% of 12th-grade students report using e-cigarettes in the prior month (CDC, 2015; Tavernise, 2015; U.S. Department of Health & Human Services, 2016).

The trend is worrisome to health experts. Although e-cigarettes do not contain the tar and other toxic chemicals found in cigarette smoke, the nicotine itself is harmful to developing adolescent brains and is an addictive substance that can become a long-term habit. Ninety percent of all smokers began smoking as teenagers, and three-quarters of teen smokers continue the habit into adulthood (CDC, 2015).

Because they are so new, little is known about the long-term effects of using e-cigarettes. Teenagers who have a clear understanding of the risks of cigarette smoking are often unsure about the risks of using e-cigarettes, and instead, they point to benefits such as looking cool and being trendy, and the flavorings.

Not surprisingly, teens who perceive e-cigarettes as being less harmful than are other forms of tobacco are more likely to use them, even if they have never tried any form of tobacco before. Although some research finds that e-cigarette use may make it easier to give up smoking of regular cigarettes, the rise in e-cigarette use remains of concern (Giovenco & Delnevo, 2018).

QUITTING SMOKING

Because smoking has both psychological and biological components, few habits are as difficult to break. Long-term successful treatment typically occurs in just 15% of those who try to stop smoking; once smoking becomes a habit, it is as hard to stop as an addiction to cocaine or heroin. In fact, some of the biochemical reactions to nicotine are similar to those to cocaine, amphetamines, and morphine. Furthermore, changes in brain chemistry brought about by smoking may make smokers more resistant to anti-smoking messages (Vanasse, Niyonsenga, & Courteau, 2004; Foulds et al., 2006; Dani & Montague, 2007).

Many people try to quit smoking but fail. The average smoker tries to quit 8–10 times before being successful, and even then, many relapse. Even long-time quitters can fall off the wagon: About 10% relapse after more than a year of avoiding cigarettes (Grady & Altman, 2008).

Among the most effective tools for ending the smoking habit are drugs that replace the nicotine found in cigarettes. Whether in the form of gum, patches, nasal sprays, or inhalers, these products provide a dose of nicotine that reduces dependence on cigarettes. Another approach is exemplified by the drugs Zyban and Chantix; rather than replacing nicotine, they reduce the pleasure from smoking and suppress withdrawal symptoms that smokers experience when they try to stop (Shiffman, 2007; Brody, 2008; Dohnke, Weiss-Gerlach, & Spies, 2011).

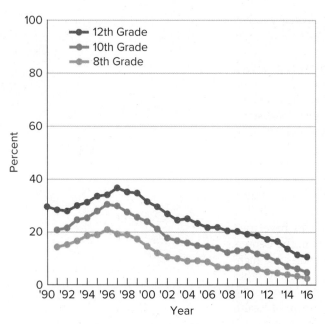

FIGURE 1 Although smoking among teenagers has declined considerably over the past several decades, a significant number still report smoking regularly. What factors might account for the continued high use of tobacco by teenagers despite the increase in antismoking advertising?

Source: Adapted from Johnston, L. D., O'Malley, P. M., Miech, R. A., Bachman, J. G., & Schulenberg, J. E. (2017). *Monitoring the Future national survey results on drug use, 1975–2016: Overview, key findings on adolescent drug use.* Ann Arbor, MI: Institute for Social Research.

Behavioral strategies, which view smoking as a learned habit and concentrate on changing the smoking response, can also be effective. Initial "cure" rates of 60% have been reported, and 1 year after treatment, more than half of those who quit have not resumed smoking. Individual or group counseling also increases the rate of success in breaking the habit. The best treatment seems to be a combination of nicotine replacement and counseling. What doesn't work? Going it alone: Only 5% of smokers who quit cold turkey on their own are successful (Rock, 1999; Woodruff, Conway, & Edwards, 2007).

In the long term, the most effective means of reducing smoking may be changes in societal norms and attitudes toward the habit. For instance, many cities and towns have made smoking in public places illegal; legislation based on strong popular sentiment that bans smoking in places such as college classrooms and buildings is being passed with increasing frequency. In addition, smokers are more likely to quit when their friends are quitting, so the social support of others quitting is helpful (Christakis & Fowler, 2008; McDermott et al., 2013; Mollen et al., 2017).

The long-term effect of the barrage of information regarding the negative consequences of smoking on people's health has been substantial; overall, smoking has declined over the last 2 decades, particularly among males. Still, more than one-fourth of students enrolled in high school are active smokers by the time they graduate, and there is evidence that the decline in smoking is leveling off. Among these students, around 10% become active smokers as early as the 8th grade (see Figure 1; Fichtenberg & Glantz, 2006; Johnston et al., 2017).

 # Exploring Diversity

Hucksters of Death: Promoting Smoking Throughout the World

A Jeep decorated with the Camel logo pulls up to a high school in Buenos Aires. A woman begins handing out free cigarettes to 15- and 16-year-olds during their lunch recess. At a video arcade in Taipei, free American cigarettes are strewn atop each game. At a disco filled with high school students, free packs of Salems are on each table. (Ecenbarger, 1993)

Because the number of smokers has steadily declined in the United States, cigarette manufacturers have turned their sights to other parts of the world, where they see a fertile market for their product. Although they must often sell cigarettes more cheaply than they do in the United States, the huge number of potential smokers still makes it financially worthwhile for the tobacco companies. The United States is now the world's largest exporter of cigarettes (Brown, 2001).

Clearly, the push into worldwide markets has been successful. In some Latin American cities, as many as 50% of teenagers smoke. Children as young as age 7 smoke in Hong Kong; 30% of children smoked their first whole cigarette before the age of 10 in India, Ghana, Jamaica, and Poland. The World Health Organization predicts that smoking will prematurely kill some 200 million of the world's children and that ultimately 10% of the world's population will die as a result of smoking. Of everyone alive today, 500 million will eventually die from tobacco use (Mackay & Eriksen, 2002).

One reason for the increase in smoking in developing countries is that their governments make little effort to discourage it. In fact, many governments are in the tobacco business themselves and rely on revenues from tobacco. For example, the world's largest manufacturer of cigarettes is the China National Tobacco Corporation, which is owned by the Chinese government (Marsh, 2008).

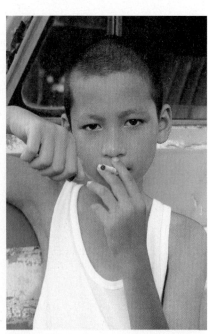

In some countries, children as young as age 6 smoke regularly.

©jan_ta_r/Shutterstock

RECAP/EVALUATE/RETHINK

RECAP

LO 35-1 How do psychological factors affect health-related problems such as coronary heart disease, cancer, and smoking?

- Hostility, a key component of the Type A behavior pattern, is linked to coronary heart disease. The Type A behavior pattern is a cluster of behaviors involving hostility, competitiveness, time urgency, and feeling driven.
- People's attitudes and emotional responses may affect the course of cancer through links to the immune system.
- Smoking, the leading preventable cause of health problems, has proved to be difficult to quit, even though most smokers are aware of the dangerous consequences of the behavior.

EVALUATE

1. Type _____ behavior is characterized by cooperativeness and by being easygoing; Type _____ behavior is characterized by hostility and competitiveness.
2. The Type A behavior pattern is known to directly cause heart attacks. True or false?

3. A cancer patient's attitude and emotions may affect that their _____ system and thus help or hinder their fight against the disease.
4. Smoking is used to regulate both nicotine levels and emotional states in smokers. True or false?

RETHINK

1. Is there a danger of "blaming the victim" when we argue that the course of cancer can be improved if a person with the disease holds positive attitudes or beliefs, particularly when we consider people with cancer who are not recovering? Explain your answer.
2. Do you think Type A or Type B behavior is more widely encouraged in the United States? Why?

Answers to Evaluate Questions

3. immune; 4. true

coronary heart disease but does not necessarily cause it directly;

1. B, A; **2.** false; Type A behavior is related to a higher incidence of

KEY TERMS

Type A behavior pattern   **Type B behavior pattern**

Module 36
Promoting Health and Wellness

LEARNING OUTCOMES

LO 36-1 How do our interactions with physicians affect our health and compliance with medical treatment?

LO 36-2 How does a sense of well-being develop?

When Stuart Grinspoon first noticed the small lump in his arm, he assumed it was just a bruise from the touch football game he had played the previous week. But as he thought about it more, he considered more serious possibilities and decided that he'd better get it checked out at the university health service. But the visit was less than satisfactory. A shy person, Stuart felt embarrassed talking about his medical condition. Even worse, after answering a string of questions, he couldn't even understand the physician's diagnosis and was too embarrassed to ask for clarification.

Many of us share Stuart Grinspoon's attitudes toward health care. We approach physicians the same way we approach auto mechanics. When something goes wrong with the car, we want the mechanic to figure out the problem and then fix it. In the same way, when something isn't working right with our bodies, we want a diagnosis of the problem and then a (we hope, quick) repair.

Yet such an approach ignores the fact that—unlike auto repair—good health care requires taking psychological factors into account. Health psychologists have sought to determine the factors involved in the promotion of good health and, more broadly, a sense of well-being and happiness. Let's take a closer look at two areas they have tackled: increasing compliance with health-related advice and identifying the determinants of well-being and happiness.

Following Medical Advice

We're not very good at following medical advice. Consider these figures:

- As many as 85% of patients do not fully comply with their physician's recommendations.
- Some 10% of adolescent pregnancies result from noncompliance with birth control practices.
- Thirty-one percent of patients don't fill their drug prescriptions.
- Forty-nine percent of patients forget to take prescribed medications.
- Thirteen percent take someone else's medicine.
- Sixty percent of all patients cannot identify their own medicines.
- From 30-50% of all patients ignore instructions or make errors in taking medication

Some of these errors are deliberate: Patients sometimes practice *creative nonadherence*, in which they alter a treatment prescribed by a physician by substituting their own medical judgment. Not surprisingly, patients' lack of medical knowledge may be harmful (Taylor, 1995; Hamani et al., 2007).

Noncompliance also can be a result of misunderstanding medical directions. For example, patients with low literacy skills may find complex instructions difficult to understand. In one study, only 34% of patients were able to understand that the direction "take two tablets by mouth twice daily" meant that they should take a total of 4 pills a day (Landro, 2011).

Whatever their causes, medical errors committed by patients and health-care providers are the third-leading cause of death in the United States. Over 250,000 Americans die annually from medical mistakes (Colland et al., 2004; Hobson, 2011; DeAngelis, 2016).

COMMUNICATING EFFECTIVELY WITH HEALTH-CARE PROVIDERS

Teresa Logan lay in the surgical ward as a her doctor drew incision lines on her chest with a felt-tipped pen. The operation would be grueling: 6 hours of surgery to use muscle tissue from her back to reconstruct her breasts, which had been removed months earlier to combat her cancer.

Teresa knew the operation wasn't the worst part; the extended recovery time would be even more grueling. She dreaded the damper it would put on her life as the mother of three young children and a serious runner and swimmer. As the doctor decorated her chest with marker ink, her husband asked a question that no one had asked before. "Is this operation really necessary?"

The answer was mind-blowing: No, it wasn't. If she left her chest as it was, she would recover in half the time with less pain and no adverse effects. The doctor had simply assumed that Teresa would want the reconstructive surgery for cosmetic reasons. Teresa and her husband looked at each other and reached a silent decision. "Get me up off this gurney, please," said Teresa.

Lack of communication between medical care providers and patients can be a major obstacle to good medical care. Such communication failures occur for several reasons. One is that physicians make assumptions about what patients prefer, or they push a specific treatment that they prefer without consulting patients.

Furthermore, the relatively high prestige of physicians may intimidate patients. Patients may also be reluctant to volunteer information that might cast them in a bad light, and physicians may have difficulties encouraging their patients to provide information. In many cases, physicians dominate an interview with questions of a technical nature, whereas patients attempt to communicate a personal sense of their illness and the impact it is having on their lives (Wain, Grammer, & Stasinos, 2006; Wallace et al., 2013; Xiang & Stanley, 2017).

Furthermore, the view many patients hold that physicians are "all knowing" can result in serious communication problems. Many patients do not understand their treatments yet fail to ask their physicians for clear explanations of a prescribed course of action. About half of all patients are unable to report accurately how long they are to continue taking a medication prescribed for them, and about a quarter do not even know the purpose of the drug. In fact, some patients are not even sure, as they are about to be rolled into the operating room, why they are having surgery (Atkinson, 1997; Halpert, 2003)!

Sometimes patient–physician communication difficulties occur because the material that must be communicated is too technical for patients, who may lack fundamental knowledge about the body and basic medical practices. In an overreaction to this problem, some health-care providers use baby talk (calling patients "honey" or telling them to go "night-night") and assume that patients cannot understand even simple information. In other cases, physicians are uncomfortable breaking bad news to patients, so they use medical jargon to avoid being direct (Mika et al., 2007; Feng et al., 2011).

To address such problems, medical schools increasingly include training to improve the communication skills of health-care providers, as we discussed in the prologue to this chapter. For example, they teach physicians to allow patients to speak first and ask questions, and how to convey empathy and honesty through their speech (Reddy, 2015).

The amount and quality of physician–patient communication also are related to the gender of a physician and patient. Overall, female primary-care physicians provide more patient-centered communications than do male primary-care physicians. Furthermore, patients often prefer same-sex physicians (Bertakis, 2009; Bertakis, Franks, & Epstein, 2009; Shin et al., 2015).

Cultural values and expectations also contribute to communication barriers between patients and their physicians. Providing medical advice to a patient whose native language is not English may be problematic. Furthermore, medical practices differ between cultures, and medical practitioners need to be familiar with a patient's culture in order to produce compliance with medical recommendations (Ho et al., 2004; Culhane-Pera, Borkan, & Patten, 2007).

Finally, the newest approaches to improving communication between health-care providers and patients is *e-health communication*, which uses technology to convey information. For example, patients may be virtually reminded using smartphone technology to take their prescribed medicines. Similarly, some health-care providers offer virtual office hours in which patients can communicate with them via Skype or Facetime (Reynolds & Maughan, 2015; Celi et al., 2017).

What can patients do to improve communication with health-care providers? Here are some tips (National Institutes of Health, 2015):

- Make a list of your medical questions and concerns before your visit.

- To prepare for a visit, write down the names and dosages of every drug you currently take.

- Take notes during your visit so you can remember what your health-care provider tells you.

- Ask how to access your medical records online and whether you can communicate with your health-care provider via e-mail and phone.

- Consider bringing a friend or relative with you. They can ask questions and in general advocate for you.

INCREASING COMPLIANCE WITH MEDICAL ADVICE

Although compliance with medical advice does not guarantee that a patient's medical problems will go away, it does optimize the possibility that the patient's condition will improve. What, then, can health-care providers do to produce greater compliance on the part of their patients? One strategy is to provide clear instructions to patients regarding drug regimens. Maintaining good, warm relations with patients also leads to increased compliance (Arbuthnott & Sharpe, 2009).

In addition, honesty helps. Patients generally prefer to be well informed—even if the news is bad; their degree of satisfaction with their medical care is linked to how well and how accurately physicians are able to convey the nature of their medical problems and treatments (Zuger, 2005).

The way in which a message is framed also can result in more positive responses to health-related information. *Positively framed messages* suggest that a change in behavior will lead to a gain and thus emphasize the benefits of carrying out a health-related

Positively framed messages suggest that a change in behavior will lead to a health-related gain.

©UpperCut Images/SuperStock

behavior. For instance, suggesting that skin cancer is curable if it is detected early and that you can reduce your chances of getting the disease by using a sunscreen places information in a positive frame. In contrast, *negatively framed messages* highlight what you can lose by not performing a behavior. For instance, a physician might say that if you don't use sunscreen, you're more likely to get skin cancer, which can kill you if it's not detected early.

What type of message is more effective? It depends on the type of health behavior the health-care provider is trying to bring about. Positively framed messages are best for motivating *preventive* behavior. However, negatively framed messages are most effective in producing behavior that will lead to the detection of a disease (McCaul, Johnson, & Rothman, 2002; Apanovich, McCarthy, & Salovey, 2003; Lee & Aaker, 2004).

From the perspective of...

A Health-Care Provider How would you try to better communicate with your patients? How might your techniques vary depending on the patient's background, gender, age, and culture?

©Tetra Images/Getty Images

Well-Being and Happiness

What makes for a good life?

This is a question that philosophers and theologians have pondered for centuries. Now health psychologists are turning their spotlight on the question by investigating **subjective well-being,** people's sense of their happiness and satisfaction with their lives (Tsaousis, Nikolaou, & Serdaris, 2007; Kesebir & Diener, 2008; Giannopoulos & Vella-Brodrick, 2011).

subjective well-being People's sense of their happiness and satisfaction with their lives. (Module 36)

WHAT ARE THE CHARACTERISTICS OF HAPPY PEOPLE?

Research on the subject of well-being shows that happy people share several characteristics (Otake, Shimai, & Tanaka-Matsumi, 2006; Nisbet, Zelenski, & Murphy, 2011; Burns, 2017):

- *Happy people have high self-esteem.* People who are happy like themselves. This is particularly true in Western cultures, which emphasize the importance of individuality. Furthermore, people who are happy see themselves as more intelligent and better able to get along with others than the average person is. In fact, they may hold *positive illusions* in which they hold moderately inflated views of themselves, believing that they are good, competent, and desirable (Taylor et al., 2000; Boyd-Wilson, McClure, & Walkey, 2004; McLeod, 2015).

- *Happy people have a firm sense of control.* They feel more in control of events in their lives, unlike those who feel they are the pawns of others and who experience learned helplessness.

- *Happy individuals are optimistic.* Their optimism permits them to persevere at tasks and ultimately to achieve more. In addition, their health is better (Peterson, 2000; Efklides & Moraitou, 2013).

- *Men and women generally are made happy by the same sorts of activities—but not always.* Most of the time, adult men and women achieve the same level of happiness from the same things, such as hanging out with friends. But there are some differences: For example, women get less pleasure from being with their parents than men do. The explanation? For women, time spent with their parents more closely resembles work, such as helping them cook or pay the bills. For men, it's more likely to involve recreational activities, such as watching a football game with their fathers. The result is that men report being slightly happier than women (Kreuger, 2007).

- *Happy people like to be around other people.* They tend to be extroverted and have a supportive network of close relationships.

Perhaps most important, most people living in a wide variety of circumstances report being at least moderately happy most of the time. Furthermore, life-altering events that one might expect would produce long-term spikes in happiness, such as winning the lottery, probably won't make you much happier than you already are, as we discuss next.

DOES MONEY BUY HAPPINESS?

If you were to win the lottery, would you be happier?

Probably not, at least in the long run. That's the implication of health psychologists' research on subjective well-being. That research shows that although winning the lottery brings an initial surge in happiness, a year later, winners' level of happiness returns to what it was before they won.

A similar pattern, although in reverse, occurs for people who have had extremely serious injuries in accidents, such as losing a limb or becoming paralyzed: Initially, they decline in happiness after the accident. But in the long run, most victims return to their prior levels of happiness after the passage of time (Priester & Petty, 2011; Weimann, Knabe, & Schöb, 2015; Wang et al., 2017).

Why is the level of subjective well-being so stable? One explanation is that people have a general *set point* for happiness, a marker that establishes the tone for one's life. Although specific events may temporarily elevate or depress one's mood (a surprise promotion or a job loss, for example), people ultimately return to their general level of happiness.

Although it is not certain how people's happiness set points are initially established, some evidence suggests that the set point is determined at least in part by genetic factors. Specifically, identical twins who grow up in widely different circumstances turn out to have very similar levels of happiness (Diener, Lucas, & Scollon, 2006; Weiss, Bates, & Luciano, 2008).

Most people's well-being set point is relatively high. For example, some 30% of people in the United States rate themselves as "very happy," and only 1 in 10 rate themselves "not too happy." Most people declare themselves to be "pretty happy." Such feelings are graphically confirmed by people who are asked to place themselves on the measure of happiness illustrated in Figure 1. The scale clearly illustrates that most people view their lives quite positively.

Study Alert

Remember the concept that individuals have a set point (a general, consistent level) relating to subjective well-being.

Faces Scale: "Which face comes closest to expressing how you feel about your life as a whole?"

| 20% | 46% | 27% | 4% | 2% | 1% | 0% |

FIGURE 1 Most people in the United States rate themselves as happy, while only a small minority indicate they are "not too happy."
Source: Adapted from Andrews, F. M., & Withey, S. B. (1976). *Social indicators of well-being: Americans' perceptions of life quality.* New York: Plenum.

Similar results are found when people are asked to compare themselves with others. For example, when asked "Who of the following people do you think is the happiest?" survey respondents answered "Oprah Winfrey" (23%), "Bill Gates" (7%), "the Pope" (12%), and "yourself" (49%), with 6% saying they didn't know (Black & McCafferty, 1998; Rosenthal, 2003).

Few differences exist between members of different demographic groups. Men and women report being equally happy, and African Americans are only slightly less likely than European Americans to rate themselves as "very happy." Furthermore, happiness is hardly unique to U.S. culture. Even countries that are not economically prosperous have, on the whole, happy residents (Diener & Clifton, 2002; Suh, 2002; Suhail & Chaudhry, 2004).

The bottom line: Money does *not* seem to buy happiness. Of course, one needs some minimal level of income; research shows that people living in extreme poverty are sadder than those with higher incomes. Furthermore, income used to purchase services that allow us more free time (someone to clean the house or bring us groceries) produces greater happiness than income spent on objects such as clothing (Kushlev, Dunn, & Lucas, 2015; Whillans et al., 2017).

Despite the ups and downs of life, then, most people tend to be reasonably happy, and they adapt to the trials and tribulations–and joys and delights–of life by returning to a steady-state level of happiness. That habitual level of happiness can have profound–and even life-prolonging–consequences (Diener & Seligman, 2004; Hecht, 2007).

RECAP/EVALUATE/RETHINK

RECAP

LO 36-1 How do our interactions with physicians affect our health and compliance with medical treatment?

- Although patients would often like physicians to base a diagnosis only on a physical examination, communicating one's problem to the physician is equally important.

- Patients may find it difficult to communicate openly with their physicians because of physicians' high social prestige and the technical nature of medical information.

LO 36-2 How does a sense of well-being develop?

- Subjective well-being, the measure of how happy people are, is highest in people with high self-esteem, a sense of control, optimism, and a supportive network of close relationships.

EVALUATE

1. Health psychologists are most likely to focus on which of the following problems with health care?
   a. Incompetent health-care providers
   b. Rising health-care costs
   c. Ineffective communication between physician and patient
   d. Scarcity of medical research funding

2. If you want people to floss more to prevent gum disease, the best approach is to
   a. Use a negatively framed message.
   b. Use a positively framed message.
   c. Have a dentist deliver an encouraging message on the pleasures of flossing.
   d. Provide people with free dental floss.
3. Winning the lottery is likely to
   a. Produce an immediate and long-term increase in the level of well-being.
   b. Produce an immediate but not lingering increase in the level of well-being.
   c. Produce a decline in well-being over the long run.
   d. Lead to an increase in greed over the long run.

RETHINK

1. Do you think stress plays a role in making communication between physicians and patients difficult? Why?
2. If money doesn't buy happiness, what *can* you do to make yourself happier? As you answer, consider the research findings on stress and coping, as well as on emotions.

Answers to Evaluate Questions

1. c; 2. b; 3. b

KEY TERMS

subjective well-being

EPILOGUE

In this set of modules, we have explored the intersection of psychology and biology. We have seen how the emotional and psychological experience of stress can lead to physical symptoms of illness, how personality factors may be related to major health problems, and how psychological factors can interfere with effective communication between physician and patient. We have also looked at the other side of the coin, noting that some relatively simple strategies can help us control stress, affect illness, and improve our interactions with physicians.

Turn back to the prologue of this set of modules, about the sessions in which medical residents practice delivering bad news to parents and patients.

1. What sorts of stressors are doctors in a hospital setting likely to experience? Do you think the training they receive in the Breaking Bad News program will help them deal with stressful situations generally or only those that involve communicating to parents and patients?
2. Think of examples of the three main types of stressors (cataclysmic events, personal stressors, and background stressors) to which hospital workers are particularly susceptible. Are they also likely to experience particular types of uplifts?
3. Is the approach of the Breaking Bad News program an example of emotion-focused coping, problem-focused coping, or both? Explain.
4. What can doctors do to encourage better communication both from and to them? Sketch out a program that builds on Breaking Bad News and aims to improve two-way communication between doctors and patients.

Design Elements: Yellow highlighter: ©luckyraccoon/Shutterstock.com; Smartphone: ©and4me/Shutterstock.com; Group of diverse hands: ©MR. Nattanon Kanchak/Shutterstock.com; Woman working on laptop: ©Dragon Images/Shutterstock.com.

VISUAL SUMMARY 11 Health Psychology

MODULE 34 Stress and Coping

<u>Stress:</u> People's response to events that threaten or challenge them
- Interpretation of events is important in determining what is stressful
  - Cataclysmic events
  - Personal stressors
  - Background stressors (daily stressors)
- Posttraumatic Stress Disorder (PTSD)

The Cost of Stress

- Psychophysiological disorders: An interaction of psychological, emotional, and physical difficulties

Direct physiological effects
- Elevated blood pressure
- Decrease in immune system functioning
- Increased hormonal activity
- Psychophysiological conditions

Stress

Harmful behaviors
- Increased smoking, alcohol use
- Decreased nutrition
- Decreased sleep
- Increased drug use

Indirect health-related behaviors
- Decreased compliance with medical advice
- Increase in delays in seeking medical advice
- Decrease in likelihood of seeking medical advice

- General Adaptation Syndrome (GAS) Model: The physiological response to stress follows the same pattern regardless of the cause of stress

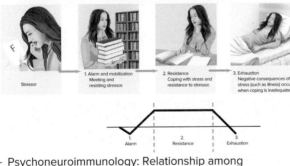

Stressor | 1. Alarm and mobilization Meeting and resisting stressor. | 2. Resistance Coping with stress and resistance to stressor. | 3. Exhaustion Negative consequences of stress (such as illness) occur when coping is inadequate.

1. Alarm | 2. Resistance | 3. Exhaustion

- Psychoneuroimmunology: Relationship among psychological factors, the immune system, and the brain

<u>Coping with Stress:</u> Emotion-focused or problem-focused coping

MODULE 35 Psychological Aspects of Illness and Well-Being

Coronary Heart Disease

- Type A behavior: A cluster of behaviors involving hostility, competitiveness, time urgency, and feeling driven
- Type B behavior: Characterized by a patient, cooperative, noncompetitive and nonaggressive manner
- Type D behavior: Insecure, anxious, and negative outlook

<u>Cancer:</u> Psychological therapy may improve quality of life

Smoking

- Over 5 million people die each year from smoking
- Heredity, in part, determines whether people will become smokers and are susceptible to harmful effects of smoking
- Few habits are as difficult to break

MODULE 36 Promoting Health and Wellness

<u>Following Medical Advice:</u> Noncompliance with medical advice takes many forms
- Communicating with health-care providers
  - Lack of communication can be a major obstacle
- Increasing compliance with medical advice
  - Patients prefer to be well informed even if the news is bad
  - Positively framed messages: most likely to motivate preventive behavior

  - Negatively framed messages: most likely to lead to the detection of a disease

<u>Well-Being and Happiness</u>
- Subjective well-being: People's own evaluation of their lives in terms of their thoughts and their emotions
- Characteristics of happy people: high self-esteem, sense of control, optimism, enjoy being with others
- Most people are moderately happy most of the time

Faces Scale: "Which face comes closest to expressing how you feel about your life as a whole?"

20%   46%   27%   4%   2%   1%   0%

(MODULE 34) Sources: (cost of stress) Adapted from Baum, A. (1994). Behavioral, biological, and environmental interactions in disease processes. In S. Blumenthal, K. Matthews, & S. Weiss Eds.), *New research frontiers in behavioral medicine: Proceedings of the National Conference*. Washington, DC: NIH Publications; (stressor) ©McGraw-Hill Global Education Holdings LLC, 1978; (MODULE 35) (photo): ©jan_ta_r/Shutterstock; (MODULE 36) (photo): ©UpperCut Images/SuperStock; (faces scale): Source: Adapted from Andrews, F. M., & Withey, S. B. (1976). *Social indicators of well-being: Americans' perceptions of life quality*. New York: Plenum.

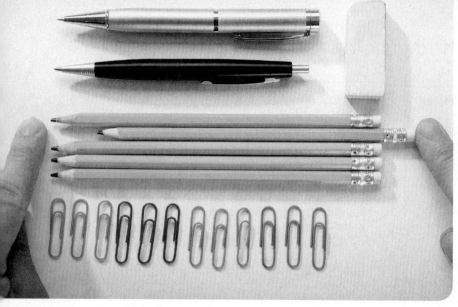

©Andrey_Popov/Shutterstock

CHAPTER 12
Psychological Disorders

LEARNING OUTCOMES FOR CHAPTER 12

MODULE 37

LO 37-1 How can we distinguish normal from abnormal behavior?

LO 37-2 What are the major perspectives on psychological disorders used by mental health professionals?

LO 37-3 What are the major categories of psychological disorders?

NORMAL VERSUS ABNORMAL: MAKING THE DISTINCTION

Defining Abnormality

Perspectives on Abnormality: From Superstition to Science

Classifying Abnormal Behavior: The ABCs of DSM

MODULE 38

LO 38-1 What are the major psychological disorders?

THE MAJOR PSYCHOLOGICAL DISORDERS

Anxiety Disorders

Obsessive-Compulsive Disorder

Somatic Symptom Disorders

Dissociative Disorders

Mood Disorders

Schizophrenia

Neuroscience in Your Life: Brain Networks Related to Memory Deficits in Schizophrenia

Personality Disorders

Disorders That Impact Childhood

Other Disorders

PROLOGUE *RUNNING SCARED*

The first time it happened, Andrea Petersen was staring at a lengthy list of classes, trying to decide which ones to take in the coming semester. One moment the college sophomore felt fine, and the next moment her world exploded. Fear spiraled up her spine. Her stomach flipped. Her heart rate rocketed. Breathing became difficult, and her vision warped. The onset, Petersen recalls, was as sudden as a car crash. All she could think was: *I'm dying. I'm dying.*

Over the next few months, the list of Petersen's symptoms grew—tingling in her feet and face, chest pains, vertigo—and her list of fears lengthened: dentists, touching dirt, licking envelopes, driving on highways. And always, the fear of death.

Petersen saw numerous doctors, and she had EKGs, blood tests, echocardiograms, and an MRI. Doctors suspected many culprits, among them a brain tumor, multiple sclerosis, and Epstein-Barr virus. But no one really knew what was wrong with Petersen. It was at that point that she remembers peering over the banister of a rooftop parking garage and thinking: *Why not jump?* (Petersen, 2017).

LOOKING *Ahead*

Andrea Petersen was losing her grip on reality. It turned out that she was suffering from an anxiety disorder, a psychological disorder that affects millions of Americans, a growing number of them college students like herself. A combination of medication, cognitive behavioral therapy, and mindfulness techniques such as yoga and meditation have helped Petersen keep her anxiety in check, but her experience raises many questions. What caused her disorder? Were genetic factors involved, or were stressors in her life primarily responsible? Were there signs that family and friends should have noticed earlier? Could her anxiety disorder have been prevented? And, more generally, how do we distinguish normal from abnormal behavior, and how can Petersen's experiences be categorized and classified in such a way as to pinpoint the specific nature of her problem?

We address the issues raised by Andrea Petersen's case in this chapter. We begin by discussing the difference between normal and abnormal behavior, which can be surprisingly indistinct. We then turn to a consideration of the most significant kinds of psychological disorders. Finally, we'll consider ways of evaluating behavior—one's own and that of others—to determine whether seeking help from a mental health professional is warranted.

Module 37

Normal Versus Abnormal: Making the Distinction

LEARNING OUTCOMES

LO 37-1 How can we distinguish normal from abnormal behavior?

LO 37-2 What are the major perspectives on psychological disorders used by mental health professionals?

LO 37-3 What are the major categories of psychological disorders?

Universally that person's acumen is esteemed very little perceptive concerning whatsoever matters are being held as most profitable by mortals with sapience endowed to be studied who is ignorant of that which the most in doctrine erudite and certainly by reason of that in them high mind's ornament deserving of veneration constantly maintain when by general consent they affirm that other circumstances being equal by no exterior splendour is the prosperity of a nation. . . .

It would be easy to conclude that these words are the musings of a madman. To most people, the passage does not seem to make any sense at all. But literary scholars would disagree. Actually, this passage is from James Joyce's classic *Ulysses*, hailed as one of the major works of 20th-century literature (Joyce, 1934).

As this example illustrates, casually examining a person's writing is insufficient to determine the degree to which that person is "normal." But even when we consider more extensive samples of a person's behavior, we will find that there may be only a fine line between behavior that is considered normal and behavior that is considered abnormal.

Defining Abnormality

Because of the difficulty in distinguishing normal from abnormal behavior, psychologists have struggled to devise a precise, scientific definition of "abnormal behavior." For instance, consider the following definitions, each of which has advantages and disadvantages:

- *Abnormality as a deviation from what is average behavior.* According to this definition, behaviors that are unusual or rare in a society or culture are considered abnormal. It is basically a statistical definition: If most people behave in a certain way, it is viewed as normal; if only a few people do it, it is considered abnormal.

  The difficulty with this definition is that some statistically unusual behaviors hardly seem abnormal. If most people eat meat, but you are a vegetarian, this deviation from the average hardly makes your behavior abnormal. Similarly, a concept of abnormality that depends on what is unusual would unreasonably label a person who has an unusually high IQ as abnormal simply because a high IQ is statistically rare. In short, a definition of abnormality that rests on deviation from the average is insufficient.

- *Abnormality as a deviation from an ideal.* An alternative definition of abnormality considers behavior in relation to some kind of ideal or morally appropriate standard toward which most people are striving.

  This sort of definition considers behavior abnormal if it is different from what society considers ideal behavior or from some moral standard. However, society has few ideals on which people universally agree. (For example, it would be hard to find agreement on whether the New Testament, the Koran, the Talmud, or the Book of Mormon provides the most appropriate ideal behavior.) Furthermore, standards that do arise change over time and vary across cultures. Thus, the deviation-from-the-ideal approach is also inadequate.

- *Abnormality as producing a sense of personal discomfort.* A more useful definition concentrates on the psychological consequences of behavior for the individual. In this

Study Alert

Remember the different definitions of abnormality (deviation from the average, deviation from the ideal, a sense of personal discomfort, inability to function effectively, and abnormality as a legal concept).

approach, behavior is considered abnormal if it produces a sense of personal distress, anxiety, or guilt in an individual–or if it is harmful to others in some way.

However, even a definition that relies on personal discomfort has drawbacks. For example, in some especially severe forms of mental disturbance, people report feeling wonderful, even though their behavior seems bizarre to others. In such cases, a person feels fine, although most people would consider the behavior abnormal. Similarly, most of us would think that a woman who says she hears uplifting messages from Martians would be displaying abnormal behavior even though she may say that the messages bring her great satisfaction.

Andrea Yates, who initially was found sane by a jury despite having drowned her five children in a bathtub, was later found innocent due to insanity.
©Brett Coomer, Pool/AP Images

- *Abnormality as the inability to function effectively.* Most people are able to feed themselves, hold a job, get along with others, and in general live as productive members of society. Yet there are those who are unable to adjust to the demands of society or function effectively.

  According to this view of abnormality, people who are unable to function effectively and to adapt to the demands of society are considered abnormal. For example, an unemployed, homeless woman living on the street may be considered unable to function effectively. Therefore, her behavior can be viewed as abnormal even if she has chosen to live this way. Her inability to adapt to the requirements of society is what makes her "abnormal," according to this approach.

- *Abnormality as a legal concept.* According to the jury that first heard her case, Andrea Yates, a woman who drowned her five children in a bathtub, was sane. She was sentenced to life in prison for her act.

  Although you might question this view (and a later appeals jury overturned the conviction), the initial verdict reflected the way in which the law defines abnormal behavior. To the judicial system, the distinction between normal and abnormal behavior rests on the definition of *insanity*, which is a legal but not a psychological term. In fact, the definition of *insanity* varies from one jurisdiction to another. In some states, *insanity* simply means that defendants cannot understand the difference between right and wrong at the time they commit a criminal act. Other states consider whether defendants are substantially incapable of understanding the criminality of their behavior or unable to control themselves. And in some jurisdictions, pleas of insanity are not allowed at all (Ferguson & Ogloff, 2011; Reisner, Piel, & Makey, 2013; Yelderman & Miller, 2017).

Clearly, none of the previous definitions is broad enough to cover all instances of abnormal behavior, and the distinction between normal and abnormal behavior often remains ambiguous even to trained professionals. Furthermore, to a large extent, cultural expectations for "normal" behavior in a particular society influence the understanding of "abnormal behavior."

Given the difficulties in precisely defining the construct, psychologists typically use a broad definition of abnormal behavior. Specifically, **abnormal behavior** is generally defined as behavior that causes people to experience distress and hinders them from functioning in their daily lives (Nolen-Hoeksema, 2007; Bassett & Baker, 2015).

abnormal behavior Behavior that causes people to experience distress and prevents them from functioning in their daily lives. (Module 46)

From the perspective of...

An Employer Imagine that you learned that a well-paid employee was arrested for shoplifting a sweater that cost only $15. Would you fire the employee if you thought the behavior was caused by a psychological disorder?

©Sam Edwards/age fotostock

Because this definition is imprecise, it's best to view abnormal behavior and normal behavior as marking two ends of a continuum rather than as absolute, precise conditions. Behavior should be evaluated in terms of gradations that range from fully normal functioning to extremely abnormal behavior. Behavior typically falls somewhere between those extremes.

Perspectives on Abnormality: From Superstition to Science

Throughout much of human history, people linked abnormal behavior to superstition, magic, and spells. Individuals who displayed abnormal behavior were accused of being possessed by the devil or some sort of demonic god. Authorities felt justified in "treating" abnormal behavior by attempting to drive out the source of the problem. This often involved whipping, immersion in hot water, starvation, or other forms of torture in which the cure was worse than the affliction (Scull, 2016).

Contemporary approaches take a more enlightened view. Today, six major perspectives are used to understand psychological disorders. These perspectives, which are discussed next, suggest not only different causes of abnormal behavior but different treatment approaches as well. Furthermore, some perspectives are more applicable to specific disorders than are others.

MEDICAL PERSPECTIVE

medical perspective The perspective that suggests that when an individual displays symptoms of abnormal behavior, the root cause will be found in a physical examination of the individual, which may reveal a hormonal imbalance, a chemical deficiency, or a brain injury. (Module 37)

When people display the symptoms of tuberculosis, medical professionals can generally find tubercular bacteria in their body tissue. Similarly, the **medical perspective** suggests that when an individual displays symptoms of a psychological disorder, the fundamental cause will be found through a physical examination of the individual, which may reveal a hormonal imbalance, a chemical deficiency, or a brain injury. Indeed, when we speak of mental "illness," "symptoms" of psychological disorders, and mental "hospitals," we are using terminology associated with the medical perspective.

Because a growing body of research shows that many forms of abnormal behavior are linked to biological causes, the medical perspective provides at least part of the explanation for psychological disorders. Yet serious criticisms have been leveled against it. For one thing, some types of abnormal behavior have no apparent biological cause. In addition, some critics have argued that the use of the term *mental illness* implies that people who display abnormal behavior have no responsibility for or control over their actions (Yang et al., 2013; Prior & Bond, 2017).

Still, recent advances in our understanding of the neurological bases of behavior underscore the importance of considering physiological factors in abnormal behavior. For instance, some of the more severe forms of psychological disorders, such as major depression and schizophrenia, clearly are influenced in important ways by genetic factors and malfunctions in neurotransmitter signals (Howes & Kapur, 2009; Li et al., 2011; Hariri, 2015).

PSYCHOANALYTIC PERSPECTIVE

psychoanalytic perspective The perspective that suggests that abnormal behavior stems from childhood conflicts over opposing wishes regarding sex and aggression. (Module 37)

Whereas the medical perspective suggests that biological causes are at the root of abnormal behavior, the **psychoanalytic perspective** holds that abnormal behavior stems from childhood conflicts over opposing wishes regarding sex and aggression. According to Freud, children pass through a series of stages in which sexual and aggressive impulses take different forms and produce conflicts that require resolution. If these childhood conflicts are not dealt with successfully, they remain unresolved in the unconscious and eventually bring about abnormal behavior during adulthood.

To uncover the roots of people's disordered behavior, the psychoanalytic perspective scrutinizes their early life history. However, there is no sure way to link what happens to people during childhood to abnormal behavior that they display as adults. Consequently, we can never be sure that specific childhood experiences can be linked to specific adult abnormal behaviors.

In addition, psychoanalytic theory paints a picture of people as having relatively little control over their behavior. Instead, the theory assumes that behavior is largely guided by unconscious impulses over which people have neither control nor awareness. Consequently, in the eyes of some critics, this perspective suggests that people have little responsibility for their own behavior.

On the other hand, the contributions of psychoanalytic theory have been significant. More than any other approach to abnormal behavior, this perspective highlights the fact that people can have a rich, involved inner life. Furthermore, it underscores that experiences that occurred long in the past can have a profound effect on current psychological functioning (Bornstein, 2003; Rangell, 2007).

BEHAVIORAL PERSPECTIVE

Both the medical and psychoanalytic perspectives look at abnormal behaviors as *symptoms* of an underlying problem. In contrast, the **behavioral perspective** looks at the rewards and punishments in the environment that determine abnormal behavior. It views the disordered behavior itself as the problem. Using the basic principles of learning, behavioral theorists see both normal and abnormal behaviors as responses to various stimuli–responses that have been learned through past experience and are guided in the present by stimuli in the individual's environment. To explain why abnormal behavior occurs, we must analyze how an individual has learned it and observe the circumstances in which it is displayed.

behavioral perspective The approach that suggests that observable, external behavior, which can be objectively measured, should be the focus of study. (Module 2)

The emphasis on observable behavior represents both the greatest strength and the greatest weakness of the behavioral approach to abnormal behavior. This perspective provides the most precise and objective approach for examining behavioral symptoms of specific disorders, such as attention-deficit hyperactivity disorder (ADHD), which we discuss in module 47. At the same time, though, critics charge that the perspective ignores the rich inner world of thoughts, attitudes, and emotions that may contribute to abnormal behavior.

COGNITIVE PERSPECTIVE

The medical, psychoanalytic, and behavioral perspectives view people's behavior as the result of factors largely beyond their control. To many critics of these views, however, people's thoughts cannot be ignored.

In response to such concerns, some psychologists employ a **cognitive perspective.** Rather than considering only external behavior, as in traditional behavioral approaches, the cognitive approach assumes that *cognitions* (people's thoughts and beliefs) are central to a person's abnormal behavior. A primary goal of treatment using the cognitive perspective is to explicitly teach new, more adaptive ways of thinking.

cognitive perspective The approach that focuses on how people think, understand, and know about the world. (Module 2)

For instance, suppose that you develop the erroneous belief that "doing well on this exam is crucial to my entire future" whenever you take an exam. Through therapy, you might learn to hold the more realistic and less anxiety-producing thought, "my entire future is not dependent on this one exam." By changing cognitions in this way, psychologists working within a cognitive framework help people free themselves from thoughts and behaviors that are potentially maladaptive (Everly & Lating, 2007; Ray et al., 2015).

The cognitive perspective also has its critics. For example, instead of maladaptive cognitions being the *cause* of a psychological disorder, they could be just another *symptom* of the disorder. Furthermore, under certain circumstances, negative beliefs may not be irrational at all but simply reflect accurately the realities of people's lives. (For example, feeling depressed because you've been found guilty of a crime may be entirely rational because you are, in fact, likely to go to jail.) Still, cognitive theorists would argue that there are adaptive ways of framing beliefs even in the most negative circumstances.

HUMANISTIC PERSPECTIVE

humanistic perspective The approach that suggests that all individuals naturally strive to grow, develop, and be in control of their lives and behavior. (Module 2)

The **humanistic perspective** emphasizes the responsibility people have for their own behavior, even when such behavior is abnormal. The humanistic perspective–growing out of the work of Carl Rogers and Abraham Maslow–concentrates on what is uniquely human–that is, it views people as basically rational, oriented toward a social world, and motivated to seek self-actualization (Rogers, 1995).

Humanistic approaches focus on the relationship of the individual to society; they consider the ways in which people view themselves in relation to others and see their place in the world. The humanistic perspective views people as having an awareness of life and of themselves that leads them to search for meaning and self-worth. Rather than assuming that individuals require a "cure," the humanistic perspective suggests that they can, by and large, set their own limits of what is acceptable behavior. As long as they are not hurting others and do not feel personal distress, people should be free to choose the behaviors in which they engage.

Although the humanistic perspective has been criticized for its reliance on unscientific, unverifiable information and its vague, almost philosophical formulations, it offers a distinctive view of abnormal behavior. It stresses the unique aspects of being human and provides a number of important suggestions for helping those with psychological problems.

SOCIOCULTURAL PERSPECTIVE

sociocultural perspective The perspective that assumes that people's behavior–both normal and abnormal–is shaped by the kind of family group, society, and culture in which they live. (Module 37)

The **sociocultural perspective** assumes that society and culture shape abnormal behavior. According to this view, societal and cultural factors such as poverty and prejudice may be at the root of abnormal behavior. Specifically, the kinds of stresses and conflicts people experience in their daily lives can promote and maintain abnormal behavior.

This perspective is supported by research showing that some kinds of psychological disorders are far more prevalent among particular social classes, races, and ethnicities than they are in others. For instance, diagnoses of schizophrenia tend to be higher among members of lower socioeconomic groups than among members of more affluent groups. Proportionally more African American individuals are hospitalized involuntarily for psychological disorders than are whites.

Furthermore, poor economic times seem to be linked to general declines in psychological functioning, and social problems such as homelessness are associated with psychological disorders. Homelessness, in particular, is linked with high levels of psychological disorder: between 20-25% of homeless people in the United States suffer

Perspectives on Psychological Disorders		
Perspective	**Description**	**Possible Application of Perspective to Andrea Petersen**
Medical	Assumes that physiological causes are at the root of psychological disorders	Examine Petersen for medical problems, such as brain tumor, chemical imbalance in the brain, or disease.
Psychoanalytic	Argues that psychological disorders stem from childhood conflicts	Seek out information about Petersen's past, considering possible childhood conflicts.
Behavioral	Assumes that abnormal behaviors are learned responses	Concentrate on rewards and punishments for Petersen's behavior, and identify environmental stimuli that reinforce her behavior.
Cognitive	Assumes that cognitions (people's thoughts and beliefs) are central to psychological disorders	Focus on Petersen's perceptions of herself and her environment.
Humanistic	Emphasizes people's responsibility for their own behavior and the need to self-actualize	Consider Petersen's behavior in terms of her choices and efforts to reach her potential.
Sociocultural	Assumes that behavior is shaped by family, society, and culture	Focus on how societal demands contributed to Petersen's disorder.

FIGURE 1 In considering the case of Andrea Petersen, discussed in the prologue, we can employ each of the perspectives on abnormal behavior. Note that because of the nature of her psychological disorder, some of the perspectives are more applicable than others.

from serious psychological disorders (Greenberg & Rosenheck, 2008; Padgett, Stanhope, & Henwood, 2011; Brown et al., 2017).

On the other hand, there are many alternative explanations for the association between abnormal behavior and social factors. For example, people from lower socioeconomic levels may be less likely than those from higher levels to seek help, gradually reaching a point where their symptoms become severe enough to warrant a serious diagnosis. Similarly, psychological disorders may cause people to become homeless, rather than homelessness producing psychological disorders.

Finally, sociocultural explanations provide relatively little specific guidance for the treatment of psychological disturbance. Because the focus is on broader societal factors, it is not obvious how to treat disorders in a specific individual (Paniagua, 2000; White et al., 2017).

Figure 1 summarizes the main perspectives on psychological disorders. In addition, it applies each of them to the case of Andrea Petersen, discussed in the chapter prologue.

Study Alert

Use Figure 1 to review the six major perspectives on abnormality and consider how they relate to the major perspectives on the field of psychology.

Classifying Abnormal Behavior: The ABCs of DSM

Crazy. Nuts. Mental. Loony. Insane. Neurotic. Psycho. Strange. Demented. Odd. Possessed.

Society has long placed labels on people who display abnormal behavior. Unfortunately, most of the time, these labels have reflected intolerance and have been used with little thought as to what each signifies.

Providing appropriate and specific names and classifications for abnormal behavior has presented a major challenge to psychologists. It is not hard to understand why, given the difficulties discussed earlier in simply distinguishing normal from abnormal behavior. Yet psychologists and other careproviders need to classify abnormal behavior in order to diagnose it and ultimately treat it.

DSM-5: DETERMINING DIAGNOSTIC DISTINCTIONS

The ***Diagnostic and Statistical Manual of Mental Disorders,*** **Fifth Edition (DSM-5)** is the most widely used system to classify and define psychological disorders (American Psychiatric Association, 2013).

The DSM-5, most recently revised in 2013, provides comprehensive and relatively precise definitions for more than 200 disorders. By following the criteria presented in the DSM-5 classification system, diagnosticians use clients' reported symptoms to identify the specific problem the clients are experiencing. Figure 2 provides a brief outline of the major diagnostic categories (American Psychiatric Association, 2013).

The authors of the newest update of DSM suggest that the manual should be viewed as the "DSM-5.0." The "5.0" name emphasizes that the DSM-5 is a work in progress, subject to revision based on users' feedback. (The next revision will be called DSM-5.1; Kupfer, Kuhl, & Regier, 2013; Wakefield, 2013).

DSM-5 takes an *atheoretical* approach to identifying psychological disorders, meaning it does not rely on any particular theoretical perspective. Consequently, it is primarily descriptive and attempts to avoid suggesting an underlying cause for an individual's behavior and problems. Instead, it seeks to paint a picture of the behavior that is being displayed.

For example, DSM does not use the term *neurotic*–a label commonly used by people in their everyday descriptions of abnormal behavior–as a category. Because the term *neurosis* refers to problems associated with a specific cause based in Freud's theory of personality, it is not included in DSM-5.

Why is this atheoretical, descriptive approach be important? For one thing, it allows communication between mental health professionals of diverse backgrounds and theoretical approaches. In addition, precise classification enables researchers to explore the causes of a problem. Without reliable descriptions of abnormal behavior, researchers would be hard pressed to find ways to investigate the disorder. Finally, DSM-5 provides a kind of

Diagnostic and Statistical Manual of Mental Disorders, Fifth Edition, (DSM-5) A system, devised by the American Psychiatric Association, used by most professionals to classify and define psychological disorders. (Module 46)

©H.S. Photos/Alamy Stock Photo

Categories of Disorders	Examples
Anxiety (problems in which anxiety impedes daily functioning)	Generalized anxiety disorder, panic disorder, phobic disorder
Somatic symptom and related disorders (psychological difficulties displayed through physical problems)	Illness anxiety disorder, conversion disorder
Dissociative (the splitting apart of crucial parts of personality that are usually integrated)	Dissociative identity disorder (multiple personality), dissociative amnesia, dissociative fugue
Mood (emotions of depression or euphoria that are so strong they intrude on everyday living)	Major depressive disorders, bipolar disorder
Schizophrenia spectrum and other psychotic disorders (declines in functioning, thought and language disturbances, perception disorders, emotional disturbances, and withdrawal from others)	Delusional disorder
Personality (problems that create little personal distress but that lead to an inability to function as a normal member of society)	Antisocial (sociopathic) personality disorder, narcissistic personality disorder
Sexual (problems related to sexual arousal from unusual objects or problems related to functioning)	Paraphilic disorders, sexual dysfunction
Substance-related (problems related to drug dependence and abuse)	Alcohol, cocaine, hallucinogens, marijuana
Neurocognitive disorders	Alzheimer's

FIGURE 2 This list of disorders represents the major categories from the DSM-5. It is only a partial list of the scores of disorders included in the diagnostic manual.

Source: Adapted from American Psychiatric Association. *Diagnostic and Statistical Manual of Mental Disorders, Fifth Edition* (DSM-5). Washington, DC: Author, 2013.

conceptual shorthand through which professionals can describe the behaviors that tend to occur together in an individual (Widiger, 2015; Busch, Morey & Hopwood, 2017).

CONNING THE CLASSIFIERS: THE SHORTCOMINGS OF DSM

When clinical psychologist David Rosenhan and eight colleagues sought admission to separate mental hospitals across the United States in the 1970s, each stated that he or she was hearing voices–"unclear voices" that said "empty," "hollow," and "thud"–and each was immediately admitted to the hospital. However, the truth was that they actually were conducting a study, and none of them was really hearing voices. Aside from these misrepresentations, *everything* else they did and said represented their true behavior, including the responses they gave during extensive admission interviews and their answers to the battery of tests they were asked to complete. In fact, as soon as they were admitted, they said they no longer heard any voices. In short, each of the pseudo-patients acted in a "normal" way (Rosenhan, 1973).

We might assume that Rosenhan and his colleagues would have been quickly discovered as the impostors they were, but this was not the case. Instead, each of them was diagnosed as severely abnormal on the basis of observed behavior. Mental health professionals labeled most as suffering from schizophrenia and kept them in the hospital 3 to 52 days, with the average stay of 19 days. Even when they were discharged, most of the "patients" left with the label *schizophrenia–in remission,* implying that the abnormal behavior had only temporarily subsided and could recur at any time. Most disturbing, no one on the hospital staff identified any of the pseudo-patients as impostors—although some of the actual patients figured out the ruse.

THE STIGMA OF LABELING

The results of Rosenhan's classic study illustrate that placing labels on individuals powerfully influences the way mental health workers perceive and interpret their actions. It also points out that determining who is psychologically disordered is not always a clear-cut or accurate process.

Gender dysphoria (in which one's gender identity is in conflict with one's biological sex) provides a modern illustration of the dilemma between the pros of a formal diagnosis and the cons of patient labeling. For example, most medical insurance providers require a formal, specific diagnosis in order to provide health-care coverage for procedures such as a sex change operation. Many individuals who experience a conflict between their gender identity and their biological sex object theoretically to the idea that their desire to be the other sex should be labeled a "disorder." Yet without a formal diagnosis, those same individuals may be forced to pay out of pocket for an expensive medical procedure.

This diagnosis-based system of insurance coverage often creates a Catch-22 for mental health-care professionals: They must decide between potentially stigmatizing their clients by providing a formal diagnosis, implying some type of disorder, or leaving patients undiagnosed and potentially without the financial support necessary to receive important procedures that will significantly improve the clients' quality of life (Kamens, 2011; Kleinplatz, Moser, & Lev, 2013).

Critics of the DSM argue that labeling an individual as abnormal provides a dehumanizing, lifelong stigma. (Think, for example, of political contenders whose candidacies have been terminated by the disclosure that they received treatment for severe psychological disorders.) Furthermore, after an initial diagnosis has been made, mental health professionals, who may concentrate on the initial diagnostic category, could overlook other diagnostic possibilities (Szasz, 2011; Frances, 2013; Kim et al., 2017).

Although the DSM-5 was developed to provide more accurate and consistent diagnoses of psychological disorders, it isn't always successful. For instance, critics charge that it relies too much on the medical perspective. Because it was drawn up by psychiatrists—who are physicians—some condemn it for viewing psychological disorders primarily in terms of the symptoms of an underlying physiological disorder. Moreover, critics suggest that DSM-5 compartmentalizes people into inflexible, all-or-none categories rather than considering the degree to which a person displays psychologically disordered behavior (Samuel & Widiger, 2006; Lasalvia, 2015).

Still, despite the drawbacks inherent in any labeling system, the DSM-5 has had an important influence on the way in which mental health professionals view psychological disorders. It has increased both the reliability and the validity of diagnostic categorization. In addition, it offers a logical way to organize examination of the major types of mental disturbances.

 Study Alert
It is important to understand the advantages and weaknesses of the DSM classification system.

RECAP/EVALUATE/RETHINK

RECAP

LO 37-1 How can we distinguish normal from abnormal behavior?

- Definitions of abnormality include deviation from the average, deviation from the ideal, a sense of personal discomfort, the inability to function effectively, and legal conceptions.
- Although no single definition is adequate, abnormal behavior can be considered to be behavior that

causes people to experience distress and prevents them from functioning in their daily lives. Most psychologists believe that abnormal and normal behavior should be considered in terms of a continuum.

LO 37-2 What are the major perspectives on psychological disorders used by mental health professionals?

- The medical perspective views abnormality as a symptom of an underlying disease.

- Psychoanalytic perspectives suggest that abnormal behavior stems from childhood conflicts in the unconscious.
- Behavioral approaches focus on the rewards and punishments in the environment that determine abnormal behavior.
- The cognitive approach suggests that abnormal behavior is the result of faulty cognitions (thoughts and beliefs). In this view, abnormal behavior can be remedied by changing one's flawed thoughts and beliefs.
- Humanistic approaches emphasize the responsibility people have for their own behavior even when such behavior is seen as abnormal.
- Sociocultural approaches view abnormal behavior in terms of difficulties arising from family and other social relationships.

LO 37-3 What are the major categories of psychological disorders?

- The most widely used system for classifying psychological disorders is DSM-5–*Diagnostic and Statistical Manual of Mental Disorders*, Fifth Edition.

EVALUATE

1. One problem in defining abnormal behavior is that
   a. Statistically rare behavior may not be abnormal.
   b. Not all abnormalities are accompanied by feelings of discomfort.
   c. Cultural standards are too general to use as a measuring tool.
   d. All of the above are correct.
2. If abnormality is defined as behavior that causes personal discomfort or harms others, which of the following people is most likely to need treatment?
   a. An executive is afraid to accept a promotion because it would require moving from his ground-floor office to the top floor of a tall office building.
   b. A woman decides to quit her job and chooses to live on the street in order to live a "simpler life."
   c. A man believes that friendly spacemen visit his house every Thursday.
   d. A photographer lives with 19 cats in a small apartment, lovingly caring for them.

3. Virginia's mother thinks that her daughter's behavior is clearly abnormal because, despite being offered admission to medical school, Virginia decides to become a waitress. What approach is Virginia's mother using to define abnormal behavior?
4. Which of the following is a strong argument against the medical perspective on abnormality?
   a. Physiological abnormalities are almost always impossible to identify.
   b. There is no conclusive way to link past experience and behavior.
   c. The medical perspective rests too heavily on the effects of nutrition.
   d. Assigning behavior to a physical problem takes responsibility away from the individual for changing his or her behavior.
5. Cheryl is painfully shy. According to the behavioral perspective, the best way to deal with her "abnormal" behavior is to
   a. Treat the underlying physical problem.
   b. Use the principles of learning theory to modify her shy behavior.
   c. Express a great deal of caring.
   d. Uncover her negative past experiences through hypnosis.

RETHINK

1. Do you agree or disagree that DSM should be updated every several years? Why? What makes abnormal behavior so variable?
2. Imagine that an acquaintance of yours was recently arrested for shoplifting a $15 necktie. Write an explanation for this behavior from *each* perspective on abnormality: the medical perspective, the psychoanalytic perspective, the behavioral perspective, the cognitive perspective, the humanistic perspective, and the sociocultural perspective.

Answers to Evaluate Questions

1. d; 2. a; 3. deviation from the ideal; 4. d; 5. b

KEY TERMS

abnormal behavior
medical perspective
psychoanalytic perspective
behavioral perspective

cognitive perspective
humanistic perspective
sociocultural perspective

Diagnostic and Statistical Manual of Mental Disorders, Fifth Edition (DSM-5)

Module 38

The Major Psychological Disorders

Sally's first panic attack was a surprise. Visiting her parents after college, she suddenly felt dizzy, broke into a cold sweat, and began hyperventilating. Her father clocked her pulse at 180 and rushed her to the hospital, where all symptoms vanished. She laughed it off and returned to her apartment.

But the panic attacks continued. At the gym, at work, in restaurants and movie theaters, Sally was never safe from them. Not just frightening, they were downright embarrassing. She quit her job to work at home. She avoided crowds and turned down dinners, parties, and movies. The only way to escape humiliation was to wall herself inside her apartment with a blanket and a pillow.

Sally suffered from panic disorder, one of the specific psychological disorders we'll consider in this module. Keep in mind that although we'll be discussing these disorders objectively, each represents a very human set of difficulties that influence and in some cases considerably disrupt people's lives.

LEARNING OUTCOME

LO 38-1 What are the major psychological disorders?

Anxiety Disorders

All of us at one time or another experience *anxiety*, a feeling of apprehension or tension, in reaction to stressful situations. There is nothing "wrong" with such anxiety. It is a normal reaction to stress that often helps rather than hinders our daily functioning. Without some anxiety, for instance, most of us probably would not have much motivation to study hard, undergo physical exams, or spend long hours at our jobs.

But some people experience anxiety in situations in which there is no apparent reason or cause for such distress. **Anxiety disorders** occur when anxiety arises without external justification and begins to affect people's daily functioning. We'll discuss three major types of anxiety disorders: phobic disorder, panic disorder, and generalized anxiety disorder.

anxiety disorder The occurrence of anxiety without an obvious external cause that affects daily functioning. (Module 38)

PHOBIC DISORDER

Forty-five-year-old Donna is terrified of electricity. She's unable to change a light bulb for fear of getting electrocuted. The thought of static electricity on clothing sends her into a panic. She can't even open a refrigerator door without being terrified a short circuit will send electricity through her body. And thunderstorms? Forget it: she is beside herself with fear of getting electrocuted by lightning (Kluger, 2001).

Donna suffers from a **specific phobia,** an intense, irrational fear of a specific object or situation. For example, claustrophobia is a fear of enclosed places, acrophobia is a fear of high places, xenophobia is a fear of strangers, social phobia is the fear of being judged or embarrassed by others, and—as in Donna's case—electrophobia is a fear of electricity.

The actual danger posed by an anxiety-producing stimulus (which can be just about anything, as you can see in Figure 1), is typically small or nonexistent. However, to someone suffering from the phobia, the danger is great, and a full-blown panic attack may follow exposure to the stimulus. Phobic disorders differ from generalized anxiety disorders and panic disorders in that there is a specific, identifiable stimulus that sets off the anxiety reaction.

specific phobia Intense, irrational fears of specific objects or situations. (Module 38)

Phobic Disorder	Description	Example
Agoraphobia	Fear of places, such as unfamiliar or crowded spaces, where help might not be available in case of emergency	Person becomes housebound because any place other than the person's home arouses extreme anxiety symptoms.
Specific phobias	Fear of specific objects, places, or situations	
Animal type	Specific animals or insects	Person has extreme fear of dogs, cats, or spiders.
Natural environment type	Events or situations in the natural environment	Person has extreme fear of storms, heights, or water.
Situational type	Public transportation, tunnels, bridges, elevators, flying, driving	Person becomes extremely claustrophobic in elevators.
Blood injection injury type	Blood, injury, injections	Person panics when viewing a child's scraped knee.
Social phobia	Fear of being judged or embarrassed by others	Person avoids all social situations and becomes a recluse for fear of encountering others' judgment.

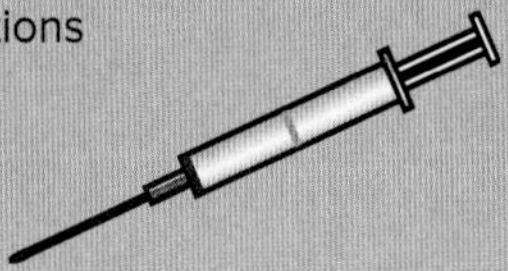

FIGURE 1 Phobic disorders differ from generalized anxiety and panic disorders because a specific stimulus can be identified. Listed here are a number of types of phobias and their triggers.
Source: Adapted from Nolen-Hoeksema, S. (2007). *Abnormal psychology* (4th ed.). New York: McGraw-Hill.

Phobias may have only a minor impact on people's lives if those who suffer from them can avoid the stimuli that trigger fear. For example, a fear of heights may have little impact on people's everyday lives (although it may prevent them from living in an apartment on a high floor)–unless they are firefighters or window washers. On the other hand, a *social phobia,* or a fear of strangers, presents a more serious problem. In one extreme case, a Washington woman left her home just three times in 30 years– once to visit her family, once for an operation, and once to purchase ice cream for a dying companion (Kimbrel, 2007; Wong, Sarver, & Beidel, 2011; Stopa et al., 2013).

PANIC DISORDER

panic disorder Anxiety disorder that takes the form of panic attacks lasting from a few seconds to several hours. (Module 38)

In another type of anxiety disorder, **panic disorder,** *panic attacks* occur that last from a few seconds to several hours. Panic disorders do not have any identifiable, specific triggers (unlike phobias, which are triggered by specific objects or situations). Instead, during an attack such as those Sally experienced in the case described earlier, anxiety suddenly–and often without warning–rises, and an individual feels a sense of impending, unavoidable doom.

Although the physical symptoms of a panic attack differ from person to person, they may include heart palpitations, shortness of breath, unusual amounts of sweating, faintness and dizziness, gastric sensations, and sometimes a sense of imminent death. After such an attack, it is no wonder that people tend to feel exhausted (Laederach-Hofmann & Messerli-Buergy, 2007; Montgomery, 2011; Carleton et al., 2014).

Panic attacks seemingly come out of nowhere and are unconnected to any specific stimulus. Because they don't know what triggers their feelings of panic, victims of panic attacks may become fearful of going places. In fact, some people with panic disorder develop a complication called *agoraphobia,* the fear of being in a situation in which escape is difficult and in which help for a possible panic attack would not be available.

In extreme cases, people with agoraphobia never leave their homes (Wittchen et al., 2008; McTeague et al., 2011; Kim & Yoon, 2017).

In addition to the physical symptoms, panic disorder affects how the brain processes information. For instance, people with panic disorder have reduced reactions in the anterior cingulate cortex to stimuli (such as viewing a fearful face) that normally produce a strong reaction in those without the disorder. It may be that recurring high levels of emotional arousal that patients with panic disorder experience desensitize them to emotional stimuli (Pillay et al., 2007; Maddock et al., 2013).

GENERALIZED ANXIETY DISORDER

People with **generalized anxiety disorder** experience long-term, persistent anxiety and uncontrollable worry. Sometimes their concerns are about identifiable issues involving family, money, work, or health. In other cases, though, people with the disorder feel that something dreadful is about to happen but can't identify the reason and thus experience "free-floating" anxiety.

Because of persistent anxiety, people with generalized anxiety disorder cannot concentrate or set their worry and fears aside; their lives become centered on their worry. Furthermore, their anxiety is often accompanied by physiological symptoms, such as muscle tension, headaches, dizziness, heart palpitations, or insomnia (Starcevic et al., 2007). Figure 2 shows the most common symptoms of generalized anxiety disorder.

Acrophobia, the fear of heights, is not an uncommon phobia. What sort of behavior-modification approaches might be used to deal with acrophobia?
©Imaginechina/AP Images

generalized anxiety disorder The experience of long-term, persistent anxiety and worry. (Module 38)

Obsessive-Compulsive Disorder

In **obsessive-compulsive disorder (OCD),** people are plagued by unwanted thoughts, called *obsessions*, or feel that they must carry out behaviors, termed *compulsions*, that they feel driven to perform.

An **obsession** is a persistent, unwanted thought or idea that keeps recurring. For example, a student may be unable to stop thinking that she has neglected to put her name on a test and may think about it constantly for the 2 weeks it takes to get the paper back. A man may go on vacation and wonder the whole time whether he locked his house. A woman may hear the same tune running through her head over and over. In each case, the thought or idea is unwanted and difficult to put out of mind. Of course, many people suffer from mild obsessions from time to time, but usually such thoughts persist only for a short period. For people with serious obsessions, however, the thoughts persist for days or months and may consist of bizarre, troubling images (Rassin & Muris, 2007; Wenzel, 2011; Iliceto et al., 2017).

As the name suggests, as part of an obsessive-compulsive disorder, people may also experience compulsions. **Compulsions** are irresistible urges to repeatedly carry out some behavior that seems strange and unreasonable even to them. Whatever the compulsive behavior is, people experience extreme anxiety if they cannot do it, even if it is something they want to stop. The acts may be relatively trivial, such as repeatedly checking the stove to make sure all the burners are turned off, or more unusual, such as washing one's hands so much that they bleed (Clark, 2007; Moretz & McKay, 2009; Gillan & Sahakian, 2015).

For example, consider this passage from the autobiography of a person with obsessive-compulsive disorder:

> I thought my parents would die if I didn't do everything in exactly the right way. When I took my glasses off at night I'd have to place them on the dresser at a particular angle. Sometimes I'd turn on the light and get out of bed seven times until I felt comfortable with the angle. If the angle wasn't right, I felt that my parents would die. The feeling ate up my insides.

obsessive-compulsive disorder (OCD) A disorder characterized by obsessions or compulsions. (Module 38)

obsession A persistent, unwanted thought or idea that keeps recurring. (Module 38)

compulsion An irresistible urge to repeatedly carry out some act that seems strange and unreasonable. (Module 38)

FIGURE 2 Frequency of symptoms in cases of generalized anxiety disorder.

Source: Adapted from Beck, A. T., & Emery, G., with Greenberg, R. L. (1985). *Anxiety disorders and phobias: A cognitive perspective.* New York: Basic Books.

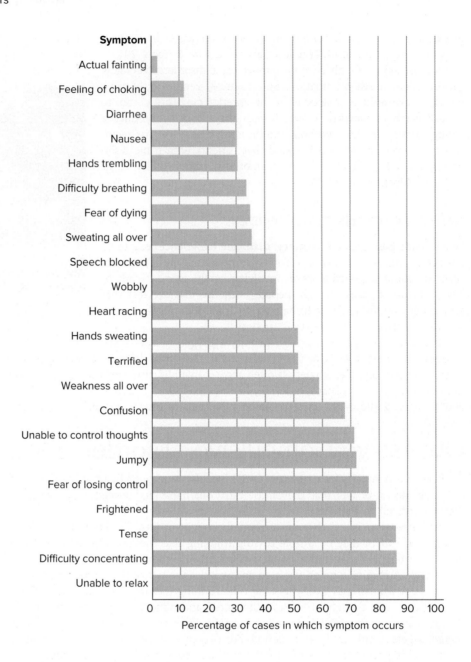

If I didn't grab the molding on the wall just the right way as I entered or exited my room; if I didn't hang a shirt in the closet perfectly; if I didn't read a paragraph a certain way; if my hands and nails weren't perfectly clean, I thought my incorrect behavior would kill my parents. (Summers, 2000)

Although carrying out compulsive rituals may lead to some immediate reduction of anxiety, in the long run the anxiety returns. In fact, people with severe cases lead lives filled with unrelenting tension (Dittrich, Johansen, & Fineberg, 2011; Kalanthroff et al., 2013).

THE CAUSES OF ANXIETY DISORDERS AND OBSESSIVE-COMPULSIVE DISORDER

We've considered several of the major types of anxiety disorders and obsessive-compulsive disorder, but there are many other related disorders. The variety of anxiety disorders means that no single explanation fits all cases.

PsychTech

Although some people seem to use the Internet compulsively, psychologists have yet to agree on whether it represents a true psychological disorder.

Genetic factors clearly are part of the picture. For example, if one member of a pair of identical twins has panic disorder, there is a 30% chance that the other twin will have it also. Furthermore, a person's characteristic level of anxiety is related to a specific gene involved in the production of the neurotransmitter serotonin. This is consistent with findings indicating that certain chemical deficiencies in the brain appear to produce some kinds of anxiety disorder (Beidel & Turner, 2007; Chamberlain et al., 2008; Yagi et al., 2017).

Some researchers believe that an overactive autonomic nervous system may be at the root of panic attacks. Specifically, they suggest that poor regulation of the brain's *locus ceruleus* may lead to panic attacks, which cause the limbic system to become overstimulated. In turn, the overstimulated limbic system produces chronic anxiety, which ultimately leads the locus ceruleus to generate still more panic attacks (Davies et al., 2008; Dresler et al., 2013).

There are also biological causes involved in obsessive-compulsive disorder. For example, researchers have found specific differences in the brains of those with the disorder compared to those without it (Christian et al., 2008; Okada et al., 2015).

Psychologists who employ the behavioral perspective have taken a different approach to explaining anxiety disorders that emphasize environmental factors. They consider anxiety to be a learned response to stress. For instance, suppose a dog bites a young girl. When the girl next sees a dog, she is frightened and runs away–a behavior that relieves her anxiety and thereby reinforces her avoidance behavior. After repeated encounters with dogs in which she is reinforced for her avoidance behavior, she may develop a full-fledged phobia regarding dogs.

Finally, the cognitive perspective suggests that anxiety disorders grow out of inappropriate and inaccurate thoughts and beliefs about circumstances in a person's world. For example, people with anxiety disorders may view a friendly puppy as a ferocious and savage pit bull, or they may see an air disaster looming every moment they are in the vicinity of an airplane. According to the cognitive perspective, people's maladaptive thoughts about the world are at the root of an anxiety disorder (Wang & Clark, 2002; Ouimet, Gawronski, & Dozois, 2009; Bouvard et al., 2017).

Somatic Symptom Disorders

Somatic symptom disorders are psychological difficulties that take on a physical (somatic) form for which there is no medical cause. Even though an individual with a somatic symptom disorder reports physical symptoms, no biological cause exists, or if there is a medical problem, the person's reaction is greatly exaggerated.

One relatively common type of somatic symptom disorder is illness anxiety disorder. Those with **illness anxiety disorder** have a constant fear of illness and a preoccupation with their health. These individuals believe that everyday aches and pains are symptoms of a dread disease. The "symptoms" are not faked; rather, they are misinterpreted as evidence of some serious illness–often in the face of inarguable medical evidence to the contrary (Abramowitz, Olatunji, & Deacon, 2007; Olatunji, 2008; Weck et al., 2011).

Conversion disorder is another somatic symptom disorder. Unlike illness anxiety disorder, in which there is no physical problem, **conversion disorders** involve an apparent physical disturbance, such as the inability to see or hear or to move an arm or leg. However, *the cause* of the physical disturbance is purely psychological; there is no biological reason for the problem. Some of Freud's classic cases involved conversion disorders. For instance, one of Freud's patients suddenly became unable to use her arm without any apparent physiological cause. Later, just as abruptly, the problem disappeared.

Conversion disorders often begin suddenly. Previously normal people wake up one day blind or deaf, or they experience numbness that is restricted to a certain part of the body. A hand, for example, may become entirely numb, while an area above the wrist, controlled by the same nerves, remains sensitive to touch–something that is physiologically implausible. Mental health professionals refer to such a condition as ·

somatic symptom disorders Psychological difficulties that take on a physical (somatic) form, but for which there is no medical cause. (Module 38)

illness anxiety disorder A disorder in which people have a constant fear of illness and a preoccupation with their health. (Module 38)

conversion disorder A major somatic symptom disorder that involves an actual physical disturbance, such as the inability to use a sensory organ or the complete or partial inability to move an arm or leg. (Module 38)

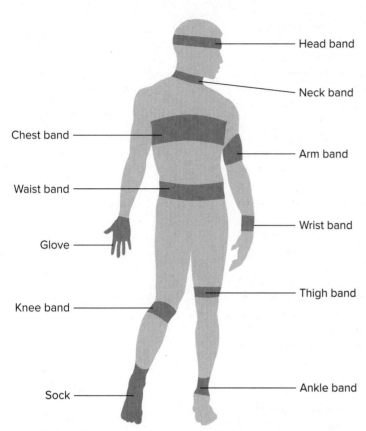

Head band

Neck band

Chest band

Arm band

Waist band

Wrist band

Glove

Knee band

Thigh band

Sock

Ankle band

FIGURE 3 Conversion disorders sometimes produce numbness in specific and isolated areas of the body (indicated by the shaded areas in the figure). For instance, in glove anesthesia, the area of the body covered by a glove feels numb. However, the condition is biologically implausible because of the nerves involved, which suggests that the problem results from a psychological disorder rather than from actual nerve damage.

dissociative disorders Psychological dysfunctions characterized by the separation of different facets of a person's personality that are normally integrated. (Module 38)

dissociative identity disorder (DID) A disorder in which a person displays characteristics of two or more distinct personalities. (Module 38)

dissociative amnesia A disorder in which a significant, selective memory loss occurs. (Module 38)

"glove anesthesia" because the numb area is the part of the hand covered by a glove and not a region related to pathways of the nervous system (see Figure 3).

Surprisingly, people who experience conversion disorders frequently remain unconcerned about symptoms that most of us would expect to be highly anxiety producing. For instance, a person in good health who wakes up blind may react in a bland, matter-of-fact way. Considering how most of us would feel if we woke up unable to see, this unemotional reaction hardly seems appropriate (Brasic, 2002; Loriedo & Leone, 2017).

Dissociative Disorders

The classic movie *The Three Faces of Eve* (about a woman with three wildly different personalities) and the book *Sybil* (about a girl who allegedly had 16 personalities) represent a highly dramatic, rare, and controversial class of disorders: dissociative disorders. **Dissociative disorders** are characterized by the separation (or dissociation) of different facets of a person's personality that are normally integrated and work together. By dissociating key parts of who they are, people are able to keep disturbing memories or perceptions from reaching conscious awareness and thereby reduce their anxiety (Houghtalen & Talbot, 2007; Laddis, Dell, & Korzekwa, 2017).

Several dissociative disorders exist, although all of them are rare. A person with a **dissociative identity disorder (DID)** (once called *multiple personality disorder*) displays characteristics of two or more distinct personalities, identities, or personality fragments. Individual personalities often have a unique set of likes and dislikes and their own reactions to situations. Some people with multiple personalities even carry several pairs of glasses because their vision changes with each personality. Moreover, each individual personality can be well adjusted when considered on its own (Stickley & Nickeas, 2006; Howell, 2011).

The diagnosis of dissociative identity disorder is controversial. It was rarely diagnosed before 1980, when it was added as a category in the third edition of DSM for the first time. At that point, the number of cases increased significantly. Some clinicians suggest the increase was due to more precise identification of the disorder. On the other hand, critics suggest that widespread publicity about cases of DID may have influenced patients to report symptoms of more common personality disorders in ways that made it more likely they would receive a diagnosis of DID (Kihlstrom, 2005a; Xiao et al., 2006; Ross, 2015).

Dissociative amnesia is another dissociative disorder in which a significant, selective memory loss occurs. Dissociative amnesia is unlike simple amnesia, which involves an actual loss of information from memory and typically results from a physiological cause. In contrast, in cases of dissociative amnesia, the "forgotten" material is still present in memory—it simply cannot be recalled. The term *repressed memories* is sometimes used to describe the lost memories of people with dissociative amnesia.

In the most severe form of dissociative amnesia, individuals cannot recall their names, are unable to recognize parents and other relatives, and do not know their addresses. In other respects, though, they may appear quite normal. Apart from an inability to remember certain facts about themselves, they may be able to recall skills and abilities that they developed earlier. For instance, even though a chef may not remember where he grew up and received training, he may still be able to prepare gourmet meals.

In some cases of dissociative amnesia, the memory loss is profound. For example, in one dramatic case, Raymond Power Jr., an attorney, husband, father of two, and Boy

Scout leader, left home to go to work one morning. Two days later, he was homeless, living a new life a thousand miles away, and had no memory of who he was or how he got there. He was found 6 months later but still had no recollection of his previous life, including any knowledge of his wife of 30 years or even that he had children (Foderaro, 2006; Dell, 2013).

Dissociative fugue is a form of amnesia in which a person leaves home suddenly and assumes a new identity. In this unusual and rare state, people take sudden, impulsive trips and adopt a new identity. After a period of time–days, months, or sometimes even years–they suddenly realize that they are in a strange place and completely forget the time they have spent wandering. Their last memories are those from the time just before they entered the fugue state (Hennig-Fast et al., 2008).

The common thread among dissociative disorders is that they allow people to escape from some anxiety-producing situation. Either the person produces a new personality to deal with stress, or the individual forgets or leaves behind the situation that caused the stress as he or she journeys to some new–and perhaps less anxiety-ridden–environment (Putnam, 2000; Brown, 2006).

dissociative fugue A form of amnesia in which a person leaves home and assumes a new identity. (Module 38)

Mood Disorders

From the time I woke up in the morning until the time I went to bed at night, I was unbearably miserable and seemingly incapable of any kind of joy or enthusiasm. Everything–every thought, word, movement–was an effort. Everything that once was sparkling now was flat. I seemed to myself to be dull, boring, inadequate, thick brained, unlit, unresponsive, chill skinned, bloodless, and sparrow drab. I doubted, completely, my ability to do anything well. It seemed as though my mind had slowed down and burned out to the point of being virtually useless. (Jamison, 1995)

We all experience mood swings. Sometimes we are happy, perhaps even euphoric; at other times, we feel upset, saddened, or depressed. Such changes in mood are a normal part of everyday life.

In some people, however, moods are so pronounced and lingering–like the feelings described above by writer (and psychiatrist) Kay Jamison–that they interfere with the ability to function effectively. **Mood disorders** are disturbances in emotional experience that are strong enough to interfere with everyday living. In extreme cases, a mood may become life threatening; in other cases, it may cause the person to lose touch with reality.

mood disorder A disturbance in emotional experience that is strong enough to intrude on everyday living. (Module 38)

MAJOR DEPRESSIVE DISORDER

President Abraham Lincoln. Queen Victoria. Newscaster Mike Wallace.

The common link among these people? Each suffered from periodic attacks of major depressive disorder. **Major depressive disorder** is a severe form of depression that interferes with concentration, decision making, and sociability.

Major depressive disorder is one of the more common forms of mood disorders. Some 15 million people in the United States suffer from major depression, and at any one time, 6-10% of the U.S. population is clinically depressed. Almost one in five people in the United States experiences major depression at some point in life, and 15% of college students have received a diagnosis of depression. The cost of depression is more than $34 billion a year in lost productivity (Scelfo, 2007; Simon et al., 2008; Edoka, Petrou, & Ramchandani, 2011).

Women are twice as likely to experience major depression as men are, with one-fourth of all females apt to encounter it at some point during their lives. Furthermore, although no one is sure why, the rate of depression is going up throughout the world. Results of in-depth interviews conducted in the United States, Puerto Rico, Taiwan, Lebanon, Canada, Italy, Germany, and France indicate that the incidence of depression has increased significantly over previous rates in every area. In fact, in some countries, the likelihood that individuals will have major depression at some point in their lives is three times higher than it was for earlier generations. In addition, people are

major depressive disorder A severe form of depression that interferes with concentration, decision making, and sociability. (Module 38)

developing major depression at increasingly younger ages (Staley, Sanacora, & Tamagnan, 2006; Sado et al., 2011; Sarubin et al., 2017).

When psychologists speak of major depressive disorder, they do not mean the sadness that accompanies one of life's disappointments, which we all have experienced. Some depression is normal after the breakup of a long-term relationship, the death of a loved one, or the loss of a job. It is normal even after less serious problems, such as doing badly on a test or having a romantic partner forget one's birthday.

People who suffer from major depressive disorder experience similar feelings, but the severity tends to be considerably greater. They may feel useless, worthless, and lonely, and they may think the future is hopeless and no one can help them. They may lose their appetite and have no energy. Moreover, they may experience such feelings for months or even years. They may cry uncontrollably, have sleep disturbances, and be at risk for suicide. The depth and duration of such behavior are the hallmarks of major depressive disorder. (Figure 4 provides a self-assessment of depression.)

MANIA AND BIPOLAR DISORDER

While depression leads to the depths of despair, mania leads to emotional heights. **Mania** is an extended state of intense, wild elation. People experiencing mania feel intense happiness, power, invulnerability, and energy. Believing they will succeed at anything they attempt, they may become involved in wild schemes. Consider, for example, the following description of an individual who experienced a manic episode:

> Mr. O'Reilly took a leave of absence from his civil service job. He purchased a large number of cuckoo clocks and then an expensive car, which he planned to use as a mobile showroom for his wares, anticipating that he would make a great deal of money. He proceeded to "tear around town" buying and selling clocks and other

Study Alert

Major depression differs from the normal depression that occasionally occurs during most people's lives; major depression is more intense, lasts longer, and may have no clear trigger.

mania An extended state of intense, wild elation. (Module 38)

FIGURE 4 This test is based on the list of signs and symptoms of depression found on the National Institute of Mental Health website at http://www.nimh.nih.gov/health/publications/depression/what-are-the-signs-and-symptoms-of-depression.shtml.

Source: National Institutes of Health, *Depression*.

A Test for Major Depression

To complete the questionnaire, count the number of statements with which you agree:

1. I feel sad, anxious, or empty.
2. I feel hopeless or pessimistic.
3. I feel guilty, worthless, or helpless.
4. I feel irritable or restless.
5. I have lost interest in activities or hobbies that were once pleasurable, including sex.
6. I feel tired and have decreased energy.
7. I have difficulty concentrating, remembering details, and making decisions.
8. I have insomnia, early-morning wakefulness, or sleep too much.
9. I overeat or have appetite loss.
10. I have thoughts of suicide or have attempted suicide.
11. I have aches or pains, headaches, cramps, or digestive problems that do not ease even with treatment.

Scoring: If you agree with at least five of the statements, including either 1 or 2, and if you have had these symptoms for at least 2 weeks, help from a professional is strongly recommended. If you answer yes to number 10, seek immediate help. And remember: These are only general guidelines. If you feel you may need help, seek it.

merchandise, and when he was not out, he was continuously on the phone making "deals." . . . He was $3,000 in debt and had driven his family to exhaustion with his excessive activity and talkativeness. He said, however, that he felt "on top of the world." (Spitzer et al., 1983)

Some people sequentially experience periods of mania and depression. This alternation of mania and depression is called **bipolar disorder** (a condition previously known as *manic-depressive disorder*). The swings between highs and lows may occur a few days apart or may alternate over a period of years. In addition, in bipolar disorder, periods of depression are usually longer than periods of mania.

Ironically, some of society's most creative individuals may have suffered from bipolar disorder. The imagination, drive, excitement, and energy that they display during manic stages allow them to make unusually creative contributions. For instance, historical analysis of the composer Robert Schumann's music shows that he was most prolific during periods of mania. In contrast, his output dropped off drastically during periods of depression (see Figure 5). On the other hand, the high output associated with mania does not necessarily lead to higher quality: Some of Schumann's greatest works were created outside his periods of mania (Szegedy Maszak, 2003; Kyaga et al., 2013).

Although creativity may be increased when someone is experiencing mania, persons who experience this disorder often show a recklessness that produces emotional and sometimes physical self-injury. They may alienate people with their talkativeness, inflated self-esteem, and indifference to the needs of others (Simonton, 2014).

bipolar disorder A disorder in which a person alternates between periods of euphoric feelings of mania and periods of depression. (Module 38)

CAUSES OF MOOD DISORDERS

Because they represent a major mental health problem, mood disorders–and, in particular, depression–have received a good deal of study. Several approaches have been used to explain the disorders.

Genetic and biological factors. Some mood disorders clearly have genetic and biological roots. In fact, most evidence suggests that bipolar disorders are caused primarily by biological factors. For instance, bipolar disorder (and some forms of major depression) clearly runs in some families, pointing to a genetic cause. Furthermore, researchers

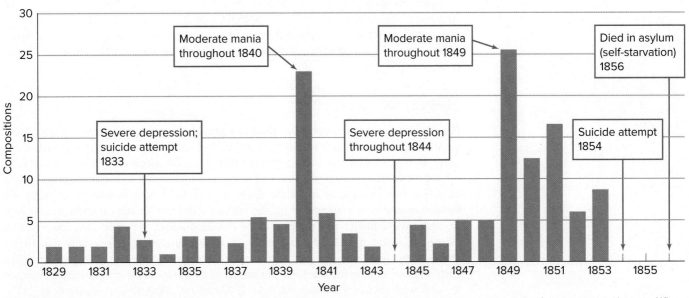

FIGURE 5 The number of pieces written by composer Robert Schumann in a given year is related to his periods of depression and mania. Why do you think mania might be associated with creative productivity in some people?

Source: Slater, E., & Meyer, A. (1959). Contributions to a pathography of the musicians: Robert Schumann. *Confinia Psychiatrica.* Reprinted in K. R. Jamison, *Touched with fire: Manic-depressive illness and the artistic temperament.* New York: Free Press; reprinted in Jamison, K. R. (1995). *An unquiet mind: A memoir of moods and madness.* New York: Knopf.

have found that several neurotransmitters play a role in depression. For example, alterations in the functioning of serotonin and norepinephrine in the brain are related to the disorder.

In addition, research on neuroimaging suggests that a brain structure called *area 25* is related to depression: When area 25 is smaller than normal, it is associated with a higher risk of depression. Furthermore, the right anterior insula, a region of the brain related to self-awareness and interpersonal experience, also appears to be related to depression (Insel, 2010; Cisler et al., 2013; Serretti, 2017).

Internal, unconscious conflicts. Supporters of psychoanalytic perspectives see depression as the result of feelings of loss (real or potential) or of anger directed inwardly at oneself. However, there is little research evidence to support this explanation (Vanheule et al., 2006; Sa, 2015).

Environmental factors. Some explanations of depression take a behavioral approach, looking to influences outside the person. For example, behavioral theories of depression argue that the stresses of life produce a reduction in positive reinforcers. As a result, people begin to withdraw, which only reduces positive reinforcers further. In addition, people receive attention for their depressive behavior, which further reinforces the depression (Lewinsohn & Essau, 2002; Lewinsohn et al., 2003; Domschke, 2013).

Cognitive and emotional factors. Some explanations for mood disorders attribute them to cognitive factors. For example, psychologist Martin Seligman suggests that depression is largely a response to learned helplessness. *Learned helplessness* is a learned expectation that events in one's life are uncontrollable and that one cannot escape from the situation. As a consequence, people simply give up fighting aversive events and submit to them, which thereby produces depression. Other theorists go a step further and suggest that depression results from hopelessness, a combination of learned helplessness and an expectation that negative outcomes in one's life are inevitable (Bjornstad, 2006; Li et al., 2011; Shirayama & Hashimoto, 2017).

Clinical psychologist Aaron Beck has proposed that faulty cognitions underlie people's depressed feelings. Specifically, his cognitive theory of depression suggests that depressed individuals typically view themselves as life's losers and blame themselves whenever anything goes wrong. By focusing on the negative side of situations, they feel inept and unable to act constructively to change their environment. In sum, their negative cognitions lead to feelings of depression (Newman et al., 2002).

Brain imaging studies suggest that people with depression experience a general blunting of emotional reactions. For example, one study found that the brains of people with depression showed significantly less activation when they viewed photos of human faces displaying strong emotions than did those without the disorder (Gotlib et al., 2004).

DEPRESSION IN WOMEN

The various theories of depression have not provided a complete answer to an elusive question that has dogged researchers: Why does depression occur in approximately twice as many women as men—a pattern that is similar across a variety of cultures?

One explanation suggests that the stress women experience may be greater than the stress men experience at certain points in their lives—such as when a woman must simultaneously earn a living and be the primary caregiver for her children. In addition, women have a higher risk for physical and sexual abuse, typically earn lower wages than men, report greater unhappiness with their marriages, and generally experience chronic negative circumstances. Furthermore, women and men may respond to stress with different coping mechanisms. For instance, men may abuse drugs, whereas women respond with depression (Hyde, Mezulis, & Abramson, 2008; Komarovskaya et al., 2011; Sun et al., 2017).

Biological factors may also explain some women's depression. For example, the rate of female depression begins to rise during puberty, so some psychologists believe that hormones make women more vulnerable to the disorder. In addition, 25-50% of women who take oral contraceptives report symptoms of depression, and depression that occurs after the birth of a child is linked to hormonal changes. Finally, structural differences in men's and women's brains may be related to gender differences in depression (Silverstein et al., 2013; Jones et al., 2017; Yang et al., 2017).

Ultimately, it is clear that researchers have discovered no definitive solutions to the puzzle of depression, and there are many alternative explanations. Most likely, a complex interaction of several factors causes mood disorders.

Schizophrenia

Things that relate, the town of Antelope, Oregon, Jonestown, Charlie Manson, the Hillside Strangler, the Zodiac Killer, Watergate, King's trial in L.A., and many more. In the last 7 years alone, over 23 Star Wars scientists committed suicide for no apparent reason. The AIDS cover-up, the conference in South America in 87 had over 1,000 doctors claim that insects can transmit it. To be able to read one's thoughts and place thoughts in one's mind without the person knowing it's being done. Realization is a reality of bioelectromagnetic control, which is thought transfer and emotional control, recording individual brainwave frequencies of thought, sensation, and emotions. (Nolen-Hoeksema, 2007)

This excerpt illustrates the efforts of a person with schizophrenia, one of the more severe forms of mental disturbance, to communicate. People with schizophrenia account for by far the largest percentage of those hospitalized for psychological disorders. They are also in many respects the least likely to recover from their difficulties.

Schizophrenia refers to a class of disorders in which severe distortion of reality occurs. Thinking, perception, and emotion may deteriorate; the individual may withdraw from social interaction; and the person may display bizarre behavior. The symptoms displayed by persons with schizophrenia may vary considerably over time. Nonetheless, a number of characteristics reliably distinguish schizophrenia from other disorders. They include the following:

schizophrenia A class of disorders in which severe distortion of reality occurs. (Module 38)

- *Decline from a previous level of functioning.* An individual can no longer carry out activities he or she was once able to do.

- *Disturbances of thought and speech.* People with schizophrenia use logic and language in a peculiar way. Their thinking often does not make sense, and their logic is frequently faulty, which is referred to as a *formal thought disorder*. They also do not follow conventional linguistic rules (Penn et al., 1997). Consider, for example, the following response to the question "Why do you think people believe in God?"

  > Uh, let's, I don't know why, let's see, balloon travel. He holds it up for you, the balloon. He don't let you fall out, your little legs sticking down through the clouds. He's down to the smokestack, looking through the smoke trying to get the balloon gassed up you know. Way they're flying on top that way, legs sticking out. I don't know, looking down on the ground, heck, that'd make you so dizzy you just stay and sleep you know, hold down and sleep there. I used to be sleep outdoors, you know, sleep outdoors instead of going home. (Chapman & Chapman, 1973)

As this selection illustrates, although the basic grammatical structure may be intact, the substance of thinking that is characteristic of schizophrenia is often illogical, garbled, and lacking in meaningful content (Holden, 2003; Heinrichs, 2005).

- *Delusions.* People with schizophrenia often have delusions—firmly held, unshakable beliefs with no basis in reality. Among the common delusions people with schizophrenia experience are the beliefs that they are being controlled by someone else, they are being persecuted by others, and their thoughts are being broadcast so that others know what they are thinking (Coltheart, Langdon, & McKay, 2007; Startup, Bucci, & Langdon, 2009; Phalen et al., 2017).

FIGURE 6 This unusual art was created by an individual suffering from a severe psychological disorder.

©Science Source

- *Hallucinations and perceptual problems.* People with schizophrenia sometimes do not perceive the world as most other people do. For example, they may have *hallucinations,* the experience of perceiving things that do not actually exist. Furthermore, they may see, hear, or smell things differently from others (see Figure 6). In fact, they may not even have a sense of their bodies in the way that others do, having difficulty determining where their bodies stop and the rest of the world begins (Botvinick, 2004; Thomas et al., 2007Bauer, Schwab, & McAdams, 2011).

- *Inappropriate emotions.* People with schizophrenia sometimes show a lack of emotion in which even the most dramatic events produce little or no emotional response. Alternately, they may display strong bursts of emotion that are inappropriate to a situation. For example, a person with schizophrenia may laugh uproariously at a funeral or react with rage when being helped by someone.

- *Withdrawal.* People with schizophrenia tend to have little interest in others. They tend not to socialize or hold real conversations with others, although they may talk at another person. In the most extreme cases, they do not even acknowledge the presence of other people and appear to be in their own isolated worlds.

Usually, the onset of schizophrenia occurs in early adulthood, and the symptoms follow one of two primary courses. In *process schizophrenia,* the symptoms develop slowly and subtly. There may be a gradual withdrawal from the world, excessive daydreaming, and a blunting of emotion until eventually the disorder reaches the point where others cannot overlook it. In other cases, known as *reactive schizophrenia,* the onset of symptoms is sudden and conspicuous. The treatment outlook for reactive schizophrenia is relatively favorable, but process schizophrenia has proved more difficult to treat.

DSM-5 classifies the symptoms of schizophrenia into two types. *Positive-symptom schizophrenia* is indicated by the presence of disordered behavior such as hallucinations, delusions, and emotional extremes. Those with positive-symptom schizophrenia clearly lose touch with reality.

In contrast, those with *negative-symptom schizophrenia* show disruptions to normal emotions and behaviors. For example, there may be an absence or loss of normal functioning, such as social withdrawal or blunted emotions (Levine & Rabinowitz, 2007; Tandon et al., 2013; Lauriello & Rahman, 2015).

The distinction between positive and negative symptoms of schizophrenia is important because it suggests that two different kinds of causes might trigger schizophrenia. Furthermore, it has implications for predicting treatment outcomes.

SOLVING THE PUZZLE OF SCHIZOPHRENIA: BIOLOGICAL CAUSES

Although schizophrenic behavior clearly departs radically from normal behavior, its causes are less apparent. It does appear, however, that schizophrenia has both biological and environmental origins (Sawa & Snyder, 2002; Pavão, Tort, & Amaral, 2015).

Let's first consider the evidence pointing to a biological cause. Because schizophrenia is more common in some families than in others, genetic factors seem to be involved in producing at least a susceptibility to or readiness for developing schizophrenia. For example, the closer the genetic link between a person with schizophrenia and another individual, the greater the likelihood that the other person will experience the disorder (see Figure 7; Plomin & McGuffin, 2003; Gottesman & Hanson, 2005; Rodrigues-Amorim et al., 2017).

However, if genetics alone were responsible for schizophrenia, the chance of both of two identical twins having schizophrenia would be 100% instead of just under 50% because identical twins have the same genetic makeup. Moreover, attempts to find a link between schizophrenia and a particular gene have been only partly successful.

Risk of Developing Schizophrenia, Based on Genetic Relatedness to a Person with Schizophrenia		
Relationship	Genetic Relatedness, %	Risk of Developing Schizophrenia, %
Identical twin	100	48
Child of two schizophrenic parents	100	46
Fraternal twin	50	17
Offspring of one schizophrenic parent	50	17
Sibling	50	9
Nephew or niece	25	4
Spouse	0	2
Unrelated person	0	1

FIGURE 7 The closer the genetic links between two people, the greater the likelihood that if one experiences schizophrenia, so will the other sometime during his or her lifetime. However, genetics is not the full story; if it were, the risk of identical twins having schizophrenia would be 100% and not the 48% shown in this figure.
Source: Adapted from Gottesman, I. I. (1991). *Schizophrenia genesis: The origins of madness.* New York: Freeman.

Apparently, genetic factors alone do not produce schizophrenia (Lenzenweger & Dworkin, 1998).; Abel & Nicki-Jochschat, 2016).

Some researchers suggest that epigenetics are involved in schizophrenia. *Epigenetics* looks at the way in which genes are expressed and influenced by the environment. In this view, genes by themselves do not invariably lead a person to display schizophrenia. Instead, they are affected by the environment. Furthermore, genes can be altered in a way that then passes on the behavior to future generations. An epigenetic explanation of schizophrenia, then, suggests that changes in gene expression may produce the disorder and that subsequently it can be passed on genetically (Alelú-Paz et al., 2017; Whitton et al., 2017).

Despite advances in our understanding of genetic and epigenetic causes of schizophrenia, most researchers agree that no single gene is responsible for the disorder. Consequently, scientists have looked to other possible biological causes (Balter, 2017).

Another biological explanation suggests that the brains of people with schizophrenia may have a biochemical imbalance. For example, the *dopamine hypothesis* suggests that schizophrenia results from excess activity in the areas of the brain that use dopamine as a neurotransmitter. This explanation came to light after the discovery that drugs that block dopamine action in brain pathways can be effective in reducing the symptoms of schizophrenia. Other research suggests that glutamate, another neurotransmitter, may contribute to the disorder, and drugs that reduce the release of glutamate in the brain show promise in alleviating symptoms of schizophrenia (Kendler & Schaffner, 2011; Beck, Javitt, & Howes, 2016; Howes et al., 2017).

Another biological explanation relates to structural abnormalities in the brains of people with schizophrenia. For example, researchers have found abnormalities in the neural circuits of the cortex and limbic systems, as well as reduced amounts of gray matter, in the brains of those with schizophrenia. Furthermore, differences exist in the way the brain functions (see *Neuroscience in Your Life;* Reichenberg & Harvey, 2007; Reichenberg et al., 2009; Bustillo et al., 2017).

Further evidence for the importance of biological factors shows that when people with schizophrenia hear voices during hallucinations, the parts of the brain responsible for hearing and language processing become active. When they have visual hallucinations, the parts of the brain involved in movement and color are active. At the same time, people with schizophrenia often have unusually low activity in the brain's frontal lobes–the parts of the brain involved with emotional regulation, insight, and the evaluation of sensory stimuli (Stern & Silbersweig, 2001; Lavigne et al., 2015).

SITUATIONAL CAUSES OF SCHIZOPHRENIA

Biological factors provide important pieces of the puzzle of schizophrenia. However, we also need to consider past and current experiences of people who develop the disturbance.

NEUROSCIENCE IN YOUR LIFE: BRAIN NETWORKS RELATED TO MEMORY DEFICITS IN SCHIZOPHRENIA

Psychological disorders are well known for their psychological symptoms, but they are also marked by significant cognitive declines. For example, patients with schizophrenia suffer from hallucinations, but they also suffer from memory deficits that can greatly impact their lives. In a recent study, neuroscientists scanned the brains of patients with schizophrenia and healthy control participants while each group attempted to memorize and later recall pictures. As you can see from the images below, healthy control participants (left) showed more activity in certain brain regions of the prefrontal cortex (indicated by more yellow) than patients with schizophrenia (right) in both the left hemisphere (top) and the right hemisphere (bottom) (Ragland et al., 2015).

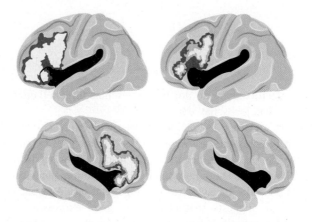

Source: Adapted from Ragland, J. D., Ranganath, C., Harms, M. P., Barch, D. M., Gold, J. M., Layher, E., . . . Carter, C. S. (2015). Functional and neuroanatomic specificity of episodic memory dysfunction in schizophrenia: A functional magnetic resonance imaging study of the relational and item-specific encoding task. *JAMA Psychiatry, 72*(9), 909–916. doi: 10.1001/jamapsychiatry.2015.0276

For instance, psychoanalytic explanations suggest that schizophrenia occurs when people experience regression to earlier stages of life. Specifically, Freud believed that people with schizophrenia lack egos that are strong enough to cope with their unacceptable impulses. They regress to the oral stage—a time when the id and ego are not yet separated. Therefore, individuals with schizophrenia essentially are presumed to act out impulses without concern for reality.

However, little research evidence supports psychoanalytic explanations. More plausible theories suggest that the emotional and communication patterns of the families of people with schizophrenia are to blame for the disorder. For instance, some researchers suggest that schizophrenia is related to a family interaction style known as expressed emotion.

Expressed emotion is an interaction style characterized by high levels of criticism, hostility, and emotional intrusiveness within a family. Other researchers suggest that faulty communication patterns lie at the heart of schizophrenia (Lobban, Barrowclough, & Jones, 2006; Nader et al., 2013).

Psychologists who take a cognitive perspective on schizophrenia suggest that the problems in thinking that people with the disorder experience point to a cognitive cause. Some suggest that schizophrenia results from *overattention* to stimuli in the environment. Rather than being able to screen out unimportant or inconsequential stimuli and focus on the most important things in the environment, people with schizophrenia may be excessively receptive to virtually everything in their environment. As a consequence of their inability to screen out noncritical information, their information-processing capabilities become overloaded and eventually break down.

Other cognitive experts argue that schizophrenia results from *underattention* to certain stimuli. According to this explanation, people with schizophrenia fail to focus sufficiently on important stimuli and pay attention to other, less important information in their surroundings (Cadenhead & Braff, 1995; Remington et al., 2014).

Although it is plausible that overattention and underattention are related to different forms of schizophrenia, these phenomena do not explain the origins of such information-processing disorders. Consequently, cognitive approaches–like other environmental explanations–do not provide a full explanation of the disorder.

PREDISPOSITIONAL MODEL OF SCHIZOPHRENIA: THE DISORDER'S MULTIPLE CAUSES

Most scientists now believe that schizophrenia is caused by biological as well as situational factors. Specifically, the *predisposition model of schizophrenia* suggests that individuals may inherit a predisposition or an inborn sensitivity to develop schizophrenia. This genetic predisposition makes them particularly vulnerable to stressors in their lives, such as social rejection, dysfunctional family communication patterns, or severe economic stress.

The stressors in people's lives may vary, but if they are strong enough and are coupled with a genetic predisposition, they result in the appearance of schizophrenia. Furthermore, a strong genetic predisposition may lead to the onset of schizophrenia even when the environmental stressors are relatively weak. On the other hand, someone with a genetic predisposition to develop schizophrenia may avoid developing the disorder if that person experiences relatively few life stressors.

In short, schizophrenia is related to several kinds of biological and situational factors. It is increasingly clear, then, that no single factor but rather a combination of interrelated variables produces schizophrenia (Opler et al., 2008; Balter, 2017).

Study Alert
Remember that the multiple causes of schizophrenia include biological and environmental factors.

Personality Disorders

I had always wanted lots of things; as a child I can remember wanting a bullet that a friend of mine had brought in to show the class. I took it and put it into my school bag and when my friend noticed it was missing, I was the one who stayed after school with him and searched the room, and I was the one who sat with him and bitched about the other kids and how one of them took his bullet. I even went home with him to help him break the news to his uncle, who had brought it home from the war for him.

But that was petty compared with the stuff I did later. I wanted a Ph.D. very badly, but I didn't want to work very hard–just enough to get by. I never did the experiments I reported; hell, I was smart enough to make up the results. I knew enough about statistics to make anything look plausible. I got my master's degree without even spending one hour in a laboratory. I mean, the professors believed anything. I'd stay out all night drinking and being with my friends, and the next day I'd get in just before them and tell 'em I'd been in the lab all night. They'd actually feel sorry for me. (Duke & Nowicki, 1979)

This excerpt provides a graphic first-person account of a person with a personality disorder. A **personality disorder** is characterized by a set of inflexible, maladaptive behavior patterns that keep a person from functioning appropriately in society.

Unlike the other disorders we have discussed, people with personality disorders typically have little sense of personal distress. Moreover, people with personality disorders frequently lead seemingly normal lives. However, just below the surface lies a set of inflexible, maladaptive personality traits that prevent them from functioning effectively as members of society (Clarkin & Lenzenweger, 2004; Friedman, Oltmanns, & Turkheimer, 2007; Anderson et al., 2015).

The best-known type of personality disorder, illustrated by the case above, is the **antisocial personality disorder** (sometimes referred to as a sociopathic personality). Individuals with this disturbance show no regard for the moral and ethical rules of society or the rights of others. Although they can appear quite intelligent and likable

personality disorder A disorder characterized by a set of inflexible, maladaptive behavior patterns that keep a person from functioning appropriately in society. (Module 38)

antisocial personality disorder A disorder in which individuals show no regard for the moral and ethical rules of society or the rights of others. (Module 38)

Study Alert
Unlike most psychological disorders, personality disorders produce little or no personal distress.

borderline personality disorder A disorder characterized by problems regulating emotions and thoughts, displaying impulsive and reckless behavior, and having unstable relationships with others. (Module 38)

narcissistic personality disorder A personality disturbance characterized by an exaggerated sense of self-importance. (Module 38)

(at least at first), upon closer examination they turn out to be manipulative and deceptive. Moreover, they lack any guilt or anxiety about their wrongdoing. When those with antisocial personality disorder behave in a way that injures someone else, they understand intellectually that they have caused harm but feel no remorse (Hilarski, 2007; Bateman, 2011; Rosenström et al., 2017).

People with antisocial personality disorder are often impulsive and lack the ability to withstand frustration. They can be extremely manipulative. They also may have excellent social skills; they can be charming, engaging, and highly persuasive. Some of the best con artists have antisocial personalities.

What causes such an unusual constellation of problem behaviors? A variety of factors have been suggested ranging from an inability to experience emotions appropriately to problems in family relationships. For example, in many cases of antisocial behavior, the individual has come from a home in which a parent has died or left or one in which there is a lack of affection, a lack of consistency in discipline, or outright rejection. Other explanations concentrate on sociocultural factors because an unusually high proportion of people with antisocial personalities come from lower socioeconomic groups. Still, no one has been able to pinpoint the specific causes of antisocial personalities, and it is likely that some combination of factors is responsible (Rosenstein & Horowitz, 1996; Costa & Widiger, 2002; Chen et al., 2011).

People with **borderline personality disorder** have problems regulating emotions and thoughts, display impulsive and reckless behavior, and have unstable relationships with others. They also have difficulty in developing a clear understanding of who they are. As a consequence, they tend to rely on relationships with others to define their identity. The problem with this strategy is that even minor rejection by others is devastating to those with borderline personality disorder. Furthermore, they generally distrust others and have difficulty controlling their anger. Their emotional volatility leads to impulsive and self-destructive behavior.

Individuals with borderline personality disorder often feel empty and alone, and they have difficulty cooperating with others. They may form intense, sudden, one-sided relationships in which they demand the attention of another person and then feel angry when they don't receive it. One reason for this behavior is that they may have a background in which others discounted or criticized their emotional reactions, and they may not have learned to regulate their emotions effectively (King-Casas et al., 2008; Hopwood et al., 2009; Samuel et al., 2013).

The narcissistic personality disorder is another type of personality disorder. The **narcissistic personality disorder** is characterized by an exaggerated sense of self-importance. Those with the disorder expect special treatment from others while also disregarding others' feelings, showing little or no sense of empathy for them.

There are several other categories of personality disorder that range in severity from individuals who may simply be regarded by others as eccentric, obnoxious, or difficult to people who act in a manner that is criminal and dangerous to others. Although they are not out of touch with reality like people with schizophrenia, people with personality disorders often lead lives that put them on the fringes of society (Trull & Widiger, 2003; Wright et al., 2016).

From the perspective of...

A Social Worker Because people with personality disorders often appear from the outside to function well in society, should you try to address their problems?

©Sam Edwards/age fotostock

Disorders That Impact Childhood

We typically view childhood as a time of innocence and relative freedom from stress. In reality, though, almost 20% of children and 40% of adolescents experience significant emotional or behavioral disorders (Romano et al., 2001; Broidy, Nagin, & Tremblay, 2003; Nolen-Hoeksema, 2007).

For example, although major depression is more prevalent in adults, around 2.5% of children and more than 8% of adolescents suffer from the disorder. In fact, by the time they reach age 20, between 15-20% of children and adolescents will experience an episode of major depression. Ten percent of adolescents will have had an episode of major depression in the previous year (Garber & Horowitz, 2002; Substance Abuse and Mental Health Services Administration, 2014; Frodl et al., 2017).

Children do not always display depression the same way adults do. Rather than showing the expression of profound sadness or hopelessness, childhood depression may produce the expression of exaggerated fears, clinginess, or avoidance of everyday activities. In older children, the symptoms may be sulking, school problems, and even acts of delinquency (Koplewicz, 2002; Seroczynski, Jacquez, & Cole, 2003).

A considerably more common childhood disorder is **attention-deficit hyperactivity disorder,** or **ADHD,** a disorder marked by inattention, impulsiveness, a low tolerance for frustration, and generally a great deal of inappropriate activity. Although all children show such behavior some of the time, it is so common in children diagnosed with ADHD that it interferes with their everyday functioning (Barkley, Knouse, & Murphy, 2011; Walton, Murphy, & Bartram, 2017).

ADHD is surprisingly widespread, with estimates ranging between 3-5% of the school-age population–or some 3.5 million children under the age of 18 in the United States. Children diagnosed with the disorder are often exhausting to parents and teachers, and even their peers find them difficult to deal with.

The cause of ADHD is not known, although most experts feel that it is produced by dysfunctions in the nervous system. For example, one theory suggests that unusually low levels of arousal in the central nervous system cause ADHD. To compensate, children with ADHD seek out stimulation to increase arousal. Still, such theories are speculative. Furthermore, because many children occasionally show behaviors characteristic of ADHD, it often is misdiagnosed or in some cases overdiagnosed. Only the frequency and persistence of the symptoms of ADHD allow for a correct diagnosis, which only a trained professional can do (Barkley, 2000; Sciutto & Eisenberg, 2007; Ketisch & Jones, 2013).

Autism spectrum disorder, a severe developmental disability that impairs one's ability to communicate and relate to others, is another disorder that usually appears in the first 3 years and typically continues throughout life. Children with autism have difficulties in both verbal and nonverbal communication, and they may avoid social contact. About 1 in 88 children are now thought to have the disorder, and its prevalence has risen significantly in the last decade. Whether the increase is the result of an actual rise in the incidence of autism or is due to better reporting is a question of intense debate among researchers (Rice, 2009; Neal, Matson, & Belva, 2013).

attention-deficit hyperactivity disorder (ADHD) A disorder marked by inattention, impulsiveness, a low tolerance for frustration, and a great deal of inappropriate activity. (Module 38)

autism A severe developmental disability that impairs children's ability to communicate and relate to others. (Module 38)

In the most severe cases of autism spectrum disorder, children display self-injurious behavior and must wear protective head gear.
©Tony Freeman/PhotoEdit

Other Disorders

It's important to keep in mind that the various forms of psychological disorders described in DSM-5 cover much more ground than we have been able to discuss in this module. Some relate to topics considered in other chapters. For example, *psychoactive substance use disorder* relates to problems that arise from the use and abuse of drugs. Furthermore, *alcohol use disorders* are among the most serious and widespread problems. Both psychoactive substance use disorder and alcohol use disorder co-occur with many other psychological disorders, such as mood disorders, trauma- and stress-or-related disorders, and schizophrenia, which complicate treatment considerably (Salgado, Quinlan, & Zlotnick, 2007).

Another widespread problem is *eating disorders*. They include such disorders as *anorexia nervosa* and *bulimia*, which we considered in the chapter on motivation and emotion, as well as *binge-eating disorder*, characterized by binge eating without behaviors designed to prevent weight gain. Finally, *sexual disorders*, in which one's sexual activity is unsatisfactory, are another important class of problems. They include *sexual desire disorders*, *sexual arousal disorders*, and *paraphilic disorders*, atypical sexual activities that may include nonhuman objects or nonconsenting partners.

Another important class of disorders is *neurocognitive disorders*, problems with a biological cause that affect thinking and behavior. We considered some of them earlier, such as Alzheimer's disease and some types of developmental disabilities that are fully the consequence of biological issues. Furthermore, there are many other disorders that we have not mentioned at all, and each of the categories of disorder we have discussed can be divided into several subcategories (Pratt et al., 2003; Reijonen et al., 2003; American Psychiatric Association, 2013).

RECAP/EVALUATE/RETHINK

RECAP

LO 38-1 What are the major psychological disorders?

- Anxiety disorders are present when a person experiences so much anxiety that it affects daily functioning. Specific types of anxiety disorders include phobic disorder, panic disorder, and generalized anxiety disorder. Also related is obsessive-compulsive disorder.
- Somatic symptom disorders are psychological difficulties that take in a physical (somatic) form but for which there is no medical cause. Examples are illness anxiety disorder and conversion disorders.
- Dissociative disorders are marked by the separation, or dissociation, of different facets of a person's personality that are usually integrated. Major kinds of dissociative disorders include dissociative identity disorder, dissociative amnesia, and dissociative fugue.
- Mood disorders are characterized by emotional states of depression or euphoria so strong that they intrude on everyday living. They include major depression and bipolar disorder.
- Schizophrenia is one of the more severe forms of mental illness. Symptoms of schizophrenia include declines in functioning, thought and language disturbances, perceptual disorders, emotional disturbance, and withdrawal from others.
- Strong evidence links schizophrenia to genetic, biochemical, and environmental factors. According to the predisposition model, an interaction among various factors produces the disorder.
- People with personality disorders experience little or no personal distress, but they do suffer from an inability to function as normal members of society. These disorders include antisocial personality disorder, borderline personality disorder, and narcissistic personality disorder.

- Childhood disorders include major depression, attention-deficit hyperactivity disorder (ADHD), and autism spectrum disorder.

EVALUATE

1. Kathy is terrified of elevators. She could be suffering from a(n)
   a. Obsessive-compulsive disorder
   b. Phobic disorder
   c. Panic disorder
   d. Generalized anxiety disorder
2. Carmen described an incident in which her anxiety suddenly rose to a peak and she felt a sense of impending doom. Carmen experienced a(n) _____ _____
3. Troubling thoughts that persist for weeks or months are known as
   a. Obsessions
   b. Compulsions
   c. Rituals
   d. Panic attacks
4. An overpowering urge to carry out a strange ritual is called a(n) _____
5. The separation of the personality, which provides escape from stressful situations, is the key factor in _____ disorders.
6. States of extreme euphoria and energy paired with severe depression characterize _____ disorder.
7. _____ schizophrenia is characterized by symptoms that are sudden and of easily identifiable onset; _____ schizophrenia develops gradually over a person's life span.
8. The _____ _____ states that schizophrenia may be caused by an excess of certain neurotransmitters in the brain.

RETHINK

1. What cultural factors might contribute to the rate of anxiety disorders found in a culture? How might the experience of anxiety differ among people of different cultures?

2. Personality disorders are often not apparent to others, and many people with these problems seem to live basically normal lives and are not a threat to others. Because these people can function well in society, why should they be considered psychologically disordered?

Answers to Evaluate Questions

1. b; 2. panic attack; 3. a; 4. compulsion; 5. dissociative; 6. bipolar; 7. Reactive, process; 8. dopamine hypothesis

KEY TERMS

anxiety disorder
specific phobias
panic disorder
generalized anxiety disorder
obsessive-compulsive
   disorder (OCD)
obsession
compulsion

somatic symptom disorders
illness anxiety disorder
conversion disorder
dissociative disorders
dissociative identity
   disorder (DID)
dissociative amnesia
dissociative fugue

mood disorder
major depressive disorder
mania
bipolar disorder
schizophrenia
personality disorder
antisocial personality
   disorder

borderline personality
   disorder
narcissistic personality
   disorder
attention-deficit
   hyperactivity disorder
   (ADHD)
autism spectrum disorder

Module 39
Psychological Disorders in Perspective

LEARNING OUTCOMES

LO 39-1 How prevalent are psychological disorders?

LO 39-2 What indicators signal a need for the help of a mental health practitioner?

Study Alert

Remember that the incidence of various psychological disorders in the general population is surprisingly high, particularly in terms of depression and alcohol dependence.

How common are the kinds of psychological disorders we've been discussing? Here's one answer: One out of two people in the United States is likely to experience a psychological disorder at some point in their lives.

That's the conclusion drawn from the most comprehensive study on the prevalence of psychological disorders conducted. In that study, researchers conducted face-to-face interviews with more than 8,000 men and women between the ages of 15 and 54. The sample was designed to be representative of the population of the United States.

According to results of the study, 48% of those interviewed had experienced a disorder at some point in their lives. In addition, 30% experienced a disorder in any particular year. Furthermore, many people experience comorbidity. *Cormorbidity* is the appearance of multiple, simultaneous psychological disorders in the same person (Welkowitz et al., 2000; Merikangas et al., 2007; Kessler & Wang, 2008).

The most common disorder reported in the study was depression. Some 17% of those surveyed reported at least one major episode. Ten percent had suffered from depression during the current year. The next most common disorder was alcohol dependence, which occurred at a lifetime incidence rate of 14%. In addition, 7% of those interviewed had experienced alcohol dependence in the previous year. Other frequently occurring psychological disorders were drug dependence, disorders involving panic (such as an overwhelming fear of talking to strangers or terror of heights), and posttraumatic stress disorder.

Although some researchers think the estimates of severe disorders may be too high (Narrow et al., 2002), the national findings are consistent with studies of college students and their psychological difficulties. For example, in one study of the problems of students who visited a college counseling center, more than 40% of students reported being depressed (see Figure 1). These figures include only students who sought help from the counseling center and not those who did not seek treatment. Consequently, the figures are not representative of the entire college population (Benton et al., 2003; also see *Applying Psychology in the 21st Century*).

From the perspective of...

A College Counselor What indicators might be most important in determining whether a college student is experiencing a psychological disorder?

©Chris Ryan/age fotostock

The significant level of psychological disorders is a problem not only in the United States; according to the World Health Organization, mental health difficulties are also a global concern. Throughout the world, psychological disorders are widespread.

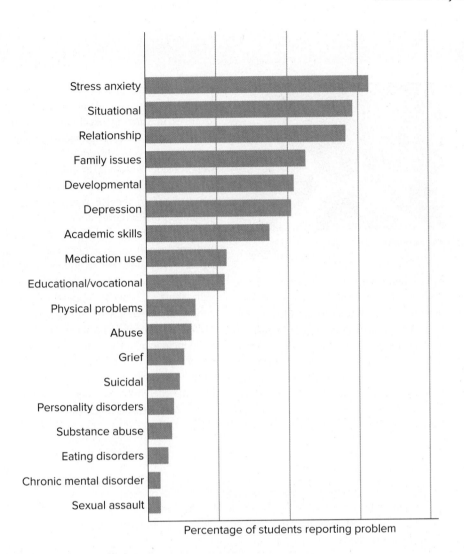

Stress anxiety
Situational
Relationship
Family issues
Developmental
Depression
Academic skills
Medication use
Educational/vocational
Physical problems
Abuse
Grief
Suicidal
Personality disorders
Substance abuse
Eating disorders
Chronic mental disorder
Sexual assault

Percentage of students reporting problem

FIGURE 1 The problems reported by students visiting a college counseling center. Would you have predicted this pattern of psychological difficulties?

Source: Adapted from Benton, S. A., Robertson, J. M., Tseng, W., Newton, F. B., & Benton, S. L. (2003). Changes in counseling center client problems across 13 years. *Professional Psychology: Research and Practice, 34*(1), 66–72.

Furthermore, there are economic disparities in treatment; more affluent people with mild disorders receive more and better treatment than do poor people who have more severe disorders. In fact, psychological disorders make up 14% of global illness, and 90% of people in developing countries receive no care at all for their disorders (see Figure 2; WHO World Mental Health Survey Consortium, 2004; Jacob et al., 2007; Wang et al., 2007).

Also, keep in mind that the incidence of specific disorders varies significantly in other cultures. For instance, cross-cultural surveys show that the incidence of major depression varies significantly from one culture to another. The probability of having at least one episode of depression is only 1.5% in Taiwan and 2.9% in Korea, compared with 11.6% in New Zealand and 16.4% in France. Such notable differences underscore the importance of considering the cultural context of psychological disorders (Weissman et al., 1997; Tseng, 2003).

The Social and Cultural Context of Psychological Disorders

In considering the nature of the psychological disorders described in DSM-5, it's important to keep in mind that the disorders that were included in the manual are a reflection of Western culture at the start of the 21st century. The classification system

APPLYING PSYCHOLOGY IN THE 21ST CENTURY

IS THE NEWEST GENERATION OF COLLEGE STUDENTS MORE PSYCHOLOGICALLY DISORDERED THAN THEIR PREDECESSORS?

If you are feeling stressed out, anxious, and maybe even depressed, you're not alone. According to the most recent annual report of the Center for Collegiate Mental Health (2017), which summarizes data provided by 139 college and university counseling centers, demand for mental health services has increased dramatically along with an ongoing increase in rates of "threat to self" incidents (including self-injury and suicidal thoughts). In fact, within the past 5 years, the average level of counseling center usage grew 30%–six times more than overall enrollment grew over the same time period.

The most common concerns for students who go in for counselling are anxiety and depression. Moreover, students' self-reported distress levels for depression and anxiety have slowly increased over recent years. Meanwhile, counselling centers are providing nearly 30% more rapid-access service hours and over 7% fewer routine

©Ingram Publishing

service hours during the past 6 years. These statistics illustrate the increase in demand by students with psychological issues.

Several reasons underlie the increase in demand for psychological services. One is that the stigma of psychological disorders is decreasing: Whereas students once may have kept their mental health concerns to themselves, they now feel more empowered to seek treatment (Itkowitz, 2016).

Another reason for the increase in demand for services relates, ironically, to advances in treating psychological disorders generally. Whereas previously, people with more severe disorders would not even consider enrolling in college, better treatment now allows them to start college and attempt to receive treatment while enrolled. Furthermore, colleges may be doing a better job of helping distressed students recognize their need for mental health services and get treatment (Center for Collegiate Mental Health, 2017).

In short, it doesn't appear that the increase in students with self-reported psychological disorders represents an increase in the incidence of those disorders. Instead, it may well be that the willingness of students to report and seek treatment for those disorders is at the root of the apparent increase (Wilson, 2015; Auerbach et al., 2016).

> **RETHINK**
>
> - Do you think it is accurate to say that the stigma of reporting a psychological disorders has declined? Why might this be the case?
> - How much responsibility do you think colleges and universities have to provide care for students with psychological disorders?

Study Alert

It is important to understand that the DSM is a living document that presents a view of disorders that reflects the culture and historical context of its authors.

provides a snapshot of how its authors viewed mental disorder when it was published. In fact, the development of the most recent version of the DSM was a source of great debate, which in part reflects issues that divide society.

One specific, newly classified disorder that was added to DSM-5 and that has caused controversy is known as disruptive mood dysregulation disorder. This particular diagnosis is characterized by temperamental outbursts grossly out of proportion to the situation, both verbally and physically, in children between the ages of 6 and 18. Some practitioners argue these symptoms simply define a child having a temper tantrum rather than a disorder (Marchand & Phillips, 2012; Frances, 2013).

Similarly, someone who overeats 12 times in 3 months can be considered to be suffering from the new classification of binge-eating disorder, which seems to some critics to be overly inclusive. Finally, hoarding behavior is now placed in its own category of psychological disorder. Some critics suggest this change is more a reflection of the rise of reality shows focusing on hoarding rather than reflecting a distinct category of psychological disturbance (Hudson et al., 2012; Racine et al., 2017; Moulding et al., 2017).

Such controversies underline the fact that our understanding of abnormal behavior reflects the society and culture in which we live. Future revisions of DSM may include a different catalog of disorders. Even now, other cultures might include a list of disorders that are very different from the list that appears in the current DSM, as we discuss next.

Developed Countries

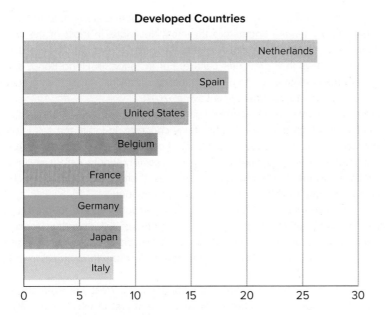

FIGURE 2 According to a global survey conducted by the World Health Organization, the prevalence of psychological disorders is widespread. These figures show the percentage of people who have experienced any psychological disorder within the prior 12-month period.

Source: Adapted from WHO World Mental Health Survey Consortium. (2004). Prevalence, severity, and unmet need for treatment of mental disorders in the World Health Organization World Mental Health Surveys. *Journal of the American Medical Association, 291*, 2581–2590.

Less-Developed Countries

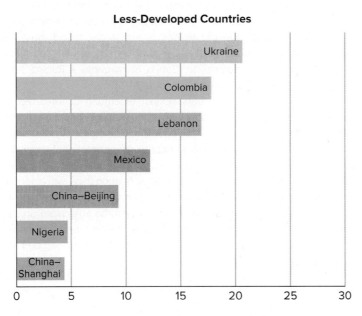

 Exploring Diversity

DSM and Culture—and the Culture of DSM

To most people raised in the United States, a person who hears voices of the recently deceased is probably a victim of a psychological disturbance. Yet some Plains Indians routinely hear the voices of the dead calling to them from the afterlife, and in their culture, that's considered perfectly normal.

The voices Plains Indians hear are only one example of the role of culture in determining what behavior should be labeled as "abnormal." In fact, among all the major adult disorders included in the DSM categorization, just a minority are found across all cultures of the world. Most others only are prevalent in North America and Western Europe (Kleinman, 1996; López & Guarnaccia, 2000; Jacob, 2014).

For instance, take anorexia nervosa, the disorder in which people become obsessed with their weight and sometimes stop eating, ultimately starving to death in the process.

It turns out that anorexia nervosa occurs most frequently in cultures that hold the societal standard that slender female bodies are the most desirable. In most of the world, where such a standard does not exist, anorexia nervosa is rare. Furthermore, the disorder may appear in specific ways in a particular culture. For instance, in Hong Kong, symptoms of one form of anorexia relate to complaints of bloated stomachs, rather than fears of becoming fat (Watters, 2010; Munro, Randell, & Lawrie, 2017).

Similarly, dissociative identity (multiple personality) disorder makes sense as a problem only in societies in which a sense of self is fairly concrete. In India, the self is based more on external factors that are relatively independent of the person. There, when an individual displays symptoms of what people in a Western society would call dissociative identity disorder, Indians assume that that person is possessed either by demons (which they view as a malady) or by gods (which does not require treatment).

Furthermore, even though disorders such as schizophrenia are found throughout the world, cultural factors influence the specific symptoms of the disorder. Hence, catatonic schizophrenia, in which unmoving patients appear to be frozen in the same position (sometimes for days), is rare in North America and Western Europe. In contrast, in India, 80% of those with schizophrenia are catatonic.

Other cultures have disorders that do not appear in the West. For example, in Malaysia, a behavior called *amok* is characterized by a wild outburst in which a usually quiet and withdrawn person kills or severely injures another. *Koro* is a condition found in Southeast Asian males who develop an intense panic that their penis is about to withdraw irretrievably into their abdomens. Finally, *ataque de nervios* is a disorder found most often among Latinos from the Caribbean. It is characterized by trembling, crying, uncontrollable screams, and incidents of verbal or physical aggression (Cohen, Slomkowski, & Robins, 1999; Adams & Dzokoto, 2007; Ebigbo, Lekwas, & Chukwunenyem, 2015).

Explanations for psychological disorders also differ among cultures. For example, in China, psychological disorders are commonly viewed as weaknesses of the heart, a concept that derives from thousands of years of traditional Chinese medicine. Chinese people are more likely than people in Western cultures to express their emotional anguish in terms of physical symptoms such as heart pain, "heart panic," or "heart vexed." They also may focus more on the effects that their symptoms have on their relationships with friends and family members than on themselves (Miller, 2006; Lee, Kleinman, & Kleinman, 2007; Watters, 2010).

In sum, we should not assume that the DSM provides the final word on psychological disorders. The disorders it includes are very much a creation and function of Western cultures at a particular moment in time, and its categories should not be seen as universally applicable (Tseng, 2003).

BECOMING AN INFORMED CONSUMER
of Psychology

Deciding When You Need Help

After you've considered the range and variety of psychological disturbances that can afflict people, you may begin to feel that you suffer from one (or more) of the problems we have discussed. In fact, this perception has a name: *medical student's disease*. Although in this case it might more aptly be labeled "psychology student's disease," the basic symptoms are the same: feeling that you suffer from the same sorts of problems you are studying.

Most often, of course, your concerns will be unwarranted. As we have discussed, the differences between normal and abnormal behavior are often so fuzzy that it is easy to jump to the conclusion that you might have the same symptoms that are involved in serious forms of mental disturbance.

Before coming to such a conclusion, though, keep in mind that from time to time, we all experience a wide range of emotions, and it is not unusual to feel deeply unhappy, fantasize about bizarre situations, or feel anxiety about life's circumstances. It is the persistence, depth, and consistency of such behavior that set normal reactions apart from abnormal ones. If you have not previously had serious doubts about the normality of your behavior, it is unlikely that reading about others' psychological disorders will prompt you to re-evaluate your earlier conclusion.

On the other hand, many people do have problems that merit concern, and in such cases, it is important to consider the possibility that professional help is warranted. The following list of symptoms can serve as a guideline to help you determine whether outside intervention might be useful (Engler & Goleman, 1992; APA, 2018).

- Long-term feelings of distress that interfere with your sense of well-being, competence, and ability to function effectively in daily activities
- Occasions in which you experience overwhelmingly high stress accompanied by feelings of inability to cope with the situation
- Prolonged depression or feelings of hopelessness, especially when they do not have any clear cause (such as the death of someone close)
- Withdrawal from other people
- Thoughts of inflicting harm on oneself or suicide
- A chronic physical problem for which no physical cause can be determined
- A fear or phobia that prevents you from engaging in everyday activities
- Feelings that other people are out to get you or are talking about and plotting against you
- Inability to interact effectively with others, preventing the development of friendships and loving relationships

This list offers a rough set of guidelines for determining when the normal problems of everyday living have escalated beyond your ability to deal with them by yourself. In such situations, the *least* reasonable approach would be to pore over the psychological disorders we have discussed in an attempt at self-diagnosis. A more reasonable strategy is to consider seeking professional help.

RECAP/EVALUATE/RETHINK

RECAP

LO 39-1 How prevalent are psychological disorders?

- About half the people in the United States are likely to experience a psychological disorder at some point in their lives; 30% experience a disorder in any specific year.

LO 39-2 What indicators signal a need for the help of a mental health practitioner?

- The signals that indicate a need for professional help include long-term feelings of psychological distress, feelings of inability to cope with stress, withdrawal from other people, thoughts of inflicting harm on oneself or suicide, prolonged feelings of hopelessness, chronic physical problems with no apparent causes, phobias and compulsions, paranoia, and an inability to interact with others.

EVALUATE

1. The latest version of DSM is considered to be the definitive guide to defining psychological disorders. True or false?

2. Match the disorder with the culture in which it is most common:

a. Amok	**a.** India
b. Anorexia nervosa	**b.** Malaysia
c. Brain fag	**c.** United States
d. Catatonic schizophrenia	**d.** West Africa

RETHINK

1. Why is inclusion in the DSM-5 of disorders such as hoarding behavior so controversial and political? What disadvantages does inclusion bring? Does inclusion bring any benefits?

2. What societal changes would have to occur for psychological disorders to be regarded as the equivalent of appendicitis or another treatable physical disorder? Do you think a person who has been treated for a psychological disorder could become president of the United States? Should such a person become president?

Answers to Evaluate Questions

2. 1-b, 2-c, 3-d, 4-a

great controversy, in part reflecting issues that divide society; **1.** false; the development of the latest version of DSM was a source of

LOOKING *Back*

EPILOGUE

We've discussed some of the many types of psychological disorders to which people are prone, noted the difficulty psychologists and physicians have in clearly differentiating normal from abnormal behavior, and looked at some of the approaches mental health professionals have taken to explain and treat psychological disorders. We considered today's most commonly used classification scheme, categorized in the DSM-5, and examined some of the more prevalent forms of psychological disorders. To gain a perspective on the topic of psychological disorders, we discussed the surprisingly broad incidence of psychological disorders in U.S. society and the cultural nature of such disorders.

Turn back to the prologue, which described the case of Andrea Petersen. Using the knowledge you've gained about psychological disorders, consider the following questions.

1. Petersen was eventually diagnosed as suffering from an anxiety disorder. What elements of her behavior do you see reflected in the three major types of this disorder? Does one type seem to prevail?
2. How might each of the perspectives on psychological disorders—medical, psychoanalytic, behavioral, cognitive, humanistic, and sociocultural—address the causes of Petersen's symptoms?
3. Which perspective do you believe provides the most useful explanation for Petersen's case? Explain your thinking.
4. The number of college students being diagnosed and treated for anxiety is increasing. Why do you think we are seeing an uptick in these numbers?

Design Elements: Yellow highlighter: ©luckyraccoon/Shutterstock.com; Smartphone: ©and4me/Shutterstock.com; Group of diverse hands: ©MR. Nattanon Kanchak/Shutterstock.com; Woman working on laptop: ©Dragon Images/Shutterstock.com.

VISUAL SUMMARY 12 Psychological Disorders

MODULE 37 Normal Versus Abnormal: Making the Distinction

Defining Abnormality

- Deviation from the average
- Deviation from the ideal
- Sense of personal discomfort
- Inability to function effectively
- Legal concept

Perspectives on Abnormality

Perspectives on Psychological Disorders

Perspective	Description	Possible Application of Perspective to Chris' Case
Medical	Assumes that physiological causes are at the root of psychological disorders	Examine Chris for medical problems, such as brain tumor, chemical imbalance in the brain, or disease
Psychoanalytic	Argues that psychological disorders stem from childhood conflicts	Seek out information about Chris' past, considering possible childhood conflicts
Behavioral	Assumes that abnormal behaviors are learned responses	Concentrate on rewards and punishments for Chris' behavior, and identify environmental stimuli that reinforce his behavior
Cognitive	Assumes that cognitions (people's thoughts and beliefs) are central to psychological disorders	Focus on Chris' perceptions of self and his environment
Humanistic	Emphasizes people's responsibility for their own behavior and the need to self-actualize	Consider Chris' behavior in terms of his choices and efforts to reach his potential
Sociocultural	Assumes that behavior is shaped by family, society, and culture	Focus on how societal demands contributed to Chris' disorder

Classifying Abnormal Behavior: DSM-5 attempts to provide comprehensive and relatively precise definitions for more than 200 disorders

MODULE 38 Major Psychological Disorders

Anxiety Disorders: Anxiety without external justification

- Phobic disorder
- Panic disorder

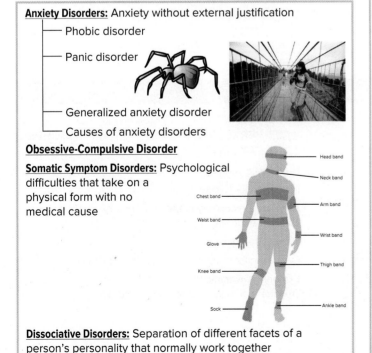

- Generalized anxiety disorder
- Causes of anxiety disorders

Obsessive-Compulsive Disorder

Somatic Symptom Disorders: Psychological difficulties that take on a physical form with no medical cause

Head band
Neck band
Chest band
Arm band
Waist band
Wrist band
Glove
Knee band
Thigh band
Sock
Ankle band

Dissociative Disorders: Separation of different facets of a person's personality that normally work together

Mood Disorders: Disturbances in emotional experience

- Major depressive disorder
- Mania and bipolar disorder
- Causes of mood disorders
  - Genetics
  - Psychological: feelings of loss or anger
  - Behavioral: stress
  - Cognitive: learned helplessness and no hope

Schizophrenia Spectrum: A class of disorders in which distortion of reality occurs

- Decline from a previous level of functioning
- Disturbances of thought and language
- Delusions
- Hallucinations and perceptual disorders
- Emotional disturbances

Personality Disorders: A set of inflexible, maladaptive behavior patterns

- Antisocial personality disorder
- Borderline personality disorder
- Narcissistic personality disorder

Childhood Disorders: Start during childhood or adolescence

- Attention-deficit hyperactivity disorder
- Autism spectrum disorder

MODULE 39 Psychological Disorders in Perspective

Social and Cultural Context: Our understanding of abnormal behavior reflects the society and culture in which we live

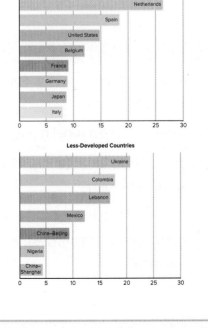

Developed Countries

Netherlands
Spain
United States
Belgium
France
Germany
Japan
Italy

0   5   10   15   20   25   30

Less-Developed Countries

Ukraine
Colombia
Lebanon
Mexico
China–Beijing
Nigeria
China–Shanghai

0   5   10   15   20   25   30

(MODULE 37) (top photo): ©Brett Coomer, Pool/AP Images; (book): ©H.S. Photos/Alamy Stock Photo Source: Adapted from Nolen-Hoeksema, S. (2007). *Abnormal psychology* (4th ed.). New York: McGraw-Hill; (MODULE 38) (China glass): ©Imaginechina/AP Images Source: Adapted from WHO World Mental Health Survey Consortium. (2004). Prevalence, severity, and unmet need for treatment of mental disorders in the World Health Organization World Mental Health Surveys. *Journal of the American Medical Association, 291,* 2581–2590.

©urbancow/Getty Images

CHAPTER 13
Treatment of Psychological Disorders

LEARNING OUTCOMES FOR CHAPTER 13

MODULE 40

LO 40-1 What are the goals of psychologically based and biologically based treatment approaches?

LO 40-2 What are the psychodynamic, behavioral, and cognitive approaches to treatment?

PSYCHOTHERAPY: PSYCHODYNAMIC, BEHAVIORAL, AND COGNITIVE APPROACHES TO TREATMENT

Psychodynamic Approaches to Therapy

Behavioral Approaches to Therapy

Cognitive Approaches to Therapy

Neuroscience in Your Life: How Cognitive Behavioral Therapy Changes Your Brain

MODULE 41

LO 41-1 What are the humanistic approaches to treatment?

LO 41-2 What is interpersonal therapy?

LO 41-3 How does group therapy differ from individual types of therapy?

LO 41-4 How effective is psychotherapy, and which kind of psychotherapy works best in a given situation?

PSYCHOTHERAPY: HUMANISTIC, INTERPERSONAL, AND GROUP APPROACHES TO TREATMENT

Humanistic Therapy

Interpersonal Therapy

Applying Psychology in the 21st Century: Click Here for Therapy

Group Therapies

Evaluating Psychotherapy: Does Therapy Work?

Exploring Diversity: Racial and Ethnic Factors in Treatment: Should Therapists Be Color-Blind?

LO 42-1 How are drug, electroconvulsive, and psychosurgical techniques used today in the treatment of psychological disorders?

PROLOGUE *GOING DEEP TO TREAT*

Deep brain stimulation (DBS) was originally developed to treat movement disorders such as Parkinson's but is still experimental for the treatment of depression. Vito Randazzo underwent a daylong operation that involved threading tiny electrodes into a mood-related part of the brain and then connecting the electrodes to a pacemaker-like device in his chest. The implant uses electrical currents to correct abnormal brain signals associated with depression.

"It's not as if DBS was a magic bullet," said Randazzo's neurosurgeon, Sameer Sheth. "Vito still had to work hard to fight through the depression, but the therapy helped him actually succeed this time." Randazzo said the operation was transformative: "I can laugh again and really enjoy life with my family" (Columbia Neurosurgery, 2017; Garcia, 2017).

LOOKING *Ahead*

Deep brain stimulation surgery is just one way in which people suffering from psychological disorders—in this instance, severe depression—can be treated. The variety of treatments available to relieve psychological pain share a common objective: to enable individuals to achieve richer, more meaningful, and more fulfilling lives.

For Vito Randazzo, the transition from a life of dark, desperate depression was by no means sudden or miraculous, but by working hard with the DBS team to confront and overcome his depression, Randazzo—while not entirely symptom-free—created a life of laughter and enjoyment with his family.

Despite their diversity, approaches to treating psychological disorders fall into two main categories: psychologically based and biologically based therapies. **Psychotherapy** is psychologically based treatment in which a trained professional—a therapist—uses psychological techniques to help someone overcome psychological difficulties and disorders, resolve problems in living, or bring about personal growth. The goal of psychotherapy is to produce lasting psychological change in a person (called a *client* or *patient*) through discussions and interactions with the therapist. In contrast, **biomedical therapy** is biologically based and relies on drugs and medical procedures to improve psychological functioning.

As we describe the various approaches to therapy, keep in mind that although the distinctions may seem clear-cut, the classifications and procedures overlap a good deal. In fact, many therapists today take an *eclectic approach* to therapy, which means they use a variety of methods with an individual patient. Assuming that psychological as well as biological processes often produce psychological disorders, eclectic therapists may draw from several perspectives simultaneously to address the psychological as well as the biological aspects of a person's problems.

psychotherapy Treatment in which a trained professional—a therapist—uses psychological techniques to help a person overcome psychological difficulties and disorders, resolve problems in living, or bring about personal growth. (Module 40)

biomedical therapy Therapy that relies on drugs and other medical procedures to improve psychological functioning. (Module 40)

Module 40

Psychotherapy: Psychodynamic, Behavioral, and Cognitive Approaches to Treatment

LEARNING OUTCOMES

LO 40-1 What are the goals of psychologically based and biologically based treatment approaches?

LO 40-2 What are the psychodynamic, behavioral, and cognitive approaches to treatment?

There are about 400 varieties of psychotherapy. Although the methods are diverse, all psychological approaches have a common perspective: They seek to solve psychological problems by modifying people's behavior and helping them obtain a better understanding of themselves and their past, present, and future.

In light of the variety of psychological approaches, it is not surprising that the people who provide therapy vary considerably in educational background and training (see Figure 1). Many have doctoral degrees in psychology, having attended graduate school, learned clinical and research techniques, and held an internship in a facility that treats people with psychological disorders. But therapy is also provided by people in fields allied with psychology, such as psychiatrists (who have a medical degree with a specialization in psychological disorders) and social workers (who have a master's degree and have specialized in psychological disorders).

The nature of the problem a person is experiencing often makes one type of therapist more appropriate than others. For example, a person who is suffering from a severe disturbance and who has lost touch with reality may typically require some sort of biologically based drug therapy. In that case, a psychiatrist–who is a physician– would be the professional of choice. In contrast, those suffering from milder disorders,

FIGURE 1 A variety of professionals provide therapy and counseling. Each could be expected to give helpful advice and direction. However, the nature of the problem a person is experiencing may make one or another therapist more appropriate.

Getting Help from the Right Person

Clinical Psychologists
Psychologists with a PhD or PsyD with about 5 years of training and who have also completed a postgraduate internship. They specialize in assessment and treatment of psychological difficulties, providing psychotherapy and, in some U.S. states, can prescribe drugs.

Counseling Psychologists
Psychologists with a PhD or EdD who typically treat day-to-day adjustment problems, often in a university mental health clinic

Psychiatrists
MDs with postgraduate training in psychological disorders. Because they can prescribe medication, they often treat the most severe disorders.

Psychoanalysts
Either MDs or psychologists who specialize in psychoanalysis, the treatment technique first developed by Freud

Licensed Professional Counselors or Clinical Mental Health Counselors
Professionals with a master's degree who provide therapy to individuals, couples, and families and who hold a national or state certification

Clinical or Psychiatric Social Workers
Professionals with a master's degree and specialized training who may provide therapy, usually regarding common family and personal problems

such as difficulty adjusting to the death of a family member, have a broader choice that might include other types of professionals listed in Figure 1.

Regardless of their specific training, all psychotherapists employ one of four major approaches to therapy that we'll consider next: psychodynamic, behavioral, cognitive, and humanistic treatment approaches. These approaches grow out of the perspectives of personality and psychological disorders developed by psychologists.

Psychodynamic Approaches to Therapy

Psychodynamic therapy seeks to bring unresolved past conflicts and unacceptable impulses from the unconscious into the conscious, where patients may deal with the problems more effectively. Although psychodynamic approaches originally derived from Freud's psychoanalytic theories of personality, today they encompass a wider range of therapies. The common assumptions behind psychodynamic therapies are that unconscious forces affect our behavior and that the goal of therapy is to try to identify and control them.

Psychodynamic approaches hold that people employ *defense mechanisms*, psychological strategies to protect themselves from unacceptable unconscious impulses. The most common defense mechanism is *repression*, which pushes threatening and unpleasant thoughts and impulses back into the unconscious. However, because people cannot completely bury their unacceptable thoughts and impulses, anxiety associated with them can produce abnormal behavior.

How do we rid ourselves of the anxiety produced by unconscious, unwanted thoughts and impulses? To Freud, the answer was to confront the conflicts and impulses by bringing them out of the unconscious part of the mind and into the conscious part. Freud assumed that this technique would reduce anxiety stemming from past conflicts and that the patient could then participate in his or her daily life more effectively.

A psychodynamic therapist, then, faces the challenge of finding a way to assist patients' attempts to explore and understand the unconscious. The technique that has evolved has a number of components, but basically it consists of guiding patients to consider and discuss their past experiences in explicit detail from the time of their first memories. This process assumes that patients will eventually stumble upon long-hidden crises, traumas, and conflicts that are producing anxiety in their adult lives. They will then be able to "work through"–understand and rectify–those difficulties.

PSYCHOANALYSIS: FREUD'S THERAPY

Psychoanalysis is Freud's specific version of psychodynamic therapy. The goal of psychoanalysis is to release hidden thoughts and feelings from the unconscious part of our mind in order to reduce their power in controlling behavior.

In traditional psychoanalysis, which tends to be a lengthy and expensive process, patients may meet with a therapist with considerable frequency, sometimes as much as 50 minutes a session, 4 to 5 days a week, for several years. In their sessions, therapists and patients typically use a technique developed by Freud called *free association*. Patients using free association say aloud whatever comes to mind, regardless of its apparent irrelevance or senselessness. The psychoanalyst then attempts to recognize and label the connections between what a patient says and the patient's unconscious.

Therapists also use *dream interpretation*, examining dreams to find clues to unconscious conflicts and problems. Moving beyond the surface description of a dream (called the *manifest content*), therapists seek its underlying meaning (the *latent content*), which supposedly reveals the true unconscious meaning of the dream (Blum, 2011; Hill et al., 2013; Sandford, 2017).

The processes of free association and dream interpretation do not always move forward easily. The same unconscious forces that initially produced repression may keep past

psychodynamic therapy Therapy that seeks to bring unresolved past conflicts and unacceptable impulses from the unconscious into the conscious, where patients may deal with the problems more effectively. (Module 40)

psychoanalysis Freud's psychotherapy in which the goal is to release hidden thoughts and feelings from the unconscious part of our minds in order to reduce their power in controlling behavior. (Module 40)

Study Alert

To better understand how psychodynamic therapy works, review Freud's psychoanalytic theory discussed in the chapter on personality.

The close and intense relationship between therapist and patient may become highly complex.

©David Buffington/Getty Images

transference The transfer of feelings to a psychoanalyst of love or anger that had been originally directed to a patient's parents or other authority figures. (Module 40)

difficulties out of the conscious mind, which produces resistance. *Resistance* is an inability or unwillingness to discuss or reveal particular memories, thoughts, or motivations.

Patients can show resistance in many ways. For instance, they may be discussing a childhood memory and suddenly forget what they were saying, or they may abruptly change the subject completely. It is the therapist's job to discern instances of resistance and interpret their meaning. The therapists also need to try to make patients return to the subject they are trying to avoid—which is likely to hold difficult or painful memories for the patients.

Because of the close, almost intimate interaction between patient and psychoanalyst, the relationship between the two often becomes emotionally charged and takes on a complexity unlike most other relationships. Patients may eventually think of the analyst as a symbol of a significant other in their past, perhaps a parent or a lover, and apply some of their feelings for that person to the analyst—a phenomenon known as transference. **Transference** is the transfer of feelings to a psychoanalyst of love or anger that had been originally directed to a patient's parents or other authority figures (Steiner, 2008; Høglend et al., 2011; Turri, 2015).

A therapist can use transference to help a patient recreate past relationships that were psychologically difficult. For instance, if a patient undergoing transference views her therapist as a symbol of her father—with whom she had a difficult relationship—the patient and therapist may "redo" an earlier interaction, this time including more positive aspects. Through this process, the patient may resolve conflicts regarding her real father—something that is beginning to happen in the following therapy session:

> Sandy: My father . . . never took any interest in any of us. . . . It was my mother—rest her soul—who loved us, not our father. He worked her to death. Lord, I miss her. . . . I must sound angry at my father. Don't you think I have a right to be angry?
> Therapist: Do you think you have a right to be angry?
> Sandy: Of course, I do! Why are you questioning? You don't believe me, do you?
> Therapist: You want me to believe you.
> Sandy: I don't care whether you believe me or not. . . . I know what you're thinking—you think I'm crazy—you must be laughing at me—I'll probably be a case in your next book! You're just sitting there—smirking—making me feel like a bad person—thinking I'm wrong for being mad, that I have no right to be mad.
> Therapist: Just like your father.
> Sandy: Yes, you're just like my father.—Oh my God! Just now—I–I—thought I was talking to him. (Sue & Sue, 1990)

CONTEMPORARY PSYCHODYNAMIC APPROACHES

Few people have the time, money, or patience to participate in years of traditional psychoanalysis. Even more important, no conclusive evidence shows that psychoanalysis, as Freud originally conceived it in the 19th century, works better than other, more recent forms of psychodynamic therapy.

Today, psychodynamic therapy tends to be of shorter duration, usually lasting no longer than 3 months or 20 sessions. Psychodynamic therapists take a more active role than Freud would have prescribed, and they prod and advise the patient with considerable directness. Finally, contemporary psychodynamic therapists put less emphasis on a patient's past history and childhood. Instead, they concentrate on an individual's current relationships and specific concerns (Wolitzky, 2006; Brafman, 2011; Dreissen et al., 2017).

EVALUATING PSYCHODYNAMIC THERAPY

Even with its current modifications, psychodynamic therapy has its critics. In its longer versions, it can be time-consuming and expensive, especially in comparison with other forms of psychotherapy, such as behavioral and cognitive approaches. Furthermore, less articulate patients may not do as well as more articulate ones.

Ultimately, the most important concern about psychodynamic treatment is whether it actually works, and there is no simple answer to this question. Psychodynamic treatment techniques have been controversial since Freud introduced them. Part of the problem is the difficulty in establishing whether patients have improved after psychodynamic therapy. Determining effectiveness depends on reports from the therapist or the patients themselves–reports that are obviously open to bias and subjective interpretation.

Furthermore, critics have questioned the entire theoretical basis of psychodynamic theory; they maintain that constructs such as the unconscious have not been scientifically confirmed. Despite the criticism, though, the psychodynamic treatment approach has remained viable. For some people, it provides solutions to difficult psychological issues, provides effective treatment for psychological disturbance, and permits the potential development of an unusual degree of insight into one's life (Anestis, Anestis, & Lilienfeld, 2011; Thase, 2013; Sell, Möller, & Taubner, 2017).

Behavioral Approaches to Therapy

behavioral treatment approaches Treatment approaches that make use of the basic processes of learning, such as reinforcement and extinction, to reduce or eliminate maladaptive behavior. (Module 40)

Perhaps, when you were a child, your parents rewarded you with an ice cream cone when you were especially good. . . or sent you to your room if you misbehaved. Sound principles back up such a child-rearing strategy: Good behavior is maintained by reinforcement, and unwanted behavior can be eliminated by punishment.

These principles represent the basic underpinnings of behavioral treatment approaches. **Behavioral treatment approaches** use the principles of learning, such as reinforcement and extinction, to reduce or eliminate maladaptive behavior. These approaches are built on a fundamental assumption: Both abnormal behavior and normal behavior are *learned*.

aversive conditioning A form of therapy that reduces the frequency of undesired behavior by pairing an aversive, unpleasant stimulus with undesired behavior. (Module 40)

In this view, people who act abnormally either have failed to learn the skills they need to cope with problems of living, or they have acquired faulty skills and patterns that are being maintained through some form of reinforcement. To modify abnormal behavior, then, proponents of these approaches propose that people must learn new behavior to replace the faulty skills they have developed, and they need to unlearn their maladaptive behavior patterns (Norton & Price, 2007; Kowalik et al., 2011; Kivlighan et al., 2015).

Behavioral psychologists do not need to delve into people's pasts or their psyches. Rather than viewing abnormal behavior as a symptom of an underlying problem, they consider the abnormal behavior as the problem in need of modification. The goal of therapy is to change people's behavior to allow them to function more effectively. In this view, then, there is no problem other than the maladaptive behavior itself; if you can change that behavior, treatment is successful.

CLASSICAL CONDITIONING TREATMENTS

Suppose you bite into your favorite candy bar and find that not only is it infested with ants, but you've also swallowed a bunch of them. You immediately become sick to your stomach and throw up. Your long-term reaction? You never eat that kind of candy bar again, and it may be months before you eat any type of candy. You have learned through the basic process of classical conditioning to avoid candy so that you will not get sick and throw up.

Aversive Conditioning This simple example illustrates how a person can be classically conditioned to modify behavior. Behavior therapists use this principle in **aversive conditioning,** which aims to reduce the frequency of undesired behavior by pairing an unpleasant stimulus with undesired behavior. For example, behavior therapists might use aversive conditioning by pairing alcohol with a drug that causes severe nausea and vomiting. After the two have been paired a few times, the person associates the alcohol alone with vomiting and finds alcohol less appealing.

Behavioral approaches to treatment would seek to modify the behavior of this couple rather than to focus on the underlying causes of the behavior.
©metinkiyak/Getty Images

Aversion therapy works reasonably well with some specific kinds of disorders, including substance-abuse problems such as alcoholism and certain kinds of sexual disorders. On the other hand, critics question the long-term effectiveness of aversion therapy because rates of relapse are significant (Waters et al., 2017).

In addition, important ethical concerns surround aversion techniques such as electric shock, even though therapists use such potent stimuli only in the most extreme cases, such as with patients who harm themselves. Clearly, though, aversion therapy offers an important procedure for eliminating maladaptive responses for some period of time—a respite that provides, even if only temporarily, an opportunity to encourage more adaptive behavior patterns (Delgado, Labouliere, & Phelps, 2006; Pautassi et al., 2011; Twining et al., 2015).

systematic desensitization

A behavioral technique based on classical conditioning in which exposure to an anxiety-producing stimulus is paired with deep relaxation to extinguish the response of anxiety. (Module 40)

Systematic Desensitization Another treatment that grew out of the classical conditioning is systematic desensitization. **Systematic desensitization** is a behavioral technique in which exposure to an anxiety-producing stimulus is paired with deep relaxation in order to reduce an anxiety response. The idea is to learn to associate relaxation with a stimulus that previously produced anxiety (Choy, Fyer, & Lipsitz, 2007; Dowling, Jackson, & Thomas, 2008; Triscari et al., 2011).

Suppose, for instance, you were extremely afraid of flying. The very thought of being in an airplane would make you begin to sweat and shake, and you couldn't get yourself near enough to an airport to know how you'd react if you actually had to fly somewhere. Using systematic desensitization to treat your problem, you would first be trained in relaxation techniques by a behavior therapist and learn to relax your body fully—a highly pleasant state, as you might imagine (see Figure 2).

The next step would involve constructing a *hierarchy of fears*—a list in order of increasing severity of the things you associate with your fears. For instance, your hierarchy might resemble this one:

1. Watching a plane fly overhead
2. Going to an airport
3. Buying a ticket
4. Stepping into the plane
5. Seeing the plane door close
6. Having the plane taxi down the runway
7. Taking off
8. Being in the air

©Picturenet/Blend Images LLC

To achieve a state of relaxation, follow these steps once or twice a day.

Step 1. Choose a word or phrase that you can repeat to achieve calm. This might be a yoga mantra (*Om* or *Om Mani Padme Hum,* for instance), a word like *Peace* or *Shalom,* or any word or phrase that sounds soft and resonant to you (such as *Peace to my heart*).

Step 2. Find a quiet and comfortable place and sit down.

Step 3. Close your eyes and try to see and feel the darkness.

Step 4. Relax your muscles one by one, starting from your toes and moving slowly up to your scalp.

Step 5. Keep your breathing steady and natural, neither deep nor shallow, and repeat your word or phrase continuously.

Step 6. Do not monitor yourself, but become passive and accepting. If outside thoughts arrive, dismiss them lightly with a smile and return to your repeated word or phrase.

Step 7. Keep this up for 15 minutes. Do not set an alarm; just open your eyes when you feel it is right. If you fall asleep, that is fine.

Step 8. When you have finished, sit quietly, eyes closed, for a minute or two, then stand up.

FIGURE 2 Following these basic steps will help you achieve a sense of calmness by employing the relaxation response.

Source: Adapted from Benson, H., Kornhaber, A., Kornhaber, C., LeChanu, M. N., Zuttermeister, P. C., Myers, P., & Friedman R. (1994). Increases in positive psychological characteristics with a new relaxation-response curriculum in high school students. *Journal of Research and Development in Education, 27,* 226–231.

From the perspective of...

A Child-Care Provider How might you use systematic desensitization to help children overcome their fears?

©Rubberball/Getty Images

Once you had developed this hierarchy and learned relaxation techniques, you would learn to associate the two sets of responses. To do this, your therapist might ask you to put yourself into a relaxed state and then imagine yourself in the first situation identified in your hierarchy. Once you could consider that first step while remaining relaxed, you would move on to the next situation. Eventually, you would move up the hierarchy in gradual stages until you could imagine yourself being in the air without experiencing anxiety. Ultimately, you would be asked to make a visit to an airport and later to take a flight.

The newest form of exposure therapy makes use of virtual reality technology. In *virtual reality exposure therapy,* clients wear virtual reality goggles that provide highly realistic depictions of stimuli that trigger anxiety. For example, someone who fears heights might be taken virtually to the top of a skyscraper. Or a person who has developed anxiety about driving after a car crash could be taken virtually to the intersection where the crash occurred. Once at the (virtual) site of the source of their anxiety, clients can be treated with traditional systematic desensitization techniques.

The extreme realism of virtual reality ensures that clients face their fears in a highly impactful manner, yet one that can be controlled more precisely than traditional means permit. The treatment is promising, although it is so new that the long-term effectiveness is not yet clear (Metz, 2017; McClay et al., 2017; North & North, 2017).

Flooding Treatments Although systematic desensitization has proven to be a successful treatment, today it is often replaced with a less-complicated form of therapy called flooding. **Flooding** is a behavioral treatment for anxiety in which people are suddenly confronted with a stimulus that they fear. However, unlike systematic desensitization, relaxation training is not included. The goal behind flooding is to allow the maladaptive response of anxiety or avoidance to become extinct (Havermans et al., 2007; Hofmann, 2007; Bush, 2008).

For example, a patient who has a deep fear of germs may be made to soil her hands in dirt and to keep them dirty for hours. For a person with a fear of germs, initially this is a highly anxiety-producing situation. After a few hours, however, the anxiety will decline, leading to extinction of the anxiety.

Flooding has proved to be an effective treatment for a number of problems, including phobias, anxiety disorders, and even impotence and fear of sexual contact. Through this technique, people can learn to enjoy the things they once feared (Franklin, March, & Garcia, 2007; Powers & Emmelkamp, 2008; Tuerk et al., 2011).

OPERANT CONDITIONING TECHNIQUES

Some behavioral approaches make use of the operant conditioning principles that we discussed in the chapter on learning. These

Study Alert
To help remember the concept of hierarchy of fears, think of something that you are afraid of and construct your own hierarchy of fears.

flooding A behavioral treatment for anxiety in which people are suddenly confronted with a stimulus that they fear. (Module 40)

Virtual reality exposure therapy immerses clients in highly realistic depictions of stimuli that trigger anxiety.
©Monika Wisniewska/Alamy Stock Photo

approaches are based on the notion that we should reward people for carrying out desirable behavior and extinguish undesirable behavior by either ignoring it or punishing it.

One example of the systematic application of operant conditioning principles is the *token system*, which rewards a person for desired behavior with a token such as a poker chip or some kind of play money. The person can later exchange the chip or play money for an actual reward, such as real money or food.

Token systems are most frequently used in institutions for people with relatively serious problems and sometimes with children as a classroom-management technique. The system resembles what parents do when they give children money for being well behaved–money that the children can later exchange for something they want. The desired behavior may range from simple things such as keeping one's room neat to personal grooming and interacting with other people. In institutions, patients can exchange tokens for some object or activity, such as snacks, new clothes, or, in extreme cases, sleeping in one's own bed rather than in a sleeping bag on the floor.

Contingency contracting is a variant of the token system that has proved quite effective in modifying behavior. In *contingency contracting*, the therapist and client prepare a written agreement, known as a contract. The contract states a series of behavioral goals the client hopes to achieve. It also specifies positive consequences for the client if she or he reaches those goals–usually an explicit reward such as money or privileges.

Contingency contracts also may state negative consequences if clients do not meet their goals. For example, clients who are trying to quit smoking might write out a check to a cause they have no interest in supporting (for instance, the National Rifle Association if they are strong supporters of gun control). If the client smokes on a given day, the therapist will mail the check.

Behavior therapists also use observational learning to systematically teach people new skills and ways of handling their fears and anxieties. *Observational learning* occurs through observing the behavior of others. For example, for clients who are socially fearful, a therapist may model and teach basic social skills, such as maintaining eye contact during conversation and acting assertively. Similarly, children with dog phobias have been able to overcome their fears by watching another child–called the "Fearless Peer"–repeatedly walk up to a dog, touch it, pet it, and finally play with it. Observational learning, then, can play a role in resolving some kinds of behavior difficulties, especially if the person being observed receives a reward for his or her behavior (Bandura, Grusec, & Menlove, 1967; Helsen, Goubert, & Vlaeyen, 2013; Waismeyer & Meltzoff, 2017).

EVALUATING BEHAVIOR THERAPY

Behavior therapy works especially well for eliminating anxiety disorders, treating phobias and compulsions, establishing control over impulses, and learning complex social skills to replace maladaptive behavior. More than any of the other therapeutic techniques, it provides methods that nonprofessionals can use to change their own behavior. Moreover, it is efficient because it focuses on solving carefully defined problems (Richard & Lauterbach, 2006; Barlow, 2007; Kertz et al., 2015).

Critics of behavior therapy believe that because it emphasizes changing external behavior, it ignores people's inner life–their thoughts and anxieties. Consequently, people do not necessarily gain insight into thoughts and expectations that may be fostering their maladaptive behavior.

On the other hand, neuroscientific evidence shows that behavioral treatments can produce actual changes in brain functioning, which suggests that behavioral treatments can produce changes beyond external behavior. For example, one experiment looked at the neurological reactions of patients with borderline personality disorder who participated in a 12-week behavioral therapy program. Compared with a control group composed of people who did not have the disorder, the patients showed significant changes in their reactions to highly arousing, emotion-evoking stimuli. Following therapy, the patients' neurological functioning was more similar to those without the disorder than it was prior to therapy (Schnell & Herpertz, 2007).

Cognitive Approaches to Therapy

If you assumed that illogical thoughts and beliefs lie at the heart of psychological disorders, wouldn't the most direct treatment route be to teach people new, more adaptive modes of thinking? The answer is yes, according to psychologists who take a cognitive approach to treatment.

Cognitive treatment approaches teach people to think in more adaptive ways by changing their dysfunctional cognitions about the world and themselves. In contrast to behavior therapists, who primarily focus on modifying external behavior, cognitive therapists focus on changing the way people think. Because they often use basic principles of learning, the methods they employ are sometimes referred to as the **cognitive-behavioral approach** (Beck & Rector, 2005; Kalodner, 2011; Sivec et al., 2017).

Although cognitive treatment approaches take many forms, they all share the assumption that anxiety, depression, and negative emotions develop from maladaptive thinking. Accordingly, cognitive treatments seek to change the thought patterns that lead to getting "stuck" in dysfunctional ways of thinking. Therapists systematically teach clients to challenge their assumptions and adopt new approaches to old problems.

Cognitive therapy is relatively short term and usually lasts a maximum of 20 sessions. Therapy tends to be highly structured and focused on concrete problems. Therapists often begin by teaching the theory behind the approach and then continue to take an active role throughout the course of therapy by acting as a combination of teacher, coach, and partner.

One example of cognitive therapy is rational-emotive behavior therapy. **Rational-emotive behavior therapy** attempts to restructure a person's belief system into a more realistic, rational, and logical set of views. By adopting more accurate thought patterns, it is assumed that people will lead more psychologically healthy lives.

Building on these views, psychologist Albert Ellis (**2004**) suggests that many people lead unhappy lives and suffer from psychological disorders because they harbor irrational, unrealistic ideas such as these:

- We need the love or approval of virtually every significant other person for everything we do.
- We should be thoroughly competent, adequate, and successful in all possible respects in order to consider ourselves worthwhile.
- It is horrible when things don't turn out the way we want them to.

Such irrational beliefs trigger negative emotions, which in turn support the irrational beliefs and lead to a self-defeating cycle. Ellis calls it the A-B-C model in which negative activating conditions (A) lead to the activation of an irrational belief system (B), which in turn leads to emotional consequences (C). For example, if a person experiences the breakup of a close relationship (A) and holds the irrational belief (B) that "I'll never be loved again," this triggers negative emotions (C) that in turn feed back into support of the irrational belief (see Figure 3).

cognitive treatment approaches
Treatment approaches that teach people to think in more adaptive ways by changing their dysfunctional cognitions about the world and themselves. (Module 40)

cognitive-behavioral approach
A treatment approach that incorporates basic principles of learning to change the way people think. (Module 40)

rational-emotive behavior therapy
A form of therapy that attempts to restructure a person's belief system into a more realistic, rational, and logical set of views by challenging dysfunctional beliefs that maintain irrational behavior. (Module 40)

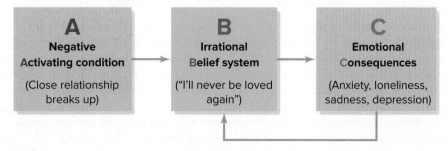

FIGURE 3 In the A-B-C model of rational-emotive behavior therapy, negative activating conditions (A) lead to the activation of an irrational belief system (B), which leads to emotional consequences (C). Those emotional consequences then feed back and support the belief system. At what steps in the model could change occur as a result of rational-emotive behavior therapy?
Source: Ellis, A. (1974). *Growth through reason.* Hollywood, CA: Wilshire Books.

The goal of rational-emotive therapy is to help clients eliminate maladaptive thoughts and beliefs and adopt more effective thinking. To accomplish this goal, therapists take an active, directive role during therapy and openly challenge patterns of thought that appear to be dysfunctional. Consider this example:

> Martha: The basic problem is that I'm worried about my family. I'm worried about money. And I never seem to be able to relax.
>
> Therapist: Why are you worried about your family?. . . What's to be concerned about? They have certain demands which you don't want to adhere to.
>
> Martha: I was brought up to think that I mustn't be selfish.
>
> Therapist: Oh, we'll have to knock that out of your head!
>
> Martha: My mother feels that I shouldn't have left home–that my place is with them. There are nagging doubts about what I should–
>
> Therapist: Why are there doubts? Why should you?
>
> Martha: I think it's a feeling I was brought up with that you always have to give of yourself. If you think of yourself, you're wrong.
>
> Therapist: That's a belief. Why do you have to keep believing that–at your age? You believed a lot of superstitions when you were younger. Why do you have to retain them? Your parents indoctrinated you with this nonsense, because that's their belief. . . . Who needs that philosophy? All it's gotten you, so far, is guilt. (Ellis, 1974)

By poking holes in Martha's reasoning, the therapist is attempting to help her adopt a more realistic view of herself and her circumstances (Ellis, 2002; Dryden & David, 2008).

Another influential form of therapy that builds on a cognitive perspective is that of Aaron Beck (Beck, 2004; Beck, Davis, & Freeman, 2015). Like rational-emotive behavior therapy, Beck's *cognitive behavior therapy* aims to change people's illogical thoughts about themselves and the world.

However, cognitive behavior therapy is considerably less confrontational and challenging than rational-emotive behavior therapy is. Instead of the therapist actively arguing with clients about their dysfunctional cognitions, cognitive behavior therapists more often play the role of teacher. Therapists urge clients to obtain information on their own that will lead them to discard their inaccurate thinking through a process of cognitive appraisal.

In *cognitive appraisal*, clients are asked to evaluate situations, themselves, and others in terms of their memories, values, beliefs, thoughts, and expectations. During the course of treatment, therapists help clients discover ways of thinking more appropriately about themselves and others (Beck, Freeman, & Davis, 2004; Moorey, 2007; Leaper, Brown, & Ayres, 2013; also see *Neuroscience in Your Life*).

Cognitive appraisal can also be used to help change students' attributions about the causes of their academic success or failure. For example, rather than attributing academic failure to a lack of intelligence, students can be helped to see that their performance is related to the amount of hard work and perseverance they invest in academic tasks (Elliot, Dweck, & Yeager, 2017).

EVALUATING COGNITIVE APPROACHES TO THERAPY

Cognitive approaches to therapy have proved successful in dealing with a broad range of disorders, including anxiety disorders, depression, substance abuse, and eating disorders. Furthermore, the willingness of cognitive therapists to incorporate additional treatment approaches (e.g., combining cognitive and behavioral techniques in cognitive behavior therapy) has made this approach a particularly effective form of treatment (Mitte, 2005; Ishikawa et al., 2007; Bhar et al., 2008).

At the same time, critics have pointed out that the focus on helping people to think more rationally ignores the fact that life is in reality sometimes irrational. Changing one's assumptions to make them more reasonable and logical thus may not always be helpful–even assuming it is possible to bring about true cognitive change. Still, the success of cognitive approaches has made it one of the most frequently employed therapies (Beck & Rector, 2005; Fresco, 2013).

PsychTech
Psychologist David Mohr found that an Internet-based treatment for depression in which patients logged into a website and also received e-mail and telephone support was effective in reducing depressive episodes.

NEUROSCIENCE IN YOUR LIFE: HOW COGNITIVE BEHAVIORAL THERAPY CHANGES YOUR BRAIN

Psychotherapy has been shown to be effective for multiple psychological disorders. But does it show measurable changes in the brain? Recent research examining the effects of psychotherapy on brain structure and function suggests that it does. Specifically, neuroscientists compared the structure and function of the amygdala, the brain area involved in fear and anxiety, in patients with social anxiety disorder before and after 9 weeks of online cognitive behavioral therapy (CBT). Compared to those who had alternative treatments, the patients who had CBT were less anxious and showed changes in brain volume and activity (see images). These results highlight the fact that psychological therapies have an impact on the brain related to the reduction of symptoms of psychological disorders (Mansson et al., 2016).

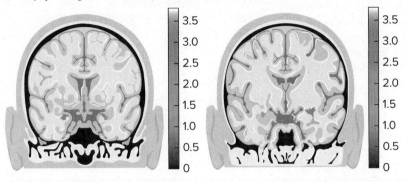

The images show that the CBT group had smaller left amygdala (shown in blue in the left image) and less active right amygdala (shown in blue in the right image) after CBT than the alternative treatment group.

Source: Adapted from Mansson, K. N., Salami, A., Frick, A., Carlbring, P., Andersson, G., Furmark, T., & Boraxbekk, C. J. (2016). Neuroplasticity in response to cognitive behavior therapy for social anxiety disorder. *Translational Psychiatry, 6,* e727. doi: 10.1038/tp.2015.218

RECAP/EVALUATE/RETHINK

RECAP

LO 40-1 What are the goals of psychologically based and biologically based treatment approaches?

- Psychotherapy (psychologically based therapy) and biomedical therapy (biologically based therapy) share the goal of resolving psychological problems by modifying people's thoughts, feelings, expectations, evaluations, and ultimately behavior.

LO 40-2 What are the psychodynamic, behavioral, and cognitive approaches to treatment?

- Psychoanalytic approaches seek to bring unresolved past conflicts and unacceptable impulses from the unconscious into the conscious, where patients may deal with the problems more effectively. To do this, therapists use techniques such as free association and dream interpretation.

- Behavioral approaches to treatment view abnormal behavior as the problem rather than viewing that behavior as a symptom of some underlying cause. To bring about a "cure," this view suggests that the outward behavior must be changed by using methods such as aversive conditioning, systematic desensitization, observational learning, token systems, and contingency contracting.

- Cognitive approaches to treatment consider that the goal of therapy is to help a person restructure his or her faulty belief system into a more realistic, rational, and logical view of the world. Two examples of cognitive treatments are the rational-emotive behavior therapy and cognitive behavior therapy.

EVALUATE

1. Match the following mental health practitioners with the appropriate description.

   1. Psychiatrist   **a.** PhD specializing in the treatment of psychological disorders
   2. Clinical psychologist   **b.** Professional specializing in Freudian therapy techniques
   3. Counseling psychologist   **c.** MD trained in abnormal behavior
   4. Psychoanalyst   **d.** PhD specializing in the adjustment of day-to-day problems

2. According to Freud, people use _____ _____ as a means of preventing unwanted impulses from intruding on conscious thought.

3. In dream interpretation, a psychoanalyst must learn to distinguish between the _____ content of a dream, which is what appears on the surface, and the _____ content, its underlying meaning.

4. Which of the following treatments deals with phobias by gradual exposure to the item producing the fear?
   a. Systematic desensitization
   b. Partial reinforcement
   c. Behavioral self-management
   d. Aversion therapy

RETHINK

1. In what ways are psychoanalysis and cognitive therapy similar, and how do they differ?
2. How might you examine the reliability of dream interpretation?

Answers to Evaluate Questions

1. 1-c, 2-a, 3-d, 4-b; 2. defense mechanisms; 3. manifest, latent; 4. a

KEY TERMS

psychotherapy	transference	systematic desensitization	cognitive-behavioral
biomedical therapy	behavioral treatment	flooding	approach
psychodynamic therapy	approaches	cognitive treatment	rational-emotive behavior
psychoanalysis	aversive conditioning	approaches	therapy

Module 41

Psychotherapy: Humanistic, Interpersonal, and Group Approaches to Treatment

Humanistic Therapy

As you know from your own experience, a student cannot master the material covered in a course without some hard work, no matter how good the teacher and the textbook are. *You must* take the time to study, memorize the vocabulary, and learn the concepts. Nobody else can do it for you. If you choose to put in the effort, you'll succeed; if you don't, you'll fail. The responsibility is primarily yours.

Humanistic therapy draws on this philosophical perspective of self-responsibility in developing treatment techniques. The many different types of therapy that fit into this category have a similar rationale: We have control of our own behavior, we can make choices about the kinds of lives we want to live, and it is up to us to solve the difficulties we encounter in our daily lives.

Humanistic therapists believe that people naturally are motivated to strive for self-actualization. As we discussed in the chapter on motivation, *self-actualization* is the term that clinical psychologist Abraham Maslow used to describe the state of self-fulfillment in which people realize their highest potentials in their own unique way.

Instead of acting in the more directive manner of some psychodynamic and behavioral approaches, humanistic therapists view themselves as guides or facilitators. Therapists using humanistic techniques seek to help people understand themselves and find ways to come closer to the ideal they hold for themselves. In this view, psychological disorders result from the inability to find meaning in life, from feelings of loneliness, and from a lack of connection to others (Watson, Goldman, & Greenberg, 2011; Lewis & Umbreit, 2015).

Humanistic approaches have produced many therapeutic techniques. Among the most important is person-centered therapy.

PERSON-CENTERED THERAPY

Consider the following therapy session excerpt:

> Alice: I was thinking about this business of standards. I somehow developed a sort of a knack, I guess, of—well—habit—of trying to make people feel at ease around me, or to make things go along smoothly. . . .
>
> Therapist: In other words, what you did was always in the direction of trying to keep things smooth and to make other people feel better and to smooth the situation.
>
> Alice: Yes. I think that's what it was. Now the reason why I did it probably was—I mean, not that I was a good little Samaritan going around making other people happy, but that was probably the role that felt easiest for me to play. . . .
>
> Therapist: You feel that for a long time you've been playing the role of kind of smoothing out the frictions or differences or what not. . . .
>
> Alice: M-hm.
>
> Therapist: Rather than having any opinion or reaction of your own in the situation. Is that it? (Rogers, 1951)

LEARNING OUTCOMES

LO 41-1 What are the humanistic approaches to treatment?

LO 41-2 What is interpersonal therapy?

LO 41-3 How does group therapy differ from individual types of therapy?

LO 41-4 How effective is psychotherapy, and which kind of psychotherapy works best in a given situation?

humanistic therapy Therapy in which the underlying rationale is that people have control of their behavior, can make choices about their lives, and are essentially responsible for solving their own problems. (Module 41)

Humanistic therapy focuses on self-responsibility.

©Don Hammond/Design Pics/Getty Images

The therapist does not interpret or answer the questions the client has raised. Instead, the therapist clarifies or reflects back what the client has said (e.g., "In other words, what you did. . . ."; "You feel that. . . ."; "Is that it?"). This therapeutic technique, known as *nondirective counseling,* is at the heart of person-centered therapy, which was first practiced by Carl Rogers in the mid-20th century (Raskin & Rogers, 1989).

person-centered therapy Therapy in which the goal is to reach one's potential for self-actualization. (Module 41)

Person-centered therapy (also called *client-centered therapy*) aims to enable people to reach their potential for self-actualization. By providing a warm and accepting environment, therapists hope to motivate clients to air their problems and feelings. In turn, this enables clients to make realistic and constructive choices and decisions about the things that bother them in their current lives (Bohart, 2006; Cooper & McLeod, 2011; McLean et al., 2017).

Instead of directing the choices clients make, therapists provide what Rogers calls unconditional positive regard. *Unconditional positive regard* involves providing wholehearted acceptance, support, and understanding, and no disapproval, no matter what feelings and attitudes a client expresses. By doing this, therapists hope to create an atmosphere that enables clients to come to decisions that can improve their lives (Vieira & Freire, 2006; Patterson & Joseph, 2013).

Study Alert

To better remember the concept of unconditional positive regard, try offering it to a friend during a conversation by showing your support, acceptance, and understanding no matter what thought or attitude your friend expresses.

Furnishing unconditional positive regard does not mean that therapists must approve of everything their clients say or do. Rather, therapists need to communicate that they are caring, nonjudgmental, and *empathetic*–that is, understanding of a client's emotional experiences (Fearing & Clark, 2000).

Today, therapists using person-centered therapy techniques are more directive with their clients. Rather than merely reflecting back their clients' statements, therapists actively nudge clients toward insights. However, therapists still view their clients' insights as central to the therapeutic process.

EVALUATING HUMANISTIC APPROACHES TO THERAPY

The notion that psychological disorders result from restricted growth potential appeals philosophically to many people. Furthermore, when humanistic therapists acknowledge that the freedom we possess can lead to psychological difficulties, clients find an unusually supportive environment for therapy. In turn, this atmosphere can help clients discover solutions to difficult psychological problems (Cooper, 2007).

However, humanistic treatments lack specificity, a problem that has troubled their critics. Humanistic approaches are not very precise and are probably the least scientifically and theoretically developed type of treatment. Moreover, this form of treatment works best for the same type of highly verbal client who profits most from psychoanalytic treatment.

Interpersonal Therapy

interpersonal therapy (IPT) Short-term therapy that focuses on the context of current social relationships, helping patients to control their moods and emotions. (Module 41)

Interpersonal therapy (IPT) is short-term therapy designed to help patients control their moods and emotions by focusing on the context of their current social relationships. Although its roots stem from psychodynamic approaches, interpersonal therapy concentrates more on the here and now with the goal of improving a client's existing relationships. It typically focuses on interpersonal issues such as conflicts with others, social skills issues, role transitions (such as divorce), or grief (Weissman, Markowitz, & Klerman, 2007; Stangier et al., 2011; Dimaggio et al., 2015).

Interpersonal therapy is more active and directive than are traditional psychodynamic approaches, and sessions are more structured. The approach makes no assumptions about the underlying causes of psychological disorders but focuses on the interpersonal context in which a disorder is developed and maintained. It also tends to be shorter than traditional psychodynamic approaches and typically lasts only 12-16 weeks. During those sessions, therapists make concrete suggestions on improving relations with others and actively offer recommendations and advice.

APPLYING PSYCHOLOGY IN THE 21ST CENTURY

CLICK HERE FOR THERAPY

You probably have an app for music, an app for ride sharing, even an app for banking. So why not one for therapy? While it may seem to trivialize the process, online therapy is real. Despite some clear limitations and potential pitfalls, it's proving to be a useful and effective channel for delivering mental health services (Novotney, 2017).

The potential benefits for online therapy clients are considerable. Therapy sessions can be scheduled with ease for convenient times, and transportation isn't an issue. Therapy is also more available to clients who work odd hours or travel frequently. Furthermore, depending on their psychological problem, some clients may lack the emotional strength to bring themselves to a real-world therapy session, in which case online therapy brings the therapist to them. Sessions can be conducted in real-time teleconferencing style, by text-based chat, or even asynchronously–that is, not in real time but, for example, by exchanging emails (Reynolds et al., 2013).

Another advantage of online therapy is that it normalizes mental health care by

©Agenturfotografin/Shutterstock

removing many of the traditional barriers and integrating it into people's daily lives. Indeed, online therapy can even act as a gateway to broader mental health services: some research shows that when clients see that therapy can be a force for positive change in their lives, they are more likely to seek out further mental health care if they need it (Jones et al., 2014).

On the other hand, online therapy has some significant limitations. For one thing, it's not the best channel for treating clients with serious mental disorders who may have difficulty adequately connecting with a therapist. Furthermore, some clients find it cold and impersonal, and therapists may find it difficult to assess clients accurately without direct face-to-face contact. Finally, conducting therapy via telecommunications companies may not be in full compliance with privacy laws and other codes of conduct for therapists (Novotney, 2017).

Despite these limitations, online therapy clearly holds great promise for making mental health services more accessible. But more research needs to be done to determine the answer to the bottom-line question: Does online therapy alleviate psychological disorders as well as more traditional, face-to-face therapy (Rozental et al., 2017)?

> **RETHINK**
> - Why might a client would prefer face-to-face therapy to an online session?
> - How would you investigate the professional qualifications of an online therapist?

Considerable research supports the effectiveness of interpersonal therapy. It is especially effective in dealing with depression, anxiety, addictions, and eating disorders (Miller et al., 2008; Bohn et al., 2013; Dimaggio et al., 2017; also see *Applying Psychology in the 21st Century*).

Group Therapies

Although most treatment takes place between a single individual and a therapist, some forms of therapy involve groups of people seeking treatment. In **group therapy,** several unrelated people meet with a therapist to discuss some aspect of their psychological functioning.

People typically discuss with the group their problems, which often center on a common difficulty, such as alcoholism or a lack of social skills. The other members of the group provide emotional support and dispense advice on ways they have coped effectively with similar problems (Scaturo, 2004; Rigby & Waite, 2007; Schachter, 2011).

Groups vary greatly in terms of the particular model they employ; there are psychoanalytic groups, humanistic groups, and groups corresponding to the other therapeutic approaches. Furthermore, groups also differ with regard to the degree of guidance the therapist provides. In some, the therapist is quite directive; in others, the members

group therapy Therapy in which people meet in a group with a therapist to discuss problems. (Module 41)

of the group set their own agenda and determine how the group will proceed (Beck & Lewis, 2000; Stockton, Morran, & Krieger, 2004; Arlo, 2017).

Because several people are treated simultaneously in group therapy, it is a much more economical means of treatment than individual psychotherapy is. On the other hand, critics argue that group settings lack the individual attention inherent in one-to-one therapy and that especially shy and withdrawn individuals may not receive the attention they need in a group setting.

FAMILY THERAPY

family therapy An approach that focuses on the family and its dynamics. (Module 41)

One specialized form of group therapy is family therapy. As the name implies, **family therapy** involves two or more family members, one (or more) of whose problems led to treatment. But rather than focusing simply on the members of the family who present the initial problem, family therapists consider the family as a unit to which each member contributes. By meeting with the entire family simultaneously, family therapists try to understand how the family members interact with one another (Strong & Tomm, 2007; Bischoff et al., 2011).

Family therapists view the family as a system, and they assume that individuals cannot improve without understanding the conflicts that exist among family members. Thus, therapists expect each member of a family to contribute to the resolution of the problem being addressed (Wretman, 2016).

Family therapists believe that family members often fall into rigid roles or patterns of behavior. For example, one person may act as the victim, another as a bully, and so forth. In their view, that system of roles supports and perpetuates family disturbances. One goal of family therapy, then, is to get family members to adopt new, more constructive patterns of behavior and to get members of the family to view others in new ways (Sori, 2006; Conoley et al., 2015).

SELF-HELP THERAPY

In self-help therapy, people with similar problems get together to discuss their shared feelings and experiences, sometimes without any formal therapist participating. For example, people who have recently experienced the death of a spouse might meet in a *bereavement support group*, or college students may get together to discuss their adjustment to college.

One of the best-known self-help groups is Alcoholics Anonymous (AA), designed to help members deal with alcohol-related problems. AA prescribes 12 steps that alcoholics must pass through on their road to recovery. Alcoholics begin with an admission that they are alcoholics and powerless over alcohol and move through additional steps in the process of recovery by attending frequent AA meetings. Proponents of AA believe that no one is fully cured of alcoholism and that members should permanently think of themselves as recovering alcoholics (Greenfield & Tonigan, 2013; Best, 2017).

Alcoholics Anonymous does not work for everyone. For one thing, there is a strong spiritual component and emphasis on the need for a higher power that do not appeal to some people. More important, some critics say that AA's requirement of total abstinence from alcohol may not be an effective or realistic approach (Kelly et al., 2012).

Still, AA provides more treatment for alcoholics than does any other therapy. Furthermore, research studies show that AA and other 12-step programs (such as Narcotics Anonymous) can be as successful in treating alcohol and other substance-abuse problems as traditional types of therapy (Galanter, 2007; Gossop, Stewart, & Marsden, 2008; Pagano et al., 2013).

In group therapy, people with psychological difficulties meet with a therapist to discuss their problems.

©Jon Bradley/The Image Bank/Getty Images

Evaluating Psychotherapy: Does Therapy Work?

Your best friend, Ben, comes to you because he just hasn't been feeling right about things lately. He's upset because he and his girlfriend aren't getting along, but his difficulties go beyond that. He can't concentrate on his studies, has a lot of trouble getting to sleep, and–this is what really bothers him–has begun to think that people are ganging up on him, talking about him behind his back. It seems that no one really cares about or understands him or makes any effort to see why he's become so miserable.

Ben knows that he ought to get *some* kind of help, but he is not sure where to turn. He is fairly skeptical of psychologists and thinks that a lot of what they say is just mumbo-jumbo, but he's willing to put his doubts aside and try anything to feel better. He also knows there are many different types of therapy, and he doesn't have a clue about which would be best for him. He turns to you for advice because he knows you are taking a psychology course. He asks, "Which kind of therapy works best?"

IS THERAPY EFFECTIVE?

This question requires a complex response. In fact, identifying the single most appropriate form of treatment is a controversial and still unresolved task for psychologists specializing in psychological disorders. In fact, even before considering whether one form of therapy works better than another, we need to determine whether therapy in any form effectively alleviates psychological disturbances.

Until the 1950s, most people simply assumed that therapy was effective. But in 1952, psychologist Hans Eysenck published an historically important study challenging that assumption. He claimed that people who received psychodynamic treatment and related therapies were no better off at the end of treatment than were people who were placed on a waiting list for treatment but never received it. Eysenck concluded that people would go into **spontaneous remission,** recovery without formal treatment, if they were simply left alone–certainly a cheaper and simpler process.

Although other psychologists quickly challenged Eysenck's conclusions, his review stimulated a continuing stream of better controlled, more carefully crafted studies on the effectiveness of psychotherapy. Today most psychologists agree: Therapy does work. Several comprehensive reviews indicate that therapy brings about greater improvement than no treatment at all, with the rate of spontaneous remission being fairly low. In most cases, then, the symptoms of abnormal behavior do not go away by themselves if left untreated–although the issue continues to be hotly debated (Lutz et al., 2006; Gaudiano & Miller, 2013; Abbass et al., 2017).

WHICH KIND OF THERAPY WORKS BEST?

Almost all psychologists agree that psychotherapeutic treatment *in general* is more effective than no treatment at all. However, the question of what specific *kind* of treatment is superior to others has not been answered definitively (Westen, Novotny, & Thompson-Brenner, 2004; Abboud, 2005; Tryer et al., 2015).

For instance, one classic study comparing the effectiveness of various approaches found that although success rates vary somewhat by treatment form, most treatments show fairly equal success rates. As Figure 1 indicates, the rates ranged from about 75–80% greater success for treated compared with untreated individuals. Behavioral and cognitive approaches tended to be slightly more successful, but that result may have been due to differences in the severity of the cases treated (Smith, Glass, & Miller, 1980; Orwin & Condray, 1984).

Other research, which relies on *meta-analysis* in which data from a large number of studies are statistically combined, yields similar general conclusions. Furthermore, a

Study Alert
Pay special attention to the discussion of (1) whether therapy is effective in general and (2) what specific types of therapy are effective because these are key issues for therapists.

spontaneous remission Recovery without formal treatment. (Module 41)

FIGURE 1 Estimates of the effectiveness of types of treatment, in comparison to control groups of untreated people. The percentage scores show how much more effective a specific type of treatment is for the average patient compared with those who have had no treatment. For example, people given psychodynamic treatment score, on average, more positively on outcome measures than do about 80% of untreated people.

Source: Adapted from Smith, M. L., Glass, G. V., & Miller, T. I. (1980). *The benefits of psychotherapy.* Baltimore: The Johns Hopkins University Press.

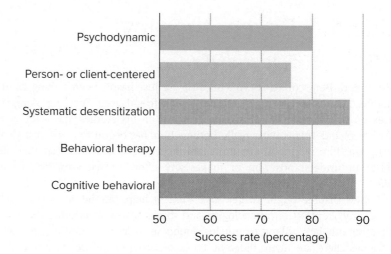

large survey of 186,000 individuals found that respondents felt they had benefited substantially from psychotherapy. However, there was little difference in "consumer satisfaction" on the basis of the specific type of treatment they had received (Seligman, 1995; Cuijpers et al., 2008; Dakin & Areán, 2013).

In short, converging evidence allows us to draw several conclusions about the effectiveness of psychotherapy:

- *For most people, psychotherapy is effective.* This conclusion holds over different lengths of treatment, specific kinds of psychological disorders, and various types of treatment. Thus, the question, "Does psychotherapy work?" appears to have been answered convincingly: It does (Westen, Novotny, & Thompson-Brenner, 2004; Payne & Marcus, 2008; Gaudiano & Miller, 2013).

- *On the other hand, psychotherapy doesn't work for everyone.* As many as 10% of people treated show no improvement–or actually deteriorated (Pretzer & Beck, 2005; Coffman et al., 2007; Lilienfeld, 2007).

- *No single form of therapy works best for every problem, and certain specific types of treatment are better, although not invariably, for specific types of problems.* For example, cognitive therapy works especially well for panic disorders, and flooding therapy relieves specific phobias effectively. However, there are exceptions to these generalizations, and often the differences in success rates for different types of treatment are not substantial (Miller & Magruder, 1999; Westen, Novotny, & Thompson-Brenner, 2004).

- *Most therapies share several basic similar elements.* Despite the fact that the specific methods used in different therapies are very different from one another, there are several common themes that lead them to be effective. These elements include the opportunity for a client to develop a positive relationship with a therapist, an explanation or interpretation of a client's symptoms, and confrontation of negative emotions. The fact that these common elements exist in most therapies makes it difficult to compare one treatment against another (Norcross, 2002; Norcross, Beutler, & Levant, 2006).

Consequently, there is no single, definitive answer to the broad question, "Which therapy works best?" because of the complexity in sorting out the various factors that enter into successful therapy. Recently, however, clinicians and researchers have reframed the question by focusing on evidence-based psychotherapy practice. *Evidence-based psychotherapy practice* seeks to use research findings to determine the best practices for treating a specific disorder. To determine best practices, researchers use clinical interviews, client self-reports of improvement in quality of life, reductions in symptoms, observations of behavior, and other outcomes to compare different therapies. By using objective research findings, clinicians are increasingly able to determine the most effective treatment for a specific disorder (American Psychological Association Presidential Task Force, 2006; Kazdin, 2008; Gaudiano & Miller, 2013).

Because no single type of psychotherapy is invariably effective for every individual, some therapists use an eclectic approach to therapy. In an *eclectic approach to therapy,* therapists use a variety of techniques, thus integrating several perspectives, to treat a person's problems. By employing more than one approach, therapists can choose the appropriate mix of evidence-based treatments to match the individual's specific needs. Furthermore, therapists with certain personal characteristics may work better with particular individuals and types of treatments, and—as we consider next—even racial and ethnic factors may be related to the success of treatment (Chambless et al., 2006; Hays, 2008; Kertz et al., 2015).

 # Exploring Diversity

Racial and Ethnic Factors in Treatment: Should Therapists Be Color-Blind?

Consider the following case report written by a school counselor about Jimmy Jones, a 12-year-old student who was referred to a counselor because of his lack of interest in schoolwork:

> Jimmy does not pay attention, daydreams often, and frequently falls asleep during class. There is a strong possibility that Jimmy is harboring repressed rage that needs to be ventilated and dealt with. His inability to directly express his anger had led him to adopt passive-aggressive means of expressing hostility, i.e., inattentiveness, daydreaming, falling asleep. It is recommended that Jimmy be seen for intensive counseling to discover the basis of the anger. (Sue & Sue, 1990)

The counselor was wrong, however. Rather than suffering from "repressed rage," Jimmy lived in a poverty-stricken and disorganized home. Because of overcrowding at his house, he did not get enough sleep and consequently was tired the next day. Frequently, he was also hungry. In short, the stresses arising from his environment and not any deep-seated psychological disturbances caused his problems.

This incident underscores the importance of taking people's environmental and cultural backgrounds into account during treatment for psychological disorders. In particular, members of racial and ethnic minority groups, especially those who are also poor, may behave in ways that help them deal with a society that discriminates against them. As a consequence, behavior that may signal psychological disorder in middle-class and upper-class whites may simply be adaptive in people from other racial and socioeconomic groups. For instance, characteristically suspicious and distrustful people may be displaying a survival strategy to protect themselves from psychological and physical injury rather than suffering from a psychological disturbance (Paniagua, 2000; Tseng, 2003; Pottick et al., 2007).

In fact, therapists must question some basic assumptions of psychotherapy when dealing with racial, ethnic, and cultural minority group members. For example, compared with the dominant culture, Asian and Latino cultures typically place much greater emphasis on the group, family, and society. When an Asian or Latino faces a critical decision, the family helps make it—a cultural practice suggesting that family members should also play a role in psychological treatment. Similarly, the traditional Chinese recommendation for dealing with depression or anxiety is to urge people who experience such problems to avoid thinking about whatever is upsetting them. Consider how this advice contrasts with treatment approaches

Therapists' interpretation of their clients' behavior is influenced by racial, ethnic, cultural, and social class backgrounds of the clients. For example, this man could be seen as lazy, drunk, or merely exhausted, depending on the context.
©Arts Illustrated Studios/Shutterstock

that emphasize the value of insight (Ponterotto, Gretchen, & Chauhan, 2001; McCarthy, 2005; Leitner, 2007).

Clearly, therapists *cannot* be "color-blind." Instead, they must take into account the racial, ethnic, cultural, and social class backgrounds of their clients in determining the nature of a psychological disorder and the course of treatment (Pedersen et al., 2002; Hays, 2008; Moodley, Gielen, & Wu, 2013).

From the perspective of...

A Social Worker How might the types of therapies you employ vary depending on a client's cultural and socioeconomic background?

©Sam Edwards/age fotostock

RECAP/EVALUATE/RETHINK

RECAP

LO 41-1 What are humanistic approaches to treatment?

- Humanistic therapy is based on the premise that people have control of their behavior, that they can make choices about their lives, and that it is up to them to solve their own problems. Humanistic therapies, which take a non-directive approach, include person-centered therapy.

LO 41-2 What is interpersonal therapy?

- Interpersonal therapy focuses on interpersonal relation-ships and strives for immediate improvement during short-term therapy.

LO 41-3 How does group therapy differ from individual types of therapy?

- In group therapy, several unrelated people meet with a therapist to discuss some aspect of their psychological functioning and often center on a common problem.

LO 41-4 How effective is psychotherapy, and which kind of psychotherapy works best in a given situation?

- Most research suggests that, in general, therapy is more effective than no therapy, although how much more effective is not known.
- The more difficult question of which therapy works best is harder to answer, but it is clear particular kinds of therapy are more appropriate for some problems than for others.

- Because no single type of psychotherapy is invariably effective, eclectic approaches in which a therapist uses a variety of techniques and thus integrates several perspectives are sometimes used.

EVALUATE

1. Match each of the following treatment strategies with the statement you might expect to hear from a therapist using that strategy.

   1. Group therapy
   2. Unconditional positive regard
   3. Behavioral therapy
   4. Nondirective counseling

   a. "In other words, you don't get along with your mother because she hates your girlfriend, is that right?"
   b. "I want you all to take turns talking about why you decided to come and what you hope to gain from therapy."
   c. "I can understand why you wanted to wreck your friend's car after she hurt your feelings. Now tell me more about the accident."
   d. "That's not appropriate behavior. Let's work on replacing it with something else."

2. _____ therapies assume that people should take responsibility for their lives and the decisions they make.

3. One of the major criticisms of humanistic therapies is that
  a. They are too imprecise and unstructured.
  b. They treat only the symptom of the problem.
  c. The therapist dominates the patient–therapist interaction.
  d. They work well only on clients of lower socioeconomic status.

4. In a controversial study, Eysenck found that some people go into _____ _____, or recovery without treatment, if they are simply left alone instead of treated.

RETHINK

1. How can people be successfully treated in group therapy when individuals with the "same" problem are so different?

What advantages might group therapy offer over individual therapy?

2. List some examples of behavior that might be considered abnormal among members of one cultural or economic group and normal by members of a different cultural or economic group. Suppose that most therapies had been developed by psychologists from minority culture groups and lower socioeconomic status; how might they differ from current therapies?

Answers to Evaluate Questions

1. 1-b, 2-c, 3-d, 4-a; **2.** Humanistic; **3.** a; **4.** spontaneous remission

KEY TERMS

humanistic therapy	**interpersonal therapy (IPT)**	**family therapy**
person-centered therapy	**group therapy**	**spontaneous remission**

Module 42
Biomedical Therapy: Biological Approaches to Treatment

LEARNING OUTCOME

LO 42-1 How are drug, electroconvulsive, and psychosurgical techniques used today in the treatment of psychological disorders?

drug therapy Treatment of psychological disorders through the use of drugs. (Module 51)

antipsychotic drugs Drugs that temporarily reduce psychotic symptoms such as agitation, hallucinations, and delusions. (Module 42)

If you get a kidney infection, your doctor gives you an antibiotic; with luck, your kidneys should be as good as new about a week later. If your appendix becomes inflamed, a surgeon removes it, and your body functions normally once more. Could a comparable approach that focuses on the body's physiology be effective for psychological disturbances?

According to biological approaches to treatment, the answer is yes. Therapists routinely use biomedical therapies that rely on drugs and medical procedures to improve psychological functioning.

The biomedical approach focuses treatment directly on altering brain chemistry or other neurological factors rather than concentrating on a patient's psychological conflicts, past traumas, or other issues of daily life that may produce psychological disorder. To do this, therapists provide treatment with drugs, electric shock, or surgery, as we will discuss.

Drug Therapy

Drug therapy is the treatment of psychological disorders using drugs. Drug therapy works by altering the operation of neurons and neurotransmitters in the brain.

Some drugs operate by *inhibiting* neurotransmitters or receptor neurons, which reduces activity at particular synapses. (Recall from our discussion of neurons in the neuroscience chapter that synapses are the gaps where nerve impulses travel from one neuron to another.) Thus, particular neurons are inhibited from firing.

Other drugs do just the opposite: They *increase* the activity of certain neurotransmitters or neurons, which allows particular neurons to fire more frequently (see Figure 1).

ANTIPSYCHOTIC DRUGS

Probably no greater change has occurred in mental hospitals than the successful introduction in the mid-1950s of **antipsychotic drugs**–drugs used to reduce severe symptoms of disturbance, such as loss of touch with reality and agitation. Previously, the typical mental hospital wasn't very different from the stereotypical 19th-century insane asylum; it gave mainly custodial care to screaming, moaning, clawing patients who displayed bizarre behaviors. However, in just a matter of days after hospital staff members administered antipsychotic drugs, the wards became considerably calmer environments in which professionals could do more than just try to get patients through the day without causing serious harm to themselves or others.

This dramatic change came about through the introduction of the drug *chlorpromazine*. Along with other similar drugs, chlorpromazine rapidly became the most popular and successful treatment for schizophrenia. Today, drug therapy is typically the preferred treatment for most cases of severely abnormal behavior and is used for most patients hospitalized with psychological disorders. The newest generation of antipsychotics, referred to as *atypical antipsychotics,* have fewer side effects; they include *risperidone, olanzapine,* and *paliperidone* (Nasrallah et al., 2008; Hattori et al., 2017).

How do antipsychotic drugs work? Most block dopamine receptors at the brain's synapses, the space between pairs of neurons that communicate via chemical messengers.

Drug Treatments			
Class of Drug	**Effects of Drug**	**Primary Action of Drug**	**Examples**
Antipsychotic Drugs, Atypical Antidepressant Drugs	Reduction in loss of touch with reality, agitation	Block dopamine receptors	Antipsychotic: chlorpromazine (Thorazine), clozapine (Clozaril), haloperidol (Haldol) Atypical antipsychotic: risperidone, olanzapine
Antipsychotic Drugs Tricyclic antidepressants	Reduction in depression	Permit rise in neurotransmitters such as norepinepherine	Trazodone (Desyrel), amitriptyline (Elavil), desipramine (Norpamin)
MAO inhibitors	Reduction in depression	Prevent MAO from breaking down neurotransmitters	Phenelzine (Nardil), tranylcypromine (Parnate)
Selective serotonin reuptake inhibitors (SSRIs)	Reduction in depression	Inhibit reuptake of serotonin	Fluoxetine (Prozac), Luvox, Paxil, Celexa, Zoloft, nefazodone (Serzone)
Mood Stabilizers Lithium	Mood stabilization	Can alter transmission of impulses within neurons	Lithium (Lithonate), Depakote, Tegretol
Antianxiety Drugs	Reduction in anxiety	Increase activity of neurotransmitter GABA	Benzodiazepines (Valium, Xanax)

FIGURE 1 The major classes of drugs used to treat psychological disorders have different effects on the brain and nervous system.

Atypical antipsychotics affect both serotonin and dopamine levels in the brain, particularly those related to planning and goal-directed activity (Sawa & Snyder, 2002; Advokat, 2005; Mizrahi et al., 2011).

Despite the effectiveness of antipsychotic drugs, they do not produce a "cure" in the same way that, say, penicillin cures an infection. Most of the time, the symptoms reappear when the drug is withdrawn. Furthermore, such drugs can have long-term side effects, such as dryness of the mouth and throat, dizziness, and sometimes tremors and loss of muscle control, which may continue after drug treatments are stopped (Voruganti et al., 2007; Pijnenborg et al., 2015).

ANTIDEPRESSANT DRUGS

As their name suggests, **antidepressant drugs** are a class of medications used in cases of severe depression to improve a patient's mood and feeling of well-being. They are also sometimes used for other disorders, such as anxiety disorders and bulimia (Walsh et al., 2006; Hedges et al., 2007; Deacon & Spielmans, 2017).

Most antidepressant drugs work by changing the concentration of specific neurotransmitters in the brain. For example, *tricyclic drugs* increase the availability of norepinephrine at the synapses of neurons, whereas *MAO inhibitors* prevent the enzyme monoamine oxidase (MAO) from breaking down neurotransmitters. Newer antidepressants–such as Lexapro–are *selective serotonin reuptake inhibitors (SSRIs)*. SSRIs target the neurotransmitter serotonin and permit it to linger at the synapse. Some antidepressants produce a combination of effects. For instance, nefazodone (Serzone) blocks serotonin at some receptor sites but not others, whereas bupropion (Wellbutrin and Zyban) affects the norepinephrine and dopamine systems (see Figure 2; Dhillon, Yang, & Curran, 2008; Harmer, Duman, & Cowen, 2017).

Finally, there are some newer drugs on the horizon. For instance, scientists have found that the anesthetic *ketamine* blocks the neural receptor NMDA, which affects the neurotransmitter *glutamate*. Glutamate plays an important role in mood regulation and the ability to experience pleasure, and researchers believe that ketamine blockers

antidepressant drugs Medications that improve a severely depressed patient's mood and feeling of well-being. (Module 42)

Study Alert

To help organize your study of different drugs used in therapy, review Figure 1, which classifies them according to the categories of antipsychotic, atypical antipsychotic, antidepressant, mood-stabilizing, and antianxiety drugs.

FIGURE 2 In (a), selective serotonin reuptake inhibitors (SSRIs) reduce depression by permitting the neurotransmitter serotonin to remain in the synapse. In (b), a newer antidepressant, nefazodone (Serzone), operates more selectively to block serotonin at some sites but not others, which helps to reduce the side effects of the drug.

Source: Adapted from Mischoulon, D. (2000, June). Anti-depressants: Choices and controversy. *HealthNews*, 4.

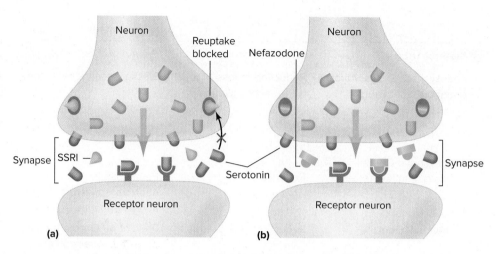

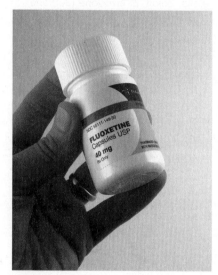

The drug fluoxetine, commonly known as Prozac, is a widely prescribed antidepressant.

©McGraw-Hill Education/Jill Braaten, photographer

may prove to be useful in the treatment of depression (Skolnick, Popik, & Trullas, 2009; Schwartzmant, Alexander, & Grothusen, 2011).

Overall, the success rates of antidepressant drugs are quite good. In fact, antidepressants can produce lasting, long-term recovery from depression. In many cases, even after patients stop taking the drugs, their depression does not return. On the other hand, antidepressant drugs may produce side effects such as drowsiness and cognitive deficits such as memory loss. Evidence also suggests that SSRI antidepressants can increase the risk of suicide in children and adolescents—clearly a significant concern (Prus et al., 2015; Shehab, Brent, & Maalouf, 2016).

Consumers spend billions of dollars each year on antidepressant drugs. Ten percent of Americans now take antidepressants, and for women in their 40s and 50s, the figure is 25%. In particular, the antidepressant *fluoxetine*, sold under the trade name *Prozac*, has been highlighted on magazine covers and has been the topic of best-selling books (Rabin, 2013).

Does Prozac deserve its acclaim? In some respects, yes. It is effective and has relatively few side effects. Furthermore, many people who do not respond to other types of antidepressants do well on Prozac. On the other hand, 20–30% of users report experiencing nausea and diarrhea, and a smaller number report sexual dysfunctions (Brambilla et al., 2005; Fenter, 2006).

Another substance that has received a great deal of publicity is *St. John's wort*, an herb that some have called a "natural" antidepressant. Although it is widely used in Europe for the treatment of depression, the U.S. Food and Drug Administration considers it a dietary supplement, and therefore, the substance is available here without a prescription.

Despite the popularity of St. John's wort, definitive clinical tests have found that the herb is ineffective in the treatment of depression. However, because some research shows that the herb successfully reduces certain psychological symptoms, some proponents argue that using it is reasonable. In any case, people should not use St. John's wort to medicate themselves without consulting a mental health-care professional (Thachil, Mohan, & Bhugra, 2007; Rapaport et al., 2011; Ng, Venkatanarayanan, & Ho, 2017).

MOOD STABILIZERS

mood stabilizers Drugs used to treat mood disorders characterized by intense mood swings, especially manic episodes in bipolar disorder. (Module 42)

Mood stabilizers are used to treat mood disorders characterized by intense mood swings, especially manic episodes in bipolar disorder. For example, the drug *lithium*, a form of mineral salts, has been used very successfully in patients with bipolar disorders. Although no one knows definitely why, lithium and other mood stabilizers such as divalproex sodium (*Depakote*) and carbamazepine (*Tegretol*) effectively reduce manic episodes. However, they do not effectively treat depressive phases of bipolar disorder, so antidepressants are usually prescribed during those phases (Smith et al., 2007; Salvi et al., 2008; Inoue et al., 2011).

Lithium and similar drugs have a quality that sets them apart from other drug treatments: They can be a *preventive* treatment that blocks future episodes of manic depression. Often, people who have had episodes of bipolar disorder can take a daily dose of lithium to prevent a recurrence of their symptoms. Most other drugs are useful only when symptoms of psychological disturbance occur.

ANTIANXIETY DRUGS

As the name implies, **antianxiety drugs** reduce the level of anxiety a person experiences and increase feelings of well-being. They are prescribed not only to reduce general tension in people who are experiencing temporary difficulties but also to aid in the treatment of more serious anxiety disorders.

Antianxiety drugs such as alprazolam and Valium are among the medications physicians most frequently prescribe. In fact, more than half of all U.S. families have someone who has taken such a drug at one time or another.

Although the popularity of antianxiety drugs suggests that they hold few risks, they can produce a number of potentially serious side effects. For instance, they can cause fatigue, and long-term use can lead to dependence. Moreover, when taken in combination with alcohol, some antianxiety drugs can be lethal. But a more important issue concerns their use to suppress anxiety. Almost every therapeutic approach to psychological disturbance views continuing anxiety as a signal of some other sort of problem. Thus, drugs that mask anxiety may simply be hiding other difficulties. Consequently, rather than confronting their underlying problems, people may be hiding from them through the use of antianxiety drugs.

> **antianxiety drugs** Drugs that reduce the level of anxiety a person experiences essentially by reducing excitability and increasing feelings of well-being. (Module 42)

Electroconvulsive Therapy (ECT)

First introduced in the 1930s, **electroconvulsive therapy (ECT)** is a procedure used in the treatment of severe depression. In the procedure, an electric current of 70–150 volts is briefly administered to a patient's head, which causes a loss of consciousness and often causes seizures. Typically, health-care professionals sedate patients and give them muscle relaxants before administering the current; such preparations help reduce the intensity of muscle contractions produced during ECT. The typical patient receives about 10 ECT treatments in the course of a month, but some patients continue with maintenance treatments for months afterward (Greenberg & Kellner, 2005; Stevens & Harper, 2007; Glass, Forester, & Hermida, 2017).

ECT is a controversial technique. Apart from the obvious distastefulness of a treatment that evokes images of electrocution, side effects occur frequently. For instance, after treatment patients often experience disorientation, confusion, and sometimes memory loss that may remain for months. Furthermore, ECT often does not produce long-term improvement; one study found that without follow-up medication, depression returned in most patients who had undergone ECT treatments. Finally, even when ECT does work, we do not know why, and some critics believe it may cause permanent brain damage (Gardner & O'Connor, 2008; Kato, 2009; Weiner & Falcone, 2011).

In light of the drawbacks to ECT, why do therapists use it at all? Basically, they use it because in many severe cases of depression, it offers the only quickly effective treatment. For instance, it may prevent depressed, suicidal individuals from committing suicide, and it can act more quickly than antidepressive medications.

The use of ECT has risen in the last decade, with more than 100,000 people undergoing it each year. Still, ECT tends to be used only when other treatments have proved ineffective, and researchers continue to search for alternative treatments (Eranti & McLoughlin, 2003; Pandya, Pozuelo, & Malone, 2007; Tokutsu et al., 2013).

One new and promising alternative to ECT is **transcranial magnetic stimulation (TMS).** TMS creates a precise magnetic pulse in a specific area of the brain. By activating particular neurons, TMS has been effective in relieving the symptoms of major depression in a number of controlled experiments. However, the therapy can produce side effects, such as seizures and convulsions, and it is still considered experimental (Kim, Pesiridou, & O'Reardon, 2009; Bentwich et al., 2011).

> **electroconvulsive therapy (ECT)** A procedure used in the treatment of severe depression in which an electric current of 70–150 volts is briefly administered to a patient's head. (Module 42)

> **transcranial magnetic stimulation (TMS)** A depression treatment in which a precise magnetic pulse is directed to a specific area of the brain. (Module 42)

Another promising therapy, still in the early stages of development, is the use of implants placed deep inside the brain to provide a short jolt of electrical stimulation, a method called *deep brain stimulation (DBS)*. Unlike ECT, which involves the entire brain, DBS (the treatment described in the chapter prologue) pinpoints specific, tiny regions of the brain and delivers a short burst of electrical stimulation to provide relief from major depression (Lipsman, Giacobbe, & Lozano, 2015; Lozano & Mayberg, 2015; Sun et al., 2015).

Because DBS treatment is so new, researchers are still trying the stimulation in different regions of the brain and fine-tuning the exact placement within given regions to get the best results. The location may vary depending on the specific symptoms the patient is experiencing. Furthermore, the optimal level, frequency, and duration of stimulation are also being explored, as are the long-term effects. Still, initial results are promising (deGusmao, Pollak, & Sharma, 2017).

Psychosurgery

psychosurgery Brain surgery once used to reduce the symptoms of mental disorder but rarely used today. (Module 42)

If ECT strikes you as a questionable procedure, the use of **psychosurgery**–brain surgery in which the object is to reduce symptoms of mental disorder–probably appears even more dubious. A technique used exceedingly rarely today, psychosurgery was introduced as a "treatment of last resort" in the 1930s.

The first form of psychosurgery to be developed was the prefrontal lobotomy. *Prefrontal lobotomy* consists of surgically destroying or removing parts of a patient's frontal brain lobes, which surgeons thought controlled emotionality. In the 1930s and 1940s, surgeons performed the procedure on thousands of patients, often with little precision. For example, in one common technique, surgeons jabbed an ice pick under a patient's eyeball and swiveled it back and forth; in other cases, they drilled into the patient's skull (Phillips, 2013; Chodakiewitz et al., 2015; Carroll, 2017).

Psychosurgery sometimes did improve a patient's behavior–but not without drastic side effects. Along with remission of the symptoms of the mental disorder, patients sometimes experienced personality changes and became bland, colorless, and unemotional. In other cases, patients became aggressive and unable to control their impulses. In the worst cases, treatment resulted in the patient's death.

With the introduction of effective drug treatments–and the obvious ethical questions regarding the appropriateness of forever altering someone's personality–psychosurgery became nearly obsolete. However, it is still used in very rare cases when all other procedures have failed and the patient's behavior presents a high risk to the patient and others. For example, surgeons sometimes use a more precise form of psychosurgery called a *cingulotomy* in rare cases of obsessive-compulsive disorder in which they destroy tissue in the *anterior cingulate* area of the brain. In another technique, *gamma knife surgery*, beams of radiation are used to destroy areas of the brain related to obsessive-compulsive disorder (Lopes et al., 2009; Wilkinson, 2009; Eljamel, 2015).

Occasionally, dying patients with severe, uncontrollable pain also receive psychosurgery. Still, even these cases raise important ethical issues, and psychosurgery remains a highly controversial treatment (Mashour, Walker, & Martuza, 2005; Steele et al., 2007; Garfield, 2014).

From the perspective of...

A Politician How would you go about regulating the use of electroconvulsive therapy and psychosurgery?

©Exactostock/SuperStock

Biomedical Therapies in Perspective

In some respects, no greater revolution has occurred in the field of mental health than biological approaches to treatment. As previously violent, uncontrollable patients have been calmed by the use of drugs, mental hospitals have been able to concentrate more on actually helping patients and less on custodial functions. Similarly, patients whose lives have been disrupted by depression or bipolar episodes have been able to function normally, and other forms of drug therapy have also shown remarkable results.

Furthermore, new forms of biomedical therapy are promising. For example, the newest treatment possibility—which remains experimental at this point—is gene therapy. Specific genes may be introduced to particular regions of the brain. These genes then have the potential to reverse or even prevent biochemical events that give rise to psychological disorders (Tuszynski, 2007; Valenzuela et al., 2016).

Another new treatment, now in its infancy, addresses disorders such as depression and anxiety using brain scan neurofeedback. In *brain scan neurofeedback*, patients are exposed to real-time brain scans showing brain activity as they recall emotion-laden memories or triggers for anxiety. By attempting to modify their brain activity, they seem to better cope with their symptoms (McDonald et al., 2017; Young et al., 2017).

Despite their current usefulness and future promise, biomedical therapies do not represent a complete cure for psychological disorders. For one thing, critics charge that biomedical therapies merely provide temporary relief of the symptoms, given that in most cases, symptoms return as soon as the drugs are withdrawn. Consequently, biomedical treatment may not solve the underlying problems that led a patient to therapy in the first place.

Study Alert
Remember that biomedical treatments have benefits as well as drawbacks.

Second, critics note that drugs may produce side effects that range from minor to serious physical reactions. In the worst case, biomedical therapies may lead to the development of new symptoms of abnormal behavior.

Finally, an overreliance on biomedical therapies may lead therapists to overlook alternative forms of treatment, such as psychotherapy, that may be helpful. In fact, new research demonstrates that adding psychotherapy involving talk sessions with a therapist to drug treatments is preferable in even severe psychological disorders such as schizophrenia (Carey, 2015; Kane et al., 2016; Browne et al., 2017).

Thus, biomedical therapies—sometimes alone and more often in conjunction with psychotherapy—have permitted millions of people to function more effectively. Furthermore, although biomedical therapy and psychotherapy appear distinct, research shows that biomedical therapies ultimately may not be as different from talk therapies as one might imagine, at least in terms of their consequences.

Specifically, measures of brain functioning as a result of drug therapy compared with psychotherapy show little difference in outcomes. For example, one study compared the reactions of patients with major depression who received either an antidepressant drug or psychotherapy. After 6 weeks of either therapy, activity in the portion of the brain related to the disorder—the basal ganglia—had changed in similar ways, and that area appeared to function more normally. Although such research is not definitive, it does suggest that at least for some disorders, psychotherapy may be just as effective as biomedical interventions—and vice versa. Research also makes it clear that no single treatment is effective universally and that each type of treatment has advantages as well as disadvantages (Greenberg & Goldman, 2009; Gaudiano & Miller, 2013).

Community Psychology: Focus on Prevention

Each of the treatments we have reviewed has a common element: It is a "restorative" treatment aimed at alleviating psychological difficulties that already exist. However, an approach known as **community psychology** has a different aim: to prevent or minimize the incidence of psychological disorders.

community psychology A branch of psychology that focuses on the prevention and minimization of psychological disorders in the community. (Module 42)

While deinstitutionalization has had many successes, it has also contributed to the release of mental patients into the community with little or no support. As a result, many have become homeless.
©McGraw-Hill Education/Gary He, photographer

deinstitutionalization The transfer of former mental patients from institutions to the community. (Module 42)

Community psychology came of age in the 1960s, when mental health professionals developed plans for a nationwide network of community mental health centers. The hope was that those centers would provide low-cost mental health services, including short-term therapy and community educational programs. In another development, the population of mental hospitals has plunged as drug treatments made physical restraint of patients unnecessary.

The community psychology movement encouraged deinstitutionalization. **Deinstitutionalization** is the process of transferring patients who have been hospitalized for long periods into less-isolated community mental health settings (see Figure 3). Proponents of deinstitutionalization wanted to ensure not only that deinstitutionalized patients received proper treatment but also that their civil rights were maintained (St. Dennis et al., 2006; Henckes, 2011; Pow et al., 2015).

Unfortunately, the promise of deinstitutionalization has not been met largely because insufficient resources are provided to deinstitutionalized patients. What started as a worthy attempt to move people out of mental institutions and into the community ended, in many cases, with former patients being dumped into the community without any real support. Many became homeless–between 15-35% of all homeless adults are thought to have a major psychological disorder–and some became involved in illegal acts caused by their disorders. In short, many people who need treatment do not get it, and in some cases, care for people with psychological disorders has simply shifted from one type of treatment site to another. In fact, for many people, the only form of mental health treatment comes in emergency rooms of hospitals, with little or no follow-up care (Dumont & Dumont, 2008; Whitaker, 2009; Searight, 2013).

On the other hand, the community psychology movement has had some positive outcomes. Its emphasis on prevention has led to new approaches to psychological disorders. Furthermore, telephone "hot lines" are now common. At any time of the day or night, people experiencing acute stress can call a trained, sympathetic listener who can provide immediate–although obviously limited–treatment (Cauce, 2007; Jarrett, 2015; Nelson & MacLeod, 2017).

College and high school crisis centers are another innovation that grew out of the community psychology movement. Modeled after suicide prevention hot-line centers, crisis centers give callers an opportunity to discuss life crises with a sympathetic listener, who is often a volunteer.

FIGURE 3 As deinstitutionalization has become prevalent over the years, the number of patients being treated in state mental hospitals declined significantly, while the number of patients being treated in outpatient facilities increased.
Source: Adapted from Doyle, R. (2002). Deinstitutionalization. *Scientific American, 287*, 38.

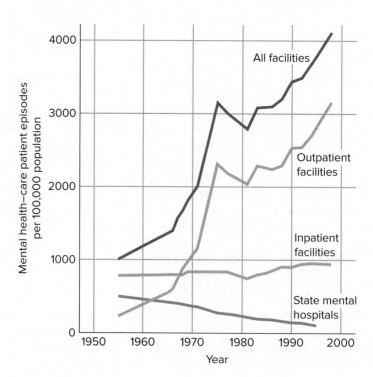

BECOMING AN INFORMED CONSUMER
of Psychology

Choosing the Right Therapist

If you decide to seek therapy, you're faced with a daunting task. Choosing a therapist is not a simple matter. One place to begin the process of identifying a therapist is at the "Help Center" of the American Psychological Association at http://www.apa.org/helpcenter. And if you start therapy, several general guidelines can help you determine whether you've made the right choice:

You and your therapist should agree on the goals for treatment. They should be clear, specific, and attainable.

- *You should feel comfortable with your therapist.* You should not be intimidated by or in awe of a therapist. Rather, you should trust the therapist and feel free to discuss the most personal issues without fearing a negative reaction. In sum, the "personal chemistry" should be right.
- *Therapists should have appropriate training and credentials and should be licensed by appropriate state and local agencies.* Check therapists' membership in national and state professional associations. In addition, the cost of therapy, billing practices, and other business matters should be clear. It is not a breach of etiquette to put these matters on the table during an initial consultation.
- *You should feel that you are making progress after therapy has begun, despite occasional setbacks.* If you have no sense of improvement after repeated visits, you and your therapist should discuss this issue frankly. Although there is no set timetable, the most obvious changes resulting from therapy tend to occur relatively early in the course of treatment. For instance, half of patients in psychotherapy improve by the 8th session and three-fourths by the 26th session. The average number of sessions with college students is just five (Lazarus, 1997; Taibbi, 2018).

Be aware that you will have to put in a great deal of effort in therapy. Although our culture promises quick cures for any problem, in reality, solving difficult problems is not easy. You must be committed to making therapy work and should know that it is you, not the therapist, who must do most of the work to resolve your problems. The effort has the potential to pay off handsomely—as you experience a more positive, fulfilling, and meaningful life.

RECAP/EVALUATE/RETHINK

RECAP

LO 42-1 How are drug, electroconvulsive, and psychosurgical techniques used today in the treatment of psychological disorders?

- Biomedical treatment approaches suggest that therapy should focus on the physiological causes of abnormal behavior rather than considering psychological factors. Drug therapy, the best example of biomedical treatments, has brought about dramatic reductions in the symptoms of mental disturbance.
- Antipsychotic drugs such as chlorpromazine very effectively reduce psychotic symptoms. Antidepressant

drugs such as Prozac reduce depression so successfully that they are used very widely. Antianxiety drugs, or minor tranquilizers, are among the most frequently prescribed medications of any sort.

- In electroconvulsive therapy (ECT), used in severe cases of depression, a patient receives a brief electric current of 70–150 volts.
- Psychosurgery typically consists of surgically destroying or removing certain parts of a patient's brain.
- The community psychology approach encouraged deinstitutionalization in which previously hospitalized mental patients were released into the community.

EVALUATE

1. Antipsychotic drugs have provided effective, long-term, and complete cures for schizophrenia. True or false?
2. One highly effective biomedical treatment for a psychological disorder that is used mainly to arrest and prevent manic-depressive episodes is
   a. Chlorpromazine
   b. Lithium
   c. Librium
   d. Valium
3. Psychosurgery has grown in popularity as a method of treatment as surgical techniques have become more precise. True or false?
4. The trend toward releasing more patients from mental hospitals and into the community is known as _____.

RETHINK

1. One of the main criticisms of biological therapies is that they treat the symptoms of mental disorder without uncovering and treating the underlying problems from which people are suffering. Do you agree with this criticism? Why?
2. If a dangerously violent person could be "cured" of violence through a new psychosurgical technique, would you approve the use of this technique? Suppose the person agreed to–or requested–the technique? What sort of policy would you develop for the use of psychosurgery?

Answers to Evaluate Questions

1. false; schizophrenia can be controlled but not cured by medication; 2. b; 3. false; psychosurgery is now used only as a treatment of last resort; 4. deinstitutionalization

KEY TERMS

drug therapy
antipsychotic drugs
antidepressant drugs
mood stabilizers

antianxiety drugs
electroconvulsive therapy (ECT)

transcranial magnetic stimulation (TMS)
psychosurgery

community psychology
deinstitutionalization

LOOKING *Back*

EPILOGUE

We have examined how psychological professionals treat people with psychological disorders. We have considered a range of approaches that include both psychologically based and biologically based therapies. Clearly, the field has made substantial progress in recent years both in treating the symptoms of mental disorders and in understanding their underlying causes.

Before we leave the topic of treating psychological disorders, turn back to the prologue describing Vito Randazzo, who underwent deep brain stimulation to treat his chronic depression. On the basis of your understanding of the treatment of psychological disorders, consider the following questions.

1. How might a psychodynamic approach, which Randazzo tried unsuccessfully, have approached the treatment of his depression?
2. In what way would behavioral therapy treat a depression like Randazzo's? Do you think this approach would have been more or less promising for Randazzo's depression than a psychodynamic approach?
3. How might a cognitive approach treat Randazzo's depression? How would humanistic therapy treat it? Under what circumstances do you think such approaches would be effective in treating depression?
4. How does deep brain stimulation differ from other forms of biomedical therapy, such as drug therapy and electroconvulsive therapy? How do you think the pacemaker-like device works to combat depression?

Design Elements: Yellow highlighter: ©luckyraccoon/Shutterstock.com; Smartphone: ©and4me/Shutterstock.com; Group of diverse hands: ©MR. Nattanon Kanchak/Shutterstock.com; Woman working on laptop: ©Dragon Images/Shutterstock.com.

VISUAL SUMMARY 13 Treatment of Psychological Disorders

MODULE 40 Psychotherapy: Psychodynamic, Behavioral, and Cognitive Approaches

Psychodynamic Therapy

- Psychoanalysis
  - Free association: say aloud whatever comes to mind
  - Dream interpretation: looking for clues to unconscious conflicts and problems in dreams
  - Frequent sessions for a long time
- Contemporary psychodynamic approaches
  - Sessions are of shorter duration
  - Therapist takes more active role: focus is more in the present

Behavioral Treatment Approaches: Help modify behavior rather than find underlying causes

- Classical conditioning treatments
  - Aversive conditioning
  - Systematic desensitization
  - Flooding
- Operant conditioning techniques
  - Token system
  - Contingency contracting
  - Observational learning

Cognitive Approaches: Teach people to think in adaptive ways

- Rational-emotive behavior therapy

A	B	C
Negative Activating condition	**Irrational Belief system**	**Emotional Consequences**
(Close relationship breaks up)	("I'll never be loved again")	(Anxiety, loneliness, sadness, depression)

MODULE 41 Psychotherapy: Humanistic, Interpersonal, and Group Approaches

Humanistic Therapy: Focuses on self-responsibility in treatment techniques

- Person-centered therapy: helps people to reach their potential for self-actualization using unconditional positive regard

Interpersonal Therapy: Focuses on interpersonal relationships and improvement through short-term therapy

Group Therapy: Several people meet with a therapist to discuss psychological functioning

- Family therapy
- Self-help therapy

Does Psychotherapy Work?

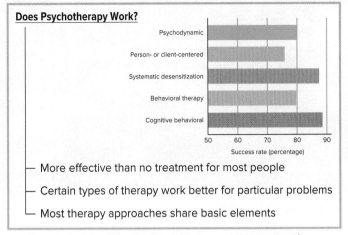

Success rate (percentage)

- More effective than no treatment for most people
- Certain types of therapy work better for particular problems
- Most therapy approaches share basic elements

MODULE 42 Biomedical Therapy: Biological Approaches to Treatment

Drug Therapy: Controlling psychological disorders with drugs

Drug Treatments			
Class of Drug	**Effects of Drug**	**Primary Action of Drug**	**Examples**
Antipsychotic Drugs, Atypical Antidepressant Drugs	Reduction in loss of touch with reality, agitation	Block dopamine receptors	Antipsychotic: chlorpromazine (Thorazine), clozapine (Clozaril), haloperidol (Haldol)
			Atypical antipsychotic: risperidone, olanzapine
Antipsychotic Drugs Tricyclic antidepressants	Reduction in depression	Permit rise in neurotransmitters such as norepinepherine	Trazodone (Desyrel), amitriptyline (Elavil), desipramine (Norpamin)
MAO inhibitors	Reduction in depression	Prevent MAO from breaking down neurotransmitters	Phenelzine (Nardil), tranylcypromine (Parnate)
Selective serotonin reuptake inhibitors (SSRIs)	Reduction in depression	Inhibit reuptake of serotonin	Fluoxetine (Prozac), Luvox, Paxil, Celexa, Zoloft, nefazodone (Serzone)
Mood Stabilizers Lithium	Mood stabilization	Can alter transmission of impulses within neurons	Lithium (Lithonate), Depakote, Tegretol
Antianxiety Drugs	Reduction in anxiety	Increase activity of neurotransmitter GABA	Benzodiazepines (Valium, Xanax)

Electroconvulsive Therapy: Used as the only quickly effective treatment for severe depression

Psychosurgery: Brain surgery to reduce symptoms of mental disorders

Community Psychology: Prevention of the incidence of psychological disorders

- Deinstitutionalization: transfer of mental patients into the community where they may not receive necessary treatment

(MODULE 40) Source: Ellis, A. (1974). *Growth through reason.* Hollywood, CA: Wilshire Books; (MODULE 41) (photo): ©Jon Bradley/The Image Bank/Getty Images; Source: Adapted from Smith, M. L., Glass, G. V., & Miller, T. I. (1980). *The benefits of psychotherapy.* Baltimore: The Johns Hopkins University Press; (MODULE 42) ©McGraw-Hill Education/Gary He, photographer

©Ingram Publishing/SuperStock

CHAPTER 14
Social Psychology

LEARNING OUTCOMES FOR CHAPTER 14

LO 46-1 Why are we attracted to certain people, and what progression do social relationships follow?

LO 46-2 What factors underlie aggression and prosocial behavior?

PROLOGUE *AN AMERICAN TERRORIST*

On a warm summer evening, Dylann Roof walked into Charleston, South Carolina's Emanuel AME Church—the South's oldest black church. The 12 church members present at that time welcomed Roof, handed him a Bible, and invited him to join their prayer meeting.

What the church members—all black—did not know was that Roof had arrived with a heart full of hate and a weapon, a Glock .45. Forty-five minutes later, during the final prayer, Roof opened fire, shooting some of his victims multiple times. Only three survived.

The 21-year-old Roof showed no remorse for his crime either at the time of his arrest or later in the courtroom. He did tell FBI agents he hoped the shootings would bring back segregation, maybe even start a race war.

Roof maintained throughout his trial (in which he acted as his own attorney during sentencing) that he was not mentally ill. "Anyone who hates anything in their mind has a good reason for it," he told the jurors. The jury responded by convicting Roof of all 33 federal charges. He became the first person to be given the death penalty for a federal hate crime (Tribune News Services, 2017).

LOOKING *Ahead*

Dylann Roof never clearly explained why he targeted the church members. He did claim to be a white supremacist and had posed with the Confederate flag in photographs. At his sentencing, he told jurors, "I still feel like I had to do it" (Tribune News Services, 2017).

What drives people like Roof to hate and distrust others of a different religion, race, or ethnicity? And conversely, why do others celebrate human diversity? More broadly, how can we improve social attitudes so that people live together in harmony?

We can fully answer these questions only by taking into account findings from the field of social psychology, the branch

that focuses on the aspects of human behavior that unite—and separate—us from one another. **Social psychology** is the scientific study of how people's thoughts, feelings, and actions are affected by others. Social psychologists consider the kinds and causes of the individual's behavior in social situations. They examine how the nature of situations in which we find ourselves influences our behavior in important ways.

The broad scope of social psychology is conveyed by the kinds of questions social psychologists ask, such as: How can we convince people to change their attitudes or adopt new ideas and values? In what ways do we come to understand what others are like? How are we influenced by what others do and think? Why do some people display so much violence, aggression, and cruelty toward others that people throughout the world live in fear of annihilation at their hands? And why, in comparison, do some people place their own lives at risk to help others? In exploring these and other questions, we also discuss strategies for confronting and solving a variety of problems and issues that all of us face—ranging from achieving a better understanding of persuasive tactics to forming more accurate impressions of others.

We begin with a look at how our attitudes shape our behavior and how we form judgments about others. We'll discuss how we are influenced by others, and we will consider prejudice and discrimination by focusing on their roots and the ways we can reduce them. After examining what social psychologists have learned about the ways people form friendships and relationships, we'll conclude with a look at the determinants of aggression and helping—two opposing sides of human behavior.

social psychology The scientific study of how people's thoughts, feelings, and actions are affected by others. (Module 43)

Module 43
Attitudes and Social Cognition

LEARNING OUTCOMES

LO 43-1 What are attitudes, and how are they formed, maintained, and changed?

LO 43-2 How do people form impressions of what others are like and the causes of their behavior?

LO 43-3 What are the biases that influence the ways in which people view others' behavior?

attitudes Evaluations of people, objects, ideas, and behavior. (Module 43)

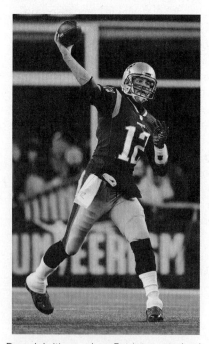

Do celebrities such as Patriot quarterback Tom Brady influence attitudes? Advertisers certainly believe this is true, investing millions of dollars in endorsement fees.
©John Cetrino/EPA-EFE/REX/Shutterstock/Shutterstock

What do Rachael Ray and Tom Brady have in common? Both have appeared in advertisements designed to mold or change our attitudes. Such commercials are part of the barrage of messages we receive each day from sources as varied as politicians, sales staff in stores, and celebrities–all of which are meant to influence us.

Persuasion: Changing Attitudes

Attitudes are one of the central concepts of social psychology. **Attitudes** are evaluations of people, objects, ideas, and behavior. We have all sorts of attitudes, ranging from those about others ("I think the president is great"), to attitudes about behavior ("I hate it when people are late for appointments"), to attitudes toward more abstract concepts ("I support affirmative action") (Hegarty & Massey, 2007; Simon & Hoyt, 2008).

Persuasion involves changing attitudes. The ease with which attitudes can be changed depends on a number of factors, including:

- *Message source.* The characteristics of a person who delivers a persuasive message, known as an *attitude communicator*, have a major impact on the effectiveness of that message. Communicators who are physically and socially attractive produce greater attitude change than do those who are less attractive. Moreover, the communicator's expertise and trustworthiness are related to the impact of a message–except in situations in which the audience believes the communicator has an ulterior motive (Messner, Reinhard, & Sporer, 2008; Bebermeier et al., 2015).

- *Characteristics of the message.* It is not just *who* delivers a message but what the message is like that affects attitudes. Generally, two-sided messages–which include both the communicator's position and the one he or she is arguing against–are more effective than one-sided messages, given the assumption that the arguments for the other side can be effectively refuted and the audience is knowledgeable about the topic. In addition, fear-producing messages ("If you don't practice safer sex, you'll get AIDS") are generally effective when they provide the audience with a means for reducing the fear. However, if the fear that is aroused is too strong, messages may evoke people's defense mechanisms and be ignored (Keer et al., 2013; Bigsby, Monahan, & Ewoldsen, 2017).

- *Characteristics of the target.* Once a communicator has delivered a message, characteristics of the *target* of the message may determine whether the message will be accepted. For example, intelligent people are more resistant to persuasion than are those who are less intelligent. Gender differences in persuadability also seem to exist. In public settings, women are somewhat more easily persuaded than men, particularly when women have less knowledge about the message's topic. However, they are as likely as men to change their private attitudes. In fact, the magnitude of the differences in resistance to persuasion between men and women is not large (Wood, 2000; Guadagno & Cialdini, 2002).

ROUTES TO PERSUASION

Recipients' receptiveness to persuasive messages relates to the type of information-processing they use. Social psychologists have discovered two primary information-processing routes to persuasion: central route and peripheral route processing. **Central route processing** occurs when the recipient thoughtfully considers the issues and arguments involved in persuasion. In central route processing, people are swayed in their judgments by the logic, merit, and strength of arguments.

In contrast, **peripheral route processing** occurs when people are persuaded on the basis of factors unrelated to the nature or quality of the content of a persuasive message. Instead, factors that are irrelevant or extraneous to the issue, such as who is providing the message, how long the arguments are, or the emotional appeal of the arguments, influence them (Warden, Wu, & Tsai, 2006; Kao, 2011; Xie & Johnson, 2015).

In general, people who are highly involved and motivated use central route processing to comprehend a message. However, if a person is disinterested, unmotivated, bored, or distracted, the characteristics of the message become less important, and peripheral factors become more influential (see Figure 1). Although both central route and peripheral route processing lead to attitude change, central route processing generally leads to stronger, more lasting attitude change.

Are some people more likely than others to habitually use central route processing rather than peripheral route processing? The answer is yes. *Need for cognition* is someone's typical level of thoughtfulness and cognitive activity. Those who have a high need for cognition are more likely to employ central route processing. In contrast, those with a low need for cognition are more likely to use peripheral route processing. See Figure 2 to get a sense of your own need for cognition (Dai & Wang, 2007; Hill et al., 2013; Luttrell, Petty, & Xu, 2017).

People who have a high need for cognition enjoy thinking, philosophizing, and reflecting on the world. Because they are more likely to reflect on persuasive messages by using central route processing, they are persuaded by complex, logical, and detailed messages. In contrast, those who have a low need for cognition become impatient when forced to spend too much time thinking about an issue. Consequently, they usually use peripheral route processing and are persuaded by factors other than the quality and detail of messages (Dollinger, 2003; Van Overwalle & Siebler, 2005).

central route processing The type of mental processing that occurs when a persuasive message is evaluated by thoughtful consideration of the issues and arguments used to persuade. (Module 43)

peripheral route processing The type of mental processing that occurs when a persuasive message is evaluated on the basis of irrelevant or extraneous factors. (Module 43)

 Study Alert
Central route processing involves the content of the message; peripheral route processing involves how the message is provided.

 ## From the perspective of...

A Sales Specialist Suppose you were selling an automobile to a customer who walked in the door. What strategies might you use to be persuasive?

©Amos Morgan/Getty Images

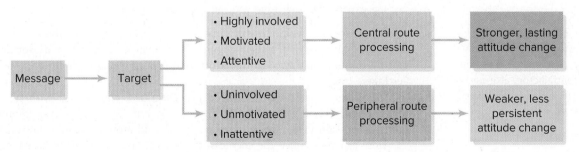

FIGURE 1 Routes to persuasion. Targets who are highly involved, motivated, and attentive use central route processing when they consider a persuasive message, which leads to a more lasting attitude change. In contrast, uninvolved, unmotivated, and inattentive targets are more likely to use peripheral route processing, and attitude change is likely to be less enduring. Can you think of specific advertisements that try to produce central route processing?

FIGURE 2 This simple questionnaire will give you a general idea of the level of your need for cognition.

Source: Adapted from Cacioppo, J. T., Berntson, G. G., & Crites, S. L., Jr. (1996). Social neuroscience: Principles of psychophysiological arousal and response. In E. T. Higgins & A. W. Kruglanski (Eds.), *Social psychology: Handbook of basic principles.* New York: Guilford.

The Need for Cognition

Which of the following statements apply to you?

1. I really enjoy a task that involves coming up with new solutions to problems.
2. I would prefer a task that is intellectual, difficult, and important to one that is somewhat important but does not require much thought.
3. Learning new ways to think doesn't excite me very much.
4. The idea of relying on thought to make my way to the top does not appeal to me.
5. I think only as hard as I have to.
6. I like tasks that require little thought once I've learned them.
7. I prefer to think about small, daily projects rather than long-term ones.
8. I would rather do something that requires little thought than something that is sure to challenge my thinking abilities.
9. I find little satisfaction in deliberating hard and for long hours.
10. I don't like to be responsible for a situation that requires a lot of thinking.

Scoring: The more you agree with statements 1 and 2, and disagree with the rest, the greater the likelihood that you have a high need for cognition.

THE LINK BETWEEN ATTITUDES AND BEHAVIOR

Not surprisingly, attitudes influence behavior. The strength of the link between particular attitudes and behavior varies, of course, but generally, people strive for consistency between their attitudes and their behavior. Furthermore, people hold fairly consistent attitudes. For instance, you would probably not hold the attitude that eating meat is immoral and still have a positive attitude toward hamburgers (Levi, Chan, & Pence, 2006; Elen et al., 2013; Rodrigues & Girandola, 2017).

Ironically, the consistency that leads attitudes to influence behavior sometimes works the other way around; in some cases, our behavior shapes our attitudes. Consider, for instance, the following incident:

> You've just spent what you feel is the most boring hour of your life turning pegs for a psychology experiment. Just as you finally finish and are about to leave, the experimenter asks you to do him a favor. He tells you that he needs a helper for future experimental sessions to introduce subsequent participants to the peg-turning task. Your specific job will be to tell them that turning the pegs is an interesting, fascinating experience. Each time you tell this tale to another participant, you'll be paid $1.

If you agree to help the experimenter, you may be setting yourself up for a state of psychological tension called cognitive dissonance. **Cognitive dissonance** occurs when a person holds two contradictory attitudes or thoughts (referred to as *cognitions*; Festinger, 1957).

If you participate in the situation just described, you are left with two contradictory thoughts: (1) I believe the task is boring, but (2) I said it was interesting with little justification ($1). These two thoughts should arouse cognitive dissonance.

How can you reduce the cognitive dissonance? You cannot deny having said that the task is interesting, because you just said it. On the other hand, it is relatively easy to change your attitude toward the task—and thus, the theory predicts that participants will reduce dissonance by adopting more positive attitudes toward the task (Rydell, McConnell, & Mackie, 2008; Dickinson & Oxoby, 2011; Harmon-Jones, Harmon-Jones, & Levy, 2015).

cognitive dissonance The mental conflict that occurs when a person holds two contradictory attitudes or thoughts (referred to as cognitions). (Module 43)

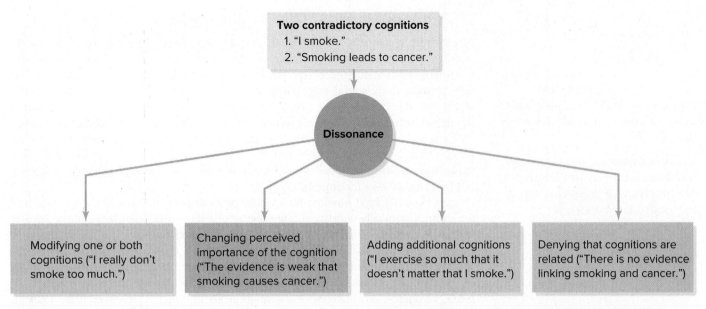

FIGURE 3 Cognitive dissonance. The simultaneous presence of two contradictory cognitions ("I smoke." and "Smoking leads to cancer.") produces dissonance, which can be reduced through several methods. What are additional ways in which dissonance can be reduced?

A classic experiment (Festinger & Carlsmith, 1959) confirmed this prediction. The experiment followed essentially the same procedure outlined earlier in which a participant was offered $1 to describe a boring task as interesting. In addition, in a comparison condition, some participants were offered $20 to say that the task was interesting. The reasoning behind this condition was that $20 was so much money that participants in this condition had a good reason to be conveying incorrect information; dissonance would not be aroused, and less attitude change would be expected. The results supported this notion. More of the participants who were paid $1 changed their attitudes (becoming more positive toward the peg-turning task) than did participants who were paid $20.

Cognitive dissonance explains many everyday events involving attitudes and behavior. For example, smokers who know that smoking leads to lung cancer hold contradictory cognitions: (1) I smoke, and (2) smoking leads to lung cancer. The theory predicts that these two thoughts will lead to a state of cognitive dissonance. More important, it predicts that smokers will be motivated to reduce their dissonance.

There are four ways to reduce the dissonance in this case:

- Modifying one or both of the cognitions (e.g., "I really don't smoke that much.")
- Changing the perceived importance of one cognition ("The link between cancer and smoking is weak.")
- Adding cognitions ("I exercise so much that I'm really a healthy person.")
- Denying that the two cognitions are related to each other ("There's no compelling evidence linking smoking and cancer.")

Whichever strategy the smoker uses results in reduced dissonance (see Figure 3).

Social Cognition: Understanding Others

Regardless of Bill Clinton's personal transgressions and impeachment trial in the late 1990s, many Americans continued to find him extremely likable throughout his presidency, and even today he is among the most popular U.S. politicians. Cases like this illustrate the power of our impressions and attest to the importance of determining how people develop an understanding of others. One of the dominant areas in social psychology during the last few years has focused on learning how we come to understand what others are like and how we explain the reasons underlying others' behavior.

UNDERSTANDING WHAT OTHERS ARE LIKE

Consider for a moment the enormous amount of information about other people to which we are exposed. How can we decide what is important and what is not and make judgments about the characteristics of others? Social psychologists interested in this question study **social cognition**–the way people understand and make sense of others and themselves. Those psychologists have learned that individuals have highly developed **schemas,** sets of cognitions about people and social experiences. Those schemas organize information stored in memory; represent in our minds the way the social world operates; and give us a framework to recognize, categorize, and recall information relating to social stimuli such as people and groups (Amodio & Ratner, 2011; Leahy, 2015; Kitayama, 2017).

We typically hold schemas for specific types of people. Our schema for "teacher," for instance, generally consists of a number of characteristics: knowledge of the subject matter he or she is teaching, a desire to impart that knowledge, and an awareness of the student's need to understand what is being said. Or we may hold a schema for "mother" that includes the characteristics of warmth, nurturance, and caring. Regardless of their accuracy, schemas are important because they organize the way in which we recall, recognize, and categorize information about others. Moreover, they help us predict what others are like on the basis of relatively little information because we tend to fit people into schemas even when we do not have much concrete evidence to go on (Ruscher, Fiske, & Schnake, 2000; Yamada & Itsukushima, 2013).

FORMING IMPRESSIONS OF OTHERS

How do we decide that Sayreeta is a flirt, Jacob is obnoxious, or Hector is a really nice guy? The earliest work on social cognition examined *impression formation*, the process by which an individual organizes information about another person to form an overall impression of that person. In a classic study, for instance, students learned that they were about to hear a guest lecturer (Kelley, 1950). Researchers told one group of students that the lecturer was "a rather warm person, industrious, critical, practical, and determined" and told a second group that he was "a rather cold person, industrious, critical, practical, and determined."

The simple substitution of "cold" for "warm" caused drastic differences in the way the students in each group perceived the lecturer even though he gave the same talk in the same style in each condition. Students who had been told he was "warm" rated him considerably more positively overall than did students who had been told he was "cold."

The findings from this experiment led to additional research on impression formation that focused on the way in which people pay particular attention to certain unusually important traits–known as **central traits**–to help them form an overall impression of others. According to this work, the presence of a central trait alters the meaning of other traits. Hence, the description of the lecturer as "industrious" presumably meant something different when it was associated with the central trait "warm" than it meant when it was associated with "cold" (Glicksohn & Nahari, 2007; McCarthy & Skowronski, 2011; Huang, Sacchi, & Sherman, 2017).

Some researchers have used information-processing approaches to develop mathematical models of how we combine individual personality traits to develop an overall impression of others. Generally, we calculate a kind of psychological "average" of the individual traits we see in a person to form an overall judgment, just as we would find the mathematical average of several numbers (Mignon & Mollaret, 2002).

We also form impressions remarkably quickly. In just a few seconds, using what have been called "thin slices of behavior," we are able to make judgments of people. Interestingly, these quick impressions are surprisingly accurate and typically match those of people who make judgments based on longer samples of behavior (Pavitt, 2007; Holleran, Mehl, & Levitt, 2009; Pretsch et al., 2013).

---

social cognition The cognitive processes by which people understand and make sense of others and themselves. (Module 43)

schemas Organized bodies of information stored in memory that bias the way new information is interpreted, stored, and recalled. (Modules 21, 52)

central traits The major traits considered in forming impressions of others. (Module 43)

Of course, as we gain more experience with people and see them exhibiting behavior in a variety of situations, our impressions of them become more complex. However, because our knowledge of others usually has gaps, we still tend to fit individuals into personality schemas that represent particular "types" of people. For instance, we may hold a "gregarious person" schema made up of the traits of friendliness, aggressiveness, and openness. The presence of just one or two of those traits may be sufficient to make us assign a person to a particular schema.

However, our schemas are susceptible to error. For example, mood affects how we perceive others. Happy people form more favorable impressions and make more positive judgments than do people who are in a bad mood (Forgas & Laham, 2005; Human & Biesanz, 2011).

Even when schemas are not entirely accurate, they serve an important function: They allow us to develop expectations about how others will behave. Those expectations permit us to plan our interactions with others more easily and serve to simplify a complex social world.

ATTRIBUTION PROCESSES: UNDERSTANDING THE CAUSES OF BEHAVIOR

> When Barbara Washington, a new employee at the Ablex Computer Company, completed a major staffing project 2 weeks early, her boss, Yolanda, was delighted. At the next staff meeting, she announced how pleased she was with Barbara and explained that *this* was an example of the kind of performance she was looking for in her staff. The other staff members looked on resentfully, trying to figure out why Barbara had worked night and day to finish the project not just on time but 2 weeks early. She must be an awfully compulsive person, they decided.

At one time or another, most of us have puzzled over the reasons behind someone's behavior. Perhaps it was in a situation similar to the one above, or it may have been in more formal circumstances, such as being a judge on a student judiciary board in a cheating case. **Attribution theory** considers how we decide, on the basis of samples of a person's behavior, what the specific causes of that behavior are. Unlike impression formation, which focuses on how people develop an overall impression of others' personality traits, attribution theory asks the "why" question: Why is someone acting in a particular way?

In seeking an explanation for behavior, we must answer one central question: Is the cause situational or dispositional? **Situational causes** are causes of behavior that are external to a person. For instance, someone who knocks over a quart of milk and then cleans it up probably does the cleaning not because he or she is necessarily a neat person but because the *situation* requires it. In contrast, a person who spends hours shining the kitchen floor probably does so because he or she is an unusually neat person. Hence, the behavior has a dispositional cause. **Dispositional causes** are causes of behavior brought about by a person's traits or personality characteristics.

In our example involving Barbara Washington, her fellow employees attributed her behavior to her disposition rather than to the situation. But from a logical standpoint, it is equally plausible that something about the situation caused the behavior. If asked, Barbara might attribute her accomplishment to situational factors and explain that she had so much other work to do she just had to get the project out of the way or that the project was not all that difficult and was easy to complete ahead of schedule. To her, then, the reason for her behavior might not be dispositional at all; it could be situational.

ATTRIBUTION BIASES: TO ERR IS HUMAN

If we always processed information in the rational manner that attribution theory suggests, the world might run a lot more smoothly. Unfortunately, although attribution theory generally makes accurate predictions, people do not always process information

attribution theory The theory that considers how we decide, on the basis of samples of a person's behavior, what the specific causes of that behavior are. (Module 52)

situational causes (of behavior) Causes of behavior that are external to a person. (Module 43)

dispositional causes (of behavior) Perceived causes of behavior brought about by a person's traits or personality characteristics. (Module 43)

Study Alert
The central question in making an attribution is whether the cause of behavior is due to situational or dispositional factors.

about others as logically as the theory seems to suggest. In fact, research reveals consistent biases in the ways people make attributions. Typical biases include the following:

- *The halo effect.* Harry is intelligent, kind, and loving. Is he also conscientious? If you were to guess, your most likely response probably would be yes. Your guess reflects the **halo effect,** a phenomenon in which an initial understanding that a person has positive traits is used to infer other uniformly positive characteristics. The opposite would also hold true. Learning that Harry was unsociable and argumentative would probably lead you to assume that he was lazy as well. However, few people have either uniformly positive or uniformly negative traits, so the halo effect leads to misperceptions of others (Dennis, 2007; Park, Park, & Dubinsky, 2011; Forgas & Laham, 2017).

- *Assumed-similarity bias.* How similar to you–in terms of attitudes, opinions, likes, and dislikes–are your friends and acquaintances? Most people believe that their friends and acquaintances are fairly similar to themselves. But this feeling goes beyond just people we know to a general tendency–known as the **assumed-similarity bias**–to think of people as being similar to oneself even when meeting them for the first time. Given the range of people in the world, this assumption often reduces the accuracy of our judgments (Lemay, Clark, & Feeney, 2007; Lemay & Clark, 2008).

- *The self-serving bias.* When their teams win, coaches usually feel that the success is due to their coaching. But when their teams lose, coaches may think it's due to their players' poor skills. Similarly, if you get an A on a test, you may think it's due to your hard work, but if you get a poor grade, it's due to the professor's inadequacies. The reason is the **self-serving bias,** the tendency to attribute success to personal factors (skill, ability, or effort) and attribute failure to factors outside oneself (Shepperd, Malone, & Sweeny, 2008; Ferring, Tournier, & Mancini, 2015).

- *The fundamental attribution error.* One of the more common attribution biases is the **fundamental attribution error,** which is the tendency to overattribute others' behavior to dispositional causes and the corresponding failure to recognize the importance of situational causes. The fundamental attribution error is prevalent in Western cultures. We tend to exaggerate the importance of personality characteristics (dispositional causes) in producing others' behavior and minimize the influence of the environment (situational factors). For example, we are more likely to jump to the conclusion that someone who is often late to work is lazy or a routinely tardy person (dispositional causes) than to assume that, perhaps, the subway they take to work frequently runs behind schedule, causing them to be late (a situational cause).

halo effect A phenomenon in which an initial understanding that a person has positive or negative traits is used to infer other uniformly positive or negative characteristics. (Module 52)

assumed-similarity bias The tendency to think of people as being similar to oneself even when meeting them for the first time. (Module 43)

self-serving bias The tendency to attribute personal success to personal factors (skill, ability, or effort) and to attribute failure to factors outside oneself. (Module 43)

fundamental attribution error A tendency to overattribute others' behavior to dispositional causes and minimize the importance of situational causes. (Module 43)

The assumed-similarity bias leads us to believe that others hold similar attitudes, opinions, and likes and dislikes.
©PhotoAlto/SuperStock

Why is the fundamental attribution error so common? One reason pertains to the nature of information available to the people making an attribution. When we view another person's behavior in a particular setting, the most conspicuous information is the person's behavior. Because the individual's immediate surroundings remain relatively unchanged and less attention grabbing, we center our attention on the person whose behavior we're considering. Consequently, we are more likely to make attributions based on personal dispositional factors and less likely to make attributions relating to the situation (Follett & Hess, 2002; Langdridge & Butt, 2004; Tal-Or & Papirman, 2007).

Social psychologists' awareness of attribution biases has led, in part, to the development of a new branch of economics called behavioral economics. *Behavioral economics* is concerned with how economic conditions are affected by individuals' biases and irrationality. Rather than viewing people as rational, thoughtful decision makers who are impartially weighing choices to draw conclusions, behavioral economists focus on the irrationality of judgments (Ariely & Norton, 2009).

 # Exploring Diversity

Attribution Biases in a Cultural Context: How Fundamental Is the Fundamental Attribution Error?

Attribution biases do not affect all of us in the same way. The culture in which we are raised clearly plays a role in the way we attribute others' behavior.

Take, for example, the fundamental attribution error: the tendency to overestimate the importance of personal, dispositional factors and underattribute situational factors in determining the causes of others' behavior. The error is pervasive in Western cultures and not in Eastern societies. For instance, adults in India were more likely to use situational attributions than to use dispositional ones in explaining events. These findings are the opposite of those for the United States, and they contradict the fundamental attribution error (Miller, 1984; Lien et al., 2006).

One reason for the difference may lie in the values of Eastern society, which emphasize social responsibility and societal obligations to a greater extent than Western societies do. In addition, the language spoken in a culture may lead to different sorts of attributions. For instance, a tardy person using English may say, "I am late"; this suggests a personal, dispositional cause ("I am a tardy person"). In contrast, speakers of Spanish who are late say, "The clock caused me to be late." Clearly, the statement in Spanish implies that the cause is situational (Macduff, 2006; Alon & Brett, 2007).

Cultural differences in attributions affect subsequent behavior. For example, parents in Asia tend to attribute good academic performance to effort and hard work (situational factors). In contrast, parents in Western cultures tend to de-emphasize the role of effort and attribute school success to innate ability (a dispositional factor). As a result, Asian students in general may strive harder to achieve and ultimately outperform U.S. students in school (Stevenson, Lee, & Mu, 2000; Lien et al., 2006).

The difference in thinking between people in Asian and Western cultures is a reflection of a broader difference in the way the world is perceived. Asian societies generally have a *collectivistic orientation,* a worldview that promotes the notion of interdependence. People with a collectivistic orientation generally see themselves as parts of a larger, interconnected social network and as responsible to others. In contrast, people in Western cultures are more likely to hold an *individualist orientation* that emphasizes personal identity and the uniqueness of the individual. They focus more on what sets them apart from others and what makes them special (Markus & Kitayama, 2003; Wang, 2004; Markus, 2007).

RECAP/EVALUATE/RETHINK

RECAP

LO 43-1 What are attitudes, and how are they formed, maintained, and changed?

- Social psychology is the scientific study of the ways in which people's thoughts, feelings, and actions are affected by others and the nature and causes of individual behavior in social situations.
- Attitudes are evaluations of a particular person, behavior, belief, or concept.
- Cognitive dissonance occurs when an individual simultaneously holds two cognitions–attitudes or thoughts–that contradict each other. To resolve the contradiction, the person may modify one cognition, change its importance, add a cognition, or deny a link between the two cognitions–thus bringing about a reduction in dissonance.

LO 43-2 How do people form impressions of what others are like and the causes of their behavior?

- Social cognition involves the way people understand and make sense of others and themselves. People develop schemas that organize information about people and social experiences in memory and allow them to interpret and categorize information about others.
- People form impressions of others in part through the use of central traits–personality characteristics that receive unusually heavy emphasis when we form an impression.
- Information-processing approaches have found that we tend to average together sets of traits to form an overall impression.
- Attribution theory tries to explain how we understand the causes of behavior, particularly with respect to situational or dispositional factors.

LO 43-3 What are the biases that influence the ways in which people view others' behavior?

- Even though logical processes are involved, attribution is prone to error. For instance, people are susceptible to the halo effect, assumed-similarity bias, self-serving bias, and fundamental attribution error (the tendency to overattribute others' behavior to dispositional causes

and the corresponding failure to recognize the importance of situational causes).

EVALUATE

1. An evaluation of a particular person, behavior, belief, or concept is called a(n) _____.
2. One brand of peanut butter advertises its product by describing its taste and nutritional value. It is hoping to persuade customers through _____ route processing. In ads for a competing brand, a popular actor happily eats the product–but does not describe it. This approach hopes to persuade customers through _____ route processing.
3. Cognitive dissonance theory suggests that we commonly change our behavior to keep it consistent with our attitudes. True or false?
4. Sopan was happy to lend his textbook to a fellow student who seemed bright and friendly. He was surprised when his classmate did not return it. His assumption that the bright and friendly student would also be responsible reflects the _____ effect.

RETHINK

1. Joan sees Annette, a new coworker, acting in a way that seems abrupt and curt. Joan concludes that Annette is unkind and unsociable. The next day, Joan sees Annette acting kindly toward another worker. Is Joan likely to change her impression of Annette? Why or why not? Finally, Joan sees several friends of hers laughing and joking with Annette, treating her in a very friendly fashion. Is Joan likely to change her impression of Annette? Why or why not?
2. Suppose you were assigned to develop a full advertising campaign for a product, including television, radio, and print ads. How might the theories in this chapter guide your strategy to suit the different media?

Answers to Evaluate Questions

1. attitude; 2. central, peripheral; 3. false; we typically change our attitudes and not our behavior to reduce cognitive dissonance; 4. halo

KEY TERMS

social psychology	cognitive dissonance	attribution theory	halo effect
attitudes	social cognition	situational causes (of behavior)	assumed-similarity bias
central route processing	schemas	dispositional causes (of behavior)	self-serving bias
peripheral route processing	central traits		fundamental attribution error

Module 44
Social Influence and Groups

You have just transferred to a new college and are attending your first class. When the professor enters, your fellow classmates instantly rise, bow to the professor, and then stand quietly with their hands behind their backs. You've never encountered such behavior, and it makes no sense to you. Is it more likely that you will (1) jump up to join the rest of the class or (2) remain seated?

Most people would probably choose the first option. As you undoubtedly know from your own experience, pressures to conform to others' behavior can be painfully strong and can bring about changes in behavior that otherwise never would have occurred.

Conformity pressures are just one type of social influence. **Social influence** is the process by which social groups and individuals exert pressure on an individual, either deliberately or unintentionally.

Social influence is so powerful in part because groups and other people generally play a central role in our lives. As defined by social psychologists, **groups** consist of two or more people who (1) interact with one another; (2) perceive themselves as part of a group; and (3) are interdependent—that is, the events that affect one group member affect other members, and the behavior of members has significant consequences for the success of the group in meeting its goals.

Groups develop and hold *norms*, informal beliefs, expectations, and standards about what is appropriate behavior for group members. Norms not only tell us how people in a group should behave ("wearing pink is fashionable this year") but also what members shouldn't do ("under no circumstances wear black"). Group members understand that not adhering to group norms can result in retaliation from other group members, ranging from being ignored to being overtly derided or even being rejected or excluded by the group. Thus, people conform to meet the beliefs and expectations of the group (Miles, Schaufeli, & van den Bos, 2011; Becker, Brackbill, & Centola, 2017).

Groups exert considerable social pressure over individuals. We'll consider three types of social pressure: conformity, compliance, and obedience.

Conformity: Following What Others Do

Conformity is a change in behavior or attitudes brought about by a desire to follow the beliefs or standards of other people. Subtle or even unspoken social pressure results in conformity.

The classic demonstration of pressure to conform comes from a series of studies carried out in the 1950s by Solomon Asch (Asch, 1951). In the experiments, the participants thought they were taking part in a test of perceptual skills with six other people. The experimenter showed the participants one card with three lines of varying length and a second card that had a fourth line that matched one of the first three (see Figure 1). The task was seemingly straightforward: Each of the participants had to announce aloud which of the first three lines was identical in length to the "standard" line on the second card. Because the correct answer was always obvious, the task seemed easy to the participants.

Indeed, because the participants all agreed on the first few trials, the procedure appeared to be simple. But then something odd began to happen. From the perspective of the participant in the group who answered last on each trial, all the answers of the

LEARNING OUTCOME

LO 44-1 What are the major sources and tactics of social influence?

social influence The process by which social groups and individuals exert pressure on an individual, either deliberately or unintentionally. (Module 44)

group Two or more people who interact with one another, perceive themselves as part of a group, and are interdependent. (Module 44)

Study Alert

The distinction between the three types of social pressure—conformity, compliance, and obedience—depends on the nature and strength of the social pressure brought to bear on a person.

conformity A change in behavior or attitudes brought about by a desire to follow the beliefs or standards of other people. (Module 44)

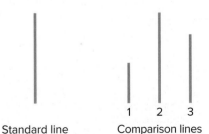

FIGURE 1 Which of the three comparison lines is the same length as the "standard" line?

first six participants seemed to be wrong—in fact, unanimously wrong. And this pattern persisted. Over and over again, the first six participants provided answers that contradicted what the last participant believed to be correct. The last participant faced the dilemma of whether to follow his or her own perceptions or follow the group by repeating the answer everyone else was giving.

As you might have guessed, this experiment was more contrived than it appeared. The first six participants were actually confederates (paid employees of the experimenter) who had been instructed to give unanimously erroneous answers in many of the trials. And the study had nothing to do with perceptual skills. Instead, the issue under investigation was conformity.

Asch found that in about one-third of the trials, the participants conformed to the unanimous but erroneous group answer; about 75% of all participants conformed at least once. However, he found strong individual differences. Some participants conformed nearly all the time, whereas others never did.

CONFORMITY CONCLUSIONS

Since Asch's pioneering work, literally hundreds of studies have examined conformity, and we now know a great deal about the phenomenon. Significant findings focus on:

status The social standing of someone in a group. (Module 44)

- *The characteristics of the group.* The more attractive a group appears to its members, the greater its ability to produce conformity. Furthermore, a person's relative **status,** the social standing of someone within a group, is critical: The lower a person's status in the group, the greater groups' power over that person's behavior (Hogg & Hains, 2001).

- *The situation in which the individual is responding.* Conformity is considerably higher when people must respond publicly than it is when they can do so privately, as the founders of the United States noted when they authorized secret ballots in voting.

- *The kind of task.* People working on ambiguous tasks and questions (those with no clear answer) are more susceptible to social pressure. When asked to give an opinion on something, such as what type of clothing is fashionable, a person will more likely yield to conformist pressures than he or she will if asked a question of fact. In addition, tasks at which an individual is less competent than others in the group make conformity more likely. For example, a person who is an infrequent computer user may feel pressure to conform to an opinion about computer brands when in a group of experienced computer users.

social supporter A group member whose dissenting views make non-conformity to the group easier. (Module 44)

- *Unanimity of the group.* Groups that unanimously support a position show the most pronounced conformity pressures. But what about the case in which people with dissenting views have an ally in the group, known as a **social supporter,** who agrees with them? Having just one person present who shares the minority point of view is sufficient to reduce conformity pressures (Goodwin, Costa, & Adonu, 2004; Levine & Moreland, 2006).

GROUPTHINK: CAVING IN TO CONFORMITY

Although we usually think of conformity in terms of our individual relations with others, in some instances, conformity pressures in organizations can lead to disastrous effects with long-term consequences. One classic example from 2003 concerns the space shuttle *Columbia* and the engineers who had to consider whether insulation that slammed into the space shuttle during takeoff would pose danger during landing. In fact, despite misgivings on the part of some engineers, a strong consensus emerged among them that the insulation would not impair the landing. Ultimately, that consensus proved wrong: The shuttle came apart as it attempted to land, killing all the astronauts on board (Schwartz & Wald, 2003; Mintz & Wayne, 2014).

Groupthink may explain the poor decision making of NASA engineers that led to the destruction of the space shuttle *Columbia*.
©Jim Sugar/Corbis/Getty Images

How could they have made such a poor decision?

A phenomenon known as groupthink may provide an explanation. **Groupthink** is a type of thinking in which group members share such a strong motivation to achieve consensus that they lose the ability to critically evaluate alternative points of view. Groupthink is most likely to occur when a popular or powerful leader is surrounded by people of lower status–which is obviously the case with any U.S. president and his advisers but is also true for leaders in a variety of other organizations.

Groupthink may have been a partial cause of numerous questionable decisions and conclusions in the political and business worlds. For example, the United States invading Iraq or the consensus among media experts that Hilary Clinton would beat Donald Trump in the 2016 presidential election can be seen at least in part as a result of groupthink (Henningsen, Henningsen, & Eden, 2006; Baumeister, Ainsworth, & Vohs, 2015).

Groupthink typically leads to poor decisions. Groups limit the list of possible solutions to just a few, and they spend relatively little time considering any alternatives once the leader seems to be leaning toward a particular solution. In addition, groups may fall prey to *entrapment*, a circumstance in which commitments to a failing point of view or course of action are increased to justify investments in time and energy that have already been made (Turner, Pratkanis, & Struckman, 2007; Willis, 2017).

Ultimately, group members may completely ignore information that challenges a developing consensus. Because historical research suggests that many disastrous decisions reflect groupthink, it is important for groups to be on guard (Chapman, 2006; Packer, 2009).

groupthink A type of thinking in which group members share such a strong motivation to achieve consensus that they lose the ability to critically evaluate alternative points of view. (Module 44)

PsychTech

Through the use of Facebook, Twitter, and other social media, social norms can develop and be rapidly communicated to others.

CONFORMITY TO SOCIAL ROLES

Another way in which conformity influences behavior is through social roles. *Social roles* are the expectations for people who occupy a given social position. For example, we expect that the role of "student" comprises behaviors such as studying, listening to an instructor, and attending class. Similarly, we expect that taxi drivers will know their way around a city and be able to find the quickest route to where we are going. Like a theatrical role, social roles tell us what behavior is associated with a given position.

In some cases, though, social roles influence us so profoundly that we engage in behavior in ways that are atypical for us. This fact was brought home in a classic experiment conducted by Philip Zimbardo and colleagues. In the study, the researchers set up a mock prison complete with cells, solitary confinement cubicles, and a small recreation area. The researchers then advertised for participants who were willing to spend 2 weeks in a study of prison life. Once they identified the study participants, a flip of a coin designated who would be prisoners and who would be prison guards. Neither prisoners nor guards were told how to fulfill their roles (Zimbardo, Maslach, & Haney, 2000; Zimbardo, 2007).

After just a few days in this mock prison, the students assigned to be guards became abusive to the prisoners by waking them at odd hours and subjecting them to arbitrary punishment. They withheld food from the prisoners and forced them to perform hard labor. On the other hand, the students assigned to the prisoner role soon became docile and submissive to the guards. They became extremely demoralized, and one slipped into a depression so severe he was released after just a few days. In fact, after only 6 days of captivity, the remaining prisoners' reactions became so extreme that the study was ended.

The experiment (which, it's important to note, drew criticism on both methodological and ethical grounds) provided a clear lesson: Conforming to a social role can have a powerful consequence on the behavior of even normal, well-adjusted people and induce them to change their behavior in sometimes undesirable ways. This phenomenon may explain how the situation in 2004 in which U.S. Army guards at the Iraqi Abu Ghraib prison found themselves could have led to their abusive behavior toward the prisoners (Haney & Zimbardo, 2009; Post, 2011; Coultas & van Leeuwen, 2015).

Compliance: Submitting to Direct Social Pressure

When we refer to conformity, we usually mean a phenomenon in which the social pressure is subtle or indirect. But in some situations, social pressure is much more obvious with direct, explicit pressure to endorse a particular point of view or behave in a certain way. **Compliance** is behavior that occurs in response to direct social pressure.

Several specific techniques represent attempts to gain compliance. Those frequently employed include:

compliance Behavior that occurs in response to direct social pressure. (Module 44)

- *Foot-in-the-door technique.* The use of the *foot-in-the-door technique* begins when someone asks a target to comply with a small, trivial request. Because such a request is easy to fulfill, the likelihood that the target of the request will comply is high. Later, though, the target is asked to comply with a significantly larger request related to the first one. It turns out that compliance with the second request increases substantially when the target has first agreed to the initial, smaller request.

  Researchers first demonstrated the foot-in-the-door phenomenon in a study in which experimenters went door to door asking residents to sign a petition in favor of safe driving (Freedman & Fraser, 1966). Almost everyone complied with that small, easy-to-agree-to request. However, a few weeks later, different experimenters contacted the residents and made a request that took considerably more effort, asking residents to erect a huge sign on their front lawns that read, "Drive Carefully." The results were clear: 55% of those who had initially signed the petition agreed to the request to put up a sign, whereas only 17% of those in a control group who initially had not been asked to sign the petition agreed to put up a sign.

  Why does the foot-in-the-door technique work? For one reason, consideration of the small request may lead to an interest in the topic of the request or issue; taking an action–any action–makes the individual more committed to the issue, thereby increasing the likelihood of future compliance. Another explanation revolves around people's self-perceptions. By complying with the initial request, individuals may come to see themselves as people who provide help when asked. Then, when confronted with the larger request, they agree in order to maintain the kind of consistency in attitudes and behavior that we described earlier. Although we don't know which of these two explanations is more accurate, it is clear that the foot-in-the-door strategy is effective (Bloom, McBride, & Pollak, 2006; Guéguen et al., 2008).

- *Door-in-the-face technique.* A fund-raiser asks for a $1,000 contribution. You laughingly refuse and tell her that the amount is way out of your league. She then asks for a $10 contribution. How would you react? If you are like most people, you'll probably be a lot more compliant than you would be if she hadn't asked for the huge contribution first. In this tactic, called the *door-in-the-face technique,* someone makes a large request, expects it to be refused, and follows it with a smaller one. This strategy, which is the opposite of the foot-in-the-door approach, has also proved to be effective (Dolinski, 2011; Cantarero, Gamian-Wilk, & Dolinski, 2017).

  In a research study that demonstrates the success of this approach, experimenters stopped college students on the street and asked them to agree to a substantial favor—acting as unpaid counselors for juvenile delinquents 2 hours a week for 2 years (Cialdini et al., 1975). Unsurprisingly, no one agreed to make such an enormous commitment. But when they were later asked the considerably smaller favor of taking a group of delinquents on a 2-hour trip to the zoo, 50% of the people complied. In comparison, only 17% of a control group of participants who had not first received the larger request agreed.

  The use of this technique is widespread. You may have tried it at some point yourself by perhaps by asking your parents for a large increase in your allowance and later settling for less. Similarly, television writers, by sometimes sprinkling their scripts with obscenities that they know network censors will cut out, hope to keep other key phrases intact (Cialdini & Sagarin, 2005).

- *That's-not-all technique.* In this technique, a salesperson offers you a deal at an inflated price. But immediately after the initial offer, the salesperson offers an incentive, discount, or bonus to clinch the deal.

  Although it sounds transparent, this practice can be quite effective. In one study, the experimenters set up a booth and sold cupcakes for 75¢ each. In one condition, the experimenters directly told customers that the price was 75¢. In another condition, they told customers that the price was originally $1 but had been reduced to 75¢. As we might predict, more people bought cupcakes at the "reduced" price—even though it was identical to the price in the other experimental condition (Burger, Reed, & DeCesare, 1999; Pratkanis, 2007).

- *Not-so-free sample.* If you ever receive a free sample, keep in mind that it comes with a psychological cost. Although they may not couch it in these terms, salespeople who provide samples to potential customers do so to bring the norm of reciprocity into play. The *norm of reciprocity* is the social standard that we should treat other people as they treat us. (It's a variant of the Golden Rule we learn as kids: "Do unto others as they will do unto you.") It's a strong cultural standard: When someone does something nice for us, we tend to feel obligated to return the favor. In the case of the *not-so-free sample,* receiving a free sample activates the norm of reciprocity and makes us feel that we should return the favor—in the form of a purchase (Cialdini, 2006; Park & Antonioni, 2007; Burger, 2009).

The persuasive techniques identified by social psychologists can be seen in practice at auto dealerships.
©kzenon/Getty Images

industrial-organizational (I/O) psychology The branch of psychology focusing on work- and job-related issues, including worker motivation, satisfaction, safety, and productivity. (Module 44)

Companies seeking to sell their products to consumers often use the techniques identified by social psychologists for promoting compliance. But employers also use them to bring about compliance and raise employees' productivity in the workplace. In fact, **industrial-organizational (I/O) psychology,** a close cousin to social psychology, considers issues such as worker motivation, satisfaction, safety, and productivity. I/O psychologists also focus on the operation and design of organizations; they ask questions such as how decision making can be improved in large organizations and how the fit between workers and their jobs can be maximized.

Obedience: Following Direct Orders

The compliance techniques that we've been discussing share a common thread: They are used to gently lead people toward agreement with a request. In some cases, however, requests are made in a strong manner. In fact, they're hardly requests at all but rather commands, aimed at producing obedience. **Obedience** is a change in behavior in response to the commands of others. Although obedience is considerably less common than conformity and compliance, it does occur in several specific kinds of relationships. For example, we may show obedience to our bosses, teachers, or parents merely because of the power they hold to reward or punish us.

obedience A change in behavior in response to the commands of others. (Module 44)

To acquire an understanding of obedience, consider for a moment how you might respond if a stranger said to you:

> I've devised a new way of improving memory. All I need is for you to teach people a list of words and then give them a test. The test procedure requires only that you give learners a shock each time they make a mistake on the test. To administer the shocks, you will use a "shock generator" that gives shocks ranging from 15 to 450 volts. You can see that the switches are labeled from "slight shock" through "danger: severe shock" at the top level, where there are three red Xs. But don't worry; although the shocks may be painful, they will cause no permanent damage.

Presented with this situation, you would be likely to think that neither you nor anyone else would go along with the stranger's unusual request. Clearly, it lies outside the bounds of what we consider good sense.

Or does it? Suppose the stranger asking for your help was a psychologist conducting an experiment. Or suppose the request came from your teacher, your employer, or your military commander—all people in authority with a seemingly legitimate reason for the request.

If you still believe it's unlikely that you would comply, think again. The situation presented above describes a classic experiment conducted by social psychologist Stanley Milgram in the 1960s. In the study, an experimenter told participants to give increasingly stronger shocks to another person as part of a study on learning (see Figure 2). In reality, the experiment had nothing to do with learning; the real issue under consideration was the degree to which participants would comply with the experimenter's requests. In fact, the "learner" supposedly receiving the shocks was a confederate who never really received any punishment (Milgram, 2005; Maher, 2015; Griggs, 2017).

Most people who hear a description of Milgram's experiment feel it is unlikely that *any* participant would give the maximum level of shock–or, for that matter, any shock at all. Even a group of psychiatrists to whom the situation was described predicted that fewer than 2% of the participants would fully comply and administer the strongest shocks.

However, the actual results contradicted both experts' and nonexperts' predictions. Some 65% of the participants eventually used the highest setting on the shock generator–450 volts–to shock the learner. This obedience occurred even though the learner, who had mentioned at the start of the experiment that he had a heart condition, demanded to be released, screaming, "Let me out of here! Let me out of here!

 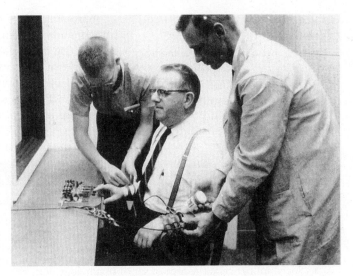

FIGURE 2 This fearsome "shock generator" led participants to believe they were administering electric shocks to another person, who was connected to the generator by electrodes attached to the skin.

(Both): From the film OBEDIENCE © 1968 by Stanley Milgram, © renewed 1993 by Alexandra Milgram. Permission granted by Alexandra Milgram.

My heart's bothering me. Let me out of here!" Despite the learner's pleas, most participants continued to administer the shocks.

Why did so many individuals comply with the experimenter's demands? The participants, who were extensively interviewed after the experiment, said they obeyed primarily because they believed that the experimenter would be responsible for any potential ill effects that befell the learner. The participants accepted the experimenter's orders, then, because they thought that they personally could not be held accountable for their actions–they could always blame the experimenter (Blass, 2004; Kaposi, 2017).

From the perspective of...

An Educator Student obedience in the elementary and secondary classroom is a major issue for many teachers. How might you promote student obedience in the classroom?

©Andersen Ross/Blend Images/Getty Images

Most participants in the Milgram experiment said later they felt the knowledge gained from the study outweighed the discomfort they may have felt. However, the experiment has been criticized for creating an extremely trying set of circumstances for the participants, thereby raising serious ethical concerns. Undoubtedly, the same experiment could not be conducted today because of ethical considerations (Perry, 2013).

Other critics have suggested that Milgram's methods were ineffective in creating a situation that actually mirrored real-world obedience. For example, how often are people placed in a situation in which someone orders them to continue hurting a victim while the victim's protests are ignored (Blass, 2004; Werhane et al., 2013)?

Despite these concerns, Milgram's research remains the strongest laboratory demonstration of obedience. And partial replications of Milgram's work, conducted in an ethically defensible way, find similar results, which adds credence to the original work (Blass, 2009; Burger, 2009; Gibson, 2013).

Study Alert

Because of its graphic demonstration of obedience to authority, the Milgram experiment is one of the most famous and influential studies in social psychology.

Furthermore, we need only consider actual instances of obedience to authority to witness some frightening real-life parallels. For instance, after World War II, the major defense that Nazi officers gave to excuse their participation in atrocities during the war was that they were "only following orders." Milgram's experiment, which was motivated in part by his desire to explain the behavior of everyday Germans during World War II, forces us to ask ourselves this question: Would we be able to withstand the intense power of authority?

RECAP/EVALUATE/RETHINK

RECAP

LO 44-1 What are the major sources and tactics of social influence?

- Social influence is the area of social psychology concerned with situations in which the actions of an individual or group affect the behavior of others.
- Conformity refers to changes in behavior or attitudes that result from a desire to follow the beliefs or standards of others.
- Compliance is behavior that results from direct social pressure. Among the ways of eliciting compliance are the foot-in-the-door, door-in-the-face, that's-not-all, and not-so-free sample techniques.
- Obedience is a change in behavior in response to the commands of others.

EVALUATE

1. A _____ _____, or person who agrees with the dissenting viewpoint, is likely to reduce conformity.
2. Who pioneered the study of conformity?
   a. Skinner
   b. Asch
   c. Milgram
   d. Fiala
3. Which of the following techniques asks a person to comply with a small initial request to enhance the likelihood that the person will later comply with a larger request?
   a. Door-in-the-face
   b. Foot-in-the-door

   c. That's-not-all
   d. Not-so-free sample
4. The _____ _____ _____ _____ technique begins with an outrageous request that makes a subsequent, smaller request seem reasonable.
5. _____ is a change in behavior that is due to another person's orders.

RETHINK

1. Why do you think the Milgram experiment is so controversial? What sorts of effects might the experiment have had on participants? Do you think the experiment would have had similar results if it had not been conducted in a laboratory setting but among members of a social group (such as a fraternity or sorority) with strong pressures to conform?
2. Imagine that you have been trained to use the various compliance techniques described in this section. Because these compliance techniques are so powerful, should the use of certain such techniques be forbidden? Should consumers be taught defenses against such techniques? Is the use of such techniques ethically and morally defensible? Why?

Answers to Evaluate Questions

1. social supporter; 2. b; 3. b; 4. door-in-the-face; 5. Obedience

KEY TERMS

social influence	social supporter	industrial-organizational
group	groupthink	(I/O) psychology
conformity	compliance	obedience
status		

Module 45
Prejudice and Discrimination

What do you think when someone says, "He's African American," "She's Chinese," or "That's a woman driver"?

If you're like most people, you'll probably automatically form some sort of impression of what each person is like. Most likely your impression is based on a **stereotype,** a set of generalized beliefs and expectations about a specific group and its members. Stereotypes grow out of our tendency to categorize and organize the vast amount of information we encounter in our everyday lives. All stereotypes share the common feature of oversimplifying the world: We view individuals not in terms of their unique, personal characteristics but also in terms of characteristics we attribute to all the members of a particular group.

Stereotypes can lead to **prejudice,** a negative (or positive) evaluation of a group and its members. For instance, racial prejudice occurs when a member of a racial group is evaluated in terms of race and not because of his or her own characteristics or abilities. Although prejudice can be positive ("I love the Irish"), social psychologists have focused on understanding the roots of negative prejudice ("I hate immigrants").

Common stereotypes and forms of prejudice involve race, religion, ethnicity, and gender. Over the years, various groups have been called "lazy" or "shrewd" or "cruel" with varying degrees of regularity by those who are not members of that group. Even today, despite major progress toward reducing legally sanctioned forms of prejudice, such as school segregation, stereotypes remain (Hunt, Seifert, & Armenta, 2006; Devos, 2011; Bhatia, 2017).

Even people who on the surface appear to be unprejudiced may harbor hidden prejudice. For example, when white participants in experiments are shown faces on a computer screen so rapidly that they cannot consciously perceive the faces, they react more negatively to black than to white faces–an example of what has been called *modern racism* (Pearson, Dovidio, & Pratto, 2007; Blanton, Jaccard, & Burrows, 2015).

Stereotypes can have harmful consequences because acting on stereotypes results in discrimination. **Discrimination** is behavior directed toward individuals on the basis of their membership in a particular group. Discrimination can lead to exclusion from jobs, neighborhoods, and educational opportunities, and it may result in lower salaries and benefits for members of specific groups. Discrimination can also result in more favorable treatment to favored groups–for example, when an employer hires a job applicant of his or her own racial group because of the applicant's race (Pager & Shepherd, 2008; Leskinen, Rabelo, & Cortina, 2015).

Stereotyping not only leads to overt discrimination but also can cause members of stereotyped groups to behave in ways that reflect the stereotype through a phenomenon known as the *self-fulfilling prophecy.* Self-fulfilling prophecies are expectations about the occurrence of a future event or behavior that act to increase the likelihood the event or behavior will occur. For example, if people think that members of a specific group lack ambition, they may treat them in a way that actually brings about a lack of ambition. Furthermore, it can lead to a self-perpetuating phenomenon that we discuss next (Madon, Willard, & Guyll, 2006; Tappin, McKay, & Abrams, 2017).

The Foundations of Prejudice

No one has ever been born disliking a specific racial, religious, or ethnic group. People learn to hate in much the same way that they learn the alphabet.

LEARNING OUTCOMES

LO 45-1 How do stereotypes, prejudice, and discrimination differ?

LO 45-2 How can we reduce prejudice and discrimination?

stereotype A set of generalized beliefs and expectations about a particular group and its members. (Module 45)

prejudice A negative (or positive) evaluation of a particular group and its members. (Module 45)

discrimination Behavior directed toward individuals on the basis of their membership in a particular group. (Module 45)

Study Alert
Remember that *prejudice* relates to *attitudes* about a group and its members, whereas *discrimination* relates to *behavior* directed to a group and its members.

According to *observational learning approaches* to stereotyping and prejudice, the behavior of parents, other adults, and peers shapes children's feelings about members of various groups. For instance, bigoted parents may commend their children for expressing prejudiced attitudes. Likewise, young children learn prejudice by imitating the behavior of adult models. Such learning starts at an early age: Children as young as 6 months judge others according to their skin color, and by 3 years of age, they begin to show preferences for members of their own race (Dovidio & Gaertner, 2006; Ponterotto, Utsey, & Pedersen, 2006; Bronson & Merryman, 2009).

The mass media also provide information about stereotypes not just for children but for adults as well. Even today, some television shows and movies portray Italians as Mafia-like mobsters, Jews as greedy bankers, and African Americans as promiscuous or lazy. When such inaccurate portrayals are the primary source of information about minority groups, they can lead to the development and maintenance of unfavorable stereotypes (Do, 2006; Scharrer & Ramasubramanian, 2015).

Other explanations of prejudice and discrimination focus on how being a member of a specific group helps to magnify one's sense of self-esteem. According to *social identity theory*, we use group membership as a source of pride and self-worth. Social identity theory suggests that people tend to be ethnocentric, viewing the world from their own perspective and judging others in terms of their group membership. Slogans such as "gay pride" and "Black is beautiful" illustrate that the groups to which we belong give us a sense of self-respect (Tajfel & Turner, 2004; Hogg, 2006; Kahn et al., 2017).

However, the use of group membership to provide social respect produces an unfortunate outcome. In an effort to maximize our sense of self-esteem, we may come to think that our own group (our *ingroup*) is better than groups to which we don't belong (our *outgroups*). Consequently, we inflate the positive aspects of our ingroup—and, at the same time, devalue outgroups. Ultimately, we come to view members of outgroups as inferior to members of our ingroup (Tajfel & Turner, 2004). The end result is prejudice toward members of groups of which we are not a part.

Neither the observational learning approach nor the social identity approach provides a full explanation for stereotyping and prejudice. For instance, some psychologists argue that prejudice results when there is perceived competition for scarce societal resources. Thus, when competition exists for jobs or housing, members of majority groups may believe (however unjustly or inaccurately) that minority group members are hindering their efforts to attain their goals; this belief can lead to prejudice. In addition, other explanations for prejudice emphasize human cognitive limitations that

Like father, like son: Social learning approaches to stereotyping and prejudice suggest that attitudes and behaviors toward members of minority groups are learned through the observation of parents and other individuals. How can this cycle be broken?

©Barbara Burnes/Science Source

lead us to categorize people on the basis of visually conspicuous physical features such as race, sex, and ethnic group. Such categorization can lead to the development of stereotypes and, ultimately, to discriminatory behavior (Weeks & Lupfer, 2004; Hugenberg & Sacco, 2008; Yoo & Pituc, 2013).

The most recent approach to understanding prejudice comes from an increasingly important area in social psychology: social neuroscience. **Social neuroscience** seeks to identify the neurological basis of social behavior. It looks at how we can illuminate our understanding of groups, interpersonal relations, and emotions by understanding their neuroscientific underpinnings (Harmon-Jones & Winkielman, 2007; Todorov, Fiske, & Prentice, 2011; Kasemsap, 2017).

In one example of the value of social neuroscience approaches, researchers examined activation of the *amygdala*, the structure in the brain that relates to emotion-evoking stimuli and situations, while people viewed white and black faces. Because the amygdala is especially responsive to threatening, unusual, or highly arousing stimuli, the researchers hypothesized greater activation of the amygdala during exposure to black faces due to negative cultural associations with racial minorities (Lieberman, 2007; Nelson, 2013).

As you can see in *Neuroscience in Your Life*, the hypothesis was confirmed: The amygdala showed more activation when participants saw a black face than when they saw a white one. Because both blacks and whites were participants in the study, it is unlikely that the amygdala activation was simply the result of the novelty of viewing members of a racial minority. Instead, the findings suggest that culturally learned societal messages about race led to the brain activation.

social neuroscience The subfield of social psychology that seeks to identify the neurological basis of social behavior. (Module 45)

NEUROSCIENCE IN YOUR LIFE: THE PREJUDICED BRAIN

Problems related to racial prejudice are ongoing in the United States. To provide insight into these problems, social neuroscientists have begun to examine how we process social information in the brain and how that processing relates to stereotypes and prejudice.

To examine a potential relationship between racial differences and threat detection, social neuroscientists scanned participants' brains while asking them to look at photos of black or white individuals, determine whether the person in the photo had a weapon, and respond by "shooting" the person in the photo if they thought a gun was present. Participants, who were white, Asian, Hispanic, and of unknown races. more quickly decided to shoot and showed greater brain activity in the parietal and visual cortexes for armed blacks than for armed whites.

In addition, as shown in the images below, greater connectivity occurred (shown in purple) between the amygdala, parietal cortex, visual cortex, and other areas when participants viewed armed blacks than when they viewed armed whites. These results demonstrate possible neural correlates contributing to the greater likelihood of treating blacks as more dangerous than whites (Senholzi et al., 2015).

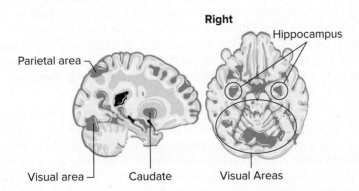

Source: Adapted from Senholzi, K. B., Depue, B. E., Correll, J., Banich, M. T., & Ito, T. A. (2015). Brain activation underlying threat detection to targets of different races. *Society for Neuroscience, 10*(6), 651–662. doi: 10.1080/17470919.2015.1091380

Measuring Prejudice and Discrimination: The Implicit Association Test

Could you be prejudiced and not even know it? Probably yes, according to the researchers who developed a test that reveals hidden prejudice.

The *Implicit Association Test*, or *IAT*, is an ingenious measure of prejudice that permits a more accurate assessment of people's discrimination between members of different groups.

The IAT uses the fact that people's automatic, instant reactions often provide the most valid indicator of what they actually believe. The test asks people questions that assess the degree to which they associate members of target groups (say, African Americans versus whites) with positive stimuli (such as a puppy) versus negative stimuli (such as a funeral). The test is based on the fact that growing up in a particular culture teaches us to unconsciously associate members of particular groups with positive or negative qualities, and we tend to absorb associations about those groups that reflect the culture without even being aware of it (Aikawa & Fujii, 2011; Blanton, Jaccard, & Burrows, 2015; Roberts, Neate, & Gierasch, 2017).

The results of the IAT show that almost 90% of test-takers have an implicit pro-white bias, and more than two-thirds of non-Arab, non-Muslim volunteers display implicit biases against Arab Muslims. Moreover, more than 80% of heterosexuals display an implicit bias against gays and lesbians (Lane et al., 2007).

So, of course, having an implicit bias does not mean that people will overtly discriminate, which is a criticism that has been made of the test. Yet it does mean that the cultural lessons to which we are exposed have a considerable unconscious influence on us. (If you would like to try a version of the IAT yourself, there is a sample test at https://implicit.harvard.edu/implicit. You may well be surprised at the results.)

Study Alert
Remember that the IAT allows measurement of attitudes about which people might not be consciously aware as well as attitudes they wish to keep hidden from others.

Reducing the Consequences of Prejudice and Discrimination

How can we diminish the effects of prejudice and discrimination? Psychologists have developed several strategies that have proved effective.

- *Increasing contact between the target of stereotyping and the holder of the stereotype.* Research consistently shows that increasing the amount of interaction between people can reduce negative stereotyping. But only certain kinds of contact are likely to reduce prejudice and discrimination. Situations in which contact is relatively intimate, the individuals are of equal status, or participants must cooperate with one another or are dependent on one another are more likely to reduce stereotyping. On the other hand, even virtual contact via social media may be sufficient to improve intergroup relations (Tropp & Pettigrew, 2005; Pettigrew & Tropp, 2006; White, Harvey, & Abu-Rayya, 2015).

- *Making values and norms against prejudice more conspicuous.* Sometimes just reminding people about the values they already hold regarding equality and fair treatment of others is enough to reduce discrimination. Similarly, people who hear others making strong, vehement antiracist statements are subsequently more likely to strongly condemn racism. Furthermore, one study found that even a short, 10-minute conversation with voters asking them to recall a time when they were judged negatively and unfairly was sufficient to reduce prejudice toward transgender people that lasted 3 months (Tropp & Bianchi, 2006; Rutland & Killen, 2015; Broockman & Kalla, 2016).

- *Providing information about the targets of stereotyping.* Probably the most direct means of changing stereotypical and discriminatory attitudes is education: teaching people to be more aware of the positive characteristics of targets of stereotyping. For instance, when the meaning of puzzling behavior is explained to people who hold stereotypes, they may come to appreciate the actual significance of the behavior (Isbell & Tyler, 2003; Banks, 2006; Nagda, Tropp, & Paluck, 2006).

- *Reducing stereotype threat.* Social psychologist Claude Steele suggests that many African Americans suffer from *stereotype vulnerability*, obstacles to performance that stem from their awareness of society's stereotypes regarding minority group members. He argues that African American students too often receive instruction from teachers who doubt their students' abilities and who set up remedial programs to assist their students. As a result of their teachers' (as well as society's) low expectations for their performance, African American students may come to accept society's stereotypes and come to believe that they are likely to fail (Aronson & Steele, 2005; Nussbaum & Steele, 2007; Aronson & Dee, 2012).

  Such beliefs can have devastating effects. When confronted with an academic task, African American students may fear that their performance will simply confirm society's negative stereotypes. The immediate consequence of this fear is anxiety that hampers performance. But the long-term consequences may be even worse: Doubting their ability to perform successfully in academic environments, African Americans may decide that the risks of failure are so great it is not worth the effort even to attempt to do well. Ultimately, they may "disidentify" with academic success by minimizing the importance of academic endeavors (Stone, 2002; Lombaard & Naudé, 2017).

  However, Steele's analysis suggests that African Americans may be able to overcome their predicament. Specifically, schools can design intervention programs to train minority group members about their vulnerability to stereotypes and provide them with self-affirmation that reinforces their confidence in their abilities and thereby inoculates them against the fear and doubt triggered by negative stereotypes (Cohen et al., 2006; Wilson, 2006; Shnabel et al., 2013).

- *Increasing the sense of social belonging of ethnic minority students.* Although almost every college student faces feelings of inadequacy and uncertainty about belonging at the start of college, such feelings are especially strong for members of groups who are underrepresented and have been the targets of prejudice and discrimination. However, research shows that a simple intervention in which members of minority groups are made to understand that feelings of inadequacy are not unique to them—and that such feelings usually diminish with time—can help minority students increase their sense of social belonging (Walton & Cohen, 2011; also see *Applying Psychology in the 21st Century*).

From the perspective of...

A Corrections Officer How might overt forms of prejudice and discrimination toward disadvantaged groups (such as African Americans) be reduced in a state or federal prison?

©Hill Street Studios/Blend Images LLC

APPLYING PSYCHOLOGY IN THE 21ST CENTURY

HELPING MORE WOMEN SUCCEED AS ENGINEERS

Majoring in a science, technology, engineering, or math (STEM) field is challenging for anyone but particularly so for women—not because women are less capable than men in these fields but because they face many additional obstacles that men don't. Chief among these is the stereotype that STEM fields are a male domain.

Female STEM students often encounter sexism, harassment, and hostility from their peers and even from their professors. In ways that are subtle and sometimes not so subtle, they are treated as if they are less capable than men and don't belong in their chosen field. Often women come to implicitly believe in these stereotypes themselves and to lose confidence in their own abilities. The result too often is that capable female students end up leaving STEM majors behind (Nosek, Banaji, & Greenwald, 2002; Dennehy et al., 2018).

Finding ways to overcome these obstacles and retain talented female students in STEM majors has therefore become an important priority of many colleges and universities. Compelling new research establishes how a relatively simple intervention is remarkably effective at achieving this goal: Pairing female STEM majors with female peer mentors. In the research, 150 incoming female engineering students were randomly paired with a female peer mentor, a male peer mentor, or no mentor for 1 year. The mentors received some training and kept a diary of their mentoring conversations, establishing that the male

©YinYang/Getty Images

mentors were as available and supportive as the female mentors. But they weren't equally effective. The female students paired with female (but not male) mentors reported a greater sense of belonging in engineering, self-efficacy, motivation, and intentions to pursue a career in engineering. They were also more likely to remain in the engineering major. Whereas 11% of the students without a mentor dropped out within that first year, *all* the students with a female mentor remained in the major—an astounding difference (Dennehy & Dasgupta, 2017).

The researchers emphasize that the key contribution of the female peer mentors was helping new female STEM undergraduates feel that they fit in and belonged. It's not about their ability; grades were in fact

not related to retention or career aspirations in their study. Feelings of belonging and confidence were, and this is what the female peer mentors reinforced. Moreover, the benefits persisted well beyond the conclusion of the mentoring period, showing up in the researchers' follow-ups throughout the second year. And these benefits are crucial, as women are most likely to withdraw from a STEM major during the first 2 years, so even a relatively short-term intervention of female peer mentoring can inoculate female students throughout this critical period.

What makes female peer mentors particularly effective at retaining female STEM students? It's not that they give better advice or care more or show greater empathy; the researchers found no evidence that their mentoring quality was better than that of men. Rather, the female mentors acted as role models. They reinforced to the incoming female STEM students that women do indeed belong in this field and that they could succeed. Beyond its important practical applications, this research provides a clear example of how social factors can be just as important determinants of success as native ability (Dennehy & Dasgupta, 2017; Dennehy et al., 2018).

> **RETHINK**
>
> - Why do you think that witnessing a similar other's success can be so crucial to one's own success?
> - Do you think that peer mentoring would work for other kinds of groups that are traditionally underrepresented in certain majors? Why or why not?

RECAP/EVALUATE/RETHINK

RECAP

LO 45-1 How do stereotypes, prejudice, and discrimination differ?

- Stereotypes are generalized beliefs and expectations about a specific group and its members. Stereotyping can lead to prejudice and self-fulfilling prophecies.

- Prejudice is the negative (or positive) evaluation of a particular group and its members.
- Stereotyping and prejudice can lead to discrimination, behavior directed toward individuals on the basis of their membership in a particular group.
- According to observational learning approaches, children learn stereotyping and prejudice by observing the

behavior of parents, other adults, and peers. Social identity theory suggests that group membership is used as a source of pride and self-worth, and this may lead people to think of their own group as better than others.

- Social neuroscientific approaches to prejudice examine the functioning of the brain and nervous system to understand the basis of prejudice.

LO 45-2 How can we reduce prejudice and discrimination?

- Among the ways of reducing prejudice and discrimination are increasing contact, demonstrating positive values against prejudice, and education.

EVALUATE

1. Any expectation–positive or negative–about an individual solely on the basis of that person's membership in a group can be a stereotype. True or false?
2. The negative (or positive) evaluation of a group and its members is called
   a. Stereotyping
   b. Prejudice
   c. Self-fulfilling prophecy
   d. Discrimination
3. Paul is a store manager who does not expect women to succeed in business. He therefore offers important, high-profile responsibilities only to men. If the female employees fail to move up in the company, it could be an example of a _____ _____ prophecy.

RETHINK

1. Do you think women can be victims of stereotype vulnerability? In what topical areas might this occur? Can men be victims of stereotype vulnerability? Why?
2. How are stereotypes, prejudice, and discrimination related? In a society committed to equality, which of the three should be changed first? Why?

Answers to Evaluate Questions

1. true; 2. b; 3. self-fulfilling

KEY TERMS

stereotype   prejudice   discrimination   social neuroscience

Module 46

Positive and Negative Social Behavior

LEARNING OUTCOMES

LO 46-1 Why are we attracted to certain people, and what progression do social relationships follow?

LO 46-2 What factors underlie aggression and prosocial behavior?

interpersonal attraction (or close relationship) Positive feelings for others; liking and loving. (Module 46)

Like philosophers and theologians, social psychologists have pondered the basic nature of humanity. Is it represented mainly by the violence and cruelty we see throughout the world, or does something special about human nature permit loving, considerate, unselfish, and even noble behavior as well?

We turn to two routes that social psychologists have followed in seeking answers to these questions. We first consider what they have learned about the sources of our attraction to others; we end with a look at two opposite sides of human behavior: aggression and helping.

Liking and Loving: Interpersonal Attraction and the Development of Relationships

Nothing is more important in most people's lives than their feelings for others. Consequently, it is not surprising that liking and loving have become a major focus of interest for social psychologists. Known more formally as the study of **interpersonal attraction or close relationships,** this area addresses the factors that lead to positive feelings for others.

HOW DO I LIKE THEE? LET ME COUNT THE WAYS

By far the greatest amount of research has focused on liking, probably because it is easier for investigators conducting short-term experiments to produce states of liking in strangers who have just met than to instigate and observe loving relationships over long periods. Consequently, research has given us a good deal of knowledge about the factors that initially attract two people to each other. The important factors social psychologists consider are the following:

- *Proximity.* If you live in a residence hall or an apartment, consider the friends you made when you first moved in. Chances are that you became friendliest with those who lived geographically nearest to you. In fact, this is one of the more firmly established findings in the research on interpersonal attraction: Proximity leads to liking (Burgoon et al., 2002; Smith & Weber, 2005; Semin & Garrido, 2013).

- *Mere exposure.* Repeated exposure to a person is often sufficient to produce attraction. Interestingly, repeated exposure to *any* stimulus–a person, picture, tweet, or virtually anything–usually makes us like the stimulus more. Becoming familiar with a person can evoke positive feelings; we then transfer the positive feelings stemming from familiarity to the person him- or herself. Of course, there are exceptions: In cases of strongly negative initial encounters, repeated exposure is unlikely to cause us to like a person more. Instead, the more we are exposed to the person, the more we are likely to dislike the individual (Zajonc, 2001; Butler & Berry, 2004).

- *Similarity.* Folk wisdom tells us that birds of a feather flock together. However, folk wisdom also maintains that opposites attract. Which is right? Social psychologists have come up with a clear verdict regarding which of the two statements is correct: We tend to like those who are similar to us. Discovering that others have similar attitudes, values, or traits promotes our liking for them. Furthermore, the more similar others are, the more we like them. One reason similarity increases the likelihood of interpersonal attraction is that we assume people with similar attitudes will evaluate us positively. Because we experience a strong **reciprocity-of-liking effect,** a tendency to like those who like us, knowing that someone evaluates us positively promotes our attraction to that person. In addition, if *we* like someone else, we tend to assume that person likes us in return (Heffernan & Fraley, 2015; Wróbel & Królewiak, 2017).

reciprocity-of-liking effect
A tendency to like those who like us. (Module 46)

- *Physical attractiveness.* For most people, the equation *beautiful = good* is quite true. As a result, physically attractive people are more popular than are physically unattractive ones, if all other factors are equal. This finding, which contradicts the values that most people say they hold, is apparent even in childhood (preschoolers' popularity is related to their attractiveness) and continues into adulthood. Indeed, physical attractiveness may be the single most important element promoting initial liking in college dating situations, although its influence eventually decreases when people get to know each other better (Little, Burt, & Perrett, 2006; Luo & Zhang, 2009).

These factors alone, of course, do not account for liking. For example, in one experiment that examined the desired qualities in a friendship, the top-rated qualities in a same-sex friend included sense of humor, warmth and kindness, expressiveness and openness, an exciting personality, and similarity of interests and leisure activities. In addition, our friendships and social networks may be related to neurological factors (Sprecher & Regan, 2002).

PsychTech
Research on Facebook and other social media sites indicates that social networking provides a less-intimidating social outlet for students who otherwise have trouble making and keeping friendships, such as those who are introverted or have low self-esteem.

Friendship and Social Networking The newest forms of friendship are found on social network sites. One out of 10 people *worldwide* belongs to Facebook, and the concentration of college students using the social network site is more than 90 percent.

For college students, the primary motivation in using social network sites is to keep in touch with their friends. In addition, younger college students use Facebook to explore their developing identities. Because users can control how they present themselves to the world on a social network profile, it is easy for college students to "try on" identities by posting selected photos of themselves, revealing specific tastes and interests, or otherwise presenting themselves in new and different ways. The feedback they get from others may help them decide which identities and forms of self-presentation suit them best (Subrahmanyam et al., 2008; Pempek, Yermolayeva, & Calvert, 2009; Phua, Jin, & Kim, 2017).

But how do social network sites affect users' nonvirtual social lives? Maintaining social connections that might otherwise have withered and died seems like a good thing, but it may be detrimental if someone spends so much time maintaining online distant or superficial friendships that they sacrifice time spent on intimate, face-to-face interactions with close friends (Steinfeld, Ellison, & Lampe, 2008).

It turns out, though, that intensity of Facebook use is positively related to college students' life satisfaction, social trust, and civic engagement. In short, research suggests that users of social network sites are not disengaged from the real world and that the benefits of social networking may outweigh the costs to real-world social lives (Valenzuela, Park, & Kee, 2009; Brandtzæg, Lüders, & Skjetne, 2010).

HOW DO I LOVE THEE? LET ME COUNT THE WAYS

Whereas our knowledge of what makes people like one another is extensive, our understanding of love is more limited in scope and recently acquired. For some time, many social psychologists believed that love was too difficult to observe and study in a controlled, scientific way. However, love is such a central issue in most people's lives that eventually social psychologists could not resist its allure.

As a first step, researchers tried to identify the characteristics that distinguish between mere liking and full-blown love. They discovered that love is not simply a greater quantity of liking but a qualitatively different psychological state. For instance, at least in its early stages, love includes relatively intense physiological arousal, an all-encompassing interest in the other individual, fantasizing about the other, and relatively rapid swings of emotion. Similarly, love, unlike liking, includes elements of passion, closeness, fascination, exclusiveness, sexual desire, and intense caring. We idealize partners by exaggerating their good qualities and minimizing their imperfections (Murray, Holmes, & Griffin, 2004; Tamini, Bojhd, & Yazdani, 2011).

Other researchers have theorized that there are two main types of love: passionate love and companionate love. **Passionate (or romantic) love** represents a state of intense absorption in someone. It includes intense physiological arousal, psychological interest, and caring for the needs of another. In contrast, **companionate love** is the strong affection we have for those with whom our lives are deeply involved. The love we feel for parents, other family members, and even some close friends falls into the category of companionate love (Regan, 2006; Loving, Crockett, & Paxson, 2009; Yildirim & Barnett, 2017).

Psychologist Robert Sternberg makes an even finer differentiation between types of love. He proposes that love consists of three parts (see Figure 1):

- *Decision/commitment*, the initial thoughts that one loves someone and the longer-term feelings of commitment to maintain love

- *Intimacy component*, feelings of closeness and connectedness

- *Passion component*, the motivational drives relating to sex, physical closeness, and romance

According to Sternberg, these three components combine to produce the different types of love. He suggests that different combinations of the three components vary over the course of relationships. For example, in strong, loving relationships, the level of commitment peaks and then remains stable. Passion, on the other hand, peaks quickly and then declines and levels off relatively early in most relationships. In addition, relationships are happiest in which the strength of the various components are similar between the two partners (Sternberg, Hojjat, & Barnes, 2001; Sternberg, 2004, 2006).

Is love a necessary ingredient in a good marriage? Yes, if you live in the United States. In contrast, it's considerably less important in other cultures. Although mutual attraction (love) is the most important characteristic men and women in the United States desire in a mate, men in China rated good health as most important, and women there rated emotional stability and maturity as most important. Among the Zulu in South Africa, men rated emotional stability first and women rated dependable character first (see Figure 2; Buss, Abbott, & Angleitner, 1990).

passionate (or romantic) love A state of intense absorption in someone that includes intense physiological arousal, psychological interest, and caring for the needs of another. (Module 46)

companionate love The strong affection we have for those with whom our lives are deeply involved. (Module 46)

FIGURE 1 According to Sternberg, love has three main components: intimacy, passion, and decision/commitment. Different combinations of these components can create other types of love. Nonlove contains none of the three components.
Source: Adapted from Sternberg, R. J. (1986). A triangular theory of love. *Psychological Review,* 93(2), 119–135.

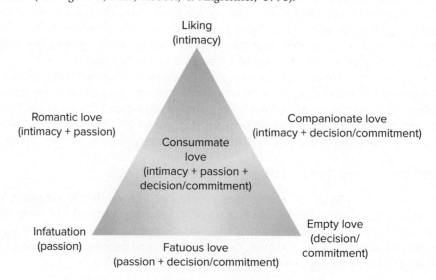

	Rank Ordering of Five Desired Characteristics in a Mate					
	United States		**China**		**South Africa Zulu**	
	Females	**Males**	**Females**	**Males**	**Females**	**Males**
Mutual attraction—love	1	1		4	5	
Emotional stability and maturity	2	2	1	5	2	1
Dependable character	3	3			1	3
Pleasing disposition	4	4			3	4
Education and intelligence	5	5	4			
Good health			3	1	4	5
Desire for home and children			2	2		
Ambition and industriousness			5			
Good cook and housekeeper						2
Chastity (no prior sexual intercourse)				3		

FIGURE 2 Although love may be an important factor in choosing a marriage partner if you live in the United States, other cultures place less importance on it.

Source: Adapted from Buss, D. M., Abbott, M., & Angleitner, A. (1990). International preferences in selecting mates: A study of 37 cultures. *Journal of Cross-Cultural Psychology, 21*, 5–47.

How we meet our romantic partners and spouses has changed drastically over the years. In the 1940s, heterosexual Americans met their future family members most often through family. Now friends and the Internet are much more frequent matchmakers (see Figure 3). The likelihood of meeting online is even greater for same-sex couples today; some 70% of gay couples report meeting online (Rosenfeld & Thomas, 2012).

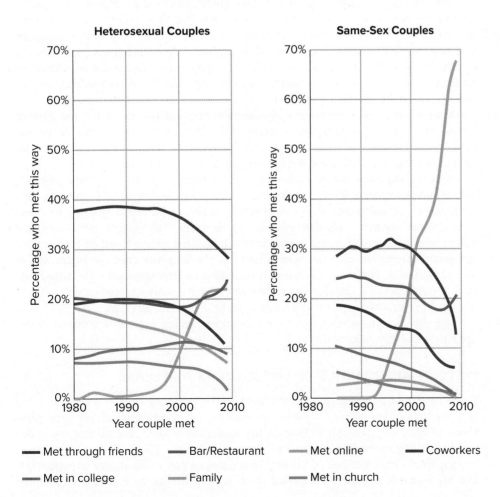

FIGURE 3 Couples are considerably more likely to meet online today than were couples in earlier generations, a change that holds true for heterosexual as well as same-sex couples.

Source: Rosenfeld, M. J., & Thomas, R. J. (2012). Searching for a mate: The rise of the Internet as a social intermediary. *American Sociological Review, 77*, 523–547.

Liking and loving clearly show a positive side of human social behavior. Now we turn to behaviors that are just as much a part of social behavior: aggression and helping behavior.

Aggression and Prosocial Behavior: Hurting and Helping Others

Drive-by shootings, carjackings, and abductions are just a few examples of the violence that seems all too common today. Yet we also find examples of generous, unselfish, thoughtful behavior that suggest a more optimistic view of humankind. Consider, for instance, people such as Mother Teresa, who ministered to the poor in India. Or contemplate the simple kindnesses of life: lending class lecture notes, stopping to help a child who has fallen off a bicycle, or merely sharing a candy bar with a friend. Such instances of helping are no less characteristic of human behavior than are the distasteful examples of aggression.

HURTING OTHERS: AGGRESSION

We need look no further than the daily news cycle to be bombarded with examples of aggression on both a societal level (war, invasion, assassination) and an individual level (crime, child abuse, and the many petty cruelties humans are capable of inflicting on one another). Is such aggression an inevitable part of the human condition? Or is aggression primarily a product of particular circumstances that, if changed, could lead to its reduction?

The difficulty of answering such knotty questions becomes apparent as soon as we consider how best to define the term *aggression*. Depending on the way we define the word, many examples of inflicted pain or injury may or may not qualify as aggression (see Figure 4). For instance, a rapist is clearly acting with aggression toward his victim. On the other hand, it is less certain that a physician carrying out an emergency medical procedure without an anesthetic, thereby causing incredible pain to the patient, should be considered aggressive.

aggression The intentional injury of, or harm to, another person. (Module 46)

Most social psychologists define aggression in terms of the intent and the purpose behind the behavior. **Aggression** is intentional injury of or harm to another person. By this definition, the rapist is clearly acting aggressively, whereas the physician causing pain during a medical procedure is not (Berkowitz, 2001).

Also, the aggression we encounter in our daily lives can take many forms. Not only do we hurt others through direct physical or verbal attacks, but we also can hurt people indirectly by doing such things as spreading rumors or purposely ignoring someone. In fact, some research finds that *microaggressions*–small, daily slights, put-downs, and insults, often perpetrated against members of marginalized groups based on race, gender, and sexual orientation–may be more harmful in the long run than are highly visible acts of aggression. However, the research findings on mircroaggressions are mixed, and more research needs to be done to understand how the daily experience of small acts of prejudice impacts recipients (Richardson, 2014; Lilienfeld, 2017; Sue, 2017).

We turn now to several approaches to understanding aggressive behavior developed by social psychologists.

INSTINCT APPROACHES: AGGRESSION AS A RELEASE

If you have ever punched an adversary in the nose, you may have experienced a certain satisfaction despite your better judgment. Instinct theories, which note the prevalence of aggression not only in humans but in animals as well, propose that aggression is primarily the outcome of innate–or inborn–urges.

Sigmund Freud was one of the first to suggest, as part of his theory of personality, that aggression is a primary instinctual drive. Konrad Lorenz, an ethologist (a scientist

Is This Aggression?

Defining aggression can be difficult. To see the challenges it raises, read each of the following scenarios and consider whether it describes an aggressive act—according to your own definition of aggressive behavior.

1. A dog chases a rabbit and kills it. Yes _____ No _____

2. A man places a live lobster into boiling water to prepare it for dinner. Yes _____ No _____

3. A war pilot bombs a village, killing both enemy soldiers and civilians. Yes _____ No _____

4. A man repairing a roof accidentally drops a hammer. The hammer hits a child in the yard below, causing permanent brain damage. Yes _____ No _____

5. A boy repeatedly yanks the leash sharply as he walks his dog, ignoring the dog's cries of pain. Yes _____ No _____

6. Mrs. X, hoping to get her son's teacher fired, spreads nasty rumors about the teacher to other parents. Yes _____ No _____

7. A woman continually threatens to spank her toddler for "acting up" while they are shopping for groceries. Yes _____ No _____

8. A man does nothing to help a drowning person at the beach, even though he is an excellent swimmer. Yes _____ No _____

9. A rock star trashes his hotel room while celebrating the success of his latest CD. Yes _____ No _____

10. A woman throws herself under a train. Yes _____ No _____

FIGURE 4 What is aggression? It depends on how the word is defined and in what context it is used.

Source: Adapted from Benjamin, L. T., Jr. (1985). Defining aggression: An exercise for classroom discussion. *Teaching of Psychology, 12*(1), 40–42.

who studies animal behavior), expanded Freud's notions by arguing that humans, along with members of other species, have a fighting instinct, which in earlier times ensured protection of food supplies and weeded out the weaker of the species (Lorenz, 1974). Lorenz's instinct approach led to the controversial notion that aggressive energy constantly builds up in an individual until the person finally discharges it in a process called **catharsis.** The longer the energy builds up, said Lorenz, the greater the amount of the aggression displayed when it is discharged.

catharsis The process of discharging built-up aggressive energy. (Module 46)

Lorenz believed that society should offer people acceptable ways of permitting catharsis. For example, he suggested that participation in aggressive sports and games would prevent the discharge of aggression in less socially desirable ways. However, little research has found evidence for the existence of a pent-up reservoir of aggression that needs to be released. In fact, some studies flatly contradict the notion of catharsis, which leads psychologists to look for other explanations for aggression (Bushman, Wang, & Anderson, 2005; Verona & Sullivan, 2008; Richardson & Hammock, 2011).

FRUSTRATION-AGGRESSION APPROACHES: AGGRESSION AS A REACTION TO FRUSTRATION

Suppose you've been working on a paper that is due for a class early the next morning, and your computer printer runs out of ink just before you can print out the paper. You rush to the store to buy more ink only to find the sales clerk locking the door for the day. Even though the clerk can see you gesturing and begging him to open the door, he refuses, shrugs his shoulders, and points to a sign that indicates when the store will open the next day. At that moment, the feelings you experience toward the sales clerk probably place you on the verge of real aggression, and you are undoubtedly seething inside.

Is road rage a result of frustration?
According to frustration-aggression
approaches, frustration is a likely cause.
©Chris Ryan/age fotostock

Frustration-aggression approaches explain how the frustration one might feel standing at that closed door could lead to aggression. According to these approaches, frustration (the experience of having one's goals thwarted or blocked) produces anger, which in turn produces a readiness to act aggressively.

But anger doesn't always lead to aggression. Whether actual aggression occurs depends on the presence of *aggressive cues*, stimuli that have been associated in the past with actual aggression or violence and that will trigger aggression again (Berkowitz, 2001; Burton et al., 2013).

What kinds of stimuli act as aggressive cues? They can range from the most explicit, such as the presence of weapons, to more subtle cues, such as the mere mention of the name of an individual who behaved violently in the past. For example, angered participants in experiments behave significantly more aggressively when in the presence of a gun than in a comparable situation in which no guns are present. Similarly, frustrated participants who view a violent movie are more physically aggressive toward a confederate with the same name as the star of the movie than they are toward a confederate with a different name (Berkowitz, 2001; Jovanović, Stanojević, & Stanojević, 2011; Wang & Zhong, 2015).

It appears, then, that frustration does lead to aggression–at least when aggressive cues are present. However, psychologists have come to realize that frustration is not the only trigger of aggression. For example, physical pain, verbal insults, and unpleasant experiences in general can also lead to aggression. Similarly, violent behavior increases when the temperature rises–suggesting that one consequence of global warming may be an increase in aggression and intergroup conflict (Barash & Lipton, 2011; Van Damme et al., 2017; Plante & Anderson, 2017).

OBSERVATIONAL LEARNING APPROACHES: LEARNING TO HURT OTHERS

Do we learn to be aggressive? The *observational learning* (sometimes called *social learning*) approach to aggression says that we do. Taking an almost opposite view from instinct theories, which focus on innate explanations of aggression, observational learning theory emphasizes that social and environmental conditions can teach individuals to be aggressive. The theory sees aggression not as inevitable but rather as a learned response that can be understood in terms of rewards and punishments.

Observational learning theory pays attention to the direct rewards and punishments that people receive for acting aggressively. For example, a father may tell his son how glad he was that he "stood up for himself" after getting into a fight, thereby rewarding aggressive behavior.

More frequently, though, people learn aggression through watching others' behavior. According to the *observational learning approach*, we learn to be aggressive by viewing the rewards and punishments that models provide. *Models* are individuals who provide a guide to appropriate behavior through their own behavior. According to observational learning theory, people observe the behavior of models and the subsequent consequences of that behavior. If the consequences are positive, the behavior is likely to be imitated when observers find themselves in a similar situation.

Suppose, for instance, a girl hits her younger brother when he damages one of her new toys. Whereas instinct theory would suggest that the aggression had been pent up and was now being discharged, and frustration-aggression theory would examine the girl's frustration at no longer being able to use her new toy, observational learning theory would look to previous situations in which the girl had viewed others being rewarded for their aggression. For example, perhaps she had watched a friend get to play with a toy after he painfully twisted it out of the hand of another child.

Observational learning theory has received wide research support. For example, children of nursery school age who have watched an adult model behave aggressively and then receive reinforcement for it later display similar behavior themselves if they have been angered, insulted, or frustrated after exposure. Furthermore, a significant

Study Alert
Understand the distinction between the instinctual, frustration-aggression, and observational learning approaches to aggression.

amount of research links watching television shows containing violence with subsequent viewer aggression (Greer, Dudek-Singer, & Gautreaux, 2006; Carnagey, Anderson, & Bartholow, 2007).

From the perspective of...

A Criminal Justice Worker How would proponents of the three main approaches to the study of aggression—instinct approaches, frustration-aggression approaches, and observational learning approaches—interpret the aggression of the killer in the Sandy Hook Elementary School shooting, in which 26 children and adults were killed?

©Deposit Photos/Glow Images

Helping Others: The Brighter Side of Human Nature

Turning away from aggression, we move now to the opposite—and brighter—side of human nature: how we provide aid to others. **Prosocial behavior,** which is the term that psychologists use for helping behavior, has been considered under many different conditions. However, the question that psychologists have looked at most closely relates to bystander intervention in emergency situations. What are the factors that lead someone to help a person in need?

One critical factor related to helping in emergency situations is the number of other individuals present. When multiple people witness an emergency situation, a sense of diffusion of responsibility can arise among the bystanders. **Diffusion of responsibility** is the belief that responsibility for intervening is shared, or diffused, among those present. The more people present in an emergency, the less personally responsible each individual feels—and therefore the less help he or she provides (Blair, Thompson, & Wuensch, 2005; Gray, 2006; Martin & North, 2015).

For example, think back to the classic case of Kitty Genovese that we described when discussing the topic of research. Genovese was stabbed multiple times, and—according to some accounts of the event—no one offered help, despite the fact that allegedly close to 40 people who lived in nearby apartments heard her screams for help. The lack of help has been attributed to diffusion of responsibility: The fact that there were so many potential helpers led each individual to feel diminished personal responsibility (Fischer et al., 2011; Gallo, 2015; Griggs, 2015).

Although most research on helping behavior supports the diffusion-of-responsibility explanation, other factors are clearly involved in helping behavior. The decision to give aid involves four basic steps (see Figure 5; Latané & Darley, 1970; Garcia et al., 2002; López-Pérez et al., 2017):

- *Noticing a person, event, or situation that may require help.* If we are to provide help, we first have to perceive that a situation is one that potentially requires our help and intervention.

- *Interpreting the event as one that requires help.* Even if we notice an event, it may be sufficiently ambiguous for us to interpret it as a nonemergency situation that requires no help. Thus, we make an interpretation as to whether or not the event requires help.

- *Assuming responsibility for helping.* It is at this key point that diffusion of responsibility is likely to occur if others are present. Moreover, a bystander's particular expertise is likely to play a role in determining whether he or she helps. For instance, if people with training in medical aid or lifesaving techniques are

prosocial behavior Helping behavior. (Module 46)

diffusion of responsibility The belief that responsibility for intervening is shared, or diffused, among those present. (Module 46)

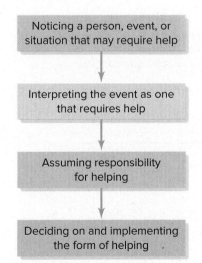

FIGURE 5 The basic steps of helping.

Source: Adapted from Latané, B., & Darley, J. M. (1970). *The unresponsive bystander: Why doesn't he help?* New York: Appleton-Century-Crofts.

present, untrained bystanders are less likely to intervene because they feel they have less expertise.

- *Deciding on and implementing the form of helping.* After we assume responsibility for helping, we must decide how to provide assistance. Helping can range from very indirect forms of intervention, such as calling the police, to more direct forms, such as giving first aid or taking the victim to a hospital. Most social psychologists use a *rewards-costs approach* for helping to predict the nature of the assistance a bystander will choose to provide. The general notion is that the bystander's perceived rewards for helping must outweigh the costs if helping is to occur, and most research tends to support this notion (Koper & Jaasma, 2001; Bartlett & DeSteno, 2006; Lin & Lin, 2007).

After determining the nature of the assistance needed, the actual help must be implemented. A rewards-costs analysis suggests that we are most likely to use the least costly form of implementation. However, this is not always the case: In some situations, the help that is provided shows altruism. **Altruism** is behavior meant to help another without regard for self-interest. It is putting the welfare of others above oneself. For example, we can see altruism in soldiers who risk their own lives to save another soldier who is wounded; a woman who jumps into an icy pond to save a drowning stranger; and everyday people who put themselves at mortal risk to help strangers escape from the burning World Trade Center towers during the 9/11 terrorist attack (Manor & Gailliot, 2007; Marshall, 2011; Xi, et al., 2017).

People who intervene in emergency situations tend to possess certain personality characteristics that differentiate them from nonhelpers. For example, helpers are more self-assured, sympathetic, emotionally understanding, and empathetic (empathy is a personality trait in which someone observing another person experiences the emotions of that person) than are nonhelpers (Walker & Frimer, 2007; Stocks, Lishner, & Decker, 2009; Batson, 2011).

Still, most social psychologists agree that no single set of attributes differentiates helpers from nonhelpers. For the most part, temporary situational factors (such as the mood we're in) determine whether we will intervene in a situation requiring aid (Dovidio et al., 2006; Sallquist et al., 2009; Snyder & Dwyer, 2013).

More generally, what leads people to make moral decisions? Clearly, situational factors make a difference. For example, one study asked people to judge the morality of plane crash survivors cannibalizing an injured boy to avoid starvation. Participants in the study were more likely to condemn the behavior if they were placed in an

altruism Behavior meant to help another person without regard for self-interest. (Module 46)

Altruism is often the only bright side of a natural disaster.
©John Glaser/CSM/REX/Shutterstock

emotional state than if they were less emotional (Schnall et al., 2008; Broeders et al., 2011).

Other psychologists, using a neuroscience perspective, believe that there's a kind of tug-of-war between emotion and rational thinking in the brain. If the rational side wins out, we're more likely to take a logical view of moral situations (if you're at risk for starving, go ahead and eat the injured boy). On the other hand, if the emotional side prevails, we're more likely to condemn the cannibalism, even if it means we may be harmed. In support of such reasoning, researchers have found that different areas of the brain are involved in moral decisions (Miller, 2008; Greene & Paxton, 2009).

Evidence also exists that our brains are hardwired to help us feel empathy for others. In this view, helping others in some ways is just as natural as other, more negative behaviors. The question becomes, then, how we balance the positive and negative behaviors that are equally the result of the functioning of the brain (Pfaff, 2014; de Waal, 2014; Fedyk, 2017).

Study Alert

The distinction between *prosocial behavior* and *altruism* is important. Prosocial behavior does not need to have a self-sacrificing component; altruism, by definition, contains an element of self-sacrifice.

BECOMING AN INFORMED CONSUMER
of Psychology

Dealing Effectively with Anger

At one time or another, almost everyone feels angry. The anger may result from a frustrating situation, or it may be due to another individual's behavior. The way we deal with anger may determine the difference between a promotion and a lost job or a broken relationship and one that mends itself.

Social psychologists who have studied the topic suggest several good strategies to deal with anger that maximize the potential for positive consequences (Nelson & Finch, 2000; Bernstein, 2011; Faupel, Herrick, & Sharp, 2018). Among the most useful strategies are the following:

- *Calm down.* Take a walk or engage in some other physical activity in order to cool down your emotional arousal.
- *Look again at the anger-provoking situation from the perspective of others.* By taking others' points of view, you may be able to understand the situation better, and with increased understanding, you may become more tolerant of the apparent shortcomings of others.
- *Minimize the importance of the situation.* Does it really matter that someone is driving too slowly and that you'll be late to an appointment as a result? Reinterpret the situation in a way that is less bothersome.
- *Use language effectively by saying "I," not "you."* Don't say *"You did _____ wrong."* Instead, say *"I felt hurt when you did _____."* When you accuse people of being wrong, they are likely to feel the need to fight back.
- *Fantasize about getting even—but don't act on it.* Fantasy provides a safety valve. In your fantasies, you can yell at that unfair professor all you want and suffer no consequences at all. However, don't spend too much time brooding: Fantasize, but then move on.
- *Relax.* By teaching yourself the relaxation techniques used in systematic desensitization (discussed in the module on treatment of psychological disorders), you can help reduce your reactions to anger. In turn, your anger may dissipate.

No matter which of these strategies you try, above all, don't ignore your anger. People who always try to suppress their anger may experience a variety of consequences, such as self-condemnation, frustration, and even physical illness (Quartana & Burns, 2007; Gardner & Moore, 2008).

RECAP/EVALUATE/RETHINK

RECAP

LO 46-1 Why are we attracted to certain people, and what progression do social relationships follow?

- The primary determinants of liking include proximity, exposure, similarity, and physical attractiveness.
- Loving is distinguished from liking by the presence of intense physiological arousal, an all-encompassing interest in another, fantasies about the other, rapid swings of emotion, fascination, sexual desire, exclusiveness, and strong feelings of caring.
- Love can be categorized as passionate or companionate. In addition, love has several components: intimacy, passion, and decision/commitment.

LO 46-2 What factors underlie aggression and prosocial behavior?

- Aggression is intentional injury of or harm to another person.
- Explanations of aggression include instinct approaches, frustration-aggression theory, and observational learning.
- Helping behavior in emergencies is determined in part by the phenomenon of diffusion of responsibility, which results in a lower likelihood of helping when more people are present.
- Deciding to help is the outcome of a four-stage process that consists of noticing a possible need for help, interpreting the situation as requiring aid, assuming responsibility for taking action, and deciding on and implementing a form of assistance.

EVALUATE

1. We tend to like people who are similar to us. True or false?

2. Which of the following sets are the three components of love proposed by Sternberg?
   a. Passion, closeness, sexuality
   b. Attraction, desire, complementarity
   c. Passion, intimacy, decision/commitment
   d. Commitment, caring, sexuality

3. Based on research evidence, which of the following might be the best way to reduce the amount of fighting a young boy does?
   a. Take him to the gym and let him work out on the boxing equipment.
   b. Make him repeatedly watch violent scenes from the film *The Matrix Reloaded* in the hope that it will provide catharsis.
   c. Reward him if he doesn't fight during a certain period.
   d. Ignore it and let it die out naturally.

4. If a person in a crowd does not help in an apparent emergency situation because many other people are present, that person is falling victim to the phenomenon of _____ _____ _____.

RETHINK

1. Can love be studied scientifically? Is there an elusive quality to love that makes it at least partially unknowable? How would you define "falling in love"? How would you study it?

2. How would the aggression of the Boston Marathon bombers be interpreted by the three main approaches to the study of aggression: instinct approaches, frustration-aggression approaches, and observational learning approaches? Do you think one of these approaches fits the bombers' case more closely than the others?

Answers to Evaluate Questions

1. true; 2. c; 3. c; 4. diffusion of responsibility

KEY TERMS

interpersonal attraction (or close relationship)	passionate (or romantic) love	aggression	diffusion of responsibility
reciprocity-of-liking effect	companionate love	catharsis	altruism
		prosocial behavior	

LOOKING *Back*

EPILOGUE

We have touched on some of the major ideas, research topics, and experimental findings of social psychology. We examined how people form, maintain, and change attitudes and how they form impressions of others and assign attributions to them. We also saw how groups, through conformity and tactics of compliance, can influence individuals' actions and attitudes. Finally, we discussed interpersonal relationships, including both liking and loving, and looked at aggression and prosocial behavior, the two sides of a coin that represent the extremes of social behavior.

Turn back to the prologue to this set of modules, which describes the massacre of nine black church members in Charleston, South Carolina, by Dylann Roof, a self-identified white supremacist. Use your understanding of social psychology to consider the following questions.

1. How might the assumed-similarity bias explain why Dylann Roof expected his actions could start a race war?
2. How susceptible to obedience is Dylann Roof in your opinion? Explain your thinking.
3. How might Dylann Roof's attitude toward black people be explained by each of the following: (1) observational learning approaches to stereotyping and prejudice, (2) social identity theory, and (3) social neuroscience? Are there other possible explanations?
4. Which do you think best explains Dylann Roof's murder of nine black people— instinct theory, frustration-aggression approaches, or observational learning theory? Why?

Design Elements: Yellow highlighter: ©luckyraccoon/Shutterstock.com; Smartphone: ©and4me/Shutterstock.com; Group of diverse hands: ©MR. Nattanon Kanchak/Shutterstock.com; Woman working on laptop: ©Dragon Images/Shutterstock.com.

VISUAL SUMMARY 14 Social Psychology

MODULE 43 Attitudes and Social Cognition

Persuasion: Attitudes: Evaluations of a particular person, behavior, belief, or concept

— Routes to persuasion

— Attitude-behavior link

Social Cognition: How people understand what others and themselves are like

— Forming impressions of others: Central traits help us form impressions of others

— Attribution theory: How we decide the specific causes of a person's behavior

- Situational causes: of behavior that are external to a person

- Dispositional causes: of behavior brought about by a person's traits or internal personality characteristics

- Attribution biases

MODULE 44 Social Influence and Groups

Conformity: A desire to follow the beliefs or standards of other people

— Groupthink: Group members want to achieve consensus and lose the ability to evaluate alternative points of view

— Social roles: Behaviors associated with people in a given position

Compliance: Social pressure to behave in a certain way

— Foot-in-the-door technique

— Door-in-the-face technique

— That's-not-all technique

— Not-so-free sample

Obedience: Behavior change in response to the commands of others

MODULE 45 Prejudice and Discrimination

Prejudice: A negative or positive evaluation of a group

Discrimination: Behavior directed toward individuals on the basis of their membership in a particular group

Stereotype: Generalized beliefs and expectations about a specific group that arise when we categorize information

Reducing Prejudice and Discrimination

— Increase contact between the target of stereotyping and the holder of the stereotype

— Make values and norms against prejudice more conspicuous

— Provide information about the targets of stereotyping

— Reduce stereotype threat

— Increase a sense of belonging

MODULE 46 Positive and Negative Social Behavior

Liking and Loving

— Determinants of liking

- Proximity
- Mere exposure
- Similarity
- Physical attractiveness

— What is love?

- Qualitatively different from liking
- Three components of love

Aggression: Intentional injury of or harm to another person

— Instinct approaches

— Frustration-aggression approach

— Observational learning approaches

Helping (Prosocial) Behavior: Actions intended to provide aid to others

(MODULE 43) Source: Adapted from Sternberg, R. J. (1986). A triangular theory of love. *Psychological Review, 93*(2), 119–135; (MODULE 44) photo (top): ©Jim Sugar/Corbis/Getty Images; (bottom): From the film OBEDIENCE © 1968 by Stanley Milgram, © renewed 1993 by Alexandra Milgram. Permission granted by Alexandra Milgram; (MODULE 45) (photo): ©Barbara Burnes/Science Source

©Shutterstock/Rawpixel.com

EPILOGUE
Diversity, Culture, Conflict, and Cooperation

LEARNING OUTCOMES FOR EPILOGUE

LO 1   What are the basic elements of diversity and culture?

DIVERSITY AND CULTURE

The Language of Diversity

Culture

Collectivism and Individualism: The Group Versus the Individual

Our View of Ourselves: Looking Inward

Exploring Diversity: The Culture of Aggression

Immigrants: The Newest Americans

LO 2   What are the roots of conflict?

CONFLICT AND COOPERATION: STRIVING FOR A JUST AND PEACEFUL WORLD

The Roots of Conflict

Misperceiving Our Enemies

Genocidal Violence and Mass Killing: Explaining the Inexplicable

LO 3   How can we reduce the risk of war and increase the chances for peace?

BECOMING AN INFORMED CONSUMER OF PSYCHOLOGY

Reducing War, Promoting Peace, and Creating a Just World

BRIDGING THE DIVIDE OF DIFFERENCE

Haifa Staiti made a friend beside a lake at a summer camp in Maine. Sitting under a canopy of trees, she spoke to another camper who, it turned out, shared many of her dreams and basic values. "I felt I was being heard, and I felt comfortable about sharing my experiences," she said (Epatko, 2018).

What made the exchange unusual was that Staiti was a Palestinian and her fellow camper was an Israeli. Although the two came from cultures that are in a perpetual state of undeclared war, they found they had much in common.

The interchange was possible due to a program called Seeds of Peace, designed to bring Israelis and Palestinians together in a neutral and supportive environment. Staiti's childhood had been difficult, with curfews and repeated imprisonment of her politically active father by the Israeli government.

Initially, the camp experience was not easy for Staiti, who was a shy 14-year-old when she began the program. But by the time her stay at the camp was over, both Staiti and her Israeli acquaintance realized that they had much in common, and they remain friends today (Epatko, 2018).

LOOKING *Ahead*

What is it about racial, ethnic, and cultural differences that evoke strong, and sometimes even deadly, responses? Why do such differences lead to prejudice, discrimination, and violence, both in the United States and across the world? And can programs such as Seeds of Peace bridge the differences that divide the diverse world in which we all live?

No principle of psychology leads us to expect that we are destined to live in constant discord. Indeed, in some communities, minorities and majorities live in tranquility, building societies that both acknowledge and welcome the differences between people.

In this module, we examine issues that shed light on psychology's role in understanding diversity and fostering a better world. In the first section, we look at how diversity and culture affect thinking and behavior in fundamental ways. In the second section, we explore issues of conflict, war, and peace. We consider why conflicts occur between people, groups, and nations. We then look at factors that sustain conflicts, such as the views people develop of enemies, and we explore some of the most extreme forms conflict can take: genocide and nuclear war. We end this epilogue on an optimistic note, considering psychological techniques for promoting peace.

Diversity and Culture

No matter where we live, we are increasingly likely to encounter people who differ from us racially, ethnically, and culturally. Technology is bringing people from across the globe into our homes, as close to us as the phone in our hand or the computer on our desk. Businesses now operate globally, so coworkers are likely to come from many countries and cultures. Being comfortable with people whose backgrounds and beliefs differ from our own is not only a social necessity, but also a requirement for career success.

Moreover, by the mid-21st century, the percentage of people in the United States of African, Latin American, Asian, and Arabic ancestry will be greater than the percentage of those of Western European ancestry–a profound statistical, and social, shift. College enrollments will mirror these changes, as populations that were minority become the majority (Alba & Barbosa, 2016; Cohn & Caumont, 2016).

More specifically, consider the following population trends (Cohn & Caumont, 2016; U.S. Census Bureau, 2017):

- By 2055, the United States will not have any single racial or ethnic majority. Put another way, we will all be members of minority groups.
- Almost 60 million immigrants have come to the United States since 1970.
- Most population growth in the United States is projected to be related to Hispanic and Asian immigration.
- Around 14% of the U.S. population is foreign-born.
- Twenty percent of U.S. residents speak a language other than English at home.

Furthermore, diversity is not just based in racial, ethnic, and cultural characteristics. The world's population is also diverse in terms of sex, gender identity, sexual orientation, age, and mental and physical abilities. Then, layer on factors such as education, religion, and income level, and you can see that each person is a complex mix of identities. The way those diverse identities overlap or interact is known as *intersectionality*. One can be, for instance, a hearing-impaired lesbian African-American woman and

Increasingly, many workplaces will include staff from a wide variety of countries and cultures, and with a wide range of customs and beliefs. What are your experiences with people who differ from you culturally?
©monkeybusinessimages/Getty Images

evoke responses from others that reflect any, all, or none of those identities (DeBlaere, Watsonk, & Langrehr, 2018; Mays & Ghavami, 2018).

The Language of Diversity

The language we use to describe others and their diversity is important, and social-cultural norms often determine what labels are appropriate. For example, should one say African American or black? Caucasian, white, or Euro-American? Hispanic or Latino? American Indian or Native American? Gay, lesbian, straight, or queer? Transgender, cisgender, male, or female? Physically challenged, differently abled, or disabled? The choice of labels matters. The subtleties of language affect how people think about members of particular groups, and how they think about themselves (Forson, 2018).

One difficulty in understanding diversity is that many of the terms we use are ill-defined and often overlapping. For example, the term **race** generally refers to obvious physical differences that set one group apart from others. But depending on how race is defined, there are between 3 and 300 races, with no race genetically distinct. And the reality is that 99.9% of our genetic makeup is similar across all human beings. Because of this, race is generally thought of as a *social construction*, something that is defined by people's attitudes and beliefs (Zuberi, Patterson, & Stewart, 2015; Gross & Weiss, 2018).

Ethnicity refers to shared national origins or cultural patterns. In the United States, for example, Puerto Rican, Irish, and Italian American typically are categorized as ethnic groups. However, ethnicity–like race–is very much in the eye of the beholder. For instance, a Cuban American who is a third-generation citizen of the United States

race Generally refers to obvious physical differences that set one group apart from others.

ethnicity Shared national origins or cultural patterns.

The term *race* is generally used to refer to obvious physical differences between groups of people. However, as you can see from these images, skin tone, hair texture, and facial features come in many varieties and combinations, so the lines between groups can't be clearly drawn.
©Shutterstock/Rawpixel.com

may feel few ties or associations to Cuba or Cuban culture. Yet whites may view her as "Hispanic," and blacks may view her as "white."

Race and ethnicity shape each of us to an enormous degree, profoundly influencing our view of others as well as ourselves. They affect how others treat us and how we treat them in turn. They can also determine a broad range of behaviors, ranging from whether we look people in the eye when we meet them (in some cultures, direct eye contact is viewed as disrespectful, so it is avoided) or how much food we eat when we're invited to dinner at a friend's house (in some cultures, it is considered impolite to leave food on one's plate (Mannarini, Talò, & Rochira, 2017; Park et al., 2018).

Even the words we use to describe others reflect our beliefs and values. For instance, the term *African American* is a label that has historical, geographical, and sociological implications. On the other hand, *black* focuses primarily on skin color.

Similarly, we do not yet have clear rules about the language to use for the varieties of gender identities and sexualities individuals may hold. For example, *transgender* refers to individuals whose sense of whether they are male or female (their *gender identity*) does not match the sex they were assigned at birth. Transgender people may refer to themselves as trans, transexual, agender, demigender, or genderqueer, and some prefer the use of gender-neutral pronouns, such as *ze, zir,* or *they.*

Furthermore, gender identity is not the same as *sexual orientation,* which describes a person's physical and emotional attraction to another person. For example, people may consider themselves straight, lesbian, gay, bisexual–or something else–depending on who they are attracted to sexually.

Culture

As a graduate student from Korea, Jung felt she was adjusting well to her psychology program in the United States. She got along well with her professors, and her officemates seemed cordial and friendly. But she felt uneasy in one area. Every Friday afternoon, other graduate students would gather at a local bar for what they called "Happy Hour," which–although Jung didn't know it–was a long-standing tradition among students in the psychology program. No one extended a personal invitation to Jung, and although she wished she could go with the other students, she felt it would be presumptuous to attend without an invitation. Since they never invited her to go along, she wondered if she had somehow insulted them.

How would you respond to Jung about her concerns? Most people familiar with the social customs of the United States would probably tell her that she needs no invitation to join her fellow students at the bar. Such gatherings are informal, and U.S. natives would neither expect nor routinely offer personal invitations to them.

Jung's confusion over the customs of public gatherings is just one example of the way in which habits differ from one culture to another. Although this problem appears to be relatively trivial, variations in such everyday behaviors indicate fundamental differences between people of diverse cultures. Furthermore, such misunderstandings may lead to stereotyping and prejudice. For example, Jung's classmates might think she was standoffish or unfriendly, and they might generalize such a view to something about Koreans. Learning about culture is essential to understanding the differences between people.

Culture comprises the learned behaviors, beliefs, and attitudes that are characteristic of an individual society or population. Culture is transmitted from one generation to another in both written and spoken form. Culture also encompasses people's creations, such as art, music, literature, and architecture. In sum, culture both shapes and reflects a society's behavior, understanding of the world, attitudes, and values (Kasser, 2011; Wan & Chiu, 2011; Han & Ma, 2015).

Despite their broad impact on people, cultural factors have traditionally received little attention from psychologists. One reason is that many psychologists have instead focused on broad universal principles of human behavior. Presumably, the thinking went, such principles should apply to all people, regardless of their culture.

culture The learned behaviors, beliefs, and attitudes that characterize an individual society or population.

Cultures vary in multiple ways, including their funeral ceremonies. In this colorful procession, family and friends accompany a loved one to burial grounds in the Vietnamese countryside. What is the funeral tradition in your culture or religion?
©Jimmy Tran/Shutterstock

Today, however, psychologists increasingly appreciate the importance of culture. Rather than considering it an obstacle to finding universal psychological principles, psychologists now view culture as a major factor in shaping our behavior. In fact, explanations for many central aspects of behavior remain elusive without an understanding of the consequences of culture. Indeed, psychologists can identify broad, universal principles of behavior only by determining which ones apply across cultures and which are specific to particular cultures. For example, a psychologist studying grief as a universal emotion would want to determine what a festive New Orleans jazz funeral has in common with a more conventional funeral at a graveside (Triandis, 2011; Rosenblatt, 2013).

Understanding the role of culture has also become increasingly important due to the growing diversity of U.S. society. The fabric of society is changing to reflect the contributions of people of diverse ethnic, racial, and religious backgrounds. We can understand the similarities and differences around us only when we consider culture. Furthermore, when we are aware of the effects of cultural differences, we may overcome our prejudices and better understand the roots of discrimination.

Furthering interest in culture is the concept of multiculturalism, which has both psychological and political implications for how members of racial, ethnic, religious, and other demographic groups are perceived. **Multiculturalism** is the view that members of all cultures deserve equal respect and that their contributions to society should be recognized. This concept not only acknowledges differences among subcultural groups, it also furthers the argument that society is stronger due to the presence of multiple groups and cultures.

Let's examine some primary psychological considerations related to culture, including differing cultural orientations and how people in different cultures vary in their view of themselves.

multiculturalism The view that members of all cultures deserve equal respect and that their contributions to society should be recognized.

Collectivism and Individualism: The Group Versus the Individual

Do you think teenagers should take their parents' views into account when choosing a career? Do you think you ought to help a neighbor who is in financial distress? Do you have an obligation to lend your class notes to a fellow student who missed a class?

If you answer yes to these questions, your responses represent values similar to those found in many Eastern cultures. On the other hand, if you reply no to these questions, your value orientation is more like that fostered in Western cultures.

These two orientations are known as *collectivism* and *individualism*. Cultures that support **collectivism** promote the idea that the well-being of the group or society is more important than that of the individual. People in collectivistic societies place the welfare of the group above their own personal well-being (Nguyen, Le, & Boles, 2010; Arpaci, Baloğlu, & Kesici, 2018).

In contrast, societies that encourage **individualism** hold as a primary value the personal identity, uniqueness, freedom, and worth of the individual person. In individualistic cultures, personal goals are viewed as more important than goals relating to society in general.

The individualistic and collectivistic tendencies of these cultures influence the way people interpret and understand behavior. For example, students and teachers in the United States tend to attribute their scholastic success to stable, internal characteristics. Consequently, a student who does well is seen as being smart, which is a stable, internal trait and is an outgrowth of an individualistic view of the world. In contrast, in China and Japan, both countries that have a more collectivistic culture than the United States, people see scholastic performance in terms of temporary, situational factors, such as how hard a student works.

The varying cultural perceptions that underlie academic success lead to different levels of scholastic motivation. Because Chinese and Japanese students are more apt to assume that academic success results from hard work, they are likely to put greater effort into their studies. U.S. students may exert less effort because they believe that their stable, unvarying level of ability underlies their school performance. After all, students who assume that their internal ability is the primary cause of their performance may not understand that studying harder may bring better results. In other words, they may feel they can't do much to change the outcome (Chen & Zhang, 2011; Fetvadjiev et al., 2018; Wu et al., 2018).

Whether a culture is collectivistic or individualistic also influences people's willingness to share scarce resources with others. For instance, people living in collectivistic cultures primarily employ the *norm of equality* to determine how rewards should be granted. The norm of equality suggests that all people ought to be rewarded equally, regardless of who they are or how competent or successful they are. In this case, an

collectivism The concept that the well-being of the group or society is more important than that of the individual.

individualism The concept that holds as a primary value the personal identity, uniqueness, freedom, and worth of the individual person.

In Eastern collectivist cultures, students are more likely to view academic achievement as tied to situational factors, such as how hard they work. In contrast, those in Western individualistic cultures tie achievement to more stable characteristics, such as how smart they think they are. How do you view academic success? ©Paul Burns/Blend Images LLC

equality norm would mean that all students working on a project together as a group would receive the same grade.

In contrast, people living in individualistic societies tend to distribute resources according to a *norm of equity,* in which rewards are based on the size of the contribution people make or the quality of their performance. Those who receive the most are the ones who have made the greatest contribution, whereas those who receive the least have made the smallest contribution. In an individualistic society, then, workers are paid according to their perceived merit. As a consequence, great discrepancies exist in the amount of rewards people receive (Boarini, Laslier, & Robin, 2009; Okely, Weiss, & Gale, 2018).

Our View of Ourselves: Looking Inward

In Western cultures, "the squeaky wheel gets the grease." In Asian cultures, "the nail that stands out gets pounded down."

The differences in these two sayings reflect profound cultural variations between the West and East in how people see themselves. In the Western perspective, people tend to differentiate themselves, making their voices heard and letting others know what their individual needs are in a situation. The Asian perspective suggests that the best approach is to blend in, to avoid being noticed (Krassner et al., 2017).

These divergent points-of-view exemplify how people in Eastern and Western cultures view the **self**, the way in which we look inward and define ourselves as individuals. Research suggests that people raised in Asian societies have an **interdependent** view of themselves, in part reflective of their collectivistic orientation. They think of themselves as members of a larger society, working together with others to achieve social harmony. In this view, people strive to fit in, to behave in a way that coincides with how others think, feel, and act (Markus & Kitayama, 2003, 2010; Levine et al., 2016).

People in Western societies, however, see themselves as **independent** of others, reflecting in part their individualistic orientation. Rather than striving to fit in, they may compete rather than cooperate with others. In many cases, they pride themselves on their uniqueness, distinctiveness, and above all, individuality.

These distinct views of the self are revealed on many levels and in all aspects of individualistic cultures. Even the languages people speak reflect the differences. For instance, the English language has more words for emotions focused on oneself, such as jealousy and anger, than the Japanese language. In contrast, the Japanese language contains many more terms for emotions involving others, such as sympathy, than the English language. In fact, the Japanese language contains words for some emotions that do not have similar words in English. *Oime,* for instance, refers to being indebted to another individual–a word for which English has nothing comparable (Markus & Kitayama, 2010; Andersen, 2017).

People in Eastern cultures also view achievement very differently than people in Western cultures. For example, Westerners assess achievement in terms of personal gains. They look at how well they are doing relative to others, comparing whether they are better or worse off. Grades, salaries, and the size of one's home or office are things that people may use to compare and measure achievements. Thus, the value they place on their success is relative to what others achieve.

In contrast, people in interdependent societies tend to measure success in terms of group achievement. Rewards are thought to be appropriate in terms of how well one's group does, rather than how one does as an individual. For example, a student's success on a group project would be measured in terms of how well the overall project turns out, rather than in terms of each student's individual contribution. Similarly, salary raises in a business might be based on the performance of the company as a whole.

Most aspects of a culture, such as the degree of its individualism and collectivism, are neither inherently good nor bad. In an absolute sense, neither individualism nor collectivism is preferable to the other. But elements in some cultures are clearly harmful. One such element is the aggressiveness of a given society, which we consider next.

self A person's essential being distinguishing themselves from others; how we define ourselves as individuals.

interdependent (view of self) To view oneself as a member of a larger society, working together with others to achieve social harmony.

independent (view of self) To view oneself as behaving independently, competing rather than cooperating with others.

 # Exploring Diversity

The Culture of Aggression

Violence is as American as apple pie. At least that's the conclusion of some observers of society in the United States, who point to the grim quantity of violence that occurs. For example, the homicide rate in the United States is four times greater than in comparable countries such as France and the United Kingdom. Even within the United States, certain segments of the population are at extraordinary risk: African Americans account for nearly half of all murder victims, yet make up only about 13% of the population. And big-city homicides rose substantially in both 2015 and 2016 (Lepore, 2009; Associated Press, 2011; Rosenfeld et al., 2017).

The United States is also an outlier when it comes to the magnitude of school violence. Since the Columbine High School shooting in 1999, 131 children, educators, and others have been killed in school shootings in 217 schools. Furthermore, 215,000 children have been witnesses to school shootings (Cox et al., 2018).

Do these figures imply that U.S. society is uniquely violent compared to other societies? Before we can answer such a question, we need to consider several factors, because comparing levels of aggression across cultures is no easy matter.

Take, for instance, the difficulty in defining the term *aggression*. Most researchers suggest that for an act to be considered aggressive, it must involve intentional injury or harm to another person; others use broader definitions. The particular definition of aggression becomes critical when comparing statistics collected from a variety of settings in very different cultures.

In addition, even when a specific definition of aggression can be agreed on, labeling a particular behavior as aggressive may prove problematic. Consider this example of observing children: One boy shoves another from behind and knocks him over; both boys laugh about the incident. Should this behavior be labeled as aggressive or as spirited play?

Finally, cultures are not necessarily homogeneous, which adds to why differences exist in the incidence of aggression. For example, there are regional differences in the United States: The rate of murder in the Texas panhandle is four times higher than the murder rate in Nebraska. Generalizing across an entire country or culture, then, may obscure important differences among subgroups (Nisbett & Cohen, 1996; Anwar, Fry, & Grigaityté, 2018; Hornsveld et al, 2018).

Despite such critical difficulties in comparing rates of violence across cultures, several researchers have attempted to identify differences between cultures in the levels of aggression. As a result, several findings have emerged.

One finding is that cultures have very different views of aggression. For instance, people in some cultures hold extremely positive attitudes about aggression. Among the Simbu of New Guinea, the most admired people are the most aggressive. The more violent a male is, the more followers he is likely to have and the higher his status. These higher-status males often seek fights and urge others to join in fighting. As a consequence, warfare is frequent (Brown, 1986; Dernbach & Marshall, 2001).

In contrast, some cultures are notably nonviolent. For instance, the Semai, who live in the Malaysian rain forest, traditionally hold negative attitudes about aggression (Bonta, 1997). They tend to deride people who are violent and hold nurturance in high esteem. Perhaps because they live in an area rich in natural resources, they generally see less practical value in antagonistic or adversarial behavior.

Other studies have focused on more direct comparisons. In one classic study, cross-cultural psychologist William Lambert (1971) examined aggression in Kenya, India, Mexico, Okinawa, the Philippines, and the United States. He looked at how mothers, the primary child-care providers in each of the cultures, reacted to their own children's aggression toward other children. The results showed that Mexican mothers were the strictest, whereas mothers in the United States showed the greatest leniency toward aggressive behavior. In contrast, mothers responded differently to acts of aggression by their children toward adults. Children who were aggressive toward adults received the greatest punishment in Kenya, the Philippines, and Mexico and the least punishment in India. U.S. children received a relatively moderate degree of punishment (Lopez, Schneider, & Dula, 2002; Stacks et al., 2009; Lansford et al., 2014).

How mothers react to aggression is ultimately reflected in overall rates of societal aggression, although the display of aggression depends on the children's activity level and opportunities for social interaction. For instance, active children who frequently interact with other children seem to learn their culture's lessons about aggression most readily. Thus, active Mexican children are relatively less aggressive than U.S. children because mothers in Mexico tend to react strongly against displays of aggressive behavior. In contrast, active children in the United States show more aggression since their aggression typically earns only a mild rebuke from their mothers.

These findings clearly demonstrate that culture plays a role in providing children with experiences that ultimately result in different levels of social aggression. How a culture trains its children, then, affects their degree of aggressiveness.

Although people in various cultures differ in levels of aggression, at least one common factor bridges across cultures: Males are more aggressive than females. In no culture do females commit more aggressive acts than males, a finding that holds for adults as well as children (Segall, 1988; Slotboom, Hendriks, & Verbruggen, 2011; Bass et al., 2018).

Why should this be true? Although we might attribute the finding to heredity—the idea that males are born with a predisposition to be more aggressive than females—this is not the only possibility. For instance, across cultures, societies may hold similar expectations about the behaviors boys and girls are taught, and it is these expectations that lead to the differences in aggression. In many cultures, boys are explicitly taught to be aggressive, whereas aggression in girls is discouraged. Related explanations suggest that boys act aggressively to accentuate their masculine identity, most likely because their societies value "strong," aggressive males (Whiting, 1965; Pellegrini et al., 2010; Bosson & Vandello, 2011; Aimé et al., 2018).

Although the universal differences in male and female aggression levels are striking, the fact that psychologists find substantial differences in levels of aggression from culture to culture is also noteworthy (Felson & Tedeschi, 1993). It suggests that aggression is not an inevitable aspect of human behavior, and it implies that people may learn to control and reduce violence in the world. In turn, it may be possible to diminish global aggression and to enhance the potential for peace in our time.

Across cultures, males tend to be more aggressive than females. Why might this be true?
©PhotoAlto/Odilon Dimier/Getty Images

Immigrants: The Newest Americans

Anti-immigrant rhetoric in the United States today describes immigrants as rapists, murders, and worse, who are straining the prison system, stealing jobs, living on welfare, and contributing little to society. However, the reality, as embodied by statistical evidence, is quite different.

For instance, consider the following data (Lazear, 2017):

- The majority of legal and illegal immigrants ultimately become financially successful. Although initially they have higher rates of poverty than native-born Americans, most immigrants eventually have higher average family incomes than native-born citizens. They have a higher rate of business startups.

- Most of the projected increase in immigration comes from increases in legal immigration, not illegal immigration.

- Few immigrants come to the United States to receive welfare. Instead, most say they come because of opportunities to work and prosper in the United States. Many come to escape political oppression and crippling poverty, and their goal is to work and earn a living. In fact, the unemployment rate for immigrants is about 10% lower than for the native-born population.

- Although they are initially more costly to the government, immigrants become increasingly productive as they get older, paying taxes that outweigh their cost to government.

Why do immigrants so often end up financially successful? One hypothesis is that those immigrants who voluntarily leave their native countries are unusually motivated to become successful, more so than immigrants who choose not to immigrate. Whatever the reason, the evidence suggests that most immigrants eventually become part of the fabric of U.S. life (Giridharadas, 2014; Bruni, 2017; López & Bialik, 2017).

Conflict and Cooperation: Striving for a Just and Peaceful World

Despite their broad cultural differences, the vast majority of the peoples of the world share some fundamental aspirations: They wish to live in peace and harmony with their neighbors and to seek a better life for themselves and their families. Unfortunately, efforts at resolving conflict often fall short of such aspirations, and we inhabit a globe where aggression and war are all too often seen as the solution to problems.

Yet, we can improve our lot. Let's consider why conflicts arise and how we can achieve cooperation and peace.

The Roots of Conflict

Conflict occurs when individuals, groups, or nations perceive that their behavior, goals, or beliefs are incompatible with those of others. What one person—or group or nation—desires, others may see as being potentially damaging. Consider these examples: Community business leaders want to erect a parking garage on land next to a residence for the elderly; the elderly fear that the increased traffic will compromise their safety, the exhaust fumes will harm their health, and the diminished green space will detract from their quality of life. On another scale, Palestinians want to establish an independent country on land currently controlled by Israelis; the Israelis fear this country will threaten their security. In the first example, the conflict may lead to a war of words, petitions, and hurt feelings; in the other, the potential for a war with lethal weapons increases.

In some cases, conflict may arise from competition over scarce resources. **Realistic conflict theory** argues that conflict is the outcome of direct competition over valued, but limited, resources. According to this perspective, the qualities we most desire, such as security, health, a good job, a safe and comfortable environment, and an adequate

realistic conflict theory The theory that conflict arises from direct competition over valued, but limited, resources.

An estimated 22.5 million people are now refugees—forced to flee their homes due to ethnic persecution, war, or violence. Many settle in refugee camps, such as the one shown here, that are intended to offer temporary shelter but may house people for decades,
©brianafrica/Alamy Stock Photo

standard of living, are limited. Consequently, we compete with others to acquire our fair share (Moghaddam, 2008; Tajfel & Turner, 2010; Densley & Peterson, 2018).

But how do we determine what's a fair share? For many people, a fair share is more than just a minimum level of resources. In reckoning how much more than a minimum level they should have, they consider what others have. According to this view, then, people consider their own level of relative deprivation to determine their level of satisfaction. **Relative deprivation** is the sense that one group lacks a desired amount of resources in comparison to another group, which the first group perceives as having more. For example, even relatively well-paid factory workers may feel underpaid when they compare their compensation to the huge salary the chief executive of the company receives (Raviallion & Lokshin, 2010; Greitemeyer & Sagioglou, 2017).

In some cases, *perceived* conflict fuels hostility among individuals and groups. Because we use group membership as a source of pride and self-worth, threats to group identity may provoke conflict. For example, the conflict between the Hutu and Tutsi clans in Rwanda in 1994 was based, primarily, on ethnic rivalries. Tragically, the focus on group membership in this situation resulted in the death or displacement of more than 2 million people (Tajfel & Turner, 2004; Staub, 2011, 2018).

Finally, conflict may occur inadvertently, with individuals pursuing a course of action that benefits them as individuals but has quite negative consequences for society as a whole. In such cases, people fall into *social traps*, situations in which individual rewards come into conflict with the optimal outcome for the group. Consider what happened to the people who fished the waters of the Georges Banks off the coast of Massachusetts in the late 1980s. Each individual sought to catch as many fish as possible—a reasonable strategy for a person seeking to maximize each day's profits. Besides, people thought that no one person could catch so many fish that the overall stock of fish would be threatened. When considered collectively, however, the behavior of the many individuals seeking to maximize their catch resulted in such rapid overfishing that the overall supply was devastated. As a consequence, Massachusetts was forced to pass laws to restrict fishing, and many fishermen went bankrupt. Ironically, their pursuit of individual goals ultimately damaged the long-term interests of all parties involved (Urlacher, 2008; Abel, 2015).

relative deprivation The sense that one lacks a desired resource in comparison to another group, which is perceived to have more.

Misperceiving Our Enemies

In 2017, during a war of words between U.S. President Donald Trump and North Korean leader Kim Jong-un, Trump called Kim "Rocket Man." In return, the North Korean leader called Trump a "mentally deranged U.S. dotard." This extraordinary public display of name-calling between world leaders illustrated how antagonism can escalate and dehumanize others. In fact, in many situations, our view of our enemies is so distorted that it causes serious strategic miscalculations. For example, psychologists suggest that several distortions in thinking influenced decision-making during the course of the war in Vietnam (White, 2004; Sang-hun, 2017):

- *An image of the enemy as diabolical.* Americans viewed the communist Vietnamese as inscrutable and deceptive, as people who were capable of horrible atrocities and fiendish aggression.

- *A virile self-image.* Americans saw themselves and their military policy as determined, correct, and strong.

- *An overconfident military.* Having never "lost" a war, Americans believed they could win any confrontation in which they participated. It always seemed that just one more battle would bring a final victory.

- *Lack of empathy for the enemy.* Political and military leaders had no clear understanding of what the enemy felt, how it perceived the situation, or even why it was fighting.

- *Selective inattention.* The U.S. government consistently ignored facts and events that might have led it to change its position on or understanding of the war. For example, widespread corruption in the South Vietnamese army, the United States' ally, was ignored, as were South Vietnam's undemocratic government policies.

- *A moral self-image.* The United States viewed itself as superior not only militarily, but morally as well.

Such misperceptions of enemies are not restricted to the war in Vietnam. Citizens and powerful world leaders still tend to mischaracterize the pronouncements of their enemies, and they base their views of other nations on stereotypes regarding national personality traits and other characteristics. Many of the mistakes in perception regarding Vietnam also apply to some degree to the U.S. military interventions in Iraq, Afghanistan, and Syria (Jost, Kay, & Thorisdotter, 2009).

Ironically, a nation's enemies are susceptible to similar misperceptions and stereotyping. Consequently, nations often hold *mirror-image perceptions*, views that duplicate those their opponents hold of them. In other words, each side sees itself as virtuous and morally just, and its enemy as evil and ruthless. Moreover, as conflicts escalate, perceptions of one's enemies grow increasingly simplistic. For example, the complexity of the images that both Israelis and Arabs use to describe each other declined as the level of conflict between them increased (Hirschberger, Pyszczynski, & Ein-Dor, 2010; Fischer, 2011; Fisher & Kelman, 2011).

Genocidal Violence and Mass Killing: Explaining the Inexplicable

The genocide of the Armenians in Turkey during World War I. The Holocaust during World War II. The massacres in Rwanda in 1994. The recent attacks on hundreds of thousands of Rohingya in Myanmar.

All these events, in which collectively *millions* of people were killed because of their religion, ethnicity, or race, represent the worst of humanity: an extinguishing of the caring and altruistic spark in human beings. How do psychologists explain such horrific behavior?

According to Ervin Staub (2018), *genocides*, in which particular demographic groups are targeted for mass killing, share certain features. They typically occur when difficult life conditions stand in the way of fulfilling some basic human needs, such as physical security and a positive social identity. When these difficult conditions occur, one group of people may blame another group of people in an effort to solve their problems, which may unleash several other processes. For example, people may elevate their own group by belittling others. Moreover, one group may identify another group as the source of the problems—the process called scapegoating. Finally, one group may develop an ideology that holds the promise of an improved future and, at the same time, accuses a particular group of blocking the success of the ideology.

Once those in power identify a group as the scapegoat, those in the more powerful group may tolerate minor acts of discrimination against them. Subsequently, these minor acts may escalate into more violent behavior, as bystanders use "just world" reasoning to conclude that the victims are merely getting the treatment they deserve because the bystanders see the world as a just and fair place. As such thinking evolves, people increasingly devalue the victims to the point that they view them as having less moral worth than the perpetrators. At the same time, perpetrators become increasingly committed to their ideology and commit higher levels of violence. Because most bystanders do not intervene, perpetrators reason that they have the tacit approval of the bystanders. Eventually, the level of violence intensifies, and societal norms change. Ultimately, full-blown genocide occurs.

Although difficult life conditions do not lead inevitably to genocide, some cultures have traditions that may increase its likelihood. These cultures have a history of devaluing

When people come together to promote caring and positive relations, they offer hope for a more peaceful world.
©Shutterstock/Rawpixel.com

other groups. Furthermore, conditions are ripe for genocide in cultures with a particularly strong respect for authority, a fairly homogeneous population, a history of aggression, and a dominant culture that sees itself as superior to other cultures.

Staub's analysis, which suggests that situational conditions combine with cultural factors to permit the development of genocide, is sobering. At the same time, though, it suggests two avenues to prevent its development. One is to deal directly with difficult life conditions by striving to help people economically and socially. The other avenue is to change cultural norms from those that permit the devaluation of others to norms that promote caring and positive relations among groups of people (Staub, Pearlman, & Bilali, 2010; Staub, 2011, 2018).

BECOMING AN INFORMED CONSUMER
of Psychology

Reducing War, Promoting Peace, and Creating a Just World

As the violence in Syria, Afghanistan, Gaza, and many other hot spots shows, the world remains a dangerous place. Although the threat of a major, all-out nuclear war has diminished, the danger remains high for smaller, more limited wars. Furthermore, other problems of the world continue unabated, such as environmental degradation, overpopulation, disease, and famine.

cross-cutting relations The links between groups in the areas of work, education, and recreation.

Yet, the world's citizens are not powerless. Several strategies, developed as a result of work conducted by psychologists, can help create a world that is safer and more just in the future. Here are some of the most promising possibilities:

- *Increase cross-cutting relations between people.* **Cross-cutting relations** are the links between groups in the areas of work, education, and recreation. By arranging opportunities for people to interact with one another, as does the Seeds of Peace program we discussed at the beginning of the chapter, cross-cutting relations can allow people to understand the underlying similarities among all the world's peoples. Ultimately, such relationships can lead to feelings of connectedness and the awareness that we all share basic needs and aspirations (Deutsch, 1994; Nowak et al., 2010).
- *Use education to overcome attitudes that devalue outgroups.* One method to reduce violence against members of minority groups and other outgroups is to extend the boundaries that delineate the people who are considered "us" to include those who are considered "them." When people become more accepting of other cultures and better understand their own, they learn that their own culture may not be the standard against which to judge all others (Staub, Pearlman, & Bilali, 2010; Staub, 2011, 2018).
- *Create a robust multicultural society.* Demographic trends show that the white majority in the United States is shrinking. Over the coming decades, the rise in the Hispanic population will be particularly dramatic. Experts estimate that by 2050, nearly one in every three Americans will be Hispanic. Whether or not the United States is prepared, it is about to become an even more deeply multicultural society with direct links to countries throughout the world. Indeed, as international travel becomes increasingly affordable and social networking tools such as Facebook and Twitter become steadily more prominent, people all over the globe will have increasing opportunities to interact (Shrestha & Heisler, 2011; Herskovits, 2018).

Increased intercultural interaction can bring several benefits. For one thing, it can reduce ingroup–outgroup bias, in which people hold more favorable opinions about members of ingroups and less favorable opinions about outgroups. By reducing this bias, people can become more flexible in their thinking and better understand the subtleties of others' behavior (Brewer, 2007; Giannakakis, & Fritsche, 2011; Jacoby-Senghor, Sinclair, & Smith, 2015).

Perhaps more important, direct interaction with people from varied racial, cultural, ethnic, and religious backgrounds, and of various sexual orientations, gender identities, and physical abilities may allow us to see the basic similarities that underlie all human behavior. Throughout this book, we discussed the broad principles that psychologists use to explain behavior. The understanding provided by this knowledge can encourage citizens to become keenly interested in the prospects for a more peaceful and just world for all the globe's inhabitants.

RECAP/EVALUATE/RETHINK

RECAP

LO 1 What are the basic elements of diversity and culture?

- Culture comprises the learned behaviors, beliefs, and attitudes that are characteristic of an individual society or population. Culture both shapes and reflects a society's behavior, understanding of the world, attitudes, and values.
- Societies that encourage individualism hold as a primary value the personal identity, uniqueness, freedom, and worth of the individual. In contrast, cultures that

support collectivism promote the idea that the well-being of the group or society is more important than that of the individual.

- Culture has an impact on people's view of themselves, meaning the way in which they look inward and define themselves as individuals. People in Eastern societies tend to have an interdependent view, perceiving themselves as members of a larger society and working together with others to achieve social harmony. In comparison, people in Western societies generally see themselves as independent. The emphasis in such societies is on competing rather than cooperating with others.

- Societies and cultures vary significantly in the degree of aggression their members display. However, at least one universal principle crosses cultures: Males are more aggressive than females.
- Despite political rhetoric to the contrary, research shows that most immigrants to the United States are productive and ultimately successful.

LO 2 What are the roots of conflict?

- Conflicts occur when individuals, groups, or nations perceive that their behavior, goals, or beliefs are incompatible with those of others. Realistic conflict theory holds that conflict stems from competition over valued, but limited, resources. The notion of relative deprivation–the perception that one group lacks a desired amount of resources in comparison to the amount held by others–adds to the idea that the sense of resource scarcity may be related to a perception of fairness.
- In some cases, perceived conflict can fuel hostility between groups. If the perception exists that group identity is threatened, conflict may occur. Conflict can also result when people fall into social traps, situations in which individual goals conflict with the optimal outcome for the group.

LO 3 How can we reduce the risk of war and increase the chances for peace?

- Psychologists have studied how people's misperceptions about their enemies act as hindrances to peace. Possible distortions include an image of the enemy as diabolical, a virile self-image, an overconfident military, lack of empathy for the enemy, selective inattention to facts, and a moralistic self-image.
- Genocide is a form of collective murder in which particular demographic groups are targeted for killing. Genocides may occur when people's basic needs are unmet because of difficult life conditions and a particular group is first belittled, then singled out as the scapegoat for those difficult conditions. Genocides are often supported by an ideology that promises a bright future and identifies the targeted group as the main obstacle to achieving that future.

- Among the ways to enhance the chances for future peace are to increase cross-cutting relations between people, to use education to overcome attitudes that devalue outgroups, and to create a robust multicultural society.

EVALUATE

1. _____ comprises the learned behaviors, beliefs, and attitudes that characterize an individual society or population.
2. In _____ cultures, personal goals are viewed as more important than goals relating to society in general.
3. Studies have shown that males are universally more aggressive than females. True or false?
4. Increasing _____ _____ relations between people can be a first step toward creating a more just, secure, and safer world in the future.

RETHINK

1. Does the global spread of Western media contribute to a sense of relative deprivation among people of less developed societies? What effect might this have?
2. Do you consider yourself an aggressive person? Are you more or less aggressive than other members of your family? In what ways and compared to which family members? Do you think you learned to be aggressive from your family or the broader culture, or do you believe you were born more or less aggressive?

Answers to Evaluate Questions

1. Culture; 2. individualistic; 3. true; 4. cross-cutting

KEY TERMS

race	collectivism	independent (view of self)	relative deprivation
ethnicity	self	realistic conflict theory	cross-cutting relations
culture	interdependent (view of self)		
multiculturalism			
individualism			

Glossary

abnormal behavior Behavior that causes people to experience distress and prevents them from functioning in their daily lives. (Module 46)

absolute threshold The smallest intensity of a stimulus that must be present for the stimulus to be detected. (Module 8)

action potential An electric nerve impulse that travels through a neuron's axon when it is set off by a "trigger," changing the neuron's charge from negative to positive. (Module 5)

activation-synthesis theory Hobson's theory that the brain produces random electrical energy during REM sleep that stimulates memories stored in the brain. (Module 12)

activity theory of aging The theory that suggests that successful aging is characterized by maintaining the interests and activities of earlier stages of life. (Module 30)

adaptation An adjustment in sensory capacity after prolonged exposure to unchanging stimuli. (Module 8)

addictive drugs Drugs that produce a biological or psychological dependence in the user so that withdrawal from them leads to a craving for the drug that, in some cases, may be nearly irresistible. (Module 14)

adolescence The developmental stage between childhood and adulthood. (Module 29)

age of viability The point at which a fetus can survive if born prematurely. (Module 27)

aggression The intentional injury of, or harm to, another person. (Module 46)

algorithm A rule that, if applied appropriately, guarantees a solution to a problem. (Module 21)

all-or-none law The rule that neurons are either on or off. (Module 5)

altruism Behavior meant to help another person without regard for self-interest. (Module 46)

Alzheimer's disease A progressive brain disorder that leads to a gradual and irreversible decline in cognitive abilities. (Modules 20, 30)

amnesia Memory loss that occurs without other mental difficulties. (Module 20)

anal stage According to Freud, a stage from age 12 to 18 months to 3 years of age, in which a child's pleasure is centered on the anus. (Module 31)

androgens Male sex hormones secreted by the testes. (Module 25)

anorexia nervosa A severe eating disorder in which people may refuse to eat while denying that their behavior and appearance—which can become skeleton-like—are unusual. (Module 25)

anterograde amnesia Amnesia in which memory is lost for events that follow an injury. (Module 20)

antianxiety drugs Drugs that reduce the level of anxiety a person experiences essentially by reducing excitability and increasing feelings of well-being. (Module 42)

antidepressant drugs Medications that improve a severely depressed patient's mood and feeling of well-being. (Module 42)

antipsychotic drugs Drugs that temporarily reduce psychotic symptoms such as agitation, hallucinations, and delusions. (Module 42)

antisocial personality disorder A disorder in which individuals show no regard for the moral and ethical rules of society or the rights of others. (Module 38)

anxiety disorder The occurrence of anxiety without an obvious external cause that affects daily functioning. (Module 38)

archetypes According to Jung, universal symbolic representations of particular types of people, objects, ideas, or experiences. (Module 31)

archival research Research in which existing data, such as census documents, college records, and newspaper articles, are examined to test a hypothesis. (Module 3)

arousal approaches to motivation The belief that we try to maintain certain levels of stimulation and activity. (Module 24)

association areas One of the major regions of the cerebral cortex; the site of the higher mental processes, such as thought, language, memory, and speech. (Module 7)

assumed-similarity bias The tendency to think of people as being similar to oneself even when meeting them for the first time. (Module 43)

attachment The positive emotional bond that develops between a child and a particular individual. (Module 28)

attention-deficit hyperactivity disorder (ADHD) A disorder marked by inattention, impulsiveness, a low tolerance for frustration, and a great deal of inappropriate activity. (Module 38)

attitudes Evaluations of people, objects, ideas, and behavior. (Module 43)

attribution theory The theory that considers how we decide, on the basis of samples of a person's behavior, what the specific causes of that behavior are. (Module 52)

authoritarian parents Parents who are rigid and punitive and value unquestioning obedience from their children. (Module 28)

authoritative parents Parents who are firm, set clear limits, reason with their children, and explain things to them. (Module 28)

autism A severe developmental disability that impairs children's ability to communicate and relate to others. (Module 38)

autobiographical memory Our recollections of our own life experiences. (Module 19)

autonomic division The part of the peripheral nervous system that controls involuntary movement of the heart, glands, lungs, and other organs. (Module 6)

autonomy-versus-shame-and-doubt stage The period during which, according to Erikson, toddlers (ages 1½ to 3 years) develop independence and autonomy if exploration and freedom are encouraged or shame and self-doubt if they are restricted and overprotected. (Module 28)

aversive conditioning A form of therapy that reduces the frequency of undesired behavior by pairing an aversive, unpleasant stimulus with undesired behavior. (Module 40)

axon The part of the neuron that carries messages destined for other neurons. (Module 5)

babble Meaningless speechlike sounds made by children from around the age of 3 months through 1 year. (Module 22)

background stressors ("daily hassles") Everyday annoyances, such as being stuck in traffic, that cause minor irritations and may have long-term ill effects if they continue or are compounded by other stressful events. (Module 34)

basilar membrane A vibrating structure that runs through the center of the cochlea, dividing it into an upper chamber and a lower chamber and containing sense receptors for sound. (Module 10)

behavior modification A technique whose goal is to increase the frequency of desirable behaviors and decrease the incidence of unwanted ones. (Module 18)

behavioral assessment Direct measures of an individual's behavior used to describe personality characteristics. (Module 33)

behavioral genetics The study of the effects of heredity on behavior. (Module 6)

behavioral neuroscientists (or biopsychologists) Psychologists who specialize in considering the ways in which the biological structures and functions of the body affect behavior. (Module 5)

behavioral perspective The approach that suggests that observable, external behavior, which can be objectively measured, should be the focus of study. (Module 2)

behavioral treatment approaches Treatment approaches that make use of the basic processes of learning, such as reinforcement and extinction, to reduce or eliminate maladaptive behavior. (Module 40)

biofeedback A procedure in which a person learns to control through conscious thought internal physiological processes such as blood pressure, heart and respiration rate, skin temperature, sweating, and the constriction of particular muscles. (Module 7)

biological and evolutionary approaches to personality Theories that suggest that important components of personality are inherited. (Module 32)

biomedical therapy Therapy that relies on drugs and other medical procedures to improve psychological functioning. (Module 40)

bipolar disorder A disorder in which a person alternates between periods of euphoric feelings of mania and periods of depression. (Module 38)

bisexuals Persons who are sexually attracted to people of the same sex and the other sex. (Module 25)

borderline personality disorder A disorder characterized by problems regulating emotions and thoughts, displaying impulsive and reckless behavior, and having unstable relationships with others. (Module 38)

bottom-up processing Perception that consists of the progression of recognizing and processing information from individual components of a stimuli and moving to the perception of the whole. (Module 11)

bulimia A disorder in which a person binges on large quantities of food, followed by efforts to purge the food through vomiting or other means. (Module 25)

Cannon-Bard theory of emotion The belief that both physiological arousal and emotional experience are produced simultaneously by the same nerve stimulus. (Module 26)

case study An in-depth, intensive investigation of an individual or small group of people. (Module 3)

cataclysmic events Strong stressors that occur suddenly and typically affect many people at once (e.g., natural disasters). (Module 34)

catharsis The process of discharging built-up aggressive energy. (Module 46)

central core The "old brain," which controls basic functions such as eating and sleeping and is common to all vertebrates. (Module 7)

central nervous system (CNS) The part of the nervous system that includes the brain and spinal cord. (Module 6)

central route processing The type of mental processing that occurs when a persuasive message is evaluated by thoughtful consideration of the issues and arguments used to persuade. (Module 43)

central traits The major traits considered in forming impressions of others. (Module 43)

cerebellum (ser-uh-BELL-um) The part of the brain that controls bodily balance. (Module 7)

cerebral cortex The "new brain," responsible for the most sophisticated information processing in the brain; contains four lobes. (Module 7)

chromosomes Rod-shaped structures that contain all basic hereditary information. (Module 27)

chunk A group of familiar stimuli stored as a single unit in short-term memory. (Module 20)

circadian rhythms Biological processes that occur regularly on approximately a 24-hour cycle. (Module 12)

classical conditioning A type of learning in which a neutral stimulus comes to bring about a response after it is paired with a stimulus that naturally brings about that response. (Module 15)

cochlea (KOKE-lee-uh) A coiled tube in the ear filled with fluid that vibrates in response to sound. (Module 10)

cognitive approaches to motivation Theories suggesting that motivation is a result of people's thoughts, beliefs, expectations, and goals. (Module 24)

cognitive development The process by which a child's understanding of the world changes due to the child's age and experience. (Module 28)

cognitive dissonance The mental conflict that occurs when a person holds two contradictory attitudes or thoughts (referred to as cognitions). (Module 43)

cognitive learning theory An approach to the study of learning that focuses on the thought processes that underlie learning. (Module 17)

cognitive perspective The approach that focuses on how people think, understand, and know about the world. (Module 2)

cognitive psychology The branch of psychology that focuses on the study of higher mental processes, including thinking, language, memory, problem solving, knowing, reasoning, judging, and decision making. (Module 21)

cognitive treatment approaches Treatment approaches that teach people to think in more adaptive ways by changing their dysfunctional cognitions about the world and themselves. (Module 40)

collective unconscious According to Jung, an inherited set of ideas, feelings, images, and symbols that are shared with all humans because of our common ancestral past. (Module 31)

collectivism An idea that the well-being of the group or society is more important than that of the individual.

community psychology A branch of psychology that focuses on the prevention and minimization of psychological disorders in the community. (Module 42)

companionate love The strong affection we have for those with whom our lives are deeply involved. (Module 46)

compliance Behavior that occurs in response to direct social pressure. (Module 44)

compulsion An irresistible urge to repeatedly carry out some act that seems strange and unreasonable. (Module 38)

concept A mental grouping of similar objects, events, or people. (Module 21)

concrete operational stage According to Piaget, the period from 7 to 12 years of age that is characterized by logical thought and a loss of egocentrism. (Module 28)

conditioned response (CR) A response that, after conditioning, follows a previously neutral stimulus (e.g., salivation at the ringing of a bell). (Module 15)

conditioned stimulus (CS) A once-neutral stimulus that has been paired with an unconditioned stimulus to bring about a response formerly caused only by the unconditioned stimulus. (Module 15)

cones Cone-shaped, light-sensitive receptor cells in the retina that are responsible for sharp focus and color perception, particularly in bright light. (Module 9)

confirmation bias The tendency to seek out and weight more heavily information that supports one's initial hypothesis and to ignore contradictory information that supports alternative hypotheses or solutions. (Module 21)

conformity A change in behavior or attitudes brought about by a desire to follow the beliefs or standards of other people. (Module 44)

consciousness The awareness of the sensations, thoughts, and feelings being experienced at a given moment. (Module 12)

constructive processes Processes in which memories are influenced by the meaning we give to events. (Module 19)

continuous reinforcement schedule A schedule in which behavior is reinforced every time the behavior occurs. (Module 16)

control group A group participating in an experiment that receives no treatment. (Module 3)

convergent thinking Thinking in which a problem is viewed as having a single answer and which produces responses that are based primarily on knowledge and logic. (Module 21)

conversion disorder A major somatic symptom disorder that involves an actual physical disturbance, such as the inability to use a sensory organ or the complete or partial inability to move an arm or leg. (Module 38)

coping The efforts to control, reduce, or learn to tolerate the threats that lead to stress. (Module 34)

correlational research Research in which the relationship between two sets of variables is examined to determine whether they are associated, or "correlated." (Module 3)

creativity The ability to generate original ideas or solve problems in novel ways. (Module 21)

cross-cutting relations The links between groups in the areas of work, education, and recreation.

cross-sectional research A research method that compares people of different ages at the same point in time. (Module 27)

crystallized intelligence The accumulation of information, knowledge, and skills that people have learned through experience and education. (Module 23)

cue-dependent forgetting Forgetting that occurs when there are insufficient retrieval cues to rekindle information that is in memory. (Module 20)

culture The learned behaviors, beliefs, and attitudes that characterize an individual society or population.

culture-fair IQ test A test trial that does not discriminate against the members of any minority group. (Module 23)

daydreams Fantasies that people construct while awake. (Module 12)

decay The loss of information in memory through its nonuse. (Module 20)

declarative memory Memory for factual information: names, faces, dates, and the like. (Module 18)

defense mechanisms In Freudian theory, unconscious strategies that people use to reduce anxiety by distorting reality and concealing the source of the anxiety from themselves. (Module 31)

deinstitutionalization The transfer of former mental patients from institutions to the community. (Module 42)

dendrite A cluster of fibers at one end of a neuron that receives messages from other neurons. (Module 5)

dependent variable The variable that is measured in an experiment. It is expected to change as a result of the experimenter's manipulation of the independent variable. (Module 3)

depressants Drugs that slow down the nervous system. (Module 14)

depth perception The ability to view the world in three dimensions and to perceive distance. (Module 11)

determinism The idea that people's behavior is produced primarily by factors outside of their willful control. (Module 2)

developmental psychology The branch of psychology that studies the patterns of growth and change that occur throughout life. (Module 27)

Diagnostic and Statistical Manual of Mental Disorders, Fifth Edition (DSM-5) A system, devised by the American Psychiatric Association, used by most professionals to classify and define psychological disorders. (Module 46)

difference threshold (just noticeable difference) The smallest level of added or reduced stimulation required to sense that a change in stimulation has occurred. (Module 10)

diffusion of responsibility The belief that responsibility for intervening is shared, or diffused, among those present. (Module 46)

discrimination Behavior directed toward individuals on the basis of their membership in a particular group. (Module 45)

disengagement theory of aging The theory that suggests that successful aging is characterized by a gradual withdrawal from the world on physical, psychological, and social levels. (Module 30)

dispositional causes (of behavior) Perceived causes of behavior brought about by a person's traits or personality characteristics. (Module 43)

dissociative amnesia A disorder in which a significant, selective memory loss occurs. (Module 38)

dissociative disorders Psychological dysfunctions characterized by the separation of different facets of a person's personality that are normally integrated. (Module 38)

dissociative fugue A form of amnesia in which a person leaves home and assumes a new identity. (Module 38)

dissociative identity disorder (DID) A disorder in which a person displays characteristics of two or more distinct personalities. (Module 38)

divergent thinking Thinking that generates unusual, yet nonetheless appropriate, responses to problems or questions. (Module 21)

double standard The view that premarital sex is permissible for males but not for females. (Module 25)

dreams-for-survival theory The theory suggesting that dreams permit information that is critical for our daily survival to be reconsidered and reprocessed during sleep. (Module 12)

drive Motivational tension, or arousal, that energizes behavior to fulfill a need. (Module 24)

drive-reduction approaches to motivation Theories suggesting that a lack of some basic biological need produces a drive to push an organism to satisfy that need. (Module 24)

drug therapy Treatment of psychological disorders through the use of drugs. (Module 51)

eardrum The part of the ear that vibrates when sound waves hit it. (Module 10)

ego The part of personality that attempts to balance the desires of the id and the realities of the objective, outside world. (Module 40)

ego-integrity-versus-despair stage According to Erikson, a period from late adulthood until death during which we review life's accomplishments and failures. (Module 29)

egocentric thought A way of thinking in which a child views the world entirely from his or her own perspective. (Module 28)

electroconvulsive therapy (ECT) A procedure used in the treatment of severe depression in which an electric current of 70–150 volts is briefly administered to a patient's head. (Module 42)

embryo A developed zygote that has a heart, a brain, and other organs. (Module 27)

emerging adulthood The period beginning in the late teenage years and extending into the mid-20s. (Module 30)

emotional intelligence The set of skills that underlie the accurate assessment, evaluation, expression, and regulation of emotions. (Module 23)

emotions Feelings that generally have both physiological and cognitive elements and that influence behavior. (Module 26)

endocrine system A chemical communication network that sends messages throughout the body via the bloodstream. (Module 6)

episodic memory Memory for events that occur in a particular time, place, or context. (Module 18)

estrogens Class of female sex hormones. (Module 25)

ethnicity Shared national origins or cultural patterns.

evolutionary psychology The branch of psychology that seeks to identify behavior patterns that are a result of our genetic inheritance from our ancestors. (Module 6)

excitatory message A chemical message that makes it more likely that a receiving neuron will fire and an action potential will travel down its axon. (Module 5)

experiment The investigation of the relationship between two (or more) variables by deliberately producing a change in one variable in a situation and observing the effects of that change on other aspects of the situation. (Module 3)

experimental bias Factors that distort how the independent variable affects the dependent variable in an experiment. (Module 4)

experimental group Any group participating in an experiment that receives a treatment. (Module 3)

experimental manipulation The change that an experimenter deliberately produces in a situation. (Module 3)

explicit memory Intentional or conscious recollection of information. (Module 19)

extinction A basic phenomenon of learning that occurs when a previously conditioned response decreases in frequency and eventually disappears. (Module 15)

extramarital sex Sexual activity between a married person and someone who is not his or her spouse. (Module 25)

facial-affect program Activation of a set of nerve impulses that make the face display the appropriate expression. (Module 26)

facial-feedback hypothesis The hypothesis that facial expressions not only reflect emotional experience but also help determine how people experience and label emotions. (Module 26)

familial intellectual disability Intellectual disability in which no apparent biological defect exists but there is a history of intellectual disability in the family. (Module 23)

family therapy An approach that focuses on the family and its dynamics. (Module 41)

feature detector Specialized neurons that are activated only by visual stimuli having specific features, such as a particular shape or pattern. (Module 9)

fetal alcohol syndrome The most common cause of intellectual disability in newborns, occurring when the mother uses alcohol during pregnancy. (Module 23)

fetus A developing individual from 8 weeks after conception until birth. (Module 27)

fixations Conflicts or concerns that persist beyond the developmental period in which they first occur. (Module 31)

fixed-interval schedule A schedule in which reinforcement is provided for a response only after a fixed time period has elapsed. (Module 16)

fixed-ratio schedule A schedule in which reinforcement is given only after a specific number of responses are made. (Module 16)

flashbulb memories Memories of a specific, important, or surprising emotionally significant event that are recalled easily and with vivid imagery. (Module 19)

flooding A behavioral treatment for anxiety in which people are suddenly confronted with a stimulus that they fear. (Module 40)

fluid intelligence Intelligence that reflects the ability to think logically, reason abstractly, and solve problems. (Module 23)

formal operational stage According to Piaget, the period from age 12 to adulthood that is characterized by abstract thought. (Module 28)

free will The idea that behavior is caused primarily by choices that are made freely by the individual. (Module 2)

frequency theory of hearing The theory that the entire basilar membrane acts like a microphone, vibrating as a whole in response to a sound. (Module 10)

functional fixedness The tendency to think of an object only in terms of its typical use. (Module 21)

functionalism An early approach to psychology that concentrated on what the mind does—the functions of mental activity—and the role of behavior in allowing people to adapt to their environments. (Module 2)

fundamental attribution error A tendency to overattribute others' behavior to dispositional causes and minimize the importance of situational causes. (Module 43)

g or g-factor The single, general factor for mental ability assumed to underlie intelligence in some early theories of intelligence. (Module 23)

gate-control theory of pain The theory that particular nerve receptors in the spinal cord lead to specific areas of the brain related to pain. (Module 10)

general adaptation syndrome (GAS) A theory developed by Selye that suggests that a person's response to a stressor consists of three stages: alarm and mobilization, resistance, and exhaustion. (Module 34)

generalized anxiety disorder The experience of long-term, persistent anxiety and worry. (Module 38)

generativity-versus-stagnation stage According to Erikson, a period in middle adulthood during which we take stock of our contributions to family and society. (Module 29)

genes The parts of the chromosomes through which genetic information is transmitted. (Module 27)

genetic preprogramming theories of aging Theories that suggest that human cells have a built-in time limit to their reproduction and that they are no longer able to divide after a certain time. (Module 30)

genital stage According to Freud, the period from puberty until death, marked by mature sexual behavior (that is, sexual intercourse). (Module 31)

genitals The male and female sex organs. (Module 25)

Gestalt (geh-SHTALLT) laws of organization A series of principles that describe how we organize bits and pieces of information into meaningful wholes. (Module 11)

Gestalt psychology An approach to psychology that focuses on the organization of perception and thinking in a "whole" sense rather than on the individual elements of perception. (Module 2)

grammar The system of rules that determine how our thoughts can be expressed. (Module 22)

group Two or more people who interact with one another, perceive themselves as part of a group, and are interdependent. (Module 44)

group therapy Therapy in which people meet in a group with a therapist to discuss problems. (Module 41)

groupthink A type of thinking in which group members share such a strong motivation to achieve consensus that they lose the ability to critically evaluate alternative points of view. (Module 44)

habituation The decrease in the response to a stimulus that occurs after repeated presentations of the same stimulus. (Module 28)

hair cells Tiny cells covering the basilar membrane that, when bent by vibrations entering the cochlea, transmit neural messages to the brain. (Module 10)

hallucinogen Drugs that are capable of producing alterations in perception, thoughts, and feelings. (Module 14)

halo effect A phenomenon in which an initial understanding that a person has positive or negative traits is used to infer other uniformly positive or negative characteristics. (Module 52)

hardiness A personality trait characterized by a sense of commitment, the perception of problems as challenges, and a sense of control. (Module 43)

health psychology The branch of psychology that investigates the psychological factors related to wellness and illness, including the prevention, diagnosis, and treatment of medical problems. (Module 34)

hemispheres Symmetrical left and right halves of the brain that control the side of the body opposite to their location. (Module 7)

heritability The degree to which a characteristic is related to genetic, inherited factors. (Module 23)

heterosexuality Sexual attraction and behavior directed to the other sex. (Module 25)

heuristic A thinking strategy that may lead us to a solution to a problem or decision but—unlike algorithms—may sometimes lead to errors. (Module 21)

homeostasis The body's tendency to maintain a steady internal state. (Module 24)

homosexuals Persons who are sexually attracted to members of their own sex. (Module 25)

hormones Chemicals that circulate through the blood and regulate the functioning or growth of the body. (Module 6)

humanistic approaches to personality Theories that emphasize people's innate goodness and desire to achieve higher levels of functioning. (Module 32)

humanistic perspective The approach that suggests that all individuals naturally strive to grow, develop, and be in control of their lives and behavior. (Module 2)

humanistic therapy Therapy in which the underlying rationale is that people have control of their behavior, can make choices about their lives, and are essentially responsible for solving their own problems. (Module 41)

hypnosis A trancelike state of heightened susceptibility to the suggestions of others. (Module 13)

hypothalamus A tiny part of the brain, located below the thalamus, that maintains homeostasis and produces and regulates vital behavior, such as eating, drinking, and sexual behavior. (Module 7)

hypothesis A prediction, stemming from a theory, stated in a way that allows it to be tested. (Module 3)

id The instinctual and unorganized part of personality whose sole purpose is to reduce tension created by primitive drives related to hunger, sex, aggression, and irrational impulses. (Module 40)

identical twins Twins who are genetically identical. (Module 27)

identification The process of wanting to be like another person as much as possible, imitating that person's behavior and adopting similar beliefs and values. (Module 31)

identity The distinguishing character of the individual: who each of us is, what our roles are, and what we are capable of. (Module 29)

identity-versus-role-confusion stage According to Erikson, a time in adolescence of major testing to determine one's unique qualities. (Module 29)

illness anxiety disorder A disorder in which people have a constant fear of illness and a preoccupation with their health. (Module 38)

implicit memory Memories of which people are not consciously aware but that can affect subsequent performance and behavior. (Module 19)

incentive approaches to motivation Theories suggesting that motivation stems from the desire to attain external rewards, known as incentives. (Module 24)

independent (view of self) To view oneself as behaving independently, competing rather than cooperating with others.

independent variable The variable that is manipulated by an experimenter. (Module 3)

individualism The idea that holds as a primary value the personal identity, uniqueness, freedom, and worth of the individual person.

industrial-organizational (I/O) psychology The branch of psychology focusing on work- and job-related issues, including worker motivation, satisfaction, safety, and productivity. (Module 44)

industry-versus-inferiority stage According to Erikson, the last stage of childhood, during which children age 6 to 12 years may develop positive social interactions with others or may feel inadequate and become less sociable. (Module 28)

information processing The way in which people take in, use, and store information. (Module 28)

informed consent A document signed by participants affirming that they have been told the basic outlines of the study and are aware of what their participation will involve. (Module 4)

inhibitory message A chemical message that prevents or decreases the likelihood that a receiving neuron will fire. (Module 5)

initiative-versus-guilt stage According to Erikson, the period during which children ages 3 to 6 years experience conflict

between independence of action and the sometimes negative results of that action. (Module 28)

insight A sudden awareness of the relationships among various elements that had previously appeared to be independent of one another. (Module 21)

instinct approaches to motivation Theories suggesting that motivation stems from the desire to attain external rewards, known as incentives. (Module 24)

instincts Inborn patterns of behavior that are biologically determined rather than learned. (Module 24)

intellectual disability A condition characterized by significant limitations both in intellectual functioning and in conceptual, social, and practical adaptive skills. (Module 23)

intellectually gifted The 2–4% segment of the population who have IQ scores greater than 130. (Module 23)

intelligence The capacity to understand the world, think rationally, and use resources effectively when faced with challenges. (Module 23)

intelligence quotient (IQ) A score that takes into account an individual's mental and chronological ages. (Module 23)

intelligence tests Tests devised to quantify a person's level of intelligence. (Module 23)

interactionist approach (to language development) The view that language development is produced through a combination of genetically determined predispositions and environmental circumstances that help teach language. (Module 22)

interdependent (view of self) To view oneself as a member of a larger society, working together with others to achieve social harmony.

interference The phenomenon by which information in memory disrupts the recall of other information. (Module 20)

interpersonal attraction (or close relationship) Positive feelings for others; liking and loving. (Module 46)

interpersonal therapy (IPT) Short-term therapy that focuses on the context of current social relationships, helping patients to control their moods and emotions. (Module 41)

intimacy-versus-isolation stage According to Erikson, a period during early adulthood that focuses on developing close relationships. (Module 29)

introspection A procedure in which people are presented with a stimulus–such as an image or sentence–and asked to describe, in their own words and in as much detail as they can, what they were experiencing. (Module 2)

James-Lange theory of emotion The belief that emotional experience is a reaction to bodily events occurring as a result of an external situation ("I feel sad because I am crying"). (Module 26)

Korsakoff's syndrome A disease that afflicts long-term alcoholics, leaving some abilities intact but including hallucinations and a tendency to repeat the same story. (Module 20)

language The communication of information through symbols arranged according to systematic rules. (Module 22)

latency period According to Freud, the period between the phallic stage and puberty during which children's sexual concerns are temporarily put aside. (Module 31)

latent learning Learning in which a new behavior is acquired but is not demonstrated until some incentive is provided for displaying it. (Module 17)

lateralization The dominance of one hemisphere of the brain in specific functions, such as language. (Module 7)

learned helplessness A state in which people conclude that unpleasant or aversive stimuli cannot be controlled–a view of the world that becomes so ingrained that they cease trying to remedy the aversive circumstances even if they actually can exert some influence on the situation. (Module 34)

learning A relatively permanent change in behavior brought about by experience. (Module 15)

learning-theory approach (to language development) The theory that language acquisition follows the principles of reinforcement and conditioning. (Module 22)

levels-of-processing theory The theory of memory that emphasizes the degree to which new material is mentally analyzed. (Module 19)

life review The process by which people examine and evaluate their lives. (Module 30)

limbic system The part of the brain that controls eating, aggression, and reproduction. (Module 7)

linguistic-relativity hypothesis The hypothesis that language shapes and may determine the way people perceive and understand the world. (Module 22)

lobes The four major sections of the cerebral cortex: frontal, parietal, temporal, and occipital. (Module 7)

long-term memory Memory that stores information on a relatively permanent basis, although it may be difficult to retrieve. (Module 18)

longitudinal research A research method that investigates behavior as participants get older. (Module 27)

major depressive disorder A severe form of depression that interferes with concentration, decision making, and sociability. (Module 38)

mania An extended state of intense, wild elation. (Module 38)

masturbation Sexual self-stimulation. (Module 25)

means-ends analysis Involves repeated tests for differences between the desired outcome and what currently exists. (Module 21)

medical perspective The perspective that suggests that when an individual displays symptoms of abnormal behavior, the root cause will be found in a physical examination of the individual, which may reveal a hormonal imbalance, a chemical deficiency, or a brain injury. (Module 37)

meditation A learned technique for refocusing attention that brings about an altered state of consciousness. (Module 13)

memory The process by which we encode, store, and retrieve information. (Module 18)

menopause The period during which women stop menstruating and are no longer fertile. (Module 30)

mental age The age for which a given level of performance is average or typical. (Module 23)

mental images Representations in the mind of an object or event. (Module 21)

mental set A framework for thinking about a problem based on our prior experience with similar problems. (Module 21)

metabolism The rate at which food is converted to energy and expended by the body. (Module 25)

metacognition An awareness and understanding of one's own cognitive processes. (Module 28)

Minnesota Multiphasic Personality Inventory-2-Restructured Form (MMPI-2-RF) A widely used self-report test that identifies people with psycholog-

ical difficulties and is employed to predict some everyday behaviors. (Module 33)

mirror neurons Specialized neurons that fire not only when a person enacts a particular behavior, but also when a person simply observes *another* individual carrying out the same behavior. (Module 5)

mood disorder A disturbance in emotional experience that is strong enough to intrude on everyday living. (Module 38)

mood stabilizers Drugs used to treat mood disorders characterized by intense mood swings, especially manic episodes in bipolar disorder. (Module 42)

motivation The factors that direct and energize the behavior of humans and other organisms. (Module 24)

motor (efferent) neurons Neurons that communicate information from the brain and nervous system to muscles and glands. (Module 6)

motor area The part of the cortex that is largely responsible for the body's voluntary movement. (Module 7)

multiculturalism The view that members of all cultures deserve equal respect and that their contributions to society should be recognized.

myelin sheath A protective coat of fat and protein that wraps around the axon. (Module 5)

narcissistic personality disorder A personality disturbance characterized by an exaggerated sense of self-importance. (Module 38)

narcotics Drugs that increase relaxation and relieve pain and anxiety. (Module 14)

nativist approach (to language development) The theory that humans are biologically prewired to learn language at certain times and in particular ways. (Module 22)

naturalistic observation Research in which an investigator simply observes some naturally occurring behavior and does not make a change in the situation. (Module 3)

nature–nurture issue The issue of the degree to which environment and heredity influence behavior. (Module 27)

need for achievement A stable, learned characteristic in which a person obtains satisfaction by striving for and achieving challenging goals. (Module 25)

need for affiliation An interest in establishing and maintaining relationships with other people. (Module 25)

need for power A tendency to seek impact, control, or influence over others and to be seen as a powerful individual. (Module 25)

negative reinforcer An unpleasant stimulus whose removal leads to an increase in the probability that a preceding response will be repeated in the future. (Module 16)

neo-Freudian psychoanalysts Psychoanalysts who were trained in traditional Freudian theory but who later rejected some of its major points. (Module 31)

neonate A newborn child. (Module 28)

neurons Nerve cells, the basic elements of the nervous system. (Module 5)

neuroplasticity Changes in the brain that occur throughout the life span relating to the addition of new neurons, new interconnections between neurons, and the reorganization of information-processing areas. (Module 7)

neuroscience perspective The approach that views behavior from the perspective of the brain, the nervous system, and other biological functions. (Module 2)

neurotransmitters Chemicals that carry messages across the synapse to the dendrite (and sometimes the cell body) of a receiver neuron. (Module 5)

neutral stimulus A stimulus that, before conditioning, does not naturally bring about the response of interest. (Module 15)

norms Standards of test performance that permit the comparison of one person's score on a test with the scores of other individuals who have taken the same test. (Module 23)

obedience A change in behavior in response to the commands of others. (Module 44)

obesity Body weight that is more than 20% above the average weight for a person of a particular height. (Module 25)

object permanence The awareness that objects–and people–continue to exist even if they are out of sight. (Module 28)

observational learning Learning by observing the behavior of another person, or model. (Module 17)

obsession A persistent, unwanted thought or idea that keeps recurring. (Module 38)

obsessive-compulsive disorder (OCD) A disorder characterized by obsessions or compulsions. (Module 38)

Oedipal conflict A child's intense, sexual interest in his or her opposite-sex parent. (Module 31)

operant conditioning Learning in which a voluntary response is strengthened or weakened, depending on its favorable or unfavorable consequences. (Module 16)

operational definition The translation of a hypothesis into specific, testable procedures that can be measured and observed. (Module 3)

opponent-process theory of color vision The theory that receptor cells for color are linked in pairs, working in opposition to each other. (Module 9)

optic nerve A bundle of ganglion axons that carry visual information to the brain. (Module 9)

oral stage According to Freud, a stage from birth to age 12 to 18 months, in which an infant's center of pleasure is the mouth. (Module 31)

overgeneralization The phenomenon by which children overapply a language rule, thereby making linguistic errors. (Module 22)

ovulation The point at which an egg is released from the ovaries. (Module 25)

panic disorder Anxiety disorder that takes the form of panic attacks lasting from a few seconds to several hours. (Module 38)

parasympathetic division The part of the autonomic division of the nervous system that acts to calm the body after an emergency has ended. (Module 6)

partial (or intermittent) reinforcement schedule Reinforcing of a behavior some but not all of the time. (Module 16)

passionate (or romantic) love A state of intense absorption in someone that includes intense physiological arousal, psychological interest, and caring for the needs of another. (Module 46)

perception The sorting out, interpretation, analysis, and integration of stimuli by the sense organs and brain. (Module 8)

perceptual constancy Our understanding that physical objects are unvarying and consistent even though sensory input about them may vary. (Module 11)

peripheral nervous system The part of the nervous system that includes the autonomic and somatic subdivisions; made up of neurons with long axons and dendrites, it branches out from the spinal cord and brain and reaches the extremities of the body. (Module 6)

peripheral route processing The type of mental processing that occurs when

a persuasive message is evaluated on the basis of irrelevant or extraneous factors. (Module 43)

permissive parents Parents who give their children relaxed or inconsistent direction and, although they are warm, require little of them. (Module 28)

person-centered therapy Therapy in which the goal is to reach one's potential for self-actualization. (Module 41)

personal stressors Major life events, such as the death of a family member, that have immediate negative consequences that generally fade with time. (Module 34)

personality The pattern of enduring characteristics that produce consistency and individuality in a given person. (Module 31)

personality disorder A disorder characterized by a set of inflexible, maladaptive behavior patterns that keep a person from functioning appropriately in society. (Module 38)

phallic stage According to Freud, a period beginning around age 3 during which a child's pleasure focuses on the genitals. (Module 31)

phonemes The smallest units of speech. (Module 22)

phonology The study of the smallest units of speech, called phonemes. (Module 22)

pituitary gland The major component of the endocrine system, or "master gland," which secretes hormones that control growth and other parts of the endocrine system. (Module 6)

place theory of hearing The theory that different areas of the basilar membrane respond to different frequencies. (Module 10)

placebo A false treatment, such as a pill, "drug," or other substance, without any significant chemical properties or active ingredient. (Module 4)

positive reinforcer A stimulus added to the environment that brings about an increase in a preceding response. (Module 16)

posttraumatic stress disorder (PTSD) A phenomenon in which victims of major catastrophes or strong personal stressors feel long-lasting effects that may include re-experiencing the event in vivid flashbacks or dreams. (Module 34)

practical intelligence According to Sternberg, intelligence related to overall success in living. (Module 23)

prejudice A negative (or positive) evaluation of a particular group and its members. (Module 45)

preoperational stage According to Piaget, the period from 2 to 7 years of age that is characterized by language development. (Module 28)

priming A phenomenon that occurs when exposure to a word or concept (called a *prime*) later makes it easier to recall information related to the prime. (Module 21)

principle of conservation The knowledge that quantity is unrelated to the arrangement and physical appearance of objects. (Module 28)

proactive interference Interference in which information learned earlier disrupts the recall of material learned later. (Module 20)

procedural memory Memory for skills and habits, such as riding a bike or hitting a baseball; sometimes referred to as *nondeclarative memory*. (Module 18)

projective personality test A test in which a person is shown an ambiguous stimulus and asked to describe it or tell a story about it. (Module 33)

prosocial behavior Helping behavior. (Module 46)

prototypes Typical, highly representative examples of a concept. (Module 21)

Prozac A widely prescribed–but still controversial–antidepressant. (Module 42)

psychoactive drugs Drugs that influence a person's emotions, perceptions, and behavior. (Module 14)

psychoanalysis Freud's psychotherapy in which the goal is to release hidden thoughts and feelings from the unconscious part of our minds in order to reduce their power in controlling behavior. (Module 40)

psychoanalytic perspective The perspective that suggests that abnormal behavior stems from childhood conflicts over opposing wishes regarding sex and aggression. (Module 37)

psychoanalytic theory Freud's theory that unconscious forces act as determinants of personality. (Module 31)

psychodynamic approaches to personality Approaches that assume that personality is primarily unconscious and motivated by inner forces and conflicts about which people have little awareness. (Module 31)

psychodynamic perspective The approach based on the view that behavior is motivated by unconscious inner forces over which the individual has little control. (Module 2)

psychodynamic therapy Therapy that seeks to bring unresolved past conflicts and unacceptable impulses from the unconscious into the conscious, where patients may deal with the problems more effectively. (Module 40)

psychological tests Standard measures devised to assess behavior objectively; used by psychologists to help people make decisions about their lives and understand more about themselves. (Module 33)

psychology The scientific study of behavior and mental processes. (Module 1)

psychoneuroimmunology (PNI) The study of the relationship among psychological factors, the immune system, and the brain. (Module 34)

psychophysics The study of the relationship between the physical aspects of stimuli and our psychological experience of them. (Module 8)

psychophysiological disorders Medical problems influenced by an interaction of psychological, emotional, and physical difficulties. (Module 34)

psychosexual stages Developmental periods that children pass through during which they encounter conflicts between the demands of society and their own sexual urges. (Module 31)

psychosocial development Development of individuals' interactions and understanding of each other and of their knowledge and understanding of themselves as members of society. (Module 28)

psychosurgery Brain surgery once used to reduce the symptoms of mental disorder but rarely used today. (Module 42)

psychotherapy Treatment in which a trained professional–a therapist–uses psychological techniques to help a person overcome psychological difficulties and disorders, resolve problems in living, or bring about personal growth. (Module 40)

puberty The period at which maturation of the sexual organs occurs, beginning at about age 11 or 12 for girls and 13 or 14 for boys. (Module 29)

punishment A stimulus that decreases the probability that a previous behavior will occur again. (Module 16)

race Generally refers to obvious physical differences that set one group apart from others.

random assignment to condition A procedure in which participants are assigned to different experimental groups or "conditions" on the basis of chance and chance alone. (Module 3)

rapid eye movement (REM) sleep Sleep occupying 20% of an adult's sleeping time, characterized by increased heart rate, blood pressure, and breathing rate; erections; eye movements; and the experience of dreaming. (Module 12)

rational-emotive behavior therapy A form of therapy that attempts to restructure a person's belief system into a more realistic, rational, and logical set of views by challenging dysfunctional beliefs that maintain irrational behavior. (Module 40)

realistic conflict theory The theory that conflict arises from direct competition over valued, but limited, resources.

recall Memory task in which specific information must be retrieved. (Module 19)

reciprocity-of-liking effect A tendency to like those who like us. (Module 46)

recognition Memory task in which individuals are presented with a stimulus and asked whether they have been exposed to it in the past or to identify it from a list of alternatives. (Module 19)

reflex An automatic, involuntary response to an incoming stimulus. (Module 6)

reflexes Unlearned, involuntary responses that occur automatically in the presence of certain stimuli. (Module 28)

rehearsal The repetition of information that has entered short-term memory. (Module 18)

reinforcement The process by which a stimulus increases the probability that a preceding behavior will be repeated. (Module 16)

reinforcer Any stimulus that increases the probability that a preceding behavior will occur again. (Module 16)

relative deprivation The sense that one lacks a desired resource in comparison to another group, which is perceived to have more.

reliability The property by which tests measure consistently what they are trying to measure. (Module 23)

replicated research Research that is repeated, sometimes using other procedures, settings, and groups of participants, to increase confidence in prior findings. (Module 3)

repression The defense mechanism in which the ego pushes unacceptable or unpleasant thoughts and impulses out of consciousness but maintains them in the unconscious. (Module 40)

resilience The ability to withstand, overcome, and actually thrive after profound adversity.

resting state The state in which there is a negative electrical charge of about −70 millivolts within a neuron. (Module 5)

reticular formation The part of the brain extending from the medulla through the pons; it is related to changes in the level of arousal of the body. (Module 7)

retina The part of the eye that converts the electromagnetic energy of light to electrical impulses for transmission to the brain. (Module 9)

retroactive interference Interference in which material that was learned later disrupts the retrieval of information that was learned earlier. (Module 20)

retrograde amnesia Amnesia in which memory is lost for occurrences prior to a certain event, but not for new events. (Module 20)

reuptake The reabsorption of neurotransmitters by a terminal button. (Module 5)

rods Thin, cylindrical receptor cells in the retina that are highly sensitive to light. (Module 9)

Rorschach test A test that involves showing a series of symmetrical visual stimuli to people who then are asked what the figures represent to them. (Module 33)

Schachter-Singer theory of emotion The belief that emotions are determined jointly by a nonspecific kind of physiological arousal and its interpretation, based on environmental cues. (Module 26)

schedules of reinforcement Different patterns of frequency and timing of reinforcement following desired behavior. (Module 16)

schemas Organized bodies of information stored in memory that bias the way new information is interpreted, stored, and recalled. (Modules 21, 52)

schizophrenia A class of disorders in which severe distortion of reality occurs. (Module 38)

scientific method The approach through which psychologists systematically acquire knowledge and understanding about behavior and other phenomena of interest. (Module 3)

self The way in which we look inward and define ourselves as individuals.

self-actualization A state of self-fulfillment in which people realize their highest potential in their own unique way. (Modules 24, 32)

self-efficacy The belief that we can master a situation and produce positive outcomes. (Module 32)

self-esteem The component of personality that encompasses our positive and negative self-evaluations. (Module 32)

self-report measures A method of gathering data about people by asking them questions about their own behavior and traits. (Module 33)

self-serving bias The tendency to attribute personal success to personal factors (skill, ability, or effort) and to attribute failure to factors outside oneself. (Module 43)

semantic memory Memory for general knowledge and facts about the world, as well as memory for the rules of logic that are used to deduce other facts. (Module 18)

semantic networks Mental representations of clusters of interconnected information. (Module 18)

semantics The meaning of words and sentences. (Module 22)

semicircular canals Three tube-like structures of the inner ear containing fluid that sloshes through them when the head moves, signaling rotational or angular movement to the brain. (Module 10)

sensation The activation of the sense organs by a source of physical energy. (Module 8)

sensorimotor stage According to Piaget, the stage from birth to 2 years, during which a child has little competence in representing the environment by using images, language, or other symbols. (Module 28)

sensory (afferent) neurons Neurons that transmit information from the perimeter of the body to the nervous system and brain. (Module 6)

sensory area The site in the brain of the tissue that corresponds to each of the senses, with the degree of sensitivity related to the amount of tissue. (Module 7)

sensory memory The initial, momentary storage of information, lasting only an instant. (Module 18)

shaping The process of teaching a complex behavior by rewarding closer and closer approximations of the desired behavior. (Module 16)

short-term memory Memory that holds information for 15 to 25 seconds. (Module 18)

significant outcome Meaningful results that make it possible for researchers to feel confident that they have confirmed their hypotheses. (Module 3)

situational causes (of behavior) Causes of behavior that are external to a person. (Module 43)

skin senses The senses of touch, pressure, temperature, and pain. (Module 10)

social cognition The cognitive processes by which people understand and make sense of others and themselves. (Module 43)

social cognitive approaches to personality Theories that emphasize the influence of a person's cognitions—thoughts, feelings, expectations, and values—as well as observation of others' behavior, in determining personality. (Module 32)

social influence The process by which social groups and individuals exert pressure on an individual, either deliberately or unintentionally. (Module 44)

social neuroscience The subfield of social psychology that seeks to identify the neurological basis of social behavior. (Module 45)

social psychology The scientific study of how people's thoughts, feelings, and actions are affected by others. (Module 43)

social support A mutual network of caring, interested others. (Module 34)

social supporter A group member whose dissenting views make non-conformity to the group easier. (Module 44)

sociocultural perspective The perspective that assumes that people's behavior—both normal and abnormal—is shaped by the kind of family group, society, and culture in which they live. (Module 37)

somatic division The part of the peripheral nervous system that specializes in the control of voluntary movements and the communication of information to and from the sense organs. (Module 6)

somatic symptom disorders Psychological difficulties that take on a physical (somatic) form, but for which there is no medical cause. (Module 38)

sound The movement of air molecules brought about by a source of vibration. (Module 10)

specific phobia Intense, irrational fears of specific objects or situations. (Module 38)

spinal cord A bundle of neurons that leaves the brain and runs down the length of the back and is the main means for transmitting messages between the brain and the body. (Module 6)

spontaneous recovery The reemergence of an extinguished conditioned response after a period of rest and with no further conditioning. (Module 15)

spontaneous remission Recovery without formal treatment. (Module 41)

stage 1 sleep The state of transition between wakefulness and sleep, characterized by relatively rapid, low-amplitude brain waves. (Module 12)

stage 2 sleep A sleep deeper than that of stage 1, characterized by a slower, more regular wave pattern, along with momentary interruptions of "sleep spindles." (Module 12)

stage 3 sleep A sleep characterized by slow brain waves, with greater peaks and valleys in the wave pattern than in stage 2 sleep. (Module 12)

status The social standing of someone in a group. (Module 44)

stereotype A set of generalized beliefs and expectations about a particular group and its members. (Module 45)

stimulants Drugs that have an arousal effect on the central nervous system, causing a rise in heart rate, blood pressure, and muscular tension. (Module 14)

stimulus Energy that produces a response in a sense organ. (Module 8)

stimulus discrimination The process that occurs if two stimuli are sufficiently distinct from one another that one evokes a conditioned response but the other does not; the ability to differentiate between stimuli. (Module 15)

stimulus generalization A process in which, after a stimulus has been conditioned to produce a particular response, stimuli that are similar to the original stimulus produce the same response. (Module 15)

stress A person's response to events that are threatening or challenging. (Module 34)

structuralism Wundt's approach, which focuses on uncovering the fundamental mental components of consciousness, thinking, and other kinds of mental states and activities. (Module 2)

subjective well-being People's sense of their happiness and satisfaction with their lives. (Module 36)

superego The part of personality that harshly judges the morality of our behavior. (Module 40)

survey research Research in which people chosen to represent a larger population are asked a series of questions about their behavior, thoughts, or attitudes. (Module 3)

sympathetic division The part of the autonomic division of the nervous system that acts to prepare the body for action in stressful situations, engaging all the organism's resources to respond to a threat. (Module 6)

synapse The space between two neurons where the axon of a sending neuron communicates with the dendrites of a receiving neuron by using chemical messages. (Module 5)

syntax Ways in which words and phrases can be combined to form sentences. (Module 22)

systematic desensitization A behavioral technique based on classical conditioning in which exposure to an anxiety-producing stimulus is paired with deep relaxation to extinguish the response of anxiety. (Module 40)

telegraphic speech Sentences in which only essential words are used. (Module 22)

temperament A basic, inborn characteristic way of responding and behavioral style. (Module 37)

teratogens Environmental agents such as drugs, chemicals, viruses, or other factors that produce birth defects. (Module 27)

terminal buttons Small bulges at the end of axons that send messages to other neurons. (Module 5)

test standardization A technique used to validate questions in personality tests by studying the responses of people with known diagnoses. (Module 33)

thalamus The part of the brain located in the middle of the central core that acts primarily to relay information about the senses. (Module 7)

Thematic Apperception Test (TAT) A test consisting of a series of pictures about which a person is asked to write a story. (Module 33)

theories Broad explanations and predictions concerning observations of interest. (Module 3)

theory of multiple intelligences Gardner's intelligence theory that proposes that there are eight distinct spheres of intelligence. (Module 23)

thinking Brain activity in which people mentally manipulate information, including words, visual images, sounds, or other data. (Module 21)

tip-of-the-tongue phenomenon The inability to recall information that one realizes one knows—a result of the difficulty of retrieving information from long-term memory. (Module 19)

top-down processing Perception that is guided by higher-level knowledge, experience, expectations, and motivations. (Module 11)

trait theory A model of personality that seeks to identify the basic traits necessary to describe personality. (Module 41)

traits Consistent, habitual personality characteristics and behaviors that are displayed across different situations. (Module 41)

transcranial magnetic stimulation (TMS) A depression treatment in which a precise magnetic pulse is directed to a specific area of the brain. (Module 42)

transference The transfer of feelings to a psychoanalyst of love or anger that had been originally directed to a patient's parents or other authority figures. (Module 40)

transgender An umbrella term for persons whose gender identity, gender expression, or behavior does not conform to that typically associated with the sex to which they were assigned at birth. (Module 25)

treatment The manipulation implemented by the experimenter. (Module 3)

trichromatic theory of color vision The theory that there are three kinds of cones in the retina, each of which responds primarily to a specific range of wavelengths. (Module 9)

trust-versus-mistrust stage According to Erikson, the first stage of psychosocial development, occurring from birth to age 1½ years, during which time infants develop feelings of trust or lack of trust. (Module 28)

Type A behavior pattern A cluster of behaviors involving hostility, competitiveness, time urgency, and feeling driven. (Module 35)

Type B behavior pattern A cluster of behaviors characterized by a patient, cooperative, noncompetitive, and nonaggressive manner. (Module 35)

unconditional positive regard An attitude of acceptance and respect on the part of an observer, no matter what a person says or does. (Module 32)

unconditioned response (UCR) A response that is natural and needs no training (e.g., salivation at the smell of food). (Module 15)

unconditioned stimulus (UCS) A stimulus that naturally brings about a particular response without having been learned. (Module 15)

unconscious A part of the personality that contains the memories, knowledge, beliefs, feelings, urges, drives, and instincts of which the individual is not aware. (Module 31)

unconscious wish fulfillment theory Sigmund Freud's theory that dreams represent unconscious wishes that dreamers desire to see fulfilled. (Module 12)

uninvolved parents Parents who show little interest in their children and are emotionally detached. (Module 28)

validity The property by which tests actually measure what they are supposed to measure. (Module 23)

variable-interval schedule A schedule by which the time between reinforcements varies around some average rather than being fixed. (Module 16)

variable-ratio schedule A schedule by which reinforcement occurs after a varying number of responses rather than after a fixed number. (Module 16)

variables Behaviors, events, or other characteristics that can change, or vary, in some way. (Module 3)

visual illusions Physical stimuli that consistently produce errors in perception. (Module 11)

wear-and-tear theories of aging Theories that suggest that the mechanical functions of the body simply stop working efficiently. (Module 30)

Weber's law A basic law of psychophysics stating that a just noticeable difference is a constant proportion to the intensity of an initial stimulus (rather than a constant amount). (Module 8)

weight set point The particular level of weight that the body strives to maintain. (Module 25)

working memory A memory system that holds information temporarily while actively manipulating and rehearsing that information. (Module 18)

zone of proximal development (ZPD) According to Vygotsky, the gap between what children already are able to accomplish on their own and what they are not quite ready to do by themselves. (Module 28)

zygote The new cell formed by the union of an egg and sperm. (Module 27)

References

Aazh, H., & Moore, B. C. J. (2007). Dead regions in the cochlea at 4 kHz in elderly adults: Relation to absolute threshold, steepness of audiogram, and pure-tone average. *Journal of the American Academy of Audiology, 18,* 97-106.

Abbass, A., Town, J., Ogrodniczuk, J., Joffres, M., & Lilliengren, P. (2017). Intensive short-term dynamic psychotherapy trial therapy: Effectiveness and role of "unlocking the unconscious". *Journal of Nervous and Mental Disease, 205,* 453-457.

Abboud, L. (2005, July 27). The next phase in psychiatry. *The Wall Street Journal,* pp. D1, D5.

Abel, D. (2015, June 16.) Panel votes to reopen Georges Bank. *Boston Globe.* Retrieved from https://www.bostonglobe.com/metro/2015/06/16/fishing-industry-body-votes-open-parts-georges-bank/c8UBRJ6zsDJbdps19Gu6VN/story.html.

Abel, T., & Nickl-Jockschat, T. (2016). *The neurobiology of schizophrenia.* San Diego, CA, US: Elsevier Academic Press.

Abramowitz, J. S., Olatunji, B. O., & Deacon, B. J. (2007). Health anxiety, hypochondriasis, and the anxiety disorders. *Behavior Therapy, 38,* 86-94.

Accardi, M., & Milling, L. (2009, August). The effectiveness of hypnosis for reducing procedure-related pain in children and adolescents: A comprehensive methodological review. *Journal of Behavioral Medicine, 32,* 328-339.

Ackerman, P. L. (2011). Intelligence and expertise. In R. J. Sternberg & S. Kaufman (Eds.), *The Cambridge handbook of intelligence.* New York: Cambridge University Press.

Acuna, D. E., Berniker, M., Fernandes, H. L., & Kording, K. P. (2015). Using psychophysics to ask if the brain samples or maximizes. *Journal of Vision, 15,* 7-18.

Adams, G., & Dzokoto, V. A. (2007). Genital-shrinking panic in Ghana: A cultural psychological analysis. *Culture & Psychology, 13,* 83-104.

Adams, K. B. (2004). Changing investment in activities and interests in elders' lives: Theory and measurement. *International Journal of Aging and Human Development, 58,* 87-108.

Adams, M., Bell, L. A., & Griffin, P. (2007). *Teaching for diversity and social justice* (2nd Ed.). New York: Routledge/Taylor & Francis Group.

Addison, A. (2017). Jung's psychoid concept: An hermeneutic understanding. *International Journal of Jungian Studies, 9,* 1-16.

Addus, A. A., Chen, D., & Khan, A. S. (2007). Academic performance and advisement of

university students: A case study. *College Student Journal, 41,* 316-326.

Adler, M. (2013). Hunger and longing: A developmental regulation model for exploring core relational needs. In S. P. Gantt & B. Badenoch (Eds.), *The interpersonal neurobiology of group psychotherapy and group process.* London: Karnac Books.

Adolph, K. E., & Berger, S. E. (2011). Physical and motor development. In M. H. Bornstein & M. E. Lamb (Eds.), *Cognitive development: An advanced textbook.* New York: Psychology Press.

Advokat, C. (2005). Differential effects of clozapine versus other antipsychotics on clinical outcome and dopamine release in the brain. *Essential Psychopharmacology, 6,* 73-90.

Ahrens, S., Pirschel, I., & Snower, D. J. (2017). A theory of price adjustment under loss aversion. *Journal of Economic Behavior & Organization, 134,* 78-95.

Aikawa, A., & Fujii, T. (2011). Using the Implicit Association Test (IAT) to measure implicit shyness. *Japanese Journal of Psychology, 82,* 41-48.

Aiken, L. R. (1997). *Psychological testing and assessment* (9th ed.). Needham Heights, MA: Allyn & Bacon.

Aimé, C., Paquette, D., Déry, M., & Verlaan, P. (2018). Predictors of childhood trajectories of overt and indirect aggression: An interdisciplinary approach. *Aggressive Behavior,* doi:10.1002/ab.21759.

Ainsworth, M. D. S., Blehar, M. C., Waters, E., & Wall, S. (1978). *Patterns of attachment: A psychological study of the strange situation.* Hillsdale, NJ: Erlbaum.

Airuehia, E., Walker, L. Y., & Nittler, J. (2015). A review of 'bath salts': Evolving designer drugs of abuse. *Journal Of Child & Adolescent Substance Abuse, 24,* 186-190.

Akil, H., & Morano, M. I. (1996). The biology of stress: From periphery to brain. In S. J. Watson (Ed.), *Biology of schizophrenia and affective disease.* Washington, DC: American Psychiatric Press.

Alampay, L. P., Godwin, J., Lansford, J. E., Bombi, A. S., Bornstein, M. H., Chang, L., . . . Bacchini, D. (2017). Severity and justness do not moderate the relation between corporal punishment and negative child outcomes: A multicultural and longitudinal study. *International Journal of Behavioral Development, 41,* 491-502.

Alba, R., & Barbosa, G. Y. (2016). Room at the top? Minority mobility and the transition to demographic diversity in the USA. *Ethnic and

Racial Studies, 39*(6), 917-938. doi:10.1080/01419870.2015.1081966.

Albanese, M., & Case, S. M. (2015). Progress testing: Critical analysis and suggested practices. *Advances In Health Sciences Education,* Accessed online, 9.1.15; http://www.ncbi.nlm.nih.gov/pubmed/25662873.

Alberts, A., Elkind, D., & Ginsberg, S. (2007). The personal fable and risk-taking in early adolescence. *Journal of Youth and Adolescence, 36,* 71-76.

Alboni, S., Di Bonaventura, M. M., Benatti, C., Giusepponi, M. E., Brunello, N., & Cifani, C. (2017). Hypothalamic expression of inflammatory mediators in an animal model of binge eating. *Behavioural Brain Research, 320,* 420-430.

Alderson-Day, B., Weis, S., McCarthy-Jones, S., Moseley, P., Smailes, D., & Fernyhough, C. (2016). The brain's conversation with itself: Neural substrates of dialogic inner speech. *Social Cognitive and Affective Neuroscience, 11*(1), 110-120.

Aleksander, I. (2013, June 23). Molly: Pure, but not so simple. *The New York Times,* p. ST1.

Alelú-Paz, R., Carmona, F. J., Sanchez-Mut, J. V., Cariaga-Martínez, A., González-Corpas, A., Ashour, N., . . . Ropero, S. (2016). Epigenetics in schizophrenia: A pilot study of global DNA methylation in different brain regions associated with higher cognitive functions. *Frontiers In Psychology, 7,* 1496.

Alexandersen, P., Karsdal, M. A., & Christiansen, C. (2009). Long-term prevention with hormone-replacement therapy after the menopause: Which women should be targeted? *Women's Health, 5,* 637-647.

Alfaro, A., Bernabeu, Á., Agulló, C., Parra, J., & Fernández, E. (2015). Hearing colors: An example of brain plasticity. *Frontiers in Systems Neuroscience, 9,* 42-50.

Alho, K., Vorobyev, V. A., Medvedev, S. V., Pakhomov, S. V., Starchenko, M. G., Terganiemi, M., & Näätänen, R. (2006). Selective attention to human voice enhances brain activity bilaterally in the superior temporal sulcus. *Brain Research, 1075,* 142-150.

Allport, G. W. (1966). Traits revisited. *American Psychologist, 21,* 1-10.

Allport, G. W., & Postman, L. J. (1958). The basic psychology of rumor. In E. D. Maccoby, T. M. Newcomb, & E. L. Hartley (Eds.), *Readings in social psychology* (3rd ed.). New York: Holt, Rinehart and Winston.

Allwood, M. A. (2007). The relations of violence exposure, trauma symptoms and aggressive cognitions to youth violent behavior. *Dissertation Abstracts International: Section B: The Sciences and Engineering, 67,* 5387.

Alon, I., & Brett, J. M. (2007). Perceptions of time and their impact on negotiations in the Arabic-speaking Islamic world. *Negotiation Journal, 23,* 55-73.

Alter, A. (2017). *Irresistible.* New York: Penguin.

Altman, N., & Stile, J. (2015). Staying alive: Freud for a new generation. *PsycCRITIQUES, 60,* 25-32.

Alzheimer's Association. (2017). *2017 Alzheimer's Disease: Facts and Figures.* Chicago, IL: Alzheimer's Association.

American Academy of Pediatrics Council on Communications and Media. (2016). Virtual violence. *Pediatrics, 138,* e20161298.

American Association of Intellectual and Developmental Disabilities. (2015). Frequently asked questions on intellectual disability and the AAIDD definition. Retrieved from http://aaidd.org/docs/default-source/sis-docs/aaiddfaqonid_template.pdf?sfvrsn=2.

American Psychiatric Association. (2013). *Diagnostic and Statistical Manual of Mental Disorders, Fifth Edition (DSM-5).* Washington, DC: Author.

American Psychiatric Association. (2018). Warning signs of mental illness. Retrieved from https://www.psychiatry.org/patients-families/warning-signs-of-mental-illness.

American Psychological Association (2015). *Demographics of the U.S. psychology workforce: Findings from the American Community Survey.* Washington, DC: Author.

American Psychological Association (APA). (2000). *Psychology careers for the twenty-first century.* Washington, DC: Author.

American Psychological Association Presidential Task Force on Evidence-Based Practice. (2006). *Evidence-based practice in psychology, 61,* 271-285.

American Psychological Association. (2002). *APA ethics code, 2002.* Washington, DC: Author.

American Psychological Association. (2016). *Breakdown of careers in psychology.* Washington, DC: APA.

Amid, P. K., & Chen, D. C. (2011). Surgical treatment of chronic groin and testicular pain after laparoscopic and open preperitoneal inguinal hernia repair. *Journal of the American College of Surgeons, 213,* 531-536.

Amodio, D. M., & Ratner, K. G. (2011). A memory systems model of implicit social cognition. *Current Directions In Psychological Science, 20,* 143-148.

Anastasi, A., & Urbina, S. (1997). *Psychological testing* (7th ed.). Englewood Cliffs, NJ: Prentice Hall.

Andersen, B. (2017). Careful words: Nursing, language, and emotion in Papua New Guinea. *Medical Anthropology, 36*(8), 758-771. doi:10.1080/01459740.2017.1317771.

Anderson, C. A., Lazard, D. S., & Hartley, D. H. (2017). Plasticity in bilateral superior temporal cortex: Effects of deafness and cochlear implantation on auditory and visual speech processing. *Hearing Research, 343,* 138-149.

Anderson, C., et al. (2015). Consensus on Media Violence Effects: Comment on Bushman, Gollwitzer, and Cruz. *Psychology of Popular Media Culture, 4,* 215-221.

Anderson, C., & Home, J. A. (2006). Sleepiness enhances distraction during monotonous task. *Sleep: Journal of Sleep and Sleep Disorders Research, 29,* 573-576.

Anderson, J. L., Sellbom, M., Pymont, C., Smid, W., De Saeger, H., & Kamphuis, J. H. (2015). Measurement of DSM-5 section II personality disorder constructs using the MMPI-2-RF in clinical and forensic samples. *Psychological Assessment, 27,* 786-800.

Anderson, J. L., Sellbom, M., Pymont, C., Smid, W., De Saeger, H., & Kamphuis, J. H. (2015). Measurement of DSM-5 section II personality disorder constructs using the MMPI-2-RF in clinical and forensic samples. *Psychological Assessment, 27,* 786-800.

Anderson, L. B., Paul, L. K., & Brown, W. S. (2017). Emotional intelligence in agenesis of the corpus callosum. *Archives of Clinical Neuropsychology, 32,* 267-279.

Andrasik, F. (2006). Psychophysiological disorders: Headache as a case in point. In F. Andrasik, *Comprehensive handbook of personality and psychopathology, Vol. 2: Adult psychopathology.* Hoboken, NJ: John Wiley & Sons.

Andrasik, F. (2007). What does the evidence show? Efficacy of behavioural treatments for recurrent headaches in adults. *Neurological Science, 28,* Supplement, S70-S77.

Anestis, M. D., Anestis, J. C., & Lilienfeld, S. O. (2011). When it comes to evaluating psychodynamic therapy, the devil is in the details. *American Psychologist, 66,* 149-151.

Anker, A. E., & Feeley, T. (2011). Are nonparticipants in prosocial behavior merely innocent bystanders? *Health Communication, 26,* 13-24.

Antonini, A., & Barone, P. (2008, December). Dopamine agonist-based strategies in the treatment of Parkinson's disease. *Neurological Sciences, 29,* S371-SS374.

Anwar, F., Fry, D. P., & Grigfaitytė, I. (2018). Aggression prevention and reduction in diverse cultures and contexts. *Current Opinion in Psychology, 19,* 49-54. doi:10.1016/j.copsyc.2017.03.029.

Apanovich, A. M., McCarthy, D., & Salovey, P. (2003). Using message framing to motivate HIV testing among low-income, ethnic minority women. *Health Psychology, 22,* 88-94.

Appel, H., Gerlach, A. L., & Crusius, J. (2016). The interplay between Facebook use, social comparison, envy, and depression. *Current Opinion in Psychology, 9,* 44-49.

Appelbaum, P. S., Scurich, N., & Raad, R. (2015). Effects of behavioral genetic evidence on perceptions of criminal responsibility and appropriate punishment. *Psychology, Public Policy, And Law, 21,* 134-144.

Apple, D. M., Fonseca, R. S., & Kokovay, E. (2017). The role of adult neurogenesis in psychiatric and cognitive disorders. *Brain Research, 1655,* 270-276.

Arafat, I., & Cotton, W. L. (1974). Masturbation practices of males and females. *Journal of Sex Research, 10,* 293-307.

Arbuthnott, A., & Sharpe, D. (2009). The effect of physician-patient collaboration on patient adherence in non-psychiatric medicine. *Patient Education and Counseling, 77,* 60-67.

Arcaro, M. J., Schade, P. F., Vincent, J. L., Ponce, C. R., & Livingstone, M. S. (2017). Seeing faces is necessary for face-domain formation. *Nature Neuroscience, 20,* 1404-1412.

Arcelus, J., Mitchell, A. J., Wales, J., & Nielsen, S. (2011). Mortality rates in patients with anorexia nervosa and other eating disorders: A meta-analysis of 36 studies. *Archives of General Psychiatry, 68,* 724-731.

Ardila, A. (2015). A proposed neurological interpretation of language evolution. *Behavioural Neurology, 20,* 15-22.

Ariely, D., & Norton, M. I. (2009). Conceptual consumption. *Annual Review of Psychology, 60,* 475-499.

Arimoto, M., Shiomi, T., Sasanabe, R., Inagawa, S., Ueda, H., & Inafuku, S. (2011). A sheet-type device for home-monitoring sleep apneas in children. *Sleep and Biological Rhythms, 9,* 103-111.

Arlo, C. (2017). Group therapy and dialectical behavior therapy: An integrative response to a clinical case. *International Journal of Group Psychotherapy, 67*(Supp1), S13-S23.

Armbruster, D., Mueller, A., Strobel, A., Lesch, K., Kirschbaum, C., & Brocke, B. (2011). Variation in genes involved in dopamine clearance influence the startle response in older adults. *Journal of Neural Transmission, 118,* 1281-1292.

Arnett, J. (2008). The neglected 95%: Why American psychology needs to become less American. *American Psychologist, 63,* 602-614.

Arnett, J. (2011). Emerging adulthood(s): The cultural psychology of a new life stage. In L. Jensen (Ed.), *Bridging cultural and developmental approaches to psychology: New syntheses in theory, research, and policy.* New York: Oxford University Press.

Arnett, J. J. (2000). Emerging adulthood. *American Psychologist, 55,* 469-480.

Arnett, J. J. (2006). *Emerging adulthood: The winding road from the late teens through the twenties.* New York: Oxford University Press.

Arnett, J. J. (2007). Afterword: Aging out of care—Toward realizing the possibilities of emerging adulthood. *New Directions for Youth Development, 113,* 151-161.

Aronson, J., & Dee, T. (2012). Stereotype threat in the real world. In M. Inzlicht & T. Schmader (Eds.), *Stereotype threat: Theory, process, and application.* New York: Oxford University Press.

Aronson, J., & Steele, Claude M. (2005). Stereotypes and the fragility of academic competence, motivation, and self-concept. In A. J. Elliot & C. S. Dweck (Eds.), *Handbook of competence and motivation.* New York, NY: Guilford Publications.

Arpaci, I., Baloğlu, M., & Kesici, Ş. (2018). The relationship among individual differences in individualism-collectivism, extraversion, and self-presentation. *Personality and Individual Differences, 121,* 89-92. doi:10.1016/j.paid.2017.09.034.

Arshamian, A., Iannilli, E., Gerber, J. C., Willander, J., Persson, J., Seo, H., & . . . Larsson, M. (2013). The functional neuroanatomy of odor evoked auto-biographical memories cued by odors and words. *Neuropsychologia, 51,* 123-131.

Artistico, D., Pinto, A., Douek, J., Black, J., & Pezzuti, L. (2013). The value of removing daily obstacles via everyday problem-solving theory: Developing an applied novel procedure to increase self-efficacy for exercise. *Frontiers In Psychology, 4.* Retrieved from http://www.ncbi.nlm.nih.gov/pubmed/23372560.

Asch, S. E. (1951). Effects of group pressure upon the modification and distortion of judgments. In H. Guetzkow (Ed.), *Groups, leadership, and men.* Pittsburgh: Carnegie Press.

Aspinwall, L. G., & Taylor, S. E. (1997). A stitch in time: Self-regulation and proactive coping. *Psychological Bulletin, 121,* 417-436.

Associated Press (2011, September 27). Study: Murder victims disproportionately black. Accessed May 2, 2018 from http://www.msnbc.msn.com/id/20203888/ns/us_news-life/t/study-murder-victims-disproportionately-black.

Atkinson, H. (Ed.). (1997, January 21). Understanding your diagnosis. *HealthNews,* p. 3.

Atkinson, R. C., & Shiffrin, R. M. (1968). Human memory: A proposed system and its control processes. In K. W. Spence & J. T. Spence (Eds.), *The psychology of learning and motivation: Advances in research and theory* (Vol. 2). New York: Academic Press.

Auerbach, R. P., Alonso, J., Axinn, W. G., Cuijpers, P., Ebert, D. D., Green, J. G., . . . Bruffaerts, R. (2016). Mental disorders among college students in the World Health Organization World Mental Health Surveys. *Psychological Medicine, 46,* 2955-2970.

Aujoulat, I., Luminet, O., & Deccache, A. (2007). The perspective of patients on their experience of powerlessness. *Quality Health Research, 17,* 772-785.

Aussilloux, C., & Bagdadli, A. (2006). Handicap mental et société: Soigner, éduquer, intégrer. Mental handicap and society. *Neuropsychiatrie de l'Enfance et de l'Adolescence, 54,* 336-340.

Averill, J. R. (1975). A semantic atlas of emotional concepts. *Catalog of Selected Documents in Psychology, 5,* 330.

Ayling, K., Bowden, T., Tighe, P., Todd, I., Dilnot, E. M., Negm, O. H., . . . Vedhara, K. (2017). The application of protein microarray assays in psychoneuroimmunology. *Brain, Behavior, and Immunity, 59,* 62-66.

Bacchiochi, J. R. (2006). Development and validation of the Malingering Discriminant Function Index (M-DFI) for the Minnesota Multiphasic Personality Inventory-2 (MMPI-2). *Dissertation Abstracts International: Section B: The Sciences and Engineering, 66*(10-B), 5673.

Baczyńska, A., & Thornton, G. C. (2017). Relationships of analytical, practical, and emotional intelligence with behavioral dimensions of performance of top managers. *International Journal of Selection and Assessment, 25,* 171-182.

Baddeley, A. D., Allen, R. J., & Hitch, G. J. (2011). Binding in visual working memory: The role of the episodic buffer. *Neuropsychologia, 49,* 1393-1400.

Baddeley, A., & Wilson, B. (1985). Phonological coding and short-term memory in patients without speech. *Journal of Memory and Language, 24,* 490-502.

Badke, M. B., Sherman, J., Boyne, P., Page, S., & Dunning, K. (2011). Tongue-based biofeedback for balance in stroke: results of an 8-week pilot study. *Archives of Physical and Medical Rehabilitation, 92,* 1364-1370.

Bagattini, C., Mele, S., Brignani, D., & Savazzi, S. (2015). No causal effect of left hemisphere hyperactivity in the genesis of neglect-like behavior. *Neuropsychologia, 72,* 12-21.

Bagge, C., & Sher, K. (2008). Adolescent alcohol involvement and suicide attempts: Toward the development of a conceptual framework. *Clinical Psychology Review, 28,* 1283-1296.

Bagnall, D. (2010). The use of spinal cord stimulation and intrathecal drug delivery in the treatment of low back-related pain. *Physical Medicine & Rehabilitation Clinics of North America, 21,* 851-858.

Bahrick, L. E., Lickliter, R., & Castellanos, I. (2013). The development of face perception in infancy: Intersensory interference and unimodal visual facilitation. *Developmental Psychology, 49,* 1919-1930.

Bai, L. (2005). Children at play: A childhood beyond the Confucian shadow. *Childhood: A Global Journal of Child Research, 12,* 9-32.

Bailey, J. M., Vasey, P. L., Diamond, L. M., Breedlove, S. M., Vilain, E., & Epprecht, M. (2016). Sexual orientation, controversy, and science. *Psychological Science in the Public Interest, 17*(2), 45-101.

Baker, J., & Berenbaum, H. (2007). Emotional approach and problem-focused coping: A comparison of potentially adaptive strategies. *Cognition and Emotion, 21,* 95-118.

Baker, S. C., & Serdikoff, S. L. (2013). Addressing the role of animal research in psychology. In D. S. Dunn, R. R. Gurung, K. Z. Naufel, & J. H. Wilson (Eds.), *Controversy in the psychology classroom: Using hot topics to foster critical thinking.* Washington, DC: American Psychological Association.

Baker, S. E., Johnson, P. J., & Slater, D. (2007). Learned food aversion with and without an odour cue for protecting untreated baits from wild mammal foraging [Special issue: Conservation, enrichment, and animal behavior]. *Applied Animal Behaviour Science, 102,* 410-428.

Balaban, C. D., McBurney, D. H., & Affeltranger, M. A. (2005). Three distinct categories of time course of pain produced by oral capsaicin. *The Journal of Pain, 6,* 315-322.

Balconi, M., Bortolotti, A., & Crivelli, D. (2013). Self-report measures, facial feedback, and personality differences (BEES) in cooperative vs. noncooperative situations: Contribution of the mimic system to the sense of empathy. *International Journal of Psychology, 48,* 631-640.

Ball, D. (2004). Genetic approaches to alcohol dependence. *British Journal of Psychiatry, 185,* 449-451.

Balter, M. (2017). Schizophrenia's unyielding mysteries. *Scientific American, 316*(5), 54-61.

Bandura, A. (1986). *Social foundations of thought and action: A social cognitive theory.* Englewood Cliffs, NJ: Prentice Hall.

Bandura, A. (1994). Social cognitive theory of mass communication. In J. Bryant & D. Zillmann (Eds.), *Media effects: Advances in theory and research: LEA's communication series.* Hillsdale, NJ: Erlbaum.

Bandura, A. (1999). Social cognitive theory of personality. In D. Cervone & Y. Shod (Eds.), *The coherence of personality.* New York: Guilford.

Bandura, A. (2000). Self-efficacy: The foundation of agency. In W. J. Perrig & A. Grob (Eds.), *Control of human behavior, mental processes, and consciousness: Essays in honor of the 60th birthday of August Flammer.* Mahwah, NJ: Erlbaum.

Bandura, A. (2004). Swimming against the mainstream: The early years from chilly tributary to transformative mainstream. *Behavior Research and Therapy, 42,* 613-630.

Bandura, A. (2009). Social cognitive theory goes global. *The Psychologist, 22,* 504-506.

Bandura, A., & Locke, E. A. (2003). Negative self-efficacy and goal effects revisited. *Journal of Applied Psychology, 88,* 87-99.

Bandura, A., Grusec, J. E., & Menlove, F. L. (1967). Vicarious extinction of avoidance behavior. *Journal of Personality and Social Psychology, 5,* 16-23.

Bandura, A., Ross, D., & Ross, S. (1963a). Imitation of film-mediated aggressive models. *Journal of Abnormal and Social Psychology, 66,* 3-11.

Bandura, A., Ross, D., & Ross, S. (1963b). Vicarious reinforcement and imitative learning. *Journal of Abnormal and Social Psychology, 67,* 601-607.

Banks, J. A. (2006). Improving race relations in schools: From theory and research to practice. *Journal of Social Issues, 62,* 607-614.

Banks, J. B., & Boals, A. (2017). Understanding the role of mind wandering in stress-related working memory impairments. *Cognition and Emotion, 31,* 1023-1030.

Barandiaran, A. A., Pascual, A. C., & Samaniego, C. M. (2006). A criticism of the Kohlberg theory: The moral development in adults and educative implications. *Revista de Psicología General y Aplicada, 59,* 165-182.

Barash, Đ. P., & Lipton, J. E. (2011). *Payback: Why we retaliate, redirect aggression, and take revenge.* New York: Oxford University Press.

Barbaro, N., Boutwell, B. B., Barnes, J. C., & Shackelford, T. K. (2017). Rethinking the transmission gap: What behavioral genetics and evolutionary psychology mean for attachment theory: A comment on Verhage et al. (2016). *Psychological Bulletin, 143,* 107-113.

Barcott, B., & Scherer, M. (2015, May 25). The great pot experiment. *Time,* pp. 38-44.

Bargh, J. A. (2014, January). Our unconscious mind. *Scientific American,* pp. 30-37.

Barke, D. B. (2011). Self-selection for stressful experiences. *Stress and Health: Journal of the International Society for the Investigation of Stress, 27,* 194-205.

Barker, J., & Jones, M. (2008). The effects of hypnosis on self-efficacy, affect, and soccer performance: A case study. *Journal of Clinical Sport Psychology, 2,* 127-147.

Barkley, R. (2000). *Taking charge of ADHD* (rev. ed.). New York: Guilford Press.

Barkley, R. A., Knouse, L. E., & Murphy, K. R. (2011). Correspondence and disparity in the self- and other ratings of current and childhood ADHD symptoms and impairment in adults with ADHD. *Psychological Assessment, 23,* 437-446.

Barlow, D. H. (2007). *Clinical handbook of psychological disorders: A step-by-step treatment manual* (4th ed.). New York: Guilford Press.

Barmeyer, C. I. (2004). Learning styles and their impact on cross-cultural training: An international comparison in France, Germany and Quebec. *International Journal of Intercultural Relations, 28,* 577-594.

Barnes, J. C., & Jacobs, B. A. (2013). Genetic risk for violent behavior and environmental exposure to disadvantage and violent crime: The case for gene-environment interaction. *Journal of Interpersonal Violence, 28,* 92-120.

Barnett, J. E., Wise, E. H., & Johnson-Greene, D. (2007). Informed consent: Too much of a good thing or not enough? *Professional Psychology: Research and Practice, 38,* 179-186.

Barnett, S. M., Rindermann, H., Williams, W. M., & Ceci, S. J. (2011). Society and intelligence. In R. J. Sternberg & S. Kaufman (Eds.), *The Cambridge handbook of intelligence.* New York: Cambridge University Press.

Barrada, J., Abad, F., & Olea, J. (2011). Varying the valuating function and the presentable bank in computerized adaptive testing. *Spanish Journal of Psychology, 14,* 500-508.

Barresi, J. (2007). Consciousness and intentionality. *Journal of Consciousness Studies, 14, Special issue: Concepts of Consciousness: Integrating an Emerging Science,* 77-93.

Barrett, L. (2011). *Beyond the brain: How body and environment shape animal and human minds.* Princeton, NJ: Princeton University Press.

Barrett, L. F., & Russell, J. A. (2015). An introduction to psychological construction. In L. F. Barrett & J. A. Russell (Eds.), *The psychological construction of emotion.* New York: Guilford Press.

Barrett, L. F., & Salovey, P. (Eds.). (2002). *The wisdom in feeling: Psychological processes in emotional intelligence.* New York: Guilford Press.

Barry, C. T., Doucette, H., Loflin, D. C., Rivera-Hudson, N., & Herrington, L. L. (2017). "Let me take a selfie": Associations between self-photography, narcissism, and self-esteem. *Psychology of Popular Media Culture, 6,* 48-60.

Barson, J. R., Morganstern, I., & Leibowitz, S. F. (2011). Similarities in hypothalamic and mesocorticolimbic circuits regulating the overconsumption of food and alcohol. *Physiology & Behavior, 104,* 128-137.

Bartlett, F. (1932). *Remembering: A study in experimental and social psychology.* Cambridge, England: Cambridge University Press.

Bartlett, M. Y., & DeSteno, D. (2006). Gratitude and prosocial behavior: Helping when it costs you. *Psychological Science, 17,* 319-325.

Bartocci, G. (2004). Transcendence techniques and psychobiological mechanisms underlying religious experience. *Mental Health, Religion and Culture, 7,* 171-181.

Bartone, P., Roland, R., Picano, J., & Williams, T. (2008). Psychological hardiness predicts success in U.S. Army Special Forces candidates. *International Journal of Selection and Assessment, 16,* 78-81.

Baruss, I. (2003). *Alterations of consciousness: An empirical analysis for social scientists.* Washington, DC: American Psychological Association.

Barzilay, S., Feldman, D., Snir, A., Apter, A., Carli, V., Hoven, C. W., . . . Wasserman, D. (2015). The interpersonal theory of suicide and adolescent suicidal behavior. *Journal of Affective Disorders, 183,* 68-74.

Bass, E. C., Saldarriaga, L., Cunha, J., Chen, B., Santo, J. B., & Bukowski, W. M. (2018). A cross-cultural analysis of the relations of physical and relational aggression with peer victimization. *International Journal of Behavioral Development, 42*(1), 132-142.

Bassett, A. M., & Baker, C. (2015). Normal or abnormal? 'Normative uncertainty' in psychiatric practice. *Journal Of Medical Humanities, 36,* 89-111.

Bassotti, G., & Villanacci, V. (2011). Can 'functional' constipation be considered as a form of enteric neuro-gliopathy? *Glia, 59,* 345-350.

Bastian, B., Jetten, J, Hornsey, M. J., & Leknes, S. (2014). The positive consequences of pain: A biopsychosocial approach. *Personality and Social Psychology Review, 18,* 256-279.

Bateman, A. W. (2011). Commentary on 'Minding the difficult patient': Mentalizing and the use of formulation in patients with borderline personality disorder comorbid with antisocial personality disorder. *Personality and Mental Health, 5,* 85-90.

Bates, E. (2005). Plasticity, localization, and language development. In S. T. Parker & J. Langer (Eds.), *Biology and knowledge revisited: From neurogenesis to psychogenesis.* Mahwah, NJ: Lawrence Erlbaum Associates.

Bates, J. E., & Pettit, G. S. (2015). Temperament, parenting, and social development. In J. E. Grusec & P. D. Hastings (Eds.), *Handbook of socialization: Theory and research* (2nd ed.). New York: Guilford Press.

Batson, C. (2011). *Altruism in humans.* New York: Oxford University Press.

Bauer, J. J., Schwab, J. R., & McAdams, D. P. (2011). Self-actualizing: Where ego development finally feels good? *Humanistic Psychologist, 39,* 121-136.

Bauer, J. J., Schwab, J. R., & McAdams, D. P. (2011). Self-actualizing: Where ego development finally feels good? *The Humanistic Psychologist, 39,* 121-136.

Bauer, P. (2008). Toward a neuro-developmental account of the development of declarative memory. *Developmental Psychobiology, 50,* 19-31.

Baum, A., Lorduy, K., & Jenkins, F. J. (2011). The molecular biology of stress: Cellular defense, immune response, and aging. In R. J. Contrada & A. Baum (Eds.), *The handbook of stress science: Biology, psychology, and health.* New York: Springer Publishing Co.

Baumeister, R. F., & Stillman, T. (2006). Erotic plasticity: Nature, culture, gender, and sexuality. In R. D. McAnulty & M. M. Burnette (Eds.), *Sex and sexuality, Vol 1: Sexuality today: Trends and controversies.* Westport, CT: Praeger Publishers/Greenwood Publishing.

Baumeister, R. F., Ainsworth, S. E., & Vohs, K. D. (2015). Are groups more or less than the sum of their members? The moderating role of individual identification. *Behavioral and Brain Sciences.* Accessed online, 10.1.15; http://www.ncbi.nlm.nih.gov/pubmed/25936575.

Baumgartner, F. (2002). The effect of hardiness in the choice of coping strategies in stressful situations. *Studia Psychologica, 44,* 69-75.

Baumrind, D. (1971). Current patterns of parental authority. *Developmental Psychology, 4,* 1-104.

Baumrind, D. (2005). Patterns of parental authority and adolescent autonomy. *New Directions for Child and Adolescent Development, 108,* 61-69.

Baumrucker, S., Mingle, P., Harrington, D., Stolick, M., Carter, G. T., & Oertli, K. A. (2011). Medical marijuana and organ transplantation: Drug of abuse, or medical necessity? *American Journal of Hospice & Palliative Medicine, 28,* 130-134.

Bautista, D. M., Wilson, S. R., & Hoon, M. A. (2014). Why we scratch an itch: The molecules, cells and circuits of itch. *Nature Neuroscience, 17*(2), 175-182.

Bavelier, D., & Green. C. S. (2016). The brain-boosting power of video games. *Scientific American, 315*(1), 27-31.

Bayliss, D. M., Jarrold, C., Baddeley, A. D., & Gunn, D. M. (2005). The relationship between short-term memory and working memory: Complex span made simple? *Memory, 13,* 414-421.

Bazalakova, M. H., Wright, J., Schneble, E. J., McDonald, M. P., Heilman, C. J., Levey, A. I., & Blakely, R. D. (2007). Deficits in acetylcholine homeostasis, receptors and behaviors in choline transporter heterozygous mice. *Genes, Brain & Behavior, 6,* 411-424.

Beam, A. (2014, August 21). Four-bit recall. *Boston Globe,* p. 1.

Beam, C. R., & Turkheimer, E. (2013). Phenotype-environment correlations in longitudinal twin models. *Development and Psychopathology, 25,* 7-16.

Bearman, C. R., Ball, L. J., & Ormerod, T. C. (2007). The structure and function of spontaneous analogising in domain-based problem solving. *Thinking & Reasoning, 13*, 273-294.

Beaudry, J. L., Lindsay, R. C. L., Leach, A-M., Mansour, J. K., Bertrand, M. I., & Kalmet, N. (2015). The effect of evidence type, identification accuracy, line-up presentation, and line-up administration on observers' perceptions of eyewitnesses. *Legal and Criminological Psychology, 20*(2), 343-364.

Bebermeier, S., Echterhoff, G., Bohner, G., & Hellmann, J. H. (2015). The generalization of shared reality: When communication about one target shapes evaluations of other targets. *European Journal of Social Psychology, 45*, 623-640.

Bechara, A., Damasio, A. R., Damasio, H., & Anderson, S. (1994). Insensitivity to future consequences following damage to human prefrontal cortex. *Cognition, 50*, 7-15.

Beck, A. P., & Lewis, C. M. (Eds.). (2000). *The process of group psychotherapy: Systems for analyzing change*. Washington, DC: American Psychological Association.

Beck, A. T. (1995). Cognitive therapy: Past, present, and future. In M. J. Mahoney (Ed.), *Cognitive and constructive psychotherapies: Theory, research, and practice*. New York: Springer.

Beck, A. T. (2004). Cognitive therapy, behavior therapy, psychoanalysis, and pharmacotherapy: A cognitive continuum. In A. Freeman, M. J. Mahoney, P. Devito, & D. Martin (Eds.), *Cognition and Psychotherapy* (2nd ed.). New York: Springer Publishing Co.

Beck, A. T., & Rector, N. A. (2005). Cognitive approaches to schizophrenia: Theory and therapy. *Annual Review of Clinical Psychology, 1*, 577-606.

Beck, A. T., Davis, D. D., & Freeman, A. (2015). *Cognitive therapy of personality disorders* (3rd ed.). New York: Guilford Press.

Beck, A. T., Freeman, A., & Davis, D. D. (2004). *Cognitive therapy of personality disorders* (2nd ed.). New York: Guilford Press.

Beck, K., Javitt, D. C., & Howes, O. D. (2016). Targeting glutamate to treat schizophrenia: Lessons from recent clinical studies. *Psychopharmacology, 233*, 2425-2428.

Beck, M. (2015, June 2). Your body's witching hours. *Wall Street Journal*, pp. D1-D2.

Becker, J., Brackbill, D., & Centola, D. (2017). Network dynamics of social influence in the wisdom of crowds. *PNAS Proceedings of the National Academy of Sciences of the United States of America, 114*, 70-76.

Becker, T. (2003). Is emotional intelligence a viable concept? *Academy of Management Review, 28*, 192-195.

Beersma, D. G. M., & Gordijn, M. C. M. (2007). Circadian control of the sleep-wake cycle. *Physiology & Behavior, 90*.

Begg, D., & Langley, J. (2001). Changes in risky driving behavior from age 21 to 26 years. *Journal of Safety Research, 32*, 491-499.

Beghetto, R. A., & Kaufman, J. C. (Eds.). (2010). *Nurturing creativity in the classroom*. New York: Cambridge University Press.

Behrendt, R. (2011). *Neuroanatomy of social behaviour: An evolutionary and psychoanalytic perspective*. London England: Karnac Books.

Behrens, M., Lendon, C., & Roe, C. (2009). A common biological mechanism in cancer and Alzheimer's disease? *Current Alzheimer Research, 6*, 196-204.

Beidel, D. C., & Turner, S. M. (2007). Etiology of social anxiety disorder. In D. C. Beidel & S. M. Turner (Eds.), *Shy children, phobic adults: Nature and treatment of social anxiety disorders* (2nd ed.). Washington, DC: American Psychological Association.

Beitel, M., Wald, L. M., Midgett, A., Green, D., Cecero, J. J., Kishon, R., & Barry, D. T. (2015). Humanistic experience and psychodynamic understanding: Empirical associations among facets of self-actualization and psychological mindedness. *Person-Centered and Experiential Psychotherapies, 14*, 137-148.

Belasen, A. T., & Fortunato, M. V. (2013). Situational motivation: Challenge the binary. In M. A. Paludi (Ed.), *Psychology for business success, Vol 1: Juggling, balancing, and integrating work and family roles and responsibilities, Vol 2: Institutional equity and compliance, Vol 3: Managing, leading, and developing employees, Vol 4: Implementing best practices in human resources*. Santa Barbara, CA: Praeger/ABC-CLIO.

Bem, D. (2012). ESP is not a psychological anomaly. *PsychCRITIQUES, 57*, 2012.

Ben-Porath, Y. S., Corey, D. M., & Tarescavage, A. M. (2017). Using the MMPI-2-RF in pre-employment evaluations of police officer candidates. In C. L. Mitchell & E. H. Dorian (Eds.), *Police psychology and its growing impact on modern law enforcement*. Hershey, PA: Information Science Reference/IGI Global.

Benderly, B. L. (2004). Looking beyond the SAT. *American Psychological Society, 17*, 12-18.

Benet-Martinez, V., Lee, F., & Leu, J. (2006). Biculturalism and cognitive complexity: Expertise in cultural representations. *Journal of Cross-Cultural Psychology, 37*, 386-407.

Benham, G., Woody, E. Z., & Wilson, K. S. (2006). Expect the unexpected: Ability, attitude, and responsiveness to hypnosis. *Journal of Personality and Social Psychology, 91*, 342-350.

Benitez, P., de CarvalhoGomes, M. L., Bondioli, R., & Domeniconi, C. (2017). Mapping of inclusive strategies for students with intellectual disabilities and autism. *Psicologia Em Estudo, 22*, 81-93.

Benson, E. (2003, April). The science of sexual arousal. *Monitor on Psychology*, 50-56.

Benton, S. A., Robertson, J. M., Tseng, W., Newton, F. B., & Benton, S. L. (2003) Changes in counseling center client problems across 13 years. *Professional Psychology: Research and Practice 34*(1) 66-72.

Bentwich, J., Dobronevsky, E., Aichenbaum, S., Shorer, R., Peretz, R., Khaigrekht, M., & . . . Rabey, J. M. (2011). Beneficial effect of repetitive transcranial magnetic stimulation combined with cognitive training for the treatment of Alzheimer's disease: A proof of concept study. *Journal of Neural Transmission, 118*, 463-471.

Beran, M. J., Smith, J., & Perdue, B. M. (2013). Language-trained chimpanzees (Pan troglodytes) name what they have seen but look first at what they have not seen. *Psychological Science, 24*, 660-666.

Berecki-Gisolf, J., McKenzie, S. J., Dobson, A. J., McFarlane, A., & McLaughlin, D. (2013). A history of comorbid depression and anxiety predicts new onset of heart disease. *Journal of Behavioral Medicine, 36*, 347-353.

Beresnevaité, M., Taylor, G. J., & Bagby, R. M. (2007). Assessing alexithymia and type A behavior in coronary heart disease patients: A multimethod approach. *Psychotherapy and Psychosomatics, 76*, 186-192.

Berk, L. E. (2005). Why parenting matters. In S. Olfman (Ed.), *Childhood lost: How American culture is failing our kids*. Westport, CT: Praeger Publishers/Greenwood Publishing Group.

Berke, D. S., Reidy, D. E., Miller, J. D., & Zeichner, A. (2017). Take it like a man: Gender-threatened men's experience of gender role discrepancy, emotion activation, and pain tolerance. *Psychology of Men & Masculinity, 18*, 62-69.

Berkman, L. F., Ertel, K. A., & Glymour, M. M. (2011). Aging and social intervention: Life course perspectives. In R. H. Binstock & L. K. George (Eds.), *Handbook of aging and the social sciences* (7th ed.). San Diego, CA: Elsevier Academic Press.

Berkowitz, L. (2001). On the formation and regulation of anger and aggression: A cognitive-neoassociationistic analysis. In W. G. Parrott (Ed.), *Emotions in social psychology: Essential readings*. New York: Psychology Press.

Bernard, L. L. (1924). *Instinct: A study in social psychology*. New York: Holt.

Bernstein, D., & Loftus, E. (2009a). How to tell if a particular memory is true or false. *Perspectives on Psychological Science, 4*, 370-374.

Bernstein, D., & Loftus, E. (2009b). The consequences of false memories for food preferences and choices. *Perspectives on Psychological Science, 4*, 135-139.

Bernstein, E. (2011, April 19). Friendly fight: A smarter way to say 'I'm angry.' *Wall Street Journal*, pp. D1, D4.

Berntsen, D., & Rubin, D. C. (2004). Cultural life scripts structure recall from autobiographical memory. *Memory and Cognition, 32*, 427-442.

Berridge, K. C. (2004). Motivation concepts in behavioral neuroscience. *Physiology and Behavior, 81*, 179-209.

Bertakis, K. (2009). The influence of gender on the doctor-patient interaction. *Patient Education and Counseling, 76*, 356-360.

Bertakis, K., Franks, P., & Epstein, R. (2009). Patient-centered communication in primary care: Physician and patient gender and gender concordance. *Journal of Women's Health, 18*, 539-545.

Berthoud, H. R. (2002). Multiple neural systems controlling food intake and body weight. *Neuroscience and Biobehavioral Reviews, 26*, 393-428.

Best, D. (2017). Why the mechanisms of 12-step behaviour change should matter to clinicians. *Addiction, 112*, 938-939.

Betley, J. N., Xu, S., Cao, Z. H., Gong, R., Magnus, C. J., Yu, Y., & Sternson, S. M. (2015). Neurons for hunger and thirst transmit a negative-valence teaching signal. *Nature, 521*, 180-185.

Betterton, R. T., Broad, L. M., Tsaneva-Atanasova, K., & Mellor, J. R. (2017). Acetylcholine modulates gamma frequency oscillations in the hippocampus by activation of muscarinic M1 receptors. *European Journal of Neuroscience, 45*, 1570-1585.

Beyene, Y., Gilliss, C., & Lee, K. (2007). "I take the good with the bad, and I moisturize": Defying middle age in the new millennium. *Menopause, 14*, 734-741.

Bhar, S., Gelfand, L., Schmid, S., Gallop, R., DeRubeis, R., Hollon, S., et al. (2008). Sequence of improvement in depressive symptoms across cognitive therapy and pharmacotherapy. *Journal of Affective Disorders, 110*, 161-166.

Bhatia, S. (2017). The semantic representation of prejudice and stereotypes. *Cognition, 164*, 46-60.

Bialystok, E. (2011). Reshaping the mind: The benefits of bilingualism. *Canadian Journal of Experimental Psychology, 65*, 229-235.

Bialystok, E., & Craik, F. I. M. (2011). Cognitive and linguistic processing in the bilingual mind. *Current Directions in Psychological Science, 19*, 19-23.

Bialystok, E., Barac, R., Blaye, A., & Poulin-Dubois, D. (2010). Word mapping and executive functioning in young monolingual and bilingual children. *Journal of Cognition and Development, 11*, 485-508.

Bianchi, S. M., & Casper, L. M. (2000). American families. *Population Bulletin, 55*(4).

Bieberstein, A., & Roosen, J. (2015). Gender differences in the meanings associated with food hazards: A means-end chain analysis. *Food Quality and Preference, 42*, 165-176.

Bienvenu, O. J., Davydow, D. S., & Kendler, K. S. (2011). Psychiatric "diseases" versus behavioral disorders and degree of genetic influence. *Psychological Medicine: A Journal of Research in Psychiatry and the Allied Sciences, 41*, 33-40.

Bigsby, E., Monahan, J. L., & Ewoldsen, D. R. (2017). An examination of adolescent recall of anti-smoking messages: Attitudes, message type, and message perceptions. *Health Communication, 32*, 409-419.

Billiard, M. (2008). Narcolepsy: Current treatment options and future approaches. *Neuropsychiatric Disease and Treatment, 4*, 557-566.

Binet, A., & Simon, T. (1916). *The development of intelligence in children (The Binet-Simon Scale).* Baltimore: Williams & Wilkins.

Bingenheimer, J. B., Brennan, R. T., & Earls, E. J. (2005, May 27). Firearm violence exposure and serious violent behavior. *Science, 308*, 1323-1327.

Bischoff, R. J., Springer, P. R., Felix, D. S., & Hollist, C. S. (2011). Finding the heart of medical family therapy: A content analysis of medical family therapy casebook articles. *Families, Systems, & Health, 29*, 184-196.

Bitterman, M. E. (2006). Classical conditioning since Pavlov. *Review of General Psychology, 10*, 365-376.

Bittles, A. H., Bower, C., & Hussain, R. (2007). The four ages of Down syndrome. *European Journal of Public Health, 17*, 121-225.

Bjork, R. A. (2015). Forgetting as a friend of learning. In D. S. Lindsay, A. P. Yonelinas, H. I. Roediger, D. S. Lindsay, A. P. Yonelinas, & H. I. Roediger (Eds.), *Remembering: Attributions, processes, and control in human memory: Essays in honor of Larry Jacoby.* New York: Psychology Press.

Bjornsdottir, E., Keenan, B. T., Eysteinsdottir, B., Arnardottir, E. S., Janson, C., Gislason, T., & . . . Benediktsdottir, B. (2015). Quality of life among untreated sleep apnea patients compared with the general population and changes after treatment with positive airway pressure. *Journal of Sleep Research, 24*, 328-338.

Bjornstad, R. (2006). Learned helplessness, discouraged workers, and multiple unemployment equilibria. *The Journal of Socio-Economics, 35*, 458-475.

Black, A. L., & McCafferty, D. (1998, July 3-5). The age of contentment. *USA Weekend*, 4-6.

Blackwell, L. S., Rodriguez, S., & Guerra-Carrillo, B. (2015). Intelligence as a malleable construct. In S. Goldstein, D. Princiotta, & J. A. Naglieri (Eds.), *Handbook of intelligence: Evolutionary theory, historical perspective, and current concepts.* New York: Springer Science + Business Media.

Blair, C. A., Thompson, L. F., & Wuensch, K. L. (2005). Electronic helping behavior: The virtual presence of others makes a difference. *Basic and Applied Social Psychology, 27*, 171-178.

Blakeslee, S. (1992, September 29). Radical brain surgery, the earlier the better, offers epileptics hope. *The New York Times.*

Blanton, H., Jaccard, J., & Burrows, C. N. (2015). Implications of the Implicit Association Test D-transformation for psychological assessment. *Assessment, 22*, 429-440.

Blass, T. (1996). Attribution of responsibility and trust in the Milgram obedience experiment. *Journal of Applied Social Psychology, 26*, 1529-1535.

Blass, T. (2004). *The man who shocked the world: The life and legacy of Stanley Milgram.* New York: Basic Books.

Blass, T. (2009). From New Haven to Santa Clara: A historical perspective on the Milgram obedience experiments. *American Psychologist, 64*, 37-45.

Blatter, K., & Cajochen, C. (2007). Circadian rhythms in cognitive performance: Methodological constraints, protocols, theoretical underpinnings. *Physiology & Behavior, 90*, 196-208.

Blechner, M. J. (2013). New ways of conceptualizing and working with dreams. *Contemporary Psychoanalysis, 49*, 259-275.

Blixen, C. E., Singh, A., & Xu, M. (2006). What women want: Understanding obesity and preferences for primary care weight reduction interventions among African-American and Caucasian women. *Journal of the National Medical Association, 98*, 1160-1170.

Bloom, P. N., McBride, C. M., & Pollak, K. I. (2006). Recruiting teen smokers in shopping malls to a smoking-cessation program using the foot-in-the-door technique. *Journal of Applied Social Psychology, 36*, 1129-1144.

Blum, D. (2002). *Love at goon park: Harry Harlow and the science of affection.* Cambridge, MA: Perseus.

Blum, H. P. (2011). To what extent do you privilege dream interpretation in relation to other forms of mental representations? *The International Journal of Psychoanalysis, 92*, 275-277.

Blumen, H. M., Rajaram, S., & Henkel, L. (2013). The applied value of collaborative memory research in aging: Considerations for broadening the scope. *Journal of Applied Research in Memory and Cognition, 2*, 133-135.

Blumenthal, H., Leen-Feldner, E. W., Babson, K. A., Gahr, J. L., Trainor, C. D., & Frala, J. L. (2011). Elevated social anxiety among early maturing girls. *Developmental Psychology, 47*, 1133-1140.

Boag, S. (2015). Repression, defence, and the psychology of science. In S. Boag, L. W. Brakel, & V. Talvitie (Eds.), *Philosophy, science, and psychoanalysis: A critical meeting.* London: Karnac Books.

Boag, S. (2017). On dreams and motivation: Comparison of Freud's and Hobson's views. *Frontiers in Psychology, 7*, 1-13.

Boag, S., Brakel, L. W., & Talvitie, V. (2015). *Philosophy, science, and psychoanalysis: A critical meeting.* London, England: Karnac Books.

Boahen, K. (2005, May). Neuromorphic microchips. *Scientific American*, pp. 56-64.

Boake, C. (2008). Clinical neuropsychology. *Professional Psychology: Research and Practice, 39*, 234-239.

Boarini, R., Laslier, J., & Robin, S. (2009). Interpersonal comparisons of utility in bargaining: Evidence from a transcontinental ultimatum game. *Theory and Decision, 67*, 341-373.

Bode, C., de Ridder, D. T., Kuijer, R. G., & Bensing, J. M. (2007). Effects of an intervention promoting proactive coping competencies in middle and late adulthood. *Gerontologist, 47*, 42-51.

Boden, J. M., Fergusson, D. M., & Horwood, L. J. (2007). Anxiety disorders and suicidal behaviours in adolescence and young adulthood: Findings from a longitudinal study. *Psychological Medicine, 37*, 431-440.

Boeve-de Pauw, J., Donche, V., & Van Petegem, P. (2011). Adolescents' environmental worldview and personality: An explorative study. *Journal of Environmental Psychology, 31*, 109-117.

Bogart, R. K., McDaniel, R. J., Dunn, W. J., Hunter, C., Peterson, A. L., & Write, E. E. (2007). Efficacy of group cognitive behavior therapy for the treatment of masticatory myo-fascial pain. *Military Medicine, 172*, 169-174.

Bohart, A. C. (2006). Understanding person-centered therapy: A review of Paul Wilkins' person-centered therapy in focus. *Person-Centered and Experiential Psychotherapies, 5*, 138-143.

Bohn, A., & Berntsen, D. (2007). Pleasantness bias in flashbulb memories: Positive and negative flashbulb memories of the fall of the Berlin Wall among East and West Germans. *Memory and Cognition, 35*, 565-577.

Bohn, C., Aderka, I. M., Schreiber, F., Stangier, U., & Hofmann, S. G. (2013). Sudden gains in cognitive therapy and interpersonal therapy for social anxiety disorder. *Journal of Consulting and Clinical Psychology, 81*, 177-182.

Boles, D. B. (2005). A large-sample study of sex differences in functional cerebral lateralization. *Journal of Clinical and Experimental Neuropsychology, 27*, 759-768.

Bolger, N., & Amarel, D. (2007). Effects of social support visibility on adjustment to stress: Experimental evidence. *Journal of Personality and Social Psychology, 92*, 458-475.

Bolkan, S. (2015). Intellectually stimulating students' intrinsic motivation: The mediating influence of affective learning and student engagement. *Communication Reports, 28*, 80-91.

Boller, F. (2004). Rational basis of rehabilitation following cerebral lesions: A review of the concept of cerebral plasticity. *Functional Neurology: New Trends in Adaptive and Behavioral Disorders, 19*, 65-72.

Bonanno, G. A. (2004). Loss, trauma, and human resilience: Have we underestimated the human capacity to thrive after extremely aversive events? *American Psychologist, 59*, 20-28.

Bonezzi, A., Brendl, C., & De Angelis, M. (2011). Stuck in the middle: The psychophysics of goal pursuit. *Psychological Science, 22*, 607-612.

Bonini, L. (2017). The extended mirror neuron network: Anatomy, origin, and functions. *The Neuroscientist, 23*, 56-67.

Bonta, B., D. (1997). Cooperation and competition in peaceful societies. *Psychological Bulletin, 121*, 299-320.

Boot, W. R., Kramer, A. F., Simons, D. J., Fabiani, M. & Gratton, G. (2008) The effects of video game playing on attention, memory, and executive control. *Acta Psychologica, 129*, 387-398.

Borghuis, J., Denissen, J. A., Oberski, D., Sijtsma, K., Meeus, W. J., Branje, S., . . . Bleidorn, W. (2017). Big Five personality stability, change, and codevelopment across adolescence and early adulthood. *Journal of Personality and Social Psychology, 113*(4), 641-657.

Bornstein, R. F. (2003). Psychodynamic models of personality. In T. Millon & M. J. Lerner (Eds.), *Handbook of psychology: Personality and social psychology* (Vol. 5). New York: Wiley.

Boroditsky, L. (2010, July 24-25). Lost in translation. *Wall Street Journal*, p. W3.

Boser, U. (2017). *Learn better: Mastering the skills for success in life, business, and school, or, how to become an expert in just about anything.* Emmaus, PA: Rodale Books. .

Bosma, H., van Boxtel, M. P. J., Ponds, R. W. H. M., Houx, P. J. H., & Jolles, J. (2003).

Education and age-related cognitive decline: The contribution of mental workload. *Educational Gerontology, 29*, 165-173.

Bossarte, R. M., & Swahn, M. H. (2011). The associations between early alcohol use and suicide attempts among adolescents with a history of major depression. *Addictive Behaviors, 36*.

Bosse, T., Gerritsen, C., & Treur, J. (2011). Combining rational and biological factors in virtual agent decision making. *Applied Intelligence, 34*, 87-101.

Bosson, J. K., & Vandello, J. A. (2011). Precarious manhood and its links to action and aggression. *Current Directions in Psychological Science, 20*, 82-86.

Botvinick, M. (2004, August 6). Probing the neural basis of body ownership. *Science, 305*, 782-783.

Bouchard, T. J., Jr. (2004). Genetic influence on human psychological traits: A survey. *Current Directions in Psychological Science, 13*, 148-151.

Bouchard, T. J., Jr., Segal, N. L., Tellegen, A., McGue, M., Keyes, M., & Krueger, R. (2004). Genetic influence on social attitudes: Another challenge to psychology from behavior genetics. In L. F. DiLalla (Ed.), *Behavior genetics principles: Perspectives in development, personality, and psychopathology.* Washington, DC: American Psychological Association.

Bourne, L. E., Dominowski, R. L., Loftus, E. F., & Healy, A. F. (1986). *Cognitive processes* (2nd ed.). Englewood Cliffs, NJ: Prentice Hall.

Bouton, C., Shaikhouni, A., Annetta, N., Bockbrader, M., Friedenberg, D. A., Nielson, D. M., . . . Rezai, A. R. (2016). Restoring cortical control of functional movement in a human with quadriplegia. *Nature, 533*, 247-250.

Bouton, M. E., Todd, T. P., Vurbic, D., & Winterbauer, N. E. (2011). Renewal after the extinction of free operant behavior. *Learning & Behavior, 39*, 57-67.

Bouvard, M., & Roulin, J. (2017). Exploratory factor analysis of the French version of the Big Five Questionnaire for Children (BFQ-C). *Swiss Journal of Psychology, 76*, 125-130.

Bouvard, M., Fournet, N., Denis, A., Sixdenier, A., & Clark, D. (2017). Intrusive thoughts in patients with obsessive compulsive disorder and non-clinical participants: A comparison using the International Intrusive Thought Interview Schedule. *Cognitive Behaviour Therapy, 46*, 287-299.

Boxer, P., Huesmann, L., Bushman, B., O'Brien, M., & Moceri, D. (2009). The role of violent media preference in cumulative developmental risk for violence and general aggression. *Journal of Youth and Adolescence, 38*, 417-428.

Boyd-Wilson, B. M., McClure, J., & Walkey, E. H. (2004). Are well-being and illusory perceptions linked? The answer may be yes, but. . . . *Australian Journal of Psychology, 56*, 1-9.

Boylan, J. M., & Ryff, C. D. (2015). Psychological well-being and metabolic syndrome: Findings from the Midlife in the United States national sample. *Psychosomatic Medicine, 77*, 548-558.

Boyle, S. H., Williams, R. B., Mark, D. B., Brummett, B. H., Siegler, I. C., & Barefoot, J. C.

(2005). Hostility, age, and mortality in a sample of cardiac patients. *American Journal of Cardiology, 96*, 64-72.

Bradford, A. C., & Bradford, W. D. (2017). Factors driving the diffusion of medical marijuana legalisation in the United States. *Drugs: Education, Prevention & Policy, 24*, 75-84.

Brafman, A. H. (2011). *Fostering independence: Helping and caring in psychodynamic therapies.* London: Karnac Books.

Brambilla, P., Cipriani, A., Hotopf, M., & Barbui, C. (2005). Side-effect profile of fluoxetine in comparison with other SSRIs, tricyclic and newer antidepressants: A meta-analysis of clinical trial data. *Pharmacopsychiatry, 38*, 69-77.

Brandao, T., Tavares, R., Schulz, M. S., & Matos, P.M. (2015, October 19). Measuring emotion regulation and emotional expression in breast cancer patients: A systematic review. *Clinical Psychology Review, 43*, 114-127.

Brandon, M., & Saffran, J. R. (2011). Apparent motion enhances visual rhythm discrimination in infancy. *Attention, Perception, & Psychophysics, 73*, 1016-1020.

Brandtzaeg, P. B., Lüders, M., Skjetne, J. H. (2010). Too many Facebook "friends"? Content sharing and sociability versus the need for privacy in social network sites. *International Journal of Human-Computer Interaction, 26*, 1006-1030.

Brang, D., Rouw, R., Ramachandran, V. S., & Coulson, S. (2011). Similarly shaped letters evoke similar colors in grapheme–color synesthesia. *Neuropsychologia, 49*, 1355-1358.

Brasic, J. R. (2002). Conversion disorder in childhood. *German Journal of Psychiatry, 5*, 54-61.

Brausch, A. M., & Gutierrez, P. M. (2009). Differences in non-suicidal self-injury and suicide attempts in adolescents. *Journal of Youth and Adolescence, 21*, 46-51.

Brazelton, T. B. (1969). *Infants and mothers: Differences in development.* New York: Dell.

Breland, K., & Breland, M. (1966). *Animal behavior.* New York: Macmillan.

Brennan, P. (2011). Pheromones: Fact or fantasy? *Ethology, 117*, 265-266.

Brennen, T., Vikan, A., & Dybdahl, R. (2007). Are tip-of-the-tongue states universal? Evidence from the speakers of an unwritten language. *Memory, 15*, 167-176.

Breslin, C. W., & Safer, M. A. (2011). Effects of event valence on long-term memory for two baseball championship games. *Psychological Science, 20*, 1-5.

Brewer, M. B. (2007). The social psychology of intergroup relations: Social categorization, ingroup bias, and outgroup prejudice. In A. W. Kruglanski & E. Higgins (Eds.), *Social psychology: Handbook of basic principles* (2nd ed.). New York: Guilford Press.

Bright, P., Buckman, J., & Fradera, A. (2006). Retrograde amnesia in patients with hippocampal, medial temporal, temporal lobe, or frontal pathology. *Learning & Memory, 13*, 545-557.

Brody, J. (2008, May 20). Trying to break nicotine's grip. *The New York Times*, p. E9.

Brody, S., & Costa, R. M. (2017). Vaginal orgasm is associated with indices of women's better psychological, intimate relationship, and psychophysiological function. *Canadian Journal of Human Sexuality, 26*, 1-4.

Broeders, R., van den Bos, K., Müller, P. A., & Ham, J. (2011). Should I save or should I not kill? How people solve moral dilemmas depends on which rule is most accessible. *Journal of Experimental Social Psychology, 47*, 923-934.

Broidy, L. M., Nagin, D. S., & Tremblay, R. E. (2003). Developmental trajectories of childhood disruptive behaviors and adolescent delinquency: A six-site, cross-national study. *Developmental Psychology, 39*, 222-245.

Bronson, P., & Merryman, A. (2009). *NurtureShock*. New York: Twelve.

Broockman, D., & Kalla, J. (2016). Durably reducing transphobia: A field experiment on door-to-door canvassing. *Science, 352*, 220-224.

Brown, E. (2001, September 17). The World Health Organization takes on big tobacco (but don't hold your breath): Anti-smoking advocates are mounting a global campaign: It's going to be a long, hard fight. *Forbes*, pp. 37-41.

Brown, M. W., & Banks, P. J. (2015). In search of a recognition memory engram. *Neuroscience and Biobehavioral Reviews, 50*, 12-28.

Brown, M., Chodzen, G., Mihelicova, M., & Collins, K. (2017). Applying a time-patterned typology of homelessness among individuals with mental illness. *American Journal of Community Psychology, 59*, 306-315.

Brown, P. (1986). Simbu aggression and the drive to win. *Anthropolitical Quarterly, 59*, 165-170.

Brown, P. K., & Wald, G. (1964). Visual pigments in single rod and cones of the human retina. *Science, 144*, 45-52.

Brown, R. (1958). How shall a thing be called? *Psychological Review, 65*, 14-21.

Brown, R. D., Goldstein, E., & Bjorklund, D. F. (2000). The history and zeitgeist of the repressed-false-memory debate: Scientific and sociological perspectives on suggestibility and childhood memory. In D. F. Bjorklund (Ed.), *False-memory creation in children and adults: Theory, research, and implications*. Mahwah, NJ: Lawrence Erlbaum.

Brown, R. J. (2006). Different types of "dissociation" have different psychological mechanisms. *Journal of Trauma Dissociation, 6*, 7-28.

Brown, S., Martinez, M. J., & Parsons, L. M. (2006). Music and language side by side in the brain: A PET study of the generation of melodies and sentences. *European Journal of Neuroscience, 23*, 2791-2803.

Browne, J., Penn, D. L., Meyer-Kalos, P. S., Mueser, K. T., Estroff, S. E., Brunette, M. F., . . . Kane, J. M. (2017). Psychological well-being and mental health recovery in the NIMH RAISE early treatment program. *Schizophrenia Research, 185*, 167-172.

Brucker, B., Ehlis, A., Häußinger, F. B., Fallgatter, A. J., & Gerjets, P. (2015). Watching corresponding gestures facilitates learning with animations by activating human mirror-neurons: An fNIRS study. *Learning And Instruction, 36*, 27-37.

Bruehl, S., Burns, J. W., Gupta, R., Buvanendran, A., Chont, M., Orlowska, D., . . . France, C. R. (2017). Do resting plasma β-endorphin levels predict responses to opioid analgesics? *Clinical Journal of Pain, 33*, 12-20.

Bruggeman, H., Yonas, A., & Konczak, J. (2007). The processing of linear perspective and binocular information for action and perception. *Neuropsychologia, 45*, 1420-1426.

Bruni, F. (2017, September 24). Want geniuses? Welcome immigrants. *The New York Times*, p. SR3.

Bruno, D. (2016, November 23). An electric shock therapy stops self-harm among the autistic, but at what cost? *Washington Post Magazine*. Accessed from https://www.washingtonpost.com/lifestyle/magazine/an-electric-shock-therapy-stops-self-harm-among-the-autistic-but-at-what-cost/2016/11/21/b9b06c44-8f2c-11e6-9c85-ac42097b8cc0_story.html?utm term=.1b9a9a3266b4.

Bryant, R. M., Coker, A. D., Durodoye, B. A., McCollum, V. J., Pack-Brown, S. P., Constantine, M. G., . . . Bryant, B. J. (2005). Having our say: African American women, diversity, and counseling. *Journal of Counseling and Development, 83*, 313-319.

Bub, K. L., Buckhalt, J. A., & El-Sheikh, M. (2011). Children's sleep and cognitive performance: A cross-domain analysis of change over time. *Developmental Psychology, 47*(6), 1504–1514.

Buchanan, T., & Selmon, N. (2008). Race and gender differences in self-efficacy: Assessing the role of gender role attitudes and family background. *Sex Roles, 58*, 822-836.

Buchert, R., Thomasius, R., Wilke, F., Petersen, K., Nebeling, B., Obrocki, J., Schulze, O., Schmidt, U., & Clausen, M. (2004). A voxel-based PET investigation of the long-term effects of "ecstasy" consumption on brain serotonin transporters. *American Journal of Psychiatry, 161*, 1181-1189.

Buckner, J. D., & Shah, S. M. (2015). Fitting in and feeling fine: Conformity and coping motives differentially mediate the relationship between social anxiety and drinking problems for men and women. *Addiction Research & Theory, 23*, 231-237.

Buerkle, C. (2011). Masters of their domain: Seinfeld and the discipline of mediated men's sexual economy. In E. Watson & M. E. Shaw (Eds.), *Performing American masculinities: The 21st-century man in popular culture*. Bloomington, IN: Indiana University Press.

Bukobza, G. (2009). Relations between rebelliousness, risk-taking behavior, and identity status during emerging adulthood. *Identity, 9*, 159-177.

Bulf, H., Johnson, S. P., & Valenza, E. (2011). Visual statistical learning in the newborn infant. *Cognition, 121*, 127-132.

Bunce, J. A. (2015). Incorporating ecology and social system into formal hypotheses to guide field studies of color vision in primates. *American Journal of Primatology, 77*, 516-526.

Bunting, M. (2006). Proactive interference and item similarity in working memory. *Journal of Experimental Psychology: Learning, Memory, and Cognition, 32*, 183-196.

Buon, M., Habib, M., & Frey, D. (2017). Moral development: Conflicts and compromises. In J. A. Sommerville & J. Decety (Eds.), *Social cognition: Development across the life span*. New York: Routledge/Taylor & Francis Group.

Burbach, M. E., Matkin, G. S., & Fritz, S. M. (2004). Teaching critical thinking in an introductory leadership course utilizing active learning strategies: A confirmatory study. *College Student Journal, 38*, 482-493.

Burchinal, M. R., Roberts, J. E., & Riggins, R., Jr. (2000). Relating quality of center-based child care to early cognitive and language development longitudinally. *Child Development, 71*, 338-357.

Bureau, J., Martin, J., Yurkowski, K., Schmiedel, S., Quan, J., Moss, E., . . . Pallanca, D. (2017). Correlates of child-father and child-mother attachment in the preschool years. *Attachment & Human Development, 19*, 130-150.

Burger, J. M. (2009). Replicating Milgram: Would people still obey today? *American Psychologist, 64*, 1-11.

Burger, J. M., Reed, M., & DeCesare, K. (1999). The effects of initial request size on compliance: More about the that's-not-all technique. *Basic and Applied Social Psychology, 21*, 243-249.

Burgoon, J. K., Bonito, J. A., Ramirez, A. J. R., Dunbar, N. E., Kam, K., & Fischer, J. (2002). Testing the interactivity principle: Effects of mediation, propinquity, and verbal and nonverbal modalities in interpersonal interaction [Special Issue: Research on the relationship between verbal and nonverbal communication: Emerging integrations]. *Journal of Communication, 52*, 657-677.

Burns, G. W. (2017). *101 stories for enhancing happiness and well-being: Using metaphors in positive psychology and therapy*. New York: Routledge/Taylor & Francis Group.

Burns, N. R., Bryan, J., & Nettelbeck, T. (2006). Ginkgo biloba: No robust effect on cognitive abilities or mood in healthy young or older adults. *Human Psychopharmacology: Clinical and Experimental, 21*, 27-37.

Burri, A., Spector, T., & Qazi, R. (2015). Common genetic factors among sexual orientation, gender nonconformity, and number of sex partners in female twins: Implications for the evolution of homosexuality. *Journal of Sexual Medicine, 12*, 1004–1011.

Burton, L., Bensimon, E., Allimant, J., Kinsman, R., Levin, A., Kovacs, L., & . . . Bahrami, J. (2013). Relationship of prosody perception to personality and aggression. *Current Psychology: A Journal for Diverse Perspectives on Diverse Psychological Issues, 32*, 275-280.

Busch, A. J., Morey, L. C., & Hopwood, C. J. (2017). Exploring the assessment of the DSM-5 alternative model for personality disorders with the personality assessment inventory. *Journal of Personality Assessment, 99*, 211-218.

Bush, J. (2008). Viability of virtual reality exposure therapy as a treatment alternative. *Computers in Human Behavior, 24*, 1032-1040.

Bushman, B. J., Wang, M. C., & Anderson, C. (2005). Is the curve relating temperature to aggression linear or curvilinear? Assaults and temperature in Minneapolis reexamined. *Journal of Personality and Social Psychology, 89*, 62-66.

Buss, A. H. (2011). *Pathways to individuality: Evolution and development of personality traits.* Washington, DC: American Psychological Association.

Buss, D. (2009). How can evolutionary psychology successfully explain personality and individual differences? *Perspectives on Psychological Science, 4*, 359-366.

Buss, D. M. (2001). Human nature and culture: An evolutionary psychological perspective. *Journal of Personality, 69*, 955-978.

Buss, D. M., Abbott, M., & Angleitner, A. (1990). International preferences in selecting mates: A study of 37 cultures. *Journal of Cross-Cultural Psychology, 21*, 5-47.

Bustillo, J. R., Jones, T., Chen, H., Lemke, N., Abbott, C., Qualls, C., . . . Gasparovic, C. (2017). Glutamatergic and neuronal dysfunction in gray and white matter: A spectroscopic imaging study in a large schizophrenia sample. *Schizophrenia Bulletin, 43*, 611-619.

Butcher, J. N. (2011). *A beginner's guide to the MMPI-2* (3rd ed.). Washington, DC US: American Psychological Association.

Butler, L. T., & Berry, D. C. (2004). Understanding the relationship between repetition priming and mere exposure. *British Journal of Psychology, 95*, 467-487.

Buysse, D. J., Germain, A., Moul, D. E., Franzen, P. L., Brar, L. K., Fletcher, M. E., et al. (2011). Efficacy of brief behavioral treatment for chronic insomnia in older adults. *Archives of Internal Medicine, 171*, 887-895.

Bylund, E., & Athanasopoulos, P. (2017). The Whorfian time warp: Representing duration through the language hourglass. *Journal of Experimental Psychology: General, 146*, 911-916.

Byne, W. (1996). Biology and homosexuality: Implications of neuroendocrinological and neuroanatomical studies. In R. P. Cabaj & T. S. Stein (Eds.), *Textbook of homosexuality and mental health.* Washington, DC: American Psychiatric Press.

Cabioglu, M., Ergene, N., & Tan, Ü. (2007, May). Smoking cessation after acupuncture treatment. *International Journal of Neuroscience, 117*, 571-578.

Cachelin, F. M., & Regan, P. C. (2006). Prevalence and correlates of chronic dieting in a multiethnic U.S. community sample. *Eating and Weight Disorders, 11*, 91-99.

Cacioppo, J. T., & Decety, J. (2009). What are the brain mechanisms on which psychological processes are based? *Perspectives on Psychological Science, 4*, 10-18.

Cadenhead, K., & Braff, D. L. (1995). Neurophysiology of schizophrenia: Attention, information processing, and inhibitory processes in schizophrenia. In J. A. Den Boer, H. G. M. Westenberg, & H. M. van Praag (Eds.), *Advances in the neurobiology of schizophrenia.* Oxford, England: John Wiley & Sons.

Caelian, C. F. (2006). The role of perfectionism and stress in the suicidal behaviour of depressed adolescents. *Dissertation Abstracts International: Section B: The Sciences and Engineering, 66*(12-B), 6915.

Calvert, S. L., Appelbaum, M., Dodge, K. A., Graham, S., Nagayama Hall, G. C., Hamby, S., . . . Hedges, L. (2017). The American Psychological Association Task Force assessment of violent video games: Science in the service of public interest. *American Psychologist, 72*, 126-143.

Camerer, C., Babcock, L., Loewenstein, G., & Thaler, R. (1997). Labor supply of New York City cabdrivers: One day at a time. *Quarterly Journal of Economics, 112*(2), 407-441.

Cameron, C. D., Spring, V. L., & Todd, A. R. (2017). The empathy impulse: A multinomial model of intentional and unintentional empathy for pain. *Emotion, 17*, 395-411.

Cameron, O. G. (2002). *Visceral sensory neuroscience: Interoception.* London: Oxford University Press.

Campos, R. C. (2011). 'It might be what I am': Looking at the use of Rorschach in psychological assessment. *Journal of Projective Psychology & Mental Health, 18*, 28-38.

Cannon, W. B. (1929). Organization for physiological homeostatics. *Physiological Review, 9*, 280-289.

Cantarero, K., Gamian-Wilk, M., & Dolinski, D. (2017). Being inconsistent and compliant: The moderating role of the preference for consistency in the door-in-the-face technique. *Personality and Individual Differences, 115*, 54-57.

Cao, R., Nosofsky, R. M., & Shiffrin, R. M. (2017). The development of automaticity in short-term memory search: Item-response learning and category learning. *Journal of Experimental Psychology: Learning, Memory, and Cognition, 43*, 669-679.

Caplan, D., Waters, G., & Dede, G. (2007). A study of syntactic processing in aphasia I: Behavioral (psycholinguistic) aspects. *Brain and Language, 101*, 103-150.

Capraro, V., & Sippel, J. (2017). Gender differences in moral judgment and the evaluation of gender-specified moral agents. *Cognitive Processing, 18*(4), 399-405.

Carbon, C., & Ditye, T. (2011). Sustained effects of adaptation on the perception of familiar faces. *Journal of Experimental Psychology: Human Perception and Performance, 37*, 615-625.

Carciofo, R., Song, N., Du, F., Wang, M. M., & Zhang, K. (2017). Metacognitive beliefs mediate the relationship between mind wandering and negative affect. *Personality and Individual Differences, 107*, 78-87.

Card, N. A. (2017). Developmental methodology: I. Developmental methodology as a central subdiscipline of developmental science. *Monographs of the Society for Research in Child Development, 82*, 7-12.

Card, N. A. (2017). Developmental methodology: VII. Replication, research accumulation, and meta-analysis in developmental science. *Monographs of the Society for Research in Child Development, 82*, 105-121.

Carels, R. A., Young, K. M., Koball, A., Gumble, A., Darby, L. A., Oehlhof, M., & . . . Hinman, N. (2011). Transforming your life: An environmental modification approach to weight loss. *Journal of Health Psychology, 16*, 430-438.

Carey, B. (2015, October 20). New approach may alleviate schizophrenia. *The New York Times*, p. A1.

Carey, B. (2016, April 14). Quadriplegic gets use of hand from chip placed in his brain. *The New York Times*, A1.

Carey, B. (2016, May 30). After thriving in combat tours, veterans are struggling at home. *The New York Times*, pp. A1, A3.

Carhart-Harris, R. (2007). Speed > Ecstasy > Ritalin: The science of amphetamines. *Journal of Psychopharmacology, 21*, 225.

Carleton, R. N., Duranceau, S., Freeston, M. H., Boelen, P. A., McCabe, R. E., & Antony, M. M. (2014). 'But it might be a heart attack': Intolerance of uncertainty and panic disorder symptoms. *Journal Of Anxiety Disorders, 28*, 463-470.

Carlstedt, R. A. (2017). Sports performance. In G. R. Elkins, G. R. Elkins (Eds.), *Handbook of medical and psychological hypnosis: Foundations, applications, and professional issues.* New York: Springer Publishing Co.

Carnagey, N., Anderson, C. A., & Bushman, B. J. (2007). The effect of video game violence on physiological desensitization to real-life violence. *Journal of Experimental Social Psychology, 43*, 489-496.

Carnagey, N., Anderson, C., & Bartholow, B. (2007). Media violence and social neuroscience: New questions and new opportunities. *Current Directions in Psychological Science, 16*, 178-182.

Carnevale, M., Luna, D., & Lerman, D. (2017). Brand linguistics: A theory-driven framework for the study of language in branding. *International Journal of Research in Marketing, 34*(2), 572-591.

Carpenter, S. (2002). What can resolve the paradox of mental health disparities? *APA Monitor, 33*, 18.

Carrillo, M., Ricci, L., Coppersmith, G., & Melloni, R. (2009, August). The effect of increased serotonergic neurotransmission on aggression: A critical meta-analytical review of preclinical studies. *Psychopharmacology, 205*, 349-368.

Carroll, D. W. (2017). The ethics of memory research. *PsycCRITIQUES, 62*, 15-22.

Carter, R. T. (2003). Becoming racially and culturally competent: The racial-cultural counseling laboratory. *Journal of Multicultural Counseling and Development, 31*, 20-30.

Cartwright, R. (2006). A neuroscientist looks at how the brain makes up our minds. *PsycCRITIQUES, 51*, 35-41.

Cartwright, R., Agargum, M. Y., & Kirkby, J. (2006). Relation of dreams to waking concerns. *Psychiatry Research, 141*, 261-270.

Caruso, E. (2008). Use of experienced retrieval ease in self and social judgments. *Journal of Experimental Social Psychology, 44*, 148-155.

Carvalho, J., & Nobre, P. (2011). Biopsychosocial determinants of men's sexual desire: Testing an integrative model. *Journal of Sexual Medicine, 8*, 754-763.

Carver, C., & Scheier, M. (2002). Coping processes and adjustment to chronic illness. In A. Christensen & M. Antoni (Eds.), *Chronic physical disorders: Behavioral medicine's perspective*. Malden, MA: Blackwell Publishers.

Casasola, M. (2011). Infant spatial categorization from an information processing approach. In L. M. Oakes, C. H. Cashon, M. Casasola, & D. H. Rakison (Eds.), *Infant perception and cognition: Recent advances, emerging theories, and future directions*. New York: Oxford University Press.

Case, R., & Okamoto, Y. (1996). The role of central conceptual structures in the development of children's thought. *Monographs of the Society for Research in Child Development, 61*, v-265.

Cassells, J. V. S. (2007). The virtuous roles of truth and justice in integral dialogue: Research, theory, and model practice of the evolution of collective consciousness. *Dissertation Abstracts International Section A: Humanities and Social Sciences, 67*(10-A), 4005.

Cattell, R. B., Cattell, A. K., & Cattell, H. E. P. (2000). *The sixteen personality factor™ (16PF ®) questionnaire*. Champaign, IL: Institute for Personality and Ability Testing.

Cauce, A. M. (2007). Bringing community psychology home: The leadership, community and values initiative. *American Journal of Community Psychology, 39*, 1-11.

Cavallini, E., Pagnin, A., & Vecchi, T. (2003). Aging and everyday memory: The beneficial effect of memory training. *Archives of Gerontology & Geriatrics, 37*, 241-257.

Celi, L.A.G., Fraser, H.S.F., Nikore, V., Osorio, J.S., & Paik, K. (2017). *Global health informatics: Principles of eHealth and mHealth to improve quality of care*. Cambridge, MA: MIT Press.

Center for Collegiate Mental Health. (2017, January). *2016 Annual Report* (Publication No. STA 17-74).

Centers for Disease Control and Prevention. (2013). Adult cigarette smoking in the United States: Current estimate. Retrieved from http://www.cdc.gov/tobacco/data statistics/fact sheets/adult data/cig smoking.

Centers for Disease Control and Prevention. (2000). *Suicide prevention fact sheet*. Atlanta: National Center for Injury Prevention and Control.

Centers for Disease Control and Prevention (CDC). (2004). Suicide and attempted suicide. *Mobidity and Mortality Weekly Report, 53*, 471.

Centers for Disease Control and Prevention. (2015, April 16). E-cigarette use triples among middle and high school students in just one year. Press release, retrieved November 23, 2015, from http://www.cdc.gov/media/releases/2015/p0416-e-cigarette-use.html.

Centers for Disease Control and Prevention Vitalsigns. (2010). *Binge Drinking*. Atlanta, GA: Centers for Disease Control.

Chamberlain, K., & Zika, S. (1990). The minor events approach to stress: Support for the use of daily hassles. *British Journal of Psychology, 81*, 469-481.

Chamberlain, S. R., Menzies, L., Hampshire, A., Suckling, J., Fineberg, N. A., del Campo, N., et al. (2008, July 18). Orbitofrontal dysfunction in patients with obsessive-compulsive disorder and their unaffected relatives. *Science, 321*, 421-422.

Chambless, D. L., Crits-Christoph, P., Wampold, B. E., Norcross, J. C., Lambert, M. J., Bohart, A. C., et al. (2006). What should be validated? In J. C. Norcross, L. E. Beutler, & R. E Levant (Eds.). *Evidence-based practices in mental health: Debate and dialogue on the fundamental questions*. Washington, DC: American Psychological Association.

Chandler, D. R. (2011). Proactively addressing the shortage of Blacks in psychology: Highlighting the school psychology subfield. *Journal of Black Psychology, 37*, 99-127.

Chandran, S., & Menon, G. (2004). When a day means more than a year: Effects of temporal framing on judgments of health risk. *Journal of Consumer Research, 31*, 375-389.

Chao, M. M., Takeuchi, R., & Farh, J. (2017). Enhancing cultural intelligence: The roles of implicit culture beliefs and adjustment. *Personnel Psychology, 70*, 257-292.

Chao, R. (2011). Managing stress and maintaining well-being: Social support, problem-focused coping, and avoidant coping. *Journal of Counseling & Development, 89*, 338-348.

Chapman, J. (2006). Anxiety and defective decision making: An elaboration of the group-think model. *Management Decision, 44*, 1391-1404.

Chapman, L. J., & Chapman, J. P. (1973). *Disordered thought in schizophrenia*. New York: Appleton-Century-Crofts.

Chapman, S. C., & Wu, L. (2015). Epidemiology and demography of illicit drug use and drug use disorders among adults aged 50 and older. In I. Crome, L. Wu, R. Rao, & P. Crome, (Eds.), *Substance use and older people*. New York: Wiley-Blackwell.

Chavez, P. R., Nelson, D. E., Naimi, T. S., & Brewer, R. D. (2011). Impact of a new gender-specific definition for binge drinking on prevalence estimates for women. *American Journal of Preventive Medicine, 40*, 468-471.

Chen, C., & Zhang, L. (2011). Temperament, personality and achievement goals among Chinese adolescent students. *Educational Psychology, 31*, 339-359.

Chen, T., Yue, G. H., Tian, Y., & Jiang, C. (2017). Baduanjin mind-body intervention improves the executive control function. *Frontiers in Psychology, 7*, 72-81.

Chen, Z., Fu, L., Peng, Y., Cai, R., & Zhou, S. (2011). The relationship among childhood abuse, parenting styles, and antisocial personality disorder tendency. *Chinese Journal of Clinical Psychology, 19*, 212-214.

Cheng, C., & Cheung, M. L. (2005). Cognitive processes underlying coping flexibility: Differentiation and integration. *Journal of Personality, 73*, 859-886.

Cheng, S., & Kwan, K. (2008). Attachment dimensions and contingencies of self-worth: The moderating role of culture. *Personality and Individual Differences, 45*, 509-514.

Cheng, Y., Diao, Q., & Behrens, J. T. (2017). A simplified version of the maximum information per time unit method in computerized adaptive testing. *Behavior Research Methods, 49*, 502-512.

Chin, J. (2013). Eastern and Western learning styles: The paradox of Asian learners. *PsycCRITIQUES, 58*, 102-111.

Chin, T. (2015). Harmony and organizational citizenship behavior in Chinese organizations. *The International Journal of Human Resource Management, 26*, 1110-1129.

Chiu, Y., Lo, S., & Hsieh, A. (2017). How colour similarity can make banner advertising effective: Insights from Gestalt theory. *Behaviour & Information Technology, 36*, 606-619.

Cho, S., Holyoak, K. J., & Cannon, T. D. (2007). Analogical reasoning in working memory: Resources shared among relational integration, interference resolution, and maintenance. *Memory & Cognition, 35*, 1445-1455.

Chodakiewitz, Y., Williams, J., Chodakiewitz, J., & Cosgrove, G. R. (2015). Ablative surgery for neuropsychiatric disorders: Past, present, future. In B. Sun & A. De Salles (Eds.), *Neurosurgical treatments for psychiatric disorders*. New York: Springer Science + Business Media.

Choi, H., Kensinger, E. A., & Rajaram, S. (2013). Emotional content enhances true but not false memory for categorized stimuli. *Memory & Cognition, 41*, 403-415.

Choi, H., Kensinger, E. A., & Rajaram, S. (2017). Mnemonic transmission, social contagion, and emergence of collective memory: Influence of emotional valence, group structure, and information distribution. *Journal of Experimental Psychology: General, 146*, 1247-1265.

Choma, B. L., Jagayat, A., Hodson, G., & Turner, R. (2018). Prejudice in the wake of terrorism: The role of temporal distance, ideology, and intergroup emotions. *Personality and Individual Differences, 123*, 65-75.

Chomsky, N. (1978). On the biological basis of language capacities. In G. A. Miller & E. Lennenberg (Eds.), *Psychology and biology of language and thought*. New York: Academic Press.

Chomsky, N. (1991). Linguistics and cognitive science: Problems and mysteries. In A. Kasher (Ed.), *The Chomskyan turn*. Cambridge, MA: Blackwell.

Chou, K. (2005). Everyday competence and depressive symptoms: Social support and sense of control as mediators or moderators? *Aging and Mental Health, 9*, 177-183.

Choubsaz, Y., & Gheitury, A. (2017). Is semantics affected by missing a critical period? Evidence from the Persian deaf. *Journal of Psycholinguistic Research, 46*, 77-88.

Choy, Y., Fyer, A. J., & Lipsitz, J. D. (2007). Treatment of specific phobia in adults. *Clinical Psychology Review, 27*, 266-286.

Christ, S. E., Steiner, R. D., & Grange, D. K. (2006). Inhibitory control in children with phenylketonuria. *Developmental Neuropsychology, 30*, 845-864.

Christakis, N. A., & Fowler, J. H. (2008). The collective dynamics of smoking in a large social network. *The New England Journal of Medicine, 358*, 2249-2258.

Christensen, K. A., Aldao, A., Sheridan, M. A., & McLaughlin, K. A. (2017). Habitual reappraisal in context: Peer victimisation moderates its association with physiological reactivity to social stress. *Cognition and Emotion, 31*, 384-394.

Christian, C. J., Lencz, T., Robinson, D. G., Burdick, K. E., Ashtari, M., Malhotra, A. K., et al. (2008). Gray matter structural alterations in obsessive-compulsive disorder: Relationship to neuropsychological functions. *Neuroimaging, 164*, 123-131.

Christoffels, I. K., de Haan, A. M., Steenbergen, L., van den Wildenberg, W. M., & Colzato, L. S. (2015). Two is better than one: Bilingual education promotes the flexible mind. *Psychological Research, 79*, 371-379.

Cialdini, R. B. (2006). *Influence: The psychology of persuasion*. New York: Collins.

Cialdini, R. B., & Sagarin, B. J. (2005). Principles of interpersonal influence. In T. C. Brock & M. C. Green (Eds.), *Persuasion: Psychological insights and perspectives* (2nd ed.). Thousand Oaks, CA: Sage Publications.

Cialdini, R. B., Schaller, M., Houlihan, D., Arps, K., Fultz, J., & Beaman, A. L. (1975). Reciprocal concessions procedure for inducing compliance: The door-in-the-face technique. *Journal of Personality and Social Psychology, 31*, 206-215.

Cisler, J. M., James, G. A., Tripathi, S., Mletzko, T., Heim, C., Hu, X. P., Mayberg, H. S., Nemeroff, C. B., & Kilts, C. D. (2013). Differential functional connectivity within an emotion regulation neural network among individuals resilient and susceptible to the depressogenic effects of early life stress. *Psychological Medicine, 43*, 507-518.

Clark, D. A. (2007). Obsessions and compulsions. In N. Kazantzis & L. L'Abate (Eds.), *Handbook of homework assignments in psychotherapy: Research, practice, prevention*. New York: Springer Science + Business Media.

Clarkin, J. F., & Lenzenweger, M. F. (Eds.). (2004). *Major theories of personality disorders* (2nd ed.). New York: Guilford.

Clay, R.A. (2017, July/August). Women outnumber men in psychology, but not in the field's top echelons. *Monitor on Psychology*, pp. 18-19.

Clements, A. M., Rimrodt, S. L., & Abel, J. R. (2006). Sex differences in cerebral laterality of language and visuospatial processing. *Brain, 8*, 150-158.

Clemons, T. L. (2006). Underachieving gifted students: A social cognitive model. *Dissertation Abstracts International Section A: Humanities and Social Sciences, 66*(9-A), 3208.

Coan, J. A., Schaefer, H. S., & Davidson, R. J. (2006). Lending a hand: Social regulation of the neural response to threat. *Psychological Science, 17*(12), 1032-1039.

Cobos, P., Sanchez, M., Garcia, C., Vera, M. N., & Vila, J. (2002). Revisiting the James versus Cannon debate on emotion: Startle and autonomic modulation in patients with spinal cord injuries. *Biological Psychology, 61*, 251-269.

Coderre, T. J. (2011). Complex regional pain syndrome: What's in a name? *The Journal of Pain, 12*, 2-12.

Coffman, S. J., Martell, C. R., Dimidjian, S., Gallop, R., & Holon, S. D. (2007). Extreme non-response in cognitive therapy: Can behavioral activation succeed where cognitive therapy fails? *Journal of Consulting Clinical Psychology, 75*, 531-545.

Cohen, B. H. (2002). *Explaining psychological statistics* (2nd ed.). New York: Wiley.

Cohen, G. L., Garcia, J., Apfel, N., & Master, A. (2006). Reducing the racial achievement gap: A social-psychological intervention. *Science, 313*, 1307-1310.

Cohen, P., Slomkowski, C., & Robins, L. N. (Eds.). (1999). *Historical and geographical influences on psychopathology*. Mahwah, NJ: Erlbaum.

Cohn, D., & Caumont, A. (2016, March 31). 10 demographic trends that are shaping the U.S. and the world. *FactTank: News in the Numbers*. Retrieved from http://www.pewresearch.org/fact-tank/2016/03/31/10-demographic-trends-that-are-shaping-the-u-s-and-the-world/.

Cole, S. W., Arevalo, J. M., Takahashi, R., Sloan, E. K., Lutgendorf, S. L., Sood, A. K., Sheridan, J. F., & Seeman, T. E. (2010). Computational identification of Gene-Social Environment interaction at the human IL6 locus. *Proceedings of the National Academy of Sciences of the USA, 107*, 5681-5686.

Coleman, E. (2002). Masturbation as a means of achieving sexual health. *Journal of Psychology and Human Sexuality, 14*, 5-16.

Colland, V. T., Van Essen-Zandvliet, L. E. M., Lans, C., Denteneer, A., Westers, P., & Brackel, H. J. L. (2004). Poor adherence to self-medication instructions in children with asthma and their parents. *Patient Education and Counseling, 55*, 416-421.

Coltheart, M., Langdon, R., & McKay, R. (2007). Schizophrenia and monothematic delusions. *Schizophrenia Bulletin, 33*, 642-647.

Columbia Neurosurgery. (2017, April). Pioneering surgical treatment for depression. Columbia Doctors: Neurological Surgery. Retrieved from http://www.columbianeurosurgery.org/2017/04/pioneering-depression-surgical-treatment/.

Colwell, M. J., & Lindsey, E. W. (2005). Preschool children's pretend and physical play and sex of play partner: Connections to peer competence. *Sex Roles, 52*, 497-509.

Commons, M. L., Adhikari, D., Giri, S., Weinberg, M., Baran, J. J., & Malik, E. (2017). Measuring developmental outcomes in autism spectrum disorder (ASD). *Behavioral Development Bulletin, 22*(1), 197-208.

Compagni, A., & Manderscheid, R. W. (2006). A neuroscientist-consumer alliance to transform mental health care. *Journal of Behavioral Health Services & Research, 33*, 265-274.

Connolly, A. C. (2007). Concepts and their features: Can cognitive science make good on the promises of concept empiricism? *Dissertation Abstracts International: Section B: The Sciences and Engineering, 67*(7-B), 4125.

Conoley, C. W., Plumb, E. W., Hawley, K. J., Spaventa-Vancil, K. Z., & Hernández, R. J. (2015). Integrating positive psychology into family therapy: Positive family therapy. *The Counseling Psychologist, 43*, 703-733.

Conway, M. A. (Ed.). (2002). *Levels of processing 30 years on special issue of memory*. Hove, UK: Psychology Press.

Cook, L. (2015, August 19). The heroin epidemic in 9 graphs. *US News & World Report*. http://www.usnews.com/news/blogs/data-mine/2015/08/19/the-heroin-epidemic-in-9-graphs.

Cook, M. (2013). *Levels of personality* (3rd ed.). New York: Cambridge University Press.

Cook-Cottone, C., & Smith, A. (2013). Eating disorders. In C. A. Noggle & R. S. Dean (Eds.), *The neuropsychology of psychopathology*. New York: Springer Publishing Co.

Coolidge, F. L., Segal, D. L., Estey, A. J., & Neuzil, P. J. (2011). Preliminary psychometric properties of a measure of Karen Horney's Tridimensional Theory in children and adolescents. *Journal of Clinical Psychology, 67*, 383-390.

Cooper, J. (2007). *Cognitive dissonance: Fifty years of a classic theory*. Thousand Oaks, CA: Sage Publications.

Cooper, M., & McLeod, J. (2011). Person-centered therapy: A pluralistic perspective. *Person-Centered and Experiential Psychotherapies, 10*, 210-223.

Cooper, Z., & Shafran, R. (2008). Cognitive behaviour therapy for eating disorders. *Behavioural and Cognitive Psychotherapy, 36*, 713-722.

Coplan, R., Reichel, M., & Rowan, K. (2009). Exploring the associations between maternal personality, child temperament, and parenting: A focus on emotions. *Personality and Individual Differences, 46*, 241-246.

Cordnoldi, C., De Beni, R., & Helstrup, T. (2007). Memory sensitivity in auto-biographical memory. In S. Magnussen & T. Helstrup (Eds.), *Everyday memory*. New York: Psychology Press.

Coren, S. (2004). Sensation and perception. In I. B. Weiner (Ed.), *Handbook of Psychology* (Vol. 1). Hoboken, NJ: John Wiley & Sons.

Cornelis, M. C., Tordoff, M. G., El-Sohemy, A., & van Dam, R. M. (2017). Recalled taste intensity, liking and habitual intake of commonly consumed foods. *Appetite, 109*, 182-189.

Cornell, C. B. (2006). A graduated scale for determining mental age. *Dissertation Abstracts International: Section B: The Sciences and Engineering, 66*(9-B), 5121.

Cornier, M. (2011). Is your brain to blame for weight regain? *Physiology & Behavior, 104*, 608-612.

Corsello, A. (2005). The wronged man. In *The best American magazine writing, 2005*. New York: Columbia University Press.

Cosmides, L., & Tooby, J. (2004). Social exchange: The evolutionary design of a neurocognitive system. In M. S. Gazzaniga (Ed.), *Cognitive neurosciences* (3rd ed.). Cambridge, MA: MIT.

Costa, P. T., Jr., & Widiger, T. A. (Eds.). (2002). *Personality disorders and the Five-Factor Model of personality* (2nd ed.). Washington, DC: American Psychological Association.

Costa, R., & Figueiredo, B. (2011). Infant's psychophysiological profile and temperament at 3 and 12 months. *Infant Behavior & Development, 34*, 270-279.

Cottencin, O., Rolland, B., & Karila, L. (2013). New designer drugs (synthetic cannabinoids and synthetic cathinones): review of literature. *Current Pharmaceutical Design*. Retrieved from http://www.ncbi.nlm.nih.gov/pubmed/24001292.

Coulson, D., & Harvey, M. (2013). Scaffolding student reflection for experience-based learning: A framework. *Teaching in Higher Education, 18*, 401-413.

Coultas, J. C., & van Leeuwen, E. C. (2015). Conformity: Definitions, types, and evolutionary grounding. In V. Zeigler-Hill, L. M. Welling, & T. K. Shackelford (Eds.), *Evolutionary perspectives on social psychology*. Cham, Switzerland: Springer International Publishing.

Couturier, J., & Lock, J. (2006). Eating-disorders: Anorexia nervosa, bulimia nervosa, and binge eating disorder. In T. G. Plante (Ed.), *Mental disorders of the new millennium: Biology and function* (Vol. 3). Westport, CT: Praeger Publishers/Greenwood Publishing.

Coventry, K. R., Venn, S. F., Smith, G. D., & Morley, A. M. (2003). Spatial problem solving and functional relations. *European Journal of Cognitive Psychology, 15*, 71-99.

Cowan, N. (2001). The magical number 4 in short-term memory: A reconsideration of mental storage capacity. *Behavioral and Brain Sciences, 24*, 97-185.

Cox, J. (2003, May 6). How far would you go to save your life? *Denver Post*, p. F1.

Cox, J. W., Rich, S., Chiu, A., Muyskens, J., & Ulmanu, M. (2018). Database: The number of children impacted by school shootings. *Washington Post*. Retrieved from https://www.washingtonpost.com/graphics/2018/local/school-shootings-database/.

Cox, R., Baker, S. E., Macdonald, D. W., & Berdoy, M. (2004). Protecting egg prey from carrion crows: The potential of aversive conditioning. *Applied Animal Behaviour Science, 87*, 325-342.

Coyle, N. (2006). The hard work of living in the face of death. *Journal of Pain and Symptom Management, 32*, 266-274.

Coyle, T. R. (2006). Test-retest changes on scholastic aptitude tests are not related to g. *Intelligence, 34*, 15-27.

Craig, P. L. (2017). Clinical neuropsychologists. In R. J. Sternberg (Ed.), *Career paths in psychology: Where your degree can take you.*

Washington, DC: American Psychological Association.

Craighero, L., Leo, I., Umilta, C., & Simion, F. (2011). Newborns' preference for goal-directed actions. *Cognition, 120*, 26-32.

Craik, F., & Lockhart, R. (2008). Levels of processing and Zinchenko's approach to memory research. *Journal of Russian & East European Psychology, 46*, 52-60.

Crano, W. D., Brewer, M. B., & Lac, A. (2015). *Principles and methods of social research* (3rd ed.). New York: Routledge/Taylor & Francis Group.

Cranston, C. C., Miller, K. E., Davis, J. L., & Rhudy, J. L. (2017). Preliminary validation of a brief measure of the frequency and severity of nightmares: The Trauma-Related Nightmare Survey. *Journal of Trauma & Dissociation, 18*, 88-99.

Creasey, G. L. (2005). *Research methods in lifespan development* (6th ed.). Boston: Allyn & Bacon.

Creel, S. C., & Bregman, M. R. (2011). How talker identity relates to language processing. *Language and Linguistics Compass, 5*, 190-204.

Crespo, R. F., & Mesurado, B. (2015). Happiness economics, eudaimonia and positive psychology: From happiness economics to flourishing economics. *Journal of Happiness Studies, 16*(4), 931-946.

Criswell, H., Ming, Z., Kelm, M., & Breese, G. (2008, August). Brain regional differences in the effect of ethanol on GABA release from presynaptic terminals. *Journal of Pharmacology and Experimental Therapeutics, 326*, 596-603.

Crockford, C., Wittig, R. M., & Zuberbühler, K. (2015). An intentional vocalization draws others' attention: A playback experiment with wild chimpanzees. *Animal Cognition, 18*, 581-591.

Croom, A. M. (2015). Aristotelian moral psychology and the situationist challenge. *Polish Psychological Bulletin, 46*, 262-277.

Crosnoe, R., & Elder, G. H., Jr. (2002). Successful adaptation in the later years: A life course approach to aging. *Social Psychology Quarterly, 65*, 309-328.

Crowne, K. (2013). Cultural exposure, emotional intelligence, and cultural intelligence: An exploratory study. *International Journal of Cross-Cultural Management, 13*(1), 5-22.

Crum, A. J., & Langer, E. J. (2007). Mind-set matters: Exercise and the placebo effect. *Psychological Science, 18*, 165-171.

Cuijpers, P., van Straten, A., Andersson, G., & van Oppen, P. (2008). Psychotherapy for depression in adults: A meta-analysis of comparative outcome studies. *Journal of Consulting and Clinical Psychology, 76*, 909-922.

Culhane-Pera, K. A., Borkan, J. M., & Patten, S. (2007). Culture and ethnicity. In O. J. Z. Sahler & J. E. Carr (Eds.), *The behavioral sciences and health care* (2nd rev. and updated ed.). Ashland, OH: Hogrefe & Huber Publishers.

Cullinane, C. A., Chu, D. Z. J., & Mamelak, A. N. (2002). Current surgical options in the control of cancer pain. *Cancer Practice, 10*, s21-s26.

Cummings, A., Ceponiene, R., & Koyama, A. (2006). Auditory semantic networks for words and natural sounds. *Brain Research, 1115*, 92-107.

Cunningham, P. (2006). Early years teachers and the influence of Piaget: Evidence from oral history. *Early Years: An International Journal of Research and Development, 26*, 5-16.

Curthoys, I. S. (2017). The new vestibular stimuli: Sound and vibration–anatomical, physiological and clinical evidence. *Experimental Brain Research, 235*, 957-972.

Cwikel, J., Behar, L., & Rabson-Hare, J. (2000). A comparison of a vote count and a meta-analysis review of intervention research with adult cancer patients. *Research on Social Work Practice, 10*, 139-158.

Cynkar, A. (2007). The changing gender composition of psychology. *Monitor on Psychology, 38*, 46-48.

Daftary, F., & Meri, J. W. (2002). *Culture and memory in medieval Islam*. London: I. B. Tauris.

Dai, D. Y., & Wang, X. (2007). The role of need for cognition and reader beliefs in text comprehension and interest development. *Contemporary Educational Psychology, 32*, 332-347.

Dakin, E. K., & Areán, P. (2013). Patient perspectives on the benefits of psychotherapy for late-life depression. *The American Journal of Geriatric Psychiatry, 21*, 155-163.

Dalal, A. K., & Misra, G. (2006). Psychology of health and well-being: Some emerging perspectives [Special issue: Psychology of health and well-being]. *Psychological Studies, 51*, 91-104.

Damaske, S. (2011). A "major career woman"? How women develop early expectations about work. *Gender & Society, 25*, 409-430.

Dani, J. A., & Montague, P. (2007). Disrupting addiction through the loss of drug-associated internal states. *Nature Neuroscience, 10*, 403-404.

Daniels, C. W., & Sanabria, F. (2017). Interval timing under a behavioral microscope: Dissociating motivational and timing processes in fixed-interval performance. *Learning & Behavior, 45*, 29-48.

Danner, D., Hagemann, D., Schankin, A., Hager, M., & Funke, J. (2011). Beyond IQ: A latent state-trait analysis of general intelligence, dynamic decision making, and implicit learning. *Intelligence, 39*, 323-334.

Dare, J. S. (2011). Transitions in midlife women's lives: Contemporary experiences. *Health Care for Women International, 32*, 111-133.

Das, A. (2007). Masturbation in the United States. *Journal of Sex & Marital Therapy, 33*, 301-317.

Das, A., Parish, W., & Laumann, E. (2009). Masturbation in urban China. *Archives of Sexual Behavior, 38*, 108-120.

Das, J. P. (2015). Search for intelligence by PASSing g. *Canadian Psychology/Psychologie Canadienne, 56*, 39-45.

Dasborough, M., & Harvey, P. (2017). Schadenfreude: The (not so) secret joy of another's misfortune. *Journal of Business Ethics, 141*, 693-707.

Datar, A. (2017). The more the heavier? Family size and childhood obesity in the U.S. *Social Science & Medicine, 180*, 143-151.

Davern, M. (2013). Nonresponse rates are a problematic indicator of nonresponse bias in survey research. *Health Services Research, 48,* 905-912.

David, E. R., & Derthick, A. O. (2018). *The psychology of oppression.* New York: Springer Publishing Co.

Davies, S., Jackson, P., Lewis, G., Hood, S., Nutt, D., & Potokar, J. (2008). Is the association of hypertension and panic disorder explained by clustering of autonomic panic symptoms in hypertensive patients? *Journal of Affective Disorders, 111,* 344-350.

Davis, J., Senghas, A., & Ochsner, K. (2009). How does facial feedback modulate emotional experience? *Journal of Research in Personality, 43,* 822-829.

Davis, K., Christodoulou, J., Seider, S., & Gardner, H. (2011). The theory of multiple intelligences. In R. J. Sternberg & S. Kaufman (Eds.), *The Cambridge handbook of intelligence.* New York: Cambridge University Press.

Davis, L. J. (2009, June 15). Sotomayor and the New Haven firefighters case: More myths than facts. *The Washington Times,* p. A04.

Davis, O., Haworth, C., & Plomin, R. (2009). Learning abilities and disabilities: Generalist genes in early adolescence. *Cognitive Neuropsychiatry, 14,* 312-331.

Davis, S. R. (2007). The nose knows best. *PsycCRITIQUES, 52,* 22-31.

Day, A. L., & Livingstone, H. A. (2003). Gender differences in perceptions of stressors and utilization of social support among university students. *Canadian Journal of Behavioural Science, 35,* 73-83.

Day, R. D., & Lamb, M. E. (2004). *Conceptualizing and measuring father involvement.* Mahwah, NJ: Lawrence Erlbaum Associates.

de Abreu, C. N., & Filho, R. C. (2017). Anorexia nervosa and bulimia nervosa–A psychotherapeutic cognitive-constructivist approach. *International Review of Psychiatry, 29,* 248-253.

De Beni, R., Pazzaglia, F., & Gardini, S. (2007). The generation and maintenance of visual mental images: Evidence from image type and aging. *Brain and Cognition, 63,* 271-278.

De Brigard, F., Brady, T. F., Ruzic, L., & Schacter, D. L. (2017). Tracking the emergence of memories: A category-learning paradigm to explore schema-driven recognition. *Memory & Cognition, 45,* 105-120.

De Dreu, C. W., Greer, L. L., Van Kleef, G. A., Shalvi, S., & Handgraaf, M. J. (2011). Oxytocin promotes human ethnocentrism. *PNAS Proceedings of the National Academy of Sciences of the United States of America, 108,* 1262-1266.

de Gusmao, C. M., Pollak, L. E., & Sharma, N. (2017). Neuropsychological and psychiatric outcome of GPi-deep brain stimulation in dystonia. *Brain Stimulation, 10,* 994-996.

de Visser, E. J., Monfort, S. S., Goodyear, K., Lu, L., O'Hara, M., Lee, M. R., . . . Krueger, F. (2017). A little anthropomorphism goes a long way: Effects of oxytocin on trust, compliance, and team performance with automated agents. *Human Factors, 59,* 116-133.

de Vivo, L., Bellesi, M., Marshall, W., Bushong, E. A., Ellisman, M. H., Tononi, G., & Cirelli, C. (2017). Ultrastructural evidence for synaptic scaling across the wake/sleep cycle. *Science, 355,* 507-510.

de Voogd, L. D., Klumpers, F., Fernández, G., & Hermans, E. J. (2017). Intrinsic functional connectivity between amygdala and hippocampus during rest predicts enhanced memory under stress. *Psychoneuroendocrinology, 75,* 192-202.

de Waal, F. B. M. (2014). Hard-wired for good? *Science, 347,* 379.

Deacon, B. J., & Spielmans, G. I. (2017). Is the efficacy of "antidepressant" medications overrated?. In S. O. Lilienfeld & I. D. Waldman (Eds.), *Psychological science under scrutiny: Recent challenges and proposed solutions.* Hoboken, NJ: Wiley-Blackwell.

DeAngelis, D., & Monahan, J. (2008). Professional credentials and professional regulations: Social work professional development. In B. W. White, K. M. Sowers, & C. N. Dulmus (Eds.), *Comprehensive handbook of social work and social welfare, Vol. 1: The profession of social work.* Hoboken, NJ: John Wiley & Sons.

DeAngelis, T. (2016). Behavioral therapy works best for insomnia. *Monitor on Psychology, 47,* 18-19.

DeAngelis, T. (2016, September). Preventing medical errors. *Monitor on Psychology,* pp. 48-52.

Dearing, E., McCartney, K., & Taylor, B. (2009). Does higher quality early child care promote low-income children's math and reading achievement in middle childhood? *Child Development, 80,* 1329-1349.

Deater-Deckard, K., Ivy, L., & Smith, J. (2005). Resilience in gene-environment transactions. In S. Goldstein & R. B. Brooks (Eds.), *Handbook of resilience in children.* New York: Kluwer Academic/Plenum Publishers.

DeBlaere, C., Watson, L. B., & Langrehr, K. J. (2018). Intersectionality applied: Intersectionality is as intersectionality does. In C. B. Travis & J. W. White (Eds.), *APA handbook of the psychology of women: Volume 1: History, theory, and battlegrounds* (pp. 567-584). Washington, DC: American Psychological Association.

deGroot, A. (1978). *Thought and choice in chess.* Paris: Mouton de Gruyter.

deGroot, A. D. (1966). Perception and memory versus thought: Some old ideas and recent findings. In B. Kleinmuntz (Ed.), *Problem solving: Research, method, and theory.* New York: Wiley.

Deisseroth, K. (2016). A look inside the brain. *Scientific American, 315,* 32-37.

Del Giudice, M. (2011). Alone in the dark? Modeling the conditions for visual experience in human fetuses. *Developmental Psychobiology, 53,* 214-219.

del Rosal, E., Alonso, L., & Moreno, R. (2006). Simulation of habituation to simple and multiple stimuli. *Behavioural Processes, 73,* 272-277.

DeLamater, J. D., & Sill, M. (2005). Sexual desire in later life. *Journal of Sex Research, 42,* 138-149.

Delgado, M. R., Labouliere, C. D., & Phelps, E. A. (2006). Fear of losing money? Aversive conditioning with secondary reinforcers [Special issue: Genetic, comparative and cognitive studies of social behavior]. *Social Cognitive and Affective Neuroscience, 1,* 250-259.

Dell, P. F. (2013). Three dimensions of dissociative amnesia. *Journal of Trauma & Dissociation, 14,* 25-39.

DeLoache, J., & LoBue, V. (2009). The narrow fellow in the grass: Human infants associate snakes and fear. *Developmental Science, 12,* 201-207.

Demaree, H. A., & Everhart, D. E. (2004). Healthy high-hostiles: Reduced para-sympathetic activity and decreased sympathovagal flexibility during negative emotional processing. *Personality and Individual Differences, 36,* 457-469.

DeMaris, A. (2013). Burning the candle at both ends: Extramarital sex as a precursor of marital disruption. *Journal of Family Issues, 34,* 1474-1499.

Dement, W. C., & Wolpert, E. A. (1958). The relation of eye movements, body mobility, and external stimuli to dream content. *Journal of Experimental Psychology, 55,* 543-553.

Deng, C., & Georgiou, G. K. (2015). Establishing measurement invariance of the cognitive assessment system across cultures. In T. C. Papadopoulos, R. K. Parrila, & J. R. Kirby (Eds.), *Cognition, intelligence, and achievement: A tribute to J. P. Das.* San Diego, CA: Elsevier Academic Press.

Denmark, G. L., & Fernandez, L. C. (1993). Historical development of the psychology of women. In F. L. Denmark & M. A. Paludi (Eds.), *A handbook of issues and theories.* Westport, CT: Greenwood Press.

Dennehy, T. C., & Dasgupta, N. (2017). Female peer mentors early in college increase women's positive academic experiences and retention in engineering. *PNAS Proceedings of the National Academy of Sciences of the United States of America, 114,* 5964-5969.

Dennehy, T. C., Smith, J. S., Moore, C., & Dasgupta, N. (2018). Stereotype threat and stereotype inoculation for underrepresented students in the first year of college. In R. S. Feldman (Ed.), *The first year of college: Research, theory, and practice on improving the student experience and increasing retention.* Cambridge, England: Cambridge University Press.

Dennis, I. (2007). Halo effects in grading student projects. *Journal of Applied Psychology, 92,* 1169-1176.

Dennis, S. (2011). Smoking causes creative responses: On state antismoking policy and resilient habits. *Critical Public Health, 21,* 25-35.

Denollet, J., & Pedersen, S. S. (2011). Type D personality in patients with cardiovascular disorders. In R. Allan & J. Fisher (Eds.), *Heart and mind: The practice of cardiac psychology* (2nd ed.) (pp. 219-247). Washington, DC: American Psychological Association.

Densley, J., & Peterson, J. (2018). Group aggression. *Current Opinion in Psychology, 19,* 43-48. doi:10.1016/j.copsyc.2017.03.031.

Denworth, L. (2017). Is there a "female" brain? *Scientific American, 317,* 38-43.

Deregowski, J. B. (1973). Illusion and culture. In R. L. Gregory & G. H. Combrich (Eds.), *Illusion in nature and art*. New York: Scribner.

Dernbach, K., & Marshall, M. (2001). Pouring beer on troubled waters: Alcohol and violence in the Papua New Guinea Highlands during the 1980s. *Contemporary Drug Problems: An Interdisciplinary Quarterly, 28*, 3-47.

Deroy, O., & Spence, C. (2013). Are we all born synaesthetic? Examining the neonatal synaesthesia hypothesis. *Neuroscience and Biobehavioral Reviews, 37*, 1240-1253.

Deshields, T., Tibbs, T., Fan, M. Y., & Taylor, M. (2006). Differences in patterns of depression after treatment for breast cancer [Electronic article published August 12, 2005]. *Psycho-Oncology, 15*(5), 398-406.

Després, O., Lithfous, S., Tromp, D., Pebayle, T., & Dufour, A. (2017). Gamma oscillatory activity is impaired in episodic memory encoding with age. *Neurobiology of Aging, 52*, 53-65.

Detterman, D. K., Gabriel, L. T., & Ruthsatz, J. M. (2000). Intelligence and mental retardation. In R. J. Sternberg (Ed.), *Handbook of intelligence*. New York: Cambridge University Press.

Deutsch, M. (1994). Constructive conflict resolution: Principles, training, and research. *Journal of Social Issues, 50*, 13-32.

Devos, T. (2011). The role of race in American politics: Lessons learned from the 2008 presidential election. In G. S. Parks & M. W. Hughey (Eds.), *The Obamas and a (post) racial America?* New York: Oxford University Press.

Dhillon, S., Yang, L., & Curran, M. (2008). Spotlight on bupropion in major depressive disorder. *CNS Drugs, 22*, 613-617.

Di Fabio, A., & Palazzeschi, L. (2009). An in-depth look at scholastic success: Fluid intelligence, personality traits or emotional intelligence? *Personality and Individual Differences, 46*, 581-585.

Di Ieva, A., Esteban, F. J., Grizzi, F., Klonowski, W., & Martín-Landrove, M. (2015). Fractals in the neurosciences, part II: Clinical applications and future perspectives. *The Neuroscientist, 21*, 30-43.

Diamond, M. (2009). Human intersexuality: Difference or disorder? *Archives of Sexual Behavior, 38*, 172.

Dias, A. M., & van Deusen, A. (2011). A new neurofeedback protocol for depression. *Spanish Journal of Psychology, 14*, 374-384.

Diaz, A., & Bell, M. (2011). Information processing efficiency and regulation at five months. *Infant Behavior & Development, 34*, 239-247.

Dickinson, D. L., & Oxoby, R. J. (2011). Cognitive dissonance, pessimism, and behavioral spillover effects. *Journal of Economic Psychology, 32*, 295-306.

Diemand-Yauman, C., et al. (2010), Fortune favors the bold (*and the italicized*): Effects of disfluency on educational outcomes. *Cognition*. Accessed online 4.19.16; https://web.princeton.edu/sites/opplab/papers/Diemand-Yauman_Oppenheimer_2010.pdf.

Diener, E., & Clifton, D. (2002). Life satisfaction and religiosity in broad probability samples. *Psychological Inquiry, 13*, 206-209.

Diener, E., & Seligman, M. E. P. (2004). Beyond money: Toward an economy of well-being. *Psychological Science in the Public Interest, 5*, 1-31.

Diener, E., Lucas, R. E., & Scollon, C. N. (2006). Beyond the hedonic treadmill: Revising the adaptation theory of well-being. *American Psychologist, 61*, 305-314.

Diener, M., Isabella, R., Behunin, M., & Wong, M. (2008). Attachment to mothers and fathers during middle childhood: Associations with child gender, grade, and competence. *Social Development, 17*, 84-101.

Dienst, J., Schreiber, K., & Valiquette, J. (2016, May 23). FBI's newest K-9 sniffs out digital evidence. Retrieved from http://www.nbcnewyork.com/news/local/New-Jersey-FBI-Dog-Electronics-Sniffing-Dog-NJ-Police-380560881.html.

Diering, G. H., Nirujogi, R. S., Roth, R. H., Worley, P. F., Pandey, A., & Huganir, R. L. (2017). Homer1a drives homeostatic scaling-down of excitatory synapses during sleep. *Science, 355*, 511-515.

Dierolf, A. M., Fechtner, J., Böhnke, R., Wolf, O. T., & Naumann, E. (2017). Influence of acute stress on response inhibition in healthy men: An ERP study. *Psychophysiology, 54*, 684-695.

Digdon, N. (2017). The Little Albert controversy: Intuition, confirmation bias, and logic. *History of Psychology*. Accessed from https://www.ncbi.nlm.nih.gov/pubmed/28125246.

DiGiovanna, A. G. (1994). *Human aging: Biological perspectives*. New York: McGraw-Hill.

Dijksterhuis, A., Chartrand, T. L., & Aarts, H. (2007). Effects of Priming and Perception on Social Behavior and Goal Pursuit. *Frontiers of Social Psychology, 17*, 33-40.

Dillard, J. P., & Shen, L. (2007). Self-report measures of discrete emotions. In R. A. Reynolds, R. Woods, & J. D. Baker (Eds.), *Handbook of research on electronic surveys and measurements*. Hershey, PA: Idea Group Reference/IGI Global, 2007.

Diller, L. (2017, January 17). The United States of Adderall. *Huffington Post*. Accessed from http://www.huffingtonpost.com/larry-diller/the-united-states-of-adderall_b_8914480.html.

Dimaggio, G., D'Urzo, M., Pasinetti, M., Salvatore, G., Lysaker, P. H., Catania, D., & Popolo, R. (2015). Metacognitive interpersonal therapy for co-occurrent avoidant personality disorder and substance abuse. *Journal Of Clinical Psychology, 71*, 157-166.

Dimaggio, G., Salvatore, G., MacBeth, A., Ottavi, P., Buonocore, L., & Popolo, R. (2017). Metacognitive interpersonal therapy for personality disorders: A case study series. *Journal of Contemporary Psychotherapy, 47*, 11-21.

Dingfelder, S. (2011). Reflecting on narcissism. *Monitor on Psychology, 42*, 64-68.

Diniz, B. S., Butters, M. A., Albert, S. M., Dew, M., & Reynolds, C. (2013). Late-life depression and risk of vascular dementia and Alzheimer's disease: Systematic review and meta-analysis of community-based cohort studies. *British Journal of Psychiatry, 202*, 329-335.

Dittrich, W. H., Johansen, T., & Fineberg, N. A. (2011). Cognitive Assessment Instrument of Obsessions and Compulsions (CAIOV-13)–A new 13-item scale for evaluating functional impairment associated with OCD. *Psychiatry Research, 187*, 283-290.

Dixon, R. A., & Cohen, A. L. (2003). Cognitive development in adulthood. In R. M. Lerner, M. A. Easterbrooks, & J. Mistry (Eds.), *Handbook of psychology: Developmental psychology* (Vol. 6). New York: Wiley.

Dixon, R. A., McFall, G., Whitehead, B. P., & Dolcos, S. (2013). Cognitive development in adulthood and aging. In R. M. Lerner, M. Easterbrooks, J. Mistry, & I. B. Weiner (Eds.), *Handbook of psychology, Vol. 6: Developmental psychology* (2nd ed.). Hoboken, NJ: John Wiley & Sons Inc.

Dixon, R. A., Rust, T. B., & Feltmate, S. E. (2007). Memory and aging: Selected research directions and application issues. *Canadian Psychology Psychologie Canadienne, 48*, 67-76.

Djapo, N., Kolenovic-Djapo, J., Djokic, R., & Fako, I. (2011). Relationship between Cattell's 16PF and fluid and crystallized intelligence. *Personality and Individual Differences, 51*, 63-67.

Do, V. T. (2006). Asian American men and the media: The relationship between ethnic identity, self-esteem, and the endorsement of stereotypes. *Dissertation Abstracts International: Section B: The Sciences and Engineering, 67*(6-B), 3446.

Dockrell, J. E., & Marshall, C. R. (2015). Measurement issues: Assessing language skills in young children. *Child and Adolescent Mental Health, 20*, 116-125.

Dodge, K. A. (2004). The nature-nurture debate and public policy [Special issue: 50th anniversary issue, part 2: The maturing of the human development sciences–Appraising past, present, and prospective agendas]. *Merrill-Palmer Quarterly: Journal of Developmental Psychology, 50*, 418-427.

Dohnke, B., Weiss-Gerlach, E., & Spies, C. D. (2011). Social influences on the motivation to quit smoking: Main and moderating effects of social norms. *Addictive Behaviors, 36*, 286-293.

Doi, T. (1990). The cultural assumptions of psychoanalysis. In J. W. Stigler, R. A. Shweder, & G. Herdt (Eds.), *Cultural psychology: Essays on comparative human development*. New York: Cambridge University Press.

Dolan, R. J. (2002). Emotion, cognition, and behavior. *Science, 298*, 1191-1194.

Dolbier, C. L., Smith, S. E., & Steinhardt, M. A. (2007). Relationships of protective factors to stress and symptoms of illness. *American Journal of Health Behavior, 31*, 423-433.

Dolinski, D. (2011). A rock or a hard place: The foot-in-the-face technique for inducing compliance without pressure. *Journal of Applied Social Psychology, 41*, 1514-1537.

Dollinger, S. J. (2003). Need for uniqueness, need for cognition and creativity. *Journal of Creative Behavior, 37*, 99-116.

Domhoff, G. W. (2011). The neural substrate for dreaming: Is it a subsystem of the default network? *Consciousness and Cognition, 20,* 1163-1174.

Domschke, K. (2013). Clinical and molecular genetics of psychotic depression. *Schizophrenia Bulletin, 39,* 766-775.

Donahoe, J. W., & Vegas, R. (2004). Pavlovian Conditioning: The CSUR Relation. *Journal of Experimental Psychology: Animal Behavior Processes, 30,* 17-33.

Doty, R. L., Green, P. A., Ram, C., & Yankell, S. L. (1982). Communication of gender from human breath odors: Relationship to perceived intensity and pleasantness. *Hormones and Behavior, 16,* 13-22.

Doty, R. L., Tourbier, I., Ng, V., Neff, J., Armstrong, D., Battistini, M., & . . . Sondheimer, S. J. (2015). Influences of hormone replacement therapy on olfactory and cognitive function in postmenopausal women. *Neurobiology of Aging, 36,* 2053-2059.

Douthit, K. Z., & Russotti, J. (2017). Biology of marginality: A neurophysiological exploration of the social and cultural foundations of psychological health. In T. A. Field, L. K. Jones, & L. A. Russell-Chapin (Eds.), *Neurocounseling: Brain-based clinical approaches.* Alexandria, VA: American Counseling Association.

Dovidio, J. F., Piliavin, J. A., Schroeder, D. A., & Penner, L. A. (2006). *The social psychology of prosocial behavior.* Mahwah, NJ: Lawrence Erlbaum Associates.

Dowling, N., Jackson, A., & Thomas, S. (2008). Behavioral interventions in the treatment of pathological gambling: A review of activity scheduling and desensitization. *International Journal of Behavioral Consultation and Therapy, 4,* 172-187.

Dresler, M., Shirer, W. R., Konrad, B. N., Muller, N. C., Wagner, I. C., Fernandez, G., . . . Greicius, M. D. (2017). Mnemonic training reshapes brain networks to support superior memory. *Neuron, 93*(5), 1227-1235.

Dresler, T., Guhn, A., Tupak, S. V., Ehlis, A., Herrmann, M. J., Fallgatter, A. J., & . . . Domschke, K. (2013). Revise the revised? New dimensions of the neuroanatomical hypothesis of panic disorder. *Journal of Neural Transmission, 120,* 3-29.

Drewes, A. A. (2005). Play in selected cultures: Diversity and universality. In E. Gil & A. A. Drewes (Eds.), *Cultural issues in play therapy.* New York: Guilford Press.

Driessen, E., Van, H. L., Peen, J., Don, F. J., Twisk, J. R., Cuijpers, P., & Dekker, J. M. (2017). Cognitive-behavioral versus psychodynamic therapy for major depression: Secondary outcomes of a randomized clinical trial. *Journal of Consulting and Clinical Psychology, 85,* 653-663.

Dryden, W., & David, D. (2008). Rational emotive behavior therapy: Current status. *Journal of Cognitive Psychotherapy, 22,* 195-209.

Dudai, Y. (2011). The engram revisited: On the elusive permanence of memory. In S. Nalbantian, P. M. Matthews, & J. L. McClelland (Eds.), *The memory process: Neuroscientific*

and humanistic perspectives. Cambridge, MA: MIT Press.

Duke, M., & Nowicki, S., Jr. (1979). *Abnormal psychology: Perspectives on being different.* Monterey, CA: Brooks/Cole.

Dumont, M., & Dumont, D. (2008). Deinstitutionalization in the United States and Italy: A historical survey. *International Journal of Mental Health, 37,* 61-70.

Duncker, K. (1945). On problem solving. *Psychological Monographs, 58* (5, whole no. 270).

Dunkley, D. M., Lewkowski, M., Lee, I. A., Preacher, K. J., Zuroff, D. C., Berg, J., . . . Westreich, R. (2017). Daily stress, coping, and negative and positive affect in depression: Complex trigger and maintenance patterns. *Behavior Therapy, 48,* 349-365.

Dunlop, W. L., Beatty, D. J., & Beauchamp, M. R. (2011). Examining the influence of other-efficacy and self-efficacy on personal performance. *Journal of Sport & Exercise Psychology, 33,* 586-593.

Dunlop, W. L., Guo, J., & McAdams, D. P. (2016). The autobiographical author through time: Examining the degree of stability and change in redemptive and contaminated personal narratives. *Social Psychological and Personality Science, 7,* 428-436.

Dweck, C. S. (2017). Is psychology headed in the right direction? Yes, no, and maybe. *Perspectives on Psychological Science, 12,* 656-659.

Diaz, E., & De la Casa, L. G. (2011). Extinction, spontaneous recovery and renewal of flavor preferences based on taste-taste learning. *Learning and Motivation, 42,* 64-75.

Eaker, E. D., Sullivan, L. M., Kelly-Hayes, M., D'Agostino, R. B., Sr., & Benjamin, E. J. (2004). Anger and hostility predict the development of atrial fibrillation in men in the Framingham Offspring Study. *Circulation, 109,* 1267-1271.

Ebigbo, P. O., Lekwas, E. C., & Chukwunenyem, N. F. (2015). Brain fag: New perspectives from case observations. *Transcultural Psychiatry, 52,* 311-330.

Ebrahimian, Z., Karimi, Z., Khoshnoud, M. J., Namavar, M. R., Daraei, B., & Haidari, M. R. (2017). Behavioral and stereological analysis of the effects of intermittent feeding diet on the orally administrated MDMA ('ecstasy') in mice. *Innovations in Clinical Neuroscience, 14,* 40-52.

Ecenbarger, W. (1993, April 1). America's new merchants of death. *Reader's Digest,* p. 50.

Eckardt, M. H. (2005). Karen Horney: A portrait: The 120th anniversary, Karen Horney, September 16, 1885. *American Journal of Psychoanalysis, 65,* 95-101.

Ecker, U. H., Tay, J., & Brown, G. A. (2015). Effects of prestudy and poststudy rest on memory: Support for temporal interference accounts of forgetting. *Psychonomic Bulletin & Review, 22,* 772-778.

Edoka, I. P., Petrou, S., & Ramchandani, P. G. (2011). Healthcare costs of paternal depression in the postnatal period. *Journal of Affective Disorders, 133,* 356-360.

Edwards, M. S., Moore, P., Champion, J. C., & Edwards, E. J. (2015). Effects of trait anxiety and situational stress on attentional shifting are buffered by working memory capacity. *Anxiety, Stress & Coping: An International Journal, 28,* 1-16.

Efklides, A., & Moraitou, D. (2013). *A positive psychology perspective on quality of life.* New York: Springer Science + Business Media.

Egan, K. (2005). Students' development in theory and practice: The doubtful role of research. *Harvard Educational Review, 75,* 25-41.

Egan, K. J., Knutson, K. L., Pereira, A. C., & von Schantz, M. (2017). The role of race and ethnicity in sleep, circadian rhythms and cardiovascular health. *Sleep Medicine Reviews, 33,* 70-78.

Egervari, G., Ciccocioppo, R., Jentsch, J. D., & Hurd, Y. L. (2017). Shaping vulnerability to addiction - the contribution of behavior, neural circuits and molecular mechanisms. *Neuroscience and Biobehavioral Reviews.* Accessed from http://www.sciencedirect.com/science/article/pii/S0149763417300866.

Ehde, D. M., Dillworth, T. M., & Turner, J. A. (2014). Cognitive-behavioral therapy for individuals with chronic pain: Efficacy, innovations, and directions for research. *American Psychologist, 69,* 153-177.

Eizenberg, M. M., & Zaslavsky, O. (2004). Students' verification strategies for combinatorial problems. *Mathematical Thinking and Learning, 6,* 15-36.

Ekman, P. (1972). Universals and cultural differences in facial expressions of emotion. In J. Cole (Ed.), *Darwin and facial expression: A century of research in review.* New York: Academic Press.

Ekman, P. (1994). Strong evidence for universals in facial expressions: A reply to Russell's mistaken critique. *Psychological Bulletin, 115,* 268-287.

Ekman, P. (2003). *Emotions revealed: Recognizing faces and feelings to improve communication and emotional life.* New York: Times Books.

Ekman, P. (2007). *Emotions revealed* (2nd ed.). New York: Holt.

Ekman, P., Levenson, R. W., & Friesen, W. V. (1983). Autonomic nervous system activity distinguishes among emotions. *Science, 223,* 1208-1210.

Ekonomou, A., Savva, G. M., Brayne, C., Forster, G., Francis, P. T., Johnson, M., & . . . Ballard, C. G. (2015). Stage-specific changes in neurogenic and glial markers in Alzheimer's disease. *Biological Psychiatry, 77,* 711-719.

Ekroll, V., & Scherzer, T. R. (2009). Apparent visual motion of the observer's own limbs. *Perception, 38,* 778-780.

Elen, M., D'Heer, E., Geuens, M., & Vermeir, I. (2013). The influence of mood on attitude-behavior consistency. *Journal of Business Research, 66,* 917-923.

Elfhag, K., Tynelius, P., & Rasmussen, F. (2007). Sugar-sweetened and artificially sweetened soft drinks in association to restrained, external and emotional eating. *Physiology & Behavior, 91,* 191-195.

Elias, V. L., Fullerton, A. S., & Simpson, J. M. (2015). Long-term changes in attitudes toward premarital sex in the United States: Re-examining the role of cohort replacement. *Journal of Sex Research, 52*, 129-139.

Eljamel, S. (2015). Ablative surgery for depression. In B. Sun & A. De Salles (Eds.), *Neurosurgical treatments for psychiatric disorders.* New York: Springer Science + Business Media.

Elkins, D. (2009). Why humanistic psychology lost its power and influence in American psychology: Implications for advancing humanistic psychology. *Journal of Humanistic Psychology, 49*, 267-291.

Elkins, G., Marcus, J., Bates, J., Hasan, R. M., & Cook, T. (2006). Intensive hypnotherapy for smoking cessation: a prospective study. *International Journal of Clinical Experimental Hypnosis, 54*, 303-315.

Ellins, E., Halcox, J., Donald, A., Field, B., Brydon, L., Deanfield, J., et al. (2008). Arterial stiffness and inflammatory response to psychophysiological stress. *Brain, Behavior, and Immunity, 22*, 941-948.

Elliot, A. J., Dweck, C. S., & Yeager, D. S. (2017). *Handbook of competence and motivation: Theory and application* (2nd ed.). New York: Guilford Press.

Ellis, A. (1974). *Growth through reason.* Hollywood, CA: Wilshire Books.

Ellis, A. (2002). *Overcoming resistance: A rational emotive behavior therapy integrated approach* (2nd ed.). New York: Springer.

Ellis, A. (2004). *Expanding the ABCs of rational emotive behavior therapy.* In A. Freeman, M. J. Mahoney, P. Devito, & D. Martin (Eds.), *Cognition and psychotherapy* (2nd ed.). New York: Springer Publishing Co.

Emmett, J., & McGee, D. (2013). Extrinsic motivation for large-scale assessments: A case study of a student achievement program at one urban high school. *High School Journal, 96*, 116-137.

Enge, L. R., Lupo, A. K., & Zárate, M. A. (2015). Neurocognitive mechanisms of prejudice formation: The role of time-dependent memory consolidation. *Psychological Science, 26*, 964-971.

Engel, U., Jann, B., Lynn, P., Scherpenzeel, A., & Sturgis, P. (2015). *Improving survey methods: Lessons from recent research.* NY: Routledge/Taylor & Francis Group.

Engen, T. (1987). Remembering odors and their names. *American Scientist, 75*, 497-503.

Engler, J., & Goleman, D. (1992). *The consumer's guide to psychotherapy.* New York: Simon & Schuster.

Epatko, L. (2018, April 16). This summer camp helps kids reach across the Israeli-Palestinian divide. *PBS News Hour.* Accessed May 2, 2018, from https://www.pbs.org/newshour/world/seeds-of-peace-empowers-its-young-leaders-to-confront-conflict-around-the-world.

Eranti, S. V., & McLoughlin, D. M. (2003). Electroconvulsive therapy: State of the art. *British Journal of Psychiatry, 182*, 8-9.

Erb, J., Henry, M. J., Eisner, F., & Obleser, J. (2013). The brain dynamics of rapid perceptual adaptation to adverse listening conditions. *The Journal of Neuroscience, 33*, 10688-10697.

Erickson, R. (2008, February). A study of the science of taste: On the origins and influence of the core ideas. *Behavioral and Brain Sciences, 31*, 59-75.

Erikson, E. H. (1963). *Childhood and society.* New York: Norton.

Ervik, S., Abdelnoor, M., & Heier, M. S. (2006). Health-related quality of life in narcolepsy. *Acta Neurologica Scandinavica, 114*, 198-204.

Espinola, M., DeVinney, H., & Steinberg, A. (. (2017). Women at midlife. In K. A. Kendall-Tackett & L. M. Ruglass (Eds.), *Women's mental health across the lifespan: Challenges, vulnerabilities, and strengths.* New York: Routledge/Taylor & Francis Group.

Etienne, J. (2013). Thoughts on how to regulate behaviours: An overview of the current debate. *British Journal of Guidance & Counselling, 41*, 36-45.

Etzrodt, C. M. (2013). Ethical considerations of therapeutic hypnosis and children. *American Journal of Clinical Hypnosis, 55*, 370-377.

Euler, M. J., Weisend, M. P., Jung, R. E., Thoma, R. J., & Yeo, R. A. (2015). Reliable activation to novel stimuli predicts higher fluid intelligence. *Neuroimage, 114*, 311-319.

Evans, D. E., & Rothbart, M. K. (2007). Developing a model for adult temperament. *Journal of Research in Personality, 41*, 868-888.

Evans, D., & Rothbart, M. (2009). A two-factor model of temperament. *Personality and Individual Differences, 47*, 565-570.

Evcik, D., Kavuncu, V., Cakir, T., Subasi, V., & Yaman, M. (2007). Laser therapy in the treatment of carpal tunnel syndrome: A randomized controlled trial. *Photomedical Laser Surgery, 25*, 34-39.

Everette, M. (2008). Gestational weight and dietary intake during pregnancy: Perspectives of African American women. *Maternal & Child Health Journal, 12*, 718-724.

Everly, G. S., Jr., & Lating, J. M. (2007). Psychotherapy: A cognitive perspective. In A. Monat, R. S. Lazarus, & G. Reevy (Eds.), *The Praeger handbook on stress and coping* (Vol. 2). Westport, CT: Praeger Publishers/Greenwood Publishing.

Eysenck, H. J. (1995). *Eysenck on extraversion.* New York: Wiley.

Fagan, J. F., & Holland, C. R. (2002). Equal opportunity and racial differences in IQ. *Intelligence, 30*, 361-387.

Fagan, J. F., & Holland, C. R. (2007). Racial equality in intelligence: Predictions from a theory of intelligence as processing. *Intelligence, 35*, 319-334.

Fagan, J. F., & Holland, C. R. (2009). Culture-fair prediction of academic achievement. *Intelligence, 37*, 62-67.

Fagan, J., & Press, J. (2008). Father influences on employed mothers' work-family balance. *Journal of Family Issues, 29*, 1136-1160.

Falasca, N. W., D'Ascenzo, S., Di Domenico, A., Onofrj, M., Tommasi, L., Laeng, B., & Franciotti, R. (2015). Hemispheric lateralization in top-down attention during spatial relation processing: A Granger causal model approach. *European Journal of Neuroscience, 41*, 912-922.

Farnsworth, D. L. (2015). Identical twins raised apart. *Teaching Statistics, 37*, 1-6.

Farrell, A. K., Simpson, J. A., Carlson, E. A., Englund, M. M., & Sung, S. (2017). The impact of stress at different life stages on physical health and the buffering effects of maternal sensitivity. *Health Psychology, 36*, 35-44.

Faupel, A., Herrick, E., & Sharp, P. M. (2018). *Anger management: A practical guide for teachers* (3rd ed.). New York: Routledge/Taylor & Francis Group.

Fayek, A. (2017). *Understanding classical psychoanalysis: Freudian concepts in contemporary practice.* New York: Routledge/Taylor & Francis Group.

Fearing, V. G., & Clark, J. (Eds.). (2000). *Individuals in context: A practical guide to client-centered practice.* Chicago: Slack Publishing.

Fedeli, A., Braconi, S., Economidou, D., Cannella, N., Kallupi, M., Guerrini, R., . . . Ciccocioppo, R. (2009). The paraventricular nucleus of the hypothalamus is a neuroanatomical substrate for the inhibition of palatable food intake by neuropeptide S. *European Journal of Neuroscience, 30*, 1594-1602.

Fedyk, M. (2017). *The social turn in moral psychology.* Cambridge, MA: MIT Press.

Feldman, D. H. (2003). Cognitive development in childhood. In R. M. Lerner, M. A. Easterbrooks, & J. Mistry (Eds.), *Handbook of psychology: Developmental psychology* (Vol. 6). New York: Wiley.

Feldman, D. H. (2004). Piaget's stages: The unfinished symphony of cognitive development. *New Ideas in Psychology, 22*, 175-231.

Feldman, R. S. (2017). *P.O.W.E.R. learning: Strategies for success in college and life.* New York: McGraw-Hill.

Feldman, R. S. (Ed.). (1993). *Applications of nonverbal behavioral theories and research.* Hillsdale, NJ: Erlbaum.

Felson, R. B., & Tedeschi, J.T. (Eds.). (1993). *Aggression and violence: Social interactionist perspectives.* Washington, DC: American Psychological Association.

Feng, B., Bell, R. A., Jerant, A. F., & Kravitz, R. L. (2011). What do doctors say when prescribing medications?: An examination of medical recommendations from a communication perspective. *Health Communication, 26*, 286-296.

Fenter, V. L. (2006). Concerns about Prozac and direct-to-consumer advertising of prescription drugs. *International Journal of Risk & Safety in Medicine, 18*, 1-7.

Ferguson, C. J. (2010). Blazing angels or resident evil? Can violent video games be a force for good? *Review of General Psychology, 14*, 68-81.

Ferguson, C. J. (2011). Video games and youth violence: A prospective analysis in adolescents. *Journal of Youth and Adolescence, 40*, 377-391.

Ferguson, C. J. (2015a). "Everybody knows psychology is not a real science": Public perceptions of psychology and how we can improve our relationship with policymakers, the scientific community, and the general public. *American Psychologist, 70*, 527-542.

Ferguson, C. J. (2015b). Does media violence predict societal violence? It depends on what you look at and when. *Journal of Communication, 65*, E1-E22.

Ferguson, C. J. (2015c). Do angry birds make for angry children? A meta-analysis of video game influences on children's and adolescents' aggression, mental health, prosocial behavior, and academic performance. *Psychological Science*, 1-22.

Ferguson, C. J., & Beresin, E. (2017). Social science's curious war with pop culture and how it was lost: The media violence debate and the risks it holds for social science. *Preventive Medicine: An International Journal Devoted to Practice and Theory, 99*, 69-76.

Ferguson, M., & Ogloff, J. P. (2011). Criminal responsibility evaluations: Role of psychologists in assessment. *Psychiatry, Psychology and Law, 18*, 79-94.

Fernald, R. D. (2015). Social behaviour: Can it change the brain? *Animal Behaviour, 103*, 259-265.

Fernyhough, C. (2017). Talking to ourselves. *Scientific American, 317*, 74-79.

Ferring, D., Tournier, I., & Mancini, D. (2015). 'the closer you get . . .': Age, attitudes and self-serving evaluations about older drivers. *European Journal of Ageing*. Accessed online, 10.1.15; http://link.springer.com/article/10.1007%2Fs10433-015-0337-0.

Feshbach, S., & Tangney, J. (2008). Television viewing and aggression: Some alternative perspectives. *Perspectives on Psychological Science, 3*, 387-389.

Festinger, D., Marlowe, D., Croft, J., Dugosh, K., Arabia, P., & Benasutti, K. (2009). Monetary incentives improve recall of research consent information: It pays to remember. *Experimental and Clinical Psychopharmacology, 17*, 99-104.

Festinger, L. (1957). *A theory of cognitive dissonance*. Stanford, CA: Stanford University Press.

Festinger, L., & Carlsmith, J. M. (1959). Cognitive consequences of forced compliance. *Journal of Abnormal and Social Psychology, 58*, 203-210.

Festini, S. B., & Reuter-Lorenz, P. A. (2017). Rehearsal of to-be-remembered items is unnecessary to perform directed forgetting within working memory: Support for an active control mechanism. *Journal of Experimental Psychology: Learning, Memory, and Cognition, 43*, 94-108.

Fetvadjiev, V. H., Meiring, D., van de Vijver, F. R., Nel, J. A., Sekaja, L., & Laher, S. (2018). Personality and behavior prediction and consistency across cultures: A multimethod study of Blacks and Whites in South Africa. *Journal of Personality and Social Psychology, 114*(3), 465-481. doi:10.1037/pspp0000129.

Fevang, S. E., Hysing, M., Sommerfelt, K., & Elgen, I. (2017). Mental health assessed by the strengths and difficulties questionnaire for children born extremely preterm without severe disabilities at 11 years of age: A Norwegian, national population-based study. *European Child & Adolescent Psychiatry, 26*(12), 1523-1531.

Fichtenberg, C. M., & Glantz, S. A. (2006). Association of the California tobacco control program with declines in cigarette consumption and mortality from heart disease. In K. E. Warner (Ed.), *Tobacco control policy*. San Francisco, CA: Jossey-Bass.

Figen, A. (2011). The relationship between test anxiety and learned helplessness. *Social Behavior and Personality, 39*, 101-112.

Filippello, P., Sorrenti, L., Buzzai, C., & Costa, S. (2015). Perceived parental psychological control and learned helplessness: The role of school self-efficacy. *School Mental Health*. Accessed online, 9.29.15; http://link.springer.com/article/10.1007%2Fs12310-015-9151-2#page-1.

Filippi, C. A., Cannon, E. N., Fox, N. A., Thorpe, S. G., Ferrari, P. F., & Woodward, A. L. (2016). Motor system activation predicts goal imitation in 7-month-old infants. *Psychological Science, 27*(5), 675-684.

Finan, P. H., Zautra, A. J., & Wershba, R. (2011). The dynamics of emotion in adaptation to stress. In R. J. Contrada & A. Baum (Eds.), *The handbook of stress science: Biology, psychology, and health*. New York: Springer Publishing Co.

Fine, R., & Fine, L. (2003). *Basic chess endings*. New York: Random House.

Fingelkurts, A., Fingelkurts, A. A., & Kallio, S. (2007). Hypnosis induces a changed composition of brain oscillations in EEG: A case study. *Contemporary Hypnosis, 24*, 3-18.

Fink, S. (2017, July 28). Two C.I.A. psychologists can face trial, judge rules. *The New York Times*, p. A18.

Finke, M. S., Howe, J. S., & Huston, S. J. (2017). Old age and the decline in financial literacy. *Management Science, 63*, 213-230.

Finkelstein, M. (2009). Intrinsic vs. extrinsic motivational orientations and the volunteer process. *Personality and Individual Differences, 46*, 653-658.

Finkler, K. (2004). Traditional healers in Mexico: The effectiveness of spiritual practices. In U. P. Gielen, J. M. Fish, & J. G. Draguns (Eds.), *Handbook of culture, therapy, and healing*. Mahwah, NJ: Lawrence Erlbaum Associates.

Finley, C. L., & Cowley, B. J. (2005). The effects of a consistent sleep schedule on time taken to achieve sleep. *Clinical Case Studies, 4*, 304-311.

Finn, A. (2011). Jungian analytical theory. In D. Capuzzi & D. R. Gross (Eds.), *Counseling and psychotherapy (5th ed.)*. Alexandria, VA: American Counseling Association.

Finn, K. (2015). Sequelae of cannabis as medicine. *Pain Medicine, 16*, 1447-1449.

Firestein, B. A. (Ed.). (1996). *Bisexuality: The psychology and politics of an invisible minority*. Thousand Oaks, CA: Sage.

Fischer, I. (2011). Several eyes for an eye: The impact of biased perceptions and noise on conflict escalation patterns. *Peace and Conflict: Journal of Peace Psychology, 17*, 77-84.

Fischer, P., Krueger, J. I., Greitemeyer, T., Vogrincic, C., Kastenmüller, A., Frey, D., & Kainbacher, M. (2011). The bystander-effect: A meta-analytic review on bystander intervention in dangerous and non-dangerous emergencies. *Psychological Bulletin, 137*, 517-537.

Fischetti, M. (2016). Fatter still. *Scientific American, 315*(2), 80.

Fisher, A. K., Moore, D. J., Simmons, C., & Allen, S. C. (2017). Teaching social workers about microaggressions to enhance understanding of subtle racism. *Journal of Human Behavior in the Social Environment, 27*(4), 346-355.

Fisher, C. B. (2003). *Decoding the ethics code: A practical guide for psychologists*. Thousand Oaks, CA: Sage.

Fisher, G. G., & Barnes-Farrell, J. L. (2013). Use of archival data in occupational health psychology research. In R. R. Sinclair, M. Wang, & L. E. Tetrick (Eds.), *Research methods in occupational health psychology: Measurement, design, and data analysis*. New York: Routledge/Taylor & Francis Group.

Fisher, R. J., & Kelman, H. C. (2011). Perceptions in conflict. In D. Bar-Tal, (Ed.), *Intergroup conflicts and their resolution: A social psychological perspective*. New York: Psychology Press.

Fiske, S. T. (2017). Going in many right directions, all at once. *Perspectives on Psychology, 12*, 652-655.

Flannelly, K. J. (2017). *Religious beliefs, evolutionary psychiatry, and mental health in America: Evolutionary threat assessment systems theory*. Cham, Switzerland: Springer International Publishing.

Fleck, J. I., Green, D. L., Payne, L., Stevenson, J. L., Bowden, E. M., Jung-Beeman, M., et al. (2008). The transliminal brain at rest: Baseline EEG, unusual experiences, and access to unconscious mental activity. *Cortex, 44*, 1353-1363.

Fleming, J. (2000). Affirmative action and standardized test scores. *Journal of Negro Education, 69*, 27-37.

Flohr, E. R., Erwin, E., Croy, I., & Hummel, T. (2017). Sad man's nose: Emotion induction and olfactory perception. *Emotion, 17*, 369-378.

Foderaro, L. W. (2006, February 16). Westchester lawyer, his memory lost, is found in Chicago shelter after 6 months. *The New York Times*, p. B3.

Foell, J., Bekrater-Bodmann, R., Diers, M., & Flor, H. (2014). Mirror therapy for phantom limb pain: Brain changes and the role of body representation. *European Journal of Pain, 18*, 729-739.

Folk, C., & Remington, R. (2008, January). Bottom-up priming of top-down attentional control settings. *Visual Cognition, 16*, 215-231.

Folkman, S., & Moskowitz, J. T. (2000). Stress, positive emotion, and coping. *Current Directions in Psychological Science, 9*, 115-118.

Folkman, S., & Moskowitz, J. T. (2004). Coping: Pitfalls and promise. *Annual Review of Psychology, 55*, 745-774.

Follett, K., & Hess, T. M. (2002). Aging, cognitive complexity, and the fundamental attribution error. *Journal of Gerontology: Series B: Psychological Sciences and Social Sciences, 57B*, P312-P323.

Forbus, K. D., Liang, C., & Rabkina, I. (2017). Representation and computation in cognitive models. *Topics in Cognitive Science, 9*(3), 694-718.

Forer, B. (1949). The fallacy of personal validation: A classroom demonstration of gullibility. *Journal of Abnormal and Social Psychology, 44,* 118-123.

Forgas, J. P., & Laham, S. M. (2005). The interaction between affect and motivation in social judgments and behavior. In J. P. Forgas, K. P. Williams, & S. M. Laham (Eds.), *Social motivation: Conscious and unconscious processes.* New York: Cambridge University Press.

Forgas, J. P., & Laham, S. M. (2017). Halo effects. In R. F. Pohl (Ed.), *Cognitive illusions: Intriguing phenomena in thinking, judgment and memory.* New York: Routledge/Taylor & Francis Group.

Forson, T.S. (2018, February 21.) Who is African-American? Definition evolves as USA does. *USA Today,* Retrieved from https://www.usatoday.com/story/news/nation-now/2018/02/21/black-history-african-american-definition/1002344001/.

Fost, J. (2015). Are there psychological species? *Review of Philosophy and Psychology, 6,* 293-315.

Foster, K. M. (2005). Introduction: John Uzo Ogbu (1939-2003): How do you ensure the fair consideration of a complex ancestor? Multiple approaches to assessing the work and legacy of John Uzo Ogbu. *International Journal of Qualitative Studies in Education, 18,* 559-564.

Fothergill, E., Guo, J., Howard, L., Kerns, J. C., Knuth, N. D., Brychta, R., . . . Hall, K. D. (2016). Persistent metabolic adaptation 6 years after "The Biggest Loser" competition. *Obesity, 24,* 1612-1619.

Foulds, J., Gandhi, K. K., Steinberg, M. B., Richardson, D. L., Williams, J. M., Burke, M. V., et al. (2006). Factors associated with quitting smoking at a tobacco dependence treatment clinic. *American Journal of Health Behavior, 30,* 400-412.

Fountas, K. N., & Smith, J. R. (2007). Historical evolution of stereotactic amygdalotomy for the management of severe aggression. *Journal of Neurosurgery, 106,* 716-713.

Fox, S., & Spector, P. E. (2000). Relations of emotional intelligence, practical intelligence, general intelligence, and trait affectivity with interview outcomes: It's not all just "G." *Journal of Organizational Behavior, 21,* 203-220.

Frances, A. (2013). *Saving Normal: An Insider's Revolt Against Out-of-Control Psychiatric Diagnosis, DSM-5, Big Pharma, and the Medicalization of Ordinary Life.* New York: Morrow.

Frank, S., Goldwater, S., & Keller, F. (2013). Adding sentence types to a model of syntactic category acquisition. *Topics in Cognitive Science, 5,* 495-521.

Franklin, A., Pilling, M., & Davies, I. (2005). The nature of infant color categorization: Evidence from eye movements on a target decision task. *Journal of Experimental Child Psychology, 91,* 227-248.

Franklin, M. E., March, J. S., & Garcia, A. (2007). Treating obsessive-compulsive disorder in children and adolescents. In C. Purdon, M. M. Antony, & L. J. Summerfeldt (Eds.), *Psychological treatment of obsessive-compulsive disorder: Fundamentals and beyond.* Washington, DC: American Psychological Association.

Franklin, T. B., & Mansuy, I. M. (2011). The involvement of epigenetic defects in mental retardation. *Neurobiology of Learning and Memory, 96,* 61-67.

Franko, D. L., & Roehrig, J. P. (2011). African American body images. In T. F. Cash & L. Smolak (Eds.), *Body image: A handbook of science, practice, and prevention* (2nd ed.). New York: Guilford Press.

Freedberg, D. (2011). Memory in art: History and the neuroscience of response. In S. Nalbantian, P. M. Matthews, & J. L. McClelland (Eds.), *The memory process: Neuroscientific and humanistic perspectives.* Cambridge, MA: MIT Press.

Freedman, D. S. (1995). The importance of body fat distribution in early life. *American Journal of the Medical Sciences, 310,* S72-S76.

Freedman, J. L., & Fraser, S. C. (1966). Compliance without pressure: The foot-in-the-door technique. *Journal of Personality and Social Psychology, 4,* 195-202.

Freedman, M. R., & Waldrop, J. (2011). Freshman orientation sessions can teach incoming students about healthful lifestyles. *Journal of Nutrition Education and Behavior, 43,* 69-70.

Fresco, D. M. (2013). Tending the garden and harvesting the fruits of behavior therapy. *Behavior Therapy, 44,* 177-179.

Freud, S. (1922/1959). *Group psychology and the analysis of the ego.* London: Hogarth.

Friborg, O., Barlaug, D., Martinussen, M., Rosenvinge, J. H., & Hjemdal, O. (2005). Resilience in relation to personality and intelligence. *International Journal of Methods in Psychiatric Research, 14,* 29-42.

Friborg, O., Hjemdal, O., & Rosenvinge, J. H. (2006). Resilience as a moderator of pain and stress. *Journal of Psychosomatic Research, 61,* 213-219.

Friedman, J. N. W., Oltmanns, T. F., & Turkheimer, E. (2007). Interpersonal perception and personality disorders: Utilization of a thin slice approach. *Journal of Research in Personality, 41,* 667-688.

Frijda, N. H. (2005). Emotion experience. *Cognition and Emotion, 19,* 473-497.

Frodl, T., Janowitz, D., Schmaal, L., Tozzi, L., Dobrowolny, H., Stein, D. J., . . . Grabe, H. J. (2017). Childhood adversity impacts on brain subcortical structures relevant to depression. *Journal of Psychiatric Research, 86,* 58-65.

Frosch, A. (2011). The effect of frequency and duration on psychoanalytic outcome: A moment in time. *Psychoanalytic Review, 98,* 11-38.

Fryling, M. J. (2017). The functional independence of Skinner's verbal operants: Conceptual and applied implications. *Behavioral Interventions, 32,* 70-78.

Fuhrman, O., McCormick, K., Chen, E., Jiang, H., Shu, D., Mao, S., & Boroditsky, L. (2011). How linguistic and cultural forces shape conceptions of time: English and Mandarin time in 3D. *Cognitive Science: A Multidisciplinary Journal, 7,* 1305-1328.

Fujita, K., Nakamura, N., Watanabe, S., & Ushitani, T. (2017). Comparative visual illusions: Evolutionary, cross-cultural, and developmental perspectives. In J. Call, G. M. Burghardt, I. M. Pepperberg, C. T. Snowdon, & T. Zentall (Eds.), *APA handbook of comparative psychology: Perception, learning, and cognition.* Washington, DC: American Psychological Association.

Fuller, A. (2006). Hypnosis and ideomotor compliance in the treatment of smoking tobacco and cannabis. *Australian Journal of Clinical Hypnotherapy and Hypnosis, 27,* 14-18.

Furumoto, L., & Scarborough, E. (2002). Placing women in the history of psychology: The first American women psychologists. In W. E. Pickren (Ed.), *Evolving perspectives on the history of psychology.* Washington, DC: American Psychological Association.

Fusari, A., & Ballesteros, S. (2008, August). Identification of odors of edible and nonedible stimuli as affected by age and gender. *Behavior Research Methods, 40,* 752-759.

Gaab, J., Rohleder, N., Nater, U. M., & Ehlert, U. (2005). Psychological determinants of the cortisol stress response: The role of anticipatory cognitive appraisal. *Psychoneuroendocrinology, 30,* 599-610.

Gabbiadini, A., & Greitemeyer, T. (2017). Uncovering the association between strategy video games and self-regulation: A correlational study. *Personality and Individual Differences, 104,* 129-136

Gadbois, S. A., & Sturgeon, R. D. (2011). Academic self-handicapping: Relationships with learning specific and general self-perceptions and academic performance over time. *British Journal of Educational Psychology, 81,* 207-222.

Gade, M., Souza, A. S., Druey, M. D., & Oberauer, K. (2017). Analogous selection processes in declarative and procedural working memory: N-2 list-repetition and task-repetition costs. *Memory & Cognition, 45,* 26-39.

Gafner, G. (2013). Review of Subliminal: How your unconscious mind rules your behavior. *American Journal of Clinical Hypnosis, 56,* 192-193.

Galambos, N. L., Fang, S., Krahn, H. J., Johnson, M. D., & Lachman, M. E. (2015). Up, not down: The age curve in happiness from early adulthood to midlife in two longitudinal studies. *Developmental Psychology, 51*(11), 1664-1671.

Galanter, M. (2007). Spirituality and recovery in 12-step programs: An empirical model. *Journal of Substance Abuse Treatment, 33,* 265-272.

Galdi, G. (2015). Celebrating the 75th anniversary of the *American Journal of Psychoanalysis. American Journal of Psychoanalysis, 75,* 1-2.

Galef, D. (2001, April 27). The information you provide is anonymous, but what was your name again? *Chronicle of Higher Education, 47,* p. B5.

Gallese, V., Gernsbacher, M. A., Heyes, C., Hickok, G., & Iacoboni, M. (2011). Mirror neuron forum. *Perspectives on Psychological Science, 6,* 369-407.

Gallo, M. M. (2015). *'No one helped': Kitty Genovese, New York City, and the myth of urban apathy.* New York: Cornell University Press.

Gallup Poll. (2005, June 16). Three in four Americans believe in paranormal.

Gandolphe, M., & El Haj, M. (2017). Flashbulb memories of the Paris attacks. *Scandinavian Journal of Psychology, 58,* 199-204.

Gangestad, S. W., Simpson, J. A., Cousins, A. J., Garver-Apgar, C. E., & Christensen, P. N. (2004). Women's preferences for male behavioral displays change across the menstrual cycle. *Psychological Science, 15,* 203-207.

Gao, Y., Schneider, B., & Li, L. (2017). The effects of the binocular disparity differences between targets and maskers on visual search. *Attention, Perception, & Psychophysics, 79,* 459-472.

Garber, J., & Horowitz, J. L. (2002). Depression in children. In I. H. Gotlib & C. L. Hammen (Eds.), *Handbook of depression.* New York: Guilford Press.

Garcia, J. (2003). Psychology is not an enclave. In R. J. Sternberg (Ed.), *Psychologists defying the crowd: Stories of those who battled the establishment and won.* Washington, DC: American Psychological Association.

Garcia, L. (2017, May 31). State of mind episode 5: Out of the depths. *CBS News.* Accessed at https://www.cbsnews.com/news/depression-neurosurgery-dbs-mental-health-uncharted-state-of-mind-episode-5/.

Garcia, S. M., Weaver, K., Moskowitz, G. B., & Darley, J. M. (2002). Crowded minds: The implicit bystander effect. *Journal of Personality and Social Psychology, 83,* 843-853.

García-Palacios, A., Hoffman, H., & Carlin, A. (2002). Virtual reality in the treatment of spider phobia: A controlled study. *Behavior Research & Therapy, 40,* 983-993.

García-Herrero, S., Mariscal, M. A., Gutiérrez, J. M., & Ritzel, D. O. (2013). Using Bayesian networks to analyze occupational stress caused by work demands: Preventing stress through social support. *Accident Analysis and Prevention, 57,* 114-123.

Gardini, S., Cornoldi, C., De Beni, R., & Venneri, A. (2009). Cognitive and neuronal processes involved in sequential generation of general and specific mental images. *Psychological Research/Psychologische Forschung, 73,* 633-643.

Gardner, B., & O'Connor, D. (2008). A review of the cognitive effects of electroconvulsive therapy in older adults. *Journal of ECT, 24,* 68-80.

Gardner, E. P., & Kandel, E. R. (2000). Touch. In E. R. Kandel, J. H. Schwartz, & T. M. Jessell (Eds.), *Principles of neural science* (4th ed.). New York: McGraw-Hill.

Gardner, F., & Moore, Z. (2008). Understanding clinical anger and violence: The anger avoidance model. *Behavior Modification, 32,* 897-912.

Gardner, H. (1999). *Intelligence reframed: Multiple intelligences for the 21st century.* New York: Basic Books.

Gardner, H. (2000). The giftedness matrix: A developmental perspective. In R. C. Friedman & B. M. Shore (Eds.), *Talents unfolding: Cognition and development.* Washington, DC: American Psychological Association.

Garfield, J. (2014). Sad psychosurgery. *Brain: A Journal of Neurology, 137,* 1262-1265.

Garfin, D. R., Holman, E. A., & Silver, R. C. (2015). Cumulative exposure to prior collective trauma and acute stress responses to the Boston marathon bombings. *Psychological Science, 26,* 675-683.

Garlow, S. J., Purselle, D. C., & Heninger, M. (2007). Cocaine and alcohol use preceding suicide in African American and White adolescents. *Journal of Psychiatric Research, 41,* 530-536.

Garrigan, P., & Kellman, P. (2008, February). Perceptual learning depends on perceptual constancy. *PNAS Proceedings of the National Academy of Sciences of the United States of America, 105,* 2248-2253.

Garwick, G. B. (2007). Intelligence-related terms in mental retardation, learning disability, and gifted/talented professional usage, 1983–2001: The 1992 mental retardation redefinition as natural experiment. *Dissertation Abstracts International Section A: Humanities and Social Sciences, 67*(9-A), 3296.

Gass, C. S., Luis, C. A., Meyers, T. L., & Kuljis, R. O. (2000). Familial Creutzfeldt-Jakob disease: A neuropsychological case study. *Archives of Clinical Neuropsychology, 15,* 165-175.

Gatchel, R. J., & Weisberg, J. N. (2000). *Personality characteristics of patients with pain.* Washington, DC: APA Books.

Gates, G.J. (2017, January 11). In U.S., more adults identifying as LGBT. Gallup Social & Policy Issues. Downloaded from http://news.gallup.com/poll/201731/lgbt-identification-rises.aspx.

Gaudiano, B. A., & Miller, I. W. (2013). The evidence-based practice of psychotherapy. *Clinical Psychology Review, 33,* 813-824.

Gazzaniga, M. S., Ivry, R. B., & Mangun, G. R. (2002). *Cognitive neuroscience: The biology of the mind* (2nd ed.). New York: W. W. Norton.

Gelbard-Sagiv, H., Mukamel, R., Harel, M., Malach, R., & Fried, I. (March 2008). Internally generated reactivation of single neurons in human hippocampus during free recall. *Science, 322,* 96-101.

Gelfand, M. M. (2000). Sexuality among older women. *Journal of Women's Health and Gender Based Medicine, 9*(Suppl. 1), S15-S20.

Geller, E. S. (2011). Psychological science and safety: Large-scale success at preventing occupational injuries and fatalities. *Psychological Science, 20,* 109-114.

Gelman, R., & Baillargeon, R. (1983). A review of some Piagetian concepts. In J. H. Flavell & E. M. Markman (Eds.), *Handbook of child psychology, Vol. 3: Cognitive development* (4th ed.). New York: Wiley.

Gelstein, S., Yeshurun, Y., Rozenkrantz, L., Shusha, S., Frumin, I., Roth, Y., & Sobel, N. (2011, January 14). Human tears contain a chemosignal. *Science, 331,* 226-230.

Genetic preprogramming

Gennaro, R. J. (2004). *Higher-order theories of consciousness: An anthology.* Amsterdam, Netherlands: John Benjamins.

Genovese, J. E. C. (2006). Piaget, pedagogy, and evolutionary psychology. *Evolutionary Psychology, 4,* 2127-2137.

Gentile, B., Grabe, S., Dolan-Pascoe, B., Twenge, J., Wells, B., & Maitino, A. (2009). Gender differences in domain-specific self-esteem: A meta-analysis. *Review of General Psychology, 13,* 34-45.

Gentner, D., Goldin, S., & Goldin-Meadow, S. (Eds.). (2003). *Language in mind: Advances in the study of language and cognition.* Cambridge, MA: MIT.

Gerdes, A., Uhl, G., & Alpers, G. (2009). Spiders are special: Fear and disgust evoked by pictures of arthropods. *Evolution and Human Behavior, 30,* 66-73.

Gershkoff-Stowe, L., Connell, B., & Smith, L. (2006). Priming overgeneralizations in two- and four-year-old children. *Journal of Child Language, 33,* 461-486.

Gerstel, N. (2005). In search of time. *Science, 308,* 204-205.

Geurten, M., Willems, S., Germain, S., & Meulemans, T. (2015). Less is more: The availability heuristic in early childhood. *British Journal of Developmental Psychology, 12,* 503-505.

Geyer, T., Gokce, A., & Müller, H. J. (2011). Reinforcement of inhibitory positional priming by spatial working memory contents. *Acta Psychologica, 137,* 235-242.

Ghahramani, Z. (2015). Probabilistic machine learning and artificial intelligence. *Nature, 521*(7553), 452-459.

Giacobbi, P. R., Jr. Lynn, T. K., Wetherington, J. M., Jenkins, J., Bodendorf, M., & Langley, B. (2004). Stress and coping during the transition to university for first-year female athletes. *Sports Psychologist, 18,* 1-20.

Giacomini, M., Baylis, F., & Robert, J. (2007). Banking on it: Public policy and the ethics of stem cell research and development. *Social Sciences Medicine, 22,* 88-84.

Gianaros, P. J., & Wager, T. D. (2015). Brain-body pathways linking psychological stress and physical health. *Current Directions in Psychological Science, 24,* 313-321.

Giannakakis, A., & Fritsche, I. (2011). Social identities, group norms, and threat: On the malleability of ingroup bias. *Personality and Social Psychology Bulletin, 37,* 82-93.

Giannopoulos, V. L., & Vella-Brodrick, D. A. (2011). Effects of positive interventions and orientations to happiness on subjective well-being. *The Journal of Positive Psychology, 6,* 95-105.

Gibb, K., Tunbridge, D., Chua, A., & Frederickson, N. (2007). Pathways to inclusion: Moving from special school to mainstream. *Educational Psychology in Practice, 23,* 109-127.

Gibbs, N. (2005, August 8). Being 13. *Time,* pp. 41-55.

Gibbs, W. W. (2002). From mouth to mind. *Scientific American, 287,* 26.

Gibson, S. (2013). Milgram's obedience experiments: A rhetorical analysis. *British Journal of Social Psychology, 52*, 290-309.

Giedd, J., Stockman, M., Weddle, C.,Liverpool, M., Alexander-Bloch, A., Wallace, G., Lee, N., Lalonde, F., & Lenroot, R. (2010). Anatomic magnetic resonance imaging of the developing child and adolescent brain and effects of genetic variation. *Neuropsychology Review, 20*, 349-361.

Gilbert, P. D. (2007). Spirituality and mental health: A very preliminary overview. *Current Opinions in Psychiatry, 20*, 594-598.

Gilboa, A., Winocur, G., & Rosenbaum, R. S. (2006). Hippocampal contributions to recollection in retrograde and anterograde amnesia. *Hippocampus, 16*, 966-980.

Gillam, B., Palmisano, S. A., & Govan, D. G. (2011). Depth interval estimates from motion parallax and binocular disparity beyond interaction space. *Perception, 40*, 39-49.

Gillan, C. M., & Sahakian, B. J. (2015). Which is the driver, the obsessions or the compulsions, in OCD? *Neuropsychopharmacology, 40*, 247-248.

Gillespie-Lynch, K., Brooks, P. J., Someki, F., Obeid, R., Shane-Simpson, C., Kapp, . . . Smith, D. S. (2015). Changing college students' conceptions of autism: An online training to increase knowledge and decrease stigma. *Journal of Autism and Developmental Disorders, 45*(8), 2553-2566.

Gilligan, C. (1996). The centrality of relationships in psychological development: A puzzle, some evidence, and a theory. In G. G. Noam & K. W. Fischer (Eds.), *Development and vulnerability in close relationships.* Hillsdale, NJ: Erlbaum.

Gilligan, C. (2004). Recovering psyche: Reflections on life-history and history. *Annual of Psychoanalysis, 32*, 131-147.

Gingrich, J.A., Malm, H., Ansorge, M.S., Brown, A., Sourander, A., Suri, D., . . . Weissman, M. M. (2017). New insights into how serotonin selective reuptake inhibitors shape the developing brain. *Brain Defects Research, 109*, 924-932.

Giovenco, D.P., & Delnevo, C.D. (2018). Prevalence of population smoking cessation by electronic cigarette use status in a national sample of recent smokers. *Addictive Behaviors, 76*, 129-134.

Giridharadas, A. (2014, May 24). The immigrant advantage. *The New York Times*, p. SR1.

Gizer, I. R., Ehlers, C. L., Vieten, C., Seaton-Smith, K. L., Feiler, H. S., Lee, J. V., & . . . Wilhelmsen, K. C. (2011). Linkage scan of alcohol dependence in the UCSF Family Alcoholism Study. *Drug and Alcohol Dependence, 113*, 125-132.

Gladwell, M. (2004, September 20). Annals of psychology: Personality, plus how corporations figure out who you are. *The New Yorker*, 42-45.

Glass, K., Flory, K., Hankin, B., Kloos, B., & Turecki, G. (2009). Are coping strategies, social support, and hope associated with psychological distress among Hurricane Katrina survivors? *Journal of Social and Clinical Psychology, 28*, 779-795.

Glass, O. M., Forester, B. P., & Hermida, A. P. (2017). Electroconvulsive therapy (ECT) for treating agitation in dementia (major neurocognitive disorder)–A promising option. *International Psychogeriatrics, 29*, 717-726.

Glicksohn, J., & Nahari, G. (2007). Interacting personality traits? Smoking as a test case. *European Journal of Personality, 21*, 225-234.

Glisky, E. L. (2007). Changes in cognitive function in human aging. In D. R. Riddle (Ed.), *Brain aging: Models, methods, and mechanisms.* Boca Raton, FL: CRC Press.

Golden, W. L. (2006). Hypnotherapy for anxiety, phobias and psychophysiological disorders. In R. A. Chapman (Ed.), *The clinical use of hypnosis in cognitive behavior therapy: A practitioner's casebook.* New York: Springer Publishing.

Golder, S. A., & Macy, M. W. (2011, September 30). Diurnal and seasonal mood vary with work, sleep, and day length across diverse cultures. *Science, 333*, 1878-1881.

Goldman, B. (2017, February 21). Brain-computer interface advance allows fast, accurate typing by people with paralysis. Retrieved from https://med.stanford.edu/news/all-news/2017/02/brain-computer-interface-allows-fast-accurate-typing-by-people-with-paralysis.html.

Goldstein, I. (2000). Female sexual arousal disorder: New insights. *International Journal of Impotence Research, 12*(Suppl. 4), S152-S157.

Goldstein, S. N. (2006). The exploration of spirituality and identity status in adolescence. *Dissertation Abstracts International: Section B: The Sciences and Engineering, 67* (6-B), 3481.

Golimbet, V. E., Alfimova, M. V., Gritsenko, I. K., & Ebstein, R. P. (2007). Relationship between dopamine system genes and extraversion and novelty seeking. *Neuroscience Behavior and Physiology, 37*, 601-606.

Gontkovsky, S. T. (2005). Neurobiological bases and neuropsychological correlates of aggression and violence. In J. P. Morgan (Ed.), *Psychology of aggression.* Hauppauge, NY: Nova Science Publishers.

Goode, E. (1999, April 13). If things taste bad, "phantoms" may be at work. *The New York Times*, pp. D1-D2.

Goodman, G., & Quas, J. (2008). Repeated interviews and children's memory: It's more than just how many. *Current Directions in Psychological Science, 17*, 386-390.

Goodwin, R., Costa, P., & Adonu, J. (2004). Social support and its consequences: 'Positive' and 'deficiency' values and their implications for support and self-esteem. *British Journal of Social Psychology, 43*, 465-474.

Gooren, L. (2006). The biology of human psychosexual differentiation. *Hormones and Behavior, 50*, 589-601.

Gopie, N., Craik, F. M., & Hasher, L. (2011). A double dissociation of implicit and explicit memory in younger and older adults. *Psychological Science, 22*, 634-640.

Gopnik, A., & Griffiths, T. (2017, August 20). What happens to creativity as we age? *The New York Times*, p. SR9.

Gopnik, A., Griffiths, T. L., & Lucas, C. G. (2015). When younger learners can be better (or at least more open-minded) than older ones. *Current Directions in Psychological Science, 24*(2), 87-92.

Gorton, R. N., & Erickson-Schroth, L. (2017). Hormonal and surgical treatment options for transgender men (female-to-male). *Psychiatric Clinics of North America, 40*, 79-97.

Gossop, M., Stewart, D., & Marsden, J. (2008). Attendance at Narcotics Anonymous and Alcoholics Anonymous meetings, frequency of attendance and substance use outcomes after residential treatment for drug dependence: A 5-year follow-up study. *Addiction, 103*, 119-125.

Goswami, I., & Urminsky, O. (2017). The dynamic effect of incentives on postreward task engagement. *Journal of Experimental Psychology: General, 146*, 1-19.

Gotlib, I. H., Krasnoperova, E., Yue, D. N., & Joorman, J. (2004). Attentional biases for negative interpersonal stimuli in clinical depression. *Journal of Abnormal Psychology, 113*, 127-135.

Goto, T., Ishibashi, Y., Kajimura, S., Oka, R., & Kusumi, T. (2015). Development of free will and determinism scale in Japanese. *Japanese Journal of Psychology, 86*, 32-41.

Gottesman, I. I., & Hanson, D. R. (2005). Human development: Biological and genetic processes. *Annual Review of Psychology, 56*, 263-286.

Gotts, S. J., Jo, H., Wallace, G. L., Saad, Z. S., Cox, R. W., & Martin, A. (2013). Two distinct forms of functional lateralization in the human brain. *PNAS Proceedings of the National Academy of Sciences of the United States of America, 110*, E3435-E3444.

Gould, R. L. (1978). *Transformations.* New York: Simon & Schuster.

Grady, C. L., St-Laurent, M., & Burianová, H. (2015). Age differences in brain activity related to unsuccessful declarative memory retrieval. *Brain Research, 161*, 230-47.

Grady, D., & Altman, L. K. (2008, December 29). Lessons for other smokers in Obama's efforts to quit. *The New York Times*, p. A12.

Grahek, N. (2007). *Feeling pain and being in pain* (2nd ed.). Cambridge, MA: MIT Press.

Granic, I., Hollenstein, T., & Dishion, T. (2003). Longitudinal analysis of flexibility and reorganization in early adolescence: A dynamic systems study of family interactions. *Developmental Psychology, 39*, 606-617.

Granic, I., Lobel, A., & Engels, R. E. (2014). The benefits of playing video games. *American Psychologist, 69*, 66-78.

Grann, J. D. (2007). Confidence in knowledge past: An empirical basis for a differential decay theory of very long-term memory monitoring. *Dissertation Abstracts International Section A: Humanities and Social Sciences, 67*, 2462.

Grant, A. (2008). Does intrinsic motivation fuel the prosocial fire? Motivational synergy in predicting persistence, performance, and productivity. *Journal of Applied Psychology, 93*, 48-58.

Grant, D. M., & Wingate, L. R. (2011). Cognitive-behavioral therapy. In C. Silverstein (Ed.), *The *initial psychotherapy interview: A gay man seeks treatment.* Amsterdam, Netherlands: Elsevier.

Gray, G. C. (2006). The regulation of corporate violations: Punishment, compliance, and the blurring of responsibility. *British Journal of Criminology, 46,* 875-892.

Green, J., Lynn, S., & Montgomery, G. (2008, January). Gender-related differences in hypnosis-based treatments for smoking: A follow-up meta-analysis. *American Journal of Clinical Hypnosis, 50,* 259-271.

Greenberg, G., & Rosenheck, R. (2008). Jail incarceration, homelessness, and mental health: A national study. *Psychiatric Services, 59,* 170-177.

Greenberg, L. S. (2015). Working with primary emotions. In *Emotion-focused therapy: Coaching clients to work through their feelings* (2nd ed.). Washington, DC: American Psychological Association.

Greenberg, R. M., & Kellner, C. H. (2005). Electroconvulsive therapy: A selected review. *The American Journal of Geriatric Psychiatry, 13,* 268-281.

Greenberg, R., & Goldman, E. (2009). Antidepressants, psychotherapy or their combination: Weighing options for depression treatments. *Journal of Contemporary Psychotherapy, 39,* 83-91.

Greene, J. D., & Paxton, J. M. (2009). Patterns of neural activity associated with honest and dishonest moral decisions. *PNAS Proceedings of the National Academy of Sciences of the United States of America, 106*(30), 12506-12511.

Greene, J. D., Sommerville, R. B., Nystrom, L. E., Darley, J. M., & Cohen, J. D. (2001). An fMRI investigation of emotional engagement in moral judgment. *Science, 293,* 2105-2108.

Greene, K. M., & Maggs, J. L. (2017). Academic time during college: Associations with mood, tiredness, and binge drinking across days and semesters. *Journal of Adolescence, 56,* 24-33.

Greenfield, B. L., & Tonigan, J. S. (2013). The general Alcoholics Anonymous tools of recovery: The adoption of 12-step practices and beliefs. *Psychology of Addictive Behaviors, 27,* 553-561.

Greenfield, S. (2002). Mind, brain and consciousness. *British Journal of Psychiatry, 181,* 91-93.

Greenspan, S. (2006). Functional concepts in mental retardation: Finding the natural essence of an artificial category. *Exceptionality, 14,* 205-224.

Greenwald, A. G., Nosek, B. A., & Sriram, N. (2006). Consequential validity of the implicit association test: Comment on Blanton and Jaccard. *American Psychologist, 61,* 56-61.

Greer, R. D., Dudek-Singer, J., & Gautreaux, G. (2006). Observational learning. *International Journal of Psychology, 41,* 486-499.

Gregory, R. L. (1978). *The psychology of seeing* (3rd ed.). New York: McGraw-Hill.

Gregory, R. L. (2008). Emmert's Law and the moon illusion. *Spatial Vision, 21,* 407-720.

Greitemeyer, T., & Sagioglou, C. (2017). Increasing wealth inequality may increase interpersonal hostility: The relationship between personal relative deprivation and aggression. *Journal of Social Psychology, 157*(6), 766-776.

Grenfell-Essam, R., Ward, G., & Tan, L. (2013). The role of rehearsal on the output order of immediate free recall of short and long lists. *Journal of Experimental Psychology: Learning, Memory, and Cognition, 39,* 317-347.

Grigg-Damberger, M. M. (2017). Ontogeny of sleep and its functions in infancy, childhood, and adolescence. In S. Nevšímalová, O. Bruni, S. Nevšímalová, & O. Bruni (Eds.), *Sleep disorders in children.* Cham, Switzerland: Springer International Publishing.

Griggs, R. A. (2015a). Psychology's lost boy: Will the real Little Albert please stand up? *Teaching Of Psychology, 42,* 14-18.

Griggs, R. A. (2015b). The Kitty Genovese story in introductory psychology textbooks: Fifty years later. *Teaching of Psychology, 42,* 149-152.

Griggs, R. A. (2017). Milgram's obedience study: A contentious classic reinterpreted. *Teaching of Psychology, 44,* 32-37.

Grigorenko, E. (2009). Speaking genes or genes for speaking? Deciphering the genetics of speech and language. *Journal of Child Psychology and Psychiatry, 50,* 116-125.

Grigorenko, E. L., & Dozier, M. (2013). Introduction to the special section on genomics. *Child Development, 84,* 6-16.

Grimes, T., & Bergen, L. (2008). The epistemological argument against a causal relationship between media violence and sociopathic behavior among psychologically well viewers. *American Behavioral Scientist, 51,* 1137-1154.

Grimm, J. W. (2011). Craving. In M. C. Olmstead (Ed.), *Animal models of drug addiction.* Totowa, NJ: Humana Press.

Gronholm, P., Rinne, J. O., Vorobyev, V., & Laine, M. (2005). Naming of newly learned objects: A PET activation study. *Brain Research and Cognitive Brain Research, 14,* 22-28.

Gross, D. M. (2006). *The secret history of emotion: From Aristotle's rhetoric to modern brain science.* Chicago: University of Chicago Press.

Gross, G., & Weiss, E. L. (2018). A call to the helping disciplines to deconstruct diversity and race: An essay on the social constructions of the "other." *International Journal for the Advancement of Counselling,* doi:10.1007/s10447-018-9344-0.

Grossberg, S. (2013). Adaptive Resonance Theory: How a brain learns to consciously attend, learn, and recognize a changing world. *Neural Networks, 47,* 88-94.

Grossmann, T., Striano, T., & Friederici, A. D. (2007). Developmental changes in infants' processing of happy and angry facial expressions: A neurobehavioral study. *Brain and Cognition, 64,* 30-41.

Grosso, M. (2015). The 'transmission' model of mind and body: A brief history. In E. F. Kelly, A. Crabtree, & P. Marshall (Eds.), *Beyond physicalism: Toward reconciliation of science and spirituality.* Lanham, MD: Rowman & Littlefield.

Groves, C. L., & Anderson, C. A. (2015). Video game violence and offline aggression. In E. Aboujaoude & V. Starcevic (Eds.), *Mental health in the digital age: Grave dangers, great promise.* New York: Oxford University Press.

Groves, R. M., Singer, E., Lepkowski, J. M., Heeringa, S. G., & Alwin, D. F. (2004). Survey methodology. In S. J. House, F. T. Juster, R. L. Kahn, H. Schuman, & E. Singer (Eds.), *A telescope on society: Survey research and social science at the University of Michigan and beyond.* Ann Arbor, MI: University of Michigan Press.

Gruber, R. P., & Block, R. A. (2017). Perception of scenes in different sensory modalities: A result of modal completion. *American Journal of Psychology, 130,* 23-34.

Gruber, T. R. (2013). Nature, nurture, and knowledge acquisition. *International Journal of Human-Computer Studies, 71,* 191-194.

Grundy, D. (2015). Principles and standards for reporting animal experiments in the *Journal of Physiology and Experimental Physiology. Journal of Physiology, 593,* 2547-2549.

Grünbaum, A. (2015). Critique of psychoanalysis. In S. Boag, L. W. Brakel, & V. Talvitie (Eds.), *Philosophy, science, and psychoanalysis: A critical meeting.* London: Karnac Books.

Grünert, U., Jusuf, P. R., Lee, S. S., & Nguyen, D. (2011). Bipolar input to melanopsin containing ganglion cells in primate retina. *Visual Neuroscience, 28,* 39-50.

Gu, C., Warkentin, S., Mais, L. A., & Carnell, S. (2017). Ethnic differences in parental feeding behaviors in UK parents of preschoolers. *Appetite, 113,* 398-404.

Guadagno, R. E., & Cialdini, R. B. (2002). Online persuasion: An examination of gender differences in computer-mediated interpersonal influence [Special issue: Groups and Internet]. *Group Dynamics, 6,* 38-51.

Guastella, A., Mitchell, P., & Dadds, M. (2008, January). Oxytocin increases gaze to the eye region of human faces. *Biological Psychiatry, 63,* 3-5.

Guiard, B. P., Chenu, F., Mansari, M., & Blier, P. (2011). Characterization of the electrophysiological properties of triple reuptake inhibitors on monoaminergic neurons. *International Journal of Neuropsychopharmacology, 14,* 211-223.

Guida, A., Tardieu, H., Le Bohec, O., & Nicolas, S. (2013). Are schemas sufficient to interpret the personalization effect? Only if long-term working memory backs up. *European Review of Applied Psychology/Revue Européenne De Psychologie Appliquée, 63,* 99-107.

Guidelines for the treatment of animals in behavioural research and teaching. (2017). *Animal Behaviour, 123,* i-ix.

Gupta, A., Love, A., Kilpatrick, L. A., Labus, J. S., Bhatt, R., Chang, L., . . . Mayer, E. A. (2017). Morphological brain measures of cortico-limbic inhibition related to resilience. *Journal of Neuroscience Research, 95*(9), 1760-1775. doi: 10.1002/jnr.24007.

Gupta, M. A. (2013). Review of somatic symptoms in post-traumatic stress disorder. *International Review of Psychiatry, 25,* 86-99.

Guttmacher Institute (2012). Facts on American teens' sources of Information about sex. Accessed at http://www.guttmacher.org/pubs/FB-Teen-Sex-Ed.html.

Guéguen, N., Marchand, M., Pascual, A., & Lourel, M. (2008). Foot-in-the-door technique using a courtship request: A field experiment. *Psychological Reports, 103*, 529-534.

Haas, H. S., Fuerst, M. P., Tönz, P., & Gubser-Ernst, J. (2015). Analyzing the psychological and social contents of evidence–Experimental comparison between guessing, naturalistic observation, and systematic analysis. *Journal of Forensic Sciences, 60*, 659-668.

Haberstick, B. C., Schmitz, S., Young, S. E., & Hewitt, J. K. (2005). Contributions of genes and environments to stability and change in externalizing and internalizing problems during elementary and middle school. *Behavior Genetics, 35*, 381-396.

Hadad, B., Maurer, D., & Lewis, T. L. (2017). The role of early visual input in the development of contour interpolation: The case of subjective contours. *Developmental Science, 20*, 25-32.

Hadiwijaya, H., Klimstra, T. A., Vermunt, J. K., Branje, S. T., & Meeus, W. J. (2017). On the development of harmony, turbulence, and independence in parent-adolescent relationships: A five-wave longitudinal study. *Journal of Youth and Adolescence, 46*, 1772-1788.

Haier, R. J., Colom, R., Schroeder, D. H., Condon, C. A., Tang, C., Eaves, E., & Head, K. (2009). Gray matter and intelligence factors: Is there a neuro-g? *Intelligence, 37*, 136-144.

Halford, S. (2006). Collapsing the boundaries? Fatherhood, organization and home-working. *Gender, Work & Organization, 13*, 383-402.

Halkitis, P. (2009). *Methamphetamine addiction: Biological foundations, psychological factors, and social consequences.* Washington, DC: American Psychological Association.

Hall, P. J., Chong, C., McNaughton, N., & Corr, P. J. (2011). An economic perspective on the reinforcement sensitivity theory of personality. *Personality and Individual Differences, 51*, 242-247.

Halpert, J. (2003, April 28). What do patients want? *Newsweek*, pp. 63-64.

Hamani, Y., Sciaki-Tamir, Y., Deri-Hasid, R., Miller-Pogrund, T., Milwidsky, A., & Haimov-Kochman, R. (2007). Misconceptions about oral contraception pills among adolescents and physicians. *Human Reproduction, 22*, 3078-3083.

Hamann, S. B., Ely, T. D., Hoffman, J. M., & Kilts, C. D. (2002). Ecstasy and agony: Activation of human amygdala in positive and negative emotion. *Psychological Science, 13*, 135-141.

Hambleton, R. K. (2006). Psychometric models, test designs and item types for the next generation of educational and psychological tests. In D. Bartram & R. K. Hambleton (Eds.), *Computer-based testing and the Internet: Issues and advances.* New York: John Wiley & Sons.

Hambleton, R. K., & Zenisky, A. L. (2013). Reporting test scores in more meaningful ways: A research-based approach to score report design. In K. F. Geisinger, B. A. Bracken, J. F. Carlson, J. C. Hansen, N. R. Kuncel, S. P. Reise, & M. C. Rodriguez (Eds.), *APA handbook of testing and assessment in psychology, Vol. 3: Testing and assessment in school psychology and education.* Washington, DC: American Psychological Association.

Hamer, M., Taylor, A., & Steptoe, A. (2006). The effect of acute aerobic exercise on stress related blood pressure responses: A systematic review and meta-analysis. *Bi Psychology, 71*, 183-190.

Hamilton, A. C., & Martin, R. C. (2007). Semantic short-term memory deficits and resolution of interference: A case for inhibition? In D. S. Gorfein & C. M. Macleod (Eds.), *Inhibition in cognition.* Washington, DC: American Psychological Association.

Hamilton, L. K., Joppé, S. E., Cochard, L. M., & Fernandes, K. L. (2013). Aging and neurogenesis in the adult forebrain: What we have learned and where we should go from here. *European Journal of Neuroscience, 37*, 1978-1986.

Hammond, D. C. (2007, April). Review of the efficacy of clinical hypnosis with headaches and migraines [Special issue: Evidence-based practice clinical hypnosis–part 1]. *International Journal of Clinical and Experimental Hypnosis 55*, 207-219.

Han, S., & Ma, Y. (2014). Cultural differences in human brain activity: a quantitative meta-analysis. *Neuroimage, 99*, 293-300.

Han, S., & Ma, Y. (2015). A culture-behavior-brain loop model of human development. *Trends in Cognitive Sciences, 19*(11), 666-676.

Haney, C., & Zimbardo, P. (2009). Persistent dispositionalism in interactionist clothing: Fundamental attribution error in explaining prison abuse. *Personality and Social Psychology Bulletin, 35*, 807-814.

Hangya, B., Tihanyi, B. T., Entz, L., Fabo, D., Erőss, L., Wittner, L., & . . . Ulbert, I. (2011). Complex propagation patterns characterize human cortical activity during slow-wave sleep. *The Journal of Neuroscience, 31*, 8770-8779.

Hanna-Pladdy, B., Pahwa, R., & Lyons, K. E. (2015). Paradoxical effect of dopamine medication on cognition in Parkinson's disease: Relationship to side of motor onset. *Journal of the International Neuropsychological Society, 21*, 259-270.

Hannon, E. E., & Johnson, S. P. (2005). Infants use meter to categorize rhythms and melodies: Implications for musical structure learning. *Cognitive Psychology, 50*, 354-377.

Hao Z., Mumphrey M. B., Townsend R. L., Morrison, C. D., Munzberg, H., Ye, J., & Berthoud, H. R. (2016). Reprogramming of defended body weight after Roux-En-Y gastric bypass surgery in diet-induced obese mice. *Obesity, 24*, 654-660.

Harden, R., Oaklander, A., Burton, A. W., Perez, R. M., Richardson, K., Swan, M., & . . . Bruehl, S. (2013). Complex regional pain syndrome: Practical diagnostic and treatment guidelines, 4th edition. *Pain Medicine, 14*, 180-229.

Harding, D. J., & Jencks, C. (2003). Changing attitudes toward premarital sex: Cohort, period, and aging effects. *Public Opinion Quarterly, 67*, 211-226.

Hardison, D. M. (2006). Review of phonetics and phonology in language comprehension and production: Differences and similarities. *Studies in Second Language Acquisition, 28*, 138-140.

Hardt, J., Sidor, A., Nickel, R., Kappis, B., Petrak, P., & Egle, U. (2008). Childhood adversities and suicide attempts: A retrospective study. *Journal of Family Violence, 23*, 713-718.

Hardt, O., Nader, K., & Nadel, L. (2013). Decay happens: The role of active forgetting in memory. *Trends in Cognitive Sciences, 17*, 111-120.

Hardy, L. T. (2007). Attachment theory and reactive attachment disorder: Theoretical perspectives and treatment implications. *Journal of Child and Adolescent Psychiatric Nursing, 20*, 27-39.

Haridi, M., Weyn Banningh, S., Clé, M., Leu-Semenescu, S., Vidailhet, M., & Arnulf, I. (2017). Is there a common motor dysregulation in sleepwalking and REM sleep behaviour disorder? *Journal of Sleep Research. 26*(5), 614-622.

Hariri, A. R. (2015). *Looking inside the disordered brain: An introduction to the functional neuroanatomy of psychopathology.* Sunderland, MA: Sinauer Associates.

Harlow, H. F., & Zimmerman, R. R. (1959). Affectional responses in the infant monkey. *Science, 130*, 421-432.

Harlow, J. M. (1869). Recovery from the passage of an iron bar through the head. *Massachusetts Medical Society Publication, 2*, 329-347.

Harmer, C. J., Duman, R. S., & Cowen, P. J. (2017). How do antidepressants work? New perspectives for refining future treatment approaches. *The Lancet Psychiatry, 4*, 409-418.

Harmon-Jones, E., & Winkielman, P. (2007). *Social neuroscience: Integrating biological and psychological explanations of social behavior.* New York, NY: Guilford Press.

Harmon-Jones, E., Harmon-Jones, C., & Levy, N. (2015). An action-based model of cognitive-dissonance processes. *Current Directions In Psychological Science, 24*, 184-189.

Harper, T. (1978, November 15). It's not true about people 65 or over. *Green Bay Press-Gazette* (Wisconsin), p. D-1.

Hart, B., & Risley, T. R. (1997). Use of language by three-year-old children. Courtesy of Drs. Betty Hart and Todd Risley, University of Kansas.

Hartshorne, J., & Germine, L. (2015). When does cognitive functioning peak? The asynchronous rise and fall of different cognitive abilities across the life span. *Psychological Science, 26*, 433-443.

Harvey, J. H., Wenzel, A., & Sprecher, S. (Eds.). (2004). *The handbook of sexuality in close relationships.* Mahwah, NJ: Lawrence Erlbaum Associates.

Harvie, D. S., Moseley, G. L., Hillier, S. L., & Meulders, A. (2017). Classical conditioning differences associated with chronic pain: A systematic review. *The Journal of Pain, 18*(8), 889-898.

Hass, R. W. (2017). Tracking the dynamics of divergent thinking via semantic distance: Analytic methods and theoretical implications. *Memory & Cognition, 45*, 233-244.

Hastings, R. P., & Oakford, S. (2003). Student teachers' attitudes towards the inclusion of children with special needs. *Educational Psychology, 23,* 87-94.

Hattori, S., Kishida, I., Suda, A., Miyauchi, M., Shiraishi, Y., Fujibayashi, M., . . . Hirayasu, Y. (2017). Effects of four atypical antipsychotics on autonomic nervous system activity in schizophrenia. *Schizophrenia Research.* Accessed at https://www.ncbi.nlm.nih.gov/pubmed/28709776.

Hauke, C. (2006). The unconscious: Personal and collective. In R. K. Papadopoulos (Ed.), *The handbook of Jungian psychology: Theory, practice and applications.* New York: Routledge.

Havermans, R. C., Mulkens, S., Nederkoorn, C., & Jansen, A. (2007). The efficacy of cue exposure with response prevention in extinguishing drug and alcohol cue reactivity. *Behavioral Interventions, 22,* 121-135.

Haviland-Jones, J. M., & Wilson, P. J. (2008). A 'nose' for emotion: Emotional information and challenges in odors and semiochemicals. In M. Lewis, J. M. Haviland-Jones, & L. G. Barrett (Eds.), *Handbook of emotions* (3rd ed.). New York: Guilford Press.

Hayes, S. C. (2015). Humanistic psychology and contextual behavioral perspectives. In K. J. Schneider, J. F. Pierson, & J. T. Bugental (Eds.), *The handbook of humanistic psychology: Theory, research, and practice* (2nd ed.). Thousand Oaks, CA: Sage Publications, Inc.

Hayflick, L. (2007). Biological aging is no longer an unsolved problem. *Annals of the New York Academy of Sciences, 1100,* 1-13.

Hays, P. A. (2008). *Addressing cultural complexities in practice: Assessment, diagnosis, and therapy* (2nd ed.). Washington, DC: American Psychological Association.

Hayward, R., & Elliott, M. (2011). Subjective and objective fit in religious congregations: Implications for well-being. *Group Processes & Intergroup Relations, 14,* 127-139.

Heath, M., & Manzone, J. (2017). Manual estimations of functionally graspable target objects adhere to Weber's law. *Experimental Brain Research, 235,* 1701-1707.

Heathcote, A., Coleman, J. R., Eidels, A., Watson, J. M., Houpt, J., & Strayer, D. L. (2015). Working memory's workload capacity. *Memory & Cognition, 43,* 973-989.

Heatherton, T., & Sargent, J. (2009). Does watching smoking in movies promote teenage smoking? *Current Directions in Psychological Science, 18,* 63-67.

Hecht, J. M. (2007). *The happiness myth: Why what we think is right is wrong. A history of what really makes us happy.* New York: HarperSanFrancisco/HarperCollins.

Hedges, D. W., Brown, B. L., Shwalk, D. A., Godfrey, K., & Larcher, A. M. (2007). The efficacy of selective serotonin reuptake inhibitors in adult social anxiety disorder: A meta-analysis of double-blind, placebo-controlled trials. *Journal of Psychopharmacology, 21,* 102-111.

Heffernan, M. E., & Fraley, R. C. (2015). How early experiences shape attraction, partner preferences, and attachment dynamics. In V. Zayas & C. Hazan (Eds.), *Bases of adult attachment: Linking brain, mind and behavior.* New York: Springer Science + Business Media.

Hegarty, P., & Massey, S. (2007). Anti-homosexual prejudice . . . as opposed to what? Queer theory and the social psychology of anti-homosexual attitudes. *Journal of Homosexuality, 52,* 47-71.

Heilman, K. M. (2005). *Creativity and the brain.* New York: Psychology Press.

Heinrichs, R. W. (2005). The primacy of cognition in schizophrenia. *American Psychologist, 60,* 229-242.

Heintz, M. M., Brander, S. M., & White, J. W. (2015). Endocrine disrupting compounds alter risk-taking behavior in guppies (Poecilia reticulata). *Ethology, 121,* 480-491.

Heitzmann, C. A., Merluzzi, T. V., Jean-Pierre, P., Roscoe, J. A., Kirsh, K. L., & Passik, S. D. (2011). Assessing self-efficacy for coping with cancer: Development and psychometric analysis of the brief version of the Cancer Behavior Inventory (CBI-B). *Psycho-Oncology, 20,* 302-312.

Helgeson, V. S., & Zajdel, M. (2017). Adjusting to chronic health conditions. *Annual Review of Psychology, 68,* 545-571.

Heller, H. C., Ruby, N. F., Rolls, A., Makam, M., & Colas, D. (2014). Adaptive and pathological inhibition of neuroplasticity associated with circadian rhythms and sleep. *Behavioral Neuroscience, 128,* 273-282.

Helsen, K., Goubert, L., & Vlaeyen, J. S. (2013). Observational learning and pain-related fear: Exploring contingency learning in an experimental study using colored warm water immersions. *The Journal of Pain, 14,* 676-688.

Henckes, N. (2011). Reforming psychiatric institutions in the mid-twentieth century: A framework for analysis. *History of Psychiatry, 22,* 164-181.

Hennessy, M. B., & Shair, H. N. (2017). Filial attachment: Development, mechanisms, and consequences. In J. Call, G. M. Burghardt, I. M. Pepperberg, C. T. Snowdon, & T. Zentall (Eds.), *APA handbook of comparative psychology: Basic concepts, methods, neural substrate, and behavior.* Washington, DC: American Psychological Association.

Hennig-Fast, K., Meister, F., Frodl, T., Beraldi, A., Padberg, F., Engel, R., et al. (2008). The case of persistent retrograde amnesia following a dissociative fugue: Neuropsychological and neurofunctional underpinnings of loss of autobiographical memory and self-awareness. *Neuropsychologia, 46*(12), 2993-3005.

Henningsen, D. D., Henningsen, M. L., & Eden, J. (2006). Examining the symptoms of groupthink and retrospective sensemaking. *Small Group Research, 37,* 36-64.

Henrich, J., Heine, S., and Norenzayan, A. (2010). The weirdest people in the world? *Behavioral and Brain Sciences, 33,* 61-83.

Henry, D., McClellen, D., Rosenthal, L., Dedrick, D., & Gosdin, M. (2008, February). Is sleep really for sissies? Understanding the role of work in insomnia in the US. *Social Science & Medicine, 66,* 715-726.

Herbenick, D., Reece, M., Sanders, S., Dodge, B., Ghassemi, A., & Fortenberry, J. (2009). Prevalence and characteristics of vibrator use by women in the United States: Results from a nationally representative study. *Journal of Sexual Medicine, 6,* 1857-1866.

Herbert, W. (2011). *On second thought: Outsmarting your mind's hard-wired habits.* New York: Broadway.

Hernández-Orallo, J. (2017). *The measure of all minds: Evaluating natural and artificial intelligence.* New York: Cambridge University Press.

Herrnstein, R. J., & Murray, D. (1994). *The bell curve.* New York: Free Press.

Herskovits, M. (2018). *Acculturation: A study of culture contact.* New York: Moat Portultis.

Herting, M. M., & Sowell, E. R. (2017). Puberty and structural brain development in humans. *Frontiers in Neuroendocrinology, 44,* 122-137.

Hertzog, C., Kramer, A., Wilson, R., & Lindenberger, U. (2008). Enrichment effects on adult cognitive development: Can the functional capacity of older adults be preserved and enhanced? *Psychological Science in the Public Interest, 9,* 1-65.

Herzberg, L. (2009). Direction, causation, and appraisal theories of emotion. *Philosophical Psychology, 22,* 167-186.

Herzog, H. (2017). The ethics of behavioral research using animals: A classroom exercise. In J. R. Stowell & W. E. Addison (Eds.), *Activities for teaching statistics and research methods: A guide for psychology instructors.* Washington, DC: American Psychological Association.

Heshka, S., Anderson, J. W., Atkinson, R. L., Greenway, F. L., Hill, J. O., Phinney, S. D., . . . Pi-Sunyer, F. X. (2003). Weight loss with self-help compared with a structured commercial program: A randomized trial. *Journal of the American Medical Association, 289,* 1792-1798.

Hess, M. J., Houg, S., & Tammaro, E. (2007). The experience of four individuals with paraplegia enrolled in an outpatient interdisciplinary sexuality program. *Sexuality and Disability, 25,* 189-195.

Hetzel-Riggin, M. D. (2017). A study of the impact of informed consent procedures on participant responses in trauma-related research. *Journal of Loss and Trauma, 22,* 36-46.

Hewitt, E. (2017, June 4). Fentanyl takes a deadly toll on Vermont. Retrieved from https://vtdigger.org/2017/06/04/hollywood-heroin-hits-vermont/.

Hickok, G. (2015, May 10). Rhythms of the brain. *New York Times,* p. SR 9.

Higgs, S. (2015). Social norms and their influence on eating behaviours. *Appetite, 86,* 38-44.

Hilarski, C. (2007). Antisocial personality disorder. In B. A. Thyer & J. S. Wodarski (Eds.), *Social work in mental health: An evidence-based approach.* Hoboken, NJ: John Wiley & Sons.

Hilbert, S., Schwaighofer, M., Zech, A., Sarubin, N., Arendasy, M., & Bühner, M. (2017). Working memory tasks train working memory but not reasoning: A material- and operation-specific investigation of transfer from working memory practice. *Intelligence, 61,* 102-114.

Hill, B. D., Foster, J. D., Elliott, E. M., Shelton, J., McCain, J., & Gouvier, W. (2013). Need for cognition is related to higher general intelligence, fluid intelligence, and crystallized intelligence, but not working memory. *Journal of Research in Personality, 47,* 22-25.

Hilton, R. C., Rengasamy, M., Mansoor, B., He, J., Mayes, T., Emslie, G. J., & . . . Brent, D. A. (2013). Impact of treatments for depression on comorbid anxiety, attentional, and behavioral symptoms in adolescents with selective serotonin reuptake inhibitor-resistant depression. *Journal of the American Academy of Child & Adolescent Psychiatry, 52,* 482-492.

Hines, M. (2004). *Brain gender.* New York: Oxford University Press.

Hinterberger, T., Schöner, J., & Halsband, U. (2011). Analysis of electrophysiological state patterns and changes during hypnosis induction. *International Journal of Clinical and Experimental Hypnosis, 59,* 165-179.

Hirschberger, G., Pyszczynski, T., & Ein-Dor, T. (2010). An ever-dying people: The existential underpinnings of Israelis' perceptions of war and conflict. *Cahiers Internationaux de Psychologie Sociale, 87*(3), 443-457. doi:10.3917/cips.087.0443.

Hirsh, I. J., & Watson, C. S. (1996). Auditory psychophysics and perception. *Annual Review of Psychology, 47,* 461-484.

Hirst, W., Phelps, E. A., Meksin, R., Vaidya, C. J., Johnson, M. K., Mitchell, K. J., & . . . Olsson, A. (2015). A ten-year follow-up of a study of memory for the attack of September 11, 2001: Flashbulb memories and memories for flashbulb events. *Journal of Experimental Psychology: General, 144,* 604-623.

Ho, S. M. Y., Saltel, P., Machavoine, J., Rapoport-Hubschman, N., & Spiegel, D. (2004). Cross-cultural aspects of cancer care. In National Institutes of Health and Stanford University School of Medicine, *Cancer, culture, and communication.* New York: Kluwer Academic/Plenum Publishers.

Hobson, J. A. (2005). In bed with Mark Solms? What a nightmare! A reply to Domhoff (2005). *Dreaming, 15,* 21-29.

Hobson, J. A. (2007). States of conciseness: Normal and abnormal variation. In P. D. Zelazo, M. Moscovitch, & E. Thompson (Eds.), *The Cambridge Handbook of Consciousness.* London: Cambridge University Press.

Hobson, K. (2011, March 28). How can you help the medicine go down? *Wall Street Journal,* R10.

Hochschild, A. (2001, February). A generation without public passion. *Atlantic Monthly,* pp. 33-42.

Hoenen, M., Lübke, K. T., & Pause, B. M. (2017). Sensitivity of the human mirror neuron system for abstract traces of actions: An EEG-study. *Biological Psychology, 124,* 57-64.

Hofeditz, M., Nienaber, A., Dysvik, A., & Schewe, G. (2017). "Want to" versus "have to": Intrinsic and extrinsic motivators as predictors of compliance behavior intention. *Human Resource Management, 56,* 25-49.

Hofer, J., Busch, H., Raihala, C., Šolcová, I. P., & Tavel, P. (2017). The higher your implicit affiliation-intimacy motive, the more loneliness can turn you into a social cynic: A cross-cultural study. *Journal of Personality, 85,* 179-191.

Hoff, E. (2003). Language development in childhood. In I. Weiner, R. M. Lerner, M. A. Easterbrooks, & J. Mistry (Eds.), *Handbook of psychology: Developmental psychology* (Vol. 6). New York: Wiley.

Hoff, E. (2008). *Language development.* New York: Wadsworth.

Hofmann, S. G. (2007). Enhancing exposure-based therapy from a translational research perspective. *Behaviour Research and Therapy, 45,* 1987-2001.

Hofmann, W., Gschwendner, T., Castelli, L., & Schmitt, M. (2008). Implicit and explicit attitudes and interracial interaction: The moderating role of situationally available control resources. *Group Processes & Intergroup Relations, 11,* 69-87.

Hogan, J., Davies, S., & Hogan, R. (2007). Generalizing personality-based validity evidence. In S. M. McPhail (Ed.), *Alternative validation strategies: Developing new and leveraging existing validity evidence.* Hoboken, NJ: John Wiley & Sons.

Hogg, M. A. (2006). Social identity theory. In P. J. Burke (Ed.), *Contemporary social psychological theories.* Palo Alto, CA: Stanford University Press.

Hogg, M. A., & Hains, S. C. (2001). Intergroup relations and group solidarity: Effects of group identification and social beliefs on depersonalized attraction. In M. A. Hogg & D. Abrams (Eds.), *Intergroup relations: Essential readings.* New York: Psychology Press.

Holden, C. (2003, January 17). Deconstructing schizophrenia. *Science, 299,* 333-335.

Holden, C. (2007, June 29). Embryonic stem cells. Stem cell science advances as politics stall. *Science, 316,* 1825.

Holland, J. C., & Lewis, S. (2001). *The human side of cancer: Living with hope, coping with uncertainty.* New York: Quill.

Holleran, S., Mehl, M., & Levitt, S. (2009). Eavesdropping on social life: The accuracy of stranger ratings of daily behavior from thin slices of natural conversations. *Journal of Research in Personality, 43,* 660-672.

Hollingworth, H. L. (1943/1990). *Leta Stetter Hollingworth: A biography.* Boston: Anker.

Hollins, K. (2007). Consequences of antenatal mental health problems for child health and development. *Current Opinions on Obstetric Gynecology, 19,* 568-573.

Holloway, L. (2000, December 16). Chief of New York City schools plans to revamp bilingual study. *The New York Times,* p. A1.

Holmes, A. (2017). Drug addictions: New insight into causes, comorbidity and potential treatments. *Genes, Brain & Behavior, 16,* 5-7.

Holowka, S., & Petitto, L. A. (2002, August 30). Left hemisphere cerebral specialization for babies while babbling. *Science, 297,* 1515.

Holtyn, A. F., & Lattal, K. A. (2013). Briefly delayed reinforcement effects on variable "ratio and yoked" interval schedule performance. *Journal of the Experimental Analysis of Behavior, 100,* 198-210.

Holtz, J. (2011). *Applied clinical neuropsychology: An introduction.* NY: Springer Publishing Co.

Holzhauer, C. G., Wemm, S., & Wulfert, E. (2017). Distress tolerance and physiological reactivity to stress predict women's problematic alcohol use. *Experimental and Clinical Psychopharmacology, 25,* 156-165.

Hongchun, W., & Ming, L. (2006). About the research on suggestibility and false memory. *Psychological Science (China), 29,* 905-908.

Hopkins, W., & Cantalupo, C. (2008, June). Theoretical speculations on the evolutionary origins of hemispheric specialization. *Current Directions in Psychological Science, 17,* 233-237.

Hopwood, C., Newman, D., Donnellan, M., Markowitz, J., Grilo, C., Sanislow, C., et al. (2009). The stability of personality traits in individuals with borderline personality disorder. *Journal of Abnormal Psychology, 118,* 806-815.

Horesh, D., Solomon, Z., Zerach, G., & Ein-Dor, T. (2011). Delayed-onset PTSD among war veterans: The role of life events throughout the life cycle. *Social Psychiatry and Psychiatric Epidemiology, 46,* 863-870.

Hori, H., Teraishi, T., Sasayama, D., Matsuo, J., Kawamoto, Y., Kinoshita, Y., & Kunugi, H. (2011). Relationships between season of birth, schizotypy, temperament, character and neurocognition in a non-clinical population. *Psychiatry Research, 189,* 388-397.

Horiguchi, H., Winawer, J., Dougherty, R. F., & Wandell, B. A. (2013). Human trichromacy revisted. *Proceedings of the National Academy of Sciences, 110,* 199-106.

Horney, K. (1937). *Neurotic personality of our times.* New York: Norton.

Hornsveld, R. J., Zwets, A. J., Leenaars, E. M., Kraaimaat, F. W., Bout, R., Lagro-Janssen, T. M., & Kanters, T. (2018). Violent female offenders compared with violent male offenders on psychological determinants of aggressive behavior. *International Journal of Offender Therapy and Comparative Criminology, 62*(2), 450-467. doi:10.1177/0306624X16648109.

Horton, C. L. (2011). Recall and recognition of dreams and waking events: A diary paradigm. *International Journal of Dream Research, 4,* 8-16.

Horton, K. D., Wilson, D. E., Vonk, J., Kirby, S. L., & Nielsen, T. (2005). Measuring automatic retrieval: A comparison of implicit memory, process dissociation, and speeded response procedures. *Acta Psychologica, 119,* 235-263.

Houghtalen, R. P., & Talbot, N. (2007). Dissociative disorders and cognitive disorders. In O. J. Z. Sahler & J. E. Carr (Eds.), *The behavioral sciences and health care* (2nd rev. and updated ed.). Ashland, OH: Hogrefe & Huber Publishers, 2007.

Hounkpatin, H. O., Wood, A. M., Boyce, C. J., & Dunn, G. (2015). An existential-humanistic view of personality change: Co-occurring changes with psychological well-being in a 10 year cohort study. *Social Indicators Research, 121,* 455-470.

Howe, M. L. (2011). The adaptive nature of memory and its illusions. *Psychological Science, 20,* 312-315.

Howell, E. F. (2011). *Understanding and treating dissociative identity disorder: A relational approach.* New York: Routledge/Taylor & Francis Group.

Howes, O. D., McCutcheon, R., Owen, M. J., & Murray, R. M. (2017). The role of genes, stress, and dopamine in the development of schizophrenia. *Biological Psychiatry, 81*(1), 9-20.

Howes, O., & Kapur, S. (2009). The dopamine hypothesis of schizophrenia: Version III—The final common pathway. *Schizophrenia Bulletin, 35,* 549-562.

Hu, E. B., Li, T. Y., Colditz, G. A., Willett, W. C., & Manson, J. E. (2003). Television watching and other sedentary behaviors in relation to risk of obesity and type 2 diabetes mellitus in women. *Journal of the American Medical Association, 289,* 1785-1791.

Huang, H., & Kashubeck-West, S. (2015). Exposure, agency, perceived threat, and guilt as predictors of posttraumatic stress disorder in veterans. *Journal of Counseling & Development, 93,* 3-13.

Huang, L. M., Sacchi, D. M., & Sherman, J. W. (2017). On the formation of context-based person impressions. *Journal of Experimental Social Psychology, 68,* 146-156.

Huang, S., Etkin, J., & Jin, L. (2017). How winning changes motivation in multiphase competitions. *Journal of Personality and Social Psychology, 112,* 813-837.

Hubbard, K., O'Neill, A., & Cheakalos, C. (1999, April 12). Out of control. *People,* 52-72.

Hubel, D. H., & Wiesel, T. N. (2004). *Brain and visual perception: The story of a 25-year collaboration.* New York: Oxford University Press.

Hudson, J. I., Coit, C. E., Lalonde, J. K., & Pope, H. G. (2012). By how much will the proposed new DSM-5 criteria increase the prevalence of binge eating disorder? *International Journal of Easting Disorders, 45,* 139-141.

Hudson, W. (1960). Pictorial depth perception in subcultural groups in Africa. *Journal of Social Psychology, 52,* 183-208.

Hudspeth, A. J. (2000). Hearing. In E. R. Kandel, J. H. Schwartz, & T. M. Jessell (Eds.), *Principles of neural science* (4th ed.). New York: McGraw-Hill.

Huesmann, L., Dubow, E. F., & Boxer, P. (2011). The transmission of aggressiveness across generations: Biological, contextual, and social learning processes. In P. R. Shaver & M. Mikulincer (Eds.), *Human aggression and violence: Causes, manifestations, and consequences.* Washington, DC: American Psychological Association.

Hugenberg, K., & Sacco, D. (2008). Social categorization and stereotyping: How social categorization biases person perception and face

memory. *Social and Personality Psychology Compass, 2,* 1052-1072.

Huijie, T. (2006). The measurement and assessment of mental health: A longitudinal and cross-sectional research on undergraduates, adults and patients. *Psychological Science (China), 29,* 419-422.

Hull, C. L. (1943). *Principles of behavior.* New York: Appleton-Century-Crofts.

Human, L. J., & Biesanz, J. C. (2011). Through the looking glass clearly: Accuracy and assumed similarity in well-adjusted individuals' first impressions. *Journal of Personality and Social Psychology, 100,* 349-364.

Hummer, T. A., & McClintock, M. K. (2009). Putative human pheromone androstadienone attunes the mind specifically to emotional information. *Hormones and Behavior, 55,* 548-559.

Humphrey, N., Curran, A., & Morris, E. (2007). Emotional intelligence and education: A critical review. *Educational Psychology, 27,* 235-254.

Hunt, E. (1994). Problem solving. In R. J. Sternberg (Ed.), *Thinking and problem solving: Handbook of perception and cognition* (2nd ed.). San Diego, CA: Academic Press.

Hunt, J. S., Seifert, A. L., & Armenta, B. E. (2006). Stereotypes and prejudice as dynamic constructs: Reminders about the nature of intergroup bias from the hurricane Katrina relief efforts. *Analyses of Social Issues and Public Policy (ASAP), 6,* 237-253.

Hunt, M. (1974). *Sexual behaviors in the 1970s.* New York: Dell.

Huprich, S. K., & Nelson, S. M. (2015). Advancing the assessment of personality pathology with the Cognitive-Affective Processing System. *Journal of Personality Assessment, 97,* 467-477.

Hurley, D. B., & Kwon, P. (2013). Savoring helps most when you have little: Interaction between savoring the moment and uplifts on positive affect and satisfaction with life. *Journal of Happiness Studies, 14,* 1261-1271.

Hurschler, M. A., Liem, F., Oechslin, M., Stämpfli, P., & Meyer, M. (2015). fMRI reveals lateralized pattern of brain activity modulated by the metrics of stimuli during auditory rhyme processing. *Brain And Language, 14,* 741-750.

Husain, O. (2015). From persecution to depression: A case of chronic depression—Associating the Rorschach, the TAT, and Winnicott. *Journal of Personality Assessment, 97,* 230-240.

Huston, J. P., Silva, M., Komorowski, M., Schulz, D., & Topic, B. (2013). Animal models of extinction-induced depression: Loss of reward and its consequences. *Neuroscience and Biobehavioral Reviews.* Retrieved from http://www.ncbi.nlm.nih.gov/pubmed/23466533.

Hwang, E., Kim, H., Lee, S., Kim, M., Lee, S., Han, S., . . . Park, J. (2017). Loganin enhances long-term potentiation and recovers scopolamine-induced learning and memory impairments. *Physiology & Behavior, 171,* 243-248.

Hyde, J., Mezulis, A. H., & Abramson, L. Y. (2008). The ABCs of depression: Integrating affective, biological, and cognitive models to explain the emergence of the gender

difference in depression. *Psychological Review, 115,* 291-313.

Hyman, B. T. (2011). Amyloid-dependent and amyloid-independent stages of Alzheimer disease. *Archives of Neurology, 68,* 1662-1664.

Høglend, P. P., Dahl, H. S., Hersoug, A. G., Lorentzen, S. S., & Perry, J. C. (2011). Long-term effects of transference interpretation in dynamic psychotherapy of personality disorders. *European Psychiatry, 26,* 419-424.

Ibbotson, P., & Tomasello, M. (2016). Language in a new key. *Scientific American, 315,* 70-75.

Iglesias, A. (2005). Awake-alert hypnosis in the treatment of panic disorder: A case report. *American Journal of Clinical Hypnosis, 47,* 249-257.

Igo, S. E. (2006). A telescope on society: Survey research and social science at the University of Michigan and beyond. *Journal of the History of the Behavioral Sciences, 42,* 95-96.

Ikonomidou, C., Bittigau, P., Ishimaru, M. J., Wozniak, D. F., Koch, C., Genz, K., . . . Olney, J. W. (2000). Ethanol-induced apoptotic neurodegeneration and fetal alcohol syndrome. *Science, 287,* 1056-1060.

Iliceto, P., D'Antuono, L., Cassarà, L., Giacolini, T., Sabatello, U., & Candilera, G. (2017). Obsessive-compulsive tendencies, self/other perception, personality, and suicidal ideation in a non-clinical sample. *Psychiatric Quarterly, 88,* 411-422.

Imamura, M., & Nakamizo, S. (2006). An empirical test of formal equivalence between Emmert's Law and the size-distance invariance hypothesis. *The Spanish Journal of Psychology, 9*(2), 295-299.

Innocenti, G. M. (2007). Subcortical regulation of cortical development: Some effects of early, selective deprivations. *Progressive Brain Research, 164,* 23-37.

Inoue, T., Abekawa, T., Nakagawa, S., Suzuki, K., Tanaka, T., Kitaichi, Y., & . . . Koyama, T. (2011). Long-term naturalistic follow-up of lithium augmentation: Relevance to bipolarity. *Journal of Affective Disorders, 129,* 64-67.

Insel, T. R. (2010, April) Faulty circuits. *Scientific American, 302*(4), 44-51.

International Human Genome Sequencing Consortium. (2003). *International Consortium completes Human Genome Project.* Bethesda, MD: National Human Genome Research Institute.

Irwin, M. (2008). Human psychoneuroimmunology: 20 years of discovery. *Brain, Behavior, and Immunity, 22,* 129-139.

Irwin, R. R. (2006). Spiritual development in adulthood: Key concepts and models. In C. Hoare (Ed.), *Handbook of adult development and learning.* New York: Oxford University Press.

Isay, R. A. (1994). *Being homosexual: Gay men and their development.* Lanham, MD: Jason Aronson.

Isbell, L. M., & Tyler, J. M. (2003). Teaching students about in-group favoritism and the minimal groups paradigm. *Teaching of Psychology, 30,* 127-130.

Ishikawa, S., Okajima, I., Matsuoka, H., & Sakano, Y. (2007). Cognitive behavioural therapy for anxiety disorders in children and adolescents: A meta-analysis. *Child and Adolescent Mental Health, 12,* 164–172.

Itkowitz, C. (2016, June 1). Unwell and unashamed. *Washington Post.* Retrieved from http://www.washingtonpost.com/sf/local/wp/2016/06/01/unwell-and-unashamed.

Iversen, S., & Iversen, L. (2007). Dopamine: 50 years in perspective. *Trends in Neurosciences, 30,* 188–193.

Iverson, P., Kuhl, P. K., Reiko, A. Y., Diesch, E., Tohkura, Y., Ketterman, A., & Siebert, C. (2003). A perceptual interference account of acquisition difficulties for non-native phonemes. *Cognition, 87,* B47–B57.

Ivtzan, I., Gardner, H. E., Bernard, I., Sekhon, M., & Hart, R. (2013). Well-being through self-fulfilment: Examining developmental aspects of self-actualization. *Humanistic Psychologist, 41,* 119–132.

Izard, C. E. (1994). Innate and universal facial expressions: Evidence from developmental and cross-cultural research. *Psychological Bulletin, 115,* 288–299.

Jablonka, E. (2017). The evolution of linguistic communication: Piagetian insights. In N. Budwig, E. Turiel, & P. D. Zelazo (Eds.), *New perspectives on human development.* New York: Cambridge University Press.

Jack, R. E., & Schyns, P. G. (2017). Toward a social psychophysics of face communication. *Annual Review of Psychology, 68,* 269–297.

Jackson, J. D. (2006). Trauma, attachment, and coping: Pathways to resilience. *Dissertation Abstracts International: Section B: The Sciences and Engineering, 67*(1-B), 547.

Jackson, M. L., Gunzelmann, G., Whitney, P., Hinson, J. M., Belenky, G., Rabat, A., & Van Dongen, H. A. (2013). Deconstructing and reconstructing cognitive performance in sleep deprivation. *Sleep Medicine Reviews, 17,* 215–225.

Jacob, K. S. (2014). DSM-5 and culture: The need to move towards a shared model of care within a more equal patient-physican partnership. *Asian Journal of Psychiatry, 7,* 89–91.

Jacob, K. S., Kumar, P. S., Gayathri, K., Abraham, S., & Prince, M. J. (2007). *The diagnosis of dementia in the community* [Special issue: Focus on psychogeriatrics in the developing world]. *International Psychogeriatrics, 19,* 669–678.

Jacobs, A. & Richtel, M. (2017, September 18). How big business got Brazil hooked on junk foods. *The New York Times.* Accessed from https://www.nytimes.com/interactive/2017/09/16/health/brazil-obesity-nestle.html?emc=edit_ta_20170917&nl=top-stories&nlid=15802952&ref=headline&r=0.

Jacobs, E. G., Kroenke, C., Lin, J., Epel, E. S., Kenna, H. A., Blackburn, E. H., & Rasgon, N. L. (2013). Accelerated cell aging in female APOE-4 carriers: Implications for hormone therapy use. *Plos ONE, 8,* 103–111.

Jacobs, J. A., & Gerson, K. (2004). *The time divide: Work, family, and gender inequality.* Cambridge, MA: Harvard University Press.

Jacobs, M., Roesch, S., Wonderlich, S., Crosby, R., Thornton, L., Wilfley, D., . . . Bulik, C. M. (2009). Anorexia nervosa trios: Behavioral profiles of individuals with anorexia nervosa and their parents. *Psychological Medicine, 39,* 451–461.

Jacobson, S. W., Stanton, M. E., Dodge, N. C., Pienaar, M., Fuller, D. S., Molteno, C. D., . . . Jacobson, J. L. (2011). Impaired delay and trace eyeblink conditioning in school-age children with fetal alcohol syndrome. *Alcoholism: Clinical and Experimental Research, 35,* 250–264.

Jacoby, J., & Schwartz, G. W. (2017). Three small-receptive-field ganglion cells in the mouse retina are distinctly tuned to size, speed, and object motion. *Journal of Neuroscience, 37,* 610–625.

Jacoby, L. L., & Wahlheim, C. N. (2013). On the importance of looking back: The role of recursive reminders in recency judgments and cued recall. *Memory & Cognition, 41,* 625–637.

Jacoby, L. L., Bishara, A. J., Hessels, S., & Hughes, A. (2007). Probabilistic retroactive interference: The role of accessibility bias in interference effects. *Journal of Experimental Psychology: General, 136,* 200–216.

Jacoby-Senghor, D. S., Sinclair, S., & Smith, C. T. (2015). When bias binds: Effect of implicit outgroup bias on ingroup affiliation. *Journal of Personality and Social Psychology, 109*(3), 415–433.

James, W. (1890). *The principles of psychology.* New York: Holt.

James, W. (2015). The principles of psychology (excerpt). In T. Alter & Y. Nagasawa (Eds.), *Consciousness in the physical world: Perspectives on Russellian monism.* New York: Oxford University Press.

Jamieson, G. A. (2007). *Hypnosis and conscious states: The cognitive neuroscience perspective.* New York: Oxford University Press.

Jamison, K. R. (1995). *An unquiet mind: A memoir of moods and madness.* New York: Knopf.

Jang, H., Reeve, J., Ryan, R. M., & Kim, A. (2009). Can self-determination theory explain what underlies the productive, satisfying learning experiences of collectivistically oriented Korean students? *Journal of Educational Psychology, 101,* pp. 644–661.

Jarlais, D. C. D., Arasteh, K., & Perlis, T. (2007). The transition from injection to non-injection drug use: Long-term outcomes among heroin and cocaine users in New York City. *Addiction, 102,* 778–785.

Jarrett, S. (2015). The meaning of 'community' in the lives of people with intellectual disabilities: An historical perspective. *International Journal Of Developmental Disabilities, 61,* 107–112.

Jarrold, C., & Tam, H. (2011). Rehearsal and the development of working memory. In P. Barrouillet & V. Gaillard (Eds.), *Cognitive development and working memory: A dialogue between neo-Piagetian theories and cognitive approaches.* New York: Psychology Press.

Jeffery, A. J. (2015). Two behavioral hypotheses for the evolution of male homosexuality in humans. In T. K. Shackelford & R. D. Hansen (Eds.), *The evolution of sexuality.* Cham, Switzerland: Springer International Publishing.

Jenkins, S. R. (1994). Need for power and women's careers over 14 years: Structural power, job satisfaction, and motive change. *Journal of Personality and Social Psychology, 66,* 155–165.

Jennings, D. J., Alonso, E., Mondragón, E., Franssen, M., & Bonardi, C. (2013). The effect of stimulus distribution form on the acquisition and rate of conditioned responding: Implications for theory. *Journal of Experimental Psychology: Animal Behavior Processes, 39,* 233–248.

Jensen, A. R. (2002). Galton's legacy to research on intelligence. *Journal of Biosocial Science, 34,* 145–172.

Jensen, M. P., & Patterson, D. R. (2014). Hypnotic approaches for chronic pain management: Clinical implications of recent research findings. *American Psychologist, 69,* 167–177.

Jensen, M. P., & Turk, D. C. (2014). Contributions of psychology to the understanding and treatment of people with chronic pain: Why it matters to ALL psychologists. *American Psychologist, 69,* 105–118.

Jequier, E. (2002). Pathways to obesity. *International Journal of Obesity and Related Metabolic Disorders, 26,* S12–S17.

Jia, C., & Hegg, C. C. (2015). Effect of IP3R3 and NPY on age-related declines in olfactory stem cell proliferation. *Neurobiology of Aging, 36,* 1045–1056.

Jia, H., Zack, M. M., & Thompson, W. W. (2011). State quality-adjusted life expectancy for U.S. adults from 1993 to 2008. *Quality of Life Research: An International Journal of Quality of Life Aspects of Treatment, Care & Rehabilitation, 20,* 853–863.

Jiang, S., Miao, B., & Chen, Y. (2017). Prolonged duration of isoflurane anesthesia impairs spatial recognition memory through the activation of JNK1/2 in the hippocampus of mice. *Neuroreport: For Rapid Communication of Neuroscience Research, 28,* 386–390.

Jin, B., & Kim, J. (2017). Grit, basic needs satisfaction, and subjective well-being. *Journal of Individual Differences, 38*(1), 29–35.

Joe, G. W., Flynn, P. M., & Broome, K. M. (2007). Patterns of drug use and expectations in methadone patients. *Addictive Behaviors, 32,* 1640–1656.

Joel, D., & McCarthy, M.M. (2017). Incorporating sex as a biological variable in neuropsychiatric research: Where are we now and where should we be. *Neuropsychopharmacology, 42,* 379–385.

John-Steiner, V., & Mahn, H. (2003). Sociocultural contexts for teaching and learning. In W. M. Reynolds & G. E. Miller (Eds.), *Handbook of psychology: Educational psychology* (Vol. 7). New York: Wiley.

Johnson, C. Y. (2014, January 17). Finding a way to erase harmful memories. *Boston Globe,* p. 1.

Johnson, G. B. (2000). *The Living World* (p. 600). Boston: McGraw-Hill.

Johnson, H. D. (2004). Gender, grade and relationship differences in emotional closeness within adolescent friendships. *Adolescence, 39,* 243–255.

Johnson, R., Stewart, C., & Bachman, C. (2015). What drives students to complete online courses? What drives faculty to teach online? Validating a measure of motivation orientation in university students and faculty. *Interactive Learning Environments, 23*, 528-543.

Johnson, W., & Deary, I. J. (2011). Placing inspection time, reaction time, and perceptual speed in the broader context of cognitive ability: The VPR model in the Lothian Birth Cohort 1936. *Intelligence, 39*, 405-417.

Johnston, E., & Olson, L. (2015). *The feeling brain: The biology and psychology of emotions.* New York: W. W. Norton & Co.

Johnston, L. D., Miech, R. A., O'Malley, P. M., Bachman, J. G., & Schulenberg, J. E. (2016, December 13). Teen use of any illicit drug other than marijuana at new low, same true for alcohol. University of Michigan News Service. Accessed from http://www.monitoringthefuture.org.

Johnston, L. D., O'Malley, P. M., Bachman, J. G., & Schulenberg, J. E. (2009). *Monitoring the future–National results on adolescent drug use; overview of key findings, 2008* (NIH Publication No. 09-7401). Bethesda, MD: National Institute on Drug Abuse.

Johnston, L. D., O'Malley, P. M., Bachman, J. G., & Schulenberg, J. E. (2013). *Monitoring the Future–National results on drug use: 2012 overview, key findings on adolescent drug use.* Ann Arbor, MI: Institute for Social Research, The University of Michigan.

Johnston, M. V. (2004). Clinical disorders of brain plasticity. *Brain and Development, 26*, 73-80.

Jokela, M., Pekkarinen, T., Sarvimäki, M., Terviö, M., & Uusitalo, R. (2017). Secular rise in economically valuable personality traits. *PNAS Proceedings of the National Academy of Sciences of the United States of America, 114*, 6527-6532.

Jones, A. L. (2006). The contemporary psychoanalyst: Karen Horney's theory applied in today's culture. *PsycCRITIQUES, 51*, 127-134.

Jones, D. (2010). A WEIRD view of human nature skews psychologists' studies. *Science, 328*, 1627.

Jones, J. E., & Corp, E. S. (2003). Effect of naltrexone on food intake and body weight in Syrian hamsters depends on metabolic status. *Physiology and Behavior, 78*, 67-72.

Jones, J. M. (2007). Exposure to chronic community violence: Resilience in African American children. *Journal of Black Psychology, 33*, 125-149.

Jones, M., Kass, A. E., Trockel, M., Glass, A. I., Wilfley, D. E., & Taylor, C. B. (2014). A population-wide screening and tailored intervention platform for eating disorders on college campuses: The Healthy Body Image program. *Journal of American College Health, 62*, 351-356.

Jones, R. K., Darroch, J. E., & Singh, S. (2005). Religious differentials in the sexual and reproductive behaviors of young women in the United States. *Journal of Adolescent Health, 36*, 279-288.

Jones, S. W., Weitlauf, J., Danhauer, S. C., Qi, L., Zaslavsky, O., Wassertheil-Smoller, S., . . . LaCroix, A. Z. (2017). Prospective data from the Women's Health Initiative on depressive symptoms, stress, and inflammation. *Journal of Health Psychology, 22*, 457-464.

Jost, J. T., Kay, A. C., & Thorisdottir, H. (2009). *Social and psychological bases of ideology and system justification.* New York: Oxford University Press.

Jovanović, D., Stanojević, P., & Stanojević, D. (2011). Motives for, and attitudes about, driving-related anger and aggressive driving. *Social Behavior and Personality, 39*, 755-764.

Joyce, J. (1934). *Ulysses.* New York: Random House.

Julien, R. M. (2001). *A primer of drug action* (9th ed.). New York: Freeman.

Jung, C. G. (1961). *Freud and psychoanalysis.* New York: Pantheon.

Jung, J. (2002). *Psychology of alcohol and other drugs: A research perspective.* Thousand Oaks, CA: Sage.

Jung, J., & Chang, D. (2017). Types of creativity–Fostering multiple intelligences in design convergence talents. *Thinking Skills and Creativity, 23*, 101-111.

Juster, E. T., Ono, H., & Stafford, E. (2002). *Report on housework and division of labor.* Ann Arbor, MI: Institute for Social Research.

Justman, S. (2011). From medicine to psychotherapy: The placebo effect. *History of the Human Sciences, 24*, 95-107.

Jylha, M. (2004). Old age and loneliness: Cross-sectional and longitudinal analyses in the Tampere longitudinal study on aging. *Canadian Journal on Aging/La Revue Canadienne du Vieillissement, 23*, 157-168.

Kadosh, R., Henik, A., & Walsh, V. (2009, May). Synaesthesia: Learned or lost? *Developmental Science, 12*, 484-491.

Kahn, K. B., Lee, J. K., Renauer, B., Henning, K. R., & Stewart, G. (2017). The effects of perceived phenotypic racial stereotypicality and social identity threat on racial minorities' attitudes about police. *Journal of Social Psychology, 157*, 416-428.

Kahn, R. E., Frick, P. J., Youngstrom, E. A., Kogos Youngstrom, J., Feeny, N. C., & Findling, R. L. (2013). Distinguishing primary and secondary variants of callous-unemotional traits among adolescents in a clinic-referred sample. *Psychological Assessment, 25*, 966-978.

Kaiser, B. L., Thomas, G. R., & Bowers, B. J. (2017). A case study of engaging hard-to-reach participants in the research process: Community Advisors on Research Design and Strategies (CARDS)®. *Research in Nursing & Health, 40*, 70-79.

Kalanthroff, E., Anholt, G. E., Keren, R., & Henik, A. (2013). What should I (not) do? Control over irrelevant tasks in obsessive-compulsive disorder patients. *Clinical Neuropsychiatry: Journal of Treatment Evaluation, 10*, Suppl. 1, 61-64.

Kalb, C. (2003, May 19). Taking a new look at pain. *Newsweek*, pp. 51-52.

Kalka, D. (2016). Quality of life and proactive coping with stress in a group of middle adulthood women with type 2 diabetes. *Polish Psychological Bulletin, 47*, 327-337.

Kalodner, C. R. (2011). Cognitive-behavioral theories. In D. Capuzzi & D. R. Gross (Eds.), *Counseling and psychotherapy* (5th ed.). Alexandria, VA: American Counseling Association.

Kamens, S. R. (2011). On the proposed sexual and gender identity diagnoses for DSM-5: History and controversies. *The Humanistic Psychologist, 39*, 37-59.

Kamimori, G. H., McLellan, T. M., Tate, C. M., Voss, D. M., Niro, P., & Lieberman, H. R. (2015). Caffeine improves reaction time, vigilance and logical reasoning during extended periods with restricted opportunities for sleep. *Psychopharmacology, 232*, 2031-2042.

Kandler, C., Riemann, R., & Angleitner, A. (2013). Patterns and sources of continuity and change of energetic and temporal aspects of temperament in adulthood: A longitudinal twin study of self- and peer reports. *Developmental Psychology, 49*, 1739-1753.

Kane, J. M., Robinson, D. G., Schooler, N. R., Mueser, K. T., Penn, D. L., Rosenheck, R. A., . . . Heinssen, R. K. (2016). Comprehensive versus usual community care for first-episode psychosis: 2-year outcomes from the NIMH RAISE Early Treatment Program. *American Journal of Psychiatry, 173*, 362-372.

Kanoski, S. E., Hayes, M. R., Greenwald, H. S., Fortin, S. M., Gianessi, C. A., Gilbert, J. R., & Grill, H. J. (2011). Hippocampal leptin signaling reduces food intake and modulates food-related memory processing. *Neuropsychopharmacology, 36*, 1859-1870.

Kantrowitz, B., & Underwood, A. (2007, June 25). The teen drinking dilemma. *Newsweek*, pp. 36-37.

Kao, D. (2011). Message sidedness in advertising: The moderating roles of need for cognition and time pressure in persuasion. *Scandinavian Journal of Psychology, 52*, 329-340.

Kaposi, D. (2017). The resistance experiments: Morality, authority and obedience in Stanley Milgram's account. *Journal for the Theory of Social Behaviour.* Accessed from http://onlinelibrary.wiley.com/doi/10.1111/jtsb.12137/abstract.

Karaszewski, B. (2008). Sub-neocortical brain: A mechanical tool for creative generation? *Trends in Cognitive Sciences, 12*, 171-172.

Karlson, C. W., Gallagher, M. W., Olson, C. A., & Hamilton, N. A. (2013). Insomnia symptoms and well-being: Longitudinal follow-up. *Health Psychology, 32*, 311-319.

Kasemsap, K. (2017). Mastering cognitive neuroscience and social neuroscience perspectives in the information age. In M. A. Dos Santos (Ed.), *Applying neuroscience to business practice.* Hershey, PA: Business Science Reference/IGI Global.

Kasof, J. (2009, May). Cultural variation in seasonal depression: Cross-national differences in winter versus summer patterns of seasonal affective disorder. *Journal of Affective Disorders, 115*, 79-86.

Kassam, K. S., Gilbert, D. T., Swencionis, J. K., & Wilson, T. D. (2009). Misconceptions of memory: The Scooter Libby effect. *Psychological Science, 20*, 551-552.

Kassel, J. D., Evatt, D. P., Greenstein, J. E., Wardle, M. C., Yates, M. C., & Veilleux, J. C. (2007).

The acute effects of nicotine on positive and negative affect in adolescent smokers. *Journal of Abnormal Psychology, 116,* 543-553.

Kasser, T. (2011). Cultural values and the well-being of future generations: A cross-national study. *Journal of Cross-Cultural Psychology, 42,* 206-215.

Kassin, S. M., Redlich, A. D., Alceste, F., & Luke, T. J. (2018). On the general acceptance of confessions research: Opinions of the scientific community. *American Psychologist, 73,* 63-80.

Kato, K., & Pedersen, N. L. (2005). Personality and coping: A study of twins reared apart and twins reared together. *Behavior Genetics, 35,* 147-158.

Kato, N. (2009). Neurophysiological mechanisms of electroconvulsive therapy for depression. *Neuroscience Research, 64,* 3-11.

Katsiyannis, A., Zhang, D., & Woodruff, N. (2005). Transition supports to students with mental retardation: An examination of data from the national longitudinal transition study 2. *Education and Training in Developmental Disabilities, 40,* 109-116.

Katz, J. (2017, June 15). Drug deaths in America are rising faster than ever. *The New York Times.* Accessed from https://www.nytimes.com/interactive/2017/06/05/upshot/opioid-epidemic-drug-overdose-deaths-are-rising-faster-than-ever.html.

Katz, M. (2001). The implications of revising Freud's empiricism for drive theory. *Psychoanalysis and Contemporary Thought, 24,* 253-272.

Kaufman, A., Johnson, C., & Liu, X. (2008). A CHC theory-based analysis of age differences on cognitive abilities and academic skills at ages 22 to 90 years. *Journal of Psychoeducational Assessment, 26,* 350-381.

Kaufman, J. C., & Baer, J. (2006). *Creativity and reason in cognitive development.* New York: Cambridge University Press.

Kaufman, J. C., & Plucker, J. A. (2011). Intelligence and creativity. In R. J. Sternberg & S. Kaufman (Eds.), *The Cambridge handbook of intelligence.* New York: Cambridge University Press.

Kaufman, J. C., Kaufman, S., & Plucker, J. A. (2013). Contemporary theories of intelligence. In D. Reisberg (Ed.), *The Oxford handbook of cognitive psychology.* New York: Oxford University Press.

Kauten, R. L., Lui, J. L., Stary, A. K., & Barry, C. T. (2015). 'Purging my friends list. Good luck making the cut': Perceptions of narcissism on Facebook. *Computers In Human Behavior, 51,* 244-254.

Kawakami, N., & Miura, E. (2015). Image or real? Altering the mental imagery of subliminal stimuli differentiates explicit and implicit attitudes. *Imagination, Cognition and Personality, 34,* 259-269.

Kawashima, H., Izaki, Y., & Grace, A. A. (2006). Co-operativity between hippocampal-pre-frontal short-term plasticity through associative long-term potentiation. *Brain Research, 1109,* 37-44.

Kazantseva, A., Gaysina, D., Kutlumbetova, Y., Kanzafarova, R., Malykh, S., Lobaskova, M., &

Khusnutdinova, E. (2015). Brain derived neurotrophic factor gene (BDNF) and personality traits: The modifying effect of season of birth and sex. *Progress in Neuro-Psychopharmacology & Biological Psychiatry, 56,* 58-65.

Kazar, D. B. (2006). Forensic psychology: Did we leave anything out? *PsycCRITIQUES, 51,* 88-97.

Kazdin, A. (2008). Evidence-based treatment and practice: New opportunities to bridge clinical research and practice, enhance the knowledge base, and improve patient care. *American Psychologist, 63,* 146-159.

Keating, D. P., & Clark, L. V. (1980). Development of physical and social reasoning in adolescence. *Developmental Psychology, 16,* 23-30.

Keer, M., van den Putte, B., Neijens, P., & de Wit, J. (2013). The influence of affective and cognitive arguments on message judgement and attitude change: The moderating effects of meta-bases and structural bases. *Psychology & Health, 28,* 895-908.

Keillor, J. M., Barrett, A. M., Crucian, G. P., Kortenkamp, S., & Heilman, K. M. (2002). Emotional experience and perception in the absence of facial feedback. *Journal of the International Neuropsychological Society, 8,* 130-135.

Kelley, H. (1950). The warm-cold variable in first impressions of persons. *Journal of Personality and Social Psychology, 18,* 431-439.

Kelly, J. B. (2000). Children's adjustment in conflicted marriage and divorce: A decade review of research. *Journal of the American Academy of Child & Adolescent Psychiatry, 39,* 963-973.

Kelly, J. F., Hoeppner, B., Stout, R. L., & Pagano, M. (2012). Determining the relative importance of the mechanisms of behavior change within Alcoholics Anonymous: A multiple mediator analysis. *Addiction, 107,* 289-299.

Keltikangas-Järvinen, L., Räikkönen, K., Ekelund, J., & Peltonen, L. (2004). Nature and nurture in novelty seeking. *Molecular Psychiatry, 9,* 308-311.

Kempermann, G. (2011). Seven principles in the regulation of adult neurogenesis. *European Journal of Neuroscience, 33,* 1018-1024.

Kemps, E., & Tiggemann, M. (2007). Reducing the vividness and emotional impact of distressing autobiographical memories: The importance of modality-specific interference. *Memory, 15,* 412-422.

Kendler, K. S., & Schaffner, K. F. (2011). The dopamine hypothesis of schizophrenia: An historical and philosophical analysis. *Philosophy, Psychiatry, & Psychology, 18,* 41-63.

Kendler, K. S., Aggen, S. H., Gillespie, N., Neale, M. C., Knudsen, G. P., Krueger, R. F., . . . Reichborn-Kjennerud, T. (2017). The genetic and environmental sources of resemblance between normative personality and personality disorder traits. *Journal of Personality Disorders, 31,* 193-207.

Kendler, K., Halberstadt, L., Butera, F., Myers, J., Bouchard, T., & Ekman, P. (2008). The similarity of facial expressions in response to emotion-inducing films in reared-apart twins. *Psychological Medicine, 38*(10), 1475-1483.

Kenett, Y. N., Levi, E., Anaki, D., & Faust, M. (2017). The semantic distance task: Quantifying semantic distance with semantic network path length. *Journal of Experimental Psychology: Learning, Memory, and Cognition, 43,* 1470-1489.

Kennedy, C. E., Moore, P. J., Peterson, R. A., Katzman, M. A., Vermani, M., & Charmak, W. D. (2011). What makes people anxious about pain? How personality and perception combine to determine pain anxiety responses in clinical and non-clinical populations. *Anxiety, Stress & Coping: An International Journal, 24,* 179-200.

Kennedy, D. O., & Haskell, C. F. (2011). Cerebral blood flow and behavioural effects of caffeine in habitual and non-habitual consumers of caffeine: A near infrared spectroscopy study. *Biological Psychology, 86,* 296-305.

Kennedy, J. E. (2004). A proposal and challenge for proponents and skeptics of psi. *Journal of Parapsychology, 68,* 157-167.

Kennison, S. M., & Bowers, J. (2011). Illustrating brain lateralisation in a naturalistic observation of cell-phone use. *Psychology Learning & Teaching, 10,* 46-51.

Keppler, J. (2017, May 3). Shedding light on the fundamental mechanism underlying hypnotic analgesia. *Annals of Palliative Medicine,* pii: apm.2017.04.03. doi: 10.21037/apm.2017.04.03.

Kertz, S. J., Koran, J., Stevens, K. T., & Björgvinsson, T. (2015). Repetitive negative thinking predicts depression and anxiety symptom improvement during brief cognitive behavioral therapy. *Behaviour Research and Therapy, 68,* 54-63.

Keränen, T., Halkoaho, A., Itkonen, E., & Pietilä, A. (2015). Placebo-controlled clinical trials: How trial documents justify the use of randomisation and placebo. *BMC Medical Ethics, 16,* 88-96.

Kesebir, P., & Diener, E. (2008). In pursuit of happiness: Empirical answers to philosophical questions. *Perspectives on Psychological Science, 3,* 117-125.

Keshavarz, M. (2017). Glial cells as key elements in the pathophysiology and treatment of bipolar disorder. *Acta Neuropsychiatrica, 29,* 140-152.

Kessler, R. C., & Wang, P. S. (2008). The descriptive epidemiology of commonly occurring mental disorders in the United States. *Annual Review of Public Health, 29,* 115-129.

Ketisch, T., & Jones, R. A. (2013). Review of 'ADHD diagnosis & management'. *American Journal of Family Therapy, 41,* 272-274.

Key, W. B. (2003). Subliminal sexuality: The fountainhead for America's obsession. In T. Reichert & J. Lambaiase (Eds.), *Sex in advertising: Perspectives on the erotic appeal. LEA's communication series.* Mahwah, NJ: Lawrence Erlbaum.

Khazaal, Y., Chatton, A., Claeys, F., Ribordy, F., Zullino, D., & Cabanac, M. (2008). Antipsychotic drug and body weight set-point. *Physiology & Behavior, 95,* 157-160.

Khedr, E. M., Omran, E. A., Ismail, N. M., El-Hammady, D. H., Goma, S. H., Kotb, H., . . .

Ahmed, G. A. (2017). Effects of transcranial direct current stimulation on pain, mood and serum endorphin level in the treatment of fibromyalgia: A double blinded, randomized clinical trial. *Brain Stimulation, 10*(5), 893-890.

Kidd, E., & Lum, J. (2008). Sex differences in past tense overregularization. *Developmental Science, 11*, 882-889.

Kiecolt, J. K. (2003). Satisfaction with work and family life: No evidence of a cultural reversal. *Journal of Marriage and Family, 65*, 23-35.

Kihlstrom, J. F. (2005a). Dissociative disorders. *Annual Review of Clinical Psychology, 1*, 227-253.

Kihlstrom, J. F. (2005b). Is hypnosis an altered state of consciousness or what? Comment. *Contemporary Hypnosis, 22*, 34-38.

Kim, D. R., Pesiridou, A., & O'Reardon, J. P. (2009). Transcranial magnetic stimulation in the treatment of psychiatric disorders. *Current Psychiatry Reports, 11*, 447-452.

Kim, H., Clark, D., & Dionne, R. (2009, July). Genetic contributions to clinical pain and analgesia: Avoiding pitfalls in genetic research. *The Journal of Pain, 10*, 663-693.

Kim, N. (2008). The moon illusion and the size-distance paradox. In Cummins-Sebree, S., Riley, M. A., & Shockley, K. (Eds.). *Studies in perception and action IX: Fourteenth International Conference on Perception and Action.* Mahwah, NJ: Lawrence Erlbaum Associates.

Kim, S., Polari, A., Melville, F., Moller, B., Kim, J., Amminger, P., & . . . Nelson, B. (2017). Are current labeling terms suitable for people who are at risk of psychosis? *Schizophrenia Research, 188*, 172-177.

Kim, Y., & Yoon, H. (2017). Common and distinct brain networks underlying panic and social anxiety disorders. *Progress In Neuro-Psychopharmacology & Biological Psychiatry.* Accessed from https://www.ncbi.nlm.nih.gov/pubmed/28642079.

Kim-Cohen, J., Caspi, A., & Moffitt, T. E. (2003). Prior juvenile diagnoses in adults with mental disorder: Developmental follow-back of a prospective-longitudinal cohort. *Archives of General Psychiatry, 60*, 709-717.

Kim-Cohen, J., Moffitt, T. E., Taylor, A., Pawlby, S. J., & Caspi, A. (2005). Maternal depression and children's antisocial behavior: Nature and nurture effects. *Archives of General Psychiatry, 62*, 173-181.

Kimbrel, N. A. (2007). A model of the development and maintenance of generalized social phobia. *Clinical Psychological Review, 8*, 69-75.

King-Casas, B., Sharp, C., Lomax-Bream, L., Lohrenz, T., Fonagy, P., & Montague, P. R. (2008, August, 8). The rupture and repair of cooperation in borderline personality disorder. *Science, 321*, 806-810.

Kirk, E. P., Jacobsen, D. J., Gibson, C., Hill, J. O., & Donnelly, J. E. (2003). Time course for changes in aerobic capacity and body composition in overweight men and women in response to long-term exercise: The Midwest Exercise Trial (MET). *International Journal of Obesity, 27*, 912-919.

Kirsch, I., Lynn, S. J., Vigorito, M., & Miller, R. R. (2004). The role of cognition in classical and operant conditioning. *Journal of Clinical Psychology, 60*, 369-392.

Kisely, S., Chang, A., Crowe, J., Galletly, C., Jenkins, P., Loi, S., . . . Macfarlane, S. (2015). Getting started in research: Systematic reviews and meta-analyses. *Australasian Psychiatry, 23*, 16-21.

Kish, S., Fitzmaurice, P., Boileau, I., Schmunk, G., Ang, L., Furukawa, Y., et al. (2009). Brain serotonin transporter in human methamphetamine users. *Psychopharmacology, 202*, 649-661.

Kitayama, S. (2017). Journal of Personality and Social Psychology: Attitudes and social cognition. *Journal of Personality and Social Psychology, 112*, 357-360.

Kivipelto, M. & Hakansson, K. (2017). A rare success against Alzheimer's. *Scientific American, 316*, 32-37.

Kivlighan, D. M., Goldberg, S. B., Abbas, M., Pace, B. T., Yulish, N. E., Thomas, J. G., & . . . Wampold, B. E. (2015). The enduring effects of psychodynamic treatments vis-à-vis alternative treatments: A multilevel longitudinal meta-analysis. *Clinical Psychology Review, 40*, 1-14.

Kizilirmak, J. M., Galvao Gomes da Silva, J., Imamoglu, F., & Richardson-Klavehn, A. (2015). Generation and the subjective feeling of "aha!" are independently related to learning from insight. *Psychological Research, 80*(6), 1059-1074.

Kleinman, A. (1996). How is culture important for DSM-IV? In J. E Mezzich, A. Kleinman, H. Fabrega, Jr., & D. L. Parron (Eds.), *Culture and psychiatric diagnosis: A DSM-IV perspective.* Washington, DC: American Psychiatric Press.

Kleinplatz, P. J., Moser, C., & Lev, A. (2013). Sex and gender identity disorders. In G. Stricker, T. A. Widiger, & I. B. Weiner (Eds.), *Handbook of psychology, Vol. 8: Clinical psychology* (2nd ed.). Hoboken, NJ: John Wiley & Sons Inc.

Kluck, A. (2008). Family factors in the development of disordered eating: Integrating dynamic and behavioral explanations. *Eating Behaviors, 9*, 471-483.

Kluger, J. (2001, April 2). Fear not! *Time*, pp. 51-62.

Kluger, J. (2006, December 4). Why we worry about the things we shouldn't and ignore the things we should. *Time*, pp. 64-71.

Kluger, J. (2013, July 29). The power of the bilingual brain. *Time*, 42-47.

Knight, S. C., & Meyer, R. G. (2007). Forensic hypnosis. In A. M. Goldstein (Ed.), *Forensic psychology: Emerging topics and expanding roles.* Hoboken, NJ: John Wiley & Sons.

Knoblich, G., & Sebanz, N. (2006). The social nature of perception and action. *Current Directions in Psychological Science, 15*, 99-111.

Kobayashi, F., Schallert, D. L., & Ogren, H. A. (2003). Japanese and American folk vocabularies for emotions. *Journal of Social Psychology, 143*, 451-478.

Koch, C., & Greenfield, S. (2007, October). How does consciousness happen? *Scientific American*, pp. 76-83.

Kochli, D. E., Thompson, E. C., Fricke, E. A., Postle, A. F., & Quinn, J. J. (2015). The amygdala is critical for trace, delay, and contextual fear conditioning. *Learning & Memory, 22*, 92-100.

Kogstad, R. E., Ekeland, T. J., & Hummelvoll, J. K. (2011). In defence of a humanistic approach to mental health care: Recovery processes investigated with the help of clients' narratives on turning points and processes of gradual change. *Journal of Psychiatric and Mental Health Nursing, 18*, 479-486.

Koh, E., Stauss, K., Coustaut, C., & Forrest, C. (2017). Generational impact of single-parent scholarships: Educational achievement of children in single-parent families. *Journal of Family Issues, 38*, 607-632

Kohlberg, L. (1984). *The psychology of moral development: Essays on moral development* (Vol. 2). San Francisco: Harper & Row.

Kohlberg, L., & Ryncarz, R. A. (1990). Beyond justice reasoning: Moral development and consideration of a seventh stage. In C. N. Alexander & E. J. Langer (Eds.), *Higher stages of human development: Perspectives on adult growth.* New York: Oxford University Press.

Kojima, M., & Kangawa, K. (2008). Structure and function of ghrelin. *Results & Problems in Cell Differentiation, 46*, 89-115.

Kolata, G. (2002, December 2). With no answers on risks, steroid users still say "yes." *The New York Times*, p. 1A.

Kolb, B., Gibb, R., & Robinson, T. E. (2003). Brain plasticity and behavior. *Current Directions in Psychological Science, 12*, 1-5.

Komarovskaya, I., Loper, A., Warren, J., & Jackson, S. (2011). Exploring gender differences in trauma exposure and the emergence of symptoms of PTSD among incarcerated men and women. *Journal of Forensic Psychiatry & Psychology, 22*, 395-410.

Koper, R. J., & Jaasma, M. A. (2001). Interpersonal style: Are human social orientations guided by generalized interpersonal needs? *Communications Reports, 14*, 117-129.

Koplewicz, H. (2002). *More than moody: Recognizing and treating adolescent depression.* New York: Putnam.

Korcha, R. A., Polcin, D. L., Bond, J. C., Lapp, W. M., & Galloway, G. (2011). Substance use and motivation: A longitudinal perspective. *The American Journal of Drug and Alcohol Abuse, 37*, 48-53.

Korotkov, D., Perunovic, M., Claybourn, M., Fraser, I., Houlihan, M., Macdonald, M., & Korotkov, K. (2011). The Type B behavior pattern as a moderating variable of the relationship between stressor chronicity and health behavior. *Journal of Health Psychology, 16*, 397-409.

Korur F, Toker S, Eryılmaz A. (2016). Effects of the integrated online advance organizer teaching materials on students' science achievement and attitude. *Journal of Science Education and Technology* [serial online], *25*(4), 628-640.

Kosambi, D. D. (1967). The Vedic "Five Tribes." *American Oriental Society, 14*, 5-12.

Kosinski, M., Matz, S. C., Gosling, S. D., Popov, V., & Stillwell, D. (2015). Facebook as a research tool for the social sciences. *American Psychologist, 70,* 543-556.

Koslowski, B. (2013). Scientific reasoning: Explanation, confirmation bias, and scientific practice. In G. J. Feist & M. E. Gorman (Eds.), *Handbook of the psychology of science.* New York: Springer Publishing Co.

Kosslyn, S. M., & Miller, G. W. (2013). *Top brain, bottom brain: Surprising insights into how you think.* New York: Simon & Schuster.

Kotre, J., & Hall, E. (1990). *Seasons of life.* Boston: Little, Brown.

Kounios, J., Fleck, J. I., Green, D. L., Payne, L., Stevenson, J. L., Bowden, E. M., et al. (2008). The origins of insight in resting-state brain activity. *Neuropsychologia, 46,* 281-291.

Kovacs, A. M., & Mehler, J. (2009). Flexible learning of multiple speech structures in bilingual infants. *Science, 325,* 611-612.

Kowalik, J., Weller, J., Venter, J., & Drachman, D. (2011). Cognitive behavioral therapy for the treatment of pediatric posttraumatic stress disorder: A review and meta-analysis. *Journal of Behavior Therapy and Experimental Psychiatry, 42,* 405-413.

Kozulin, A., Gindis, B., Ageyev, V. S., & Miller, S. M. (2003). *Vygotsky's educational theory in cultural context.* New York: Cambridge University Press.

Koçak, O., Özpolat, A., Atbaşoğlu, C., & Çiçek, M. (2011). Cognitive control of a simple mental image in patients with obsessive-compulsive disorder. *Brain and Cognition, 76,* 390-399.

Krassner, A. M., Gartstein, M. A., Park, C., Dragan, W. Ł., Lecannelier, F., & Putnam, S. P. (2017). East-west, collectivist-individualist: A cross-cultural examination of temperament in toddlers from Chile, Poland, South Korea, and the U.S. *European Journal of Developmental Psychology, 14*(4), 449-464. doi:10.1080/17405629.2016.1236722.

Kreher, D., Holcomb, P., Goff, D., & Kuperberg, G. (2008). Neural evidence for faster and further automatic spreading activation in schizophrenic thought disorder. *Schizophrenia Bulletin, 34,* 473-482.

Kreppner, J., Rutter, M., Marvin, R., O'Connor, T., & Sonuga-Barke, E. (2011). Assessing the concept of the "insecure-other" category in the Cassidy-Marvin scheme: Changes between 4 and 6 years in the English and Romanian adoptee study. *Social Development, 20,* 1-16.

Kreuger, A. (2007). Are we having fun yet? Categorizing and evaluating changes in time allocation. *Brookings Papers on Economic Activity,* (Vol. 2), 38, 193-218.

Krueger, K., & Dayan, P. (2009). Flexible shaping: How learning in small steps helps. *Cognition, 110,* 380-394.

Krumhuber, E. G., & Scherer, K. R. (2011). Affect bursts: Dynamic patterns of facial expression. *Emotion, 11,* 825-841.

Krüger, O., Korsten, P., & Hoffman, J. I. (2017). The rise of behavioral genetics and the transition to behavioral genomics and beyond. In J. Call, G. M. Burghardt, I. M. Pepperberg, C. T. Snowdon, & T. Zentall (Eds.), *APA handbook of comparative psychology: Basic concepts, methods, neural substrate, and behavior.* Washington, DC: American Psychological Association.

Kubanek, J., Snyder, L. H., & Abrams, R. A. (2015). Reward and punishment act as distinct factors in guiding behavior. *Cognition, 139,* 154-167.

Kulik, L., & Sadeh, I. (2015). Explaining fathers' involvement in childcare: An ecological approach. *Community, Work & Family, 18,* 19-40.

Kumari, S., & Joshi, S. (2013). Neonatal outcomes in women with depression during pregnancy. *Journal of Projective Psychology & Mental Health, 20,* 141-145.

Kuncel, N. R., & Beatty, A. S. (2013). Thinking at work: Intelligence, critical thinking, job knowledge, and reasoning. In K. F. Geisinger, B. A. Bracken, J. F. Carlson, J. C. Hansen, N. R. Kuncel, S. P. Reise, & M. C. Rodriguez (Eds.), *APA handbook of testing and assessment in psychology, Vol. 1: Test theory and testing and assessment in industrial and organizational psychology.* Washington, DC: American Psychological Association.

Kuo, L. J. (2007). Effects of bilingualism on development of facets of phonological competence (China). *Dissertation Abstracts International Section A: Humanities and Social Sciences, 67* (11-A), 4095.

Kupfer, D. J., Kuhl, E. A., & Regier, D. A. (2013). DSM-5—The future arrived. *JAMA: Journal of the American Medical Association, 309,* 1691-1692.

Kuppens, P., Ceulemans, E., Timmerman, M. E., Diener, E., & Kim-Prieto, C. (2006). Universal intracultural and intercultural dimensions of the recalled frequency of emotional experience. *Journal of Cross Cultural Psychology, 37,* 491-515.

Kurdziel, L., Duclos, K., & Spencer, R. M. C. (2013). Sleep spindles in midday naps enhance learning in preschool children. *PNAS Early Edition,* 1-6.

Kuriyama, K., Stickgold, R., & Walker, M. P. (2004). Sleep-dependent learning and motor-skill complexity. *Learning and Memory, 11,* 705-713.

Kushlev, K., Dunn, E. W., & Lucas, R. E. (2015). Higher income is associated with less daily sadness but not more daily happiness. *Social Psychological and Personality Science, 6,* 483-489.

Kuther, T. L. (2003). *Your career in psychology: Psychology and the law.* New York: Wadsworth.

Kwon, P. (2013). Resilience in lesbian, gay, and bisexual individuals. *Personality and Social Psychology Review, 17,* 371-383.

Kyaga, S., Landén, M., Boman, M., Hultman, C. M., Långström, N., & Lichtenstein, P. (2013). Mental illness, suicide and creativity: 40-year prospective total population study. *Journal of Psychiatric Research, 47,* 83-90.

Kyllonen, P., & Kell, H. (2017). What is fluid intelligence? Can it be improved?. In M. Rosén, K. Yang Hansen, & U. Wolff (Eds.), *Cognitive abilities and educational outcomes: A festschrift in honour of Jan-Eric Gustafsson.* Cham, Switzerland: Springer International Publishing.

Köhler, W. (1927). *The mentality of apes.* London: Routledge & Kegan Paul.

Kübler-Ross, E. (1969). *On death and dying.* New York: Macmillan.

LaBar, K. (2007). Beyond fear: Emotional memory mechanisms in the human brain. *Current Directions in Psychological Science, 16,* 173-177.

Labrecque, L. T., & Whisman, M. A. (2017). Attitudes toward and prevalence of extramarital sex and descriptions of extramarital partners in the 21st century. *Journal of Family Psychology, 31*(7), 952-957.

Labrecque, N., & Cermakian, N. (2015). Circadian clocks in the immune system. *Journal Of Biological Rhythms, 30,* 277-290.

Laddis, A., Dell, P. F., & Korzekwa, M. (2017). Comparing the symptoms and mechanisms of "dissociation" in dissociative identity disorder and borderline personality disorder. *Journal of Trauma & Dissociation, 18,* 139-173.

Laederach-Hofmann, K., & Messerli-Buergy, N. (2007). Chest pain, angina pectoris, panic disorder, and Syndrome X. In J. Jordan, B. Barde, & A. M. Zeiher (Eds.), *Contributions toward evidence-based psychocardiology: A systematic review of the literature.* Washington, DC: American Psychological Association.

Lagacé-Séguin, D. G., & d'Entremont, M. L. (2006). The role of child negative affect in the relations between parenting styles and play. *Early Child Development and Care, 176,* 461-477.

Lahti, J., Räikkönen, K., Ekelund, J., Peltonen, L., Raitakari, O. T., & Keltikangas-Järvinen, L. (2005). Novelty seeking: Interaction between parental alcohol use and dopamine D4 receptor gene exon III polymorphism over 17 years. *Psychiatric Genetics, 15,* 133-139.

Lal, S. (2002). Giving children security: Mamie Phipps Clark and the racialization of child psychology. *American Psychologist, 57,* 20-28.

LaLumiere, R. T., & Kalivas, P. W. (2013). Motivational systems: Rewards and incentive value. In R. J. Nelson, S. Y. Mizumori, & I. B. Weiner (Eds.), *Handbook of psychology, Vol. 3: Behavioral neuroscience* (2nd ed.). New York: John Wiley & Sons Ltd.

Lambert, W. W. (1971). *Comparative perspectives on social psychology.* Boston: Little, Brown.

Lamborn, S. D., & Groh, K. (2009). A four-part model of autonomy during emerging adulthood: Associations with adjustment. *International Journal of Behavioral Development, 33,* 393-401.

Lampard, A. M., Byrne, S. M., McLean, N., & Fursland, A. (2011). An evaluation of the enhanced cognitive-behavioural model of bulimia nervosa. *Behaviour Research and Therapy, 49,* 529-535.

Lanciano, T., Curci, A., Mastandrea, S., & Sartori, G. (2013). Do automatic mental associations detect a flashbulb memory? *Memory, 21,* 482-493.

Lancy, D. F. (2015). *The anthropology of childhood: Cherubs, chattel, changelings* (2nd ed.). New York: Cambridge University Press.

Landro, L. (2010, May 11). New ways to treat pain. *Wall Street Journal,* p. D1-D2.

Landro, L. (2011, April 26). 'Use only as directed' isn't easy. *Wall Street Journal,* p. D1-D2.

Landry, S. H., Zucker, T. A., Taylor, H. B., Swank, P. R., Williams, J. M., Assel, M., . . . Klein, A. (2013). Enhancing early child care quality and learning for toddlers at risk: the responsive early childhood program. *Developmental Psychology, 50*(2), 526-541.

Lane, K. A., Banaji, M. R., Nosek, B. A., & Greenwald, A. G. (Eds.). (2007). Understanding and using the implicit association test: IV: What we know (so far) about the method. In B. Wittenbrink & N. Schwarz (Eds.), *Implicit measures of attitudes*. New York: Guilford Press.

Lane, S. D., Cherek, D. R., & Tcheremissine, O. V. (2007). Response perseveration and adaptation in heavy marijuana-smoking adolescents. *Addictive Behaviors, 32*, 977-990.

Lang, A. J., Sorrell, J. T., & Rodgers, C. S. (2006). Anxiety sensitivity as a predictor of labor pain. *European Journal of Pain, 10*, 263-270.

Lang, P. J., & Bradley, M. M. (2013). Appetitive and defensive motivation: Goal-directed or goal-determined? *Emotion Review, 5*, 230-234.

Langan-Fox, J., & Grant, S. (2006). The Thematic Apperception Test: Toward a standard measure of the big three motives. *Journal of Personality Assessment, 87*, 277-291.

Langdridge, D., & Butt, T. (2004). The fundamental attribution error: A phenomenological critique. *British Journal of Social Psychology, 43*, 357-369.

Langley, Liz. (2016, March 19). How dogs can sniff out diabetes and cancer. *National Geographic*. Retrieved from http://news.national-geographic.com/2016/03/160319-dogs-diabetes-health-cancer-animals-science/.

Langlois, F., Langlois, M., Carpentier, A. C., Brown, C., Lemieux, S., & Hivert, M. (2011). Ghrelin levels are associated with hunger as measured by the Three-Factor Eating Questionnaire in healthy young adults. *Physiology & Behavior, 104*, 373-377.

Langreth, R. (2000, May 1). Every little bit helps: How even moderate exercise can have a big impact on your health. *The Wall Street Journal*, p. R5.

Lankov, A. (2004). The dawn of modern Korea: Changes for better or worse. *The Korea Times*, p. A1.

Lansford, J. E., Sharma, C., Malone, P. S., Woodlief, D., Dodge, K. A., Oburu, P., . . . Di Giunta, L. (2014). Corporal punishment, maternal warmth, and child adjustment: A longitudinal study in eight countries. *Journal of Clinical Child and Adolescent Psychology, 43*(4), 670-685.

Lanza, S. T., & Collins, L. M. (2002). Pubertal timing and the onset of substance use in females during early adolescence. *Prevention Science, 3*, 69-82.

LaPointe, L. L. (2013). *Paul Broca and the origins of language in the brain*. San Diego, CA: Plural Publishing.

Larsen, E. F. (2014). Good teens turned addicts. *Choices*. Accessed from http://www.huffing-tonpost.com/2014/09/24/teens-turned-drug-addicts.n_5877306.html.

Larsen, R. J., & Buss, D. M. (2006). *Personality psychology: Domains of knowledge about human nature with PowerWeb* (2nd ed.). New York: McGraw-Hill.

Lasalvia, A. (2015). DSM-5 two years later: Facts, myths and some key open issues. *Epidemiology and Psychiatric Sciences, 24*, 185-187.

Lascaratos, G., Ji, D., & Wood, J. P. (2007). Visible light affects mitochondrial function and induces neuronal death in retinal cell cultures. *Vision Research, 47*, 1191-1201.

Latané, B., & Darley, J. M. (1970). *The unresponsive bystander: Why doesn't he help?* New York: Appleton-Century-Crofts.

Lattal, K. A., Cançado, C. X., Cook, J. E., Kincaid, S. L., Nighbor, T. D., & Oliver, A. C. (2017). On defining resurgence. *Behavioural Processes, 141*(Part 1), 85-91.

Laugharne, J., Janca, A., & Widiger, T. (2007). Posttraumatic stress disorder and terrorism: 5 years after 9/11. *Current Opinion in Psychiatry, 20*, 36-41.

Lauriello, J., & Rahman, T. (2015). Schizophrenia spectrum and other psychotic disorders. In L. W. Roberts & A. K. Louie (Eds.), *Study Guide to DSM-5®*. Arlington, VA: American Psychiatric Publishing, Inc.

Lavazza, A., & Manzotti, R. (2013). An externalist approach to creativity: Discovery versus recombination. *Mind & Society, 12*, 61-72.

Lavenex, P., & Lavenex, P. (2009). Spatial memory and the monkey hippocampus: Not all space is created equal. *Hippocampus, 19*, 8-19.

Lavigne, K. M., Rapin, L. A., Metzak, P. D., Whitman, J. C., Jung, K., Dohen, M., & . . . Woodward, T. S. (2015). Left-dominant temporal-frontal hypercoupling in schizophrenia patients with hallucinations during speech perception. *Schizophrenia Bulletin, 41*, 259-267.

Lazarus, A. A. (1997). *Brief but comprehensive psychotherapy: The multimodal way*. New York: Springer.

Lazarus, R. S. (1995). Emotions express a social relationship, but it is an individual mind that creates them. *Psychological Inquiry, 6*, 253-265.

Lazear, E.P. (2017, June 26). The surprising factor for immigrant success. *Wall Street Journal*. Accessed from https://www.wsj.com/articles/the-surprising-factor-for-immigrant-success-1498517898.

Leahy, R. L. (2015). Emotional schema therapy. In N. C. Thoma & D. McKay (Eds.), *Working with emotion in cognitive-behavioral therapy: Techniques for clinical practice*. New York: Guilford Press.

Leaper, C., Brown, C., & Ayres, M. M. (2013). Adolescent girls' cognitive appraisals of coping responses to sexual harassment. *Psychology in the Schools, 50*, 969-986.

Leclair-Visonneau, L., Oudiette, D., Gaymard, B., Leu-Semenescu, S., & Arnulf, I. (2011). Do the eyes scan dream images during rapid eye movement sleep? Evidence from the rapid eye movement sleep behaviour disorder model: Corrigendum. *Brain: A Journal of Neurology, 134*, 88-97.

Lee, A. Y., & Aaker, J. L. (2004). Bringing the frame into focus: The influence of regulatory fit on processing fluency and persuasion. *Journal of Personality and Social Psychology, 86*, 205-218.

Lee, A., Isaac, M., & Janca, A. (2007). Posttraumatic stress disorder and terrorism. In A. Monat, R. S. Lazarus, & G. Reevy (Eds.), *The Praeger handbook on stress and coping* (Vol. 1). Westport, CT: Praeger Publishers/Greenwood Publishing Group.

Lee, D., Kleinman, J., & Kleinman, A. (2007). Rethinking depression: An ethnographic study of the experiences of depression among Chinese. *Harvard Review of Psychiatry, 15*, 1-8.

Lee, F. H., & Raja, S. N. (2011). Complementary and alternative medicine in chronic pain. *Pain, 152*, 28-30.

Lee-Chiong, T. L. (2006). *Sleep: A comprehensive handbook*. New York: Wiley-Liss.

Leeman, R. F., Fischler, C., & Rozin, P. (2011). Medical doctors' attitudes and beliefs about diet and health are more like those of their lay countrymen (France, Germany, Italy, UK and USA) than those of doctors in other countries. *Appetite, 56*, 558-563.

Lehman, D. R., & Taylor, S. E. (1988). Date with an earthquake: Coping with a probable, unpredictable disaster. *Personality and Social Psychology Bulletin, 13*, 546-555.

Lehrer, J. (2012, April 13). When memory commits an injustice. *Wall Street Journal*, p. C18.

Lehrman, S. (2007). Going beyond X and Y. *Scientific American*, pp. 40-41.

Leib, J. R., Gollust, S. E., Hull, S. C., & Wilfond, B. S. (2005). Carrier screening panels for Ashkenazi Jews: Is more better? *Genetic Medicine, 7*, 185-190.

Leibel, R. L., Rosenbaum, M., & Hirsch, J. (1995, March 9). Changes in energy expenditure resulting from altered body. *New England Journal of Medicine, 332*, 621-628.

Leiblum, S. R., & Chivers, M. L. (2007). Normal and persistent genital arousal in women: New perspectives. *Journal of Sex & Marital Therapy, 33*, 357-373.

Leigh, J. H., Zinkhan, G. M., & Swaminathan, V. (2006). Dimensional relationships of recall and recognition measures with selected cognitive and affective aspects of print ads. *Journal of Advertising, 35*, 105-122.

Leising, D., Scharloth, J., Lohse, O., & Wood, D. (2014). What types of terms do people use when describing an individual's personality? *Psychological Science, 25*, 1787-1794.

Leiter, S., & Leiter, W. M. (2003). *Affirmative action in antidiscrimination law and policy: An overview and synthesis. SUNY series in American constitutionalism*. Albany: State University of New York Press.

Leitner, L. M. (2007). Diversity issues, postmodernism, and psychodynamic therapy. *PsycCRITIQUES, 52*, n.p.

Lemay, E. P., Jr., Clark, M. S., & Feeney, B. C. (2007). Projection of responsiveness to needs and the construction of satisfying communal relationships. *Journal of Personality and Social Psychology, 92*, 834-853.

Lemay, E., & Clark, M. (2008). How the head liberates the heart: Projection of communal responsiveness guides relationship promotion. *Journal of Personality and Social Psychology, 94*, 647-671.

Lemogne, C., Consoli, S. M., Geoffroy-Perez, B., Coeuret-Pellicer, M., Nabi, H., Melchior, M., & . . . Cordier, S. (2013). Personality and the risk of cancer: A 16-year follow-up study of the GAZEL cohort. *Psychosomatic Medicine, 75*, 262-271.

Lenzenweger, M. F., & Dworkin, R. H. (Eds.). (1998). *The origins and development of schizophrenia: Advances in experimental psychopathology.* Washington, DC: American Psychological Association.

Leong, C., Alessi-Severini, S., Enns, M. W., Nie, Y., Sareen, J., Bolton, . . . Chateau, D. (2017). Cerebrovascular, cardiovascular, and mortality events in new users of selective serotonin reuptake inhibitors and serotonin norepinephrine reuptake inhibitors: A propensity score-matched population-based study. *Journal of Clinical Psychopharmacology, 37*, 332-340.

Lepore, J. (2009, November 9). Why is American history so murderous? *The New Yorker.*

Leppänen, J. M., Moulson, M. C., Vogel-Farley, V. K., & Nelson, C. A. (2007). An ERP study of emotional face processing in the adult and infant brain. *Child Development, 78*, 232-245.

Leskinen, E. A., Rabelo, V. C., & Cortina, L. M. (2015). Gender stereotyping and harassment: A 'catch-22' for women in the workplace. *Psychology, Public Policy, and Law, 21*, 192-204.

Lester, K. J., Coleman, J. I., Roberts, S., Keers, R., Breen, G., Bögels, S., . . . Eley, T. C. (2017). Genetic variation in the endocannabinoid system and response to cognitive behavior therapy for child anxiety disorders. *American Journal of Medical Genetics Part B: Neuropsychiatric Genetics, 174*, 144-155.

Leung, A.K., & Chiu, C. (2010). Multicultural experience, idea receptiveness, and creativity. *Journal of Cross-Cultural Psychology, 41*, 721-741.

LeVay, S. (2011). *Gay, straight, and the reason why: The science of sexual orientation.* New York: Oxford University Press.

Levi, A., Chan, K. K., & Pence, D. (2006). Real men do not read labels: The effects of masculinity and involvement on college students' food decisions. *Journal of American College Health, 55*, 91-98.

Levin, R. J. (2007). Sexual activity, health and well-being—the beneficial roles of coitus and masturbation. *Sexual and Relationship Therapy, 22*, 135-148.

Levine, C. S., Miyamoto, Y., Markus, H. R., Rigotti, A., Boylan, J. M., Park, J., & . . . Ryff, C. D. (2016). Culture and healthy eating: The role of independence and interdependence in the United States and Japan. *Personality and Social Psychology Bulletin, 42*(10), 1335-1348.

Levine, J. M., & Moreland, R. L. (2006). Small groups: An overview. In J. M. Levine & R. L. Moreland (Eds.), *Small groups.* New York: Psychology Press.

Levine, L. E., & Munsch, J. (2011). *Child development: An active learning approach.* Thousand Oaks, CA: Sage Publications, Inc.

Levine, S. Z. (2011). Elaboration on the association between IQ and parental SES with subsequent crime. *Personality and Individual Differences, 50*, 1233-1237.

Levine, S. Z., & Rabinowitz, J. (2007). Revisiting the 5 dimensions of the Positive and Negative Syndrome Scale. *Journal of Clinical Psychopharmacology, 27*, 431-436.

Levinson, D. (1992). *The seasons of a woman's life.* New York: Knopf.

Levinson, D. J. (1990). A theory of life structure development in adulthood. In C. N. Alexander & E. J. Langer (Eds.), *Higher stages of human development: Perspectives on adult growth.* New York: Oxford University Press.

Levy, B. (1996). Improving memory in old age through implicit self-stereotyping. *Journal of Personality and Social Psychology, 71*, 1092-1107.

Levy, B. R., & Myers, L. M. (2004). Preventive health behaviors influenced by self-perceptions of aging. *Preventive Medicine: An International Journal Devoted to Practice and Theory, 39*, 625-629.

Levy, B. R., Slade, M. D., Kunkel, S. R., & Kasl, S. V. (2002). Longevity increased by positive self-perceptions of aging. *Journal of Personality & Social Psychology, 83*, 261-270.

Lewin, T. (2003, December 22). For more people in their 20s and 30s, going home is easier because they never left. *The New York Times*, p. A27.

Lewinsohn, P. M., & Essau, C. A. (2002). Depression in adolescents. In I. H. Gotlib & C. L. Hammen (Eds.), *Handbook of depression.* New York: Guilford Press.

Lewinsohn, P. M., Petit, J. W., Joiner, T. E., Jr., & Seeley, J. R. (2003). The symptomatic expression of major depressive disorder in adolescents and young adults. *Journal of Abnormal Psychology, 112*, 244-252.

Lewis, C. E., Thomas, K. F., Dodge, N. C., Molteno, C. D., Meintjes, E. M., Jacobson, J. L., & Jacobson, S. W. (2015). Verbal learning and memory impairment in children with fetal alcohol spectrum disorders. *Alcoholism: Clinical and Experimental Research, 39*, 724-732.

Lewis, C., & Lamb, M. (2011). The role of parent-child relationships in child development. In M. E. Lamb & M. H. Bornstein (Eds.), *Social and personality development: An advanced textbook.* New York: Psychology Press.

Lewis, D. G., Al-Shawaf, L., Conroy-Beam, D., Asao, K., & Buss, D. M. (2017). Evolutionary psychology: A how-to guide. *American Psychologist, 72*(4), 353-373.

Lewis, T., & Umbreit, M. (2015). A humanistic approach to mediation and dialogue: An evolving transformative practice. *Conflict Resolution Quarterly.* Accessed online, 9.30.15; http://onlinelibrary.wiley.com/doi/10.1002/crq.21130/abstract.

Li, B., Piriz, J., Mirrione, M., Chung, C., Proulx, C. D., Schulz, D., & . . . Malinow, R. (2011). Synaptic potentiation onto habenula neurons in learned helplessness model of depression. *Nature, 470*, 535-539.

Li, M. D., Cheng, R., Ma, J. Z., & Swan, G. E. (2003). A meta-analysis of estimated genetic and environmental effects on smoking behavior in male and female adult twins. *Addiction, 98*, 23-31.

Li, M. D., Lou, X., Chen, G., Ma, J. Z., & Elston, R. C. (2008). Gene-gene interactions among CHRNA4, CHRNB2, BDNF, and NTRK2 in nicotine dependence. *Biological Psychiatry, 64*, 951-957.

Li, T. K., Volkow, N. D., & Baler, R. D. (2007). The biological bases of nicotine and alcohol co-addiction. *Biological Psychiatry, 61*, 1-3.

Li, Y., Hofstetter, C. R., Wahlgren, D., Irvin, V., Chhay, D., & Hovell, M. F. (2015). Social networks and immigration stress among first-generation mandarin-speaking Chinese immigrants in Los Angeles. *International Journal of Social Welfare, 24*, 170-181.

Li, Y., Zuo, Y., Yu, P., Ping, X., & Cui, C. (2015). Role of basolateral amygdala dopamine D2 receptors in impulsive choice in acute cocaine-treated rats. *Behavioural Brain Research, 287*, 187-195.

Liang, K. A. (2007). Acculturation, ambivalent sexism, and attitudes toward women who engage in premarital sex among Chinese American young adults. *Dissertation Abstracts International: Section B: The Sciences and Engineering, 67*(10-B), 6065.

Libedinsky, C., & Livingstone, M. (2011). Role of prefrontal cortex in conscious visual perception. *The Journal of Neuroscience, 31*, 64-69.

Licis, A. K., Desruisseau, D. M., Yamada, K. A., Duntley, S. P., & Gurnett, C. A. (2011). Novel genetic findings in an extended family pedigree with sleepwalking. *Neurology, 76*, 49-52.

Lick, D. J., Durso, L. E., & Johnson, K. L. (2013). Minority stress and physical health among sexual minorities. *Perspectives on Psychological Science, 8*, 521-548.

Lieberman, M. D. (2007). Social cognitive neuro-science: A review of core processes. *Annual Review of Psychology, 58*, 259-289.

Lieberman, P. (2015). A tangled tale of circuits, evolution, and language. *Psyccritiques, 60*, 88-97.

Liechti, M. E., Dolder, P. C., & Schmid, Y. (2017). Alterations of consciousness and mystical-type experiences after acute LSD in humans. *Psychopharmacology, 234*, 1499-1510.

Liedl, A., Müller, J., Morina, N., Karl, A., Denke, C., & Knaevelsrud, C. (2011). Physical activity within a CBT intervention improves coping with pain in traumatized refugees: results of a randomized controlled design. *Pain Medicine, 12*, 138-145.

Liem, G. D. (2015). Academic and social achievement goals: Their additive, interactive, and specialized effects on school functioning. *British Journal of Educational Psychology, 86*(1), 37-56.

Lien, Y. W., Chu, R. L., Jen, C. H., & Wu, C. H. (2006). Do Chinese commit neither fundamental attribution error nor ultimate attribution error? *Chinese Journal of Psychology, 48*, 163-181.

Lilienfeld, S. O. (2007). Psychological treatments that cause harm. *Perspectives on Psychological Science, 2*, 53-58.

Lilienfeld, S. O. (2012). Further sources of our field's embattled public reputation. *American Psychologist*, 808-809.

Lilienfeld, S. O. (2017). Microaggressions: Strong claims, inadequate evidence. *Perspectives on Psychological Science, 12*, 138-169.

Lillard, A. S., & Woolley, J. D. (2015). Grounded in reality: How children make sense of the unreal. *Cognitive Development, 34*, 111-114.

Lim, A., & Okuno, H. G. (2015). A recipe for empathy: Integrating the mirror system, insula, somatosensory cortex and motherese. *International Journal of Social Robotics, 7*, 35-49.

Limberg, B. (2015). Nature vs. nurture . . . again: Examining the interplay between genetics and the environment. *PsycCRITIQUES, 60*, 88-98.

Lin, C. H., & Lin, H. M. (2007). What price do you ask for the 'extra one'? A social value orientation perspective. *Social Behavior and Personality, 35*, 9-18.

Lin, I., Wang, S., Chu, I., Lu, Y., Lee, C., Lin, T., & Fan, S. (2017). The association of Type D personality with heart rate variability and lipid profiles among patients with coronary artery disease. *International Journal of Behavioral Medicine, 24*, 101-109.

Lin, J., Arthurs, J., & Reilly, S. (2017). Conditioned taste aversions: From poisons to pain to drugs of abuse. *Psychonomic Bulletin & Review, 24*, 335-351.

Lin, L., McCormack, H., Kruczkowski, L., & Berg, M. B. (2015). How women's perceptions of peer weight preferences are related to drive for thinness. *Sex Roles, 72*, 117-126.

Lin, Y., Li, K., Sung, W., Ko, H., Tzeng, O. L., Hung, D. L., & Juan, C. (2011). The relationship between development of attention and learning in children: A cognitive neuroscience approach. *Bulletin of Educational Psychology, 42*, 517-542.

Lindblad, F., Lindahl, M., & Theorell, T. (2006). Physiological stress reactions in 6th and 9th graders during test performance. *Stress and Health: Journal of the International Society for the Investigation of Stress, 22*, 189-195.

Lindemann, O., & Bekkering, H. (2009). Object manipulation and motion perception: Evidence of an influence of action planning on visual processing. *Journal of Experimental Psychology: Human Perception and Performance, 35*, 1062-1071.

Lindh-Astrand, L., Brynhildsen, J., & Hoffmann, M. (2007). Attitudes towards the menopause and hormone therapy over the turn of the century. *Maturitas, 56*, 12-20.

Lindley, L. D. (2006). The paradox of self-efficacy: Research with diverse populations. *Journal of Career Assessment, 14*, 143-160.

Lindorff, M. (2005). Determinants of received social support: Who gives what to managers? *Journal of Social and Personal Relationships, 22*, 323-337.

Lindsay, P. H., & Norman, D. A. (1977). *Human information processing* (2nd ed.). New York: Academic Press.

Lindsey, E., & Colwell, M. (2003). Preschoolers' emotional competence: Links to pretend and physical play. *Child Study Journal, 33*, 39-52.

Linley, P. (2013). Human strengths and well-being: Finding the best within us at the intersection of eudaimonic philosophy, humanistic psychology, and positive psychology. In A. S. Waterman (Ed.), *The best within us: Positive psychology perspectives on eudaimonia*. Washington, DC: American Psychological Association.

Lipsman, N., Giacobbe, P., & Lozano, A. M. (2015). Deep brain stimulation for the management of treatment-refractory major depressive disorder. In B. Sun & A. De Salles (Eds.), *Neurosurgical treatments for psychiatric disorders* (pp. 95-104). New York, NY, US: Springer Science + Business Media.

Little, A., Burt, D. M., & Perrett, D. I. (2006). What is good is beautiful: Face preference reflects desired personality. *Personality and Individual Differences, 41*, 1107-1118.

Little, K., Ramssen, E., Welchko, R., Volberg, V., Roland, C., & Cassin, B. (2009). Decreased brain dopamine cell numbers in human cocaine users. *Psychiatry Research, 168*, 173-180.

Liu, J., Ying, Z., & Zhang, S. (2015). A rate function approach to computerized adaptive testing for cognitive diagnosis. *Psychometrika, 80*, 468-490

Liu, L., He, S-Z., & Wu, Y. (2007). An analysis of the characteristics of single parent families with different structures and their children. *Chinese Journal of Clinical Psychology, 15*, 68-70.

Livingstone, A. G., Spears, R., Manstead, A. R., Bruder, M., & Shepherd, L. (2011). We feel, therefore we are: Emotion as a basis for self-categorization and social action. *Emotion, 11*, 754-767.

Llorca-Mestre, A., Samper-García, P., Malonda-Vidal, E., & Cortés-Tomás, M. T. (2017). Parenting style and peer attachment as predictors of emotional instability in children. *Social Behavior And Personality, 45*, 677-694.

Lobato, M. I., Koff, W. J., & Manenti, C. (2006). Follow-up of sex reassignment surgery in transsexuals: A Brazilian cohort. *Archives of Sexual Behavior, 35*, 711-715.

Lobban, F., Barrowclough, C., & Jones, S. (2006). Does expressed emotion need to be understood within a more systemic framework? An examination of discrepancies in appraisals between patients diagnosed with schizophrenia and their relatives. *Social Psychiatry and Psychiatric Epidemiology, 41*, 50-55.

Lobo, I., & Harris, R. (2008, July). GABA$_a$ receptors and alcohol. *Pharmacology, Biochemistry and Behavior, 90*, 90-94.

Lockl, K., & Schneider, W. (2007). Knowledge about the mind: Links between theory of mind and later metamemory. *Child Development, 78*, 148-167.

Loehlin, J. C., Bartels, M., Boomsma, D. I., Bratko, D., Martin, N. G., Nichols, R. C., & Wright, M. J. (2015). Is there a genetic correlation between general factors of intelligence and personality? *Twin Research and Human Genetics, 18*, 234-242.

Lofholm, N. (2003, May 6). Climber's kin share relief: Ralston saw 4 options, they say; death wasn't one of them. *Denver Post*, p. A1.

Loftus, E. F., & Palmer, J. C. (1974). Reconstruction of automobile destruction: An example of the interface between language and memory. *Journal of Verbal Learning and Verbal Behavior, 13*, 585-589.

Loitfelder, M., Fazekas, F., Petrovic, K., Fuchs, S., Ropele, S., Wallner-Blazek, M., & . . . Enzinger, C. (2011). Reorganization in cognitive networks with progression of multiple sclerosis: Insights from fMRI. *Neurology, 76*, 526-533.

Lombaard, N., & Naudé, L. (2017). "Breaking the cycle": Black adolescents' experiences of being stereotyped during identity development. *Journal of Psychology in Africa, 27*, 185-190.

Longo, M. R., Trippier, S., Vagnoni, E., & Lourenco, S. F. (2015). Right hemisphere control of visuospatial attention in near space. *Neuropsychologia, 70*, 350-357.

Lopes, A. C., Greenberg, B. D., Noren, G., Canteras, M. M., Busatto, G. F. de Mathis, et al. (2009). Treatment of resistant obsessive-compulsive disorder with ventral capsular/ventral striatal gamma capsulotomy: A pilot prospective study. *The Journal of Neuropsychiatry and Clinical Neurosciences, 21*, 381-392.

Lopez, N. L., Schneider, H. G., & Dula, C. S. (2002). Parent Discipline Scale: Discipline choice as a function of transgression type. *North American Journal of Psychology, 4*, 381-393.

Lorenz, K. (1966). *On aggression*. New York: Harcourt Brace Jovanovich.

Lorenz, K. (1974). *Civilized man's eight deadly sins*. New York: Harcourt Brace Jovanovich.

Loriedo, C., & Di Leone, F. G. (2017). Conversion disorder. In G. R. Elkins (Ed.), *Handbook of medical and psychological hypnosis: Foundations, applications, and professional issues*. New York: Springer Publishing Co.

Loving, T., Crockett, E., & Paxson, A. (2009). Passionate love and relationship thinkers: Experimental evidence for acute cortisol elevations in women. *Psychoneuroendocrinology, 34*, 939-946.

Lowe, P., Humphreys, C., & Williams, S. J. (2007). Night terrors: Women's experiences of (not) sleeping where there is domestic violence. *Violence against Women, 13*, 549-561.

Lozano, A., & Mayberg, H. (2015, February). Treating depression at the source: Electrical stimulation deep within the brain may alleviate devastating mood. *Scientific American*, 68-73.

Lu, S. (2015, February.) Erasing bad memories. *Monitor on Psychology*, pp. 41-45.

Lubell, K. M., Swahn, M. H., Crosby, A. E., & Kegler, S. R. (2004). Methods of suicide among persons aged 10-19 years–United States, 1992-2001. *Morbidity and Mortality Weekly Report, 53*, 471-473.

Lucas, W. (2008). Parents' perceptions of the Drug Abuse Resistance Education program (DARE). *Journal of Child & Adolescent Substance Abuse, 17*, 99-114.

Luchins, A. S. (1946). Classroom experiments on mental set. *American Journal of Psychology, 59*, 295-298.

Lun, V. M., & Bond, M. H. (2006). Achieving relationship harmony in groups and its consequence for group performance. *Asian Journal of Social Psychology, 9*, 195-202.

Luo, S., & Zhang, G. (2009). What leads to romantic attraction: Similarity, reciprocity, security, or beauty? Evidence from a speed-dating study. *Journal of Personality, 77*, 933-964.

Luong, G., Rauers, A., & Fingerman, K. L. (2015). The multifaceted nature of late-life socialization: Older adults as agents and targets of socialization. In J. E. Grusec & P. D. Hastings (Eds.), *Handbook of socialization: Theory and research* (2nd ed.). New York: Guilford Press.

Luria, A. R. (1968). *The mind of a mnemonist.* Cambridge, MA: Basic Books.

Ślusarczyk, E., & Niedźwieńska, A. (2013). A naturalistic study of prospective memory in preschoolers: The role of task interruption and motivation. *Cognitive Development, 28*, 179-192.

Lutgendorf, S. K., & Andersen, B. L. (2015). Biobehavioral approaches to cancer progression and survival: Mechanisms and interventions. *American Psychologist, 70*, 186-197.

Luttrell, A., Petty, R. E., & Xu, M. (2017). Replicating and fixing failed replications: The case of need for cognition and argument quality. *Journal of Experimental Social Psychology, 69*, 178-183.

Lutz, C. K., & Novak, M. A. (2005). Environmental enrichment for nonhuman primates: theory and application. *ILAR Journal, 46*, 178-191.

Lutz, W., Lambert, M. J., Harmon, S. C., Tschitsaz, A., Schurch, E., & Stulz, N. (2006). The probability of treatment success, failure and duration—What can be learned from empirical data to support decision making in clinical practice? *Clinical Psychology & Psychotherapy, 13*, 223-232.

Lynn, S. J., Kirsch, I., Barabasz, A., Cardena, E., & Patterson, D. (2000). Hypnosis as an empirically supported clinical intervention: The state of the evidence and a look to the future. *International Journal of Clinical and Experimental Hypnosis, 48*, 239-259.

Lynn, S. J., Krackow, E., Loftus, E. F., Locke, T. G., & Lilienfeld, S. O. (2015). Constructing the past: Problematic memory recovery techniques in psychotherapy. In S. O. Lilienfeld, S. J. Lynn, & J. M. Lohr (Eds.), *Science and pseudoscience in clinical psychology (2nd ed.).* New York: Guilford Press.

Lynn, S. J., Laurence, J., & Kirsch, I. (2015). Hypnosis, suggestion, and suggestibility: An integrative model. *American Journal of Clinical Hypnosis, 57*, 314-329.

Lyons, H., Giordano, P. C., Manning, W. D., & Longmore, M. A. (2011). Identity, peer relationships, and adolescent girls' sexual behavior: An exploration of the contemporary double standard. *Journal of Sex Research, 48*, 437-449.

López, G., & Bialik, K. (2017, May 3.). Key findings about U.S. immigrants. *Fact Tank: News in the Numbers.* http://www.pewresearch.org/fact-tank/2017/05/03/key-findings-about-u-s-immigrants/.

López, S. R., & Guarnaccia, P. J. J. (2000). Cultural psychopathology: Uncovering the social world of mental illness. *Annual Review of Psychology, 51*, 571-598.

López-Pérez, B., & Ambrona, T. (2015). The role of cognitive emotion regulation on the vicarious emotional response. *Motivation and Emotion, 39*, 299-308.

López-Pérez, B., Carrera, P., Oceja, L., Ambrona, T., & Stocks, E. (2017). Sympathy and tenderness as components of dispositional empathic concern: Predicting helping and caring behaviors. *Current Psychology: A Journal for Diverse Perspectives on Diverse Psychological Issues.* Accessed from https://link.springer.com/article/10.1007/s12144-017-9615-7.

Macaluso, E., & Driver, J. (2005). Multisensory spatial interactions: a window onto functional integration in the human brain. *Trends in Neurosciences, 28, Issue 5*, 264-271.

Macaluso, E., Frith, C. D., & Driver, J. (2000, August 18). Modulation of human visual cortex by crossmodal spatial attention. *Science, 289*, 1206-1208.

Macduff, I. (2006). Your pace or mine? Culture, time and negotiation. *Negotiation Journal, 22*, 31-45.

Mace, J. H., Bernas, R. S., & Clevinger, A. (2015). Individual differences in recognising involuntary autobiographical memories: Impact on the reporting of abstract cues. *Memory, 23*, 445-452.

Mack, J. (2003). *The museum of the mind.* London: British Museum Publications.

Mack, M. L., Love, B. C., & Preston, A. R. (2016). Dynamic updating of hippocampal object representations reflects new conceptual knowledge. *PNAS Proceedings of the National Academy of Sciences of the United States of America, 113*, 13203-13208.

Mackay, J., & Eriksen, M. (2002). *The tobacco atlas.* Geneva, Switzerland: World Health Organization.

Mackey, A. P., Finn, A. S., Leonard, J. A., Jacoby-Senghor, D. S., West, M. R., Gabrieli, C. F. O., . . . Gabrieli, J. D. (2015). Neuroanatomical correlates of the income-achievement gap. *Psychological Science*, 1-9.

MacLean, L., Edwards, N., Garrard, M., Sims-Jones, N., Clinton, K., & Ashley, L. (2009). Obesity, stigma and public health planning. *Health Promotion International, 24*, 88-93.

MacLennan, A. (2009). Evidence-based review of therapies at the menopause. *International Journal of Evidence-Based Healthcare, 7*, 112-123.

MacNeilage, P. F., Rogers, L. J., & Vallortigara, G. (2009, July). Origins of the left & right brain. *Scientific American*, pp. 60-67.

Macur, J. (2017, July 18). Honest tour analysis from a familiar, though hardly trusted, voice. *The New York Times*, p. B7.

Madden, D. J. (2007). Aging and visual attention. *Current Directions in Psychological Science, 16*, 70-74.

Maddi, S. R. (2007). The story of hardiness: Twenty years of theorizing, research, and practice. In A. Monat, R. S. Lazarus, & G. Reevy (Eds.), *The Praeger handbook on stress and coping* (Vol. 2). Westport, CT: Praeger Publishers/Greenwood Publishing.

Maddi, S. R., Khoshaba, D. M., Harvey, R. H., Fazel, M., & Resurreccion, N. (2011). The personality construct of hardiness, V: Relationships with the construction of existential meaning in life. *Journal of Humanistic Psychology, 51*, 369-388.

Maddock, R. J., Buonocore, M. H., Miller, A. R., Yoon, J. H., Soosman, S. K., & Unruh, A. M. (2013). Abnormal activity-dependent brain lactate and glutamate + glutamine responses in panic disorder. *Biological Psychiatry, 73*, 1111-1119.

Mader, S. S. (2000). *Biology* (6th ed.). Boston: McGraw-Hill.

Madon, S., Willard, J., & Guyll, M. (2006). Self-fulfilling prophecy effects of mothers' beliefs on children's alcohol use: Accumulation, dissipation, and stability over time. *Journal of Personality and Social Psychology, 90*, 911-926.

Magee, S. R., Bublitz, M. H., Orazine, C., Brush, B., Salisbury, A., Niaura, R., & Stroud, L. R. (2013). The relationship between maternal-fetal attachment and cigarette smoking over pregnancy. *Maternal and Child Health Journal, 18*(4), 1017-1022.

Magida, A. J. (2006). *Opening the doors of wonder: Reflections on religious rites of passage.* Berkeley, CA: University of California Press.

Magis, D., & Schoenen, J. (2011). Treatment of migraine: update on new therapies. *Current Opinions in Neurology, 24*, 203-210.

Magoni, M., Bassani, L., Okong, P., Kituuka, P., Germinario, E. P., Giuliano, M., & Vella, S. (2005). Mode of infant feeding and HIV infection in children in a program for prevention of mother-to-child transmission in Uganda. *AIDS, 19*, 433-437.

Magoon, M., & Critchfield, T. (2008). Concurrent schedules of positive and negative reinforcement: Differential-impact and differential-outcomes hypotheses. *Journal of the Experimental Analysis of Behavior, 90*, 1-22.

Magruder, K., & Yeager, D. (2009). The prevalence of PTSD across war eras and the effect of deployment on PTSD: A systematic review and meta-analysis. *Psychiatric Annals, 39*, 778-788.

Maher, B. (2015). The anatomy of obedience. *Nature, 523*, 408-409.

Majeres, R. L. (2007). Sex differences in phonological coding: Alphabet transformation speed. *Intelligence, 35*, 335-346.

Major, J. T., Johnson, W., & Bouchard, T. J. (2011). The dependability of the general factor of intelligence: Why small, single-factor models do not adequately represent g. *Intelligence, 39*, 418-433.

Majorano, M., & D'Odorico, L. (2011). The transition into ambient language: A longitudinal study of babbling and first word production of Italian children. *First Language, 31*, 47-66.

Malin, D. H., Schaar, K. L., Izygon, J. J., Nghiem, D. M., Jabitta, S. Y., Henceroth, M. M., & . . . Ward, C. P. (2015). Validation and scopolamine-reversal of latent learning in the water maze utilizing a revised direct platform placement procedure. *Pharmacology, Biochemistry And Behavior, 13*, 590-96.

Malouff, J. M., & Rooke, S. E. (2013). Expert-recommended warnings for medical marijuana. *Substance Abuse, 34*, 92-93.

Mancinelli, R., Binetti, R., & Ceccanti, M. (2007). Woman, alcohol and environment: Emerging risks for health. *Neuroscience & Biobehavioral Reviews, 31*, 246-253.

Manjhi, A., & Purty, S. (2017). Response to the blank card of Thematic Apperception Test (TAT) and its correlation with personality factors. *Journal of Projective Psychology & Mental Health, 24*, 52-56.

Manly, J. J. (2005). Advantages and disadvantages of separate norms for African Americans. *Clinical Neuropsychologist, 19*, 270-275.

Manly, J., & Echemendia, R. (2007). Race-specific norms: Using the model of hypertension to understand issues of race, culture, and education in neuropsychology. *Archives of Clinical Neuropsychology, 22*, 319-325.

Mannarini, T., Talò, C., & Rochira, A. (2017). How diverse is this community? Sense of community, ethnic prejudice, and perceived ethnic heterogeneity. *Journal of Community and Applied Social Psychology, 27*(3), 181-195.

Manni, R., & Terzaghi, M. (2013). Dreaming and enacting dreams in nonrapid eye movement and rapid eye movement parasomnia: A step toward a unifying view within distinct patterns? *Sleep Medicine, 14*, 387-388.

Manor, J. K., & Gailliot, M. T. (2007). Altruism and egoism: Prosocial motivations for helping depend on relationship context. *European Journal of Social Psychology*, Retrieve from http://onlinelibrary.wiley.com/doi/10.1002/ejsp.364/abstract.

Mansson, K. N., Salami, A., Frick, A., Carlbring, P., Andersson, G., Furmark, T., & Boraxbekk, C. J. (2016). Neuroplasticity in response to cognitive behavior therapy for social anxiety disorder. *Translational Psychiatry, 6*, e727. doi: 10.1038/tp.2015.218.

Manstead, A. S. R., & Wagner, H. L. (2004). *Experience emotion.* Cambridge, England: Cambridge University Press.

Manstead, A. S. R., Frijda, N., & Fischer, A. H. (Eds.). (2003). *Feelings and emotions: The Amsterdam Symposium.* Cambridge, England: Cambridge University Press.

Manzo, L., Gómez, M. J., Callejas-Aguilera, J. E., Fernández-Teruel, A., Papini, M. R., & Torres, C. (2015). Partial reinforcement reduces vulnerability to anti-anxiety self-medication during appetitive extinction. *International Journal Of Comparative Psychology, 28*, 22-30.

Marchand, S., & Phillips, G. E. (2012). Hoarding's place in the DSM-5: Another symptom, or a newly listed disorder? *Issues in Mental Health Nursing, 33*, 591-597.

Marks, I. M. (2004). The Nobel prize award in physiology to Ivan Petrovich Pavlov-1904. *Australian and New Zealand Journal of Psychiatry, 38*, 674-677.

Markus, H. R. (2007). Sociocultural psychology: The dynamic interdependence among self systems and social systems. In S. Kitayama & D. Cohen (Eds.), *Handbook of cultural psychology.* New York: Guilford Press.

Markus, H. R., & Kitayama, S. (2003). Models of agency: Sociocultural diversity in the construction of action. In V. Murphy-Berman & J. J. Berman (Eds.), *Cross-cultural differences in perspectives on the self.* Lincoln, NE: University of Nebraska Press.

Markus, H., & Kitayama, S. (2003). Culture, self, and the reality of the social. *Psychological Inquiry, 14*, 277-283.

Markus, H., & Kitayama, S. (2010). Cultures and selves: A cycle of mutual constitution. *Perspectives on Psychological Science, 5*, 420-430.

Markus, K. A., & Borsboom, D. (2013). *Frontiers of test validity theory: Measurement, causation, and meaning.* New York: Routledge/Taylor & Francis Group.

Marques, A. H., Bjørke-Monsen, A., Teixeira, A. L., & Silverman, M. N. (2015). Maternal stress, nutrition and physical activity: Impact on immune function, CNS development and psychopathology. *Brain Research, 161*, 728-746.

Marsh, B. (2008, February 24). A growing cloud over the planet. *The New York Times,* p. WK4.

Marsh, H. W., Hau, K. T., & Sung, R. Y. T. (2007). Childhood obesity, gender, actual-ideal body image discrepancies, and physical self-concept in Hong Kong children: Cultural differences in the value of moderation. *Developmental Psychology, 43*, 647-662.

Marshall, J. R. (2011). Ultimate causes and the evolution of altruism. *Behavioral Ecology and Sociobiology, 65*, 503-512.

Marshall, K., Laing, D. G., & Jinks, A. L. (2006). The capacity of humans to identify components in complex odor-taste mixtures. *Chemical Senses, 31*, 539-545.

Marshall, L., & Born, J. (2007, October). The contribution of sleep to hippocampus-dependent memory consolidation. *Trends in Cognitive Sciences, 11*(10), 442-450.

Marshall, M. K. (2007). The critical factors of coaching practice leading to successful coaching outcomes. *Dissertation Abstracts International: Section B: The Sciences and Engineering, 67*(7-B), 4092.

Marshall, R. D., Bryant, R. A., Amsel, L., Suh, E. J., Cook, J. M., & Neria, Y. (2007). The psychology of ongoing threat: Relative risk appraisal, the September 11 attacks and terrorism-related fears. *American Psychologist, 62*, 304-316.

Martelle, S., Hanley, C., & Yoshino K. (2003, January 28). "Sopranos" scenario in slaying? *Los Angeles Times,* p. B1.

Martin, E. A., & Kerns, J. G. (2011). The influence of positive mood on different aspects of cognitive control. *Cognition and Emotion, 25*, 265-279.

Martin, K. K., & North, A. C. (2015). Diffusion of responsibility on social networking sites. *Computers In Human Behavior, 44*, 124-131.

Martin, L., & Pullum, G. K. (1991). *The great Eskimo vocabulary hoax.* Chicago: University of Chicago Press.

Mashour, G. A., Walker, E. E., & Martuza, R. L. (2005). Psychosurgery: Past, present, and future. *Brain Research Reviews, 48*, 409-419.

Masi, S., Asselain, N., Robelin, L., Bourgeois, A., Hano, C., Dousseau, G., & . . . Krief, S. (2013). Response to bitter substances in primates: Roles of diet tendency and weaning age. *Cognitive, Affective & Behavioral Neuroscience.* Retrieved from http://www.ncbi.nlm.nih.gov/pubmed/23712664.

Maslow, A. H. (1970). *Motivation and personality.* New York: Harper & Row.

Maslow, A. H. (1987). *Motivation and personality* (3rd ed.). New York: Harper & Row.

Mason, T. B., Maduro, R. S., Derlega, V. J., Hacker, D. S., Winstead, B. A., & Haywood, J. E. (2017). Individual differences in the impact of vicarious racism: African American students react to the George Zimmerman trial. *Cultural Diversity and Ethnic Minority Psychology, 23*, 174-184.

Massadi, O. A., López, M., Tschöp, M., Diéguez, C., & Nogueiras, R. (2017). Current understanding of the hypothalamic ghrelin pathways inducing appetite and adiposity. *Trends In Neurosciences, 40*, 167-180.

Massé-Alarie, H., Beaulieu, L., Preuss, R., & Schneider, C. (2017). The side of chronic low back pain matters: Evidence from the primary motor cortex excitability and the postural adjustments of multifidi muscles. *Experimental Brain Research, 235*, 647-659.

Mast, F. W., & Kosslyn, S. M. (2002). Visual mental images can be ambiguous: Insights from individual differences in spatial transformation abilities. *Cognition, 86*, 57-70.

Masters, W. H., & Johnson, V. E. (1979). *Homosexuality in perspective.* Boston: Little, Brown.

Matchock, R. L., & Mordkoff, J. T. (2009). Chronotype and time-of-day influences on the alerting, orienting, and executive components of attention. *Experimental Brain Research, 192*, 189-198.

Mathews, H. L., & Janusek, L. (2011). Epigenetics and psychoneuroimmunology: Mechanisms and models. *Brain, Behavior, and Immunity, 25*, 25-39.

Maton, K. I., Kohout, J. L., Wicherski, M., Leary, G. E., & Vinokurov, A. (2006). Minority students of color and the psychology graduate pipeline. *American Psychologist, 61*, 117-131.

Matsumoto, D. (2002). Methodological requirements to test a possible in-group advantage in judging emotions across cultures: Comment on Elfenbein and Ambady (2002) and evidence. *Psychological Bulletin, 128*, 236-242.

Mattan, B. D., Kubota, J. T., & Cloutier, J. (2017). How social status shapes person perception and evaluation: A social neuroscience perspective. *Perspectives on Psychological Science, 12*, 468-507.

Mattys, S. L., Seymour, F. F., Attwood, A. S., & Munafò, M. R. (2013). Effects of acute anxiety induction on speech perception: Are anxious listeners distracted listeners? *Psychological Science, 24*, 1606-1608.

Maturana, M. J., Pudell, C., Targa, A. S., Rodrigues, L. S., Noseda, A. D., Fortes, M. H., & . . . Lima, M. S. (2015). REM sleep deprivation reverses neurochemical and other depressive-like alterations induced by olfactory bulbectomy. *Molecular Neurobiology, 51*, 349-360.

Maurer, D., Lewis, T. L., Brent, H. P., & Levin, A. V. (1999). Rapid improvement in the acuity of infants after visual input. *Science, 286*, 108-110.

Maxson, S. C. (2013). Behavioral genetics. In R. J. Nelson, S. Y. Mizumori, & I. B. Weiner (Eds.), *Handbook of psychology, Vol. 3: Behavioral neuroscience (2nd ed.)*. New York: John Wiley & Sons Ltd.

Maxwell, S. E., Lau, M. Y., & Howard, G. S. (2015). Is psychology suffering from a replication crisis? *American Psychologist, 70*, 487-498.

Maybin, S. (2017, March 10). Busting the attention span myth. *BBC World News*. Retrieved from http://www.bbc.com/news/health-38896790.

Mayer, D., Simetin, I. P., Rodin, U., Benjak, T., Puntarić, E., & Puntarić, I. (2015). The impacts of media messaging and age and sex variance on adolescent smoking habits in Croatia. *Journal of Addiction Medicine, 9*, 147-154.

Mayer, J. D., Salovey, P., & Caruso, D. R. (2004). Emotional intelligence: Theory, findings, and implications. *Psychological Inquiry, 15*, 197-215.

Mayer, J. D., Salovey, P., & Caruso, D. R. (2008). Emotional intelligence: New ability or eclectic traits? *American Psychologist, 63*, 503-517.

Mayer, R. E. (2013). Problem solving. In D. Reisberg (Ed.), *The Oxford handbook of cognitive psychology*. New York: Oxford University Press.

Maynard, A. E., & Martini, M. I. (2005). *Learning in cultural context: Family, peers, and school*. New York: Kluwer Academic/Plenum Publishers.

Mays, V. M., & Ghavami, N. (2018). History, aspirations, and transformations of intersectionality: Focusing on gender. In C. B. Travis & J. W. White (Eds.), *APA handbook of the psychology of women: Volume 1: History, theory, and battlegrounds* (pp. 541-566). Washington, DC: American Psychological Association.

McAdams, D. P., Diamond, A., de St. Aubin, E., & Mansfield, E. (1997). Stories of commitment: The psychosocial construction of generative lives. *Journal of Personality and Social Psychology, 72*, 678-694.

McCabe, C., & Rolls, E. T. (2007). Umami: A delicious flavor formed by convergence of taste and olfactory pathways in the human brain. *European Journal of Neuroscience, 25*, 1855-1864.

McCann, J. T., Lynn, S. J., Lilienfeld, S. O., Shindler, K. L., & Hammond Natof, T. R. (2015). The science and pseudoscience of expert testimony. In S. O. Lilienfeld, S. J. Lynn, & J. M. Lohr (Eds.), *Science and pseudoscience in clinical psychology (2nd ed.)*. New York: Guilford Press.

McCarrey, A. C., & Resnick, S. M. (2015). Postmenopausal hormone therapy and cognition. *Hormones and Behavior, 74*, 167-172.

McCarthy, J. (2005). Individualism and collectivism: What do they have to do with counseling? *Journal of Multicultural Counseling and Development, 33*, 108-117.

McCarthy, J., & Brown, A. (2015, March 2). Getting more sleep linked to higher well-being. Gallup Poll. http://www.gallup.com/poll/1181583/getting-sleep-linked-higher.aspx.

McCarthy, R. J., & Skowronski, J. J. (2011). You're getting warmer: Level of construal affects the impact of central traits on impression formation. *Journal of Experimental Social Psychology, 47*, 1304-1307.

McCaul, K. D., Johnson, R. J., & Rothman, A. J. (2002). The effects of framing and action instructions on whether older adults obtain flu shots. *Health Psychology, 21*, 624-628.

McCauley, R. N., & Henrich, J. (2006). Susceptibility to the Müller-Lyer illusion, theory-neutral observation, and the diachronic penetrability of the visual input. *Philosophical Psychology, 19*, 79-101.

McClelland, D. C. (1985). How motives, skills, and values determine what people do. *American Psychologist, 40*, 812-825.

McClelland, D. C. (1993). Intelligence is not the best predictor of job performance. *Current Directions in Psychological Research, 2*, 5-8.

McClelland, D. C., Atkinson, J. W., Clark, R. A., & Lowell, E. L. (1953). *The achievement motive*. New York: Appleton-Century-Crofts.

McCrae, R. R., & Costa, P. T. (1994). The stability of personality: Observation and evaluations. *Current Directions in Psychological Science, 3*, 173-175.

McCrae, R. R., Kurtz, J. E., Yamagata, S., & Terracciano, A. (2011). Internal consistency, retest reliability, and their implications for personality scale validity. *Personality and Social Psychology Review, 15*, 28-50.

McCrink, K., & Wynn, K. (2007). Ratio abstraction by 6-month-old infants. *Psychological Science, 18*, 740-745.

McCulloch, K., Lachner Bass, N., Dial, H., Hiscock, M., & Jansen, B. (2017). Interaction of attention and acoustic factors in dichotic listening for fused words. *Laterality: Asymmetries of Body, Brain and Cognition, 22*, 473-494.

McDaniel, M. A., Maier, S. F., & Einstein, G. O. (2002). "Brain specific" nutrients: A memory cure? *Psychological Science in the Public Interest, 3*, 12-18.

McDermott, M. S., Beard, E., Brose, L. S., West, R., & McEwen, A. (2013). Factors associated with differences in quit rates between 'specialist' and 'community' stop-smoking practitioners in the English stop-smoking services. *Nicotine & Tobacco Research, 15*, 1239-1247.

McDonald, A. R., Muraskin, J., Van Dam, N. T., Froehlich, C., Puccio, B., Pellman, J., . . . Craddock, R. C. (2017). The real-time fMRI neurofeedback based stratification of Default Network Regulation Neuroimaging data repository. *Neuroimage, 146*, 157-170.

McDonald, H. E., & Hirt, E. R. (1997). When expectancy meets desire: Motivational effects in reconstructive memory. *Journal of Personality and Social Psychology, 72*, 5-23.

McDougall, W. (1908). *Introduction to social psychology*. London: Methuen.

McElreath, R., Wallin, A., & Fasolo, B. (2013). The evolutionary rationality of social learning. In R. Hertwig & U. Hoffrage (Eds.), *Simple heuristics in a social world*. New York: Oxford University Press.

McEwen, B. S. (1998, January 15). Protective and damaging effects of stress mediators [Review article]. *New England Journal of Medicine, 338*, 171-179.

McGaugh, J.L, & LePort, A. (2014, February.) Remembrance of all things past. *Scientific American*, pp. 41-45.

McGilvray, J. (Ed.). (2004). *The Cambridge companion to Chomsky*. Oxford, England: Cambridge University Press.

McGinn, D. (2003, June 9). Testing, testing: The new job search. *Time*, pp. 36-38.

McGregor, K. K., & Capone, N. C. (2004). Genetic and environmental interactions in determining the early lexicon: Evidence from a set of tri-zygotic quadruplets. *Journal of Child Language, 31*, 311-337.

McIntyre, K., Korn, J., & Matsuo, H. (2008). Sweating the small stuff: How different types of hassles result in the experience of stress. *Stress and Health: Journal of the International Society for the Investigation of Stress, 24*, 383-392.

McKinley, J. C. Jr. (2013, September 12). Overdoses of 'Molly' led to Electric Zoo deaths. *The New York Times*. Retrieved from http://artsbeat.blogs.nytimes.com/2013/09/12/overdoses-of-molly-led-to-electric-zoo-deaths/.

McLay, R. N., Baird, A., Webb-Murphy, J., Deal, W., Tran, L., Anson, H., . . . Johnston, S. (2017). A randomized, head-to-head study of virtual reality exposure therapy for posttraumatic stress disorder. *Cyberpsychology, Behavior, and Social Networking, 20*, 218-224.

McLean, C. P., Su, Y., Carpenter, J. K., & Foa, E. B. (2017). Changes in PTSD and depression during prolonged exposure and client-centered therapy for PTSD in adolescents. *Journal of Clinical Child And adolescent Psychology, 46*, 500-510.

McLeod, J. (2015). Happiness, wellbeing and self-esteem: Public feelings and educational projects. In K. Wright & J. McLeod (Eds.), *Rethinking youth wellbeing: Critical perspectives*. New York: Springer Science + Business Media.

McMurtray, A. M., Licht, E., Yeo, T., Krisztal, E., Saul, R. E., & Mendez, M. F. (2007). Positron emission tomography facilitates diagnosis of early-onset Alzheimer's disease. *European Neurology, 59*, 31-37.

McNamara, T. P. (2013). Semantic memory and priming. In A. F. Healy, R. W. Proctor, & I. B. Weiner (Eds.), *Handbook of psychology, Vol. 4: Experimental psychology* (2nd ed.). Hoboken, NJ: John Wiley & Sons Inc.

McRobbie, L. R. (2017, February 8). Total recall: The people who never forget. *The Guardian*. Retrieved from https://www.theguardian.

com/science/2017/feb/08/total-recall-the-people-who-never-forget.

McSpadden, K. (2015, May 14). You now have a shorter attention span than a goldfish. *Time.*

McTeague, L. M., Lang, P. J., Laplante, M., & Bradley, M. M. (2011). Aversive imagery in panic disorder: Agoraphobia severity, comorbidity, and defensive physiology. *Biological Psychiatry, 70,* 415-424.

Medeiros, R., Prediger, R. D. S., Passos, G. F., Pandolfo, P., Duarte, F. S., Franco, J. L., . . . Calixto, J. B. (2007). Connecting TNF-alpha signaling pathways to iNOS expression in a mouse model of Alzheimer's disease: Relevance for the behavioral and synaptic deficits induced by amyloid beta protein. *Journal of Neuroscience, 27,* 5394-5404.

Meeter, M., & Murre, J. M. J. (2004). Consolidation of long-term memory: Evidence and alternatives. *Psychological Bulletin, 130,* 843-857.

Megill, J. (2013). Emotion, cognition and artificial intelligence. *Minds and Machines,* 1-11.

Meier, B., & Rothen, N. (2015). Developing synaesthesia: A primer. *Frontiers in Human Neuroscience, 9,* I 37-47.

Meltzer, A. L., Makhanova, A., Hicks, L. L., French, J. E., McNulty, J. K., & Bradbury, T. N. (2017). Quantifying the sexual afterglow: The lingering benefits of sex and their implications for pair-bonded relationships. *Psychological Science, 28*(5), 587-598.

Meltzoff, A. N. (1996). The human infant as imitative generalist: A 20-year progress report on infant imitation with implications for comparative psychology. In C. M. Heyes & B. G. Galef, Jr. (Eds.), *Social learning in animals: The roots of culture.* San Diego, CA: Academic Press.

Melzack, R., & Katz, J. (2001). The McGill Pain Questionnaire: Appraisal and current status. In D. Turk & R. Melzack (Eds.), *Handbook of pain assessment* (2nd ed.). New York: Guilford Press.

Melzack, R., & Katz, J. (2004). *The gate control theory: Reaching for the brain.* Mahwah, NJ: Lawrence Erlbaum Associates.

Mendle, J., Moore, S. R., Briley, D. A., & Harden, K. P. (2016). Puberty, socioeconomic status, and depression in girls: Evidence for gene × environment interactions. *Clinical Psychological Science, 4*(1), 3-16.

Mensah, F. K., Bayer, J. K., Wake, M., Carlin, J. B., Allen, N. B., & Patton, G. C. (2013). Early puberty and childhood social and behavioral adjustment. *Journal of Adolescent Health, 53,* 118-124.

Mercadillo, R. E., Díaz, J., Pasaye, E. H., & Barrios, F. A. (2011). Perception of suffering and compassion experience: Brain gender disparities. *Brain and Cognition, 76,* 5-14.

Mercier, H. (2017). Confirmation bias–Myside bias. In R. F. Pohl (Ed.), *Cognitive illusions: Intriguing phenomena in thinking, judgment and memory.* New York: Routledge/Taylor & Francis Group.

Merikangas, K. R., Ames, M., Cui, L., Stang, P. E., Ustun, T. B., VonKorff, M., et al. (2007). The impact of comorbidity of mental and physical conditions on role disability in the US

adult household population. *Archives of General Psychiatry, 64,* 1180-1188.

Merrill, Everett. (2016, June 26). Meet Iris the FBI dog. Retrieved from http://www.mycentraljersey.com/story/news/crime/jersey-mayhem/2016/06/26/meet-iris-fbi-dog/84770556/.

Mesoudi, A. (2011). Evolutionary psychology meets cultural psychology. *Journal of Evolutionary Psychology, 9,* 83-87.

Messner, M., Reinhard, M., & Sporer, S. (2008). Compliance through direct persuasive appeals: The moderating role of communicator's attractiveness in interpersonal persuasion. *Social Influence, 3,* 67-83.

Metz, C. (2017, July 31). Therapy in a dose of illusion. *The New York Times,* pp. B1, B4.

Michael, R. T., Gagnon, J. H., Laumann, E. O., & Kolata, G. (1994). *Sex in America: A definitive survey.* Boston: Little, Brown.

Micheau, J., & Marighetto, A. (2011). Acetylcholine and memory: A long, complex and chaotic but still living relationship. *Behavioural Brain Research, 221,* 424-429.

Midanik, L. T., Tam, T. W., & Weisner, C. (2007). Concurrent and simultaneous drug and alcohol use: Results of the 2000 national alcohol survey. *Drug and Alcohol Dependence, 90,* 72-80.

Mifflin, L. (1998, January 14). Study finds a decline in TV network violence. *The New York Times,* p. A14.

Mignon, A., & Mollaret, P. (2002). Applying the affordance conception of traits: A person perception study. *Personality and Social Psychology Bulletin, 28,* 1327-1334.

Miguez, G., Witnauer, J. E., & Miller, R. R. (2011). The role of contextual associations in producing the partial reinforcement acquisition deficit. *Journal of Experimental Psychology: Animal Behavior Processes, 37,* 88-97.

Mihalca, L., Mengelkamp, C., & Schnotz, W. (2017). Accuracy of metacognitive judgments as a moderator of learner control effectiveness in problem-solving tasks. *Metacognition and Learning, 12*(3), 357-379.

Mika, V. S., Wood, P. R., Weiss, B. D., & Trevino, L. (2007). Ask Me 3: Improving communication in a Hispanic pediatric outpatient practice. *American Journal of Behavioral Health, 31,* S115-S121.

Miles, P., Schaufeli, W. B., & van den Bos, K. (2011). When weak groups are strong: How low cohesion groups allow individuals to act according to their personal absence tolerance norms. *Social Justice Research, 24,* 207-230.

Milgram, S. (2005). *Obedience to authority.* Pinter & Martin: New York.

Miller, C., & Williams, A. (2011). Ethical guidelines in research. In J. C. Thomas & M. Hersen (Eds.), *Understanding research in clinical and counseling psychology* (2nd ed.). New York: Routledge/Taylor & Francis Group.

Miller, G. (2006). A spoonful of medicine–and a steady diet of normalcy. *Science, 311,* 464-465.

Miller, G. (2008, May 9). The roots of morality. *Science, 320,* 734-737.

Miller, G. E., Chen, E., & Parker, K. J. (2011). Psychological stress in childhood and susceptibility to the chronic diseases of aging: Moving toward a model of behavioral and biological mechanisms. *Psychological Bulletin, 137,* 959-997.

Miller, G. F., & Penke, L. (2007). The evolution of human intelligence and the coefficient of additive genetic variance in human brain size. *Intelligence, 35,* 97-114.

Miller, J. A., & Leffard, S. A. (2007). Behavioral assessment. In S. R. Smith & L. Handler (Eds.), *The clinical assessment of children and adolescents: A practitioner's handbook.* Mahwah, NJ: Lawrence Erlbaum Associates.

Miller, J. G. (1984). Culture and the development of everyday social explanation. *Journal of Personality and Social Psychology, 46,* 961-978.

Miller, L. A., McIntire, S. A., & Lovler, R. L. (2011). *Foundations of psychological testing: A practical problem* (3rd ed.). Thousand Oaks, CA: Sage Publications, Inc.

Miller, L., Gur, M., Shanok, A., & Weissman, M. (2008). Interpersonal psychotherapy with pregnant adolescents: Two pilot studies. *Journal of Child Psychology and Psychiatry, 49,* 733-742.

Miller, N. E., & Magruder, K. M. (Eds.). (1999). *Cost-effectiveness of psychotherapy: A guide for practitioners, researchers, and policymakers.* New York: Oxford University Press.

Miller, Naseem S. (2016, January 18). Doctors learn how to give bad news to patients. *Orlando Sentinel.* Retrieved from http://www.orlandosentinel.com/health/os-breaking-bad-news-residents-ormc-20160118-story.html.

Miller-Perrin, C., Perrin, R., & Kocur, J. (2009). Parental physical and psychological aggression: Psychological symptoms in young adults. *Child Abuse & Neglect, 33,* 1-11.

Mills, J. (2013). Jung's metaphysics. *International Journal of Jungian Studies, 5,* 19-43.

Mills, M. J. (2011). Associations among achievement measures and their collective prediction of work involvement. *Personality and Individual Differences, 50,* 360-364.

Milner, B. (1966). Amnesia following operation on temporal lobes. In C. W. M. Whitty & P. Zangwill (Eds.), *Amnesia.* London: Butterworth.

Milner, B. (2005). The medial temporal-lobe amnesic syndrome. *Psychiatric Clinics of North America, 28,* 599-611.

Milos, G., Baur, V., Schumacher, S., Kuenzli, C., Schnyder, U., Mueller-Pfeiffer, C., & Martin-Soelch, C. (2017). How fat will it make me? Estimation of weight gain in anorexia nervosa. *Appetite, 114,* 368-373.

Miner, J., & Clarke-Stewart, K. (2008). Trajectories of externalizing behavior from age 2 to age 9: Relations with gender, temperament, ethnicity, parenting, and rater. *Developmental Psychology, 44,* 771-786.

Miner-Rubino, K., Winter, D. G., & Stewart, A. J. (2004). Gender, social class, and the subjective experience of aging: Self-perceived personality change from early adulthood to late midlife. *Personality and Social Psychology Bulletin, 30,* 1599-1610.

Minică, C. C., Mbarek, H., Pool, R., Dolan, C. V., Boomsma, D. I., & Vink, J. M. (2017). Pathways to smoking behaviours: Biological insights from the Tobacco and Genetics Consortium meta-analysis. *Molecular Psychiatry, 22,* 82-88.

Mintz, A., & Wayne, C. (2014). Group decision making in conflict: From groupthink to polythink in the war in Iraq. In P. T. Coleman, M. Deutsch, & E. C. Marcus (Eds.), *The handbook of conflict resolution: Theory and practice* (3rd ed.). San Francisco, CA: Jossey-Bass.

Miquel, J. (2006). Integración de teorías del envejecimiento (parte I). Integration of theories of ageing. *Revista Espanola de Geriatriay Gerontologia, 41,* 55-63.

Mirzairad, R., Haydari, A., Pasha, R., Ehteshamzadeh, P., & Makvandi, B. (2017). The relationship between perfectionism and psychological distress with the mediation of coping styles and self-esteem. *International Journal of Mental Health and Addiction, 15,* 614-620.

Mischel, W. (2004). Toward an integrative science of the person. *Annual Review of Psychology, 55,* 1-22.

Mischel, W. (2009). From Personality and Assessment (1968) to Personality Science, 2009. *Journal of Research in Personality, 43,* 282-290.

Mischel, W., & Shoda, Y. (2008). Toward a unified theory of personality: Integrating dispositions and processing dynamics within the cognitive-affective processing system. In O. P. Oliver, R. W. Robins & L. A. Pervin (Eds.), *Handbook of personality psychology: Theory and research* (3rd ed.). New York: Guilford Press.

Mitchell, D. B., & Schmitt, F. A. (2006). Short- and long-term implicit memory in aging and Alzheimer's disease. *Neuropsychological Development and Cognition, B, Aging and Neuropsychological Cognition, 13,* 611-635.

Mitte, K. (2005). Meta-analysis of cognitive-behavioral treatments for generalized anxiety disorder: A comparison with pharmacotherapy. *Psychological Bulletin, 131,* 785-795.

Mizrahi, R., Agid, O., Borlido, C., Suridjan, I., Rusjan, P., Houle, S., & . . . Kapur, S. (2011). Effects of antipsychotics on D3 receptors: A clinical PET study in first episode antipsychotic naive patients with schizophrenia using [11C]-(+)-PHNO. *Schizophrenia Research, 131,* 63-68.

Moen, K. C., Miller, J. K., & Lloyd, M. E. (2017). Selective attention meets spontaneous recognition memory: Evidence for effects at retrieval. *Consciousness and Cognition: An International Journal, 49,* 181-189.

Moffitt, T. E., Caspi, A., & Rutter, M. (2006). Measured gene-environment interactions in psychopathology: Concepts, research strategies, and implications for research, intervention, and public understanding of genetics. *Perspectives on Psychological Science, 1,* 5-27.

Moghaddam, F. M. (2008). The materialist view: From realistic conflict theory to evolutionary psychology. In F. M. Moghaddam (Ed.), *Multiculturalism and intergroup relations: Psychological implications for democracy in global.* Washington, DC: American Psychological Association.

Mograss, M., Guillem, F., Brazzini-Poisson, V., & Godbout, R. (2009, May). The effects of total sleep deprivation on recognition memory processes: A study of event-related potential. *Neurobiology of Learning and Memory, 91,* 343-352.

Mohan, A., Sharma, R., & Bijlani, R. L. (2011). Effect of meditation on stress-induced changes in cognitive functions. *The Journal of Alternative and Complementary Medicine, 17,* 207-212.

Moher, C., Gould, D., Hegg, E., & Mahoney, A. (2008). Non-generalized and generalized conditioned reinforcers: Establishment and validation. *Behavioral Interventions, 23,* 13-38.

Mohr, C., & Messina, S. (2015). Brain dysfunctions, psychopathologies, and body image distortions: Propositions for a possible common cause. *European Psychologist, 20,* 72-81.

Mokdad, A. H., Brewer, R. D., & Naimi, T. (2007). Binge drinking is a problem that cannot be ignored. *Preventive Medicine: An International Journal Devoted to Practice and Theory, 44,* 303-304.

Molina, M., Sann, C., David, M., Touré, Y., Guillois, B., & Jouen, F. (2015). Active touch in late-preterm and early-term neonates. *Developmental Psychobiology, 57,* 322-335.

Mollen, S., Engelen, S., Kessels, L. E., & van den Putte, B. (2017). Short and sweet: The persuasive effects of message framing and temporal context in antismoking warning labels. *Journal of Health Communication, 22,* 20-28.

Monk, T. H., Buysse, D. J., Billy, B. D., Fletcher, M. E., Kennedy, K. S., Schlarb, J. E., & Beach, S. R. (2011). Circadian type and bed-timing regularity in 654 retired seniors: Correlations with subjective sleep measures. *Sleep, 34,* 235-239.

Monteleone, P., Martiadis, V., & Maj, M. (2011). Circadian rhythms and treatment implications in depression. *Progress in Neuro-Psychopharmacology & Biological Psychiatry, 35,* 1569-1574.

Montgomery, K. L. (2011). Living with panic, worry, and fear: Anxiety disorders. In C. Franklin & R. Fong (Eds.), *The church leader's counseling resource book: A guide to mental health and social problems.* New York: Oxford University Press.

Moodley, R., Gielen, U. P., & Wu, R. (2013). *Handbook of counseling and psychotherapy in an international context.* New York: Routledge/Taylor & Francis Group.

Moody, H. R. (2000). *Aging: Concepts and controversies.* Thousand Oaks, CA: Sage.

Moody, R. L., Starks, T. J., Grov, C., & Parsons, J. T. (2017). Internalized homophobia and drug use in a national cohort of gay and bisexual men: Examining depression, sexual anxiety, and gay community attachment as mediating factors. *Archives of Sexual Behavior.* Accessed from https://www.ncbi.nlm.nih.gov/pubmed/28608294.

Moon, C., Lagercrantz, H., & Kuhl, P. (2013). Language experienced in utero affects vowel perception after birth: A two-country study. *Acta Paediatrica, 102,* 156-160.

Moore, D. G., Goodwin, J. E., & George, R. (2007). Infants perceive human point-light displays as solid forms. *Cognition, 104,* 377-396.

Moore, E. S., Wilkie, W. L., & Desrochers, D. M. (2017). All in the family? Parental roles in the epidemic of childhood obesity. *Journal of Consumer Research, 43,* 824-859.

Moorey, S. (2007). Cognitive therapy. In W. Dryden (Ed.), *Dryden's handbook of individual therapy* (5th ed.). Thousand Oaks, CA: Sage Publications.

Mora-Giral, M., Raich-Escursell, R. M., Segues, C. V., Torras-Claras, A. J., & Huon, G. (2004). Bulimia symptoms and risk factors in university students. *Eating and Weight Disorders, 9,* 163-169.

Morad, Y., Barkana, Y., Zadok, D., Hartstein, M., Pras, E., & Bar-Dayan, Y. (2009, July). Ocular parameters as an objective tool for the assessment of truck drivers fatigue. *Accident Analysis and Prevention, 41,* 856-860.

Moran, A. (2009). Cognitive psychology in sport: Progress and prospects. *Psychology of Sport and Exercise, 10,* 420-426.

Morcom, A. M., & Friston, K. J. (2011, September 1). Decoding episodic memory in ageing: A Bayesian analysis of activity patterns predicting memory. *Neuroimagel, 33,* 88-91.

Moreno-Gómez, F. N., Véliz, G., Rojas, M., Martínez, C., Olmedo, R., Panussis, F., . . . Delano, P. H. (2017). Music training and education slow the deterioration of music perception produced by presbycusis in the elderly. *Frontiers in Aging Neuroscience, 9,* 1-10.

Moretz, M., & McKay, D. (2009). The role of perfectionism in obsessive-compulsive symptoms: 'Not just right' experiences and checking compulsions. *Journal of Anxiety Disorders, 23,* 640-644.

Morgan, A. A., Marsiske, M., & Whitfield, K. E. (2008). Characterizing and explaining differences in cognitive test performance between African American and European American older adults. *Experimental Aging Research, 34,* 80-100.

Morone, N. E., & Greco, C. M. (2007). Mind-body interventions for chronic pain in older adults: A structured review. *Pain Medicine, 8,* 359-375.

Morris, S. Y. (2017, May 25). What does it mean to have hyperthymesia or highly superior autobiographical memory (HSAM)? *HealthLine.* Retrieved from http://www.healthline.com/health/hyperthymesia#overview1.

Morrone, A. S., & Pintrich, P. R. (2006). Achievement motivation. In G. G. Bear & K. M. Minke (Eds.), *Children's needs III: Development, prevention, and intervention.* Washington, DC: National Association of School Psychologists.

Moscoso, S. C., Chaves, S. S., & Argilaga, M. T. A. (2013). Reporting a program evaluation: Needs, program plan, intervention, and decisions. *International Journal of Clinical and Health Psychology, 13,* 58-66.

Mosher, C. E., Winger, J. G., Given, B. A., Helft, P. R., & O'Neil, B. H. (2015). Mental health outcomes during colorectal cancer survivorship: A review of the literature. *Psycho-Oncology.*

Accessed online, 9.29.15; http://onlinelibrary.wiley.com/doi/10.1002/pon.3954/abstract.

Moshman, D. (2011). *Adolescent rationality and development: Cognition, morality, and identity* (3rd ed.). New York: Psychology Press.

Motley, M. T. (1987, February). What I meant to say. *Psychology Today*, pp. 25–28.

Moulding, R., Nedeljkovic, M., Kyrios, M., Osborne, D., & Mogan, C. (2017). Short-term cognitive–behavioural group treatment for hoarding disorder: A naturalistic treatment outcome study. *Clinical Psychology & Psychotherapy, 24*, 235–244.

Moynihan, A. B., Igou, E. R., & van Tilburg, W. P. (2017). Free, connected, and meaningful: Free will beliefs promote meaningfulness through belongingness. *Personality and Individual Differences, 107*, 54–65.

Muammar, O. M. (2007). An integration of two competing models to explain practical intelligence. *Dissertation Abstracts International: Section B: The Sciences and Engineering, 67(7-B)*, 4128.

Mueller, C. E. (2009). Protective factors as barriers to depression in gifted and nongifted adolescents. *Gifted Child Quarterly, 53*, 3–14.

Mullane, M. P., Martens, B. K., Baxter, E. L., & Steeg, D. V. (2017). Children's preference for mixed- versus fixed-ratio schedules of reinforcement: A translational study of risky choice. *Journal of the Experimental Analysis of Behavior, 107*, 161–175.

Mungan, E., Peynircioğlu, Z. F., & Halpern, A. R. (2011). Levels-of-processing effects on 'remember' responses in recognition for familiar and unfamiliar tunes. *American Journal of Psychology, 124*, 37–48.

Munjiza, J., Britvic, D., Radman, M., & Crawford, M. J. (2017). Severe war-related trauma and personality pathology: A case-control study. *BMC Psychiatry, 17*, 22–28.

Munro, C., Randell, L., & Lawrie, S. M. (2017). An integrative bio-psycho-social theory of anorexia nervosa. *Clinical Psychology & Psychotherapy, 24*, 1–21.

Murayama, K., & Kitagami, S. (2013). Consolidation Power of Extrinsic Rewards: Reward Cues Enhance Long-Term Memory for Irrelevant Past Events. *Journal of Experimental Psychology: General*. Retrieved from http://www.ncbi.nlm.nih.gov/pubmed/23421444.

Murphy, S. T., & Zajonc, R. B. (1993). Affect, cognition, and awareness: Affective priming with optimal and suboptimal stimulus exposures. *Journal of Personality and Social Psychology, 64*, 723–739.

Murray, B. (2002, June). Good news for bachelor's grads. *Monitor on Psychology*, 30–32.

Murray, R., Lappin, J., & Di Forti, M. (2008). Schizophrenia: From developmental deviance to dopamine dysregulation. *European Neuropsychopharmacology, 18*, S129–SS134.

Murray, S. L., Holmes, J. G., & Griffin, D. W. (2004). The benefits of positive illusions: Idealization and the construction of satisfaction in close relationships. In H. T. Reis & C. E. Rusbult (Eds.), *Close relationships: Key readings*. Philadelphia, PA: Taylor & Francis.

Murthy, P., Kudlur, S., George, S., & Mathew, G. (2009). A clinical overview of fetal alcohol syndrome. *Addictive Disorders & Their Treatment, 8*, 1–12.

Myers, L. L. (2007). Anorexia nervosa, bulimia nervosa, and binge eating disorder. In B. A. Thyer & J. S. Wodarski (Eds.), *Social work in mental health: An evidence-based approach*. Hoboken, NJ: John Wiley & Sons.

Myrtek, M. (2007). Type A behavior and hostility as independent risk factors for coronary heart disease. In J. Jordan, B. Barde, & A. M. Zeiher (Eds.), *Contributions toward evidence-based psychocardiology: A systematic review of the literature*. Washington, DC: American Psychological Association.

Møller, A. R. (2011). Anatomy and physiology of the auditory system. In A. R. Møller, B. Langguth, . . . T. Kleinjung (Eds.), *Textbook of tinnitus*. New York: Springer Science + Business Media.

Nabi, R. L., Prestin, A., & So, J. (2013). Facebook friends with (health) benefits? Exploring social network site use and perceptions of social support, stress, and well-being. *Cyberpsychology, Behavior, and Social Networking, 16*, 721–727.

Nader, E. G., Kleinman, A., Gomes, B., Bruscagin, C., Santos, B., Nicoletti, M., & Caetano, S. C. (2013). Negative expressed emotion best discriminates families with bipolar disorder children. *Journal of Affective Disorders, 148*, 418–423.

Nagda, B. A., Tropp, L. R., & Paluck, E. L. (2006). Looking back as we look ahead: Integrating research, theory, and practice on intergroup relations. *Journal of Social Research, 62*, 439–451.

Nagesh, A. (2017, July 9). Instagram star's "healthy food" obsession was actually a dangerous eating disorder. *Metro.co.uk*. Retrieved from http://metro.co.uk/2017/07/09/instagram-stars-healthy-food-obsession-was-actually-a-dangerous-eating-disorder-6766434/.

Naglieri, J. A., LeBuffe, P. A., & Ross, K. M. (2013). Measuring resilience in children: From theory to practice. In S. Goldstein & R. B. Brooks (Eds.), *Handbook of resilience in children* (2nd ed.). New York: Springer Science + Business Media.

Nagy, T. F. (2011). Informed consent. In T. F. Nagy (Ed.), *Essential ethics for psychologists: A primer for understanding and mastering core issues*. Washington, DC: American Psychological Association.

Najman, J. M., Aird, R., Bor, W., O'Callaghan, M., Williams, G. M., & Shuttlewood, G. J. (2004). The generational transmission of socioeconomic inequalities in child cognitive development and emotional health. *Social Science and Medicine, 58*, 1147–1158.

Nakamura, Y., Goto, T. K., Tokumori, K., Yoshiura, T., Kobayashi, K., Nakamura, Y., & . . . Yoshiura, K. (2011). Localization of brain activation by umami taste in humans. *Brain Research, 1390*, 156–163.

Nalbantian, S. (2011). Autobiographical memory in modernist literature and neuroscience. In S. Nalbantian, P. M. Matthews, & J. L.

McClelland (Eds.), *The memory process: Neuroscientific and humanistic perspectives*. Cambridge, MA: MIT Press.

Narrow, W. E., Rae, D. S., Robins, L. N., & Regier, D. A. (2002). Revised prevalence estimates of mental disorders in the United States: Using a clinical significance criterion to reconcile 2 surveys' estimates. *Archives of General Psychiatry, 59*, 115–123.

Nasrallah, H., Black, D., Goldberg, J., Muzina, D., & Pariser, S. (2008). Issues associated with the use of atypical antipsychotic medications. *Annals of Clinical Psychiatry, 20*, S24–S29.

National Adolescent Health Information Center. (2003). *Fact Sheet on Demographics: Adolescents*. San Francisco: University of California, San Francisco.

National Association for the Education of Young Children. (2005). *Position statements of the NAEYC*. Washington, DC: National Association for the Education of Young Children

National Institute of Child Health and Human Development (NICHD) Early Child Care Research Network. (1999). Child care and mother-child interaction in the first 3 years of life. *Psychology, 35*, 1399–1413.

National Institute of Child Health and Human Development (NICHD) Early Child Care Research Network. (2001). Child-care and family predictors of preschool attachment and stability from infancy. *Development Psychology, 37*, 847–862.

National Institute of Child Health and Human Development (NICHD) Early Child Care Research Network. (2002). Child-care structure– process–outcome: Direct and indirect effects of child-care quality on young children's development. *Psychological Science, 13*, 199–206.

National Institute of Child Health and Human Development (NICHD) Early Child Care Research Network. (2006). Child-care effect sizes for the NICHD study of early child care and youth development. *American Psychologist, 61*, 99–116.

National Institute on Drug Abuse. (2000). *Monitoring the future study*. Bethesda, MD: National Institutes of Health.

National Institute on Drug Abuse. (2018). What is the scope of cocaine use in the United States? Downloaded from https://www.drugabuse.gov/publications/research-reports/cocaine/what-scope-cocaine-use-in-united-states.

National Institutes of Health. (2015, November 24). Talking to your doctor. Downloaded from https://www.nih.gov/institutes-nih/nih-office-director/office-communications-public-liaison/clear-communication/talking-your-doctor.

National Research Council. (2001). *Eager to learn: Educating our preschoolers*. Washington, DC: National Academy Press.

Natsuaki, M. N., Samuels, D., & Leve, L. D. (2015). Puberty, identity, and context: A biopsychosocial perspective on internalizing psychopathology in early adolescent girls. In K. C.

McLean & M. Syed (Eds.), *The Oxford hand-book of identity development*. New York: Oxford University Press.

Naveh-Benjamin, M., Guez, J., & Sorek, S. (2007). The effects of divided attention on encoding processes in memory: Mapping the locus of interference. *Canadian Journal of Experimental Psychology, 61*, 1-12.

Neal, D., Matson, J. L., & Belva, B. C. (2013). An examination of the reliability of a new observation measure for Autism spectrum disorders: The autism spectrum disorder observation for children. *Research in Autism Spectrum Disorders, 7*, 29-34.

Nedelec, J. L. (2017). A multi-level analysis of the effect of interviewer characteristics on survey respondents' reports of sensitive topics. *Personality and Individual Differences, 107*, 96-101.

Neher, A. (2006). Evolutionary psychology: Its programs, prospects, and pitfalls. *American Journal of Psychology, 119*, 517-566.

Nelson, D. L., Kitto, K., Galea, D., McEvoy, C. L., & Bruza, P. D. (2013). How activation, entanglement, and searching a semantic network contribute to event memory. *Memory & Cognition, 41*, 797-819.

Nelson, G., & MacLeod, T. (2017). The evolution of housing for people with serious mental illness. In J. Sylvestre, G. Nelson, & T. Aubry (Eds.), *Housing, citizenship, and communities for people with serious mental illness: Theory, research, practice, and policy perspectives*. New York: Oxford University Press.

Nelson, T. D. (2013). The neurobiology of stereotyping and prejudice. In D. D. Franks & J. H. Turner (Eds.), *Handbook of neurosociology*. New York: Springer Science + Business Media.

Nelson, W. M., III, & Finch, A. J., Jr. (2000). Managing anger in youth: A cognitive-behavioral intervention approach. In P. C. Kendall (Ed.), *Child & adolescent therapy: Cognitive-behavioral procedures* (2nd ed.). New York: Guilford Press.

Neria, Y., DiGrande, L., & Adams, G. G. (2011). Postraumatic stress disorder following the September 11, 2001, terrorist attacks. *American Psychologist, 66*, 429-446.

Nesheim, S., Henderson, S., Lindsay, M., Zuberi, J., Grimes, V., Buehler, J., & Bulterys, M. (2004). *Prenatal HIV testing and antiretroviral prophylaxis at an urban hospital-Atlanta, Georgia, 1997-2000*. Atlanta, GA: Centers for Disease Control.

Nestler, E. J., & Malenka, R. C. (2004, March). The addicted brain. *Scientific American*, 78-83.

Nestoriuc, Y., Martin, A., Rief, W., & Andrasik, F. (2008, September). Biofeedback treatment for headache disorders: A comprehensive efficacy review. *Applied Psychophysiology and Biofeedback, 33*, 125-140.

Neumark-Sztainer, D. (2009). Preventing obesity and eating disorders in adolescents: What can health care providers do? *Journal of Adolescent Health, 44*, 206-213.

Newby-Clark, I. R., & Ross, M. (2003). Conceiving the past and future. *Personality and Social Psychology Bulletin, 29*, 807-818.

Newman, C. F., Leahy, R. L., Beck, A. T., Reilly-Harrington, N. A., & Gyulai, L. (2002). *Bipolar disorder: A cognitive therapy approach*. Washington, DC: American Psychological Association.

Newman, M., & Bakay, R. (2008, April). Therapeutic potentials of human embryonic stem cells in Parkinson's disease. *Neurotherapeutics, 5*, 237-251.

Newman, S. D., Willoughby, G., & Pruce, B. (2011). The effect of problem structure on problem-solving: An fmri study of word versus number problems. *Brain Research, 30*, 88-96.

Ng, Q. X., Venkatanarayanan, N., & Ho, C. X. (2017). Clinical use of Hypericum perforatum (St. John's wort) in depression: A meta-analysis. *Journal of Affective Disorders, 210*, 211-221.

Nguyen, H. D., Le, H., & Boles, T. (2010). Individualism-collectivism and co-operation: A cross-society and cross-level examination. *Negotiation and Conflict Management Research, 3*, 179-204.

Niccols, A. (2007). Fetal alcohol syndrome and the developing socio-emotional brain. *Brain Cognition, 65*, 135-142.

Nichols, S. (2011). Experimental philosophy and the problem of free will. *Science, 331*, 1401-1403.

Niedenthal, P. M. (2007). Embodying emotion. *Science, 316*, 1002-1005.

Nielsen, T., O'Reilly, C., Carr, M., Dumel, G., Godin, I., Solomonova, E., & . . . Paquette, T. (2015). Overnight improvements in two REM sleep-sensitive tasks are associated with both REM and NREM sleep changes, sleep spindle features, and awakenings for dream recall. *Neurobiology of Learning and Memory, 122*, 88-97.

Nijboer, T. C. W., te Pas, S. F., & van der Smagt, M. J. (2011). Detecting gradual visual changes in colour and brightness agnosia: A double dissociation. *NeuroReport: For Rapid Communication of Neuroscience Research, 22*, 175-180.

Nimrod, G., & Kleiber, D. A. (2007). Reconsidering change and continuity in later life: Toward an innovation theory of successful aging. *International Journal of Human Development, 65*, 1-22.

Nisbet, E. K., Zelenski, J. M., & Murphy, S. A. (2011). Happiness is in our nature: Exploring nature relatedness as a contributor to subjective well-being. *Journal of Happiness Studies, 12*, 303-322.

Nisbett, R. E. (2007, December 9). All brains are the same color. *The New York Times*, p. E11.

Nisbett, R. E. (2009). All brains are the same color. *Association for Psychological Science Observer, 22*(3), 20-21.

Nisbett, R.E., & Cohen, D. (1996). *Culture of honor: The psychology of violence in the South*. Boulder, CO: Westview Press.

Nishida, M., Pearsall, J., Buckner, R., & Walker, M. (2009). REM sleep, prefrontal theta, and the consolidation of human emotional memory. *Cerebral Cortex, 19*, 1158-1166.

Nishimura, T., Kawamura, S., & Sakurai, S. (2011). Autonomous motivation and meta-cognitive strategies as predictors of academic performance: Does intrinsic motivation predict academic performance? *Japanese Journal of Educational Psychology, 59*, 77-87.

Nishino, S. (2007). Clinical and neurobiological aspects of narcolepsy. *Sleep Medicine, 8*, 373-399.

Nittrouer, S., & Lowenstein, J. H. (2007). Children's weighting strategies for word-final stop voicing are not explained by auditory sensitivities. *Journal of Speech, Language, and Hearing Research, 50*, 58-73.

Nolen-Hoeksema, S. (2007). *Abnormal psychology* (4th ed.). New York: McGraw-Hill.

Norcia, A. M., Pei, F., Bonneh, Y., Hou, C., Sampath, V., & Petter, M. W. (2005). Development of sensitivity to texture and contour information in the human infant. *Journal of Cognitive Neuroscience, 17*, 569-579.

Norcross, J. C. (2002). Empirically supported therapy relationships. In J. C. Norcross (Ed.), *Psychotherapy relationships that work: Therapist contributions and responsiveness to patients*. New York: Oxford University Press.

Norcross, J. C., Beutler, L. E., & Levant, R. F. (2006). *Evidence-based practices in mental health: Debate and dialogue on the fundamental questions*. Washington, DC: American Psychological Association.

Norlander, T., Von Schedvin, H., & Archer, T. (2005). Thriving as a function of affective personality: Relation to personality factors, coping strategies and stress. *Anxiety, Stress & Coping: An International Journal, 18*, 105-116.

North, M. M., & North, S. M. (2017). Virtual reality therapy for treatment of psychological disorders. In M. M. Maheu, K. P. Drude, & S. D. Wright (Eds.), *Career paths in telemental health* (pp. 263-268). Cham, Switzerland: Springer International Publishing.

Norton, D., Heath, D., & Ventura, D. (2013). Finding creativity in an artificial artist. *Journal of Creative Behavior, 47*, 106-124.

Norton, P. J., & Price, E. C. (2007). A meta-analytic review of adult cognitive-behavioral treatment outcome across the anxiety disorders. *Journal of Nervous and Mental Disease, 195*, 521-531.

Nosek, B. A., Banaji, M. R., & Greenwald, A. G. (2002). Math = male, me = female, therefore math ≠ me. *Journal of Personality and Social Psychology, 83*, 44-59.

Nosek, C. L., Kerr, C. W., Woodworth, J., Wright, S. T., Grant, P. C., Kuszczak, S. M., & . . . Depner, R. M. (2015). End-of-life dreams and visions: A qualitative perspective from hospice patients. *American Journal of Hospice & Palliative Medicine, 32*, 269-274.

Nourouzpour, N., Salomonczyk, D., Cressman, E. K., & Henriques, D. Y. (2015). Retention of proprioceptive recalibration following visuomotor adaptation. *Experimental Brain Research, 233*, 1019-1029.

Nouwens, P. G., Lucas, R., Embregts, P. M., & van Nieuwenhuizen, C. (2017). In plain sight but still invisible: A structured case analysis of people with mild intellectual disability or borderline intellectual functioning. *Journal of Intellectual and Developmental Disability, 42,* 36-44.

Novotney, A. (2017). A growing wave of online therapy. *Monitor on Psychology, 48*(2), 48.

Nowak, A., Deutsch, M., Bartkowski, W., & Solomon, S. (2010). From crude law to civil relations: The dynamics and potential resolution of intractable conflict. *Peace and Conflict: Journal of Peace Psychology, 16,* 189-209.

Noy, V. M. (2006). A psychoneuroimmunology program for Hispanic women with stage I–H breast cancer. *Dissertation Abstracts International: Section B: The Sciences and Engineering, 66*(11-B), 6287.

Nurnberger, J. I., Jr., & Bierut, L. J. (2007, April). Seeking the connections: Alcoholism and our genes. *Scientific American,* pp. 46-53.

Nussbaum, A. D., & Steele, C. M. (2007). Situational disengagement and persistence in the face of adversity. *Journal of Experimental Social Psychology, 43,* 127-134.

Nyaradi, A., Li, J., Hickling, S., Foster, J., & Oddy, W. H. (2013). The role of nutrition in children's neurocognitive development, from pregnancy through childhood. *Frontiers in Human Neuroscience, 7,* 97.

Nygaard, E., Slinning, K., Moe, V., & Walhovd, K. B. (2017). Cognitive function of youths born to mothers with opioid and poly-substance abuse problems during pregnancy. *Child Neuropsychology, 23,* 159-187.

Nærland, T., Bakke, K. A., Storvik, S., Warner, G., & Howlin, P. (2017). Age and gender-related differences in emotional and behavioural problems and autistic features in children and adolescents with Down syndrome: A survey-based study of 674 individuals. *Journal of Intellectual Disability Research, 61,* 594-603.

O'Leary, A. P., & Sloutsky, V. M. (2017). Carving metacognition at its joints: Protracted development of component processes. *Child Development, 88,* 1015-1032.

Oberauer, K., Awh, E., & Sutterer, D. W. (2017). The role of long-term memory in a test of visual working memory: Proactive facilitation but no proactive interference. *Journal of Experimental Psychology: Learning, Memory, and Cognition, 43,* 1-22.

Occhionero, M. (2004). Mental processes and the brain during dreams. *Dreaming, 14,* 54-64.

Occhionero'Brien, W. H., & Young, K. M. (2013). Assessment of psychopathology: Behavioral approaches. In J. R. Graham, J. A. Naglieri, & I. B. Weiner (Eds.), *Handbook of psychology, Vol. 10: Assessment psychology* (2nd ed.). Hoboken, NJ: John Wiley & Sons Inc.

Offer, D., Kaiz, M., Howard, K. I., & Bennett, E. S. (2000). The altering of reported experiences. *Journal of the American Academy of Child & Adolescent Psychiatry, 39,* 735-742.

Ogbu, J. U. (2003). *Black American students in an affluent suburb: A study of academic disengagement.* New Jersey: Lawrence Erlbaum.

Ogden, C.L., Carroll, M.D, Kit, B.K., & Flegal, K.M. (2014). Prevalence of childhood and adult obesity in the United States, 2011-2012.

Journal of the American Medical Association, 311, 806-814.

Ohira, T., Hozawa, A., Iribarren, C., Daviglus, M. L., Matthews, K. A., Gross, M. D., et al. (2007). Longitudinal association of serum carotenoids and tocopherols with hostility: The CARDIA study. *American Journal of Epidemiology, 18,* 235-241.

Ojha, H., & Pramanick, M. (2009). Effects of age on intensity and priority of life needs. *Journal of the Indian Academy of Applied Psychology, 35,* 131-136.

Okada, K., Nakao, T., Sanematsu, H., Murayama, K., Honda, S., Tomita, M., & . . . Kanba, S. (2015). Biological heterogeneity of obsessive-compulsive disorder: A voxel-based morphometric study based on dimensional assessment. *Psychiatry and Clinical Neurosciences, 69,* 411-421

Okely, J. A., Weiss, A., & Gale, C. R. (2018). The interaction between individualism and well-being in predicting mortality: Survey of Health Ageing and Retirement in Europe. *Journal of Behavioral Medicine, 41*(1), 1-11. doi:10.1007/s10865-017-9871-x.

Olatunji, B. (2008). New directions in research on health anxiety and hypochondriasis: Commentary on a timely special series. *Journal of Cognitive Psychotherapy, 22,* 183-190.

Oliver, M. B., & Hyde, J. S. (1993). Gender differences in sexuality: A meta-analysis. *Psychological Bulletin, 114,* 29-51.

Olson, D. H., & DeFrain, J. (2005). *Marriages and families: Intimacy, diversity, and strengths with PowerWeb.* New York: McGraw-Hill.

Olulade, O. A., Jamal, N. I., Koo, P. S., Perfetti, C. A., LaSasso, C., & Eden, G. F. (2016). Neuroanatomical evidence in support of the bilingual advantage theory. *Cerebral Cortex, 26,* 3196-3204.

Ong, J. C. (2017). Insomnia: The problem of sleeplessness. In J. C. Ong, *Mindfulness-based therapy for insomnia.* Washington, DC: American Psychological Association.

Open Science Collaboration. (2015). Estimating the reproducibility of psychological science. *Science, 349.*

Opendak, M., Gould, E., & Sullivan, R. (2017). Early life adversity during the infant sensitive period for attachment: Programming of behavioral neurobiology of threat processing and social behavior. *Developmental Cognitive Neuroscience, 25,* 145-159.

Opler, M., Perrin, M., Kleinhaus, K., & Malaspina, D. (2008). Factors in the etiology of schizophrenia: Genes, parental age, and environment. *Primary Psychiatry, 15,* 37-45.

Ornat, S. L., & Gallo, P. (2004). Acquisition, learning, or development of language? Skinner's "verbal behavior" revisited. *Spanish Journal of Psychology, 7,* 161-170.

Orwin, R. G., & Condray, D. S. (1984). Smith and Glass' psychotherapy conclusions need further probing: On Landman and Dawes' re-analysis. *American Psychologist, 39,* 71-72.

Otake, K., Shimai, S., & Tanaka-Matsumi, J. (2006). Happy people become happier through kindness: A counting kindnesses intervention. *Journal of Happiness Studies, 7,* 361-375.

Otgaar, H., Howe, M. L., & Muris, P. (2017). Maltreatment increases spontaneous false memories but decreases suggestion-induced false memories in children. *British Journal of Developmental Psychology, 35*(3), 376-391.

Otters, R. V., & Hollander, J. F. (2015). Leaving home and boomerang decisions: A family simulation protocol. *Marriage & Family Review, 51,* 39-58.

Ouimet, A., Gawronski, B., & Dozois, D. (2009). Cognitive vulnerability to anxiety: A review and an integrative model. *Clinical Psychology Review, 29,* 459-470.

Oviedo-Joekes, E., et al. (2009). Diacetylmorphine versus methadone for the treatment of opioid addiction. *The New England Journal of Medicine, 361,* 777-786.

O'Brien, K. M., & LeBow, M. D. (2007). Reducing maladaptive weight management practices: Developing a psychoeducational intervention program. *Eating Behaviors, 8,* 195-210.

Özdemir, V., Dove, E. S., Gürsoy, U. K., Şardaş, S., Yıldırım, A., Yılmaz, Ş. G., . . . Srivastava, S. (2017). Personalized medicine beyond genomics: Alternative futures in big data–Proteomics, environtome and the social proteome. *Journal of Neural Transmission, 124,* 25-32.

Paciorek, A., & Williams, J. N. (2015). Semantic generalization in implicit language learning. *Journal of Experimental Psychology: Learning, Memory, and Cognition, 41,* 989-1002.

Packer, D. (2009). Avoiding groupthink: Whereas weakly identified members remain silent, strongly identified members dissent about collective problems. *Psychological Science, 20,* 546-548.

Padgett, D. K., Stanhope, V., & Henwood, B. F. (2011). Housing-first services for homeless adults with co-occurring disorders: An evidence-based practice. In M. Roberts-DeGennaro & S. J. Fogel (Eds.), *Using evidence to inform practice for community and organizational change.* Chicago: Lyceum Books.

Pagano, M. E., White, W. L., Kelly, J. F., Stout, R. L., & Tonigan, J. S. (2013). The 10-year course of Alcoholics Anonymous participation and long-term outcomes: A follow-up study of outpatient subjects in Project MATCH. *Substance Abuse, 34,* 51-59.

Pager, D., & Shepherd, H. (2008). The sociology of discrimination: Racial discrimination in employment, housing, credit, and consumer markets. *Annual Review of Sociology, 34,* 181-209.

Pagonis, T. A., Angelopoulos, N., & Koukoulis, G. N. (2006). Psychiatric side effects induced by supraphysiological doses of combinations of anabolic steroids correlate to the severity of abuse. *European Psychiatry, 21,* 551-562.

Pallanti, S., & Bernardi, S. (2009, July). Neurobiology of repeated transcranial magnetic stimulation in the treatment of anxiety: A critical review. *International Clinical Psychopharmacology, 24,* 163-173.

Palmiter, R. (2015). Hunger logic. *Nature Neuroscience, 18,* 789-791.

Pandya, M., Pozuelo, L., & Malone, D. (2007). Electroconvulsive therapy: What the internist needs to know. *Cleveland Clinic Journal of Medicine, 74*, 679-685.

Paniagua, F. A. (2000). *Diagnosis in a multicultural context: A casebook for mental health professionals.* Thousand Oaks, CA: Sage.

Papoiu, A., Nattkemper, L., Sanders, K., Kraft, R., Chan, Y-H, Coghill, R., & Yosipovitch, G. (2013). Brain's reward circuits mediate itch relief. A functional MRI study of active scratching. *PLoS ONE 8(12):* e82389.

Pardini, D., White, H. R., Xiong, S., Bechtold, J., Chung, T., Loeber, R., & Hipwell, A. (2015). Unfazed or dazed and confused: Does early adolescent marijuana use cause sustained impairments in attention and academic functioning? *Journal of Abnormal Child Psychology.* Accessed online, 8.30.15; http://www.ncbi.nlm.nih.gov/pubmed/25862212.

Parish, C. L., & Arenas, E. (2007). Stem-cell-based strategies for the treatment of Parkinson's disease. *Neurodegenerative Disease, 4*, 339-347.

Park, A. (2011, March 7). Healing the hurt. *Time,* 64-71.

Park, A. (2015, May 7). Exclusive: Meet the world's first baby born with an assist from stem cells. *Time.* Retrieved from http://time.com/3849127/baby-stem-cells-augment-ivf/.

Park, D. C. (2007). Eating disorders: A call to arms. *American Psychologist, 62*, 158.

Park, E., McCoy, T. P., Erausquin, J. T., & Bartlett, R. (2018). Trajectories of risk behaviors across adolescence and young adulthood: The role of race and ethnicity. *Addictive Behaviors, 76*, 1-7.

Park, H., & Antonioni, D. (2007). Personality, reciprocity, and strength of conflict resolution strategy. *Journal of Research in Personality, 41*, 110-125.

Park, H., & Raymo, J. M. (2013). Divorce in Korea: Trends and educational differentials. *Journal of Marriage and Family, 75*, 110-126.

Park, H., Yun, I., & Walsh, A. (2017). Early puberty, school context, and delinquency among South Korean girls. *International Journal of Offender Therapy and Comparative Criminology, 61*, 795-818.

Park, J., Park, K., & Dubinsky, A. J. (2011). Impact of retailer image on private brand attitude: Halo effect and summary construct. *Australian Journal of Psychology, 63*, 173-183.

Parke, M. R., Seo, M., & Sherf, E. N. (2015). Regulating and facilitating: The role of emotional intelligence in maintaining and using positive affect for creativity. *Journal of Applied Psychology, 100*, 917-934.

Parker-Pope, T. (2003, April 22). The diet that works. *The Wall Street Journal,* pp. R1, R5.

Parkinson, J., Garfinkel, S., Critchley, H., Dienes, Z., & Seth, A. K. (2017). Don't make me angry, you wouldn't like me when I'm angry: Volitional choices to act or inhibit are modulated by subliminal perception of emotional faces. *Cognitive, Affective & Behavioral Neuroscience, 17*, 252-268.

Parra, A., & Argibay, J. C. (2007). Comparing psychics and non-psychics through a 'token-object' forced-choice ESP test. *Journal of the Society for Psychical Research, 71*, 80-90.

Parris, B. A. (2017). The role of frontal executive functions in hypnosis and hypnotic suggestibility. *Psychology of Consciousness: Theory, Research, and Practice, 4*, 211-229.

Parrott, A. C., Downey, L. A., Roberts, C. A., Montgomery, C., Bruno, R., & Fox, H. C. (2017). Recreational 3,4-methylenedioxymethamphetamine or 'ecstasy': Current perspective and future research prospects. *Journal of Psychpharmacology,* 269881117711922. doi: 10.1177/0269881117711922.

Paterson, H. M., Kemp, R. I., & Ng, J. R. (2011). Combating co-witness contamination: Attempting to decrease the negative effects of discussion on eyewitness memory. *Applied Cognitive Psychology, 25*, 43-52.

Patten, S. B., Williams, J. A., Lavorato, D. H., Bulloch, A. M., Fiest, K. M., Wang, J. L., . . . Sajobi, T. T. (2017). Seasonal variation in major depressive episode prevalence in Canada. *Epidemiology and Psychiatric Sciences, 26*, 169-176.

Patterson, T. G., & Joseph, S. (2013). Unconditional positive self-regard. In M. E. Bernard (Ed.), *The strength of self-acceptance: Theory, practice and research.* New York: Springer Science + Business Media.

Paul, A. M. (2004). *Cult of personality: How personality tests are leading us to miseducate our children, mismanage our companies and misunderstand ourselves.* New York: Free Press.

Paulmann, S., Jessen, S., & Kotz, S. A. (2009). Investigating the multimodal nature of human communication: Insights from ERPs. *Journal of Psychophysiology, 23*, 63-76.

Pautassi, R., Myers, M., Spear, L., Molina, J., & Spear, N. E. (2011). Ethanol induces second-order aversive conditioning in adolescent and adult rats. *Alcohol, 45*, 45-55.

Pavitt, C. (2007). Impression formation. In B. B. Whaley & W. Samter (Eds.), *Explaining communication: Contemporary theories and exemplars.* Mahwah, NJ: Lawrence Erlbaum Associates.

Pavot, W., & Diener, E. (2013). Happiness experienced: The science of subjective well-being. In S. A. David, I. Boniwell, & A. Conley Ayers (Eds.), *The Oxford handbook of happiness.* New York: Oxford University Press.

Pavão, R., Tort, A. L., & Amaral, O. B. (2015). Multifactoriality in psychiatric disorders: A computational study of schizophrenia. *Schizophrenia Bulletin, 41*, 980-988.

Payne, K., & Marcus, D. (2008). The efficacy of group psychotherapy for older adult clients: A meta-analysis. *Group Dynamics: Theory, Research, and Practice, 12*, 268-278.

Pearson, A. R., Dovidio, J. F., & Pratto, E. (2007). Racial prejudice, intergroup hate, and blatant and subtle bias of whites toward blacks in legal decision making in the United States. *International Journal of Psychology & Psychological Therapy, 7*, 125-134.

Pedersen, P. B., Draguns, J. G., Lonner, W. J., & Trimble, J. E. (Eds.). (2002). *Counseling across cultures* (5th ed.). Thousand Oaks, CA: Sage.

Pedraza, O., & Mungas, D. (2008). Measurement in cross-cultural neuropsychology. *Neuropsychology Review, 18*, 184-193.

Pekrun, R. (2017). Emotion and achievement during adolescence. *Child Development Perspectives, 11*(3), 215-221.

Pell, M. D., Monetta, L., Paulmann, S., & Kotz, S. A. (2009). Recognizing emotions in a foreign language. *Journal of Nonverbal Behavior, 33*, 107-120.

Pellegrini, A. D., Bohn-Gettler, C. M., Dupuis, D., Hickey, M., Roseth, C., & Solberg, D. (2010). An empirical examination of sex differences in scoring preschool children's aggression. *Journal of Experimental Child Psychology, 109*, 232-238.

Pellis, S. M., & Pellis, V. C. (2007). Rough-and-tumble play and the development of the social brain. *Current Directions in Psychological Science, 16*, 95-97.

Pelphrey, K., & Shultz, S. (2013). Brain mechanisms for social perception: Moving toward an understanding of autism. In K. L. Johnson & M. Shiffrar (Eds.), *People watching: Social, perceptual, and neurophysiological studies of body perception.* New York: Oxford University Press.

Pempek, T., Yermolayeva, Y., & Calvert, S. (2009). College students' social networking experiences on Facebook. *Journal of Applied Developmental Psychology, 30*, 227-238.

Pendyam, S., Bravo-Rivera, C., Burgos-Robles, A., Sotres-Bayon, F., Quirk, G. J., & Nair, S. S. (2013). Fear signaling in the prelimbic-amygdala circuit: A computational modeling and recording study. *Journal of Neurophysiology, 110*, 844-861.

Penhollow, T. M., Young, M., & Nnaka, T. (2017). Alcohol use, hooking-up, condom use: Is there a sexual double standard? *American Journal of Health Behavior, 41*, 92-103.

Penley, J. A., Tomaka, J., & Wiebe, J. S. (2002). The association of coping to physical and psychological health outcomes: A meta-analytic review. *Journal of Behavioral Medicine, 25*, 551-603.

Penn, D. L., Corrigan, P. W., Bentall, R. P., Racenstein, J. M., & Newman, L. (1997). Social cognition in schizophrenia. *Psychological Bulletin, 121*, 114-132.

Perogamvros, L., & Schwartz, S. (2015). Sleep and emotional functions. In P. Meerlo, R. M. Benca, & T. Abel (Eds.), *Sleep, neuronal plasticity and brain function.* New York: Springer-Verlag Publishing.

Perovic, S., & Radenovic, L. (2011). Fine-tuning nativism: The "nurtured nature" and innate cognitive structures. *Phenomenology and the Cognitive Sciences, 10*, 399-417.

Perrier, M., & Ginis, K. M. (2017). Narrative interventions for health screening behaviours: A systematic review. *Journal of Health Psychology, 22*, 375-393.

Perry, G. (2013). *Behind the shock machine.* New York: New Press.

Perry, J., Presniak, M. D., & Olson, T. R. (2013). Defense mechanisms in schizotypal, borderline, antisocial, and narcissistic personality disorders. *Psychiatry: Interpersonal and Biological Processes, 76,* 32-52.

Pert, C. B. (2002). The wisdom of the receptors: Neuropeptides, the emotions, and body-mind. *Advances in Mind-Body Medicine, 18,* 30-35.

Pervin, L. A. (2003). *The science of personality* (2nd ed.). London: Oxford University Press.

Pesmen, C. (2006). Health and wealth techniques to help keep chronic pain from taking over. *Money Builder, 35,* 48.

Pessoa, L. (2011). Reprint of: Emotion and cognition and the amygdala: From "what is it?" to "what's to be done?" *Neuropsychologia, 49,* 681-694.

Peterfi, Z., McGinty, D., Sarai, E., & Szymusiak, R. (2010). Growth hormone-releasing hormone activates sleep regulatory neurons of the rat preoptic hypothalamus. *American Journal of Physiology: Regulatory, Integrative and Comparative Physiology, 298,* R147-R156.

Peters, E. N., Rosenberry, Z. R., Schauer, G. L., O'Grady, K. E., & Johnson, P. S. (2017). Marijuana and tobacco cigarettes: Estimating their behavioral economic relationship using purchasing tasks. *Experimental and Clinical Psychopharmacology, 25*(3), 208-215.

Peters, E., Hess, T. M., Västfjäll, D., & Auman, C. (2007). Adult age differences in dual information processes. *Perspectives on Psychological Science, 2,* 1-23.

Peters, J., Suchan, B., Koster, O., & Daum, I. (2007). Domain-specific retrieval of source information in the medial temporal lobe. *European Journal of Neuroscience, 26,* 1333-1343.

Petersen, A. (2011, August 23). A sleep battle of the sexes. *Wall Street Journal,* pp. D1, D4.

Petersen, A. (2017, April 28). My escape from anxiety. *Wall Street Journal.* Retrieved from https://www.wsj.com/articles/my-escape-from-anxiety-1493391641.

Peterson, C. (2000). The future of optimism. *American Psychologist, 55,* 44-55.

Peterson, L. R., & Peterson, M. J. (1959). Short-term retention of individual items. *Journal of Experimental Psychology, 58,* 193-198.

Petersson, K. M., Silva, C., Castro-Caldas, A., Ingvar, M., & Reis, A. (2007). Literacy: A cultural influence on functional left-right differences in the inferior parietal cortex. *European Journal of Neuroscience, 26,* 791-799.

Petrill, S. A., & Deater-Deckard, K. (2004). The heritability of general cognitive ability: A within-family adoption design. *Intelligence, 32,* 403-409.

Pettigrew, T. F., & Tropp, L. R. (2006). A meta-analytic test of intergroup contact theory. *Journal of Personality and Social Psychology, 90,* 751-783.

Pettito, L. A. (1993). On the ontogenetic requirements for early language acquisition. In B. de Boysson-Bardies, S. de Schonen, P. W. Jusczyk, P. McNeilage, & J. Morton (Eds.), *Developmental neurocognition: Speech and face processing in the first year of life. NATO ASI series D: Behavioural and social sciences* (Vol. 69). Dordrecht, Netherlands: Kluwer Academic.

Pezoulas, V. C., Zervakis, M., Michelogiannis, S., & Klados, M. A. (2017). Resting-state functional connectivity and network analysis of cerebellum with respect to crystallized IQ and gender. *Frontiers in Human Neuroscience, 11,* 1-10.

Pfaff, D. W. (2014). *The altruistic brain: How we are naturally good.* Oxford: Oxford University Press.

Phalen, P. L., Dimaggio, G., Popolo, R., & Lysaker, P. H. (2017). Aspects of Theory of Mind that attenuate the relationship between persecutory delusions and social functioning in schizophrenia spectrum disorders. *Journal of Behavior Therapy and Experimental Psychiatry, 56,* 65-70.

Phillips, M. (2013, December 12). The Lobotomy Files. *Wall Street Journal,* p. A1.

Phua, J., Jin, S. V., & Kim, J. (. (2017). Uses and gratifications of social networking sites for bridging and bonding social capital: A comparison of Facebook, Twitter, Instagram, and Snapchat. *Computers in Human Behavior, 72,* 115-122.

Pi-Sunyer, X. (2003). A clinical view of the obesity problem. *Science, 299,* 859-860.

Piaget, J. (1970). Piaget's theory. In P. H. Mussen (Ed.), *Carmichael's manual of child psychology* (3rd ed., Vol. I). New York: Wiley.

Piaget, J., & Inhelder, B. (1958). *The growth of logical thinking from childhood to adolescence* (A. Parsons & S. Seagrin, Trans.). New York: Basic Books.

Pickel, K. (2009). The weapon focus effect on memory for female versus male perpetrators. *Memory, 17,* 664-678.

Pickering, G. J., & Gordon, R. (2006). Perception of mouthfeel sensations elicited by red wine are associated with sensitivity to 6-N-propylthiouracil. *Journal of Sensory Studies, 21,* 249-265.

Pickrell, J. E., McDonald, D., Bernstein, D. M., & Loftus, E. F. (2017). Misinformation effect. In R. F. Pohl (Ed.), *Cognitive illusions: Intriguing phenomena in thinking, judgment and memory* (pp. 406-423). New York: Routledge/Taylor & Francis Group.

Pietarinen, A.-V. (2006). The evolution of semantics and language-games for meaning. *Interaction Studies: Social Behaviour and Communication in Biological and Artificial Systems, 7,* 79-104.

Pietromonaco, P., & Collins, N.L. (2017). Interpersonal mechanisms linking close relationships to health. *American Psychologist, 72,* 531-542.

Pijnenborg, G. M., Timmerman, M. E., Derks, E. M., Fleischhacker, W. W., Kahn, R. S., & Aleman, A. (2015). Differential effects of antipsychotic drugs on insight in first episode schizophrenia: Data from the European First-Episode Schizophrenia Trial (EUFEST). *European Neuropsychopharmacology, 25,* 808-816.

Pillay, S. S., Rogowska, J., Gruber, S. A., Simpson, N., & Yurgelun-Todd, D. A. (2007). Recognition of happy facial affect in panic disorder: an fMRI study. *Journal of Anxiety Disorders, 21,* 381-393.

Pinal, D., Zurrón, M., & Díaz, F. (2015). Age-related changes in brain activity are specific for high

order cognitive processes during successful encoding of information in working memory. *Frontiers in Aging Neuroscience, 7,* 88-97.

Pincus, T., & Morley, S. (2001). Cognitive processing bias in chronic pain: A review and integration. *Psychological Bulletin, 127,* 599-617.

Pinker, S. (1994). *The language instinct.* New York: William Morrow.

Pinker, S. (2004). Clarifying the logical problem of language acquisition. *Journal of Child Language, 31,* 949-953.

Pinker, S., & Jackendoff, R. (2005). The faculty of language: What's special about it? *Cognition, 96,* 201-236.

Pinkerton, S. D., Bogart, L. M., Cecil, H., & Abramson, P. R. (2002). Factors associated with masturbation in a collegiate sample. *Journal of Psychology and Human Sexuality, 14,* 103-121.

Pinquart, M., & Kauser, R. (2017). Do the associations of parenting styles with behavior problems and academic achievement vary by culture? Results from a meta-analysis. *Cultural Diversity and Ethnic Minority Psychology.* Accessed at https://www.ncbi.nlm.nih.gov/pubmed/28394165.

Pisarik, C. T., Rowell, P., & Currie, L. K. (2013). Work-related daydreams: A qualitative content analysis. *Journal of Career Development, 40,* 87-106.

Plante, C., & Anderson, C.A. (2017). Global warming and violent behavior. *APS Observer,* pp. 29-32.

Plomin, R. (2003). 50 years of DNA: What it has meant to psychological science. *American Psychological Society, 16,* 7-8.

Plomin, R. (2005). Finding genes in child psychology and psychiatry: When are we going to be there? *Journal of Child Psychology and Psychiatry, 46,* 1030-1038.

Plomin, R. (2009). The nature of nurture. In K. McCartney & R. A. Weinberg (Eds.), *Experience and development: A festschrift in honor of Sandra Wood Scarr.* New York: Psychology Press.

Plomin, R., & McGuffin, P. (2003). Psychopathology in the postgenomic era. *Annual Review of Psychology, 54,* 205-228.

Pluess, M., & Belsky, J. (2009). Differential susceptibility to rearing experience: The case of childcare. *Journal of Child Psychology and Psychiatry, 50,* 396-404.

Plötner, M., Over, H., Carpenter, M., & Tomasello, M. (2015). Young children show the bystander effect in helping situations. *Psychological Science, 26*(4), 499-506.

Poirier, M., Saint-Aubin, J., Mair, A., Tehan, G., & Tolan, A. (2015). Order recall in verbal short-term memory: The role of semantic networks. *Memory & Cognition, 43,* 489-499.

Pole, N. (2007).The psychophysiology of post-traumatic stress disorder: A meta-analysis. *Psychological Bulletin, 133,* 34-45.

Polgár, Z., Kinnunen, M., Újváry, D., Miklósi, Á., & Gácsi, M. (2016). A test of canine olfactory capacity: Comparing various dog breeds and wolves in a natural detection task. *Plos ONE, 11*(5).

Polivy, J., Herman, C. P., & Boivin, M. (2005). Eating disorders. In J. E. Maddux & B. A.

Winstead (Eds.), *Psychopathology: Foundations for a contemporary understanding.* Mahwah, NJ: Lawrence Erlbaum Associates.

Polonsky, D. C. (2006). Review of The Big Book of Masturbation: From angst to zeal. *Journal of Sex & Marital Therapy, 32,* 75-78.

Ponterotto, J. G., Gretchen, D., & Chauhan, R. V. (2001). Cultural identity and multicultural assessment: Quantitative and qualitative tools for the clinician. In L. A. Suzuki & J. G. Ponterotto (Eds.), *Handbook of multicultural assessment: Clinical, psychological, and educational applications* (2nd ed.). San Francisco: Jossey-Bass/Pfeiffer.

Ponterotto, J. G., Utsey, S. O., & Pedersen, P. B. (2006). *Preventing prejudice: A guide for counselors, educators, and parents.* Thousand Oaks, CA: Sage Publications.

Pontzer, H. (2017). Exercise paradox. *Scientific American, 316*(2), 28-31.

Pool, E., Rehme, A. K., Fink, G. R., Eickhoff, S. B., & Grefkes, C. (2013). Network dynamics engaged in the modulation of motor behavior in healthy subjects. *Neuroimage, 88,* 68-76.

Popa, D., Léna, C., Alexandre, C., & Adrien, J. (2008). Lasting syndrome of depression produced by reduction in serotonin uptake during postnatal development: Evidence from sleep, stress, and behavior. *Journal of Neuroscience, 28,* 88-97.

Porcerelli, J. H., Bornstein, R.F., Porcerelli, D., & Arterbery, V.E. (2015). The complex role of personality in cancer treatment: Impact of dependency-detachment on health status, distress, and physician-patient relationship. *Journal of Nervous and Mental Disease, 203,* 264-268.

Porkka-Heiskanen, T. (2013). Sleep homeostasis. *Current Opinion in Neurobiology, 23,* 799-805.

Porkka-Heiskanen, T., & Kalinchuk, A. V. (2011). Adenosine, energy metabolism and sleep homeostasis. *Sleep Medicine Reviews, 15,* 123-135.

Posada, G., & Trumbell, J. M. (2017). Universality and cultural specificity in child-mother attachment relationships: In search of answers. In S. Gojman-de-Millan, C. Herreman, & L. A. Sroufe (Eds.), *Attachment across clinical and cultural perspectives: A relational psychoanalytic approach.* New York: Routledge/Taylor & Francis Group.

Post, J. M. (2011). Crimes of obedience: 'Groupthink' at Abu Ghraib. *International Journal of Group Psychotherapy, 61,* 49-66.

Post, J. M. (2015). Terrorism and rightwing extremism: The changing face of terrorism and political violence in the 21st century: The virtual community of hatred. [Special issue: Violence in America: Part II.] *International Journal of Group Psychotherapy, 65*(2), 243-271.

Potash, J. S. (2015). Archetypal aesthetics: Viewing art through states of consciousness. *International Journal of Jungian Studies, 7,* 139-153.

Pottick, K. J., Kirk, S. A., Hsieh, D. K., & Tian, X. (2007). Judging mental disorder in youths: Effects of client, clinician, and contextual differences. *Journal of Consulting Clinical Psychology, 75,* 1-8.

Pow, A. M., & Cashwell, C. S. (2017). Posttraumatic stress disorder and emotion-focused coping among disaster mental health counselors. *Journal of Counseling & Development, 95*(3), 322-331.

Pow, J. L., Baumeister, A. A., Hawkins, M. F., Cohen, A. S., & Garand, J. C. (2015). Deinstitutionalization of American public hospitals for the mentally ill before and after the introduction of antipsychotic medications. *Harvard Review of Psychiatry, 23,* 176-187.

Powell, L. H. (2006). Review of marital and sexual lifestyles in the United States: Attitudes, behaviors, and relationships in social context. *Family Relations, 55,* 149.

Powell, L. H., Shahabi, L., & Thoresen, C. E. (2003). Religion and spirituality: Linkages to physical health. *American Psychology, 58,* 36-52.

Powell, R. A., Digdon, N., Harris, B., & Smithson, C. (2014). Correcting the record on Watson, Rayner, and Little Albert: Albert Barger as "Psychology's Lost Boy." *American Psychologist, 69,* 600-611.

Powers, M., & Emmelkamp, P. (2008). Virtual reality exposure therapy for anxiety disorders: A meta-analysis. *Journal of Anxiety Disorders, 22,* 561-569.

Pozzan, L., & Valian, V. (2017). Asking questions in child English: Evidence for early abstract representations. *Language Acquisition: A Journal of Developmental Linguistics, 24,* 209-233.

Prasser, J., Schecklmann, M., Poeppl, T. B., Frank, E., Kreuzer, P. M., Hajak, G., & . . . Langguth, B. (2015). Bilateral prefrontal rTMS and theta burst TMS as an add-on treatment for depression: A randomized placebo controlled trial. *The World Journal of Biological Psychiatry, 16,* 57-65.

Pratkanis, A. R. (2007). Social influence analysis: An index of tactics. In A. R. Pratkanis (Ed.), *The science of social influence: Advances and future progress.* New York: Psychology Press.

Pratkanis, A. R., Epley, N., & Savitsky, K. (2007). Issue 12: Is subliminal persuasion a myth? In J. A. Nier, *Taking sides: Clashing views in social psychology* (2nd ed.). New York: McGraw-Hill.

Pratt, H. D., Phillips, E. L., Greydanus, D. E., & Patel, D. R. (2003). Eating disorders in the adolescent population: Future directions [Special issue: Eating disorders in adolescents]. *Journal of Adolescent Research, 18,* 297-317.

Pratto, F., Lee, I., Tan, J. Y., & Pitpitan, E. Y. (2011). Power basis theory: A psychoecological approach to power. In D. Dunning (Ed.), *Social motivation.* New York: Psychology Press.

Pretsch, J., Heckmann, N., Flunger, B., & Schmitt, M. (2013). Agree or disagree?: Influences on consensus in personality judgments. *European Journal of Psychological Assessment.* Retrieved from http://psycnet.apa.org/psycinfo/2013-30588-001/.

Pretzer, J. L., & Beck, A. T. (2005). A cognitive theory of personality disorders. In M. F. Lenzenweger & J. F. Clarkin (Eds.), *Major theories of personality disorder* (2nd ed.). New York: Guilford Press.

Price, M. (2008, September). Against doctors' orders. *Monitor on Psychology,* pp. 34-36.

Priester, J. R., & Petty, R. E. (2011). The potholed path to happiness, possibly paved with money: A research dialogue. *Journal of Consumer Psychology, 21,* 113-114.

Prince, C. V. (2005). Homosexuality, transvestism and transsexuality: Reflections on their etymology and differentiation. *International Journal of Transgenderism, 8,* 15-18.

Prinz, J. J. (2007). Emotion: Competing theories and philosophical issues. In P. Thagard (Ed.), *Philosophy of psychology and cognitive science.* Amsterdam, Netherlands: North Holland/Elsevier.

Prior, K. N., & Bond, M. J. (2017). Patterns of "abnormal" illness behavior among healthy individuals. *American Journal of Health Behavior, 41,* 139-146.

Proffitt, D. R. (2006). Distance perception. *Current Directions in Psychological Science, 15,* 131-139.

Prohovnik, I., Skudlarski, P., Fulbright, R. K., Gore, J. C., & Wexler, B. E. (2004). Functional MRI changes before and after onset of reported emotions. *Psychiatry Research: Neuroimaging, 132,* 239-250.

Proudfoot, D. (2009). Meaning and mind: Wittgenstein's relevance for the "does language shape thought?" debate. *New Ideas in Psychology, 27,* 163-183.

Proyer, R. T., Gander, F., Wellenzohn, S., & Ruch, W. (2013). What good are character strengths beyond subjective well-being? The contribution of the good character on self-reported health-oriented behavior, physical fitness, and the subjective health status. *Journal of Positive Psychology, 8,* 222-232.

Prus, A. J., Mooney-Leber, S. M., Berquist, M. I., Pehrson, A. L., Porter, N. P., & Porter, J. H. (2015). The antidepressant drugs fluoxetine and duloxetine produce anxiolytic-like effects in a schedule-induced polydipsia paradigm in rats: Enhancement of fluoxetine's effects by the α_2 adrenoceptor antagonist yohimbine. *Behavioural Pharmacology, 26,* 489-494.

Puca, R. M. (2005). The influence of the achievement motive on probability estimates in pre- and post-decisional action phases. *Journal of Research in Personality, 39,* 245-262.

Puhl, R. M., & Liu, S. (2015). A national survey of public views about the classification of obesity as a disease. *Obesity, 23*(6), 1288-1295.

Purdy, S. C., Sharma, M. M., Munro, K. J., & Morgan, C. A. (2013). Stimulus level effects on speech-evoked obligatory cortical auditory evoked potentials in infants with normal hearing. *Clinical Neurophysiology, 124,* 474-480.

Putnam, E. W. (2000). Dissociative disorders. In A. J. Sameroff & M. Lewis (Eds.), *Handbook of developmental psychopathology* (2nd ed.). Dordrecht, Netherlands: Kluwer Academic Publishers.

Pérez-Leroux, A. T., Pirvulescu, M., & Roberge, Y. (2011). Topicalization and object omission in child language. *First Language, 31,* 280-299.

Qu, C., Zhang, A., & Chen, Q. (2013). Monetary effects on fear conditioning. *Psychological Reports, 112,* 353-364.

Quartana, P. J., & Burns, J. W. (2007). Painful consequences of anger suppression. *Emotion, 7,* 400-414.

Quinn, K., Pacella, M. L., Dickson-Gomez, J., & Nydegger, L. A. (2017). Childhood adversity and the continued exposure to trauma and violence among adolescent gang members. *American Journal of Community Psychology, 59,* 36-49.

Quintana, S. M., Aboud, F. E., & Chao, R. K. (2006). Race, ethnicity, and culture in child development: Contemporary research and future directions. *Child Development, 77,* 1129-1141.

Rabin, J. (2004). Quantification of color vision with cone contrast sensitivity. *Visual Neuroscience, 21,* 483-485.

Rabin, R. C. (2013, August 13). A glut of antidepressants. *The New York Times,* p. D4.

Racine, S. E., VanHuysse, J. L., Keel, P. K., Burt, S. A., Neale, M. C., Boker, S., & Klump, K. L. (2017). Eating disorder-specific risk factors moderate the relationship between negative urgency and binge eating: A behavioral genetic investigation. *Journal of Abnormal Psychology, 126,* 481-494.

Radvansky, G. A. (2010). *Human memory.* N.Y.: Psychology Press.

Radvansky, G. A., Pettijohn, K. A., & Kim, J. (2015). Walking through doorways causes forgetting: Younger and older adults. *Psychology And Aging, 30,* 259-265.

Raffin, E., Richard, N., Giraux, P., & Reilly, K. T. (2016). Primary motor cortex changes after amputation correlate with phantom limb pain and the ability to move the phantom limb. *Neuroimage, 130,* 134-144.

Ragland, J. D., Layher, E., Hannula, D. E., Niendam, T.A., Lesh, T.A., Solomon, M., Carter, C. S., & Ranganath, C. (2015). Impact of schizophrenia on anterior and posterior hippocampus during memory for complex scenes. *Neuroimage Clinics, 13,* 82-88.

Rahman, Q., & Yusuf, S. (2015). Lateralization for processing facial emotions in gay men, heterosexual men, and heterosexual women. *Archives of Sexual Behavior, 44,* 1405-1413.

Rahman, Q., Kumari, V., & Wilson, G. D. (2003). Sexual orientation-related differences in prepulse inhibition of the human startle response. *Behavioral Neuroscience, 117,* 1096-1102.

Rajagopal, S. (2006). The placebo effect. *Psychiatric Bulletin, 30,* 185-188.

Rajecki, D. W., & Borden, V. M. H. (2011). Psychology degrees: Employment, wage, and career trajectory consequences. *Perspectives on Psychological Science, 6,* 321-335.

Rajsic, J., Wilson, D. E., & Pratt, J. (2015). Confirmation bias in visual search. *Journal of Experimental Psychology: Human Perception and Performance, 41*(5), 1353-1364.

Ramachandra, V. (2009, February). On whether mirror neurons play a significant role in processing affective prosody. *Perceptual and Motor Skills, 108,* 30-36.

Ramachandran, V. S., & Hubbard, E. M. (2006). Hearing colors, tasting shapes. *Scientific American, 16,* 76-83

Ramos, R. A., Ferguson, C. J., Frailing, K., & Romero-Ramirez, M. (2013). Comfortably numb or just yet another movie? Media violence exposure does not reduce viewer empathy for victims of real violence among primarily Hispanic viewers. *Psychology of Popular Media Culture, 2,* 2-10.

Ramus, F. (2006). Genes, brain, and cognition: A roadmap for the cognitive scientist. *Cognition, 101,* 247-269.

Randall, D. K. (2012, August 4-5). Decoding the science of sleep. *Wall Street Journal,* pp. C1-C2.

Randolph-Seng, B., & Nielsen, M. E. (2009). Opening the doors of perception: Priming altered states of consciousness outside of conscious awareness. *Archivfür Religionspsychologie/Archive for the Psychology of Religions, 31,* 237-260.

Rangell, L. (2007). *The road to unity in psychoanalytic theory.* Lanham, MD: Jason Aronson.

Rapaport, M., Nierenberg, A. A., Howland, R., Dording, C., Schettler, P. J., & Mischoulon, D. (2011). The treatment of minor depression with St. John's wort or citalopram: Failure to show benefit over placebo. *Journal of Psychiatric Research, 45,* 931-941.

Raskin, N. J., & Rogers, C. R. (1989). Person-centered therapy. In R. J. Corsini & D. Wedding (Eds.), *Current psychotherapies* (4th ed.). Itasca, IL: F. E. Peacock.

Rassin, E., & Muris, P. (2007). Abnormal and normal obsessions: A reconsideration. *Behaviour Research and Therapy, 45,* 1065-1070.

Ravallion, M., & Lokshin, M. (2010). Who cares about relative deprivation? *Journal of Economic Behavior & Organization, 73*(2), 171-185. doi:10.1016/j.jebo.2009.08.008.

Ravicz, M.M., Perdue, K.L., Westerlund, A., Vanderwert, R.E. and Nelson, C.A. (2015). Infants' neural responses to facial emotion in the prefrontal cortex are correlated with temperament: a functional near-infrared spectroscopy study. *Frontiers in Psychology, 6,* 922. Retrieved from https://doi.org/10.3389/fpsyg.2015.00922.

Ray, J. V., Thornton, L. C., Frick, P. J., Steinberg, L., & Cauffman, E. (2015). Impulse control and callous-unemotional traits distinguish patterns of delinquency and substance use in justice involved adolescents: Examining the moderating role of neighborhood context. *Journal Of Abnormal Child Psychology.* Accessed online, 9.29.15; http://www.ncbi.nlm.nih.gov/pubmed/26201308.

Ray, L. A., & Hutchison, K. E. (2007). Effects of naltrexone on alcohol sensitivity and genetic moderators of medication response: a double-blind placebo-controlled study. *Archives of General Psychiatry, 64,* 1069-1077.

Ray, L., Bryan, A., MacKillop, J., McGeary, J., Hesterberg, K., & Hutchison, K. (2009). The dopamine D4 receptor gene exon III polymorphism, problematic alcohol use and novelty seeking: Direct and mediated genetic effects. *Addiction Biology, 14,* 238-244.

Ray, R., et al. (2008). Neuroimaging, genetics and the treatment of nicotine addiction. *Behavioural Brain Research, 193,* 159-169.

Raz, A. (2007). Suggestibility and hypnotizability: Mind the gap. *American Journal of Clinical Hypnosis, 49,* 205-210.

Raznahan, A., Lee, Y., Stidd, R., Long, R., Greenstein, D., Clasen, L., Addington, A., Gogtay, N., Rapoport, J., & Giedd, J. (2010). Longitudinally mapping the influence of sex and androgen signaling on the dynamics of human cortical maturation in adolescence. *Proceedings of the National Academy of Sciences, 107,* 16988-16993.

Reddy, S. (2013(a), March 19). People who taste too much. *Wall Street Journal,* p. D1.

Reddy, S. (2013(b), September 3). A field guide to the perfect nap. *Wall Street Journal,* pp. D1-D2.

Reddy, S. (2015, May 19.) How doctors break bad news. *Wall Street Journal,* pp. D1, D4.

Reddy, S. (2016, May 10). When daydreaming becomes a problem. *Wall Street Journal,* pp. D1, D4.

Reddy, S. (2017, January 17.) A disorder that blurs the senses. *Wall Street Journal,* pp. A13-A14.

Redford, M. A. (2017). Sound categories or phonemes? *British Journal of Psychology, 108,* 34-36.

Redish, A. D. (2004). Addiction as a computational process gone awry. *Science, 306,* 1944-1947.

Redshaw, M., & Martin, C. (2013). Babies, "bonding" and ideas about parental "attachment." *Journal of Reproductive and Infant Psychology, 31,* 219-221.

Reece, M., Herbenick, D., Sanders, S., Dodge, B., Ghassemi, A., & Fortenberry, J. (2009). Prevalence and characteristics of vibrator use by men in the United States. *Journal of Sexual Medicine, 6,* 1867-1874.

Reed, P. (2007). Response rate and sensitivity to the molar feedback function relating response and reinforcement rate on VI+ schedules of reinforcement. *Journal of Experimental Psychology: Animal Behavior Processes, 33,* 428-439.

Reed, P., & Morgan, T. (2008). Effect on subsequent fixed-interval schedule performance of prior exposure to ratio and interval schedules of reinforcement. *Learning & Behavior, 36,* 82-91.

Reed, S. K. (2017). Problem solving. In S. F. Chipman, S. F. Chipman (Eds.) , *The Oxford handbook of cognitive science.* New York: Oxford University Press.

Rees, P., & Seaton, N. (2011). Psychologists' response to crises: International perspectives. *School Psychology International, 32,* 73-94.

Reeve, J.M. (2014). *Understanding Motivation and Emotion* (6th ed.). New York: Wiley.

Regan, P. C. (2006). Love. In R. D. McAnulty & M. M. Burnette (Eds.), *Sex and sexuality, Vol. 2: Sexual function and dysfunction.* Westport, CT: Praeger Publishers/Greenwood Publishing.

Regnerus, M., Price, J., & Gordon, D. (2017). Masturbation and partnered sex: Substitutes or complements? *Archives of Sexual Behavior, 46*(7), 2111-2121.

Reichenberg, A., & Harvey, P. D. (2007). Neuro-psychological impairments in schizophrenia: Integration of performance-based and brain imaging findings. *Psychological Bulletin, 133,* 212-223.

Reichenberg, A., Harvey, P., Bowie, C., Mojtabai, R., Rabinowitz, J., Heaton, R., et al. (2009). Neuropsychological function and dysfunction in schizophrenia and psychotic affective disorders. *Schizophrenia Bulletin, 35*, 1022-1029.

Reid, J. L., Martin, A., & Brooks-Gunn, J. (2017). Low-income parents' adult interactions at childcare centres. *Early Child Development and Care, 187*, 138-151.

Reid, J. R., MacLeod, J., & Robertson, J. R. (2010). Cannabis and the lung. *Journal of the Royal College of Physicians, 40*, 328 -334.

Reijonen, J. H., Pratt, H. D., Patel, D. R., & Greydanus, D. E. (2003). Eating disorders in the adolescent population: An overview [Special issue: Eating disorders in adolescents]. *Journal of Adolescent Research, 18*, 209-222.

Reilly, M. T., Noronha, A., Goldman, D., & Koob, G. F. (2017). Genetic studies of alcohol dependence in the context of the addiction cycle. *Neuropharmacology, 12*, 23-21.

Reilly, T., & Waterhouse, J. (2007). Altered sleep-wake cycles and food intake: The Ramadan model. *Physiology & Behavior, 90*, 219-228.

Reiner, R. (2008, March). Integrating a portable biofeedback device into clinical practice for patients with anxiety disorders: Results of a pilot study. *Applied Psychophysiology and Biofeedback, 33*, 55-61.

Reinisch, J. M., Mortensen, E. L., & Sanders, S. A. (2017). Prenatal exposure to progesterone affects sexual orientation in humans. *Archives of Sexual Behavior, 46*(5), 1239-1249.

Reisberg, D. (1997). *Cognition: Exploring the science of the mind.* New York: Norton.

Reisberg, D. (2009). *Cognition: Exploring the science of the mind.* New York: Norton.

Reisberg, D. (2013). Mental images. In D. Reisberg (Ed.), *The Oxford handbook of cognitive psychology.* New York: Oxford University Press.

Reisner, A. D., Piel, J., & Makey, M. (2013). Competency to stand trial and defendants who lack insight into their mental illness. *Journal of the American Academy of Psychiatry and the Law, 41*, 85-91.

Reks, S., Sheaves, B., & Freeman, D. (2017, July 15.) Nightmares in the general population: Identifying potential causal factors. *Social Psychiatry and Psychiatric Epidemiology.* doi: 10.1007/s00127-017-1408-7.

Remington, G., Foussias, G., Fervaha, G., & Agid, O. (2014). Schizophrenia, cognition, and psychosis. *JAMA Psychiatry, 71*, 336-337.

Ren, X., Wang, T., & Jarrold, C. (2016). Individual differences in frequency of inner speech: Differential relations with cognitive and non-cognitive factors. *Frontiers in Psychology, 7*, 1675.

Repp, B. H., & Knoblich, G. (2007). Action can affect auditory perception. *Psychological Science, 18*, 6-7.

Reynolds, C. A., & Maughan, E. D. (2015). Telehealth in the school setting: An integrative review. *Journal of School Nursing, 31*, 44-53.

Reynolds, C. R., & Ramsay, M. C. (2003). Bias in psychological assessment: An empirical review and recommendations. In J. R. Graham & J. A. Naglieri (Eds.), *Handbook of psychology: Assessment psychology* (Vol. 10). New York: Wiley.

Reynolds, d. J., Stiles, W. B., Bailer, A. J., & Hughes, M. R. (2013). Impact of exchanges and client-therapist alliance in online-text psychotherapy. *Cyberpsychology, Behavior, and Social Networking, 16*, 370-377.

Reznikova, T. N., Seliverstova, N. A., Kataeva, G. V., Aroev, R. A., Ilves, A. G., Kuznetsova, A. K., & Makeeva, E. (2015). Functional activity of brain structures and predisposition to aggression in patients with lingering diseases of the CNS. *Human Physiology, 41*, 27-33.

Riccelli, R., Toschi, N., Nigro, S., Terracciano, A. & Passamonti, L. (2017). Surface-based morphometry reveals the neuroanatomical basis of the five-factor model of personality. *Social Cogniitive and Affective Neuroscience, 12*, 671-684

Rice, C. (2009, December 18). Prevalence of Autism Spectrum Disorders–Autism and Developmental Disabilities Monitoring Network, United States, 2006. *MMWR, 58*(SS10), 1-20.

Richard, D. C. S., & Lauterbach, D. (Eds.). (2006). *Handbook of exposure therapies.* New York: Academic Press.

Richards, C. (2011). Transsexualism and existentialism. *Existential Analysis, 22*(2), 272-279.

Richards, R. (2006). Frank Barron and the study of creativity: A voice that lives on. *Journal of Humanistic Psychology, 46*, 352-370.

Richardson, D. S. (2014). Everyday aggression takes many forms. *Current Directions in Psychological Science, 23*, 220-224.

Richardson, D., & Hammock, G. S. (2011). Is it aggression?: Perceptions of and motivations for passive and psychological aggression. In J. P. Forgas, A. W. Kruglanski, & K. D. Williams (Eds.), *The psychology of social conflict and aggression.* New York: Psychology Press.

Richmond, A. S., Broussard, K. A., Sterns, J. L., Sanders, K. K., & Shardy, J. C. (2015). Who are we studying? Sample diversity in teaching of psychology research. *Teaching of Psychology, 42*, 218-226.

Rieber, R. W., & Robinson, D. K. (2006). Review of the essential Vygotsky. *Journal of the History of the Behavioral Sciences, 42*, 178-180.

Rigby, L., & Waite, S. (2007). Group therapy for self-esteem: Using creative approaches and metaphor as clinical tools. *Behavioural and Cognitive Psychotherapy, 35*, 361-364.

Rimmele, J. M., Sussman, E., & Poeppel, D. (2015). The role of temporal structure in the investigation of sensory memory, auditory scene analysis, and speech perception: A healthy-aging perspective. *International Journal of Psychophysiology, 95*, 175-183.

Rinaman, L., Banihashemi, L., & Koehnle, T. J. (2011). Early life experience shapes the functional organization of stress-responsive visceral circuits. *Physiology & Behavior, 104*, 632-640.

Rindone, H. G. (2015). Methamphetamine addiction. In R. L. Smith (Ed.), *Treatment strategies for substance and process addictions.* Alexandria, VA: American Counseling Association.

Riniolo, T. C., Koledin, M., Drakulic, G. M., & Payne, R. A. (2003). An archival study of eyewitness memory of the Titanic's final plunge. *Journal of General Psychology, 130*, 89-95.

Rinn, W. E. (1984). The neuropsychology of facial expression: A review of neurological and psychological mechanisms for producing facial expressions. *Psychological Bulletin, 95*, 52-77.

Rinn, W. E. (1991). Neuropsychology of facial expression. In R. S. Feldman & B. Rimé (Eds.), *Fundamentals of non-verbal behavior.* Cambridge, England: Cambridge University Press.

Risen, J. (2015, August 8). Association bars psychologists from ties to U.S. national security interrogations. *The New York Times*, p. A11.

Rivera-Gaxiola, M., Klarman, L., Garcia-Sierra, A., & Kuhl, P. K. (2005). Neural patterns to speech and vocabulary growth in American infants. *Neuroreport: For Rapid Communication of Neuroscience Research, 16*, 495-498.

Rizzi, T. S., & Posthuma, D. (2013). Genes and intelligence. In D. Reisberg (Ed.), *The Oxford handbook of cognitive psychology.* New York: Oxford University Press.

Robert, S. (2006). Deictic space in Wolof: Discourse, syntax and the importance of absence. In M. Hickman & S. Robert (Eds.), *Space in languages: Linguistic systems and cognitive categories.* Amsterdam, Netherlands: John Benjamins.

Roberts, M. E., Moore, S. D., & Beckham, J. C. (2007). Post-traumatic stress disorder and substance use disorders. In M. Al'bsi (Ed.), *Stress and addiction: Biological and psychological mechanisms.* San Diego, CA: Elsevier Academic Press.

Roberts, R. M., Neate, G. M., & Gierasch, A. (2017). Implicit attitudes towards people with visible difference: Findings from an Implicit Association Test. *Psychology, Health & Medicine, 22*, 352-358.

Robinson, D. N. (2007). Theoretical psychology: What is it and who needs it? *Theory & Psychology, 17*, 187-198.

Robinson-Papp, J., George, M. C., Dorfman, D., & Simpson, D. M. (2015). Barriers to chronic pain measurement: A qualitative study of patient perspectives. *Pain Medicine, 16*, 1256-1264.

Robson, H., Grube, M., Lambon Ralph, M. A., Griffiths, T. D., & Sage, K. (2013). Fundamental deficits of auditory perception in Wernicke's aphasia. *Cortex: A Journal Devoted to the Study of the Nervous System and Behavior, 49*, 1808-1822.

Rock, A. (1999, January). Quitting time for smokers. *Money*, pp. 139-141.

Rodrigues, L., & Girandola, F. (2017). Self-prophecies and cognitive dissonance: Habit, norms and justification of past behavior. *North American Journal of Psychology, 19*, 65-86.

Rodrigues-Amorim, D., Rivera-Baltanás, T., López, M., Spuch, C., Olivares, J. M., & Agís-Balboa, R. C. (2017). Schizophrenia: A review of potential biomarkers. *Journal of Psychiatric Research, 93*, 37-49.

Rodriguez, D. N., & Strange, D. (2015). False memories for dissonance inducing events. *Memory, 23*, 203-212.

Roets, A., & Van Hiel, A. (2011). An integrative process approach on judgment and decision making: The impact of arousal, affect, motivation, and cognitive ability. *The Psychological Record, 61,* 497-520.

Roffman, R. A. (2013). Legalization of marijuana: Unraveling quandaries for the addiction professional. *Frontiers in Psychiatry, 4,* 88-93.

Rogalsky, C., Love, T., Driscoll, D., Anderson, S. W., & Hickok, G. (2011). Are mirror neurons the basis of speech perception? Evidence from five cases with damage to the purported human mirror system. *Neurocase, 17,* 178-187.

Rogers, B., & Naumenko, O. (2015). The new moon illusion and the role of perspective in the perception of straight and parallel lines. *Attention, Perception, & Psychophysics, 77,* 249-257.

Rogers, C. R. (1951). *Client-centered therapy.* Boston: Houghton-Mifflin.

Rogers, C. R. (1971). A theory of personality. In S. Maddi (Ed.), *Perspectives on personality.* Boston: Little, Brown.

Rogers, C. R. (1995). *A way of being.* Boston: Houghton Mifflin.

Rogers, J. M. (2009). Tobacco and pregnancy: Overview of exposures and effects. *Birth Defects Research Part C: Embryo Today, 84,* 152-160.

Rogers, S. (2007). The underlying mechanisms of semantic memory loss in Alzheimer's disease and semantic dementia. *Dissertation Abstracts International: Section B: The Sciences and Engineering, 67*(10-B), 5591.

Roid, G., Nellis, L., & McLellan, M. (2003). Assessment with the Leiter International Performance Scale–Revised and the S-BIT. In R. S. McCallum & R. Steve (Eds.), *Handbook of nonverbal assessment.* New York: Kluwer Academic/Plenum Publishers.

Roizen, N. J., & Patterson, D. (2003). Down's syndrome. *Lancet, 361,* 1281-1289.

Rolls, E. T. (2011). Functions of human emotional memory: The brain and emotion. In S. Nalbantian, P. M. Matthews, & J. L. McClelland (Eds.), *The memory process: Neuroscientific and humanistic perspectives.* Cambridge, MA: MIT Press.

Rom, S. A., Miller, L., & Peluso, J. (2009). Playing the game: Psychological factors in surviving cancer. *International Journal of Emergency Mental Health, 11,* 25-36.

Romani, C., Palermo, L., MacDonald, A., Limback, E., Hall, S. K., & Geberhiwot, T. (2017). The impact of phenylalanine levels on cognitive outcomes in adults with phenylketonuria: Effects across tasks and developmental stages. *Neuropsychology, 31,* 242-254.

Romano, E., Tremblay, R. E., Vitaro, E., Zoccolillo, M., & Pagani, L. (2001). Prevalence of psychiatric diagnoses and the role of perceived impairment: Findings from an adolescent community sample. *Journal of Child Psychology and Psychiatry and Allied Disciplines, 42,* 451-461.

Romero-Guevara, R., Cencetti, F., Donati, C., & Bruni, P. (2015). Sphingosine 1-phosphate signaling pathway in inner ear biology. New therapeutic strategies for hearing loss? *Frontiers in Aging Neuroscience, 7,* 101-111.

Roncero, C., Daigre, C., Gonzalvo, B., Valero, S., Castells, X., Grau-López, L., & . . . Casas, M. (2013). Risk factors for cocaine-induced psychosis in cocaine-dependent patients. *European Psychiatry, 28,* 141-146.

Ronconi, L., Casartelli, L., Carna, S., Molteni, M., Arrigoni, F., & Borgatti, R. (2017). When one is enough: Impaired multisensory integration in cerebellar agenesis. *Cerebral Cortex, 27,* 2041-2051

Rooke, S. E., & Hine, D. W. (2011). A dual process account of adolescent and adult binge drinking. *Addictive Behaviors, 36,* 341-346.

Roos, V., & Zaaiman, R. (2017). Active ageing as positive intervention: Some unintended consequences. In C. Proctor (Ed.), *Positive psychology interventions in practice.* Cham, Switzerland: Springer International Publishing.

Rorschach, H. (1924). *Psychodiagnosis: A diagnostic test based on perception.* New York: Grune & Stratton.

Rose, N., & Blackmore, S. (2002). Horses for courses: Tests of a psychic claimant. *Journal of the Society for Psychical Research, 66,* 29-40.

Rosellini, A. J., Stein, M. B., Colpe, L. J., Heeringa, S. G., Petukhova, M. V., Sampson, N. A., & . . . Kessler, R. C. (2015). Approximating a DSM-5 diagnosis of PTSD using DSM-IV criteria. *Depression and Anxiety, 32,* 493-501.

Rosenblat, A., & Stark, L. (2016). Algorithmic labor and information assymetries: A case study of Uber's drivers. *International Journal of Communication, 10,* 3758-3784.

Rosenblatt, P. C. (2013). The concept of complicated grief: Lessons from other cultures. In M. Stroebe, H. Schut, & J. van den Bout (Eds.), *Complicated grief: Scientific foundations for health care professionals* (pp. 27-39). New York: Routledge/Taylor & Francis Group.

Rosenbloom, T., & Wolf, Y. (2002). Sensation seeking and detection of risky road signals: A developmental perspective. *Accident Analysis and Prevention, 34,* 569-580.

Rosenfeld, , R., Gaston, S., Spivak, H., & Irazola, S. (2017, November.) Assessing and responding to the recent homicide rise in the United States. Washington, DC: National Institute of Justice.

Rosenfeld, M. J., & Thomas, R. J. (2012). Searching for a mate: The rise of the Internet as a social intermediary. *American Sociological Review, 77,* 523-547.

Rosenhan, D. L. (1973). On being sane in insane places. *Science, 179,* 250-258.

Rosenstein, D. S., & Horowitz, H. A. (1996). Adolescent attachment and psychopathology. *Journal of Consulting and Clinical Psychology, 64,* 244-253.

Rosenström, T., Ystrom, E., Torvik, F. A., Czajkowski, N. O., Gillespie, N. A., Aggen, S. H., . . . Reichborn-Kjennerud, T. (2017). Genetic and environmental structure of DSM-IV criteria for antisocial personality disorder: A twin study. *Behavior Genetics, 47,* 265-277.

Rosenthal, N. F. (2003). *The emotional revolution: How the new science of feeling can transform your life.* New York: Citadel.

Rosenthal, R. (2002). Covert communication in classrooms, clinics, courtrooms and cubicles. *American Psychologist, 57,* 838-849.

Rosenthal, R. (2003). Covert communication in laboratories, classrooms, and the truly real world. *Current Directions in Psychological Science, 12,* 151-154.

Ross, C. A. (2015). When to suspect and how to diagnose dissociative identity disorder. *Journal of EMDR Practice and Research, 9,* 114-120.

Ross, J. (2006). Sleep on a problem . . . It works like a dream. *The Psychologist, 19,* 738-740.

Ross, L. A., Molholm, S., Blanco, D., Gomez-Ramirez, M., Saint-Amour, D., & Foxe, J. J. (2011). The development of multisensory speech perception continues into the late childhood years. *European Journal of Neuroscience, 33,* 2329-2337.

Ross, P. E. (2004). Draining the language out of color. *Scientific American, 290,* 46-51.

Rossato, M., Pagano, C., & Vettor, R. (2008). The cannabinoid system and male reproductive functions. *Journal of Neuroendocrinology, 20,* 90-93.

Rossi-Arnaud, C., Cestari, V., Marques, V. S., Gabrielli, G. B., & Spataro, P. (2017). Collaboration in implicit memory: Evidence from word-fragment completion and category exemplar generation. *Psychological Research, 81,* 55-65.

Rotan, L. W., & Ospina-Kammerer, V. (2007). *Mindbody medicine: Foundations and practical applications.* New York: Routledge/Taylor & Francis Group.

Rouder, J. N., Morey, R. D., & Province, J. M. (2013). A Bayes factor meta-analysis of recent extrasensory perception experiments: Comment on Storm, Tressoldi, and Di Risio (2010). *Psychological Bulletin, 139,* 241-247.

Roughton, R. E. (2002). Rethinking homosexuality: What it teaches us about psychoanalysis. *Journal of the American Psychoanalytic Association, 50,* 733-763.

Routtenberg, A., & Lindy, J. (1965). Effects of the availability of rewarding septal and hypothalamic stimulation on bar pressing for food under conditions of deprivation. *Journal of Comparative and Physiological Psychology, 60,* 158-161.

Royzman, E. B., Cassidy, K. W., & Baron, J. (2003). "I know, you know": Epistemic egocentrism in children and adults. *Review of General Psychology, 7,* 38-65.

Rozental, A., Shafran, R., Wade, T., Egan, S., Nordgren, L. B., Carlbring, P., . . . Andersson, G. (2017). A randomized controlled trial of Internet-Based Cognitive Behavior Therapy for perfectionism including an investigation of outcome predictors. *Behaviour Research and Therapy, 95,* 79-86.

Rozin, P., Kabnick, K., Pete, E., Fischler, C., & Shields, C. (2003). The ecology of eating: Smaller portion sizes in France than in the United States help explain the French paradox. *Psychological Science, 14,* 450-454.

Rubichi, S., Ricci, F., Padovani, R., & Scaglietti, L. (2005). Hypnotic susceptibility, baseline attentional functioning, and the Stroop task. *Consciousness and Cognition: An International Journal, 14,* 296-303.

Rubin, D. C., Schrauf, R. W., Gulgoz, S., & Naka, M. (2007). Cross-cultural variability of component processes in autobiographical remembering: Japan, Turkey, and the USA. *Memory, 15*, 536-547.

Ruiz, M. R. (2015). Behaviourisms: Radical behaviourism and critical inquiry. In I. Parker & I. Parker (Eds.), *Handbook of critical psychology*. NY: Routledge/Taylor & Francis Group.

Ruscher, J. B., Fiske, S. T., & Schnake, S. B. (2000). The motivated tactician's juggling act: Compatible vs. incompatible impression goals. *British Journal of Social Psychology, 39*, 241-256.

Rushton, J. P., & Jensen, A. R. (2006). The totality of available evidence shows the race IQ gap still remains. *Psychological Science, 17*, 921-922.

Russo, N. (1981). Women in psychology. In L. T. Benjamin, Jr. & K. D. Lowman (Eds.), *Activities handbook for the teaching of psychology*. Washington, DC: American Psychological Association.

Rutherford, B., Rose, S., Sneed, J., & Roose, S. (2009). Study design affects participant expectations: A survey. *Journal of Clinical Psychopharmacology, 29*, 179-181.

Rutland, A., & Killen, M. (2015). A developmental science approach to reducing prejudice and social exclusion: Intergroup processes, social-cognitive development, and moral reasoning. *Social Issues And Policy Review, 9*, 121-154.

Rutter, M. (2002). Nature, nurture, and development: From evangelism through science toward policy and practice. *Child Development, 73*, 1-21.

Ryan, R. M., & Deci, E. L. (2011). A self-determination theory perspective on social, institutional, cultural, and economic supports for autonomy and their importance for well-being. In V. I. Chirkov, R. M. Ryan, & K. M. Sheldon (Eds.), *Human autonomy in cross-cultural context: Perspectives on the psychology of agency, freedom, and well-being*. New York: Springer Science + Business Media.

Ryan, R. M., & Deci, E. L. (2017). *Self-determination theory: Basic psychological needs in motivation, development, and wellness*. New York: Guilford Press.

Rydell, R., McConnell, A., & Mackie, D. (2008). Consequences of discrepant explicit and implicit attitudes: Cognitive dissonance and increased information processing. *Journal of Experimental Social Psychology, 44*, 1526-1532.

Rymer, R. (1994). *Genie: A scientific tragedy*. New York: Penguin.

Sa, M. (2015). Mood and personality disorders. In G. M. Kapalka (Ed.), *Treating disruptive disorders: A guide to psychological, pharmacological, and combined therapies*. New York: Routledge/ Taylor & Francis Group.

Saarimäki, H., Gotsopoulos, A., Jääskelainen, I. P., Lampinen, J., Vuilleumier, P., Hari, R., . . . Nummenmaa, L. (2016). Discrete neural signatures of basic emotions. *Cerebral Cortex , 26*(6), 2563-2573.

Sachs-Ericsson, N., Joiner, T., Plant, E. A., & Blazer, D. G. (2005). The influence of depression on cognitive decline in community-dwelling elderly persons. *American Journal of Geriatric Psychiatry, 13*, 402-408.

Sachse, P., Beermann, U., Martini, M., Maran, T., Domeier, M., & Furtner, M. R. (2017). "The world is upside down"–The Innsbruck Goggle Experiments of Theodor Erismann (1883-1961) and Ivo Kohler (1915-1985). *Cortex: A Journal Devoted to the Study of the Nervous System and Behavior, 92*, 222-232.

Sachser, R. M., Haubrich, J., Lunardi, P. S., & de Oliveira Alvares, L. (2017). Forgetting of what was once learned: Exploring the role of postsynaptic ionotropic glutamate receptors on memory formation, maintenance, and decay. *Neuropharmacology, 112*(Part A), 94-103.

Sacks, O. (2003, July 28). The mind's eye. *The New Yorker*, pp. 48-59.

Sado, M., Yamauchi, K., Kawakami, N., Ono, Y., Furukawa, T. A., Tsuchiya, M., & . . . Kashima, H. (2011). Cost of depression among adults in Japan in 2005. *Psychiatry and Clinical Neurosciences, 65*, 442-450.

Salazar, L. F., Crosby, R. A., & DiClemente, R. J. (2015). Experimental research designs. In L. F. Salazar, R. A. Crosby, & R. J. DiClemente (Eds.), *Research methods in health promotion* (2nd ed.). San Francisco: Jossey-Bass.

Salgado, D. M., Quinlin, K. J., & Zlotnick, C. (2007). The relationship of lifetime polysubstance dependence to trauma exposure, symptomatology, and psychosocial functioning in incarcerated women with comorbid PTSD and substance use disorder. *Journal of Trauma Dissociation, 8*, 9-26.

Sallquist, J., Eisenberg, N., Spinrad, T. L., Eggum, N. D., & Gaertner, B. (2009). Assessment of preschoolers' positive empathy: Concurrent and longitudinal relations with positive emotion, social competence, and sympathy. *The Journal of Positive Psychology, 4*, 223-233.

Salvi, V., Fagiolini, A., Swartz, H., Maina, G., & Frank, E. (2008). The use of antidepressants in bipolar disorder. *Journal of Clinical Psychiatry, 69*, 1307-1318.

Sammut, G., & Buhagiar, L. J. (2017). The sociocultural determination of planned behaviour. *Integrative Psychological & Behavioral Science, 51*, 164-170.

Samoilov, V., & Zayas, V. (2007). Ivan Petrovich Pavlov (1849–1936). *Journal of the History of the Neurosciences, 16*, 74-89.

Samuel, D. B., & Widiger, T. A. (2006). Differentiating normal and abnormal personality from the perspective of the DSM. In S. Strack (Ed.), *Differentiating normal and abnormal personality* (2nd ed.). New York: Springer Publishing.

Samuel, D. B., Carroll, K. M., Rounsaville, B. J., & Ball, S. A. (2013). Personality disorders as maladaptive, extreme variants of normal personality: Borderline personality disorder and neuroticism in a substance using sample. *Journal of Personality Disorders, 27*, 625-635.

Sandford, S. (2017). Freud, Bion and Kant: Epistemology and anthropology in The Interpretation of Dreams. *International Journal of Psychoanalysis, 98*, 91-110.

Sandman, C. A. (2015). Mysteries of the human fetus revealed. *Monographs of the Society for Research in Child Development, 80*, 124-137.

Sandomir, R. (2007, July 17). W. W. E.'s testing is examined after Benoit murder-suicide. *The New York Times*, p. S3.

Sanes, J. R., & Masland, R. H. (2015). The types of retinal ganglion cells: Current status and implications for neuronal classification. *Annual Review of Neuroscience, 38*, 221-246.

Sang-hun, C. (2017, September 21). Kim's rejoinder to Trump's rocket man: "Mentally deranged U.S. dotard." *The New York Times*. Retrieved from https://www.nytimes.com/2017/09/21/world/asia/kim-trump-rocketman-dotard.html.

Santelli, J., Carter, M., Orr, M., & Dittus, P. (2009). Trends in sexual risk behaviors, by nonsexual risk behavior involvement, U.S. high school students, 1991-2007. *Journal of Adolescent Health, 44*, 372-379.

Santos, B. G., Carey, R. J., & Carrera, M. P. (2017). The acquisition, extinction and spontaneous recovery of Pavlovian drug conditioning induced by post-trial dopaminergic stimulation/inhibition. *Pharmacology, Biochemistry and Behavior, 156*, 24-29.

Saper, C. B. (2013). The neurobiology of sleep. *CONTINUUM: Lifelong Learning in Neurology, 19*, 19-31.

Sarsour, K., Sheridan, M., Jutte, D., Nuru-Jeter, A., Hinshaw, S., & Boyce, W. (2011). Family socioeconomic status and child executive functions: The roles of language, home environment, and single parenthood. *Journal of the International Neuropsychological Society, 17*, 120-132.

Sarubin, N., Hilbert, S., Naumann, F., Zill, P., Wimmer, A., Nothdurfter, C., . . . Schüle, C. (2017). The sex-dependent role of the glucocorticoid receptor in depression: Variations in the NR3C1 gene are associated with major depressive disorder in women but not in men. *European Archives of Psychiatry and Clinical Neuroscience, 267*, 123-133.

Saucier, G., & Srivastava, S. (2015). What makes a good structural model of personality? Evaluating the big five and alternatives. In M. Mikulincer, P. R. Shaver, M. L. Cooper, & R. J. Larsen (Eds.), *APA handbook of personality and social psychology, Volume 4: Personality processes and individual differences*. Washington, DC: American Psychological Association.

Saunders, B. T., Yager, L. M., & Robinson, T. E. (2013). Preclinical studies shed light on individual variation in addiction vulnerability. *Neuropsychopharmacology, 38*, 249-250.

Sauter, S. L., & Hurrell, J. J. (2017). Occupational health contributions to the development and promise of occupational health psychology. *Journal of Occupational Health Psychology, 22*, 251-258.

Savage, J., & Yancey, C. (2008). The effects of media violence exposure on criminal aggression: A meta-analysis. *Criminal Justice and Behavior, 35*, 772-791.

Savage-Rumbaugh, E. S., Toth, N., & Schick, K. (2007). Kanzi learns to knap stone tools. In

D. A. Washburn (Ed.), *Primate perspectives on behavior and cognition*. Washington, DC: American Psychological Association.

Savazzi, S., Fabri, M., Rubboli, G., Paggi, A., Tassinari, C. A., & Marzi, C. A. (2007). Interhemispheric transfer following callosotomy in humans: Role of the superior colliculus. *Neuropsychologia, 45*, 2417-2427.

Saville, B. (2009). Performance under competitive and self-competitive fixed-interval schedules of reinforcement. *The Psychological Record, 59*, 21-38.

Sawa, A., & Snyder, S. H. (2002, April 26). Schizophrenia: Diverse approaches to a complex disease. *Science, 296*, 692-695.

Scalzo, S., Bowden, S., & Hillbom, M. (2015). Wernicke-Korsakoff syndrome. In J. Svanberg, A. Withall, B. Draper, S. Bowden, J. Svanberg, A. Withall, . . . S. Bowden (Eds.) , *Alcohol and the adult brain*. New York: Psychology Press.

Scarr, S., & Weinberg, R. A. (1976). I.Q. test performance of black children adopted by white families. *American Psychologist, 31*, 726-739.

Scaturo, D. J. (2004). Fundamental clinical dilemmas in contemporary group psychotherapy. *Group Analysis, 37*, 201-217.

Scelfo, J. (2007, February 26). Men & depression: Facing darkness. *Newsweek*, pp. 43-50.

Scelfo, J. (2015, February 8). They. *The New York Times*, p. ED18.

Schachter, R. (2011). Using the group in cognitive group therapy. *Group, 35*, 135-149.

Schachter, S., & Singer, J. E. (1962). Cognitive, social, and physiological determinants of emotional state. *Psychological Review, 69*, 379-399.

Schachter, S., & Singer, J. E. (2001). Cognitive, social, and psychological determinants of emotional state. In W. G. Parrott, (Ed.), *Emotions in social psychology: Essential readings* (pp. 76-93). New York: Psychology Press.

Schacter, D. L., Dobbins, I. G., & Schnyer, D. M. (2004). Specificity of priming: A cognitive neuroscience perspective. *Nature Reviews Neuroscience, 5*, 853-862.

Schacter, D. L., Guerin, S. A., & St. Jacques, P. L. (2011). Memory distortion: An adaptive perspective. *Trends in Cognitive Sciences, 15*, 467-474.

Schaefer, E. G., Halldorson, M. K., & Dizon-Reynante, C. (2011). TV or not TV? Does the immediacy of viewing images of a momentous news event affect the quality and stability of flashbulb memories? *Memory, 19*, 251-266.

Schaie, K. W. (2005b). What can we learn from longitudinal studies of adult development? *Research in Human Development, 2*, 133-158.

Schaller, M., & Crandall, C. S. (Eds.). (2004). *The psychological foundations of culture*. Mahwah, NJ: Lawrence Erlbaum Associates.

Scharrer, E., & Ramasubramanian, S. (2015). Intervening in the media's influence on stereotypes of race and ethnicity: The role of media literacy education. *Journal of Social Issues, 71*, 171-185.

Schechter, T., Finkelstein, Y., & Koren, G. (2005). Pregnant "DES daughters" and their offspring. *Canadian Family Physician, 51*, 493-494.

Schepers, P., & van den Berg, P. T. (2007). Social factors of work-environment creativity. *Journal of Business and Psychology, 21*, 407-428.

Schermer, J., Johnson, A. M., Vernon, P. A., & Jang, K. L. (2011). The relationship between personality and self-report abilities: A behavior-genetic analysis. *Journal of Individual Differences, 32*, 47-53.

Schieber, E. (2006). Vision and aging. In J. E. Birren & K. W. Schaire (Eds.), *Handbook of the psychology of aging* (6th ed.). Amsterdam, Netherlands: Elsevier.

Schiff, R., & Vakil, E. (2015). Age differences in cognitive skill learning, retention and transfer: The case of the Tower of Hanoi puzzle. *Learning and Individual Differences, 39*, 164-171.

Schilling, O. K., & Diehl, M. (2015). Psychological vulnerability to daily stressors in old age: Results of short-term longitudinal studies. *Zeitschrift Für Gerontologie Und Geriatrie, 48*, 517-523.

Schlinger, H. D. (2015). Behavior analysis and behavioral neuroscience. *Frontiers in Human Neuroscience, 9*, 98-105

Schlinger, H. R. (2011). Skinner as missionary and prophet: A review of Burrhus F. Skinner: Shaper of behaviour. *Journal of Applied Behavior Analysis, 44*, 217-225.

Schmidt, J. P. (2006). The discovery of neurotransmitters: A fascinating story and a scientific object lesson. *PsycCRITIQUES, 61*, 101-115.

Schmidt, J., Klusmann, U., Lüdtke, O., Möller, J., & Kunter, M. (2017). What makes good and bad days for beginning teachers? A diary study on daily uplifts and hassles. *Contemporary Educational Psychology, 48*, 85-97.

Schnall, S., Haidt, J., Clore, G. L., & Jordan, A. H. (2008). Disgust as embodied moral judgment. *Personality and Social Psychology Bulletin, 34*, 1096-1109.

Schneider, D. W., & Logan, G. D. (2015). Chunking away task-switch costs: A test of the chunk-point hypothesis. *Psychonomic Bulletin & Review, 22*, 884-889.

Schnell, K., & Herpertz, S. C. (2007). Effects of dialectic-behavioral-therapy on the neural correlates of affective hyperarousal in borderline personality disorder. *Journal of Psychiatric Research, 41*, 837-847.

Schnupp, J., Nelken, I., & King, A. (2011). *Auditory neuroscience: Making sense of sound*. Cambridge, MA: MIT Press.

Schoofs, H., Hermans, D., Griffith, J. W., & Raes, F. (2013). Self-discrepancy and reduced autobiographical memory specificity in ruminating students and depressed patients. *Cognition and Emotion, 27*, 245-262.

Schooler, L. J., & Hertwig, R. (2012). How forgetting aids heuristic inference. In G. Gigerenzer, R. Hertwig, & T. Pachur (Eds.), *Heuristics: The foundations of adaptive behavior*. New York: Oxford University Press.

Schredl, M., & Piel, E. (2005). Gender differences in dreaming: Are they stable over time? *Personality and Individual Differences, 39*, 309-316.

Schredl, M., & Reinhard, I. (2011). Gender differences in nightmare frequency: A meta-analysis. *Sleep Medicine Reviews, 15*, 115-121.

Schreurs, B. G., Smith-Bell, C. A., & Burhans, L. B. (2011). Classical conditioning and conditioning-specific reflex modification of rabbit heart rate as a function of unconditioned stimulus location. *Behavioral Neuroscience, 125*, 604-612.

Schroers, M., Prigot, J., & Fagen, J. (2007, December). The effect of a salient odor context on memory retrieval in young infants. *Infant Behavior & Development, 30*, 685-689.

Schrotenboer, B. (2016, July 12). Feds call Lance Armstrong "a doper, dealer and liar" in scathing new rebuke. *USA Today*. Retrieved from https://www.usatoday.com/story/sports/cycling/2016/07/12/feds-lance-armstrong-rebuke-doper-dealer-liar/86978852/.

Schultheiss, O. C., & Schiepe-Tiska, A. (2013). The role of the dorsoanterior striatum in implicit motivation: The case of the need for power. *Frontiers in Human Neuroscience, 7*, Retrieved from http://www.ncbi.nlm.nih.gov/pubmed/23626531.

Schurger, A., Sarigiannidis, I., Naccache, L., Sitt, J. D., & Dehaene, S. (2015). Cortical activity is more stable when sensory stimuli are consciously perceived. *PNAS Proceedings of the National Academy of Sciences of the United States of America, 112*, E2083-E2092.

Schwartz, B. (2008). Working memory load differentially affects tip-of-the-tongue states and feeling-of-knowing judgments. *Memory & Cognition, 36*, 9-19.

Schwartz, B. L. (2002). The phenomenology of naturally-occurring tip-of-the-tongue states: A diary study. In S. P. Shohov (Ed.), *Advances in psychology research* (Vol. 8). Huntington, NY: Nova.

Schwartz, B. L., & Metcalfe, J. (2011). Tip-of-the-tongue (TOT) states: Retrieval, behavior, and experience. *Memory & Cognition, 39*, 737-749.

Schwartz, J., & Wald, M. L. (2003). NASA's curse? "Groupthink" is 30 years old, and still going strong. *The New York Times*, p. C1.

Schwartz, P., Maynard, A., & Uzelac, S. (2008). Adolescent egocentrism: A contemporary view. *Adolescence, 43(171)*, 441-448.

Schwartz, S. J., Donnellan, M., Ravert, R. D., Luyckx, K., & Zamboanga, B. L. (2013). Identity development, personality, and well-being in adolescence and emerging adulthood: Theory, research, and recent advances. In R. M. Lerner, M. Easterbrooks, J. Mistry, & I. B. Weiner (Eds.), *Handbook of psychology, Vol. 6: Developmental psychology* (2nd ed.). Hoboken, NJ: John Wiley & Sons Inc.

Schwartzmant, R. J., Alexander, G. M., & Grothusen, J. R. (2011). The use of ketamine in complex regional pain syndrome: Possible mechanisms. *Expert Review of Neurotherapeutics, 11*, 719-734.

Schwarzer, R., & Luszczynska, A. (2013). Stressful life events. In A. M. Nezu, C. Nezu, P. A. Geller, & I. B. Weiner (Eds.), *Handbook of psychology, Vol. 9: Health psychology* (2nd ed.). Hoboken, NJ: John Wiley & Sons Inc.

Schwenkreis, P., El Tom, S., Ragert, P., Pleger, B., Tegenthoff, M., & Dinse, H. (2007, December). Assessment of sensorimotor cortical representation asymmetries and motor skills in violin players. *European Journal of Neuroscience, 26,* 3291-3302.

Sciutto, M., & Eisenberg, M. (2007). Evaluating the evidence for and against the overdiagnosis of ADHD. *Journal of Attention Disorders, 11,* 106-113.

Scull, A. (2015). *Madness in civilization: A cultural history of insanity, from the Bible to Freud, from the madhouse to modern medicine.* Princeton, NJ: Princeton University Press.

Searight, H. (2013). Deinstitutionalization of people with mental illness: A failed policy that could have succeeded. *PsycCRITIQUES, 58,* 88-94.

Searls, D. (2017). *The inkblots: Hermann Rorschach, his iconic test, and the power of seeing.* New York: Crown Publishers/Random House.

Sebastiani, L., Castellani, E., & D'Alessandro, L. (2011). Emotion processing without awareness: Features detection or significance evaluation? *International Journal of Psychophysiology, 80,* 150-156.

Sebel, P. S., Bonke, B., & Winograd, E. (Eds.). (1993). *Memory and awareness in anesthesia.* Englewood Cliffs, NJ: Prentice-Hall.

Seeman, P. (2011). All roads to schizophrenia lead to dopamine supersensitivity and elevated dopamine D2[sup]High[/sup] receptors. *CNS Neuroscience & Therapeutics, 17,* 118-132.

Sefcek, J. A., Brumbach, B. H., & Vasquez, G. (2007). The evolutionary psychology of human mate choice: How ecology, genes, fertility, and fashion influence mating strategies. *Journal of Psychology & Human Sexuality, 18,* 125-182.

Segall, M. H. (1988). Cultural roots of aggressive behavior. In M. Bond (Ed.), *The cross-cultural challenge to social psychology.* Newbury Park, CA: Sage.

Segall, M. H., Campbell, D. T., & Herskovits, M. J. (1966). *The influence of culture on visual perception.* New York: Bobbs-Merrill.

Seligman, M. E. (2007). *What you can change . . . and what you can't: The complete guide to successful self-improvement.* New York: Vintage.

Seligman, M. E. P. (1995, December). The effectiveness of psychotherapy: The *Consumer Reports* study. *American Psychologist, 50,* 965-974.

Sell, C., Möller, H., & Taubner, S. (2017). Effectiveness of integrative Imagery- and trance-based psychodynamic therapies: Guided imagery psychotherapy and hypnopsychotherapy. *Journal of Psychotherapy Integration.* Accessed at http://psycnet.apa.org/record/2017-07863-001.

Sellbom, M., Fischler, G., & Ben-Porath, Y. (2007). Identifying MMPI-2 Predictors of police officer integrity and misconduct. *Criminal Justice and Behavior, 34,* 985-1004.

Sells, R. (1994, August). *Homosexuality study.* Paper presented at the annual meeting of the American Statistical Association, Toronto.

Selove, R. (2007). The glass is half full: Current knowledge about pediatric cancer and sickle cell anemia. *PsycCRITIQUES, 52,* 88-99.

Selsky, A. (1997, February 16). African males face circumcision rite. *The Boston Globe,* p. C7.

Selye, H. (1976). *The stress of life.* New York: McGraw-Hill.

Selye, H. (1993). History of the stress concept. In L. Goldberger & S. Breznitz (Eds.), *Handbook of stress: Theoretical and clinical aspects* (2nd ed.). New York: Free Press.

Semin, G. R., & Garrido, M. V. (2013). A systemic approach to impression formation: From verbal to multimodal processes. In J. P. Forgas, K. Fiedler, & C. Sedikides (Eds.), *Social thinking and interpersonal behavior.* New York: Psychology Press.

Semler, C. N., & Harvey, A. G. (2005). Misperception of sleep can adversely affect daytime functioning in insomnia. *Behaviour Research and Therapy, 43,* 843-856.

Semykina, A., & Linz, S. J. (2007). Gender differences in personality and earnings: Evidence from Russia. *Journal of Economic Psychology, 28,* 387-410.

Senholzi, K. B., Depue, B. E., Correll, J., Banich, M. T., & Ito, T. A. (2015). Brain activation underlying threat detection to targets of different races. *Social Neuroscience, 10,* 651-662.

Seroczynski, A. D., Jacquez, F. M., & Cole, D. A. (2003). Depression and suicide during adolescence. In G. R. Adams & M. D. Berzonsky (Eds.), *Blackwell handbook of adolescence.* Malden, MA: Blackwell Publishers.

Serretti, A. (2017). Genetics and pharmacogenetics of mood disorders. *Psychiatria Polska, 51,* 197-203.

Servick, K. (2014). New support for "gay gene." *Science, 346,* 900.

Seymour, B. (2006). Carry on eating: Neural pathways mediating conditioned potentiation of feeding. *Journal of Neuroscience, 26,* 1061-1062.

Sezgin, F., & Erdogan, O. (2015). Academic optimism, hope and zest for work as predictors of teacher self-efficacy and perceived success. *Kuram Ve Uygulamada Eğitim Bilimleri, 15,* 7-19.

Shafer, V. L., & Garrido-Nag, K. (2007). The neurodevelopmental bases of language. In E. Hoff & M. Shatz (Eds.), *Blackwell handbook of language development.* Malden, MA: Blackwell Publishing.

Shah, A. S., Young, J., & Vieira, K. (2014). Long-term Suboxone treatment and its benefit on long-term remission for opiate dependence. *African Journal of Psychiatry, 17,* 1-4.

Shaikholeslami, R., & Khayyer, M. (2006). Intrinsic motivation, extrinsic motivation, and learning English as a foreign language. *Psychological Reports, 99,* 813-818.

Shaked, A., & Clore, G. (2017). Breaking the world to make it whole again: Attribution in the construction of emotion. *Emotion Review, 9*(1), 27-35.

Shakya, H., & Christakis, N. (2017). Association of Facebook use with compromised well-being: A longitudinal study. *American Journal of Epidemiology, 185,* 203-211.

Shanahan, L., Copeland, W. E., Worthman, C. M., Erkanli, A., Angold, A., & Costello, E. (2013). Sex-differentiated changes in C-reactive protein from ages 9 to 21: The contributions of BMI and physical/sexual maturation. *Psychoneuroendocrinology, 38,* 2209-2217.

Shaner, L., Kelly, L., Rockwell, D., & Curtis, D. (2017). Calm abiding: The lived experience of the practice of long-term meditation. *Journal of Humanistic Psychology, 57,* 98-121.

Sharpe, Lindsey. (2013, November 1). U.S. obesity rate climbing in 2013. Gallup Poll.

Shea, A., & Steiner, M. (2008). Cigarette smoking during pregnancy. *Nicotine & Tobacco Research, 10,* 267-278.

Sheahan, C. L., Pozzulo, J. D., Reed, J. E., & Pica, E. (2017). The role of familiarity with the defendant, type of descriptor discrepancy, and eyewitness age on mock jurors' perceptions of eyewitness testimony. *Journal of Police and Criminal Psychology.* Accessed from https://link.springer.com/article/10.1007/s11896-017-9232-2.

Shehab, A. S., Brent, D., & Maalouf, F. T. (2016). Neurocognitive changes in selective serotonin reuptake inhibitors–Treated adolescents with depression. *Journal of Child and Adolescent Psychopharmacology, 26,* 713-720.

Shehata-Dieler, W., Ehrmann-Mueller, D., Wermke, P., Voit, V., Cebulla, M., & Wermke, K. (2013). Pre-speech diagnosis in hearing-impaired infants: How auditory experience affects early vocal development. *Speech, Language and Hearing, 16,* 99-106.

Shellenbarger, S. (2012, August 22). Are you a hero or a bystander? *Wall Street Journal,* D1.

Shellenbarger, S. (2013, April 3). Tactics to spark creativity. *Wall Street Journal,* pp. D1-D2.

Shepperd, J., Malone, W., & Sweeny, K. (2008). Exploring causes of the self-serving bias. *Social and Personality Psychology Compass, 2,* 895-908.

Sherblom, S. (2008). The legacy of the "care challenge": Re-envisioning the outcome of the justice-care debate. *Journal of Moral Education, 37,* 81-98.

Sherman, S. L., Allen, E. G., Bean, L. H., & Freeman, S. B. (2007). Epidemiology of Down syndrome [Special issue: Down syndrome]. *Mental Retardation and Developmental Disabilities Research Reviews, 13,* 221-227.

Shibata, K., Sasaki, Y., Bang, J. W., Walsh, E. G., Machizawa, M. G., Tamaki, M., . . . Watanabe, T. (2017). Overlearning hyperstabilizes a skill by rapidly making neurochemical processing inhibitory-dominant. *Nature Neuroscience, 20,* 470-475.

Shiffman, S. (2007). Use of more nicotine lozenges leads to better success in quitting smoking. *Addiction, 102,* 809-814.

Shimono, K., & Wade, N. J. (2002). Monocular alignment in different depth planes. *Vision Research, 42,* 1127-1135.

Shin, D. W., Roter, D. L., Roh, Y. K., Hahm, S. K., Cho, B., & Park, H. (2015). Physician gender and patient centered communication: The moderating effect of psychosocial and biomedical case characteristics. *Patient Education and Counseling, 98,* 55-60.

Shin, H. B., & Kominski, R. A. 2010. *Language Use in the United States: 2007.* American

Community Survey Reports, ACS-12. Washington, DC: U.S. Census Bureau.

Shirai, F., & Hayashi-Takagi, A. (2017). Optogenetics: Applications in psychiatric research. *Psychiatry and Clinical Neurosciences, 71,* 363–372.

Shirayama, Y., & Hashimoto, K. (2017). Effects of a single bilateral infusion of R-ketamine in the rat brain regions of a learned helplessness model of depression. *European Archives of Psychiatry and Clinical Neuroscience, 267,* 177–182.

Shnabel, N., Purdie-Vaughns, V., Cook, J. E., Garcia, J., & Cohen, G. L. (2013). Demystifying values-affirmation interventions: Writing about social belonging is a key to buffering against identity threat. *Personality and Social Psychology Bulletin, 39,* 663–676.

Shogren, K. A., & Wehmeyer, M. L. (2017). Problem solving. In M. L. Wehmeyer, K. A. Shogren, T. D. Little, & S. J. Lopez (Eds.), *Development of self-determination through the life-course.* New York: Springer Science + Business Media.

Shors, T. J. (2009, March). Saving new brain cells. *Scientific American,* pp. 47–54.

Shrestha, L. B., & Heisler, E. J. (2011). The changing demographic profile of the United States. Congressional Research Service. Retrieved from www.fas.org/sgp/crs/misc/RL32701.pdf.

Shweder, R. A. (1994). You're not sick, you're just in love: Emotion as an interpretive system. In P. Ekman & R. J. Davidson (Eds.), *The nature of emotion: Fundamental questions.* New York: Oxford.

Sibunruang, H., Capezio, A., & Restubog, S. D. (2015). In pursuit of success: The differential moderating effects of political skill on the relationships among career-related psychological needs and ingratiation. *Journal of Career Assessment, 23,* 336–348.

Sidman, M. (2006). The distinction between positive and negative reinforcement: Some additional considerations. *Behavior Analyst, 29,* 135–139.

Sielski, R., Rief, W., & Glombiewski, J. A. (2017). Efficacy of biofeedback in chronic back pain: A meta-analysis. *International Journal of Behavioral Medicine, 24,* 25–41.

Siemer, M., Mauss I., & Gross, J. J. (2007). Same situation–different emotions: How appraisals shape our emotions. *Emotion, 7,* 592–600.

Sifrit, K. J. (2006). The effects of aging and cognitive decrements on simulated driving performance. *Dissertation abstracts international: Section B: The sciences and engineering, 67,* 2863.

Sikka, P., Revonsuo, A., Sandman, N., Tuominen, J., & Valli, K. (2017). Dream emotions: A comparison of home dream reports with laboratory early and late REM dream reports. *Journal of Sleep Research.* Accessed from https://www.ncbi.nlm.nih.gov/pubmed/28568911.

Sikkema, K. J., Ranby, K. W., Meade, C. S., Hansen, N. B., Wilson, P. A., & Kochman, A. (2013). Reductions in traumatic stress following a coping intervention were mediated by decreases in avoidant coping for people living with HIV/AIDS and childhood sexual abuse. *Journal of Consulting and Clinical Psychology, 81,* 274–283.

Silva, M. T. A., Gonçalves, E. L., & Garcia-Mijares, M. (2007). Neural events in the reinforcement contingency. *Behavior Analyst, 30,* 17–30.

Silverstein, B., Edwards, T., Gamma, A., Ajdacic-Gross, V., Rossler, W., & Angst, J. (2013). The role played by depression associated with somatic symptomatology in accounting for the gender difference in the prevalence of depression. *Social Psychiatry and Psychiatric Epidemiology, 48,* 257–263.

Silverstein, M. L. (2007). Rorschach test findings at the beginning of treatment and 2 years later, with a 30-year follow-up. *Journal of Personality Assessment, 88,* 131–143.

Simon, E. B., Maron-Katz, A., Lahav, N., Shamir, R., & Hendler, T. (2017). Tired and misconnected: A breakdown of brain modularity following sleep deprivation. *Human Brain Mapping, 38,* 3300–3314.

Simon, E. B., Oren, N., Sharon, H., Kirschner, A., Goldway, N., Okon-Singer, H., . . . Hendler, T. (2015). Losing neutrality: The neural basis of impaired emotional control without sleep. *Journal of Neuroscience, 35*(38), 13194–13205.

Simon, G., Ludman, E., Unützer, J., Operskalski, B., & Bauer, M. (2008). Severity of mood symptoms and work productivity in people treated for bipolar disorder. *Bipolar Disorders, 10,* 718–725.

Simon, S., & Hoyt, C. (2008). Exploring the gender gap in support for a woman for president. *Analyses of Social Issues and Public Policy (ASAP), 8,* 157–181.

Simonton, D. K. (2009). Varieties of (scientific) creativity: A hierarchical model of domain-specific disposition, development, and achievement. *Perspectives on Psychological Science, 4,* 441–452.

Simonton, D. K. (2014). The mad-genius paradox: Can creative people be more mentally healthy but highly creative people more mentally ill? *Perspectives on Psychological Science, 9,* 470–480.

Sinclair, R. R., Waitsman, M. C., Oliver, C. M., & Deese, M. (2013). Personality and psychological resilience in military personnel. In R. R. Sinclair & T. W. Britt (Eds.), *Building psychological resilience in military personnel: Theory and practice.* Washington, DC: American Psychological Association.

Singer, B. F., Bryan, M. A., Popov, P., Robinson, T. E., & Aragona, B. J. (2017). Rapid induction of dopamine sensitization in the nucleus accumbens shell induced by a single injection of cocaine. *Behavioural Brain Research, 324,* 66–70.

Singer, J. L. (2006). Why imagery, personal memories, and daydreams matter. In J. L. Singer (Ed.), *Imagery in psychotherapy.* Washington, DC: American Psychological Association.

Singer, L. T., & Richardson, G. A. (2011). Introduction to "understanding developmental consequences of prenatal drug exposure: Biological and environmental effects and their interactions." *Neurotoxicology and Teratology, 33,* 5–8.

Singh, R. D., Jimerson, S. R., Renshaw, T., Saeki, E., Hart, S. R., Earhart, J., & Stewart, K. (2011). A summary and synthesis of contemporary empirical evidence regarding the effects of the Drug Abuse Resistance Education Program (D.A.R.E.). *Contemporary School Psychology, 15,* 93–102.

Sininger, Y. S., & Cone-Wesson, B. (2004, September 10). Asymmetric cochlear processing mimics hemispheric specialization. *Science, 305,* 1581.

Sininger, Y. S., & Cone-Wesson, B. (2006). Lateral asymmetry in the ABR of neonates: evidence and mechanisms. *Hearing Research, 212,* 203–211.

Sivec, H. J., Montesano, V. L., Skubby, D., Knepp, K. A., & Munetz, M. R. (2017). Cognitive behavioral therapy for psychosis (CBT-p) delivered in a community mental health setting: A case comparison of clients receiving CBT informed strategies by case managers prior to therapy. *Community Mental Health Journal, 53,* 134–142.

Skinner, B. F. (1957). *Verbal behavior.* New York: Appleton-Century-Crofts.

Skinner, B. F. (1975). The steep and thorny road to a science of behavior. *American Psychologist, 30,* 42–49.

Skolnick, P., Popik, P., & Trullas, R. (2009). Glutamate-based antidepressants: 20 years on. *Trends in Pharmacological Science, 30,* 563–569.

Slocombe, K. E., Waller, B. M., & Liebal, K. (2011). The language void: The need for multimodality in primate communication research. *Animal Behaviour, 81,* 919–924.

Slotboom, A., Hendriks, J., & Verbruggen, J. (2011). Contrasting adolescent female and male sexual aggression: A self-report study on prevalence and predictors of sexual aggression. *Journal of Sexual Aggression, 17,* 15–33.

Šmigelskas, K., Žemaitienė, N., Julkunen, J., & Kauhanen, J. (2015). Type A behavior pattern is not a predictor of premature mortality. *International Journal of Behavioral Medicine, 22,* 161–169.

Smart, R. G. (2007). Review of introduction to addictive behaviours. *Addiction, 102,* 831.

Smetana, J. B. (2007). Strategies for understanding archetypes and the collective unconscious of an organization. *Dissertation Abstracts International Section A: Humanities and Social Sciences, 67* (12-A), 4714.

Smetana, J. G. (2005). Adolescent-parent conflict: Resistance and subversion as developmental process. In L. Nucci (Ed.), *Conflict, contradiction, and contrarian elements in moral development and education.* Mahwah, NJ: Lawrence Erlbaum Associates.

Smetana, J., Daddis, C., & Chuang, S. (2003). "Clean your room!" A longitudinal investigation of adolescent-parent conflict and conflict resolution in middle-class African American families. *Journal of Adolescent Research, 18,* 631–650.

Smith, C. (2006). Symposium V–Sleep and learning: New developments [Special issue: Methods and learning in functional MRI]. *Brain and Cognition, 60,* 331–332.

Smith, C. A., & Lazarus, R. S. (2001). Appraisal components, core relational themes, and the emotions. In W. G. Parrott (Ed.), *Emotions in social psychology: Essential readings* (pp. 94–114). Philadelphia: Psychology Press.

Smith, C. D., Chebrolu, J., Wekstein, D. R., Schmitt, F. A., & Markesbery, W. R. (2007). Age and gender effects on human brain anatomy: A voxel-based morphometric study in healthy elderly. *Neurobiology of Aging, 28,* 1057–1087.

Smith, D. E., Springer, C. M., & Barrett, S. (2011). Physical discipline and socioemotional adjustment among Jamaican adolescents. *Journal of Family Violence, 26,* 51–61.

Smith, E. P., Witherspoon, D. P., Hart, M., & Davidson, W. S. (2017). The dynamic and interactive role of theory in community psychology research, practice, and policy. In M. A. Bond, I. Serrano-García, C. B. Keys, & M. Shinn (Eds.), *APA handbook of community psychology: Methods for community research and action for diverse groups and issues.* Washington, DC: American Psychological Association.

Smith, E. S., Geissler, S. A., Schallert, T., & Lee, H. J. (2013). The role of central amygdala dopamine in disengagement behavior. *Behavioral Neuroscience, 127,* 164–174.

Smith, M. L., Glass, G. V., & Miller, T. I. (1980). *The benefits of psychotherapy.* Baltimore: The Johns Hopkins University Press.

Smith, N. A., Folland, N. A., Martinez, D. M., & Trainor, L. J. (2017). Multisensory object perception in infancy: 4-month-olds perceive a mistuned harmonic as a separate auditory and visual object. *Cognition, 164,* 1–7.

Smith, R. A., & Weber, A. L. (2005). Applying social psychology in everyday life. In F. W. Schneider, J. A. Gruman, & L. M. Coutts (Eds.), *Applied social psychology: Understanding and addressing social and practical problems.* Thousand Oaks, CA: Sage Publications.

Smith, T. W., & Son, J. (2013). *Trends in public attitudes about sexual morality.* Chicago: NORC at the University of Chicago.

Smith, W. B. (2007). Karen Horney and psychotherapy in the 21st century. *Clinical Social Work Journal, 35,* 57–66.

Smrtnik-Vitulić, H., & Zupančič, M. (2011). Personality traits as a predictor of academic achievement in adolescents. *Educational Studies, 37,* 127–140.

Snowdon, C. T. (2017). Learning from monkey "talk." *Science, 355,* 1120–1122.

Snyder, J., Cramer, A., & Afrank, J. (2005). The contributions of ineffective discipline and parental hostile attributions of child misbehavior to the development of conduct problems at home and school. *Developmental Psychology, 41,* 30–41.

Snyder, M. (2002). Applications of Carl Rogers' theory and practice to couple and family therapy: A response to Harlene Anderson and David Bott. *Journal of Family Therapy, 24,* 317–325.

Snyder, M. D., & Dwyer, P. C. (2013). Altruism and prosocial behavior. In H. Tennen, J. Suls, & I. B. Weiner (Eds.). *Handbook of psychology, Vol. 5: Personality and social psychology* (2nd ed.). Hoboken, NJ: John Wiley & Sons.

Society for Personality Assessment. (2005). The status of Rorschach in clinical and forensic practice: An official statement by the board

of trustees of the Society for Personality Assessment. *Journal of Personality Assessment, 85,* 219–237.

Sodian, B. (2011). Theory of mind in infancy. *Child Development Perspectives, 5,* 39–43.

Sohr-Preston, S. L., & Scaramella, L. V. (2006). Implications of timing of maternal depressive symptoms for early cognitive and language development. *Clinical Child and Family Psychology Review, 9,* 65–83.

Šolcová, I. P., & Lačev, A. (2017). Differences in male and female subjective experience and physiological reactions to emotional stimuli. *International Journal of Psychophysiology, 117,* 75–82.

Solesio-Jofre, E., Lorenzo-López, L., Gutiérrez, R., López-Frutos, J., Ruiz-Vargas, J., & Maestú, F. (2011). Age effects on retroactive interference during working memory maintenance. *Biological Psychology, 88,* 72–82.

Solomonia, R. O., & McCabe, B. J. (2015). Molecular mechanisms of memory in imprinting. *Neuroscience and Biobehavioral Reviews, 50,* 56–69.

Somers, T. J., Moseley, G., Keefe, F. J., & Kothadia, S. M. (2011). Neuroimaging of pain: A psychosocial perspective. In R. A. Cohen & L. H. Sweet (Eds.), *Brain imaging in behavioral medicine and clinical neuroscience.* New York: Springer Science + Business Media.

Sommer, R., & Sommer, B. (2001). *A practical guide to behavioral research: Tools and techniques* (5th ed.). New York: Oxford University Press.

Soorya, L. V., Carpenter, L., & Romanczyk, R. G. (2011). Applied behavior analysis. In E. Hollander, A. Kolevzon, & J. T. Coyle (Eds.), *Textbook of autism spectrum disorders.* Arlington, VA: American Psychiatric Publishing, Inc.

Sori, C. E. (Ed.). (2006). *Engaging children in family therapy: Creative approaches to integrating theory and research in clinical practice.* New York: Routledge/Taylor & Francis Group.

Soussignan, R. (2002). Duchenne smile, emotional experience, and automatic reactivity: A test of the facial feedback hypothesis. *Emotion, 2,* 52–74.

South, S. C., Reichborn-Kjennerud, T., Eaton, N. R., & Krueger, R. F. (2013). Genetics of personality. In H. Tennen, J. Suls, & I. B. Weiner (Eds.), *Handbook of psychology, Vol. 5: Personality and social psychology* (2nd ed.). Hoboken, NJ: John Wiley & Sons Inc.

South, S., & Krueger, R. (2008). An interactionist perspective on genetic and environmental contributions to personality. *Social and Personality Psychology Compass, 2,* 929–948.

Spackman, M. P., Fujiki, M., & Brinton, B. (2006). Understanding emotions in context: The effects of language impairment on children's ability to infer emotional reactions. *International Journal of Language & Communication Disorders, 41,* 173–188.

Sparrow, B., Liu, J., & Wegner, D. M. (2011, August 5). Google effects on memory: cognitive consequences of having information at our fingertips. *Science, 333,* 776–778.

Spaulding, S. (2013). Mirror neurons and social cognition. *Mind & Language, 28,* 233–257.

Special issue: The dopamine hypothesis of schizophrenia. (2017). *Biological Psychiatry, 81*(1), 1.

Speirs-Neumeister, K. L., & Finch, H. (2006). Perfectionism in high-ability students: Relational precursors and influences on achievement motivation. *Gifted Child Quarterly, 50,* 238–251.

Spence, C., Auvray, M., & Smith, B. (2015). Confusing tastes with flavours. In D. Stokes, M. Matthen, & S. Biggs (Eds.), *Perception and its modalities.* New York: Oxford University Press.

Spence, M. J., & DeCasper, A. J. (1982, March). *Human fetuses perceive maternal speech.* Paper presented at the meeting of the International Conference on Infant Studies, Austin, TX.

Spencer, S. J., Fein, S., Zanna, M. P., & Olson, J. M. (Eds.). (2003). *Motivated social perception: The Ontario Symposium* (Vol. 9). Mahwah, NJ: Erlbaum.

Sperling, G. (1960). The information available in brief visual presentation. *Psychological Monographs, 74,* pp. 29.

Sperner-Unterweger, B., & Fuchs, D. (2015). Schizophrenia and psychoneuroimmunology: An integrative view. *Current Opinion in Psychiatry, 28,* 201–206.

Sperry, R. (1982). Some effects of disconnecting the cerebral hemispheres. *Science, 217,* 1223–1226.

Spiegel, D. (2014). Minding the body: Psychotherapy and cancer survival. *British Journal of Health Psychology, 19,* 465–485.

Spiegel, D. (2015). Hypnosis and pain control. In T. R. Deer, M. S. Leong, & A. L. Ray (Eds.), *Treatment of chronic pain by integrative approaches: The American Academy of Pain Medicine textbook on patient management.* New York: Springer Science + Business Media.

Spitzer, R. L., Skodol, A. E., Gibbon, M., & Williams, J. B. W. (1983). *Psychopathology: A case book.* New York: McGraw-Hill.

Sprecher, S., & Regan, P. C. (2002). Liking some things (in some people) more than others: Partner preferences in romantic relationships and friendships. *Journal of Social and Personal Relationships, 19,* 436–481.

Sprecher, S., Treger, S., & Sakaluk, J. K. (2013). Premarital sexual standards and sociosexuality: Gender, ethnicity, and cohort differences. *Archives of Sexual Behavior, 42*(8), 1395–1405.

Squire, L. R., Clark, R. E., & Bayley, P. J. (2004). Medial temporal lobe function and memory. In M. S. Gazzaniga (Ed.), *Cognitive neurosciences* (3rd ed.). Cambridge, MA: MIT.

Srinivasan, M., Al-Mughairy, S., Foushee, R., & Barner, D. (2017). Learning language from within: Children use semantic generalizations to infer word meanings. *Cognition, 159,* 11–24.

St. Dennis, C., Hendryx, M., Henriksen, A. L., Setter, S. M., & Singer, B. (2006). Postdischarge treatment costs following closure of a state geropsychiatric ward: Comparison of 2 levels of community care. *Primary Care Companion Journal of Clinical Psychiatry, 8,* 279–284.

St. Jacques, P. L., & Levine, B. (2007). Ageing and autobiographical memory for emotional and neutral events. *Memory, 15,* 129–144.

Stacks, A., Oshio, T., Gerard, J., & Roe, J. (2009). The moderating effect of parental warmth on the association between spanking and child aggression: A longitudinal approach. *Infant and Child Development, 18,* 178-194.

Staley, J. K., Sanacora, G., & Tamagnan, G. (2006). Sex differences in diencephalon serotonin transporter availability in major depression. *Biological Psychiatry, 59,* 40-47.

Stam, G. (2015). Changes in thinking for speaking: A longitudinal case study. *Modern Language Journal, 99*(Suppl 1), 83-99.

Stangier, U., Schramm, E., Heidenreich, T., Berger, M., & Clark, D. M. (2011). Cognitive therapy vs interpersonal psychotherapy in social anxiety disorder: A randomized controlled trial. *Archives of General Psychiatry, 68,* 692-700.

Stankov, L. (2003). Complexity in human intelligence. In R. J. Sternberg & J. Lautrey (Eds.), *Models of intelligence: International perspectives.* Washington, DC: American Psychological Association.

Stanley, M. L., Henne, P., Iyengar, V., Sinnott-Armstrong, W., & De Brigard, F. (2017). I'm not the person I used to be: The self and autobiographical memories of immoral actions. *Journal of Experimental Psychology: General, 146,* 884-895.

Stanojevic, S., Mitic, K., & Vujic, V. (2007). Exposure to acute physical and psychological stress alters the response of rat macrophages to corticosterone, neuropeptide Y and beta-endorphin. *International Journal on the Biology of Stress, 10,* 65-73.

Stanton, A. L., Danoff-Burg, S., Cameron, C. L., Bishop, M., Collins, C. A., Kirk, S. B., et al. (2000). Emotionally expressive coping predicts psychological and physical adjustment to breast cancer. *Journal of Consulting and Clinical Psychology, 68,* 875-882.

Starcevic, V., Berle, D., Milicevic, D., Hannan, A., Pamplugh, C., & Eslick, G. D. (2007). Pathological worry, anxiety disorders and the impact of co-occurrence with depressive and other anxiety disorders. *Journal of Anxiety Disorders, 21,* 1016-1027.

Startup, M., Bucci, S., & Langdon, R. (2009). Delusions of reference: A new theoretical model. *Cognitive Neuropsychiatry, 14,* 110-126.

Staub, E. (2011). *Overcoming evil: Genocide, violent conflict, and terrorism.* New York: Oxford University Press.

Staub, E. (2018). Preventing violence and promoting active bystandership and peace: My life in research and applications. *Peace and Conflict: Journal of Peace Psychology, 24*(1), 95-111.

Staub, E., Pearlman, L., & Bilali, R. (2010). Understanding the roots and impact of violence and psychological recovery as avenues to reconciliation after mass violence and intractable conflict: Applications to national leaders, journalists, community groups, public education through radio, and children. In G. Salomon & E. Cairns (Eds.), *Handbook on peace education.* New York: Psychology Press.

Steele, J. D., Christmas, D., Eljamel, M. S., & Matthews, K. (2007). Anterior cingulotomy for major depression: clinical outcome and relationship to lesion characteristics. *Biological Psychiatry, 12,* 127-134.

Steiger, A. (2007). Neurochemical regulation of sleep. *Journal of Psychiatric Research, 41,* 537-552.

Stein, L. A. R., & Graham, J. R. (2005). Ability of substance abusers to escape detection on the Minnesota Multiphasic Personality Inventory- Adolescent (MMPI-A) in a juvenile correctional facility. *Assessment, 12,* 28-39.

Steinbeis, N., Crone, E., Blakemore, S., & Kadosh, K. C. (2017). Development holds the key to understanding the interplay of nature versus nurture in shaping the individual. *Developmental Cognitive Neuroscience, 25,* 1-4.

Steinberg, L. (2007). Risk taking in adolescence: New perspectives from brain and behavioral science. *Current Directions in Psychological Science, 16,* 55-59.

Steinberg, L. (2016). Commentary on special issue on the adolescent brain: Redefining adolescence. *Neuroscience and Biobehavioral Reviews, 70,* 343-346.

Steiner, J. (2008). Transference to the analyst as an excluded observer. *The International Journal of Psychoanalysis, 89,* 39-54.

Steinfeld, C., Ellison, N., & Lampe, C. (2008). Social capital, self-esteem, and use of online social network sites: A longitudinal analysis. *Journal of Applied Developmental Psychology, 29,* 434-445.

Steinhubl, S. R., Wineinger, N. E., Patel, S., Boeldt, D. L., Mackellar, G., Porter, V., & . . . Topol, E. J. (2015). Cardiovascular and nervous system changes during meditation. *Frontiers in Human Neuroscience, 9,* 88-97.

Steinmetz, Katy. (2015, March 6). States battle over bathroom access for transgender people. *Time.* Accessed at http://time.com/3734714/transgender-bathroom-bills-lgbtdiscrimination/.

Stemler, S. E., & Sternberg, R. J. (2006). Using situational judgment tests to measure practical intelligence. In J. A. Weekley & R. E. Ployhart (Eds.), *Situational judgment tests: Theory, measurement, and application.* Mahwah, NJ: Lawrence Erlbaum Associates.

Stemler, S. E., Sternberg, R. J., Grigorenko, E. L., Jarvin, L., & Sharpes, K. (2009). Using the theory of successful intelligence as a framework for developing assessments in AP physics. *Contemporary Educational Psychology, 34,* 195-209.

Stenbacka, L., & Vanni, S. (2007). fMRI of peripheral visual field representation. *Clinical Neurophysiology, 108,* 1303-1314.

Stern, E., & Silbersweig, D. A. (2001). Advances in functional neuroimaging methodology for the study of brain systems underlying human neuropsychological function and dysfunction. In D. A. Silbersweig & E. Stern (Eds.), *Neuropsychology and functional neuroimaging: Convergence, advances and new directions.* Amsterdam, Netherlands: Swets and Zeitlinger.

Sternberg, R. J. (1998). *Successful intelligence: How practical and creative intelligence determine success in life* (p. 17). New York: Plume.

Sternberg, R. J. (2000). Intelligence and wisdom. In R. J. Sternberg et al. (Eds.), *Handbook of intelligence.* New York: Cambridge University Press.

Sternberg, R. J. (2004). A triangular theory of love. In H. T. Reis & C. E. Rusbult (Eds.), *Close relationships: Key readings.* Philadelphia, PA: Taylor & Francis.

Sternberg, R. J. (2006). A duplex theory of love. In R. J. Sternberg (Ed.), *The new psychology of love.* New Haven, CT: Yale University Press.

Sternberg, R. J. (2011). Individual differences in cognitive development. In U. Goswami (Ed.), *The Wiley-Blackwell handbook of childhood cognitive development* (2nd ed.). New York: Wiley-Blackwell.

Sternberg, R. J. (2011). Individual differences in cognitive development. In U. Goswami (Ed.), *The Wiley-Blackwell handbook of childhood cognitive development (2nd ed.).* NY: Wiley-Blackwell.

Sternberg, R. J. (2013). What is cognitive education? *Journal of Cognitive Education and Psychology, 12*(1), 45-58.

Sternberg, R. J. (2015). Multiple intelligences in the new age of thinking. In S. Goldstein, D. Princiotta, & J. A. Naglieri (Eds.), *Handbook of intelligence: Evolutionary theory, historical perspective, and current concepts.* New York: Springer Science + Business Media.

Sternberg, R. J. (2017). *Career paths in psychology: Where your degree can take you* (3rd ed.). Washington, DC: American Psychological Association.

Sternberg, R. J., & Jarvin, L. (2003). Alfred Binet's contributions as a paradigm for impact in psychology. In R. J. Sternberg (Ed.), *The anatomy of impact: What makes the great works of psychology great.* Washington, DC: American Psychological Association.

Sternberg, R. J., & Pretz, J. E. (2005). *Cognition and intelligence: Identifying the mechanisms of the mind.* New York: Cambridge University Press.

Sternberg, R. J., Grigorenko, E. L., & Kidd, K. K. (2005). Intelligence, race, and genetics. *American Psychologist, 60,* 46-59.

Sternberg, R. J., Hojjat, M., & Barnes, M. L. (2001). Empirical aspects of a theory of love as a story. *European Journal of Personality, 15,* 1-20.

Sternberg, R. J., Jarvin, L., & Grigorenko, E. L. (2011). *Explorations in giftedness.* New York: Cambridge University Press.

Sternberg, R. J., Kaufman, J. C., & Pretz, J. E. (2004). A propulsion model of creative leadership [Special issue: Creativity in the workplace]. *Creativity and Innovation Management, 13,* 145-153.

Sternson, S. M., Betley, J., & Cao, Z. (2013). Neural circuits and motivational processes for hunger. *Current Opinion in Neurobiology, 23,* 353-360.

Stettler, N., Stallings, V. A., Troxel, A. B., Zhao, J. Z., Schinnar, R., Nelson, S. E., . . . Strom, B. L. (2005). Weight gain in the first week of life and overweight in adulthood. *Circulation, 111,* 1897-1903.

Stevens, C. F. (2015). Novel neural circuit mechanism for visual edge detection. *PNAS Proceedings of the National Academy of Sciences of the United States of America, 112,* 875-880.

Stevens, G. (2015). Black psychology: Resistance, reclamation, and redefinition. In I. Parker & I.

Parker (Eds.), *Handbook of critical psychology*. New York: Routledge/Taylor & Francis Group.

Stevens, P., & Harper, D. J. (2007). Professional accounts of electroconvulsive therapy: A discourse analysis. *Social Science & Medicine, 64*, 1475-1486.

Stevens, S. S., & Pashler, H. E. (2002). *Steven's handbook of experimental psychology: Learning, motivation, and emotion*. New York: Wiley.

Stevens, T., Brevers, D., Chambers, C. D., Lavric, A., McLaren, I. L., Mertens, M., . . . Verbruggen, F. (2015). How does response inhibition influence decision making when gambling? *Journal of Experimental Psychology: Applied, 21*, 15-36.

Stevenson, H. W., Lee, S., & Mu, X. (2000). Successful achievement in mathematics: China and the United States. In C. F. M. van Lieshout & P. G. Heymans (Eds.), *Developing talent across the life span*. New York: Psychology Press.

Stewart, C. E., Lee, S. Y., Hogstrom, A., & Williams, M. (2017). Diversify and conquer: A call to promote minority representation in clinical psychology. *The Behavior Therapist, 40*, 74-79.

Stey, P. C., Lapsley, D., & McKeever, M. O. (2013). Moral judgement in adolescents: Age differences in applying and justifying three principles of harm. *European Journal of Developmental Psychology, 10*, 206-220.

Stickgold, R. (2015, October). Why we sleep. *Scientific American*, 52-57.

Stickgold, R., Hobson, J. A., Fosse, R., & Fosse, M. (2001, November 2). Sleep, learning, and dreams: Off-line memory reprocessing. *Science, 294*, 1052-1057.

Stickley, T., & Nickeas, R. (2006). Becoming one person: Living with dissociative identity disorder. *Journal of Psychiatric and Mental Health Nursing, 13*, 180-187.

Stifter, C. A., Dollar, J. M., & Cipriano, E. A. (2011). Temperament and emotion regulation: The role of autonomic nervous system reactivity. *Developmental Psychobiology, 53*, 266-279.

Stix, G. (2011, March). The neuroscience of true grit. *Scientific American*, 29-33.

Stocks, E., Lishner, D., & Decker, S. (2009). Altruism or psychological escape: Why does empathy promote prosocial behavior? *European Journal of Social Psychology, 39*, 649-665.

Stockton, R., Morran, D. K., & Krieger, K. (2004). An overview of current research and best practices for training beginning group leaders. In J. L. DeLucia-Waack, D. A. Gerrity, C. R. Kalodner, & M. T. Riva (Eds.), *Handbook of group counseling and psychotherapy*. Thousand Oaks, CA: Sage Publications.

Stolorow, R. D., & Stolorow, B. A. (2013). Blues and emotional trauma. *Clinical Social Work Journal, 41*, 5-10.

Stone, D. L., & Rosopa, P. J. (2017). The advantages and limitations of using meta-analysis in human resource management research. *Human Resource Management Review, 27*, 1-7.

Stone, J. (2002). Battling doubt by avoiding practice: The effects of stereotype threat on self-handicapping in white athletes. *Personality and Social Psychology Bulletin, 28*, 1667-1678.

Stopa, L., Denton, R., Wingfield, M., & Taylor, K. (2013). The fear of others: A qualitative analysis of interpersonal threat in social phobia and paranoia. *Behavioural and Cognitive Psychotherapy, 41*, 188-209.

Stoppelbein, L., McRae, E., & Greening, L. (2017). A longitudinal study of hardiness as a buffer for posttraumatic stress symptoms in mothers of children with cancer. *Clinical Practice in Pediatric Psychology, 5*, 149-160.

Storm, L., & Ertel, S. (2001). Does psi exist? Comments on Milton and Wiseman's (1999) meta-analysis of Ganzfeld's research. *Psychological Bulletin, 127*, 424-433.

Storm, L., & Rock, A. J. (2015). Dreaming of psi: A narrative review and meta-analysis of dream-ESP studies at the Maimonides Dream Laboratory and beyond. In J. A. Davies & D. B. Pitchford (Eds.), *Stanley Krippner: A life of dreams, myths, and visions: Essays on his contributions and influence*. New York: University Professors Press.

Stowell, J. R., Robles, T. F., & Kane, H. S. (2013). Psychoneuroimmunology: Mechanisms, individual differences, and interventions. In A. M. Nezu, C. Nezu, P. A. Geller, & I. B. Weiner (Eds.), *Handbook of psychology, Vol. 9: Health psychology* (2nd ed.). Hoboken, NJ: John Wiley & Sons Inc.

Strange, D., Clifasefi, S., & Garry, M. (2007). False memories. In M. Garry & H. Hayne (Eds.), *Do justice and let the sky fall: Elizabeth Loftus and her contributions to science, law, and academic freedom*. Mahwah, NJ: Lawrence Erlbaum Associates.

Strathern, A., & Stewart, P. J. (2003). *Landscape, memory and history: Anthropological perspectives*. London: Pluto Press.

Strayer, D. L., & Drews, F. A. (2007). Cell-phone-induced driver distraction. *Current Directions in Psychological Science, 16*, 128-131.

Strenze, T. (2015). Intelligence and success. In S. Goldstein, D. Princiotta, & J. A. Naglieri (Eds.), *Handbook of intelligence: Evolutionary theory, historical perspective, and current concepts* (pp. 405-413). New York: Springer Science + Business Media.

Striano, T., & Vaish, A. (2006). Seven- to 9-month-old infants use facial expressions to interpret others' actions. *British Journal of Developmental Psychology, 24*, 753-760.

Striegel, R. H., Bedrosian, R., Wang, C., & Schwartz, S. (2011). Why men should be included in research on binge eating: Results from a comparison of psychosocial impairment in men and women. *International Journal of Eating Disorder, 45*(2), 233-240.

Striegel-Moore, R., & Bulik, C. M. (2007). Risk factors for eating disorders. *American Psychologist, 62*, 181-198.

Strong, T., & Tomm, K. (2007). Family therapy as re-coordinating and moving on together. *Journal of Systemic Therapies, 26*, 42-54.

Stålhammar, J., Nordlund, A., & Wallin, A. (2015). An example of exceptional practice effects in the verbal domain. *Neurocase, 21*, 162-168.

Subrahmanyam, K., Reich, S., Waechter, N., & Espinoza, G. (2008). Online and offline social networks: Use of social networking sites by emerging adults. *Journal of Applied Developmental Psychology, 29*, 420-433.

Substance Abuse and Mental Health Services Administration. (2014). *Results from the 2013 National Survey on Drug Use and Health: Mental Health Findings*, NSDUH Series H-49, HHS Publication No. (SMA) 14-4887. Rockville, MD: Substance Abuse and Mental Health Services Administration.

Sue, D. W. (2017). Microaggressions and "evidence": Empirical or experiential reality? *Perspectives on Psychological Science, 12*, 170-172.

Sue, D. W., & Sue, D. (1990). *Counseling the culturally different: Theory and practice* (2nd ed.). Oxford, England: John Wiley & Sons.

Suh, E. M. (2002). Culture, identity consistency, and subjective well-being. *Journal of Personality & Social Psychology, 83*, 1378-1391.

Suhail, K., & Chaudhry, H. R. (2004). Predictors of subjective well-being in an Eastern Muslim culture. *Journal of Social and Clinical Psychology, 23*, 359-376.

Suizzo, M.-A., & Bornstein, M. H. (2006). French and European American child-mother play: Culture and gender considerations. *International Journal of Behavioral Development, 30*, 498-508.

Sullivan, E. L., Smith, S. M., & Grove, K. L. (2011). Perinatal exposure to high-fat diet programs energy balance, metabolism and behavior in adulthood. *Neuroendocrinology, 93*, 1-8.

Sullivan, J., Riccio, C., & Reynolds, C. (2008). Variations in students' school- and teacher-related attitudes across gender, ethnicity, and age. *Journal of Instructional Psychology, 35*, 296-305.

Summa, K. C., & Turek, F. W. (2015, February). The clocks within us. *Scientific American*, pp. 51-55.

Summers, M. (2000). *Everything in its place*. New York: Putnam.

Summers, S. J., Schabrun, S. M., Marinovic, W., & Chipchase, L. S. (2017). Peripheral electrical stimulation increases corticomotor excitability and enhances the rate of visuomotor adaptation. *Behavioural Brain Research, 322* (Part A), 42-50.

Sun, X., Niu, G., You, Z., Zhou, Z., & Tang, Y. (2017). "Gender, negative life events and coping on different stages of depression severity: A cross-sectional study among Chinese university students": Corrigendum. *Journal of Affective Disorders, 215*, 102.

Sun, Y., Giacobbe, P., Tang, C. W., Barr, M. S., Rajji, T., Kennedy, S. H., Fitzgerald, P. B., Lozano, A. M., Wong, W., & Daskalakis, Z. J. (2015, June 26). Deep brain stimulation modulates gamma oscillations and theta-gamma coupling in treatment resistant depression. *Brain Stimulation, 6*, 1033-1042.

Super, C. M. (1980). Cognitive development: Looking across at growing up. In C. M. Super & S. Harkness (Eds.), *New directions for child development: Anthropological perspectives on child development*. San Francisco: Jossey-Bass.

Sutherland, S. (2016). The maddening sensation of itch. *Scientific American, 314,* 39-43.

Sutin, A. R., & Robins, R. W. (2007). Phenomenology of autobiographical memories: The Memory Experiences Questionnaire. *Memory, 15,* 390-411.

Suzuki, L. A., Short, E. L., & Lee, C. S. (2011). Racial and ethnic group differences in intelligence in the United States: Multicultural perspectives. In R. J. Sternberg & S. Kaufman (Eds.), *The Cambridge handbook of intelligence.* New York: Cambridge University Press.

Swain, P. I. (2006). *New developments in eating disorders research.* Hauppauge, NY: Nova Science Publishers.

Swain, R. A., Kerr, A. L., & Thompson, R. F. (2011). The cerebellum: A neural system for the study of reinforcement learning. *Frontiers in Behavioral Neuroscience, 18,* 89-96.

Szasz, T. S. (2011). *The myth of mental illness: Foundations of a theory of personal conduct.* New York: HarperCollins.

Szegedy Maszak, M. (2003, January 13). The sound of unsound minds. *U.S. News & World Report,* pp. 45-46.

Tadmor, C. T. (2007). Biculturalism: The plus side of leaving home? The effects of second-culture exposure on integrative complexity and its consequences for overseas performance. *Dissertation Abstracts International Section A: Humanities and Social Sciences, 67*(8-A), 3068.

Taibbi, R. (2018). *Brief therapy with couples and families in crisis.* New York, NY, US: Routledge/Taylor & Francis Group.

Tajfel, H., & Turner, J. C. (2004). The social identity theory of intergroup behavior. In J. T. Jost & J. Sidanius (Eds.), *Political psychology: Key readings.* New York: Psychology Press.

Tajfel, H., & Turner, J. C. (2010). An integrative theory of intergroup conflict. In T. Postmes & N. R. Branscombe (Eds.), *Rediscovering social.* New York: Psychology Press.

Takahashi, M., Nakata, A., Haratani, T., Ogawa, Y., & Arito, H. (2004). Post-lunch nap as a worksite intervention to promote alertness on the job. *Ergonomics, 47,* 1003-1013.

Taki, Y., Thyreau, B., Kinomura, S., Sato, K., Goto, R., Wu, K., & . . . Fukuda, H. (2013). A longitudinal study of age and gender related annual rate of volume changes in regional gray matter in healthy adults. *Human Brain Mapping, 34,* 2292-2301.

Takizawa, T., Kondo, T., & Sakihara, S. (2007). Stress buffering effects of social support on depressive symptoms in middle age: Reciprocity and community mental health: Corrigendum. *Psychiatry and Clinical Neurosciences, 61,* 336-337.

Takooshian, H., Gielen, U.P., Plous, S., Rich, G.J., & Velayo, R.S. (2016). Internationalizing undergraduate psychology education: Trends, techniques, and technologies. *American Psychologist, 71,* 136-147.

Tal-Or, N., & Papirman, Y. (2007). The fundamental attribution error in attributing fictional figures' characteristics to the actors. *Media Psychology, 9,* 331-345.

Talarico, J. (2009). Freshman flashbulbs: Memories of unique and first-time events in starting college. *Memory, 17,* 256-265.

Talarico, J., & Rubin, D. (2007). Flashbulb memories are special after all; in phenomenology, not accuracy. *Applied Cognitive Psychology, 21,* 557-578.

Talmi, D., Anderson, A., Riggs, L., Caplan, J., & Moscovitch, M. (2008). Immediate memory consequences of the effect of emotion on attention to pictures. *Learning & Memory, 15, 172-182.*

Talukdar, S., & Shastri, J. (2006). Contributory and adverse factors in social development of young children. *Psychological Studies, 51,* 294-303.

Tam, S. E., Bonardi, C., & Robinson, J. (2015). Relative recency influences object-in-context memory. *Behavioural Brain Research, 281,* 250-257.

Tamini, B., Bojhd, F., & Yazdani, S. (2011). Love types, psychological well-being and self-concept. *Journal of the Indian Academy of Applied Psychology, 37,* 169-178.

Tan, G., Rintala, D. H., Jensen, M. P., Richards, J. S., Holmes, S. A., Parachuri, R., Lashgari-Saegh, S., & Price, L. R. (2011). Efficacy of cranial electrotherapy stimulation for neuropathic pain following spinal cord injury: a multi-site randomized controlled trial with a secondary 6-month open-label phase. *Journal of Spinal Cord Medicine, 34,* 285-296.

Tan, L., Chan, A., Kay, P., Khong, P., Yip, L., & Luke, K. (2008). Language affects patterns of brain activation associated with perceptual decision. *PNAS Proceedings of the National Academy of Sciences of the United States of America, 105*(10), 4004-4009.

Tan, L., Yu, J., & Tan, L. (2015). Causes and consequences of microRNA dysregulation in neurodegenerative diseases. *Molecular Neurobiology, 51,* 1249-1262.

Tandon, R., Gaebel, W., Barch, D. M., Bustillo, J., Gur, R. E., Heckers, S., & . . . Carpenter, W. (2013). Definition and description of schizophrenia in the DSM-5. *Schizophrenia Research.* Retrieved from http://ccpweb.wustl.edu/pdfs/2013.defdes.pdf.

Tanner, J. M. (1990). *Foetus into man: Physical growth from conception to maturity* (rev. ed.). Cambridge, MA: Harvard University Press.

Tappin, B. M., McKay, R. T., & Abrams, D. (2017). Choosing the right level of analysis: Stereotypes shape social reality via collective action. *Behavioral and Brain Sciences, 40.* Accessed from https://www.ncbi.nlm.nih.gov/pubmed/28327226.

Tasker, F. (2005). Lesbian mothers, gay fathers, and their children: A review. *Journal of Developmental and Behavioral Pediatrics, 26,* 224-240.

Tavernise, S. (2015, April 17). Teenagers pick up e-cigarettes as old-school smoking declines. *The New York Times,* A1.

Taylor, F., & Bryant, R. A. (2007). The tendency to suppress, inhibiting thoughts, and dream rebound. *Behaviour Research and Therapy, 45,* 163-168.

Taylor, S. (2003). Anxiety sensitivity and its implications for understanding and treating PTSD. *Journal of Cognitive Psychotherapy, 17,* 179-186.

Taylor, S. (2015). *Health psychology* (9th ed.). New York: McGraw-Hill.

Taylor, S. E. (1995). Quandary at the crossroads: Paternalism versus advocacy surrounding end-of-treatment decisions. *American Journal of Hospital Palliatory Care, 12,* 43-46.

Taylor, S. E., Kemeny, M. E., Reed, G. M., Bower, J. E., & Gruenewald, T. L. (2000). Psychological resources, positive illusions, and health. *American Psychologist, 55,* 99-109.

Teague, R. (2013). The American view of Freud's couch. *PsycCRITIQUES, 58,* 12-21.

Tedeschi, R. G., Blevins, C. L., & Riffle, O. M. (2017). Posttraumatic growth: A brief history and evaluation. In M. A. Warren & S. I. Donaldson (Eds.), *Scientific advances in positive psychology* (pp. 131-163). Santa Barbara, CA: Praeger/ABC-CLIO. ten Cate, C. (2017). Assessing the uniqueness of language: Animal grammatical abilities take center stage. *Psychonomic Bulletin & Review, 24,* 91-96.

Teodorov, E., Salzgerber, S. A., Felicio, L. F., Varolli, F. M. F., & Bernardi, M. M. (2002). Effects of perinatal picrotoxin and sexual experience on heterosexual and homosexual behavior in male rats. *Neurotoxicology and Teratology, 24,* 235-245.

Thachil, A. F., Mohan, R., & Bhugra, D. (2007). The evidence base of complementary and alternative therapies in depression. *Journal of Affective Disorders, 97,* 23-35.

Thaler, L. (2015). Using sound to get around: Discoveries in human echolocation. *APS Observer, 28,* 24-27.

Thaler, N. S., Thames, A. D., Cagigas, X. E., & Norman, M. A. (2015). IQ testing and the African American client. In L. T. Benuto & B. D. Leany (Eds.), *Guide to psychological assessment with African Americans.* New York: Springer Science + Business Media.

Thanos, P. K., Robison, L. S., Robinson, J. K., Michaelides, M., Wang, G., & Volkow, N. D. (2013). Obese rats with deficient leptin signaling exhibit heightened sensitivity to olfactory food cues. *Synapse, 67,* 171-178.

Tharp, R. G. (1989). Psychocultural variables and constants: Effects on teaching and learning in schools [Special issue: Children and their development: Knowledge base, research agenda, and social policy application]. *American Psychologist, 44,* 349-359.

Thase, M. E. (2013). Comparative effectiveness of psychodynamic psychotherapy and cognitive-behavioral therapy: It's about time, and what's next? *The American Journal of Psychiatry, 170,* 953-956.

Thatcher, D. L., & Clark, D. B. (2006). Adolescent alcohol abuse and dependence: Development, diagnosis, treatment and outcomes. *Current Psychiatry Reviews, 2,* 159-177.

Theriault, J., Krause, P., & Young, L. (2017). Know thy enemy: Education about terrorism improves social attitudes toward terrorists.

Journal of Experimental Psychology: General, 146(3), 305-317.

Thomas, P., Mathur, P., Gottesman, I. I., Nagpal, R., Nimgaonkar, V. L., & Deshpande, S. N. (2007). Correlates of hallucinations in schizophrenia: A cross-cultural evaluation. *Schizophrenia Research, 92,* 41-49.

Thompson, A. K., & Wolpaw, J. R. (2015). Restoring walking after spinal cord injury: Operant conditioning of spinal reflexes can help. *The Neuroscientist, 21*(2), 203-215.

Thompson, M. (2015, April 6.) Unlocking the secrets of PTSD. *Time,* pp. 41-43.

Thorkildsen, T. A. (2006). An empirical exploration of language and thought. *PsycCRITIQUES, 51,* n.p.

Thorndike, E. L. (1932). *The fundamentals of learning.* New York: Teachers College.

Thornton, A., & Young-DeMarco, L. (2001). Four decades of trends in attitudes toward family issues in the United States: The 1960s through the 1990s. *Journal of Marriage and the Family, 63,* 1009-1017.

Thrailkill, E. A., & Bouton, M. E. (2017). Effects of outcome devaluation on instrumental behaviors in a discriminated heterogeneous chain. *Journal of Experimental Psychology: Animal Learning and Cognition, 43,* 88-95.

Thrash, T. M., & Elliot, A. J. (2002). Implicit and self-attributed achievement motives: Concordance and predictive validity. *Journal of Personality, 70,* 729-755.

Thurman, S. M., & Lu, H. (2013). Physical and biological constraints govern perceived animacy of scrambled human forms. *Psychological Science, 24,* 1133-1141.

Tingley, K. (2016, March 20). Sixth sense. *The New York Times Magazine,* p. MM52.

Tippin, J., Sparks, J., & Rizzo, M. (2009, August). Visual vigilance in drivers with obstructive sleep apnea. *Journal of Psychosomatic Research, 67,* 143-151.

Tirri, K., & Nokelainen, P. (2008). Identification of multiple intelligences with the Multiple Intelligence Profiling Questionnaire III [Special issue: High-ability assessment]. *Psychology Science, 50,* 206-221.

Todorov, A. (Ed.), Fiske, S. (Ed.), & Prentice, D. (Ed.). (2011). *Social neuroscience: Toward understanding the underpinnings of the social mind.* New York: Oxford University Press.

Toft, A., Tome, M., Barnett, S. C., & Riddell, J. S. (2013). A comparative study of glial and non neural cell properties for transplant mediated repair of the injured spinal cord. *Glia, 61,* 513-528.

Tokutsu, Y., Umene-Nakano, W., Shinkai, T., Yoshimura, R., Okamoto, T., Katsuki, A., & . . . Nakamura, J. (2013). Follow-up study on electroconvulsive therapy in treatment-resistant depressed patients after remission: A chart review. *Clinical Psychopharmacology and Neuroscience, 11,* 34-38.

Tolman, E. C., & Honzik, C. H. (1930). Introduction and removal of reward and maze performance in rats. *University of California Publications in Psychology, 4,* 257-275.

Tolnai, S., Beutelmann, R., & Klump, G. M. (2017). Effect of preceding stimulation on sound localization and its representation in the auditory midbrain. *European Journal of Neuroscience, 45,* 460-471.

Tommasi, L. (2009). Mechanisms and functions of brain and behavioural asymmetries. *Philosophical Transactions of the Royal Society B, 364,* 855-859.

Tononi, G., & Cirelli, C. (2013, August). Perchance to prune. *Scientific American,* 34-39.

Tononi, G., & Koch, C. (2008). The neural correlates of consciousness: An update. In A Kingstone & M. B. Miller (Eds.), *The year in cognitive neuroscience.* Malden, MA: Blackwell Publishing.

Tosto, M. G., Hayiou-Thomas, M. E., Harlaar, N., Prom-Wormley, E., Dale, P. S., & Plomin, R. (2017). The genetic architecture of oral language, reading fluency, and reading comprehension: A twin study from 7 to 16 years. *Developmental Psychology, 53,* 1115-1129.

Toth, J. P., & Daniels, K. A. (2002). Effects of prior experience on judgments of normative word frequency: Automatic bias and correction. *Journal of Memory and Language, 46,* 845-874.

Touhara, K. (2007). Molecular biology of peptide pheromone production and reception in mice. *Advanced Genetics, 59,* 147-171.

Towns, C. R. (2017). The science and ethics of cell-based therapies for Parkinson's disease. *Parkinsonism & Related Disorders, 34,* 1-6.

Tracy, J. L., & Robins, R. W. (2004). Show your pride: Evidence for a discrete emotion expression. *Psychological Science, 15,* 194-197.

Trafton, A. (2015). It's not all downhill after 20. *MIT Technology Review, 118*(4), 8-9.

Tramontana, J. (2011). *Sports hypnosis in practice: Scripts, strategies and case examples.* Norwalk, CT: Crown House Publishing Limited.

Tranter, L. J., & Koutstaal, W. (2008). Age and flexible thinking: An experimental demonstration of the beneficial effects of increased cognitively stimulating activity on fluid intelligence in healthy older adults. *Neuropsychology and Cognition, 15,* 184-207.

Travis, F. (2006). From I to I: Concepts of self on a object-referral/self-referral continuum. In A. P. Prescott (Ed.), *The concept of self in psychology.* Hauppauge, NY: Nova Science Publishers.

Travis, F., et al. (2009, February). Effects of transcendental meditation practice on brain functioning and stress reactivity in college students. *International Journal of Psychopathy, 71,* 170-176.

Tremblay, A. (2004). Dietary fat and body weight set point. *Nutrition Review, 62*(7, Pt 2), S75-S77.

Triandis, H. C. (2011). Culture and self-deception: A theoretical perspective. *Social Behavior and Personality, 39,* 3-14.

Tribune News Services. (2017, January 10). Dylann Roof sentenced to death for killing 9 black church members in South Carolina. *Chicago Tribune.* Retrieved from http://www.chicagotribune.com/news/nationworld/ct-dylann-roof-sentencing-20170110-story.html.

Triscari, M., Faraci, P., D'Angelo, V., Urso, V., & Catalisano, D. (2011). Two treatments for fear of flying compared: Cognitive behavioral therapy combined with systematic desensitization or eye movement desensitization and reprocessing (EMDR). *Aviation Psychology and Applied Human Factors, 1,* 9-14.

Tropp, L. R., & Bianchi, R. A. (2006). Valuing diversity and interest in intergroup contact. *Journal of Social Issues, 62,* 533-551.

Tropp, L. R., & Pettigrew, T. F. (2005). Differential relationships between intergroup contact and affective and cognitive dimensions of prejudice. *Personality and Social Psychology Bulletin, 31,* 1145-1158.

Trujillo-Pisanty, I., Hernandez, G., Moreau-Debord, I., Cossette, M. P., Conover, K., Cheer, J. F., & Shizgal, P. (2011). Cannabinoid receptor blockade reduces the opportunity cost at which rats maintain operant performance for rewarding brain stimulation. *Journal of Neuroscience, 31,* 5426-5430.

Trull, T. J., & Widiger, T. A. (2003). Personality disorders. In G. Stricker, T. A. Widiger, et al. (Eds.), *Handbook of psychology: Clinical psychology* (Vol. 8). New York: Wiley.

Tsaousis, I., Nikolaou, I., & Serdaris, N. (2007). Do the core self-evaluations moderate the relationship between subjective well-being and physical and psychological health? *Personality and Individual Differences, 42,* 1441-1452.

Tschentscher, N., & Hauk, O. (2017). Frontal cortex supports the early structuring of multiple solution steps in symbolic problem-solving. *Journal of Cognitive Neuroscience, 29,* 114-124.

Tseng, W. S. (2003). *Clinician's guide to cultural psychiatry.* San Diego, CA: Elsevier Publishing.

Tsenkova, V., Boylan, J., & Ryff, C. (2013). Stress eating and health. Findings from MIDUS, a national study of US adults. *Appetite, 69,* 151-155.

Tsuchida, K., Ueno, K., & Shimada, S. (2015). Motor area activity for action-related and nonaction-related sounds in a three-dimensional sound field reproduction system. *Neuroreport: For Rapid Communication of Neuroscience Research, 26,* 291-295.

Tsukasaki, T., & Ishii, K. (2004). Linguistic-cultural relativity of cognition: Rethinking the Sapir-Whorf hypothesis. *Japanese Psychological Review, 47,* 173-186.

Tuckey, M. R., Searle, B. J., Boyd, C. M., Winefield, A. H., & Winefield, H. R. (2015). Hindrances are not threats: Advancing the multidimensionality of work stress. *Journal of Occupational Health Psychology, 20,* 131-147.

Tuerk, P. W., Yoder, M., Grubaugh, A., Myrick, H., Hamner, M., & Acierno, R. (2011). Prolonged exposure therapy for combat-related posttraumatic stress disorder: An examination of treatment effectiveness for veterans of the wars in Afghanistan and Iraq. *Journal of Anxiety Disorders, 25,* 397-403.

Tuerlinckx, F., De Boeck, P., & Lens, W. (2002). Measuring needs with the Thematic Apperception Test: A psychometric study. *Journal of Personality and Social Psychology, 82,* 448-461.

Tugay, N., et al. (2007). Effectiveness of transcutaneous electrical nerve stimulation and interferential current in primary dysmenorrhea. *Pain Medicine, 8,* 295-300.

Tulving, E. (2002). Episodic memory and common sense: How far apart? In A. Baddeley & J. P. Aggleton (Eds.), *Episodic memory: New directions in research.* London: Oxford University Press.

Tummala-Narra, P. (2016). *Psychoanalytic theory and cultural competence in psychotherapy.* Washington, DC: American Psychological Association.

Tunstall, B. J., Verendeev, A., & Kearns, D. N. (2013). Outcome specificity in deepened extinction may limit treatment feasibility: Co-presentation of a food cue interferes with extinction of cue-elicited cocaine seeking. *Drug and Alcohol Dependence.* Retrieved from http://www.ncbi.nlm.nih.gov/pubmed/24071568.

Turner, M. E., Pratkanis, A. R., & Struckman, C. K. (2007). Groupthink as social identity maintenance. In C. K. Struckman (Ed.), *The science of social influence: Advances and future progress.* New York: Psychology Press.

Turri, M. G. (2015). Transference and katharsis, Freud to Aristotle. *International Journal of Psychoanalysis, 96,* 369-387.

Tuszynski, M. H. (2007). Nerve growth factor gene therapy in Alzheimer's disease. *Alzheimer's Disease and Associated Disorders, 21,* 179-189.

Tutwiler, S., Lin, M., & Chang, C. (2013). The use of a gesture-based system for teaching multiple intelligences: A pilot study. *British Journal of Educational Technology, 44,* E133-E138.

Tversky, A., & Kahneman, D. (1987). Rational choice and the framing of decisions. In R. Hogarth & M. Reder (Eds.), *Rational choice: The contrast between economics and psychology.* Chicago: University of Chicago Press.

Twenge, J. M. (2013). Does online social media lead to social connection or social disconnection? *Journal of College and Character, 14,* 11-20.

Twenge, J. M., & Kasser, T. (2013). Generational changes in materialism and work centrality, 1976-2007: Associations with temporal changes in societal insecurity and materialistic role-modeling. *Personality and Social Psychology Bulletin.* Retrieved from http://psp.sagepub.com/content/early/2013/05/01/0146167213484586.

Twenge, J. M., Campbell, W. K., & Gentile, B. (2013). Changes in pronoun use in American books and the rise of individualism, 1960-2008. *Journal of Cross-Cultural Psychology, 44,* 406-415.

Twining, R. C., Wheeler, D. S., Ebben, A. L., Jacobsen, A. J., Robble, M. A., Mantsch, J. R., & Wheeler, R. A. (2015). Aversive stimuli drive drug seeking in a state of low dopamine tone. *Biological Psychiatry, 77,* 895-902.

Tydgat, I., & Grainger, J. (2009). Serial position effects in the identification of letters, digits, and symbols. *Journal of Experimental Psychology: Human Perception and Performance, 35,* 480-498.

Tyrer, H., Tyrer, P., Lisseman-Stones, Y., McAllister, S., Cooper, S., Salkovskis, P., & . . . Wang, D. (2015). Therapist differences in a randomised trial of the outcome of cognitive behaviour therapy for health anxiety in medical patients. *International Journal of Nursing Studies, 52,* 686-694.

U.S. Bureau of Labor Statistics. (2007). *American time use survey.* Washington, DC: Bureau of Labor Statistics.

U.S. Bureau of Labor Statistics. (2013, April 26). Employment characteristics of families—2012. Washington, DC: Bureau of Labor Statistics.

U.S. Bureau of the Census. (2000). *Census 2000.* Retrieved from American Fact Finder http://factfinder.census.gov/servlet/BasicFactsServlet.

U.S. Census Bureau. (2017, September 14). New American community survey statistics for income, poverty and health insurance available for states and local areas. Release Number CB17-157. Retrieved from https://www.census.gov/newsroom/press-releases/2017/acs-single-year.html?CID=CBSM+ACS16.

U.S. Department of Health and Human Services. (2016). E-cigarette use among youth and young adults. A report of the Surgeon General. Atlanta, GA: U.S. Department of Health and Human Services, Centers for Disease Control and Prevention, National Center for Chronic Disease Prevention and Health Promotion, Office on Smoking and Health.

U.S. Senate Select Committee on Intelligence. (2004, July 9). *Report of the U.S. intelligence community's prewar intelligence assessments on Iraq.* Retrieved from https://nsarchive2.gwu.edu/NSAEBB/NSAEBB254/doc12.pdf.

Uchino, B. N. (2006). Social support and health: A review of physiological processes potentially underlying links to disease outcomes. *Journal of Behavioral Medicine, 29,* 377-387.

Underwood, A. (2005, October 3). The good heart. *Newsweek,* p. 49.

Unsworth, N., & Engle, R. W. (2005). Individual differences in working memory capacity and learning: Evidence from the serial reaction time task. *Memory and Cognition, 33,* 213-220.

Updegraff, K. A., Helms, H. M., McHale, S. M., Crouter, A. C., Thayer, S. M., & Sales, L. H. (2004). Who's the boss? Patterns of perceived control in adolescents' friendships. *Journal of Youth & Adolescence, 33,* 403-420.

Urlacher, B. R. (2008). Walking out of two-level social traps (with a little help from my friends). *Simulation & Gaming, 39,* 453-464.

Ursprung, W. W., Sanouri, A., & DiFranza, J. R. (2009). The loss of autonomy over smoking in relation to lifetime cigarette consumption. *Addictive Behaviors, 22,* 12-19.

Uylings, H. B. M. (2006). Development of the human cortex and the concept of "critical" or "sensitive" periods. *Language Learning, 56,* 59-90.

Vaillant, G. E., & Vaillant, C. O. (1990). Natural history of male psychological health: XII. A 46-year study of predictors of successful aging at age 65. *American Journal of Psychiatry, 147,* 31-37.

Valencia, R. R., & Suzuki, L. A. (2003). *Intelligence testing and minority students: Foundations, performance factors, and assessment issues.* Thousand Oaks, CA: Sage.

Valenzuela, S., Park, N., & Kee, K. F. (2009). Is there social capital in a social network site? Facebook use and college students' life satisfaction, trust, and participation. *Journal of Computer-Mediated Communications, 14,* 875-901.

Valenzuela, V., Martínez, G., Duran-Aniotz, C., & Hetz, C. (2016). Gene therapy to target ER stress in brain diseases. *Brain Research, 1648*(Part B), 561-570.

Valois, R. F., Zullig, K. J., & Hunter, A. A. (2013). Association between adolescent suicide ideation, suicide attempts and emotional self-efficacy. *Journal of Child and Family Studies, 24,* 237-248.

Valsecchi, M., Caziot, B., Backus, B. T., & Gegenfurtner, K. R. (2013). The role of binocular disparity in rapid scene and pattern recognition. *I-Perception, 4*(2), 254-262.

Valyear, M. D., Villaruel, F. R., & Chaudhri, N. (2017). Alcohol-seeking and relapse: A focus on incentive salience and contextual conditioning. *Behavioural Processes, 141*(Part 1), 26-32.

Van Belle, V., Pelckmans, K., Suykens, J. A. K., & Van Huffel, S. (2011). Learning transformation models for ranking and survival analysis. *Journal of Machine Learning Research, 12,* 819-862.

Van Damme, C., Deschrijver, E., Van Geert, E., & Hoorens, V. (2017). When praising yourself insults others: Self-superiority claims provoke aggression. *Personality and Social Psychology Bulletin, 43,* 1008-1019.

Van den Wildenberg, W. P. M., & Van der Molen, M. W. (2004). Developmental trends in simple and selective inhibition of compatible and incompatible responses. *Journal of Experimental Child Psychology, 87,* 201-220.

Van der Zee, E. A., Platt, B. B., & Riedel, G. G. (2011). Acetylcholine: Future research and perspectives. *Behavioural Brain Research, 221,* 583-586.

van Dijk, W. W., Ouwerkerk, J. W., Wesseling, Y. M., & van Koningsbruggen, G. M. (2011). Towards understanding pleasure at the misfortunes of others: The impact of self-evaluation threat on schadenfreude. *Cognition and Emotion, 25,* 360-368.

van Hooren, S. A. H., Valentijn, A. M., & Bosma, H. (2007). Cognitive functioning in healthy older adults aged 64-81: A cohort study into the effects of age, sex, and education. *Aging, Neuropsychology, and Cognition, 14,* 40-54.

van Marle, K., & Wynn, K. (2009). Infants' auditory enumeration: Evidence for analog magnitudes in the small number range. *Cognition, 111,* 302-316.

van Nieuwenhuijzen, M., Vriens, A., Scheepmaker, M., Smit, M., & Porton, E. (2011). The development of a diagnostic instrument to measure social information processing in children with mild to borderline intellectual disabilities. *Research in Developmental Disabilities, 32,* 358-370.

Van Overwalle, F., & Siebler, F. (2005). A connectionist model of attitude formation and change. *Personality and Social Psychology Review, 9,* 231-274.

Van Rosmalen, L., Van Der Veer, R., & Van Der Horst, F. (2015). Ainsworth's strange situation procedure: The origin of an instrument. *Journal of the History of the Behavioral Sciences, 51,* 261-284.

van Soelen, I. C., Brouwer, R. M., van Leeuwen, M., Kahn, R. S., Pol, H., & Boomsma, D. I. (2011). Heritability of verbal and performance intelligence in a pediatric longitudinal sample. *Twin Research and Human Genetics, 14,* 119-128.

van Wesel, F., Boeije, H., & Hoijtink, H. (2013). Use of hypotheses for analysis of variance models: Challenging the current practice. *Quality & Quantity: International Journal of Methodology, 47,* 137-150.

Vanasse, A., Niyonsenga, T., & Courteau, J. (2004). Smoking cessation within the context of family medicine: Which smokers take action? *Preventive Medicine: An International Journal Devoted to Practice and Theory, 38,* 330-337.

Vandell, D. L., Burchinal, M. R., Belsky, J., Owen, M. T., Friedman, S. L., Clarke-Stewart, A., . . . Weinraub, M. (2005). *Early child care and children's development in the primary grades: Follow-up results from the NICHD Study of Early Child Care.* Paper presented at the biennial meeting of the Society for Research in Child Development, Atlanta, GA.

Vandervert, L. R., Schimpf, P. H., & Liu, H. (2007). How working memory and the cerebellum collaborate to produce creativity and innovation. *Creativity Research Journal, 19,* 1-18.

Vandierendonck, A., & Szmalec, A. (Eds.). (2011). *Spatial working memory.* New York: Psychology Press.

Vanheule, S., Desmet, M., Rosseel, Y., & Meganck, R. (2006). Core transference themes in depression. *Journal of Affective Disorders, 91,* 71-75.

Varma, S. (2007). A computational model of Tower of Hanoi problem solving. *Dissertation Abstracts International: Section B: The Sciences and Engineering, 67*(8-B), 4736.

Vasudeva, K., Vodovotz, Y., Azhar, N., Barclay, D., Janjic, J. M., & Pollock, J. A. (2015). In vivo and systems biology studies implicate IL-18 as a central mediator in chronic pain. *Journal of Neuroimmunology, 28,* 343-49.

Vecchione, M., Schoen, H., Castro, J., Cieciuch, J., Pavlopoulos, V., & Caprara, G. (2011). Personality correlates of party preference: The Big Five in five big European countries. *Personality and Individual Differences, 51,* 737-742.

Vega, C. P. (2006). The effects of therapeutic components on at-risk middle school children's grades and attendance: An archival study of an after-school prevention program. *Dissertation Abstracts International: Section B: The Sciences and Engineering, 66,* 4504.

Velentzas, K., Heinen, T., & Schack, T. (2011). Routine integration strategies and their effects on volleyball serve performance and players' movement mental representation. *Journal of Applied Sport Psychology, 23,* 209-222.

Vellacott, J. (2007). Resilience: A psychoanalytic exploration. *British Journal of Psychotherapy, 23,* 163-170.

Veltman, M. W. M., & Browne, K. D. (2001). Three decades of child maltreatment research: Implications for the school years. *Trauma, Violence, and Abuse, 2,* 215-239.

Vera-Estay, E., Dooley, J. J., & Beauchamp, M. H. (2015). Cognitive underpinnings of moral reasoning in adolescence: The contribution of executive functions. *Journal of Moral Education, 44,* 17-33.

Verdejo, A., Toribio, I., & Orozco, C. (2005). Neuropsychological functioning in methadone maintenance patients versus abstinent heroin abusers. *Drug and Alcohol Dependence, 78,* 283-288.

Verdon, B. (2011). The case of thematic tests adapted to older adults: On the importance of differentiating latent and manifest contents in projective tests. *Rorschachiana, 32,* 46-71.

Verfaellie, M., & Keane, M. M. (2002). Impaired and preserved memory processes in amnesia. In L. R. Squire & D. L. Schacter (Eds.), *Neuropsychology of memory* (3rd ed.). New York: Guilford Press.

Vernon, P., Villani, V., Vickers, L., & Harris, J. (2008). A behavioral genetic investigation of the Dark Triad and the Big 5. *Personality and Individual Differences, 44,* 445-452.

Verona, E., & Sullivan, E. (2008). Emotional catharsis and aggression revisited: Heart rate reduction following aggressive responding. *Emotion, 8,* 331-340.

Verschueren, M., Rassart, J., Claes, L., Moons, P., & Luyckx, K. (2017). Identity statuses throughout adolescence and emerging adulthood: A large-scale study into gender, age, and contextual differences. *Psychologica Belgica, 57,* 32-42.

Vesely, A. K., Saklofske, D. H., & Leschied, A. W. (2013). Teachers—The vital resource: The contribution of emotional intelligence to teacher efficacy and well-being. *Canadian Journal of School Psychology, 28,* 71-89.

Vicari, S., Pontillo, M., & Armando, M. (2013). Neurodevelopmental and psychiatric issues in Down's syndrome: Assessment and intervention. *Psychiatric Genetics, 23,* 95-107.

Vieira, E. M., & Freire, J. C. (2006). Alteridade e psicologia humanista: Uma leitura ética da abordagem centrada na pessoa. Alterity and humanistic psychology: An ethical reading of the person-centered approach. *Estudos de Psicologia, 23,* 425-432.

Villemure, C., Slotnick, B. M., & Bushnell, M. C. (2003). Effects of odors on pain perception: Deciphering the roles of emotion and attention. *Pain, 106,* 101-108.

Vincus, A. A., Ringwalt, C., Harris, M. S., & Shamblen, S. R. (2010). A short-term, quasi-experimental evaluation of D.A.R.E.'s revised elementary school curriculum. *Journal of Drug Education, 40,* 37-49.

Vitaro, F., Brendgen, M., & Arseneault, L. (2009). Methods and measures: The discordant MZ-twin method: One step closer to the holy

grail of causality. *International Journal of Behavioral Development, 33,* 376-382.

Vitello, P. (2006, June 12). A ring tone meant to fall on deaf ears. *The New York Times,* A1.

Vitiello, A. L., Bonello, R. P., & Pollard, H. P. (2007). The effectiveness of ENAR® for the treatment of chronic neck pain in Australian adults: A preliminary single-blind, randomised controlled trial. *Chiropractic Osteopathology, 9,* 9.

Vlassova, A., & Pearson, J. (2013). Look before you leap: Sensory memory improves decision making. *Psychological Science, 24,* 1635-1643.

Vleioras, G., & Bosma, H. A. (2005). Are identity styles important for psychological well-being? *Journal of Adolescence, 28,* 397-409.

Vogt, D., Rizvi, S., Shipherd, J., & Resick, P. (2008). Longitudinal investigation of reciprocal relationship between stress reactions and hardiness. *Personality and Social Psychology Bulletin, 34,* 61-73.

Volterra, V., Caselli, M. C., Capirci, O., Tonucci, F., & Vicari, S. (2003). Early linguistic abilities of Italian children with Williams syndrome [Special issue: Williams syndrome]. *Developmental Neuropsychology, 23,* 33-58.

Voruganti, L. P., Awad, A. G., Parker, B., Forrest, C., Usmani, Y., Fernando, M. L. D., et al. (2007). Cognition, functioning and quality of life in schizophrenia treatment: Results of a one-year randomized controlled trial of olanzapine and quetiapine. *Schizophrenia Research, 96,* 146-155.

Vrieze, S. I., McGue, M., Miller, M. B., Hicks, B. M., & Iacono, W. G. (2013). Three mutually informative ways to understand the genetic relationships among behavioral disinhibition, alcohol use, drug use, nicotine use/dependence, and their co-occurrence: Twin biometry, GCTA, and genome-wide scoring. *Behavior Genetics, 43,* 97-107.

Vukasović, T., & Bratko, D. (2015). Heritability of personality: A meta-analysis of behavior genetic studies. *Psychological Bulletin, 141,* 769-785.

Vygotsky, L. S. (1926/1997). *Educational psychology.* Delray Beach, FL: St. Lucie Press.

Vöhringer, I. A., Kolling, T., Graf, F., Poloczek, S., Fassbender, I., Freitag, C., . . . Knopf, M. (2017). The development of implicit memory from infancy to childhood: On average performance levels and interindividual differences. *Child Development.* Accessed from https://www.ncbi.nlm.nih.gov/pubmed/28220933.

Wabitsch, M., Funcke, J., Lennerz, B., Kuhnle-Krahl, U., Lahr, G., Debatin, K., & Fischer-Posovszky, P. (2015). Biologically inactive leptin and early-onset extreme obesity. *New England Journal of Medicine, 372,* 48-54.

Waddell, J., & Shors, T. J. (2008). Neurogenesis, learning and associative strength. *European Journal of Neurosciences, 27,* 3020-3028.

Wagemans, J., Elder, J. H., Kubovy, M., Palmer, S. E., Peterson, M. A., Singh, M., & von der Heydt, R. (2012). A century of Gestalt psychology in visual perception: I. Perceptual grouping and figure–ground organization. *Psychological Bulletin, 138,* 1172-1217.

Wagner, R. K. (2002). Smart people doing dumb things: The case of managerial incompetence. In R. J. Sternberg (Ed.), *Why smart people can be so stupid.* New Haven, CT: Yale University Press.

Wagner, R. K. (2011). Practical intelligence. In R. J. Sternberg & S. Kaufman (Eds.), *The Cambridge handbook of intelligence.* New York: Cambridge University Press.

Wagstaff, G. (2009, January). Is there a future for investigative hypnosis? *Journal of Investigative Psychology and Offender Profiling, 6,* 43-57.

Wagstaff, G. F., Wheatcroft, J. M., & Jones, A. (2011). Are high hypnotizables especially vulnerable to false memory effects? A sociocognitive perspective. *International Journal of Clinical and Experimental Hypnosis, 59,* 310-326.

Wain, H. J., Grammer, G. G., & Stasinos, J. (2006). Psychiatric intervention for medical and surgical patients following traumatic injuries. In E. C. Ritchie, P. J. Watson, & M. J. Friedman (Eds.), *Interventions following mass violence and disasters: Strategies for mental health practice.* New York: Guilford Press.

Waismeyer, A., & Meltzoff, A. N. (2017). Learning to make things happen: Infants' observational learning of social and physical causal events. *Journal of Experimental Child Psychology, 162,* 58-71.

Wakefield, J. C. (2013). DSM-5: An overview of changes and controversies. *Clinical Social Work Journal, 41,* 139-154.

Walker, L. J., & Frimer, J. A. (2007). Moral personality of brave and caring exemplars. *Journal of Personality and Social Psychology, 93,* 845-860.

Walker, L., & Frimer, J. (2009). The song remains the same: Rebuttal to Sherblom's re-envisioning of the legacy of the care challenge. *Journal of Moral Education, 38,* 53-68.

Walker, M. P., & van der Helm, E. (2009). Overnight therapy? The role of sleep in emotional brain processing. *Psychological Bulletin, 135,* 731-748.

Walker, W. R., Skowronski, J. J., & Thompson, C. P. (2003). Consolidation of long-term memory: Evidence and alternatives. *Review of General Psychology, 7,* 203-210.

Wallace, L. S., Chisolm, D. J., Abdel-Rasoul, M., & DeVoe, J. E. (2013). Survey mode matters: Adults' self-reported statistical confidence, ability to obtain health information, and perceptions of patient-health-care provider communication. *Journal of Health Psychology, 18,* 1036-1045.

Wallerstein, J. S., Lewis, J., Blakeslee, S., & Lewis, J. (2000). *The unexpected legacy of divorce.* New York: Hyperion.

Walsh, B. T., Kaplan, A. S., Attia, E., Olmstead, M., Parides, M., Carter, J. C., et al. (2006). Fluoxetine after weight restoration in anorexia nervosa: A randomized controlled trial. *JAMA: Journal of the American Medical Association, 295,* 2605-2612.

Walsh, R., & Shapiro, S. L. (2006). The meeting of meditative disciplines and western psychology. *American Psychologist, 61,* 227-239.

Walton, G. M., & Cohen, G. L. (2011, March 18). A brief social-belonging intervention improves academic and health outcomes of minority students. *Science, 331,* 1447-1451.

Walton, J. R., Murphy, C., & Bartram, L. (2017). Childhood behavioral problems–Attention-deficit/hyperactivity disorder (ADHD). In W. O'Donohue, L. James, & C. Snipes (Eds.), *Practical strategies and tools to promote treatment engagement.* Cham, Switzerland: Springer International Publishing.

Wan, C., & Chiu, C. (2011). Culture as intersubjective representations of values. In A. Y. Leung, C. Chiu, & Y. Hong (Eds.), *Cultural processes: A social psychological perspective.* New York: Cambridge University Press.

Wang, A., & Clark, D. A. (2002). Haunting thoughts: The problem of obsessive mental intrusions [Special issue: Intrusions in cognitive behavioral therapy]. *Journal of Cognitive Psychotherapy, 16,* 193-208.

Wang, F., Kameda, M., Yasuhara, T., Tajiri, N., Kikuchi, Y., Liang, H. B., & . . . Date, I. (2011). Gdnf-pretreatment enhances the survival of neural stem cells following transplantation in a rat model of Parkinson's disease. *Neuroscience Research, 18,* 202-211.

Wang, J. X., Rogers, L. M., Gross, E. Z., Ryals, A. J., Dokucu, M. E., Brandstatt, K. L., . . . Voss, J. L. (2014). Targeted enhancement of cortical-hippocampal brain networks and associative memory. *Science, 345*(6200), 1054-1057.

Wang, M. T., & Kenny, S. (2013). Longitudinal links between fathers' and mothers' harsh verbal discipline and adolescents' conduct problems and depressive symptoms. *Child Development.* Retrieved from http://onlinelibrary.wiley.com/doi/10.1111/cdev.12143/abstract.

Wang, M., Chen, W., Zhang, C., & Deng, X. (2017). Personality types and scholarly creativity in undergraduate students: The mediating roles of creative styles. *Personality and Individual Differences, 105,* 170-174.

Wang, P. S., Aguilar-Gaxiola, S., Alonso, J., Angermeyer, M. C., Borges, G., Bromet, E. J., et al. (2007, September 8). Use of mental health services for anxiety, mood, and substance disorders in 17 countries in the WHO world mental health surveys. *Lancet, 370,* 841-850.

Wang, Q. (2004). The emergence of cultural self-constructs: Autobiographical memory and self-description in European American and Chinese children. *Developmental Psychology, 40,* 3-15.

Wang, Q., & Conway, M. A. (2006). Autobiographical memory, self, and culture. In L-G. Nilsson & N. Ohta, *Memory and society: Psychological perspectives.* New York: Psychology Press.

Wang, R., Liu, H., Jiang, J., & Song, Y. (2017). Will materialism lead to happiness? A longitudinal analysis of the mediating role of psychological needs satisfaction. *Personality and Individual Differences, 105,* 312-317.

Wang, X., Lu, T., Snider, R. K., & Liang, L. (2005). Sustained firing in auditory cortex evoked by preferred stimuli. *Nature, 435,* 341-346.

Wang, Y., & Zhong, Z. (2015). Effects of frustration situation and resilience on implicit aggression. *Chinese Journal of Clinical Psychology, 23,* 209-212.

Wannez, S., Heine, L., Thonnard, M., Gosseries, O., & Laureys, S. (2017). The repetition of behavioral assessments in diagnosis of disorders of consciousness. *Annals of Neurology, 81,* 883-889.

Ward, L. M. (2011). The thalamic dynamic core theory of conscious experience. *Consciousness and Cognition: An International Journal, 20,* 464-486.

Ward-Baker, P. D. (2007). The remarkable oldest old: A new vision of aging. *Dissertation Abstracts International Section A: Humanities and Social Sciences, 67*(8-A), 3115.

Warden, C. A., Wu, W. Y., & Tsai, D. (2006). Online shopping interface components: Relative importance as peripheral and central cues. *CyberPsychology & Behavior, 9,* 285-296.

Wark, B., Lundstrom, B., & Fairhall, A. (2007, August). Sensory adaptation. *Current Opinion in Neurobiology, 17,* 423-429.

Warmbold-Brann, K., Burns, M. K., Preast, J. L., Taylor, C. N., & Aguilar, L. N. (2017). Meta-analysis of the effects of academic interventions and modifications on student behavior outcomes. *School Psychology Quarterly, 32*(3), 291-305.

Warne, R. T., & Liu, J. K. (2017). Income differences among grade skippers and non-grade skippers across genders in the Terman sample, 1936-1976. *Learning and Instruction, 47,* 1-12.

Waters, A. M., Theresiana, C., Neumann, D. L., & Craske, M. G. (2017). Developmental differences in aversive conditioning, extinction, and reinstatement: A study with children, adolescents, and adults. *Journal of Experimental Child Psychology, 159,* 263-278.

Watson, J. B. (1924). *Behaviorism.* New York: Norton.

Watson, J. C., Goldman, R. N., & Greenberg, L. S. (2011). Humanistic and experiential theories of psychotherapy. In J. C. Norcross, G. R. VandenBos, & D. K. Freedheim (Eds.), *History of psychotherapy: Continuity and change* (2nd ed.). Washington, DC: American Psychological Association.

Watson, P. J., Brymer, M. J., & Bonanno, G. A. (2011). Postdisaster psychological intervention since 9/11. *American Psychologist, 66,* 482-494.

Watters, E. (2010, January 10). The Americanization of mental illness. *The New York Times,* p. C2.

Waxman, S. (2009). Learning from infants' first verbs. *Monographs of the Society for Research in Child Development, 74,* 127-132.

Weber, L., & Dwoskin, E. (2014, September 30). As personality tests multiply, employers are split. *Wall Street Journal,* pp. A1, A12.

Wechsler, H., Lee, J. E., Nelson, T. F., & Kuo, M. (2002). Underage college students' drinking behavior, access to alcohol, and the influence of deterrence policies. *Journal of American College Health, 50,* 223-236.

Weck, F., Bleichhardt, G., Witthöft, M., & Hiller, W. (2011). Explicit and implicit anxiety: Differences between patients with hypochondriasis, patients with anxiety disorders, and healthy controls. *Cognitive Therapy and Research, 35,* 317-325.

Weeks, M., & Lupfer, M. B. (2004). Complicating race: The relationship between prejudice, race, and social class categorizations. *Personality and Social Psychology Bulletin, 30*, 972-984.

Wehrle, R., Kaufmann, C., Wetter, T. C., Holsboer, F., Auer, D. P., Pollmacher, T., & Czisch, M. (2007). Functional microstates within human REM sleep: First evidence from fMRI of a thalamocortical network specific for phasic REM periods. *European Journal of Neuroscience, 25*, 863-871.

Weimann, J., Knabe, A., & Schöb, R. (2015). *Measuring happiness: The economics of well-being.* Cambridge, MA: MIT Press.

Weinberg, M. S., Williams, C. J., & Pryor, D. W. (1991, February 27). Personal communication. Indiana University, Bloomington.

Weiner, R. D., & Falcone, G. (2011). Electroconvulsive therapy: How effective is it? *Journal of the American Psychiatric Nurses Association, 17*, 217-218.

Weinstein, L. (2007). Selected genetic disorders affecting Ashkenazi Jewish families. *Family & Community Health, 30*, 50-62.

Weinstein, M., Glei, D. A., Yamazaki, A., & Ming-Cheng, C. (2004). The role of intergenerational relations in the association between life stressors and depressive symptoms. *Research on Aging, 26*, 511-530.

Weir, K. (2016). The science of naps. *Monitor on Psychology, 47*, 48-51.

Weir, K. (2016, April). New insights on eating disorders. *Monitor on Psychology*, 36-40.

Weir, K. (2016, March). The risks of earlier puberty. *Monitor on Psychology*, 41-44.

Weiss, A., Bates, T., & Luciano, M. (2008). Happiness is a personal(ity) thing: The genetics of personality and well-being in a representative sample. *Psychological Science, 19*, 205-210.

Weissman, M. M., Bland, R. C., Canino, G. J., Faravelli, C., Greenwald, S., Hwu, H. G., et al. (1997, July 24-31). Cross-national epidemiology of major depression and bipolar disorder. *Journal of the American Medical Association, 276*, 293-299.

Weissman, M., Markowitz, J., & Klerman, G. L. (2007). *Clinician's quick guide to interpersonal psychotherapy.* New York: Oxford University Press.

Welkowitz, L. A., Struening, E. L., Pittman, J., Guardino, M., & Welkowitz, J. (2000). Obsessive-compulsive disorder and comorbid anxiety problems in a national anxiety screening sample. *Journal of Anxiety Disorders, 14*, 471-482.

Weller, P.D., Anderson, M.C., Gomez-Ariza, C.J., & Bajo, M.T. (2013). On the status of cue independence as a criterion for memory inhibition. *Journal of Experimental Psychology: Learning, Memory, and Cognition, 39*, 1232-1245.

Wells, R., Phillips, R. S., & McCarthy, E. P. (2011). Patterns of mind-body therapies in adults with common neurological conditions. *Neuroepidemiology, 36*, 46-51.

Wen, M., Butler, L. T., & Koutstaal, W. (2013). Improving insight and noninsight problem solving with brief interventions. *British Journal of Psychology, 104*, 97-118.

Wenzel, A. (2011). Obsessions and compulsions. In A. Wenzel & S. Stuart (Eds.), *Anxiety in childbearing women: Diagnosis and treatment.* Washington, DC: American Psychological Association.

Wenzel, A., Zetocha, K., & Ferraro, R. F. (2007). Depth of processing and recall of threat material in fearful and nonfearful individuals. *Anxiety, Stress & Coping: An International Journal, 20*, 223-237.

Werhane, P. H., Pincus Hartman, L., Archer, C., Englehardt, E. E., & Pritchard, M. S. (2013). *Obstacles to ethical decision-making: Mental models, Milgram and the problem of obedience.* New York: Cambridge University Press.

Werker, J. F., & Tees, R. C. (2005). Speech perception as a window for understanding plasticity and commitment in language systems of the brain. *Developmental Psychobiology, 46*, 233-234.

Werner, J. S., Pinna, B., & Spillmann, L. (2007, March). Illusory color and the brain. *Scientific American*, 90-96.

Wertheimer, M. (1923). Untersuchungen zur Lehre von der Gestalt, II. *Psychol. Forsch., 5*, 301-350. In R. Beardsley & M. Wertheimer (Eds.) (1958), *Readings in perception.* New York: Van Nostrand.

West, D. S., Harvey-Berino, J., & Raczynski, J. M. (2004). Behavioral aspects of obesity, dietary intake, and chronic disease. In J. M. Raczynski & L. C. Leviton (Eds.), *Handbook of clinical health psychology: Vol. 2. Disorders of behavior and health.* Washington, DC: American Psychological Association.

West, R. L., Bagwell, D. K., & Dark-Freudeman, A. (2007). Self-efficacy and memory aging: The impact of a memory intervention based on self-efficacy. *Neuropsychological Development and Cognition, B, Aging and Neuropsychological Cognition, 14*, 1-28.

Westen, D., Novotny, C. M., & Thompson-Brenner, H. (2004). The empirical status of empirically supported psychotherapies: Assumptions, findings, and reporting in controlled clinical trials. *Psychological Bulletin, 130*, 631-663.

Wester, A. J., van Herten, J. C., Egger, J. M., & Kessels, R. C. (2013). Applicability of the Rivermead Behavioural Memory Test-Third Edition (RBMT-3) in Korsakoff's syndrome and chronic alcoholics. *Neuropsychiatric Disease and Treatment, 9*, 202-212.

Westerhausen, R., Moosmann, M., Alho, K., Medvedev, S., Hämäläinen, H., & Hugdahl, K. (2009, January). Top-down and bottom-up interaction: Manipulating the dichotic listening ear advantage. *Brain Research, 1250*, 183-189.

Westerterp, K. R. (2006). Perception, passive overfeeding and energy metabolism. *Physiology & Behavior, 89*, 62-65.

Whillans, A.V., Dunn, E.W., Smeets, Pl., Bekkers, R., & Norton, M.I. (2017). Buying time promotes happiness, *PNAS, 114*, 8523-8527.

Whisman, M., & Snyder, D. (2007). Sexual infidelity in a national survey of American women: Differences in prevalence and correlates as a function of method of assessment. *Journal of Family Psychology, 21*, 14-154.

Whitaker, R. (2009). Deinstitutionalization and neuroleptics: The myth and reality. In Y. O. Alanen, M. González de Chávez, A. S. Silver, B. Martindale, Y. O. Alanen, M. González de Chávez, . . . B. Martindale (Eds.) , *Psychotherapeutic approaches to schizophrenic psychoses: Past, present and future.* New York: Routledge/Taylor & Francis Group.

Whitbourne, S. (2010). *The search for fulfillment.* New York: Ballantine.

Whitbourne, S. K. (2000). The normal aging process. In S. K. Whitbourne & S. Krauss (Eds.), *Psychopathology in later adulthood.* New York: Wiley.

Whitbourne, S. K., Zuschlag, M. K., Elliot, L. B., & Waterman, A. S. (1992). Psychosocial development in adulthood: A 22-year sequential study. *Journal of Personality and Social Psychology, 63*, 260-271.

White, F. A., Harvey, L. J., & Abu-Rayya, H. M. (2015). Improving intergroup relations in the Internet Age: A critical review. *Review of General Psychology, 19*, 129-139.

White, K. (2013). Remembering and forgetting. In G. J. Madden, W. V. Dube, T. D. Hackenberg, G. P. Hanley, & K. A. Lattal (Eds.), *APA handbook of behavior analysis, Vol. 1: Methods and principles.* Washington, DC: American Psychological Association.

White, L. (2007). Linguistic theory, universal grammar, and second language acquisition. In B. Van Patten & J. Williams (Eds.), *Theories in second language acquisition: An introduction.* Mahwah, NJ: Lawrence Erlbaum Associates.

White, R. G., Jain, S., Orr, D. R., & Read, U. M. (2017). *The Palgrave handbook of sociocultural perspectives on global mental health.* New York: Palgrave Macmillan.

White, R. K. (2004). Misperception and war. *Peace and Conflict: Journal of Peace Psychology, 10*, 399-409.

Whitebread, D., Coltman, P., Jameson, H., & Lander, R. (2009). Play, cognition and self-regulation: What exactly are children learning when they learn through play? *Educational and Child Psychology, 26*, 40-52.

Whitehouse, W. G., Orne, E. C., Dinges, D. F., Bates, B. L., Nadon, R., & Orne, M. T. (2005). The cognitive interview: Does it successfully avoid the dangers of forensic hypnosis? *American Journal of Psychology, 118*, 213-234.

Whiting, B. B. (1965). Sex identity conflict and physical violence: A comparative study. *American Anthropologist, 67*, 123-140.

Whitney, P. G., & Green, J. A. (2011). Changes in infants' affect related to the onset of independent locomotion. *Infant Behavior & Development, 34*, 459-466.

Whitton, L., Cosgrove, D., Clarkson, C., Harold, D., Kendall, K., Richards, A., . . . Morris, D. W. (2016). Cognitive analysis of schizophrenia risk genes that function as epigenetic regulators of gene expression. *American Journal of Medical Genetics Part B: Neuropsychiatric Genetics, 171*, 1170-1179.

WHO World Mental Health Survey Consortium. (2004). Prevalence, severity, and unmet need for treatment of mental disorders in the World Health Organization World Mental Health Surveys. *Journal of the American Medical Association, 291,* 2581-2590.

Whorf, B. L. (1956). *Language, thought, and reality.* New York: Wiley.

Wickelgren, E. A. (2004). Perspective distortion of trajectory forms and perceptual constancy in visual event identification. *Perception and Psychophysics, 66,* 629-641.

Widaman, K. (2009). Phenylketonuria in children and mothers: Genes, environments, behavior. *Current Directions in Psychological Science, 18,* 48-52.

Widiger, T. A. (2015). Assessment of DSM-5 personality disorder. *Journal of Personality Assessment, 97,* 456-466.

Wiech, K. (2016). Deconstructing the sensation of pain: The influence of cognitive processes on pain perception. *Science, 354,* 584-587.

Wieth, M., & Zacks, R. (2011). Time of day effects on problem solving: When the non-optimal is optimal. *Thinking & Reasoning, 17,* 387-401.

Wiggins, J. S. (2003). *Paradigms of personality assessment.* New York: Guilford Press.

Wilcox, C. E., Calhoun, V. D., Rachakonda, S., Claus, E. D., Littlewood, R. A., Mickey, J., . . . Hutchinson, K. E. (2017). Functional network connectivity predicts treatment outcome during treatment of nicotine use disorder. *Psychiatry Research: Neuroimaging, 26,* 545-53.

Wildavsky, B. (2000, September 4). A blow to bilingual education. *U.S. News & World Report,* 22-28.

Wilde, D. J. (2011). *Jung's personality theory quantified.* New York: Springer-Verlag Publishing.

Wiley, J., & Jarosz, A. F. (2012). Working memory capacity, attentional focus, and problem solving. *Current Directions in Psychological Science, 21,* 258-262.

Wilkin, L., & Haddock, B. (2011). Functional fitness of older adults. *Activities, Adaptation & Aging, 35,* 197-209.

Wilkinson, H. A. (2009). Cingulotomy. *Journal of Neurosurgery, 110,* 607-611.

Wilkinson, L., & Olliver-Gray, Y. (2006). The significance of silence: Differences in meaning, learning styles, and teaching strategies in cross-cultural settings [Special issue: Child language]. *Psychologia: An International Journal of Psychology in the Orient, 49,* 74-88.

Willander, J., & Larsson, M. (2006). Smell your way back to childhood: Autobiographical odor memory. *Psychonomic Bulletin & Review, 13,* 240-244.

Williams, C. L., & Butcher, J. N. (2011). The nuts and bolts: Administering, scoring, and augmenting MMPI-A assessments. In C. L. Williams & J. N. Butcher (Eds.), *A beginner's guide to the MMPI–A.* Washington, DC: American Psychological Association.

Williams, J. E., Paton, C. C., Siegler, I. C., Eigenbrodt, M. L., Nieto, F. J., & Tyroler, H. A. (2000). Anger proneness predicts coronary heart disease risk: Prospective analysis from the Atherosclerosis Risk in Communities (ARIC) Study. *Circulation, 101,* 2034-2039.

Williamson, P., McLeskey, J., & Hoppey, D. (2006). Educating students with mental retardation in general education classrooms. *Exceptional Children, 72,* 347-361.

Willis, J. (2017). Moving toward extremism: Group polarization in the laboratory and the world. In S. C. Cloninger & S. A. Leibo, S. C. (Eds.), *Understanding angry groups: Multidisciplinary perspectives on their motivations and effects on society.* Santa Barbara, CA: Praeger/ABC-CLIO.

Wills, K. E. (2013). Sickle cell disease. In I. Baron & C. Rey-Casserly (Eds.), *Pediatric neuropsychology: Medical advances and lifespan outcomes.* New York: Oxford University Press.

Wills, T., Sargent, J., Stoolmiller, M., Gibbons, F., & Gerrard, M. (2008). Movie smoking exposure and smoking onset: A longitudinal study of mediation processes in a representative sample of U.S. adolescents. *Psychology of Addictive Behaviors, 22,* 269-277.

Willyard, C. (2011, January). Men: A growing minority? Women earning doctoral degrees in psychology outnumber men three to one. What does this mean for the future of the field? *GradPsych, 40.*

Wilson, J. H., & Joye, S. W. (2017). Demonstrating interobserver reliability in naturalistic settings. In J. R. Stowell & W. E. Addison (Eds.), *Activities for teaching statistics and research methods: A guide for psychology instructors.* Washington, DC: American Psychological Association.

Wilson, R. (2015, August 31). An epidemic of anguish: overwhelmed by demand for mental-health care, colleges face conflicts in choosing how to respond. *Chronicle of Higher Education,* p. 38.

Wilson, T. D. (2006, September 1). The power of social psychological interventions. *Science, 313,* 1251-1252.

Wilson, T. G., Grilo, C. M., & Vitousek, K. M. (2007). Psychological treatment of eating disorders [Special issue: Eating disorders]. *American Psychologist, 62,* 199-216.

Wimmer, M. C., Maras, K. L., Robinson, E. J., & Thomas, C. (2016). The format of children's mental images: Evidence from mental scanning. *Cognition, 154,* 49-54.

Winner, E. (2003). Creativity and talent. In M. H. Bornstein & L. Davidson (Eds.), *Well-being: Positive development across the life course.* Mahwah, NJ: Lawrence Erlbaum.

Winstead, B. A., & Sanchez, A. (2005). Gender and psychopathology. In J. E. Maddux & B. A. Winstead (Eds.), *Psychopathology: Foundations for a contemporary understanding.* Mahwah, NJ: Lawrence Erlbaum Associates.

Winston, C. N., Maher, H., & Easvaradoss, V. (2017). Needs and values: An exploration. *Humanistic Psychologist, 45*(3), 295-311.

Winter, D. G. (2007). The role of motivation, responsibility, and integrative complexity in crisis escalation: Comparative studies of war and peace crises. *Journal of Personality and Social Psychology, 92,* 920-937.

Winter, D.G. (2016). Taming power: generative historical consciousness. *American Psychologist, 71,* 160-174.

Winters, B. D., & Bussey, T. J. (2005). Glutamate receptors in perirhinal cortex mediate encoding, retrieval, and consolidation of object recognition memory. *Journal of Neuroscience, 25,* 4243-4251.

Wiseman, R., & Greening, E. (2002). The mind machine: A mass participation experiment into the possible existence of extra-sensory perception. *British Journal of Psychology, 93,* 487-499.

Wishart, D., Somoray, K., & Rowland, B. (2017). Role of thrill and adventure seeking in risky work-related driving behaviours. *Personality and Individual Differences, 104,* 362-367.

Witelson, S., Kigar, D., Scamvougeras, A., Kideckel, D., Buck, B., Stanchev, P., . . . Black, S. (2008). Corpus callosum anatomy in right-handed homosexual and heterosexual men. *Archives of Sexual Behavior, 37,* 857-863.

Witt, C. M., Jena, S., & Brinkhaus, B. (2006). Acupuncture for patients with chronic neck pain. *Pain, 125,* 98-106.

Wittchen, H., Nocon, A., Beesdo, K., Pine, D., Hofler, M., Lieb, R., et al. (2008). Agoraphobia and panic. *Psychotherapy and Psychosomatics, 77,* 147-157.

Wixted, J. T., & Carpenter, S. K. (2007). The Wickelgren Power Law and the Ebbinghaus Savings Function. *Psychological Science, 18,* 133-134.

Wixted, J. T., & Wells, G. L. (2017). The relationship between eyewitness confidence and identification accuracy: A new synthesis. *Psychological Science in the Public Interest, 18*(1), 10-65.

Wixted, J. T., Mickes, L., Clark, S. E., Gronlund, S. D., & Roediger, H. L., III. (2015). Initial eyewitness confidence reliably predicts eyewitness identification accuracy. *American Psychologist, 70*(6), 515-526.

Wlodarczyk, A., Basabe, N., Páez, D., Villagrán, L., & Reyes, C. (2017). Individual and collective posttraumatic growth in victims of natural disasters: A multidimensional perspective. *Journal of Loss and Trauma, 22*(5), 371-384.

Wojciechowska, L. (2017). Subjectivity and generativity in midlife. *Polish Psychological Bulletin, 48,* 38-43.

Wolf, A. J., Guyer, M. J., & Sharpe, L. (2010). Repressed memories in a controversial conviction. *Journal of the American Academy of Psychiatry Law, 38,* 607-609.

Wolfe, M. S. (2006). Shutting down Alzheimer's. *Scientific American, 294*(5), 72-79.

Wolitzky, D. L. (2006). Psychodynamic theories. In J. C. Thomas, D. L. Segal, & M. Hersen (Eds.), *Comprehensive handbook of personality and psychopathology, Vol. 1: Personality and everyday functioning.* Hoboken, NJ: John Wiley & Sons.

Wolk, D. A., Das, S. R., Mueller, S. G., Weiner, M. W., & Yushkevich, P. A. (2017). Medial temporal lobe subregional morphometry using high resolution MRI in Alzheimer's disease. *Neurobiology of Aging, 49,* 204-213.

Wolman, D. (2012, March 15). The split brain: A tale of two halves. *Nature, 483,* 260-263.

Wong, N., Sarver, D. E., & Beidel, D. C. (2011). Quality of life impairments among adults with social phobia: The impact of subtype. *Journal of Anxiety Disorders, 14,* 88-95.

Wood, W. (2000). Attitude change: Persuasion and social influence. *Annual Review of Psychology, 51*, 539-570.

Woodruff, S. I., Conway, T. L., & Edwards, C. C. (2007). Sociodemographic and smoking-related psychosocial predictors of smoking behavior change among high school smokers. *Addictive Behaviors, 33*, 354-358.

Woods, S. C., Schwartz, M. W., Baskin, D. G., & Seeley, R. J. (2000). Food intake and the regulation of body weight. *Annual Review of Psychology, 51*, 255-277.

Woodson, S. R. J. (2006). Relationships between sleepiness and emotion experience: An experimental investigation of the role of subjective sleepiness in the generation of positive and negative emotions. *Dissertation Abstracts International: Section B: The Sciences and Engineering, 67*(5-B), 2849.

Woollett, K., & Maguire, E. (2009). Navigational expertise may compromise anterograde associative memory. *Neuropsychologia, 47*, 1088-1095.

World Health Organization. (2017, May). Smoking fact sheet. Retrieved from http://www.who.int/mediacentre/factsheets/fs339/en/.

Wretman, C. J. (2016). Saving Satir: Contemporary perspectives on the change process model. *Social Work, 61*, 61-68.

Wright, A. C. (2017). The current state and future of factor analysis in personality disorder research. *Personality Disorders: Theory, Research, and Treatment, 8*, 14-25.

Wright, A. C., Zalewski, M., Hallquist, M. N., Hipwell, A. E., & Stepp, S. D. (2016). Developmental trajectories of borderline personality disorder symptoms and psychosocial functioning in adolescence. *Journal of Personality Disorders, 30*, 351-372.

Wright, D. S., Nash, R. A., & Wade, K. A. (2015). Encouraging eyewitnesses to falsely corroborate allegations: Effects of rapport-building and incriminating evidence. *Psychology, Crime & Law, 21*, 648-660.

Wrosch, C., Bauer, I., & Scheier, M. (2005). Regret and quality of life across the adult life span: The influence of disengagement and available future goals. *Psychology and Aging, 20*, 657-670.

Wrzesniewski, K., & Chylinska, J. (2007). Assessment of coping styles and strategies with school-related stress. *School Psychology International, 28*, 179-194.

Wróbel, M., & Królewiak, K. (2017). Do we feel the same way if we think the same way? Shared attitudes and the social induction of affect. *Basic and Applied Social Psychology, 39*, 19-37.

Wu, L.-T., Schlenger, W. E., & Galvin, D. M. (2006). Concurrent use of methamphetamine, MDMA, LSD, ketamine, GHB, and flunitrazepam among American youths. *Drug and Alcohol Dependence, 84*, 102-113.

Wu, N., Hou, Y., Wang, Q., & Yu, C. (2018). Intergenerational transmission of educational aspirations in Chinese families: Identifying mediators and moderators. *Journal of Youth and Adolescence*, doi:10.1007/s10964-018-0820-y.

Wu, Y. (2013). An empirical study of narrative imagery in implicit and explicit contexts. *Computers in Human Behavior, 29*, 1580-1589.

Wynn, K., Bloom, P., & Chiang, W. C. (2002). Enumeration of collective entities by 5-month-old infants. *Cognition, 83*, B55-B62.

Wyra, M., Lawson, M. J., & Hungi, N. (2007). The mnemonic keyword method: The effects of bidirectional retrieval training and of ability to image on foreign language vocabulary recall. *Learning and Instruction, 17*, 360-371.

Xi, J., Lee, M., LeSuer, W., Barr, P., Newton, K., & Poloma, M. (2017). Altruism and existential well-being. *Applied Research in Quality of Life, 12*, 67-88.

Xiang, J., & Stanley, S. J. (2017). From online to offline: Exploring the role of e-health consumption, patient involvement, and patient-centered communication on perceptions of health care quality. *Computers in Human Behavior, 70*, 446-452.

Xiao, N. G., Quinn, P. C., Liu, S., Ge, L., Pascalis, O., & Lee, K. (2015). Eye tracking reveals a crucial role for facial motion in recognition of faces by infants. *Developmental Psychology, 51*, 744-757.

Xiao, Z., Yan, H., Wang, Z., Zou, Z., Xu, Y., Chen, J., et al. (2006). Trauma and dissociation in China. *American Journal of Psychiatry, 163*, 1388-1391.

Xie, G., & Johnson, J. Q. (2015). Examining the third-person effect of baseline omission in numerical comparison: The role of consumer persuasion knowledge. *Psychology & Marketing, 32*, 438-449.

Yadav, R., Yadav, R. K., Sarvottam, K. & Netam, R. (2017). Framingham Risk Score and estimated 10-year cardiovascular disease risk reduction by a short-term yoga-based life-style intervention. *Journal of Alternative Complement Medicine, 23*(9), 730-737.

Yagi, M., Hirano, Y., Nakazato, M., Nemoto, K., Ishikawa, K., Sutoh, C., . . . Nakagawa, A. (2017). Relationship between symptom dimensions and white matter alterations in obsessive-compulsive disorder. *Acta Neuropsychiatrica, 29*, 153-163.

Yamada, R., & Itsukushima, Y. (2013). The schema provokes a disparity of false recollection between actions and objects in an everyday scene. *Scandinavian Journal of Psychology, 54*, 276-282.

Yang, C., Crain, S., Berwick, R. C., Chomsky, N., & Bolhuis, J. J. (2017). The growth of language: Universal grammar, experience, and principles of computation. *Neuroscience and Biobehavioral Reviews, 81*(Part B), 103-119.

Yang, D., Bushnell, E. W., Buchanan, D. W., & Sobel, D. M. (2013). Infants' use of contextual cues in the generalization of effective actions from imitation. *Journal of Experimental Child Psychology, 116*, 510-531.

Yang, N., Gelaye, B., Zhong, Q., Rondon, M. B., Sanchez, S. E., & Williams, M. A. (2016). Serum brain-derived neurotrophic factor (BDNF) concentrations in pregnant women with post-traumatic stress disorder and comorbid depression. *Archives of Women's Mental Health, 19*, 979-986.

Yang, Q., Song, D., & Qing, H. (2017). Neural changes in Alzheimer's disease from circuit to molecule: Perspective of optogenetics. *Neuroscience and Biobehavioral Reviews, 79*, 110-118.

Yao, S.-Q., Zhour, Y.-H., & Jiang, L. (2006). The intelligence scale for Chinese adults: Item analysis, reliability and validity. *Chinese Journal of Clinical Psychology, 14*, 441-445.

Yapko, M. D. (2006). Utilizing hypnosis in addressing ruminative depression-related insomnia. In M. D. Yapko (Ed.), *Hypnosis and treating depression: Applications in clinical practice*. New York: Routledge/Taylor & Francis Group.

Yardley, L., & Moss-Morris, R. (2009, January). Current issues and new directions in psychology and health: Increasing the quantity and quality of health psychology research. *Psychology & Health, 24*, 1-4.

Yarkoni, T. (2015). Neurobiological substrates of personality: A critical overview. In M. Mikulincer, P. R. Shaver, M. L. Cooper, & R. J. Larsen (Eds.), *APA handbook of personality and social psychology, Volume 4: Personality processes and individual differences*. Washington, DC: American Psychological Association.

Yelderman, L. A., & Miller, M. K. (2017). Religious fundamentalism, religiosity, and priming: Effects on attitudes, perceptions, and mock jurors' decisions in an insanity defense case. *Psychology, Crime & Law, 23*, 147-170.

Yeomans, M. R., Tepper, B. J., & Ritezschel, J. (2007). Human hedonic responses to sweetness: Role of taste genetics and anatomy. *Physiology & Behavior, 91*, 264-273.

Yesilyaprak, B., Kisac, I., & Sanlier, N. (2007). Stress symptoms and nutritional status among survivors of the Marmara region earthquakes in Turkey. *Journal of Loss & Trauma, 12*, 1-8.

Yi, X., Plucker, J. A., & Guo, J. (2015). Modeling influences on divergent thinking and artistic creativity. *Thinking Skills and Creativity, 16*, 62-68.

Yildirim, F., & Barnett, R. V. (2017). Comparing the effects of specific variables on passionate love among young people: A cross-cultural study. In N. R. Silton (Ed.), *Family dynamics and romantic relationships in a changing society*. Hershey, PA: Information Science Reference/ IGI Global.

Yim, D., & Rudoy, J. (2013). Implicit statistical learning and language skills in bilingual children. *Journal of Speech, Language, and Hearing Research, 56*, 310-322.

Yoder, R. M., Goebel, E. A., Köppen, J. R., Blankenship, P. A., Blackwell, A. A., & Wallace, D. G. (2015). Otolithic information is required for homing in the mouse. *Hippocampus, 25*, 890-899.

Yoo, H., & Pituc, S. T. (2013). Assessments of perceived racial stereotypes, discrimination, and racism. In K. F. Geisinger, B. A. Bracken, J. F.

Carlson, J. C. Hansen, N. R. Kuncel, S. P. Reise, & M. C. Rodriguez (Eds.), *APA handbook of testing and assessment in psychology, Vol. 2: Testing and assessment in clinical and counseling psychology.* Washington, DC: American Psychological Association.

Young, K. D., Misaki, M., Harmer, C. J., Victor, T., Zotev, V., Phillips, R., . . . Bodurka, J. (2017). Real-time functional magnetic resonance imaging amygdala neurofeedback changes positive information processing in major depressive disorder. *Biological Psychiatry, 82*(8), 578-586.

Young, N. L., Kuss, D. J., Griffiths, M. D., & Howard, C. J. (2017). Passive Facebook use, Facebook addiction, and associations with escapism: An experimental vignette study. *Computers in Human Behavior, 71,* 24–31.

Young, R., Subramanian, R., Miles, S., Hinnant, A., & Andsager, J. L. (2017). Social representation of cyberbullying and adolescent suicide: A mixed-method analysis of news stories. *Health Communication, 32*(9), 1082-1092.

Zacks, J. (2008). Neuroimaging studies of mental rotation: A meta-analysis and review. *Journal of Cognitive Neuroscience, 20,* 1-19.

Zahn, N., Sellbom, M., Pymont, C., & Schenk, P. W. (2017). Associations between MMPI-2-RF scale scores and self-reported personality disorder criteria in a private practice sample. *Journal of Psychopathology and Behavioral Assessment, 39*(4), 723-741.

Zahnow, R., McVeigh, J., Ferris, J., & Winstock, A. (2017). Adverse effects, health service engagement, and service satisfaction among anabolic androgenic steroid users. *Contemporary Drug Problems: An Interdisciplinary Quarterly, 44,* 69-83.

Zaitsu, W. (2007). The effect of fear on eyewitness' retrieval in recognition memory. *Japanese Journal of Psychology, 77,* 504–511.

Zajonc, R. B. (2001). Mere exposure: A gateway to the subliminal. *Current Directions in Psychological Science, 10,* 224-228.

Zamarian, L., Högl, B., Delazer, M., Hingerl, K., Gabelia, D., Mitterling, T., & . . . Frauscher, B. (2015). Subjective deficits of attention, cognition and depression in patients with narcolepsy. *Sleep Medicine, 16,* 45-51.

Zeigler, D. W., et al. (2005). The neurocognitive effects of alcohol on adolescents and college students. *Preventive Medicine: An International Journal Devoted to Practice and Theory, 40,* 23-32.

Zeng, L., Proctor, R. W., & Salvendy, G. (2011). Can traditional divergent thinking tests be trusted in measuring and predicting real-world creativity? *Creativity Research Journal, 23,* 24-37.

Zhang, D., He, Z., Chen, Y., & Wei, Z. (2016). Deficits of unconscious emotional processing in patients with major depression: An ERP study. *Journal of Affective Disorders, 199,* 13-20.

Zhang, W., & Guo, B. (2017). Resolving defence mechanisms: A perspective based on dissipative structure theory. *International Journal of Psychoanalysis, 98,* 457-472.

Zhao, K., & Smillie, L. D. (2015). The role of interpersonal traits in social decision making: Exploring sources of behavioral heterogeneity in economic games. *Personality and Social Psychology Review, 19,* 277-302.

Zhou, Y., Li, H., Siddiqui, N., Caudle, Y., Zhang, H., Elgazzar, M., & Yin, D. (2017). Hematopoietic stem progenitor cells prevent chronic stress-induced lymphocyte apoptosis. *Journal of Neuroimmunology, 309*72-76.

Zhou, Z., & Buck, L. B. (2006, March 10). Combinatorial effects of odorant mixes in olfactory cortex. *Science,* 1477-1481.

Zhou, Z., Liu, Q., & Davis, R. L. (2005). Complex regulation of spiral ganglion neuron firing patterns by neurotrophin-3. *Journal of Neuroscience, 25,* 7558-7566.

Zickar, M. J. (2015). Digging through dust: Historiography for the organizational sciences. *Journal of Business and Psychology, 30,* 1-14.

Zigler, E., Bennett-Gates, D., Hodapp, R., & Henrich, C. (2002). Assessing personality traits of individuals with mental retardation. *American Journal on Mental Retardation, 107,* 181-193.

Zimbardo, P. (2007). *The Lucifer effect: Understanding how good people turn evil.* New York: Random House.

Zimbardo, P. G. (1973). On the ethics of intervention in human psychological research: With special reference to the Stanford Prison Experiment. *Cognition, 2,* 243-256.

Zimbardo, P. G. (2004). Does psychology make a significant difference in our lives? *American Psychologist, 59,* 339-351.

Zimbardo, P. G., Maslach, C., & Haney, C. (2000). Reflections on the Stanford Prison Experiment: Genesis, transformations, consequences. In T. Blass (Ed.), *Obedience to authority: Current perspectives on the Milgram Paradigm.* Mahwah, NJ: Lawrence Erlbaum Associates.

Zizzari, Z. V., Engl, T., Lorenz, S., van Straalen, N. M., Ellers, J., & Groot, A. T. (2017). Love at first sniff: A spermatophore-associated pheromone mediates partner attraction in a collembolan species. *Animal Behaviour, 124,* 221-227.

Zuberi, T., Patterson, E. J., & Stewart, Q. T. (2015). Race, methodology, and social construction in the genomic era. *Annals of the American Academy of Political and Social Science, 661*(1), 109-127.

Zuger, A. (2005, November 10). Doctors learn how to say what no one wants to hear. *The New York Times,* p. S1.

Zvyagintsev, M., Clemens, B., Chechko, N., Mathiak, K. A., Sack, A. T., & Mathiak, K. (2013). Brain networks underlying mental imagery of auditory and visual information. *European Journal of Neuroscience, 37,* 1421-1434.

Name Index

Subject Index

Note: Page numbers followed by *f* indicate figures.